# Visit classzone.com
# and get connected

## Online resources for students and parents

*ClassZone* resources are linked together and provide instruction, practice, and learning support.

### eEdition Plus
ONLINE

This interactive version of the text encourages students to explore mathematics.

### eWorkbook

Interactive practice, correlated to the text, provides support for key concepts and skills.

### @HomeTutor

This interactive tutorial reinforces key skills and helps students prepare for tests.

### Chapter–Based Support

State test practice, quizzes, vocabulary support, activities, and examples help students succeed.

**Now it all clicks!**™

CLASSZONE.COM

McDougal Littell

D0803361

## McDougal Littell
# MATH
### Course 3

TEXAS

# McDougal Littell
# MATH
## Course 3

*Ron Larson*
*Laurie Boswell*
*Timothy D. Kanold*
*Lee Stiff*

TEXAS

Complete listing of

Grade 8 TEKS for Mathematics
and TAKS Objectives for Mathematics

on pages TEKS1–TEKS4
at the back of the book

McDougal Littell
A DIVISION OF HOUGHTON MIFFLIN COMPANY
Evanston, Illinois • Boston • Dallas

# McDougal Littell MATH

## *About Course 3*

*McDougal Littell Math Course 3* provides you with the skills you need to master the Texas Essential Knowledge and Skills (TEKS) for Grade 8. TEKS references appear at the beginning of each lesson and activity, and a full-page "Mixed Review for TEKS" appears twice each chapter.

The focus of the early chapters in *McDougal Littell Math Course 3* is on rational numbers and their operations, equations and inequalities. You will build your understanding of these concepts using models, such as algebra tiles, number lines, and verbal models. You will also apply your skills to problem-solving situations and use estimation to check reasonableness. Topics from other math strands, such as real number properties, geometric formulas, and averages, are introduced early in the course and then integrated and expanded upon throughout.

Later chapters in *McDougal Littell Math Course 3* include topics such as linear equations and their graphs, properties of right triangles, geometric transformations, and probability. The number and variety of problems, ranging from basic to challenging, give you the practice you need to develop your math skills.

Every lesson in *McDougal Littell Math Course 3* has both skill practice and problem-solving exercises. Many of these exercises are especially designed to help you prepare for the Grade 8 Texas Assessment of Knowledge and Skills (TAKS). *McDougal Littell Math Course 3* provides instruction for the TAKS objectives in the "TAKS Preparation" pages of each chapter, with additional exercises in the "TAKS Practice" pages in each chapter. Technology suport for course content and standardized test preparation is available at classzone.com.

ISBN-13: 978-0-618-63830-7
ISBN-10: 0-618-63830-X    123456789—DWO—09 08 07 06 05

Internet Web Site: http://www.mcdougallittell.com

# About the Authors

**Ron Larson** is a professor of mathematics at Penn State University at Erie, where he has taught since receiving his Ph.D. in mathematics from the University of Colorado. Dr. Larson is well known as the author of a comprehensive program for mathematics that spans middle school, high school, and college courses. Dr. Larson's numerous professional activities keep him in constant touch with the needs of teachers and supervisors. He closely follows developments in mathematics standards and assessment.

**Laurie Boswell** is a mathematics teacher at The Riverside School in Lyndonville, Vermont, and has taught mathematics at all levels, elementary through college. A recipient of the Presidential Award for Excellence in Mathematics Teaching, she was also a Tandy Technology Scholar. She served on the NCTM Board of Directors (2002–2005), and she speaks frequently at regional and national conferences on topics related to instructional strategies and course content.

**Timothy D. Kanold** is the superintendent of Adlai E. Stevenson High School District 125 in Lincolnshire, Illinois. Dr. Kanold served as a teacher and director of mathematics for 17 years prior to becoming superintendent. He is the recipient of the Presidential Award for Excellence in Mathematics and Science Teaching, and a past president of the Council for Presidential Awardees in Mathematics. Dr. Kanold is a frequent speaker at national and international mathematics meetings.

**Lee Stiff** is a professor of mathematics education in the College of Education and Psychology of North Carolina State University at Raleigh and has taught mathematics at the high school and middle school levels. He served on the NCTM Board of Directors and was elected President of NCTM for the years 2000–2002. He is a recipient of the W. W. Rankin Award for Excellence in Mathematics Education presented by the North Carolina Council of Teachers of Mathematics.

# Advisers and Reviewers

## Teacher Panels

### Texas Panel

**Judy Carlin**
Mathematics Teacher
Brown Middle School
McAllen, TX

**Judith Cody**
Mathematics Teacher
Deady Middle School
Houston, TX

**Lisa Hiracheta**
Mathematics Teacher
Irons Junior High School
Lubbock, TX

**Kay Neuse**
Mathematics Teacher
Wilson Middle School
Plano, TX

**Louise Nutzman**
Mathematics Teacher
Sugar Land Middle School
Sugar Land, TX

**Clarise Orise**
Mathematics Teacher
Tafolla Middle School
San Antonio, TX

**Wonda Webb**
Mathematics Teacher
William H. Atwell Middle School
  and Law Academy, Dallas, TX

**Karen West-Young**
Mathematics Teacher
Murchison Elementary School
Pflugerville, TX

### Kansas and Missouri Panel

**Linda Cordes**
Department Chair
Paul Robeson Middle School
Kansas City, MO

**Linda Dodd**
Mathematics Department Chair
Argentine Middle School
Kansas City, KS

**Melanie Dowell**
Mathematics Teacher
Raytown South Middle School
Raytown, MO

**Rhonda Foote**
Mathematics Department Chair
Maple Park Middle School
North Kansas City, MO

**Cas Kyle**
District Math Curriculum Coordinator
Richard A. Warren Middle School
Leavenworth, KS

**Jan Rase**
Mathematics Teacher
Moreland Ridge Middle School
Blue Springs, MO

**Dan Schoenemann**
Mathematics Teacher
Raytown Middle School
Kansas City, MO

## Curriculum Advisers and Reviewers

**Margarita Figueredo**
Mathematics Teacher
Cummings Middle School
Brownsville, TX

**Wendy Loeb**
Mathematics Teacher
Twin Groves Junior High School
Buffalo Grove, IL

**Tom Scott**
Resource Teacher
Duval County Public Schools
Jacksonville, FL

**Donna Foley**
Curriculum Specialist for Math
Chelmsford Middle School
Chelmsford, MA

**Barbara Nunn**
Secondary Mathematics Specialist
Broward County Schools
Fort Lauderdale, FL

**Reginald Taylor**
Mathematics Teacher
Ryan Middle School
Houston, TX

## Field Test Teachers

**Kathryn Chamberlain**
Mathematics Teacher
McCarthy Middle School
Chelmsford, MA

**Jill Leone**
Mathematics Teacher
Twin Groves Junior High School
Buffalo Grove, IL

**Deb Mueth**
Mathematics Teacher
St. Aloysius School
Springfield, IL

**Sheree Daily**
Mathematics Teacher
Canal Winchester Middle School
Canal Winchester, OH

**Wendy Loeb**
Mathematics Teacher
Twin Groves Junior High School
Buffalo Grove, IL

**Gail Sigmund**
Mathematics Teacher
Charles A. Mooney Middle School
Cleveland, OH

**Deborah Kebe**
Mathematics Teacher
Canal Winchester Middle School
Canal Winchester, OH

**Melissa McCarty**
Mathematics Teacher
Canal Winchester Middle School
Canal Winchester, OH

## Reviewers

**Chris Acosta**
Grand Bay Middle School
Grand Bay, AL

**Dorene Ellis**
Kimpton Middle School
Munroe Falls, OH

**Myrna McNaboe**
Immaculate Conception High School
East Aurora, NY

**Jennifer Clark**
Mayfield Middle School
 (Putnam City Schools)
Oklahoma City, OK

**Shannon Galamore**
Clay-Chalkville Middle School
Pinson, AL

**James Richardson**
Booker T. Washington Middle School
Mobile, AL

**James Cussen**
Candlewood Middle School
Dix Hills, NY

**Tricia Highland**
Moon Area Middle School
Moon Tap, PA

**Ray Scacalossi**
Hauppauge High School
Hauppauge, NY

**Kristen Dailey**
Boardman Center Middle School
Boardman, OH

**Jessica Kent**
Westside Middle School
Omaha, NE

**Wendee Siegel**
Orchard Park Middle School
Orchard Park, NY

# Course 3 Overview

## Number and Operations

## Algebra

## Geometry and Measurement

## Data Analysis and Probability

## Problem Solving

# Number Sense, Patterns, and Algebraic Thinking

Evaluating Expressions, p. 13
$5 + 6(t)$

*Animated* **Math** Activities........ 8, 9, 14, 19, 20, 21, 28, 35, 38, 39
classzone.com

## Chapter 1 Highlights

**STUDENT HELP**

- Homework Help, 5, 10, 15, 21, 28, 34, 40
  At classzone.com:
  Texas@HomeTutor, Online Quiz, eWorkbook, Hints and Homework
- Reading and Vocabulary, 2, 3, 8, 13, 14, 19, 26, 27, 32, 33, 37, 38, 45
- Notetaking, 8, 20, 32, 33, 38
- Avoid Errors, 4, 19

**🔻 ASSESSMENT**

- TAKS Practice Examples, 28, 34
- Mixed Review for TAKS, 7, 11, 18, 24, 30, 36, 43
- TAKS Reasoning, 6, 7, 10, 11, 16, 17, 18, 21, 22, 24, 25, 28, 29, 30, 34, 35, 36, 40, 41, 43, 44
- Writing, 11, 17, 30, 35, 41

**PROBLEM SOLVING**

- Real Life Examples, 3, 4, 9, 13, 15, 20, 27, 33, 34, 39
- Mixed Review for TEKS, 25, 44
- Multi-Step Problems, 4, 5, 11, 17, 22, 25, 28, 30, 36, 39, 42, 44
- Challenge, 7, 11, 18, 23, 30, 36, 42, 43

# Integer Operations

**Ordering Integers, p. 57**
$-154, -86, 0, 90, 115$

## Chapter 2 Highlights

| STUDENT HELP | 🔽 ASSESSMENT | PROBLEM SOLVING |
|---|---|---|
| • Homework Help, 59, 65, 70, 75, 79, 85, 90, 96<br>  At classzone.com:<br>  Texas@HomeTutor, Online Quiz, eWorkbook, Hints and Homework<br>• Reading and Vocabulary, 56, 57, 58, 63, 68, 73, 77, 83, 85, 88, 94, 95, 102<br>• Notetaking, 64, 68, 73, 74, 77, 83, 84, 88, 89<br>• Avoid Errors, 74, 77, 90 | • TAKS Practice Examples, 69. 95<br>• Mixed Review for TAKS, 61, 67, 81, 87, 92, 100<br>• TAKS Reasoning, 59, 60, 61, 65, 66, 67, 69, 70, 71, 72, 75, 76, 79, 80, 81, 86, 87, 90, 91, 92, 95, 96, 97, 98, 99<br>• Writing, 60, 62, 66, 72, 76, 80, 87, 91, 98 | • Real Life Examples, 57, 58, 65, 69, 73, 78, 83, 88<br>• Mixed Review for TEKS, 82, 101<br>• Multi-Step Problems, 61, 67, 72, 76, 78, 80, 82, 87, 92, 95, 98, 101<br>• Challenge, 61, 67, 72, 76, 81, 87, 92, 99, 100 |

# Solving Equations and Inequalities

**Using Area Formula, p. 144**
Total area $= lw + r$

## Chapter 3 Highlights

**STUDENT HELP**

- Homework Help, 119, 124, 131, 136, 145, 150, 156
    At classzone.com:
    Texas@HomeTutor, Online Quiz, eWorkbook, Hints and Homework
- Reading, Vocabulary, and Notetaking, 114, 117, 118, 122, 123, 129, 130, 134, 142, 143, 148, 149, 154, 155, 161
- Avoid Errors, 118, 123, 130

**🟤 ASSESSMENT**

- TAKS Practice Examples, 134, 143
- Mixed Review for TAKS, 121, 126, 133, 139, 147, 153, 159
- TAKS Reasoning, 119, 120, 121, 124, 125, 126, 131, 132, 133, 134, 136, 138, 139, 143, 144, 145, 146, 147, 151, 152, 153, 156, 157, 158, 159
- Writing, 121, 126, 128, 133, 137, 146, 152, 157

**PROBLEM SOLVING**

- Real Life Examples, 118, 123, 129, 134, 135, 143, 144, 150, 155
- Mixed Review for TEKS, 141, 160
- Multi-Step Problems, 121, 125, 133, 138, 141, 147, 152, 157, 160
- Challenge, 121, 126, 133, 138, 139, 147, 153, 158, 159

# Factors, Fractions, and Exponents

Least Common Multiples, p. 197
3, 6, 9, (12)
4, 8, (12)

## Chapter 4 Highlights

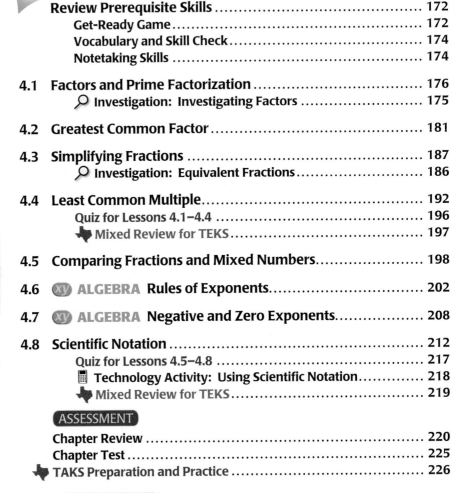

| STUDENT HELP | 🪶 ASSESSMENT | PROBLEM SOLVING |
|---|---|---|
| • Homework Help, 178, 183, 189, 194, 200, 204, 210, 214 <br> At classzone.com: <br> Texas@HomeTutor, Online Quiz, eWorkbook, Hints and Homework <br> • Reading and Vocabulary, 174, 176, 181, 187, 192, 198, 202, 208, 212, 220 <br> • Notetaking, 189, 202, 203, 208, 209, 212 <br> • Avoid Errors, 176, 181, 182, 193, 203, 204, 209, 214 | • TAKS Practice Examples, 182, 199, 213 <br> • Mixed Review for TAKS, 180, 191, 196, 201, 207, 211, 217 <br> • TAKS Reasoning, 179, 180, 184, 185, 190, 191, 194, 195, 196, 199, 200, 201, 205, 206, 207, 210, 211, 213, 214, 215, 216, 217, 219 <br> • Writing, 180, 185, 191, 195, 201, 216 | • Real Life Examples, 176, 182, 187, 192, 199, 208, 212, 213 <br> • Mixed Review for TEKS, 197, 219 <br> • Multi-Step Problems, 176, 180, 181, 182, 185, 191, 193, 195, 197, 198, 199, 201, 206, 211, 216, 219 <br> • Challenge, 180, 185, 191, 196, 201, 207, 211, 217 |

# Rational Number Operations

**Subtracting Decimals, p. 263**
time (sec) $= 58.01 - 55.48$

## Chapter 5 Highlights

| STUDENT HELP |
| --- |
| • Homework Help, 235, 240, 245, 249, 257, 262, 267, 274<br>  At classzone.com:<br>  Texas@HomeTutor, Online Quiz, eWorkbook, Hints and Homework |
| • Reading and Vocabulary, 232, 233, 234, 238, 243, 247, 248, 249, 255, 260, 265, 272, 280 |
| • Notetaking, 233, 243, 247, 257, 265, 266, 272 |
| • Avoid Errors, 234, 239, 244, 266, 273 |

| ASSESSMENT |
| --- |
| • TAKS Practice Examples, 262, 273 |
| • Mixed Review for TAKS, 237, 242, 246, 252, 259, 264, 271, 278 |
| • TAKS Reasoning, 236, 237, 240, 241, 242, 245, 246, 250, 251, 252, 258, 259, 262, 263, 264, 267, 268, 269, 273, 274, 276, 278 |
| • Writing, 237, 241, 251, 259, 264, 268, 271, 275 |

| PROBLEM SOLVING |
| --- |
| • Real Life Examples, 234, 239, 244, 249, 256, 260, 261, 262, 265, 272, 273 |
| • Mixed Review for TEKS, 254, 279 |
| • Multi-Step Problems, 237, 242, 246, 251, 254, 257, 259, 261, 264, 269, 276, 279 |
| • Challenge, 237, 242, 246, 252, 259, 264, 269, 277, 278 |

# Multi-Step Equations and Inequalities

*Getting Ready*

**Using Circumference Formula, p. 313**
$423.9 \text{ ft} = \pi d$

## Chapter 6 Highlights

**STUDENT HELP**

- Homework Help, 295, 300, 305, 314, 320, 326
  At classzone.com:
  Texas@HomeTutor, Online Quiz, eWorkbook, Hints and Homework
- Reading and Vocabulary, 292, 293, 298, 300, 303, 312, 318, 324, 325, 331
- Notetaking, 303, 312
- Avoid Errors, 294, 304, 319

**ASSESSMENT**

- TAKS Practice Examples, 299, 313
- Mixed Review for TAKS, 297, 302, 308, 317, 322, 329
- TAKS Reasoning, 295, 296, 297, 301, 302, 305, 306, 307, 313, 315, 316, 320, 321, 322, 327, 328, 329
- Writing, 297, 301, 306, 316, 317, 328

**PROBLEM SOLVING**

- Real Life Examples, 293, 295, 300, 303, 313, 314, 319, 324, 325
- Mixed Review for TEKS, 309, 330
- Multi-Step Problems, 297, 302, 307, 309, 316, 322, 328, 330
- Challenge, 297, 302, 307, 308, 317, 322, 329

# Ratio, Proportion, and Percent

*Getting Ready*

*Animated* **Math** Activities ............. 344, 349, 361, 376, 379, 383
classzone.com

**Using Percent Equation, p. 375**
$a = 26.7\% \cdot 2000$

## Chapter 7 Highlights

**STUDENT HELP**

- Homework Help, 345, 350, 356, 361, 368, 372, 377, 383
  At classzone.com:
  Texas@HomeTutor, Online Quiz, eWorkbook, Hints and Homework

- Reading and Vocabulary, 342, 343, 348, 349, 354, 359, 366, 370, 375, 376, 381, 382, 388

- Notetaking, 349, 354, 355, 360, 366, 375, 376, 381

- Avoid Errors, 360, 367, 371, 372

**ASSESSMENT**

- TAKS Practice Examples, 350, 372, 382

- Mixed Review for TAKS, 346, 353, 364, 369, 374, 379, 386

- TAKS Reasoning, 345, 346, 350, 352, 353, 354, 356, 357, 358, 363, 364, 368, 369, 373, 374, 377, 378, 379, 384, 385, 386

- Writing, 346, 347, 352, 357, 363, 369, 374, 378, 385

**PROBLEM SOLVING**

- Real Life Examples, 344, 348, 350, 354, 361, 366, 367, 370, 372, 376, 382

- Mixed Review for TEKS, 365, 387

- Multi-Step Problems, 346, 353, 358, 361, 363, 365, 367, 369, 370, 371, 372, 374, 378, 382, 385, 387

- Challenge, 346, 353, 358, 364, 369, 374, 379, 386

# Polygons and Transformations

Finding Angle Measures, p. 408
$2(m\angle 1) = 135°$

## Chapter 8 Highlights

| STUDENT HELP | 🔖 ASSESSMENT | PROBLEM SOLVING |
|---|---|---|
| • Homework Help, 406, 413, 417, 422, 429, 435, 441, 450<br>  At classzone.com:<br>  Texas@HomeTutor, Online Quiz, eWorkbook, Hints and Homework<br>• Reading and Vocabulary, 402, 403, 405, 411, 416, 420, 427, 428, 433, 439, 440, 445, 447, 456<br>• Notetaking, 405, 411, 416, 421, 434, 440, 441, 447, 449<br>• Avoid Errors, 435 | • TAKS Practice Examples, 404, 434, 448<br>• Mixed Review for TAKS, 408, 415, 419, 424, 432, 438, 444, 454<br>• TAKS Reasoning, 406, 407, 408, 414, 415, 418, 419, 422, 423, 424, 430, 431, 434, 436, 437, 438, 444, 448, 451, 452, 453<br>• Writing, 414, 419, 426, 431, 432, 437, 443, 453 | • Real Life Examples, 404, 421, 429, 435, 447, 448<br>• Mixed Review for TEKS, 425, 455<br>• Multi-Step Problems, 404, 408, 409, 410, 415, 419, 424, 425, 431, 438, 444, 447, 453, 455<br>• Challenge, 408, 415, 419, 424, 432, 438, 444, 453, 454 |

# Real Numbers and Right Triangles

**Using Irrational Numbers, p. 477**

$$s = \sqrt{\frac{95}{0.019}}$$

## Chapter 9 Highlights

**STUDENT HELP**

- Homework Help, 472, 477, 484, 489, 495, 503
  At classzone.com:
  Texas@HomeTutor, Online Quiz, eWorkbook, Hints and Homework
- Reading and Vocabulary, 468, 469, 471, 475, 482, 487, 493, 500, 509
- Notetaking, 482, 493, 494, 500
- Avoid Errors, 476, 488, 501

**ASSESSMENT**

- TAKS Practice Examples, 470, 483
- Mixed Review for TAKS, 474, 480, 486, 491, 497, 506
- TAKS Reasoning, 470, 472, 473, 474, 478, 479, 483, 484, 485, 486, 489, 491, 492, 496, 497, 503, 505, 506, 508
- Writing, 473, 479, 480, 486, 490, 497, 504

**PROBLEM SOLVING**

- Real Life Examples, 471, 477, 483, 487, 493, 495, 502
- Mixed Review for TEKS, 492, 508
- Multi-Step Problems, 492, 508, 474, 476, 480, 486, 488, 491, 492, 494, 495, 497, 505, 508
- Challenge, 474, 480, 486, 491, 497, 505, 506

# Measurement, Area, and Volume

**Area of Circles, p. 528**
$$A = 2\pi(15)^2$$

*Animated* **Math** Activities... **522, 527, 528, 534, 535, 554, 556, 563**
classzone.com

## Chapter 10 Highlights

### STUDENT HELP

- Homework Help, 523, 529, 536, 545, 550, 557, 563
  At classzone.com:
  Texas@HomeTutor, Online Quiz, eWorkbook, Hints and Homework
- Reading and Vocabulary, 520, 521, 522, 527, 534, 535, 539, 542, 548, 554, 556, 561, 567, 569
- Notetaking, 521, 522, 527, 543, 544, 548, 550, 554, 555, 561, 562, 567
- Avoid Errors, 528, 554

### 🔻 ASSESSMENT

- TAKS Practice Examples, 523, 528, 545, 556
- Mixed Review for TAKS, 526, 532, 538, 547, 552, 559, 566
- TAKS Reasoning, 523, 524, 525, 526, 629, 530, 532, 537, 538, 541, 545, 546, 547, 550, 551, 552, 556, 558, 559, 564, 565, 566, 568
- Writing, 526, 531, 537, 547, 552, 559

### PROBLEM SOLVING

- Real Life Examples, 522, 528, 543, 544, 556, 563
- Mixed Review for TEKS, 541, 568
- Multi-Step Problems, 523, 526, 528, 531, 535, 538, 541, 547, 549, 552, 556, 559, 565, 568
- Challenge, 526, 532, 538, 547, 552, 559, 566

# Linear Equations and Graphs

**Using Intercepts, p. 607**
$$4x + 2y = 8$$

## Chapter 11 Highlights

**STUDENT HELP**

- Homework Help, 585, 590, 600, 608, 614, 624, 631
　At classzone.com:
　Texas@HomeTutor, Online Quiz, eWorkbook, Hints and Homework
- Reading and Vocabulary, 582, 583, 584, 588, 593, 598, 606, 612, 618, 622, 627, 629, 630, 636
- Notetaking, 600, 606, 607, 612, 614, 622, 630
- Avoid Errors, 583, 599, 600, 613

**ASSESSMENT**

- TAKS Practice Examples, 585, 593
- Mixed Review for TAKS, 587, 592, 597, 603, 609, 617, 626, 634
- TAKS Reasoning, 585, 586, 587, 592, 593, 595, 596, 597, 600, 602, 603, 608, 609, 615, 616, 617, 625, 626, 632, 633
- Writing, 587, 592, 596, 609, 616, 625, 632

**PROBLEM SOLVING**

- Real Life Examples, 584, 588, 589, 593, 599, 607, 612, 623, 631
- Mixed Review for TEKS, 605, 635
- Multi-Step Problems, 584, 585, 587, 588, 589, 592, 594, 597, 599, 602, 605, 606, 607, 609, 617, 623, 626, 627, 628, 630, 633, 635
- Challenge, 587, 592, 597, 603, 609, 617, 626, 633, 634

# Data Analysis and Probability

**Box-and-Whisker Plots, p. 654**

$$\text{median} = \frac{1377 + 1385}{2}$$

## Chapter 12 Highlights

**STUDENT HELP**

- Homework Help, 651, 656, 661, 672, 677, 682, 687, 697
  At classzone.com:
  Texas@HomeTutor, Online Quiz, eWorkbook, Hints and Homework

- Reading and Vocabulary, 648, 649, 654, 659, 667, 670, 675, 680, 682, 685, 686, 690, 694, 701, 704

- Notetaking, 660, 671, 676, 681, 690, 695, 696

- Avoid Errors, 650, 660, 661

**ASSESSMENT**

- TAKS Practice Examples, 672, 695

- Mixed Review for TAKS, 653, 658, 664, 674, 679, 684, 689, 700

- TAKS Reasoning, 651, 652, 653, 656, 657, 658, 662, 663, 664, 673, 673, 674, 677, 678, 679, 683, 684, 688, 689, 695, 697, 699, 700

- Writing, 653, 658, 663, 673, 678, 684, 689, 699

**PROBLEM SOLVING**

- Real Life Examples, 649, 650, 654, 655, 659, 660, 671, 675, 676, 680, 682, 685, 687, 695, 696

- Mixed Review for TEKS, 669, 703

- Multi-Step Problems, 649, 653, 657, 659, 660, 664, 669, 670, 672, 674, 678, 684, 689, 691, 698, 703

- Challenge, 653, 658, 664, 674, 679, 684, 689, 699, 700

Unit 4: Advanced Algebra Topics

# Polynomials and Functions

**Evaluating Polynomials, p. 720**
$-16t^2 + 88t + 2$

## Chapter 13 Highlights

**STUDENT HELP**
- Homework Help, 719, 723, 728, 736, 741
  At classzone.com:
  Texas@HomeTutor, Online Quiz, eWorkbook, Hints and Homework
- Reading and Vocabulary, 716, 717, 721, 726, 734, 735, 739, 748
- Notetaking, 727, 728, 734
- Avoid Errors, 717, 722, 723, 739, 741

**ASSESSMENT**
- TAKS Practice Example, 740
- Mixed Review for TAKS, 720, 725, 731, 738, 745
- TAKS Reasoning, 719, 720, 724, 725, 729, 730, 736, 737, 738, 740, 743, 743, 744, 745
- Writing, 720, 725, 730, 737, 743

**PROBLEM SOLVING**
- Real Life Examples, 718, 723, 727, 735, 739
- Mixed Review for TEKS, 732, 747
- Multi-Step Problems, 720, 722, 725, 730, 732, 738, 740, 745, 747
- Challenge, 720, 725, 730, 731, 738, 745

# Contents of Student Resources

# McDougal Littell
# MATH
## Course 3

TEXAS

# 1

# Variables and Equations

TEXAS

## Before

In previous courses you've . . .

• Compared quantities
• Performed operations on numbers

## Now

**TEKS** you'll study . . .

| 8.12.C | 1.1 Interpreting graphs |
| 8.2.B | 1.2 Order of operations |
| 8.4 | 1.3 Variable expressions |
| 8.2.B | 1.4 Powers and exponents |
| 8.5.A | 1.5 Equations and solutions |
| 8.5.A | 1.6 Familiar formulas |
| 8.14.B | 1.7 Problem solving |

## Why?

So you can solve real-world problems about . . .

• volcanoes, p. 3
• cliff diving, p. 22
• tiger beetles, p. 35
• parachuting, p. 36

 **Math**

at *classzone.com*

• Mountain Climbing Substitution Race, p. 14
• Powers and Exponents, p. 19
• Perimeter and Area, p. 35

## Get-Ready Games

**Review Prerequisite Skills** by playing *Vacation Views* and *Next Stop*.

VACATION VIEWS

| Kim | Dave | Ann | Sam |
|-----|------|-----|-----|
| 9 | 4 | 7.9 | 8.2 |
| 2 | 8 | 5.3 | 4.1 |
| 5 | 6 | 4.8 | 6.5 |
| 7 | 3 | 9.6 | 9.2 |
| 6 | 7 | 2.1 | 1.6 |

**Skill Focus:** Finding the sums of whole numbers and decimals

On a family vacation trip, the first stop is a mountain lookout tower. The four ladders lead to the top of the tower. Which child gets to the top first?

• Find the sum of the numbers on the rungs of each ladder.

• The ladder with the least sum is where the fastest person climbs.

## NEXT STOP

| | 415.79 | | Tens |
|---|---|---|---|
| 410 M | 420 U | 430 E | ? |

| | 19.45 | | Ones |
|---|---|---|---|
| 17 D | 18 A | 19 N | ? |

| | 8.178 | | Hundredths |
|---|---|---|---|
| 8.16 A | 8.17 T | 8.18 H | ? |

| | 589.63 | | Tenths |
|---|---|---|---|
| 589.6 C | 589.7 R | 589.8 S | ? |

| | 627.4 | | Hundreds |
|---|---|---|---|
| 600 L | 700 E | 899 N | ? |

**Skill Focus:** Rounding and identifying place value

Help the kids figure out what the next stop is on the family trip by solving the puzzle.

- Each number has been rounded to one of its digits. Select the answer that shows the number rounded correctly.

- On the right, write each letter below the place value it was rounded to.

- Put letters in correct place value order to figure out the next stop.

### Stop and Think

1. **CRITICAL THINKING** List the names in *Vacation Views* from who gets to the top first to who gets there last (the least sum to the greatest). Whose name is first on this list?

2. **WRITING** In *Next Stop*, a student thinks that the result of rounding 8.178 is 8.17 because the last digit is removed. What is wrong with the student's reasoning?

# Review Prerequisite Skills

**REVIEW WORDS**
- **whole number,** *p. 759*
- **sum,** *p. 764*
- **difference,** *p. 764*
- **product,** *p. 768*
- **quotient,** *p. 770*

## VOCABULARY CHECK

Copy and complete using a review word from the list at the left.

1. When you add two numbers, the result is called the __?__.

2. When you multiply two numbers, the result is called the __?__.

3. When you split up an amount into equal parts, the result is called the __?__.

## SKILL CHECK

Write the place value of the red digit. *(p. 759)*

4. 26.10
5. 45.901
6. 139.07
7. 6.394

Find the sum, difference, product, or quotient.

8. $12.7 - 9.4$ *(p. 764)*
9. $17.8 + 26.3$ *(p. 764)*
10. $9.64 + 6.36$ *(p. 764)*
11. $20.24 - 16.5$ *(p. 764)*
12. $1.3 \times 3$ *(p. 769)*
13. $9.6 \div 6$ *(p. 770)*

14. You are shopping for new clothes. If you have $75.00 and buy a pair of jeans for $37.75, how much money do you have left? *(p. 767)*

**TEXAS @HomeTutor** Prerequisite skills practice at classzone.com

## Notetaking Skills — Keeping a Notebook

In each chapter you will learn a new notetaking skill. In Chapter 1 you will apply the strategy of keeping a notebook to Example 3 on p. 20.

Your math notebook is an important tool for learning and reviewing the topics of this course. Here are some tips for organizing your notes. Organize your notes in the same way for each lesson.

Start with the date and topic.

September 7    Decimals

To add decimals, line up the decimal points.

Copy examples shown in class.

Example: Adding Decimals

$$
\begin{array}{r}
23.40 \\
+ 36.15 \\
\hline
59.55
\end{array}
$$

# 1.1 Interpreting Graphs

TEKS *8.12.C, 8.15.A*

| Before | You compared quantities. |
| Now | You'll use graphs to analyze data. |
| Why? | So you can make conclusions about data, as in Example 1. |

**KEY VOCABULARY**
- **bar graph,** *p. 3*
- **data,** *p. 3*
- **frequency table,** *p. 4*
- **histogram,** *p. 4*

**Volcanoes** The *bar graph* at the right shows the number of historically active volcanoes in four countries. Which country has the most historically active volcanoes?

A **bar graph** is a type of graph in which the lengths of bars are used to represent and compare *data* in categories. **Data** are facts, numbers, or numerical information.

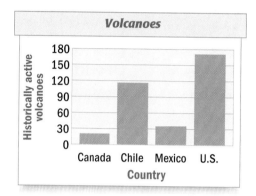

---

## EXAMPLE 1 Interpreting a Bar Graph

**Use the bar graph above about volcanoes. Answer the question or explain why you can't answer the question using the graph.**

**a.** Which country has the most historically active volcanoes?

**b.** Which country has the most volcanic eruptions in a given year?

**SOLUTION**

*READING MATH*
Read carefully to make sure you don't misinterpret the graph. Just because the U.S. has the most active volcanoes of the countries shown does not mean it has the most in the world.

**a.** The vertical axis in the bar graph is labeled *Historically active volcanoes*, so the tallest bar represents the country with the most historically active volcanoes. Because the United States has the tallest bar, it has the most historically active volcanoes.

**b.** Having more historically active volcanoes doesn't necessarily mean having more eruptions, so you can't answer this question from the bar graph.

---

## ✓ GUIDED PRACTICE for Example 1

**Use the bar graph above about historically active volcanoes.**

**1.** About how many more historically active volcanoes does Chile have than Mexico?

**2.** Which country has the least number of historically active volcanoes?

**3.** About how many historically active volcanoes do Canada, Mexico, and the U.S. have altogether?

**Histograms** A large set of data values can be grouped into intervals in a **frequency table**. The *frequency* of data in an interval is the number of values in the interval. You can graph data organized in equal intervals in a **histogram**, where the height of each bar indicates its frequency.

**EXAMPLE 2** Making a Frequency Table

**Roller Coasters** The data show the heights, in meters, of some of the tallest roller coasters in the world. Make a frequency table of the data.

66.4, 94.5, 68.3, 115, 62.5, 97, 66.4, 126.5, 63.4, 74.7, 63.4, 70.1, 66.4, 64.9, 63.7, 79, 63.4, 63.1, 62.5, 61.9, 71.6

**SOLUTION**

*AVOID ERRORS*
Make sure that the intervals do not overlap.

**STEP 1** **Choose** intervals of equal size for the data. The intervals should include numbers from 61.9 to 126.5.

**STEP 2** **Tally** the data in each interval. Use tally marks to record each occurrence of a height in its interval.

**STEP 3** **Write** the frequency for each interval by totaling the tally marks.

| Height (m) | Tally | Frequency |
|------------|-------|-----------|
| 60–69.9 | ЖЖ ЖЖ III | 13 |
| 70–79.9 | IIII | 4 |
| 80–89.9 | | 0 |
| 90–99.9 | II | 2 |
| 100–109.9 | | 0 |
| 110–119.9 | I | 1 |
| 120–129.9 | I | 1 |

**EXAMPLE 3** Making a Histogram

**Make a histogram of the data in the frequency table above.**

**STEP 1** **Draw** and label the horizontal and vertical axes. Start the vertical scale at 0 and end at a point greater than 13. Use equal increments.

**STEP 2** **Draw** a bar to represent the frequency of each interval. The bars of neighboring intervals should touch.

**STEP 3** **Write** a title for the histogram.

**GUIDED PRACTICE** for Examples 2 and 3

4. **What If?** Using the data from Example 2, make a new frequency table using 6 intervals. Then make a histogram from your frequency table.

## 1.1 EXERCISES

HOMEWORK KEY

🚩 = **TAKS Practice and Reasoning**
Exs. 13, 14, 18, 21, 22, 24, and 25

◯ = **HINTS AND HOMEWORK HELP**
for Exs. 3, 5, 7, 13, 15 at classzone.com

### SKILL PRACTICE

1. **VOCABULARY** Copy and complete: A histogram is a graph that shows data that are divided into equal __?__.

2. **VOCABULARY** Copy and complete: The lengths of bars are used to represent and compare data in categories in a __?__.

**INTERPRETING A GRAPH Use the bar graph. It shows the number of businesses at a mall by category.**

*Mall Businesses*

| | 0 | 10 | 20 | 30 |
Businesses

*SEE EXAMPLE 1*
*on p. 3*
*for Exs. 3–6*

3. Which category has the greatest number of businesses?

4. Which category has the least number of businesses?

5. About how many more shoe stores are there than jewelry stores?

6. Can you tell from the graph which category of businesses uses the most floor space in the mall? Why or why not?

*SEE EXAMPLE 2*
*on p. 4*
*for Ex. 7*

7. **MULTI-STEP PROBLEM** The data show the numbers of hours 30 students in a class spent on the Internet in a week.

  4, 2.5, 5.7, 1.8, 3.7, 5.4, 5.5, 11.6, 3.7, 6.5, 2, 10, 0.5, 4.5,
  5, 9.5, 2.1, 4.5, 7.5, 2.5, 8, 1, 9, 4.2, 8, 7, 3, 7, 5, 6

  a. **Make a Frequency Table** Make a frequency table of the data. Use 0–1.9 as the first interval.

  b. **Make a Frequency Table** Make a frequency table of the data. Use 0–2.9 as the first interval.

  c. **Compare** Does the frequency table in part (a) or part (b) give a clearer representation of the data? *Explain* your reasoning.

*SEE EXAMPLE 3*
*on p. 4*
*for Exs. 8–9*

8. **ERROR ANALYSIS** Jack used the intervals 0–2, 2–4, 4–6, 6–8, and 8–10 to make a histogram. Describe the error Jack made.

9. **GRAPHING DATA** The frequency table shows when new states were added to the United States. Make a histogram of the data.

| Year | 1787–1836 | 1837–1886 | 1887–1936 | 1937–1986 |
|---|---|---|---|---|
| States | 25 | 13 | 10 | 2 |

10. **CHALLENGE** *Explain* why a frequency table and a histogram aren't appropriate to show the data: 1, 23, 97, 184, 551, 2097, 9143 and 12,221.

11. **GUIDED PROBLEM SOLVING** The table shows the numbers of movies released in the United States from 1998 through 2003. Use a bar graph to help you describe how the data have changed from year to year.

a. **Choose** intervals for the scale for a bar graph.

b. **Make** a bar graph.

c. **Compare** the values for different years to describe how they've changed.

| Year | Movies |
|------|--------|
| 1998 | 357 |
| 1999 | 438 |
| 2000 | 502 |
| 2001 | 477 |
| 2002 | 473 |
| 2003 | 492 |

**MEDIA** In Exercises 12–14, use the triple bar graph. It shows how many U.S. high schools (per 100 schools) have the given media activities.

SEE EXAMPLE 1
on p. 3
for Exs. 12–14

12. Which of the given media did the greatest number of schools offer in each of the 3 years?

13. ⬥ **TAKS REASONING** Which of the media saw the most growth from 1991 to 2002? *Explain* how you can tell that from the graph.

14. ⬥ **TAKS REASONING** In 1998, how did the number of high schools with newspapers compare to the number of high schools with radio or TV stations?

Ⓐ About $\frac{1}{4}$ as many had newspapers

Ⓑ About $\frac{1}{2}$ as many had newspapers

Ⓒ About twice as many had newspapers

Ⓓ About 4 times as many had newspapers

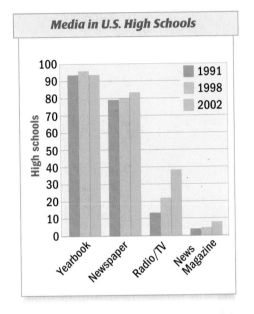

**HURRICANES** In Exercises 15–17 the histogram shows the numbers of hurricanes in the Atlantic Ocean from 1950 through 1999.

15. How many years of data does this graph show?

16. Can you determine the number of hurricanes in the Atlantic Ocean in 1965? *Explain*.

17. Can you use the histogram to predict the number of hurricanes in 2000–2009? Why or why not?

18. ⬥ **TAKS REASONING** Give an example of a set of data that can be graphed with a bar graph but not with a histogram.

19. **REASONING** You are looking for data on high tides. Is it easier to find the exact number of high tides between 2:00 A.M. and 2:59 A.M. last year from a frequency table or a histogram? *Explain*.

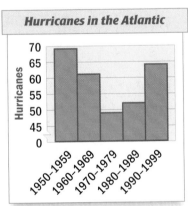

**20.** ◆ **MULTIPLE REPRESENTATIONS** The data show the average numbers of meteors that fall per hour during 39 annual meteor showers. For example, in the first meteor shower, an average of 60 meteors fall each hour.

**Meteor shower**

> 60, 4, 1, 5, 5, 1, 40, 4, 5, 20, 2, 15, 8, 6, 21, 15, 20, 30, 3, 15, 10, 62, 25, 26, 50, 12, 20, 12, 15, 30, 10, 10, 20, 12, 12, 60, 10, 12, 20

  **a. Frequency Table** Make a frequency table of the data. Use intervals of 10 starting with 0–9.

  **b. Histogram** Make a histogram of the data from your frequency table.

  **c. Compare** Compare the displays. *Discuss* one thing that is easier to tell about the data from each display.

**21.** 🏴 **TAKS REASONING** You want to collect data about the pets owned by students in your class. What data would you collect to make a bar graph? Could you use the same data to make a histogram? *Explain* your reasoning.

**22.** 🏴 **TAKS REASONING** The data below are the number of medals the United States won in each of the Winter Olympic Games as of 2002.

> 4, 7, 12, 4, 9, 11, 7, 10, 6, 7, 8, 10, 12, 8, 6, 11, 13, 13, 34

  **a.** Create a histogram of the data with intervals of 5 and a second histogram with intervals of 10.

  **b.** Which histogram gives a clearer picture of how many medals you can expect the U.S. to win in future Winter Olympics? What might account for the 34 medals?

**23.** **CHALLENGE** Use the graph at the right. *Describe* how the data changed during the years shown. What might explain the rapid growth in sales of DVD players? What might cause the growth to slow down in the future? *Explain* your reasoning.

---

## 🏴 MIXED REVIEW FOR TAKS
**TAKS** PRACTICE at classzone.com

*REVIEW*
Skills Review Handbook, p. 772; TAKS Workbook

**24.** 🏴 **TAKS PRACTICE** Tom and three friends shared the cost of dinner evenly. They bought 2 pizzas and 2 bottles of soda water for a total of $22. Tax on the purchase was about $2. About how much did they each pay? *TAKS Obj. 1*

  Ⓐ $3    Ⓑ $4    Ⓒ $6    Ⓓ $8

*REVIEW*
Skills Review Handbook, p. 766; TAKS Workbook

**25.** 🏴 **TAKS PRACTICE** Adam bought a book for $18 using a $25 gift card. What did Adam do next to find the money he had left on his card? *TAKS Obj. 6*

  Ⓕ Add 18 and 25    Ⓖ Subtract 18 from 25

  Ⓗ Multiply 18 by 25    Ⓙ Divide 25 by 18

# 1.2 Order of Operations

TEKS *8.2.B, 8.14.A*

| Before | You performed operations on numbers. |
| Now | You'll use order of operations to evaluate numerical expressions. |
| Why? | So you can find total costs, as in the aquarium visit in Example 3. |

## KEY VOCABULARY
- **numerical expression,** *p. 8*
- **evaluate,** *p. 8*
- **order of operations,** *p. 8*
- **verbal model,** *p. 9*

**Visiting an Aquarium** You and four friends visit an aquarium, but only three of you go to the movie at the aquarium. What is the total cost of the visit? You will find the total cost of the visit using the prices in the table on the right in Example 3 and applying the *order of operations*.

| Aquarium Prices | |
|---|---|
| Admission | $13.50 |
| Sea Lion show | Free |
| Movie | $8.00 |

A **numerical expression** consists of numbers and operations. To find the value of a numerical expression is to **evaluate** it. When a numerical expression has more than one operation, use a set of rules called the **order of operations**.

---

### KEY CONCEPT                    *For Your Notebook*

**Order of Operations**

To evaluate an expression that has more than one operation:

1. Evaluate expressions inside grouping symbols.
2. Multiply and divide from left to right.
3. Add and subtract from left to right.

---

### EXAMPLE 1  Using the Order of Operations

**Evaluate the expression $7 + 16 \div 4 \times 2$.**

*INTERPRET SYMBOLS*
You can express multiplication by using parentheses or the symbols $\cdot$ or $\times$.
$3(4) = 12$
$3 \cdot 4 = 12$
$3 \times 4 = 12$

$$7 + 16 \div 4 \times 2 = 7 + 4 \times 2 \qquad \text{Divide 16 by 4.}$$
$$= 7 + 8 \qquad \text{Multiply 4 by 2.}$$
$$= 15 \qquad \text{Add 7 and 8.}$$

*Animated* **Math**
at classzone.com

---

✓ **GUIDED PRACTICE**  for Example 1

**Evaluate the expression.**

**1.** $14 - 6 \div 2 + 12$     **2.** $20 - 7 \times 2 + 1$     **3.** $2 \cdot 13 - 2 \cdot 7$

**Grouping Symbols** The most common grouping symbols are parentheses ( ), brackets [ ], and fraction bars.

**EXAMPLE 2** **Using Grouping Symbols**

**a.** $(14 + 6) \cdot 8 = 20 \cdot 8$      Add inside parentheses first.

$= 160$      Then multiply.

**b.** $\dfrac{9 \times 8}{4 + 8} = \dfrac{72}{4 + 8}$      Evaluate numerator.

$= \dfrac{72}{12}$      Evaluate denominator.

$= 6$      Divide.

**c.** $45 \div [63 \div (56 \div 8)] = 45 \div [63 \div 7]$      Divide inside the innermost set of grouping symbols.

$= 45 \div 9$      Divide inside brackets.

$= 5$      Divide.

*Animated* **Math** at classzone.com

*ANOTHER WAY*
You can express division using either ÷ or a fraction bar. To evaluate an expression with a fraction bar, evaluate the numerator and the denominator before you divide.

**Verbal Model** When you solve a problem, it may help to write a **verbal model**. Use symbols for operations, and use words to label necessary information.

**EXAMPLE 3** **Using a Verbal Model**

To find the total cost of the visit to the aquarium described on the previous page, you can use a verbal model to write and evaluate an expression.

| Total cost of visit | = | Admission price | × | Number of people | + | Movie price | × | Number of people |
|---|---|---|---|---|---|---|---|---|

$= 13.50 \times 5 + 8 \times 3$      Substitute values.

$= 67.50 + 24$      Multiply first.

$= 91.50$      Then add.

▶ **Answer** The total cost of the visit is $91.50.

*REVIEW DECIMALS*
Need help with decimal operations? See pp. 764, 769, and 770.

✓ **GUIDED PRACTICE** for Examples 2 and 3

**Evaluate the expression.**

**4.** $35 \div (9 - 4)$      **5.** $3 \cdot [(11 - 1) \div 5]$      **6.** $\dfrac{45 + 19}{2 \times 8}$

**7.** **What If?** Suppose 50 students go to the aquarium and movie in Example 3. It costs $35 to park their school bus. Use a verbal model to write and evaluate an expression for the total cost of their visit.

# 1.2 EXERCISES

HOMEWORK KEY

= TAKS Practice and Reasoning
Exs. 3, 25, 36, 38, 39, 43, and 44

= HINTS AND HOMEWORK HELP
for Exs. 5, 7, 9, 11, 37 at classzone.com

## SKILL PRACTICE

1. **VOCABULARY** Use the order of operations to list, in order, the steps needed to evaluate the following expression: $8 + 2 \times 5 - 4$.

2. **VOCABULARY** Copy and complete: A(n) __?__ consists of numbers and operations.

*SEE EXAMPLES 1 AND 2*
on pp. 8–9
for Exs. 3–24

3. ✦ **TAKS REASONING** In what order should the operations be performed to evaluate the expression $2 \times 4 - 6 \div 3 + 1$?

   (A) $\times, \div, -, +$    (B) $\times, -, \div, +$    (C) $\times, \div, +, -$    (D) $\times, +, -, \div$

**USING ORDER OF OPERATIONS** Evaluate the expression.

4. $12 - 10 + 4$

5. $7 + 3 - 2 + 4$

6. $18 + 6 \div 3 \times 2$

7. $16 - 6 + 2 \times 4$

8. $26 - 15 + 8 \div 2$

9. $18 \div (8 + 4 - 9)$

10. $\dfrac{8 + 2}{5 - 3}$

11. $\dfrac{16}{7 - 3}$

12. $8 \times [6 \div (5 - 3)]$

13. $120 \div [(6 + 2) \cdot 3]$

14. $9 \div \left[3 \cdot \left(\dfrac{5}{3} + \dfrac{4}{3}\right)\right]$

15. $3 \cdot \left(\dfrac{7}{2} + \dfrac{1}{2}\right)$

16. $(1.5 - 0.5) \times 2$

17. $4 + 3.9 \div 1.3$

18. $9.4 + 4.2 \div 6$

19. $6 \times (2.4 - 0.4 + 3)$

20. $7.8 \times (5 + 2)$

21. $8.4 \div (21 - 14)$

22. $3 \cdot (12 - 5) + \dfrac{23 - 9}{7}$

23. $\dfrac{41 - 2(3 + 4)}{(36 \div 4)}$

24. $\dfrac{62 - (3 + 4)}{3 + (4 \times 2)}$

25. ✦ **TAKS REASONING** Which operation should be performed first when finding *the sum of twenty and the quotient of eighteen and six*?

   (A) $20 + 18$    (B) $18 \div 6$    (C) $20 + 6$    (D) $20 \div 6$

26. **ERROR ANALYSIS** Describe and correct the error made in the solution.

   $$3 \times 3 + 63 \div 9 = 9 + 63 \div 9$$
   $$= 72 \div 9$$
   $$= 8$$

**NUMBER SENSE** Insert parentheses to make the statement true.

27. $5 \cdot 2 + 3 - 8 = 17$

28. $12 \div 6 + 4 - 7 = 4$

29. $13 - 5 \times 8 - 6 = 3$

30. $7 - 2 \times 3 + 12 = 27$

31. $12 \div 3 \times 4 + 1 = 20$

32. $24 \div 10 - 3 + 1 = 3$

**CHALLENGE** Copy and complete the statement using one of the operations $+, -, \times,$ and $\div$, and one set of parentheses to obtain the greatest possible value of the expression.

33. $12 \underline{\ ?\ } 4 + 2$

34. $15 \underline{\ ?\ } 5 - 2$

35. $12 + 9 \underline{\ ?\ } 3$

**SEE EXAMPLE 3**
on p. 9
for Exs. 36–40

**36.** 🔻 **TAKS REASONING** Your friend pledges $10 to you for a fundraising walk and $.25 for each mile you walk. You walk 6 miles. Which expression could you use to find your friend's contribution?

**(A)** $10 + 0.25(6)$  **(B)** $6 \times (10 + 0.25)$  **(C)** $10(6) + 0.25$  **(D)** $10(6)(0.25)$

**37.** **WRITING**   You buy 3 notebooks at $2 each and 4 pens at $1.50 each. *Explain* how to find the total cost.

**38.** 🔻 **TAKS REASONING** Your school softball team has 25 members. The school contributes $30 toward each $40 uniform. Write and evaluate a verbal model to find how much money the team needs to raise to buy uniforms for every member. Is more than one model possible? *Explain.*

**39.** 🔻 **TAKS REASONING**   Write a verbal model and an expression for a real-world problem whose answer is 25. Use at least three operations.

**40.** **MULTI-STEP PROBLEM** Liz and Ty are baking for the school bake sale. Liz makes 5 batches of 3 dozen cookies, and Ty makes 4 batches of 4 dozen cookies.

   **a.** **Verbal Model** Write a verbal model for the total number of cookies baked.

   **b.** **Evaluate** Evaluate the expression.

   **c.** **Extend** Liz and Ty decide to make packages of three cookies. Write and evaluate an expression to find the number of packages they can make.

**41.** **CHALLENGE** To make the statement below true, copy and complete using one or more of the operators ×, ÷, −, and +: 8 ? 6 ? 3 ? 7 ? 1 = 5

**42.** **CHALLENGE** Your sister is 14 years old. Your brother is 10 years less than twice your sister's age. Your cousin is half of your brother's age. Write and evaluate an expression to find your cousin's age.

**REVIEW**
Skills Review
Handbook,
p. 772;
TAKS Workbook

**43.** 🔻 **TAKS PRACTICE** Ben is riding a bicycle at an average speed of 18 miles per hour. How far will he travel in 2 hours? *TAKS Obj. 1*

  **(A)** 9 mi                 **(B)** 16 mi

  **(C)** 20 mi               **(D)** 36 mi

**REVIEW**
Skills Review
Handbook,
p. 763;
TAKS Workbook

**44.** 🔻 **TAKS PRACTICE** A champion in a hot-dog-eating contest ate about 8 hot dogs every 2 minutes. How long, on average, did it take the champion to eat 1 hot dog? *TAKS Obj. 1*

  **(F)** 4 sec                 **(G)** 15 sec

  **(H)** 30 sec               **(J)** 120 sec

**TEKS** *8.2.B, 8.14.D*

# 1.2 Using Order of Operations

**EXAMPLE** You and three friends are ordering a pizza. The cost of the pizza is $15.90, but you have a coupon for $1.50 off. How much should each of you pay if you want to divide the total cost equally?

**SOLUTION**

$$\text{Cost per person} = \frac{\text{Price of a pizza} - \text{Coupon}}{\text{Number of friends} + \text{Yourself}}$$   Write a verbal model.

$$= \frac{15.90 - 1.50}{3 + 1}$$   Substitute.

To find the cost per person, use the order of operations. Use parentheses to separate expressions that should be grouped together.

**Keystrokes**                                    **Display**

( 15.90 − 1.50 ) ÷ ( 3 + 1 ) =                    **3.6**

▸ **Answer** Each person should pay $3.60 for the pizza.

**PRACTICE** Use a calculator to evaluate the expression.

**1.** $62 + 7 \times 6.4$

**2.** $8.32 - 9 \div 2$

**3.** $6.8 \div 4 + 15.9 \div 3$

**4.** $36.2 - 4.3 \cdot 5$

**5.** $\dfrac{14 + 11}{4 + 1}$

**6.** $\dfrac{20 - 3.5}{10.3 - 7}$

**7.** $\dfrac{10}{3.8 + 1.2}$

**8.** $\dfrac{17.7 - 13.7}{0.2 + 4.8}$

**9.** **SNACKS** You buy 3 bags of snack mix for $1.49 each, 2 boxes of raisins for $1.79 each, and lemonade for $2.39. Find the total cost using the expression $3 \cdot 1.49 + 2 \cdot 1.79 + 2.39$.

**10.** **CLOTHING** You buy 3 T-shirts at $9.99 each, a pair of sneakers for $44.89, a hat for $10.59, and a pair of socks at a cost of 4 pairs for $8.60. Find the total cost.

**11.** **MUSIC** You pick out 2 CDs for $12.99 each, 3 CDs for $9.49 each, and a CD for $15.97. At the register, you find out that, when you buy 5 CDs, you get the sixth CD for half off. Find the total cost if you get the least expensive CD for half off. Round to the nearest cent.

# 1.3 Variables and Expressions

 TEKS 8.4

| Before | You evaluated numerical expressions. |
| Now | You'll write and evaluate variable expressions. |
| Why? | So you can find total distances traveled, as in Example 1. |

**KEY VOCABULARY**
• **variable,** *p. 13*
• **variable expression,** *p. 13*

A **variable** is a symbol, usually a letter, that represents one or more numbers. A **variable expression** consists of numbers, variables, and operations. To evaluate a variable expression, substitute a number for each variable. Then find the value of the numerical expression.

You can write the product of a number and a variable by writing the number next to that variable. For example, you can write $5 \cdot n$ as $5n$.

---

### EXAMPLE 1  Using a Variable Expression

 **Hot Air Balloons** You are riding in a hot air balloon. After traveling 5 miles, the balloon speed changes to 6 miles per hour. So, the total distance traveled is *original distance + speed · time*, which is $5 + 6t$, where $t$ is the number of hours traveled at 6 mi/h.

What is the total distance you travel if the balloon moves at this speed for 1 hour? for 2 hours?

*READING*

The speed 6 mi/h is read "six miles per hour."

**SOLUTION**

| STEP 1 | STEP 2 | STEP 3 |
|---|---|---|
| **Write** hours traveled $t$. | **Substitute** for $t$ in the expression $5 + 6t$. | **Evaluate** to find total distance. |
| 1 | $5 + 6(\mathbf{1})$ | 11 |
| 2 | $5 + 6(\mathbf{2})$ | 17 |

▶ **Answer** If the balloon travels at 6 miles per hour for 1 hour, you travel a total of 11 miles. After 2 hours you travel a total of 17 miles.

---

✔ **GUIDED PRACTICE**    for Example 1

**What If?  Use the information above about hot air balloons.**

**1.** If you travel at 6 miles per hour for 3 hours, what is the total distance?

**2.** If you travel at 6 miles per hour for $\frac{1}{2}$ hour, what is the total distance?

**3.** If you travel at 3 miles per hour for 2 hours, what is the total distance?

**EXAMPLE 2**    Evaluating Variable Expressions

**Evaluate the expression when** $x = 8$ **and** $y = 2$.

  **a.**   $3x - 5y = 3(8) - 5(2)$      Substitute 8 for $x$ and 2 for $y$.

               $= 24 - 10$          Multiply.

               $= 14$             Subtract.

  **b.**   $5(x + y) = 5(8 + 2)$      Substitute 8 for $x$ and 2 for $y$.

               $= 5(10)$         Add.

               $= 50$           Multiply.

**Animated Math**
at classzone.com

**Writing Expressions**   Many words and phrases suggest mathematical operations. The following common words and phrases indicate addition, subtraction, multiplication, and division.

| Addition | Subtraction | Multiplication | Division |
|---|---|---|---|
| plus | minus | times | divided by |
| the sum of | the difference of | the product of | the quotient of |
| increased by | decreased by | multiplied by | separate into equal parts |
| total | fewer than | of | |
| more than | less than | twice | |
| added to | subtracted from | | |

**EXAMPLE 3**    Translating Verbal Phrases

**READING**
...........................
Order is important when translating subtraction and division expressions. The *difference of a number and 6* means $n - 6$, not $6 - n$. The *quotient of a number and 10* means $n \div 10$, not $10 \div n$.

| Verbal Phrase | Variable Expression |
|---|---|
| The sum of a number and 9 | $n + 9$ |
| The difference of a number and 21 | $n - 21$ |
| The product of 6 and a number | $6n$ |
| The quotient of 48 and a number | $\dfrac{48}{n}$ |
| One third of a number | $\dfrac{1}{3}n$ |

**Animated Math**
at classzone.com

✓   **GUIDED PRACTICE**    for Examples 2 and 3

**Evaluate the expression when** $a = 12$ **and** $b = 3$.

  **4.** $9a$            **5.** $ab$            **6.** $b(a - 6)$         **7.** $\dfrac{6a}{a - b}$

**Write the phrase as a variable expression using** $x$.

  **8.** a number increased by 15         **9.** 8 times a number

**EXAMPLE 4** Writing and Evaluating an Expression

**Heart Rate** To measure your heart rate, count the number of heartbeats *n* in 15 seconds. Then multiply by 4 to find your heart rate in beats per minute.

  **a.** Use *n* to write an expression for heart rate in beats per minute.

  **b.** After exercising, you count 24 beats in 15 seconds. Find your heart rate.

**SOLUTION**

  **a.** The phrase *multiply by* suggests multiplication. So, multiply the number of heart beats *n* by 4.

    ▸**Answer** A variable expression for heart rate in beats per minute is $4n$.

  **b.** Substitute 24 for *n* in the expression $4n$ to find your heart rate.

$$4n = 4(24) = 96$$

    ▸**Answer** Your heart rate is 96 beats per minute.

---

✓ **GUIDED PRACTICE**    for Example 4

**10. Savings** You have $25 saved. You save $4 more per week for *n* weeks. Write and evaluate an expression for your total savings after 8 weeks.

---

# 1.3 EXERCISES

HOMEWORK KEY    ✖ = **TAKS Practice and Reasoning**
     Exs. 22, 44, 45, 47, and 54

○ = **HINTS AND HOMEWORK HELP**
     for Exs. 7, 11, 15, 19, 43 at classzone.com

## SKILL PRACTICE

**VOCABULARY** Copy and complete the statement.

**1.** $3t - 4$ is a(n) __?__ expression and $5 + 13$ is a(n) __?__ expression.

**2.** A(n) __?__ is a symbol, usually a letter, that represents one or more numbers.

**EVALUATING EXPRESSIONS** Evaluate the expression for the given value(s) of the variable(s).

*SEE EXAMPLE 2*
on p. 14
for Exs. 3–12

**3.** $4x - 5$, $x = 7$

**4.** $10n + 115$, $n = 9$

**5.** $3(c - d)$, $c = 12$, $d = 7$

**6.** $4(f + g)$, $f = 10$, $g = 6$

**(7.)** $7p + 6q$, $p = 3$, $q = 1.5$

**8.** $8a - 3b$, $a = 3$, $b = 8$

**9.** $3x + 4y$, $x = 6$, $y = 2.5$

**10.** $6r + 4q$, $q = 6$, $r = 5$

**(11.)** $\dfrac{d + 10}{c - d}$, $c = 14$, $d = 8$

**12.** $\dfrac{50 - s}{p + 3}$, $p = 6$, $s = 5$

**SEE EXAMPLE 1**
on p. 13
for Ex. 13

**13. ERROR ANALYSIS** Describe and correct the error made in evaluating $5 + 4 \cdot x$ when $x = 7$.

$$\times \quad \begin{array}{l} 5 + 4 \cdot x = 5 + 4 \cdot 7 \\ \quad\quad\quad\; = 9 \cdot 7 \\ \quad\quad\quad\; = 63 \end{array}$$

**TRANSLATING VERBAL PHRASES** Write the phrase as a variable expression. Let $x$ represent the variable.

**SEE EXAMPLE 3**
on p. 14
for Exs. 14–21

**14.** two fifths of a number

**15.** a number subtracted from 10

**16.** 12 increased by a number

**17.** the quotient of a number and 7

**18.** the sum of a number and 11

**19.** a number decreased by 15

**20.** 8 times a number

**21.** the product of a number and 22

**22.** ⬇ **TAKS REASONING** Which values make the expression $x \cdot [4 + (y \div 5)]$ have a value of 18?

**A** $x = 10, y = 20$ **B** $x = 3, y = 30$ **C** $x = 2, y = 50$ **D** $x = 3, y = 10$

**REASONING** Evaluate the expression when $x = 2.4$ and $y = 8$. Then tell whether swapping the values of $x$ and $y$ will *increase, decrease,* or *not change* the value of the expression. *Explain* your reasoning.

**23.** $7x + 2y$      **24.** $10(x + y)$      **25.** $5xy$      **26.** $x(y - 2)$

**27.** $4x - y$      **28.** $7.2y \div x$      **29.** $\dfrac{3y}{x}$      **30.** $x - \dfrac{y}{4}$

**EVALUATING EXPRESSIONS** Evaluate the expression when $x = 1.05$, $y = 7$, and $z = 0.65$. Round to the nearest hundredth.

**31.** $\dfrac{5(3x + 2z + 0.14)}{xy + z}$      **32.** $\dfrac{2x - 4y - 41.6 + 2z}{y - 5z}$      **33.** $\dfrac{5y + 3z + x}{x + 2yz}$

**CHALLENGE** Tell whether there is a whole number $x$ that will make the statement true. If so, find the value of $x$.

**34.** $2x + 4 = 4$      **35.** $x \div 9 = 9 \div x$      **36.** $8 - 5x = 8 + 5x$      **37.** $4 + x = 3x$

## PROBLEM SOLVING

**SEE EXAMPLE 1**
on p. 13
for Exs. 38–39

**BICYCLES** Evaluate the expression $9t$ to find how many miles you go if you ride your bike for $t$ hours at 9 miles per hour.

**38.** How far do you go if you ride your bike for 2 hours?

**39.** How far do you go if you ride your bike for $3\frac{1}{2}$ hours?

**SEE EXAMPLE 4**
on p. 15
for Ex. 40

**40. GUIDED PROBLEM SOLVING** You buy a hat for $8 and rent videos for $3.80 each. How much do you spend altogether if you rent 5 videos?

   **a.** Write a variable expression for the cost to rent $m$ videos.

   **b.** Add the cost of the hat to this expression.

   **c.** Evaluate the expression for $m = 5$.

⬇ = **TAKS Practice and Reasoning**     ◯ = **HINTS AND HOMEWORK HELP** *at classzone.com*

SEE EXAMPLE 4
on p. 15
for Exs. 41–44

**41. TELEVISION** You watch $x$ thirty-minute TV shows and $y$ sixty-minute TV shows in one week, but you don't watch $z$ three-minute commercial breaks during the shows. Write a variable expression representing the total number of minutes you spend watching television that week.

**42. NUTRITION** Rice has 13 grams of protein per serving, beans have 15 grams per serving, and an orange has 2 grams per serving. Write a variable expression for the total grams of protein in $x$ servings of rice, $y$ servings of beans, and $z$ oranges.

**43. MOVIES** At the movies, popcorn costs $2.75 and drinks cost $2.50. Write an expression to find the change you will receive from $20 if you buy $p$ popcorns and $d$ drinks. Find your change from $20 if you treat 3 people to popcorn and 4 people to drinks.

**44. TAKS REASONING** A personal CD player costs $35 and CDs cost $15 each. Write an expression to represent the total cost of the CD player and $n$ CDs. How much will you spend for a personal CD player and 4 CDs? Will you spend twice as much for 8 CDs? *Explain.*

**45. TAKS REASONING** You are saving money to buy a bike that costs $152.88. You want to buy the bike in $n$ weeks by saving the same amount of money each day. How much money should you save each day?

**(A)** $\dfrac{152.88(7)}{n}$   **(B)** $\dfrac{152.88}{7n}$   **(C)** $\dfrac{152.88n}{7}$   **(D)** $\dfrac{152.88}{n}$

**46. MEASUREMENT** The vine shown below grows the same distance every week. Measure the vine's current length in centimeters. Write a variable expression for the length of the vine $w$ weeks from now. Then estimate the vine's length in centimeters 19 weeks from now.

1 week from now    2 weeks from now

**47. TAKS REASONING** *Describe* a real-world situation that can be modeled by the expression $98 - 8d$. Choose one reasonable value for $d$ and evaluate the expression. Then choose one unreasonable value for $d$ and *explain* why it is unreasonable.

**48. WRITING** An Internet music club offers unlimited downloads for $14.85 per month. Another club offers downloads for $.99 per song. Write an expression for the difference in cost between a 2 month subscription and the purchase of $n$ downloaded songs. *Explain* what it means when the expression has a value of zero.

**Ice Sculptures** Ice sculptures can be beautiful additions to special parties and large celebrations. The sculptures can last a surprisingly long time indoors. After 4 to 6 hours, the sculpture will begin to lose its detail. To melt an entire 122 cm thick ice sculpture would take about 192 hours at room temperature. It melts at a constant rate of about 0.6 cm in one hour.

49. **Estimate** How much does the sculpture described above melt in 3 hours? In 6 hours?

50. **Write and Evaluate** Write and evaluate an expression for how long it would take a sculpture $y$ centimeters thick to melt if it melts at the same rate. Then evaluate when $y = 64$ cm. Round to the nearest hour.

51. **Reasoning** What factors might affect the melting rate of the ice sculpture?

52. **CHALLENGE** Jim's car gets 18 miles per gallon in city traffic and 26 miles per gallon on the highway. He has 22 gallons of gasoline in his tank and is going on a trip.

   a. Write an expression for the amount of gas Jim uses driving $h$ highway miles and $c$ city miles.

   b. Can Jim make a 480 mile trip with 90 miles of city traffic without buying more gasoline? *Explain* your reasoning.

53. **CHALLENGE** The population of Amesville can be represented by $6800 - 120x$, and the population of Boomville can be represented by $4200 + 80x$, where $x$ is the number of years after 2006. In how many years will the population of the two towns be equal? What will the population of each town be in the year 2030?

## MIXED REVIEW FOR TAKS

**TAKS** PRACTICE at classzone.com

*REVIEW*
Lesson 1.2;
TAKS Workbook

54. **TAKS PRACTICE** Two families go to an amusement park together. One family has 5 members and the other family has 3 members. It costs $15 per person for entry, regardless of age. To find the total spent by both families, first you find the sum of 5 and 3. What is your next step? *TAKS Obj. 6*

   (A) Add the sum to 15

   (B) Subtract the sum from 15

   (C) Multiply the sum by 15

   (D) Divide the sum by 15

# 1.4 Powers and Exponents

TEKS 8.2.B, 8.14.A

**Before** You evaluated numerical and variable expressions.

**Now** You'll evaluate expressions with powers.

**Why?** So you can calculate speed, as in Ex. 61.

**KEY VOCABULARY**
• **power,** *p. 19*
• **exponent,** *p. 19*
• **base,** *p. 19*

**Waterfall** A stone falls over the edge of a cliff next to a waterfall. The stone hits the water 5 seconds later. How tall is the cliff?

You will find the height of the cliff in Example 3 using an expression with a *power*. A **power** is a product made of repeated factors. The **exponent** tells how many times the **base** is used as a factor.

Base        Exponent

$$b^8 = \underbrace{b \cdot b \cdot b \cdot b \cdot b \cdot b \cdot b \cdot b}_{b \text{ is a factor } 8 \text{ times.}}$$

Power

---

### EXAMPLE 1    Reading Powers

| Power | Repeated Multiplication | Description in Words |
|-------|------------------------|----------------------|
| $4^2$ | $4 \cdot 4$ | 4 to the *second power*, or 4 *squared* |
| $9^3$ | $9 \cdot 9 \cdot 9$ | 9 to the *third power*, or 9 *cubed* |
| $y^5$ | $y \cdot y \cdot y \cdot y \cdot y$ | $y$ to the *fifth power* |

*AVOID ERRORS*
Make sure that you write $4^2$ and not $4 \cdot 2$.

---

### EXAMPLE 2    Evaluating a Power

**Evaluate five cubed.**

$$5^3 = 5 \cdot 5 \cdot 5 \qquad \text{Write 5 as a factor 3 times.}$$
$$= 125 \qquad \text{Multiply.}$$

*Animated* Math
at classzone.com

---

✓ **GUIDED PRACTICE**    for Examples 1 and 2

**Write the product as a power.**

**1.** $7 \times 7 \times 7 \times 7 \times 7 \times 7$    **2.** $10 \cdot 10 \cdot 10 \cdot 10$    **3.** $w \cdot w$

**Describe the power in words and then evaluate.**

**4.** $6^3$    **5.** $2^5$    **6.** $13^2$    **7.** $3^1$

**Order of Operations** When you evaluate expressions with powers, evaluate any powers before multiplying or dividing.

> **KEY CONCEPT** *For Your Notebook*
>
> ## Order of Operations
>
> 1. Evaluate expressions inside grouping symbols.
>
> 2. Evaluate powers.
>
> 3. Multiply and divide from left to right.
>
> 4. Add and subtract from left to right.

**EXAMPLE 3** Using a Power

**Cliff Height** To find the height of the cliff from the previous page, use the expression $16t^2$, the distance in feet that an object falls in $t$ seconds after it begins to fall.

*TAKE NOTES*
In your notes, you may want to label each example that you copy with a title so that you can tell what it is about.

$$16t^2 = 16(5)^2 \qquad \text{Substitute 5 for } t.$$
$$= 16(25) \qquad \text{Evaluate the power.}$$
$$= 400 \qquad \text{Multiply.}$$

▶**Answer** The height of the cliff is 400 feet.

**EXAMPLE 4** Using the Order of Operations

**Evaluate the expression.**

a. $(6 - 4)^3 + 3 - 2^2 = 2^3 + 3 - 2^2$     **Evaluate inside grouping symbols.**
$$= 8 + 3 - 4 \qquad \text{Evaluate powers.}$$
$$= 7 \qquad \text{Add and subtract from left to right.}$$

b. $3.3 \cdot (7 + 1)^2 \div 4^2 = 3.3 \cdot 8^2 \div 42$     **Evaluate inside grouping symbols.**
$$= 3.3 \cdot 64 \div 16 \qquad \text{Evaluate powers.}$$
$$= 13.2 \qquad \text{Multiply and divide from left to right.}$$

*Animated* **Math** at classzone.com

✓ **GUIDED PRACTICE** for Examples 3 and 4

**Evaluate the expression.**

**8.** $(5 - 2)^3 - 7 + 4^3$     **9.** $12.3 + (4 + 2)^2 - 2^4$     **10.** $7^3 + 24 \div (7 - 6)^4$

**11. What If?** Suppose the falling stone in Example 3 took 8 seconds to hit the water. Evaluate the expression to find the height of the cliff.

# 1.4 EXERCISES

HOMEWORK KEY

🔷 = **TAKS Practice and Reasoning**
Exs. 37, 54, 56, 58, 63, 67, and 68

◯ = **HINTS** AND **HOMEWORK HELP**
for Exs. 3, 9, 21, 25, 53 at classzone.com

## SKILL PRACTICE

1. **VOCABULARY** Write a power and label the base and the exponent.

2. **VOCABULARY** Using the order of operations, what should you do first before evaluating powers?

**SEE EXAMPLE 1**
on p. 19
for Exs. 3–5

**READING POWERS** Write the product as a power and describe it in words.

**3.** $9 \cdot 9 \cdot 9 \cdot 9 \cdot 9$      **4.** $3 \cdot 3 \cdot 3$      **5.** $n \cdot n \cdot n \cdot n \cdot n \cdot n$

**EVALUATING A POWER** Evaluate the power.

**SEE EXAMPLE 2**
on p. 19
for Exs. 6–18

**6.** three squared      **7.** eleven cubed      **8.** one to the ninth

**9.** $2^6$      **10.** $5^5$      **11.** $0^7$

**12.** $6^1$      **13.** $11^2$      **14.** $2^7$

**15.** $10^3$      **16.** $1^8$      **17.** $20^2$

**18. ERROR ANALYSIS** Describe and correct the error made in evaluating $7^2$.

$$7^2 = 7 \times 2$$
$$= 14$$ ✗

**XY** **ALGEBRA** Evaluate the expression when $g = 4$.

**SEE EXAMPLE 3**
on p. 20
for Exs. 19–24

**19.** $g^4 \div 16$      **20.** $(3 + g)^3$      **21.** $(3g)^2 - 25$

**22.** $(g - 1)^5 \div 9$      **23.** $2 \times (g + 2)^3$      **24.** $(2g + 3)^2 + 12$

**USING THE ORDER OF OPERATIONS** Evaluate the expression.

**SEE EXAMPLE 4**
on p. 20
for Exs. 25–36

**25.** $(2 + 1)^4 \div 9 - 4$      **26.** $48 \div (9 - 7)^3$      **27.** $(5 \times 3)^2 - 4$

**28.** $(2 \times 5)^2 + 9$      **29.** $500 \div (12 - 7)^1$      **30.** $6 \times 18 \div 3^2$

**31.** $(9 - 7)^5 + 17$      **32.** $108 \div (5 + 1)^2$      **33.** $9^2 - 3^3$

**34.** $(8 - 5)^3 - 6.2 \times 3$      **35.** $\frac{3}{4} \times 4 + 6^2 \div 9$      **36.** $10.7 - 0.8 + 4^4 \div 2^3$

 **Animated Math** at classzone.com

**37.** 🔷 **TAKS REASONING** Which operation should be done last when evaluating $5^3 - 2^4 \div 4$?

     **A** Find $5^3$      **B** Find $2^4$      **C** Subtract      **D** Divide

**COMPARING VALUES** Copy and complete the statement using <, >, or =.

**38.** $3^2 \underline{\ ?\ } 2^3$      **39.** $5^4 \underline{\ ?\ } 4^5$      **40.** $10^1 \underline{\ ?\ } 1^{10}$

**41.** $\left(\frac{1}{4}\right)^4 \underline{\ ?\ } \left(\frac{1}{3}\right)^4$      **42.** $\left(\frac{5}{2}\right)^1 \underline{\ ?\ } \left(\frac{2}{5}\right)^5$      **43.** $\left(\frac{1}{4}\right)^3 \underline{\ ?\ } \left(\frac{1}{2}\right)^6$

**XV** **ALGEBRA** Evaluate the expression when $a = 2$, $b = 4$, and $c = 5$.

**44.** $a^3 b^2 + 4.2$

**45.** $5.9 \times (c - a)^3$

**46.** $2 \cdot (b + 2)^2 \div (3a)$

**47. LOOK FOR A PATTERN** Evaluating $2^1, 2^2, 2^3, 2^4, 2^5, 2^6, 2^7$, and $2^8$ gives the sequence 2, 4, 8, 16, 32, 64, 128, and 256. Find the pattern with the ones' digits. Predict the ones' digit in $2^{14}$.

**48. LOOK FOR A PATTERN** Evaluate $3^1, 3^2, 3^3, 3^4, 3^5, 3^6, 3^7$, and $3^8$. Predict the ones' digit in $3^{15}$. *Justify* your reasoning.

**49. LOOK FOR A PATTERN** Evaluate $4^1, 4^2, 4^3, 4^4, 4^5$, and $4^6$. Predict the ones' digit in $4^{24}$, and in $4^{87}$. *Justify* your reasoning.

**CHALLENGE** Find the value of $x$.

**50.** $3^x = 9^4$

**51.** $6^{10} = 36^x$

**52.** $4^x = 64^3$

## PROBLEM SOLVING

SEE EXAMPLE 3
on p. 20
for Exs. 53–55

**53. GEOMETRY** The *area* of a square is $s^2$, where $s$ is the length of one side of the square. Find the area of a square that has a side length of 17 inches.

**54. TAKS REASONING** The *volume* of a cube is $s^3$, where $s$ is the length of one side of the cube. A cube has a side length of 14 centimeters. What is the volume of the cube in cubic centimeters?

**(A)** 42          **(B)** 196          **(C)** 1400          **(D)** 2744

**55. MULTI-STEP PROBLEM** At Kaunolo in Hawaii, divers jump from a platform on top of a cliff 82 feet above the water. At time $t$ seconds, a diver has fallen $16t^2$ feet.

a. Does a diver reach the surface of the water in 2 seconds? *Explain* your reasoning.

b. How much lower would a diver be after 3 seconds than after 2 seconds? *Explain*.

**56. TAKS REASONING** *Describe* how to find the value of $3^9$ using the fact that $3^8 = 6561$. *Explain* your reasoning.

**57. LOOK FOR A PATTERN** Write an expression for the $n$th number of the sequence of numbers 1, 4, 9, 16, . . . .

**58. TAKS REASONING** Joe puts $1275 into a retirement account that earns interest so that the account has two times the value every 15 years. What expression represents the amount of money in the account after 45 years?

**(A)** $1275 \times 2^2$     **(B)** $1275 \times 2^3$     **(C)** $1275 \times 2^{15}$     **(D)** $1275 \times 2^{45}$

**59. WRITING** *Explain* why $4x^2 < (4x)^2$ for $x \neq 0$.

**60. FOOTBALL** The season attendance at your school's football games is 1000 people one year. For the next 3 years, the attendance is double the previous year's attendance. Write an expression with a power that shows the season attendance at the football games after 3 years.

**61. INLINE SKATING** An inline skater is at the top of a hill. The hill is 30 feet long and is angled such that the speed of a skater going down the hill doubles every 6 feet. A skater is going 3 miles per hour after the first 6 feet. What is the speed of the skater when the skater reaches the bottom of the hill?

**62.** ◆ **MULTIPLE REPRESENTATIONS** At an archeological dig, the lead scientist decides that the dig should be organized by repeatedly dividing the square area into four smaller squares as shown.

Stage 1          Stage 2          Stage 3

   **a. Make a Table** Make a table that shows the number of squares at each stage from the 1st stage through the 6th stage.

   **b. Write an Expression** Write an expression as a power for the number of squares in the dig at the 7th stage.

   **c. Write a Description** If the whole dig is 64 feet on a side, how many squares are along each side of the dig at the 7th stage? What is the side length of each individual square at the 7th stage?

**63.** 🢃 **TAKS REASONING** On an ostrich farm a single breeding pair hatches 30 eggs per season. These hatchlings will form breeding pairs the following season. Each new breeding pair will hatch about 30 eggs per season. How many breeding pairs would be on the farm after 1 breeding season, assuming all survive? after 2 seasons? after $n$ seasons? *Explain* your answer.

**64. EVALUATING POWERS** Some powers of 11 read the same forward and backward. For example $11^1 = 11$, $11^2 = 121$. What is the smallest $n$ such that $11^n$ does *not* read the same forward and backward?

**65. REASONING** Evaluate $7^4$, $7^3$, $7^2$, and $7^1$. Based on this pattern, what is the value of $7^0$? *Predict* the value of $x^0$, where $x$ is a whole number greater than 0. *Explain* your reasoning.

**66. CHALLENGE** The personal computers of the early 1980s had 64 kilobytes of memory. Today they have more than one gigabyte of memory. Use the table. Write, as a power, the number of bytes of memory that personal computers of the early 1980s had.

| Name | Bytes |
|------|-------|
| Kilobyte | $2^{10}$ |
| Megabyte | $2^{20}$ |
| Gigabyte | $2^{30}$ |

*REVIEW*
Lesson 1.2;
TAKS Workbook

**67.** ✈ **TAKS PRACTICE** Liz and her two sisters went to a country music festival. Entry to the festival cost $14 per person. Liz also used a coupon for $5 off. Which expression shows the total amount they paid in dollars? *TAKS Obj. 1*

(A) $14 \times (3 - 5)$

(B) $14 \times 3 - 5$

(C) $14 - 5 \times 3$

(D) $(14 - 5) \times 3$

*REVIEW*
Lesson 1.3;
TAKS Workbook

**68.** ✈ **TAKS PRACTICE** The expression $7x$ can be used to find the number of students allowed on a field trip if $x$ adults go. Which table shows possible values for the number of students and adults on a field trip? *TAKS Obj. 2*

(F)

| Adults | Students |
|--------|----------|
| 2      | 7        |
| 3      | 8        |
| 4      | 9        |

(G)

| Adults | Students |
|--------|----------|
| 2      | 9        |
| 3      | 10       |
| 4      | 11       |

(H)

| Adults | Students |
|--------|----------|
| 2      | 14       |
| 3      | 21       |
| 4      | 28       |

(J)

| Adults | Students |
|--------|----------|
| 2      | 15       |
| 3      | 22       |
| 4      | 29       |

## QUIZ *for Lessons 1.1–1.4*

**HOME RUNS** In Exercises 1–2, use the table at the right. It shows the record number of home runs hit in a single season by position as of 2005. *(p. 3)*

| Position  | Home Runs |
|-----------|-----------|
| Catcher   | 42        |
| 1st base  | 69        |
| Pitcher   | 9         |
| 2nd base  | 42        |
| Shortstop | 57        |
| 3rd base  | 48        |
| Outfield  | 71        |

1. Make a bar graph that displays the data.

2. How many more home runs is the record for outfield than for pitcher?

**Evaluate the expression.** *(p. 8)*

**3.** $21 - 2 \cdot 7$

**4.** $8 \times 10 - 40 + 25$

**5.** $24 - (9 + 7) \div 4$

**6.** $(3 + 1)^2 - 1^5$

**7.** $10^4 \div 5^3$

**8.** $3^4 + 7 \cdot 5$

**9. PLANTS** A plant is 14 inches tall and grows 4 inches each year. Another plant is 8 inches tall and grows 6 inches each year. Write a variable expression for each plant's height in $x$ years. Then evaluate the expressions to find the heights in 5 years. *Compare* the results. *(p. 13)*

**Evaluate the expression for the given value of the variable.** *(p. 19)*

**10.** $5a - 3 + 7$ when $a = 4$

**11.** $8 + b + 4 \cdot 11$ when $b = 3$

**12.** $2 \cdot z^4 \div 8$ when $z = 4$

**13.** $(9 - x)^5 \cdot 3 - 16$ when $x = 7$

## Lessons 1.1–1.4

**MULTIPLE CHOICE**

1. **STUDENT HEIGHTS** The frequency table shows the heights of 30 students. Which of the following statements is NOT necessarily true according to the table? *TEKS 8.5.A*

| Height (inches) | Frequency |
|---|---|
| 56–57.9 | 2 |
| 58–59.9 | 5 |
| 60–61.9 | 5 |
| 62–63.9 | 7 |
| 64–65.9 | 6 |
| 66–67.9 | 3 |
| 68–69.9 | 2 |

(A) The greatest number of students have heights between 62 and 63.9 inches.

(B) If the students line up from shortest to tallest, the two students in the middle will have heights between 62 and 63.9 inches.

(C) The difference between the tallest student and the shortest student is 13.9 inches.

(D) Fewer than one-quarter of the students are under 5 feet tall.

2. **FUNDRAISERS** You participate in a 20-mile fundraising walk. People can contribute a certain amount per mile that you walk, or just make a contribution. The direct contributions you collect total $150. The per-mile contributions total $15 per mile. Which expression can be used to find the amount that you raise if you walk all 20 miles? *TEKS 8.2.A*

(F) $150(15 \times 20)$

(G) $150(15 + 20)$

(H) $150 + 15(20)$

(J) $150(20) + 15$

3. **METAL ALLOYS** Muntz metal is an alloy of copper and zinc. A sample of Muntz metal has a volume of 15 cubic centimeters. The volume of the copper in the sample is $x$ cubic centimeters. The mass of this copper is 80.1 grams. Assuming that 1 cubic centimeter of zinc has a mass of 7.1 grams, which expression shows the total mass of the sample in terms of $x$? *TEKS 8.15.A*

(A) $7.1(15 - x)$

(B) $80.1 + 7.1(15 - x)$

(C) $80.1(15 - x)$

(D) $80.1 + 7.1(15 + x)$

4. **TRIP TO DALLAS** Your car's fuel gauge is broken. The car can go 22 miles on one gallon of gasoline. You start a trip to Dallas with 13 gallons of gasoline. You want to have at least a gallon in the tank at all times. What is the farthest you can drive before stopping for gasoline? *TEKS 8.14.A*

(F) 264 mi     (G) 273 mi

(H) 286 mi     (J) 308 mi

**GRIDDED ANSWER** ⊙①●③④⑤⑥⑦⑧⑨

5. **FALLING OBJECTS** The expression $16t^2$ is used to find the distance in feet that an object has fallen $t$ seconds after being dropped. You drop a rock off of a 512 foot cliff. How many feet farther will the rock fall in 4 seconds than in 3 seconds? *TEKS 8.14.B*

# 1.5 Equations and Solutions

TEKS 8.4, 8.5.A

| Before | You wrote and evaluated variable expressions. |
| Now | You'll write and solve equations using mental math. |
| Why? | So you can find unknown measures, as in Ex. 47. |

**KEY VOCABULARY**
- **equation,** *p. 26*
- **solution,** *p. 26*
- **solving an equation,** *p. 26*

## ACTIVITY

**You can use algebra tiles to solve equations.**

In an *equation*, the quantities on each side of the equal sign have the same value. The algebra tile model below represents the equation $x + 2 = 6$.

**STEP 1** With how many 1-tiles should you replace the *x*-tile so that the quantities on both sides of the equal sign have the same value? *Explain.*

**STEP 2** What value of *x* makes the equation $x + 2 = 6$ a true statement?

**Make a model to represent the equation. Then tell what value of *x* makes the equation a true statement.**

**1.** $x + 3 = 8$          **2.** $x + 4 = 5$          **3.** $6 + x = 10$

An **equation** is a mathematical sentence formed by placing an equal sign (=) between two expressions.

A **solution** of a variable equation is a number that you can substitute for a variable to make the equation true. Finding all the solutions of an equation is called **solving an equation**.

### EXAMPLE 1  Using Mental Math to Solve Equations

**Solve the equation using mental math.**

**a.** $15 - n = 4$          **b.** $8x = 32$          **c.** $r \div 12 = 4$

**SOLUTION**

To solve an equation using mental math, think of the equation as a question.

**a.** 15 minus **what number** equals 4?          $15 - 11 = 4$, so $n = 11$.

**b.** 8 times **what number** equals 32?          $8(4) = 32$, so $x = 4$.

**c.** **What number** divided by 12 equals 4?    $48 \div 12 = 4$, so $r = 48$.

**EXAMPLE 2** Checking Solutions

**Tell whether the value of the variable is a solution of $n - 8 = 20$.**

 **a.** $n = 12$                          **b.** $n = 28$

**SOLUTION**

Substitute for $n$ and then simplify.

 **a.**  $n - 8 = 20$                       **b.**  $n - 8 = 20$

   $12 - 8 \overset{?}{=} 20$                         $28 - 8 \overset{?}{=} 20$

     $4 \neq 20$                                  $20 = 20$

▶ **Answer** 12 is not a solution.          ▶ **Answer** 28 is a solution.

*READING*

The $\overset{?}{=}$ symbol means *are these values equal?* The $\neq$ symbol means *is not equal to.*

**EXAMPLE 3** Writing an Equation

**Times Square** The Times Square New Year's Eve Ball drops a total of 77 feet in 60 seconds. After 54 seconds it has dropped 69 feet. How many more feet will it drop?

**SOLUTION**

You can use a verbal model to write an equation. Let $d$ represent the distance left to drop.

| Total distance ball drops | = | Distance ball has dropped | + | Distance left to drop | | Write a verbal model. |
|---|---|---|---|---|---|---|
| 77 | = | 69 | + | $d$ | | Substitute. |
| 77 | = | 69 | + | **8** | | Use mental math. |

▶ **Answer** Because $d = 8$, the ball will drop 8 more feet.

**Check** You can check your answer by finding the sum of 8 and 69.

   $8 + 69 \overset{?}{=} 77$

     $77 = 77$ ✓

✓ **GUIDED PRACTICE** for Examples 1, 2, and 3

**Solve the equation using mental math.**

 **1.** $5x = 45$          **2.** $16 + n = 21$          **3.** $t \div 6 = 9$

**Tell whether the value of the variable is a solution of the equation.**

 **4.** $a + 9 = 16; a = 7$      **5.** $88 \div y = 8; y = 8$      **6.** $7n = 13, n = 2$

 **7. Laundry** Julie has $9 to wash her clothes at the laundromat. Each load costs $1.75 to wash and $1.25 to dry. How many loads can she do?

**EXAMPLE 4** **TAKS PRACTICE: Multiple Choice**

**Soccer Goals** Ira, Luis, and Marco are high scorers in soccer. In a recent game, the difference of Ira's and Marco's goals scored was 2. Luis scored 1 more goal than Ira. Marco scored 3 goals. How many goals did Luis score?

   Ⓐ 3         Ⓑ 4         Ⓒ 5         Ⓓ 6

**ELIMINATE CHOICES**
Luis scored 1 more goal than Ira, and Ira scored more goals than Marco, who scored 3 goals. So, you can eliminate choice A.

**SOLUTION**

**STEP 1** **Write** and solve an equation to find the goals scored by Ira.

| Ira's goals − Marco's goals = 2 | **Write a verbal model.** |
| $i$    −    3    = 2 | **Substitute 3 for Marco's goals.** |
| 5    −    3    = 2 | **Use mental math.** |

Ira scored 5 goals.

**STEP 2** **Use** Ira's goals scored to find Luis's goals scored. Add: $1 + 5 = 6$.

▶ **Answer** Luis scored 6 goals. The correct answer is D. Ⓐ Ⓑ Ⓒ ⬤

✓ **GUIDED PRACTICE**    **for Example 4**

8. **What If?** In Example 4, suppose the difference of Ira's and Marco's goals scored was 3. How many goals did Luis score?

# 1.5 EXERCISES

**HOMEWORK KEY**

 = **TAKS Practice and Reasoning**
Exs. 25, 49, 50, 51, 57, and 58

◯ = **HINTS AND HOMEWORK HELP**
for Exs. 3, 11, 19, 21, 45 at classzone.com

**SKILL PRACTICE**

**VOCABULARY** **Copy and complete the statement.**

1. The process of finding all possible values that make a mathematical sentence true is __?__ .

2. A(n) __?__ is a mathematical sentence formed by placing an equal sign between two expressions.

**SEE EXAMPLE 1**
on p. 26
for Exs. 3–18

**SOLVING EQUATIONS** **Solve the equation using mental math.**

3. $9 + p = 31$      4. $y - 10 = 34$      5. $7x = 77$      6. $56 \div k = 8$

7. $z + 8 = 19$      8. $6m = 48$      9. $c - 16 = 13$      10. $51 \div k = 3$

11. $\dfrac{32}{n} = 16$      12. $26 - r = 17$      13. $10y = 150$      14. $7 + x = 31$

15. $z - 5 = 12$      16. $6x = 42$      17. $22 \div c = 11$      18. $3 + a = 19$

 **Animated Math** at classzone.com

SEE EXAMPLE 2
on p. 27
for Exs. 19–26

**CHECKING SOLUTIONS** Tell whether the given value is a solution.

**19.** $35 - x = 21$; $x = 16$

**20.** $75 \div x = 5$; $x = 15$

**21.** $7x = 84$; $x = 14$

**22.** $x + 29 = 42$; $x = 13$

**23.** $15 + b = 28$; $b = 13$

**24.** $37 - d = 14$; $d = 21$

**25.** ⬥ **TAKS REASONING** Which of the following is a solution of $63 \div x = 9$?

Ⓐ 6          Ⓑ 7          Ⓒ 9          Ⓓ 54

**26. ERROR ANALYSIS** A student says that a solution of $5 \div x = 10$ is 2. *Explain* why the student's solution is incorrect.

**TRANSLATING EQUATIONS** Write the equation as a question in words. Then solve the equation.

**27.** $24 \div t = 8$

**28.** $t + 8 = 24$

**29.** $24t = 8$

**30.** $\dfrac{t}{24} = 8$

**IDENTIFYING SOLUTIONS** Tell which of the given values is a solution of the equation.

**31.** $3x + 6 = x + 12$; $x = 1, 2, 3$

**32.** $2x - 7 = x + 1$; $x = 8, 9, 10$

**33.** $8 - 4x = 4x$; $x = 0, 1, 2$

**34.** $2x - 4.5 = x \div 2$; $x = 3, 4, 5$

**35.** $5x + 1 = x + 17$; $x = 3, 4, 5$

**36.** $12 - 3x = 3x$; $x = 0, 1, 2$

**CHALLENGE** Find the value of $x$ that makes the equation true.

**37.** $[(x + 3) \cdot 4 - 7] \div 3 = 3$

**38.** $[(x + 3) \cdot 3 - 6] \div 5 = 3$

**39.** $[(x - 2) \cdot 6 - 2] \div 5 = 2$

**40.** $[(x - 2) \cdot 5 + 8] \div 4 = 2$

**CHALLENGE** Solve the equation.

**41.** $\dfrac{x - 8}{6} = 12$

**42.** $\dfrac{71 - x}{7} = 8$

**43.** $\dfrac{x + 6}{9} = 5$

**44.** $\dfrac{64 - x}{4} = 10$

## PROBLEM SOLVING

SEE EXAMPLE 3
on p. 27
for Exs. 45–47

**45. RAINFALL** The greatest recorded rainfall in the United States in a 24 hour period is 43 inches. At your location, 14 inches has already fallen in 7 hours. Write an equation to find how much more rain needs to fall in the next 17 hours to equal the record. Then solve the equation.

**46. MEASUREMENT** Write and solve an equation to find the number of feet $f$ in 3600 inches.

**47. ELEPHANTS** A baby elephant at the Bronx Zoo would get on a scale only with its mother. The zoo weighed the mother as 5033 pounds. They weighed the mother and the baby together as 5396 pounds. Write and solve an equation to find the weight of the baby elephant.

**SEE EXAMPLE 3**
on p. 27
for Exs. 48–49

48. **WRITING**  *Explain* how you can tell if 5 is a solution of $4x = 20$.

49. ✦ **TAKS REASONING** You are writing invitations to a party. It takes you four minutes to complete each invitation. What is the equation for finding $x$, the number of invitations you can complete in one hour?

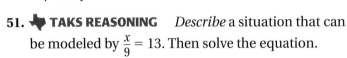

(A) $\frac{4}{x} = 60$　　　(B) $\frac{x}{4} = 60$　　　(C) $4x = 60$　　　(D) $x - 4 = 60$

**SEE EXAMPLE 4**
on p. 28
for Ex. 50

50. ✦ **TAKS REASONING** Your town's fireworks show lasted 20 minutes. The total cost was $25,000. Use a verbal model to write and solve an equation to find the cost per minute. What is the cost of a show at the same rate per minute that lasts twice as long? *Explain* your answer.

51. ✦ **TAKS REASONING**  *Describe* a situation that can be modeled by $\frac{x}{9} = 13$. Then solve the equation.

52. **MARATHON** To qualify for the Boston Marathon, Maria needs to run a qualifying time of 3 hours 40 minutes or less. Her best time so far is 4 hours 5 minutes. Write and solve an equation to find the fewest minutes by which Maria must improve her time to qualify.

53. **VOLUNTEERING** You want to volunteer a total of 200 hours at a zoo. After 5 weeks, you have worked 80 hours. Write and solve an equation to find how many hours you will work per week over 8 weeks total.

54. **CONSECUTIVE NUMBERS** Consecutive numbers are numbers that follow one after another, such as 1, 2, and 3. The sum of two consecutive numbers divided by 3 is 71. What are the two numbers?

55. **CHALLENGE** Joe had a box of gumballs. He gave half of them to Antowain, one sixth to Shaniqua, and one fourth to Naresh. He has 4 left. How many gumballs did Joe have before he gave some away?

56. **CHALLENGE** Jen has $\frac{4}{5}$ as much money as Bob. Tim has $50 more than Jen. Rita has $150, which is $35 more than Bob. How much money does Tim have?

---

🔷 **MIXED REVIEW FOR TAKS**　　　　**TAKS** **PRACTICE** at classzone.com

**REVIEW**
Lesson 1.3;
TAKS Workbook

57. ✦ **TAKS PRACTICE** In February, Mrs. Galvez parked her car for 160 hours in a parking garage. Her monthly parking fee can be found by evaluating $25 + 0.5h$, where $h$ is the total number of hours her car was parked. Find Mrs. Galvez's monthly parking fee for February. *TAKS Obj. 2*

(A) $25.50　　　(B) $37.50　　　(C) $80　　　(D) $105

**REVIEW**
Problem Solving
Handbook,
p. 791;
TAKS Workbook

58. ✦ **TAKS PRACTICE** Which expression shows the next term in the pattern to the right? *TAKS Obj. 6*

| 4 | 16 | 64 | 256 | ? |

(F) $4 \times 256$　　　(G) $12 + 256$　　　(H) $256 \times 256$　　　(J) $48 + 256$

# INVESTIGATION
*Use before Lesson 1.6*

**GOAL**
Develop formulas for finding the areas of rectangles and squares.

**MATERIALS**
• square tiles

**TEKS** *8.15.A, 8.16.A*

# 1.6 Modeling Area

You can use square tiles to find the *areas* of rectangles and squares.

**EXPLORE** **Find the area of a 5-unit by 3-unit rectangle.**

**STEP 1** Use square tiles to make a rectangle with side lengths of 5 units and 3 units.

1 unit     **One square unit**
1 unit

**STEP 2** The *area* of the rectangle is equal to the number of square unit tiles that cover it. Count the square tiles to find the area of the rectangle.

width = 3 units

length = 5 units

**PRACTICE**

1. Use square tiles to make rectangles that have the dimensions given in the table. Copy and complete the table.

| Dimensions | Length | Width | Number of square tiles | Area of rectangle |
|------------|--------|-------|------------------------|-------------------|
| 3 by 4 | ? | ? | ? | ? |
| 4 by 4 | ? | ? | ? | ? |
| 5 by 6 | ? | ? | ? | ? |
| 3 by 3 | ? | ? | ? | ? |

**DRAW CONCLUSIONS**

2. **WRITING A FORMULA** Write a variable equation to find the area of a rectangle and explain what each variable represents.

3. **WRITING A FORMULA** Write a different equation to find the area of a square and explain what each variable represents.

4. **REASONING** Area is measured in square units. Perimeter is the distance around a figure. Is perimeter measured in square units? Why or why not?

# 1.6 Variables in Familiar Formulas

TEKS 8.5.A, 8.14.A

| Before | You evaluated variable expressions. |
| Now | You'll use formulas to find unknown values. |
| Why? | So you can calculate distances, as in Ex. 31. |

**KEY VOCABULARY**
- **formula,** *p. 32*
- **perimeter,** *p. 32*
- **area,** *p. 32*

A **formula** is an equation that relates two or more quantities such as *perimeter*, length, and width. The **perimeter** of a figure is the sum of the lengths of its sides. The amount of surface the figure covers is called its **area**.

Perimeter is measured in linear units such as feet. Area is measured in square units such as square feet, written as $ft^2$. You may have found the formula for area in the Investigation on p. 31.

## KEY CONCEPT — *For Your Notebook*

### Perimeter and Area Formulas

| | Diagram | Perimeter | Area |
|---|---|---|---|
| **Rectangle** | | $P = l + w + l + w$ or $P = 2l + 2w$ | $A = lw$ |
| **Square** | | $P = 4s$ | $A = s^2$ |

## EXAMPLE 1 Finding Perimeter and Area

**Find the perimeter and area of the rectangle.**

5 ft

8 ft

**SOLUTION**

Find the perimeter.

| $P = 2l + 2w$ | Write formula. |
| $= 2(8) + 2(5)$ | Substitute. |
| $= 26$ | Multiply, then add. |

Find the area.

| $A = lw$ | Write formula. |
| $= (8)(5)$ | Substitute. |
| $= 40$ | Multiply. |

▶ **Answer** The perimeter is 26 feet, and the area is 40 square feet.

**EXAMPLE 2** Finding Side Length

Find the side length of a square with an area of 81 square feet.

$A = s^2$    **Write formula for area of a square.**

$81 = s^2$    **Substitute 81 for $A$.**

$9 = s$    **Use mental math: $9^2 = 81$.**

$A = 81 \text{ ft}^2$   s

s

▶ **Answer** The side length of the square is 9 feet.

**Distance Formula** Another useful formula is the distance formula. You can use the distance formula to find distance traveled.

---

**KEY CONCEPT**        *For Your Notebook*

**Distance Formula**

**Words**    The distance traveled $d$ is the product of the rate $r$ and the time $t$.

**Algebra**    $d = r \cdot t$, or $d = rt$

**Numbers**    $d = 45 \, \dfrac{\text{miles}}{\text{hour}} \cdot 3 \, \text{hours} = 135 \, \text{miles}$

---

**EXAMPLE 3** Using the Distance Formula

**Rabbits** A rabbit is running at a rate of 26.4 feet per second. How far does the rabbit travel in 5 seconds?

**SOLUTION**

*VOCABULARY*

In the formula $d = rt$, the rate $r$ is the speed of travel.

$d = r \cdot t$    **Write distance formula.**

$= 26.4 \cdot 5$    **Substitute 26.4 for $r$ and 5 for $t$.**

$= 132$    **Multiply.**

▶ **Answer** The rabbit travels 132 feet in 5 seconds.

---

✓ **GUIDED PRACTICE**    for Examples 1, 2, and 3

**Find the perimeter and area of the figure.**

**1.** rectangle: $l = 25$ in., $w = 14$ in.

**2.** square: $s = 7$ in.

**Find the side length of the figure.**

**3.** rectangle: $A = 91 \text{ cm}^2$, $l = 13$ cm, $w = \underline{\ ?\ }$

**4.** square: $A = 100 \text{ yd}^2$, $s = \underline{\ ?\ }$

**5. Distance** How far does a car travel in 2 hours at a rate of 40 mi/h?

**Rewriting the Distance Formula** You can write the distance formula in different forms to find rate or time. Use $t = \frac{d}{r}$ to find the time and $r = \frac{d}{t}$ to find the rate.

**TAKS**

**EXAMPLE 4** **TAKS PRACTICE: Multiple Choice**

**Running Times** How long will it take a rabbit to travel 352 feet at a rate of 22 feet per second?

Ⓐ 7744 sec   Ⓑ 374 sec

Ⓒ 16 sec   Ⓓ 0.063 sec

**ELIMINATE CHOICES**
Since 352 feet is more than 22 feet, 0.063 seconds is unreasonable. So, you can eliminate choice D.

**SOLUTION**

$t = \dfrac{d}{r}$   Write distance formula.

$= \dfrac{352}{22}$   Substitute 264 for *d* and 22 for *r*.

$= 16$   Divide.

▶ **Answer** It will take a rabbit 16 seconds to travel 352 feet. The correct answer is C. Ⓐ Ⓑ Ⓒ Ⓓ

✓ **GUIDED PRACTICE** **for Example 4**

6. **Running Speeds** How fast is a rabbit running if it travels 192 feet in 8 seconds?

## 1.6 EXERCISES

**HOMEWORK KEY**  = **TAKS Practice and Reasoning**
Exs. 20, 23, 32, 33, 34, 36, and 37

◯ = **HINTS AND HOMEWORK HELP**
for Exs. 3, 9, 13, 15, 27 at classzone.com

### SKILL PRACTICE

1. **VOCABULARY** Describe the difference between area and perimeter.

2. **VOCABULARY** Write the three forms of the distance formula.

**FINDING PERIMETER AND AREA** **Find the perimeter and area of the figure.**

**SEE EXAMPLE 1**
on p. 32
for Exs. 3–7

3.

6 yd
9 yd

4.
8 cm
3 cm

5.
5 m
5 m

6.
12 ft
12 ft

7. **ERROR ANALYSIS** Describe and correct the error made in finding the area.

$A = s^2$
$= 4^2$
$= 16$ meters

4 m
4 m

**ALGEBRA** **Find the unknown value.**

SEE EXAMPLES
1 AND 2
on pp. 32–33
for Exs. 8–13

8. square: $A = 36$ yd$^2$, $s = $ _?_

9. square: $P = 24$ m, $s = $ _?_

10. square: $A = 144$ ft$^2$, $s = $ _?_

11. square: $A = $ _?_ , $s = 18$ in.

12. rectangle: $A = $ _?_ , $l = 17$ m, $w = 9$ m

13. rectangle: $A = 88$ in.$^2$, $l = $ _?_ , $w = 8$ in.

**USING FORMULAS** **Use the distance formula to find the unknown value.**

SEE EXAMPLES
3 AND 4
on pp. 33–34
for Exs. 14–19

14. $d = 36$ km, $r = $ _?_ , $t = 4$ h

15. $d = $ _?_ , $r = 0.5$ mi/min, $t = 10$ min

16. $d = $ _?_ , $r = 7$ mi/h, $t = 1.5$ h

17. $d = 40$ ft, $r = 5$ ft/sec, $t = $ _?_

18. $d = 130$ mi, $r = 65$ mi/h, $t = $ _?_

19. $d = 75$ ft, $r = $ _?_ , $t = 5$ sec

20. ◆ **TAKS REASONING** Which pair of dimensions for a rectangle does *not* yield a perimeter of 16 feet?

Ⓐ 1 ft by 7 ft   Ⓑ 2 ft by 8 ft   Ⓒ 3 ft by 5 ft   Ⓓ 4 ft by 4 ft

**COMPOSITE FIGURES** **Find the perimeter and area of the figure.**

21.

6 in.
12 in.
9 in.
12 in.

22.

10 cm
10 cm
10 cm
3 cm   4 cm   3 cm

**Animated Math** at classzone.com

23. ◆ **TAKS REASONING** Give the dimensions of 6 rectangles, 3 with a perimeter of 24 centimeters and 3 with an area of 24 square centimeters.

24. **FINDING SIDE LENGTHS** A rectangle has an area of 60 square inches and a perimeter of 38 inches. Find the length and width of the rectangle.

25. **CHALLENGE** A rectangular box has a length of 10 centimeters, a width of 6 centimeters, and a height of 5 centimeters. Find the area of all six sides.

## PROBLEM SOLVING

SEE EXAMPLE 4
on p. 34
for Ex. 26

26. **TIGER BEETLES** A tiger beetle runs 210 centimeters in 4 seconds. How fast is the beetle running?

27. **MEASUREMENT** To convert from degrees Celsius $C$ to degrees Fahrenheit $F$, you can use the formula $F = \frac{9}{5}C + 32$. Convert 20°C to degrees Fahrenheit.

28. **WRITING** *Describe* how to find the width of a rectangle when you know its area and length.

**29. ESTIMATION** The driving distance between Dallas and Houston is 240 miles. Suppose a car travels at an average rate of 55 miles per hour. Estimate the time it takes to travel from Houston to Dallas.

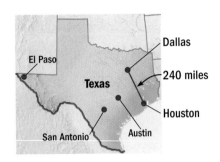

**30. MEASUREMENT** Write a formula for converting meters to centimeters in words and in symbols.

**31. PARACHUTING** A parachutist falls for 2 minutes at a speed of 13 feet per second. How far does the parachutist fall during this time?

**32. TAKS REASONING** You drive 50 miles per hour for 1 hour 30 minutes. Which expression can be used to find how many miles you travel?

   **A** $50 \times 130$    **B** $50 \times 90$    **C** $50 \times 1.5$    **D** $50 \div 90$

**33. TAKS REASONING** A train travels from New York to Philadelphia to Washington, D.C., a total of 226 miles. It travels 1 hour 13 minutes, makes one stop, and continues for 1 hour 44 minutes. Find the average speed of the train to the nearest mile per hour. *Explain* how you found your answer.

**34. TAKS REASONING** The table shows information about two rectangular swimming pools. Copy and complete the table. *Compare* the dimensions of the two pools. What is the relationship between their areas? Their perimeters?

| | Length | Width | Area | Perimeter |
|---|---|---|---|---|
| **Pool A** | 60 ft | 22 ft | ? | ? |
| **Pool B** | ? | 44 ft | 5280 ft² | ? |

**35. CHALLENGE** Your rectangular yard is twice as long as it is wide. You fenced in the yard using 240 feet of fencing. You want to fertilize your yard. Each bag of fertilizer covers 2000 square feet. How many bags should you buy? *Justify* your answer.

---

### MIXED REVIEW FOR TAKS    TAKS PRACTICE at classzone.com

REVIEW
Lesson 1.5;
TAKS Workbook

**36. TAKS PRACTICE** Tim, Ed, and Sam compete in a race. Ed crossed the finish line 5 seconds after Tim. Sam's time was 2 seconds shorter than Ed's time. Sam completed the race in 50 seconds. How long did it take Tim to finish the race? *TAKS Obj. 6*

   **A** 43 sec    **B** 47 sec    **C** 52 sec    **D** 57 sec

REVIEW
Problem Solving
Handbook,
p. 790;
TAKS Workbook

**37. TAKS PRACTICE** In an election for class president, Erin had more votes than Lynn, Maria had more votes than Ben, and Lynn had fewer votes than Ben. Which of the following is definitely true? *TAKS Obj. 6*

   **F** Maria won.    **G** Erin won.    **H** Lynn came in last.    **J** Ben was second.

**EXTRA PRACTICE** for Lesson 1.6, p. 801

**ONLINE QUIZ** at classzone.com

# 1.7 A Problem Solving Plan

TEKS *8.14.B, 8.14.C*

| **Before** | You used problem solving strategies to solve problems. |
|---|---|
| **Now** | You'll use a problem solving plan to solve problems. |
| **Why?** | So you can predict future events, as in Ex. 30. |

**KEY VOCABULARY**
• unit analysis,
  *p. 39*

**Triathlon**  You and a friend decide to compete in a triathlon. You both swim 200 meters, bike 10 kilometers, and then run 2 kilometers.

The table shows your speeds for swimming in meters per minute, and biking in kilometers per minute. Who has the better total time after these two stages?

| | Swimming (m/min) | Biking (km/min) |
|---|---|---|
| **You** | 76.9 | 0.43 |
| **Friend** | 82.6 | 0.41 |

### EXAMPLE 1  Understanding and Planning

To solve the triathlon problem, you need to make sure you understand the problem. Then make a plan for solving the problem.

**READ AND UNDERSTAND**

**What do you know?**

The table displays your speeds for each stage.

You both swim 200 meters and bike 10 kilometers.

**What do you want to find out?**

Who has the better total time for swimming and biking?

**MAKE A PLAN**

**How can you relate what you know to what you want to find out?**

Find each of your swimming and biking times. You can organize this information in a table.

Find each of your total times and then compare these times.

You will solve the problem in Example 2.

---

✓ **GUIDED PRACTICE**  for Example 1

**1.** Which formula would you use to find swimming and running times? *Explain* your reasoning.

**A.** $distance = rate \cdot time$   **B.** $time = \dfrac{distance}{rate}$   **C.** $rate = \dfrac{distance}{time}$

**EXAMPLE 2** Solving and Looking Back

Carry out the plan from Example 1. Check the answer.

**SOLVE THE PROBLEM**

Use the formula $time = \frac{distance}{rate}$.

| | Swimming | Biking |
|---|---|---|
| **You** | $t = \frac{d}{r}$ $= \frac{200}{76.9}$ $\approx 2.60$ min | $t = \frac{d}{r}$ $= \frac{10}{0.43}$ $\approx 23.26$ min |
| **Friend** | $t = \frac{d}{r}$ $= \frac{200}{82.6}$ $\approx 2.42$ min | $t = \frac{d}{r}$ $= \frac{10}{0.41}$ $\approx 24.39$ min |

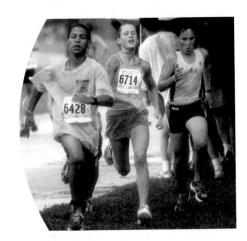

**READING**

The symbol $\approx$ means *is approximately equal to.*

Add to find the total time.

**You**     $2.60 + 23.26 = 25.86$ min

**Friend**     $2.42 + 24.39 = 26.81$ min

▶ **Answer** You have the better total time after the two stages.

*Animated* **Math**
at classzone.com

**LOOK BACK**

**Does your answer make sense?**

You swim slower than your friend, so your swimming time should be greater. You bike faster than your friend, so your biking time should be less. So the calculations are reasonable.

---

 **GUIDED PRACTICE**     **for Example 2**

2. **What If?** Suppose in Example 2 that your friend biked at a rate of 0.44 km/min. Who had the better total time after two stages?

---

**KEY CONCEPT**                                        *For Your Notebook*

**A Problem Solving Plan**

1. **Read and Understand** Read the problem carefully. Identify the question and any important information.

2. **Make a Plan** Decide on a problem solving strategy.

3. **Solve the Problem** Use the strategy to answer the question.

4. **Look Back** Check that your answer is reasonable.

---

**Unit Analysis**  You can use **unit analysis** to evaluate expressions with units of measure and to check that your answer uses the correct units.

For example, when you find the product of rate (miles per hour) and time (hours), the units for distance will be in miles: $\dfrac{\text{miles}}{\cancel{\text{hour}}} \cdot \cancel{\text{hour}} = \text{miles}$.

❖ ◆ **EXAMPLE 3**  **Using a Problem Solving Plan**

**City Blocks**  In parts of New York City, the blocks between avenues are called *long blocks*. There are 4 long blocks per mile. Blocks between streets are called *short blocks*. There are 20 short blocks per mile. You walk 40 short blocks and 6 long blocks. How many miles do you walk?

**SOLUTION**

*REVIEW PROBLEM
SOLVING STRATEGIES*
Need help with problem solving strategies? See pp. 786–795.

**Read and Understand**  You walk 40 short blocks and 6 long blocks. There are 20 short blocks per mile and 4 long blocks per mile. You are asked to find how many miles you walk.

**Make a Plan**  Convert short blocks to miles and long blocks to miles using unit analysis. Then add to find the total miles.

**Solve the Problem**  Because 20 short blocks equal one mile, you can multiply the number of short blocks by $\dfrac{1\text{ mile}}{20\text{ short blocks}}$ to convert to miles.

$$40 \ \cancel{\text{short blocks}} \times \frac{1\text{ mile}}{20 \ \cancel{\text{short blocks}}} = 2 \text{ miles}$$

You can convert long blocks to miles by multiplying by $\dfrac{1\text{ mile}}{4\text{ long blocks}}$.

$$6 \ \cancel{\text{long blocks}} \times \frac{1\text{ mile}}{4 \ \cancel{\text{long blocks}}} = 1.5 \text{ miles}$$

▶ **Answer**  You walk a total of $2 + 1.5 = 3.5$ miles.

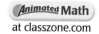
at classzone.com

**Look Back**  Check your answer by drawing a diagram.

From the diagram you can see that 40 short blocks are 2 miles and 6 long blocks are 1.5 miles, which totals 3.5 miles. So, your answer checks.

✓ **GUIDED PRACTICE**   **for Example 3**

3. **What If?**  In Example 3, how many miles do you walk if you walk 50 short blocks and 12 long blocks?

# 1.7 EXERCISES

HOMEWORK KEY

↖ = **TAKS Practice and Reasoning**
Exs. 8, 17, 18, 21, 34, and 35

○ = **HINTS** AND **HOMEWORK HELP**
for Exs. 3, 5, 7, 17, 19 at classzone.com

## SKILL PRACTICE

*SEE EXAMPLE 1*
on p. 37
for Exs. 3–4

1. **VOCABULARY**  List the four steps of the problem solving plan.

2. **VOCABULARY**  Copy and complete: You can use __?__ to evaluate expressions with units of measure and to check for the correct units.

3. **READ AND UNDERSTAND**  A customer bought a lunch that cost $3.99 and a drink that cost $.99. The customer paid with a $10 bill. You are the cashier. Identify what you know and what you need to find out.

4. **MAKE A TABLE**  You have a handful of quarters, nickels, and dimes that totals 75 cents. Make a table listing all possible combinations.

*SEE EXAMPLE 2*
on p. 38
for Exs. 5–6

5. **LOOK BACK**  The cost of a ticket to a baseball game is $10. The cost of a hot dog is $2. Matt goes to the game and has 3 hot dogs. One of your friends says that Matt spent $16. *Explain* how to check the answer.

6. **ERROR ANALYSIS**  Daniel can take 96 photos on a 5 day trip. He takes 45 photos in 2 days. He wants to take an equal number of photos each of the last 3 days. *Describe* and correct the error in the solution.

$$\times \quad \frac{96}{3} = 32$$

Daniel can take 32 pictures each day.

*SEE EXAMPLE 3*
on p. 39
for Ex. 7

7. **USING A PLAN**  You are selling bags of microwavable popcorn as a fundraiser. Each bag costs $2. A neighbor wants to buy 5 bags. Use the verbal model to find out how much money the neighbor will give you.

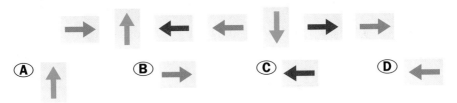

| Dollars Raised | = | dollars/bag | × | Number of bags |

8. ↖ **TAKS REASONING**  Which represents the 15th arrow in the pattern?

→ ↑ ← ← ↓ → →

Ⓐ ↑    Ⓑ →    Ⓒ ←    Ⓓ ←

9. **IDENTIFYING UNNECESSARY INFORMATION**  You buy 3 packs of pens for $12. Each pack of pens contains 12 pens. How much does each pack of pens cost? Identify the unnecessary information in this problem.

⑭ **LOOK FOR A PATTERN**  Complete the pattern.

10. $7x^2, 15x^2, 23x^2,$ __?__, __?__

11. $81x, 78x^2, 75x^3, 72x^4,$ __?__, __?__

**CHALLENGE**  What are the next three numbers? Describe the rule.

12. 11, 7, 14, 10, 20, 16, . . .  13.  7, 20, 46, 98, 202, 410, . . .  14.  1.5, 1.5, 3, 4.5, 7.5, 12, . . .

**15. GUIDED PROBLEM SOLVING** A monorail ride at an amusement park has 5 cars in each train, and each car can hold 4 passengers. In one hour, 900 people can ride the monorail. How many trains run in one hour?

  **a.** Write a verbal model of the problem.

  **b.** Use the model to find the number of trains that run in one hour.

  **c.** Check your answer.

**16. MUSIC** You practice piano for 50 minutes each weekday and for 40 minutes on each weekend day. How many hours per week do you practice?

**17. TAKS REASONING** You pay $15 a ticket for 4 tickets and a service charge of $2 for every ticket after the second one. You are charged $64 for this order. *Describe* a way to check that this is the correct price.

*SEE EXAMPLE 3*
on p. 39
for Exs. 18–23

**18. TAKS REASONING** You are trying to earn 4000 points in a computer game. In the first round you get 1540 points. In the next round you get 780 points. How many more points do you need?

  **(A)** 760 **(B)** 1680 **(C)** 1760 **(D)** 2680

**19. BICYCLE RACE** A Tour de France bicycle race covered 3462 kilometers in 21 days. Riders traveled 3152 kilometers during the first 19 racing days and 160 kilometers the next day. How long was the ride on the last day?

**20. SALES** During a 4 week period, a salesperson at a photography studio wants to sell photography packages worth a total of $16,000. What does the sales amount need to be in week 4 to reach the $16,000 goal?

| Week | 1 | 2 | 3 | 4 |
|------|------|------|------|------|
| Sales | $1240 | $3720 | $5980 | ? |

**21. TAKS REASONING** You are making lasagna for 30 people at a shelter. You need 8 ounces of mozzarella cheese to make enough for 10 people. You have 12 ounces. How many more ounces do you need?

  **(A)** 0 **(B)** 4 **(C)** 12 **(D)** 24

**22. WRITING** Is there enough information to answer the question? *Explain* how to solve the problem, or tell what information is needed.

> *Amanda has sold magazine subscriptions worth $330 for a school fundraiser. If she reaches a total of $500, she wins a gift certificate. How many more subscriptions does she need to sell to reach $500?*

**23. HOMEWORK** You need to read 60 pages for English and 20 pages for History by Friday. You have read 16 pages on Monday. How much do you need to read each day to complete the assignment on time?

**24. SAVING** Fran is saving for a printer that costs $210. Her mom will pay $120. Fran makes $6 an hour baby-sitting. Use the problem solving plan to find how many hours she needs to baby-sit to earn enough to buy the printer.

**25. GUESS, CHECK, AND REVISE** You know you have 15 coins in your pocket, 5 of them are nickels, and the rest are dimes and quarters. The total amount is $2.30. How many dimes do you have? How many quarters?

**26. VENN DIAGRAMS** There are 48 students on the track team, 16 on the wrestling team, and 117 on neither team. There are 171 students total. How many students are on both teams? Solve using a Venn Diagram.

**27. MAKE A TABLE** Your school talent show allows people to sign up for 3 or 5 minute acts. There is one minute between acts. The talent show has 15 acts and lasts for 79 minutes. How many 3 minute acts are there?

**28. GARDEN** You have 28 yards of fencing and want to construct a rectangular garden with the largest possible area with whole number dimensions. Find the side lengths of the largest garden. What is its area?

**29. NUMBER SENSE** The product of two numbers is 104. Their difference is 5. Find the two numbers.

**30. BASKETBALL** The table shows the numbers of people who attended Women's National Basketball Association (WNBA) games from 2000 through 2004. *Describe* a strategy to predict the attendance for WNBA games in 2005. Use your strategy to predict the 2005 attendance.

| Year | 2000 | 2001 | 2002 | 2003 | 2004 |
|------|------|------|------|------|------|
| Attendance | 2,322,429 | 2,323,161 | 2,391,972 | 2,100,630 | 1,898,077 |

**31. USE A DIAGRAM** John lives 1.2 miles west of the library and his school is 0.6 miles east of the library on the same road. The distance between the school and the post office is twice the distance between John's home and school. How far is John's home from the post office using the diagram below? Suppose the post office is west of John's home. How far from John's home would the post office be then?

**32. SOLVE A SIMPLER PROBLEM** At summer camp, 12 campers in a group each shake hands with every other camper once as they introduce themselves. How many handshakes occur?

**33. CHALLENGE** Bill's house is third in a row of 12 houses. There are 5 houses between Chris's house and Audrey's house, and 2 between Chris's house and Bill's house. How many houses are between Audrey's house and the first house? *Explain* how you found your answer.

**PROBLEM SOLVING**

Need help with problem solving strategies? See p. 793.

= TAKS Practice and Reasoning     = **HINTS AND HOMEWORK HELP** *at classzone.com*

*REVIEW*
Lesson 1.6;
TAKS Workbook

**34.** 🔷 **TAKS PRACTICE** A rectangular print of a painting by Degas has an area of 864 square inches. The width of the print is 24 inches. How can you find the print's length? *TAKS Obj. 6*

**(A)** Multiply 24 by itself

**(B)** Subtract 24 from 864

**(C)** Multiply 864 by 24

**(D)** Divide 864 by 24

*REVIEW*
Skills Review
Handbook,
p.772;
TAKS Workbook

**35.** 🔷 **TAKS PRACTICE** Adela buys a dozen pieces of candy to share with her friends. She gives each person, including herself, the same number of candy pieces. What additional information is needed to find how many pieces of candy each friend receives? *TAKS Obj. 6*

**(F)** Total cost of the candy

**(G)** Number of friends

**(H)** Number of candy pieces bought

**(J)** Cost of each piece of candy

---

**QUIZ** *for Lessons 1.5–1.7*

**Solve the equation using mental math.** *(p. 26)*

**1.** $h + 12 = 21$

**2.** $22 - y = 8$

**3.** $54 = 6x$

**4.** $\dfrac{108}{r} = 9$

**5.** **VIDEO GAMES** You have $24 to spend on video game rentals. Each rental costs $3. How many video games can you rent? *(p. 26)*

**6.** **GEOMETRY** Find the perimeter and area of a rectangle 14 feet by 11 feet. *(p. 32)*

**7.** **DRIVING** On the highway you drive at a speed of 55 miles per hour for 3 hours. How far do you drive? *(p. 32)*

**8.** **EXERCISE** You plan to exercise 200 minutes over 5 days. The first four days you exercise 45 minutes, 30 minutes, 20 minutes, and 1 hour. Use a problem solving plan to find the number of minutes you need to exercise on the fifth day to meet your goal. *(p. 37)*

---

**Brain Game**

### What's Happening?

Scott, John, Annie, and Rebecca are each doing a different activity (debate, art club, student council, or tutoring). Who is doing what?

- Annie is not going to student council or to art club.
- Rebecca and Scott are not members of the student council.
- Annie and Rebecca do not tutor.

---

## Lessons 1.5–1.7

**MULTIPLE CHOICE**

1. **FOOTWEAR** A store has 10 pairs of black shoes and three times as many pairs of brown shoes as black. There are 10 more pairs of sandals than black shoes. What is the total number of pairs of sandals and shoes together? *TEKS 8.14.C*

   (A) 20 pairs        (B) 30 pairs

   (C) 50 pairs        (D) 60 pairs

2. **TRIATHLONS** The table shows the times, rounded to the nearest minute, that it took Renee and Beth to complete the running and swimming parts of a triathlon. Which conclusion is true? *TEKS 8.5.A*

   |  | Run 10 kilometers | Swim 1000 meters |
   |---|---|---|
   | **Renee** | 49 min | 22 min |
   | **Beth** | 46 min | 23 min |

   (F) Beth completed the two parts of the triathlon about 1 minute before Renee.

   (G) Beth ran twice as far as she swam.

   (H) Renee swam approximately 2 times as fast as she ran.

   (J) On average, Renee ran 0.2 kilometer per minute.

3. **ICE CREAM** An ice cream shop offers week-long specials when you purchase a large ice cream cake. They offer a free small ice cream cake every fifth week, a free pint of ice cream every sixth week, and a free ice cream cone every third week. How many times in one year will they offer all three specials in the same week if they offer all three specials on the first week of the year? *TEKS 8.14.B*

   (A) 1        (B) 2

   (C) 3        (D) 4

4. **AREA** The area of the rectangle below is 120 square centimeters. Which equation can you use to find the width, *w*? *TEKS 8.4.A*

   $A = 120 \text{ cm}^2$    *w*

   15 cm

   (F) $120 = 15w$

   (G) $120 = 15 + w$

   (H) $15 = 120w$

   (J) $120 = 2(15) + 2w$

**GRIDDED ANSWER** ⊘①②●④⑤⑥⑦⑧⑨

5. **GRAVEL** One ton of gravel will fill 16 cubic feet of space. Marcus wants to cover a driveway that is 12 feet wide and 60 feet long with 4 inches of gravel. The formula for volume is $V = lwh$. How many tons of gravel should he order? *TEKS 8.5.A*

6. **MODELS** A model of a building is given below. What is the area, in square feet, of the model? *TEKS 8.7.B*

   3 ft

   10 ft

   3 ft  8 ft

   4 ft        4 ft

## REVIEW KEY VOCABULARY

- bar graph, *p. 3*
- data, *p. 3*
- frequency table, histogram, *p. 4*
- numerical expression, *p. 8*
- evaluate, *p. 8*

- order of operations, *p. 8*
- verbal model, *p. 9*
- variable, variable expression, *p. 13*
- power, exponent, base, *p. 19*

- equation, solution, *p. 26*
- solving an equation, *p. 26*
- formula, *p. 32*
- perimeter, area, *p. 32*
- unit analysis, *p. 39*

### VOCABULARY EXERCISES

1. You can graph data organized in a frequency table using a(n) __?__.

2. __?__ is the amount of surface covered by a figure.

3. To evaluate an expression that has more than one operation, use the __?__.

4. A power has an exponent and a(n) __?__.

## REVIEW EXAMPLES AND EXERCISES

### 1.1 Interpreting Graphs

*pp. 3–7*

**EXAMPLE**

The bar graph displays the number of times each country has won the World Cup in soccer. How many more times has Italy won than England?

**SOLUTION**

Italy has won the World Cup 3 times and England once. Italy has won 2 more times.

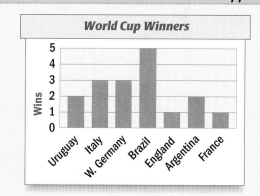

**World Cup Winners**

### EXERCISES

**Volunteering** Use the table that shows the number of volunteers at a local animal shelter.

*SEE EXAMPLE 2*
on p. 4
for Exs. 5–6

5. Which age group has the most volunteers? Which age group has the fewest volunteers?

6. Can you determine the number of volunteers who are teenagers? *Explain.*

| Age Group | Volunteers |
|-----------|------------|
| 15–24 | 24 |
| 25–34 | 30 |
| 35–44 | 31 |
| 45–54 | 30 |
| 55–64 | 27 |
| 65+ | 23 |

## 1.2 Order of Operations

pp. 8–11

### EXAMPLE

**Evaluate the expression $5 + 12 \cdot 5 \div 4$.**

$$5 + 12 \cdot 5 \div 4 = 5 + 60 \div 4 \qquad \text{Multiply 12 by 5.}$$
$$= 5 + 15 \qquad \text{Divide 60 by 4.}$$
$$= 20 \qquad \text{Add 5 and 15.}$$

### EXERCISES

**Evaluate the expression.**

**SEE EXAMPLES**
**1, 2, AND 3**
on pp. 8–9
for Exs. 7–10

**7.** $16 + 5 \times 3 + 8$

**8.** $40 \div [(14 + 6) \cdot 2]$

**9.** $10 + \dfrac{60}{31 - 26}$

**10. Electricians** An electrician charges \$50 to come to your house plus \$40 per hour of work. To find how much the electrician charges for 2 hours of work, evaluate the expression $50 + 40 \cdot 2$.

## 1.3 Variables and Expressions

pp. 13–18

### EXAMPLE

**Evaluate the expression when $x = 6$ and $y = 5$.**

$$4x - 3y = 4(6) - 3(5) \qquad \text{Substitute 6 for } x \text{ and 5 for } y.$$
$$= 24 - 15 \qquad \text{Multiply.}$$
$$= 9 \qquad \text{Subtract.}$$

### EXERCISES

**Evaluate the expression when $x = 4$ and $y = 9$.**

**SEE EXAMPLES**
**1, 2, AND 3**
on p. 14
for Exs. 11–21

**11.** $\dfrac{xy}{3x}$

**12.** $\dfrac{y + 19}{x + 3}$

**13.** $5y - 6x$

**14.** $3xy - xy$

**15.** $\dfrac{x + y}{y - x}$

**16.** $\dfrac{x + y}{2xy}$

**17.** $4x + 6y$

**18.** $5xy + \dfrac{9x}{y}$

**Write the phrase as a variable expression using $n$.**

**19.** the sum of a number and 12

**20.** one fifth of a number

**21. Clothes** You are saving money to buy two sweaters. Each one costs \$28.50. You have saved \$20. To find out how much more money you need to save, translate *20 less than the product of 2 and 28.5* into an expression and then evaluate.

## 1.4 Powers and Exponents

*pp. 19–24*

### EXAMPLE

Evaluate the expression.

$$(5 - 2)^2 + 7 - 2^2 = 3^2 + 7 - 2^2 \quad \text{Evaluate inside grouping symbols.}$$

$$= 9 + 7 - 4 \quad \text{Evaluate powers.}$$

$$= 12 \quad \text{Add and subtract from left to right.}$$

### EXERCISES

Evaluate the power.

SEE EXAMPLES
2 AND 4
on pp. 19–20
for Exs. 22–29

**22.** $15^2$     **23.** $4^5$     **24.** $10^4$     **25.** $9^4$

Evaluate the expression.

**26.** $(5 + 4)^2 \div 3$     **27.** $5 \cdot (6 - 3)^5 + 45$     **28.** $[10 + (4 \times 2)^3] \div 2$

**29. Icicles** An icicle falls from the roof of a building. It hits the ground in 3 seconds. Use the expression $16t^2$ to find the distance in feet that the icicle falls in $t$ seconds to find the height of the building.

## 1.5 Equations and Solutions

*pp. 26–30*

### EXAMPLE

Solve the equation $18 - n = 13$ using mental math.

To solve a simple equation using mental math, you can think of the equation as a question.

18 minus **what number** equals 13?     $18 - 5 = 13$, so $n = 5$.

### EXERCISES

Solve the equation using mental math.

SEE EXAMPLES
1, 2, AND 3
on pp. 26–27
for Exs. 30–36

**30.** $7b = 56$     **31.** $\dfrac{84}{x} = 12$     **32.** $98 - t = 35$

Tell whether the value of the variable is a solution of the equation.

**33.** $t + 11 = 30; t = 29$     **34.** $48 \div k = 12; k = 4$     **35.** $8m = 68, m = 8$

**36. River Speed** A log travels 50 feet down a river in 20 seconds. After 15 seconds it has traveled 40 feet. How many more feet will it travel in the remaining 5 seconds?

## 1.6 Variables in Familiar Formulas

*pp. 32–36*

**EXAMPLE**

**Find the length and perimeter of the rectangle. Its area is 54 square feet.**

6 ft

9 ft

For area use the formula $A = lw$.

| | |
|---|---|
| $A = lw$ | Write formula. |
| $54 = l(6)$ | Substitute. |
| $9 = l$ | Use mental math. |

For perimeter use the formula $P = 2l + 2w$.

| | |
|---|---|
| $P = 2l + 2w$ | Write formula. |
| $= 2(9) + 2(6)$ | Substitute. |
| $= 30$ | Multiply, then add. |

▶ **Answer** The length is 9 feet and the perimeter is 30 feet.

### EXERCISES

**Find the unknown value for the rectangle or square.**

*SEE EXAMPLES 1 AND 3*
on pp. 32–33
for Exs. 37–39

**37.** rectangle: $P = 56$ cm, $l = 12$ cm, $w = \underline{\ ?\ }$

**38.** square: $A = 121$ ft$^2$, $s = \underline{\ ?\ }$

**39. Cars** A car travels at an average rate of 50 miles per hour for 3 hours. How far does it travel?

## 1.7 A Problem Solving Plan

*pp. 37–42*

**EXAMPLE**

You need 3 pitcherfuls to fill a 5-gallon aquarium with a pitcher. How many trips will you need to fill a 55-gallon aquarium with the same pitcher?

**Read and Understand and Make a Plan** Find how many times as great the capacity of the larger tank is than the smaller tank. Compare using division. Then multiply that number by 3, because it takes 3 pitcherfuls to make 5 gallons.

**Solve the Problem** $\dfrac{55 \text{ gal}}{5 \text{ gal}} \cdot 3 \text{ trips} = 11 \cdot 3 \text{ trips}$

$= 33 \text{ trips}$

▶ **Answer** You need 33 pitcherfuls to fill the larger aquarium.

### EXERCISES

*SEE EXAMPLE 3*
on p. 39
for Ex. 40

**40. Sugar** You like 2 teaspoons of sugar in an 8-ounce glass of iced tea. How much sugar should you add to a 36-ounce thermos of iced tea?

**Evaluate the expression.**

1. $20 + 12 \div 4$

2. $6 \times 5 - 20 \div 2$

3. $(3 + 7) \div 5 + 10$

4. $(2 + 3)^4 \div 5$

5. $10^2 - 3^4 + 22$

6. $(11 - 5)^4 - 300 \div 12$

**Solve the equation using mental math.**

7. $17 - t = 5$

8. $9n = 72$

9. $49 \div b = 7$

10. $21 + a = 27$

**Tell whether the value of the variable is a solution of the equation.**

11. $z + 2 = 15; z = 13$

12. $65 \div y = 16; y = 4$

13. $11x = 45; x = 4$

**XY** **ALGEBRA** **Find the unknown value for the variable.**

14. square: $A = 64 \text{ yd}^2$, $s = \underline{\phantom{?}}$

15. square: $P = 44 \text{ m}$, $s = \underline{\phantom{?}}$

16. rectangle: $A = \underline{\phantom{?}}$, $l = 12 \text{ m}$, $w = 9 \text{ m}$

17. rectangle: $A = 128 \text{ in.}^2$, $l = \underline{\phantom{?}}$, $w = 8 \text{ in.}$

**SPORTS** **In a survey, 3000 people in Japan were asked about their participation in ten sports. The results for four sports are in the table.**

18. Make a bar graph of the data.

19. Is it possible to make a histogram of the data? *Explain.*

20. **PLUMBING** A plumber charges a flat rate of $25 plus an additional $55 for each hour of work. To find how much money the plumber makes in 5 hours at one location, evaluate the expression $25 + 55 \cdot 5$.

| Sport | Participants |
|---|---|
| Gymnastics | 1002 |
| Bowling | 996 |
| Jogging | 807 |
| Swimming | 717 |

21. **FRUIT** You are buying 3 apples and 4 oranges for a fruit salad. The cost of one apple is $x$ dollars. The cost of one orange is $y$ dollars. Write a variable expression to represent the cost of 3 apples and 4 oranges. If one apple costs $.75 and one orange costs $.50, what is the total cost?

22. **HORSES** A horse travels at a rate of 30 feet per second. How far does the horse travel in 4 seconds?

23. **COURT AREA** The lengths and widths of three types of courts are listed in the table. Find the area of each court. Which court has the largest area? Which court has the smallest area?

| Court | Length | Width |
|---|---|---|
| Squash | 32 feet | 21 feet |
| Tennis | 78 feet | 27 feet |
| Racquetball | 40 feet | 20 feet |

24. **PARK** A rectangular park that is 90 feet long and 60 feet wide needs to be planted with sod. A roll of sod covers 1 square yard. Use a problem solving plan to find how many rolls of sod are needed to cover the park.

TEXAS TAKS Objs. 2, 5
TEKS 8.5.A,
8.12.C

## REVIEWING DATA DISPLAY PROBLEMS

There are many different ways to display data, such as bar graphs, histograms, circle graphs, and tables. It is important to be careful to interpret these displays correctly.

**EXAMPLE**

**Dance School** The table shows the number of students studying certain styles of dance at a local studio. Which circle graph best represents the data?

| Ballet | Ballroom | Hip-hop | Quick Step | Salsa |
|--------|----------|---------|------------|-------|
| 20 | 20 | 30 | 20 | 30 |

A.

B.

C.

D.

## Solution

A circle graph represents data as parts of a whole.

**STEP 1** **Find** the total number of dance students by adding the number of students studying each style: $20 + 20 + 30 + 20 + 30 = 120$. There are 120 dance students.

**STEP 2** **Compare** the number of students studying each style of dance to the total.

- Ballet, ballroom dance, and quick step each have 20 students out of 120 total students. So $\frac{1}{6}$ of all students study ballet, $\frac{1}{6}$ study ballroom dance, and $\frac{1}{6}$ study quick step.

- Hip-hop and salsa each have 30 dance students out of 120 total students. So $\frac{1}{4}$ of the students study hip-hop and $\frac{1}{4}$ study salsa.

▶ **Answer** The circle graph that shows the correct fractions of the whole for each category is B.

# DATA DISPLAY PROBLEMS ON TAKS

Below are examples of problems in multiple choice format. Try solving the problems before looking at the solutions. (Cover the solutions with a piece of paper.) Then check your solutions against the ones given.

1. Julie recorded her heart rate and the heart rates of her pets. The results are shown in the bar graph below. Which statement is NOT supported by the bar graph?

**A** The cat has the highest heart rate.

**B** Julie's heart beats about 90 times each minute.

**C** The dog has the lowest heart rate.

**D** The cat's heart rate is three times as fast as the dog's heart rate.

**Solution**

The bar representing the cat's heart rate appears three times higher than the bar representing the dog's heart rate. However, notice that the vertical scale starts at 60.

According to the graph, the cat's heart beats 160 times each minute, and the dog's heart beats 80 times each minute.

Compare heart rates:

$$\frac{160}{80} = 2$$

The cat's heart rate is twice as fast, *not* three times as fast, as the dog's heart rate.

So, the correct answer is D.

2. Alex is driving his car at a constant rate. The line graph shows the distances Alex traveled in different amounts of time. How long will it take Alex to travel 225 miles?

**F** 1 hour

**G** 5 hours

**H** 7 hours

**J** 9 hours

**Solution**

According to the line graph, Alex travels 45 miles in one hour, 90 miles in two hours, and so forth. So, he travels at a constant rate of 45 miles per hour.

Use the distance formula to solve the problem.

$$t = \frac{d}{r} = \frac{225}{45} = 5$$

It will take Alex 5 hours to travel 225 miles.

So, the correct answer is G.

## PRACTICE FOR TAKS OBJECTIVES 2 AND 5

**1.** A store manager is trying to determine the most common age group that shops between 10 A.M. and 2 P.M. The ages of all the customers who entered the store during that time period are:

15, 21, 65, 40, 46, 48, 36, 18, 60, 58, 28, 50, 49, 12, 30, 42, 55

Which intervals would be the best to use when creating a histogram of the data?

**A** 0–35, 36–70

**B** 0–20, 21–40, 41–60

**C** 0–18, 19–30, 31–50, 51–68

**D** 0–15, 16–30, 31–45, 46–60, 61–75

**2.** Use the data from Exercise 1. People in what age group entered the store the most between 10 A.M. to 2 P.M.?

**F** Twenties

**G** Thirties

**H** Forties

**J** Fifties

**3.** Some animals can sprint at fast rates of speed for short periods of time. The table below shows the sprinting speeds, in feet per second, for a few animals.

| Animal | Sprinting speed |
|---|---|
| Grizzly Bear | 44 ft per sec |
| Hyena | 59 ft per sec |
| Antelope | 88 ft per sec |
| Elephant | 37 ft per sec |

When sprinting, how far can a grizzly bear travel in 5.5 seconds?

**A** 8 ft

**B** 24.2 ft

**C** 220 ft

**D** 242 ft

**4.** Which animal shown in Exercise 3 can travel 143 feet in 3.25 seconds?

**F** Grizzly bear

**G** Hyena

**H** Antelope

**J** Elephant

**5.** The bar graph shows the total number of players in two different recreational leagues for the years 2002 to 2005. If the trend shown in the graph continues, how many more football players than baseball players will there be in 2006?

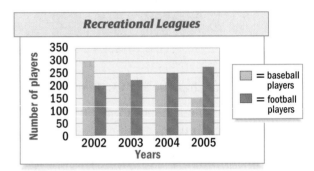

**A** 125

**B** 150

**C** 175

**D** 200

## MIXED TAKS PRACTICE

**6.** Four roommates split the cost of electricity, gas, and rent evenly. One month, they spent $110 on gas and $880 for rent. They spent $75.60 less on electricity than on gas that month. How much should each roommate pay? *TAKS Obj. 1*

**F** $256.10

**G** $266.40

**H** $293.90

**J** $448.60

## MIXED TAKS PRACTICE

**7.** Chris, Tom, and Erin are in a chess club. Chris won twice as many chess matches as Erin. Tom won $1\frac{1}{6}$ as many matches as Chris. Erin won 12 matches. How many matches did Tom win? *TAKS Obj. 6*

  **A** 14

  **B** 24

  **C** 28

  **D** 30

**8.** The length of a rectangle is 3 times longer than its width. The perimeter of the rectangle is 40 feet. What are the dimensions of the rectangle? *TAKS Obj. 6*

  **F** 3 ft by 17 ft

  **G** 4 ft by 10 ft

  **H** 5 ft by 15 ft

  **J** 10 ft by 30 ft

**9.** What effect would doubling the dimensions have on the perimeter of the rectangle shown below? *TAKS Obj. 4*

4 cm

14 cm

  **A** The perimeter would increase by a factor of 2.

  **B** The perimeter would increase by a factor of 4.

  **C** The perimeter would increase by a factor of 18.

  **D** The perimeter would increase by a factor of 36.

**10.** Elsa is sketching a picture on the rectangular mat shown below.

14 in.

$A = 280$ in.$^2$

What is the length of the mat? *TAKS Obj. 3*

  **F** 20 in.

  **G** 28 in.

  **H** 40 in.

  **J** 126 in.

**11.** The director of a charity group plans to buy 2 wristbands per volunteer for the next fundraiser. If 50 people volunteer for the next fundraiser and the director can buy wristbands in bags of 6, what other information is needed to find the cost of all of the wristbands? *TAKS Obj. 6*

  **A** The number of fundraisers held in one year.

  **B** The total amount of money raised for the fundraiser.

  **C** The price of a bag of wristbands.

  **D** The total number of wristbands needed for the volunteers.

**12.** **GRIDDED ANSWER** Kylie hiked through the rainforest in Borneo following a 12-kilometer trail. She trod 7 kilometers, crossed a bridge for 34 meters, and hiked another 150 meters until she saw a wild orangutan. How many meters were left to go on the trail? *TAKS Obj. 1*

*Record your answer and fill in the bubbles on your answer document. Be sure to use the correct place value.*

# 2 Integer Operations

## Before

In previous chapters you've . . .

- Performed operations on whole numbers
- Evaluated expressions

## Now

## Why?

So you can solve real-world problems about . . .

- space shuttles, p. 60
- dinosaurs, p. 72
- diving, p. 73

 **Math**

*at classzone.com*

- Adding Integers, p. 66
- Multiplying Integers, p. 74
- The Coordinate Plane, p. 97

## Get-Ready Games

**Review Prerequisite Skills** by playing *Four in a Row*.

**Skill Focus:** Multiplying whole numbers

### FOUR IN A ROW

**MATERIALS**

- 2 Answer Cards
- 24 Expression Cards
- 24 Markers

$$32 \times 26$$

**HOW TO PLAY**  Fill in your Answer Card with 16 of the 24 answers given below. Place the Expression Cards face down in a pile. On each turn follow the steps on the next page.

| | | | | | |
|---|---|---|---|---|---|
| 168 | 196 | 240 | 315 | 338 | 342 |
| 352 | 361 | 405 | 414 | 418 | 441 |
| 516 | 522 | 529 | 595 | 720 | 792 |
| 832 | 851 | 918 | 961 | 975 | 1020 |

**① FLIP** over an Expression Card. Both players solve the expression.

**② LOOK** for the answer on your Answer Card. If you find it, place a marker over the answer.

**HOW TO WIN** Mark 4 answers in a row across, up and down, or diagonally.

**Stop and Think**

1. **CRITICAL THINKING** How many ways can you get 4 answers in a row on your card?

2. **CRITICAL THINKING** How many squares can you mark without winning?

# Review Prerequisite Skills

## VOCABULARY CHECK

**REVIEW WORDS**

- **variable,** *p. 13*
- **variable expression,** *p. 13*
- **perimeter,** *p. 32*
- **area,** *p. 32*

Copy and complete using a review word from the list at the left.

**1.** A symbol that represents one or more numbers is called a(n)   ?  .

**2.** The measure of the surface enclosed by a figure in a plane is its   ?  .

## SKILL CHECK

**Round the decimal to the nearest whole number.** *(p. 760)*

**3.** 10.61    **4.** 134.7    **5.** 0.25    **6.** 12.86

**Evaluate the expression.** *(p. 8)*

**7.** $32 - 27 + 14$    **8.** $4 \cdot 12 \div 6$    **9.** $6 + 34 \div 2$

**Evaluate the expression when $s = 4$ and $t = 16$.** *(p. 13)*

**10.** $(t - 9) + s$    **11.** $s(t - 5)$    **12.** $\frac{1}{4}t - 4$

**Solve the equation using mental math.** *(p. 26)*

**13.** $3x = 39$    **14.** $x - 6 = 12$    **15.** $x + 13 = 17$

**TEXAS @HomeTutor**   Prerequisite skills practice at classzone.com

# Notetaking Skills   Including Vocabulary Notes

In each chapter you will learn a new notetaking skill. In Chapter 2 you will apply the strategy of including vocabulary notes on p. 89.

When you write down new vocabulary words, you should also write examples of how they are used. Label the examples with the new words.

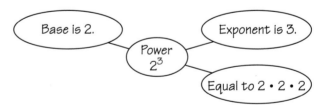

$5^2$ is read "five squared"

$5^3$ is read "five cubed"

$5^4$ is read "five to the fourth power"

As you work through Chapter 2, label examples of new vocabulary in your notes.

# 2.1 Integers and Absolute Value

TEKS 8.1.A, 8.15.A

| Before | You studied whole numbers. |
| Now | You'll study integers. |
| Why? | So you can order elevations, as in Example 1. |

**KEY VOCABULARY**
- **integers,** *p. 57*
- **negative integers,** *p. 57*
- **positive integers,** *p. 57*
- **absolute value,** *p. 58*
- **opposites,** *p. 58*

**Geography** The Global Positioning System (GPS) can be used to determine elevations. The table shows the lowest elevations of several countries. Which country in the table has the lowest elevation?

Each number in the table is an *integer*. The following numbers are **integers**.

$$\ldots, -5, -4, -3, -2, -1, 0, 1, 2, 3, 4, 5, \ldots$$

| Lowest Elevations | |
| --- | --- |
| *Country* | *Elevation (m)* |
| United States | $-86$ |
| Canada | 0 |
| China | $-154$ |
| Bolivia | 90 |
| Czech Republic | 115 |

**Negative integers** are less than 0. They lie *to the left* of 0 on a number line. **Positive integers** are greater than 0. They lie *to the right* of 0 on a number line. Zero is neither positive nor negative. When you use a number line to compare numbers, numbers increase as you move to the right.

---

**EXAMPLE 1** Graphing and Ordering Integers

To find which country in the table above has the lowest elevation, graph each integer on a number line.

▶ **Answer** China has the lowest elevation, at $-154$ meters.

---

✓ **GUIDED PRACTICE** for Example 1

**Order the integers from least to greatest.**

**1.** $-7, 2, -1, 0, -2$      **2.** $9, -4, 12, -11, -1$      **3.** $0, -99, 44, -60, 16$

**Absolute Value** The **absolute value** of a number is the distance between the number and zero on a number line. The absolute value of a number $n$ is written as $|n|$. The absolute value of 0 is 0.

The distance between 4 and 0 is 4. So, $|4| = 4$.

The distance between $-5$ and 0 is 5. So, $|-5| = 5$.

**EXAMPLE 2** **Finding Absolute Value**

**Eyeglasses** An eyeglass prescription is given as a positive or negative number. A prescription for a person who is farsighted is positive. A prescription for a person who is nearsighted is negative. The greater the absolute value, the stronger the prescription. Which prescription is stronger, $-3$ or 2?

**SOLUTION**

$|-3| = 3$ and $|2| = 2$.

▶ **Answer** The prescription of $-3$ is stronger because $3 > 2$.

**READING**
The integer $-2$ can be read "negative 2" or "the opposite of 2."

**Opposites** Two numbers are **opposites** if they have the same absolute value but different signs. Opposites are the same distance from 0 on a number line but on opposite sides of 0. The opposite of 0 is 0.

$-2$ and $2$ are *opposites*.

**EXAMPLE 3** **Finding Opposites**

Write the opposite of the integer.

**a.** 5      The opposite of 5 is $-5$.

**b.** $-12$      The opposite of $-12$ is 12.

**c.** $|-9|$      Because $|-9| = 9$, the opposite of $|-9|$ is $-9$.

✓ **GUIDED PRACTICE**     for Examples 2 and 3

Write the absolute value and the opposite of the integer.

**4.** $-16$           **5.** 140           **6.** $-1$           **7.** 0

# 2.1 EXERCISES

HOMEWORK KEY

= TAKS Practice and Reasoning
Exs. 15, 46, 47, 55, and 56

◯ = HINTS AND HOMEWORK HELP
for Exs. 3, 13, 17, 19, 45 at classzone.com

## SKILL PRACTICE

**VOCABULARY** Copy and complete the statement.

**1.** The __?__ of a number is its distance from zero on a number line.

**2.** Two integers are __?__ if their sum is zero.

**SEE EXAMPLE 1**
on p. 57
for Exs. 3–16

**COMPARING INTEGERS** Copy and complete the statement with < or >.

**3.** $4 \; \underline{?} \; -6$     **4.** $-12 \; \underline{?} \; 1$     **5.** $-9 \; \underline{?} \; -2$     **6.** $0 \; \underline{?} \; -5$

**7.** $5 \; \underline{?} \; -5$     **8.** $-17 \; \underline{?} \; 2$     **9.** $34 \; \underline{?} \; -29$     **10.** $-20 \; \underline{?} \; -14$

**ORDERING INTEGERS** Use a number line to order the integers from least to greatest.

**11.** $5, -10, 15, 27, -20, 13$     **12.** $120, 62, 0, -56, 74, -130$

**13.** $64, -12, 18, 59, -20, 44$     **14.** $278, 121, -301, 262, -155$

**15.** ⬥ **TAKS REASONING** Which list orders the integers from least to greatest?

   **A** $-1, -6, -12, -34$     **B** $-1, -12, -34, -6$

   **C** $-34, -12, -6, -1$     **D** $-34, -6, -12, -1$

**16.** **ERROR ANALYSIS** A student was asked to order the integers $3, 1, 0, -9, -2,$ and $5$ from least to greatest. Describe and correct the error in the solution.

$$\times \quad 0, 1, -2, 3, 5, -9$$

**SEE EXAMPLES
2 AND 3**
on p. 57
for Exs. 17–20

**ABSOLUTE VALUE** Write the absolute value and the opposite of the integer.

**17.** $19$     **18.** $-8$     **19.** $-740$     **20.** $1327$

**READING VERBAL EXPRESSIONS** Match the integer expression with the verbal expression.

**21.** $-|7|$     **A.** the opposite of negative seven

**22.** $|-7|$     **B.** the opposite of the absolute value of seven

**23.** $-|-7|$     **C.** the absolute value of negative seven

**24.** $-(-7)$     **D.** the opposite of the absolute value of negative seven

**SIMPLIFYING EXPRESSIONS** Simplify the expression.

**25.** $|-32|$     **26.** $-|9|$     **27.** $-|29|$     **28.** $-(-5)$

**29.** $-(-81)$     **30.** $-|-17|$     **31.** $-|-3|$     **32.** $-(-(-4))$

**COMPARING VALUES** Copy and complete the statement with <, >, or =.

**33.** $|4| \; \underline{?} \; |-4|$     **34.** $|-6| \; \underline{?} \; -|6|$     **35.** $-|-9| \; \underline{?} \; -(-9)$     **36.** $|-2| \; \underline{?} \; -(-2)$

**ORDERING INTEGERS** Order the numbers from least to greatest.

**37.** $-28, -(-73), |-65|, |95|, -|47|$

**38.** $|-19|, -74, -|12|, -(-56), -|-58|$

**39.** $-|6|, -8, -(-5), -14, |-1|$

**40.** $|38|, -37, -|-42|, -(-29), |-49|$

**CHALLENGE** Tell whether the statement is *always*, *sometimes*, or *never* true. *Justify* your answer.

**41.** The absolute value of a number $x$ is greater than or equal to $x$.

**42.** The opposite of a number $y$ is greater than or equal to $y$.

**43.** The absolute value of a number $z$ is less than the opposite of $z$.

## PROBLEM SOLVING

**ELEVATION** In Exercises 44 and 45, use the table at the right showing elevations of lakes.

*SEE EXAMPLE 1*
on p. 57
for Exs. 44–45

**44.** Which lake is at a lower elevation, Gieselmann Lake or Silver Lake?

**45.** Arrange the lakes in order from least to greatest elevation.

| Lakes | Elevation (ft) |
|---|---|
| Jones Lake | −30 |
| Silver Lake | 90 |
| Gieselmann Lake | −162 |
| Seneca Lake | 445 |
| Craigs Pond | 0 |

**46.** ⬥ **TAKS REASONING** What numbers have opposites that are the same as their absolute values? What numbers have opposites that are different from their absolute values? Use examples to support your answer.

**47.** ⬥ **TAKS REASONING** The Java Trench in the Indian Ocean lies 7725 meters below sea level. Which number represents this elevation in meters?

**A** $-7725$ **B** $-(-7725)$ **C** $|-7725|$ **D** $|7725|$

**48.** **LAUNCH COUNTDOWN** Put the following activities for a shuttle launch in the order in which they occur. "T−5 minutes" means 5 minutes before liftoff.

| Count | Activity |
|---|---|
| T−5 minutes | Pilot starts auxiliary power units. |
| T+7 seconds | Shuttle clears launch tower, and control switches to the Mission Control Center. |
| T−2 hours, 55 minutes | Flight crew departs for launch pad. |
| T−6 seconds | Main engine starts. |
| T−0 | Liftoff. |

*Animated* Math at classzone.com

**49.** **NUMBER SENSE** $A$ is a point on a number line halfway between $-11$ and 5. $B$ is a point halfway between $A$ and 3. What point on the number line is $B$?

⬥ = TAKS Practice and Reasoning ◯ = **HINTS AND HOMEWORK HELP** *at classzone.com*

**50. WRITING** *Explain* why no value of $x$ makes the equation $|x| = -8$ true.

**51. REASONING** Suppose $|a| < |b|$. What are the possible relationships between $a$ and $b$?

**52. MULTI-STEP PROBLEM** The bar graph shows the quarterly earnings at a store in four quarters of one year.

a. Which quarters showed gains? Write a positive integer to represent these earnings.

b. Which quarters showed losses? Write a negative integer to represent these earnings.

c. Did the gains balance the losses? Did the store make a profit for the year? *Explain* your reasoning.

*Quarterly Earnings*

**53. BOILING POINTS** The table below shows the substances in a solution and their boiling points in degrees Celsius. Order the substances from lowest boiling point to highest boiling point. If you heat the solution, which substance will you expect to be left at the end of the heating? *Explain* your reasoning.

| Solution | Ethanol | Water | Propanol | Methanol |
|---|---|---|---|---|
| Boiling Point | $|-78|$ | $-(-100)$ | 97 | $|-65|$ |

**54. CHALLENGE** A newspaper reports these changes in the price of a stock during a 5 month period: $-1$, $-8$, $+2$, $-4$, and $+6$. The stock price ended at \$35 in the fifth month. Use a number line to show the price of the stock at the beginning of the 5 month period.

---

## MIXED REVIEW FOR TAKS

**TAKS PRACTICE** at classzone.com

*REVIEW*
Lesson 1.6;
TAKS Workbook

**55. TAKS PRACTICE** The table shows the height of a rollercoaster $s$ seconds into its climb. What is a reasonable prediction for its height after 40 seconds, assuming the rollercoaster continues to rise? *TAKS Obj. 2*

| Seconds, s | 0 | 10 | 20 | 30 |
|---|---|---|---|---|
| Height (ft) | 15 | 50 | 85 | 120 |

**A** 135 ft  **B** 150 ft  **C** 155 ft  **D** 190 ft

*REVIEW*
Lesson 1.2;
TAKS Workbook

**56. TAKS PRACTICE** Lisa and Meg split the cost of a hotel one night. The room cost \$80 and the tax was \$6.40. How much did each pay? *TAKS Obj. 1*

**F** \$43.20  **G** \$46.40  **H** \$73.60  **J** \$86.40

# INVESTIGATION
*Use before Lesson 2.2*

**GOAL**
Model integer addition on a number line.

**MATERIALS**
• pencil
• paper

**TEKS** *8.15.A, 8.16.A*

## 2.2 Adding Integers

You can model addition of integers by using a number line.

**EXPLORE** **Find the sum −15 + 11.**

**STEP 1** **Draw** a number line, place a pencil at 0, and move 15 units to the left to show −15.

**STEP 2** **Move** 11 units to the right to show the sum of −15 and 11.

**STEP 3** The final position is −4. So, −15 + 11 = −4.

**PRACTICE** **Write an addition expression to represent the figure. Then evaluate the expression.**

1.

2.

**Use a number line to find the sum.**

3. −7 + (−14)    4. 20 + (−25)    5. −10 + 15    6. −7 + (−33)

7. 11 + (−13)    8. −23 + 5    9. −18 + (−12)    10. 16 + (−17)

**DRAW CONCLUSIONS**

11. The sum of two positive integers is always positive. What is the sign of the sum of two negative integers? *Explain* your answer using a number line.

12. **REASONING** How can you predict the sign of the sum of a positive integer and a negative integer before you add the numbers?

13. **WRITING** Write the steps you use to evaluate 25 + (−13) + 5 + (−20). Then evaluate the expression.

# 2.2 Adding Integers

**TEKS** *8.2.B, 8.4*

| | |
|---|---|
| **Before** | You added whole numbers. |
| **Now** | You'll add integers. |
| **Why?** | So you can find total scores, as in Ex. 57. |

**KEY VOCABULARY**
- **integer,** *p. 57*
- **absolute value,** *p. 58*
- **additive identity,** *p. 64*
- **additive inverse,** *p. 64*
- **sum,** *p. 764*

You can use a number line to add integers.

To add a positive integer, move to the right.

To add a negative integer, move to the left.

## EXAMPLE 1  Adding Integers Using a Number Line

**Use a number line to find the sum.**

   **a.** $5 + (-8)$          **b.** $-6 + 10$          **c.** $-4 + (-3)$

**a.** Start at 0. Move **5** units to the right. Then move **8** units to the left.

▶ **Answer** The final position is $-3$. So, $5 + (-8) = -3$.

**b.** Start at 0. Move **6** units to the left. Then move **10** units to the right.

▶ **Answer** The final position is 4. So, $-6 + 10 = 4$.

**c.** Start at 0. Move **4** units to the left. Then move **3** units to the left.

▶ **Answer** The final position is $-7$. So, $-4 + (-3) = -7$.

---

✓ **GUIDED PRACTICE**  for Example 1

   **1.** Use a number line. Find $-8 + 4$.       **2.** Find $-1 + (-6)$.

## KEY CONCEPT
*For Your Notebook*

### Adding Integers

You can add integers without using a number line by following these rules.

**Same sign**

Add the absolute values and use the common sign.

**Different signs**

Subtract the lesser absolute value from the greater absolute value. Use the sign of the number with the greater absolute value.

---

**EXAMPLE 2** **Adding Integers**

**Find the sum** $-12 + 4$.

$$-12 + 4 = -8 \longleftarrow \text{Different signs, so subtract } |4| \text{ from } |-12|.$$
$$\text{Use sign of number with greater absolute value.}$$

**Check** Use a number line to find the sum.

---

## KEY CONCEPT
*For Your Notebook*

### Addition Properties

**Identity Property of Addition**

**Words**  The sum of a number and the **additive identity**, 0, is the number.

**Numbers**  $-3 + 0 = -3$    **Algebra**  $a + 0 = a$

**Inverse Property of Addition**

**Words**  The sum of a number and its **additive inverse**, or opposite, is 0.

**Numbers**  $5 + (-5) = 0$    **Algebra**  $a + (-a) = 0$

---

**EXAMPLE 3** **Adding More Than Two Integers**

**Find the sum using the order of operations.**

| | |
|---|---|
| $(-7 + 7) + (-8) + (-5) = 0 + (-8) + (-5)$ | **Inverse property of addition** |
| $= -8 + (-5)$ | **Identity property of addition** |
| $= -13$ | **Same sign, so sum has common sign** |

---

EXAMPLE 4 Adding More Than Two Integers

**School Fair** Your class has a fair to raise money for a field trip. The table shows the incomes and expenses for the fair. How much money was raised?

| Games | $750 |
|---|---|
| Display tables | $625 |
| Donations | $36 |
| Advertising | −$16 |
| Decorations | −$60 |
| Game rentals | −$500 |

**ANOTHER WAY**
You can also add the numbers in order from left to right or look for compatible numbers, such as 750 and −500, to make the calculation easier.

**SOLUTION**

First, add the positive integers. Then add the negative integers.

$$750 + 625 + 36 + (-16) + (-60) + (-500) = 1411 + (-576)$$
$$= 835$$

▸ **Answer** Your class raised $835.

✓ **GUIDED PRACTICE** for Examples 2, 3, and 4

**Find the sum. Identify any addition properties you use.**

**3.** −20 + (−15)

**4.** 18 + 0 + (−54)

**5.** 300 + 111 + (−44) + (−256)

**6.** −230 + (−512) + 178 + 94

**7. What If?** Suppose in Example 4 that games made $825 and the decorations cost $100. How much money did your class raise?

## 2.2 EXERCISES

HOMEWORK KEY

= TAKS Practice and Reasoning
Exs. 11, 36, 53, 56, and 59

= HINTS AND HOMEWORK HELP
for Exs. 3, 9, 13, 17, 53 at classzone.com

**SKILL PRACTICE**

**1. VOCABULARY** Copy and complete: To add two integers with the same sign, add the _?_ and use the common sign.

**ADDING WITH A NUMBER LINE** Use a number line to find the sum.

SEE EXAMPLE 1
on p. 63
for Exs. 2–10

**2.** −6 + 8

**3.** −3 + (−9)

**4.** 5 + (−7)

**5.** −4 + 4

**6.** −2 + (−1)

**7.** −10 + (−9)

**8.** −3 + 7

**9.** 7 + (−5)

**10. ERROR ANALYSIS** Describe and correct the error made in finding the sum of −8 and 5.

 −8 + 5 = −13

SEE EXAMPLES
2, 3, AND 4
on pp. 64–65
for Exs. 11–23

**11.** ★ **TAKS REASONING** Evaluate $-8 + 3$.

    Ⓐ $-11$       Ⓑ $-5$       Ⓒ $5$       Ⓓ $11$

**ADDING INTEGERS** Find the sum. Identify any addition properties you use.

**12.** $42 + (-23)$       **13.** $-63 + (-49)$       **14.** $-93 + (-16)$

**15.** $25 + (-25)$       **16.** $0 + (-82)$       **17.** $98 + (-128)$

**18.** $-9 + 9 + (-14)$       **19.** $-12 + 9 + (-5)$       **20.** $20 + (-15) + (-22)$

**21.** $-12 + (-25) + 8$       **22.** $-21 + (-15) + (-25)$       **23.** $-17 + 8 + 16$

*Animated* **Math** at classzone.com

**EVALUATING EXPRESSIONS** Evaluate when $a = -13$, $b = 24$, and $c = -27$.

**24.** $a + b$       **25.** $b + c$       **26.** $-b + c$       **27.** $a + (-b)$

**28.** $a + |c|$       **29.** $b + |a|$       **30.** $|a| + |c|$       **31.** $|c| + |b|$

**ALGEBRA** Evaluate $x + (-478)$ using the given value of $x$.

**32.** $x = 806$       **33.** $x = -729$       **34.** $x = |-349|$       **35.** $x = -|-521|$

**36.** ★ **TAKS REASONING** Name two integers with the same sign that have a sum of $-28$. Name two integers with different signs that have a sum of $-28$.

**REASONING** Tell whether the sum of the two integers is *always*, *sometimes*, or *never* negative. *Justify* your answer.

**37.** two negative integers       **38.** two positive integers

**39.** a positive integer and a negative integer       **40.** a negative integer and zero

**MENTAL MATH** Solve the equation using mental math.

**41.** $-92 + k = 102$     **42.** $-6 = x + (-7)$     **43.** $-9 = 5 + j$     **44.** $-81 + b = -90$

**CHALLENGE** Find the value(s) of $x$ that make the equation true.

**45.** $|x| + (-13) = 29$       **46.** $|x| + (-45) = -12$       **47.** $-123 + |x| = -98$

## PROBLEM SOLVING

**CHEMISTRY** A proton has a charge of $+1$, and an electron has a charge of $-1$. Find the sum of the charges.

**48.** Sodium: 11 protons, 10 electrons       **49.** Chlorine: 17 protons, 17 electrons

**50.** Oxide: 8 protons, 10 electrons       **51.** Phosphorus: 15 protons, 12 electrons

**52.** **ELEVATORS** You enter an elevator on the sixth floor. The elevator goes up 3 floors and then down 5 floors, where you exit. Write and evaluate an addition expression to find the floor on which you exit.

★ = TAKS Practice and Reasoning       ◯ = **HINTS AND HOMEWORK HELP** *at classzone.com*

**53.** **TAKS REASONING** A bank statement for January is shown. What is the sum of the transactions in this month?

| $\overset{\text{Central}}{\text{Savings}}$ | |
|---|---|
| January 5 | +$25 |
| January 6 | −$30 |
| January 15 | +$35 |

Ⓐ −$30    Ⓑ $30

Ⓒ $20    Ⓓ $90

**54.** **WRITING**  You want to add a positive integer and a negative integer. How do you choose the sign of your answer? *Explain.*

**55.** **MULTI-STEP PROBLEM** The classic Mexican period began around 200 B.C. and lasted for 1100 years. The classic Greek period began in 500 B.C. and lasted for 200 years.

**a.** About what year did the classic Mexican period end?

**b.** About what year did the classic Greek period end?

**c.** About how many years after the classic Greek period ended did the classic Mexican period end?

**Classical Mexican art**

*SEE EXAMPLE 4*
on p. 65 for
Ex. 56–57

**56.** **TAKS REASONING** A football team gained 7 yards on the first play, lost 9 yards on the second play, and gained 6 yards on the third play. To get a first down, they must gain 10 yards in 4 plays. How many yards must they gain on the fourth play to get a first down? *Explain* your reasoning.

**57.** **MINIATURE GOLF** *Par* is the number of strokes considered necessary to get the ball in the hole. A player's score for each hole is the number of strokes above or below par. The total score is the sum of the scores for each hole. Is Jill's score for the first 8 holes *above par, under par,* or *at par*? What score does she need next to be at par for the first 9 holes?

| HOLE | 1 | 2 | 3 | 4 | 5 | 6 | 7 | 8 | 9 | OUT |
|---|---|---|---|---|---|---|---|---|---|---|
| PAR | 4 | 5 | 3 | 3 | 5 | 4 | 3 | 5 | 3 | 35 |
| Jill | 0 | +1 | −2 | −1 | 0 | +1 | +2 | +1 | ? | |

**58.** **CHALLENGE** Does $|x + y| = |x| + |y|$ if $x$ and $y$ are both positive? both negative? What if $x$ is positive and $y$ is negative? *Explain.*

**MIXED REVIEW FOR TAKS**    **TAKS** **PRACTICE** at classzone.com

*REVIEW*
Lesson 2.1;
TAKS Workbook

**59.** **TAKS PRACTICE** A geologist measured the elevations, in feet, of a few locations compared to sea level. Choose the group of elevations that is listed in order from least to greatest. *TAKS Obj. 1*

Ⓐ 0, 3, −6, −11, −22, 26

Ⓑ −22, −11, −6, 0, 3, 26

Ⓒ 26, 3, 0, −6, −11, −22

Ⓓ −6, −11, −22, 0, 3, 26

## 2.3 Subtracting Integers

TEKS 8.2.B, 8.16.A

| Before | You added integers. |
|---|---|
| Now | You'll subtract integers. |
| Why? | So you can find lengths of time, as in Ex. 49. |

**KEY VOCABULARY**
- integer, *p. 57*
- opposite, *p. 58*
- difference, *p. 764*

### ACTIVITY

**You can use patterns to discover a rule for subtracting integers.**

**STEP 1** **Copy** the table below. In the second column, write the answer to the subtraction problem. Use a pattern to find the differences involving negative integers.

**STEP 2** **Complete** the addition problem in the third column so the sum is equal to the number in the difference column.

| Subtraction Problem | Difference | Addition Problem |
|---|---|---|
| 3 − 3 | 0 | 3 + (−3) |
| 3 − 2 | ? | 3 + ? |
| 3 − 1 | ? | 3 + ? |
| 3 − 0 | ? | 3 + ? |
| 3 − (−1) | ? | 3 + ? |
| 3 − (−2) | ? | 3 + ? |
| 3 − (−3) | ? | 3 + ? |

**STEP 3** **Tell** how the second number in the addition problems relates to the second number in the subtraction problems.

**STEP 4** **Describe** how to use addition to subtract integers.

In the activity above, you may have observed that when you subtract integers you can write the expression as an addition expression and then use the rules for adding integers.

### KEY CONCEPT                    *For Your Notebook*

#### Subtracting Integers

**Words**      To subtract an integer, add its opposite.

**Numbers**    $3 - 7 = 3 + (-7) = -4$     **Algebra**    $a - b = a + (-b)$

            $2 - (-6) = 2 + 6 = 8$                   $a - (-b) = a + b$

**EXAMPLE 1** Subtracting Integers

**a.** $-56 - (-9) = -56 + 9$      Add the opposite of $-9$.

              $= -47$      Add.

**b.** $-14 - 21 = -14 + (-21)$      Add the opposite of 21.

              $= -35$      Add.

**EXAMPLE 2** Evaluating a Variable Expression

Evaluate $15 - a - b$ when $a = 24$ and $b = -36$.

$$15 - a - b = 15 - 24 - (-36)$$      Substitute 24 for $a$ and $-36$ for $b$.

              $= 15 + (-24) + 36$      Add the opposite of 24 and of $-36$.

              $= -9 + 36$      Add 15 and $-24$.

              $= 27$      Add $-9$ and 36.

 **EXAMPLE 3** TAKS PRACTICE: Multiple Choice

**Outer Core** The outer core is a layer of the Earth below the Earth's crust and mantle, as shown in the diagram. What is the vertical height of the outer core?

*ELIMINATE CHOICES*
A height is always a positive number. So, you can eliminate choices A and B.

(A) $-8000$ km    (B) $-2200$ km

(C) $2200$ km    (D) $8000$ km

**SOLUTION**

The vertical height is the difference of the upper and lower elevations.

     Vertical height $= -2900 - (-5100)$      Write subtraction statement.

                   $= -2900 + 5100$      Add the opposite of $-5100$.

                   $= 2200$      Add.

▶ **Answer** The vertical height of the outer core is 2200 meters. The correct answer is C. (A) (B) (C) (D)

 ✓ **GUIDED PRACTICE**    for Examples 1, 2, and 3

**Evaluate the expression.**

**1.** $15 - 41$      **2.** $-16 - 8$      **3.** $a - b - (-6); a = 8, b = -15$

**4. Distance** What is the difference in elevation between 4 feet above sea level and 30 feet below sea level?

# 2.3 EXERCISES

HOMEWORK KEY

= TAKS Practice and Reasoning
Exs. 27, 36, 43, 47, 54, and 55

◯ = HINTS AND HOMEWORK HELP
for Exs. 5, 13, 19, 25, 43 at classzone.com

## SKILL PRACTICE

**VOCABULARY** **Write the verbal phrase as a numerical expression.**

1. The difference of negative two and six

2. The difference of the opposite of five and the opposite of three

**SUBTRACTING INTEGERS** **Find the difference.**

*SEE EXAMPLE 1*
on p. 69
for Exs. 3–18

3. $5 - 12$

4. $6 - (-16)$

5. $-11 - (-7)$

6. $-13 - 12$

7. $-14 - (-14)$

8. $11 - (-6)$

9. $9 - 17$

10. $-18 - (-12)$

11. $-20 - 7$

12. $32 - 40$

13. $28 - (-16)$

14. $-39 - (-13)$

15. $-5 - (-5) - (-5)$

16. $8 - 2 - 6 - 10$

17. $-52 - (-18) - 37$

18. **ERROR ANALYSIS** Describe and correct the error made in finding the difference between the opposite of 12 and 5.

$-12 - 5 = -7$

**ALGEBRA** **Evaluate the expression when $a = -9$, $b = 18$, and $c = -4$.**

*SEE EXAMPLE 2*
on p. 69
for Exs. 19–27

19. $a - 6$

20. $b - c$

21. $a - c$

22. $14 - a - b$

23. $a - b - c$

24. $c - a - b$

25. $a + b - c$

26. $c - a + b$

27. **TAKS REASONING** Evaluate the expression $-c + 2a - b$ when $a = 5$, $b = -9$, and $c = 3$.

  **A** $-2$       **B** 4       **C** 16       **D** 22

**SOLVING EQUATIONS** **Use mental math to solve the equation.**

28. $35 - x = 45$

29. $-32 - x = -37$

30. $-49 = 50 - x$

31. $x - 11 = -3$

32. $-56 = x - 52$

33. $-36 = x - 24$

34. $16 = 12 - x$

35. $64 - x = -37$

36. **TAKS REASONING** Give an example of two integers with the same sign that have a difference of $-9$. Give an example of two integers with different signs that have a difference of $-9$.

37. **REASONING** Are the expressions $x - y$ and $y - x$ always opposites? *Explain* your reasoning.

**CHALLENGE** **Copy and complete the statement using *always, sometimes,* or *never*. *Justify* your reasoning.**

38. A positive number minus a negative number is ___?___ negative.

39. A negative number minus a negative number is ___?___ positive.

**SEE EXAMPLE 3**
on p. 69
for Exs. 40, 43

**40. GUIDED PROBLEM SOLVING** Find the distances between the bird and the boat, the boat and the reef, and the bird and the reef.

**a.** Identify which elevation is greater for each situation above.

**b.** Subtract the lesser elevation from the greater elevation.

**c.** Answer the original question by completing each statement.

The bird is __?__ feet above the boat.

The boat is __?__ feet above the reef.

The bird is __?__ feet above the reef.

**GAME SHOW** Bobby Joe is on a game show and has −400 points. He has one question left. Find his total score after the given scenario.

**41.** He answers the question incorrectly and loses 600 points.

**42.** He answers the question correctly and gains 600 points.

**43. TAKS REASONING** A whale that is 660 feet below sea level rises up and breaches out of the water to a height of 32 feet above sea level. What is the vertical distance the whale travels?

**A** −628 feet  **B** 628 feet

**C** 660 feet  **D** 692 feet

**44. REASONING** *Explain* how you can find the distance between the points on the number line using subtraction.

**Animated Math** at classzone.com

**TEMPERATURES** In Exercises 45–47, use the given table.

**45.** How much colder is Alaska's coldest temperature than Kentucky's?

**46.** How much colder is Colorado's coldest temperature than Mississippi's?

**47. TAKS REASONING** Which two states have the greatest difference in coldest temperatures? Which two states have the least difference in coldest temperatures? *Justify* your answer.

| Coldest Recorded Temperatures | |
|---|---|
| **State** | **Temperature** |
| Alaska | −80°F |
| Colorado | −61°F |
| Kentucky | −37°F |
| Mississippi | −19°F |

**48. WRITING** *Explain* why you add an integer's opposite when you are subtracting integers.

**49. DINOSAURS** The table shows the ranges of three dinosaur periods during the Mesozoic Era. Which period lasted 64 million years? About what fraction of the three periods did that period last?

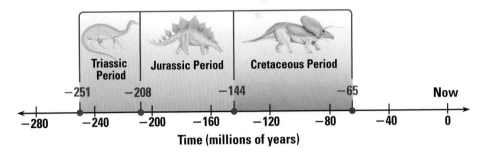

**Time (millions of years)**

Triassic Period | Jurassic Period | Cretaceous Period
−251  −208  −144  −65  Now

−280  −240  −200  −160  −120  −80  −40  0

**READING _IN_ MATH** Read the information below for Exercises 50–52.

**Lunar Temperatures** The Moon has no atmosphere, which results in the Moon experiencing extreme temperatures. During the day, it can reach a high temperature of 265°F. At night, the temperature can reach a low of −170°F. The highest temperature ever recorded on Earth is 136°F and the lowest temperature recorded on Earth is −129°F.

**50. Compare** What is the difference between the high temperatures on the Moon and on Earth?

**51. Compare** What is the difference between the low temperatures on the Moon and on Earth?

**52. Interpret** What is the range of temperatures on the Moon? How does this compare with the range of temperatures on Earth? *Explain* how the lack of an atmosphere might cause the greater range of temperatures on the Moon.

**53. CHALLENGE** Craig had $150 in his checking account on April 1. He wrote 3 checks in April, one for $47 and another for $63. He did not record the amount of the third check. He received a statement stating that he overdrew his account by $23. What was the amount on the third check that he wrote?

## MIXED REVIEW FOR TAKS
**TAKS PRACTICE** at classzone.com

*REVIEW*
Lesson 2.2;
TAKS Workbook

**54. TAKS PRACTICE** John developed his own scoring system for darts. His first three throws are worth −10, −5, and 35 points. What is his total score for the three throws? *TAKS Obj. 1*

(A) −50    (B) −15    (C) 20    (D) 50

*REVIEW*
Lesson 1.6;
TAKS Workbook

**55. TAKS PRACTICE** The side lengths of a square are doubled. If the square's original area was *a*, what is its area after the change? *TAKS Obj. 6*

(F) 2*a*    (G) 4*a*    (H) *a* + *a*    (J) 2 + *a*

# 2.4 Multiplying Integers

TEKS *8.2.B, 8.14.A*

| Before | You added and subtracted integers. |
| Now | You'll multiply integers. |
| Why? | So you can find positions of objects, as in Example 1. |

**KEY VOCABULARY**
- integer, *p. 57*
- multiplicative identity, *p. 74*
- product, *p. 768*

**Diving** A diver is swimming downward to explore a coral reef. The diver's depth is changing by −2 feet per second. The diver started at sea level. What is the diver's position relative to sea level after 10 seconds? after 30 seconds?

To find the position, you can multiply integers. When you multiply integers, the sign of the product depends on the signs of the factors.

---

### KEY CONCEPT                                *For Your Notebook*

## Multiplying Integers

| Words | Numbers |
|---|---|
| **Same Sign** The product of two integers with the same sign is positive. | $4 \cdot 2 = 8$ <br> $-3 \cdot (-7) = 21$ |
| **Different Sign** The product of two integers with different signs is negative. | $4 \cdot (-2) = -8$ <br> $-3 \cdot 7 = -21$ |

---

### EXAMPLE 1   Multiplying Integers

**a.** To find the diver's position relative to sea level after 10 seconds, use the distance formula $d = rt$.

$d = rt$        **Write the distance formula.**

$d = -2(10)$    **Substitute −2 for *r* and 10 for *t*.**

$d = -20$       **Different signs, so product is negative.**

▶ **Answer** The diver's position relative to sea level is −20 feet.

**b.** Find the diver's position relative to sea level after 30 seconds.

$d = rt$        **Write the distance formula.**

$d = -2(30)$    **Substitute −2 for *r* and 30 for *t*.**

$d = -60$       **Different signs, so product is negative.**

▶ **Answer** The diver's position relative to sea level is −60 feet.

**Properties** You can use the following properties when multiplying.

> ### KEY CONCEPT
> *For Your Notebook*
>
> ## Multiplication Properties
>
> **Multiplication Property of Zero**
>
> **Words** The product of a number and 0 is 0.
>
> **Numbers** $-4 \cdot 0 = 0$    **Algebra** For any value of $a$, $a \cdot 0 = 0$.
>
> **Identity Property of Multiplication**
>
> **Words** The product of a number and the **multiplicative identity**, 1, is the number.
>
> **Numbers** $4(1) = 4$    **Algebra** For any value of $a$, $a(1) = a$.

---

### **EXAMPLE 2** Multiplying Two or More Integers

*AVOID ERRORS*
........................
If a product has an even number of negative factors, it is positive. If a product has an odd number of negative factors, it is negative.

**a.** $-1(6) = -6$    Different signs, so product is negative.

**b.** $-8(-2) = 16$    Same sign, so product is positive.

**c.** $-15(0) = 0$    Product of an integer and 0 is 0.

**d.** $4(-10)(-12) = -40(-12)$    Multiply from left to right.

$\qquad\qquad\quad = 480$    Multiply.

---

### **EXAMPLE 3** Evaluating an Expression with Integers

 Evaluate $a^2 + 3b$ when $a = -5$ and $b = -11$.

$a^2 + 3b = (-5)^2 + 3(-11)$    Substitute $-5$ for $a$ and $-11$ for $b$.

$\qquad\quad = 25 + 3(-11)$    Evaluate the power.

$\qquad\quad = 25 + (-33)$    Multiply.

$\qquad\quad = -8$    Add.

*Animated* **Math**
at classzone.com

---

✓ **GUIDED PRACTICE** for Examples 1, 2, and 3

1. **What If?** In Example 1, what is the diver's position relative to sea level after 13 seconds?

**Find the product.**

**2.** $-1(4)$    **3.** $7(0)$    **4.** $-6(-11)$    **5.** $-1(-12)(-9)$

**Evaluate the expression when $a = 3$, $b = -4$, and $c = -8$.**

**6.** $ac - b$    **7.** $ac + b$    **8.** $a^2 + bc$    **9.** $ab - c^2$

## 2.4 EXERCISES

HOMEWORK KEY

 = TAKS Practice and Reasoning
Exs. 40, 56, 59, and 62

○ = HINTS AND HOMEWORK HELP
for Exs. 5, 17, 25, 31, 55 at classzone.com

### SKILL PRACTICE

1. **VOCABULARY** Copy and complete: The product of a positive integer and a negative integer is a __?__ integer.

2. **VOCABULARY** Copy and complete: The product of two integers with the same sign is __?__ .

**MULTIPLYING INTEGERS** Find the product. Identify any properties you use.

*SEE EXAMPLES 1 AND 2*
on pp. 73–74
for Exs. 3–23

3. $-4(-7)$
4. $0(-9)$
5. $-3(6)$
6. $8(-5)$

7. $-6(7)$
8. $-1(-17)$
9. $0(-13)$
10. $-4(-11)$

11. $9(-2)$
12. $3(-5)$
13. $-15(-12)$
14. $1(-32)$

15. $-1(-2)(-3)$
16. $2(-4)(5)$
17. $10(-9)(-3)$
18. $-7(-9)(-6)$

19. $-2(5)(-6)$
20. $6(-4)(12)$
21. $-8(-7)(-5)$
22. $12(0)(-45)$

23. **ERROR ANALYSIS** Describe and correct the error made in finding the product of $-8$ and $-12$.

$$-8(-12) = -96$$

**EVALUATING EXPRESSIONS** Evaluate the expression when $x = -9$, $y = -7$, and $z = -4$.

*SEE EXAMPLE 3*
on p. 74
for Exs. 24–35

24. $xy$
25. $y^2$
26. $2xyz$
27. $-3z^2$

28. $-x(-x)$
29. $z(-y^2)$
30. $3xy - yz$
31. $x + 2y^2 - z$

32. $x^2 + y$
33. $z - y^2$
34. $[x + (-x)y]^2$
35. $xz^2 - (-y)^2z$

**USING ABSOLUTE VALUE** Find the product.

36. $-12 \cdot |11|$
37. $-7(-8) \cdot |-4|$
38. $10(-4) \cdot |13|$
39. $|8| \cdot |-14| \cdot 3$

40. ★ **TAKS REASONING** What is the value of the expression $-4(-8) \cdot |-3|$?

 (A) $-96$
 (B) $-36$
 (C) $12$
 (D) $96$

**MENTAL MATH** Use mental math to solve the equation.

41. $2x = -8$
42. $-21y = 63$
43. $-5(-4)z = -80$
44. $-4a = -20$

45. $130 = -13b$
46. $6(-8)k = -96$
47. $-36 = 9a$
48. $7(-3)m = -21$

49. **REASONING** Does $(-3)^2$ equal $-3^2$? *Explain* your reasoning.

**CHALLENGE** What are the next three numbers of the sequence? Write a rule using the variable $n$ for the $n$th number in the list.

50. $-2, 4, -6, 8, \ldots$
51. $5, 10, 15, 20, \ldots$
52. $-3, 9, -27, 81, \ldots$

**SEE EXAMPLE 1**
on p. 73
for Ex. 53

**53. FINDING DEPTH** A coin is tossed off a boat into the ocean. The coin's depth changes by $-8$ inches per second. Determine the depth of the coin 12 seconds after it hits the water.

**54. BANKING** You have $500 in a savings account. Over a 2 month period, you make 9 withdrawals of $30 each. What is your new balance?

**55. VIDEO GAME** David is playing a video game. If he falls into a pit, he loses 125 points. He has 400 points before he falls into 5 pits. Write and evaluate an expression to find how many points he now has.

**56. TAKS REASONING** A coconut falls 64 feet from a palm tree. The equation $h = -16t^2 + 64$ gives the height $h$, in feet, of the coconut after falling for $t$ seconds. Evaluate the equation when $t$ equals 1, 2, and 3 seconds. After how many seconds does the coconut hit the ground?

**57. LOOK FOR A PATTERN** Evaluate $(-10)^1$, $(-10)^2$, $(-10)^3$, $(-10)^4$, and $(-10)^5$. How is the exponent related to the sign of the power?

**58. WRITING** When multiplying integers other than zero, explain why the product is negative when there is an odd number of negative factors. Why is it positive when there is an even number of negative factors?

**59. TAKS REASONING** When you multiply an integer less than 1 and an integer less than $-1$, the product is which of the following?

　Ⓐ less than zero
　Ⓑ greater than zero
　Ⓒ less than or equal to zero
　Ⓓ greater than or equal to zero

**60. STOCK MARKET** Your uncle owns 25 shares of stock A, 45 shares of stock B, and 60 shares of stock C. In one day, the price per share changed by $+56¢$ for stock A, $-\$2$ for stock B, and $-56¢$ for stock C. Find the total change, in dollars, of the value of your uncle's stock.

**61. CHALLENGE** Mount Everest is 8850 meters tall. The temperature falls at a rate of 1°C per 100 meters. The base is at an elevation of 5400 meters and its temperature is $-3$°C. Write and evaluate an expression to find the temperature at the top of the mountain. What is the temperature?

## MIXED REVIEW FOR TAKS          **TAKS** PRACTICE at classzone.com

**REVIEW**
Lesson 2.2;
TAKS Workbook

**62. TAKS PRACTICE** Dan accepted a loan of $200 from his cousin to pay for job training. He pays $10 back each week. His debt, $d$, can be written as $d = -200 + 10w$, where $w$ is the number of weeks since Dan started paying off the debt. What is Dan's debt after he pays it off for 6 weeks? *TAKS Obj. 2*

　Ⓐ $-260$　　　Ⓑ $-190$　　　Ⓒ $-140$　　　Ⓓ $-60$

# 2.5 Dividing Integers

TEKS 8.2.B, 8.14.A

| | |
|---|---|
| **Before** | You added, subtracted, and multiplied integers. |
| **Now** | You'll divide integers. |
| **Why?** | So you can find means of profits, as in Ex. 38. |

**KEY VOCABULARY**
• **mean,** *p. 78*

You will use the rules for dividing integers to find an average temperature in Example 2. Because division is the opposite of multiplication, these rules are similar to the rules for multiplying integers.

---

### KEY CONCEPT
*For Your Notebook*

#### Dividing Integers

**Words**

**Numbers**

**Same Sign** The quotient of two integers with the same sign is positive.

$\dfrac{12}{6} = 2$ $\qquad$ $\dfrac{-12}{-6} = 2$

**Different Sign** The quotient of two integers with different signs is negative.

$\dfrac{12}{-6} = -2$ $\qquad$ $\dfrac{-12}{6} = -2$

**Zero** The quotient of 0 and any nonzero integer is 0.

$\dfrac{0}{12} = 0$ $\qquad$ $\dfrac{0}{-12} = 0$

---

### EXAMPLE 1 Dividing Integers

**a.** $\dfrac{-40}{-8} = 5$ $\qquad$ **Same sign, so quotient is positive.**

**b.** $\dfrac{-14}{2} = -7$ $\qquad$ **Different signs, so quotient is negative.**

**c.** $\dfrac{36}{-9} = -4$ $\qquad$ **Different signs, so quotient is negative.**

**d.** $\dfrac{0}{-7} = 0$ $\qquad$ **Dividend is 0 so quotient is 0.**

*AVOID ERRORS*
You cannot divide a number by 0. Any number divided by 0 is *undefined*.

✓ **GUIDED PRACTICE** for Example 1

**Find the quotient, if possible.**

**1.** $\dfrac{-33}{11}$ $\qquad$ **2.** $\dfrac{-25}{-5}$ $\qquad$ **3.** $\dfrac{0}{-4}$

**4.** $\dfrac{72}{-9}$ $\qquad$ **5.** $\dfrac{-36}{18}$ $\qquad$ **6.** $\dfrac{-28}{0}$

The **mean** of a data set is the sum of the values divided by the number of values.

$$\text{mean} = \frac{\text{sum of values}}{\text{number of values}}$$

## EXAMPLE 2 Finding a Mean

**Temperatures** One of the coldest places on Earth is the Russian town of Verkhoyansk, located near the Arctic Circle. Find the mean of the average high temperatures during winter in Verkhoyansk. Use the data in the table.

| Winter Temperatures | | | | |
|---|---|---|---|---|
| **Month** | Dec | Jan | Feb | Mar |
| **Average High** | −41°F | −40°F | −48°F | −18°F |

**SOLUTION**

**STEP 1** **Find** the sum of the temperatures.

$$-41 + (-40) + (-48) + (-18) = -147$$

**STEP 2** **Divide** the sum by the number of temperatures. $\frac{-147}{4} = -36.75$

▶ **Answer** The mean of the temperatures is about −37°F.

## EXAMPLE 3 Evaluating Expressions

 Evaluate the expression when $a = -24$, $b = 8$, and $c = -4$.

**SOLUTION**

**a.** $\frac{a}{b} = \frac{-24}{8}$  Substitute values.

$\quad = -3$  Different signs, so quotient is negative.

**b.** $\frac{ab}{c} = \frac{-24 \cdot 8}{-4}$  Substitute values.

$\quad = \frac{-192}{-4}$  Multiply.

$\quad = 48$  Same sign, so quotient is positive.

---

✓ **GUIDED PRACTICE** for Examples 2 and 3

Find the mean of the data.

**7.** −16, 17, 8, −23, −31

**8.** 0, −4, −10, 4, 11, −9, −13

**9.** Evaluate $\frac{a}{bc}$ when $a = -42$, $b = -3$, and $c = 7$.

# 2.5 EXERCISES

HOMEWORK KEY

⬥ = **TAKS Practice and Reasoning**
Exs. 34, 39, 41, 44, 48, and 49

◯ = **HINTS AND HOMEWORK HELP**
for Exs. 9, 11, 15, 21, 39 at classzone.com

## SKILL PRACTICE

1. **VOCABULARY** Copy and complete: To find the __?__ of three numbers, add them and divide the sum by three.

*SEE EXAMPLE 1*
on p. 77
for Exs. 2–13

**DIVIDING INTEGERS** Find the quotient if possible.

2. $\dfrac{-44}{4}$     3. $\dfrac{0}{-7}$     4. $\dfrac{-81}{-9}$     5. $\dfrac{50}{-10}$

6. $\dfrac{-49}{-7}$     7. $\dfrac{-28}{2}$     8. $\dfrac{36}{-4}$     9. $\dfrac{-19}{-1}$

10. $\dfrac{-66}{-11}$     11. $\dfrac{-27}{0}$     12. $\dfrac{-9}{6}$     13. $\dfrac{-6}{-30}$

*SEE EXAMPLE 2*
on p. 78
for Exs. 14–17

**FINDING A MEAN** Find the mean of the data.

14. $-12, 5, -9, 10, 16, -8, -2, 8$

15. $4, -3, -8, 7, -1, 4, -2, -9, -1$

16. $-18, 14, 16, -24, 31, -8, -19$

17. $-38, 32, 41, -45, 39, -21, -24$

*SEE EXAMPLE 3*
on p. 78
for Exs. 18–25

**ALGEBRA** Evaluate the expression when $x = 18$, $y = -12$, and $z = -6$.

18. $\dfrac{y}{z}$     19. $\dfrac{x}{z}$     20. $\dfrac{xz}{y}$     21. $\dfrac{z^2}{y}$

22. $\dfrac{x}{y+z}$     23. $\dfrac{x-yz}{x}$     24. $\dfrac{x^2+y}{z}$     25. $\dfrac{y-z^2}{y}$

**ORDER OF OPERATIONS** Evaluate the expression.

26. $2 + 3(-4) \div 6$     27. $5 + 6 \cdot 8 \div 4 - 3$     28. $12 \div 3 + 3 \cdot (-4)$     29. $16 + 8(-2) - 4$

30. $7 - 10 \div 2$     31. $5 \cdot 6 - 2(6) \div 4$     32. $-14 - 6 \div 2 + 7$     33. $7 \cdot 3 - 12 \div 6$

34. ⬥ **TAKS REASONING** You multiply the quotient of a negative integer and a positive integer by $-1$. What is the sign of the product?

Ⓐ negative     Ⓑ positive     Ⓒ zero     Ⓓ can't be determined

35. **WHICH ONE DOESN'T BELONG?** Suppose that $a > 0$ and $b > 0$. Which expression has a value that doesn't belong?

**A.** $-a \cdot (-b)$     **B.** $b \div (-a)$     **C.** $-ab$     **D.** $a \div (-b)$

36. **ERROR ANALYSIS** On three SCUBA dives, John once reached a depth of 85 feet below sea level, and twice reached a depth of 95 feet below sea level. Describe and correct the error made in finding the mean of the depths.

$$\cancel{\quad\dfrac{-(85 + 95)}{2} = -90}$$

37. **CHALLENGE** Use the number line shown to determine the sign of the quotient $\dfrac{a-b}{ab}$. *Explain* your reasoning.

SEE EXAMPLE 2
on p. 78
for Exs. 38–40

**38. GUIDED PROBLEM SOLVING** Will opened a musical instrument shop. The table shows his profits for the first three months. Find his mean profit for these months.

| Month | Profit |
|---|---|
| October | −$172 |
| November | −$203 |
| December | $157 |

  **a.** Add the profits.

  **b.** Count the number of months given.

  **c.** Divide the sum in part (a) by the number in part (b).

**39. TAKS REASONING** Over a 6 month period a bookstore has earnings of $400, −$76, −$139, $526, $650, and −$17. What is the mean of the monthly earnings for the 6 months?

  **A** $224  **B** $268.80  **C** $301.33  **D** $361.60

**40. TEMPERATURES** The temperatures during a 5 day period in Center City were −19°F, −14°F, −8°F, 13°F, and 18°F. What was the mean temperature for these 5 days?

**41. TAKS REASONING** The table shows the temperatures in Fairbanks, Alaska during a 5 day period. Find the mean. Suppose the temperature on Tuesday was 5°F lower than shown. How would this affect the mean? *Explain* your reasoning.

| Day | Mon | Tues | Wed | Thu | Fri |
|---|---|---|---|---|---|
| Temperature | −8°F | −1°F | −6°F | −21°F | −31°F |

**42. WRITING** Is the mean of a set of negative numbers *always*, *sometimes*, or *never* negative? *Explain* your reasoning, and include examples.

**43. BASKETBALL** In 3 basketball games, a player records the statistics shown in the table. Find the mean of each of the categories. *Explain* why there is always at least one actual value above and below the mean for each category.

| Points | 18 | 26 | 19 |
|---|---|---|---|
| Assists | 3 | 6 | 3 |
| Rebounds | 13 | 14 | 6 |

**44. TAKS REASONING** The table shows your test scores for 5 tests. You can use integers to find the mean of these scores quickly. Begin by choosing an integer close to what you think the mean might be. In this case, try 85.

  **a.** Find the difference between each test score and 85. For scores less than 85, record the difference as negative. Complete the third column of the table.

  **b.** What is the mean of the differences? Look for groups of numbers that are opposites to make your calculation easier.

  **c.** Use your answer to part (b) to adjust the "close to mean" that you started with. What is the exact mean of all the test scores?

| Test | Score | Difference |
|---|---|---|
| 1 | 81 | ? |
| 2 | 83 | ? |
| 3 | 92 | ? |
| 4 | 88 | ? |
| 5 | 79 | ? |

= TAKS Practice and Reasoning       = HINTS AND HOMEWORK HELP *at classzone.com*

**45. TEMPERATURE CONVERSION** The natural habitat of reindeer is the Arctic tundra. The mean temperature during the winter in the Arctic tundra is $-34°$C. You can convert degrees Celsius $C$ to degrees Fahrenheit $F$ by using the formula $F = \frac{9}{5}C + 32$. What is the mean temperature in degrees Fahrenheit?

**46. REASONING** Is it possible to work backward from the mean in Exercise 45 to determine the high and low winter temperatures? *Explain* your reasoning.

**47. CHALLENGE** The mean of five daily high temperatures is $-2°$F. Four of the temperatures are shown. Find the fifth temperature.

$$-4°F \qquad -6°F \qquad 3°F \qquad -1°F$$

## MIXED REVIEW FOR TAKS

**TAKS PRACTICE** at classzone.com

*REVIEW*
Lesson 2.3;
TAKS Workbook

**48. ✈ TAKS PRACTICE** The SOFAR (*SO*und *F*ixing *A*nd *R*anging) channel is a layer of water in the oceans that allows sounds to travel extremely long distances. It begins 600 meters below sea level and ends 1200 meters below sea level. What is the vertical height of the SOFAR channel? *TAKS Obj. 1*

**(A)** $-1800$ m   **(B)** $-600$ m   **(C)** $600$ m   **(D)** $1800$ m

*REVIEW*
Lesson 1.6;
TAKS Workbook

**49. ✈ TAKS PRACTICE** A square courtyard outside an apartment complex is 30 feet wide. What is the area of the courtyard? *TAKS Obj. 3*

**(F)** $60$ ft$^2$   **(G)** $120$ ft$^2$   **(H)** $300$ ft$^2$   **(J)** $900$ ft$^2$

## QUIZ *for Lessons 2.1–2.5*

**Copy and complete the statement with < or >.** *(p. 57)*

**1.** $-8 \; \underline{?} \; 8$    **2.** $0 \; \underline{?} \; -14$    **3.** $-20 \; \underline{?} \; \left|-30\right|$    **4.** $\left|-7\right| \; \underline{?} \; 5$

**Find the sum, difference, product, or quotient.**

**5.** $-6 + 1$ *(p. 63)*   **6.** $-20 + (-10)$ *(p. 63)*   **7.** $-4 - (-3)$ *(p. 68)*   **8.** $\frac{36}{-9}$ *(p. 77)*

**9.** $-6(-8)$ *(p. 73)*   **10.** $-12(4)$ *(p. 73)*   **11.** $\frac{-48}{-8}$ *(p. 77)*   **12.** $-11 - 8$ *(p. 68)*

**Find the mean of the data.** *(p. 77)*

**13.** $-9, -15, 16, 4, 2, -10, 8, 20$     **14.** $-10, 6, -11, -6, -7, 3, -4, 1, 1$

**15. GRAVITY** You drop a ball out of a window that is 144 feet above the ground. The equation $h = -16t^2 + 144$ gives the height $h$, in feet, of the ball after falling for $t$ seconds. Find the height of the ball after 1, 2, and 3 seconds. After how many seconds does the ball hit the ground? *(p. 73)*

## Lessons 2.1–2.5

**MULTIPLE CHOICE**

1. **THEATER** The table shows the earnings and expenses for the Theater Club during the year. How much money did the Theater Club make or lose during the year? *TEKS 8.2.B*

| Event | Fall play | Winter play | Musical |
|---|---|---|---|
| Earnings | $500 | $800 | $1500 |
| Expenses | $800 | $600 | $900 |

   Ⓐ −$2300     Ⓑ $500

   Ⓒ $2800     Ⓓ $5100

2. **FALLING OBJECTS** A rock is dropped from a height of 256 feet above the ground. The equation $h = -16t^2 + 256$ gives the rock's height $h$ in feet above the ground after falling for $t$ seconds. Which statement describes the rock's position when $t = 4$? *TEKS 8.5.A*

   Ⓕ The rock is 192 feet above ground level.

   Ⓖ The rock is 128 feet above ground level.

   Ⓗ The rock is at ground level.

   Ⓙ The rock is 192 feet below ground level.

3. **FALLING OBJECTS** Use the equation given in Exercise 2 above. Find the rock's height after falling for 1, 2, and 3 seconds. Which of the following is true? *TEKS 8.5.A*

   Ⓐ The rock falls the same distance each second until hitting the ground.

   Ⓑ The distance that the rock falls each second increases until it hits the ground.

   Ⓒ The distance that the rock falls each second decreases until it hits the ground.

   Ⓓ The rock always travels at the same speed during the time that it is falling.

4. **STAIRS** Pia walks up and down stairs. A move on the stairs is defined as an up and down pair. For example, (3, −2) means she goes up 3 steps and down 2 steps. Pia starts on the eighth step. Which move will NOT result in her ending on the second step? *TEKS 8.14.C*

   Ⓕ (1, −7)

   Ⓖ (3, −9)

   Ⓗ (0, −6)

   Ⓙ (2, −4)

5. **GOLF** The table shows golf scores for six students. If Irma's score was 66 instead of 72, how would the mean of the scores change? *TEKS 8.14.C*

| Player | Score |
|---|---|
| Elliot | 84 |
| Louisa | 76 |
| Chad | 68 |
| Mark | 71 |
| Irma | 72 |
| Petra | 65 |

   Ⓐ The mean would decrease by 11.

   Ⓑ The mean would decrease by 6.

   Ⓒ The mean would decrease by 4.

   Ⓓ The mean would decrease by 1.

**GRIDDED ANSWER** ⓪①②●④⑤⑥⑦⑧⑨

6. **STOCK** Last week's daily changes in cents of the price per share of a stock were: +125, −105, −24, −67, and +11. Based on the mean of these changes, how many weekdays would it take for the price to fall by $1.80? *TEKS 8.14.B*

# 2.6 Number Properties

 **TEKS** *8.2.A, 8.16.B*

| **Before** | You evaluated expressions. |
| **Now** | You'll use properties to evaluate expressions. |
| **Why?** | So you can find total distance traveled, as in Example 1. |

**KEY VOCABULARY**
- **sum,** *p. 764*
- **product,** *p. 768*
- **identity property of addition,** *p. 63*
- **inverse property of addition,** *p. 63*
- **identity property of multiplication,** *p. 73*

You can use the commutative properties of addition and multiplication to easily evaluate expressions using mental math.

---

**KEY CONCEPT**                                    *For Your Notebook*

**The Commutative Property**

|  | **Addition** | **Multiplication** |
|---|---|---|
| **Words** | You can add numbers of a sum in any order. | You can multiply factors of a product in any order. |
| **Numbers** | $3 + (-8) = -8 + 3$ | $5(-6) = -6(5)$ |
| **Algebra** | $a + b = b + a$ | $ab = ba$ |

---

**EXAMPLE 1** **Using the Commutative Property**

**Tour Biking** You are going on a 400 mile bike trip. You plan to cycle at an average speed of 12 miles per hour for 7 hours a day. Can you complete the trip in 5 days?

**SOLUTION**

Write a verbal model to find the total distance you can cycle in 5 days.

| Total distance | = | Average speed | • | Hours per day | • | Number of days |

$= 12 \cdot 7 \cdot 5$      **Substitute known values.**

$= 12 \cdot 5 \cdot 7$      **Commutative property of multiplication**

$= 60 \cdot 7$      **Multiply.**

$= 420$      **Multiply.**

The unit for the result is miles.    $\dfrac{\text{miles}}{\text{hour}} \cdot \dfrac{\text{hours}}{\text{day}} \cdot \text{days} = \text{miles}$

▶ **Answer** Because 400 miles is less than the 420 miles you can cycle in 5 days, you can complete the trip in 5 days.

**Properties and Subtraction** Subtracting a number is the same as adding its opposite. So you can rewrite subtraction expressions using the commutative property of addition to simplify them.

**EXAMPLE 2** Using the Commutative Property

*SIMPLIFY COMPUTATIONS*

When deciding what numbers to add or multiply first, look for pairs whose sum or product ends in zero, because multiples of 10 are easier to work with.

$$-54 + 35 - 16 = -54 + 35 + (-16)$$   Change subtraction to addition.

$$= -54 + (-16) + 35$$   Commutative property of addition

$$= -70 + 35$$   Add $-54$ and $-16$.

$$= -35$$   Add $-70$ and $35$.

✓ **GUIDED PRACTICE**   for Examples 1 and 2

1. **What If?** Suppose in Example 1 you only want to bike for 6 hours a day at an average speed of 14 miles per hour. Can you complete the trip in 6 days?

**Use the commutative property to evaluate the expression.**

2. $4 \cdot (-9) \cdot 25$   3. $-13 + 34 - 7$   4. $\dfrac{3}{7} + \left(8 + \dfrac{4}{7}\right)$

**Associative Properties** You can also use the associative properties of addition and multiplication to evaluate expressions more easily using mental math.

**KEY CONCEPT**   *For Your Notebook*

**The Associative Property**

|  | Addition | Multiplication |
|---|---|---|
| **Words** | Changing the grouping of numbers will not change their sum. | Changing the grouping of factors will not change their product. |
| **Numbers** | $(2 + 3) + 4 = 2 + (3 + 4)$ | $(7 \cdot 4) \cdot 5 = 7 \cdot (4 \cdot 5)$ |
| **Algebra** | $(a + b) + c = a + (b + c)$ | $(ab)c = a(bc)$ |

**EXAMPLE 3** Using the Associative Property

*REVIEW ADDING FRACTIONS*

Grouping fractions can make adding them easier. For help adding fractions with common denominators, see p. 765.

$$\dfrac{3}{5} + \left(\dfrac{2}{5} + 3\right) = \left(\dfrac{3}{5} + \dfrac{2}{5}\right) + 3$$   Associative property of addition

$$= \dfrac{5}{5} + 3$$   Add fractions.

$$= 1 + 3$$   Write $\dfrac{5}{5}$ as 1.

$$= 4$$   Add.

**EXAMPLE 4** Using the Associative Property

*VOCABULARY*
*Commute* means change locations. *Associate* means group together. These words can help you remember which property is which.

| | |
|---|---|
| $5 \cdot (11 \cdot 2) = 5 \cdot (2 \cdot 11)$ | Commutative property of multiplication |
| $= (5 \cdot 2) \cdot 11$ | Associative property of multiplication |
| $= 10 \cdot 11$ | Multiply inside grouping symbols. |
| $= 110$ | Multiply. |

✓ **GUIDED PRACTICE** for Examples 3 and 4

Use properties to evaluate the expression.

**5.** $18 + (-34 + 12)$  **6.** $\frac{4}{5} + \left(8 + \frac{1}{5}\right)$  **7.** $12\left(6 \cdot \frac{1}{12}\right)$  **8.** $\frac{5}{6}\left(3 \cdot \frac{6}{5}\right)$

Evaluate the expression using mental math.

**9.** $4\left(\frac{1}{4} \cdot 23\right)$  **10.** $-2(46 \cdot 50)$  **11.** $[-21 \cdot (-29)] \cdot 0$  **12.** $10(-6)\left(\frac{1}{10}\right)$

## 2.6 EXERCISES

**HOMEWORK KEY**

🔻 = **TAKS Practice and Reasoning**
Exs. 22, 45, 48, 50, and 51

◯ = **HINTS** AND **HOMEWORK HELP**
for Exs. 7, 13, 17, 23, 41 at classzone.com

### SKILL PRACTICE

VOCABULARY **Match the equation with the property it illustrates.**

**1.** $(x + 9) + 1 = x + (9 + 1)$  **A.** Identity property of addition

**2.** $12(1) = 12$  **B.** Commutative property of multiplication

**3.** $8a = a \cdot 8$  **C.** Commutative property of addition

**4.** $-16 + 0 = -16$  **D.** Associative property of multiplication

**5.** $(5 \cdot 7)y = 5(7y)$  **E.** Associative property of addition

**6.** $-24 + a = a + (-24)$  **F.** Identity property of multiplication

MENTAL MATH **Evaluate the expression using mental math. Identify any property you used.**

*SEE EXAMPLES 1, 2, 3, AND 4*
on pp. 83–85
for Exs. 7–21

**7.** $17 + 15 + 13$  **8.** $-27 + 43 - 13$  **9.** $5 \cdot (-29) \cdot 2$

**10.** $-53 + (-27 + 44)$  **11.** $(-39 + 48) + 12$  **12.** $-2(-9 \cdot 50)$

**13.** $[-4 \cdot (-7)](-5)$  **14.** $[25 \cdot (-7)]4$  **15.** $(-20 \cdot 9) \cdot 5$

USING PROPERTIES **Copy and complete the statement using the property indicated.**

**16.** $28 + 65 = \underline{\ ?\ }$; commutative  **17.** $54 \cdot 16 = \underline{\ ?\ }$; commutative

**18.** $(7 \cdot 3)3 = \underline{\ ?\ }$; associative  **19.** $4 + (9 + 2) = \underline{\ ?\ }$; commutative

**20.** $5(11 \cdot 2) = \underline{\ ?\ }$; commutative  **21.** $(8 + 16) + 2 = \underline{\ ?\ }$; commutative

SEE EXAMPLES
1, 2, 3, AND 4
on pp. 83–85
for Exs. 22–34

**22.** ⬥ **TAKS REASONING** Which expression is equivalent to $7 + 5 - 17$?

Ⓐ $7 + 17 - 15$ Ⓑ $17 - 7 + 5$ Ⓒ $7 - 17 + 5$ Ⓓ $7 - 5 + 17$

**EVALUATING EXPRESSIONS** Evaluate the expression. Show and justify each step.

**23.** $45 - (-68) - 44$

**24.** $-57 - 38 - (-57)$

**25.** $(-26 + 33) + (-4)$

**26.** $(0.5)(45 \cdot 2)$

**27.** $\left(\frac{2}{7} + 5\right) + \frac{5}{7}$

**28.** $\left(\frac{2}{3} \cdot 7\right) \cdot 21$

**29.** $12 \cdot (7 \cdot 1 \cdot 5)$

**30.** $-2 \cdot (19 \cdot 15) \cdot 1$

**31.** $36 + 57 + (-36)$

**32.** $17 + 0 + (-19)$

**33.** $24 + (-12 - 8) + 6$

**34.** $5(7 \cdot 4)(0.25)$

🅧🆈 **ALGEBRA** Simplify the expression.

**35.** $7 \cdot x \cdot 10$

**36.** $-67 + [x + (-13)]$

**37.** $(52 + x) + 18$

**38.** **ERROR ANALYSIS** Describe and correct the error made in evaluating the expression.

$$\begin{aligned} 15 - (5 + 3) &= (15 - 5) + 3 \\ &= 10 + 3 \\ &= 13 \end{aligned}$$

**39.** **CHALLENGE** Use the commutative properties of addition and multiplication to write three expressions equivalent to $4 \cdot 8 + 5$.

## PROBLEM SOLVING

SEE EXAMPLE 1
on p. 83
for Exs. 40–42

**40.** **SUPER BOWL** During Super Bowl XXXVI, six New England Patriots rushed the football for 92 yards, 22 yards, 15 yards, 5 yards, 3 yards, and $-4$ yards. What was the total number of their rushing yards?

**41.** **JUICE BOX** You have a juice box that is 2.5 inches long, 1.5 inches wide, and 4 inches high. The formula for the *volume* of a box is $V = lwh$. How much juice could the box hold, in cubic inches? How can you verify that cubic units are appropriate?

**42.** **PAYCHECK** The table shows the hours you worked during one week. Your hourly wage is $8 per hour. Write a multiplication model to find the amount you earned for the week. Then find the amount.

| Time Card | | | | | | |
|---|---|---|---|---|---|---|
| **Day** | Monday | Tuesday | Wednesday | Thursday | Friday | Saturday |
| **Time in** | 4 P.M. | 4 P.M. | did not work | 3 P.M. | 3 P.M. | 11 A.M. |
| **Time out** | 6 P.M. | 6 P.M. | | 5 P.M. | 5 P.M. | 1 P.M. |

**43.** **REASONING** Is the expression $-15 + 34 - 44 - 19 + 51$ equivalent to the expression $34 - 19 + 15 - 44 + 51$? *Explain* your reasoning.

**44. WRITING** You need to find the sum of 52, 99, 65, 38, and 11. *Describe* how the commutative and associative properties of addition can help you find the sum using mental math.

**45. ⚑ TAKS REASONING** Show how to use order of operations to simplify the product $25 \cdot 6 \cdot 4 \cdot 7$. *Describe* how the commutative and associative properties of multiplication can help you find the product using mental math. Then find the product.

**46. REASONING** Is division commutative? *Justify* your answer with an example.

**47. SALE PRICE** You are buying 9 yards of fabric that costs $5.25 per yard. You have a coupon for one third off the original price. What is the discount? What is the price of your purchase after the discount?

**48. ⚑ TAKS REASONING** *Explain* how a student used the properties of addition to go from the first expression to the second expression below. Use the same method to find the sum of the numbers from 1 to 19. *Describe* how to use this method to find the sum of the numbers from 1 to 99.

$$1 + 2 + 3 + 4 + 5 + 6 + 7 + 8 + 9 = 10 + 10 + 10 + 10 + 5$$
$$= 45$$

**49. CHALLENGE** The shortest side length of a four-sided figure is $a$ feet. The second side is 4 feet longer than the first side. The third side is 8 feet longer than the second side. The fourth side is 6 feet shorter than the third side. Write and simplify an expression to find the perimeter of the figure. Then evaluate when $a = 6$ feet. Find the perimeter.

---

## ◗ MIXED REVIEW FOR TAKS          TAKS PRACTICE at classzone.com

*REVIEW*
Skills Review
Handbook,
p. 772;
TAKS Workbook

**50. ⚑ TAKS PRACTICE** Patty has read 110 pages of a book. She sees that she has read less than half of the book. Why does she believe the book has more than 200 pages? *TAKS Obj. 6*

**(A)** Because the product of 110 and $\frac{1}{2}$ is greater than 200.

**(B)** Because half of 200 is greater than 110.

**(C)** Because the sum of 110 and $\frac{1}{2}$ is greater than 200.

**(D)** Because 110 is half of 220, and 220 is greater than 200.

*REVIEW*
Lesson 1.3;
TAKS Workbook

**51. ⚑ TAKS PRACTICE** Party cups and balloons each cost $2 per package. Oliver buys 3 packages of balloons and 2 packages of cups. Which expression can be used to find the amount of dollars he spent? *TAKS Obj. 6*

**(F)** $3(3) + 2(2)$     **(G)** $3(2) + 2(2)$     **(H)** $2(3) + 2(3)$     **(J)** $2(2) + 2(2)$

---

# 2.7 The Distributive Property

TEKS 8.7.B, 8.16.B

**Before** You used addition and multiplication properties.

**Now** You'll use the distributive property.

**Why?** So you can find areas, as for murals in Ex. 46.

**KEY VOCABULARY**
- **distributive property,** *p. 88*
- **terms,** *p. 89*
- **like terms,** *p.89*
- **coefficient,** *p. 89*
- **constant term,** *p. 89*

**Architecture** A replica of the Parthenon, a temple in ancient Greece, was built in Nashville, Tennessee, in 1897. The diagram below shows the approximate dimensions of two adjacent rooms inside the replica. You can find the total area in two ways as shown in Example 1.

**EXAMPLE 1** Finding a Combined Area

Two methods can be used to find the total area of the two rooms.

**METHOD 1** **Find** the area of each room, and then find the total area.

$$\text{Area} = 63(44) + 63(98)$$
$$= 2772 + 6174$$
$$= 8946 \text{ square feet}$$

**METHOD 2** **Find** the total length, and then multiply by the common width.

$$\text{Area} = 63(44 + 98)$$
$$= 63(142)$$
$$= 8946 \text{ square feet}$$

▸**Answer** The total area of the two rooms is 8946 square feet.

Example 1 demonstrates the distributive property.

**KEY CONCEPT** *For Your Notebook*

**The Distributive Property**

**Words** You can multiply a number and a sum by multiplying the number by each part of the sum and then adding these products. The same property applies to subtraction.

**Algebra** $a(b + c) = ab + bc$   **Numbers** $6(4 + 3) = 6(4) + 6(3)$
$a(b - c) = ab - bc$                    $7(8 - 5) = 7(8) - 7(5)$

**Distributive Property** You can apply the distributive property to expressions with a sum or difference of two or more numbers or variable expressions. Applying the distributive property produces an equivalent expression.

### EXAMPLE 2   Using the Distributive Property

**a.** $-5(x + 10) = -5x + (-5)(10)$     Distributive property

$\phantom{-5(x + 10)} = -5x + (-50)$     Multiply.

$\phantom{-5(x + 10)} = -5x - 50$     Simplify.

**b.** $3[1 - 20 + (-5)] = 3(1) - 3(20) + 3(-5)$     Distributive property

$\phantom{3[1 - 20 + (-5)]} = 3 - 60 + (-15)$     Multiply.

$\phantom{3[1 - 20 + (-5)]} = 3 + (-60) + (-15)$     Add the opposite of 60.

$\phantom{3[1 - 20 + (-5)]} = -72$     Add.

✓ **GUIDED PRACTICE**   for Examples 1 and 2

Use the distributive property to find the area of the figure.

**1.**
10 ft

12 ft     22 ft

**2.**
3 m

14 m

9 m

Use the distributive property to evaluate or write an equivalent expression.

**3.** $-2(5 + 12)$     **4.** $-4(-7 - 10)$     **5.** $2(w - 8)$     **6.** $-8(z + 25)$

**Combining Like Terms** In an expression, **terms** are separated by addition and subtraction symbols. You can use the distributive property to combine *like terms*. **Like terms** have identical variable parts raised to the same power. In a term, the number multiplied by the variable is the **coefficient** of the variable. A term that has no variable is a **constant term**.

Coefficients are 4 and 8.     Constant term is 1.

$$4x + 8x + 1$$

4x and 8x are like terms.

### EXAMPLE 3   Combining Like Terms

**a.** $3x + 4x = (3 + 4)x$     Distributive property

$\phantom{3x + 4x} = 7x$     Add inside grouping symbols.

**b.** $-9y + 7y + 5z = (-9 + 7)y + 5z$     Distributive property

$\phantom{-9y + 7y + 5z} = -2y + 5z$     Add inside grouping symbols.

## EXAMPLE 4 Simplifying an Expression

**a.** $2(4 + x) + x = 8 + 2x + x$     Distributive property

$\quad\quad\quad\quad\quad\quad = 8 + 3x$     Combine like terms.

**b.** $-5(3x - 6) + 7x = -15x + 30 + 7x$     Distributive property

$\quad\quad\quad\quad\quad\quad\quad = -8x + 30$     Combine like terms.

✓ **GUIDED PRACTICE**    for Examples 3 and 4

Simplify the expression by combining like terms.

**7.** $2(x + 4) + 3x - 5$     **8.** $5y + 9z - 7 - 3y$     **9.** $-3(6x + 2y) + 22x$

# 2.7 EXERCISES

HOMEWORK KEY

 = **TAKS Practice and Reasoning**
Exs. 15, 37, 45, 48, 49, 52, and 53

○ = **HINTS** AND **HOMEWORK HELP**
for Exs. 9, 21, 23, 45 at classzone.com

## SKILL PRACTICE

**VOCABULARY Identify the following in the expression** $7x - 3y - 6y + x + 2$.

**1.** the coefficient of the third term     **2.** the coefficient of the fourth term

**3.** a like term for the second term     **4.** a constant term

**MATCHING EXPRESSIONS Match the expression with its equivalent expression.**

**5.** $3(x + 4)$     **6.** $4(x + 3)$     **7.** $2(2x - 6)$     **8.** $x(4 + 9)$

**A.** $4x - 12$     **B.** $3x + 12$     **C.** $13x$     **D.** $4x + 12$

**WRITING EQUIVALENT EXPRESSIONS Use the distributive property to write a sum that is equivalent to the expression. Then find the sum.**

**9.** $4(7 + 8)$     **10.** $-7(3 + 2)$     **11.** $3(5 + 6)$

**12.** $-13(-12 + 9)$     **13.** $6(-5 + 10 + 2)$     **14.** $-4(3 + 6 + -8)$

**15.**  **TAKS REASONING** Which expression is equivalent to $-3(2x + 4)$?

    **(A)** $-6x + 4$     **(B)** $-6x + 12$     **(C)** $-6x - 12$     **(D)** $-6x - 3$

**USING THE DISTRIBUTIVE PROPERTY Use the distributive property to simplify.**

**16.** $9(x - 3)$     **17.** $-8(5 - x)$     **18.** $-12(4 + 5 + y)$

**19.** $19[7 + w + (-2)]$     **20.** $-34(z - 21 - 5)$     **21.** $-2[4 - x + (-7)]$

**COMBINING LIKE TERMS Simplify the expression by combining like terms.**

**22.** $r + 2s + 3r$     **23.** $11w + 9z + 3z + 5w$     **24.** $7a - 2a + 8b - 2b$

**25.** $3x + 2x + y + 2y - 3$     **26.** $-3x + 2x - 9y - 2x$     **27.** $r + 2s - (-3r) - s$

**28. ERROR ANALYSIS** Describe and correct the error made in simplifying the expression $4x + 2y - 7y - 2x$.

$$
\begin{aligned}
4x + 2y - 7y - 2x &= 4x - 2x + 2y - 7y \\
&= 2x - 5y \\
&= -3xy
\end{aligned}
$$

**SIMPLIFYING EXPRESSIONS** Simplify by combining like terms.

SEE EXAMPLE 4
on p. 90
for Exs. 29–37

**29.** $5(z + 2z) - 4z$

**30.** $2(2x + 1) + 3x - 5x$

**31.** $4(3c - 4) + 2 - 4c$

**32.** $8d - 2(3d - 5d)$

**33.** $3(a + 4) + b - 5 - a + 7(b - 3)$

**34.** $7(y - 1.3) + 2.4 - 5.3y$

**35.** $3.2(2z - 3x) + 4(1.1y + x) - 2z$

**36.** $5(x + 2) - 5(y + 3) - 2x + 5y$

**37.** **TAKS REASONING** Which expression is equivalent to $5 - 4x + 2(2 - y)$?

    **A** $2x + 2y - x$     **B** $9 - 4x - 2y$     **C** $2x + y$     **D** $9 - 2x - 2y$

**Animated Math** at classzone.com

**MENTAL MATH** Use the distributive property and mental math to find the product. *Explain* your reasoning.

**38.** $4(34)$        **39.** $9(19)$        **40.** $24(12)$        **41.** $65(24)$

**42. REASONING** Are $3xy$ and $4yx$ like terms? *Explain* your reasoning.

**43. CHALLENGE** Simplify the expression $7[6 - 2(x + 3)]$ using the order of operations. Show and justify each step. Then show how to get the same result by first distributing the 7. *Explain* why the second method works.

## PROBLEM SOLVING

**44. GUIDED PROBLEM SOLVING** You are buying three pairs of flip-flops that cost $12.90 each. Use mental math and the distributive property to find the total cost of the flip-flops.

  **a.** Copy and complete: $3(12.90) = 3(13 - \underline{\phantom{?}})$.

  **b.** Find the products $3(13)$ and $3(0.10)$.

  **c.** Find the difference of the products.

**45. TAKS REASONING** You are going to the store to purchase 6 pounds each of bird seed, cat food, and dog bones. Prices per pound are $.30 for bird seed, $.70 for cat food, and $.90 for dog bones. *Explain* how to use mental math to find how much money you will need.

**46. WRITING** Some students have been given permission to paint murals on 5 walls around your school. The walls are each 8 feet tall. The mural widths are 21.5 feet, 35 feet, 27.5 feet, 33.5 feet, and 22.5 feet. *Describe* two methods for finding the total area of the murals. Then find the total area.

**47. GEOMETRY** A floor plan of a house is shown. You want to carpet the family room and the living room. The carpeting you want to use in these two rooms sells for $3.12 per square foot. How much will the carpet cost?

**48.** **TAKS REASONING** Which is an appropriate expression to model the area of a room that is 23 feet by 35 feet?

&#9400; $20(30 + 5) + 3(20 + 3)$      &#9399; $30(20 + 3) + 5(20 + 3)$

&#9402; $35(20 + 3) + 23(30 + 5)$      &#9401; $35(30 + 5) + 23(20 + 3)$

**49.** **TAKS REASONING** The perimeter of the entire stage, including backstage, is 200 feet. Find the value of $x$. Show your work. *Explain* two different ways to find the area of the stage. Use either method to find the area.

**50. EXAMPLES AND NONEXAMPLES** *Explain* what you should consider when deciding which expression is easier to evaluate, $8(1000 - 2)$ or $8 \cdot 1000 - 8 \cdot 2$. Give an example of a problem you think is easier to solve using the distributive property and an example you think is more difficult to solve using the distributive property.

**51. CHALLENGE** You are ordering T-shirts with your school logo. Each T-shirt costs $7.25. There is a $25 setup fee for silk screening and a screening charge of $1.85 per shirt. Write an expression to find the total cost for $x$ T-shirts. What is the total cost for 75 T-shirts? What is the total cost for 170 T-shirts? How does the distributive property apply?

---

## MIXED REVIEW FOR TAKS

**TAKS PRACTICE** at classzone.com

**52.** **TAKS PRACTICE** How long will it take a three-toed sloth to travel 156 feet at a rate of 12 feet per minute? *TAKS Obj. 2*

&#9400; 0.08 min     &#9399; 13 min     &#9402; 168 min     &#9401; 1872 min

**53.** **TAKS PRACTICE** The table below shows the temperatures at four different times in the day. How many degrees did the temperature rise from 8 A.M. to 4 P.M.? *TAKS Obj. 1*

| Time | 8 A.M. | 12 P.M. | 4 P.M. | 8 P.M. |
|------|--------|---------|--------|--------|
| Temperature | −7°C | 4°C | 5°C | −1°C |

&#9403; −2°C     &#9404; 6°C     &#9405; 11°C     &#9406; 12°C

**TEKS** *8.2.B, 8.14.D*

# 2.7 Using Integer Operations

**EXAMPLE** Use a calculator to evaluate the expression.

**a.** $-900{,}018 + (-805{,}560)$

**b.** $\dfrac{-278 \cdot (-640)}{-139}$

**SOLUTION**

Use the following keystrokes to find your answer.

**Keystrokes**          **Display**

**a.** (−) 900018 + (−) 805560 =     **−1705578**

▶ **Answer** $-900{,}018 + (-805{,}560) = -1{,}705{,}578$

**Keystrokes**          **Display**

**b.** (−) 278 × (−) 640 ÷ (−) 139 =     **−1280**

▶ **Answer** $\dfrac{-278 \cdot (-640)}{-139} = -1280$

**PRACTICE** Use a calculator to evaluate the expression.

**1.** $18{,}432 + (-46{,}978)$

**2.** $-50{,}215 + 1315$

**3.** $7010 - (-3999)$

**4.** $-14{,}300 - (-500)$

**5.** $-751 \cdot 2804$

**6.** $-1940 \cdot (-689)$

**7.** $3336(-198 \cdot 398)$

**8.** $\dfrac{-105{,}638}{-221}$

**9.** $\dfrac{-67{,}771}{671}$

**10. EARTH** The diameter of Earth is about 4 times the diameter of the Moon. The diameter of the Moon is 3476 kilometers. What is the diameter of Earth? Find the difference of the diameter of Earth and the diameter of the Moon.

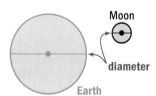

Moon

diameter

Earth

**11. BLUEBERRIES** Blueberries are purchased in a six ounce package and the manufacturer guarantees about 170 blueberries in each package. You purchase three packages of blueberries and count the number of blueberries in each package.

Package 1: 12 blueberries below average
Package 2: 8 blueberries below average
Package 3: 16 blueberries above average

Is the manufacturer's guarantee accurate? *Justify* your reasoning.

# 2.8 The Coordinate Plane

TEKS 8.7.D

| | |
|---|---|
| **Before** | You used number lines. |
| **Now** | You'll identify and plot points in a coordinate plane. |
| **Why?** | So you can find patterns in real-world data, as in Ex. 41. |

**KEY VOCABULARY**
- **coordinate plane,** p. 94
- ***x*-axis, *y*-axis,** p. 94
- **origin,** p. 94
- **quadrant,** p. 94
- **ordered pair,** p. 94
- ***x*- and *y*-coordinates,** p. 94

A **coordinate plane** is formed by the intersection of a horizontal number line called the ***x*-axis** and a vertical number line called the ***y*-axis**. The axes meet at the point (0, 0), called the **origin**, and divide the coordinate plane into four **quadrants**.

Points in a coordinate plane are represented by **ordered pairs**. The first number is the ***x*-coordinate**. The second number is the ***y*-coordinate**. Point $P$ is represented by the ordered pair $(-2, 1)$.

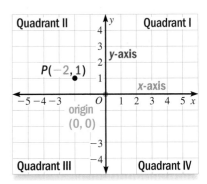

*x*-coordinate      *y*-coordinate

$P(-2, 1)$

---

**EXAMPLE 1** Naming Points in a Coordinate Plane

Give the coordinates of the point.

**a.** $A$          **b.** $B$          **c.** $C$

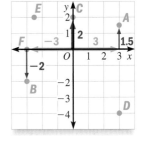

**SOLUTION**

**a.** Point $A$ is 3 units to the right of the origin and 1.5 units up. So, the *x*-coordinate is 3 and the *y*-coordinate is 1.5. The coordinates of $A$ are (3, 1.5).

**b.** Point $B$ is 3 units to the left of the origin and 2 units down. So, the *x*-coordinate is $-3$ and the *y*-coordinate is $-2$. The coordinates of $B$ are $(-3, -2)$.

**c.** Point $C$ is 2 units up from the origin. So, the *x*-coordinate is 0 and the *y*-coordinate is 2. The coordinates of $C$ are (0, 2).

---

✔ **GUIDED PRACTICE** for Example 1

Use the graph in Example 1. Give the coordinates of the point.

**1.** $D$          **2.** $E$          **3.** $F$

**EXAMPLE 2** Graphing Points in a Coordinate Plane

**Plot the point and describe its location.**

   **a.** $A(4, -2)$     **b.** $B(-1, 2.5)$     **c.** $C(0, -3)$

**SOLUTION**

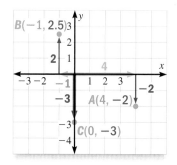

   **a.** Begin at the origin, move 4 units to the right, then 2 units down. Point $A$ lies in Quadrant IV.

*VOCABULARY*
Points on the *x*-axis or *y*-axis do not lie in any quadrant.

   **b.** Begin at the origin, move 1 unit to the left, then 2.5 units up. Point $B$ lies in Quadrant II.

   **c.** Begin at the origin, move 3 units down. Point $C$ lies on the *y*-axis.

---

**TAKS**

**EXAMPLE 3** TAKS REASONING: Multi-Step Problem

**Archaeology** On a field trip, students are exploring an archaeological site. They rope off an area of land to explore. Identify the figure of the region they are exploring and find its perimeter.

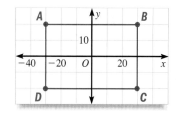

**SOLUTION**

*FINDING DISTANCES*
You can find the distance *d* between two points *a* and *b* on a number line. Use the formula $d = |a - b|$.

**STEP 1** **Notice** that points *A, B, C,* and *D* form a rectangle. Find the coordinates of the vertices.

$$A(-30, 20), B(30, 20), C(30, -20), D(-30, -20)$$

**STEP 2** **Find** the *horizontal* distance from *A* to *B* to find the length *l*.

$$l = |\; x\text{-coordinate of } A - x\text{-coordinate of } B\;|$$
$$= |-30 - 30| = |-60| = 60$$

**STEP 3** **Find** the *vertical* distance from *A* to *D* to find the width *w*.

$$w = |\; y\text{-coordinate of } A - y\text{-coordinate of } D\;|$$
$$= |20 - (-20)| = |40| = 40$$

**STEP 4** **Find** the perimeter: $2l + 2w = 2(60) + 2(40) = 200$

▶ **Answer** The region's perimeter is 200 units · 10 feet per unit = 2000 feet.

---

✓ **GUIDED PRACTICE**   for Examples 2 and 3

**Plot the point and describe its location.**

   **4.** $R(-3, 4)$     **5.** $S(1, -2.5)$     **6.** $T(0.5, 3)$     **7.** $U(-4, 0)$

   **8.** Move points *A* and *B* in Example 3 to form a new rectangle. Find the perimeter.

# 2.8 EXERCISES

HOMEWORK KEY

🔶 = **TAKS Practice and Reasoning**
**Exs. 28, 36, 38, 41, 46, 51, and 52**

◯ = **HINTS AND HOMEWORK HELP**
**for Exs. 3, 7, 15, 21, 39 at classzone.com**

## SKILL PRACTICE

**1. VOCABULARY** Draw a coordinate plane and label the *x*-axis, *y*-axis, each quadrant, and the origin.

**2. VOCABULARY** Identify the *y*-coordinate in the ordered pair $(3, -4)$.

**NAMING POINTS** Give the coordinates of the point.

*SEE EXAMPLE 1*
on p. 94
for Exs. 3–10

**3.** *A*          **4.** *B*

**5.** *C*          **6.** *D*

**7.** *E*          **8.** *F*

**9.** *G*          **10.** *H*

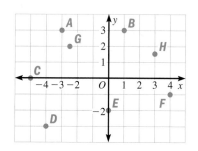

**PLOTTING POINTS** Plot the point in a coordinate plane and describe its location.

*SEE EXAMPLE 2*
on p. 95
for Exs. 11–23

**11.** $(4, 1)$          **12.** $(2, -3)$          **13.** $(-3, 0)$          **14.** $(-2, -1)$

**15.** $(-2, 3)$          **16.** $(3, -1)$          **17.** $(0, -5)$          **18.** $(-3, -4)$

**19.** $(-8.2, 6.1)$          **20.** $(-0.4, -9.6)$          **21.** $(2.4, 0)$          **22.** $(4.3, -1.8)$

**23. ERROR ANALYSIS** Describe and correct the error made in plotting the points $P(2, 3)$ and $Q(1, -1)$.

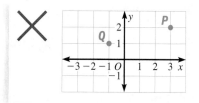

**FINDING PERIMETER** Plot and connect the given points. Identify the resulting figure and find its perimeter.

*SEE EXAMPLE 3*
on p. 95
for Exs. 24–27

**24.** $A(-2, 6), B(2, 6), C(2, -6), D(-2, -6)$

**25.** $E(4, -2), F(4, 3), G(-1, 3), H(-1, -2)$

**26.** $J(5, 4), K(5, -2), L(-1, -2), M(-1, 4)$

**27.** $N(-5, 4), O(8, 4), P(8, -1), Q(-5, -1)$

**28.** 🔶 **TAKS REASONING** Which pair of points have *x*-coordinates that are opposites?

Ⓐ *M* and *N*          Ⓑ *M* and *P*

Ⓒ *R* and *N*          Ⓓ *R* and *P*

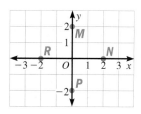

**GEOMETRY** Plot and connect the given points. Find the perimeter and area of the figure formed.

**29.** $A(1, 1), B(4, 1), C(4, -1), D(-3, -1), E(-3, 1), F(-2, 1), G(-2, 2), H(1, 2)$

**30.** $J(-4, 1), K(-4, -2), L(0, -2), M(0, 0.5), N(4, 0.5), P(4, 1)$

**31.** $W\left(-\frac{1}{2}, -7\right), X\left(-\frac{1}{2}, 3\right), Y(2, 3), Z(2, -7)$

**FINDING SIDE LENGTH** The perimeter and the coordinates of two vertices for a side of a rectangle are given. Find the other side length. Give the possible coordinates for the other vertices of the rectangle.

**32.** Perimeter = 22 units, $R(4, -5), S(-1, -5)$

**33.** Perimeter = 36 units, $R(2, 1), S(9, 1)$

**34.** Perimeter = 68 units, $R(-4, -2), S(10, -2)$

**35. CHALLENGE** Two vertices of a rectangle are $(-8, 5)$ and $(4, -5)$. The vertices do not share a common side. Find two other vertices that will form a rectangle. Then find the area and perimeter of the rectangle.

## PROBLEM SOLVING

**36. TAKS REASONING** The grid at the right shows the streets of a town. What are the coordinates of the intersection of Eagle Road and Deer Lane?

**(A)** (2, 3)  **(B)** (3, 2)

**(C)** (2, 2)  **(D)** (3, 3)

*Animated Math* at classzone.com

**37. SEGMENTS** Draw four horizontal or vertical line segments that start at the point $(2, -1)$ and have a length of 6 units. What are the endpoints of the four segments?

**38. TAKS REASONING** Rectangle $ABCD$ has a length of 8 units and one vertex at $B(2, 5)$. Its other vertices are in other quadrants. Give two sets of possible coordinates of the other three vertices of the rectangle. What are the perimeters and areas in each case?

**39. CITY PARK** The rectangle with vertices $A$, $B$, $C$, and $D$ represents a city park. The length and width of each small square on the coordinate grid represents 100 feet. Find the distance around the city park.

**40. RUNWAYS** Two runways at an airport are shown. Plane 1 needs 1500 meters to take off and plane 2 needs 2500 meters to take off. Planes 1 and 2 are both scheduled to leave on different runways. Which runway will each plane use? What are the coordinates of the point at which each plane takes off, if each starts at the labeled end of its runway?

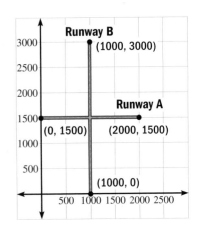

**41. ✈ TAKS REASONING** The following ordered pairs represent the cost of buying several weights of pineapple from a fruit stand. The *x*-coordinate represents the number of pounds and the *y*-coordinate represents the cost.

(1, $3.50), (2, $7.00), (3, $10.50), (4, $14.00)

Plot the points in a coordinate plane. *Identify* the pattern. *Explain* how to use the pattern to estimate the cost of $2\frac{1}{2}$ pounds of pineapple.

**42. WRITING** On a coordinate plane, sketch a figure with at least 8 sides. Write instructions telling a friend how to draw the figure that you drew. Then have your friend follow your instructions to draw the figure, without looking at your sketch. Compare your friend's drawing with yours. Do they match? How could you improve your instructions?

**43. MULTI-STEP PROBLEM** The table below shows the number of minutes used on a telephone call.

| | Length of a call |
|---|---|
| **Jane** | 10 minutes |
| **Tom** | 20 minutes |
| **Chris** | 30 minutes |

a. **Calculate** It costs 7 cents per minute to make a phone call using a phone card. Using the table above, find the cost of each of the phone calls.

b. **Graph** Plot the costs you found in part (a) in a coordinate plane, where the *x*-coordinate represents the length, in minutes, of the call and the *y*-coordinate represents the total cost of the call, in dollars.

c. **Estimate** Draw a line through the points. Use the line to estimate the cost of a 1 hour call.

**44. FURNITURE** The center of the top of a desk is at the origin of a coordinate plane. Each grid represents 1 inch. The screws, which attach the desk to the frame, are located at (0, −11), (−8, −11), (−8, 0), (−8, 11), (0, 11), (8, 11), (8, 0), and (8, −11). Each screw is 1 inch from the closest edge of the desk. The corner screws are 1 inch from each edge. What is the perimeter of the desk top?

**45. TRANSFORMATIONS** Copy the figure shown. Move the figure 2 units to the left and 3 units up. Give the new coordinates of *A*, *B*, *C*, *D*, and *E*.

**46.** ⬤ **TAKS REASONING** Plot the points *A*(−3, −4), *B*(2, −4), *C*(2, −2), *D*(5, −2), *E*(5, 3) and *F*(−3, 3) in a coordinate plane. Connect the points. Find the perimeter of the figure. Move the figure 4 units up. Write the new coordinates for points *A*, *B*, *C*, *D*, *E*, and *F*, and find the perimeter. Compare the results.

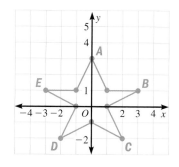

**47. GEOMETRY** Draw a rectangle that has one vertex in each quadrant. Multiply each coordinate by 2 and draw the resulting figure. Compare the new figure with the original figure and compare their perimeters. What do you find?

**48. TRANSFORMATIONS** Plot and connect the points (0, 0), (0, 3), (1, 3), (1, 1), (3, 1), and (3, 0) on a coordinate plane. Multiply each coordinate by −2 and draw the resulting figure. *Compare* this figure with the original figure and compare their perimeters. What do you find?

**49. GEOMETRY** A rectangle has a width of *x* centimeters and a length of 8 centimeters. Copy and complete the table using this information. Graph the data. Is there a pattern in the graph? *Explain.*

| Width x (cm) | 1 | 2 | 3 | 4 | 5 | 6 | 7 | 8 |
|---|---|---|---|---|---|---|---|---|
| Perimeter P (cm) | ? | ? | ? | ? | ? | ? | ? | ? |

**50. CHALLENGE** (8, 1), (5, 6), (−5, 0), (−2, −5) are the vertices of a rectangle. Find the area of the rectangle. *Explain* how you found your answer.

---

## MIXED REVIEW FOR TAKS

**TAKS** PRACTICE at classzone.com

REVIEW
Lesson 1.6;
TAKS Workbook

**51.** ⬤ **TAKS PRACTICE** Mr. Vila is renovating his house. His living room is currently 14 feet wide and 12 feet long. He is adding 2 feet to the width and 4 feet to the length. Which expression can he use to find the new perimeter of the living room? *TAKS Obj. 3*

Ⓐ 2(14) + 2(12) + 2 + 4

Ⓑ (14 + 2) × (12 + 4)

Ⓒ 2(14 + 2) + 2(12 + 4)

Ⓓ 2(28 + 4) + 2(24 + 8)

REVIEW
Lesson 1.7;
TAKS Workbook

**52.** ⬤ **TAKS PRACTICE** Becky, Brian, and Jeremy are siblings. Jeremy was born six years after Brian. Becky was born 2 years before Brian. Jeremy is 24 years old. How old is Becky? *TAKS Obj. 6*

Ⓕ 20 years old      Ⓖ 26 years old      Ⓗ 30 years old      Ⓙ 32 years old

**Evaluate the expression.** *Justify* **each step.** *(p. 83)*

**1.** $(19 + 33) + 11$

**2.** $(25 \cdot 16)(-4)$

**3.** $5(-4 \cdot 9)$

**Simplify the expression.** *(p. 88)*

**4.** $9x + 22x$

**5.** $3a - 2b + 6 - a$

**6.** $8(y + 2) - 4y$

**In Exercises 7–9, use the coordinate plane.** *(p. 94)*

**7.** Write the coordinates of points *A*, *B*, *C*, *D*, and *E*.

**8.** Which point lies on the *y*-axis?

**9.** Which point lies in Quadrant II?

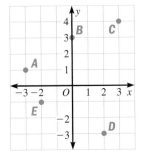

**10.** **BASKETBALL**  In the first basketball game, Joe scored 13 points in the first half and 6 points in the second half. In the second game, he scored 7 points in the first half and 14 points in the second half. How many total points did Joe score? *Explain* how to use properties to find the answer using mental math. *(p. 83)*

## Brain Game

# Spatial Delivery

Jack delivers balloons in a city. Below is a grid of Jack's city and a list of the deliveries he made today. Copy the diagram on graph paper and plot each stop. How many blocks did Jack travel?

**Delivery Stops**

Began at Main and State Street

**1.** E 3rd St. and Main

**2.** E 3rd St. and N 2nd Ave.

**3.** E 1st St. and N 2nd Ave.

**4.** E 1st St. and S 2nd Ave.

**5.** W 2nd St. and S 3rd Ave.

**6.** W 3rd St. and S 1st Ave.

**7.** W 3rd St. and N 2nd Ave.

**8.** W 1st St. and N 2nd Ave.

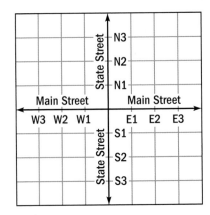

## Lessons 2.6–2.8

**MULTIPLE CHOICE**

1. **AREA** What is the area of the rectangle shown in the coordinate plane? *TEKS 8.5.A*

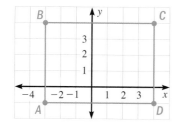

Ⓐ 21 square units

Ⓑ 24 square units

Ⓒ 35 square units

Ⓓ 42 square units

2. **VILLAGE WALK** The coordinate grid models the streets of a vacation village where Paulo stays. Each side of a grid square is 100 yards. A statue is at the origin of the grid. Paulo stays at the cottage and wants to walk exactly 2200 yards daily. He will start at the cottage and walk a single rectangular path that passes or encloses both the statue and the park, and ends back at the cottage. With the cottage as a vertex, which other points may be the vertices of his rectangular walk? *TEKS 8.7.D*

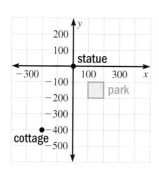

Ⓕ (300, −400), (300, 100), (−200, 100)

Ⓖ (400, −400), (400, 100), (−200, 100)

Ⓗ (300, −400), (300, 0), (−200, 0)

Ⓙ (300, −400), (300, 100), (−200, 0)

3. **PRINTED SHIRTS** You belong to a group that is selling printed shirts at a fair. Total expenses are $12 per shirt. Which expression can NOT be used to find the profit made by selling $x$ shirts for $20 each? *TEKS 8.4.A*

Ⓐ $8x$          Ⓑ $20x - 12$

Ⓒ $20x - 12x$   Ⓓ $x(20 - 12)$

4. **FIELD TRIP** You are planning a field trip to a museum. The cost for the bus is $250. The admission is $8 per person. Lunch is $5 per person. Which expression shows the cost in dollars if 20 students go on the trip? *TEKS 8.14.C*

Ⓕ $250 + 20 \times 8 + 5$   Ⓖ $20(250 + 8 + 5)$

Ⓗ $250 + 8 + 5 \times 20$   Ⓙ $20(8 + 5) + 250$

**GRIDDED ANSWER** ⓪①②●④⑤⑥⑦⑧⑨

5. **GIFTS** You buy gifts for 3 friends while on vacation. For each friend, you buy a keychain that costs $3.25, a miniature statue that costs $7.95, and a postcard that costs $1. How much money, in dollars and cents, do you spend on gifts for your friends? *TEKS 8.14.B*

6. **PAINTING** Olivia plans to paint four walls in a gallery. The walls are all 6 feet high. The lengths of the walls are 42 feet, 87 feet, 22 feet, and 29 feet. What is the total area, in square feet, of the walls that Olivia plans to paint? *TEKS 8.7.B*

## REVIEW KEY VOCABULARY

- integer, *p. 57*
- negative integer, *p. 57*
- positive integer, *p. 57*
- absolute value, *p. 58*
- opposite, *p. 58*
- mean, *p. 78*

- distributive property, *p. 88*
- terms, *p. 89*
- like terms, *p. 89*
- coefficient, *p. 89*
- constant term, *p. 89*
- coordinate plane, *p. 94*

- *x*-axis, *y*-axis, *p. 94*
- origin, *p. 94*
- quadrant, *p. 94*
- ordered pair, *p. 94*
- *x*-coordinate, *p. 94*
- *y*-coordinate, *p. 94*

### VOCABULARY EXERCISES

1. How many numbers have an absolute value of 15? List them.

2. Copy the expression. List the terms and the coefficients.

   $$-6y + 8 - 7x + 17x - 21y$$

3. How many quadrants are in a coordinate plane? Draw a coordinate plane and label each quadrant.

4. A point in a coordinate plane is represented by a(n) __?__ .

5. A(n) __?__ is formed by the intersection of a horizontal number line and a vertical number line.

6. The __?__ is the sum of the values divided by the number of values.

## REVIEW EXAMPLES AND EXERCISES

**2.1** **Integers and Absolute Value**                     *pp. 57–61*

**EXAMPLE**

**Write the opposite of the integer.**

a. 8            The opposite of 8 is $-8$.

b. $-3$        The opposite of $-3$ is 3.

c. $\left|-22\right|$     Because $\left|-22\right| = 22$, the opposite of $\left|-22\right|$ is $-22$.

**EXAMPLE**

Use a number line to order the integers from least to greatest: $2, -8, -6, 4, -1$.

Ordered least to greatest: $-8, -6, -1, 2, 4$

## EXERCISES

**Order the integers from least to greatest.**

**SEE EXAMPLES 1, 2, AND 3**
on pp. 57–58
for Exs. 7–16

**7.** $-42, 53, 8, -31, -5, 11$　　　　　　　**8.** $-56, -102, 98, -58, 114$

**Write the opposite and the absolute value of the integer.**

**9.** $22$　　　　　　**10.** $-13$　　　　　　**11.** $-512$　　　　　　**12.** $102$

**13.** $-92$　　　　　　**14.** $76$　　　　　　**15.** $147$　　　　　　**16.** $-250$

---

## 2.2 Adding Integers

*pp. 63–67*

### EXAMPLE

**Find the sum $-9 + 6$.**

$-9 + 6 = -3$ ← Different signs, so subtract $|6|$ from $|-9|$.

Use sign of number with greater absolute value.

**Check** Use a number line to check.

### EXERCISES

**Find the sum.**

**SEE EXAMPLE 2**
on p. 64
for Exs. 17–28

**17.** $-81 + (-91)$　　**18.** $32 + (-79)$　　**19.** $-324 + 500$　　**20.** $-468 + (-196)$

**21.** $752 + (-351)$　　**22.** $-96 + (-11)$　　**23.** $-246 + 198$　　**24.** $-28 + (-59)$

**25.** $-34 + 68$　　**26.** $471 + (-504)$　　**27.** $-101 + (-235)$　　**28.** $97 + (-41)$

---

## 2.3 Subtracting Integers

*pp. 68–72*

### EXAMPLE

**a.** $-62 - (-8) = -62 + 8$　　　Add the opposite of $-8$.

$\qquad\qquad\quad = -54$　　　Add.

**b.** $-12 - 43 = -12 + (-43)$　　　Add the opposite of $43$.

$\qquad\qquad\quad = -55$　　　Add.

**Find the difference.**

*SEE EXAMPLE 1*
on p. 69
for Exs. 29–36

**29.** $-29 - 57$      **30.** $62 - (-58)$      **31.** $-43 - (-122)$      **32.** $31 - 108$

**33.** $88 - (-49)$      **34.** $-56 - (-32)$      **35.** $-50 - 84$      **36.** $61 - 28$

## 2.4 Multiplying Integers
*pp. 73–76*

**EXAMPLE**

**a.** $-3(5) = -15$      Different signs, so product is negative.

**b.** $-6(-2) = 12$      Same sign, so product is positive.

**c.** $-22(0) = 0$      Product of an integer and 0 is 0.

**d.** $5(-9)(-8) = -45(-8)$      Multiply from left to right.

             $= 360$      Multiply.

**EXERCISES**

**Find the product.**

*SEE EXAMPLES*
*1, 2, AND 3*
on pp. 73–74
for Exs. 37–49

**37.** $-6(9)$      **38.** $31(-4)$      **39.** $-9(-23)(0)$      **40.** $-2(-3)(6)(-8)$

**Evaluate the expression when $x = -6$, $y = -4$, and $z = -8$.**

**41.** $xyz$      **42.** $9z - 2x$      **43.** $11y - 2xz$      **44.** $2x + 3yz$

**45.** $2xy - z$      **46.** $3y + 4x$      **47.** $2yz + 3yz$      **48.** $9z - 4xy$

**49. Hot Air Balloon** A hot air balloon at a height of 110 feet rises for 6 minutes at a rate of 18 feet per minute, then drops 22 feet per minute for 3 minutes. What is the height of the balloon?

## 2.5 Dividing Integers
*pp. 77–81*

**EXAMPLE**

**a.** $\dfrac{-96}{-16} = 6$      Same sign, so quotient is positive.

**b.** $\dfrac{-36}{4} = -9$      Different signs, so quotient is negative.

**c.** $\dfrac{24}{-4} = -6$      Different signs, so quotient is negative.

## EXERCISES

**Find the quotient.**

**SEE EXAMPLES
1 AND 2**

on pp. 77–78
for Exs. 50–61

**50.** $\dfrac{-26}{2}$      **51.** $\dfrac{-98}{-7}$      **52.** $\dfrac{-120}{-15}$      **53.** $\dfrac{63}{-7}$

**54.** $\dfrac{-56}{-14}$      **55.** $\dfrac{-84}{12}$      **56.** $\dfrac{45}{-9}$      **57.** $\dfrac{-48}{-16}$

**Find the mean of the data.**

**58.** $5, 7, -9, -2, -6, 8, -9, 6$      **59.** $15, -9, 6, -14, -18, 12, 7, 5, -2, 8$

**60.** $-11, 15, 26, 12, -8, 0, 1$      **61.** $24, -23, -17, -13, 27, 31, -44, -9$

---

## 2.6   Number Properties

*pp. 83–87*

**EXAMPLE**

$$5 \cdot (13 \cdot 4) = 5 \cdot (4 \cdot 13)$$    **Commutative property of multiplication**

$$= (5 \cdot 4) \cdot 13$$    **Associative property of multiplication**

$$= 20 \cdot 13$$    **Multiply inside grouping symbols.**

$$= 260$$    **Multiply.**

## EXERCISES

**Evaluate the expression using mental math. Name the property or
properties used.**

**SEE EXAMPLES
2 AND 4**

on pp. 84–85
for Exs. 62–70

**62.** $19 - (-58 - 81)$      **63.** $(-28 - 95 + 85) + (-62)$      **64.** $(-45 + 97) - (-45)$

**65.** $4(19 \cdot 25)$      **66.** $[-54 \cdot (-56)] \cdot 0 \cdot (-17)$      **67.** $(-15 \cdot 5) \cdot (-20)$

**68.** $(-19 - 56) + 19$      **69.** $12 \cdot 96 \cdot 0 + 3$      **70.** $(-92 + 47) - (-92)$

---

## 2.7   The Distributive Property

*pp. 88–93*

**EXAMPLE**

**a.** $3(5 + x) + x = 15 + 3x + x$    **Distributive property**

$$= 15 + 4x$$    **Combine like terms.**

**b.** $-2(5x - 8) + 4x = -10x + 16 + 4x$    **Distributive property**

$$= -6x + 16$$    **Combine like terms.**

## EXERCISES

**Use the distributive property to simplify the expression.**

SEE EXAMPLES
2, 3, AND 4
on pp. 89–90
for Exs. 71–83

**71.** $5(12x - 20)$

**72.** $7(9 + 11y)$

**73.** $4(25z - 30)$

**74.** $12(6y - 4)$

**75.** $9(15 - 12t)$

**76.** $15(4r + 15)$

**Simplify the expression by combining like terms.**

**77.** $14x - 3y - 7x + y$

**78.** $4x - 11y + 2(1 - x)$

**79.** $5x + 2y - 9x - 8y$

**80.** $6a + 2a - 5b - 11a$

**81.** $9(4a - 2b) + 13a + 19b$

**82.** $-2(5 - y) + 11y + 12$

**83. Baseball Caps** Use mental math and the distributive property to find the total price of 5 baseball caps that cost \$16.90 each.

---

## 2.8 The Coordinate Plane

pp. 94–100

### EXAMPLE

**Give the coordinates of the point.**

**a.** $A$  **b.** $B$  **c.** $C$

### SOLUTION

**a.** Point $A$ is 2 units to the right of the origin and 2 units up. So, the $x$-coordinate is 2 and the $y$-coordinate is 2. The coordinates of $A$ are $(2, 2)$.

**b.** Point $B$ is 2 units to the left of the origin and 4 units down. So, the $x$-coordinate is $-2$ and the $y$-coordinate is $-4$. The coordinates of $B$ are $(-2, -4)$.

**c.** Point $C$ is 3 units down from the origin. So, the $x$-coordinate is 0 and the $y$-coordinate is $-3$. The coordinates of $C$ are $(0, -3)$.

### EXERCISES

**Give the coordinates of the point.**

SEE EXAMPLES
1 AND 3
on pp. 94–95
for Exs. 84–88

**84.** $A$

**85.** $B$

**86.** $C$

**87.** $D$

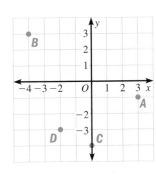

**88. Geometry** Plot, label, and connect in order the following points in a coordinate plane. Find the perimeter of the figure.

$A(0, 7)$, $B(4, 7)$, $C(4, 4)$, $D(8, 4)$, $E(8, 0)$, $F(0, 0)$

**Order the integers from least to greatest.**

**1.** $-9, 8, 14, -11, 0, -1$

**2.** $123, 87, -59, -12, -111, 22$

**Evaluate.**

**3.** $|x|$ when $x = 2$ and when $x = -4$.

**4.** $-(-x)$ when $x = -1$ and when $x = 7$.

**Find the sum or difference.**

**5.** $17 + (-9)$

**6.** $-8 + (-14)$

**7.** $-2 + (-21)$

**8.** $-33 + 26$

**9.** $1 - 19$

**10.** $-4 - 17$

**11.** $10 - (-15)$

**12.** $-7 - (-18)$

**13.** $17 + 35 - 3$

**14.** $-16 + 14 - 12$

**15.** $11 + (-1 + 32)$

**16.** $(-26 + 17) + 4$

**Find the product or the quotient.**

**17.** $-5(14)$

**18.** $-12(-20)$

**19.** $\dfrac{-152}{-19}$

**20.** $\dfrac{-132}{6}$

**Evaluate the expression when $a = 3$, $b = -15$, and $c = 15$.**

**21.** $\dfrac{c}{-a}$

**22.** $\dfrac{6b}{2c}$

**23.** $\dfrac{c}{-5a}$

**24.** $\dfrac{b^2}{a^2}$

**Simplify the expression by combining like terms.**

**25.** $3x + 4 - x + 1$

**26.** $2x - 3y + 5x - (-9y)$

**27.** $2(9x - 22y) + 4x$

**Plot the point in a coordinate plane and describe its location.**

**28.** $(-3, 3)$

**29.** $(6, 0)$

**30.** $(-4, -8)$

**31.** $(5, -2)$

**32. TEMPERATURE** The following temperatures were taken during a week in December in Nome, Alaska. What is the mean temperature, to the nearest degree?

$$-5°F, -8°F, -13°F, -16°F, -8°F, 11°F, 0°F$$

**33. GROCERIES** You are purchasing a loaf of bread for $2.16, a box of cereal for $3.25, and two cans of soup for $.42 each. Write an expression to find the total cost. Then evaluate your expression.

**34. XY ALGEBRA** Copy and complete the table for the equation $y = |x|$. Then plot the points on a coordinate plane.

| x | −3 | −2 | −1 | 0 | 1 | 2 | 3 |
|---|----|----|----|---|---|---|---|
| y | ? | ? | ? | ? | ? | ? | ? |

**TAKS Obj. 1**
**TEKS 8.2.A,
8.2.B**

# REVIEWING AVERAGE PROBLEMS

To find the mean of a set of data, you find the sum of the data values and divide by the number of data values. You can use this concept to find the mean of a data set when you add a new data value.

**EXAMPLE**

*READING*

In this Example, the word *average* is used in place of the more specific word *mean*.

**Temperature** The average low temperature over the last 6 days was −15°C. Today's low temperature is −8°C. What is the average low temperature over all 7 days including today?

## Solution

### METHOD 1

**STEP 1** **Work backwards** to find the sum of the average temperatures for the first 6 days.

You divide the sum by 6 to get the average temperature of −15°C. To find the sum, multiply the mean by 6.

$$-15 \cdot 6 = -90$$

**STEP 2** **Find** the new mean.

$$\text{mean} = \frac{\text{sum of values}}{\text{number of values}} \qquad \text{Write formula.}$$

$$= \frac{-90 + (-8)}{7} \qquad \text{Substitute values.}$$

$$= \frac{-98}{7} \qquad \text{Add.}$$

$$= -14 \qquad \text{Divide.}$$

### METHOD 2

**Write** and evaluate an expression.

$$\frac{6(-15) + (-8)}{7} \qquad \text{Write expression.}$$

$$= \frac{-90 + (-8)}{7} \qquad \text{Multiply.}$$

$$= -14 \qquad \text{Add and divide.}$$

▶ **Answer** The average low temperature over all 7 days is −14°C.

# AVERAGE PROBLEMS ON TAKS

Below are examples of average problems in multiple choice format. Try solving the problems before looking at the solutions. (Cover the solutions with a piece of paper.) Then check your solutions against the ones given.

**1.** Ten golfers play a round of golf. The average score of the ten players is $-3$. The average of the five worst scores is $+2$. Which expression can be used to find the average of the top five scores?

  **A** $\dfrac{10(-3) - 5(2)}{5}$

  **B** $\dfrac{10(-3) - 5(2)}{10}$

  **C** $\dfrac{10(-3) + 5(2)}{10}$

  **D** $10(-3) - \dfrac{5(2)}{5}$

**Solution**

To find the average, find the sum of the top five scores and divide by 5.

To find the sum of the top five scores, subtract the sum of the five worst scores from the sum of all ten scores. The average score of the ten golfers is $-3$, so the sum of all ten scores is $10(-3)$. The average of the five worst scores is $+2$, so the sum of the five worst scores is $5(2)$.

The sum of the top five scores is $10(-3) - 5(2)$. Divide this difference by 5 to find the average.

The expression is $\dfrac{10(-3) - 5(2)}{5}$, so the correct answer is A.

  Ⓐ    Ⓑ    Ⓒ    Ⓓ

**2.** The table shows the change in value for 1 share of stock in each of two companies, and the amount of each stock Jerry owns.

|  | Company A | Company B |
|---|---|---|
| **Shares owned** | 70 | 30 |
| **Change in value** | $-\$0.40$ | $\$0.90$ |

Jerry says that the average change in value of his shares across both companies is $\$1.30$. Why is his answer unreasonable?

  **F** The average should be exactly halfway between $-\$0.40$ and $\$0.90$.

  **G** The average should be between $-\$0.40$ and $\$0.90$.

  **H** The average should be either $-\$0.40$ or $\$0.90$.

  **J** The average should be less than $-\$0.40$.

**Solution**

There are 100 stocks in total. To find the average change in value for the stocks, find the sum of the change in value of each stock and divide this sum by 100.

The sum of the change in value for the 70 stocks of Company A is $70(-0.4)$. The sum of the change in value for the 30 stocks of Company B is $30(0.9)$. So, the sum of the change in value for all 100 stocks is $70(-0.4) + 30(0.9)$. Divide this sum by 100 to find the average change in value for all of the stocks.

$$\dfrac{70(-0.4) + 30(0.9)}{100} = -0.01$$

The average is between the two values, but not exactly halfway between the numbers. So, the correct answer is G.

  Ⓕ    Ⓖ    Ⓗ    Ⓙ

# 2 TAKS PRACTICE

## PRACTICE FOR TAKS OBJECTIVE 1

1. Eight scuba divers are at an elevation of
   −10 feet below the ocean's surface. Six
   other people stayed on the divers' boat at
   an elevation of 4 feet. What is the average
   elevation of all 14 people?

   **A** −14 ft

   **B** −6 ft

   **C** 4 ft

   **D** 2 ft

2. Charlize made four transactions involving
   her checking account this month. First,
   she withdrew money three times, taking
   out a total of $548 from the account. Then
   she made one deposit of $600 into the
   account. Which equation can be used to
   find $t$, the mean dollar amount of the four
   transactions?

   **F** $t = \dfrac{-548 + 600}{4}$

   **G** $t = \dfrac{548 - 600}{4}$

   **H** $t = 600 + \dfrac{-548}{3}$

   **J** $t = -548 + \dfrac{600}{4}$

3. Tamara receives an average of 8 emails per
   day for 9 consecutive days in September.
   On the tenth day, she receives 18 emails.
   How many emails, on average, did she
   receive each day over all 10 days?

   **A** 7

   **B** 8

   **C** 9

   **D** 10

4. The mean daily low temperature from
   December 1 to December 31 was −3°C.
   The mean daily low temperature from
   December 1 to January 31 was 2°C. Which
   expression can be used to find the mean
   daily low temperature from January 1 to
   January 31?

   **F** $\dfrac{31(2) - 62(-3)}{31}$

   **G** $\dfrac{62(2) - 31(-3)}{31}$

   **H** $\dfrac{31(2) + 31(-3)}{62}$

   **J** $\dfrac{31(-3) + 62(2)}{62}$

## MIXED TAKS PRACTICE

5. The bar graph shows the change in value of
   4 vehicles after 1 year. Which statement is
   NOT supported by the graph? *TAKS Obj. 5*

   **A** Car A lost more value than Car D.

   **B** Car A lost the same value as Car C and
   Car D together.

   **C** The value in dollars lost by Car A,
   Car C, and Car D together is more
   than the value lost by Car B.

   **D** Car B lost 8 times more value than
   Car C.

## MIXED TAKS PRACTICE

**6.** Find the area of the figure below, then find the area after doubling the dimensions. What conclusion can you make about the areas? *TAKS Obj. 4*

2 ft
4 ft
13 ft

    **F** The doubling of the dimensions doubled the area.

    **G** The doubling of the dimensions tripled the area.

    **H** The doubling of the dimensions quadrupled the area.

    **J** The doubling of the dimensions did not change the area.

**7.** Rose completes the statement $\left| -6 \right|$ ? $\left| 5 \right|$ with <. Why is her answer unreasonable? *TAKS Obj. 1*

    **A** Because −6 is to the left of 0 on a number line.

    **B** Because 6 is greater than −5.

    **C** Because 5 is to the right of −6 on a number line.

    **D** Because the distance from 6 to 0 is greater than the distance from 5 to 0 on a number line.

**8.** A penny is dropped over a sidewalk from a height of 36 feet. The equation $h = -16t^2 + 36$ gives the height $h$ of the penny, in feet, after $t$ seconds. What is the height of the penny after 2 seconds? *TAKS Obj. 2*

    **F** −28 ft

    **G** 0 ft

    **H** 20 ft

    **J** 10 ft

**9.** A duck flew from Ontario, Canada, and was spotted in Mississippi 12 days later. The duck's average rate of speed when flying was 41.5 miles per hour. What information could be used to find the total distance of the flight? *TAKS Obj. 6*

    **A** The average number of hours that the duck flew each day

    **B** The time that the duck left Ontario

    **C** The time that the duck arrived in Mississippi

    **D** The number of times that the duck stopped flying

**10.** What are the new coordinates of *A*, *B*, and *C* when the triangle shown below is moved 2 units to the right and 1 unit down? *TAKS Obj. 3*

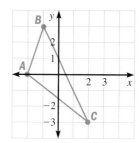

    **F** $A(-4, -1)$, $B(-3, 2)$, $C(0, -4)$

    **G** $A(-3, 2)$, $B(-2, 5)$, $C(1, -1)$

    **H** $A(-1, 2)$, $B(0, 5)$, $C(3, -1)$

    **J** $A(0, -1)$, $B(1, 2)$, $C(4, -4)$

**11. GRIDDED ANSWER** What is the value of $\dfrac{x^2 + 5y}{10}$ when $x = -5$ and $y = 6$? *TAKS Obj. 1*

*Record your answer and fill in the bubbles on your answer document. Be sure to use the correct place value.*

# 3 Solving Equations and Inequalities

## Before

In previous chapters you've...

- Evaluated expressions
- Solved word problems

## Now

 you'll study...

## Why?

So you can solve real-world problems about...

- sea lions, p. 121
- illustrators, p. 132
- biplane rides, p. 152
- DJs, p. 157

 **Math**

*at classzone.com*

- Algebra Tiles, p. 117
- Solving Two-Step Equations, p. 128
- Inequalities, p. 150

## Get-Ready Games

**Review Prerequisite Skills** by playing *Name that Planet!* and *Planet Pinball.*

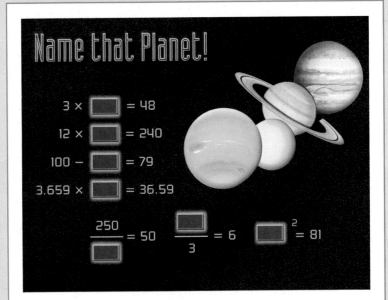

**Skill Focus:** Solving mental math equations

- Use mental math to find the missing number.

- Match each answer with the corresponding letter of the alphabet. (1 = A, 2 = B, etc.)

- Rearrange the letters to find the name of a planet.

**Planet Pinball**

**Skill Focus:** Operations with integers

**Materials:** coin

- Both players start at the top planet with 36 points.

- On your turn, toss a coin. If you get heads, go to the planet on the left. If you get tails, go to the planet on the right.

- Perform the operation written on the planet. The result is your current score.

- Take turns moving until both players reach the bottom row.

- The player with the higher score wins.

### Stop and Think

1. **WRITING** Without tossing the coin, work with your partner to find the route through the planets in the *Planet Pinball* that gives the highest score. *Explain* how you know you have found the best route.

2. **EXTENSION** Choose another planet name. Write a puzzle like *Name that Planet!* with that name as the solution.

# Review Prerequisite Skills

**REVIEW WORDS**
• **variable,** *p. 13*
• **equation,** *p. 26*
• **solution,** *p. 26*
• **opposite,** *p. 58*
• **like terms,** *p. 89*
• **coefficient,** *p. 89*

## VOCABULARY CHECK

Copy and complete using a review word from the list at the left.

**1.** 5 is the __?__ of $-5$.

**2.** In the expression $6x$, 6 is the __?__.

**3.** A statement with an equal sign between two expressions is a(n) __?__.

**4.** __?__ have identical variable parts raised to the same power.

## SKILL CHECK

Solve the equation using mental math. *(p. 26)*

**5.** $x - 1 = 5$  **6.** $x - 2 = 9$  **7.** $4 + x = 12$  **8.** $10 = x + 3$

**9.** $5x = 20$  **10.** $x \div 3 = 1$  **11.** $x \div 7 = 5$  **12.** $3x = 51$

In Exercises 13–20, evaluate the expression. *(pp. 63, 68, 73, 77)*

**13.** $-3 - 2 + 8$  **14.** $3 - 7 + 2 - 1$  **15.** $-2(3 + 1) + 2$  **16.** $8(1 - 4) - 9$

**17.** $-5 \times 4 + 2$  **18.** $7(3 + 1) \div 2$  **19.** $-8 \div 2 + 4 \times 6$  **20.** $6(2 - 5) \times 3$

**21.** **AIRPLANE SPEED** A jet airplane cruises at a speed of 540 mi/h. Write and solve an equation to find how far it travels at that cruising speed in 15 minutes. *(p. 32)*

**TEXAS @HomeTutor** Prerequisite skills practice at classzone.com

## Notetaking Skills   Organizing Information

In each chapter you will learn a new notetaking skill. In Chapter 3 you will apply the strategy of organizing information to the Key Concept on p. 155.

Sometimes you can organize information in a table to make it easier to understand and remember.

Multiplying Integers

| × | Positive | Negative |
|---|---|---|
| Positive | + | − |
| Negative | − | + |

**GOAL**
Solve addition and subtraction equations using algebra tiles.

**MATERIALS**
• algebra tiles

  *8.4, 8.15.A*

## 3.1 Modeling One-Step Equations

You can use algebra tiles to model and solve one-step addition equations and one-step subtraction equations.

**+**

*x*-tile
represents the
variable *x*

**+**

1-tile
represents a positive
unit, or 1

**–**

−1-tile
represents a negative
unit, or −1

**EXPLORE 1** Model and solve $x + 3 = 8$.

**STEP 1** Model $x + 3 = 8$ using algebra tiles.

**STEP 2** Remove three 1-tiles from each side so the *x*-tile is by itself.

**STEP 3** Write the solution.
The solution of the equation is 5.

**PRACTICE**

1. Use algebra tiles to model each step below. Draw a picture of each step.

   **Step 1** **Model** the equation $x + 5 = 7$.

   **Step 2** **Remove** five 1-tiles from each side.

   **Step 3** **Find** the solution.

**Use algebra tiles to model and solve the equation.**

2. $x + 4 = 9$     3. $5 + x = 7$     4. $6 = x + 2$     5. $7 + x = 9$

*Continued on next page*

When you combine a 1-tile and a −1-tile, the result is zero. This pair of tiles is called a *zero pair* and may be removed from the model.

 $= 0$

**EXPLORE 2** Model and solve $x - 5 = -3$. Write the equation at each step.

| Tile Model | Algebra |
|---|---|

**STEP 1** Model $x - 5 = -3$ using algebra tiles.

$x - 5 = -3$

**STEP 2** **Add** the same number of 1-tiles to each side to create zero pairs. Add five 1-tiles to each side and then remove zero pairs from each side, to get the $x$-tile by itself.

$x - 5 + 5 = -3 + 5$

**STEP 3** **Write** the solution. The solution is 2.

$x = 2$

**Animated Math** at classzone.com

**PRACTICE** Use algebra tiles to model and solve the equation. Write the equation at each step.

**6.** $x - 3 = 6$     **7.** $x - 5 = 5$     **8.** $x + 6 = 2$     **9.** $8 + x = 1$

**10.** $x - 4 = -2$     **11.** $x - 7 = -3$     **12.** $x + 8 = 4$     **13.** $x - 3 = -6$

**DRAW CONCLUSIONS**

**14. REASONING** Give an example of an equation that requires you to create zero pairs to solve it. How do you know that zero pairs are required?

# 3.1 Solving Equations Using Addition or Subtraction

**TEKS** *8.4, 8.5.A*

**Before** You solved equations using mental math.

**Now** You'll solve equations using addition or subtraction.

**Why?** So you can solve problems, such as finding distances in Example 3.

**KEY VOCABULARY**
• **equivalent equations,** *p. 117*
• **inverse operation,** *p. 117*

You can model and solve an equation by thinking of the equation as a "balanced" set of numbers, as shown below.

$$x + 3 = 5 \qquad\qquad x = 2$$

In the model above, removing three 1-tiles from each side of the scale keeps the scale in balance.

When you perform the same operation on each side of an equation, the result is a new equation that has the same solution. Equations that have the same solution(s) are **equivalent equations**.

You solve an equation by using *inverse operations* to write equivalent equations. An **inverse operation** is an operation that "undoes" another operation. Addition and subtraction are inverse operations.

## KEY CONCEPT *For Your Notebook*

### Subtraction Property of Equality

**Words** Subtracting the same number from each side of an equation produces an equivalent equation.

**Numbers** If $x + 5 = 7$, then $x + 5 - 5 = 7 - 5$.

**Algebra** If $x + a = b$, then $x + a - a = b - a$.

## EXAMPLE 1 Solving an Equation Using Subtraction

$$
\begin{array}{ll}
x + 8 = -15 & \text{Original equation} \\
\underline{\phantom{x}-8 \quad -8} & \text{Subtract 8 from each side to undo addition.} \\
x \phantom{+8} = -23 & \text{Simplify. } x \text{ is by itself.}
\end{array}
$$

▶ **Answer** The solution is $-23$.

*Animated* Math
at classzone.com

You can also use the *addition property of equality* to solve an equation.

**KEY CONCEPT** For Your Notebook

**Addition Property of Equality**

**Words**  Adding the same number to each side of an equation produces an equivalent equation.

**Numbers**  If $x - 2 = 6$, then $x - 2 + 2 = 6 + 2$.

**Algebra**  If $a = b$, then $a + c = b + c$.

**EXAMPLE 2** Solving an Equation Using Addition

*AVOID ERRORS*

You can add or subtract horizontally or vertically to solve equations. Either way, you must remember to perform the same operation on *each* side.

| | |
|---|---|
| $c - 4.5 = 13$ | Original equation |
| $c - 4.5 + 4.5 = 13 + 4.5$ | Add 4.5 to each side to undo subtraction. |
| $c = 17.5$ | Simplify. *c* is by itself. |
| **Check**  $17.5 - 4.5 \stackrel{?}{=} 13$ | Substitute 17.5 for *c* in original equation. |
| $13 = 13 ✓$ | |

*Animated* **Math**
at classzone.com

**EXAMPLE 3** Using a Model

**Rock Climbing**  A cliff has a height of about 1500 feet. If you have already climbed 675 feet, how much farther do you have to climb to reach the top?

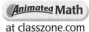

**SOLUTION**

Use the diagram to help you write an algebraic model. Let *x* represent the distance left to climb.

| | |
|---|---|
| $1500 = x + 675$ | Write an algebraic model. |
| $1500 - 675 = x + 675 - 675$ | Subtract 675 from each side. |
| $825 = x$ | Simplify. *x* is by itself. |

▶ **Answer**  You have about 825 feet left to climb.

✓ **GUIDED PRACTICE**  for Examples 1, 2, and 3

Solve the equation. Check your solution.

**1.** $x + 9 = 20$     **2.** $-10 = 3 + y$     **3.** $m - 14 = -15$     **4.** $2 = z - 6.4$

**5. Seashells**  Lucinda combines her 49 seashells with Jerry's seashells, for a total of 162. Write and solve an addition equation to find how many seashells *s* Jerry had before their collections were combined.

# 3.1 EXERCISES

HOMEWORK KEY

= TAKS Practice and Reasoning
Exs. 22, 51, 52, 56, 60, and 61

= HINTS AND HOMEWORK HELP
for Exs. 3, 9, 11, 19, 49 at classzone.com

## SKILL PRACTICE

**VOCABULARY** Copy and complete the statement.

1. Addition and subtraction are __?__ operations.

2. Equations that have the same solution(s) are called __?__.

**SOLVING EQUATIONS** Solve the equation. Check your solution.

*SEE EXAMPLES 1 AND 2*
on pp. 117–118
for Exs. 3–28

3. $x + 10 = 16$

4. $12 = x - 8$

5. $43 = a - 21$

6. $r + 2 = 7$

7. $t - 5 = 2$

8. $z + 9 = 11$

9. $23 = 6 + n$

10. $y - 15 = 9$

11. $13 = d - 27$

12. $24 = 52 + n$

13. $-204 = m - 41$

14. $11 = c + 48$

15. $p + 3.4 = 4.4$

16. $1.76 = a - 2.94$

17. $3.777 + c = 3.977$

18. $x + \frac{1}{2} = \frac{1}{2}$

19. $\frac{2}{3} = d + \frac{1}{3}$

20. $y - \frac{3}{4} = \frac{1}{4}$

21. **ERROR ANALYSIS** Describe and correct the error made in solving the equation.

$$x + 1000 = 5000$$
$$x + 1000 + 1000 = 5000 + 1000$$
$$x = 6000$$

22. **TAKS REASONING** What is the solution of $-4 + x = 8$?

   (A) $-12$   (B) $-4$   (C) $4$   (D) $12$

**SOLVING EQUATIONS** Solve the equation. Check your solution.

23. $m + (-20) = -12$

24. $-2 = b + (-4)$

25. $r - (-36) = 5$

26. $2 + x - 4 = 12$

27. $m - 5 - 9 = 21$

28. $d + 6(3) = -11$

**MODELING** Write and solve an equation to model the statement.

*SEE EXAMPLE 3*
on p. 118
for Exs. 29–34

29. The sum of a number $n$ and twelve is twenty-five.

30. Thirty-five is the sum of a number $n$ and eight.

31. Three less than a number $n$ is negative sixteen.

**GEOMETRY** Write and solve an equation to find the length of the fourth side.

32. Perimeter = 16 ft

2 ft
3 ft
$x$
6 ft

33. Perimeter = 97 cm

24 cm
$k$
38 cm
16 cm

34. Perimeter = 40 m

11 m
7 m
8 m
$y$

**CHOOSE A METHOD** Tell whether you would use *mental math* or *paper and pencil* to solve the equation. Then solve.

**35.** $x + 367 = 426$

**36.** $y + 4 = 6$

**37.** $m - \dfrac{8001}{21} = 792$

**REASONING** Without solving the equation, decide whether the solution is *positive* or *negative*. *Explain* your reasoning.

**38.** $27 + m = 6$

**39.** $-50 = p - 12$

**40.** $-10 + y = 5$

**SIMPLIFY AND SOLVE** Solve the equation.

**41.** $3x - 2x + 8 - 10 = 7$

**42.** $0.2x + 3.4 + 0.8x = 4$

**43.** $7.3x + 9 - 6.3x = 12$

**CHALLENGE** Find the solutions of the equation.

**44.** $|x| - 3 = 14$

**45.** $|x| + 5 = 25$

**46.** $|x - 2| = 7$

## PROBLEM SOLVING

**SEE EXAMPLE 3**
on p. 118
for Exs. 47–51

**47. GUIDED PROBLEM SOLVING** You need to buy new school supplies. The price of the items is $54.99, but after sales tax is added, the cost is $58.29. How much is the sales tax?

  **a.** Copy and complete the verbal model.

   Price + _?_ = Total cost

  **b.** Substitute numbers and variables in the verbal model to write an algebraic model.

  **c.** Solve the algebraic model. Check your solution.

**ERROR ANALYSIS** In Exercises 48–50, tell whether the equation correctly represents the situation. If not, correct the equation. Then answer the question.

**48.** At 62 inches tall, you are 5 inches taller than your sister. What is your sister's height $h$? Equation: $62 = h + 5$.

**49.** The mean temperature for February 4 in Chicago is 3°F below the mean temperature of 29°F for all of February in Chicago. What is the mean temperature $t$ for February 4? Equation: $t - 3 = 29$.

**50.** An item that usually costs $2.29 will cost $1.79 with a coupon. How much is the coupon $c$ worth? Equation: $2.29 - c = 1.79$.

**51. ⬥ TAKS REASONING** Five less than the total number of students $x$ is twenty-four. Which equation represents the statement?

  **Ⓐ** $5 - x = 24$    **Ⓑ** $24 - 5 = x$    **Ⓒ** $x + 24 = 5$    **Ⓓ** $x - 5 = 24$

**52. ⬥ TAKS REASONING** *Explain* how to use inverse operations to solve an addition or subtraction equation. Give two examples.

**Sea Lions** Steller sea lions live in the northern Pacific Ocean. Pups are about 45 inches long at birth. Their diet of fish, squid, and octopus help them to grow much larger. Female sea lions reach their full adult size of about 104 inches in seven years. Male sea lions reach their full size of about 128 inches in 12 years. These lengths (and also their weights) make the Steller sea lion the largest of all the eared seals.

53. **Calculate** Write and solve an addition equation to find the number of inches a female Steller sea lion grows between birth and adulthood.

54. **Calculate** Write and solve an addition equation to find the number of inches a male Steller sea lion grows between birth and adulthood.

55. **Predict** What is the average growth per year between birth and adulthood for a female and a male Steller sea lion? Round to the nearest inch. After five years, which is longer, a male or a female?

56. **TAKS REASONING**   *Describe* a real-word situation that can be represented by the equation $s + 13 = 55$.

57. **WRITING**   *Explain* why $24 = x + 21$ and $27 + x = 30$ are equivalent equations.

58. **COST** You spent a total of $11.09 at the store. You bought two bottles of water for $1.29 each, a magazine for $3.50, trail mix for $1.49, and a package of 10 markers for $m$ dollars. Write an addition equation for the situation. (Assume there is no sales tax.) Solve the equation and find the cost of a marker.

59. **CHALLENGE** The cost $b$ of a book bag is $3 more than the cost $s$ of a pair of sneakers. The cost of the sneakers is $6 more than the cost $c$ of a CD, which is $8 less than the cost $t$ of a T-shirt. The sneakers cost $18. Write and solve three equations to find the cost of the book bag, the CD, and the T-shirt.

## MIXED REVIEW FOR TAKS

**TAKS** PRACTICE at classzone.com

*REVIEW*
Lesson 1.5;
TAKS Workbook

60. **TAKS PRACTICE** A grocery store allows you to purchase a maximum of 10 cases of water priced at $6 for 2 cases. Which equation can be used to find $c$, the cost of buying the maximum number of cases? *TAKS Obj. 1*

   **A** $c = 20 \cdot 6$   **B** $c = 10 \cdot 6$   **C** $c = 10 \cdot 3$   **D** $c = 5 \cdot 3$

*REVIEW*
Lesson 1.6;
TAKS Workbook

61. **TAKS PRACTICE** A painting of shapes done in 1962 has a blue rectangle 4 inches wide and 2.6 inches long. What is the rectangle's area? *TAKS Obj. 3*

   **F** 6.6 in.   **G** 13.2 in.   **H** 10.4 in.$^2$   **J** 104 in.$^2$

# 3.2 Solving Equations Using Multiplication or Division

TEKS *8.4, 8.5.A*

| | |
|---|---|
| **Before** | You solved equations using addition or subtraction. |
| **Now** | You'll solve equations using multiplication or division. |
| **Why?** | So you can find unknown values, such as rows in Exercise 43. |

**KEY VOCABULARY**
- **equivalent equations,** *p. 117*
- **inverse operations,** *p. 117*

## ACTIVITY

**You can use multiplication to solve equations.**

$$\frac{x}{2} = 5 \qquad \text{Multiply each side by 2.} \qquad \frac{x}{2} \cdot 2 = 5 \cdot 2 \qquad \text{Simplify.} \qquad x = 10$$

**Solve the equations.**

1. $\dfrac{y}{5} = 4$    2. $\dfrac{h}{6} = 9$    3. $\dfrac{m}{6} = -3$

4. What operation did you use to solve each division equation? How did you use that operation? Write a rule for solving division equations.

In the activity, you used multiplication to solve equations involving division. Multiplication and division are inverse operations.

---

### KEY CONCEPT                                          *For Your Notebook*

**Multiplication Property of Equality**

**Words**   Multiplying each side of an equation by the same nonzero number produces an equivalent equation.

**Numbers**   If $\dfrac{x}{3} = 4$, then $\dfrac{x}{3} \cdot 3 = 4 \cdot 3$.

**Algebra**   If $a = b$ and $c \neq 0$, then $ac = bc$.

---

### EXAMPLE 1   Solving an Equation Using Multiplication

$$\frac{y}{3} = 5 \qquad \text{Original equation}$$

$$\frac{y}{3} \cdot 3 = 5 \cdot 3 \qquad \text{Multiply each side by 3 to undo division.}$$

$$y = 15 \qquad \text{Simplify. } y \text{ is by itself.}$$

**Check**   $\dfrac{15}{3} = 5 \checkmark$   Substitute 15 for *y* in original equation.

**CHECK ANSWERS**
Remember to check your answer by substituting it in the original equation.

You can use division to solve equations involving multiplication.

---

**KEY CONCEPT**                      *For Your Notebook*

**Division Property of Equality**

**Words**       Dividing each side of an equation by the same nonzero number produces an equivalent equation.

**Numbers**    If $2x = 24$, then $\dfrac{2x}{2} = \dfrac{24}{2}$.

**Algebra**     If $a = b$ and $c \neq 0$, then $\dfrac{a}{c} = \dfrac{b}{c}$.

---

**EXAMPLE 2**    **Solving an Equation Using Division**

**DIVIDING**

Need help dividing negatives and decimals? See pp. 70 and 770.

$-2.5x = 20$        **Original equation**

$\dfrac{-2.5x}{-2.5} = \dfrac{20}{-2.5}$       **Divide each side by −2.5 to undo multiplication.**

$x = -8$        **Simplify. *x* is by itself.**

---

**EXAMPLE 3**    **Writing and Solving an Equation**

**Sports** Ninety basketball players show up for a tournament. Write and solve an equation to find how many five-person teams can be formed.

**SOLUTION**

Let $t$ be the number of five-person teams that can be formed.

| Total number of people | = | Number per team | • | Number of teams |
|---|---|---|---|---|

$90 = 5t$        **Write an algebraic model.**

$\dfrac{90}{5} = \dfrac{5t}{5}$       **Divide each side by 5.**

$18 = t$        **Simplify.**

▶ **Answer** Eighteen five-person teams can be formed.

---

✓   **GUIDED PRACTICE**    **for Examples 1, 2, and 3**

**Solve the equation. Check your solution.**

**1.** $21 = \dfrac{x}{9}$      **2.** $\dfrac{x}{3.5} = 14$      **3.** $9x = 54$      **4.** $48 = -3x$

**5. Team Size** A teacher divided a class into four teams, with 6 students per team. Write and solve a division equation to find the class size.

# 3.2 EXERCISES

HOMEWORK KEY

✦ = TAKS Practice and Reasoning
Exs. 27, 29, 36–39, 44, 52, 55, and 56

○ = HINTS AND HOMEWORK HELP
for Exs. 5, 9, 13, 21, 45 at classzone.com

## SKILL PRACTICE

**VOCABULARY** Copy and complete the statement.

**1.** To solve $6x = 36$, __?__ each side of the equation by 6.

**2.** Multiplying each side of an equation by __?__ produces an equivalent equation.

**INVERSE OPERATIONS** Describe an inverse operation that will undo the operation.

SEE EXAMPLES
1 AND 2
on pp. 122–123
for Exs. 3–28

**3.** Multiplying by 5

**4.** Dividing by $-9$

**5.** Adding $-6$

**6.** Subtracting 10

**7.** Multiplying by $-3$

**8.** Subtracting $-4$

**SOLVING EQUATIONS** Solve the equation. Check your solution.

**9.** $\frac{p}{2} = 9$

**10.** $18 = 6g$

**11.** $3b = 39$

**12.** $48 = 96z$

**13.** $\frac{z}{1.8} = 5$

**14.** $14 = \frac{x}{5}$

**15.** $44 = 4.4p$

**16.** $25 = \frac{h}{14}$

**17.** $14h = 35$

**18.** $\frac{r}{18} = 12$

**19.** $12m = -25.2$

**20.** $7 = \frac{k}{15}$

**21.** $1368 = 456x$

**22.** $\frac{h}{6} = -36$

**23.** $12 = -2z$

**24.** $-2.4k = 48$

**25.** $\frac{y}{-1.5} = 21$

**26.** $-21 = -0.7p$

**27.** ✦ **TAKS REASONING** What is the solution of $-3 = 0.3a$?

Ⓐ 30　　　　Ⓑ 3　　　　Ⓒ $-10$　　　　Ⓓ $-30$

**28.** **ERROR ANALYSIS** Describe and correct the error made in solving the equation represented by the verbal sentence.

*The quotient of a number and the opposite of 7 is 56.*

$$\frac{x}{-7} = 56$$
$$\frac{x}{-7} \cdot 7 = 56 \cdot 7$$
$$x = 392$$

**29.** ✦ **TAKS REASONING** Which operation should you perform to solve the equation represented by the verbal sentence?

*The quotient of a number and four is the opposite of two.*

Ⓐ Divide each side by 4.

Ⓑ Multiply each side by 4.

Ⓒ Divide each side by $-4$.

Ⓓ Multiply each side by $-4$.

**SOLVING EQUATIONS** Solve the equation. Explain each step.

**30.** $-x = -8$

**31.** $-b = 12 - 4$

**32.** $15 - 21 = -n$

**33.** $\dfrac{m}{6} = \dfrac{2}{3}$

**34.** $\dfrac{a}{3} = 5\dfrac{1}{3}$

**35.** $\dfrac{t}{4} = 3\dfrac{1}{6}$

**TAKS REASONING** Write a multiplication equation and a division equation such that each has the given solution.

**36.** $-7$

**37.** $2$

**38.** $9$

**39.** $-2.5$

**CHALLENGE** Rewrite the formula so that the indicated variable is by itself.

**40.**

$$A = \dfrac{1}{2}bh$$

$$b = \underline{\phantom{?}}$$

**41.**

$$V = \dfrac{1}{3}Bh$$

$$h = \underline{\phantom{?}}$$

**42.**

$$V = \pi r^2 h$$

$$h = \underline{\phantom{?}}$$

## PROBLEM SOLVING

SEE EXAMPLE 3
on p. 123
for Exs. 43–46

**43. THEATER** A movie theater has 1950 seats. Each row has 30 seats. Use the verbal model to write and solve an equation to find how many rows of seats there are.

**44. TAKS REASONING** A pizza shop cuts a pizza into 8 slices. One slice costs $1.10. Which equation can you use to find the cost $x$ of the whole pizza?

**A** $1.10x = 8$   **B** $8x = 1.10$   **C** $\dfrac{x}{8} = 1.10$   **D** $x = \dfrac{1.10}{8}$

**45. MOWING LAWNS** Your friend charged your neighbors $56 for mowing their lawn 7 times. Write and solve a multiplication equation to find the amount $a$ your friend charged for mowing the lawn once.

**46. MULTI-STEP PROBLEM** Joanne drove for three hours at a constant speed $r$. She traveled a total of 174 miles.

**a. Write an Equation** Write a multiplication equation that represents the situation.

**b. Solve the Equation** Solve the equation to find her speed.

**c. Apply the Result** Can Joanne travel 100 miles farther in two hours at the same speed? *Justify* your answer.

**47. WRITING** *Describe* how algebra tiles could be used as an alternative way to solve Example 3.

**WATERFALLS** In Exercises 48–50, use the graph below. Write and solve a multiplication equation for the unknown height. Use the graph to check whether your solution is reasonable.

48. The height of Angel Falls in Venezuela is 20 times the height of Niagara Falls in Canada and the United States.

49. The height of Comet Falls in Washington is $\frac{1}{5}$ the height of Takkakaw Falls in British Columbia.

50. The height of Skykje Falls in Norway is 1.25 times the height of Feather Falls in California.

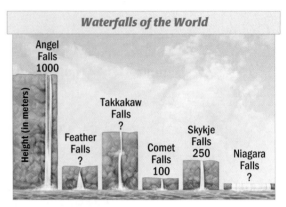

*Waterfalls of the World*

51. **EGG PRODUCTION** About 285 million laying hens produce about 76 billion eggs each year in the United States. About how many eggs does each hen lay in a month? in a week?

52. **TAKS REASONING** A basketball team plays 20 games and averages 65 points per game. Write a verbal model involving division for finding the total number of points for the season. Write and solve a related equation. The team's goal for next season is to score 5 more points per game for 20 games. *Explain* how to adjust the model to find the total number of points for next season. Then solve.

53. **CHALLENGE** A hardcover book sells for $19.50. The same title in paperback sells for $t$ times the price. The price for 26 paperbacks equals the price for 12 hardcover books. Find the price of one paperback.

54. **CHALLENGE** Find the dimensions of a rectangle whose perimeter is 36 inches and whose length is three times its width.

---

## MIXED REVIEW FOR TAKS

**TAKS** PRACTICE at classzone.com

*REVIEW*
Lesson 3.1;
TAKS Workbook

55. **TAKS PRACTICE** Which procedure can be used to solve the equation $x + 2 = 3$? *TAKS Obj. 6*

　Ⓐ Add 2 to each side 　　　　Ⓑ Subtract 2 from each side

　Ⓒ Add 3 to each side 　　　　Ⓓ Subtract 3 from each side

*REVIEW*
Lesson 1.7;
TAKS Workbook

56. **TAKS PRACTICE** Mr. Lee joins a discount shopping club by paying an annual fee. He then buys jars of olives in bulk for $35.55. What information is needed to find how much he paid for each jar of olives? *TAKS Obj. 6*

　Ⓕ The amount of the annual fee 　　Ⓖ The sum of the annual fee and $35.55

　Ⓗ The capacity of each jar 　　　　Ⓙ The number of jars bought

**TEKS** *8.4, 8.15.A*

# 3.3 Modeling Two-Step Equations

A *two-step equation* is an equation you solve using two operations. You can use algebra tiles to model and solve two-step equations.

**EXPLORE 1**  Model and solve $2x + 3 = 7$.

**STEP 1**  **Model** the equation $2x + 3 = 7$.

**STEP 2**  **Remove** three 1-tiles from each side.

**STEP 3**  **Notice** there are two $x$-tiles, and the coefficient of $x$ is 2, so divide the remaining tiles on each side into 2 identical groups.

**STEP 4**  **Compare** one group from each side. One $x$-tile is equal to two 1-tiles. So, the solution is 2.

**PRACTICE**

1. Model each step described below. Draw a picture of each step.

   **Step 1**  **Use** algebra tiles to model the equation $3x + 1 = 10$.

   **Step 2**  **Remove** one 1-tile from each side.

   **Step 3**  **Divide** the remaining tiles into three identical groups.

   **Step 4**  **Solve** the equation. Then check your solution by substituting in the original equation.

**Use algebra tiles to model and solve the equation.**

2. $3x + 1 = 7$      3. $2x + 4 = 10$      4. $2x + 3 = 5$      5. $4x + 1 = 9$

*Continued on next page*

**EXPLORE 2** Model and solve $3x - 4 = 5$. Write the equation at each step.

**Tile Model**       **Algebra**

**STEP 1**

$3x - 4 = 5$

**STEP 2** **Add** four 1-tiles to each side. Then remove zero pairs.

$3x - 4 + 4 = 5 + 4$

**STEP 3**

$$\frac{3x}{3} = \frac{9}{3}$$

**STEP 4**

$x = 3$

**Animated Math** at classzone.com

**PRACTICE** Use algebra tiles to model and solve the equation. Write the equation at each step.

**6.** $3x - 6 = 6$      **7.** $2x - 3 = 7$      **8.** $4x + 2 = -10$      **9.** $2x - 5 = -9$

**DRAW CONCLUSIONS**

**10.** **REASONING** *Explain* what kinds of equations are difficult or impossible to solve using algebra tiles. Give an example.

**11.** **WORK BACKWARD** Use algebra tiles to write a two-step equation whose solution is 1.

# 3.3 Solving Two-Step Equations

TEKS *8.2.A, 8.2.B*

| **Before** | You solved one-step equations. |
| **Now** | You'll solve two-step equations. |
| **Why?** | So you can find costs, as for using a pool in Ex. 45. |

**KEY VOCABULARY**
- **equation,** *p. 26*
- **solution,** *p. 26*

**Music Club** You pay $9.95 to join an Internet music club. You pay $.99 for each song that you download. Your cost for joining and downloading some songs is $17.87. How many songs did you download? Example 1 answers this question using a two-step equation.

## EXAMPLE 1  Solving a Real-World Problem

 The model below represents a way of finding how many songs you downloaded. You can use $x$ to represent the number of songs.

| Cost to join | $+$ | Cost per song | $\cdot$ | Number of songs | $=$ | Total cost |

| | |
|---|---|
| $9.95 + 0.99x = 17.87$ | **Write an algebraic model.** |
| $\underline{-9.95} \qquad \underline{-9.95}$ | **Subtract 9.95 from each side to undo addition.** |
| $0.99x = 7.92$ | **Simplify.** |
| $\dfrac{0.99x}{0.99} = \dfrac{7.92}{0.99}$ | **Divide each side by 0.99 to undo multiplication.** |
| $x = 8$ | **Simplify. $x$ is by itself.** |

▶ **Answer** You downloaded 8 songs.

 **GUIDED PRACTICE**   **for Example 1**

**1.** Show how to check the solution in Example 1.

**2. What If?** Suppose the cost to join and download some songs is $26.78. How does this change the equation in Example 1? Find the number of songs.

**3. Film** You pay $35 in dues to a photo club and $10 per roll you have developed. If you spend $225 during the year, how many rolls of film do you have developed? Use $10x + 35 = 225$ and solve for $x$.

### Solving a Two-Step Equation

Some equations require two inverse operations to solve.

| | |
|---|---|
| $2x + 1 = 5$ | **Original equation** |
| $2x + 1 - 1 = 5 - 1$ | **Undo addition or subtraction.** |
| $2x = 4$ | **Simplify.** |
| $\dfrac{2x}{2} = \dfrac{4}{2}$ | Undo multiplication **or division.** |
| $x = 2$ | **Simplify.** |

---

**EXAMPLE 2**  Solving with a Variable in the Numerator

| | |
|---|---|
| $\dfrac{x}{2} - 14 = 8$ | **Original equation** |
| $\underline{\phantom{xx}+14 \quad +14}$ | **Add 14 to each side to undo subtraction.** |
| $\dfrac{x}{2} = 22$ | **Simplify.** |
| $\dfrac{x}{2} \cdot 2 = 22 \cdot 2$ | **Multiply each side by 2 to undo division.** |
| $x = 44$ | **Simplify.** |

**Check**  $\dfrac{44}{2} - 14 \overset{?}{=} 8$    **Substitute 44 for *x* in original equation.**

$22 - 14 = 8 \checkmark$

---

**EXAMPLE 3**  Solving with a Negative Coefficient

*ANOTHER WAY*

Remember that you can solve an equation horizontally, as shown here, or vertically, as shown in Example 2.

| | |
|---|---|
| $8 = 12 - 2x$ | **Original equation** |
| $8 - 12 = 12 - 2x - 12$ | **Subtract 12 from each side to undo addition.** |
| $-4 = -2x$ | **Simplify.** |
| $\dfrac{-4}{-2} = \dfrac{-2x}{-2}$ | **Divide each side by −2 to undo multiplication.** |
| $2 = x$ | **Simplify.** |

---

✓ **GUIDED PRACTICE**    for Examples 2 and 3

*AVOID ERRORS*

Recall from Lesson 2.7 that $a = 1 \cdot a$, so *a* has a coefficient of 1.

**Solve the equation. Check your answer.**

**4.** $13 = 11 + \dfrac{y}{3}$    **5.** $\dfrac{z}{5} - 3 = 4$    **6.** $-6x + 5 = 23$    **7.** $6 = 16 - a$

**8.** $10 - 4a = 34$    **9.** $8w - 3 = 21$    **10.** $7x + 3 = 17$    **11.** $\dfrac{3}{4}m + 1 = 7$

# 3.3 EXERCISES

HOMEWORK KEY

🔷 = **TAKS Practice and Reasoning**
**Exs. 21, 40, 41, 45, 47, and 48**

⭕ = **HINTS** AND **HOMEWORK HELP**
for **Exs. 3, 5, 13, 17, 39** at classzone.com

## SKILL PRACTICE

1. **VOCABULARY** Copy and complete: A number that you can substitute for a variable to make an equation true is a(n) __?__ of the equation.

2. **VOCABULARY** Copy and complete: A mathematical sentence formed by placing an equal sign (=) between two expressions is a(n) __?__ .

**SOLVING EQUATIONS** Solve the equation. Check your answer.

**SEE EXAMPLES 1, 2, AND 3**
on pp. 129–130
for Exs. 3–22

3. $2x + 1 = 7$

4. $3y - 4 = 2$

5. $10 - 7z = 3$

6. $15 = -4p + 7$

7. $9 - 2k = 25$

8. $11 = \dfrac{h}{6} + 8$

9. $\dfrac{x}{9} - 4 = 5$

10. $6 + 2c = 15$

11. $29 = -5a + 4$

12. $7 + 5b = -23$

13. $100 - 7r = 44$

14. $20 - 6w = 14$

15. $-32 = -17 - \dfrac{d}{2}$

16. $\dfrac{c}{3} - 7 = 5.3$

17. $-7 + \dfrac{z}{4} = 5.2$

18. $\dfrac{3x}{5} = 12$

19. $\dfrac{2x}{3} = -8$

20. $-\dfrac{5m}{2} = 35$

21. 🔷 **TAKS REASONING** What is the solution of the equation $21 = 3x + 9$?

Ⓐ $-2$　　　Ⓑ $4$　　　Ⓒ $10$　　　Ⓓ $16$

22. **ERROR ANALYSIS** Describe and correct the error made in solving the equation.

$$
\begin{aligned}
3x - 9 &= 18 \\
3x &= 9 \\
x &= 3
\end{aligned}
$$

**REASONING** In Exercises 23 and 24, two methods for solving the equation $2(m + 3) = 18$ are shown. *Justify* each step of the solution.

23.
$$
\begin{aligned}
2(m + 3) &= 18 \\
2m + 6 &= 18 \\
2m + 6 - 6 &= 18 - 6 \\
2m &= 12 \\
\dfrac{2m}{2} &= \dfrac{12}{2} \\
m &= 6
\end{aligned}
$$

24.
$$
\begin{aligned}
2(m + 3) &= 18 \\
\dfrac{2(m + 3)}{2} &= \dfrac{18}{2} \\
m + 3 &= 9 \\
m + 3 - 3 &= 9 - 3 \\
m &= 6
\end{aligned}
$$

**CHOOSE A METHOD** Use one of the methods in Exercises 23 and 24 to solve. *Explain* your choice of method.

25. $3(r + 1) = 9$

26. $4 = -1(z + 11)$

27. $6\left(\dfrac{1}{3} + h\right) = 20$

**GEOMETRY** Write and solve equations to find the values of the variables.

**28.**

10

10      10

$3x - 8$

**29.**

5

2      $3y - 10$

$4x + 9$

**30.**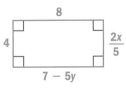

8

4      $\dfrac{2x}{5}$

$7 - 5y$

**APPLYING PROPERTIES** Solve the equation. *Justify* each step.

**31.** $\dfrac{4h - 6}{8} = -3$

**32.** $\dfrac{3a + 4}{5} = 11$

**33.** $\dfrac{2w - 3}{9} = 5$

**34.** $\dfrac{2(h + 12)}{5} = 10$

**35.** $\dfrac{2(4t - 7)}{3} = -22$

**36.** $\dfrac{6(4h + 5)}{7} = -6$

**37. CHALLENGE** The perimeter of a rectangle is found by the formula $P = 2l + 2w$, where $l$ is the length and $w$ is the width.

    **a.** Rewrite this formula with $w$ alone on one side.

    **b.** Rewrite this formula with $l$ alone on one side.

## PROBLEM SOLVING

*SEE EXAMPLE 1*
on p. 129
for Exs. 38–40

**38. GUIDED PROBLEM SOLVING** You draw illustrations. You charge $50 per illustration and $12 per hour to make changes. You get a check for $198 to pay for three illustrations and changes. How many hours did you spend making changes to the illustrations?

    **a.** Read the problem. What is the main idea? What do you know and what do you need to find?

    **b.** You can use the equation $3(50) + 12n = 198$ to find the number of hours you spent making changes to the illustrations. Why is the value of $n$ the number of hours you spent making changes?

    **c.** Solve the equation and check your answer.

**39. WALKING DOGS** You earn money by walking dogs in your neighborhood. Each neighbor pays you $5 per walk and you spend $4 per week on dog treats. If your goal is to earn $51 per week, how many walks do you need to do at $5 each? To answer this question, solve the equation $5w - 4 = 51$.

**40. TAKS REASONING** Students are cleaning up 11 miles of trails in a local park. After an hour, they have cleaned about 3 miles of trails. Solve the two-step equation $3h + 3 = 11$. *Explain* why the value of $h$ is an estimate of the number of hours it will take to finish.

**41. TAKS REASONING** *Describe* a real-world situation that can be solved using a two-step equation involving subtraction and multiplication. Write and solve the equation.

**42. WRITING** Jamie is a certified youth soccer referee. After completing a course that cost $35, she earned $15 per game. Her profit in the first season was $280. Which equation should you use to find *g*, the number of games Jamie worked? *Explain.*

(**A**) $15g + 35 = 280$  (**B**) $15g - 35 = 280$

**43. PHONE CARDS** You have $2.10 remaining on your phone card. You pay 7 cents for each minute of a call and a 75 cent charge for using a pay phone. If you make a call from a pay phone, what is the maximum whole number of minutes that you can talk? (*Hint:* The cost is the sum of the pay phone charge and 7 cents per minute for your call.)

**44. REASONING** Ted has $12 more than Carla, and Carla has $8 more than Devon. Together they have $73. How much money does each person have? Write an equation in terms of *D* to represent the situation.

**45. TAKS REASONING** Use the given information about the cost of using the city pool.

**a. Evaluate and Explain** Evaluate the expression $3(40) + 12$. What does the value of the expression represent?

**b. Interpret** Solve the two-step equation $3x + 12 = 100$. What does the answer tell you about the payment plans?

**c. Compare and Contrast** For each payment plan, give one reason why you might choose it.

**CITY POOL RATES**

**SUMMER PASS** $100
unlimited visits – including registration

**DAY PASS** $3
additional $12 registration

**46. CHALLENGE** The length of a rectangle is 5 meters less than twice its width. If each dimension is reduced by 6 meters, the rectangle has a perimeter of 38 meters. What are the dimensions of the original rectangle?

## MIXED REVIEW FOR TAKS

TAKS PRACTICE at classzone.com

REVIEW
Lesson 3.2;
TAKS Workbook

**47. TAKS PRACTICE** Gail buys 5 greeting cards for $5.50 including tax. Why does she think she can buy 1 more card for a dollar and a dime? *TAKS Obj. 1*

(**A**) Because the solution to $x + 5 = 6.10$ is $x = 1.10$.

(**B**) Because the solution to $x - 5 = -3.90$ is $x = 1.10$.

(**C**) Because the solution to $5x = 5.50$ is $x = 1.10$.

(**D**) Because the solution to $x + 5.50 = 6.60$ is $x = 1.10$.

REVIEW
Lesson 2.8;
TAKS Workbook

**48. TAKS PRACTICE** Mrs. Carr draws a coordinate plane and plots a point in the second quadrant that she labels point *A*. She then plots point *B* two units down and two units to the right of point *A*. Point *B* lies in the fourth quadrant. Which ordered pair might be the coordinates of point *A*? *TAKS Obj. 3*

(**F**) $(-1, 1)$   (**G**) $(1, 1)$   (**H**) $(-3, 1)$   (**J**) $(2, 1)$

ONLINE QUIZ at classzone.com   **133**

# 3.4 Writing Two-Step Equations

TEKS 8.4, 8.5.A

| Before | You solved two-step equations. |
| Now | You'll solve problems by writing two-step equations. |
| Why? | So you can find additional quantities, as in Example 1. |

**KEY VOCABULARY**
- equation, *p. 26*
- solution, *p. 26*

You can solve some problems by writing and solving two-step equations. You can use a verbal model to help you write a two-step equation.

**EXAMPLE 1** **TAKS PRACTICE: Multiple Choice**

> **American Flamingos** A zoo currently spends $1620 to feed its American flamingos. Next year, its budget for feeding the flamingos will be $2790 and it will cost $390 to feed each additional flamingo. Which equation can be used to find $n$, the number of additional flamingos the zoo can buy?
>
> **(A)** $1620 + 2790 = n$   **(B)** $2790 = 390n + 1620$
>
> **(C)** $1620 + 2790 = 390n$   **(D)** $2790 = n + 390$

**ELIMINATE CHOICES**
Each additional flamingo costs $390 to feed. So, you need to multiply the number of flamingos by 390. This eliminates choices A and D.

**SOLUTION**

Write and solve a two-step equation to find the number of flamingos. Write a verbal model. Let $n$ be the number of additional flamingos.

| Budget available | = | Cost of each new flamingo | · | Number of new flamingos | + | Cost of existing flamingos |
|---|---|---|---|---|---|---|

$$2790 = 390n + 1620 \qquad \textbf{Write an algebraic model.}$$

$$2790 - 1620 = 390n + 1620 - 1620 \qquad \textbf{Subtract 1620 from each side.}$$

$$1170 = 390n \qquad \textbf{Simplify.}$$

$$\frac{1170}{390} = \frac{390n}{390} \qquad \textbf{Divide each side by 390.}$$

$$3 = n \qquad \textbf{Simplify.}$$

▶ **Answer** The zoo can buy 3 new flamingos next year. An equation for finding the number of flamingos is $2370 = 390n + 1620$. The correct answer is B. Ⓐ **Ⓑ** Ⓒ Ⓓ

---

✓ **GUIDED PRACTICE** for Example 1

1. **Feeding Costs** It costs a zoo $1150 this year to feed tortoises. Each new tortoise costs $575 to feed. A zoo's budget for tortoise food next year is $2875. How many new tortoises can the zoo buy next year?

## EXAMPLE 2 Writing and Solving a Two-Step Equation

**The sum of 4 times a number plus −6 is 14. What is the number?**

| | |
|---|---|
| 4 times **a number** and −6 is 14. | **Write a verbal model.** |
| $4 \cdot n + (-6) = 14$ | **Translate.** |
| $4n - 6 = 14$ | **Write equation.** |
| $4n - 6 + 6 = 14 + 6$ | **Add 6 to each side.** |
| $4n = 20$ | **Simplify.** |
| $\dfrac{4n}{4} = \dfrac{20}{4}$ | **Divide each side by 4.** |
| $n = 5$ | **Simplify.** |

▸ **Answer** The number is 5.

**REWRITE SUMS**
Remember that adding −6 is the same as subtracting 6.

## EXAMPLE 3 Writing and Solving a Two-Step Equation

**Reading** You want to find how many pages you need to read per week in order to finish several books in six weeks. The books have a total of 1244 pages. You have already read 500 pages. How many pages do you have to read per week?

### SOLUTION

Let $p$ be the number of pages to read per week.

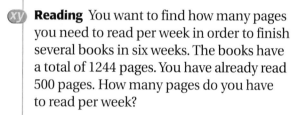

| | |
|---|---|
| $1244 = 6p + 500$ | **Write an algebraic model.** |
| $1244 - 500 = 6p + 500 - 500$ | **Subtract 500 from each side.** |
| $744 = 6p$ | **Simplify.** |
| $\dfrac{744}{6} = \dfrac{6p}{6}$ | **Divide each side by 6.** |
| $124 = p$ | **Simplify.** |

▸ **Answer** You have to read 124 pages per week.

✓ **GUIDED PRACTICE** for Examples 2 and 3

**2.** The difference of six times a number and 9 is −3. What is the number?

**3.** **What If?** Suppose in Example 3 that you have read 714 pages and have five weeks left. How many pages do you have to read per week?

# 3.4 EXERCISES

## SKILL PRACTICE

**VOCABULARY** **Copy and complete the statement.**

1. You use two inverse operations to solve a(n) __?__ .

2. A(n) __?__ model uses symbols for operations and words to label information.

**TRANSLATING STATEMENTS** **Match the statement with the correct equation.**

*SEE EXAMPLE 2*
on p. 135
for Exs. 3–16

3. The sum of 3 and a number is 16.    **A.** $3n - 2 = 16$

4. The product of 3 and a number is 16.    **B.** $3(2n) = 16$

5. The difference of 3 times a number and 2 is 16.    **C.** $3n = 16$

6. The product of 3 and twice a number is 16.    **D.** $3 + n = 16$

7. ✦ **TAKS REASONING** The sum of twice a number and 5 is 13. Which equation matches this statement?

   **Ⓐ** $2x + 5 = 13$    **Ⓑ** $2x - 5 = 13$    **Ⓒ** $x + 5 = 13$    **Ⓓ** $5x + 13 = 2$

8. **ERROR ANALYSIS** Describe and correct the error made in translating the statement into an equation.
   *The difference of 3 times a number and −2 is 4.*

$3n - 2 = 4$

**WRITING AND SOLVING TWO-STEP EQUATIONS** **Translate the statement into an equation. Then solve the equation.**

9. The sum of 5 times a number and 4 is 9.

10. Seven subtracted from the quotient of a number and 2 is −6.

11. The sum of −2 times a number and 3.5 is 7.5.

12. The difference of 3 times a number and $-\frac{1}{2}$ is $-\frac{5}{2}$.

13. The absolute value of a number divided by 6 is 4.

14. Two times the absolute value of a number is 8.

15. The sum of the absolute value of a number and 6 is 12.

16. Five less than the product of 2 and the absolute value of a number is 3.

**CHALLENGE** **Translate the statement into an equation. Then solve.**

17. The product of a number divided by 5 and 2 is 1.

18. The sum of 2 and 3, plus 3 times a number, is −4.

19. The quotient of −36 and 9 exceeds 4 times a number by 8.

20. The product of 8 squared divided by 16 and a number is 24.

SEE EXAMPLES
1 AND 3
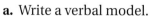
on pp. 134–135
for Exs. 21–29

**21. GUIDED PROBLEM SOLVING** You and your friends decide to have a car wash as a fundraiser for the school chorus. You spend $15 on supplies and charge $6 per car. At the end of the day your profit is $93. How many cars did you and your friends wash?

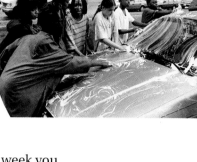

   **a.** Write a verbal model.

   **b.** Translate your verbal model into an algebraic model.

   **c.** Solve the equation.

   **d.** Check that your answer is reasonable.

**22. HOURLY WAGE** You earn $70 per week mowing lawns. One week you work 10 hours during the week and spend $20 on gasoline for your mower. How much do you earn each hour?

**23. CANDLE SALES** You make candles and sell them for $15 each. The materials to make up to 20 candles cost $20. How many candles must you sell to have a profit of $85 after expenses?

**24. TAKS REASONING** A bicycle rental shop charges $5 per hour plus a fee of $10 each time you rent a bicycle. Which equation can you use to find the number of hours you can rent a bicycle for $45?

   **Ⓐ** $5h + 10 = 45$         **Ⓑ** $10h + 5 = 45$

   **Ⓒ** $5 + h + 10 = 45$     **Ⓓ** $15h = 45$

**25. MAGAZINE SUBSCRIPTION** You subscribe to a magazine that costs $26 yearly. You make an initial payment of $5 and then make three equal payments. How much is each payment?

**26. RUNNING TIME** How long will it take the dog to be 0.7 mile away from the owner? Use $d = 35t + 0.1$, where $d$ is the distance the dog is from the owner after $t$ hours.

35 miles per hour

0    0.1 mi              0.7 mi

**27. TAKS REASONING** Write two different two-step equations that both have 8 as a solution.

**28. WRITING** Write a word problem that can be modeled by the equation $5x - 6 = 9$. Interpret the solution in terms of your problem.

**29. RESTAURANT** At a restaurant one day, 60 sandwiches were sold in all, some on rye bread and 28 on white bread. The number of sandwiches sold on rye bread was twice the number sold the day before. How many sandwiches on rye bread were sold the day before?

**30. PARTY SUPPLIES** You need 124 plastic forks for a party. At one store you buy the last 5 boxes, and each box contains 8 forks. At another store you find boxes that each contain 12 forks. How many of these boxes do you need to buy?

**31. SCHOOL FAIR** The senior class at your school made a $300 profit at the school fair by having a dunk tank. The dunk tank cost $135 to rent, and the senior class charged $5 for each person to play. If one third of people who participated were adults, how many adults participated?

**32. GEOMETRY** The sum of the angles of a triangle is 180°. In triangle *ABC*, the measure of angle *A* is 12° greater than the measure of angle *C*, and the measure of angle *B* is 4 times as great as the measure of angle *C*. Write an equation where each angle is expressed in terms of the measure of angle *C*. Find the measure of each angle. Show your work.

**33. ⬇ TAKS REASONING** A taxicab costs $2 plus an additional $1.50 for every mile. Your ride cost $17 before the tip. How many miles did you go? Will it cost twice as much to go twice as far? *Explain.*

**REASONING** **Exercises 34 and 35 are missing information. Tell what information is needed to solve the problems.**

**34.** You jog for 5 minutes and then you run for 20 minutes. For each week after, you jog for 5 minutes, but increase the time that you run. After how many weeks will you be training for a total of 85 minutes?

**35.** You have a job in which you make $6 per hour plus tips. You made a total of $34 yesterday. How much did you make in tips?

**36. GEOMETRY** The length of a rectangle is 15 feet more than three times its width. The perimeter is 94 feet. What is the area of the rectangle?

**37. ⬇ TAKS REASONING** The table shows how much it costs to rent videos, including $5 for snacks. Write an equation for finding the cost of renting *x* videos. *Explain* how you found your equation. Find the cost of renting 12 videos.

| Videos | 1 | 2 | 3 | 4 | 5 | 6 |
|--------|------|------|------|------|------|------|
| Price | $8 | $11 | $14 | $17 | $20 | $23 |

**38. CHALLENGE** Amanda takes her car to the repair shop. The mechanic starts working on her car at 10:30 A.M., takes a 45 minute lunch break, and then continues working into the afternoon. The parts to fix the car cost $350 and the labor costs $80 per hour. Amanda pays $730 in all. At what time does the mechanic finish the work?

⬇ = TAKS Practice and Reasoning      ◯ = **HINTS AND HOMEWORK HELP** *at classzone.com*

*REVIEW*
Lesson 3.3;
TAKS Workbook

**39.** 🔻 **TAKS PRACTICE** The equation $3p + 76 = 100$ models the number of points, $p$, that Kyle must score in each of his last three basketball games to score 100 points for the season. Which procedure can be used to solve the equation? *TAKS Obj. 6*

(A) Divide each side by 3, then add 76 to each side.

(B) Add 76 to each side, then divide each side by 3.

(C) Divide each side by 3, then subtract 76 from each side.

(D) Subtract 76 from each side, then divide each side by 3.

*REVIEW*
Lesson 1.6;
TAKS Workbook

**40.** 🔻 **TAKS PRACTICE** Which could be the area and perimeter of a square? *TAKS Obj. 6*

(F) $25 \text{ ft}^2$ and 25 ft

(G) $2.5 \text{ ft}^2$ and 2 ft

(H) $6.25 \text{ ft}^2$ and 10 ft

(J) $144 \text{ ft}^2$ and 44 ft

## QUIZ *for Lessons 3.1–3.4*

**Solve the equation.**

**1.** $x - 16 = 8$ *(p. 117)*

**2.** $8 + x = 3$ *(p. 117)*

**3.** $19r = 76$ *(p. 122)*

**4.** $\dfrac{y}{-1.4} = -5$ *(p. 122)*

**5.** $3x - 8 = 7$ *(p. 129)*

**6.** $14 = 2 + \dfrac{x}{3}$ *(p. 129)*

**Translate the statement into an equation. Then solve.** *(p. 134)*

**7.** The sum of 10 times a number and 5 is $-15$.

**8.** The difference of 4 times a number and $-7$ is 39.

**9.** BICYCLE Mary wants to buy a bicycle that costs $280. Her parents agree to pay $100. Mary will save $20 a week. Write and solve an equation to find how long it will take her to save enough money. *(p. 134)*

## Brain Game

### *Behind the Magic*

Choose any number. Multiply the number by **2**. Add **14**. Divide by **2**. Subtract the number you started with. Multiply by **3**. Your answer is **21**.

To figure out why the answer is always **21**, let $x$ be the number you choose and write an algebraic expression that shows all of the steps. Then simplify the expression. What is your answer?

**TEKS** *8.4, 8.14.D*

# 3.4 Searching for Information

### EXAMPLE

A class is planning a trip to the Naismith Memorial Basketball Hall of Fame in Springfield, Massachusetts. The class has $310 to spend on admission. There are 35 students in the class. How many adults can they afford to bring?

#### SOLUTION

Follow these steps to perform a search on the Internet:

**STEP 1** **Pick** a search engine.

**STEP 2** **Type** keywords that cover the topic you would like to search. Then select Search.

**STEP 3** **Pick** a site from the results that is likely to have the information you need.

Use the steps described above to find the prices for students and adults. (*Hint:* There are over 35 people going, so the group rates would apply.)

| Amount to spend | = | Number of students | · | Price per student | + | Number of adults | · | Price per adult |

### PRACTICE  Use the results of your search.

**1.** Write and solve an equation to solve the problem in the example.

**2.** Your class is planning a trip to a museum. Use the Internet to research prices for student and adult tickets at a nearby museum. If your class has $350 to spend on admission, how many adults can you afford to bring?

## Lessons 3.1–3.4

**MULTIPLE CHOICE**

1. **DRAWING BLUEPRINTS** An architect drawing blueprints sketches a rectangle and accurately labels the rectangle's width as $x$ and its length as $x + 7$. The rectangle's perimeter is 46 inches. What is its area? *TEKS 8.7.B*

   (A) 8 in.$^2$

   (B) 15 in.$^2$

   (C) 120 in.$^2$

   (D) 516 in.$^2$

2. **SEARS TOWER** The Empire State Building in New York is 1250 feet tall. The difference between the height of the CN Tower in Toronto, Canada, and the height of the Empire State building is 565 feet. The height of the CN Tower is 365 feet more than the height of the Sears Tower in Chicago. Which equation can be solved to find the height, $S$, of the Sears Tower? *TEKS 8.4.A*

   (F) $S = 1250 + 565 + 365$

   (G) $S = 1250 + 365 - 565$

   (H) $S = 1250 + 565 - 365$

   (J) $S = 1250 - 565 - 365$

3. **JOB INTERVIEW** It takes Jesse 60 minutes to drive 20 miles to an important job interview during rush hour. If Jesse can travel 1.5 times as fast on the way home, how many minutes will it take him to return home? $[d = rt]$ *TEKS 8.5.A*

   (A) 30 min     (B) 40 min

   (C) 45 min     (D) 120 min

4. **MODELING** Which situation might be represented by the equation $93 = \dfrac{y}{16}$? *TEKS 8.15.A*

   (F) A football team plays 16 games and averages 93 rushing yards per game. The variable $y$ is the total number of rushing yards over all games.

   (G) A student takes 16 exams and averages 93 on the exams. The variable $y$ is the student's score on one exam.

   (H) Maria divides $93 among 16 relatives. The variable $y$ is the amount of money that each relative receives.

   (J) Tammy bicycles 16 miles in 93 minutes. The variable $y$ is the speed that she traveled measured in miles per minute.

**GRIDDED ANSWER** ⊙①②●③④⑤⑥⑦⑧⑨

5. **TRUCK DRIVING** Jen's truck gets 5 miles per gallon of diesel fuel. She drove 3400 miles to deliver a shipment. She left with a full tank and used 80 gallons of fuel between each stop at a gas station to fill up her fuel tank. How many times did Jen have to stop for fuel during the 3400 miles? *TEKS 8.2.B*

6. **BUS RIDE** Kevin traveled from his house to the city library by bus. He took one bus 3 miles. Then he changed buses. The second bus traveled at an average speed of 45 miles per hour. Kevin's entire trip covered 18 miles. How many minutes did he spend on the second bus? *TEKS 8.2.B*

# 3.5 Applying Geometric Formulas

TEKS 8.5.A, 8.7.B

| | |
|---|---|
| **Before** | You measured rectangles. |
| **Now** | You'll use formulas for perimeter and area. |
| **Why?** | So you can find areas, as for exhibits in Example 5. |

**KEY VOCABULARY**
- **base,** *p. 142*
- **height,** *p. 142*

## ACTIVITY

**You can use a model to find the area of a triangle.**

**STEP 1** **Copy** the diagram on graph paper.

**STEP 2** **Cut** out the three pieces.

**STEP 3** **Arrange** the pieces to make two equal-sized triangles.

**STEP 4** **Compare** the height of triangle 2 to the height of the original rectangle. What is the area of the rectangle? of triangle 2?

**STEP 5** **Draw** your own triangle on graph paper so that its longest side is a side of a rectangle and the opposite vertex touches the opposite side of the rectangle. Find its area by following the steps above.

**STEP 6** **Write** a formula for the area of a triangle.

To find the area of a triangle, you need to know the *base* and the *height*. Any side of a triangle can be labeled as the triangle's **base**. The perpendicular distance from a base to its opposite vertex is the **height** of a triangle.

## KEY CONCEPT — For Your Notebook

### Area and Perimeter of a Triangle

**Words** The *area* of a triangle is one half the product of its base *b* and height *h*.

The *perimeter* of a triangle is the sum of the lengths of all three sides *a*, *b*, and *c*.

**Algebra** $A = \frac{1}{2}bh$

$P = a + b + c$

**Diagram**

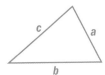

## EXAMPLE 1 Finding Area and Perimeter of a Triangle

**VOCABULARY**

Remember that *perimeter* is measured in linear units, such as feet, and *area* is measured in square units, such as square feet, or ft².

**Find the area and perimeter of the triangle.**

$$A = \frac{1}{2}bh \qquad\qquad P = a + b + c$$

$$= \frac{1}{2}(14)(12) \qquad\qquad = 13 + 14 + 15$$

$$= 84 \text{ in.}^2 \qquad\qquad = 42 \text{ in.}$$

## EXAMPLE 2 Finding the Area of a Triangle

**Sailboats** Find the area of the sail.

**SOLUTION**

$$A = \frac{1}{2}bh \qquad\qquad \text{Write area formula.}$$

$$= \frac{1}{2}(171)(134) \qquad \text{Substitute values.}$$

$$= 11{,}457 \qquad\qquad \text{Multiply.}$$

▶ **Answer** The area of the sail is 11,457 square inches.

## ✓ GUIDED PRACTICE for Examples 1 and 2

1. A triangle's height is 9 inches and its base is 10 inches. Find its area.

2. A triangle's side lengths are 4 feet, 6 feet, and 2.5 feet. Find its perimeter.

**Unknown Dimensions** Now that you can solve equations, you can use area and perimeter formulas to find unknown dimensions of geometric shapes.

## EXAMPLE 3 TAKS PRACTICE: Multiple Choice

**Renovation** An interior designer renovates a rectangular sunroom with an area of 96 square feet and a length of 12 feet. What is the room's width?

Ⓐ 8 feet     Ⓑ 12 feet     Ⓒ 36 feet     Ⓓ 1152 feet

**ELIMINATE CHOICES**

Since $A = lw$, the width has to be less than 96. So, you can eliminate choice D.

**SOLUTION**

$$A = lw \qquad\qquad \text{Write area formula.}$$

$$96 = 12w \qquad\quad \text{Substitute values.}$$

$$\frac{96}{12} = \frac{12w}{12} \qquad\quad \text{Divide each side by 12.}$$

$$8 = w \qquad\qquad \text{Simplify.}$$

▶ **Answer** The width is 8 feet. The correct answer is A. Ⓐ Ⓑ Ⓒ Ⓓ

**EXAMPLE 4** Finding an Unknown Length

The rectangle at the right has a perimeter of 20 inches. Find the length of the rectangle.

4 in.

$l$

$$P = 2l + 2w$$      Write perimeter formula.

$$20 = 2l + 2(4)$$      Substitute 20 for *P* and 4 for *w*.

$$20 = 2l + 8$$      Multiply.

$$20 - 8 = 2l + 8 - 8$$      Subtract 8 from each side.

$$12 = 2l$$      Simplify.

$$\frac{12}{2} = \frac{2l}{2}$$      Divide each side by 2.

$$6 = l$$      Simplify.

▶ **Answer** The length of the rectangle is 6 inches.

**EXAMPLE 5** Using an Area Formula

**Zoo Exhibit** A polar bear exhibit includes a rectangular pool and rocks. Find the area of the region with rocks.

20 ft

pool

40 ft

32 ft

rocks

56 ft

**SOLUTION**

Let *r* be the area of the region with rocks.

| Total area | = | Area of pool | + | Area of rock region |
|:---:|:---:|:---:|:---:|:---:|

$$40 \cdot 56 = 20 \cdot 32 + r$$

$$2240 = 640 + r$$      Write an algebraic model.

$$2240 - 640 = 640 - 640 + r$$      Subtract 640 from each side.

$$1600 = r$$      Simplify.

▶ **Answer** The area of the region with rocks is 1600 square feet.

**Animated Math**
at classzone.com

✓ **GUIDED PRACTICE** for Examples 3, 4, and 5

Find the unknown dimension.

**3.** Perimeter = 36 feet

8 ft

$l$

**4.** Area = 32 mm$^2$

$h$

8 mm

**5.** Area = 6 in.$^2$

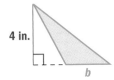

4 in.

$b$

**6. What If?** In Example 5, suppose the length of the exhibit area was 64 feet instead of 56 feet. Find the area of the region with rocks.

# 3.5 EXERCISES

HOMEWORK KEY

🟥 = **TAKS Practice and Reasoning**
Exs. 10, 13–15, 24, 25, 27, 33, and 36

◯ = **HINTS AND HOMEWORK HELP**
for Exs. 3, 5, 7, 9, 27 at classzone.com

## SKILL PRACTICE

**VOCABULARY** **Copy and complete the statement.**

1. In order to find the area of a triangle, you need to know the length of a(n) __?__ and the __?__ .

2. The __?__ of a triangle is the sum of the lengths of all three of its sides.

**FINDING AREA AND PERIMETER** **Find the area and perimeter of the triangle.**

SEE EXAMPLES
1 AND 2
on p. 143
for Exs. 3–6

3.

4.

5.

6. **ERROR ANALYSIS** Describe and correct the error made in finding the area of a triangle with a base of 5 inches and a height of 4 inches.

$$A = \frac{1}{2}(5 \text{ in.})(4 \text{ in.})$$
$$A = \frac{1}{2}(20 \text{ in.})$$
$$A = 10 \text{ in.}$$

**FINDING DIMENSIONS** **Find the unknown dimension.**

SEE EXAMPLES
3 AND 4
on pp. 143–144
for Exs. 7–10

7. $A = 18 \text{ ft}^2$

8. $A = 49 \text{ in.}^2$

9. $P = 60 \text{ m}$

10. 🟥 **TAKS REASONING** What is the length, in feet, of a rectangle that has a perimeter of 24 feet and a width of 4 feet?

(A) 4 feet (B) 8 feet (C) 12 feet (D) 32 feet

**FINDING COMBINED AREA** **Find the area of the figure.**

11.

12.

🟥 **TAKS REASONING** Draw and label two triangles with different dimensions that have the given area.

13. 36 square feet   14. 20 square inches   15. 9 square meters

**USING PERIMETER AND AREA** **Find the unknown dimension.**

**16.** A rectangle has a perimeter of 146 inches, a length of 49 inches, and a width of $2x$. What is the value of $x$?

**17.** A triangle has an area of 36 square meters, a height of 8 meters, and a base of $3y$. What is the value of $y$?

**18.** A triangle has an area of 5 square meters and a base of $2x$. What is the height of the triangle in terms of $x$?

**19.** A rectangle has an area of 70 square inches and a width of $3.5w$ inches. What is the length of the rectangle in terms of $w$?

**CHALLENGE** **Find the value of the variable in the rectangular figures, given the area of the shaded region.**

**20.** $A = 16 \text{ m}^2$

**21.** $A = 76 \text{ cm}^2$

**22.** $A = 180 \text{ ft}^2$

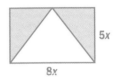

---

## PROBLEM SOLVING

**SEE EXAMPLES 3, 4, AND 5**
on p. 144
for Exs. 23–27

**23. GUIDED PROBLEM SOLVING** Find the area of the stone patio inside the backyard.

  **a.** Find the area of the rectangular portion of the patio.

  **b.** Find the area of the square portion of the patio.

  **c.** Add the two areas.

**24. TAKS REASONING** A rectangular garden has an area of 64 square feet. Its length is 16 feet. Which equation can you use to find the width?

  **(A)** $16 = 64 - x$    **(B)** $32 = x + 16$    **(C)** $16 = 64x$    **(D)** $64 = 16x$

**25. TAKS REASONING** What is the length of a rectangular room that is 22 feet wide and has a perimeter of 114 feet?

  **(A)** 20 feet    **(B)** 25 feet    **(C)** 30 feet    **(D)** 35 feet

**26. WRITING** In Example 2 on page 143, the bottom of the triangle has a length of 159 inches. *Explain* why this is not used as the base.

**27. TAKS REASONING** Michelle and Kate share a bedroom that is 18 feet by 14 feet. They want to divide the room so that each sister has half the area. Kate jokingly marks a square with sides 11 feet long in the center of the room. Does Kate have half the area of the room? *Explain.*

**28. GEOMETRY** Find the area of the regular *hexagon*. All the triangles are congruent.

2 mm
1.732 mm

**REASONING** Draw a triangle with a right angle at *A* on graph paper. Make the lengths of the sides through *A* whole numbers. Find the area. *Describe* how the area of the triangle changes if you change the triangle as described below.

**29.** Double the height.

**30.** Double the base.

**31.** Double both the height and the base.

**32.** Change its shape, but not its base or height.

**33.** ![TAKS] **TAKS REASONING** Use the advertisement shown.

   **a. Calculate** Find the area of the tent floor.

   **b. Estimate** Estimate the dimensions of a rectangular sleeping bag and find its area.

   **c. Analyze** Could four sleeping bags fit in the tent without overlapping? *Explain* your reasoning. Include a diagram.

**34. WINDOWS** A roll of weather stripping for windows is 108 inches long and costs $4. You need enough to go around three square windows that measure 3 feet on each side and one rectangular window that measures 3 feet by 5 feet. Is $25 enough money? *Explain.*

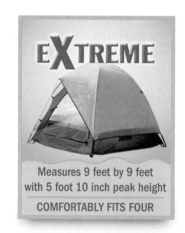

Measures 9 feet by 9 feet with 5 foot 10 inch peak height

COMFORTABLY FITS FOUR

**35. CHALLENGE** The distance between lines *a* and *b* is constant. *Explain* why triangles *VYZ*, *WYZ*, and *XYZ* have the same area.

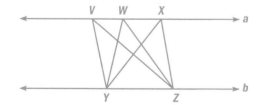

## MIXED REVIEW FOR TAKS

**TAKS** PRACTICE at classzone.com

*REVIEW*
Lesson 3.4;
TAKS Workbook

**36.** ![TAKS] **TAKS PRACTICE** In October, Gervace has money in a savings account. In November, he earns exactly enough to double his savings, and in December he saves another $110. He then has $480. Which equation can be used to find the amount of money he had in savings back in October? *TAKS Obj. 2*

  **(A)** $m + 110 = 480$

  **(B)** $2m + 480 = 110$

  **(C)** $480 - 110 = m + 2$

  **(D)** $2m + 110 = 480$

# 3.6 Solving Inequalities Using Addition or Subtraction

TEKS *8.4, 8.15.A*

| | |
|---|---|
| **Before** | You solved equations using addition or subtraction. |
| **Now** | You'll solve inequalities using addition or subtraction. |
| **Why?** | So you can find a minimum throwing distance, as in Example 3. |

**KEY VOCABULARY**
- **inequality,** *p. 148*
- **solution of an inequality,** *p. 148*
- **equivalent inequalities,** *p. 149*

**Disc Golf** In a game of disc golf, the target is beyond a pond, the far end of which is 300 feet away. Your first throw travels 134 feet. How long does your second throw have to be in order to clear the pond? You will use an inequality to answer this question in Example 3.

An **inequality**, such as $x \leq 6$, is a statement formed by placing an inequality symbol between two expressions. The **solution of an inequality** is the set of numbers that you can substitute for the variable to make the inequality true. To translate sentences into inequalities, look for the following phrases:

| Phrase | Symbol |
|---|---|
| is less than | < |
| is less than or equal to | ≤ |
| is greater than | > |
| is greater than or equal to | ≥ |

You can graph the solution of an inequality using a number line. When graphing inequalities with > or <, use an open circle. When graphing inequalities with ≥ or ≤, use a closed circle.

### EXAMPLE 1 Graphing Inequalities

| Inequality | Graph | Verbal Phrase |
|---|---|---|
| **a.** $y < 7$ | 2 3 4 5 6 7 8 | **All numbers less than 7** |
| **b.** $q \leq 3$ | −2 −1 0 1 2 3 4 | **All numbers less than or equal to 3** |
| **c.** $x > -5$ | −6 −4 −2 0 | **All numbers greater than −5** |
| **d.** $h \geq 2\frac{1}{2}$ | 0 1 2 3 | **All numbers greater than or equal to $2\frac{1}{2}$** |

**Solving Inequalities** When you solve an inequality, you find all solutions of the inequality. Inequalities that have the same solutions are **equivalent inequalities.** You can solve some inequalities by adding or subtracting.

## KEY CONCEPT

*For Your Notebook*

### Addition and Subtraction Properties of Inequality

**Words**  Adding or subtracting the same number on each side of an inequality produces an equivalent inequality.

**Algebra**  If $a > b$, then $a + c > b + c$.

If $a > b$, then $a - c > b - c$.

---

**EXAMPLE 2**  Solving Inequalities

> **VOCABULARY**
> Just as with equations, you can solve inequalities by using *inverse operations* to write equivalent inequalities.

**Solve the inequality. Then graph its solution.**

**a.**

| | |
|---|---|
| $x - 5 < 8$ | Original inequality |
| $x - 5 + 5 < 8 + 5$ | Add 5 to each side. |
| $x < 13$ | Simplify. |

```
◄──┼──┼──┼──┼──⊕──┼──┼──►
   9  10 11 12 13 14 15
```

**b.**

| | |
|---|---|
| $y - 7 \geq -10$ | Original inequality |
| $y - 7 + 7 \geq -10 + 7$ | Add 7 to each side. |
| $y \geq -3$ | Simplify. |

```
◄──┼──┼──●──┼──┼──┼──┼──►
  -5 -4 -3 -2 -1  0  1
```

> **AVOID ERRORS**
> The graph of $m > 7$ starts just after 7, not at 8, because numbers such as 7.01 are also solutions.

**c.**

| | |
|---|---|
| $8 + m > 15$ | Original inequality |
| $8 - 8 + m > 15 - 8$ | Subtract 8 from each side. |
| $m > 7$ | Simplify. |

```
◄──┼──┼──┼──⊕──┼──┼──┼──►
   4  5  6  7  8  9  10
```

---

✓ **GUIDED PRACTICE**  for Examples 1 and 2

**Graph and write a verbal phrase for the inequality.**

**1.** $z \geq -1$  **2.** $4 > p$  **3.** $k \leq -3.5$  **4.** $m > \dfrac{1}{2}$

**Solve the inequality. Then graph its solution.**

**5.** $x - 3 > -2$  **6.** $6 > t - 1$  **7.** $12 \geq p + 14$

**8.** $x + 5 < 10$  **9.** $t + 9 \leq 6$  **10.** $-4 < k - 3$

**EXAMPLE 3** Writing and Solving an Inequality

**Disc Golf** Using an inequality, you can find the distance the second throw must travel to clear the pond described on page 148. Let $d$ be the distance of your second throw.

| Distance of 2nd throw | $+$ | Distance of 1st throw | $>$ | Distance to far end of pond |
|---|---|---|---|---|

| | |
|---|---|
| $d + 134 > 300$ | Write an algebraic model. |
| $d + 134 - 134 > 300 - 134$ | Subtract 134 from each side. |
| $d > 166$ | Simplify. |

▶ **Answer** Your second throw needs to travel more than 166 feet.

*Animated* **Math**
at classzone.com

---

✓ **GUIDED PRACTICE**    for Example 3

**11. What If?** Suppose in Example 3 that your first throw went 155 feet. How far does your second throw have to go to clear the pond?

---

## 3.6 EXERCISES

**HOMEWORK KEY** ✦ = **TAKS Practice and Reasoning**
Exs. 20, 25–28, 40, 44, 47, 49, and 50

◯ = **HINTS AND HOMEWORK HELP**
for Exs. 7, 11, 13, 17, 39 at classzone.com

### SKILL PRACTICE

**1. VOCABULARY** Copy and complete: $-4 + x < -6$ and $x < -2$ are ___?___ .

**MATCHING** Match the inequality with its graph.

*SEE EXAMPLE 1*
on p. 148
for Exs. 2–10

**2.** $x < -1$

**3.** $x \le 1$

**4.** $x \ge 1$

**5.** $x > -1$

A. [number line: −2 −1 0 1 2, closed dot at 1 pointing left]

B. [number line: −2 −1 0 1 2, closed dot at 1 pointing right]

C. [number line: −2 −1 0 1 2, open dot at −1 pointing right]

D. [number line: −2 −1 0 1 2, open dot at −1 pointing left]

**WRITING INEQUALITIES** Write the inequality and the verbal phrase represented by the graph.

**6.** [number line: −3 −2 −1 0 1 2, open dot at −2 pointing right]

**7.** [number line: −10 −5 0 5 10 15, closed dot at −5 pointing right]

**8.** [number line: −2 −1 0 1 2 3, closed dot at 2 pointing left]

**9.** [number line: −2 0 2 4 6 8, open dot at 6 pointing left]

**10. ERROR ANALYSIS** Describe and correct the error made in graphing $x \geq -6$.

**SEE EXAMPLE 2**
on p. 149
for Exs. 11–20

**SOLVING INEQUALITIES** Solve the inequality. Then graph its solution.

**11.** $12 + p < 7$  **12.** $k + 4 \leq 11$  **13.** $n - 6 > 3$

**14.** $17 + r \geq 25$  **15.** $-8 \geq m - 19$  **16.** $-3.5 < w - 9$

**17.** $5.45 + b < -3.55$  **18.** $\frac{2}{3} \leq p - 2\frac{1}{3}$  **19.** $t + \frac{1}{4} > 5$

**20.** **TAKS REASONING** Which inequality has 23 for a solution?

**(A)** $x - 3 > 20$  **(B)** $x - 3 \geq 20$  **(C)** $x - 3 < 20$  **(D)** $x + 3 \leq 20$

**SOLUTIONS** Tell which positive integers less than 10 are solutions.

**21.** $-8 + x \leq 2$  **22.** $x - 20 > -15$  **23.** $-10 - x \leq -4$  **24.** $5 + x \leq 9$

**TAKS REASONING** Write two equivalent inequalities for the phrase.
Then graph the solution.

**25.** all real numbers less than 4  **26.** all real numbers greater than $-10$

**27.** all real numbers greater than 19  **28.** all real numbers less than $-7$

**29. REASONING** Are the inequalities $x < 2$ and $2 > x$ equivalent? *Explain.*

**CHALLENGE** *Describe* the values of $x$ that will make the statement true.

**30.** $|x| < 3$  **31.** $|x| > 2$  **32.** $|x| + 1 \leq 5$  **33.** $|x| + 1 \geq 7$

In Exercises 34–36, write two verbal sentences that describe the
*compound inequality.*

---

**EXTENSION** Compound Inequalities

The set of all real numbers greater than or equal to 0 *and* less than 4
can be represented by the following graph.

This set of numbers can be written as two inequalities or as a single
*compound inequality.*

two inequalities          compound inequality
$0 \leq x$ and $x < 4$          $0 \leq x < 4$

The compound inequality can be read in these two ways:
$x$ is greater than or equal to 0 and $x$ is less than 4.
$x$ is between 0 and 4, including 0.

---

**34.** $-2 < y < 1$  **35.** $7 \leq t < 9$  **36.** $4 \leq m \leq 11$

*SEE EXAMPLE 3*
on p. 150
for Exs. 37–39

**37. GUIDED PROBLEM SOLVING** On four tests you scored 90, 85, 98, and 87. To earn a B in math class, you need at least 425 points on five tests. Write and solve an inequality that represents the possible test scores you could get on your fifth test and still get at least a B in the class.

   **a.** Add your current scores.

   **b.** Let $x$ represent the fifth score. Write and solve the inequality.

   **c.** Graph the possible test scores.

**38. BANKING** You have $33.96 in a savings account. At your bank, you must have a minimum balance of $50 in your account to avoid a fee. Write and solve an inequality to represent the amount of money you must deposit in order to equal or exceed the minimum balance.

**39. SKI JUMPING** In a ski jumping competition, the top four jumpers perform as shown. How much farther does the fourth place jumper need to jump in order to place first? Write and solve an addition inequality that describes the situation.

| Name | Distance |
|---------|----------|
| Cara | 57 m |
| Jason | 91.5 m |
| Marisa | 85 m |
| Mitchell | 93.5 m |

**40. TAKS REASONING** Write and solve a real-world problem that can be solved using the inequality $p + 4 < 10$.

**41. WRITING** *Explain* why $x - 3 \geq 10$ and $x \geq 13$ are equivalent inequalities. Then explain why 13 and 20 would be useful values to substitute for $x$ to check the solution.

**42. BIPLANE RIDE** Your family bought your grandmother a biplane ride for her sixtieth birthday. The flight can last up to 1 hour 15 minutes.

The ride has 10 minutes of corkscrew rolls, 15 minutes of hammerheads, and 30 minutes of over-water flying. Write and solve an addition inequality to find how much time can be used for scenic low-altitude flying without going over the time limit.

**43. RACING** You run a race in 2.5 hours. The record winning time is 1.9 hours. Write and solve an inequality to find the numbers of minutes you can improve by and break the record.

**44. TAKS REASONING** The frequency $f$ of the human singing voice is between about 81 hertz and about 1100 hertz. Which statement is *not* true about $f$?

   **A** $f \geq 81$     **B** $f \leq 1100$     **C** $81 \leq f$     **D** $f \geq 1100$

**45. TIGER POPULATION** The map shows the tiger population in India around 1900. The population dropped to below 2000 in 1972 but has rebounded since then, increasing by about 2200 animals. Write and solve an inequality to find the number of tigers today. How many whole tiger icons would be on the map today?

**Indian Tiger Population, 1900**

= 4000 tigers

**46. ADVERTISING** During the first Super Bowl in 1967, a 30 second television commercial cost about $42,000. In 2005, advertisers paid about $2.4 million for a 30 second commercial. Assuming those were the least and greatest costs during that period, write two inequalities that together describe the cost $c$ of 30 seconds of commercial time during the Super Bowl from 1967 through 2005.

**47. ✦ TAKS REASONING** Lauren can spend at most $75 at the mall. She plans to buy a backpack on sale for between $25 and $35. She'll spend the remaining money on gifts. Let $x$ represent the cost of the gifts. Write and solve an addition equation to find the least amount Lauren will be able to spend on gifts. Repeat this to find the greatest amount Lauren can spend. *Describe* possible values for $x$ using inequalities.

**48. CHALLENGE** The *triangle inequality theorem* states that the sum of the lengths of any two sides of a triangle is greater than the length of the third side. A side of a triangle is 13 inches. Another side measures 6 inches. What values can the length $x$ of the third side be? *Explain* your reasoning.

## MIXED REVIEW FOR TAKS

TAKS PRACTICE at classzone.com

REVIEW
Lesson 3.2;
TAKS Workbook

**49. ✦ TAKS PRACTICE** Which procedure can be used to solve the equation $-\frac{1}{2}x = 9$? *TAKS Obj. 6*

(A) Add $\frac{1}{2}$ to each side

(B) Subtract 9 from each side

(C) Multiply each side by $-2$

(D) Divide each side by $-2$

REVIEW
Lesson 1.7;
TAKS Workbook

**50. ✦ TAKS PRACTICE** Of four friends, Lance is older than Greg and Greg is younger than Britney. Alex is younger than Britney and older than Lance. Which shows the four in order from youngest to oldest? *TAKS Obj. 6*

(F) Greg, Alex, Britney, Lance

(G) Lance, Alex, Britney, Greg

(H) Britney, Greg, Alex, Lance

(J) Greg, Lance, Alex, Britney

# 3.7 Solving Inequalities Using Multiplication or Division

TEKS 8.4

| **Before** | You solved equations using multiplication or division. |
| **Now** | You'll solve inequalities using multiplication or division. |
| **Why?** | So you can find measurements, as in Example 3. |

**KEY VOCABULARY**
- **inequality,** *p. 148*
- **solution of an inequality,** *p. 148*
- **equivalent inequalities,** *p. 149*

Solving inequalities and solving equations have one important difference. Look at what happens when you multiply each side of the inequality $3 > 1$ by $-1$.

$$3 > 1$$

$$3(-1) \underset{?}{} 1(-1)$$

$$-3 < -1$$

You can use a number line to check this.

From the number line you know that $-3 < -1$. So when multiplying or dividing each side of an inequality by a negative number, you must *reverse the direction of the inequality symbol.*

---

**KEY CONCEPT**            *For Your Notebook*

### Multiplication Properties of Inequality

| **Words** | **Algebra** |
|---|---|
| **Multiplying by a positive** Multiplying each side of an inequality by a *positive* number produces an equivalent inequality. | $4x < 10$ $\left(\dfrac{1}{4}\right)(4x) < \left(\dfrac{1}{4}\right)(10)$ |
| **Multiplying by a negative** Multiplying each side of an inequality by a *negative* number and *reversing the direction of the inequality symbol* produces an equivalent inequality. | $-5x < 10$ $\left(-\dfrac{1}{5}\right)(-5x) > \left(-\dfrac{1}{5}\right)(10)$ |

---

### EXAMPLE 1   Solving an Inequality Using Multiplication

| | |
|---|---|
| $-\dfrac{1}{8}n \geq 2$ | **Original inequality** |
| $-8 \cdot \left(-\dfrac{1}{8}\right)n \leq -8 \cdot 2$ | **Multiply each side by −8. Reverse inequality symbol.** |
| $n \leq -16$ | **Simplify.** |

## Division Properties of Inequality

| Words | Algebra |
|---|---|

**Dividing by a positive** Dividing each side of an inequality by a *positive* number produces an equivalent inequality.

$2x < 10$

$\dfrac{2x}{2} < \dfrac{10}{2}$

**Dividing by a negative** Dividing each side of an inequality by a *negative* number and *reversing the direction of the inequality symbol* produces an equivalent inequality.

$-5x < 15$

$\dfrac{-5x}{-5} > \dfrac{15}{-5}$

---

**EXAMPLE 2**   Solving an Inequality Using Division

$15 > -3m$      **Original inequality**

$\dfrac{15}{-3} < \dfrac{-3m}{-3}$      **Divide each side by −3. Reverse inequality symbol.**

$-5 < m$      **Simplify.**

---

**EXAMPLE 3**   Using the Division Property of Inequality

**Biology** About 15,000 fruit-eating bats live on Barro Colorado Island. Yearly they eat up to 61,440,000 grams of fruit. Write and solve an inequality to find about how many grams *g* of fruit each bat eats yearly.

**SOLUTION**

$15{,}000g \le 61{,}440{,}000$      **Write an algebraic model.**

$\dfrac{15{,}000g}{15{,}000} \le \dfrac{61{,}440{,}000}{15{,}000}$      **Divide each side by 15,000.**

$g \le 4096$      **Simplify.**

▶**Answer** Each bat eats up to 4096 grams of fruit in a year.

---

✓ **GUIDED PRACTICE**   for Examples 1, 2, and 3

**Solve the inequality.**

**1.** $\dfrac{t}{6} > 4$      **2.** $-\dfrac{1}{2}x \le 10$      **3.** $27 > -3t$      **4.** $9n < 63$

**5. Fruit Bats** A bat that weighs about 25 grams can eat up to 2.5 times its body mass in figs in one night. How many grams *g* of figs can it eat?

# 3.7 EXERCISES

HOMEWORK KEY

 = TAKS Practice and Reasoning
Exs. 29, 36, 37, 52, 53, 58, and 59

◯ = HINTS AND HOMEWORK HELP
for Exs. 5, 11, 23, 25, 43 at classzone.com

## SKILL PRACTICE

1. **VOCABULARY** Copy and complete: When you multiply both sides of an inequality by a negative number, you need to __?__ the inequality symbol.

2. **VOCABULARY** Copy and complete: Dividing each side of an inequality by a __?__ number makes an equivalent equation.

**PROPERTIES OF INEQUALITIES** Tell whether you would reverse the inequality symbol when solving. Write *Yes* or *No*. Do not solve.

*SEE EXAMPLES 1 AND 2*
on pp. 154–155
for Exs. 3–29

3. $\frac{1}{3}y < 18$

4. $-6x \geq 24$

⑤ $\frac{m}{-8} > 3$

6. $2b \leq -14$

**MATCHING** Solve the inequality. Match the inequality with the graph of its solution.

7. $\frac{1}{4}x \leq 8$

8. $-4x \geq 8$

9. $4x \geq -8$

10. $-\frac{1}{4}x \leq 8$

A. ![number line with closed point at -2, shaded left; marks -8 -6 -4 -2 0 2]

B. ![number line with closed point at -32, shaded right; marks -40 -32 -24 -16 -8 0]

C. ![number line with closed point at -2, shaded right; marks -8 -6 -4 -2 0 2]

D. ![number line with closed point at 32, shaded left; marks 0 8 16 24 32 40]

**SOLVING INEQUALITIES** Solve the inequality. Then graph its solution.

⑪ $\frac{1}{2}x < 4$

12. $\frac{m}{-7} \geq 6$

13. $9 \leq 3z$

14. $30 > -6p$

15. $\frac{1}{4}x > 1$

16. $-\frac{1}{7}t \geq -3$

17. $-\frac{1}{5}b \geq 72$

18. $\frac{1}{3}d < -33$

19. $4g < 24$

20. $12 \geq -3s$

21. $-9c \leq 54$

22. $5z < -15$

㉓ $7 > -\frac{1}{8}r$

24. $-6t \geq 36$

㉕ $-39 \leq 13k$

26. $-\frac{1}{6}a < -54$

**ERROR ANALYSIS** Describe and correct the error made in solving the inequality.

27.
✗
$-12 < 4x$
$\frac{-12}{4} > \frac{4x}{4}$
$-3 > x$

28.
✗
$-7x \geq 35$
$\frac{-7x}{-7} \geq \frac{35}{-7}$
$x \geq -5$

29.  **TAKS REASONING** Which inequality is represented by the graph?

(A) $2x \geq -8$     (B) $3x < -12$     (C) $\frac{1}{2}x > -2$     (D) $\frac{x}{4} \leq -1$

**SOLVING INEQUALITIES** Solve the inequality. Then graph its solution.

**30.** $12 > 6 - 2x$

**31.** $4p - 9 \geq -1$

**32.** $5(5 - 2x) > 15$

**33.** $8g + 6 < 24$

**34.** $\frac{8}{3}y + 3 \leq 51$

**35.** $\frac{5}{6}(a - 12) \leq 20$

**36.** ⚑ **TAKS REASONING** What is the solution of the inequality $-4 > 26 + 2x$?

    Ⓐ $x < -15$      Ⓑ $x > -15$      Ⓒ $x \leq 11$      Ⓓ $x < 11$

**37.** ⚑ **TAKS REASONING** Write an inequality where you reverse the inequality symbol to solve. Write another inequality where you do *not* reverse the inequality symbol to solve.

**NUMBER SENSE** *Describe* all the numbers that satisfy both inequalities.

**38.** $\frac{n}{2} < 2$ and $-6n \leq -6$

**39.** $3n + 4 < 52$ and $4n - 7 > 25$

**CHALLENGE** Solve the compound inequality.

**40.** $-6 < 2x < 10$

**41.** $-35 \leq 7x \leq -14$

**42.** $10 < 5x < 100$

## PROBLEM SOLVING

*SEE EXAMPLE 3*
on p. 155
for Exs. 43–44

**43.** **DANCE** The student council must pay a disc jockey $275 to work at a dance. A ticket to the dance costs $5.50. Write and solve an inequality that gives the numbers of tickets that can be sold to cover the cost of the disc jockey.

**44.** **FUNDRAISING** Students are having a car wash. They want to raise at least $300 for disaster relief work. The profit is $5 per car. How many cars must they wash?

**45.** **COMPARE AND CONTRAST** How is solving an inequality similar to solving an equation? How is solving an inequality different from solving an equation?

**46.** **WRITING** A friend says that the solution of $-x < 0$ is all numbers greater than zero. Do you agree? *Explain.*

**47.** **MULTI-STEP PROBLEM** An elevator can hold a maximum of 2000 pounds. The average weight of a person is 150 pounds. Let $p$ be the number of people the elevator can hold.

    **a.** Write an inequality involving multiplication that models the situation.

    **b.** Solve the inequality.

    **c.** What does the answer tell you about the number of people who can ride in the elevator?

**48. BORROWING MONEY** You borrow $200 from your aunt to buy a new surfboard. You pay her back $12 per week. Write and solve an inequality to find when you will owe her less than $60.

**49. GEOMETRY** The width of a rectangle is 12 meters and its area is greater than 228 square meters. Write and solve an inequality for the length *l*.

**50. TICKETS** Concert tickets are sold for $15 in advance and $20 at the door. There were 120 advance tickets sold. Write and solve an inequality to find how many tickets must be sold at the door for total ticket revenue to be at least $4000.

**51. EXAMPLES AND NONEXAMPLES** *Describe* a real-world situation for which you can list all solutions of an inequality and a situation for which you cannot list all solutions of an inequality.

**52.** ⬇ **TAKS REASONING** John has test scores of 75, 84, 88, and 77 on four of his five science tests. He wants to get at least an average of 80 on his five tests. What is the lowest score that John can get on his last test to achieve his goal?

    **(A)** 76        **(B)** 79        **(C)** 80        **(D)** 81

**53.** ⬇ **TAKS REASONING** Joe has *x* baseball cards. If he had 6 more than twice as many, he would have more than 20. If he had 10 fewer than three times as many, he would have fewer than 17. Write and solve two inequalities to find how many baseball cards Joe has.

**54. BICYCLE RACING** A professional bicycle racer trains by biking at least 50 miles a day. The racer starts by biking at a rate of 13 miles per hour for 2 hours. Then the racer bikes at a rate of 8 miles per hour. How long does the racer bike at this rate?

**55. COMPUTER SCREEN** The height of a rectangular computer screen is 20 inches less than twice the width. The perimeter is at least 53 inches. Write and solve an inequality to find the minimum dimensions of the screen if each dimension is an integer.

**56.** **CHALLENGE** Your neighbor is a real estate agent and earns a $50 commission for every $1000 in house sales, rounded to the nearest $1000. For what range of prices will the neighbor earn a commission between $4000 and $5000?

**57.** **CHALLENGE** Let $a$, $b$, $c$, and $d$ be positive integers. Show that for fractions $\frac{a}{b}$ and $\frac{c}{d}$, if $ad > bc$, then $\frac{a}{b} > \frac{c}{d}$. Use this property to compare the fractions $\frac{3}{5}, \frac{5}{8}, \frac{7}{8}$, and $\frac{9}{11}$. If any of the integers are negative, is the statement still true?

## MIXED REVIEW FOR TAKS

**TAKS** PRACTICE at classzone.com

*REVIEW*

Lesson 2.2;
TAKS Workbook

**58.** **TAKS PRACTICE** Stefan lives in Amsterdam on a street that is about $\frac{1}{2}$ meter below sea level. His bedroom is on the second floor of his house. His bedroom floor is about 2 meters above sea level. How far above the street is his bedroom floor? *TAKS Obj. 1*

  (A) $-2\frac{1}{2}$ m      (B) $-1\frac{1}{2}$ m      (C) $1\frac{1}{2}$ m      (D) $2\frac{1}{2}$ m

*REVIEW*

Lesson 1.7;
TAKS Workbook

**59.** **TAKS PRACTICE** Wesley has written down two numbers, and says that the following statements are true about the numbers.

  • They are factors of 80.
  • Their sum is less than 24.
  • They are even numbers.

Which two numbers might be those that Wesley wrote down? *TAKS Obj. 6*

  (F) 4, 10      (G) 5, 10      (H) 4, 20      (J) 10, 12

## QUIZ *for Lessons 3.5–3.7*

**Find the length of each side.** *(p. 142)*

**1.** A rectangle has a perimeter of 30 millimeters and a width of 6 millimeters. Find the length.

**2.** A triangle has an area of 26 square yards and a height of 4 yards. Find the length of the base.

**Solve the inequality. Then graph its solution.**

**3.** $a + 9 \geq -1$ *(p. 148)*   **4.** $16 > y - 12$ *(p. 148)*   **5.** $\frac{x}{3} < -3$ *(p. 154)*   **6.** $-7x > 42$ *(p. 154)*

**7.** **APPLES** An empty basket weighs 2 pounds. When filled with apples, the basket weighs more than 13 pounds. Write and solve an inequality that represents this situation. What does the variable represent? *(p. 148)*

**8.** **CALLING CARD** You have $9.50 with which to recharge your phone card. Write and solve an inequality to find how many minutes you can add to your phone card if each minute costs $.10. *(p. 154)*

## Lessons 3.5–3.7

**MULTIPLE CHOICE**

1. **CLASSROOMS** The Uniform Building Code requires at least 20 square feet of space for each person in a classroom. A classroom is 28 feet long and 18 feet wide. Which inequality models the number of people, $x$, that can be in the classroom according to the Uniform Building Code? *TEKS 8.5.A*

   Ⓐ $20x \leq 28 \times 18$

   Ⓑ $x + 20 \leq 28 \times 18$

   Ⓒ $20x \geq 28 \times 18$

   Ⓓ $x + 20 \geq 28 \times 18$

2. **GAMES** Amy, Fred, and Megan are playing a board game. The sum of Amy's score and Fred's score is less than Megan's score. Fred's score is 30 and Megan's score is 75. Based on this information, which statement is true? *TEKS 8.15.A*

   Ⓕ Fred's score is greater than Amy's score.

   Ⓖ Amy's score must be more than 30 and less than 45.

   Ⓗ The difference between Megan's score and Amy's score is Fred's score.

   Ⓙ If Amy doubles her score on her next turn, it is possible that she will have more points than Megan.

3. **PLATFORM** The figure below shows the top of a platform on a stage. What is the area of the platform? *TEKS 8.7.B*

   Ⓐ 36 ft²      Ⓑ 54 ft²

   Ⓒ 67.5 ft²     Ⓓ 108 ft²

4. **FLOOR PLAN** Which expression shows the area of the floor plan below? *TEKS 8.7.B*

   Ⓕ $12(2x + 5 + x)$

   Ⓖ $12 \times 5 + 12(2x + 4x)$

   Ⓗ $12(4x + 5 + 2x)$

   Ⓙ $\frac{1}{2} \times 12(4x + 5 + 2x)$

**GRIDDED ANSWER** ⊙①●③④⑤⑥⑦⑧⑨

5. **GIFTS** Mike and his sister Rebecca plan to buy a gift for their parents. Rebecca can contribute up to one third of the $27 she has saved. Mike can contribute no more than twice the amount his sister contributes. What is the greatest amount, in dollars, that they can spend together on a gift? *TEKS 8.14.B*

6. **FENCING** A rancher uses 6000 feet of fence to enclose a rectangular part of a pasture for a horse. The rancher sets up the fence to enclose the largest rectangular area possible. What is the area, in thousands of square feet, of the pasture enclosed by the rancher's fence? *TEKS 8.14.C*

## REVIEW KEY VOCABULARY

- equivalent equations, *p. 117*
- inverse operation, *p. 117*
- base, height, *p. 142*
- inequality, *p. 148*
- solution of an inequality, *p. 148*
- equivalent inequalities, *p. 149*

### VOCABULARY EXERCISES

1. List two pairs of inverse operations. *Explain* why these are called inverse operations.

2. How can two inequalities be equivalent? Give an example of equivalent inequalities.

**Copy and complete the statement.**

3. Two equations that have the same solution are __?__.

4. A(n) __?__ is a statement formed by placing an inequality symbol between two expressions.

## REVIEW EXAMPLES AND EXERCISES

### 3.1 Solving Equations Using Addition or Subtraction
*pp. 117–121*

**EXAMPLE**

**Solve the equation.**

$$
\begin{aligned}
x - 23 &= \phantom{0}9 \\
+ 23 \phantom{} &\phantom{=} + 23
\end{aligned}
$$
Add 23 to each side.

$$x = \phantom{0}32$$ Simplify.

$$
\begin{aligned}
y + 17.3 &= 68.8 \\
- 17.3 \phantom{} &\phantom{=} - 17.3
\end{aligned}
$$
Subtract 17.3 from each side.

$$y = \phantom{0}51.5$$ Simplify.

### EXERCISES

**Solve the equation.**

*SEE EXAMPLES 1, 2, AND 3* on pp. 117–118 for Exs. 5–14

5. $c + 14 = 3$

6. $y - 31 = 11$

7. $7.7 = s - 4.3$

8. $29 = 40 + p$

9. $b + 3.09 = -5.91$

10. $v + 13 = 29$

11. $t - \dfrac{3}{7} = \dfrac{1}{7}$

12. $x + (-5) = -8$

13. $y - 3.9 = 10.9$

14. Last year Marguerite had 12 elm trees in her yard. This year she has 17 elm trees. Write an equation and solve it to find how many elm trees she planted this year.

## 3.2 Solving Equations Using Multiplication or Division

pp. 122–126

### EXAMPLE

**Solve the equation.**

$$\frac{y}{4} = -8 \qquad \text{Original equation}$$

$$\frac{y}{4} \cdot 4 = -8 \cdot 4 \qquad \text{Multiply each side by 4.}$$

$$y = -32 \qquad \text{Simplify.}$$

$$-7x = -56 \qquad \text{Original equation}$$

$$\frac{-7x}{-7} = \frac{-56}{-7} \qquad \text{Divide each side by } -7.$$

$$x = 8 \qquad \text{Simplify.}$$

### EXERCISES

**Solve the equation.**

**SEE EXAMPLES 1 AND 2**
on pp. 122–123
for Exs. 15–20

**15.** $\frac{m}{3} = 9$

**16.** $\frac{z}{-7} = 23$

**17.** $-5 = \frac{w}{-11}$

**18.** $-25x = 0$

**19.** $7 = 3.5t$

**20.** $-9.5m = -22.8$

## 3.3 Solving Two-Step Equations

pp. 129–133

### EXAMPLE

**Solve the equation.**

$$3x + 10 = -20 \qquad \text{Original equation}$$

$$3x + 10 - 10 = -20 - 10 \qquad \text{Subtract 10 from each side to undo addition.}$$

$$3x = -30 \qquad \text{Simplify.}$$

$$\frac{3x}{3} = \frac{-30}{3} \qquad \text{Divide each side by 3 to undo multiplication.}$$

$$x = -10 \qquad \text{Simplify.}$$

### EXERCISES

**Solve the equation.**

**SEE EXAMPLES 1, 2, AND 3**
on pp. 129–130
for Exs. 21–27

**21.** $2p - 5 = 13$

**22.** $19 + 8v = 43$

**23.** $\frac{g}{9} + 6 = -2$

**24.** $\frac{c}{-10} + 26 = 46$

**25.** $-82 = 53 - 5t$

**26.** $-33 = -15t - 12$

**27.** Ralph is putting pictures in a scrapbook. He puts four pictures on each page and has three pictures left over. If he starts with 55 pictures, write and solve an equation to find how many pages have four pictures on them.

## 3.4 Writing Two-Step Equations

*pp. 134–139*

### EXAMPLE

A catering company charges $100 for setup plus $15 per guest. How many guests can be served within a $1000 budget?

| Setup | + | Cost per guest | · | Number of guests | = | Budget |
|---|---|---|---|---|---|---|

$$100 + 15n = 1000 \quad \textbf{Write an algebraic model.}$$
$$15n = 900 \quad \textbf{Subtract 100 from each side.}$$
$$n = 60 \quad \textbf{Divide each side by 15.}$$

▶ **Answer** 60 guests can be served within a $1000 budget.

### EXERCISES

*SEE EXAMPLES 2 AND 3*
on p. 135 for
Exs. 28–31

**28.** The sum of 3 times a number and 6 is 12. What is the number?

**29.** Four less than 2 times a number is 20. What is the number?

**30. Fruit Baskets** Your class spends $26 on supplies for fruit baskets. How many baskets must your class sell at $7 each to make a profit of $100?

**31. Attendance** A small college has 1250 students. There are 30 more women than men. How many women attend the college?

## 3.5 Applying Geometric Formulas

*pp. 142–147*

### EXAMPLE

**Find the height of the triangle. Its area is 21 square inches.**

$$A = \frac{1}{2}bh \quad \textbf{Write area formula.}$$
$$21 = \frac{1}{2}(6)(h) \quad \textbf{Substitute known values.}$$
$$7 = h \quad \textbf{Solve for } h.$$

6 in.

▶ **Answer** The height of the triangle is 7 inches.

### EXERCISES

*SEE EXAMPLE 4*
on p. 144 for
Exs. 32 and 33

**Find the unknown dimension of the triangle.**

**32.** $b = 10$ cm, $h = 5$ cm, $A = \underline{\ ?\ }$ cm$^2$    **33.** $A = 45$ ft$^2$, $h = 10$ ft, $b = \underline{\ ?\ }$

**Solving Inequalities Using Addition or Subtraction**          *pp. 148–153*

**EXAMPLE**

Solve the inequality.

$$x - 9 \leq -4 \qquad \text{Original inequality}$$
$$x - 9 + 9 \leq -4 + 9 \qquad \text{Add 9 to each side.}$$
$$x \leq 5 \qquad \text{Simplify.}$$

**EXERCISES**

Solve the inequality. Then graph its solution.

**SEE EXAMPLES
2 AND 3**
on pp. 149–150
for Exs. 34–42

**34.** $h - 12 > 12$    **35.** $-4 + k \leq 6$    **36.** $7 < 15 + p$    **37.** $d + 11 \geq 5$

**38.** $m - 10 > 21$    **39.** $b + 13 \leq 11$    **40.** $k - 8 \geq 2\frac{1}{2}$    **41.** $p - 2.5 < 7.7$

**42. CDs** Mary claims that she has at least 50 CDs at home and she just got 4 more for her birthday. Write an inequality for the number of CDs she has now.

**3.7** **Solving Inequalities Using Multiplication or Division**          *pp. 154–159*

**EXAMPLE**

Solve the inequality.

$$\frac{t}{7} > 2 \qquad \text{Original inequality} \qquad\qquad -12k \leq 60 \qquad \text{Original inequality}$$

$$\frac{t}{7} \cdot 7 > 2 \cdot 7 \qquad \text{Multiply each side by 7.} \qquad \frac{-12k}{-12} \geq \frac{60}{-12} \qquad \begin{array}{l}\text{Divide each side by} \\ -12. \text{ Reverse} \\ \text{inequality symbol.}\end{array}$$

$$t > 14 \qquad \text{Simplify.} \qquad\qquad\qquad k \geq -5 \qquad \text{Simplify.}$$

**EXERCISES**

Solve the inequality.

**SEE EXAMPLES
1 AND 2**
on pp. 154–155
for Exs. 43–50

**43.** $\dfrac{d}{6} \leq 34$    **44.** $-\dfrac{1}{5}x \geq 20$    **45.** $-15b < 60$    **46.** $5c > 25$

**47.** $-4k \leq -36$    **48.** $\dfrac{2}{3}y > -12$    **49.** $16z < 32$    **50.** $\dfrac{m}{5} \geq -11$

**Solve the equation.**

**1.** $s - 6 = 39$     **2.** $x + 12 = -2$     **3.** $14.6 = \dfrac{k}{2.5}$     **4.** $24v = 288$

**5.** $\dfrac{1}{9} = t + \dfrac{1}{9}$     **6.** $-9.8 = \dfrac{y}{-4.7}$     **7.** $5b - 7 = 120$     **8.** $-236 = 29 - 5g$

**Translate the statement into an equation. Then solve the equation.**

**9.** A number times 3 subtracted from 20 is $-4$.

**10.** The sum of 5 times a number and 14 is 9.

**Find the unknown dimension.**

**11.** Perimeter = 62 in.     **12.** Area = 72 in.$^2$     **13.** Area = 200 cm$^2$

**Solve the inequality.**

**14.** $y + 78 < -124$     **15.** $-8.56 + k \geq 5.32$     **16.** $-8x < 64$

**17.** $-\dfrac{1}{6}x > 5$     **18.** $3x \leq 12$     **19.** $m - 9 \leq 19$

**20. HIKING** You go on a 20 mile hike. In the morning you hike 8.3 miles, and by 2:00 P.M. you have hiked 7.5 more miles. Write and solve an equation to find how many miles you have left to hike.

**In Exercises 21 and 22, write and solve an equation.**

**21. BOOK SALES** A bookstore offers three books in a set for $21.75. Each book costs the same amount. How much does each book cost?

**22. WEIGHT** A calf weighs 220 pounds. The calf gains about 22 pounds a month for the next 4 months. In how many months will the calf weigh 550 pounds?

**23. LUNCH** You and a friend are having lunch together. You can spend no more than $30 on both meals. The total cost of your friend's meal is $14.78. Write and solve an inequality to determine how much you can spend on your meal.

**24. FIGURE SKATING** You are taking figure skating lessons. You can rent skates for $5 per lesson. You can buy skates for $75. Write and solve an inequality to find the number of lessons for which it is cheaper to buy skates than to rent.

# 3 TAKS PREPARATION

## REVIEWING EQUATION AND INEQUALITY PROBLEMS

You can use equations and inequalities to make or verify conclusions in real-life problems.

> ### EXAMPLE
>
> **ART** The following statements are true about the painting at the right.
>
> - The length is 1.5 times the width.
>
> - The perimeter of the painting is at least 120 inches.
>
> Leo says that the statements above indicate that the length of the painting is greater than or equal to 36 inches. Is Leo correct?

### Solution

**ANOTHER WAY**

Redraw the rectangular painting shown. Label the width of the rectangle $w$ and the length $1.5w$. The perimeter of the rectangle, it can then be seen, will be $5w$. So $5w$ must be at least 120 inches. Use mental math to judge whether Leo's answer is correct.

**STEP 1** **Use** the first statement to write an equation relating length and width.

The length $l$ is 1.5 times the width $w$, so $l = 1.5w$.

**STEP 2** **Use** the second statement to write an equation about the perimeter.

| | |
|---|---|
| $2l + 2w = P$ | **Equation for the perimeter of a rectangle.** |
| $2l + 2w \geq 120$ | **The perimeter is at least 120 inches, so use $\geq$.** |

**STEP 3** **Combine** information from the equations in Step 1 and Step 2.

| | |
|---|---|
| $2l + 2w \geq 120$ | **Equation from Step 2.** |
| $2(1.5w) + 2w \geq 120$ | **Substitute $1.5w$ for $l$.** |
| $3w + 2w \geq 120$ | **Multiply.** |
| $5w \geq 120$ | **Combine like terms.** |
| $w \geq 24$ | **Divide each side by 5.** |

**STEP 4** **Make** a conclusion about the length.

The width is greater than or equal to 24 inches. So the length, which is 1.5 times the width, must be at least $1.5 \cdot (24)$ inches.

$l \geq 1.5 \cdot 24$

$l \geq 36$

▶ **Answer** The length is greater than or equal to 36 inches, so Leo is correct.

# EQUATION AND INEQUALITY PROBLEMS ON TAKS

Below are examples of equation and inequality problems in multiple choice format. Try solving the problems before looking at the solutions. (Cover the solutions with a piece of paper.) Then check your solutions against the ones given.

1. Mr. McMullen paid $15 for a yearly membership to a nutrition store. With the membership, he spent $18 each month on products that would cost him $22 without the membership. Why did Mr. McMullen believe he saved $33 over the year by paying for the membership?

   **A**   The cost of the membership and one month of products is $33.

   **B**   The cost of the membership and one month of products without the membership is more than $33.

   **C**   The savings with the membership were $4 each month, or more than $33 for the entire year.

   **D**   The savings with the membership were $4 each month. Over 12 months, the savings minus the cost of the membership was $33.

**Solution**

You can see that the membership saves Mr. McMullen $4 per month.

Because there are 12 months in a year and his membership cost was $15, Mr. McMullen's yearly savings, $s$, can be found using the equation $s = 12(4) - 15$.

Solve the equation.

$$s = 12(4) - 15$$
$$s = 48 - 15$$
$$s = 33$$

Mr. McMullen saved $33 over 12 months, or one year, by paying for the membership.

The correct answer is D.

Ⓐ      Ⓑ      Ⓒ      **Ⓓ**

2. The area of the triangle below represents the portion of Mrs. Simpson's driveway in which cement is to be poured. The area of the region is 73.5 square feet. Mrs. Simpson wants to surround the region with caution tape. How much tape does she need?

   **F**   10.5 ft

   **G**   31.75 ft

   **H**   39.9 ft

   **J**   42 ft

**Solution**

The height of the triangle is 14 feet. Use the area formula to find the base of the triangle.

$$A = \frac{1}{2}bh$$
$$73.5 = \frac{1}{2}b(14)$$
$$73.5 = 7b$$
$$10.5 = b$$

The base is 10.5 feet. Find the perimeter.

$$P = 14 + 10.5 + 17.5 = 42$$

The perimeter is 42 feet, so the correct answer is J.

Ⓕ      Ⓖ      Ⓗ      **Ⓙ**

## PRACTICE FOR TAKS OBJECTIVE 6

1. Which equation can be used to find the perimeter $P$ of a square whose area is $s^2$?

   **A** $P = 2s$

   **B** $P = 2s^2$

   **C** $P = 4s$

   **D** $P = 4s^2$

2. The following statements are true about the envelope below.

   - The area of the envelope's triangular flap is 84 square centimeters.

   - The perimeter of the rectangle that the whole envelope forms is between 66 and 70 centimeters.

   Which possible width $w$ for the rectangle fits both statements?

   **F** 8 cm

   **G** 10 cm

   **H** 12 cm

   **J** 13 cm

3. Bob told his friend that he was thinking of a number with these properties:

   - Its absolute value is greater than 9.

   - It is divisible by 3.

   - It is less than $-1$.

   Which number might be the one he has in mind?

   **A** $-12$

   **B** $-10$

   **C** $-6$

   **D** 15

4. Karl tells his friend that his sister Wanda paid between $15 and $20 for 5 used books. Why is it possible that each book Wanda bought cost $3.10?

   **F** Because $15 \leq 5(3.10)$.

   **G** Because $20 \geq 5(3.10)$.

   **H** Because $15 \leq 5(3.10)$ and $20 \geq 5(3.10)$.

   **J** Because all 5 books must have cost the same amount.

## MIXED TAKS PRACTICE

5. Ten hammers are available at a hardware store. The hammers all have prices less than or equal to $30. Why is the range of the prices of the hammers misrepresented in the graph below? *TAKS Obj. 5*

   **A** The graph includes unrealistic dollar amounts.

   **B** The graph should not include 30.

   **C** The graph should point to the right.

   **D** The graph should start at 10.

6. Kevin traveled from his house to the city library by bus. He took one bus 3 miles, then changed buses. The second bus averaged 30 miles per hour. His entire trip covered 18 miles. How long did he spend on the second bus? *TAKS Obj. 2*

   **F** 6 min

   **G** 30 min

   **H** 36 min

   **J** 42 min

## MIXED TAKS PRACTICE

**7.** A section of a sidewalk has an area of 13.5 square feet and a width of 3 feet. What is the length of the section? *TAKS Obj. 3*

**A** 3.75 ft

**B** 4.5 ft

**C** 7.5 ft

**D** 40.5 ft

**8.** Find the area of the triangle shown. How does the area change when the base and height are doubled? *TAKS Obj. 4*

**F** The area increases by a factor of 2.

**G** The area increases by a factor of 4.

**H** The area increases by a factor of 6.

**J** The area increases by a factor of 8.

**9.** The solution to which inequality is represented by the graph below? *TAKS Obj. 2*

**A** $-10x \le 40$

**B** $-12x \le 108 - 60$

**C** $-5(3 - x) \ge -11$

**D** $5(3 - x) \ge 19$

**10.** The cost to organize a fundraiser was $2000. Tickets cost $50 each. Which equation can be used to find the number of tickets, $x$, that must be sold for the fundraiser to make a $2500 profit? *TAKS Obj. 2*

**F** $50x = 2500$

**G** $50x = 2500 - 2000$

**H** $50x = 2500 + 2000$

**J** $50x = 2000 - 2500$

**11.** The height of a person is related to the length of the femur bone in that person's thigh. The person's height in inches can be approximated by adding 32 to the product of 1.9 and the length of that person's femur bone in inches. Which equation can be used to approximate the length, $l$, of the femur bone in a person who is 72 inches tall? *TAKS Obj. 6*

**A** $32 = 1.9(l + 72)$

**B** $72 = 1.9(l + 32)$

**C** $72 = 1.9l + 32$

**D** $72 = 32 + 1.9l$

**12.** Mr. Wong asks his class to plot a triangle that has an area of 12 square units. Which of the following points on the coordinate plane does NOT form a triangle of area 12 square units with the points $A$ and $B$ shown below? *TAKS Obj. 3*

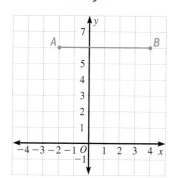

**F** $(-3, 2)$

**G** $(3, 2)$

**H** $(2, 3)$

**J** $(0, 2)$

**13. GRIDDED ANSWER** A bird at a height of 100 feet rises for 4 seconds at a rate of 6 feet per second, then drops 10 feet per second for 6 seconds. What is the height of the bird in feet? *TAKS Obj. 2*

*Record your answer and fill in the bubbles on your answer document. Be sure to use the correct place value.*

**Evaluate the expression.**

**1.** $8 + 6 \div 2$ *(p. 8)*

**2.** $15 - 9 \div 3$ *(p. 8)*

**3.** $3 \times (1.8 + 5 - 0.6)$ *(p. 8)*

**4.** $9 \times 2^3 - 15$ *(p. 19)*

**5.** $(2^5 + 8) \cdot 5^2$ *(p. 19)*

**6.** $(18 \div 6)^3 + (11 - 4)^3$ *(p. 19)*

**Solve the equation using mental math.** *(p. 26)*

**7.** $x + 3 = 9$

**8.** $3w = 33$

**9.** $24 \div r = 6$

**10.** $34 - z = 21$

**Find the perimeter and area of the rectangle or square.** *(p. 32)*

**11.** length = 12 m, width = 7 m

**12.** length = 18 cm, width = 14 cm

**13.** side length = 9 in.

**14.** length = 13 ft, width = 11 ft

**Use a number line to order the integers from least to greatest.** *(p. 57)*

**15.** $-15, 16, 1, -5, 4, 8$

**16.** $40, -60, 98, -85, -6, 42$

**Find the sum or difference.**

**17.** $29 + (-18)$ *(p. 63)*

**18.** $-8 - 9$ *(p. 68)*

**19.** $44 - (-11)$ *(p. 68)*

**Find the product or quotient.**

**20.** $-5(4)$ *(p. 73)*

**21.** $-12(-8)$ *(p. 73)*

**22.** $\frac{42}{-3}$ *(p. 77)*

**Evaluate the expression when $a = 4$, $b = -16$, and $c = 12$.** *(p. 83)*

**23.** $\frac{-c}{a}$

**24.** $\frac{3b}{2c}$

**25.** $\frac{b}{-4a}$

**Simplify the expression by combining like terms.** *(p. 88)*

**26.** $9(3a + 11) - 4$

**27.** $-8b + 12(7b + 3)$

**28.** $2c - 8(9c - 5)$

**Plot the point in a coordinate plane and describe its location.** *(p. 94)*

**29.** $L(3, -5)$

**30.** $M(0, -1)$

**31.** $N(6, 0)$

**Solve the equation.**

**32.** $n + 8 = 15$ *(p. 117)*

**33.** $z + 12 = 3$ *(p. 117)*

**34.** $4r = -32$ *(p. 122)*

**35.** $\frac{k}{7} = 5$ *(p. 122)*

**36.** $8 = 7y - 13$ *(p. 129)*

**37.** $\frac{a}{6} + 4 = -8$ *(p. 129)*

**38.** A triangle has an area of 48 square meters and a height of 6 meters. What is the length of its base? *(p. 142)*

**Solve the inequality. Then graph its solution.**

**39.** $96 \geq -12 + c$ *(p. 148)*

**40.** $-\frac{1}{3}x > 4$ *(p. 154)*

**41.** $-96 < 24h$ *(p. 154)*

**HEIGHTS**  The frequency table shows the heights of 30 students. *(p. 3)*

| Height (inches) | Frequency |
|---|---|
| 54–55.9 | 1 |
| 56–57.9 | 2 |
| 58–59.9 | 4 |
| 60–61.9 | 5 |
| 62–63.9 | 7 |
| 64–65.9 | 6 |
| 66–67.9 | 3 |
| 68–69.9 | 2 |

**42.** Make a histogram of the data shown in the frequency table.

**43.** Which height interval has the most students?

**44.** Can you use the histogram to determine the number of students who are between 60 and 69.9 inches tall? *Explain.*

**45. DOLPHINS**  After swimming 22 miles, a dolphin changes direction and swims at a rate of 18 miles per hour. Use the expression $22 + 18t$, where $t$ is the number of hours, to find the total distance traveled by the dolphin after 2.4 more hours. *(p. 13)*

**46. RADIO**  You are the disc jockey for a 15 minute radio show at your school. You must leave 3 minutes open for announcements, and you want to play 3 songs. Use the table at the right to determine the 3 songs you can play. *(p. 37)*

| Song | A | B | C | D | E |
|---|---|---|---|---|---|
| Length (minutes) | 6 | 4 | 3 | 5 | 6 |

**47. CHECKBOOK**  The balance of a checkbook is $225. There are deposits of $80 and $40 and withdrawals of $100 and $25. What is the new balance of the checkbook? *(p. 63)*

**48. FALLING ROCK**  A rock falls 144 feet from a ledge. The equation $h = -16t^2 + 144$ gives the height $h$, in feet, of the rock after falling for $t$ seconds. Evaluate the equation when $t$ equals 2.5, 3, and 3.5 seconds. When does the rock hit the ground? What is the actual height of the rock after 3.5 seconds? *(p. 73)*

**49. FUEL**  You rent an all-terrain vehicle that has $\frac{5}{8}$ of a tank of fuel. When you are done riding, $\frac{3}{8}$ of a tank is left. Write a verbal model to represent the fraction of a tank of fuel you used. Then write and solve an algebraic model. *(p. 117)*

**50. INTRAMURALS**  A college brochure states that 215 students participate in intramural sports. This is one third of the students. How many students attend the college? *(p. 122)*

**51. GROUNDSKEEPING**  You need to buy enough bags of grass seed to cover a field that is 300 feet long and 150 feet wide. One bag of seed covers 5000 square feet. How many bags do you need? *(p. 142)*

# 4

## Factors, Fractions, and Exponents

TEXAS

### Before

In previous chapters you've . . .

- **Multiplied numbers**
- **Compared integers**

### Now

TEKS **you'll study . . .**

| 8.15.A | **4.1** | **Factors** |
| 8.14.A | **4.2** | **Greatest common factors** |
| 8.1.B | **4.3** | **Simplifying fractions** |
| 8.14.C | **4.4** | **Least common multiples** |
| 8.1.A | **4.5** | **Comparing fractions** |
| 8.16.A | **4.6** | **Rules of exponents** |
| 8.16.B | **4.7** | **Negative exponents** |
| 8.1.D | **4.8** | **Scientific notation** |

### Why?

So you can solve real-world problems about . . .

- **geography, p. 190**
- **orangutans, p. 199**
- **bubbles, p. 213**

**Math**

at classzone.com

- **Creating a Factor Tree, p. 177**
- **Simplifying Fractions, p. 186**
- **Mixed Numbers and Improper Fractions, p. 199**

## Get-Ready Games

**Review Prerequisite Skills** by playing *Bicycle Math.*

**Skill Focus:** Whole number division

### BICYCLE MATH

**HOW TO PLAY**

**1** **PICK** the number with each letter that divides evenly into the bold number in the matching fact.

   **A** 4, 8, 42    **B** 7, 13, 23    **C** 15, 17, 21

**2** **USE** the answer for each letter to evaluate the expression below. The value of the expression is the world record bicycle speed in miles per hour, set by Fred Rompelberg in 1995.

A(B + C) + 30.9

In **1884**, the "safety bicycle," a bicycle resembling the ones we use today, was invented.

**A**

In 2001, **39,000,000** people in the United States rode a bicycle more than once.

**B**

In 2002, **189** cyclists competed in the Tour de France.

**C**

## Stop and Think

1. **WRITING** A student thinks that 42 divides evenly into 1884 because 42 divides evenly into 84. *Explain* what is wrong with the student's reasoning.

2. **CRITICAL THINKING** What number will divide evenly into any even number? *Explain*.

# Review Prerequisite Skills

## VOCABULARY CHECK

Copy and complete using a review word from the list at the left.

**1.** In the expression $2^6$, 2 is called the __?__ .

**2.** The expression $3^7$ is a(n) __?__ of 3.

**3.** In the expression $5^4$, 4 is called the __?__ .

## SKILL CHECK

Evaluate the expression. *(p. 19)*

**4.** $3^2 \cdot 3$     **5.** $(2 + 3)^2$     **6.** $4^2 \div 4^2$     **7.** $(6 - 5)^7$

**8.** $3^2 + 4 \cdot 5$     **9.** $12 - 8 \div 2^2$     **10.** $7^2 - 3^3$     **11.** $6^2 \div 2^2$

Simplify the expression by combining like terms. *(p. 88)*

**12.** $7x + 4 - 3x$     **13.** $-2x + 5x - x$

**14.** $x + 4 - 12x$     **15.** $6x - 5 + x$

**16.** $15y + 9x - 6x - y$     **17.** $-13y + 8x - 2x + 3y - 10$

Solve the equation. Check your answer. *(p. 129)*

**18.** $2a + 6 = 14$     **19.** $8 - 4m = 20$     **20.** $-7 + 5c = -32$

**TEXAS @HomeTutor**     Prerequisite skills practice at classzone.com

## Notetaking Skills     Preview the Chapter

In each chapter you will learn a new notetaking skill. In Chapter 4 you will apply the strategy of previewing the chapter to Example 5 on p. 189.

Skim the content of the chapter you are about to study. If you already know something about the topic, outline what you know in your notes.

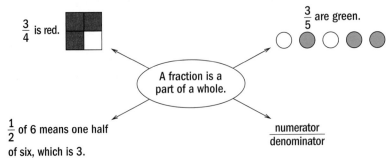

$\frac{3}{4}$ is red.

$\frac{3}{5}$ are green.

A fraction is a part of a whole.

$\frac{1}{2}$ of 6 means one half of six, which is 3.

$\frac{\text{numerator}}{\text{denominator}}$

In Chapter 4, you will learn more things about fractions that you can add to your outline.

**GOAL**
Introduce prime and composite numbers.

**MATERIALS**
• paper
• colored pencils

TEKS *8.16.A*

# 4.1 Investigating Factors

A *prime* number is a whole number that has exactly two factors: 1 and itself. A *composite* number has more than two factors. In this activity, you will look at a number pattern attributed to Eratosthenes, a mathematician who lived in Alexandria, Egypt, around 230 B.C.

**EXPLORE** Create the Sieve of Eratosthenes with the integers 1 to 60.

**STEP 1** **Write** the whole numbers 1 to 60 in a rectangular array as shown at the right.

| 1 | 2 | 3 | 4 | 5 | 6 | 7 | 8 | 9 | 10 |
|---|---|---|---|---|---|---|---|---|----|
| 11 | 12 | 13 | 14 | 15 | 16 | 17 | 18 | 19 | 20 |
| 21 | 22 | 23 | 24 | 25 | 26 | 27 | 28 | 29 | 30 |
| 31 | 32 | 33 | 34 | 35 | 36 | 37 | 38 | 39 | 40 |
| 41 | 42 | 43 | 44 | 45 | 46 | 47 | 48 | 49 | 50 |
| 51 | 52 | 53 | 54 | 55 | 56 | 57 | 58 | 59 | 60 |

**STEP 2** **Start** with the number 2. Circle it and cross out every multiple of 2 after 2.

**STEP 3** **Move** to the next number that is not crossed out, 3. Circle it and cross out every multiple of 3 after 3.

**STEP 4** **Move** to the next number that is not crossed out. Circle it and cross out all other multiples of that number.

Skip the numbers that have already been crossed out.

**STEP 5** **Repeat** Step 4 until every number except 1 is either crossed out or circled.

**PRACTICE**

1. What type of numbers are circled in your array?

2. What type of numbers are crossed out in your array?

**DRAW CONCLUSIONS**

3. **WRITING** If you continued this process with the numbers 61 to 100, what type of numbers would you expect to be circled? Why?

# 4.1 Factors and Prime Factorization

TEKS 8.15.A

| | |
|---|---|
| **Before** | You multiplied and divided numbers. |
| **Now** | You'll write the prime factorization of numbers. |
| **Why?** | So you can find different arrangements of rows and columns, as in Example 1. |

**KEY VOCABULARY**
- prime number, composite number, prime factorization, factor tree, *p. 177*
- monomial, *p. 178*

**Lettering** Members of the art club are learning to do calligraphy. Their first project is to make posters to display their new lettering style. A poster will display 36 characters in order: the 26 uppercase letters of the alphabet and the digits 0 through 9.

The art club members want the characters arranged in a rectangular display with the same number of characters in each row. You can use the factors of 36 to determine how many arrangements are possible.

## EXAMPLE 1 Writing Factors

In the situation above, how many ways can the art club arrange the 36 characters in a rectangular display with rows of equal length?

**SOLUTION**

**STEP 1** **List** the factors of 36 by writing 36 as a product of two numbers in all possible ways.

$$1 \times 36 \qquad 2 \times 18 \qquad 3 \times 12 \qquad 4 \times 9 \qquad 6 \times 6$$

The factors of 36 are 1, 2, 3, 4, 6, 9, 12, 18, and 36.

**AVOID ERRORS**
Because you are looking for arrangements of rows and columns, $1 \times 36$ is different from $36 \times 1$. Each product except $6 \times 6$ is listed twice.

**STEP 2** **Use** these factors to find all the possible rectangular arrangements of rows and columns.

$$1 \times 36 \qquad 2 \times 18 \qquad 3 \times 12 \qquad 4 \times 9 \qquad 6 \times 6$$
$$36 \times 1 \qquad 18 \times 2 \qquad 12 \times 3 \qquad 9 \times 4$$

▶ **Answer** There are nine possible rectangular arrangements.

---

✓ **GUIDED PRACTICE** for Example 1

**Write all the factors of the number.**

**1.** 20      **2.** 29      **3.** 42      **4.** 57

**5.** **What If?** Suppose the poster in Example 1 was to include both uppercase and lowercase letters as well as the digits 0–9. How many ways can the 62 characters be arranged in rows of equal length?

**Primes and Composites** A **prime number** is a whole number greater than 1 whose only positive factors are 1 and itself. A **composite number** is a whole number greater than 1 that has positive factors other than 1 and itself. The number 1 is neither prime nor composite.

---

**EXAMPLE 2** Identifying Prime and Composite Numbers

Write all the factors of the number and tell whether it is *prime* or *composite*.

**FIND FACTORS**
You can use divisibility tests to help find all the factors of a composite number. For help with divisibility tests, see p. 761.

| Number | Factors | Prime or Composite? |
|---|---|---|
| **a.** 32 | 1, 2, 4, 8, 16, 32 | composite |
| **b.** 39 | 1, 3, 13, 39 | composite |
| **c.** 43 | 1, 43 | prime |
| **d.** 76 | 1, 2, 4, 19, 38, 76 | composite |
| **e.** 149 | 1, 149 | prime |
| **f.** 121 | 1, 11, 121 | composite |

---

**Prime Factorization** When you write a whole number as the product of prime numbers, you are writing its **prime factorization**. One way to find the prime factorization of a number is to use a **factor tree**.

---

**EXAMPLE 3** Writing Prime Factorization

**Write the prime factorization of 450.**

Three factor trees are shown. Notice that each factor tree produces the same prime factorization, differing only in the order of the factors.

**ORDER FACTORS**
When writing the prime factorization, write the factors in order from least to greatest.

So, $450 = 2 \cdot 3 \cdot 3 \cdot 5 \cdot 5$.

▶ **Answer** Using exponents, the prime factorization of 450 is $2 \cdot 3^2 \cdot 5^2$.

*Animated* Math at classzone.com

---

✔ **GUIDED PRACTICE** for Examples 2 and 3

Tell whether the number is *prime* or *composite*. If it is composite, write its prime factorization using exponents.

**6.** 24 **7.** 51 **8.** 73 **9.** 560

**Factoring Monomials** A **monomial** is a number, a variable, or a product of a number and one or more variables. To factor a monomial means to write the monomial as a product of prime numbers and variables with exponents of 1.

**EXAMPLE 4** Factoring a Monomial

 Factor the monomial $12x^2y$.

$$12x^2y = 2 \cdot 2 \cdot 3 \cdot x^2 \cdot y \qquad \text{Factor 12.}$$
$$= 2 \cdot 2 \cdot 3 \cdot x \cdot x \cdot y \qquad \text{Write } x^2 \text{ as } x \cdot x.$$

✓ **GUIDED PRACTICE** for Example 4

**Factor the monomial.**

**10.** $3mn$ **11.** $18t^2$ **12.** $14x^2y^3$ **13.** $54w^3z^4$

# 4.1 **EXERCISES**

HOMEWORK KEY

 = **TAKS Practice and Reasoning**
Exs. 30, 50, 51, 53, 55, and 59

○ = **HINTS AND HOMEWORK HELP**
for Exs. 3, 17, 25, 33, 51 at classzone.com

## SKILL PRACTICE

**1. VOCABULARY** Copy and complete: The only positive factors of a(n) _?_ number are the number itself and one.

**2. VOCABULARY** What is the prime factorization of a number?

**WRITING FACTORS** Write all the factors of the number.

*SEE EXAMPLES 1 AND 2*
on pp. 176–177
for Exs. 3–18

**3.** 18 **4.** 27 **5.** 34 **6.** 41

**7.** 29 **8.** 64 **9.** 108 **10.** 175

**11.** 299 **12.** 336 **13.** 400 **14.** 512

**IDENTIFYING PRIMES** Tell whether the number is *prime* or *composite*.

**15.** 21 **16.** 45 **17.** 59 **18.** 91

**USING FACTOR TREES** Copy and complete the factor tree. Then write the prime factorization of the number.

*SEE EXAMPLE 3*
on p. 177
for Exs. 19–21

**19.**
```
        88
      /    \
    ?   •   11
   / \       |
  2 • 4  •  11
     / \     |
  ? • ? • ? • ?
```

**20.**
```
    95
   /  \
  5 • ?
```

**21.**
```
        210
       /    \
     ?   •   105
     |      /    \
     ? •  5   •   ?
     |    |      / \
     2 • ? • ? • ?
```

**PRIME FACTORIZATION** **Write the prime factorization of the number.**

**SEE EXAMPLE 3**
on p. 177
for Exs. 22–30

**22.** 28   **23.** 55   **24.** 97   **25.** 96

**26.** 280   **27.** 396   **28.** 1125   **29.** 2000

**30.** **TAKS REASONING** What is the prime factorization of 405?

**(A)** $9 \cdot 9 \cdot 5$   **(B)** $3^3 \cdot 5^2$   **(C)** $3^4 \cdot 5$   **(D)** $3^3 \cdot 15$

**XY** **ALGEBRA** **Factor the monomial.**

**SEE EXAMPLE 4**
on p. 178
for Exs. 31–39

**31.** $15cd$   **32.** $40pq$   **33.** $9x^2y$   **34.** $24g^2h^3$

**35.** $48n^3m^3$   **36.** $144n^2m^5$   **37.** $20ab^4c^2$   **38.** $99r^3s^2t$

**39.** **ERROR ANALYSIS** Your friend says that the factored form of the monomial $18x^2y$ is $1 \cdot 3 \cdot 6 \cdot x \cdot y$. Describe and correct your friend's error.

**MAKE A LIST** **Show how the prime factorization of the number can be used to find all of its factors besides 1 and itself.**

**40.** 24   **41.** 56   **42.** 102   **43.** 225

**REWRITING NUMBERS** **Many even numbers are the sum of two primes. For example, $8 = 3 + 5$. Write the number as the sum of two primes.**

**44.** 10   **45.** 16   **46.** 28   **47.** 30

**48.** **CHALLENGE** Some numbers have an odd number of factors. For example, the factors of 4 are 1, 2, and 4. Find three more numbers that have an odd number of factors. What do the numbers have in common?

## PROBLEM SOLVING

**SEE EXAMPLE 1**
on p. 176
for Exs. 49–51

**49.** **GUIDED PROBLEM SOLVING** You are making a quilt out of 120 square patches. What are the two most reasonable rectangular arrangements of the patches for the quilt?

   **a.** List all of the factors of 120.

   **b.** List all the pairs of factors from part (a) that have a product of 120. These are the possible arrangements of the patches.

   **c.** List the two most reasonable arrangements of the patches. *Explain* why the other arrangements are not reasonable.

**50.** **TAKS REASONING** The director of a baseball league must divide 180 players into teams of equal size. List all the possible combinations of number of teams and team sizes of 9 to 50. The director wants an even number of teams. Which two sizes are most reasonable? *Explain.*

**51.** **TAKS REASONING** Several teachers at a school are rearranging the desks in their classrooms. Which number of desks *cannot* be arranged in a rectangular arrangement with two or more rows all of equal length?

   **(A)** 20   **(B)** 23   **(C)** 25   **(D)** 27

**52. WRITING** *Explain* how you can create two different factor trees for 540. Do both factor trees result in the same prime factorization?

**53.**  **TAKS REASONING** You are in charge of a ring toss game at a school fair. In this game, players try to throw a small ring over a bottle that is in a rectangular display. You have 140 bottles to arrange in equal rows. Can you have 40 equal rows? *Explain.* You are setting the display on a square table that can fit at most 15 bottles across. Which rectangular arrangements of the 140 bottles will fit on the table? *Explain.*

**54. NUMBER SENSE** Name two prime numbers that have a difference of 1. Are there others? *Explain* your reasoning.

**55.** **TAKS REASONING** Find dimensions in whole inches.

    **a. Calculate** The area of a rectangle is 24 square inches. Find all possible dimensions of the rectangle. Which dimensions produce the rectangle with the least perimeter?

    **b. Calculate** Repeat step (a) for a rectangle with an area of 36 square inches and a rectangle with an area of 40 square inches.

    **c. Predict** A rectangle has an area of 100 square inches. Without making any calculations, which dimensions produce the rectangle with the least perimeter? *Explain* your reasoning.

**56. GEOMETRY** The *volume* of a box can be found by using the formula Volume = length $\times$ width $\times$ height. A box has a volume of 200 cubic inches. Find all the possible whole-number dimensions of the box.

**57. CHALLENGE** *Twin primes* are prime numbers with a difference of 2. For example, 5 and 7 are twin primes. List five other pairs of twin primes.

**58. CHALLENGE** A *perfect number* is a number that is equal to the sum of all its factors excluding itself. For example, 6 is a perfect number because 6 = 1 + 2 + 3. Find the next perfect number.

---

**MIXED REVIEW FOR TAKS**     **TAKS PRACTICE** at classzone.com

*REVIEW*
Lesson 3.6;
TAKS Workbook

**59.** **TAKS PRACTICE** Tyrone found that more than $\frac{3}{5}$ of the students in his math class ask questions of the teacher at least once every two days. There are 29 students in his math class. Which statement is NOT true? *TAKS Obj. 6*

   Ⓐ At least 18 students ask questions in class at least twice in a five day week.

   Ⓑ Fewer than 12 students do not ask any questions in a five day week.

   Ⓒ More than half the students ask questions at least once every two days.

   Ⓓ It is impossible to know from this data how many students ask questions daily.

# 4.2 Greatest Common Factor

TEKS *8.1.B, 8.14.A*

| **Before** | You found the factors of a number. |
| **Now** | You'll find the greatest common factor of two or more numbers. |
| **Why?** | So you can find compatible dimensions, as for pens in Ex. 46. |

**KEY VOCABULARY**
- **common factor,** *p. 181*
- **greatest common factor (GCF),** *p. 181*
- **relatively prime,** *p. 182*

### ACTIVITY

The table at the right shows the factors of 24, 20, and 18.

**STEP 1** Which number(s) are factors of 18 and 24?

**STEP 2** Which number(s) are factors of 20 and 24?

**STEP 3** Which number(s) are factors of 18, 20, and 24?

**STEP 4** What is the greatest factor that is in all three lists?

| *Number* | *Factors* |
|----------|-----------|
| 24 | 1, 2, 3, 4, 6, 8, 12, 24 |
| 20 | 1, 2, 4, 5, 10, 20 |
| 18 | 1, 2, 3, 6, 9, 18 |

**VOCABULARY**

The GCF is sometimes called the *greatest common divisor* (GCD) because it is the greatest number that divides the given numbers.

A **common factor** is a whole number that is a factor of two or more nonzero whole numbers. The greatest of the common factors is the **greatest common factor (GCF)**. One way to find the GCF of two or more numbers is to multiply the common prime facors.

### EXAMPLE 1  Finding the Greatest Common Factor

**Find the greatest common factor of 56 and 84.**

**SOLUTION**

**STEP 1** Write the prime factorization of each number.

$$56 = 2 \times 2 \times 2 \times 7 \qquad 84 = 2 \times 2 \times 3 \times 7$$

**AVOID ERRORS**

2 appears twice in each prime factorization. So it must be used twice when computing the GCF.

**STEP 2** Find the common prime factors. They are 2, 2, and 7. The GCF of 56 and 84 is the product of these factors.

▸ **Answer** The GCF of 56 and 84 is 2 • 2 • 7, or 28.

✓ **GUIDED PRACTICE**  for Example 1

**Find the greatest common factor of the numbers.**

**1.** 12, 32  **2.** 42, 60  **3.** 36, 90  **4.** 96, 120

**Relatively Prime Numbers** Two numbers are **relatively prime** if their greatest common factor is 1. For example, 8 and 15 are relatively prime.

### EXAMPLE 2 Identifying Relatively Prime Numbers

**Tell whether the numbers 112 and 45 are relatively prime.**

**SOLUTION**

Write the prime factorization of each number. Then look for all the common prime factors.

$$112 = 2^4 \cdot 7 \qquad 45 = 3^2 \cdot 5$$

There are no common prime factors. However, two numbers always have 1 as a common factor. So, the GCF is 1.

▶ **Answer** The numbers 112 and 45 are relatively prime.

### EXAMPLE 3 TAKS REASONING: Multi-Step Problem

**Pep Rally** Students at your school are planning to hand out pep rally packs to support your school's athletic program. The students have 240 bumper stickers, 360 pennants, and 720 pencils. Every pack must have the same contents, and no items should be left over. What is the greatest number of packs that can be made? What will each pack contain?

**STEP 1** **Find** the greatest number of pep rally packs by finding the GCF.

$$240 = 2^4 \cdot 3 \cdot 5 \qquad 360 = 2^3 \cdot 3^2 \cdot 5 \qquad 720 = 2^4 \cdot 3^2 \cdot 5$$

The common prime factors are $2^3$, 3, and 5. The GCF is $2^3 \cdot 3 \cdot 5$, or 120. So, 120 pep rally packs can be made.

**STEP 2** **Divide** the number of items by the number of pep rally packs.

$$240 \div 120 = 2 \qquad 360 \div 120 = 3 \qquad 720 \div 120 = 6$$

▶ **Answer** The greatest number of pep rally packs is 120. Each pack will contain 2 bumper stickers, 3 pennants, and 6 pencils.

✓ **GUIDED PRACTICE** for Examples 2 and 3

**Tell whether the numbers are relatively prime. If they are not relatively prime, find the GCF.**

**5.** 48, 72 **6.** 124, 128 **7.** 39, 44 **8.** 200, 63

**9. What If?** In Example 3, suppose the students have 240 bumper stickers and 360 pennants, but only 600 pencils. How many pep rally packs can be made? What items will each pack contain?

**GCF of Monomials** You can find the greatest common factor of two monomials by factoring the monomials.

---

**EXAMPLE 4** **Finding the GCF of Monomials**

 Find the greatest common factor of $12a^3$ and $9a^2$.

**STEP 1** **Write** the prime factorization of each expression.

$$12a^3 = 2 \cdot 2 \cdot 3 \cdot a \cdot a \cdot a \qquad 9a^2 = 3 \cdot 3 \cdot a \cdot a$$

**STEP 2** **Find** the common factors, 3 and $a^2$. The GCF is their product.

▶ **Answer** The GCF of $12a^3$ and $9a^2$ is $3 \cdot a^2$, or $3a^2$.

---

✓ **GUIDED PRACTICE** **for Example 4**

**Find the greatest common factor of the monomials.**

**10.** $6x, 18x$     **11.** $6xy, 4xy^2$     **12.** $15y, 9x^2y^2$     **13.** $5xy^3, 10x^2y^2$

---

# 4.2 EXERCISES

HOMEWORK KEY

 = **TAKS Practice and Reasoning**
Exs. 20, 30–33, 41, 42, 44, 49, and 50

◯ = **HINTS** AND **HOMEWORK HELP**
for Exs. 3, 9, 13, 21, 41 at classzone.com

## SKILL PRACTICE

**VOCABULARY** Copy and complete the statement.

**1.** Six is the __?__ of 12 and 18.

**2.** Two numbers are __?__ if their GCF is 1.

*SEE EXAMPLE 1*
on p. 181
for Exs. 3–11

**FINDING THE GCF** Find the GCF of the numbers.

**3.** 14, 70     **4.** 38, 51     **5.** 24, 196     **6.** 42, 184

**7.** 3, 9, 27     **8.** 21, 28, 56     **9.** 17, 18, 20     **10.** 24, 36, 180

**11. ERROR ANALYSIS** Describe and correct the error made in finding the GCF of 140 and 440.

$140 = 2 \cdot 2 \cdot 5 \cdot 7$
$440 = 2 \cdot 2 \cdot 2 \cdot 5 \cdot 11$
The GCF is $2 \cdot 5 = 10$.

*SEE EXAMPLE 2*
on p. 182
for Exs. 12–19

**RELATIVELY PRIME NUMBERS** Tell whether the numbers are relatively prime. If not, find the GCF.

**12.** 5, 16     **13.** 10, 25     **14.** 28, 42     **15.** 55, 72

**16.** 21, 66     **17.** 18, 216     **18.** 212, 312     **19.** 268, 515

*SEE EXAMPLE 4*
on p. 183
for Ex. 20

**20.** ⬥ **TAKS REASONING** What is the GCF of $4x^2$ and $6x$?

**(A)** $x$     **(B)** $2x$     **(C)** $4x$     **(D)** $2x^2$

**SEE EXAMPLE 4**
on p. 183
for Exs. 21–29

**XY ALGEBRA** Find the GCF of the monomials.

**21.** $3x^2, 9x$        **22.** $4z^3, 2z^2$        **23.** $5t^4, 15t^5$

**24.** $12x^2y^2, 16xy^3$        **25.** $18rs^2, 30st^2$        **26.** $15bc^3, 75b^3c$

**27.** $9t^3, 33t, 27t^4$        **28.** $12x^2y^3, 42x^3y^2, 36x^2y^3$        **29.** $63mn, 42m^3, 32n^2$

**TAKS REASONING** Find two numbers or monomials with the given GCF.

**30.** 16        **31.** 21        **32.** $18x^2$        **33.** $15sc^3$

**REASONING** Copy and complete the statement using *always*, *sometimes*, or *never*. *Explain* your reasoning.

**34.** The greatest common factor of two numbers is __?__ greater than both of the numbers.

**35.** The greatest common factor of two numbers is __?__ equal to one of the two numbers.

**36.** The greatest common factor of two numbers is __?__ prime.

**37.** The greatest common factor of relatively prime numbers is __?__ 1.

**XY CHALLENGE** Describe the pattern and find the next three monomials. What is the GCF of the list of monomials?

**38.** $5x, 10x^2, 20x^3, \ldots$        **39.** $4r^2s, 16r^3s^3, 64r^4s^5, \ldots$

## PROBLEM SOLVING

**SEE EXAMPLE 3**
on p. 182
for Exs. 40–42

**40. GUIDED PROBLEM SOLVING** In a youth sports league, 60 girls and 66 boys will be divided into teams. Each team will have an equal number of players and will have the same number of girls. What is the greatest number of teams that can be formed?

   **a.** Write the prime factorizations of 60 and 66.

   **b.** What are the common prime factors of the two numbers?

   **c.** Multiply the common prime factors to find the GCF. What meaning does the GCF have in the situation?

**41. TAKS REASONING** You must cut four pieces of wood that measure 36 inches, 45 inches, 81 inches, and 108 inches into smaller, equally sized pieces. What is the longest each piece can be so that each piece is the same length?

   **(A)** 3 in.       **(B)** 9 in.       **(C)** 18 in.       **(D)** 36 in.

**42. TAKS REASONING** A florist is making identical bouquets from 360 tulips, 270 roses, and 180 lilies. No flowers should be left over. What is the greatest number of bouquets that the florist can make? What will each bouquet contain? *Explain* your reasoning.

**43. WRITING** Can two even numbers be relatively prime? *Explain* why or why not.

**44.** ★ **TAKS REASONING** Name three composite numbers that are relatively prime.

**45. REASONING** *Explain* why any two prime numbers are always relatively prime. Give two examples to justify your reasoning.

**46. MULTI-STEP PROBLEM** A farmer needs to build two adjacent rectangular pens for his sheep as shown. Fence lengths are available in one-foot increments. What is the greatest length $x$ the farmer can make the fence that is shared by the two pens? What are the dimensions of each pen? How many feet of fence are needed to build the two pens?

| | | |
|---|---|---|
| $x$ ft | $A = 156 \text{ ft}^2$ | $A = 204 \text{ ft}^2$ |

**47. REASONING** Three numbers $x$, $y$, and $z$ are each multiplied by a constant $c$. Compare the GCF of $x$, $y$, and $z$ to the GCF of $cx$, $cy$, and $cz$. *Explain* your reasoning.

**48. CHALLENGE** *Describe* a process for finding the GCF of two monomials that involves comparing exponents.

## MIXED REVIEW FOR TAKS

TAKS PRACTICE at classzone.com

REVIEW
Lesson 3.5;
TAKS Workbook

**49.** ★ **TAKS PRACTICE** An artist created a mural on a rectangular concrete wall that has an area of 180 square feet. What is the width of the wall if the length is 20 feet? *TAKS Obj. 3*

**(A)** 9 ft          **(B)** 70 ft          **(C)** 90 ft          **(D)** 3600 ft

REVIEW
Lesson 1.3;
TAKS Workbook

**50.** ★ **TAKS PRACTICE** A group of twelve people went to a music festival. They paid a total of $192 in entrance fees. Which equation shows the dollar amount, $d$, that four people would pay to enter the festival? *TAKS Obj. 1*

**(F)** $d = 192 - 12 \times 4$          **(G)** $d = 192 \div 12 \times 4$

**(H)** $d = 192 \div 4 \times 12$          **(J)** $d = 4(192 - 12)$

## Brain Game

### Marble Mystery

You have a bucket full of marbles. If the marbles in the bucket are counted by twos, threes, fives, and sevens, there is exactly one left over each time. What is the fewest number of marbles that could be in the bucket?

**GOAL**
Use area models to find equivalent fractions.

**MATERIALS**
• graph paper
• colored pencils

**TEKS** *8.1.A, 8.15.A*

# 4.3 Equivalent Fractions

You can use area models to find equivalent fractions that represent the same number.

**EXPLORE** Find two fractions equivalent to $\frac{6}{8}$.

**STEP 1** **Draw** a rectangle on a piece of graph paper. Divide the rectangle into 8 equal parts and shade 6 of the parts.

**STEP 2** **Look** for other ways of dividing the rectangle into equal parts.

There are 4 parts and 3 are shaded.

There are 16 parts and 12 are shaded.

**STEP 3** **Write** the equivalent fractions.

The fractions $\frac{3}{4}$ and $\frac{12}{16}$ are equivalent to $\frac{6}{8}$.

*Animated* **Math** at classzone.com

**PRACTICE** Draw a model of the given fraction. Then find two equivalent fractions.

1. $\frac{4}{6}$
2. $\frac{10}{12}$
3. $\frac{4}{16}$
4. $\frac{10}{16}$

**DRAW CONCLUSIONS**

5. **WRITING** Look at the fractions in Step 3. How can factoring both the numerator and denominator of a fraction help to write an equivalent fraction?

# 4.3 Simplifying Fractions

**TEKS** *8.1.A, 8.1.B*

**Before** You evaluated numerical expressions.

**Now** You'll simplify fractions.

**Why?** So you can find fractions of an amount, as in Example 1.

**KEY VOCABULARY**
- simplest form, *p. 187*
- equivalent fractions, *p. 187*

A *fraction* is a number of the form $\frac{a}{b}$ ($b \neq 0$) where $a$ is called the numerator and $b$ is called the denominator. A fraction is in **simplest form** if its numerator and denominator have 1 as their GCF.

**Equivalent fractions** represent the same number. They have the same simplest form.

---

**EXAMPLE 1** Writing a Fraction in Simplest Form

**History** One of the Czech Republic's royal coronation jewels is the St. Wenceslas crown. It was made around 1345 and is decorated with 44 spinels, 30 emeralds, 22 pearls, 19 sapphires, and 1 ruby. Write the fraction of jewels in the crown that are emeralds in simplest form.

**SOLUTION**

Write the fraction of jewels in the crown that are emeralds. Then simplify.

$$\frac{\text{Number of emeralds}}{\text{Total number of jewels in the crown}} = \frac{30}{116}$$

**Sapphire**

**Ruby**

**METHOD 1** Find and use the GCF of 30 and 116.

$$30 = 2 \cdot 3 \cdot 5 \qquad 116 = 2^2 \cdot 29$$

The GCF of 30 and 116 is 2.

$$\frac{30}{116} = \frac{30 \div 2}{116 \div 2} \qquad \text{Divide numerator and denominator by GCF.}$$

$$= \frac{15}{58} \qquad \text{Simplify.}$$

**Pearl**

**APPLY PROPERTIES**

You can use the identity property of multiplication to understand dividing out common factors.

$$\frac{2 \cdot 3 \cdot 5}{2 \cdot 2 \cdot 29} = \frac{2}{2} \cdot \frac{3 \cdot 5}{2 \cdot 29}$$

$$= 1 \cdot \frac{3 \cdot 5}{2 \cdot 29}$$

$$= \frac{3 \cdot 5}{2 \cdot 29}$$

**METHOD 2** Use prime factorization.

$$\frac{30}{116} = \frac{2 \cdot 3 \cdot 5}{2 \cdot 2 \cdot 29} \qquad \text{Write prime factorizations.}$$

$$= \frac{\overset{1}{\cancel{2}} \cdot 3 \cdot 5}{\underset{1}{\cancel{2}} \cdot 2 \cdot 29} \qquad \text{Divide out common factor.}$$

$$= \frac{15}{58} \qquad \text{Simplify.}$$

**Spinel**

**Emerald**

▶ **Answer** The fraction of jewels that are emeralds is $\frac{15}{58}$.

Use the information from Example 1. Write the fraction of jewels in the crown that are the given jewel. Simplify if possible.

**1.** pearls          **2.** sapphires          **3.** spinels

---

**EXAMPLE 2** Identifying Equivalent Fractions

Tell whether the fractions $\frac{3}{8}$ and $\frac{18}{48}$ are equivalent.

**SOLUTION**

Write each fraction in simplest form.

$\frac{3}{8}$ is in simplest form.          $\frac{18}{48} = \frac{18 \div 6}{48 \div 6} = \frac{3}{8}$

▶ **Answer** The fractions have the same simplest form, so they are equivalent.

---

**EXAMPLE 3** Writing Equivalent Fractions

Write two fractions that are equivalent to $\frac{4}{10}$.

**SOLUTION**

Multiply or divide the numerator and denominator by the same nonzero number.

$\frac{4}{10} = \frac{4 \times 3}{10 \times 3} = \frac{12}{30}$     **Multiply numerator and denominator by 3.**

$\frac{4}{10} = \frac{4 \div 2}{10 \div 2} = \frac{2}{5}$     **Divide numerator and denominator by 2, a common factor of 4 and 10.**

*OTHER SOLUTIONS*
Many other equivalent fractions can be found by multiplying the numerator and denominator by other numbers.

▶ **Answer** The fractions $\frac{12}{30}$ and $\frac{2}{5}$ are equivalent to $\frac{4}{10}$.

---

✓ **GUIDED PRACTICE** for Examples 2 and 3

Tell whether the fractions are equivalent.

**4.** $\frac{1}{6}, \frac{4}{24}$     **5.** $\frac{3}{7}, \frac{10}{21}$     **6.** $\frac{24}{30}, \frac{4}{6}$     **7.** $\frac{15}{35}, \frac{3}{7}$

Write two fractions that are equivalent to the given fraction.

**8.** $\frac{8}{16}$     **9.** $\frac{9}{15}$     **10.** $\frac{10}{12}$     **11.** $\frac{21}{24}$

**Variable Expressions** You can use prime factorization to simplify fractions that contain variable expressions, as you will see in the next example.

**EXAMPLE 4** Simplifying a Variable Expression

$\dfrac{14x}{7xy} = \dfrac{2 \cdot 7 \cdot x}{7 \cdot x \cdot y}$    **Factor numerator and denominator.**

$= \dfrac{2 \cdot \overset{1}{\cancel{7}} \cdot \overset{1}{\cancel{x}}}{\underset{1}{\cancel{7}} \cdot \underset{1}{\cancel{x}} \cdot y}$    **Divide out common factors.**

$= \dfrac{2}{y}$    **Simplify.**

 **EXAMPLE 5** Evaluating a Variable Expression

**Evaluate the expression $\dfrac{-4x^3}{2x}$ when $x = 5$.**

**TAKE NOTES**
You may want to add information on simplifying fractions with variable expressions to the outline that you started on page 174.

$\dfrac{-4x^3}{2x} = \dfrac{-1 \cdot 2 \cdot 2 \cdot x \cdot x \cdot x}{2 \cdot x}$    **Factor numerator and denominator.**

$= \dfrac{-1 \cdot 2 \cdot \overset{1}{\cancel{2}} \cdot \overset{1}{\cancel{x}} \cdot x \cdot x}{\underset{1}{\cancel{2}} \cdot \underset{1}{\cancel{x}}}$    **Divide out common factors.**

$= -2x^2$    **Simplify.**

$= -2(5)^2$    **Substitute 5 for $x$.**

$= -50$    **Evaluate powers and simplify.**

✓ **GUIDED PRACTICE**    for Examples 4 and 5

**Simplify the variable expression. Then evaluate for $x = -2$ and $y = 3$.**

**12.** $\dfrac{4xy}{6x}$      **13.** $\dfrac{32x}{8xy}$      **14.** $\dfrac{2x^3y}{6x}$      **15.** $\dfrac{5x^2y}{10xy}$

# 4.3 EXERCISES

HOMEWORK KEY    **= TAKS Practice and Reasoning**
     **Exs. 21, 48, 49, 50, 51, and 54**

○ **= HINTS AND HOMEWORK HELP**
     **for Exs. 3, 7, 13, 27, 45** at classzone.com

## SKILL PRACTICE

**VOCABULARY Copy and complete the statement.**

**1.** The GCF of the numerator and denominator of a fraction in __?__ is 1.

**2.** Fractions with the same simplest form are __?__.

**WRITING IN SIMPLEST FORM Write the fraction in simplest form.**

**SEE EXAMPLE 1**
on p. 187
for Exs. 3–12

**3.** $\dfrac{21}{49}$      **4.** $\dfrac{-9}{72}$      **5.** $\dfrac{10}{15}$      **6.** $\dfrac{16}{20}$      **7.** $\dfrac{-25}{40}$

**8.** $\dfrac{-36}{72}$      **9.** $\dfrac{39}{52}$      **10.** $\dfrac{18}{27}$      **11.** $\dfrac{-49}{56}$      **12.** $\dfrac{33}{121}$

**EQUIVALENT FRACTIONS** Tell whether the fractions are equivalent.

**SEE EXAMPLE 2**
on p. 188
for Exs. 13–21

**13.** $\dfrac{4}{5}, \dfrac{20}{25}$

**14.** $\dfrac{21}{28}, \dfrac{1}{3}$

**15.** $\dfrac{24}{40}, \dfrac{30}{50}$

**16.** $\dfrac{30}{60}, \dfrac{27}{54}$

**17.** $\dfrac{30}{75}, \dfrac{75}{105}$

**18.** $\dfrac{45}{54}, \dfrac{90}{108}$

**19.** $\dfrac{54}{96}, \dfrac{144}{256}$

**20.** $\dfrac{84}{112}, \dfrac{168}{192}$

**21.** ◆ **TAKS REASONING** Which pair of fractions are equivalent?

(A) $\dfrac{6}{10}, \dfrac{9}{25}$  (B) $\dfrac{3}{8}, \dfrac{15}{35}$  (C) $\dfrac{14}{21}, \dfrac{12}{18}$  (D) $\dfrac{2}{5}, \dfrac{5}{20}$

**SEE EXAMPLE 3**
on p. 188
for Exs. 22–25

**WRITING FRACTIONS** Write two fractions equivalent to the given fraction.

**22.** $\dfrac{45}{90}$

**23.** $\dfrac{36}{81}$

**24.** $\dfrac{24}{60}$

**25.** $\dfrac{48}{140}$

(xy) **EVALUATING EXPRESSIONS** Write the fraction in simplest form. Then evaluate the expression when $x = 3$ and $y = 5$.

**SEE EXAMPLES
4 AND 5**
on p. 189
for Exs. 26–33

**26.** $\dfrac{3x}{x^3}$

**27.** $\dfrac{2y^2}{-5y}$

**28.** $\dfrac{5y}{y^2}$

**29.** $\dfrac{4x^4}{24x^3}$

**30.** $\dfrac{-18x^2y}{24x}$

**31.** $\dfrac{35xy^2}{7x^2y^4}$

**32.** $\dfrac{6x^3y^2}{21xy^4}$

**33.** $\dfrac{-20x^2y}{8x^4y^3}$

**34. WHICH ONE DOESN'T BELONG?** Which fraction is *not* equivalent to the other fractions?

**A.** $\dfrac{180}{320}$  **B.** $\dfrac{9}{16}$  **C.** $\dfrac{81}{144}$  **D.** $\dfrac{14}{25}$

(xy) **ALGEBRA** Find the value of $x$ that makes the fractions equivalent.

**35.** $\dfrac{x}{140} = \dfrac{1}{10}$

**36.** $\dfrac{x}{5} = \dfrac{42}{70}$

**37.** $\dfrac{8}{18} = \dfrac{x}{54}$

**38.** $\dfrac{36}{78} = \dfrac{x}{13}$

(xy) **VARIABLE EXPRESSIONS** Tell whether the expressions are equivalent.

**39.** $\dfrac{4abc}{5ab}, \dfrac{4c}{5a}$

**40.** $\dfrac{3a}{5}, \dfrac{6a^2}{10a}$

**41.** $\dfrac{2a}{3b}, \dfrac{10a^2b}{15ab^2}$

**42.** $\dfrac{7a}{9b}, \dfrac{21a^4b^3}{27a^5b^4}$

**43. CHALLENGE** The product of the integers from $n$ down to 1 is called *n factorial* and is written $n! = n \cdot (n-1) \cdot (n-2) \cdot \ldots \cdot 1$. Simplify the expression $\dfrac{12!}{3! \cdot 4!}$.

## PROBLEM SOLVING

**SEE EXAMPLE 1**
on p. 187
for Exs. 44–47

**GEOGRAPHY** Write the number of states in the region as a fraction of all the states. Write your answer in simplest form.

**44.** Northeast: 9

**45.** Midwest: 12

**46.** South: 16

**47.** West: 13

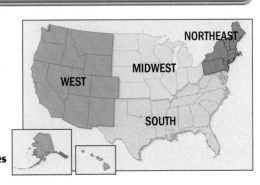

The U.S. Census Bureau divides the 50 states into 4 regions.

◆ = TAKS Practice and Reasoning   ◯ = **HINTS AND HOMEWORK HELP** *at classzone.com*

**48. ➤ TAKS REASONING** Mr. Wilkens has attended 18 of his daughter's 24 basketball games. What fraction of the games has he *missed*?

(A) $\frac{1}{4}$       (B) $\frac{2}{3}$       (C) $\frac{3}{4}$       (D) $\frac{4}{3}$

**49. ➤ TAKS REASONING** You buy two dozen eggs. In one carton, 1 egg is broken. In the other, 2 are broken. What fraction of all the eggs are broken? What fraction of all the eggs are unbroken? Write your answers in simplest form. *Explain* your reasoning.

**50. ➤ TAKS REASONING** The table gives information about animals in Peru.

   **a. Calculate** Find the fraction of threatened species in each group (mammals, birds, and reptiles). Write your answers in simplest form.

   **b. Estimate** Round the number of known bird species to 1500 and the number of threatened bird species to 60. Approximately what fraction of bird species are threatened?

   **c. Mental Math** Use mental math and your fraction from part (b) to find which group has the greatest fraction of threatened species and which group has the least. *Explain* your reasoning.

**Yellow-faced parrot**

| Peruvian Animal Species | | | |
|---|---|---|---|
| | **Mammals** | **Birds** | **Reptiles** |
| **Known** | 460 | 1541 | 360 |
| **Threatened** | 46 | 64 | 9 |

**51. ➤ TAKS REASONING** Your class of 30 students votes on what type of fundraiser to have this year: a car wash, a fair, or a dance. Eight students choose a car wash and 12 students choose a fair. Find the fraction of students who choose to have a dance. Write your answer in simplest form. *Explain* how you found your answer.

**52. WRITING** If you divide the numerator and denominator of a fraction by a common factor, will the resulting fraction always be in simplest form? *Explain* your reasoning and give an example to justify your answer.

**53. CHALLENGE** Jason believes that if the numerator or the denominator of a fraction is prime, then the fraction is in simplest form. *Explain* why this is not always true.

---

### MIXED REVIEW FOR TAKS

**TAKS** PRACTICE at classzone.com

REVIEW
Lesson 2.5;
TAKS Workbook

**54. ➤ TAKS PRACTICE** Ms. Jackson made 4 deposits of $750 each into her bank account. She also made 3 withdrawals of $80 each. Which expression can be used to find the average amount of money involved in each of the transactions? *TAKS Obj. 1*

(A) $\dfrac{4(750) - 3(-80)}{4}$       (B) $\dfrac{3(750) + 4(-80)}{4}$

(C) $\dfrac{4(750) + 3(-80)}{7}$       (D) $\dfrac{3(750) - 4(-80)}{7}$

---

# 4.4 Least Common Multiple

TEKS *8.14.A, 8.14.C*

**Before**  You found the greatest common factor of two numbers.

**Now**  You'll find the least common multiple of two numbers.

**Why?**  So you can plan a schedule, as in Example 1.

**KEY VOCABULARY**
- **multiple,** *p. 192*
- **common multiple,** *p. 192*
- **least common multiple (LCM),** *p. 192*

A **multiple** of a number is the product of the number and any nonzero whole number. A multiple that is shared by two or more numbers is a **common multiple**. The least of the common multiples of two or more whole numbers is the **least common multiple (LCM)**.

**EXAMPLE 1**  Finding the Least Common Multiple

 **Animal Clinic**  A veterinarian at an animal clinic is on call every four days. Today is Saturday, and the veterinarian is on call. In how many more days will the veterinarian be on call on a Saturday again?

**SOLUTION**

The veterinarian is on call every 4 days. A Saturday occurs every 7 days. Find the least common multiple of 4 and 7.

**READING**
Read the problem above carefully to determine what you know and what you need to find out.

**METHOD 1**  Use a calendar. Start with a Saturday and circle every 4 days on a calendar. You can see that the veterinarian will be on call on a Saturday in 28 days.

June 29 is 28 days after June 1.

**METHOD 2**  Make a list.

List the multiples of each number.

**Multiples of 4:** 4, 8, 12, 16, 20, 24, **28**, 32, . . .

**Multiples of 7:** 7, 14, 21, **28**, 35, 42, 49, 56, . . .

The least common multiple is the first number that appears in both lists. The LCM of 4 and 7 is 28.

**METHOD 3**  Use prime factorization.

Write the prime factorization of each number.   $4 = 2^2$   $7 = 7$

Circle the greatest power of each prime factor.   $4 = \boxed{2^2}$   $7 = \boxed{7}$

The LCM of 4 and 7 is the product of the circled numbers:   $2^2 \cdot 7 = 28$

▶ **Answer**  In 28 days, the veterinarian will be on call on a Saturday.

EXAMPLE 2 **Finding the Least Common Multiple**

**Find the LCM of 32, 96, and 120 using prime factorization.**

**SOLUTION**

**STEP 1** **Write** the prime factorization of each number and circle the greatest power of each prime factor.

$$32 = \boxed{2^5}$$
$$96 = 2^5 \cdot \boxed{3}$$
$$120 = 2^3 \cdot 3 \cdot \boxed{5}$$

**STEP 2** **Find** the product of the circled factors.

$$2^5 \cdot 3 \cdot 5 = 480$$

▶ **Answer** The LCM of 32, 96, and 120 is 480.

*AVOID ERRORS*

Make sure you circle the greatest power of each prime factor only once in *all* of the prime factorizations. $2^5$ occurs in both 32 and 96, but it is only circled once.

*Animated* **Math**
at classzone.com

**Monomials** The factoring method used in Example 2 is also useful for finding the least common multiples of monomials.

**EXAMPLE 3** **Finding the LCM of Monomials**

 **Find the LCM of $6x^2y$ and $9x^4z$.**

**SOLUTION**

**STEP 1** **Factor** each expression using exponents and circle the greatest power of each factor.

$$6x^2y = \boxed{2} \cdot 3 \cdot x^2 \cdot \boxed{y}$$
$$9x^4z = \boxed{3^2} \cdot \boxed{x^4} \cdot \boxed{z}$$

**STEP 2** **Find** the product of the circled factors.

$$2 \cdot 3^2 \cdot x^4 \cdot y \cdot z = 18x^4yz$$

▶ **Answer** The LCM of $6x^2y$ and $9x^4z$ is $18x^4yz$.

✓ **GUIDED PRACTICE** **for Examples 1, 2, and 3**

1. **What If?** In Example 1, suppose the veterinarian is on call every 3 days. In how many more days will the vet be on call on a Saturday again?

**Find the least common multiple of the numbers.**

**2.** 6, 15      **3.** 4, 20      **4.** 12, 28      **5.** 24, 36, and 72

**Find the least common multiple of the monomials.**

**6.** $8x^3, 20x^7$      **7.** $12y^4, 36y^8$      **8.** $4ab^2, 10a^2b$      **9.** $6m^3np^2, 8mp^3$

# 4.4 EXERCISES

## SKILL PRACTICE

**VOCABULARY Copy and complete the statement.**

**1.** A(n) ? of 6 and 9 is 54.

**2.** The ? of 6 and 9 is 18.

**LISTING MULTIPLES Find the LCM of the numbers by listing multiples.**

*SEE EXAMPLE 1*
on p. 192
for Exs. 3–10

**3.** 6, 8

**4.** 6, 21

**5.** 8, 10

**6.** 10, 15

**7.** 18, 36

**8.** 45, 75

**9.** 6, 8, 12

**10.** 3, 6, 15

**USING PRIME FACTORIZATION Find the LCM of the numbers by using prime factorization.**

*SEE EXAMPLE 2*
on p. 193
for Exs. 11–19

**11.** 14, 21

**12.** 7, 56

**13.** 15, 55

**14.** 36, 90

**15.** 42, 105

**16.** 90, 108

**17.** 10, 12, 14

**18.** 16, 20, 40

**19. ERROR ANALYSIS** Describe and correct the error made in finding the LCM.

Find the LCM of 12 and 24.
$12 = 2 \cdot 2 \cdot 3$    $24 = 2 \cdot 2 \cdot 2 \cdot 3$
The LCM is $2 \cdot 2 \cdot 3$, or 12.

**CHOOSE A METHOD Tell whether you would find the LCM of the numbers by *using mental math, listing multiples* or *using prime factorization*. *Explain* your choice and find the LCM.**

*SEE EXAMPLES 1 AND 2*
on pp. 192–193
for Exs. 20–27

**20.** 17, 57

**21.** 125, 500

**22.** 8, 16, 32

**23.** 6, 15, 45

**24.** 30, 75, 100

**25.** 36, 54, 72

**26.** 10, 12, 30, 60

**27.** 21, 42, 63, 105

**XV ALGEBRA Find the LCM of the monomials.**

*SEE EXAMPLE 3*
on p. 193
for Exs. 28–36

**28.** $4x, 16x^3$

**29.** $9y^4, 12y$

**30.** $24t, 60st$

**31.** $5ab, 7ab^2$

**32.** $7s^3t, 49st^2$

**33.** $4x^3y^3, 18xy^5$

**34.** $18x^2y, 24x^4y, 30y^7$

**35.** $24c^2d^3, 30c^3d^2, 60c^2d^6$

**36.** $33g^4hk^3, 36g^3h^7k, 45gh^5k^3$

**37. TAKS REASONING** Which statement is *always* true?

Ⓐ The LCM of two prime numbers is 1.

Ⓑ The LCM of two numbers is greater than or equal to both numbers.

Ⓒ The LCM of two different numbers is the product of the two numbers.

Ⓓ The LCM of a prime number and a composite number is the product of the two numbers.

**TAKS REASONING Find a pair of numbers that have the given LCM.**
*Explain* how you found your answer.

**38.** 30

**39.** 70

**40.** 105

**41.** 150

**42. NUMBER SENSE** What is the *least* possible number for which the LCM of the number and 15 is 105? What is the *greatest* number for which the LCM of the number and 15 is 105? *Explain* your reasoning.

**43. CHALLENGE** Could the GCF of two different numbers also be the LCM of those numbers? *Explain.*

## PROBLEM SOLVING

SEE EXAMPLES
*1 AND 2*
on pp. 192–193
for Exs. 44–46

**44. SCHEDULE** Your schedule changes on a three-day rotation. Your math class is the last period of every third day. This week, your math class is on Friday. In how many more school days will you again have math on Friday?

**45. TRAFFIC LIGHTS** One traffic light turns red every 45 seconds. Another traffic light turns red every 60 seconds. Both traffic lights just turned red. In how many seconds will they turn red at the same time again?

**46. CLASS SIZES** A teacher can arrange a class into groups of 2, 5, or 6 students with no one left out. What is the least number of students that the teacher can have in class to do this? *Explain* your reasoning.

**47. WRITING** Could you find the *greatest* common multiple of two numbers? *Explain* your reasoning.

**48. COOKING** Zoe is making lasagna for a family reunion. Her recipe calls for 12 noodles for each batch of lasagna. One box of lasagna noodles contains 14 noodles. What is the least number of batches of lasagna that Zoe can make without having any noodles left over? *Explain.*

**49. REASONING** You are asked to find the LCM of two numbers. One of the numbers is a factor of the other. Is there a shortcut to finding their LCM? *Explain.*

**50. TAKS REASONING** You are forming sets of plastic utensils for a party that include one spoon, one fork, and one knife. Spoons come in packs of 24, forks come in packs of 36, and knives come in packs of 20. What is the least number of sets you can make without having any utensils left over? How many packs of each utensil will you need to make the sets? *Explain.*

**51. LOOK FOR A PATTERN** What is the number of the next figure that will be identical to Figure 1 in color and orientation? *Explain.*

| 1 | 2 | 3 | 4 | 5 | 6 | 7 |

**52. TAKS REASONING** Becky and Tonya are running laps. Becky runs one lap in 4 minutes. Tonya runs one lap in 3 minutes. They start at 4:00 P.M. from the same point. At which time will they *not* both be at the starting point?

   **A** 4:12 P.M.     **B** 4:18 P.M.     **C** 4:24 P.M.     **D** 4:36 P.M.

**53. CHALLENGE** Will swims one pool length in 45 seconds, while Martin swims one length in 40 seconds. The boys start at the same time from the same end of the pool and maintain their pace.

  **a.** When will they both be at their starting place at the same time again? Write your answer in seconds and in minutes.

  **b.** Kyle swims at a constant rate of 75 lengths per hour. Assume Kyle started swimming at the same time from the same end of the pool as Will and Martin. Will Kyle end up at the starting place at the same time as in part (a)? *Explain.*

  **c.** Kyle swims a total of 45 lengths. How many times will Kyle end up at the starting place at the same time as Will and Martin? *Explain* how you found your answer.

**MIXED REVIEW FOR TAKS**   **TAKS** PRACTICE at classzone.com

*REVIEW*
Lesson 2.2;
TAKS Workbook

**54.** **TAKS PRACTICE** In the first round of an academic challenge, a team scored +940 points. The team scored −450 points on the first 5 turns of the second round. What is the team's overall score? *TAKS Obj. 1*

  (A) −1390       (B) 490       (C) 510       (D) 1390

*REVIEW*
Lesson 2.1;
TAKS Workbook

**55.** **TAKS PRACTICE** A mechanical engineer took a series of measurements in liters. Which list shows some of the engineer's measurements ordered from greatest to least? *TAKS Obj. 1*

  (F) 14.010, 14.013, 14.020, 14.3       (G) 9.10, 9.09, 9.8, 9.07

  (H) 4.303, 4.299, 4.028, 4.1       (J) 12.12, 12.1, 12.06, 12.009

**QUIZ** *for Lessons 4.1–4.4*

**1.** Write the prime factorization of 1620. *(p. 176)*

**Find the GCF of the numbers or monomials.** *(p. 181)*

**2.** 24, 90       **3.** 36, 72, 108       **4.** $20c^3, 48c^2$       **5.** $64m^2, 80m^5$

**Find the LCM of the numbers or monomials.** *(p. 192)*

**6.** 88, 99       **7.** 36, 96       **8.** $7xy, 21y^3$       **9.** $6ab^2, 30ab$

**Tell whether the fractions are equivalent.** *(p. 187)*

**10.** $\frac{9}{27}, \frac{60}{180}$       **11.** $\frac{39}{91}, \frac{42}{56}$       **12.** $\frac{40}{48}, \frac{70}{84}$       **13.** $\frac{108}{120}, \frac{189}{210}$

**14. SUPERMARKET** A supermarket gives every tenth customer a coupon and every twenty-fifth customer a gift. Which of the first 200 customers receive both a coupon and a gift? *(p. 176)*

## Lessons 4.1–4.4

**MULTIPLE CHOICE**

1. **THE ORB OF 1661** The Orb of 1661 is a gold sphere displayed at the Tower of London. It is set with 365 diamonds, 363 cultured pearls, 18 rubies, 9 emeralds, 9 sapphires, and 1 amethyst. Which is *not* a reasonable conclusion? *TEKS 8.2.C*

   (A) More than $\frac{1}{3}$ of the jewels are cultured pearls.

   (B) About $\frac{3}{4}$ of the jewels are not emeralds.

   (C) Exactly $\frac{2}{85}$ of the jewels are rubies.

   (D) Less than $\frac{1}{2}$ of the jewels are diamonds.

2. **CORPORATE STUDY** A company needs to find at least 32 but no more than 45 people to participate in a scientific study. The company wants to be able to divide the people into groups and have between 8 and 10 groups of equal size. Which number of people would *not* satisfy the company's needs? *TEKS 8.1.B*

   (F) 32 people     (G) 36 people

   (H) 42 people     (J) 45 people

3. **SETS** Which set of numbers includes only prime numbers? *TEKS 8.16.B*

   (A) {2, 4, 6, 8}     (B) {3, 7, 11, 15}

   (C) {1, 3, 5, 7}     (D) {3, 7, 13, 17}

4. **ASSEMBLY** Two fifths of the students at an assembly are girls. Suppose there are between 400 and 500 students at the assembly. How many could be girls? *TEKS 8.2.B*

   (F) 159 students

   (G) 170 students

   (H) 201 students

   (J) 210 students

5. **TENNIS MATCH** Every fourth Saturday, Alana visits her aunt. Alana and a friend want to start playing tennis every third Saturday. She visits her aunt this Saturday and wants to begin playing tennis one of the three following Saturdays. After visiting her aunt, on which Saturday should she start playing tennis to postpone the first conflict of schedules as long as possible? *TEKS 8.14.A*

   (A) First Saturday

   (B) Second Saturday

   (C) Third Saturday

   (D) The first and third Saturdays will postpone the conflict by the same amount.

**GRIDDED ANSWER** ⊙①●③④⑤⑥⑦⑧⑨

6. **TEXTILES** A bolt of cloth is 48 inches wide and 120 feet long. What is the least number of identical square pieces it can be divided into so all of the cloth is used? *TEKS 8.14.C*

7. **PARTY** At a block party, party hats are bought in packages of 8 and party favors in packages of 6. Each guest gets 1 hat and 1 favor. After the party, Bo sees that no hats or favors from opened packages remain. Over 60 people were at the party. What is the least number of people who could have attended? *TEKS 8.1.B*

# 4.5 Comparing Fractions and Mixed Numbers

TEKS *8.1.A, 8.1.B*

| | |
|---|---|
| **Before** | You compared and ordered integers. |
| **Now** | You'll compare and order fractions and mixed numbers. |
| **Why?** | So you can compare statistics, as for sports in Ex. 43. |

**KEY VOCABULARY**
- **least common denominator (LCD),** *p. 198*

You can use models to compare the fractions $\frac{2}{3}$ and $\frac{3}{4}$.

 =       =

$$\frac{2}{3} = \frac{2 \cdot 4}{3 \cdot 4} = \frac{8}{12}$$

$$\frac{3}{4} = \frac{3 \cdot 3}{4 \cdot 3} = \frac{9}{12}$$

In the diagram above, $\frac{8}{12} < \frac{9}{12}$, so $\frac{2}{3} < \frac{3}{4}$.

The **least common denominator (LCD)** of two or more fractions is the least common multiple of the denominators. You can compare fractions by using the least common denominator to write equivalent fractions.

---

**EXAMPLE 1** Comparing Fractions Using the LCD

Compare $\frac{3}{8}$ and $\frac{5}{12}$.

**SOLUTION**

**STEP 1** **Find** the least common denominator of the fractions.
The LCM of 8 and 12 is 24, so the least common denominator is 24.

**STEP 2** **Use** the least common denominator to write equivalent fractions.

$$\frac{3}{8} = \frac{3 \cdot 3}{8 \cdot 3} = \frac{9}{24} \qquad\qquad \frac{5}{12} = \frac{5 \cdot 2}{12 \cdot 2} = \frac{10}{24}$$

**STEP 3** **Compare** the numerators: $9 < 10$, so $\frac{9}{24} < \frac{10}{24}$.

▶ **Answer** Because $\frac{9}{24} < \frac{10}{24}$, you can write $\frac{3}{8} < \frac{5}{12}$.

---

✓ **GUIDED PRACTICE** for Example 1

Copy and complete the statement with <, >, or =.

1. $\frac{2}{3} \; \underline{?} \; \frac{5}{8}$

2. $\frac{2}{4} \; \underline{?} \; \frac{15}{20}$

3. $\frac{3}{10} \; \underline{?} \; \frac{2}{4}$

4. $\frac{9}{16} \; \underline{?} \; \frac{11}{18}$

**Mixed Numbers** To compare or order improper fractions and mixed numbers, first write any mixed numbers as improper fractions.

**EXAMPLE 2** **TAKS PRACTICE: Multiple Choice**

> What is the order of $5\frac{9}{16}$, $\frac{11}{2}$, and $\frac{45}{8}$ from least to greatest?
>
> **(A)** $\frac{45}{8}$, $\frac{11}{2}$, $5\frac{9}{16}$  **(B)** $\frac{45}{8}$, $5\frac{9}{16}$, $\frac{11}{2}$  **(C)** $\frac{11}{2}$, $\frac{45}{8}$, $5\frac{9}{16}$  **(D)** $\frac{11}{2}$, $5\frac{9}{16}$, $\frac{45}{8}$

*ELIMINATE CHOICES*
Using mental math, you can see that $\frac{11}{2} = \frac{44}{8}$. So, choices A and B can be eliminated.

**SOLUTION**

**STEP 1** **Find** the least common denominator of the fractions. The LCM of 16, 2, and 8 is 16, so the LCD is 16.

**STEP 2** **Use** the least common denominator to write equivalent fractions.

$$5\frac{9}{16} = \frac{5 \cdot 16 + 9}{16} = \frac{89}{16} \qquad \frac{11}{2} = \frac{11 \cdot 8}{2 \cdot 8} = \frac{88}{16} \qquad \frac{45}{8} = \frac{45 \cdot 2}{8 \cdot 2} = \frac{90}{16}$$

**STEP 3** **Compare** numerators: $88 < 89$, $89 < 90$, so $\frac{88}{16} < \frac{89}{16}$ and $\frac{89}{16} < \frac{90}{16}$.

▶ **Answer** From least to greatest, the numbers are $\frac{11}{2}$, $5\frac{9}{16}$, and $\frac{45}{8}$. The correct answer is D. **(A) (B) (C) (D)**

**EXAMPLE 3** **Comparing Mixed Numbers**

**Orangutans** A female orangutan is about $3\frac{3}{7}$ feet tall. A male is about $3\frac{2}{5}$ feet tall. Which of the two orangutans is taller?

*ANOTHER WAY*
When the whole parts of two mixed numbers are equal, you can just compare the fraction parts. Because $\frac{3}{7} > \frac{2}{5}$, $3\frac{3}{7} > 3\frac{2}{5}$.

**SOLUTION**

**STEP 1** **Write** equivalent fractions using the LCD, 35.

$$3\frac{3}{7} = \frac{24}{7} = \frac{24 \cdot 5}{7 \cdot 5} = \frac{120}{35} \qquad 3\frac{2}{5} = \frac{17}{5} = \frac{17 \cdot 7}{5 \cdot 7} = \frac{119}{35}$$

**STEP 2** **Compare** the fractions: $\frac{120}{35} > \frac{119}{35}$, so $3\frac{3}{7} > 3\frac{2}{5}$.

▶ **Answer** The female orangutan is taller.

**Animated Math** at classzone.com

✓ **GUIDED PRACTICE** for Examples 2 and 3

Copy and complete the statement with <, >, or =.

**5.** $\frac{16}{5}$ _?_ $3\frac{1}{3}$  **6.** $1\frac{4}{5}$ _?_ $\frac{21}{12}$  **7.** $2\frac{2}{3}$ _?_ $4\frac{5}{6}$

**8.** Order the numbers $2\frac{7}{9}$, $2\frac{5}{12}$, and $\frac{11}{4}$ from least to greatest.

## 4.5 EXERCISES

HOMEWORK
KEY

🔶 = **TAKS Practice and Reasoning**
**Exs. 24, 29, 30, 31, 32, 38, 39, and 44**

◯ = **HINTS AND HOMEWORK HELP**
**for Exs. 3, 7, 9, 17, 37 at classzone.com**

### SKILL PRACTICE

**1. VOCABULARY** Copy and complete: The least common denominator of two fractions is the ___?___ of their denominators.

**2. VOCABULARY** *Explain* how to compare fractions using the LCD.

**FINDING LCDs Find the LCD of the fractions.**

*SEE EXAMPLES 1 AND 3*
on pp. 198–199
for Exs. 3–15

**(3.)** $\frac{1}{2}, \frac{2}{3}$

**4.** $\frac{3}{4}, \frac{7}{20}$

**5.** $\frac{11}{24}, \frac{5}{6}$

**6.** $\frac{5}{12}, \frac{7}{18}$

**COMPARING NUMBERS Copy and complete the statement with <, >, or =.**

**(7.)** $\frac{7}{18} \underset{?}{} \frac{5}{9}$

**8.** $\frac{24}{32} \underset{?}{} \frac{3}{4}$

**(9.)** $\frac{5}{8} \underset{?}{} \frac{9}{16}$

**10.** $\frac{165}{36} \underset{?}{} 4\frac{5}{12}$

**11.** $2\frac{4}{5} \underset{?}{} \frac{7}{3}$

**12.** $\frac{31}{6} \underset{?}{} 5\frac{2}{12}$

**13.** $3\frac{1}{4} \underset{?}{} \frac{13}{14}$

**14.** $\frac{5}{9} \underset{?}{} \frac{16}{24}$

**15. ERROR ANALYSIS** A classmate says that $\frac{3}{5} < \frac{4}{7}$ because 3 < 4.
Describe and correct your classmate's error.

**ORDERING NUMBERS Order the numbers from least to greatest.**

*SEE EXAMPLE 2*
on p. 199
for Exs. 16–24

**16.** $\frac{1}{2}, \frac{1}{8}, \frac{3}{4}, \frac{5}{16}$

**(17.)** $1\frac{1}{2}, \frac{5}{4}, \frac{11}{6}$

**18.** $\frac{5}{3}, \frac{35}{15}, 2\frac{2}{5}, \frac{15}{16}$

**19.** $\frac{3}{4}, \frac{5}{9}, 1\frac{1}{3}$

**20.** $\frac{19}{6}, 3\frac{1}{2}, \frac{11}{4}$

**21.** $1\frac{3}{5}, \frac{7}{3}, 2\frac{1}{4}, \frac{19}{12}$

**22.** $\frac{15}{4}, 3\frac{2}{3}, \frac{25}{7}$

**23.** $\frac{34}{3}, 11\frac{7}{12}, \frac{47}{4}$

**24.** 🔶 **TAKS REASONING** Which list of fractions is in order from least to greatest?

**Ⓐ** $\frac{12}{18}, \frac{13}{30}, \frac{8}{15}$

**Ⓑ** $\frac{4}{18}, \frac{9}{15}, \frac{18}{27}$

**Ⓒ** $\frac{6}{10}, \frac{4}{18}, \frac{16}{24}$

**Ⓓ** $\frac{7}{11}, \frac{7}{8}, \frac{15}{25}$

**MENTAL MATH Copy and complete the statement with <, >, or = by first comparing each fraction to $\frac{1}{2}$.**

**25.** $\frac{25}{50} \underset{?}{} \frac{37}{74}$

**26.** $\frac{17}{30} \underset{?}{} \frac{10}{33}$

**27.** $\frac{23}{100} \underset{?}{} \frac{19}{36}$

**28.** $\frac{105}{210} \underset{?}{} \frac{13}{27}$

🔶 **TAKS REASONING** Name a fraction $\frac{a}{b}$ between the given pair, where $a$ and $b$ are positive integers.

**29.** $\frac{1}{3}, \frac{1}{2}$

**30.** $\frac{3}{4}, \frac{4}{5}$

**31.** $\frac{5}{8}, \frac{2}{3}$

**32.** $\frac{3}{5}, \frac{1}{2}$

**(XV) CHALLENGE** Copy and complete the statement with <, >, or =, where $a > b$ and $b > 0$. *Explain* your reasoning.

**33.** $\frac{a}{b} \underset{?}{} \frac{b}{a}$

**34.** $\frac{1}{a} \underset{?}{} \frac{1}{b}$

**35.** $\frac{a}{a+1} \underset{?}{} \frac{b}{b+1}$

**36.** $\frac{a+1}{a} \underset{?}{} \frac{b+1}{b}$

SEE EXAMPLE 1
on p. 198
for Ex. 37–39

**37.** WALKERS Sarah walks two thirds mile to school every day. Amy walks five eighths mile to school. Who walks the greater distance to school?

**38.** TAKS REASONING During a 30 minute TV show, there are 8 minutes of commercials. During a 2 hour movie, there are 31 minutes of commercials. Which TV program has a greater fraction of commercial time? *Explain.*

**39.** TAKS REASONING In a class of 32 people, 28 were at school. Which fraction is *less* than the fraction of people in the class who were at school?

**A** $\frac{27}{30}$     **B** $\frac{24}{27}$     **C** $\frac{21}{24}$     **D** $\frac{24}{28}$

**40.** WRITING *Explain* how comparing fractions with like denominators differs from comparing fractions with like numerators.

**41.** ELEPHANTS Which elephant's trunk represents a greater fraction of the elephant's weight? *Explain* how you can answer this question without writing the fractions with a common denominator.

| Elephant | Trunk |
|---|---|
| 10,000 lb | 350 lb |
| 13,200 lb | 430 lb |

**42.** WRITING In Exercises 25–28, why does it help to compare each number to $\frac{1}{2}$ first? Will this step always work? *Explain.*

**43.** CHALLENGE Teams from California have played in the world championship game of the Little League World Series 20 times and won 5 times. Texas teams have appeared in 7 world championship games and won twice.

 **a.** Which state has won a greater fraction of their world championship games? What is the fraction?

 **b.** What is the *least* number of future wins the other state needs in order to have won a *greater* fraction of their games than the fraction in part (a)? *Explain.*

REVIEW
Lesson 4.3;
TAKS Workbook

**44.** TAKS PRACTICE Vikram's grandmother gave him $4 for lunch on Monday. On Tuesday, she gave him 1.5 times the amount she gave him on Monday. On Wednesday, she gave him $\frac{4}{3}$ of the amount she gave him on Tuesday. Which expression does NOT represent the amount of money he was given on Wednesday? *TAKS Obj. 6*

**A** $4(1.5)\left(\frac{4}{3}\right)$          **B** $1.5(4)\left(\frac{4}{3}\right)$

**C** $\frac{4}{3}(1.5)(4)$          **D** $4(1.5) + 4\left(\frac{4}{3}\right)$

# 4.6 Rules of Exponents

TEKS *8.16.A, 8.16.B*

| Before | You multiplied and divided numerical expressions. |
| Now | You'll multiply and divide expressions with exponents. |
| Why? | So you can represent large amounts, such as distance in Ex. 89. |

**KEY VOCABULARY**
- **exponent,** *p. 19*
- **power,** *p. 19*

## ACTIVITY

**Use patterns to discover rules for multiplying powers.**

**STEP 1** **Copy** and complete the table.

| Expression | Expanded Expression | Number of Factors | Product as a Power |
|---|---|---|---|
| $2^2 \cdot 2^4$ | $(2 \cdot 2) \cdot (2 \cdot 2 \cdot 2 \cdot 2)$ | 6 | $2^6$ |
| $3^3 \cdot 3^1$ | $(3 \cdot 3 \cdot 3) \cdot 3$ | ? | $3^?$ |
| $7^2 \cdot 7^3$ | ? | ? | ? |

**STEP 2** **Explain** how the exponents in the first and last columns are related.

**Write the product as a single power.**

1. $3^4 \cdot 3^3$     2. $6^5 \cdot 6^{11}$     3. $10^7 \cdot 10^{13}$

As you saw in the activity, you can expand expressions to find their product. The following equation suggests a rule for multiplying powers with the same base.

$$\overbrace{a^4}^{\text{4 factors}} \cdot \overbrace{a^2}^{\text{2 factors}} = \underbrace{(a \cdot a \cdot a \cdot a) \cdot (a \cdot a)}_{\text{6 factors}} = a^{4+2} = a^6$$

---

**KEY CONCEPT**                                      *For Your Notebook*

### Product of Powers Property

**Words**    To multiply powers with the same base, add their exponents.

**Algebra**   $a^m \cdot a^n = a^{m+n}$     **Numbers**   $5^6 \cdot 5^3 = 5^{6+3} = 5^9$

---

## EXAMPLE 1 Using the Product of Powers Property

 **Simplify** $x^4 \cdot x^7$.

$$x^4 \cdot x^7 = x^{4+7} \qquad \text{Product of powers property}$$
$$= x^{11} \qquad \text{Add exponents.}$$

✓ **GUIDED PRACTICE** for Example 1

**Simplify the expression. Write your answer as a power.**

**1.** $4^6 \cdot 4^4$      **2.** $9^8 \cdot 9$      **3.** $a^6 \cdot a^9$      **4.** $c \cdot c^{12} \cdot c^3$

## EXAMPLE 2 Using the Product of Powers Property

 **Simplify** $3^2 x^2 \cdot 3x^3$.

**AVOID ERRORS**
Remember that numbers raised to the first power are usually written without an exponent. For example, $3 = 3^1$.

$$3^2 x^2 \cdot 3x^3 = (3^2 \cdot 3) \cdot (x^2 \cdot x^3) \qquad \text{Use properties of multiplication.}$$
$$= 3^{2+1} \cdot x^{2+3} \qquad \text{Product of powers property}$$
$$= 3^3 x^5 \qquad \text{Add exponents.}$$
$$= 27x^5 \qquad \text{Evaluate the power.}$$

✓ **GUIDED PRACTICE** for Example 2

**Simplify the expression.**

**5.** $10^2 s^4 \cdot 10^4 s^2$    **6.** $6^3 t^5 \cdot 6^2 t^8$    **7.** $7x^2 \cdot 7x^4$    **8.** $5^2 z \cdot 5z^7 \cdot z^2$

**Dividing Powers** The following equation suggests a rule for dividing powers with the same base when the exponents are integers.

5 factors           2 factors

$$\frac{a^5}{a^3} = \frac{\overbrace{a \cdot a \cdot a \cdot a \cdot a}}{\underbrace{a \cdot a \cdot a}} = \frac{a \cdot a \cdot \overset{1}{\cancel{a}} \cdot \overset{1}{\cancel{a}} \cdot \overset{1}{\cancel{a}}}{\underset{1}{\cancel{a}} \cdot \underset{1}{\cancel{a}} \cdot \underset{1}{\cancel{a}}} = \overbrace{a \cdot a} = a^{5-3} = a^2$$

3 factors

---

### KEY CONCEPT          *For Your Notebook*

#### Quotient of Powers Property

**Words**    To divide two powers with the same nonzero base, subtract the exponent of the denominator from the exponent of the numerator.

**Algebra**   $\dfrac{a^m}{a^n} = a^{m-n}$      **Numbers**   $\dfrac{4^7}{4^4} = 4^{7-4} = 4^3$

**EXAMPLE 3** Using the Quotient of Powers Property

Simplify the expression. Write your answer as a power.

**a.** $\dfrac{x^{12}}{x^7} = x^{12-7}$      Quotient of powers property

        $= x^5$      Subtract exponents.

**b.** $\dfrac{9^7}{9^3} = 9^{7-3}$      Quotient of powers property

        $= 9^4$      Subtract exponents.

---

**EXAMPLE 4** Simplifying Fractions with Powers

Simplify the expression.

*AVOID ERRORS*

The bases of the powers must be the same to use the product or quotient property. In part (b) of Example 4, you cannot simplify the numerator any further because the bases, $x$ and $y$, are different.

**a.** $\dfrac{y^4 \cdot y}{y^3} = \dfrac{y^5}{y^3}$      Simplify numerator using product of powers property.

        $= y^{5-3}$      Quotient of powers property

        $= y^2$      Subtract exponents.

**b.** $\dfrac{xy^4}{y^3} = xy^{4-3}$      Quotient of powers property

        $= xy$      Subtract exponents.

---

✓ **GUIDED PRACTICE**    for Examples 3 and 4

Simplify the expression. Write your answer as a power.

**9.** $\dfrac{a^6}{a^4}$       **10.** $\dfrac{10^9}{10^6}$       **11.** $\dfrac{q^3 \cdot q^5}{q^4}$       **12.** $\dfrac{a^2 b^8}{b^2}$

---

# 4.6 EXERCISES

HOMEWORK KEY

 = **TAKS Practice and Reasoning**
Exs. 31, 54, 88, 90, 96, 97, and 98

◯ = **HINTS AND HOMEWORK HELP**
for Exs. 3, 17, 23, 33, 83 at classzone.com

## SKILL PRACTICE

**VOCABULARY** Copy and complete the statement.

**1.** Three is the __?__ of the power $3^4$.      **2.** Seven is the __?__ of the power $4^7$.

**SIMPLIFYING PRODUCTS** Simplify the product. Write your answer as a power.

*SEE EXAMPLE 1*
on p. 203
for Exs. 3–14

**3.** $4^2 \cdot 4^4$     **4.** $8 \cdot 8^3$     **5.** $a^5 \cdot a^7$     **6.** $b^9 \cdot b^9$

**7.** $u^7 \cdot u$     **8.** $v^2 \cdot v^{10}$     **9.** $b^9 \cdot b^6$     **10.** $m^{11} \cdot m^8$

**11.** $3^2 \cdot 3^5$     **12.** $7^2 \cdot 7^2$     **13.** $(-4)^2 \cdot (-4)^3$     **14.** $(-5)^4 \cdot (-5)$

SEE EXAMPLE 2
on p. 203
for Exs. 15–22

**XY SIMPLIFYING EXPRESSIONS** Simplify the product.

**15.** $3a^3 \cdot 3a^2$

**16.** $2y^3 \cdot 2y^2$

**17.** $3^2x^5 \cdot 3^3x^4$

**18.** $4a^3b^4 \cdot 4^2a^4b^6$

**19.** $5x^7 \cdot 5x^9$

**20.** $7^2b^3 \cdot 7^5b^8$

**21.** $6^2x^2y \cdot 6x^4y^3$

**22.** $10c^4 \cdot 10c^2$

**SIMPLIFYING QUOTIENTS** Simplify the quotient. Write your answer as a power.

SEE EXAMPLES
3 AND 4
on p. 204
for Exs. 23–39

**23.** $\dfrac{5^8}{5^4}$

**24.** $\dfrac{8^7}{8^2}$

**25.** $\dfrac{d^8}{d}$

**26.** $\dfrac{a^4}{a}$

**27.** $\dfrac{w^{15}}{w^9}$

**28.** $\dfrac{y^{20}}{y^{18}}$

**29.** $\dfrac{(-7)^7}{(-7)^4}$

**30.** $\dfrac{(-2)^{13}}{(-2)^3}$

**31.** ★ **TAKS REASONING** Which expression is equivalent to $\dfrac{a^9 \cdot a^6}{a^5}$?

(A) $a^3$ (B) $a^5$ (C) $a^{10}$ (D) $a^{15}$

**XY SIMPLIFYING EXPRESSIONS** Simplify the quotient.

**32.** $\dfrac{p^5q^9}{pq^5}$

**33.** $\dfrac{z^6 \cdot z^3}{z^4}$

**34.** $\dfrac{3^3m^9}{3^2m^5}$

**35.** $\dfrac{5^5n^{15}}{5^3n^{12}}$

**36.** $\dfrac{6^4k^5}{6k^3}$

**37.** $\dfrac{7^9r^{12}}{7^5r^8}$

**38.** $\dfrac{a^{11} \cdot b^7}{a^{10} \cdot b}$

**39.** $\dfrac{y^6 \cdot y^{13}}{y^9}$

**ERROR ANALYSIS** Describe and correct the error made in simplifying the expression.

SEE EXAMPLES
1 AND 4
on pp. 203–204
for Exs. 40–41

**40.**
$$2^2 \cdot 2^4 = (2 \cdot 2)^{2+4}$$
$$= 4^6$$

**41.**
$$\dfrac{x^{20}y^6}{x^5y^3} = x^4y^2$$

**XY ALGEBRA** Simplify the expression when $x = 2$, $y = 3$, and $z = 4$. Write your answer as a power.

**42.** $\dfrac{3^x \cdot 3^y}{3^z}$

**43.** $\dfrac{(-2)^{2z}}{(-2)^x}$

**44.** $\dfrac{(-6)^{2y}}{(-6)^z}$

**45.** $\dfrac{2^{2x}}{2^y}$

**46.** $\dfrac{5^x \cdot 5^z}{5^y}$

**47.** $\dfrac{(-3)^{3y}}{(-3)^z}$

**48.** $\dfrac{7^{3z}}{7^{2y}}$

**49.** $\dfrac{w^{x+y+z}}{w^{3y}}$

**50.** $\dfrac{64a^z}{4a^y}$

**51.** $\dfrac{-20b^{2y+z}}{5b^{3x}}$

**52.** $\dfrac{12m^{x+y}}{6m^{z-y}}$

**53.** $\dfrac{27n^{x+y}}{3n^x}$

**54.** ★ **TAKS REASONING** Write three variable expressions that simplify to $x^4y^4$. Write three variable expressions that simplify to $\dfrac{2b^3}{5a}$.

**NUMBER SENSE** Find the number that correctly completes the equation.

**55.** $2^3 \cdot 2^? = 2^{11}$

**56.** $5^4 \cdot ?^5 = 5^9$

**57.** $12^3 \cdot ?^{13} = 12^{16}$

**58.** $3^2 \cdot 3^? = 3^7$

**59.** $\dfrac{8^7}{8^?} = 8^3$

**60.** $\dfrac{7^4}{7^?} = 7$

**61.** $\dfrac{13^?}{13^9} = 13^2$

**62.** $9^3 \cdot 9^? = 9^{20}$

**63.** $\dfrac{6^{14}}{6^?} = 6^6$

**64.** $\dfrac{12^?}{12^5} = 12^4$

**65.** $4^? \cdot 4^7 = 4^{19}$

**66.** $\dfrac{11^3}{11^?} = 11^2$

**XY** **ALGEBRA** Write and solve an equation to find the value of $x$ that makes the statement true.

**67.** $4^{2x} \cdot 4^{x-3} = 4^{12}$    **68.** $5^{x-3} \cdot 5^{3x} = 5^{13}$    **69.** $8^{3x+4} \cdot 8^x = 8^{12}$    **70.** $2^{22} = 2^{2x-2} \cdot 2^{4x-6}$

**71.** $\dfrac{3^{2x-1}}{3^{x+4}} = 3^3$    **72.** $7^8 = \dfrac{7^{3x-2}}{7^x}$    **73.** $9^2 = \dfrac{9^{5x}}{9^{x+2}}$    **74.** $\dfrac{11^{6x+1}}{11^{3x-7}} = 11^{17}$

**EVALUATING EXPRESSIONS** Write the expression as a power and evaluate.

**75.** $(3^2 \cdot 3)^2$    **76.** $(2^3 \cdot 2^2)^3$    **77.** $\left(\dfrac{4^7}{4^5}\right)^2$    **78.** $\left(\dfrac{5^8}{5^7}\right)^4$

**XY** **CHALLENGE** Simplify the expression.

**79.** $4y^3 + \dfrac{6y^5}{2y^2} - 3y(y^2)$    **80.** $\dfrac{9s^4t^2}{3st} + \dfrac{6s^2t^5}{2t^2} - \dfrac{s^5t^2}{s^2t}$    **81.** $\dfrac{x^{n+1}}{x^n}$

## PROBLEM SOLVING

**METRIC UNITS** In Exercises 82–87, use the table. It shows the number of meters in some metric measures written as powers of ten. Write your answers as powers of 10.

**82.** How many decameters are in a yottameter?

**83.** How many kilometers are in a petameter?

**84.** How many gigameters are in a zettameter?

**85.** How many terameters are in a yottameter?

**86.** How many megameters are in an exameter?

**87.** How many petameters are in a zettameter?

| Metric Units | |
|---|---|
| **Unit** | **Meters** |
| yottameter | $10^{24}$ |
| zettameter | $10^{21}$ |
| exameter | $10^{18}$ |
| petameter | $10^{15}$ |
| terameter | $10^{12}$ |
| gigameter | $10^{9}$ |
| megameter | $10^{6}$ |
| kilometer | $10^{3}$ |
| decameter | $10^{1}$ |

**88.** ⬇ **TAKS REASONING** The product of 1 kilometer and which power of 10 yields 1 exameter? Use the table at the right.

   **A** $10^6$      **B** $10^9$

   **C** $10^{15}$     **D** $10^{18}$

**The historical standard platinum iridium meter bar**

**89.** **MULTI-STEP PROBLEM** The distance to the Andromeda Galaxy is 21 quintillion kilometers, which is 21 followed by 18 zeros. Refer to the table above to answer the questions.

   **a.** How many exameters are in 1 quintillion kilometers?

   **b.** Use your answer to part (a) to find the number of exameters in 21 quintillion kilometers.

   **c.** How many gigameters are in 1 exameter?

   **d.** Use your answers to parts (b) and (c) to find the number of gigameters in 21 quintillion kilometers.

90. ⚓ **TAKS REASONING** *Describe* two ways to evaluate the expression $\dfrac{6y^{10}}{3y^8}$ when $y = 5$. Evaluate the expression using both methods. Which method do you prefer? Why?

91. **WRITING** *Explain* why it is not necessary to multiply to evaluate powers of 10. Include an example with your answer.

92. **CHECKING REASONABLENESS** It takes you $5^2$ seconds to run $x$ feet. If your speed remains constant, is it reasonable to say that it will take you $5^3$ seconds to run $5x$ feet? *Justify* your answer.

93. **LAND AREA** A square field has sides of length $3^8$ millimeters. Find the area of the field. A larger field has side lengths 9 times those of the smaller field. How many times greater is the area of the large field? *Explain.*

94. **COMPUTERS** A friend tells you that his family first bought a computer in 1979. It had $2^3$ KB (kilobytes) of available memory.

    **a.** Your family's first computer was purchased in 1987 and had 64 times the amount of memory of your friend's. How much memory did your computer have? Express your answer as a power of 2.

    **b.** A typical computer purchased in 2005 had at least $2^9$ MB (megabytes) of memory. A MB is equal to $2^{10}$ KB. How many times the amount of the memory in your friend's 1979 computer is this? *Explain.*

95. **CHALLENGE** A number $x$ is $c$ followed by $b$ zeros. Another number $y$, which is smaller than $x$, is $d$ followed by $b$ zeros. How many times greater is $x$ than $y$? *Explain* your reasoning.

## MIXED REVIEW FOR TAKS

**TAKS** PRACTICE at classzone.com

REVIEW
Lesson 4.5;
TAKS Workbook

96. ⚓ **TAKS PRACTICE** What is the order of $\dfrac{23}{3}$, $7\dfrac{11}{18}$, and $\dfrac{70}{9}$ from least to greatest? *TAKS Obj. 1*

   **A** $\dfrac{23}{3}, 7\dfrac{11}{18}, \dfrac{70}{9}$    **B** $\dfrac{23}{3}, \dfrac{70}{9}, 7\dfrac{11}{18}$    **C** $7\dfrac{11}{18}, \dfrac{70}{9}, \dfrac{23}{3}$    **D** $7\dfrac{11}{18}, \dfrac{23}{3}, \dfrac{70}{9}$

REVIEW
Lesson 4.3;
TAKS Workbook

97. ⚓ **TAKS PRACTICE** A newspaper conducted a restaurant survey of 320 people. Of those surveyed, 60 of them preferred Chinese food, 40 preferred Indian food, 80 preferred Mexican food, and 140 preferred typical American fare such as steaks and hamburgers. Which statement is supported by the survey data? *TAKS Obj. 5*

   **F** Less than a quarter of those surveyed preferred either Chinese or Indian food.

   **G** More than half of those surveyed preferred American fare.

   **H** More than one quarter of those surveyed preferred Mexican food.

   **J** Less than one fifth of those surveyed preferred Chinese food.

REVIEW
Lesson 4.5;
TAKS Workbook

98. ⚓ **TAKS PRACTICE** Which fraction is between $\dfrac{2}{5}$ and $\dfrac{3}{7}$? *TAKS Obj. 1*

   **A** $\dfrac{1}{2}$      **B** $\dfrac{1}{3}$      **C** $\dfrac{6}{35}$      **D** $\dfrac{5}{12}$

**EXTRA PRACTICE** for Lesson 4.6, p. 804

⚙ **ONLINE QUIZ** at classzone.com

# 4.7 Negative and Zero Exponents

TEKS *8.1.B, 8.16.B*

| **Before** | You simplified expressions with positive exponents. |
| **Now** | You'll simplify expressions with negative exponents. |
| **Why?** | So you can describe very quick events, as the flash in Example 1. |

**KEY VOCABULARY**
- **exponent,** *p. 19*
- **common factor,** *p. 181*

You have seen two ways to evaluate expressions involving division of powers. Compare the results of the two methods when the denominator contains the greater power.

**Divide out common factors.**

$$\frac{x^5}{x^7} = \frac{\cancel{x}^1 \cdot \cancel{x}^1 \cdot \cancel{x}^1 \cdot \cancel{x}^1 \cdot \cancel{x}^1}{\cancel{x}_1 \cdot \cancel{x}_1 \cdot \cancel{x}_1 \cdot \cancel{x}_1 \cdot \cancel{x}_1 \cdot x \cdot x} = \frac{1}{x^2}$$

**Quotient of powers property**

$$\frac{x^5}{x^7} = x^{5-7} = x^{-2}$$

So $\frac{1}{x^2} = x^{-2}$. This suggests the following definition for negative exponents.

---

**KEY CONCEPT** *For Your Notebook*

### Negative Exponents

**Words** For any integer $n$ and any number $a \neq 0$, $a^{-n}$ is equal to $\frac{1}{a^n}$.

**Algebra** $a^{-n} = \frac{1}{a^n}$ **Numbers** $2^{-3} = \frac{1}{2^3}$

---

**EXAMPLE 1** Using a Negative Exponent

**Strobes** The picture of the golf ball was taken using a strobe light. Each flash of the strobe light lasted about 1 microsecond. How can you write this time in seconds as a power of ten?

**SOLUTION**

The flash lasts 1 microsecond. Because the prefix *micro* means one millionth of a unit, you know that 1 microsecond is equal to $\frac{1}{1,000,000}$ second.

$$\frac{1}{1,000,000} = \frac{1}{10^6} \qquad \text{Write 1,000,000 as } 10^6.$$

$$= 10^{-6} \qquad \text{Definition of negative exponent}$$

▶**Answer** One flash of the strobe light lasts about $10^{-6}$ second.

**EXAMPLE 2** Evaluating a Numerical Expression

**Evaluate the expression.**

$$5^2 \cdot 5^{-5} = 5^{2 + (-5)}$$  **Product of powers property**

$$= 5^{-3}$$  **Simplify.**

$$= \frac{1}{5^3}$$  **Definition of negative exponent**

$$= \frac{1}{125}$$  **Evaluate the power.**

---

**KEY CONCEPT**                          *For Your Notebook*

**Zero Exponents**

**Words**     For any number $a \neq 0$, $a^0$ is equal to 1.

**Algebra**   $a^0 = 1$                **Numbers**   $2^0 = 1$

---

**EXAMPLE 3** Simplifying Variable Expressions

**Simplify. Write the expression using only positive exponents.**

*AVOID ERRORS*

In expressions such as $-2n^0$ and $4n^{-5}$, the exponent is applied only to the variable, not to the coefficient. $-2n^0 \neq -2^0 \cdot n^0$

**a.** $-2n^0 = -2 \cdot n^0$     **Zero exponent applies only to *n*.**

$$= -2 \cdot 1$$     **Definition of zero exponent**

$$= -2$$     **Multiply.**

**b.** $\dfrac{8x^{-3}}{x} = \dfrac{8 \cdot x^{-3}}{x^1}$     **Exponent applies only to *x*.**

$$= 8 \cdot x^{-3 - 1}$$     **Quotient of powers property**

$$= 8 \cdot x^{-4}$$     **Simplify.**

$$= \dfrac{8}{x^4}$$     **Definition of negative exponent**

**Animated Math** at classzone.com

---

✓ **GUIDED PRACTICE**   for Examples 1, 2, and 3

1. **What If?** In Example 1, suppose the flash of a light lasted about one thousandth of a second. Write this time in seconds as a power of 10.

**Evaluate the expression.**

**2.** $7^{-2}$          **3.** $(-2)^{-5}$          **4.** $6 \cdot 6^{-3}$          **5.** $10^{-5} \cdot 10^5$

**Simplify. Write the expression using only positive exponents.**

**6.** $-6m^{-1}$     **7.** $b^2 \cdot b^{-2}$     **8.** $\dfrac{5x^4}{x^{-7}}$     **9.** $\dfrac{10a^{-3}}{a^4}$

# 4.7 EXERCISES

HOMEWORK KEY

🟫 = **TAKS Practice and Reasoning**
Exs. 20, 37, 43, and 46

⭕ = **HINTS AND HOMEWORK HELP**
for Exs. 3, 5, 13, 15, 39 at classzone.com

## SKILL PRACTICE

**VOCABULARY** Copy and complete the statement.

**1.** The power $x^0$ is equal to __?__.

**2.** The power $x^{-h}$ is equal to __?__.

**EVALUATING EXPRESSIONS** Evaluate the expression.

*SEE EXAMPLES*
*1 AND 2*
on pp. 208–209
for Exs. 3–11

**(3.)** $3^{-4}$

**4.** $12^0$

**(5.)** $-2^{-4}$

**6.** $(-4)^{-3}$

**7.** $(-6)^{-2} \cdot (-6)^0$

**8.** $-2 \cdot 2^{-6}$

**9.** $-5^4 \cdot 5^{-8}$

**10.** $9^0 \cdot 9^{-2}$

**11.** **ERROR ANALYSIS** Describe and correct the error made in evaluating $5^{-3}$.

$$\times \quad 5^{-3} = (-5)(-5)(-5)$$
$$= -125$$

**XV SIMPLIFYING EXPRESSIONS** Simplify. Write the expression using only positive exponents.

*SEE EXAMPLE 3*
on p. 209
for Exs. 12–20

**12.** $m^{-9} \cdot m^5$

**(13.)** $x^5 \cdot x^{-5}$

**14.** $9n^{-3}$

**(15.)** $c^{-1} \cdot c^{-2} \cdot c^{-4}$

**16.** $b^3 \cdot b^{-4} \cdot b^{-5}$

**17.** $\dfrac{4z^{-2}}{z^4}$

**18.** $\dfrac{a^{-5}}{a^8}$

**19.** $\dfrac{18r^{-6}}{3r^3}$

**20.** 🟫 **TAKS REASONING** Simplify the expression $\dfrac{-3x^{-4}}{x^2}$.

**A** $\dfrac{-3}{x^6}$

**B** $-3x^6$

**C** $\dfrac{-3}{x^{-6}}$

**D** $\dfrac{-3x}{x^6}$

**XV MENTAL MATH** Find the missing exponent.

**21.** $(4x^5)^? = 1$

**22.** $15a^? = \dfrac{15}{a^8}$

**23.** $y^? \cdot y^4 = \dfrac{1}{y}$

**24.** $\dfrac{x^{-3}}{x^?} = \dfrac{1}{x^{13}}$

**25.** $\dfrac{5x^?}{x^{-5}} = 5x^3$

**26.** $(2y^8)^? = 1$

**27.** $9b^? = \dfrac{9}{b^7}$

**28.** $a^6 \cdot a^? = \dfrac{1}{a^2}$

**REASONING** Copy and complete the statement using *always, sometimes,* or *never. Explain* your reasoning.

**29.** A power with an exponent of zero is __?__ positive.

**30.** A power with a positive base and a negative exponent is __?__ negative.

**31.** A power with a negative base and a positive exponent is __?__ positive.

**32.** A power with an integer base and a negative exponent can __?__ be written as a fraction.

**XV CHALLENGE** Simplify. Write the expression using only positive exponents.

**33.** $c^{-1} \cdot (b^2c)^{-2}$

**34.** $\dfrac{x^6 y^4}{(x^3 y^{-4})^{-2}}$

**35.** $(2t)^{-3} \cdot 4t^3 \cdot (4t^{-3})^0$

**SEE EXAMPLES 1 AND 3**
on pp. 208–209
for Exs. 36–37

**36.** **BIOLOGY** Phytoplankton are tiny plants that live in the ocean. One type has a length of about 0.2 micrometer. A micrometer is $10^{-6}$ meter. What part of a meter is this phytoplankton? Use a positive exponent to write your answer.

**37.** **TAKS REASONING** The time it takes a decaying radioactive substance to be reduced by half is known as its *half-life*. An equation to find the fraction $r$ of a substance remaining after $t$ half-lives is $r = 2^{-t}$. What fraction of the substance remains after 4 half-lives? After how many half-lives does $\frac{1}{64}$ of the original amount remain? *Explain*.

**Single-celled alga**

**38.** **PHYSICS** Pressure is measured in *pascals*. This unit can be expressed as $\text{kg} \cdot \text{m}^{-1} \cdot \text{s}^{-2}$. Write the unit without negative exponents.

**MEASUREMENT** **In Exercises 39–42, use the table. It shows the number of meters in some metric measures written as powers of ten.**

**39.** How many picometers are in a decimeter?

**40.** How many yoctometers are in a picometer?

**41.** How many nanometers are in a decimeter?

**42.** How many attometers are in a centimeter?

| Unit | Meter |
|---|---|
| decimeter | $10^{-1}$ |
| centimeter | $10^{-2}$ |
| nanometer | $10^{-9}$ |
| picometer | $10^{-12}$ |
| attometer | $10^{-18}$ |
| yoctometer | $10^{-24}$ |

**43.** **TAKS REASONING** What is the area of a rectangle with a length of $2^3$ meters and a width of $4^{-2}$ meters?

**(A)** $\frac{1}{2}\,\text{m}^2$ **(B)** $2\,\text{m}^2$ **(C)** $4\,\text{m}^2$ **(D)** $128\,\text{m}^2$

**44.** **MULTIPLE REPRESENTATIONS** The expanded form of 389.602 is

$$3 \times 100 + 8 \times 10 + 9 \times 1 + 6 \times 0.1 + 2 \times 0.001.$$

Write this expanded form using positive or zero powers of 10 and then using positive, negative, or zero powers of 10.

**45.** **CHALLENGE** Use the product of powers property to show why $a^0 = 1$, when $a$ is a nonzero number.

**MIXED REVIEW FOR TAKS** **TAKS** **PRACTICE** at classzone.com

**REVIEW**
Lesson 3.4;
TAKS Workbook

**46.** **TAKS PRACTICE** Herbert has a collection of four coins. He adds three new coins to his collection every year. Which equation can be used to find the number of years, $y$, it will take for Herbert's collection to have three times as many coins as those he started with? *TAKS Obj. 2*

**(A)** $y + 4 = 4$ **(B)** $y + 4 = 12$

**(C)** $3y + 4 = 12$ **(D)** $4y + 3 = 12$

# 4.8 Scientific Notation

TEKS 8.1.B, 8.1.D

**Before** You multiplied numbers by powers of 10.

**Now** You'll read and write numbers using scientific notation.

**Why?** So you can express small measurements, as bubbles in Example 2.

**KEY VOCABULARY**
• scientific notation, p. 212

One way to write very small numbers like the thickness of a soap bubble or very large numbers like the number of stars in the galaxy is to use powers of ten. This can be done by writing numbers using *scientific notation*.

---

### KEY CONCEPT
*For Your Notebook*

#### Using Scientific Notation

A number is written in **scientific notation** if it has the form $c \times 10^n$ where $c \geq 1$, $c < 10$, and $n$ is an integer.

| Standard form | Product form | Scientific notation |
|---|---|---|
| 325,000 | $3.25 \times 100,000$ | $3.25 \times 10^5$ |
| 0.0005 | $5 \times 0.0001$ | $5 \times 10^{-4}$ |

---

### EXAMPLE 1  Writing Numbers in Scientific Notation

**POWERS OF 10**
$10^5 = 100,000$
$10^4 = 10,000$
$10^3 = 1000$
$10^2 = 100$
$10^1 = 10$
$10^0 = 1$
$10^{-1} = 0.1$
$10^{-2} = 0.01$
$10^{-3} = 0.001$
$10^{-4} = 0.0001$
$10^{-5} = 0.00001$

**Stars** There are over 300,000,000,000 stars in the Andromeda Galaxy. Write the number of stars in scientific notation.

**SOLUTION**

| Standard form | Product form | Scientific notation |
|---|---|---|
| 300,000,000,000 | $3 \times 100,000,000,000$ | $3 \times 10^{11}$ |

Move decimal point 11 places to the left.        Exponent is 11.

▶ **Answer** The number in scientific notation is $3 \times 10^{11}$.

---

✓ **GUIDED PRACTICE**  for Example 1

**Write the number in scientific notation.**

1. 4000
2. 7,300,000
3. 63,000,000,000
4. 230,000
5. 2,420,000
6. 105

**EXAMPLE 2** TAKS PRACTICE: Multiple Choice

**Bubbles** The thickness of a soap bubble is about 0.0004 centimeter. What is the thickness of a soap bubble written in scientific notation?

(A) $4 \times 10^{-3}$ cm      (B) $4 \times 10^{-4}$ cm

(C) $4 \times 10^{-5}$ cm      (D) $40 \times 10^{5}$ cm

*ELIMINATE CHOICES*
A correct answer must be in the form $c \times 10^{n}$ where the greatest place value for $c$ is the ones place. Choice D is not in this form, so it can be eliminated.

**SOLUTION**

| Standard form | Product form | Scientific notation |
|---|---|---|
| 0.0004 | $4 \times 0.0001$ | $4 \times 10^{-4}$ |
| Move decimal point 4 places to the right. | | Exponent is $-4$. |

▶ **Answer** The thickness of the bubble is $4 \times 10^{-4}$ meter. The correct answer is B. (A) (B) (C) (D)

✓ **GUIDED PRACTICE** for Example 2

**Write the number in scientific notation.**

**7.** 0.00475          **8.** 0.00000526          **9.** 0.0000000082

**10.** 0.0237          **11.** 0.000097          **12.** 0.0003141

**Standard Form** A number in scientific notation can be written in standard form by using the exponent. Move the decimal point the appropriate number of places left or right, depending on the sign of the exponent.

**EXAMPLE 3** Writing Numbers in Standard Form

| | Scientific notation | Product form | Standard form |
|---|---|---|---|
| **a.** | $7.2 \times 10^{5}$ | $7.2 \times 100,000$ | 720,000 |
| | Exponent is 5. | | Move decimal point 5 places to the right. |
| **b.** | $4.65 \times 10^{-7}$ | $4.65 \times 0.0000001$ | 0.000000465 |
| | Exponent is $-7$. | | Move decimal point 7 places to the left. |

✓ **GUIDED PRACTICE** for Example 3

**Write the number in standard form.**

**13.** $3.5 \times 10^{3}$     **14.** $2.48 \times 10^{6}$     **15.** $5.1 \times 10^{-4}$     **16.** $9.16 \times 10^{-2}$

**Products in Scientific Notation** You can use the product of powers property to multiply two numbers written in scientific notation.

---

**EXAMPLE 4** Multiplying Numbers in Scientific Notation

**Find the product $(4.5 \times 10^3) \times (6.3 \times 10^7)$.**

$(4.5 \times 10^3) \times (6.3 \times 10^7)$

$= 4.5 \times 6.3 \times 10^3 \times 10^7$      **Commutative property of multiplication**

$= (4.5 \times 6.3) \times (10^3 \times 10^7)$     **Associative property of multiplication**

$= 28.35 \times 10^{10}$     **Product of powers property**

$= 2.835 \times 10^1 \times 10^{10}$     **Write 28.35 in scientific notation.**

$= 2.835 \times 10^{11}$     **Product of powers property**

*AVOID ERRORS*
Make sure the product is written in proper scientific notation. The number $28.35 \times 10^{10}$ is not written in scientific notation because $28.35 \geq 10$.

---

✓ **GUIDED PRACTICE**    for Example 4

**Write the product in scientific notation.**

**17.** $(1.25 \times 10^6) \times (7.6 \times 10^{12})$        **18.** $(8 \times 10^5) \times (5.65 \times 10^4)$

---

# 4.8 EXERCISES

 = **TAKS Practice and Reasoning**
Exs. 13, 46, 49, 51, 59, 60, and 61

○ = **HINTS AND HOMEWORK HELP**
for Exs. 5, 7, 15, 17, 23, 47 at classzone.com

## SKILL PRACTICE

**VOCABULARY** Tell whether the number is expressed in scientific notation. *Explain* why or why not.

**1.** $9.32 \times 10^5$      **2.** $56.8 \times 10^2$      **3.** $7 \times 10^{-4}$

**SCIENTIFIC NOTATION** Write the number in scientific notation.

*SEE EXAMPLES 1 AND 2*
on pp. 212–213
for Exs. 4–13

**4.** 7900      **5.** 0.468      **6.** 0.0000671

**7.** 89,200,000,000      **8.** 8,100,000,000      **9.** 2,130,000

**10.** 0.0312      **11.** 0.000000415      **12.** 0.0000000342

**13.**  **TAKS REASONING** What is 0.000000765 written in scientific notation?

  **(A)** $7.65 \times 10^{-9}$    **(B)** $76.5 \times 10^{-8}$    **(C)** $7.65 \times 10^{-7}$    **(D)** $7.65 \times 10^{-6}$

**STANDARD FORM** Write the number in standard form.

*SEE EXAMPLE 3*
on p. 213
for Exs. 14–22

**14.** $5.72 \times 10^{-3}$      **15.** $4.35 \times 10^6$      **16.** $9.62 \times 10^7$

**17.** $8.71 \times 10^{-2}$      **18.** $6.35 \times 10^{-6}$      **19.** $1.76 \times 10^{-9}$

**20.** $4.13 \times 10^9$      **21.** $2.83 \times 10^{12}$      **22.** $3.61 \times 10^7$

**MULTIPLYING** Write the product in scientific notation.

**SEE EXAMPLE 4**
on p. 214
for Exs. 23–31

**23.** $(3 \times 10^3) \times (2 \times 10^5)$

**24.** $(2 \times 10^{-6}) \times (4 \times 10^{-4})$

**25.** $(1.5 \times 10^{-2}) \times (3.9 \times 10^{-5})$

**26.** $(3.6 \times 10^8) \times (2.4 \times 10^5)$

**27.** $(7.8 \times 10^6) \times (8.4 \times 10^7)$

**28.** $(7.6 \times 10^{-8}) \times (4.8 \times 10^{-6})$

**29.** $(2.6 \times 10^7) \times (4.1 \times 10^{-3})$

**30.** $(5.4 \times 10^5) \times (3.6 \times 10^{-9})$

**31. ERROR ANALYSIS** Describe and correct the error made in writing the product in scientific notation.

$$\begin{aligned}
(3 \times 10^2) \times (6.2 \times 10^3) \\
= (3 \times 6.2) \times (10^2 \times 10^3) \\
= 18.6 \times 10^6
\end{aligned}$$

**COMPARING** Copy and complete the statement with <, >, or =.

**32.** $6.92 \times 10^{11}$ ? $6.92 \times 10^{12}$

**33.** $1.06 \times 10^6$ ? $9.98 \times 10^5$

**34.** $3.67 \times 10^{-3}$ ? $3.76 \times 10^{-4}$

**35.** $3.4 \times 10^{-20}$ ? $4.1 \times 10^{-21}$

**DIVIDING** Find the quotient. Write your answer in scientific notation.

**36.** $\dfrac{4.08 \times 10^6}{3.4 \times 10^2}$

**37.** $\dfrac{2.765 \times 10^{21}}{7.9 \times 10^9}$

**38.** $\dfrac{5.46 \times 10^{28}}{6.5 \times 10^{24}}$

**39.** $\dfrac{2.015 \times 10^7}{6.2 \times 10^3}$

**40. ORDERING** Order the numbers from least to greatest.

$3.75 \times 10^8$ $\qquad$ $37{,}500{,}000$ $\qquad$ $3.57 \times 10^9$ $\qquad$ $5.37 \times 10^7$

**CHALLENGE** Find the sum or difference. Write your answer in scientific notation.

**41.** $(3.2 \times 10^5) + (8.1 \times 10^3)$

**42.** $(5 \times 10^{-1}) + (9.8 \times 10^{-3})$

**43.** $(4.1 \times 10^8) - (7.7 \times 10^6)$

**44.** $(6.4 \times 10^4) - (5.9 \times 10^{-2})$

## PROBLEM SOLVING

**45. GUIDED PROBLEM SOLVING** The mass of Earth is about $1.3 \times 10^{25}$ pounds. The mass of Jupiter is about $4.2 \times 10^{27}$ pounds. About how many times Earth's mass is Jupiter's mass?

  **a.** Write the quotient of 4.2 and 1.3 as a decimal rounded to the nearest tenth.

  **b.** Write the quotient of $10^{27}$ and $10^{25}$.

  **c.** Write the product of the quotients from parts (a) and (b) in scientific notation.

**SEE EXAMPLE 1**
on p. 212
for Exs. 46–47

**46. ◆ TAKS REASONING** In 2000, there were approximately 281,000,000 people in the United States. Which of the following is *not* another way of expressing the number 281,000,000?

  **(A)** 28.1 million   **(B)** 0.281 billion   **(C)** $28.1 \times 10^7$   **(D)** $2.81 \times 10^8$

**47.** **WELL WATER** In the United States, 15,000,000 households use private wells for their water supply. Write this number in scientific notation.

*SEE EXAMPLE 3*
on p. 213
for Ex. 48

**48.** **STATE PARKS** The United States has a total of $1.2916 \times 10^7$ acres of land reserved for state parks. Write this number in standard form.

**49.** ⬥ **TAKS REASONING** The masses of an oxygen atom and a hydrogen atom are shown below. Write these numbers in standard form. Which atom has a greater mass? Approximately how many times greater? *Explain.*

**Oxygen**

mass $\approx 2.6561 \times 10^{-23}$ g

**Hydrogen**

mass $\approx 1.6735 \times 10^{-24}$ g

**50.** **SCIENCE** The radius of a proton is about 1.2 Fermis. One *Fermi* is equal to $10^{-15}$ meter. How many centimeters is the radius of a proton? Write your answer in scientific notation.

**51.** ⬥ **TAKS REASONING** A space probe travels about $1.5 \times 10^6$ kilometers per day to its destination 21 million kilometers away. After traveling 9 million kilometers, about how many days of travel remain? *Explain.*

**52.** **WRITING** *Explain* how to compare numbers written in scientific notation.

---

**READING *IN* MATH** Read the information below for Exercises 53–56.

**U.S. Currency Facts** The United States Bureau of Engraving and Printing is responsible for printing new money. In 2004, the Bureau printed about 23.9 million bills daily for a face value of about $351 million. More than half of these were $1 and $5 bills. About 11.4 million were $1 bills and about 1.72 million were $5 bills. The average life of a bill depends on its denomination. A $1 bill lasts an average of about 22 months, while a $100 bill lasts an average of 8.5 years.

**53.** **Calculate** About how many $1 bills were printed in one week during 2004? one year? Write your answers in scientific notation.

**54.** **Calculate** About how many $5 bills were printed in one week during 2004? one year? Write your answers in scientific notation.

**55.** **Compare** What is the total value of the number of $5 bills that were printed each day? each week? each year? Write your answers in standard form.

**56.** **Compare** What is greater, the value of the $5 bills printed in 2004 or the value of the $1 bills? How much greater? Write your answer in standard form.

**57. CHALLENGE** Light travels approximately $1.86 \times 10^5$ miles in 1 second. About how far does light travel in one year? Write your answer in scientific notation.

**58. CHALLENGE** It takes about 8.3 minutes for sunlight to reach the Earth. Find the approximate distance, in miles, from the Earth to the sun. Use the speed of light given in Exercise 57. Write your answer in standard form.

## MIXED REVIEW FOR TAKS

**TAKS PRACTICE** at classzone.com

*REVIEW*
Lesson 3.5;
TAKS Workbook

**59. TAKS PRACTICE** An engineer designs a triangular pool that has a triangular floor with an area of 200 square feet and a height of 20 feet. What is the length of the base of the pool floor? *TAKS Obj. 3*

(A) 5 ft      (B) 10 ft      (C) 20 ft      (D) 40 ft

*REVIEW*
Lesson 4.5;
TAKS Workbook

**60. TAKS PRACTICE** Which fraction is between $\frac{1}{3}$ and $\frac{1}{2}$? *TAKS Obj. 1*

(F) $\frac{1}{4}$      (G) $\frac{2}{5}$      (H) $\frac{2}{3}$      (J) $\frac{4}{7}$

*REVIEW*
Lesson 4.4;
TAKS Workbook

**61. TAKS PRACTICE** A car stops every 300 minutes for gasoline. Another car stops every 225 minutes for gasoline or food. If both cars just stopped at the same time, which procedure can be used to find the next time both cars will stop at the same time again? *TAKS Obj. 6*

(A) Multiply 225 by 300.

(B) Find the greatest common prime factor of 225 and 300.

(C) Find the least common multiple of 225 and 300.

(D) Find the greatest common factor of 225 and 300.

## QUIZ *for Lessons 4.5–4.8*

**Copy and complete the statement with <, >, or =.** *(p. 198)*

**1.** $\frac{2}{5} \underline{\ ?\ } \frac{6}{15}$      **2.** $\frac{5}{6} \underline{\ ?\ } \frac{4}{9}$      **3.** $\frac{99}{15} \underline{\ ?\ } 6\frac{5}{9}$      **4.** $4\frac{35}{40} \underline{\ ?\ } 4\frac{21}{24}$

**Order the numbers from least to greatest.** *(p. 198)*

**5.** $\frac{2}{3}, \frac{5}{6}, \frac{1}{2}, \frac{5}{12}$      **6.** $\frac{3}{5}, \frac{7}{10}, \frac{3}{4}, \frac{7}{8}$      **7.** $1\frac{4}{7}, 1\frac{5}{14}, \frac{5}{4}, 1\frac{5}{8}$      **8.** $4\frac{8}{9}, 4\frac{17}{18}, \frac{65}{14}, 4\frac{6}{7}$

**Multiply or divide. Write your answer as a power using only positive exponents.**

**9.** $b^2 \cdot b^4$ *(p. 202)*      **10.** $c^5 \cdot c^{-2}$ *(p. 208)*      **11.** $\dfrac{a^7}{a^2}$ *(p. 202)*      **12.** $\dfrac{n^{-2}}{n^3}$ *(p. 208)*

**13. POPCORN** People in the United States eat approximately 1,120,000,000 pounds of popcorn a year. Write this number in scientific notation. *(p. 212)*

**TEKS** *8.1.D, 8.14.D*

# 4.8 Using Scientific Notation

**EXAMPLE** The Sun is about $1.5 \times 10^8$ kilometers from Earth, and Proxima Centauri is about $2.5 \times 10^5$ times farther from Earth than the Sun. How far is Proxima Centauri from Earth?

**SOLUTION**

To find how far Proxima Centauri is from Earth, multiply the distance between the Sun and Earth by $2.5 \times 10^5$.

**Keystrokes**

1.5 [EE] 8 [×] 2.5 [EE] 5 [=]

**Display**

$3.75 \times 10^{13}$

The [EE] key on a calculator means "times 10 raised to the power of."

▶ **Answer** Proxima Centauri is approximately $3.75 \times 10^{13}$ kilometers from Earth.

**PRACTICE** Use a calculator to evaluate the expression. Write your answer in scientific notation.

**1.** $(3.19 \times 10^7) \times (8.5 \times 10^6)$

**2.** $(6.7 \times 10^{-3}) \times (1.12 \times 10^{15})$

**3.** $(3.3 \times 10^{-3}) \times (4.8 \times 10^{-9})$

**4.** $(7.1 \times 10^{-9}) \times (2.05 \times 10^6)$

**5.** $\dfrac{1.681 \times 10^{10}}{2.05 \times 10^3}$

**6.** $\dfrac{1.44 \times 10^{-15}}{1.2 \times 10}$

**7.** $\dfrac{8.241 \times 10^{-11}}{2.05 \times 10^{-4}}$

**8.** $\dfrac{6.25 \times 10^{-8}}{1.25 \times 10^{-12}}$

**9.** $\dfrac{1.26 \times 10^9}{2.8 \times 10^2}$

**10.** $\dfrac{2.64 \times 10^{-8}}{2.2 \times 10^{-13}}$

**11.** $\dfrac{2.59 \times 10^{-6}}{1.85 \times 10^3}$

**12.** $\dfrac{3 \times 10^{16}}{3.75 \times 10^{-16}}$

**13.** **WATER** About 110 billion gallons of water flow through Lake Erie each day. How many gallons of water flow through Lake Erie in a week? in a year? Write your answers in scientific notation.

**14.** **BIOLOGY** The nucleus of a human cell is about $7 \times 10^{-6}$ meter in diameter. A ribosome, another part of a cell, is about $3 \times 10^{-8}$ meter in diameter. Approximately how many times larger is a nucleus than a ribosome?

## Lessons 4.5–4.8

**MULTIPLE CHOICE**

1. **VOLUME** The formula for the volume of a cube is given by $V = s^3$, where $s$ is the side length. The side lengths of two cubes are listed below.

   **Cube A:** $s = 2$ meters

   **Cube B:** $s = 2^2$ meters

   How many times greater is the volume of cube B than cube A? *TEKS 8.10.B*

   Ⓐ 2 times     Ⓑ 4 times

   Ⓒ 5 times     Ⓓ 8 times

2. **LAND AREA** The table shows the approximate land areas in square kilometers of several countries.

   | Country | Area (km²) |
   |---|---|
   | Antarctica | 14,000,000 |
   | Canada | $10 \times 10^6$ |
   | Egypt | 1,000,000 |
   | India | $0.33 \times 10^7$ |
   | Russia | $1.7 \times 10^7$ |
   | United States | 9,600,000 |

   Which country has the least land area? *TEKS 8.1.A*

   Ⓕ Russia     Ⓖ Canada

   Ⓗ Egypt     Ⓙ India

3. **ASTRONOMY** A light-year is equal to $9.5 \times 10^{12}$ kilometers. The Andromeda galaxy is approximately 2.3 million light-years away. How far is this in kilometers? *TEKS 8.1.D*

   Ⓐ $2.185 \times 10^{12}$ km

   Ⓑ $2.185 \times 10^{13}$ km

   Ⓒ $2.185 \times 10^{18}$ km

   Ⓓ $2.185 \times 10^{19}$ km

4. **BASKETBALL** The table shows the number of baskets Hope made and the number of baskets she attempted in five basketball games.

   | Game | 1 | 2 | 3 | 4 | 5 |
   |---|---|---|---|---|---|
   | Baskets made | 10 | 9 | 6 | 15 | 9 |
   | Attempts | 22 | 12 | 18 | 25 | 18 |

   In which game did Hope make the greatest fraction of her baskets? *TEKS 8.1.A*

   Ⓕ Game 1     Ⓖ Game 2

   Ⓗ Game 4     Ⓙ Game 5

5. **TEDDY BEAR** In 1997, German teddy bear specialist Hanne Schramm made one of the smallest teddy bears in the world. It measures 0.47 inch, or about 12 millimeters long. A nanometer is $10^{-6}$ millimeter. How many nanometers long is the bear? *TEKS 8.1.D*

   Ⓐ $1.2 \times 10^{-7}$ nm

   Ⓑ $1.2 \times 10^{-6}$ nm

   Ⓒ $1.2 \times 10^6$ nm

   Ⓓ $1.2 \times 10^7$ nm

**GRIDDED ANSWER** ⊙①②③④⑤⑥⑦⑧⑨

6. **LAOS** Niyana keeps a wallet-sized photo of her grandfather, who lives in Savannakhet, Laos. The photo is about $6.3 \times 10^{-2}$ meters wide. How many centimeters wide is Niyana's photo? Write your answer in standard form. *TEKS 8.1.B*

## REVIEW KEY VOCABULARY

- prime number, *p. 177*
- composite number, *p. 177*
- prime factorization, *p. 177*
- factor tree, *p. 177*
- monomial, *p. 178*
- common factor, *p. 181*

- greatest common factor (GCF), *p. 181*
- relatively prime, *p. 182*
- simplest form, *p. 187*
- equivalent fractions, *p. 187*
- multiple, *p. 192*

- common multiple, *p. 192*
- least common multiple (LCM), *p. 192*
- least common denominator (LCD), *p. 198*
- scientific notation, *p. 212*

### VOCABULARY EXERCISES

1. Describe the difference between the *greatest common factor* and the *least common multiple* of two numbers.

2. Give three examples of prime numbers greater than 20.

3. Give three examples of monomials.

4. Describe what it means for two numbers to be relatively prime.

**Copy and complete the statement.**

5. A fraction is in __?__ if its numerator and denominator have 1 as their GCF.

6. A(n) __?__ is a whole number that has positive factors other than 1 and itself.

7. Two fractions are __?__ if they represent the same number.

## REVIEW EXAMPLES AND EXERCISES

### 4.1 Factors and Prime Factorization

*pp. 176–180*

**EXAMPLE**

**Write the prime factorization of 504.**

$$504$$
$$8 \cdot 63$$
$$2 \cdot 4 \cdot 9 \cdot 7$$
$$2 \cdot 2 \cdot 2 \cdot 3 \cdot 3 \cdot 7$$

$504 = 2 \cdot 2 \cdot 2 \cdot 3 \cdot 3 \cdot 7$, or $2^3 \cdot 3^2 \cdot 7$

▶ **Answer** The prime factorization of 504 is $2^3 \cdot 3^2 \cdot 7$.

## EXERCISES

**Tell whether the number is *prime* or *composite*.**

SEE EXAMPLES
2, 3, AND 4

on pp. 177–178
for Exs. 8–20

**8.** 24 **9.** 91 **10.** 53 **11.** 197

**Write the prime factorization of the number.**

**12.** 40 **13.** 7 **14.** 85 **15.** 120

**Factor the monomial.**

**16.** $19a^2b$ **17.** $28xy^3$ **18.** $56u^2v^2$ **19.** $80p^4q^3$

**20. Planting Trees** A conservation group wants to plant 48 trees in a rectangular arrangement so that each row has the same number of trees. How many trees can be planted in each row? List all possibilities.

---

## 4.2 Greatest Common Factor

pp. 181–185

**EXAMPLE**

**Find the GCF of 36 and 60.**

Begin by writing the prime factorization of each number. Look for the common prime factors.

$$36 = 2 \times 2 \times 3 \times 3 \qquad 60 = 2 \times 2 \times 3 \times 5$$

The common prime factors are 2, 2, and 3. The GCF of 36 and 60 is the product of these factors. $2 \cdot 2 \cdot 3 = 12$.

▶ **Answer** The GCF of 36 and 60 is 12.

## EXERCISES

**Find the GCF of the numbers or monomials.**

SEE EXAMPLES
1, 2, 3, AND 4

on pp. 181–183
for Exs. 21–33

**21.** 48, 80 **22.** 60, 100 **23.** $14a^3, 21a$ **24.** $20y^4, 60y^5$

**25.** 20, 40, 90 **26.** 48, 60, 165 **27.** $2x, x^2, x^3$ **28.** $54s^4t^4, 164st^3$

**Determine whether the numbers are relatively prime.**

**29.** 11, 15 **30.** 92, 115 **31.** 72, 176 **32.** 30, 91

**33. Food Baskets** Your class is making Thanksgiving baskets for a food bank. You have 60 cans of cranberry sauce, 120 cans of fruit, 90 cans of corn, and 60 boxes of muffin mix. You want every basket to be the same with no leftover items. What is the greatest number of baskets you can assemble? What will each basket contain?

## 4.3 Simplifying Fractions

pp. 187–191

**EXAMPLE**

Write $\frac{48}{72}$ in simplest form.

Write the prime factorization of each number.

$48 = 2 \cdot 2 \cdot 2 \cdot 2 \cdot 3$
$72 = 2 \cdot 2 \cdot 2 \cdot 3 \cdot 3$

The GCF of 48 and 72 is $2 \cdot 2 \cdot 2 \cdot 3 = 24$.

$\frac{48}{72} = \frac{48 \div 24}{72 \div 24}$      **Divide numerator and denominator by GCF.**

$= \frac{2}{3}$      **Simplify.**

### EXERCISES

**SEE EXAMPLES
1 AND 4**
on pp. 187, 189
for Exs. 34–37

**Write the fraction in simplest form.**

**34.** $\frac{15}{45}$      **35.** $\frac{12}{80}$      **36.** $\frac{9ab}{27a}$      **37.** $\frac{18n^3}{54n}$

## 4.4 Least Common Multiple

pp. 192–196

**EXAMPLE**

Find the LCM of 20 and 48.

**STEP 1** **Write** the prime factorization of each number and circle the greatest power of each prime factor.

$20 = 2^2 \cdot \boxed{5}$          $48 = \boxed{2^4} \cdot \boxed{3}$

**STEP 2** **Find** the product of the circled numbers.

$2^4 \cdot 3 \cdot 5 = 240$

▶ **Answer** The LCM of 20 and 48 is 240.

### EXERCISES

**Find the LCM of the numbers or monomials.**

**SEE EXAMPLES
1 AND 3**
on pp. 192–193
for Exs. 38–42

**38.** 28, 42      **39.** 54, 90      **40.** $10cd, 25c^2$      **41.** $9n^3, 12n^2$

**42. Fitness** Yolanda has a yoga class every 4 days and a pilates class every 3 days. If she has both classes today, in how many days will both classes be on the same day again?

## 4.5 Comparing Fractions and Mixed Numbers

pp. 198–201

### EXAMPLE

Compare $\frac{11}{18}$ and $\frac{3}{4}$.

The LCM of 18 and 4 is 36, so the least common denominator is 36. Write each fraction using the LCD.

$$\frac{11}{18} = \frac{11 \cdot 2}{18 \cdot 2} = \frac{22}{36} \qquad\qquad \frac{3}{4} = \frac{3 \cdot 9}{4 \cdot 9} = \frac{27}{36}$$

▶ **Answer** Because $\frac{22}{36} < \frac{27}{36}$, you can write $\frac{11}{18} < \frac{3}{4}$.

### EXERCISES

Copy and complete the statement with <, >, or =.

*SEE EXAMPLES 1, 2, AND 3*
on pp. 198–199
for Exs. 43–51

**43.** $\frac{79}{16} \; \underline{?} \; \frac{35}{8}$

**44.** $6\frac{2}{3} \; \underline{?} \; \frac{81}{12}$

**45.** $\frac{161}{9} \; \underline{?} \; 17\frac{8}{9}$

**46.** $\frac{223}{15} \; \underline{?} \; 14\frac{4}{5}$

Order the numbers from least to greatest.

**47.** $\frac{7}{11}, \frac{2}{3}, \frac{5}{8}$

**48.** $9\frac{1}{2}, \frac{29}{3}, \frac{37}{4}$

**49.** $5\frac{7}{8}, \frac{53}{9}, \frac{17}{3}$

**50.** $\frac{25}{6}, \frac{49}{12}, 4\frac{1}{10}$

**51. Gardening** Joe picked $4\frac{7}{8}$ cups of green beans and Sarah picked $\frac{29}{6}$ cups. Who picked more beans? How many cups more?

## 4.6 Rules of Exponents

pp. 202–207

### EXAMPLE

Multiply or divide. Write your answer as a power.

**a.** $x^7 \cdot x^8 = x^{7+8}$
$$= x^{15}$$

**b.** $\dfrac{a^6}{a^3} = a^{6-3}$
$$= a^3$$

### EXERCISES

Simplify the expression. Write your answer as a power.

*SEE EXAMPLES 1, 2, 3, AND 4*
on pp. 203–204
for Exs. 52–63

**52.** $n^4 \cdot n^9$

**53.** $9^6 \cdot 9^3$

**54.** $5^4 \cdot 5^7$

**55.** $a^{12} \cdot a^{11}$

**56.** $\dfrac{x^7}{x^5}$

**57.** $\dfrac{5^{10}}{5^7}$

**58.** $\dfrac{11^9}{11^3}$

**59.** $\dfrac{b^{15}}{b^8}$

**60.** $\dfrac{x^5 \cdot x^4}{x^8}$

**61.** $\dfrac{y^{20}}{y^3 \cdot y^9}$

**62.** $\dfrac{2^5 \cdot x^7}{2^3 \cdot x}$

**63.** $\dfrac{y^6 \cdot x^{12}}{y^4 \cdot x^9}$

## 4.7 Negative and Zero Exponents
pp. 208–211

**EXAMPLE**

Write $x^{-4} \cdot x^{-3}$ using only positive exponents.

$$x^{-4} \cdot x^{-3} = x^{-4 + (-3)}$$
$$= x^{-7}$$
$$= \frac{1}{x^7}$$

**EXERCISES**

Simplify. Write the expression using only positive exponents.

SEE EXAMPLES 2 AND 3
on p. 209
for Exs. 64–71

**64.** $12a^{-5} \cdot a^0$

**65.** $n^7 \cdot n^{-10}$

**66.** $\dfrac{m^{-6}}{m^5}$

**67.** $\dfrac{18c^{-9}}{6c^4}$

**68.** $b^5 \cdot b^2$

**69.** $\dfrac{9z^{-4}}{6z^{-2}}$

**70.** $\dfrac{8y^5}{12y^{-11}}$

**71.** $5x^3 \cdot 4x^{-3}$

## 4.8 Scientific Notation
pp. 212–217

**EXAMPLE**

Write the number in scientific notation.

**a.** $980,000,000 = 9.8 \times 100,000,000$
$$= 9.8 \times 10^8$$

**b.** $0.000012 = 1.2 \times 0.00001$
$$= 1.2 \times 10^{-5}$$

**EXERCISES**

Write the number in scientific notation.

SEE EXAMPLES 1, 2, 3, AND 4
on pp. 212–214
for Exs. 72–82

**72.** $34,600,000,000$

**73.** $0.0000009$

**74.** $0.000000000502$

Write the number in standard form.

**75.** $2.36 \times 10^8$

**76.** $0.015 \times 10^5$

**77.** $9.4 \times 10^{-3}$

Write the product in scientific notation.

**78.** $(3 \times 10^{16}) \times (5 \times 10^{-5})$

**79.** $(6.2 \times 10^{-4}) \times (2.6 \times 10^{12})$

**80.** $(1.08 \times 10^7) \times (2.09 \times 10^{-2})$

**81.** $(7.63 \times 10^{11}) \times (4.8 \times 10^{-3})$

**82. Niagara Falls** In tourist season, the water at Niagara Falls flows at a rate of 100,000 cubic feet per second during the day. How fast does it flow per minute? per hour? Write your answers in scientific notation.

**Write the prime factorization of the number.**

**1.** 49　　　　　**2.** 68　　　　　**3.** 95　　　　　**4.** 112

**Find the greatest common factor of the numbers or monomials.**

**5.** 36, 84　　　　**6.** 45, 117　　　　**7.** $2z^3, 3z^2$　　　**8.** $14r^2, 42r$

**Find the least common multiple of the numbers or monomials.**

**9.** 4, 16, 32　　**10.** 18, 24, 36　　**11.** $5x^2y, 21xy^3$　　**12.** $54pq^2, 63p^3q^3$

**Copy and complete the statement with <, >, or =.**

**13.** $\dfrac{11}{12} \underline{\ ?\ } \dfrac{41}{48}$　　**14.** $4\dfrac{3}{6} \underline{\ ?\ } \dfrac{9}{2}$　　**15.** $8\dfrac{7}{16} \underline{\ ?\ } \dfrac{17}{2}$　　**16.** $\dfrac{35}{7} \underline{\ ?\ } 5\dfrac{1}{7}$

**Simplify the expression. Write your answer using only positive exponents.**

**17.** $m^8 \cdot m^3$　　**18.** $6^2 \cdot 6^6 \cdot 6^0$　　**19.** $\dfrac{n^{16}}{n^{10}}$　　**20.** $\dfrac{p^4 \cdot p^6}{p^2 \cdot p^7}$

**21.** $5x^{-3}$　　**22.** $c^{-1} \cdot c^{-7}$　　**23.** $\dfrac{-4u^{-9}}{u^3}$　　**24.** $\dfrac{16a^2b^5}{8a^4b}$

**Write the number in scientific notation.**

**25.** 200,400　　　　**26.** 0.000005126　　　　**27.** 42,000

**Write the number in standard form.**

**28.** $7.72 \times 10^6$　　**29.** $1.46 \times 10^{-6}$　　**30.** $8.22 \times 10^{-4}$

**Write the product in scientific notation.**

**31.** $(6 \times 10^5) \times (5 \times 10^7)$　　　　**32.** $(8.1 \times 10^4) \times (9.2 \times 10^8)$

**33.** $(4.2 \times 10^{-5}) \times (6 \times 10^{-2})$　　　　**34.** $(3.8 \times 10^{-4}) \times (2.9 \times 10^7)$

**35. CAKE** Three identical round layer cakes are served at a party. Each cake is cut into a different number of equal-sized slices. After the guests leave, $\dfrac{1}{8}$ of the yellow cake, $\dfrac{3}{16}$ of the chocolate cake, and $\dfrac{1}{6}$ of the carrot cake remain. Which type of cake has the least amount left over? Which has the most? *Explain* your reasoning.

**36. SCIENCE** Scientists have created a microfabric using molded plastic. Its narrowest links are $\dfrac{1}{1,000,000}$ meter across. Write this fraction as a power of ten.

**37. ENVIRONMENT** In the United States, approximately 120,000 aluminum cans are recycled each minute. Write this number in scientific notation.

**38. BIRTH WEIGHT** The western harvest mouse weighs approximately $1.5 \times 10^{-3}$ kilograms at birth. Write this number in standard form.

TEXAS TAKS Obj. 6
TEKS 8.14.A,
8.14.C

## REVIEWING FACTOR AND FRACTION PROBLEMS

You can compare and order fractions to reach conclusions from a table of data. To do so, use the GCF to simplify fractions and the LCD to compare fractions.

**EXAMPLE**

**Clubs** The student government of a middle school wants to find out whether at least three quarters of the students in each grade are involved in clubs after school. A student committee takes a poll and returns with the table shown at the right. In which grades are at least three quarters of the students in clubs?

| Grade | Total Number of Students | Number of Students in Clubs |
|-------|--------------------------|------------------------------|
| 6 | 108 | 72 |
| 7 | 96 | 64 |
| 8 | 120 | 90 |

## Solution

**STEP 1** **Write** the fraction of students in clubs from each grade and simplify.

6th grade: $\dfrac{\text{Number of students in clubs}}{\text{Total number of students}} = \dfrac{72}{108} = \dfrac{72 \div 36}{108 \div 36} = \dfrac{2}{3}$

7th grade: $\dfrac{\text{Number of students in clubs}}{\text{Total number of students}} = \dfrac{64}{96} = \dfrac{64 \div 32}{96 \div 32} = \dfrac{2}{3}$

8th grade: $\dfrac{\text{Number of students in clubs}}{\text{Total number of students}} = \dfrac{90}{120} = \dfrac{90 \div 30}{120 \div 30} = \dfrac{3}{4}$

**STEP 2** **Compare** the fraction of students in clubs from each grade with $\dfrac{3}{4}$.

For grades six and seven, compare $\dfrac{2}{3}$ with $\dfrac{3}{4}$. The LCM of 3 and 4 is 12, so the LCD is 12. Write equivalent fractions.

$$\dfrac{2}{3} = \dfrac{2 \cdot 4}{3 \cdot 4} = \dfrac{8}{12} \qquad\qquad \dfrac{3}{4} = \dfrac{3 \cdot 3}{4 \cdot 3} = \dfrac{9}{12}$$

Compare the numerators. $8 < 9$, so $\dfrac{2}{3} < \dfrac{3}{4}$.

For grade eight, notice that exactly $\dfrac{3}{4}$ of the students are in clubs.

▶ **Answer** At least three quarters of students in eighth grade belong to clubs.

# FACTOR AND FRACTION PROBLEMS ON TAKS

Below are examples of factor and fraction problems in multiple choice format.
Try solving the problems before looking at the solutions. (Cover the solutions
with a piece of paper.) Then check your solutions against the ones given.

1. Alexander is asked by his teacher to order fractions, but he is unsure of how to do so. Which procedure can he use to order the numbers $2\frac{5}{6}$, $\frac{10}{3}$, and $\frac{11}{4}$ from least to greatest?

   **A** Use the LCD to write equivalent fractions, then compare the denominators.

   **B** Use the LCD to write equivalent fractions, then compare the numerators.

   **C** Use the GCF to write equivalent fractions, then compare the denominators.

   **D** Use the GCF to write equivalent fractions, then compare the numerators.

**Solution**

Compare the fractions using the LCD. The LCM of 6, 3, and 4 is 12, so the least common denominator is 12. Write equivalent fractions.

$$2\frac{5}{6} = \frac{34}{12} \qquad \frac{10}{3} = \frac{40}{12} \qquad \frac{11}{4} = \frac{33}{12}$$

Compare numerators.

$$33 < 34 < 40, \text{ so } \frac{11}{4} < 2\frac{5}{6} < \frac{10}{3}$$

The correct procedure is to use the LCD to write equivalent fractions, and then compare the numerators.

So, the correct answer is B.

Ⓐ ⬤B Ⓒ Ⓓ

2. The table at the right shows the fraction of males and females finishing among the top 30 racers for different parts of an aquathlon. Based on the data, which statement is true?

| *Aquathlon* | | |
|---|---|---|
| | *Male* | *Female* |
| *Swim* | $\frac{11}{15}$ | $\frac{4}{15}$ |
| *Run* | $\frac{4}{5}$ | $\frac{1}{5}$ |

   **F** More males finished in the top 30 of the swim than in the top 30 of the run.

   **G** More females finished in the top 30 of the swim than in the top 30 of the run.

   **H** The same number of males finished in the top 30 of the run as females who finished in the top 30 of the swim.

   **J** More females finished in the top 30 of the run than males who finished in the top 30 of the swim.

**Solution**

Compare the fractions using the LCD. The LCM of 5 and 15 is 15, so the least common denominator is 15.

Male swim: $\frac{11}{15}$

Female swim: $\frac{4}{15}$

Male run: $\frac{4}{5} = \frac{4 \cdot 3}{5 \cdot 3} = \frac{12}{15}$

Female run: $\frac{1}{5} = \frac{1 \cdot 3}{5 \cdot 3} = \frac{3}{15}$

Because $\frac{4}{15} > \frac{3}{15}$, more females finished in the top 30 of the swim than in the top 30 of the run.

So, the correct answer is G.

Ⓕ ⬤G Ⓗ Ⓙ

## PRACTICE FOR TAKS OBJECTIVE 6

1. Deidre says that $10 \times 10^{-4}$ is not written in scientific notation, $c \times 10^n$. Why is she correct?

   **A** Because $11 \geq 10$.

   **B** Because 10 is not a decimal.

   **C** Because $-4 < 0$.

   **D** Because $-4$ is not an integer.

2. In May, Tammy spent 6 hours per week practicing piano, 45 minutes jogging daily, more than 1 hour per day doing homework, and 30 hours over the 31 days reading for fun. Assume that she practices piano for the same amount of time each day, and that she reads for the same amount of time each day. Order the activities from the one she spent the least time doing to the one she spent the most time doing each day.

   **F** Piano, jogging, homework, reading

   **G** Jogging, piano, reading, homework

   **H** Piano, jogging, reading, homework

   **J** Jogging, reading, piano, homework

3. Which of the following is NOT a common multiple of two integers $a$ and $b$?

   **A** Greatest common factor of $a$ and $b$

   **B** Least common multiple of $a$ and $b$

   **C** The product $ab$

   **D** The product $2ab$

4. Which procedure can be used to write $8.6 \times 10^6$ in standard form?

   **F** Multiply 8.6 by 100,000

   **G** Multiply 8.6 by 1,000,000

   **H** Multiply 8.6 by 10,000,000

   **J** Multiply 8.6 by 0.000001

5. Yolanda says the least common multiple (LCM) of two different whole numbers is $x$ and the greatest common factor (GCF) of the same two numbers is $2x$. Why is her answer incorrect?

   **A** The LCM and the GCF may be the same.

   **B** The LCM may not exist.

   **C** The two numbers may not have a greatest common factor.

   **D** The GCF must be less than the LCM.

6. Juan goes to the grocery store every Sunday. Suzie goes to the grocery store every ten days. She just went to the store today, Monday. In how many days will Juan and Suzie both go to the store on the same day?

   **F** 6 days

   **G** 10 days

   **H** 20 days

   **J** 30 days

## MIXED TAKS PRACTICE

7. Which graph is represented by the equation $2x - 4 > 0$? *TAKS Obj. 2*

   **A**
   $$-4 \quad -2 \quad 0 \quad 2 \quad 4 \quad 6 \quad 8 \quad 10$$

   **B**
   $$-4 \quad -2 \quad 0 \quad 2 \quad 4 \quad 6 \quad 8 \quad 10$$

   **C**
   $$-4 \quad -2 \quad 0 \quad 2 \quad 4 \quad 6 \quad 8 \quad 10$$

   **D**
   $$-4 \quad -2 \quad 0 \quad 2 \quad 4 \quad 6 \quad 8 \quad 10$$

## MIXED TAKS PRACTICE

8. The table shows the fraction of free throws made by Ed, Al, Jay, and Jen during a competition. Which conclusion is reasonable according to the data? *TAKS Obj. 2*

| Name | Ed | Al | Jay | Jen |
|---|---|---|---|---|
| Fraction made | $\frac{7}{10}$ | $\frac{3}{4}$ | $\frac{3}{5}$ | $\frac{9}{10}$ |

**F** If Ed and Al each try 20 free throws, Ed will sink more baskets than Al.

**G** If all four try the same number of free throws, Ed and Al will sink fewer baskets than Jay and Jen.

**H** Jen sinks on average 3 times as many free throws as Jay.

**J** If Ed and Jen try 15 free throws, it is impossible to estimate who will sink more baskets.

9. A frame is built for the painting of the Roman Coliseum below. The frame extends 2 inches farther than the painting in each direction. What is the total area of the frame and the painting? *TAKS Obj. 3*

**15 in.**

**14 in.**

**A** 74 in.²

**B** 210 in.²

**C** 272 in.²

**D** 342 in.²

10. Lenny has two bottles. One bottle holds 12 fluid ounces and the other holds 16 fluid ounces. He fills a container by emptying full water bottles into it. Which container can be completely filled using either bottle or both bottles so that neither bottle holds excess water when he is finished? *TAKS Obj. 6*

**F** 42 fl oz container

**G** 46 fl oz container

**H** 54 fl oz container

**J** 68 fl oz container

11. The square below is shrunk so that the perimeter is half of the original perimeter. What is the effect on its side length? *TAKS Obj. 4*

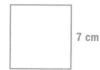

**7 cm**

**A** The side length decreases by a factor of $\frac{1}{2}$.

**B** The side length decreases by a factor of $\frac{1}{3}$.

**C** The side length decreases by a factor of $\frac{1}{4}$.

**D** The side is $\frac{1}{4}$ shorter.

12. **GRIDDED ANSWER** Four roommates agreed to split the cost of food, rent, and electricity evenly. Last month they spent a total of $472.63 for food, $315 each for rent, and a total of $132.21 for electricity. How much, in dollars, did each roommate pay? *TAKS Obj. 1*

*Record your answer and fill in the bubbles on your answer document. Be sure to use the correct place value.*

# 5 Rational Number Operations

TEXAS

## Before

In previous chapters you've . . .

- Performed operations on integers
- Interpreted tables and graphs

## Now

TEKS you'll study . . .

| | | |
|---|---|---|
| 8.2.B | 5.1 | Common denominators |
| 8.1.B | 5.2 | Different denominators |
| 8.2.B | 5.3 | Multiplying fractions |
| 8.15.A | 5.4 | Dividing fractions |
| 8.1.A | 5.5 | Fractions and decimals |
| 8.14.D | 5.6 | Adding and subtracting |
| 8.2.C | 5.7 | Multiplying and dividing |
| 8.12.A | 5.8 | Mean, median, mode |

## Why?

So you can solve real-world problems about . . .

- sledding, p. 241
- rafting, p. 265
- deep sea jellies, p. 272

 **Math**

*at classzone.com*

- Fractions with Different Denominators, p. 240
- Penalty Shot, p. 249
- Mean, Median, and Mode, p. 275

## Get-Ready Games

**Review Prerequisite Skills** by playing *Scale the Cliff* and *Tangled Fractions.*

| | | | |
|---|---|---|---|
| $\frac{7}{32}$ | $\frac{1}{3}$ | $\frac{2}{7}$ | $\frac{3}{11}$ |
| $\frac{7}{17}$ | $\frac{4}{9}$ | $\frac{4}{15}$ | $\frac{11}{25}$ |
| $\frac{6}{11}$ | $\frac{13}{21}$ | $\frac{4}{7}$ | $\frac{3}{8}$ |
| $\frac{1}{2}$ | $\frac{5}{8}$ | $\frac{7}{11}$ | $\frac{9}{14}$ |
| $\frac{3}{4}$ | $\frac{5}{6}$ | $\frac{3}{5}$ | $\frac{5}{7}$ |
| $\frac{2}{3}$ | | | |

Scale the Cliff

**Skill Focus:** Comparing fractions

Find the handholds you can use to scale the cliff.

- Start at $\frac{2}{3}$ and move up, selecting a handhold in each row.

- The value of each handhold must be less than the value of the handhold below it.

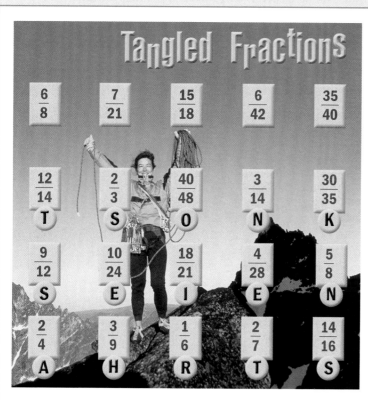

**Skill Focus:** Identifying equivalent fractions

Susan is going rock climbing. Help her figure out what equipment she is missing.

- In each column, find a fraction equivalent to the top one to decode the name of the equipment Susan is missing.

## Stop and Think

1. **CRITICAL THINKING** A student thinks that a fraction cannot be smaller than another fraction if the first fraction's denominator is greater than the second fraction's denominator. *Explain* why the student is wrong.

2. **WRITING** Explain how to tell whether fractions with different denominators are equivalent.

# Review Prerequisite Skills

**REVIEW WORDS**
- **like terms,** *p. 89*
- **simplest form,** *p. 187*
- **least common denominator (LCD),** *p. 198*
- **improper fraction,** *p. 762*
- **mixed number,** *p. 762*

## VOCABULARY CHECK

**Copy and complete using a review word from the list at the left.**

1. If 1 is the greatest common factor of the numerator and the denominator, then the fraction is in __?__.

2. A number like $3\frac{4}{7}$, whose value is the sum of a whole number and a fraction, is a(n) __?__.

3. A fraction whose numerator is greater than or equal to its denominator is a(n) __?__.

## SKILL CHECK

**Find the product or quotient.** *(pp. 73, 77)*

4. $-125 \cdot 2$   5. $-4 \cdot (-23)$   6. $20 \cdot (-6)$   7. $-8 \cdot (-7)$

8. $-39 \div 3$   9. $-136 \div (-17)$   10. $64 \div (-16)$   11. $-27 \div (-9)$

**Write the fraction in simplest form.** *(p. 187)*

12. $\frac{4}{12}$   13. $\frac{-35}{50}$   14. $\frac{24}{52}$   15. $\frac{14}{49}$

16. $\frac{-34}{51}$   17. $\frac{26}{65}$   18. $\frac{56}{72}$   19. $\frac{-16}{96}$

20. You bought a sweater for $15.65 and a pair of jeans for $23.95. What was the total cost of your purchase? *(p. 764)*

**TEXAS @HomeTutor**   Prerequisite skills practice at classzone.com

# Notetaking Skills     Writing Helpful Hints

In each chapter you will learn a new notetaking skill. In Chapter 5 you will apply the strategy of writing helpful hints to Example 1 on p. 233.

In your notebook, write down any hints your teacher or your textbook gives you for solving problems.

Equivalent Fractions

Write equivalent fractions by multiplying by a fraction that is equal to 1.

$$\frac{3}{5} \times \frac{4}{4} = \frac{12}{20} \qquad \frac{3}{5} \times \frac{9}{9} = \frac{27}{45} \qquad \frac{3}{5} \times \frac{100}{100} = \frac{300}{500}$$     ← A fraction has many equivalent forms.

You can rename a mixed number as an equivalent improper fraction.

$$3\frac{5}{6} = \frac{3 \cdot 6 + 5}{6} = \frac{23}{6}$$

# 5.1 Fractions with Common Denominators

TEKS *8.1.B, 8.2.B*

| **Before** | You added and subtracted whole numbers and integers. |
|---|---|
| **Now** | You'll add and subtract fractions with common denominators. |
| **Why?** | So you can interpret survey results, as in Ex. 44. |

**KEY VOCABULARY**
- **order of operations,** *p. 8*
- **like terms,** *p. 89*
- **numerator,** *p. 762*
- **denominator,** *p. 762*

You may have used a model, such as the one below, to add or subtract fractions with common denominators.

$$\frac{2}{5} \quad + \quad \frac{1}{5} \quad = \quad \frac{3}{5}$$

The model illustrates the following rules for adding and subtracting fractions.

---

### KEY CONCEPT *For Your Notebook*

**Adding and Subtracting Fractions**

**Words**  To add fractions or subtract fractions with a common denominator, write the sum or difference of the numerators over the denominator.

**Numbers**  $\dfrac{3}{9} + \dfrac{5}{9} = \dfrac{8}{9}$   **Algebra**  $\dfrac{a}{c} + \dfrac{b}{c} = \dfrac{a+b}{c}$  $(c \neq 0)$

$\dfrac{3}{5} - \dfrac{2}{5} = \dfrac{1}{5}$   $\dfrac{a}{c} - \dfrac{b}{c} = \dfrac{a-b}{c}$  $(c \neq 0)$

---

To add or subtract negative fractions or mixed numbers, apply the rules you learned for integers in Chapter 2. Interpret negative signs as follows.

$$-\frac{11}{13} = \frac{-11}{13} \text{ or } \frac{11}{-13} \qquad \text{and} \qquad -5\frac{6}{7} = -5 - \frac{6}{7} \text{ or } -5 + \frac{-6}{7}$$

---

### EXAMPLE 1  Fractions and Mixed Numbers

*TAKE NOTES*
You may wish to copy Example 1 and the helpful hint above about negative fractions into your notebook.

**a.**  $-\dfrac{11}{13} + \dfrac{8}{13} = \dfrac{-11+8}{13}$

$= -\dfrac{3}{13}$

**b.**  $-5\dfrac{6}{7} + 3\dfrac{2}{7} = -5 - \dfrac{6}{7} + 3 + \dfrac{2}{7}$

$= -5 + 3 - \dfrac{6}{7} + \dfrac{2}{7}$

$= -2\dfrac{4}{7}$

**EXAMPLE 2** Simplifying Fractions with Variables

**a.** $-\dfrac{a}{9} + \dfrac{7a}{9} = \dfrac{-a + 7a}{9}$     Write sum over common denominator.

$= \dfrac{6a}{9}$     Combine like terms.

$= \dfrac{\overset{2}{\cancel{6}}a}{\underset{3}{\cancel{9}}}$     Divide out common factor.

$= \dfrac{2a}{3}$     Simplify.

**VOCABULARY**

Recall that *like terms* are terms that have identical variable parts raised to the same power.

**b.** $\dfrac{6x}{11y} - \dfrac{10x}{11y} = \dfrac{6x - 10x}{11y}$     Write difference over common denominator.

$= \dfrac{-4x}{11y}$, or $-\dfrac{4x}{11y}$     Combine like terms.

---

✓ **GUIDED PRACTICE**     for Examples 1 and 2

**Find the sum or difference. Then simplify if possible.**

**1.** $\dfrac{1}{12} + \dfrac{5}{12}$     **2.** $\dfrac{3}{8} - 2\dfrac{1}{8}$     **3.** $-\dfrac{t}{3} - \dfrac{2t}{3}$     **4.** $\dfrac{y}{8a} + \dfrac{-5y}{8a}$

---

**EXAMPLE 3** Solving an Equation with Mixed Numbers

**Biology** A corn snake that is $14\dfrac{3}{4}$ inches long grows $g$ inches to a length of $27\dfrac{1}{4}$ inches. How much does it grow?

**SOLUTION**

To find the amount of growth, subtract the original length from the current length.

**AVOID ERRORS**

When you subtract mixed numbers, compare their fraction parts. If the first fraction part is less, rename the mixed number before you subtract.

$g = 27\dfrac{1}{4} - 14\dfrac{3}{4}$     Original equation.

$= 26\dfrac{5}{4} - 14\dfrac{3}{4}$     Rename $27\dfrac{1}{4}$ so its fraction part is greater than $\dfrac{3}{4}$.

$= \left(26 + \dfrac{5}{4}\right) - \left(14 + \dfrac{3}{4}\right)$     Write mixed numbers in expanded form.

$= 26 + \dfrac{5}{4} - 14 - \dfrac{3}{4}$     Distribute the subtraction.

$= (26 - 14) + \left(\dfrac{5}{4} - \dfrac{3}{4}\right)$     Group whole numbers and fractions.

$= 12 + \dfrac{2}{4}$     Subtract whole numbers and fractions.

$= 12\dfrac{1}{2}$     Simplify and write as a mixed number.

▶ **Answer** The snake grows $12\dfrac{1}{2}$ inches.

**Order of Operations** The rules for adding and subtracting fractions can be applied to evaluate longer expressions. Remember to always use the order of operations.

**EXAMPLE 4** Evaluating Longer Expressions

**ANOTHER WAY**
You can also write the mixed numbers as improper fractions and then evaluate:
$\frac{27}{7} - \frac{17}{7} + \frac{33}{7} = \frac{43}{7}$, or $6\frac{1}{7}$.

a. $\frac{2}{11} - \frac{5}{11} + \frac{9}{11} = \frac{2 - 5 + 9}{11}$   Write $2 - 5 + 9$ over common denominator.

$= \frac{6}{11}$   Evaluate numerator from left to right.

b. $3\frac{6}{7} - 2\frac{3}{7} + 4\frac{5}{7} = (3 - 2 + 4) + \left(\frac{6}{7} - \frac{3}{7} + \frac{5}{7}\right)$   Group whole numbers and fractions.

$= 5\frac{8}{7}$   Evaluate inside parentheses.

$= 6\frac{1}{7}$   Rename.

✓ **GUIDED PRACTICE** for Examples 3 and 4

5. **Gardening** A plant that is $5\frac{7}{8}$ inches high grows $x$ inches to a height of $8\frac{3}{8}$ inches. Write and solve an equation to find the amount of growth.

**Evaluate. Then simplify if possible.**

6. $\frac{3}{4} + \frac{7}{4} + \frac{5}{4}$

7. $\frac{15}{8} - \frac{7}{8} + \frac{3}{8}$

8. $2\frac{1}{3} - \frac{2}{3} + 3\frac{2}{3}$

# 5.1 EXERCISES

HOMEWORK KEY

 = TAKS Practice and Reasoning
Exs. 42, 46, 47, 49, and 50

◯ = HINTS AND HOMEWORK HELP
for Exs. 9, 11, 19, 23, 43 at classzone.com

**SKILL PRACTICE**

1. **VOCABULARY** Copy and complete: In the fraction $\frac{4}{9}$, 9 is the __?__ and 4 is the __?__.

**FRACTION OPERATIONS** Find the sum or difference. Then simplify if possible.

**SEE EXAMPLE 1**
on p. 233
for Exs. 2–9

2. $\frac{5}{18} + \frac{7}{18}$

3. $\frac{5}{21} + \frac{2}{21}$

4. $\frac{3}{10} - \frac{7}{10}$

5. $\frac{7}{18} - \frac{5}{18}$

6. $-4\frac{2}{7} - 4\frac{2}{7}$

7. $-4\frac{9}{14} + 3\frac{5}{14}$

8. $2\frac{7}{9} + \frac{8}{9}$

9. $-7\frac{3}{5} - \frac{4}{5}$

 **SIMPLIFYING EXPRESSIONS** Simplify the expression.

**SEE EXAMPLE 2**
on p. 234
for Exs. 10–17

10. $\frac{h}{13} + \frac{6h}{13}$

11. $-\frac{8n}{21} + \frac{5n}{21}$

12. $\frac{-8p}{9} - \frac{-p}{9}$

13. $\frac{12}{a} + \frac{3}{a}$

14. $\frac{4x}{5y} - \frac{9x}{5y}$

15. $\frac{9a}{20b} - \frac{7a}{20b}$

16. $-\frac{5q}{18p} - \frac{13q}{18p}$

17. $\frac{5a}{2b} - \frac{a}{2b}$

**EVALUATING EXPRESSIONS** Evaluate the expression.

SEE EXAMPLES
1 AND 4
on pp. 233, 235
for Exs. 18–27

**18.** $7\frac{1}{3} - 3\frac{2}{3}$

**19.** $19\frac{1}{4} - 17\frac{3}{4}$

**20.** $1\frac{4}{15} + \left(-\frac{11}{15}\right)$

**21.** $\frac{13}{18} + \frac{5}{18} + \frac{11}{18}$

**22.** $-\frac{4}{5} - \frac{1}{5} - \frac{2}{5}$

**23.** $4\frac{5}{12} - \left(1\frac{11}{12} - \frac{7}{12}\right)$

**24.** $-5\frac{4}{15} - \left(3\frac{7}{15} + \frac{8}{15}\right)$

**25.** $-\frac{3}{16} - 2\frac{1}{16} - \frac{15}{16}$

**26.** $1\frac{3}{8} + \frac{5}{8} - 1\frac{7}{8}$

**27. ERROR ANALYSIS** Describe and correct the error made in subtracting the fractions.

$$2\frac{4}{9} - 1\frac{1}{9} = (2 - 1) + \left(\frac{4}{9} + \frac{1}{9}\right)$$
$$= 1\frac{5}{9}$$

**ALGEBRA** Solve the equation.

**28.** $x + \frac{5}{8} = 0$

**29.** $\frac{7}{17} + k = \frac{9}{17}$

**30.** $z - \frac{9}{15} = \frac{11}{15}$

**31.** $m - \frac{6}{9} = \frac{2}{9}$

**32.** $j + \frac{2}{13} + \frac{5}{13} = \frac{8}{13}$

**33.** $\frac{1}{7} + a + \frac{3}{7} = \frac{4}{7}$

**34.** $\frac{7}{16} + b - \frac{2}{16} = \frac{5}{16}$

**35.** $\frac{10}{11} - y = \frac{2}{11}$

**36.** $\frac{3}{19} - c = 0$

**37. EXAMPLES AND NONEXAMPLES** Give an example of a pair of mixed numbers whose sum is a mixed number. Then give an example of a pair of mixed numbers whose sum is *not* a mixed number.

**CHALLENGE** Solve the equation.

**38.** $\frac{a}{10} + \frac{2a}{10} = -\frac{9}{10}$

**39.** $\frac{-3b}{15} + \frac{7b}{15} = \frac{8}{15}$

**40.** $\frac{5}{4c} - \frac{13}{4c} = -\frac{1}{3}$

## PROBLEM SOLVING

SEE EXAMPLE 3
on p. 234
for Exs. 41–43

**41. KNITTING** You find a mistake after knitting $21\frac{3}{8}$ inches of a scarf. You have to pull out $2\frac{5}{8}$ inches of the scarf. How many inches of the scarf are left?

**42. TAKS REASONING** You are fencing a rectangular plot of land. The plot and its dimensions are shown. How many feet of fencing do you need in total?

**A** $26\frac{3}{4}$ feet

**B** $52\frac{1}{2}$ feet

**C** $53\frac{1}{4}$ feet

**D** $53\frac{1}{2}$ feet

**43. EUROS** A 2-euro coin is $25\frac{3}{4}$ millimeters wide. A 1-euro coin is $23\frac{1}{4}$ millimeters wide. How much wider is a 2-euro coin than a 1-euro coin?

**44. WRITING** One hundred people were asked to name their favorite pet. The results are shown in the circle graph at the right.

Your friend says that if you make each number the numerator in a fraction with a denominator of 100, the sum of these fractions must be 1. Is your friend correct? *Explain*.

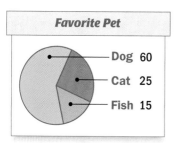

**Favorite Pet**

Dog 60
Cat 25
Fish 15

**45. LONG JUMP RECORD** You want to match your school's long jump record of 17 feet $8\frac{1}{4}$ inches. Your best long jump so far is 15 feet $11\frac{3}{4}$ inches. How much farther do you need to jump to match the school record?

**46. TAKS REASONING** You did volunteer work for $6\frac{1}{6}$ hours the first week of the month, $8\frac{5}{6}$ hours the second week, and $5\frac{1}{6}$ hours the third week. Your volunteer group gives awards to those who volunteer at least 25 hours per month. How many hours do you have to volunteer the last week of the month to win the award? *Explain* your reasoning.

**47. TAKS REASONING** Some cars in a race were allowed to reduce the height of their rear spoilers by one fourth of an inch to reduce drag and increase speed. After the change, one car's spoiler was $6\frac{1}{4}$ inches tall.

— spoiler

**a.** How tall was the spoiler before the change in height? *Justify* your answer.

**b.** What fraction of the original height was removed? *Explain* how you found your answer.

**48. CHALLENGE** Bill is 1 foot $3\frac{1}{4}$ inches taller than Hollie. Hollie is $6\frac{1}{8}$ inches taller than Chris. Amanda is $4\frac{7}{8}$ inches shorter than Chris. Amanda is 4 feet $2\frac{1}{4}$ inches tall. How tall is each person in feet and inches?

## MIXED REVIEW FOR TAKS

TAKS PRACTICE at classzone.com

*REVIEW*
Lesson 1.5;
TAKS Workbook

**49. TAKS PRACTICE** A patient starts a diet recommended by a doctor and loses 3 pounds per month. The patient's weight in pounds, $a$, can be represented by $a = -3t + 190$, where $t$ is the number of months the patient diets. What is the patient's weight after 4 months of dieting? *TAKS Obj. 2*

(A) 178 lb    (B) 183 lb    (C) 187 lb    (D) 202 lb

*REVIEW*
Lesson 3.5;
TAKS Workbook

**50. TAKS PRACTICE** A rectangle 8 inches long and 5 inches wide is divided into two triangles by a diagonal line. What is the area of each triangle? *TAKS Obj. 6*

(F) 10 in.$^2$    (G) 20 in.$^2$    (H) 40 in.$^2$    (J) 80 in.$^2$

## 5.2 Fractions with Different Denominators

TEKS 8.1.B, 8.2.B

| Before | You added and subtracted with common denominators. |
| Now | You'll add and subtract with different denominators. |
| Why? | So you can find length, as of a wooden board in Example 3. |

**KEY VOCABULARY**
- **least common denominator (LCD),** *p. 198*

**Carpentry** A board is $36\frac{5}{8}$ inches long. You cut off a piece $12\frac{3}{4}$ inches long. The saw blade destroys an additional $\frac{1}{16}$ inch of wood which is equal to its width. What is the length of the remaining piece of wood? You will solve this problem in Example 3 on page 239 by adding and subtracting mixed numbers and fractions with different denominators.

To add or subtract fractions with different denominators, first rewrite the fractions so the denominators are the same. Choose a denominator that is the least common multiple of denominators in the problem.

---

### EXAMPLE 1  Adding and Subtracting Fractions

*REVIEW LCD*

Need help rewriting fractions with common denominators? See p. 198.

**a.** $\dfrac{7}{8} + \dfrac{-2}{5} = \dfrac{35}{40} + \dfrac{-16}{40}$    **Rewrite fractions using LCD of 40.**

$\qquad = \dfrac{35 + (-16)}{40}$    **Write sum over LCD.**

$\qquad = \dfrac{19}{40}$    **Evaluate numerator.**

**b.** $\dfrac{3}{10} - \dfrac{5}{6} = \dfrac{9}{30} - \dfrac{25}{30}$    **Rewrite fractions using LCD of 30.**

$\qquad = \dfrac{9 - 25}{30}$    **Write difference over LCD.**

$\qquad = \dfrac{-16}{30}$    **Evaluate numerator.**

$\qquad = -\dfrac{8}{15}$    **Simplify.**

---

✓ **GUIDED PRACTICE**   **for Example 1**

**Find the sum or difference. Then simplify if possible.**

**1.** $\dfrac{1}{3} + \dfrac{3}{8}$

**2.** $\dfrac{3}{4} - \dfrac{9}{10}$

**3.** $\dfrac{5}{12} + \dfrac{-7}{9}$

**4.** $\dfrac{2}{8} + \dfrac{7}{16}$

**5.** $\dfrac{1}{6} - \dfrac{11}{15}$

**6.** $\dfrac{-4}{33} - \dfrac{1}{11}$

## EXAMPLE 2 Simplifying Variable Expressions

 **Simplify the expression.**

**a.** $\dfrac{2x}{5} - \dfrac{x}{6} = \dfrac{12x}{30} - \dfrac{5x}{30}$     **Rewrite fractions using LCD of 30.**

$= \dfrac{12x - 5x}{30}$     **Write difference over LCD.**

$= \dfrac{7x}{30}$     **Combine like terms.**

> **AVOID ERRORS**
> Notice in part (b) that
> $\dfrac{40 + 7y}{8y} \neq \dfrac{47y}{8y}$,
> because 40 and $7y$ are *not* like terms. The expression is already in simplest form.

**b.** $\dfrac{5}{y} + \dfrac{7}{8} = \left( \dfrac{5}{y} \cdot \dfrac{8}{8} \right) + \left( \dfrac{7}{8} \cdot \dfrac{y}{y} \right)$     **Multiply $\dfrac{5}{y}$ by $\dfrac{8}{8}$ and $\dfrac{7}{8}$ by $\dfrac{y}{y}$ for LCD of 8y.**

$= \dfrac{40}{8y} + \dfrac{7y}{8y}$     **Multiply inside parentheses.**

$= \dfrac{40 + 7y}{8y}$     **Write sum over LCD.**

## EXAMPLE 3 Modeling with Mixed Numbers

To find the length of the remaining piece of wood described on page 238, first write a verbal model.

$$\boxed{\text{Remaining length } L} = \boxed{\text{Original length}} - \left( \boxed{\text{Length cut off}} + \boxed{\text{Blade width}} \right)$$

$L = 36\dfrac{5}{8} - \left( 12\dfrac{3}{4} + \dfrac{1}{16} \right)$     **Write an algebraic model.**

$= 36\dfrac{10}{16} - \left( 12\dfrac{12}{16} + \dfrac{1}{16} \right)$     **Rewrite fractions using LCD of 16.**

$= 36\dfrac{10}{16} - 12\dfrac{13}{16}$     **Add inside parentheses.**

$= 35\dfrac{26}{16} - 12\dfrac{13}{16}$     **Rename $36\dfrac{10}{16}$ as $35\dfrac{26}{16}$.**

$= (35 - 12) + \left( \dfrac{26}{16} - \dfrac{13}{16} \right)$     **Group whole numbers and fractions.**

$= 23\dfrac{13}{16}$     **Subtract whole numbers and fractions.**

> **CHECK REASONABLENESS**
> You can check that the sum or difference of mixed numbers is reasonable by rounding each number to the nearest whole number. In Example 3,
> $36\dfrac{5}{8} - \left( 12\dfrac{3}{4} + \dfrac{1}{16} \right) \approx$
> $37 - 13 = 24$.

▶ **Answer** The remaining piece of wood is $23\dfrac{13}{16}$ inches long.

### ✓ GUIDED PRACTICE for Examples 2 and 3

**7.** Find the sum and difference of $\dfrac{2}{5}$ and $\dfrac{2}{z}$.

**8. What If?** In Example 3 suppose you cut $4\dfrac{5}{6}$ inches off the original piece of wood. What is the length of the remaining piece of wood?

# 5.2 EXERCISES

## SKILL PRACTICE

1. **VOCABULARY** Copy and complete: To add fractions with different denominators, rewrite the fractions using the __?__ of the fractions.

**SEE EXAMPLE 1**
on p. 238
for Exs. 2–7, 22

**ADDING AND SUBTRACTING FRACTIONS** Find the sum or difference. Simplify if possible.

2. $\frac{1}{2} + \frac{1}{3}$

3. $\frac{7}{8} - \frac{1}{4}$

4. $\frac{1}{8} - \frac{5}{32}$

5. $\frac{5}{9} + \frac{1}{6}$

**SEE EXAMPLE 3**
on p. 239
for Exs. 8–13

6. $-\frac{7}{12} + \frac{4}{15}$

7. $\frac{-3}{8} + \frac{-9}{20}$

8. $4\frac{5}{8} - 2\frac{2}{3}$

9. $5\frac{1}{2} - \frac{7}{10}$

10. $7\frac{4}{5} + 5\frac{3}{7}$

11. $12\frac{5}{18} - \frac{3}{4}$

12. $12 - 16\frac{3}{7}$

13. $-7\frac{3}{11} - (-8)$

**SIMPLIFYING VARIABLE EXPRESSIONS** Simplify the expression.

**SEE EXAMPLE 2**
on p. 239
for Exs. 14–21

14. $-\frac{7y}{12} + \frac{4y}{15}$

15. $\frac{-3w}{8} + \frac{-9w}{20}$

16. $\frac{2x}{7} - \frac{x}{2}$

17. $\frac{9s}{4} - \frac{7s}{5}$

18. $\frac{4}{x} + \frac{1}{9}$

19. $\frac{16}{25n} - \frac{9}{10n}$

20. $\frac{16}{25n} + \frac{9}{10n}$

21. $\frac{18}{7a} + \frac{11}{21}$

22. **TAKS REASONING** What is the value of $\frac{5}{6} + \frac{1}{9} - \frac{2}{3}$?

(A) $\frac{1}{6}$

(B) $\frac{2}{9}$

(C) $\frac{5}{18}$

(D) $\frac{1}{3}$

**CHOOSE A METHOD** Use *estimation, mental math,* or *pencil and paper* to tell whether the statement is *true* or *false*. Identify your choice of method.

23. $\frac{1}{4} - \frac{6}{7} + \frac{3}{14} = -\frac{11}{28}$

24. $\frac{3}{4} + 2\frac{1}{2} - \frac{1}{4} = 3$

25. $\frac{4}{9} + \frac{7}{8} + \frac{1}{24} = \frac{7}{8}$

26. $3\frac{4}{9} - 1\frac{1}{2} - \frac{1}{3} = 2\frac{5}{18}$

27. $1\frac{1}{3} - \frac{2}{9} - \frac{5}{6} = \frac{7}{18}$

28. $10\frac{7}{8} - 3\frac{1}{10} = 5\frac{31}{40}$

**ALGEBRA** Solve the equation.

29. $z + 3\frac{4}{7} - 5\frac{2}{5} = 1\frac{1}{2}$

30. $2\frac{3}{5} + w - 4\frac{1}{3} = 7\frac{8}{15}$

31. $6\frac{3}{8} + 2\frac{5}{12} - x = 4\frac{3}{4}$

32. $7\frac{7}{8} - 6\frac{5}{9} - y = \frac{1}{6}$

**Animated Math** at classzone.com

**CHALLENGE** *Describe* the pattern. Then write the next three fractions in the pattern.

33. $1\frac{7}{10}, 2, 2\frac{3}{10}, 2\frac{3}{5}, \ldots$

34. $5\frac{3}{4}, 4\frac{5}{8}, 3\frac{1}{2}, 2\frac{3}{8}, \ldots$

35. $\frac{11}{12}, \frac{19}{24}, \frac{2}{3}, \frac{13}{24}, \ldots$

*SEE EXAMPLE 3*
on p. 239
for Exs. 36–41

**36.** **GUIDED PROBLEM SOLVING** You are building a stone wall 13 feet long. You build $4\frac{1}{3}$ feet of wall on Monday and $5\frac{3}{4}$ feet on Tuesday. How much wall do you have left to build?

  **a.** Write a verbal model to describe the problem.

  **b.** Substitute the given values into the model.

  **c.** Solve the equation to find the length left to build.

**37.** **OLYMPIC SLEDDING** What is the difference in the lengths of the skeleton sleds below?

$31\frac{1}{2}$ in.        $47\frac{1}{4}$ in.

**38.** **TAKS REASONING** A board $2\frac{1}{4}$ inches thick is placed on top of a board $\frac{5}{6}$ inch thick. What is the combined thickness of the boards?

  **(A)** $1\frac{5}{12}$ in.    **(B)** $2\frac{1}{12}$ in.    **(C)** $2\frac{3}{5}$ in.    **(D)** $3\frac{1}{12}$ in.

**39.** **TAKS REASONING** You bike $1\frac{5}{8}$ miles from school to the store, $\frac{1}{2}$ mile more to the post office, and then $2\frac{3}{4}$ miles home. *Explain* how to estimate the total distance traveled. Is it more or less than 5 miles?

**40.** **POLE VAULT** The gold medal winning men's pole vault at the 2004 Athens Summer Olympics was $5\frac{19}{20}$ meters. The world record, set in 1994, is $6\frac{7}{50}$ meters. How much higher is the world record than the gold medal winning vault at the 2004 Summer Olympics?

**41.** **TREE REMOVAL** A dead tree is being cut down in three parts. The lengths of the first and second cuts are shown at the right. Write and solve an equation to find how many feet of the tree remain to be cut down.

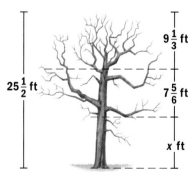

$9\frac{1}{3}$ ft

$25\frac{1}{2}$ ft

$7\frac{5}{6}$ ft

$x$ ft

**42.** **WRITING** *Describe* two strategies to evaluate the sum of two mixed numbers. In one strategy, use improper fractions. *Explain* when it might be better to use one strategy and when it might be better to use the other strategy.

**43.** **TAKS REASONING** Write an addition or subtraction expression containing three fractions, with different denominators, that you can easily evaluate using mental math. *Explain* why you think it is appropriate.

**44. MULTI-STEP PROBLEM** The table shows the results of an annual softball throwing contest. The player with the greatest combined distance wins.

**a.** Who won the contest?

**b.** What was the difference between the winner's combined distance and the 3rd place player's combined distance?

**c.** What distance would the 2nd place player need on his or her 3rd throw to *tie* the winner's combined distance? *Explain* how you found your answer.

| | Distance Thrown (feet) | | |
|---|---|---|---|
| | **1st throw** | **2nd throw** | **3rd throw** |
| **Curtis** | $51\frac{1}{3}$ | $85\frac{1}{2}$ | $80\frac{1}{4}$ |
| **Shanee** | $102\frac{1}{2}$ | $54\frac{2}{3}$ | $57\frac{3}{4}$ |
| **Dave** | $71\frac{1}{3}$ | $72\frac{3}{4}$ | $67\frac{1}{6}$ |

**45.** 🔹 **TAKS REASONING** The fractions in the diagram are fractions of the total distance around Earth on the equator.

**a.** What fraction of the equator do you cover if you travel east from the Galápagos Islands to Singapore?

**b.** Is traveling from the Galápagos Islands to Singapore a shorter trip if you travel *east* or *west*? *Explain.*

**46. CLOCKS** You put a cake in the oven to bake and notice that the hour hand on the oven's clock is broken. At the same time, you hear a radio announcer mention that it is 3:17 P.M. The minute hand on the clock makes $\frac{5}{8}$ revolution before you check the cake. The minute hand makes another $\frac{13}{24}$ revolution before you take the baked cake out of the oven. What time is it when the cake is done?

**47.** ⓍⓎ **CHALLENGE** Write the expression $\frac{a}{b} + \frac{c}{d}$ ($b, d \neq 0$) as a single fraction.

---

**MIXED REVIEW FOR TAKS**                    **TAKS** **PRACTICE** at classzone.com

*REVIEW*
Lesson 4.8;
TAKS Workbook

**48.** 🔹 **TAKS PRACTICE** The mass of a proton is about $1.67 \times 10^{-27}$ gram. The mass of a million protons is one million times the mass of one proton. What is the approximate mass of a million protons expressed in scientific notation? *TAKS Obj. 1*

**A** $1.67 \times 10^{-21}$ g

**B** $1.67 \times 10^{-33}$ g

**C** $16.7 \times 10^{-22}$ g

**D** $16.7 \times 10^{-34}$ g

*REVIEW*
Lesson 2.4;
TAKS Workbook

**49.** 🔹 **TAKS PRACTICE** A small business owner owes $4500 to a supplier. The owner represents this as $-4500$ in the spreadsheet which the owner uses to track the monthly budget. The owner owes 5 times this amount to a bank. How should the owner enter this amount into the spreadsheet? *TAKS Obj. 1*

**F** $-22,500$     **G** $-4,505$     **H** $4,505$     **J** $22,500$

🔸 **ONLINE QUIZ** at classzone.com

# 5.3 Multiplying Fractions

Utah

TEKS 8.1.B, 8.2.B

**Before** You added and subtracted fractions and mixed numbers.

**Now** You'll multiply fractions and mixed numbers.

**Why?** So you can find area, as of a postcard in Example 2.

**KEY VOCABULARY**
• numerator, *p. 762*
• denominator, *p. 762*

You can use the model at the right or the rule below to find the product of two fractions such as $\frac{5}{8}$ and $\frac{3}{4}$. When a product involves negative fractions, you can apply the rules for multiplying integers that you learned in Lesson 2.4.

$\frac{5}{8}$

$\frac{3}{4}$ of $\frac{5}{8}$

---

**KEY CONCEPT** *For Your Notebook*

**Multiplying Fractions**

**Words** The product of two or more fractions is equal to the product of the numerators divided by the product of the denominators.

**Numbers** $\frac{3}{4} \cdot \frac{5}{8} = \frac{3 \cdot 5}{4 \cdot 8} = \frac{15}{32}$  **Algebra** $\frac{a}{b} \cdot \frac{c}{d} = \frac{a \cdot c}{b \cdot d}$ $(b, d \neq 0)$

---

**EXAMPLE 1** Multiplying Fractions

**REVIEW MULTIPLICATION**
Remember that the product of two numbers with the same sign is positive. The product of two numbers with different signs is negative.

**a.** $-\frac{2}{5} \cdot \left(-\frac{2}{3}\right) = \frac{-2 \cdot (-2)}{5 \cdot 3}$  Use rule for multiplying fractions.

$= \frac{4}{15}$  Evaluate numerator and denominator.

**b.** $-\frac{3}{10} \cdot \frac{5}{6} = \frac{-3 \cdot 5}{10 \cdot 6}$  Use rule for multiplying fractions.

$= \frac{\overset{-1}{-3} \cdot \overset{1}{5}}{\underset{2}{10} \cdot \underset{2}{6}}$  Divide out common factors.

$= -\frac{1}{4}$  Multiply.

---

✓ **GUIDED PRACTICE** for Example 1

**Find the product. Simplify if possible.**

**1.** $-\frac{5}{12} \cdot \frac{9}{10}$   **2.** $\frac{-5}{6} \cdot \frac{-7}{9}$   **3.** $\frac{1}{6} \cdot \frac{12}{17}$   **4.** $\frac{7}{12} \cdot -15$

**Mixed Numbers** To multiply mixed numbers, first write them as improper fractions.

---

### EXAMPLE 2    Multiplying Mixed Numbers

**Postcards** A postcard is $5\frac{1}{2}$ inches long and $3\frac{3}{4}$ inches wide. Find the area of the postcard.

**SOLUTION**

Area = length $\cdot$ width     **Write formula for area of a rectangle.**

$= 5\frac{1}{2} \cdot 3\frac{3}{4}$       **Substitute values.**

$= \dfrac{11}{2} \cdot \dfrac{15}{4}$       **Write as improper fractions.**

$= \dfrac{11 \cdot 15}{2 \cdot 4}$       **Use rule for multiplying fractions.**

$= \dfrac{165}{8}$, or $20\frac{5}{8}$       **Multiply.**

▶ **Answer** The area of the postcard is $20\frac{5}{8}$ square inches.

---

### EXAMPLE 3    Evaluating a Variable Expression

 Evaluate $x^2y$ when $x = -\frac{4}{5}$ and $y = \frac{2}{3}$.

$x^2y = \left(-\dfrac{4}{5}\right)^2 \cdot \dfrac{2}{3}$       **Substitute $-\frac{4}{5}$ for $x$ and $\frac{2}{3}$ for $y$.**

$= \left(-\dfrac{4}{5}\right) \cdot \left(-\dfrac{4}{5}\right) \cdot \dfrac{2}{3}$       **Write $-\frac{4}{5}$ as a factor 2 times.**

$= \dfrac{-4 \cdot (-4) \cdot 2}{5 \cdot 5 \cdot 3}$       **Use rule for multiplying fractions.**

$= \dfrac{32}{75}$       **Multiply.**

---

✓ **GUIDED PRACTICE**    for Examples 2 and 3

**AVOID ERRORS**

Be careful when you write a negative mixed number as an improper fraction.

$-1\dfrac{5}{6} = \dfrac{-1 \cdot 6 + (-5)}{6}$

**Find the product. Simplify if possible.**

**5.** $1\frac{2}{5} \cdot 3\frac{1}{2}$      **6.** $5\frac{1}{2} \cdot \left(-1\frac{5}{6}\right)$      **7.** $-5\frac{3}{4} \cdot 2\frac{3}{5}$      **8.** $-2\frac{1}{3} \cdot \left(-\frac{3}{4}\right)$

**Evaluate the expression when $x = -\frac{3}{4}$ and $y = \frac{5}{6}$. Simplify if possible.**

**9.** $\frac{2}{3}x$           **10.** $2y$           **11.** $xy$           **12.** $xy^2$

# 5.3 EXERCISES

HOMEWORK KEY

🟋 = **TAKS Practice and Reasoning**
Exs. 22, 36, 38, 40, and 41

◯ = **HINTS AND HOMEWORK HELP**
for Exs. 3, 9, 11, 17, 33 at classzone.com

## SKILL PRACTICE

1. **VOCABULARY** Copy and complete: The product of two or more fractions is equal to the product of the fractions' __?__ divided by the product of the fractions' __?__ .

**MULTIPLYING FRACTIONS** Find the product. Simplify if possible.

*SEE EXAMPLE 1*
on p. 243
for Exs. 2–9

2. $\dfrac{5}{8} \cdot \dfrac{7}{16}$

3. $-\dfrac{9}{4} \cdot \dfrac{5}{6}$

4. $\dfrac{7}{11} \cdot \dfrac{1}{6}$

5. $\dfrac{4}{5} \cdot \dfrac{3}{10}$

6. $-\dfrac{3}{4} \cdot \left(-\dfrac{2}{9}\right)$

7. $-\dfrac{5}{6} \cdot \dfrac{5}{12}$

8. $-4 \cdot \dfrac{3}{5}$

9. $12 \cdot \dfrac{3}{8}$

*SEE EXAMPLE 2*
on p. 244
for Exs. 10–14

10. $-4 \cdot 2\dfrac{9}{16}$

11. $6\dfrac{3}{16} \cdot \left(-3\dfrac{1}{5}\right)$

12. $-9\dfrac{2}{7} \cdot 1\dfrac{2}{5}$

13. $5\dfrac{2}{3} \cdot (-6)$

14. **ERROR ANALYSIS** Alexia wants to multiply $2\dfrac{2}{3}$ by $3\dfrac{3}{4}$. She says she will multiply 2 by 3 and $\dfrac{2}{3}$ by $\dfrac{3}{4}$ and then add the results. Describe and correct the error in Alexia's method for multiplying the mixed numbers.

*SEE EXAMPLE 3*
on p. 244
for Exs. 15–18

**ⅩⅤ ALGEBRA** Evaluate the expression when $a = \dfrac{5}{8}$, $b = -\dfrac{7}{6}$, and $c = -1\dfrac{1}{2}$.

15. $ac$

16. $bc$

17. $ab^2$

18. $16c^3$

**GEOMETRY** Find the area of the figure.

19.
$\dfrac{15}{16}$ in.
2 in.

20.
$\dfrac{4}{5}$ ft
$1\dfrac{2}{3}$ ft

21.
$3\dfrac{5}{11}$ m
$3\dfrac{5}{11}$ m

22. 🟋 **TAKS REASONING** Let $n$ represent the position number in the pattern below. Which expression can be used to find any number in the pattern?

$$\dfrac{1}{3}, \ \dfrac{2}{3}, \ 1, \ 1\dfrac{1}{3}, \ 1\dfrac{2}{3}, \ \dots$$

Ⓐ $\dfrac{1}{3}n$

Ⓑ $\dfrac{2}{3}n$

Ⓒ $2n$

Ⓓ $3n$

**EVALUATING EXPRESSIONS** Evaluate the expression.

23. $\dfrac{2}{5} \cdot 1\dfrac{1}{5} \cdot \left(-4\dfrac{7}{12}\right)$

24. $-\dfrac{7}{8} + 5\dfrac{1}{2} \cdot \dfrac{11}{15}$

25. $\dfrac{5}{2} \cdot \left(\dfrac{8}{9} - \dfrac{5}{12}\right)$

26. $5 - \left(\dfrac{1}{3} + \dfrac{1}{6}\right)^2$

27. $4 - \left(\dfrac{3}{4} + \dfrac{7}{8}\right)$

28. $\dfrac{2}{3}\left(\dfrac{3}{5} - \dfrac{7}{12}\right)$

29. $\dfrac{-7}{16} + 8\dfrac{1}{3} \cdot \dfrac{3}{5}$

30. $\dfrac{2}{9}\left(-2\dfrac{1}{5}\right)\left(3\dfrac{3}{10}\right)$

**ⅩⅤ CHALLENGE** List the expressions in the order of their values from least to greatest when $a = 2\dfrac{3}{4}$, $b = \dfrac{2}{3}$, and $c = 3$.

31. $2bc, \ bc^2, \ a^2b, \ a + bc$

32. $-b^2 + 2ac, \ -a + 5c, \ a^2bc$

*SEE EXAMPLE 1*
on p. 243
for Exs. 33–35

**33.** **MOON CRATERS** The depth of a simple impact crater on the moon is about $\frac{1}{5}$ of its width. One simple impact crater, Moltke Crater, is 7 kilometers wide. About how deep is Moltke Crater?

**34.** **SNACK MIX** A serving of a snack mix is $\frac{7}{8}$ cup. You need to take 15 servings to your friend's party. How many cups of snack mix should you take? *Explain* how you can use estimation to check your answer.

**35.** **COMPUTERS** One of the first computers, the ENIAC, took $\frac{1}{5000}$ second to perform one operation. How long did it take to perform 11,000 operations?

**36.** **TAKS REASONING** You run 1 mile in 8 minutes at a constant speed. How far do you run in 1 minute? Write an equation to represent how far you can run in *m* minutes. *Explain* how you can use your equation to find how far you can run in 11 minutes.

**37.** **MOSAICS** You have mosaic tiles that measure $1\frac{2}{5}$ inch by $1\frac{2}{5}$ inch. How many square feet will 1000 mosaic tiles cover? Write your answer in simplest form.

**38.** **TAKS REASONING** A poster measures $8\frac{1}{2}$ inches by 11 inches. You enlarge it by increasing each dimension by a factor of $1\frac{1}{2}$. What is the area of the new poster?

**(A)** $93\frac{1}{2}$ in.$^2$   **(B)** $140\frac{1}{4}$ in.$^2$

**(C)** $210\frac{3}{8}$ in.$^2$   **(D)** $280\frac{1}{2}$ in.$^2$

**39.** **CHALLENGE** To present a petition to the student council, $\frac{1}{8}$ of the student/teacher population of 1200 must sign the petition. Also, $\frac{1}{25}$ of the signatures must be from teachers. A petition currently has 150 signatures of which $\frac{73}{75}$ are student signatures. Can this petition be presented? *Explain*.

*REVIEW*
Lesson 5.2;
TAKS Workbook

**40.** **TAKS PRACTICE** Kat ran $2\frac{3}{4}$ miles on Monday and $1\frac{4}{5}$ miles on Tuesday. Which estimate is closest to the total distance Kat ran? *TAKS Obj. 1*

**(A)** 4 mi   **(B)** $4\frac{1}{4}$ mi   **(C)** $4\frac{1}{2}$ mi   **(D)** $4\frac{2}{3}$ mi

*REVIEW*
Lesson 4.5;
TAKS Workbook

**41.** **TAKS PRACTICE** A carpenter has a pipe that is between $\frac{1}{2}$ inch and $\frac{7}{8}$ inch long. Which might be the pipe's length? *TAKS Obj. 1*

**(F)** $\frac{3}{8}$ in.   **(G)** $\frac{5}{12}$ in.   **(H)** $\frac{3}{5}$ in.   **(J)** $\frac{8}{9}$ in.

# 5.4 Dividing Fractions

TEKS 8.1.B, 8.15.A

| **Before** | You added, subtracted, and multiplied fractions. |
| **Now** | You'll divide fractions. |
| **Why?** | So you can calculate weight, as in pounds of chicken feed in Ex. 57. |

**KEY VOCABULARY**

- **reciprocal,** *p. 247*
- **multiplicative inverse,** *p. 247*

## ACTIVITY

**You can use models to divide fractions.**

**STEP 1** The model shows that $\frac{3}{4}$ is a part of 6 eight times, so $6 \div \frac{3}{4} = 8$.

**STEP 2** Calculate $6 \cdot \frac{4}{3}$. Compare the values of $6 \div \frac{3}{4}$ and $6 \cdot \frac{4}{3}$.

**STEP 3** Use the model below to evaluate $4 \div \frac{2}{5}$.

**STEP 4** Calculate $4 \cdot \frac{5}{2}$. Compare the values of $4 \div \frac{2}{5}$ and $4 \cdot \frac{5}{2}$.

**STEP 5** What fraction can you multiply by 5 to evaluate $5 \div \frac{2}{3}$?

**Reciprocals** As the activity suggests, dividing a number by a fraction and multiplying the number by the fraction's *reciprocal* give the same result. Two nonzero numbers are **reciprocals** if their product is 1.

Reciprocals, like $\frac{3}{7}$ and $\frac{7}{3}$, are also called **multiplicative inverses**.

---

### KEY CONCEPT
*For Your Notebook*

## Dividing Fractions

**Words**  To divide by a fraction, multiply by its reciprocal.

**Numbers**  $\frac{3}{10} \div \frac{4}{7} = \frac{3}{10} \cdot \frac{7}{4} = \frac{21}{40}$

**Algebra**  $\frac{a}{b} \div \frac{c}{d} = \frac{a}{b} \cdot \frac{d}{c}$  $(b, c, d \neq 0)$

## EXAMPLE 1  Dividing a Fraction by a Fraction

**a.** $\dfrac{5}{6} \div \dfrac{10}{21} = \dfrac{5}{6} \cdot \dfrac{21}{10}$

$= \dfrac{\overset{1}{\cancel{5}} \cdot \overset{7}{\cancel{21}}}{\underset{2}{\cancel{6}} \cdot \underset{2}{\cancel{10}}}$

$= \dfrac{7}{4}, \text{ or } 1\dfrac{3}{4}$

**b.** $\dfrac{9}{14} \div \dfrac{-2}{7} = \dfrac{9}{14} \cdot \dfrac{7}{-2}$

$= \dfrac{9 \cdot \overset{1}{\cancel{7}}}{\underset{2}{\cancel{14}} \cdot (-2)}$

$= \dfrac{9}{-4}, \text{ or } -2\dfrac{1}{4}$

## EXAMPLE 2  Dividing a Fraction by a Whole Number

$\dfrac{6}{13} \div 3 = \dfrac{6}{13} \cdot \dfrac{1}{3}$     $3 \cdot \dfrac{1}{3} = 1$, so the reciprocal of 3 is $\dfrac{1}{3}$.

$= \dfrac{\overset{2}{\cancel{6}} \cdot 1}{13 \cdot \underset{1}{\cancel{3}}}$     **Multiply fractions. Divide out common factor.**

$= \dfrac{2}{13}$     **Multiply.**

 **GUIDED PRACTICE**  for Examples 1 and 2

**Find the quotient. Simplify if possible.**

**1.** $\dfrac{5}{8} \div \left(-\dfrac{7}{10}\right)$     **2.** $\dfrac{2}{15} \div 8$     **3.** $-\dfrac{3}{4} \div \dfrac{-7}{12}$     **4.** $\dfrac{6}{7} \div 2$

## EXAMPLE 3  Dividing Mixed Numbers

$6\dfrac{1}{3} \div \left(-2\dfrac{5}{6}\right) = \dfrac{19}{3} \div \left(-\dfrac{17}{6}\right)$     **Write $6\dfrac{1}{3}$ and $-2\dfrac{5}{6}$ as improper fractions.**

$= \dfrac{19}{3} \cdot \left(-\dfrac{6}{17}\right)$     **Multiply by $-\dfrac{6}{17}$, the reciprocal of $-\dfrac{17}{6}$.**

$= \dfrac{19 \cdot (\overset{-2}{\cancel{-6}})}{\underset{1}{\cancel{3}} \cdot 17}$     **Multiply. Divide out common factor.**

$= -\dfrac{38}{17}, \text{ or } -2\dfrac{4}{17}$     **Multiply.**

**Check**  Use estimation to check your answer. Replace the divisor and dividend with compatible whole numbers. Because $6 \div (-3) = -2$, you know that $-2\dfrac{4}{17}$ is a reasonable answer.

 **GUIDED PRACTICE**  for Example 3

**Find the quotient. Simplify if possible.**

**5.** $6\dfrac{2}{7} \div 4$     **6.** $-12\dfrac{1}{4} \div 7$     **7.** $10 \div 3\dfrac{1}{3}$     **8.** $-15\dfrac{3}{4} \div \left(-2\dfrac{5}{8}\right)$

**EXAMPLE 4** Solving an Equation with a Fraction

 **Photography** You take 16 of the 24 pictures of a roll of film on your first day of vacation. At this rate, how many days will 4 rolls of film last?

**SOLUTION**

Write a verbal model to describe the problem. Let $d$ represent the number of days.

| Number of rolls of film | = | Fraction of pictures taken each day | · | Number of days |
|---|---|---|---|---|

$$4 = \frac{16}{24}d \qquad \text{Write an algebraic model.}$$

$$4 \cdot \frac{24}{16} = \frac{24}{16} \cdot \frac{16}{24}d \qquad \text{The multiplicative inverse of } \frac{16}{24} \text{ is } \frac{24}{16}.$$

$$\overset{1}{\underset{1}{\cancel{4}}} \cdot \frac{24}{\underset{4}{\cancel{16}}} = 1 \cdot d \qquad \text{Divide out common factor.}$$

$$6 = d \qquad \text{Simplify.}$$

**VOCABULARY**

The product of a number and its multiplicative inverse is 1. You can use this fact to solve equations. This property is called the *inverse property of multiplication*.

▶ **Answer** Four rolls of film will last 6 days.

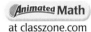 at classzone.com

✓ **GUIDED PRACTICE** for Example 4

9. **What If?** In Example 4, suppose you take 20 of the 24 pictures on the first day. At this rate, how many days will 5 rolls of film last?

## 5.4 EXERCISES

HOMEWORK KEY

🟐 = **TAKS Practice and Reasoning**
Exs. 36, 58, 60, 61, 63, and 65

◯ = **HINTS AND HOMEWORK HELP**
for Exs. 9, 11, 29, 53, 57 at classzone.com

### SKILL PRACTICE

1. **VOCABULARY** What is the multiplicative inverse of a number?

2. **VOCABULARY** Write the reciprocal of each of the numbers: $\frac{1}{2}, \frac{4}{7}, -8, 1\frac{1}{2}$.

**DIVIDING FRACTIONS** Find the quotient. Simplify if possible.

**SEE EXAMPLES 1 AND 2**
on p. 248
for Exs. 3–14

3. $\frac{3}{4} \div \frac{1}{8}$

4. $\frac{11}{12} \div \frac{11}{16}$

5. $\frac{5}{6} \div \left(-\frac{1}{3}\right)$

6. $-\frac{7}{10} \div \frac{4}{5}$

7. $\frac{4}{9} \div \frac{4}{7}$

8. $-\frac{3}{8} \div \frac{7}{12}$

9. $\frac{9}{14} \div \left(-\frac{3}{26}\right)$

10. $-\frac{21}{22} \div \frac{-7}{11}$

11. $-\frac{5}{6} \div (-2)$

12. $\frac{2}{3} \div 3$

13. $\frac{3}{5} \div (-4)$

14. $-\frac{8}{5} \div 12$

**SEE EXAMPLES 1 AND 2**
on p. 248
for Exs. 15–23

**15. ERROR ANALYSIS** Describe and correct the error made in dividing the fractions.

$$\times \quad -\frac{3}{10} \div \left(-\frac{4}{5}\right) = \frac{\overset{-2}{\cancel{-10}}}{3} \cdot \frac{-4}{\underset{1}{\cancel{5}}} = \frac{8}{3}, \text{ or } 2\frac{2}{3}$$

**MENTAL MATH** Use mental math to find the quotient.

**16.** $\frac{1}{2} \div 3$  **17.** $4 \div \frac{1}{2}$  **18.** $1 \div \frac{4}{7}$  **19.** $\frac{2}{3} \div \frac{3}{2}$

**20.** $9 \div \frac{1}{3}$  **21.** $\frac{5}{6} \div \frac{6}{5}$  **22.** $6 \div \frac{2}{3}$  **23.** $10 \div \frac{1}{10}$

**DIVIDING MIXED NUMBERS** Find the quotient. Simplify if possible.

**SEE EXAMPLE 3**
on p. 248
for Exs. 24–35

**24.** $5\frac{1}{4} \div 2\frac{1}{3}$  **25.** $12\frac{1}{7} \div 5\frac{5}{6}$  **26.** $7\frac{7}{8} \div \left(-2\frac{1}{4}\right)$  **27.** $-22\frac{2}{3} \div 3\frac{1}{5}$

**28.** $(-8) \div -9\frac{3}{5}$  **29.** $8\frac{4}{13} \div 6\frac{3}{4}$  **30.** $1\frac{5}{7} \div (-6)$  **31.** $15 \div 4\frac{1}{6}$

**32.** $2 \div 1\frac{1}{3}$  **33.** $6\frac{4}{7} \div (-4)$  **34.** $13\frac{1}{6} \div \frac{2}{5}$  **35.** $-9\frac{5}{6} \div 1\frac{2}{3}$

**SEE EXAMPLE 4**
on p. 249
for Ex. 36

**36. ★ TAKS REASONING** By what do you multiply each side to solve the equation $\frac{5}{6}a = -15$?

(A) $\frac{5}{6}$  (B) $\frac{6}{5}$  (C) $\frac{-1}{15}$  (D) $-15$

**INTERPRETING MODELS** Write and evaluate the division expression illustrated by the model.

**37.**

**38.**

**DRAWING MODELS** Draw a model to show how to divide the fractions.

**39.** $3 \div \frac{1}{2}$  **40.** $2 \div \frac{2}{3}$  **41.** $5 \div \frac{2}{5}$  **42.** $4 \div \frac{3}{4}$

**ALGEBRA** Solve the equation.

**SEE EXAMPLE 4**
on p. 249
for Ex. 43–50

**43.** $\frac{3}{4}a = 15$  **44.** $\frac{7}{10}b = 28$  **45.** $-\frac{9}{17}r = 3$  **46.** $-11 = -9\frac{1}{6}h$

**47.** $\frac{-8}{11}k = -48$  **48.** $\frac{2}{5}m = -18$  **49.** $42 = -5\frac{1}{4}p$  **50.** $9 = \frac{-9}{10}t$

**51. REASONING** Juan says, "To divide a fraction by another fraction, rewrite the fractions with common denominators. Then use the formula $\frac{a}{c} \div \frac{b}{c} = \frac{a}{b}$." Does Juan's method work? *Explain* your reasoning.

**52. CHALLENGE** Find the quotient. Then go back and divide the numerators across and divide the denominators across in the original problem. Make and prove a generalization based on the results.

**a.** $\frac{10}{21} \div \frac{2}{3}$  **b.** $\frac{9}{20} \div \frac{3}{4}$  **c.** $\frac{15}{16} \div \frac{5}{8}$  **d.** $\frac{24}{25} \div \frac{4}{5}$

**CHOOSE AN OPERATION** In Exercises 53–57, tell which operation you would use to solve the problem and why. Then solve the problem.

**53.** **SERVING SIZES** How many hamburgers can you make from 5 pounds of hamburger if you use $\frac{1}{4}$ pound of meat per hamburger?

**54.** **CD PLAYER** Your CD player runs for about $6\frac{1}{2}$ hours on new batteries. The average length of the CDs in your collection is about $\frac{5}{6}$ hour. How many CDs can you expect to listen to using one new set of batteries?

**55.** **TRIPLE JUMP** Jasmine did the triple jump in gym class. What total distance did she cover?

**56.** **BOOKSHELVES** You have 4 bookshelves, each $2\frac{1}{3}$ feet wide. How many feet of wall space will all 4 take up if they are placed end to end?

**57.** **FARMING** You have 6 chickens and each chicken eats about 85 pounds of feed per year. How many pounds of feed will they eat in $1\frac{1}{2}$ years?

**58.** **TAKS REASONING** Haley has a summer job at which she normally works $7\frac{1}{2}$ hours a day, 3 days per week. She plans to work for 7 weeks.

  **a.** Haley earns $180 per week. How much does she earn per hour?

  **b.** How much will Haley earn weekly if she works an extra 3 hour shift?

  **c.** How many extra 3 hour shifts does Haley need to work in order to earn a total of $1356 for the summer? *Explain* how you found your answer.

**59.** **WRITING** *Explain* how to find the reciprocal of a positive fraction and the reciprocal of a negative fraction.

**60.** **TAKS REASONING** Use the formula $C = (F - 32) \div \frac{9}{5}$. What is 77°F in degrees Celsius?

  **(A)** 20°C **(B)** 25°C **(C)** 30°C **(D)** 81°C

**61.** **TAKS REASONING** You are creating a board game. You want to cut square game pieces that measure $1\frac{1}{4}$ inches on each side from a piece of paper that measures $8\frac{1}{2}$ inches by 11 inches. How many game pieces can you cut from the paper? How many square inches of paper are left over? *Explain* how you found your answer.

**62. ENROLLMENT** Two fifths of the students in your school, which is 270 students, are taking an art class. How many students are in your school? *Explain* how you got your answer.

**63.** 🌟 **TAKS REASONING** *Describe* a real-world situation that can be modeled by the equation $\frac{1}{2}\left(\frac{4}{9}x\right) = 28$. Then solve the equation.

**64. CHALLENGE** Students were asked whether they preferred watching fall, winter, or spring school sports. Then they were asked to choose their favorite sport from their preferred season. One third of the students chose fall sports. Of those students, two sevenths chose soccer. One half of the students chose spring sports. Of those students, three fifths chose baseball. The number of students who chose baseball was how many times the number who chose soccer?

---

## MIXED REVIEW FOR TAKS

**TAKS** PRACTICE at classzone.com

*REVIEW*
Lesson 5.3;
TAKS Workbook

**65.** 🌟 **TAKS PRACTICE** Jim had 5 hours worth of homework. He spent 45 minutes on math homework and used one third of the remaining time to work on his history project. To find the amount of time Jim has left to work on homework, convert 5 hours to 300 minutes, subtract 45, and then — *TAKS Obj. 6*

- **Ⓕ** convert the result back to hours.

- **Ⓖ** subtract 20 from the result.

- **Ⓗ** divide the result by 20.

- **Ⓙ** multiply the result by two thirds.

---

## QUIZ for Lessons 5.1–5.4

**Evaluate the expression.** *(pp. 233, 238)*

**1.** $1\frac{5}{8} - \frac{7}{8}$    **2.** $-\frac{4}{9} + 3\frac{5}{9}$    **3.** $\frac{x}{12} + \frac{5x}{12}$    **4.** $\frac{4}{9} - \frac{8}{9} + \frac{5}{9}$

**5.** $\frac{2}{3} + \frac{9}{6}$    **6.** $\frac{6y}{21} - \frac{2y}{7}$    **7.** $-5\frac{3}{4} - 2\frac{1}{3}$    **8.** $\frac{3}{10} + 4\frac{2}{5} - 1\frac{1}{2}$

**9. RECIPE** A recipe uses $4\frac{2}{3}$ cups of flour. Another recipe uses $4\frac{1}{4}$ cups. You have 9 cups of flour. Can you make both recipes? *Explain.* *(p. 238)*

**Find the product or quotient.** *(pp. 243, 247)*

**10.** $\frac{7}{12} \cdot \frac{8}{21}$    **11.** $-\frac{11}{12} \cdot \left(-\frac{3}{10}\right)$    **12.** $-\frac{14}{5} \cdot 2\frac{6}{7}$    **13.** $1\frac{1}{8} \cdot (-3)$

**14.** $\frac{1}{2} \div \frac{5}{6}$    **15.** $\frac{4}{9} \div 8$    **16.** $-\frac{4}{5} \div \frac{3}{2}$    **17.** $-1\frac{3}{4} \div \left(-\frac{7}{12}\right)$

**18. BIOLOGY** An average human hair grows about $\frac{1}{2}$ inch per month. How much does a human hair grow in $3\frac{1}{2}$ months? *(p. 243)*

---

TEKS *8.1.B, 8.14.D*

# 5.4 Operations with Fractions

You can use a calculator to evaluate expressions with fractions. First, set your calculator to display the answers as fractions or mixed numbers in simplest form.

Press **2nd** [FracMode]. Select $A \sqcup b/c$ and press **=** to set the calculator to mixed number mode.

Press **2nd** [FracMode]. Select *Auto* and press **=** to set the calculator to automatically simplify fractions.

**EXPLORE** Use a calculator to evaluate the expression.

| | | **Keystrokes** | **Display** | **Answer** |
|---|---|---|---|---|
| a. | $\frac{2}{3} - 4\frac{6}{7}$ | **2** [/] **3** [−] **4** [UNIT] **6** [/] **7** [=] | $-4 \sqcup 4/21$ | $-4\frac{4}{21}$ |
| b. | $-\frac{5}{17} \cdot \left(-\frac{8}{35}\right)$ | [(−)] **5** [/] **17** [×] [(−)] **8** [/] **35** [=] | $8/119$ | $\frac{8}{119}$ |
| c. | $\frac{3}{10} \div \left(-1\frac{4}{5}\right)$ | **3** [/] **10** [÷] [(−)] **1** [UNIT] **4** [/] **5** [=] | $-1/6$ | $-\frac{1}{6}$ |

**PRACTICE** Use a calculator to evaluate the expression.

**1.** $\frac{5}{11} + \frac{2}{5}$  **2.** $3\frac{1}{4} + \left(-\frac{6}{7}\right)$  **3.** $7\frac{1}{2} - 6\frac{5}{6}$  **4.** $\frac{2}{5} - \frac{2}{3}$

**5.** $\frac{7}{9} \cdot 1\frac{1}{3}$  **6.** $\frac{2}{5} \cdot \left(-\frac{3}{4}\right)$  **7.** $\frac{4}{7} \cdot \frac{1}{2}$  **8.** $2\frac{2}{3} \cdot \left(-\frac{1}{4}\right)$

**9.** $9\frac{4}{5} \div \frac{7}{8}$  **10.** $-10\frac{2}{13} \div \left(-3\frac{1}{3}\right)$  **11.** $1\frac{7}{9} \div \frac{1}{3}$  **12.** $\frac{5}{8} \div \left(-\frac{1}{7}\right)$

**13. PAPER DRIVE** A community center's members are having a newspaper drive. Their goal is to collect 1000 pounds of newspaper to be recycled. They have already collected $625\frac{3}{8}$ pounds. How many more pounds do they need to reach their goal?

**14. CAR CARE** Rosa's car needs $4\frac{1}{4}$ quarts of oil to run properly. She notices her car has only $\frac{3}{4}$ of the amount of oil that it needs. How much oil should she add for her car to run properly?

## Lessons 5.1–5.4

**MULTIPLE CHOICE**

1. **BEADS** Anna takes $\frac{1}{6}$ of the 24 beads in a bowl. Then John takes 2 beads. Lena takes $\frac{1}{9}$ of what Anna and John left. Dawn takes $\frac{1}{4}$ of what Lena left, and then Jamal takes 5 beads. What fraction of the original beads is left in the bowl? *TEKS 8.14.A*

   Ⓐ $\frac{1}{6}$          Ⓑ $\frac{1}{4}$

   Ⓒ $\frac{7}{24}$         Ⓓ $\frac{17}{24}$

2. **RIBBON** You buy a roll of ribbon 20 yards long to make gift bows. The amounts of ribbon you use for a gift are shown below. You tie and decorate 5 gifts. How many extra bows can you make with the ribbon you have left? *TEKS 8.2.B*

    $2\frac{1}{6}$ yards     $1\frac{1}{2}$ yards

   Ⓕ 0          Ⓖ 1

   Ⓗ 2          Ⓙ 3

3. **RECIPES** A recipe for making rolls calls for $5\frac{2}{3}$ cups of flour. Each batch of the recipe makes $3\frac{1}{2}$ dozen rolls. How many rolls can you make with 17 cups of flour? *TEKS 8.1.B*

   Ⓐ $9\frac{1}{6}$ dozen     Ⓑ $9\frac{1}{2}$ dozen

   Ⓒ $10\frac{1}{2}$ dozen    Ⓓ 14 dozen

4. **NUMBER PUZZLE** A fraction and a mixed number has a sum that is greater than 1, a product that is less than 1, and a difference that is less than $\frac{1}{2}$. What are possible values of the fraction and mixed number? *TEKS 8.14.B*

   Ⓕ $\frac{1}{2}$ and $1\frac{1}{4}$     Ⓖ $\frac{2}{3}$ and $1\frac{1}{4}$

   Ⓗ $\frac{2}{5}$ and $1\frac{1}{3}$     Ⓙ $\frac{3}{4}$ and $1\frac{1}{6}$

5. **BACKPACKING** Bill packs $8\frac{1}{2}$ pounds of food and $13\frac{1}{2}$ pounds of equipment in a $2\frac{1}{4}$ pound backpack. The total recommended weight of a backpack and its contents should not exceed $\frac{1}{5}$ of the carrier's bodyweight. Bill weighs 100 pounds. How much more does Bill's backpack weigh than is recommended? *TEKS 8.2.B*

   Ⓐ $3\frac{1}{4}$ lb       Ⓑ $4\frac{1}{4}$ lb

   Ⓒ $4\frac{17}{20}$ lb     Ⓓ $6\frac{3}{4}$ lb

6. **TRAILS** A fitness trail is divided into five segments, as shown below. You run the first segment of the trail, and walk the next. You continue to alternate between running and walking until you finish the trail. What fraction of the trail do you run? *TEKS 8.14.B*

   **Fitness Trail**
   $1\frac{1}{2}$ mi   $1\frac{1}{4}$ mi   $1\frac{1}{6}$ mi   $\frac{4}{3}$ mi   $\frac{5}{4}$ mi   Start   End

   Ⓕ $\frac{5}{13}$        Ⓖ $\frac{7}{12}$

   Ⓗ $\frac{8}{13}$        Ⓙ 4

**GRIDDED ANSWER** ⓪①②●④⑤⑥⑦⑧⑨

7. **JOBS** Two sevenths of the students in your school, or 400 students, have a part-time job. How many students in your school do *not* have a part-time job? *TEKS 8.3.B*

# 5.5 Fractions and Decimals

**TEKS** *8.1.A, 8.1.B*

| | |
|---|---|
| **Before** | You divided whole numbers. |
| **Now** | You'll write fractions as decimals and decimals as fractions. |
| **Why?** | So you can compare lengths, as with caterpillars in Ex. 57. |

**KEY VOCABULARY**
- **rational number,** *p. 255*
- **terminating decimal,** *p. 255*
- **repeating decimal,** *p. 255*

A **rational number** is a number that can be written as a quotient $\frac{a}{b}$, where $a$ and $b$ are integers and $b \neq 0$. The diagram below shows how rational numbers, integers, and whole numbers are related.

Rational numbers include integers. ⟶

Integers include whole numbers. ⟶

**Rational numbers**

**Integers**
−3  −2  −1

**Whole numbers**
3  1
0  2

Numbers like 2, −6, −5$\frac{3}{5}$, and −8.73 are rational numbers.

To write any rational number $\frac{a}{b}$ as a decimal, divide $a$ by $b$. If the quotient has a remainder of zero, the result is a **terminating decimal**. If the quotient has a digit or group of digits that repeats without end, the result is a **repeating decimal**.

## EXAMPLE 1  Writing Fractions as Decimals

**Write the fraction as a decimal.**

**WRITE REPEATING DECIMALS**
You can use an ellipsis or an overbar to show that one or more digits repeat.

$0.333 \ldots = 0.\overline{3}$

**a.** $\frac{5}{11} \longrightarrow$
$$
\begin{array}{r}
0.4545\ldots \\
11\overline{)5.0000\ldots} \\
\underline{4\,4} \\
60 \\
\underline{55} \\
50 \\
\underline{44} \\
60 \\
\underline{55}
\end{array}
$$
⟵ Repeating decimal

▶ **Answer** $\frac{5}{11} = 0.4545\ldots = 0.\overline{45}$

**b.** $\frac{7}{20} \longrightarrow$
$$
\begin{array}{r}
0.35 \\
20\overline{)7.00} \\
\underline{6\,0} \\
1\,00 \\
\underline{1\,00} \\
0
\end{array}
$$
⟵ Terminating decimal

▶ **Answer** $\frac{7}{20} = 0.35$

✓ **GUIDED PRACTICE**  for Example 1

**1.** Write $\frac{8}{25}$ as a decimal.

**2.** Write $\frac{1}{6}$ as a decimal.

## EXAMPLE 2 Ordering Rational Numbers

**Biology** The table lists the mean lengths of five species of finches. Order the finch species from shortest to longest.

| *Finch species* | House Finch | Indigo Bunting | Lazuli Bunting | Painted Bunting | Purple Finch |
|---|---|---|---|---|---|
| *Length (inches)* | $5\frac{5}{8}$ | 5.5 | $5\frac{7}{16}$ | 5.25 | $5\frac{3}{4}$ |

**Indigo bunting**

### SOLUTION

Write all of the lengths as decimals. The **ones** digits are all the same, so order according to the **tenths** digits.

*KNOW COMMON CONVERSIONS*

With practice, you'll recognize common equivalent fractions and decimals. For a table of these pairs, see page 820.

$$5\frac{5}{8} = 5.625 \qquad 5.5 \qquad 5\frac{7}{16} = 5.4375 \qquad 5.25 \qquad 5\frac{3}{4} = 5.75$$

▶ **Answer** From shortest to longest the species are Painted Bunting, Lazuli Bunting, Indigo Bunting, House Finch, and Purple Finch.

**Check** Graph the finches' lengths on a number line.

These lengths, from left to right, correspond to the answer.

## ✓ GUIDED PRACTICE for Example 2

**Order the numbers from least to greatest.**

**3.** $0.51, \frac{3}{5}, \frac{11}{20}, \frac{2}{3}, 0.62$

**4.** $-1\frac{1}{8}, -1\frac{3}{7}, -1.1, -1.43, -1\frac{4}{15}$

**Terminating Decimals** To write a terminating decimal as a fraction or mixed number, use the place value of the decimal's last digit as the denominator. For example, write 0.37 as $\frac{37}{100}$ because 7 is in the hundredths' place.

## EXAMPLE 3 Writing Terminating Decimals as Fractions

**Write the decimal as a fraction or mixed number in simplest form.**

*REVIEW PLACE VALUE*

Need help with place value? See the Skills Review Handbook, p. 759.

**a.** $0.4 = \frac{4}{10}$ ◀— 4 is in the tenths' place.

$= \frac{2}{5}$ **Simplify.**

**b.** $-1.905 = -1\frac{905}{1000}$ ◀— 5 is in the thousandths' place.

$= -1\dfrac{\overset{181}{\cancel{905}}}{\underset{200}{\cancel{1000}}}$

$= -1\frac{181}{200}$ **Simplify.**

**Repeating Decimals** To write a repeating decimal as a fraction or mixed number, let the decimal equal $x$. Then form an equivalent equation by multiplying both sides of the equation by $10^n$, where $n$ is the number of repeating digits. Then subtract the equations.

**EXAMPLE 4** Writing Repeating Decimals as Fractions

**TAKE NOTES**
You may wish to copy examples into your notebook that show writing repeating decimals as fractions. Include examples with one, two, and three repeating digits.

**STEP 1** Write $0.\overline{48}$ as a fraction by first letting $x = 0.\overline{48}$ or $0.484848\ldots$.

**STEP 2** Multiply by $10^2$, or 100, because the number has 2 repeating digits. You get $100x = 48.\overline{48}$, or $48.484848\ldots$.

**STEP 3** Subtract $x$ from $100x$.

$$
\begin{array}{r}
100x = 48.484848\ldots \\
-\quad x = \phantom{0}0.484848\ldots \\
\hline
99x = 48.000000\ldots
\end{array}
$$

**STEP 4** Solve for $x$ and simplify.
$$x = \frac{48}{99} = \frac{16}{33}$$

▶ **Answer** The decimal $0.\overline{48}$ is equivalent to the fraction $\frac{16}{33}$.

✓ **GUIDED PRACTICE** for Examples 3 and 4

**Write the decimal as a fraction or mixed number.**

**5.** $0.62$      **6.** $-2.45$      **7.** $-0.\overline{7}$      **8.** $0.\overline{36}$

# 5.5 EXERCISES

**HOMEWORK KEY**
🔷 = **TAKS Practice and Reasoning**
Exs. 55, 61, 62, and 64

◯ = **HINTS AND HOMEWORK HELP**
for Exs. 13, 15, 27, 35, 55 at classzone.com

## SKILL PRACTICE

**VOCABULARY** Tell whether the number is included in each of the following number sets: *rational number, integer, whole number.*

**1.** $0$      **2.** $0.55$      **3.** $-14$      **4.** $0.\overline{3}$

**FRACTIONS AS DECIMALS** Write the fraction or mixed number as a decimal.

**SEE EXAMPLE 1**
on p. 255
for Exs. 5–17

**5.** $\frac{3}{4}$      **6.** $-\frac{1}{9}$      **7.** $-\frac{12}{25}$      **8.** $\frac{7}{12}$

**9.** $-\frac{4}{25}$      **10.** $\frac{27}{50}$      **11.** $3\frac{11}{16}$      **12.** $-4\frac{33}{80}$

**13.** $-\frac{14}{33}$      **14.** $\frac{27}{44}$      **15.** $6\frac{8}{15}$      **16.** $-14\frac{7}{11}$

**17. ERROR ANALYSIS** Describe and correct the error made in writing the mixed number as a decimal.

$$\cancel{2\frac{3}{10} = 2.03}$$

SEE EXAMPLE 2
on p. 256
for Exs. 18–28

**COMPARING NUMBERS** Complete the statement using <, >, or =.

**18.** 1.1 ? 1.09

**19.** $-4.29$ ? $-4.3$

**20.** $-\frac{7}{15}$ ? $-\frac{3}{8}$

**21.** $-\frac{11}{20}$ ? $-\frac{5}{9}$

**22.** $\frac{11}{18}$ ? $0.6\overline{1}$

**23.** $0.857$ ? $\frac{6}{7}$

**24.** $-0.71$ ? $-\frac{17}{24}$

**25.** $-\frac{23}{30}$ ? $-0.7\overline{6}$

**ORDERING NUMBERS** Order the numbers from least to greatest.

**26.** $7\frac{4}{5}, 7\frac{2}{3}, 7.6, 7.71, 7\frac{8}{21}$

**(27.)** $0.1, \frac{5}{6}, \frac{3}{10}, -\frac{2}{7}, -0.4$

**28.** $9\frac{3}{4}, 9.74, 9\frac{5}{7}, 9.72, 9\frac{9}{13}$

SEE EXAMPLES
3 AND 4
on pp. 256–257
for Exs. 29–44

**DECIMALS AS FRACTIONS** Write the decimal as a fraction or mixed number.

**29.** $0.6$

**30.** $-6.4$

**31.** $0.48$

**32.** $-2.79$

**33.** $0.365$

**34.** $7.253$

**(35.)** $-5.0032$

**36.** $-0.0012$

**37.** $0.\overline{8}$

**38.** $0.\overline{53}$

**39.** $0.\overline{21}$

**40.** $0.\overline{6}$

**41.** $0.6\overline{35}$

**42.** $-0.1\overline{87}$

**43.** $-0.1\overline{5}$

**44.** $4.0\overline{25}$

**ORDERING EXPRESSIONS** Order the values from greatest to least.

**45.** $1.21, \left(\frac{1}{3}\right)^3, 3^{-2}, 1.\overline{21}$

**46.** $2.411, \frac{13}{5}, 2\frac{2}{5}, 2.4\overline{1}$

**47.** $\left(\frac{1}{5}\right)^2, 0.\overline{4}, \frac{3}{7}, 4^{-2}$

**48.** $-3.\overline{4}, -3.4\overline{2}, \left(\frac{1}{3}\right)^{-1}, -3\frac{2}{5}$

**49.** $2^{-4}, \frac{-1}{15}, -0.\overline{6}, 0.66$

**50.** $\left(\frac{2}{3}\right)^{-2}, -2.2, -2.\overline{25}, \frac{-9}{4}$

**51. REASONING** In the following expressions, $x > 0$. Order the expressions from least to greatest. *Explain* your reasoning.

$$x, \quad \frac{x}{5}, \quad \frac{x}{3}, \quad \frac{x}{7}, \quad \frac{x}{8}, \quad \frac{x}{6}, \quad \frac{x}{2}, \quad \frac{x}{4}$$

**CHALLENGE** Solve the equation.

**52.** $\frac{y}{15} = 2.\overline{45}$

**53.** $\frac{x}{12} = 0.41\overline{6}$

**54.** $\frac{z}{20} = 0.\overline{27}$

## PROBLEM SOLVING

SEE EXAMPLE 1
on p. 255
for Exs. 55–56

**(55.)** ⬆ **TAKS REASONING** In a class, $\frac{22}{25}$ of the students are right-handed. What is another way to express this number?

**(A)** 0.22

**(B)** 0.25

**(C)** 0.47

**(D)** 0.88

**56. STOCK LISTINGS** The New York Stock Exchange once used fractions to list the values of its stocks. It switched to decimals in 2001. Write the following stock prices as decimals rounded to the nearest cent.

$$\$5\frac{1}{4}, \quad \$44\frac{1}{2}, \quad \$53\frac{3}{8}, \quad \$17\frac{7}{16}$$

SEE EXAMPLES
1 AND 2
on pp. 255–256
for Ex. 57

**57. CATERPILLARS** Write the following lengths of caterpillars in order from shortest to longest. Express the lengths as decimals, in inches. (*Hint:* Convert from feet to inches first.)

$$1\frac{7}{8} \text{ inches}, \quad \frac{3}{20} \text{ foot}, \quad 2\frac{1}{9} \text{ inches}, \quad \frac{7}{40} \text{ foot}$$

⬆ = **TAKS Practice and Reasoning** ⭘ = **HINTS AND HOMEWORK HELP** *at classzone.com*

**58. WRITING** Lake Superior has a surface area of about 32,000 square miles. About what fraction of the 182,000 square miles of U.S. water surface area is this? Write this fraction as a decimal. *Explain* how you can use estimation to check that the answer is reasonable.

**59. NUMBER SENSE** Is the number 0.1010010001 . . . a rational number? *Explain.*

**60. LOOK FOR A PATTERN** Write the fractions $\frac{1}{11}$, $\frac{2}{11}$, and $\frac{3}{11}$ as decimals. *Predict* the decimal forms of $\frac{4}{11}$ and $\frac{5}{11}$ using your results. Check your predictions.

**Lake Superior**

**61. TAKS REASONING** The table below lists the fraction of 1200 students in a survey that named each breakfast food as their favorite.

| Breakfast food | bagels | bacon | eggs | cereal | pancakes |
|---|---|---|---|---|---|
| Fraction of students | $\frac{1}{8}$ | $\frac{1}{12}$ | $\frac{3}{16}$ | $\frac{1}{4}$ | $\frac{3}{25}$ |

**a.** Write each fraction as a decimal and order the foods from most popular to least popular.

**b.** How many more students picked the most popular food than the least popular food? *Explain* how you found your answer.

**c.** How many of the 1200 students did not choose any of the foods listed?

**62. TAKS REASONING** Find a rational number between $-\frac{1}{64}$ and $-\frac{1}{63}$. Write your answer as a decimal and as a fraction.

**63. CHALLENGE** At the end of a race, all of the runners' times are posted as decimals rounded to the nearest thousandth of an hour. Kim finished the race in 1 hour, 22 minutes, and 34 seconds. What was Kim's posted time? If no two runners finished at the same time, how many runners could have the same *posted* time as Kim? *Explain.*

---

## MIXED REVIEW FOR TAKS
**TAKS PRACTICE** at classzone.com

*REVIEW*
Lesson 5.2;
TAKS Workbook

**64. TAKS PRACTICE** Lily subscribes to a news Website. The first month costs half the standard monthly subscription rate, *r*. If she subscribes for six months, she also gets one third of one month's cost back.

Which expression shows the amount she will pay for a six month subscription? *TAKS Obj. 2*

**Ⓐ** $6r - \frac{1}{2} - \frac{1}{3}$

**Ⓑ** $\frac{1}{2}\left(6r - \frac{1}{3}\right)$

**Ⓒ** $\frac{1}{2}r + 5r - \frac{1}{3}r$

**Ⓓ** $\frac{1}{2}\left(5r - \frac{1}{3}\right)$

---

# 5.6 Adding and Subtracting Decimals

TEKS *8.2.B, 8.14.D*

| Before | You added and subtracted fractions. |
| Now | You'll add and subtract decimals. |
| Why? | So you can compare spending, as in Example 1. |

**KEY VOCABULARY**
• front-end estimation, *p. 261*

You can use a vertical format to add or subtract decimals. Begin by lining up the decimal points. Then add or subtract as with whole numbers. Be sure to include the decimal point in your answer.

**EXAMPLE 1** Adding and Subtracting Decimals

**Dancing** The table shows the amounts of money (in billions of dollars) that people in the United States spent on dance studios, schools, and halls. How much was spent in 1995 and 1996? How much more was spent in 1998 than in 1997?

| Money Spent on Dancing | |
|---|---|
| **Year** | **Dollars (billions)** |
| 1994 | 0.906 |
| 1995 | 0.947 |
| 1996 | 1.046 |
| 1997 | 1.08 |
| 1998 | 1.138 |

**SOLUTION**

a. To find how many billions of dollars were spent in 1995 and 1996, add the values from the table for 1995 and 1996.

$$\begin{array}{r} \overset{1}{0.947} \\ +1.046 \\ \hline 1.993 \end{array}$$

▸ **Answer** In 1995 and 1996, $1.993 billion was spent.

b. To find how much more was spent in 1998 than in 1997, subtract the value for 1997 from the value for 1998.

$$\begin{array}{r} 1.138 \\ -1.080 \\ \hline 0.058 \end{array}$$

Use a zero as a placeholder.

▸ **Answer** In 1998, $0.058 billion more was spent than in 1997.

**ADD AND SUBTRACT INTEGERS**
Need help adding and subtracting integers? See Lessons 2.2 and 2.3.

In Chapter 2, you learned rules for adding and subtracting positive and negative integers. You can apply the same rules to adding and subtracting positive and negative decimals.

✓ **GUIDED PRACTICE** for Example 1

**Find the sum or difference.**

**1.** $-12.5 + (-4.55)$  **2.** $8.93 + 0.367$  **3.** $7.624 + (-0.05)$

**4.** $8.91 - 2.745$  **5.** $-5.3 - 11.49$  **6.** $5.376 - (-0.8)$

## EXAMPLE 2 Solving Equations with Decimals

**a.**

$$y - 1.537 = 6.48 \qquad \text{Original equation}$$

$$y - 1.537 + \mathbf{1.537} = 6.48 + \mathbf{1.537} \qquad \text{Add 1.537 to each side.}$$

$$y = 8.017 \qquad \text{Simplify.}$$

**b.**

$$x + (-0.34) = 4.27 \qquad \text{Original equation}$$

$$x + (-0.34) + \mathbf{0.34} = 4.27 + \mathbf{0.34} \qquad \text{Add 0.34 to each side.}$$

$$x = 4.61 \qquad \text{Simplify.}$$

**Estimating** You can estimate sums using **front-end estimation**. Add the front-end digits to get a low estimate. Then use the remaining digits to adjust the sum to a closer estimate.

## EXAMPLE 3 Using Front-End Estimation

**Theater** You want to estimate the cost of supplies for a play. Is the cost of the items shown (excluding tax) more or less than your $50 budget?

**SOLUTION**

Use front-end estimation.

| Play supplies | Cost |
|---|---|
| cowboy hat | $18.97 |
| cotton fabric | $9.49 |
| rope | $3.49 |
| safety pins | $2.19 |
| picnic basket | $16.77 |

**STEP 1**
**Add** the **front-end digits**: the dollars.

$18.97
$9.49
$3.49
$2.19
$16.77
$48

**STEP 2**
**Estimate** the sum of the remaining digits: the cents.

$18.97 —— $1
$9.49
$3.49 > $1
$2.19
$16.77 > $1
$3

**STEP 3**
**Add** the results.

$48
+ $3
$51

▶ **Answer** The cost of the items is more than your $50 budget.

✓ **GUIDED PRACTICE** for Examples 2 and 3

**Solve the equation.**

**7.** $x + 1.38 = 2.55$  **8.** $z - 5.3 = 16.29$  **9.** $y - (-0.83) = 0.48$

**10.** Use front-end estimation to estimate the sum $1.95 + $7.49 + $3.50.

**EXAMPLE 4** TAKS PRACTICE: Multiple Choice

**Kelvins** The Kelvin scale for temperature is used by chemists. The formula $K = C + 273.15$ is used to convert from degrees Celsius to kelvins, where $C$ is the degrees Celsius and $K$ is kelvins. The boiling point of liquid nitrogen is approximately $-196°C$. What is this temperature in kelvins?

(A) 77.15 K     (B) 253.55 K     (C) 271.19 K     (D) 469.15 K

**SOLUTION**

To find the temperature in kelvins, substitute the Celsius temperature into the equation.

$K = C + 273.15$     **Original equation**

$K = -196 + 273.15$     **Substitute -196 for C.**

$K = 77.15$     **Add.**

▶ **Answer** The temperature in kelvins is 77.15 K.
The correct answer is A. (A) (B) (C) (D)

✓ **GUIDED PRACTICE**    **for Example 4**

**11.** What is 29°C in kelvins?       **12.** What is 324.15 K in degrees Celsius?

# 5.6 EXERCISES

HOMEWORK KEY

✎ = **TAKS Practice and Reasoning**
Exs. 18, 46, 47, and 52

○ = **HINTS AND HOMEWORK HELP**
for Exs. 9, 13, 25, 29, 45 at classzone.com

## SKILL PRACTICE

**1. VOCABULARY** Copy and complete: You can get a low estimate of $13.56 + 11.42 + 25.94$ by adding the front-end digits ___?___ , ___?___ , and ___?___ .

**EVALUATING EXPRESSIONS** Find the sum or difference.

*SEE EXAMPLE 1*
on p. 260
for Exs. 2–18

**2.** $30.193 + 7.91$      **3.** $2.507 + 0.586$      **4.** $-6.08 + 2.661$

**5.** $-0.37 + (-1.8)$      **6.** $6.8 + (-1.812)$      **7.** $-12.09 + 1.20$

**8.** $3.28 + (-4.91)$      **9.** $1.46 + (-1.564)$      **10.** $1.57 - 9.28$

**11.** $68.79 - 9.18$      **12.** $15.7 - (-6.4)$      **13.** $-0.99 - 0.304$

**14.** $25.885 - 6.9$      **15.** $29.1 - (-3.05)$      **16.** $-4.22 - 0.807$

**17. ERROR ANALYSIS** Describe and correct the error made in the solution.

$$\begin{array}{r} 10.43 \\ +\ 7.521 \\ \hline 8.564 \end{array}$$

**18.** ⬥ **TAKS REASONING** An item costs $9.87 plus sales tax of $.49. What is the total cost of the item?

    **(A)** $8.38        **(B)** $9.36        **(C)** $9.38        **(D)** $10.36

**SEE EXAMPLE 2**
on p. 261
for Exs. 19–27

**XY** **ALGEBRA** **Solve the equation.**

**19.** $x + 2.9 = 5.3$      **20.** $y - 4.15 = -4.26$      **21.** $z - (-7.7) = 13.31$

**22.** $y + 1.5 = 37$      **23.** $-2.8 + x = 4.51$      **24.** $10.4 = 12.46 + z$

**25.** $7.81 = 7.98 + y$      **26.** $z + (-3.19) = 5.83$      **27.** $x - 0.013 = -6.36$

**SEE EXAMPLE 3**
on p. 261
for Exs. 28–31

**ESTIMATING SUMS** **Use front-end estimation to estimate the sum.**

**28.** $2.32 + 6.69 + 8.50 + 4.46$      **29.** $10.23 + 6.98 + 9.05 + 5.80$

**30.** $5.62 + 4.89 + 3.44 + 9.98$      **31.** $23.70 + 16.12 + 5.96 + 14.18$

**XY** **ALGEBRA** **Evaluate the expression when $a = 6.28$ and $b = -0.35$. Write your answer as a decimal.**

**32.** $a - \dfrac{5}{2}$      **33.** $\dfrac{3}{8} + a$      **34.** $b - \dfrac{3}{4}$      **35.** $\dfrac{9}{20} + b$

**GEOMETRY** **Find the perimeter of the figure.**

**36.**
28.4 ft, 19 ft, 20.35 ft

**37.**
3.05 cm, 5.8 cm, 5.8 cm, 6.25 cm

**38.**
3.2 m, 7.41 m, 3.2 m, 3.2 m, 9.41 m

**39.** **GEOMETRY** Plot the following points in a coordinate plane. Then connect the points to form a rectangle and find its perimeter.

     $A(1.25, 3.5)$, $B(4.25, 3.5)$, $C(4.25, 6.75)$, $D(1.25, 6.75)$

**CHALLENGE** **Find the sum.**

**40.** $0.\overline{67} + 0.\overline{6}$      **41.** $5.\overline{345} + 0.\overline{87}$      **42.** $1.\overline{7} + 1.\overline{876621}$      **43.** $3.\overline{19} + 7.\overline{91}$

## PROBLEM SOLVING

**44.** **TRACK** You run 400 meters in 58.01 seconds. What is the difference of your time and the school record of 55.49 seconds?

**45.** **SHOT PUT** The world record for men's shot put is 23.12 meters. The Olympic record is 22.47 meters. The gold medal winning throw at the 2004 Summer Olympics was 21.16 meters.

  **a.** How much longer was the world record throw than the gold medal winning throw at the 2004 Olympics?

  **b.** How much longer is the Olympic record throw than the gold medal winning throw at the 2004 Olympics?

46. ➤ **TAKS REASONING** The formula $K = (F - 32)\frac{5}{9} + 273.15$ converts degrees Fahrenheit to kelvins. The boiling point of water is 212° F. What is this temperature in kelvins?

(A) 390.93 K     (B) 373.15 K     (C) 273.15 K     (D) 100 K

47. ➤ **TAKS REASONING** A city had 4.52 inches of rain in April, 5.23 inches of rain in May, and 3.41 inches of rain in June. During this three-month period, did the city have more than 12 inches of rain? *Explain* why an estimate is sufficient to answer the question.

48. **WRITING** What do you know about the sum of two positive decimals that are less than 1? What do you *not* know about this sum? *Explain.*

49. **MULTI-STEP PROBLEM** Use the January bank record below. The beginning balance was $83.47.

    **a.** Estimate the balance at the end of the month.

    **b.** Find the exact balance.

    **c.** After the next transaction, the new balance is $101.25. Was the transaction a deposit or withdrawal? How much was the deposit or withdrawal?

| Date | Transaction | Deposit | Withdrawal |
|------|-------------|---------|------------|
| 1/02 | deposit | $50 | |
| 1/10 | groceries | | $75.35 |
| 1/16 | bookstore | | $12.95 |
| 1/22 | deposit | $112.81 | |
| 1/29 | movie rentals | | $13.08 |
| 1/31 | computer game | | $21.98 |

50. **CHEMISTRY** One *mole* of hydrogen atoms has a mass of 1.0079 grams. One mole of oxygen atoms has a mass of 15.9994 grams. A mole of water is made up of 2 moles of hydrogen and 1 mole of oxygen. What is the mass of a mole of water?

51. **CHALLENGE**

    **a.** Copy and complete the table.

    **b.** Use the results of your table. What is another name for $0.\overline{9}$?

| Fraction pair | $\frac{1}{3}, \frac{2}{3}$ | $\frac{1}{6}, \frac{5}{6}$ | $\frac{4}{9}, \frac{5}{9}$ | $\frac{3}{11}, \frac{8}{11}$ |
|---------------|------|------|------|------|
| Decimal pair | ? | ? | ? | ? |
| Fraction sum | ? | ? | ? | ? |
| Decimal sum | ? | ? | ? | ? |

## MIXED REVIEW FOR TAKS

TAKS PRACTICE at classzone.com

52. ➤ **TAKS PRACTICE** Eva compares 2 triangles, $\triangle ABC$ and $\triangle DEF$. The base of $\triangle ABC$ is half the base of $\triangle DEF$. She decides that the area of $\triangle ABC$ must also be half the area of $\triangle DEF$. Why is she incorrect? *TAKS Obj. 6*

(A) The perimeter of $\triangle ABC$ may not be half the perimeter of $\triangle DEF$.

(B) The area of $\triangle ABC$ must be one quarter the area of $\triangle DEF$.

(C) The area of $\triangle ABC$ must be twice the area of $\triangle DEF$.

(D) The height of $\triangle ABC$ may not be equal to the height of $\triangle DEF$.

# 5.7 Multiplying and Dividing Decimals

TEKS *8.2.B, 8.2.C*

| Before | You multiplied and divided integers and fractions. |
| Now | You'll multiply and divide decimals. |
| Why? | So you can find distance traveled, as in Example 1. |

**KEY VOCABULARY**
• leading digit, *p. 265*

**Rafting** You travel downstream in a raft at a rate of about 4.3 miles per hour. How far will you travel in 2.5 hours? To answer this question, you need to multiply decimals.

---

**KEY CONCEPT**                                            *For Your Notebook*

**Multiplying Decimals**

**Words**   Multiply decimals as you do whole numbers. Then place the decimal point. The number of decimal places in the product is the total number of decimal places in the factors.

**Numbers**   2.25   ×   8.9   =   20.025
             2 places    1 place    3 places

---

**EXAMPLE 1**   Multiplying Decimals

To find how far you travel in the rafting problem above, substitute the given values into the distance formula: distance = rate • time.

$d = rt$
$\quad = 4.3 \cdot 2.5$
$\quad = 10.75$

$$\begin{array}{r} 4.3 \\ \times\ 2.5 \\ \hline 215 \\ 86\phantom{0} \\ \hline 10.75 \end{array}$$

1 decimal place
+ 1 decimal place

2 decimal places

▶ **Answer** You will travel about 10.75 miles.

**Check** A number's **leading digit** is its leftmost nonzero digit. To check for reasonableness, round each factor to its leading digit and multiply.

4.3 • 2.5   **Round factors to leading digit.** ▷   4 • 3 = 12

---

✓ **GUIDED PRACTICE**   for Example 1

**Find the product. Check that the answer is reasonable.**

**1.** $-7.39 \cdot 2.1$ **2.** $19.62 \cdot 5.07$ **3.** $1.13 \cdot 0.04$ **4.** $-0.85 \cdot (-8)$

## Dividing Decimals

**Words**  When you divide by a decimal, multiply both the divisor and the dividend by the power of ten that will make the divisor an integer. Then divide.

**Numbers**  $2.75\overline{)15.125}$  **Multiply by 100.**  $2.75\overline{)1512.5}$ with quotient $5.5$

---

**EXAMPLE 2**  **Dividing Decimals**

To find the quotient $60.102 \div 6.3$, multiply the divisor and dividend by 10. Move the decimal points 1 place to the right.

$6.3\overline{)60.102}$  **Move decimal points.**  $6.3\overline{)601.02}$

$63\overline{)601.02}$ with quotient $9.54$    Then divide.

**AVOID ERRORS**
When checking your work, remember to use the *original* divisor, *not* the divisor you used after moving the decimal points.

**Check**  To check that the quotient is reasonable, round the quotient and the divisor to the leading digit. Then multiply and compare to the dividend.

$9.54 \cdot 6.3$  **Round.**  $10 \cdot 6 = 60 \approx 60.102$

*Animated* Math
at classzone.com

---

**EXAMPLE 3**  **Using Zeros as Placeholders**

To find some quotients, you may need to use zeros as placeholders.

**Placeholder in Dividend**          **Placeholder in Quotient**

$6 \div 1.2$                           $0.0126 \div 1.8$

$1.2\overline{)6.0}$ ← Zero as placeholder      $1.8\overline{)0.0126}$

$12\overline{)60}$ with quotient $5$           $18\overline{)0.126}$ with quotient $0.007$ ← Zeros as placeholders
$\underline{60}$                              $\underline{126}$
$0$                                           $0$

---

✓ **GUIDED PRACTICE**  for Examples 2 and 3

**REVIEW DIVISION**
Need help dividing negative numbers? See p. 77.

**Find the quotient. Check that the answer is reasonable.**

**5.** $1.6 \div 0.04$  **6.** $0.632 \div 0.79$  **7.** $-13 \div (-0.65)$

**8.** $-4.365 \div (-4.5)$  **9.** $0.3744 \div 1.56$  **10.** $-0.0108 \div 2.7$

# 5.7 EXERCISES

HOMEWORK KEY

= TAKS Practice and Reasoning
Exs. 26, 48, 50, 58 and 59

○ = HINTS AND HOMEWORK HELP
for Exs. 3, 9, 19, 21, 47 at classzone.com

## SKILL PRACTICE

1. **VOCABULARY** Copy and complete: In 0.0745, the digit "_?_" is the leading digit.

2. **VOCABULARY** Copy and complete the division problem. Use *quotient*, *dividend*, and *divisor* as labels.

**MULTIPLYING AND DIVIDING DECIMALS** Find the product or quotient. Check that the answer is reasonable.

*SEE EXAMPLES 1, 2, AND 3*
on pp. 265–266
for Exs. 3–24

3. $7.8 \cdot 2.6$
4. $3.75 \cdot (-0.4)$
5. $-8.2 \cdot 0.7$
6. $0.5 \div 1.25$

7. $25 \cdot 0.2$
8. $2.4 \cdot 0.3$
9. $13.2 \div 1.1$
10. $13.65 \cdot 1.1$

11. $4.8 \div 1.2$
12. $4.9 \div 0.07$
13. $-8 \div (-3.2)$
14. $5 \div (-0.1)$

15. $5.41 \cdot 0.35$
16. $4.844 \div 0.56$
17. $-0.57 \div 0.38$
18. $-2.687 \cdot (-9)$

19. $-37.41 \div 4.3$
20. $0.098 \cdot -0.55$
21. $6.025 \cdot 48.2$
22. $1.11 \div 0.925$

**ERROR ANALYSIS** In Exercises 23 and 24, describe and correct the error made in evaluating the product or quotient.

23.

$$\begin{array}{r} 9.78 \\ \times\ 3.4 \\ \hline 3912 \\ 2934 \\ \hline 332.52 \end{array}$$

24.

$$\begin{array}{r} 0.24 \\ 8\overline{)0.192} \end{array}$$

25. **WHICH ONE DOESN'T BELONG?** Which expression is *not* equivalent to the other expressions?

**A.** $3.5 \cdot 0.2$
**B.** $0.35 \cdot 2$
**C.** $3.5 \div 5$
**D.** $35 \div 0.5$

26. **TAKS REASONING** The quotient of $-0.67$ and $0.42$ is _?_.

Ⓐ more than 1   Ⓑ between 0 and 1   Ⓒ between 0 and $-1$   Ⓓ less than $-1$

**ALGEBRA** Solve the equation.

27. $9 = \dfrac{a}{-0.9}$
28. $\dfrac{c}{4.5} = 0.16$
29. $-2.8 = \dfrac{p}{6.2}$

30. $-5t = 0.085$
31. $1.2w = 0.321$
32. $-8.2y = -3.3$

33. $0.13z = -0.0544$
34. $\dfrac{g}{-7.2} = -0.022$
35. $-25.2z = 15.0012$

**ESTIMATING QUOTIENTS** Estimate each quotient. Then copy and complete the statement using < or >.

36. $105.4 \div 29.8$ _?_ $20.4 \div 5.1$

37. $3.8 \div (-2.1)$ _?_ $-1.8 \div 6.4$

**EVALUATING EXPRESSIONS** Evaluate the expression.

**38.** $3.4^3 + 5.1 \div 1.7 - 4.89$

**39.** $6.2 \cdot (18.77 - 6.27) + 9.1^2$

**NUMBER SENSE** *Describe* the pattern. Then write the next two numbers.

**40.** $125, 100, 80, 64, \ldots$

**41.** $1, -0.5, 0.25, -0.125, \ldots$

**CHALLENGE** You can write the expression $\frac{1.6}{2.4}$ in rational form by multiplying by $\frac{10}{10}$, a form of 1, to get $\frac{16}{24} = \frac{2}{3}$. Write the expression as a fraction in rational form $\frac{a}{b}$, where $a$ and $b$ are integers, and then in simplest form. Tell by what form of 1 you multiplied.

**42.** $\frac{0.5}{2}$

**43.** $\frac{1.75}{3.5}$

**44.** $\frac{0.75}{2.25}$

**45.** $\frac{4.8}{12}$

## PROBLEM SOLVING

SEE EXAMPLE 1
on p. 265
for Ex. 46

**46. GUIDED PROBLEM SOLVING** A mother rhinoceros weighs 3600 pounds. Her baby weighs 0.038 of her weight. How much does the baby weigh? *Explain* why your answer is reasonable.

  **a.** Write a verbal model to describe the problem.

  **b.** Substitute the given values and solve.

  **c.** Check that the answer is reasonable. Show your work.

**47. LOOK FOR A PATTERN** Copy and complete the table by multiplying each number in the left column by the number at the top of each other column. *Describe* the pattern.

| x | 1 | 0.1 | 0.01 | 0.001 | 0.0001 |
|---|---|-----|------|-------|--------|
| 87 | 87 | 8.7 | ? | ? | ? |
| 356 | 356 | ? | ? | ? | ? |
| 1200 | ? | ? | ? | ? | ? |

SEE EXAMPLE 2
on p. 266
for Ex. 48

**48. TAKS REASONING** You are buying balloons that cost $.89 per package, including tax. You have $14.75 to spend. How many packages of balloons can you buy?

  **(A)** 13.13    **(B)** 16    **(C)** 16.57    **(D)** 17

SEE EXAMPLE 3
on p. 266
for Ex. 49

**49. WRITING** *Explain* how 4.6 divided by 0.23 is related to 460 divided by 23. Are the quotients equal? *Explain* why or why not.

**50. TAKS REASONING** You have $75 to spend on daffodil bulbs.

  **a.** Boxes of bulbs cost $19.95 per box, including tax. How many boxes can you buy? Estimate to check that your answer is reasonable.

  **b.** Individual bulbs cost $1.20 each. How many bulbs can you buy with the money left over from purchasing the boxes of bulbs? *Explain*.

 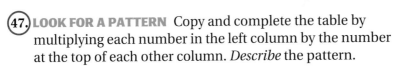

**51. REASONING** How many decimal places does $1.3^1$ have? $1.3^2$? $1.3^3$? $1.3^7$? *Explain* your reasoning.

**52. LAVA FLOWS** A lava flow is a stream of molten rock that pours from an erupting vent of a volcano. A lava flow travels 15.5 miles down a steep slope in 2.5 hours. Find the average rate at which the flow travels. Write your answer in miles per hour. *Explain* why your answer is reasonable.

**53. AIR TRAVEL** A plane travels from Boston to London in 6.25 hours, a distance of about 3285 miles. The return trip takes 7.5 hours. How many miles per hour faster is the faster speed than the slower speed? How many times as fast?

**54. POSTAL RATES** The table shows rates to mail a first class letter at one time. How much did it cost to mail a first class letter weighing 3.5 ounces?

| First ounce or fraction of ounce | $.37 |
| Each additional ounce or fraction | $.23 |

**55. POOLS** A rectangular deck surrounds a swimming pool on all four sides. The deck has the dimensions shown. What is the area of the water?

**56. CHALLENGE** One micrometer is equal to 0.001 millimeter. A bacterium is 4 micrometers wide. How many times would you have to magnify it for the bacterium to appear 1 millimeter wide?

**57. CHALLENGE** One inch is equal to 2.54 centimeters. The volume of a cube is 8 cubic inches. What is the volume of the cube in cubic centimeters? Round your answer to the nearest tenth.

---

## MIXED REVIEW FOR TAKS

**TAKS** PRACTICE at classzone.com

REVIEW
Lesson 1.7;
TAKS Workbook

**58. TAKS PRACTICE** Study participants are divided into 5 groups of 8 people each. Eight more participants arrive and the groups are reformed. What other information is needed to find the number of groups? *TAKS Obj. 6*

   **A** The number of people per group

   **B** Whether each group has an equal number of people

   **C** The factors of 48

   **D** The least common multiple of 5 and 8

REVIEW
Lesson 2.3;
TAKS Workbook

**59. TAKS PRACTICE** What is the difference of $-6$ and $-12$? *TAKS Obj. 1*

   **F** $-18$      **G** $-6$      **H** 6      **J** 18

**GOAL**
Collect and analyze data.

**MATERIALS**
• number cubes

TEKS **8.12.A**

# 5.8 Collecting and Analyzing Data

You can collect data and find a number that represents the data. The *median* is the middle value when the values are written in order. The *mode* is the value that occurs most often.

**EXPLORE 1** Collect data by rolling two number cubes to explore how often each sum occurs.

**STEP 1** **Roll** a pair of number cubes eleven times and record the results.

| | | | | | |
|---|---|---|---|---|---|
| $3 + 2 = 5$ | $4 + 4 = 8$ | $6 + 6 = 12$ | $1 + 2 = 3$ | $1 + 6 = 7$ | $2 + 1 = 3$ |
| $5 + 3 = 8$ | $4 + 1 = 5$ | $1 + 5 = 6$ | $2 + 6 = 8$ | $2 + 2 = 4$ | |

**STEP 2** **Add** the sums together. Divide by the number of rolls to find the mean.

$$\frac{5 + 8 + 12 + 3 + 7 + 3 + 8 + 5 + 6 + 8 + 4}{11} = \frac{69}{11} \approx 6.3$$

**STEP 3** **Order** the sums. Find the median and the mode.

3, 3, 4, 5, 5, 6, 7, 8, 8, 8, 12

middle number    most frequent number

The median is 6, and the mode is 8.

**STEP 4** **Compare** your results with the results of other groups. Which sum occurs most often?

**PRACTICE** Find the mean, median, and mode of the data.

1. 4.2, 6.1, 3.8, 4.1, 10.2, 9.6, 6.1, 7.3, 2.1, 2.4, 9.8

2. 105, 121, 42, 78, 77, 63, 108, 32, 33, 121, 64

3. $2\frac{1}{2}, 7\frac{3}{4}, 9\frac{1}{4}, 7\frac{1}{2}, 4\frac{3}{8}, 7\frac{3}{4}, 3\frac{7}{8}$

4. 56.4, 25.1, 24.3, 56.4, 48.7, 59.2, 37.9

**EXPLORE 2** **Collect data about the number of letters in the last name of each student in your class.**

**STEP 1** **Find** the shortest and longest names so you can make a frequency table.

Cho = 3
Fitzpatrick = 11

Number of Letters

| 3 | 4 | 5 | 6 | 7 | 8 | 9 | 10 | 11 |
|---|---|---|---|---|---|---|----|----|
| ‖ | ⫼ | ⊪⊩ | ⊪⊩ | ⊪⊩ | | ‖ | | |

**STEP 2** **Count** the number of letters in each name. Make a tally mark for each name.

$$\begin{array}{cccccc} 3 & 4 & 5 & 6 & 7 & 8 \\ \times 2 & \times 3 & \times 5 & \times 5 & \times 6 & \times 2 \\ \hline \end{array}$$

→ $6 + 12 + 25 + 30 + 42 + 16 + 9 + 0 + 11 = 151$

**STEP 3** **Find** the mean number of letters in the last names.

You can multiply to count the number of letters for each column. Then add the column totals.

Divide by the number of students. The mean is $151 \div 25 \approx 6$.

**STEP 4** **Find** the most frequent name length. This is the mode.

Number of Letters

| 3 | 4 | 5 | 6 | 7 | 8 | 9 | 10 | 11 |
|---|---|---|---|---|---|---|----|----|
| ‖ | ⫼ | ⊪⊩ | ⊪⊩ | ⊪⊩ ⏐ | ‖ | ⏐ | | ⏐ |

The mode is 7.

**STEP 5** **Decide** whether you can use the mean to describe the average length of a last name in your class. Then decide whether you can use the mode. *Explain* your choices.

**PRACTICE**

5. A new student whose last name has 16 letters joins your class. If you add "16" to your data, how does this affect the mean and the mode? *Explain.*

**DRAW CONCLUSIONS**

6. **WRITING** You are designing a form to collect data. Students will write their last names in a row of small boxes, one letter per box. How many boxes do you think the form should provide? *Explain.*

# 5.8 Mean, Median, and Mode

TEKS *8.12.A, 8.14.A*

| | |
|---|---|
| **Before** | You used tables and graphs to analyze data sets. |
| **Now** | You'll describe data sets using mean, median, mode, and range. |
| **Why?** | So you can describe data, such as the location of jellyfish in Example 1. |

**KEY VOCABULARY**
- **mean,** *p. 78*
- **median,** *p. 272*
- **mode,** *p. 272*
- **range,** *p. 273*

Three averages can be used to describe a data set. In Lesson 2.5, you learned how to find the *mean* of a data set. Investigation 5.8, on pages 270–271, explores the *median* and the *mode* of a data set. In this lesson, you will use these averages to describe data sets. You will also learn how to choose which average best represents a data set.

---

### KEY CONCEPT                         *For Your Notebook*

#### Averages

The **mean** of a data set is the sum of the values divided by the number of values.

The **median** of a data set is the middle value when the values are written in numerical order. If a data set has an even number of values, the median is the mean of the two middle values.

The **mode** of a data set is the value that occurs most often. A data set can have no mode, one mode, or more than one mode.

---

### EXAMPLE 1   Finding a Mean

**Biology** A marine biologist records the following locations of 6 deep sea jellyfish in relation to the ocean surface: $-2278$ feet, $-1875$ feet, $-3210$ feet, $-2755$ feet, $-2407$ feet, and $-2901$ feet. What is the mean location of the deep sea jellies?

$$\textbf{Mean} = \frac{-2278 + (-1875) + (-3210) + (-2755) + (-2407) + (-2901)}{6}$$

$$= \frac{-15{,}426}{6} = -2571$$

▸**Answer** The mean location in relation to the ocean surface is $-2571$ feet.

---

✓ **GUIDED PRACTICE**   **for Example 1**

**Find the mean of the data.**

**1.** $-3°\,C, 44°\,C, -11°\,C, 9°\,C, -21°\,C$

**2.** $12\frac{1}{2}$ in., $14\frac{3}{4}$ in., $20\frac{1}{2}$ in., $16\frac{3}{4}$ in.

**Range** The **range** of a data set is the difference of the greatest value and the least value. The range measures how spread out the data are. An *outlier* is a value in a data set that is much greater or much less than the other values.

**EXAMPLE 2** Finding Median, Mode, and Range

**Find the median, mode(s), and range of the prices.**

$7.20, $13.25, $14.94, $16.56, $18.74, $19.99, $19.99, $29.49

**AVOID ERRORS**
If the data are not ordered, you need to order the data to find the median.

**Median:** The data set has an even number of prices, so the median is the mean of the two middle values, $16.56 and $18.74.

$$\text{Median} = \frac{\$16.56 + \$18.74}{2} = \frac{\$35.30}{2} = \$17.65$$

**Mode:** The price that occurs most often is $19.99. This is the mode.

**Range:** Find the difference of the greatest and the least values.

$$\text{Range} = \$29.49 - \$7.20 = \$22.29$$

**EXAMPLE 3** TAKS PRACTICE: Multiple Choice

**Ice Cream** Twelve people try a new ice cream flavor and rate it on a scale of 1 to 20. The ratings are shown below. Which averages best represent the data?

1, 1, 2, 2, 3, 3, 3, 4, 4, 5, 18, 20

**A** mean and median      **B** mode and median

**C** mean and mode      **D** mean, median, and mode

**ELIMINATE CHOICES**
By inspection, you can see that the mode is 3 and does represent the data well. Choice A does not include the mode. So, it can be eliminated.

**SOLUTION**

$$\textbf{Mean} = \frac{66}{12} = 5.5$$

$$\textbf{Median} = \frac{3 + 3}{2} = \frac{6}{2} = 3$$

**Mode:** 3

▶ **Answer** Because 18 and 20 are outliers, the mean is higher than all but two ratings. It does not represent the data well. The mode and median best represent the data. The correct answer is B.   Ⓐ **Ⓑ** Ⓒ Ⓓ

✓ **GUIDED PRACTICE** for Examples 2 and 3

**Find the median, mode(s), and range of the data.**

**3.** 14, 13, 20, 24, 15, 10, 22, 17, 18      **4.** 9, 7, 4, 9, 4, 10, 5, 14, 9, 4

**5. What If?** Suppose another group of ten people tries the new ice cream flavor from Example 3 and their ratings are: 1, 1, 1, 2, 3, 4, 4, 9, 10, 10. Which average or averages best represent the data?

# 5.8 EXERCISES

## SKILL PRACTICE

**VOCABULARY** In Exercises 1–3, use the data set 6, 12, 4, 15, 10, 6, 2, and 9. **Copy and complete the statement using *mean*, *median*, *mode*, or *range*.**

1. The __?__ is 8.

2. The __?__ is 6.

3. The __?__ is 13.

**FINDING AVERAGES AND RANGE** Find the mean, median, mode(s), and range of the data.

*SEE EXAMPLES 1 AND 2*
on pp. 272–273
for Exs. 4–14

4. Weekly hits at a Web site: 115, 157, 289, 185, 164, 225, 185, 208

5. Distances: 16 km, 23 km, 11 km, 6 km, 15 km, 23 km, 17 km, 16 km

6. Depths of fish: $-71$ in., $-56$ in., $-62$ in., $-44$ in., $-56$ in., $-47$ in.

7. Golf scores relative to par: $-2, 0, 3, 1, 0, -1, 2, -2, -3, 0, 4, 1$

8. Elevations: 127 ft, $-8$ ft, 436 ft, 508 ft, $-23$ ft, 47 ft

9. Daily calories: 2000, 1872, 2112, 2255, 2080, 1795, 1977

10. Shoe lengths: $10\frac{3}{4}$ in., $9\frac{1}{2}$ in., $8\frac{7}{8}$ in., $10\frac{1}{2}$ in., $8\frac{3}{8}$ in., $10\frac{1}{2}$ in.

11. Temperatures (°F): $20°, -11°, 72°, -1°, 9°, 51°, 17°, -5°$

12. Pages in a book: 156, 212, 538, 77, 388, 419, 212

13. **ERROR ANALYSIS** Describe and correct the error made in the solution.

3, 6, 5, 2, 8, 9, 5, 8, 1, 5, 10, 8
The mode of the data set is 5.

14. **TAKS REASONING** Which has the same value as the median of the following data set: 45, 56, 50, 43, 56, 64, 36?

   (A) mean         (B) mode         (C) range         (D) none

**CHOOSING AN AVERAGE** Tell which average(s) best represent(s) the data.

*SEE EXAMPLE 3*
on p. 273
for Exs. 15–18

15. 23, 20, 30, 22, 24, 23, 24

16. 94, 47, 34, 45, 48, 38

17. 25, 58, 88, 74, 21, 20, 72, 22, 24

18. 124, 152, 108, 159, 116, 142, 175, 167, 119, 127, 112

**EXAMINING OUTLIERS** Find the mean, median, mode(s), and range of the data with and without the number(s) in red. *Describe* the effect of the red data value(s) on the averages and on the range.

19. 19, 16, 23, 35, 28, 20, 16, 36, **98**, 13, 26, 29, 31

20. 58, 67, 94, 85, 78, 76, **6**, 99, 100, 88, 76, **2**, 82, 81, 94, 98

**ALGEBRA** Find the unknown number in the data set. Then find the mean, median, mode, and range, if not given.

**21.** 63, 52, 49, *b*, 68, 75 (greatest value), 57, range = 31

**22.** 17 (least value), 96, 54, 48, *d*, 27, range = 81

**23.** 6, 8, 14, 9, 3, *c*, 12, 5, median = 7.5

**24.** 11, *z*, 30, 42, 7, 39, 22, median = 28

**25.** 32, 18, 16, *a*, 23, 41, mean = 28

*Animated* Math
at classzone.com

**26.** **ALGEBRA** Find the mean of 3*b*, 5*b*, *b*, 6*b*, −6*b*, and −2*b*.

**CHALLENGE** Find a data set of five numbers with the given characteristics.

**27.** Mean: 11
Median: 12
Mode: 17
Range: 13

**28.** Mean: 16
Median: 15
Mode: 15
Range: 22

**29.** Mean: 5
Median: 1
Mode: −4
Range: 26

## PROBLEM SOLVING

*SEE EXAMPLE 1*
on p. 272
for Ex. 30

**30. GUIDED PROBLEM SOLVING** Shana is training to run in a 5K race. Her practice times (in minutes and seconds) are 22:45, 21:56, 21:03, 20:33, and 20:28. Find her mean practice time.

**a.** Change Shana's practice times to seconds.

**b.** Find the sum of the practice times. Divide by the number of times.

**c.** Convert your answer to part (b) to minutes and seconds.

*SEE EXAMPLES
1, 2, AND 3*
on pp. 272–273
for Ex. 31

**31. BASEBALL** The attendance for the 2001 World Series is shown in the table below. Find the mean, median, and mode(s) of the data. Which average do you think best represents the attendance data? *Explain.*

| Game | 1 | 2 | 3 | 4 | 5 | 6 | 7 |
|---|---|---|---|---|---|---|---|
| Attendance | 49,646 | 49,646 | 55,820 | 55,863 | 56,018 | 49,707 | 49,589 |

**32. BASKETBALL** In basketball practice, the numbers of free throws made out of 20 shots are listed below. Find the mean, median, mode, and range of each set of data. Who is the more consistent player? *Justify* your reasoning.

Kendra: 8, 10, 9, 9, 10, 12, 10, 11          Jade:  8, 5, 9, 12, 13, 10, 7, 11

**33. WRITING** You are researching the average salaries for several careers. Would you rather know the mean, median, or mode(s) of the salaries for each career? *Explain* your reasoning.

**SEE EXAMPLE 3**
on p. 273
for Ex. 34

**34.** ⚓ **TAKS REASONING** The scores on a 20-point quiz in math class are 8, 9, 11, 12, 14, 14, 15, 16, 17, 17, 18, and 20. Which averages best represent the data?

**Ⓐ** mean and median      **Ⓑ** mode and median

**Ⓒ** mean and mode      **Ⓓ** mean, median, and mode

**㉟ ICEBERGS** An iceberg's depth can be 3 to 9 times its height above the water surface. The image below shows the distances, in meters, below the water surface that six icebergs reach. What is the mean distance below the water surface these icebergs reach?

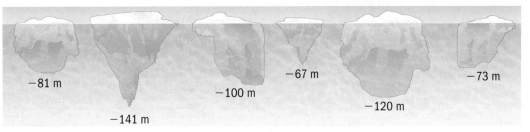

**36.** ⚓ **TAKS REASONING** Write an example of a data set whose mode is greater than its mean.

**37. COMPARE AND CONTRAST** Jerry and Roberta both find the mean of $-2a$, $a$, $3a$, $6a$, and $9a$ when $a = 2.5$, as shown below. *Describe* each method. How are they similar? How are they different?

Jerry
$$-2a = -5 \qquad a = 2.5 \qquad 3a = 7.5$$
$$6a = 15 \qquad 9a = 22.5$$
$$\frac{-5 + 2.5 + 7.5 + 15 + 22.5}{5} = \frac{42.5}{5}$$
$$= 8.5$$

Roberta
$$\frac{-2a + a + 3a + 6a + 9a}{5} = \frac{17a}{5}$$
$$= \frac{17 \cdot 2.5}{5}$$
$$= 8.5$$

**38. BOWLING** You are bowling three games. In the first two games, you score 125 and 113 points. How many points do you need in the third game to have a mean score of 126 points?

**39. STREAMS** You want to know if you can wade across a local stream. The average depth of the stream is reported to be 2 feet. What information might be concealed when depth is reported as an average?

**40.** ⚓ **TAKS REASONING** Find the outlier in the data set: 318, 390, 592, 388, 375, 350, 410, 395. Find the mean, median, and mode of the data set with the outlier and without the outlier. Which average is most affected by the outlier? *Explain.*

**Read the information below for Exercises 41–43.**

**Gymnastics** At Ramsey High's last gymnastics meet, the Rams overran the competition once again. They were lead by their top scorers on the rings. The scores for this event from each of the 6 judges are shown below. The final score for each gymnast is calculated by dropping the highest and lowest scores and taking the mean of the remaining 4 scores.

|  | *Judge 1* | *Judge 2* | *Judge 3* | *Judge 4* | *Judge 5* | *Judge 6* |
|---|---|---|---|---|---|---|
| **Isaac** | 9.600 | 9.600 | 9.600 | 9.650 | 9.800 | 9.650 |
| **Carl** | 9.800 | 9.800 | 9.700 | 9.700 | 9.700 | 9.800 |
| **Kurt** | 9.550 | 9.400 | 9.800 | 9.750 | 9.800 | 9.600 |

**41. Calculate** Find the final score for each gymnast. Who was awarded first, second, and third places on the rings?

**42. Investigate** Find the mean score for each gymnast that includes all 6 judges' scores. If these averages were used as the final scores, would the top three gymnasts be the same? *Explain.*

**43. Interpret** *Explain* why it may be more fair to rank the gymnasts according to a final score that omits the highest and lowest scores.

**44. TELEVISION SURVEY** Ten people rate a television show on a scale from 1 to 10. The ratings are 1, 7, 7, 8, 8, 8, 8, 8, 9, and 9.

  **a.** Find the mean, median, and mode of the data with and without the outlier.

  **b.** *Describe* the effect on the averages.

**45. ⬥ TAKS REASONING** The table shows attendance at 6 school dances.

  **a.** Make a bar graph of the data.

  **b.** Find the mean and median attendance.

  **c.** The student council wants to find the total amount of money collected for admission to the dances. Would the bar graph, the mean, or the median be most useful? *Explain.*

  **d.** What other information is also needed to find how much money was collected?

| Dance | Number of students |
|---|---|
| Fall | 97 |
| Winter Ball | 88 |
| Valentine's Day | 133 |
| Spring Fling | 210 |
| End of Year | 198 |

**46. CHALLENGE** The table below shows the numbers of points you scored during the first 14 basketball games of a 15-game season. By halftime of the final game, you score 7 points. How many points do you need to score in the second half to have a mean of 10 points per game?

| Game | 1 | 2 | 3 | 4 | 5 | 6 | 7 | 8 | 9 | 10 | 11 | 12 | 13 | 14 |
|---|---|---|---|---|---|---|---|---|---|---|---|---|---|---|
| Points | 15 | 8 | 7 | 10 | 12 | 4 | 20 | 13 | 7 | 7 | 5 | 3 | 10 | 14 |

*REVIEW*
Lesson 5.6;
TAKS Workbook

**47.** ⬥ **TAKS PRACTICE** Jerry ran a 5 kilometer race. For the first 2.3 kilometers he was in first place. For the next 0.15 kilometer he was in second place. Then for 1.1 kilometers he was in third place. After running those distances, how much farther did he have to run to finish the race? *TAKS Obj. 1*

   **A** 0.1 km     **B** 1.45 km     **C** 1.585 km     **D** 3.55 km

*REVIEW*
Lesson 5.5;
TAKS Workbook

**48.** ⬥ **TAKS PRACTICE** Which list shows the heights of 4 students, in inches, in order from greatest to least? *TAKS Obj. 1*

  **F** $47\frac{7}{8}$, 47.87, $47\frac{13}{16}$, $47\frac{1}{4}$       **G** 47.87, $47\frac{13}{16}$, $47\frac{7}{8}$, $47\frac{1}{4}$

  **H** $47\frac{7}{8}$, $47\frac{13}{16}$, 47.87, $47\frac{1}{4}$       **J** $47\frac{1}{4}$, $47\frac{13}{16}$, 47.87, $47\frac{7}{8}$

---

## QUIZ *for Lessons 5.5–5.8*

**Write the fraction as a decimal or the decimal as a fraction.** *(p. 255)*

**1.** 4.25       **2.** $\frac{4}{9}$       **3.** 0.58       **4.** $0.\overline{2}$

**Find the sum or difference.** *(p. 260)*

**5.** $-2.301 + 8.4$   **6.** $15.25 + 9.636$   **7.** $14.65 - 3.608$   **8.** $3.02 - (-0.225)$

**Find the product or quotient.** *(p. 265)*

**9.** $-15.3 \cdot 0.48$   **10.** $3.88 \cdot 0.9$   **11.** $0.162 \div 2.7$   **12.** $2.07 \div 0.225$

**13. RACING** A racing camel can travel at a speed of 11.75 miles per hour. How far does it travel in 0.02 hour at this speed? *(p. 265)*

**14. TORNADOES** The table shows the numbers of tornadoes in the United States from 1998–2004. Find the mean, median, mode(s), and range of the data. *(p. 272)*

| Year | 1998 | 1999 | 2000 | 2001 | 2002 | 2003 | 2004 |
|------|------|------|------|------|------|------|------|
| Tornadoes | 1424 | 1342 | 1071 | 805 | 941 | 1376 | 1819 |

---

## Brain Game

### The Prize is Right!

You are a contestant on a television game show. To win a trip you must find the prices of the five items in a shopping cart. The game show host gives you four hints about the prices.

- The mean of the prices is $1.68
- The mode of the prices is $1.50
- The median of the prices is $1.65
- One item costs $.10 more than the median.

List the prices of the items in the cart in order from least to greatest.

---

**EXTRA PRACTICE** for Lesson 5.8, p. 805      ➤ **ONLINE QUIZ** at classzone.com

## Lessons 5.1–5.8

**MULTIPLE CHOICE**

1. **MOVIES** The table below shows the fraction of 800 people in a survey that named their favorite type of movie. Only the top three are shown.

| Movie type | Comedy | Drama | Action |
|---|---|---|---|
| Fraction of students | $\frac{2}{5}$ | $\frac{1}{8}$ | $\frac{5}{16}$ |

Which expression can be used to find the number of people who picked the most popular movie type? *TEKS 8.5.A*

Ⓐ $800(0.125)$    Ⓑ $800(0.2)$

Ⓒ $800(0.3125)$    Ⓓ $800(0.4)$

2. **PHONE CALLS** Gareth's long distance plan charges \$.10 per minute before 7:00 P.M. and \$.05 per minute after 7:00 P.M. Gareth makes a long distance call at 6:39 P.M. and talks for 18 minutes. At 7:15, he makes another long distance call for 18 minutes. What is the price difference between the two calls? *TEKS 8.2.B*

Ⓕ \$.05    Ⓖ \$.15

Ⓗ \$.90    Ⓙ \$2.70

3. **INSTANT MESSAGING** You spend the following minutes instant messaging at different times: 18, 15, 7, 10, 32, 17, 32, 21, 94. You want to present the average time of your sessions so that it appears you spend as little time instant messaging as possible. Which measure of data should you use? *TEKS 8.12.A*

Ⓐ mean    Ⓑ median

Ⓒ mode    Ⓓ range

4. **NUMBER SENSE** Which decimals have a sum greater than one and a product less than two fifths? *TEKS 8.16.A*

Ⓕ 0.4 and 0.6    Ⓖ 0.5 and 0.7

Ⓗ 0.5 and 0.8    Ⓙ 0.5 and 0.9

5. **RECTANGLES** Rectangle $X$ has a length of 9.3 feet and a width of 7.5 feet. The length and width of rectangle $Y$ are 3 times the length and width of rectangle $X$. Which equations show the area, $a$, and the perimeter, $p$, of rectangle $Y$? *TEKS 8.10.A*

Ⓐ $a = 3(9.3)(7.5)$, $p = 3(2(9.3) + 2(7.5))$

Ⓑ $a = 3(9.3)(7.5)$, $p = 9(2(9.3) + 2(7.5))$

Ⓒ $a = 9(9.3)(7.5)$, $p = 3(2(9.3) + 2(7.5))$

Ⓓ $a = 9(9.3)(7.5)$, $p = 9(2(9.3) + 2(7.5))$

6. **TAXIS** Numbered streets of a city are perpendicular to lettered streets. Each block is 0.2 mile long. A taxi costs \$2.50 for the first fifth of a mile and \$.40 for each additional fifth of a mile. A taxi takes you from Fourth and A to Third and D using the shortest route. How much does the ride cost? *TEKS 8.14.C*

Ⓕ \$3.20    Ⓖ \$3.70

Ⓗ \$4.10    Ⓙ \$4.50

7. **GARDENING** A rectangular garden has a length of 3.2 meters and an area of 8.96 square meters. What is the width of the garden? *TEKS 8.7.B*

Ⓐ 2.56 m    Ⓑ 2.80 m

Ⓒ 5.76 m    Ⓓ 28.672 m

**GRIDDED ANSWER** ⓪①②●③④⑤⑥⑦⑧⑨

8. **GRAPES** Grapes cost \$1.30 per pound. You buy 2.3 pounds for yourself and 1.5 pounds for your friend. How much, in dollars, do you spend on grapes? *TEKS 8.3.B*

## REVIEW KEY VOCABULARY

- reciprocal, *p. 247*
- multiplicative inverse, *p. 247*
- rational number, *p. 255*
- terminating decimal, *p. 255*
- repeating decimal, *p. 255*
- front-end estimation, *p. 261*
- leading digit, *p. 265*
- mean, median, mode, *p. 272*
- range, *p. 273*

### VOCABULARY EXERCISES

**Copy and complete the statement.**

1. The fractions $\frac{3}{5}$ and $\frac{5}{3}$ are __?__ or __?__ because their product is 1.

2. If the remainder of the quotient $\frac{a}{b}$ is 0, then the decimal form of $\frac{a}{b}$ is a __?__.

3. You can use __?__ when you do not need to find an exact sum of a group of decimals.

4. A value that occurs most often in a data set is a __?__.

5. A number that can be written as $\frac{a}{b}$, where $a$ and $b$ are integers and $b \neq 0$, is a __?__.

## REVIEW EXAMPLES AND EXERCISES

### 5.1 Fractions with Common Denominators
*pp. 233–237*

**EXAMPLE**

**Find the sum.**

$$\frac{2}{9} + 3\frac{4}{9} = 3 + \left(\frac{2}{9} + \frac{4}{9}\right) \qquad \text{Group fractions.}$$

$$= 3\frac{6}{9} \qquad \text{Add fractions.}$$

$$= 3\frac{2}{3} \qquad \text{Simplify.}$$

**EXERCISES**

**Find the sum or difference.**

**SEE EXAMPLES 1 AND 2**
on pp. 233–234
for Exs. 6–13

6. $\frac{8}{9} + \frac{4}{9}$

7. $3\frac{5}{8} - 1\frac{7}{8}$

8. $\frac{3}{10} - \frac{7}{10} - \frac{9}{10}$

9. $\frac{4}{7} + \frac{2}{7} + \frac{6}{7}$

10. $\frac{6n}{18} - \frac{2n}{18}$

11. $-\frac{4n}{6} + \frac{3n}{6}$

12. $\frac{8n}{11} + \frac{4n}{11}$

13. $-\frac{7n}{9} - \frac{5n}{9}$

## 5.2 Fractions with Different Denominators

pp. 238–242

**EXAMPLE**

**Find the difference.**

$$2\frac{9}{14} - \frac{6}{7} = 2\frac{9}{14} - \frac{12}{14} \qquad \text{Rewrite fractions using LCD of 14.}$$

$$= 1\frac{23}{14} - \frac{12}{14} \qquad \text{Rename } 2\frac{9}{14} \text{ as } 1\frac{23}{14}.$$

$$= 1 + \left(\frac{23}{14} - \frac{12}{14}\right) \qquad \text{Group fractions.}$$

$$= 1\frac{11}{14} \qquad \text{Subtract inside parentheses.}$$

### EXERCISES

**Find the sum.**

*SEE EXAMPLES 1, 2, AND 3*
on pp. 238–239
for Exs. 14–22

**14.** $\frac{3}{5} + \frac{2}{3}$      **15.** $\frac{3}{5} + \frac{1}{4}$      **16.** $6\frac{2}{7} + \left(-7\frac{1}{8}\right)$      **17.** $\frac{5v}{3} + \frac{4v}{5}$

**Find the difference.**

**18.** $\frac{8}{9} - \frac{2}{5}$      **19.** $\frac{7}{12} - \left(-\frac{5}{8}\right)$      **20.** $3\frac{1}{3} - 1\frac{1}{4}$      **21.** $\frac{8x}{17} - \frac{x}{2}$

**22. Robots** It took Central High's robot team $107\frac{1}{3}$ hours of labor to build their robot. East High built their robot in $111\frac{5}{6}$ hours. How much longer did East High School take to build their robot?

## 5.3 Multiplying Fractions

pp. 243–246

**EXAMPLE**

**Find the product.**

$$3\frac{3}{5} \cdot \frac{4}{9} = \frac{18}{5} \cdot \frac{4}{9} \qquad \text{Write } 3\frac{3}{5} \text{ as an improper fraction.}$$

$$= \frac{18 \cdot 4}{5 \cdot 9} \qquad \text{Use rule for multiplying fractions.}$$

$$= \frac{\overset{2}{\cancel{18}} \cdot 4}{5 \cdot \underset{1}{\cancel{9}}} \qquad \text{Divide out common factor.}$$

$$= \frac{8}{5}, \text{ or } 1\frac{3}{5} \qquad \text{Multiply and write as a mixed number.}$$

## EXERCISES

**Find the product.**

SEE EXAMPLES
1 AND 2
on pp. 243–244
for Exs. 23–30

**23.** $-\dfrac{5}{8} \cdot \dfrac{2}{5}$

**24.** $-\dfrac{9}{5} \cdot \left(-\dfrac{11}{15}\right)$

**25.** $-\dfrac{1}{3} \cdot \dfrac{2}{7}$

**26.** $\dfrac{3}{8} \cdot \left(-\dfrac{12}{13}\right)$

**27.** $8\dfrac{2}{3} \cdot (-3)$

**28.** $-7\dfrac{4}{9} \cdot \left(-\dfrac{1}{4}\right)$

**29.** $-6\dfrac{3}{7} \cdot 2\dfrac{1}{2}$

**30.** $4 \cdot \left(-3\dfrac{5}{12}\right)$

## 5.4 Dividing Fractions

pp. 247–252

### EXAMPLE

**Find the quotient.**

$$\dfrac{1}{3} \div \dfrac{5}{6} = \dfrac{1}{3} \cdot \dfrac{6}{5} \qquad \dfrac{5}{6} \cdot \dfrac{6}{5} = 1, \text{ so the reciprocal of } \dfrac{5}{6} \text{ is } \dfrac{6}{5}.$$

$$= \dfrac{1 \cdot \overset{2}{\cancel{6}}}{\underset{1}{\cancel{3}} \cdot 5} \qquad \text{Divide out common factor.}$$

$$= \dfrac{2}{5} \qquad \text{Multiply.}$$

### EXAMPLE

**Find the quotient.**

$$2\dfrac{1}{5} \div 2\dfrac{3}{4} = \dfrac{11}{5} \div \dfrac{11}{4} \qquad \text{Write } 2\dfrac{1}{5} \text{ and } 2\dfrac{3}{4} \text{ as improper fractions.}$$

$$= \dfrac{11}{5} \cdot \dfrac{4}{11} \qquad \dfrac{11}{4} \cdot \dfrac{4}{11} = 1, \text{ so the reciprocal of } \dfrac{11}{4} \text{ is } \dfrac{4}{11}.$$

$$= \dfrac{\overset{1}{\cancel{11}} \cdot 4}{5 \cdot \underset{1}{\cancel{11}}} \qquad \text{Divide out common factor.}$$

$$= \dfrac{4}{5} \qquad \text{Multiply.}$$

## EXERCISES

**Find the quotient.**

SEE EXAMPLES
1, 2, AND 3
on p. 248
for Exs. 31–39

**31.** $\dfrac{13}{18} \div \dfrac{5}{6}$

**32.** $\dfrac{7}{22} \div \dfrac{1}{11}$

**33.** $\dfrac{2}{3} \div \left(-\dfrac{1}{6}\right)$

**34.** $-\dfrac{4}{5} \div \left(-\dfrac{1}{2}\right)$

**35.** $2\dfrac{3}{4} \div 1\dfrac{1}{3}$

**36.** $\dfrac{9}{21} \div 5$

**37.** $5\dfrac{8}{11} \div \left(-\dfrac{3}{4}\right)$

**38.** $12\dfrac{1}{2} \div 4\dfrac{1}{6}$

**39. Relay** You participate in a $12\dfrac{1}{2}$ mile relay run for charity. Your team has 8 people and each person runs the same distance. How many miles does each person run?

## 5.5 Fractions and Decimals

**EXAMPLE**

Write $\frac{2}{5}$ as a decimal.

$$\frac{2}{5} = 5\overline{\smash{)}2.0}$$
$$\frac{2\ 0}{0}$$

**EXAMPLE**

Write $2.\overline{8}$ as a fraction.

Let $x = 2.\overline{8}$ or $2.888.\ldots$

The number has 1 repeating digit, so multiply by 10. Let $10x = 28.\overline{8}$ or $28.888.\ldots$

Subtract the two equations.

$$\begin{array}{r} 10x = 28.888\ldots \\ -\quad x = \phantom{2}2.888\ldots \\ \hline 9x = 26.000\ldots \end{array}$$

Then solve for $x$.    $x = \dfrac{26}{9}$, or $2\dfrac{8}{9}$.

### EXERCISES

Write the fraction as a decimal or the decimal as a fraction or mixed number.

SEE EXAMPLES
1, 3, AND 4
on pp. 255–257
for Exs. 40–47

**40.** $\dfrac{3}{5}$        **41.** $-\dfrac{7}{8}$        **42.** $-0.\overline{23}$        **43.** $3.45$

**44.** $\dfrac{2}{9}$        **45.** $2.\overline{65}$        **46.** $0.16$        **47.** $-\dfrac{3}{11}$

## 5.6 Adding and Subtracting Decimals

pp. 260–264

**EXAMPLE**

a. Find the sum of 14.02 and 9.81.

$$\begin{array}{r} 14.02 \\ +\ 9.81 \\ \hline 23.83 \end{array}$$

b. Find the difference of 20.5 and 3.764.

$$\begin{array}{r} 20.500 \\ -\ 3.764 \\ \hline 16.736 \end{array}$$

Use zeros as placeholders.

### EXERCISES

Find the sum or difference.

SEE EXAMPLE 1
on p. 260
for Exs. 48–55

**48.** $1.2 + 0.67$        **49.** $33.2 + 9.398$        **50.** $3.16 - 1.845$        **51.** $90.3 - (-7.81)$

**52.** $5.2 + 20.68$        **53.** $0.103 + 0.7$        **54.** $9.6 - 3.555$        **55.** $-4.23 - 8.093$

## 5.7 Multiplying and Dividing Decimals

*pp. 265–269*

**EXAMPLE**

**a. Find the product of 14.75 and 1.3.**

$$
\begin{array}{r}
14.75 \\
\times\ \ 1.3 \\
\hline
4425 \\
1475 \\
\hline
19.175
\end{array}
\qquad
\begin{array}{l}
\text{2 decimal places} \\
\text{+ 1 decimal place} \\
\\
\\
\text{3 decimal places}
\end{array}
$$

**b. Find the quotient of 21.726 and 4.26.**

$$4.26\overline{)21.726} \qquad 426\overline{)2172.6}\ \ \ \ 5.1$$

### EXERCISES

**Find the product or quotient.**

**SEE EXAMPLES
1, 2, AND 3**
on pp. 265–266
for Exs. 56–60

**56.** $6.24 \cdot 0.375$     **57.** $3.348 \cdot 0.9$     **58.** $66.96 \div (-2.7)$     **59.** $18.91 \div 9.455$

**60. Cats** A tiger at a zoo has a mass of 144.9 kilograms. This is 40.25 times the mass of a house cat. What is the mass of a house cat?

## 5.8 Mean, Median, and Mode

*pp. 272–278*

**EXAMPLE**

**Find the mean, median, mode(s), and range of the following ordered set of data.**

$$4, 5, 6, 6, 7, 9, 11, 12$$

$$\text{Mean} = \frac{4 + 5 + 6 + 6 + 7 + 9 + 11 + 12}{8} = \frac{60}{8} = 7.5$$

$$\text{Median} = \frac{6 + 7}{2} = \frac{13}{2} = \frac{6}{5}$$

$$\text{Mode} = 6$$

$$\text{Range} = 12 - 4 = 8$$

### EXERCISES

**Find the mean, median, mode(s), and range of the data set.**

**SEE EXAMPLES
1 AND 2**
on pp. 272–273
for Exs. 61–64

**61.** Temperatures (°C): $-7, -1, 0, 8, 4, 2, -7, 2$

**62.** Length of jumps (meters): 14.6, 19.2, 11, 16.5, 12, 11, 10.9

**63.** Length of bike trails (km): 7, 8.3, 17.1, 4.8, 3.9, 7, 4.8, 13.1

**64.** Thickness of books (inches): 2.4, 1, 3.7, 1.4, 1.3, 2.5, 2, 2.5

**Find the sum or difference.**

**1.** $4\frac{5}{11} - 2\frac{6}{11}$   **2.** $\frac{9}{16} - \left(-\frac{11}{16}\right)$   **3.** $-\frac{5}{6} + \frac{1}{8}$   **4.** $\frac{3}{7} + \left(-\frac{8}{21}\right) + \frac{2}{3}$

**Find the product or quotient.**

**5.** $\frac{2}{9} \cdot (-4)$   **6.** $\frac{5}{2} \cdot \frac{4}{15}$   **7.** $3\frac{1}{2} \div 2$   **8.** $7\frac{3}{4} \div 2\frac{7}{12}$

**Write the fraction as a decimal or the decimal as a fraction.**

**9.** $\frac{7}{20}$   **10.** $\frac{3}{40}$   **11.** $0.0082$   **12.** $0.\overline{4}$

**Find the sum, difference, product, or quotient.**

**13.** $6.2 - 5.984$   **14.** $2.608 + 12.93$   **15.** $0.7992 \div 0.333$   **16.** $-34.69 \cdot 12.7$

**17.** $3.64 + 14.2$   **18.** $0.123 \cdot 4.53$   **19.** $15.68 - 4.94$   **20.** $3.7611 \div 0.597$

**21.** ⓧ **ALGEBRA** Evaluate $0.2x$ and $\frac{x}{0.2}$ when $x = -4.1$, $0.06$, and $1.8$.

**22. HOMEWORK** Yesterday you spent $3\frac{1}{4}$ hours on homework. Today you will spend $1\frac{4}{5}$ hours. How many more hours did you spend yesterday? How many minutes is this?

**23. BOOK CLUB** You are reading a novel for your book club. You can read one chapter in $\frac{5}{12}$ hour. How many chapters can you read in $3\frac{3}{4}$ hours?

**BAGELS** In Exercises 24 and 25, use the table. It shows the approximate supermarket sales of three types of bagels (in billions of dollars) in 2003.

**24.** How much greater were the sales for frozen bagels than the sales for refrigerated bagels?

**25.** What is the total amount of sales of all three types of bagels?

| Bagels | Sales (billions) |
|---|---|
| Frozen | $.086 |
| Refrigerated | $.077 |
| Fresh | $.43 |

**26. ENERGY BILL** A gas supplier charges 64.5 cents per therm of gas used. How much does it cost for 116 therms of gas?

**27. STUDYING** Last week, twelve students spent the following hours studying. Find the mean, median, mode(s), and range of the data.

$$2, 5, 3, 7, 10, 9, 8, 7, 6, 7, 6, 2$$

**28. THEME PARKS** The mean number per week of theme park visitors over a four week period was 15,271. The numbers of visitors in each of the first three weeks were 15,514, 17,328, and 13,697. How many people visited the park in the fourth week?

# 5 TAKS PREPARATION

**TAKS Obj. 1
TEKS 8.2.B,
8.2.C**

## REVIEWING RATIONAL NUMBER PROBLEMS

You may need to perform operations on rational numbers to find an actual or estimated solution to a real-life problem, and to justify or check the reasonableness of a solution.

In the following example, you will estimate shared monetary contributions for a family reunion and then check the reasonableness of your estimate.

> **EXAMPLE**
>
> **Family Reunion** The Cohen family has a family reunion. Twelve adults and fifteen children attend. Dinner costs $247.73 with tax included. Movie and music concert tickets for everyone cost $407.21. The adults share the costs of entertainment and dinner. What is a reasonable estimate for the amount each adult family member must contribute?

### Solution

To find the amount of money each adult must contribute, $c$, divide the combined cost of dinner and entertainment by the number of adults.

$$c = (247.73 + 407.21) \div 12 \qquad \text{Write an equation.}$$

$$= 654.94 \div 12 \qquad \text{Add.}$$

$$\approx 54.58 \qquad \text{Divide and round.}$$

$$\approx 55 \qquad \text{Estimate.}$$

▶ **Answer** Each adult must contribute about $55.

**Check** To see if your answer is reasonable, compare the total amount of money generated by the 12 estimated contributions to the estimated cost of dinner and entertainment.

| Total of 12 estimated contributions: | $55 \times 12 = 660$ |
|---|---|
| Estimated cost of dinner and entertainment: | $\begin{array}{r} 248 \\ + 407 \\ \hline 655 \end{array}$ |

Because $655 \approx 660$, you know that a contribution of $55 by each adult is a reasonable estimate.

# RATIONAL NUMBER PROBLEMS ON TAKS

Below are examples of rational number problems in multiple choice format. Try solving the problems before looking at the solutions. (Cover the solutions with a piece of paper.) Then check your solutions against the ones given.

**1.** Mr. Shepard's class is hoping to raise $120 during a fund drive. They wash cars for five days and raise these amounts:

$15.75, $25.00, $22.75, $19.50, $26.50

Some members of the class round the amounts and estimate that they have raised about $120. Which statement best describes their estimate?

**A** They rounded amounts to the nearest dollar.

**B** They rounded amounts to the nearest five dollars.

**C** They rounded amounts to the nearest ten dollars.

**D** They rounded amounts to the nearest twenty dollars.

**Solution**

Four possible estimates are suggested by the answers given. Check each estimation method to see which one yields $120.

Estimate rounded to nearest dollar:
16 + 25 + 23 + 20 + 27 = 111

Estimate rounded to nearest 5 dollars:
15 + 25 + 25 + 20 + 25 = 110

Estimate rounded to nearest 10 dollars:
20 + 30 + 20 + 20 + 30 = 120

Estimate rounded to nearest 20 dollars:
20 + 20 + 20 + 20 + 20 = 100

They rounded to the nearest $10. So, the correct answer is C.

Ⓐ Ⓑ Ⓒ Ⓓ

**2.** One ton of apples is divided into bags that hold twelve apples each. Each bag weighs at least four pounds and at most five pounds. What is a reasonable estimate for the number of bags filled?

**F** 167

**G** 320

**H** 450

**J** 520

**Solution**

Convert the amount of apples from tons to pounds. One ton equals 2000 pounds.

The least number of bags, $l$, are filled when each bag holds 5 pounds. Solve the equation:

$$5l = 2000$$
$$5l \div 5 = 2000 \div 5$$
$$l = 400$$

The greatest number of bags, $g$, are filled when each bag holds 4 pounds. Solve the equation:

$$4g = 2000$$
$$4g \div 4 = 2000 \div 4$$
$$g = 500.$$

From 400 to 500 bags can be filled. So, the correct answer is H.

Ⓕ Ⓖ Ⓗ Ⓙ

## PRACTICE FOR TAKS OBJECTIVE 1

**1.** Lin has five half-gallon bottles of apple juice. She fills glasses so that each glass is mostly full, pouring from eight to ten fluid ounces into each glass. Which is NOT a reasonable estimate for the number of glasses she might fill?

  **A** 42

  **B** 40

  **C** 37

  **D** 32

**2.** The dimensions of a television screen are given below. What is the best estimate for the area of the screen?

  **F** 70 in.$^2$

  **G** 200 in.$^2$

  **H** 300 in.$^2$

  **J** 350 in.$^2$

**3.** At a school fundraiser, Mrs. Dooley contributed between two thirds and four fifths of the amount that her sister contributed. If her sister contributed $40, how much might Mrs. Dooley have contributed?

  **A** $70

  **B** $35

  **C** $27

  **D** $14

**4.** Tim bought sneakers and a belt. He told his friend that the sneakers were about $50 and the belt about $20. Assuming that he rounded to the nearest ten dollars, what are possible exact prices for the sneakers and belt?

  **F** $55.45 and $18.99

  **G** $54.99 and $24.75

  **H** $49.99 and $14.70

  **J** $56.25 and $21.25

## MIXED TAKS PRACTICE

**5.** A traveler packs a bag with a pair of pants, two shirts, and a book. The book weighs $2\frac{1}{2}$ pounds. The pants weigh $\frac{5}{7}$ pound. The shirts weigh $\frac{3}{4}$ pound each. What is the total weight of the contents of the bag? *TAKS Obj. 1*

  **A** $4\frac{9}{28}$ lb

  **B** $4\frac{5}{14}$ lb

  **C** $4\frac{11}{14}$ lb

  **D** $4\frac{5}{7}$ lb

**6.** Mr. McConnell tells a class during study period that students will be able to have free time after they have finished at least four sevenths of their homework. Who will have free time? *TAKS Obj. 1*

  **F** Stacy who finished three of her five English essay questions.

  **G** Aaron who finished five of his nine science lab assignment sections.

  **H** Keith who finished six of his eleven math exercises.

  **J** Julia who finished defining and using eleven of her twenty vocabulary words.

## MIXED TAKS PRACTICE

**7.** Which procedure will equal the area of the triangle shown below? *TAKS Obj. 6*

1.25 cm   1 cm

0.75 cm

**A** Adding 0.75, 1, and 1.25

**B** Multiplying 0.75 by 1

**C** Dividing 0.75 by 2

**D** Multiplying 0.75 by 1.25 and dividing the result by 2

**8.** Latoya thought that her last five bowling scores were 195, 172, 200, 165, and 183. But she finds that she remembered her highest score incorrectly. She actually scored 195 not 200. Which measure of her bowling score data will NOT change when Latoya corrects the value of her highest score? *TAKS Obj. 5*

**F** Mode

**G** Median

**H** Mean

**J** Range

**9.** Juhi wants to buy 4 Mexican rugs and 2 Mexican paintings with a certain amount of money. Each painting costs twice as much as each rug. How much must each rug cost for her to be able to afford the purchase? *TAKS Obj. 6*

**A** At most one fourth of Juhi's money

**B** At most one sixth of Juhi's money

**C** At most one eighth of Juhi's money

**D** At most one tenth of Juhi's money

**10.** Al is asked to evaluate $-\dfrac{2}{x} \div \dfrac{6}{x}$ when $x = 5$. What should his answer be? *TAKS Obj. 1*

**F** $-12$

**G** $-3$

**H** $-\dfrac{12}{25}$

**J** $-\dfrac{1}{3}$

**11.** It took Ms. Davis 4 hours 48 minutes to drive to her summer beach house, driving an average of 50 miles per hour. She wants to drive home in exactly 4 hours. At what constant rate should she travel? *TAKS Obj. 2*

**A** 50 mph

**B** 60 mph

**C** 62.5 mph

**D** 80 mph

**12.** The table shows the cost, including shipping, of buying shoulder bags from a catalog company. Which equation shows the relationship between the quantity of bags purchased, $Q$, and the total cost in dollars, $C$? *TAKS Obj. 1*

| Quantity | 2 | 3 | 4 |
|---|---|---|---|
| Cost | $12.50 | $17.50 | $22.50 |

**F** $C = 5Q + 2.5$

**G** $C = 25 \div Q$

**H** $C = 6.25Q$

**J** $C = 12.5 + 5Q$

**13.** **GRIDDED ANSWER** One morning Charlotte and her 3 brothers share a gallon of milk equally. How many fluid ounces of milk does each person drink? *TAKS Obj. 1*

*Record your answer and fill in the bubbles on your answer document. Be sure to use the correct place value.*

# 6 Multi-Step Equations and Inequalities

TEXAS

## Before

**In previous chapters you've ...**

- Solved equations by using one or two steps
- Solved one-step inequalities

## Now

TEKS **you'll study ...**

| 8.5.A | 6.1 Multi-step equations |
| 8.4 | 6.2 Collecting like terms |
| 8.2.A | 6.3 Fractions and decimals |
| 8.7.B | 6.4 Circumference |
| 8.4 | 6.5 Multi-step inequalities |
| 8.5.A | 6.6 Problem solving |

## Why?

**So you can solve real-world problems about ...**

- fundraising, p. 297
- drumming, p. 300
- bowling, p. 319

 **Math**
*at classzone.com*

- Solving Multi-Step Equations, p. 295
- Solving Inequalities, p. 318
- Problem Solving and Inequalities, p. 325

## Get-Ready Games

**Review Prerequisite Skills** by playing *Treasure Hunt*.

**Skill Focus:** Solving one- and two-step equations

### TREASURE HUNT

**MATERIALS**

- 1 number cube
- 1 Treasure Hunt board
- 20 red markers
- 20 yellow markers

**HOW TO PLAY** Each player gets 20 markers of the same color. On your turn, follow the steps on the next page. You can challenge the other player when you believe they have covered an incorrect space.

$\dfrac{14x}{5} = 14$

$5x + 1 = 21$

$-9x$

$7x + 8 = 50$

$x - 9 = -8$

$-12x = -7$

$\dfrac{5x}{2} = 15$

$\dfrac{9x}{-3} = -6$

$-7 - x = -9$

$29 + x = 33$

$\dfrac{15x}{3} = 5$

**1** **ROLL** a number cube. This is your solution.

**2** **COVER** an equation that has your solution with a marker. If there are no equations that have your solution, you cannot place a marker and it is the next player's turn. Each space you cover is a piece of treasure.

**3** **CHECK** that you cover a correct space for your roll. If you cover an incorrect space, then you must remove your marker and it is the next player's turn.

**HOW TO WIN** Be the player with the most spaces covered (the most treasure collected) when all spaces on the board are covered.

## Stop and Think

1. **WRITING** If the only spaces left on the board are $5x + 1 = 21$, $-7 - x = 29$, and $11 - 2x = 3$, what is the best number to roll? What is the second best number to roll? *Explain.*

2. **CRITICAL THINKING** How many spaces on the board have a solution of 5? *Explain* how you found your answer.

# Review Prerequisite Skills

## VOCABULARY CHECK

**Copy and complete using a review word from the list at the left.**

1. The ___?___ of a figure is the sum of its side lengths.

2. The four ___?___ symbols are <, >, ≤, and ≥.

3. To divide by a fraction, you multiply by its ___?___.

4. Terms that have identical variable parts raised to the same power are ___?___.

## SKILL CHECK

**Simplify the expression by combining like terms.** *(p. 88)*

5. $3 - 2x + 4$      6. $4x + 5 + x - 1$     7. $-2(3x + 1) - 2$    8. $5(x - 4) - x$

**Solve the equation. Check your answer.** *(p. 129)*

9. $2x - 1 = 3$     10. $-3x - 2 = 7$     11. $4 - x = 12$     12. $13 = 2x + 3$

13. $-5x + 6 = -9$    14. $8 - x = -3$     15. $17 = 4x + 1$    16. $3x - 5 = 10$

**Solve the inequality. Then graph its solution.** *(pp. 148, 154)*

17. $x + 5 < 18$     18. $x - 4 \geq -6$     19. $17 + x > 19$     20. $-4 + x \leq -9$

21. $5x \geq 30$      22. $-6x \leq 54$      23. $\frac{4}{5}x > 20$      24. $\frac{2}{3}x \leq 12$

**TEXAS @HomeTutor**  Prerequisite skills practice at classzone.com

## Notetaking Skills    Recording the Process

In each chapter you will learn a new notetaking skill. In Chapter 6 you will apply the strategy of recording the process to Example 1 on p. 303.

Copy examples your teacher explains during class. Be sure to record each step of the solution to help you remember the process.

Solving Two-Step Equations

| | |
|---|---|
| $-2x - 3 = 11$ | Original equation |
| $-2x - 3 + 3 = 11 + 3$ | Add 3 to each side. |
| $-2x = 14$ | Simplify. |
| $\dfrac{-2x}{-2} = \dfrac{14}{-2}$ | Divide each side by $-2$. |
| $x = -7$ | Simplify. |

Call attention to important steps in examples.

# 6.1 Solving Multi-Step Equations

TEKS *8.4, 8.5.A*

| | |
|---|---|
| **Before** | You solved equations by using one or two steps. |
| **Now** | You'll solve equations by using two or more steps. |
| **Why?** | So you can plan science experiments, as in Example 1. |

**KEY VOCABULARY**
- **distributive property,** *p. 88*
- **like terms,** *p. 89*

**Science** For a science fair, you perform an experiment to see how the number of Venus flytrap seeds planted in a cup affects plant growth. In each cup, you plant either 5 seeds or 10 seeds. You want to use an equal number of cups for each seed amount. You have 75 seeds. How many cups do you need? You can use an equation to solve this problem.

Before using inverse operations to solve an equation, check to see if you can simplify one or both sides of the equation by combining like terms.

**EXAMPLE 1** Writing and Solving a Multi-Step Equation

To find the number of cups for each seed amount, first write a verbal model. Let *c* represent the number of cups for each seed amount.

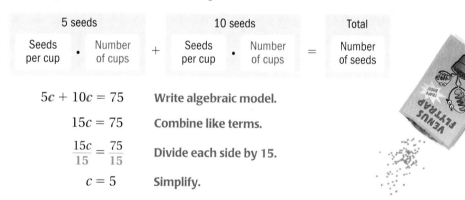

| 5 seeds | | 10 seeds | | Total |
|---|---|---|---|---|
| Seeds per cup · Number of cups | + | Seeds per cup · Number of cups | = | Number of seeds |

$$5c + 10c = 75 \qquad \text{Write algebraic model.}$$
$$15c = 75 \qquad \text{Combine like terms.}$$
$$\frac{15c}{15} = \frac{75}{15} \qquad \text{Divide each side by 15.}$$
$$c = 5 \qquad \text{Simplify.}$$

▶ **Answer** You can plant five cups with 5 seeds and five cups with 10 seeds.

**Check** Substitute 5 for *c* in the original equation.

$$5(5) + 10(5) \stackrel{?}{=} 75$$
$$25 + 50 \stackrel{?}{=} 75$$
$$75 = 75 \checkmark$$

 **GUIDED PRACTICE** for Example 1

1. **Flowers** A pack of petunia seeds costs $3 and a pack of balloon flower seeds costs $4. You buy the same number of packs of each type of flower and pay $42. How many packs of each do you buy?

## EXAMPLE 2 Combining Like Terms

| | |
|---|---|
| $3x + 12 - 4x = 20$ | Original equation |
| $-x + 12 = 20$ | Combine like terms. |
| $-x + 12 - 12 = 20 - 12$ | Subtract 12 from each side. |
| $-x = 8$ | Simplify. |
| $\dfrac{-x}{-1} = \dfrac{8}{-1}$ | Divide each side by $-1$. |
| $x = -8$ | Simplify. |

**Grouping Symbols** When an equation involves parentheses, as in Example 3 below, you can use the distributive property before you combine like terms. When an equation involves a fraction, as in Example 4 on page 295, you can multiply each side of the equation by the same number to *clear* the fraction. This will allow you to write an equivalent equation without a fraction.

## EXAMPLE 3 Using the Distributive Property

**AVOID ERRORS**
When distributing a negative number, remember to distribute the negative sign to *each* term inside the parentheses. For help with the distributive property, see p. 88.

| | |
|---|---|
| $6n - 2(n + 1) = 26$ | Original equation |
| $6n - 2n - 2 = 26$ | Distributive property |
| $4n - 2 = 26$ | Combine like terms. |
| $4n - 2 + 2 = 26 + 2$ | Add 2 to each side. |
| $4n = 28$ | Simplify. |
| $\dfrac{4n}{4} = \dfrac{28}{4}$ | Divide each side by 4. |
| $n = 7$ | Simplify. |

**Check** Substitute 7 for $n$ in the original equation.

$$6(7) - 2(7 + 1) \stackrel{?}{=} 26$$
$$6(7) - 2(8) \stackrel{?}{=} 26$$
$$42 - 16 \stackrel{?}{=} 26$$
$$26 = 26 \checkmark$$

✓ **GUIDED PRACTICE** for Examples 2 and 3

**Solve the equation. Then check the solution.**

**2.** $-6 = 11w - 5w$

**3.** $4p + 10 + p = 25$

**4.** $-8r - 2 + 7r = -9$

**5.** $3(x - 9) = -39$

**6.** $z + 4(6 - z) = 21$

**7.** $8 = -7(y + 1) + 2y$

**EXAMPLE 4** **TAKS PRACTICE: Multiple Choice**

**Volunteering** Volunteers originally form 4 groups containing $x$ volunteers each. Then 5 more volunteers arrive. The volunteers regroup into 5 groups containing 9 members each. The equation $\frac{4x + 5}{5} = 9$ models this situation, where $x$ represents the original group size. What could you do first to produce a simpler, equivalent equation?

> **A** Divide by 4.    **B** Multiply by 5.    **C** Multiply by 9.    **D** Subtract 5.

*ELIMINATE CHOICES*
It's simplest to "undo" division before doing any operations in the numerator. So, choices A and D can be eliminated.

**SOLUTION**

| | |
|---|---|
| $\frac{4x + 5}{5} = 9$ | Original equation |
| $\frac{4x + 5}{5} \cdot 5 = 9 \cdot 5$ | Multiply each side by 5. |
| $4x + 5 = 45$ | Simplify. |
| $4x = 40$ | Subtract 5 from each side. |
| $x = 10$ | Divide each side by 4. |

▶ **Answer** The first step is to multiply each side by 5. The correct answer is B. Ⓐ Ⓑ Ⓒ Ⓓ

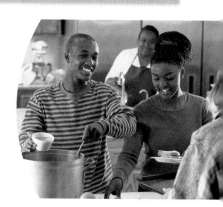

*Animated* **Math**
at classzone.com

✓ **GUIDED PRACTICE** for Example 4

**Solve the equation. Then check the solution.**

**8.** $\frac{2y + 4}{5} = 6$    **9.** $\frac{3x - 1}{8} = 4$    **10.** $\frac{9 - z}{8} = 3$

# 6.1 EXERCISES

HOMEWORK KEY

🔲 = **TAKS Practice and Reasoning**
Exs. 16, 38, 40, 44, and 45

◯ = **HINTS AND HOMEWORK HELP**
for Exs. 5, 13, 23, 37 at classzone.com

## SKILL PRACTICE

**1. VOCABULARY** Identify the like terms in the expression $5x + 6 - 2 - 9x$.

**2. VOCABULARY** Rewrite $3(x + 4)$ using the distributive property.

**SOLVING EQUATIONS** Solve the equation. Then check the solution.

*SEE EXAMPLES 1, 2, AND 3*
on pp. 293–294
for Exs. 3–14

**3.** $8b + 2b = 10$    **4.** $-n + 8n = 35$    **⑤** $7y - 3y - 8 = -32$

**6.** $4x - 7 - 7x = -1$    **7.** $-2z + 6z - 9 = 15$    **8.** $-22 + 3k + 6 = -28$

**9.** $5(w - 7) = -15$    **10.** $-2(m + 7) = -22$    **11.** $5(3 - 2n) + 5n = 65$

**12.** $m + 3(m - 4) = 16$    **⑬** $-4 = -1 - 3(2p + 3)$    **14.** $2z - 4(9 - 3z) = 62$

**SEE EXAMPLES 2 AND 3**
on p. 294
for Exs. 15–16

**15. ERROR ANALYSIS** Describe and correct the error made in solving the equation.

$$3x - 2(x - 4) = 5$$
$$3x - 2x - 8 = 5$$
$$x - 8 = 5$$
$$x = 13$$

**16.** ⬥ **TAKS REASONING** What is the value of $v$ in the equation $3 + 8v - 9v = 21$?

**(A)** $-24$    **(B)** $-18$    **(C)** $18$    **(D)** $24$

**CLEARING FRACTIONS** Solve the equation by first clearing fractions.

**SEE EXAMPLE 4**
on p. 295
for Exs. 17–24

**17.** $\dfrac{6k + 2}{4} = 2$    **18.** $\dfrac{2b + 8}{5} = -12$    **19.** $\dfrac{-c - 5}{8} = 4$    **20.** $\dfrac{-g + 4}{7} = 6$

**21.** $\dfrac{5 - 2d}{7} = 7$    **22.** $\dfrac{9 - 3h}{5} = -6$    **(23.)** $\dfrac{5a - 2}{3} = -9$    **24.** $\dfrac{4m - 16}{12} = -3$

**SOLVING EQUATIONS** Solve the equation. Then check the solution.

**25.** $5y + 8 - 2y + 9y = -16$          **26.** $8k - 7k - 16 - 3k = -21$

**27.** $7(t + 4) - 3(1 + t) = -19$          **28.** $-(6 - c) + 3(2c - 7) = 1$

**29.** $9z + 5(8 + z) - 6(2z - 7) = 40$          **30.** $4a + 7(2a - 5) - 5(3a + 1) = 50$

**GEOMETRY** Write an equation for the area of the triangle. Then solve for $x$.

**31.**  **19 in.** Area = 228 in.$^2$

$(x + 11)$ in.

**32.** $(x - 9)$ m  Area = 918 m$^2$

**51 m**

**33. GEOMETRY** Find the values of $x$ and $y$ so that the rectangle and the triangle have the same perimeter. What is the perimeter?

13
$x - 1$
$x + 8$
$y - 1$
$y + 5$
$y + 6$

**34. CHALLENGE** The sum of 5 consecutive integers divided by 4 is 60. What are the integers?

---

## PROBLEM SOLVING

**SEE EXAMPLES 1 AND 3**
on pp. 293–294
for Ex. 35

**35. GUIDED PROBLEM SOLVING** Tickets to the county fair cost $8 each. Seventy people bought their tickets in advance and the rest bought them at the gate. The revenue from ticket sales is $2560. How many people bought their tickets at the gate?

**a.** Use the verbal model to write an equation to find the number of tickets bought at the gate.

| Price per ticket | · | ( Tickets bought in advance | + | Tickets bought at gate ) | = | Total revenue |

**b.** Solve the equation. Then check the solution.

⬥ = TAKS Practice and Reasoning          ◯ = **HINTS AND HOMEWORK HELP** *at classzone.com*

**SEE EXAMPLE 1**
on p. 293
for Ex. 36

**36. FUNDRAISER** Student council members raised money selling T-shirts. Shirt sales numbers were: Maria, 13; Kevin, 9; and Emma, 10. The total raised was $352. Write and solve an equation to find the price of one T-shirt.

**(37.) MEASUREMENT** The perimeter of the rectangle is $4(x - 8)$ millimeters. Use a ruler to measure the perimeter of the rectangle. Then find the value of $x$.

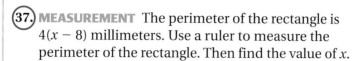

**38.** ⬥ **TAKS REASONING** You charge $x$ dollars per hour for painting and $(x + 5)$ dollars per hour for hanging wallpaper. In one week you earn $1020 painting for 12 hours and hanging wallpaper for 15 hours. Which equation represents this situation?

**(A)** $12x + 15(x + 5) = 1020$   **(B)** $x + (x + 5) + 12 + 15 = 1020$

**(C)** $15x + 12(x + 5) = 1020$   **(D)** $27(x + x + 5) = 1020$

**39. WRITING** You volunteered at a senior citizens' center for 9 hours last month and 14 hours this month. *Describe* how you would use a division equation to find the number of hours you need to volunteer next month if you want your monthly mean to be 10 hours.

**40.** ⬥ **TAKS REASONING** Sara has $26 to spend at a yard sale. She decides to buy a $5 teapot and as many pairs of teacups and saucers as she can afford, plus one spare teacup. The teacups are $2 each and the saucers are $1 each. How many pairs can she buy? Can she also afford a $.50 teaspoon? *Explain.*

**41. SAVING PLAN** You are saving to buy a mountain bike that costs $235. You already have $25. Each week, you earn $15 babysitting and $25 as a cashier, but you spend $10 on lunches. Write and solve an equation to find in how many weeks you will have enough money saved.

**42. REASONING** Use the distributive property to solve the equation $3(x + 2) - 3 = 9$. Is it possible to solve this equation without distributing a 3? *Explain* your reasoning.

**43. CHALLENGE** Write an equation that has a solution of $-2$ and fits this description: The final step in solving the equation is dividing both sides by $-18$. Before that, 12 is added to both sides. The first step is distributing $-3$.

## MIXED REVIEW FOR TAKS

**TAKS PRACTICE** at classzone.com

**REVIEW**
Lesson 1.7;
TAKS Workbook

**44.** ⬥ **TAKS PRACTICE** Jake had 4 hits in a baseball game. Marc had two more hits than Nathan. Nathan had fewer than one third as many hits as Jake. What is the greatest number of hits Marc could have had? *TAKS Obj. 6*

**(A)** 2   **(B)** 3   **(C)** 4   **(D)** 13

**REVIEW**
Lesson 4.7;
TAKS Workbook

**45.** ⬥ **TAKS PRACTICE** Which of the following is true when $x = 4$? *TAKS Obj. 1*

**(F)** $-2x \geq -10$   **(G)** $-x \leq -2^{-3}$

**(H)** $3x \geq 33$   **(J)** $4x \leq 2^3$

## 6.2 Solving Equations with Variables on Both Sides

TEKS 8.4, 8.5.A

**Before**  You solved equations that had variables on one side.

**Now**  You'll solve equations that have variables on both sides.

**Why?**  So you can compare costs, as for drum lessons in Example 4.

**KEY VOCABULARY**
- **perimeter,** *p. 32*
- **distributive property,** *p. 88*
- **like terms,** *p. 89*

---

### ACTIVITY

**Use algebra tiles to model and solve an equation.**

**STEP 1**
**Represent** the equation $2x + 3 = x + 5$ using algebra tiles.

**STEP 2**
**Remove** one *x*-tile and three 1-tiles from each side.

**STEP 3**
**Interpret** the remaining tiles. The solution is 2.

**Use algebra tiles to solve the equation.**

**1.** $2x + 7 = 3x + 2$      **2.** $4x - 1 = x - 7$      **3.** $5x - 2 = 3x + 6$

---

**Collecting like Terms** To solve an equation with variables on both sides, as in the activity above, collect like terms on the same side.

### EXAMPLE 1  Collecting Like Terms

| | |
|---|---|
| $x + 2 = 3x$ | **Original equation** |
| $x + 2 - x = 3x - x$ | **Subtract *x* from each side.** |
| $2 = 2x$ | |
| $\dfrac{2}{2} = \dfrac{2x}{2}$ | **Divide both sides by 2.** |
| $1 = x$ | |

 **Math** at classzone.com

**EXAMPLE 2** TAKS REASONING: Multi-Step Problem

 **Each side of the triangle has the same length. What is the perimeter of the triangle?**

**SOLUTION**

| $5x + 9 = 7x + 5$ | Write an equation. |
|---|---|
| $5x + 9 - 5x = 7x + 5 - 5x$ | Subtract 5x from each side. |
| $9 = 2x + 5$ | Simplify. |
| $9 - 5 = 2x + 5 - 5$ | Subtract 5 from each side. |
| $4 = 2x$ | Simplify. |
| $\dfrac{4}{2} = \dfrac{2x}{2}$ | Divide each side by 2. |
| $2 = x$ | Simplify. |

**ANOTHER WAY**

You can also begin by subtracting 5 from each side, and then subtracting 5x from each side.

$5x + 9 = 7x + 5$
$5x + 4 = 7x$
$4 = 2x$
$2 = x$

Because $5x + 9 = 5(2) + 9 = 19$, each side of the triangle is 19 units long. Since each side of the triangle has the same length, the perimeter is $3 \cdot 19$, or 57, units.

▶ **Answer** The perimeter of the triangle is 57 units.

**Using the Distributive Property** Sometimes you may have to use the distributive property to simplify one or both sides of an equation before you solve.

**EXAMPLE 3** Using the Distributive Property

| $21x = 3(2x + 30)$ | Original equation |
|---|---|
| $21x = 6x + 90$ | Distributive property |
| $21x - 6x = 6x + 90 - 6x$ | Subtract 6x from each side. |
| $15x = 90$ | Simplify. |
| $\dfrac{15x}{15} = \dfrac{90}{15}$ | Divide each side by 15. |
| $x = 6$ | Simplify. |

✓ **GUIDED PRACTICE** for Examples 1, 2, and 3

**Solve the equation.**

**1.** $55 + 3x = 8x$     **2.** $9x = 12x - 9$     **3.** $-15x + 120 = 15x$

**4.** $4a + 5 = a + 11$     **5.** $3n + 7 = 2n - 1$     **6.** $-6c + 1 = -9c + 7$

**7.** $28 - 3s = 5s - 12$     **8.** $4(w - 9) = 7w + 18$     **9.** $2(y + 4) = -3y - 7$

6.2 Solving Equations with Variables on Both Sides     **299**

**EXAMPLE 4** Using a Verbal Model

 **Music** You pay $20 for a youth center membership. Drum lessons at the center cost $8 each for members and $12 each for nonmembers. You take two more lessons than your friend, a nonmember. For what number of lessons will your friend pay the same total amount as you?

**SOLUTION**

Let $n$ represent the number of lessons your friend takes.

| Cost for friend | | | | Cost for you | | |
|---|---|---|---|---|---|---|
| Price per lesson | · | Number of lessons | = | Price per lesson | · | Number of lessons | + | Membership fee |

$$12n = 8(n + 2) + 20 \quad \text{Write algebraic model.}$$
$$12n = 8n + 16 + 20 \quad \text{Distributive property}$$
$$12n = 8n + 36 \quad \text{Simplify.}$$
$$4n = 36 \quad \text{Subtract } 8n \text{ from each side.}$$
$$n = 9 \quad \text{Divide each side by 4.}$$

▶ **Answer** Your friend pays the same total amount as you for 9 lessons.

✓ **GUIDED PRACTICE** for Example 4

**10. What If?** In Example 4, suppose your friend takes 4 fewer lessons than you. For what number of lessons will your friend pay as much as you?

# 6.2 EXERCISES

**HOMEWORK KEY**

🪁 = **TAKS Practice and Reasoning**
Exs. 14, 31, 36, 39, and 40

○ = **HINTS AND HOMEWORK HELP**
for Exs. 3, 11, 15, 21, 33 at classzone.com

## SKILL PRACTICE

1. **VOCABULARY** What is the perimeter of a figure?

**SOLVING EQUATIONS** Solve the equation.

**2.** $7x = x + 18$

**3.** $7m = 4m + 21$

**4.** $30 - 2s = 4s$

**5.** $81 + 2k = 5k$

**6.** $13q - 48 = -3q$

**7.** $-11r = -4r + 56$

**8.** $5z - 43 = 2z + 80$

**9.** $16y - 43 = 4y + 65$

**10.** $8f + 11 = -7f - 19$

**11.** $-1 + 11a = 6 - 3a$

**12.** $9b - 10 = -b - 18$

**13.** $14s - 28 = 4s + 7$

**14.** 🪁 **TAKS REASONING** What is the value of $x$ in $5x + 14 = 3x - 12$?

(A) 1     (B) $-1$     (C) $-13$     (D) $-26$

**GEOMETRY** Find the perimeter. The triangles' sides are equal in length.

**SEE EXAMPLE 2**
on p. 299
for Exs. 15–18

**15.**
$2x - 3$
$7$ $7$
$3x - 10$

**16.**
$7x - 12$
$3x$

**17.**
$2x + 10$
$3x - 7$

**18. ERROR ANALYSIS** Describe and correct the error made in finding the perimeter $P$ of the rectangle.

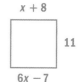
$3x + 6$
$20$ $20$
$4x - 2$

$3x + 6 = 4x - 2$
$6 = x - 2$
$8 = x$
$P = 2(20) + 2(8) = 56$ units

**USING THE DISTRIBUTIVE PROPERTY** Solve the equation.

**SEE EXAMPLE 3**
on p. 299
for Exs. 19–26

**19.** $3(t - 7) = 6t$

**20.** $-3h = 9(2 - 3h)$

**21.** $3(j + 4) = -2j + j$

**22.** $5(t + 7) = 2(2t + 7)$

**23.** $2(c + 6) = 5(c + 12)$

**24.** $6(s - 4) = 3(s + 9)$

**25.** $-2.5(2g + 6) = 3g - 6g$

**26.** $2(p + 2) = 1.8p - 2 - 0.2(p + 5)$

**REASONING** Use the rectangle at the right to decide whether the statement is *true* or *false*. *Justify* your reasoning.

$x + 8$
$11$
$6x - 7$

**27.** The rectangle is a square.

**28.** The area of the rectangle is 33 square units.

**29. WHICH ONE DOESN'T BELONG?** Which of the following triangles *cannot* have all three sides equal in length? (*Note:* Figures may not be to scale.)

**A.**
$11$ $3x + 2$
$5x - 4$

**B.**
$3x - 1$
$23$
$2x + 7$

**C.**
$5.8 - 3x$
$9x - 0.2$
$5x + 0.8$

**D.**
$9x - 1$ $5x + 3$
$2x + 6$

**30. CHALLENGE** Try to solve the equation $2(5x + 1) = -7x + 2 + 17x$. What do you notice? *Explain* what this tells you about the number of solutions of the equation.

## PROBLEM SOLVING

**SEE EXAMPLE 4**
on p. 300
for Ex. 31

**31. TAKS REASONING** One phone card charges $.018 per minute with a $.25 weekly fee. Another card charges $.029 per minute with no weekly fee. You need a card for 4 weeks. Which equation could you use to find the number of minutes for which both cards cost the same?

**(A)** $0.018x = 0.029x + 4(0.25)$

**(B)** $0.018x + 4(0.25) = 0.029x$

**(C)** $0.018x = 0.029x$

**(D)** $0.018x + 0.25 = 0.029x$

**32. WRITING** Your friend says that when you solve an equation with the same variable on both sides, you must always begin by collecting the variable terms on the same side. Do you agree? *Explain* why or why not.

**SEE EXAMPLE 4**
on p. 300
for Ex. 33

**33.** **CONCERT TICKETS** Tickets to a concert cost $30 for fan club members and $35 for nonmembers. Fan club membership is $25 per person. Write and solve an equation to find the number of tickets for which a member and a nonmember pay the same amount.

**34.** **ASSEMBLY LINE** Nia and Joseph are making fruit bowls. Joseph cuts the fruit and Nia distributes the fruit into the bowls. Joseph had already cut 72 pieces of fruit when Nia started. Joseph continues to cut fruit at the same rate. How many minutes will it take for Nia to catch up to Joseph?

Joseph cuts 3 pieces of fruit per minute.

Nia distributes 9 pieces of fruit per minute.

**35.** **DECORATIONS** You are decorating for a school dance. Balloons cost $8 per dozen but cost more if bought singly. You have the exact amount of money for either 7 dozen and 5 single balloons or 75 single balloons. What is the cost of a single balloon? How much money do you have? *Explain.*

**36.** **TAKS REASONING** David has $26 and saves $8 each week. Emily has $56 and saves $4 each week. How many weeks will it take for David and Emily to have the same amount of money? Will David ever have twice the amount of money that Emily has? *Justify* your answer.

**37.** **CHALLENGE** The sum of two numbers is 30. Three times one number is 6 more than 4 times the other number. What are the two numbers?

**38.** **CHALLENGE** Let $a$, $b$, $c$, and $d$ be any numbers. What must be true about the relationship between $a$ and $c$ and the relationship between $b$ and $d$ for the equation $ax + b = cx + d$ to have *no* solution?

## MIXED REVIEW FOR TAKS
**TAKS PRACTICE** at classzone.com

**REVIEW**
Lesson 3.4;
TAKS Workbook

**39.** **TAKS PRACTICE** Isaac knows 32 German words. Since he started German lessons, he learns an additional 4 new words a day. Which equation can be used to find the number of days, $d$, that it will take Isaac to know 300 German words? *TAKS Obj. 2*

(A) $32 + 4d = 300$

(B) $4 = 300 - 32d$

(C) $32d + 4 = 300$

(D) $32d + 4d = 300$

**REVIEW**
Lesson 5.8;
TAKS Workbook

**40.** **TAKS PRACTICE** Sue polled audience opinions of seven new summer movies. The percentage of people polled who liked each movie "very much" were 52%, 87%, 16%, 4%, 73%, 24%, and 32%. An eighth movie came out and the percentage of people polled who liked that movie "very much" was 65%. Which measure of data changed the most after Sue added the results of the poll of the eighth movie? *TAKS Obj. 5*

(F) Mean     (G) Median     (H) Mode     (J) Range

# 6.3 Solving Equations Involving Fractions and Decimals

TEKS *8.2.A, 8.2.B*

| | |
|---|---|
| **Before** | You solved equations involving whole numbers. |
| **Now** | You'll solve equations with fractions and decimals. |
| **Why?** | So you can compare heights, as with coral in Example 1. |

**KEY VOCABULARY**
• **least common denominator (LCD),** *p. 198*

You may have noticed that equations sometimes have coefficients and constant terms that are not integers. In this lesson, you will solve multi-step equations that have fractions and decimals.

---

### EXAMPLE 1  Solving an Equation Involving Decimals

**Environment** A colony of coral is 0.17 meter high and is growing at a rate of 0.025 meter per year. Another colony is 0.11 meter high and is growing at a rate of 0.041 meter per year. In how many years will the colonies be the same height?

**SOLUTION**

First write a verbal model. Let $n$ represent the number of years.

**TAKE NOTES**
Some of the steps in Example 1 are not shown. Identify these steps and include them in your notes.

| | |
|---|---|
| $0.17 + 0.025n = 0.11 + 0.041n$ | **Write algebraic model.** |
| $0.17 = 0.11 + 0.016n$ | **Subtract 0.025n from each side.** |
| $0.06 = 0.016n$ | **Subtract 0.11 from each side.** |
| $\dfrac{0.06}{0.016} = \dfrac{0.016n}{0.016}$ | **Divide each side by 0.016.** |
| $3.75 = n$ | **Simplify.** |

▶ **Answer** The colonies will be the same height in 3.75 years.

---

✔ **GUIDED PRACTICE**  **for Example 1**

1. **Snowboarding** You and a friend are buying snowboarding gear. You buy a pair of goggles that costs $39.95 and 4 tubes of wax. Your friend buys a helmet that costs $54.95 and 2 tubes of wax. You each spend the same amount. Write and solve an equation to find the price of one tube of wax.

**Clearing Decimals** The multiplication property of equality allows you to multiply each side of an equation by the same number. You can use this property to clear decimals from an equation. Multiply each side of the equation by a power of ten that makes all coefficients and constants integers.

**EXAMPLE 2** Solving an Equation Involving Decimals

| | |
|---|---|
| $1.4x - 1.8 + 2.35x = 0.21$ | **Original equation** |
| $(1.4x - 1.8 + 2.35x)100 = (0.21)100$ | **Multiply each side by 100 to clear decimals.** |
| $140x - 180 + 235x = 21$ | **Simplify.** |
| $375x - 180 = 21$ | **Combine like terms.** |
| $375x = 201$ | **Add 180 to each side.** |
| $\dfrac{375x}{375} = \dfrac{201}{375}$ | **Divide each side by 375.** |
| $x = 0.536$ | **Simplify.** |

**Clearing Fractions** When you solve an equation with fractions, you can multiply each side by the LCD to clear the fractions.

**EXAMPLE 3** Solving an Equation Involving Fractions

**AVOID ERRORS**
When multiplying both sides of an equation by the same number, be sure to multiply *each* term by that number.

| | |
|---|---|
| $\dfrac{3}{10}x = -\dfrac{1}{6}x + \dfrac{7}{10}$ | **Original equation** |
| $\left(\dfrac{3}{10}x\right)30 = \left(-\dfrac{1}{6}x + \dfrac{7}{10}\right)30$ | **Multiply each side by the LCD, 30.** |
| $\left(\dfrac{3}{10}x\right)30 = \left(-\dfrac{1}{6}x\right)30 + \left(\dfrac{7}{10}\right)30$ | **Distributive property** |
| $\dfrac{3 \cdot \overset{3}{\cancel{30}}}{\underset{1}{\cancel{10}}}x = -\dfrac{1 \cdot \overset{5}{\cancel{30}}}{\underset{1}{\cancel{6}}}x + \dfrac{7 \cdot \overset{3}{\cancel{30}}}{\underset{1}{\cancel{10}}}$ | **Divide out common factors.** |
| $9x = -5x + 21$ | **Simplify.** |
| $14x = 21$ | **Add 5x to each side.** |
| $x = \dfrac{21}{14} = \dfrac{3}{2}, \text{ or } 1\dfrac{1}{2}$ | **Divide each side by 14. Simplify.** |

✓ **GUIDED PRACTICE** for Examples 2 and 3

**Solve the equation.**

**2.** $-1.7k + 6.7k = 13.1$     **3.** $1.2n - 0.24 = 0.7n$     **4.** $8.3 - 8y = 1.2y + 6$

**5.** $\dfrac{4}{5}x + 3 = -\dfrac{7}{10}$     **6.** $2s - 1\dfrac{1}{4}s = \dfrac{1}{3}$     **7.** $\dfrac{5}{6}v + \dfrac{5}{8} = \dfrac{3}{8}v$

# 6.3 EXERCISES

HOMEWORK KEY

= **TAKS Practice and Reasoning**
Exs. 20, 29, 34, 37, 40, 42, 45, and 46

= **HINTS** AND **HOMEWORK HELP**
for Exs. 5, 11, 17, 35 at classzone.com

## SKILL PRACTICE

**VOCABULARY  Copy and complete the statement.**

1. Twenty-four is the __?__ of $\frac{1}{4}, \frac{5}{6}$, and $\frac{3}{8}$.

2. The process of multiplying both sides of the equation $2.4 + 0.2x = 5$ by 10 is used to __?__ decimals.

**SOLVING EQUATIONS  Solve the equation.**

SEE EXAMPLES
1 AND 2
on pp. 303–304
for Exs. 3–10, 19

3. $1.5a - 1.2 = 1.8a$

4. $5.85b = 8.68 + 3.68b$

5. $0.5c + 3.49 - 2c = 4$

6. $r + 8.2 + 0.4r = -8.6$

7. $1.5s - 1.2 - s = 0.5$

8. $5.3 + u = 3.2u - 2.7$

9. $4.93 - 9.20v = 0.66v$

10. $7.6a + 9.6 = 1.2a$

SEE EXAMPLE 3
on p. 304
for Exs. 11–18

11. $\frac{3}{8}m + \frac{7}{8} = 2m$

12. $\frac{3}{4} - \frac{1}{2}b = -3b$

13. $-\frac{4}{15}n + \frac{2}{3} = \frac{2}{5}n$

14. $p - \frac{4}{9}p = -\frac{7}{9}$

15. $-\frac{1}{5}p + \frac{3}{4}p = 11$

16. $\frac{1}{6}x + \frac{2}{3}x = 1$

17. $\frac{3}{10} - w = \frac{4}{5} - \frac{3}{5}w$

18. $\frac{7}{4}z - \frac{1}{6} = \frac{17}{6} + \frac{3}{4}z$

19. **ERROR ANALYSIS**  Describe and correct the error made in the solution.

$$\times \quad \begin{aligned} 1.5x + 0.25 &= 1.6x \\ 15x + 25 &= 16x \\ 25 &= x \end{aligned}$$

20. **TAKS REASONING**  By what do you multiply each side of the equation $3.75x - \frac{1}{2} = 1.125 - \frac{9}{4}x$ to clear all fractions and decimals?

(A) 2      (B) 4      (C) 8      (D) 100

**CLEARING DECIMALS AND FRACTIONS  Tell what number you multiply each side of the equation by to clear the decimals and fractions. Then solve.**

21. $-4.42x + 0.9 = -9.070 - 0.432x$

22. $0.025(x + 4) = 1.2415$

23. $6\frac{4}{5}n - \frac{8}{9} = \frac{7}{15}n$

24. $\frac{3}{8} + \frac{9}{20}m = \frac{23}{20} + \frac{7}{8}m$

25. $5\frac{3}{10} - 0.2x = \frac{1}{5}x + 0.8$

26. $1.25(x - 9) = \frac{13}{4}$

27. $\frac{1}{2}x - 3 + 0.625x = 5$

28. $2.25 - 3z = 0.375 - \frac{3}{4}z$

**29.** ![texas] **TAKS REASONING** Write three equivalent equations for $\frac{5}{6}x - \frac{1}{2} = 3$.

**CHALLENGE** Solve the equation. Then check the solution.

**30.** $\frac{7}{2a} - \frac{5}{4} = \frac{1}{a}$

**31.** $\frac{3}{4x} = \frac{1}{2x} - \frac{7}{12}$

**32.** $1.8 - \frac{3}{8y} = \frac{9}{10y} - 6$

**33.** $3\frac{4}{9} - \frac{2}{3c} = 6\left(\frac{1}{c} + 3\right)$

## PROBLEM SOLVING

SEE EXAMPLES
1 AND 2
on pp. 303–304
for Exs. 34–36

**34.** ![texas] **TAKS REASONING** At a basketball game, you buy 10 raffle tickets. Your friend buys a T-shirt for $13.50 and 1 raffle ticket. If you each spend the same amount, which equation can you use to find the cost $x$ of one ticket?

(**A**) $11x = 13.5$

(**B**) $13.5 = 10x + x$

(**C**) $10x + 13.5 = x$

(**D**) $10x = 13.5 + x$

**35.** **DELI PRICES** At the deli, Swiss cheese costs $3.96 per pound and turkey costs $4.76 per pound. You buy the same amount of each and spend $13.08. Write and solve an equation to find how many pounds of each you buy.

**36.** **PICNIC** Rosa and Arlene are shopping for a neighborhood picnic. Rosa buys paper plates and cups for $19.10 and 5 pints of potato salad. Arlene buys watermelons for $15.55 and 6 pints of potato salad. They each spend the same total amount and each pint of potato salad costs the same amount. Write and solve an equation to find the cost of one pint of potato salad.

**37.** ![texas] **TAKS REASONING** Write a real-world problem that can be solved using the equation $2.1r + 0.4r = 127.5$. The units for $r$ should be miles per hour and the units for the constant term should be miles. What does the solution represent?

SEE EXAMPLE 3
on p. 304
for Ex. 38

**38.** **SEWING SUPPLIES** You buy a clothes pattern for $7 at a fabric store. You also buy $\frac{3}{4}$ yard of red fabric, $2\frac{1}{2}$ yards of purple fabric, and $\frac{7}{8}$ yard of blue fabric. The total cost is $23.50. All three fabrics cost the same per yard.

   **a.** Write and solve an equation to find the price per yard.

   **b.** How much do you spend on each fabric? *Explain.*

**39.** **WRITING** Suppose you multiply each side of an equation containing fractions by a common multiple of the denominators that is the product of all the denominators. Will you still get the correct answer? *Describe* advantages and disadvantages of this method.

![texas] = **TAKS Practice and Reasoning** ◯ = **HINTS AND HOMEWORK HELP** *at classzone.com*

**40.** ✦ **TAKS REASONING** Use the equation $6.95x - 2.13 = 1.8x + 3.07$.

    **a. Solve** Solve the equation.

    **b. Estimate** *Describe* a way to estimate the solution. Then estimate the solution. *Explain* how this estimation method might be useful.

**41.** **GEOMETRY** You mow $\frac{1}{3}$ of the lawn, and your sister mows $\frac{2}{5}$ of the lawn. What is the area of the entire lawn? What is the length of the section left to mow?

**42.** ✦ **TAKS REASONING** You deposit half of your money in the bank. You spend half of the remaining amount on a movie ticket, and you spend another four dollars on popcorn. You have five dollars left.

    **a.** Write an equation to model this situation.

    **b.** How much money did you start with?

    **c.** *Describe* another method for solving the problem that does not involve writing and solving an equation.

    **d.** *Compare* the methods. How are they alike? How are they different?

**43.** **CHALLENGE** The mean rainfall in Honolulu, Hawaii, from January through the end of May was 3.756 inches. The mean rainfall from January through the end of June was 2.872 inches more than the amount of rain that fell in June. How many inches of rain fell in June? Round your answer to the nearest hundredth.

**44.** **CHALLENGE** The length of a rectangle is $2\frac{2}{3}$ times the width. The perimeter of the rectangle is $2\frac{1}{2}$ units less than 3 times the length. Find the width and the area of the rectangle.

## MIXED REVIEW FOR TAKS

**TAKS** **PRACTICE** at classzone.com

*REVIEW*

Skills Review Handbook, p. 780; TAKS Workbook

**45.** ✦ **TAKS PRACTICE** A clerk at a gift wrapping booth had 2 spools of ribbon. Each spool has 5.4 meters of ribbon. The clerk had no ribbon left after he wrapped 12 identical gifts using an equal amount of ribbon for each gift. How many centimeters of ribbon was used for each gift? *TAKS Obj. 1*

    **(A)** 0.9 cm     **(B)** 9 cm     **(C)** 90 cm     **(D)** 900 cm

*REVIEW*

Lesson 3.5; TAKS Workbook

**46.** ✦ **TAKS PRACTICE** An urban community center designs a mural on a rectangular concrete wall that has an area of 180 square feet. What is the width of the wall if the length is 20 feet? *TAKS Obj. 3*

    **(F)** 8 ft     **(G)** 9 ft     **(H)** 90 ft     **(J)** 3600 ft

**Solve the equation.**

**1.** $2(x + 16) = 46$ *(p. 293)*

**2.** $79 = 10x - 23 + 7x$ *(p. 293)*

**3.** $-108 - 9x = -16(x + 5)$ *(p. 298)*

**4.** $12n = 17 - 22n$ *(p. 298)*

**5.** $\dfrac{x + 8}{3} = -4$ *(p. 293)*

**6.** $\dfrac{2x - 1}{5} = 7$ *(p. 293)*

**7.** $27.2m + 15.7 = -85.94 + 0.8m$ *(p. 303)*

**8.** $14.6p + 34.25 = 11.8p + 45.45$ *(p. 303)*

**9.** $\dfrac{1}{2}v + \dfrac{11}{12} - \dfrac{5}{4}v = -\dfrac{5}{12}$ *(p. 303)*

**10.** $2\dfrac{5}{6} - \dfrac{1}{3}w = w + \dfrac{1}{6}$ *(p. 303)*

**11. GEOMETRY** Find the perimeter of the rectangle. The length and width are measured in feet. *(p. 298)*

4y − 12

2x − 3  |  7x − 18

y + 3

**12. COLOR PRINTER** You have \$445 to buy a printer. You find one that costs \$235. It uses a black ink cartridge that costs \$30 and a color ink cartridge that costs \$40. You buy the same number of each type of cartridge.

**a.** Write and solve an equation to determine how many pairs of ink cartridges you can buy for the printer. *(p. 293)*

**b.** How much money will you spend on color ink cartridges?

## Brain Game

### City Solutions

Solve the equations. Then fill in each blank with the variable that corresponds to the solution. When you are finished, the letters will spell out the name of a city found in 19 states.

$$\frac{?}{-5} \quad \frac{?}{4} \quad \frac{?}{6} \quad \frac{?}{-1} \quad \frac{?}{2} \quad \frac{?}{5} \quad \frac{?}{-4} \quad \frac{?}{-2} \quad \frac{?}{1}$$

**1.** $2g - 7 - 3g = -12$

**2.** $4n + 1 = 9n - 4$

**3.** $1.6o + 13 = 5 - 2.4o$

**4.** $12 = -2r - 12 + 8r$

**5.** $\dfrac{9}{16}l - \dfrac{9}{8} = \dfrac{3}{8}l$

**6.** $a - 2(a + 1) = 3$

**7.** $\dfrac{9}{10}n + \dfrac{1}{5} = \dfrac{7}{10}n + \dfrac{3}{5}$

**8.** $i + 4 - 7i = 10$

**9.** $7 - 2.65t = -4.4t$

## Lessons 6.1–6.3

**MULTIPLE CHOICE**

1. **CELL PHONES** Frank buys 5 ringtones and a $9.99 cover for his cell phone. His friend Kaylee buys 3 ringtones. Kaylee also buys a flashing antenna top costing $15.97 for her phone. They each spend the same amount of money. The ringtones are all the same price. What is the cost of one ringtone? *TEKS 8.5.A*

   (A) $0.75      (B) $1.99

   (C) $2.99      (D) $5.95

2. **TREES** Over the next 10 years, a bald cypress tree will grow at a rate of about 30 inches per year and a bur oak tree will grow at a rate of about 10 inches per year. The bald cypress is presently 15 feet tall and the bur oak is 22 feet tall. How many years will it take for the trees to be the same height? *TEKS 8.5.A*

   (F) 2.1 years

   (G) 4.2 years

   (H) 8.4 years

   (J) 22.2 years

3. **ROAD TRIP** Lisa and two friends took a road trip to Miami. One friend drove $\frac{1}{3}$ of the distance and the other friend drove $\frac{1}{2}$ of the distance. The two friends drove a total of 900 miles. Lisa drove the remaining distance. How far did Lisa drive? *TEKS 8.2.B*

   (A) 150 mi      (B) 180 mi

   (C) 200 mi      (D) 250 mi

4. **GARDEN** Jené plants a garden in a corner of her yard. She encloses the garden with two logs and a fence as shown. One log is 9 feet long. How long must the other log be if the garden covers 138 square feet? *TEKS 8.7.B*

   (F) 14 ft      (G) 15 ft

   (H) 16 ft      (J) 17 ft

5. **SHOPPING** You bought *n* pairs of shorts for $8 per pair. Every pair of shorts after the second pair was $3 off the original price. You spent $36. How many pairs of shorts did you buy? *TEKS 8.14.C*

   (A) 4      (B) 5

   (C) 6      (D) 7

**GRIDDED ANSWER** ⊙①●③④⑤⑥⑦⑧⑨

6. **SAVINGS** Ben has $20 saved. He earns $40 a day at his job. He needs $150 to buy a new ski jacket. What is the least number of days Ben must work to have enough money to buy the jacket? *TEKS 8.5.A*

7. **PERIMETER** Each side of the triangle has the same length. How many units is the perimeter of the triangle? *TEKS 8.5.A*

# INVESTIGATION
*Use before Lesson 6.4*

**GOAL**
Find the relationship between diameter and circumference.

**MATERIALS**
• metric tape measure or ruler
• string
• paper and pencil

**TEKS** *8.1.C, 8.16.A*

# 6.4 Diameter and Circumference

In this Investigation, you will explore the relationship between the diameter and circumference of a circle.

The *diameter* is the distance across a circle through the center.

diameter

The *circumference* is the distance around a circle.

circumference

**EXPLORE 1**  Find the diameter and circumference of circular objects.

**STEP 1**  **Measure** the diameter and circumference of several circular objects. If necessary, wrap a string around the object and measure the length of the string with a ruler.

**STEP 2**  **Record** the measurements in a table like the one below.

| Object | Diameter | Circumference | Circumference / Diameter |
|---|---|---|---|
| water bottle | 65 mm | 206 mm | ? |
| tuna can | 84 mm | 264 mm | ? |
| clock | 174 mm | 549 mm | ? |
| quarter | 24 mm | 74 mm | ? |
| mug | 82 mm | 261 mm | ? |

**PRACTICE**

1. Find the quotient of the circumference and the diameter for each object you measured. Round to the nearest hundredth, if necessary. Record the quotients in another column of the table.

2. What do you notice about the numbers in the new column of your table?

**EXPLORE 2** **Write a circumference formula.**

**STEP 1** **Find** the mean of the quotients $\dfrac{\text{circumference}}{\text{diameter}}$ in your table. How does your mean compare with the means found by the other students in your class?

**STEP 2** **Find** the mean of the quotients $\dfrac{\text{circumference}}{\text{diameter}}$ collected by your whole class.

**STEP 3** **Use** the result in Step 2 to write a formula for the circumference $C$ of a circle in terms of the diameter $d$.

**PRACTICE** **Use the formula you wrote in Step 3 above to calculate the circumference of the circle given its diameter $d$.**

**3.** $d = 64$ mm

**4.** $d = 140$ mm

**5.** $d = 36$ cm

**6.** $d = 20$ cm

**7.** $d = 4$ in.

**8.** $d = 1.25$ in.

**DRAW CONCLUSIONS**

**9.** **WRITING A FORMULA** Write a formula for the diameter $d$ of a circle in terms of the circumference $C$.

# 6.4 Solving Equations Involving Circumference

TEKS *8.1.C, 8.7.B*

| | |
|---|---|
| **Before** | You solved equations involving fractions and decimals. |
| **Now** | You'll solve equations involving the circumference of a circle. |
| **Why?** | So you can find a diameter, as of a Ferris wheel in Example 3. |

**KEY VOCABULARY**
- **circle,** *p. 312*
- **center,** *p. 312*
- **radius,** *p. 312*
- **diameter,** *p. 312*
- **circumference,** *p. 312*
- **pi (π),** *p. 312*

A **circle** is the set of all points in a plane that are the same distance from a fixed point called the **center**. The distance from the center to any point on the circle is the **radius**. The **diameter** is the distance across the circle through the center, or twice the radius.

*radius r*

*circumference C*

*diameter d*

*VOCABULARY*
Even though π is a Greek letter, remember that π is *not* a variable. It has a specific value.

The **circumference** of a circle is the distance around the circle. For every circle, the quotient of its circumference and its diameter is the same: about 3.14159. This constant is represented by the Greek letter **pi**, π. You can approximate π using 3.14, $\frac{22}{7}$, or the π key on a calculator.

---

### KEY CONCEPT    *For Your Notebook*

**Circumference of a Circle**

**Words**    The circumference of a circle is the product of π and the diameter.

$d = 2r$

**Algebra**    $C = \pi d$    or    $C = 2\pi r$

---

### EXAMPLE 1    Using Radius to Find Circumference

**Find the circumference of a circle with a radius of 11 meters.**

**SOLUTION**

$$C = 2\pi r \qquad \text{Circumference formula}$$
$$\approx 2(3.14)(11) \qquad \text{Substitute 3.14 for } \pi \text{ and 11 for } r.$$
$$= 69.08 \qquad \text{Multiply.}$$

▶ **Answer** The circumference is about 69.08 meters.

**Check** Estimate: $2(3.14)(11) \approx 2(3)(11) = 66$, so 69.08 is reasonable.

EXAMPLE 2 **Using Diameter to Find Circumference**

**Find the circumference of the circle.**

21 ft

**SOLUTION**

The measure shown is a diameter, so use the circumference formula that involves the diameter.

$$C = \pi d \qquad \text{Circumference formula}$$

$$\approx \frac{22}{7} \cdot \overset{3}{\underset{1}{21}} \qquad \text{Substitute. Use } \frac{22}{7} \text{ for } \pi \text{ because 21 is divisible by 7.}$$

$$= 66 \qquad \text{Multiply.}$$

▶ **Answer** The circumference is about 66 feet.

---

*SUBSTITUTE FOR $\pi$*
When considering whether to use $\frac{22}{7}$ for $\pi$, look for numbers that are divisible by 22 or 7.

---

**TAKS** **EXAMPLE 3** **TAKS PRACTICE: Multiple Choice**

**Ferris Wheel** A Ferris wheel has a circumference of about 392.5 feet. What is the diameter of the Ferris wheel? Use 3.14 for $\pi$.

**A** 12.5 feet  **B** 62.5 feet  **C** 125 feet  **D** 1250 feet

*ELIMINATE CHOICES*
The diameter of a circle cannot be greater than the circumference of the circle. So, choice D can be eliminated.

**SOLUTION**

You are asked to find the diameter, so use the circumference formula that involves diameter.

$$C = \pi d \qquad \text{Circumference formula}$$

$$392.5 \approx 3.14d \qquad \text{Substitute 392.5 for } C \text{ and 3.14 for } \pi.$$

$$\frac{392.5}{3.14} \approx \frac{3.14d}{3.14} \qquad \text{Divide each side by 3.14.}$$

$$125 \approx d \qquad \text{Simplify.}$$

▶ **Answer** The diameter is about 125 feet.
   The correct answer is C. Ⓐ Ⓑ Ⓒ Ⓓ

---

✓ **GUIDED PRACTICE** for Examples 1, 2, and 3

**Find the circumference of the circle. Use 3.14 or $\frac{22}{7}$ for $\pi$. Explain your choice of $\pi$.**

**1.**

28 mi

**2.**

9.5 m

**3.**

16 cm

**4.** diameter = 32 in.   **5.** diameter = 140 ft   **6.** radius = 1.5 km

**7. What If?** In Example 3, suppose the circumference of the Ferris wheel is 462 feet. What is the diameter of the Ferris wheel?

**EXAMPLE 4**  **Using Circumference to Find the Radius**

 **A pottery wheel has a circumference of 44 inches. Find the radius.**

**SOLUTION**

$C = 2\pi r$ — Circumference formula

$44 \approx 2\left(\dfrac{22}{7}\right)r$ — Use $\dfrac{22}{7}$ for $\pi$.

$44 = \dfrac{44}{7}r$ — Simplify.

$\overset{1}{44} \cdot \dfrac{7}{\underset{1}{44}} = \dfrac{44}{7}r \cdot \dfrac{7}{44}$ — Multiply each side by $\dfrac{7}{44}$, the reciprocal of $\dfrac{44}{7}$.

$7 = r$ — Simplify.

*REVIEW RECIPROCALS*
Need help with reciprocals? See p. 247.

▶ **Answer** The radius is about 7 inches.

---

✓ **GUIDED PRACTICE**  **for Example 4**

8. **What If?** In Example 4, suppose the pottery wheel has a circumference of 38 inches. Find the radius to the nearest hundredth. Explain your choice of $\pi$.

---

# 6.4 EXERCISES

HOMEWORK KEY

= **TAKS Practice and Reasoning**
Exs. 22, 41, 43, 44, 46, 49, and 50

○ = **HINTS AND HOMEWORK HELP**
for Exs. 7, 11, 15, 19, 39 at classzone.com

## SKILL PRACTICE

1. **VOCABULARY** Draw and label a circle with a radius and a diameter.

2. **VOCABULARY** Copy and complete: The distance around a circle is its ___?___.

**FINDING CIRCUMFERENCE** Find the circumference of a circle with the given radius or diameter. Use 3.14 or $\dfrac{22}{7}$ for $\pi$. *Explain* your choice.

*SEE EXAMPLES 1 AND 2*
on pp. 312–313 for Exs. 3–12

3. $r = 10$ mm

4. $r = 3\dfrac{1}{2}$ ft

5. $d = 100$ cm

6. $r = 21$ ft

7. $d = 14$ in.

8. $d = 20$ mi

9. $d = 63$ mm

10. $d = 56$ m

11. $r = 42$ ft

12. **ERROR ANALYSIS** Describe and correct the error made in finding the circumference of the circle.

$C = 2 \cdot \pi \cdot \text{radius}$
$\approx 2(3.14)(4.5)$
$= 28.26$ inches

4.5 in

**314**   Chapter 6   Multi-Step Equations and Inequalities

**XY FINDING RADIUS OR DIAMETER** Find the radius or diameter of the circle with the given circumference. Use 3.14 or $\frac{22}{7}$ for $\pi$.

**SEE EXAMPLES
3 AND 4**
on pp. 313–314
for Exs. 13–22

**13.** $C = 66$ in., $d = \underline{\ ?\ }$

**14.** $C = 3.14$ m, $r = \underline{\ ?\ }$

**15.** $C = 33$ km, $d = \underline{\ ?\ }$

**16.** $C = 628$ cm, $r = \underline{\ ?\ }$

**17.** $C = 9.42$ cm, $r = \underline{\ ?\ }$

**18.** $C = 330$ yd, $d = \underline{\ ?\ }$

**19.** $C = 157$ yd, $r = \underline{\ ?\ }$

**20.** $C = 235.5$ cm, $d = \underline{\ ?\ }$

**21.** $C = 44$ m, $r = \underline{\ ?\ }$

**22.** ✦ **TAKS REASONING** Which circle has a circumference of 50.24 feet? Use 3.14 for $\pi$.

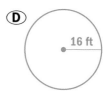

Ⓐ 4 ft  Ⓑ 4 ft  Ⓒ 8 ft  Ⓓ 16 ft

**MEASUREMENT** Use a ruler to measure the unknown dimension. Then find the circumference of the circle. Use 3.14 for $\pi$. Estimate to check.

**SEE EXAMPLES
1 AND 2**
on pp. 312–313
for Exs. 23–25

**23.**

$d = ?$ cm

**24.**

$d = ?$ in.

**25.**
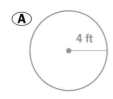
$r = ?$ mm

**PERIMETER** Find the perimeter of the figure. Use 3.14 for $\pi$.

**26.**

5 cm

**27.**

6 ft
3 ft

**28.**

9 in.
7 in.

**REWRITE
FORMULAS**
Need help
rewriting
formulas?
See p. 32.

**XY ALGEBRA** In Chapter 1 you learned three ways to write the distance formula. Copy and complete each statement by using the properties of equality to rewrite the circumference formula. *Justify* each step.

**29.** If $C = \pi d$, then $\pi = \underline{\ ?\ }$.

**30.** If $C = \pi d$, then $d = \underline{\ ?\ }$.

**31.** If $C = 2\pi r$, then $r = \underline{\ ?\ }$.

**32.** If $C = 2\pi r$, then $\pi = \underline{\ ?\ }$.

**CHALLENGE** Two circles are *concentric* if they share a center, as in the diagrams below. The circumference of the outer circle is given. Find the value of $x$. Use 3.14 for $\pi$. (All measures are in meters.)

**33.** $C = 75.36$ m

**34.** $C = 109.9$ m

**35.** $C = 94.2$ m

9
$x$

$x$ 17 $x$

$x$
10

## PROBLEM SOLVING

**SEE EXAMPLES
1 AND 2**

on pp. 312–313
for Exs. 36–37

**36. ARCHITECTURE** The diameter of the U.S. Capitol Building's dome is 96 feet at its widest point. Find its circumference. Use 3.14 for $\pi$.

**37. GEARS** One circular gear has a radius of 3.5 inches. It meshes with another gear that has a radius 3 times as great. What is the circumference of each gear? How do the circumferences compare? Use $\frac{22}{7}$ for $\pi$.

**SEE EXAMPLES
3 AND 4**

on pp. 313–314
for Exs. 38–39,
42

**38. CHECKING REASONABLENESS** The circumference of a circular fountain is 35.5 feet. A friend says that the diameter of the fountain is approximately 12 feet. Is this approximation reasonable? *Explain.*

**39. ESTIMATION** The Great Clock of Westminster rings the bell known as "Big Ben" in London, England. The circumference of the clock face is about 72 feet 3 inches. Estimate the diameter of the clock face.

**40. WRITING** Look up *circumnavigate* in the dictionary. *Describe* how the definition is similar to the definition of *circumference*.

**41. ✦ TAKS REASONING** Find a circular object in your house. Measure the diameter of the object. Then calculate the circumference.

**42. FASHION** To measure the leg opening of a pair of flared jeans, you flatten them out and measure the width. The width is 12 inches, which is half the circumference. What is the diameter of the leg opening? Use 3.14 for $\pi$. Round your answer to the nearest hundredth.

**43. ✦ TAKS REASONING** A basketball hoop has a circumference of about 56.5 inches. A basketball has a circumference of about 28.5 inches. What is the approximate difference between the diameter of the hoop and the diameter of the basketball? Use 3.14 for $\pi$.

C = 28.5 in.    C = 56.5 in.

    **(A)** 4.5 in.       **(B)** 9 in.

    **(C)** 18 in.      **(D)** 27 in.

**44. ✦ TAKS REASONING** Find the circumferences of circles with radii 1, 2, 4, 8, and 16 meters. Leave your answers in terms of $\pi$. *Compare* the circumferences. What happens to the circumference of a circle as its radius doubles? What do you think happens as the radius triples? *Explain* your reasoning.

**45. REASONING** The circumference of the larger circle is approximately 37.7 centimeters. Between what two whole numbers of centimeters is the perimeter of the square? Which of these numbers do you think the perimeter of the square is closer to? *Explain.*

2 cm

**46.** ![TAKS icon] **TAKS REASONING** Adventurer Mike Horn traveled around the world as close to the equator as possible without using any motorized transportation.

 **a. Calculate** The radius of Earth is about 3963 miles. Approximate its circumference. Use 3.14 for $\pi$.

 **b. Compare** Mike Horn actually traveled a total of 29,000 miles. About how much farther did Mike Horn travel than if he had followed the equator exactly?

 **c. Analyze** To the nearest mile, find what the radius of Earth would be if its circumference were 29,000 miles. Use 3.14 for $\pi$. *Compare* this radius to the actual radius.

 **d. Draw Conclusions** Why do you think the circumference of Earth is different from the distance Mike Horn traveled?

**47.** **CHALLENGE** A single rotation of a car's wheel is shown below. How many rotations will the wheel make if the car travels 6 miles? Round your answer to the nearest whole number.

**48.** ![XY icon] **CHALLENGE** Each circle below is divided into equal sections. The radius of each circle is 5 units. Write your answers in terms of $\pi$.

 **a.** Find the length of the blue portion of each circle.

 **b.** Write a formula for the length of the blue portion of the *n*th circle.

 **c.** Find the length of the blue portion of the 11th circle.

---

**MIXED REVIEW FOR TAKS**  **TAKS** PRACTICE at classzone.com

*REVIEW*
Lesson 6.3;
TAKS Workbook

**49.** ![TAKS icon] **TAKS PRACTICE** Claire buys 5 shirts and Cindy buys a book for $12.99 and 2 shirts. They each spend the same amount of money. To find the cost of one shirt, you write an equation and find that 3 shirts cost $12.99. What is the next step to find the cost of each shirt? *TAKS Obj. 6*

 **(A)** Add 3 and 12.99      **(B)** Subtract 3 from 12.99

 **(C)** Multiply 12.99 by 3      **(D)** Divide 12.99 by 3

---

# 6.5 Solving Multi-Step Inequalities

TEKS 8.4, 8.16.A

**Before** You solved multi-step equations and one-step inequalities.

**Now** You'll use two or more steps to solve inequalities.

**Why?** So you can analyze event fundraising, as in Ex. 33.

**KEY VOCABULARY**
- distributive property, *p. 88*
- like terms, *p. 89*
- inequality, *p. 148*

## ACTIVITY

**Use a table to solve the inequality $x + 4 \geq 3x$.**

**STEP 1** **Copy** and complete the table.

**STEP 2** **Find** the values of $x$ that make the inequality true. What do you think is the solution of the inequality? *Explain* your reasoning.

**STEP 3** **Make** a similar table to find the solution of $4x + 3 > 9x - 7$.

How is this solution different from the solution in Step 2?

**STEP 4** **Determine** if the inequalities above are true when you substitute a number less than $-1$ for $x$. *Explain.*

| $x$ | $x + 4$ | $3x$ | Is $x + 4 \geq 3x$? |
|-----|---------|------|---------------------|
| $-1$ | 3 | $-3$ | Yes |
| 0 | ? | ? | ? |
| 1 | ? | ? | ? |
| 2 | ? | ? | ? |
| 3 | ? | ? | ? |
| 4 | ? | ? | ? |

In Lessons 6.1 through 6.3, you solved multi-step equations algebraically. You can use many of the same steps to solve multi-step inequalities.

## EXAMPLE 1 Solving and Graphing a Two-Step Inequality

| | |
|---|---|
| $10 + 4y < 18$ | **Original inequality** |
| $10 + 4y - 10 < 18 - 10$ | **Subtract 10 from each side.** |
| $4y < 8$ | **Simplify.** |
| $\dfrac{4y}{4} < \dfrac{8}{4}$ | **Divide each side by 4.** |
| $y < 2$ | **Simplify.** |

**CHECK SOLUTIONS**
To check your solution, try three values for the variable in the original inequality. In Example 1, choose a value less than 2, a value greater than 2, and 2.

Number line graph showing values 0 1 2 3 4 5 with open circle at 2 and arrow to the left.

**Use an open circle and draw the arrow to the left.**

**Animated Math** at classzone.com

**EXAMPLE 2** Combining Like Terms

$$3x - 8 < -x + 4$$      Original inequality

$$3x - 8 - 3x < -x + 4 - 3x$$      Subtract 3x from each side.

$$-8 < -4x + 4$$      Combine like terms.

*AVOID ERRORS*
Remember to reverse the inequality symbol when multiplying or dividing both sides of an inequality by a negative number. For help, see p. 154.

$$-8 - 4 < -4x + 4 - 4$$      Subtract 4 from each side.

$$-12 < -4x$$      Simplify.

$$\frac{-12}{-4} > \frac{-4x}{-4}$$      Divide each side by −4 and reverse the inequality symbol.

$$3 > x$$      Simplify.

**EXAMPLE 3** Writing and Solving a Multi-Step Inequality

**Charity Bowling** You are organizing a bowling night for charity. Each ticket costs $10 and includes shoe rental. Shoe rental costs you $5 per pair, and door prizes cost you $50. What are the possible numbers of people who need to attend for you to make a profit of at least $200?

**SOLUTION**

To find the amount you can raise, subtract the total costs from the total ticket sales. Let $x$ represent the number of people.

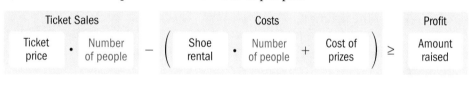

| Ticket Sales | | Costs | | | Profit |
|---|---|---|---|---|---|
| Ticket price | · Number of people | − ( Shoe rental | · Number of people | + Cost of prizes ) | ≥ Amount raised |

$$10x - (5x + 50) \geq 200$$      **Write an inequality.**

$$10x - 5x - 50 \geq 200$$      **Distributive property**

$$5x - 50 \geq 200$$      **Combine like terms.**

$$5x \geq 250$$      **Add 50 to each side.**

$$x \geq 50$$      **Divide each side by 5.**

▶ **Answer** At least 50 people need to attend the bowling night.

✓ **GUIDED PRACTICE**    for Examples 1, 2, and 3

**Solve the inequality. Then graph the solution.**

  **1.** $-7z + 15 \geq 57$        **2.** $11n + 36 < 3n - 4$        **3.** $9(y - 2) > -16$

  **4. What If?** In Example 3, suppose that each ticket also includes a $1 beverage. How many people need to attend for you to make a profit of at least $200?

# 6.5 EXERCISES

## SKILL PRACTICE

1. **VOCABULARY** Write the meanings of the symbols $<$, $>$, $\le$ and $\ge$.

2. **VOCABULARY** Copy and complete: When you solve an inequality, you reverse the inequality symbol when multiplying or dividing by a __?__ number.

**SOLVING INEQUALITIES** Solve the inequality. Then graph the solution.

*SEE EXAMPLES 1 AND 2*
on pp. 318–319
for Exs. 3–19

3. $4a + 7 \ge 11$

4. $16 < 3b + 22$

5. $7 - 2p \ge -5$

6. $-3y + 2 < -16$

7. $-2w + 6 < 2$

8. $26s \le 3s + 69$

9. $12c + 12 > 48c$

10. $5x - 14 \le 2x + 7$

11. $5 - 4z > 17 - z$

12. $10 \ge 5(3 + t)$

13. $2(5 + n) \le 6$

14. $-3(d + 2) < -3$

15. $10a > -5(a + 6)$

16. $2(5x - 4) \le 8(x + 1)$

17. $4(6k - 4) \ge 7k - (2k - 3)$

18. ✦ **TAKS REASONING** Solve the inequality $-3b + 9 - 11b < 65$.

   (A) $b < -4$
   (B) $b > -4$
   (C) $b < 4$
   (D) $b > 4$

19. **ERROR ANALYSIS** Describe and correct the error made in the solution.

   $9 - 2x \le 3$
   $-2x \le -6$
   $\dfrac{-2x}{-2} \le \dfrac{-6}{-2}$
   $x \le 3$ ✗

**CLEARING RATIONALS** Tell what number you should multiply each side of the inequality by to clear the decimals and fractions. Then solve.

20. $\frac{2}{3}x + \frac{4}{3} - \frac{3}{4}x < -\frac{3}{4}$

21. $\frac{2}{3}y + 18 \ge 5 - \frac{4}{7}y$

22. $\frac{1}{2}k - 6 \ge -\frac{1}{6}k$

23. $\frac{1}{3}m - \frac{1}{2}m > -4$

24. $3.7z \le 33.32 - 3.1z$

25. $-0.6y - 3.79 + 5.2y < 19.67$

26. $0.05a + 9.367 - 1.65a \le 4.183$

27. $2.3x - 52.46 \le -0.9(x - 117)$

28. **EXAMPLES AND NONEXAMPLES** You want to create circles that have a circumference that is less than 5 units plus twice the radius. Write an inequality that represents the situation. Use 3.14 for $\pi$. Solve the inequality and use the solution to give two examples and two nonexamples of radii for the circles.

*REVIEW COMPOUND INEQUALITIES*
Need help with compound inequalities? See p. 151.

**GRAPHING INEQUALITIES** Solve and graph the compound inequality.

29. $-13 < 3x - 4 < 8$

30. $9 < -x + 6 \le 17$

31. $2 \le 2(x + 4) < 20$

32. **CHALLENGE** Solve $|a| \ge 2$. Then graph the solution.

## PROBLEM SOLVING

**SEE EXAMPLE 3**
on p. 319
for Exs. 33–35

**33. GUIDED PROBLEM SOLVING** You agree to raise at least $2500 for charity to enter the Boston Marathon. You've already raised $925 by asking people to pledge $25 each. How many more $25 pledges do you need?

| Amount already raised | + | Amount per pledge | · | Additional pledges | ≥ | Minimum required |

**a.** Use the verbal model to write an inequality for the number $p$ of additional pledges that will satisfy the donation requirement.

**b.** Solve the inequality. *Interpret* the solution.

**34.** ✒ **TAKS REASONING** While at camp, you call your parents from a pay phone. The first minute costs you $.25 and each additional minute costs $.10. You have $1.65 in change. Solve the inequality $0.25 + 0.10m \le 1.65$ to find the number of additional minutes $m$ you can talk.

   **A** less than 14   **B** no more than 14   **C** at most 19   **D** fewer than 19

**35. VIDEO GAMES** You are approaching the high score of 18,550 on a video game in which you have to catch discs for 150 points each. Your current score is 16,000. Use the verbal model to write and solve an inequality to find how many more discs you need to catch to have a new high score. *Interpret* the solution.

| Current score | + | Points earned per disc | · | Discs caught | > | Current high score |

**36. WRITING** How is solving a multi-step inequality similar to solving a multi-step equation? How is it different?

**37.** ✒ **TAKS REASONING** Jade works in a clothing store and earns $350 per week, plus $.20 for every dollar of clothing she sells. Solve the inequality $350 + 0.2x \ge 500$ to find how much she has to sell in one week to earn at least $500. *Explain* what the solution means in this situation. How would the solution change if she earns only $.15 for every dollar? *Explain*.

**38.** ✒ **TAKS REASONING** It costs a magazine publisher $1.20 to produce each magazine. Overhead costs, such as salaries and office space, are $25,000 per month. The publisher sells the magazine for $3.95.

| Price per magazine | · | Number of magazines | − | Cost per magazine | · | Number of magazines | ≥ | Overhead costs |

**a.** *Explain* what the verbal model represents in this situation.

**b.** Write and solve an inequality. *Interpret* the solution.

**c.** If the magazine publisher cuts costs to $1.10 per magazine and $24,000 in overhead, what effect will this have? *Explain*.

**Clouds** Clouds form when the air is cooled to its dew point or when the air reaches saturation. The three basic cloud types stem from Latin words that are related to their heights above the ground. *Cirro* is the prefix given to high level clouds that have bases at or above 20,000 feet above the ground. *Alto* is the prefix given to mid-level clouds. *Strato* is the prefix given to low-level clouds that can cover the entire sky like a blanket.

39. **Solve** The minimum base height of a *Cirro* cloud is more than 3500 feet above 2.75 times the base height *h* of a *Strato* cloud. Solve the inequality $20,000 > 2.75h + 3500$. What does this solution say about the base height of a *Strato* cloud?

40. **Apply** A cloud base forms at 6300 feet. How would you classify this cloud? *Explain* your reasoning.

41. **Interpret** *Describe* the range of base heights for the cloud type in Exercise 40.

**NUMBER SENSE** In Exercises 42–44, use the information below. Tell why the given solution *cannot* be correct.

You and your sisters have $25 to spend at a baseball game. You buy 3 ice creams for $4 each, and then use the rest for drinks that cost $3 each. You write and solve an inequality to find the number of drinks *d* you can afford.

42. $d < 120$          43. $d \leq 0$          44. $d \geq 4$

45. **CHALLENGE** Solve the inequality $ax + b < c$ to find the value of *x* in terms of *a*, *b*, and *c*. *Justify* each step.

## MIXED REVIEW FOR TAKS

**TAKS** PRACTICE at classzone.com

*REVIEW*
Lesson 6.4;
TAKS Workbook

46. **TAKS PRACTICE** A dollhouse collector owns a miniature car. The collector makes a mark on the bottom of the wheel and rolls the car so that the mark travels exactly once around, ending in the same position. The wheel has made one full rotation. The car travels about 5 inches during this time. What is the diameter of the wheel, to the nearest tenth of an inch? *TAKS Obj. 3*

(A) 0.8 in.          (B) 1.6 in.          (C) 15.7 in.          (D) 31.4 in.

*REVIEW*
Lesson 3.5;
TAKS Workbook

47. **TAKS PRACTICE** Two triangular minimalist paintings by a famous artist have heights of 9.25 inches. They have bases of 4.5 inches and 5 inches. Which expression shows the total area of both paintings? *TAKS Obj. 2*

(F) $0.5(9.25 \times 4.5 + 5)$          (G) $0.5 \times 9.25 \times 4.5 \times 5$

(H) $0.5 \times 9.25 \times 4.5 + 5$          (J) $0.5 \times 9.25(4.5 + 5)$

**Technology ACTIVITY** *Use after Lesson 6.5*

**GOAL**
Use a spreadsheet and truth functions to solve inequalities.

**TEKS** *8.5.A, 8.14.D*

# 6.5 Solving Inequalities

**EXAMPLE** Use spreadsheet software to solve $3x + 2 < 2x - 6$.

**SOLUTION**

**STEP 1** **Enter** the integers $-10$ to $10$ in column A. Column A contains possible solutions of the inequality.

| B2 | = 3*A2 + 2 | | | |
|---|---|---|---|---|
| | *A* | *B* | *C* | *D* |
| **1** | *x*-values | $3x + 2$ | | |
| **2** | $-10$ | $-28$ | | |
| **3** | $-9$ | $-25$ | | |
| **4** | $-8$ | $-22$ | | |
| **5** | $-7$ | $-19$ | | |

**STEP 2** **Type** the formula "=3*A2 + 2" in cell B2. Use the fill down feature. Column B contains calculated values of the left side of the inequality.

**STEP 3** **Type** the formula "=2*A2 − 6" in cell C2. Use the fill down feature. Column C contains values of the right side of the inequality.

| C4 | = 2*A2 − 6 | | | |
|---|---|---|---|---|
| | *A* | *B* | *C* | *D* |
| **1** | *x*-values | $3x + 2$ | $2x - 6$ | B < C? |
| **2** | $-10$ | $-28$ | $-26$ | True |
| **3** | $-9$ | $-25$ | $-24$ | True |
| **4** | $-8$ | $-22$ | $-22$ | False |
| **5** | $-7$ | $-19$ | $-20$ | False |

**STEP 4** **Type** the *truth function* "=B2 < C2" in cell D2. Use the fill down feature. Column D tells whether the inequality is true or false for the *x*-value in that row.

A *truth function* compares values and returns *True* or *False*.

▶ **Answer** The solution is all numbers less than $-8$.

**PRACTICE** Use spreadsheet software to solve the inequality.

**1.** $13 - 3y > -2y$  **2.** $7 - 2s < s - 2$  **3.** $2n - 10 \geq 12n$

**4.** $p + 16 \leq -3p$  **5.** $-2t + 9 > -5t$  **6.** $x - 3 < 5x + 1$

**7.** **SHOPPING** Dani has at most $10 to buy school supplies. A notebook costs $1.50, a pencil costs $.25, and a pen costs $.95. She needs two notebooks, three pens, and some pencils. What are the possible numbers of pencils she can buy?

# 6.6 Problem Solving and Inequalities

TEKS *8.5.A, 8.15.A*

| | |
|---|---|
| **Before** | You solved multi-step inequalities. |
| **Now** | You'll write and solve multi-step inequalities. |
| **Why?** | So you can solve real world problems, as in Example 1. |

**KEY VOCABULARY**
• **inequality,** *p. 148*

**Season Tickets** Individual tickets for a college hockey game cost $8 each plus a one-time transaction fee of $5. You can buy a season ticket for $99. How many games would you have to attend so that buying a season ticket is a better value than buying individual tickets?

### EXAMPLE 1  Writing and Solving an Inequality

**xy** To solve the problem above, write and solve an inequality. Let *x* represent the number of games.

| Price of single ticket | • | Number of games | + | Transaction fee | > | Price of season ticket |

$8x + 5 > 99$      **Write an inequality.**

$8x > 94$      **Subtract 5 from each side.**

$x > 11.75$      **Divide each side by 8.**

▶ **Answer** It doesn't make sense to attend 11.75 games. So, you would have to attend 12 or more games to make buying a season ticket the better value.

**Check** Try three values for *x*. Use 11.75, and one value on either side of it.

When $x = 10$
$8(10) + 5 = 80 + 5 < 99$
not a solution

When $x = 11.75$
$8(11.75) + 5 = 94 + 5 = 99$
not a solution

When $x = 15$
$8(15) + 5 = 120 + 5 > 99$
a solution

*ANOTHER WAY*

You can use guess-and-check to solve the problem.

| Games | Cost |
|---|---|
| 10 | 85 |
| 11 | 93 |
| 12 | 101 |

**Writing Inequalities** The following common sentences indicate the four types of inequalities.

| $a < b$ | $a > b$ |
|---|---|
| *a* is less than *b*.<br>*a* is fewer than *b*. | *a* is greater than *b*.<br>*a* is more than *b*. |
| $a \leq b$ | $a \geq b$ |
| *a* is less than or equal to *b*.<br>*a* is at most *b*.<br>*a* is no more than *b*. | *a* is greater than or equal to *b*.<br>*a* is at least *b*.<br>*a* is no less than *b*. |

**EXAMPLE 2** **Translating Verbal Sentences**

 **Write the sentence as an inequality.**

**a.** Six times the difference of a number and 3 is more than 24.

**b.** Nine more than 4 times a number is at least 30 plus 11 times the number.

**c.** Three times a number divided by 4 is no more than 5 plus twice the number.

> **READING**
> The phrase "*a* more than *b*" means *b* + *a*, or *a* + *b*, while "*a* is more than *b*" means *a* > *b*.

**SOLUTION**

First decide which inequality symbol to use. Then substitute numbers, variables, and operation symbols.

**a.** The phrase "is more than" means >.

6 times the difference of a number and 3 **is more than** 24.

6 · (x − 3) > 24

▶ **Answer** The inequality is $6(x - 3) > 24$.

**b.** The phrase "is at least" means ≥.

9 more than 4 times a number **is at least** 30 plus 11 times the number.

9 + 4x ≥ 30 + 11x

▶ **Answer** The inequality is $9 + 4x \geq 30 + 11x$.

**c.** The phrase "is no more than" means ≤.

3 times a number divided by 4 **is no more than** 5 plus twice the number.

3x ÷ 4 ≤ 5 + 2x

▶ **Answer** The inequality is $\frac{3x}{4} \leq 5 + 2x$.

 at classzone.com

✓ **GUIDED PRACTICE** **for Examples 1 and 2**

**1. Basketball** Individual tickets for a college basketball game cost $12 each plus a one-time transaction fee of $8. A season ticket costs $125. How many games would you have to attend so that buying a season ticket is a better value than buying individual tickets?

**Write the sentence as an inequality. Let *x* represent the unknown number.**

**2.** The difference of a number and 4 is less than 10 more than 3 times the number.

**3.** Six times the sum of a number and 8 is no more than 12 less than twice the number.

6.6 Problem Solving and Inequalities 325

**EXAMPLE 3** Writing and Solving an Inequality

**Owning a Business** You use the Internet to sell mousepads. You pay a wholesaler $6 for each mousepad. You then sell the mousepads for $10 each. You pay $21 per month for Web page hosting. How many mousepads should you sell each month to earn a profit?

**SOLUTION**

To earn a profit, your revenue must be greater than your expenses.

| Selling price | $\cdot$ | Number of mousepads | > | Wholesale price | $\cdot$ | Number of mousepads | + | Web page cost |

$10x > 6x + 21$     **Write an inequality.**

$4x > 21$     **Subtract 6x from each side.**

$x > 5.25$     **Divide each side by 4.**

▶ **Answer** You cannot sell part of a mousepad. So, you should sell at least 6 mousepads per month to earn a profit.

---

✓ **GUIDED PRACTICE**    **for Example 3**

4. **Nutrition** A membership at a nutrition store costs $20 per year. You can buy vitamins for $18 a bottle without a membership, and $15 a bottle with a membership. How many bottles of vitamins do you need to buy each year to make a membership worthwhile?

---

## 6.6 EXERCISES

HOMEWORK KEY

🔶 = **TAKS Practice and Reasoning**
Exs. 11, 19, 23, 24, 28, 30, and 31

⚪ = **HINTS AND HOMEWORK HELP**
for Exs. 5, 9, 19, 21 at classzone.com

### SKILL PRACTICE

**VOCABULARY** Tell whether the sentence can be translated as an inequality. *Explain* your reasoning.

1. A number is at least 5.

2. A number plus 5 is 9.

3. Eight more than a number is equal to 6.

4. Four times a number is less than 28.

**TRANSLATING VERBAL SENTENCES** Write the sentence as an inequality. Let *x* represent the unknown number. Then solve the inequality.

*SEE EXAMPLE 2*
on p. 325
for Exs. 5–10

5. A number plus 2 is at most 6.

6. Nine is less than a number plus 1.

7. Six less than a number is more than 14.

8. Eight times a number is at least 40.

9. Twelve more than a number is less than 4.

10. Seven is more than a number minus 5.

**SEE EXAMPLE 2**
on p. 325
for Exs. 11–12

**11.** ⚐ **TAKS REASONING** Match the verbal sentence with the inequality: The sum of 4 times a number and 2 is fewer than 18.

(A) $4(x + 2) < 18$    (B) $4x + 2 < 18$    (C) $2x - 4 > 18$    (D) $2(x - 4) \leq 18$

**12. ERROR ANALYSIS** Describe and correct the error made in translating the verbal sentence. Then solve the inequality.

Three times the sum of a number and 5 is at least 26.

$$3(x + 5) \leq 26$$
$$3x + 15 \leq 26$$
$$3x \leq 11$$
$$x \leq 3\tfrac{2}{3}$$

**NUMBER SENSE** Tell whether it makes sense for the variable in red to have a value that is *not* a whole number. *Explain* your reasoning.

**13.**

| Entrance fee | + | Ride ticket price | · | Number of ride tickets | ≤ | $20 |

**14.**

| Cost per pound of ham | · | Pounds of ham | + | Cost of a loaf of bread | ≤ | $15 |

**15.**

| Number of hot dogs | · | Cost per hot dog | + | Cost of a ticket | ≤ | $30 |

**CHALLENGE** Write the sentence as a compound inequality. Then solve.

**16.** Eight times the sum of a number and 3 is at least −16 and less than 72.

**17.** 12 is less than the difference of 6 times a number and 4, which is at most 26.

## PROBLEM SOLVING

**SEE EXAMPLES**
**1 AND 3**
on p. 324
for Exs. 18–19

**18.** ◆ **MULTIPLE REPRESENTATIONS** You have at most $200 to spend on a health club membership. The initial fee to join is $50. There is a monthly fee of $32.

   **a.** Write a verbal model for the total cost of a health club membership.

   **b.** Write and solve an inequality to find the number of months you can be a member without spending more than $200.

   **c.** Graph the solution and check that the answer makes sense. *Explain* what the solution means in the situation.

**19.** ⚐ **TAKS REASONING** You are making craft items to sell for $2 each. The materials cost you $55. You want to make a profit of at least $100. Which inequality can you use to find the number of items you need to sell?

(A) $2x - 55 \leq 100$    (B) $2x - 55 \geq 100$    (C) $2x + 55 \geq 100$    (D) $2x + 55 \leq 100$

SEE EXAMPLES
1 AND 3
.................
on p. 324
for Exs. 20–21

**20. BUYING CDs** Each CD you order online costs $12. Shipping charges are $4. You have at most $50 to spend. Copy and complete the verbal model. Write and solve an inequality to find how many CDs you can buy.

| Cost of CD | • | Number of CDs | + | Shipping charges | ? | Money you have |
|---|---|---|---|---|---|---|

**21. TEEN CLUB** A teen club has weekly dances. You can become a member of the club for $30 a year and pay only $4 to attend each dance. Otherwise, each dance costs $6. Write and solve an inequality to find how many dances you have to attend so that becoming a member will cost less than paying the nonmember rate.

**22. WRITING** *Explain* the difference between *3 less than a number* and *3 is less than a number*. Include examples.

**23. ☞ TAKS REASONING** *Describe* a real-world problem that can be solved using the inequality $5 + 8x \le 31$. Solve the inequality and explain what the solution means in the situation.

**24. ☞ TAKS REASONING** School will be cancelled if there are at least 6 inches of snow at 6 A.M. At 7 P.M. the night before, 2 inches of snow has covered the ground. Snow is predicted to continue falling at a rate of 0.5 inch per hour. Write an inequality to represent the situation. At what time will there be at least 6 inches of snow? Will school be held the next day? *Explain.*

**25. BOWLING** Your scores on the last 3 bowling games are 90, 92, and 115. Write and solve an inequality to find the score you need in the next game to have a mean score of at least 100.

**26. SUMMER JOB** You earn $6.50 an hour working at the snack bar at a community pool. You earn time and a half for any hours you work over 30 hours. Write and solve an inequality to find how many hours over 30 you must work to make more than $273 in a week.

**27. EXPRESS MAIL** A package sent via express mail must be no more than 108 inches in total length and girth. You want to wrap as many boxes together as possible to send as one package. Each box is the same size. Write and solve an inequality to find how many boxes you could wrap as one package if they are arranged as shown.

girth = 2h + 2w

h = 15 in.

w = 12 in.

l = 6 in.

**28.** ✈ **TAKS REASONING**   Town Taxi charges $2.00 plus $.40 for every $\frac{1}{5}$ mile. City Cab charges $2.50 plus $.15 for every $\frac{1}{10}$ mile.

   **a. Interpret**   Write algebraic expressions for the total cost of a ride with Town Taxi and the total cost of a ride with City Cab.

   **b. Compare**   Your friends decide that Town Taxi is the better deal, because Town Taxi charges only $2 initially and City Cab charges $2.50. Is your friends' reasoning valid? *Explain.*

   **c. Analyze**   For what distances is the total cost for City Cab less than the total cost for Town Taxi? *Explain* your reasoning.

**29. CHALLENGE**   The sum of two consecutive odd integers is no more than 232 and no less than 216. Use inequalities to find all possible pairs of consecutive odd integers. *Justify* your answer.

## MIXED REVIEW FOR TAKS

TAKS PRACTICE at classzone.com

REVIEW
Lesson 4.8;
TAKS Workbook

**30.** ✈ **TAKS PRACTICE**   A company lost 88.4 million dollars over 3 years. Which expression represents this monetary loss in scientific notation? *TAKS Obj. 2*

   **A** $-8.84 \times 10^{-7}$        **B** $-8.84 \times 10^{-6}$

   **C** $-8.84 \times 10^{6}$         **D** $-8.84 \times 10^{7}$

REVIEW
Lesson 5.8;
TAKS Workbook

**31.** ✈ **TAKS PRACTICE**   Linda scored 95, 84, 68, 80, and 68 on Biology exams during her first semester. Her biology teacher averaged her exam scores using the measure that gave Linda the highest average score possible. Which measure did her biology teacher use? *TAKS Obj. 2*

   **F** Mean      **G** Median      **H** Mode      **J** Range

## QUIZ for Lessons 6.4–6.6

Find the unknown measurement, where *r* = radius, *d* = diameter, and *C* = circumference. Use 3.14 or $\frac{22}{7}$ for $\pi$. Round to the nearest hundredth if necessary. *(p. 312)*

   **1.** $d = 28$ in., $C = \underline{\ ?\ }$     **2.** $C = 132$ ft, $d = \underline{\ ?\ }$     **3.** $C = 150$ cm, $r = \underline{\ ?\ }$

Solve the inequality. *(p. 318)*

   **4.** $-8a - 10 > 14$      **5.** $3z \le 35 - 2z$      **6.** $5b \ge 2(b + 2.25)$

Write the sentence as an inequality. Then solve. *(p. 324)*

   **7.** Two less than 6 times a number is at least 40.

   **8.** Five times the sum of 4 and a number is greater than 10.

   **9. VIDEO GAMES**   Your current score in a video game is 33,600 points. At the end of each level you earn 2500 points for catching objects and 1700 points for overcoming the obstacles. How many more levels must you go through to beat your high score of 54,000? *(p. 324)*

## Lessons 6.4–6.6

**MULTIPLE CHOICE**

1. **BICYCLES** A penny-farthing bicycle has a front wheel diameter of 50 inches and a rear wheel diameter of 17 inches. About how many rotations will the rear wheel take during one rotation of the front wheel? *TEKS 8.14.A*

   Ⓐ 3                Ⓑ 5

   Ⓒ 9                Ⓓ 11

2. **TRACK** The diagram shows the approximate measures of a track. What is the approximate perimeter of the track? *TEKS 8.14.C*

   Ⓕ 317 m            Ⓖ 402 m

   Ⓗ 550 m            Ⓙ 635 m

3. **CHAIRS** Mr. Rohr makes chairs in a small shop for which he pays $760 per month in rent. The materials cost $70 per chair. He sells the chairs for $380 each. Mr. Rohr's other monthly expenses total $720. How many chairs must Mr. Rohr sell monthly to turn a profit? *TEKS 8.5.A*

   Ⓐ 3                Ⓑ 4

   Ⓒ 5                Ⓓ 6

4. **NESTING DOLLS** The largest doll in a set of nesting dolls has a circumference of 24 centimeters. The radius of each doll inside is three fourths the radius of the doll that encloses it. What is the approximate radius of the fifth doll? *TEKS 8.7.B*

   Ⓕ 1.2 cm           Ⓖ 2.4 cm

   Ⓗ 4.5 cm           Ⓙ 7.6 cm

5. **BUS PASS** One bus ride costs $1.25. If you buy a monthly pass for $47, you can ride as often as you want. What is the fewest number of times you must ride the bus so that buying a pass costs less than paying for each ride? *TEKS 8.2.B*

   Ⓐ 35               Ⓑ 36

   Ⓒ 37               Ⓓ 38

6. **MUSEUMS** You pay $30 per year for a museum membership. As a member you pay $2 to see an exhibit. Otherwise, it costs $6 to see an exhibit. How many exhibits must you see to make buying a membership worthwhile? *TEKS 8.5.A*

   Ⓕ 5                Ⓖ 6

   Ⓗ 7                Ⓙ 8

**GRIDDED ANSWER** ⊙①●③④⑤⑥⑦⑧⑨

7. **PRETZELS** A pretzel shop sells large pretzels for $2.50 each and pretzel bites for $0.50 each. One week, the shop sells 130 large pretzels. What is the least number of pretzel bites the shop needs to sell to take in $668? *TEKS 8.14.B*

## REVIEW KEY VOCABULARY

- circle, *p. 312*
- center, *p. 312*
- radius, *p. 312*
- diameter, *p. 312*
- circumference, *p. 312*
- pi ($\pi$), *p. 312*

### VOCABULARY EXERCISES

**1.** The set of all points in a plane that are the same distance from a fixed point called the center is a __?__.

**2.** You can approximate __?__ with the decimal 3.14 or the fraction $\frac{22}{7}$.

**Matching** Match the word with the correct definition.

**3.** diameter

**4.** circumference

**5.** radius

**A.** the distance around a circle

**B.** the distance across a circle through the center

**C.** the distance from the center to any point on the circle

## REVIEW EXAMPLES AND EXERCISES

### 6.1 Solving Multi-Step Equations
*pp. 293–297*

**EXAMPLE**

Solve the equation.

**a.** $5x + 8 - 4x = 17$    Original equation

$x + 8 = 17$    Combine like terms.

$x = 9$    Subtract 8 from each side.

**b.** $4(x - 4) = -12$    Original equation

$4x - 16 = -12$    Distributive property

$4x = 4$    Add 16 to both sides.

$x = 1$    Divide each side by 4.

**EXERCISES**

Solve the equation.

*SEE EXAMPLES 2, 3, AND 4 on pp. 294–295 for Exs. 6–11*

**6.** $6a + 8 - 14a = 96$

**7.** $18 + 4(p - 9) = 6$

**8.** $4(12 + z) - z = -192$

**9.** $12 + 5(b - 7) = 2$

**10.** $\dfrac{a + 4}{3} = 10$

**11.** $\dfrac{-5c - 12}{4} = 2$

## 6.2 Solving Equations with Variables on Both Sides

pp. 298–302

### EXAMPLE

| | |
|---|---|
| $4(x - 8) = -x + 4 + 7x$ | Original equation |
| $4x - 32 = 6x + 4$ | Use the distributive property and combine like terms. |
| $-32 = 2x + 4$ | Subtract 4x from each side. |
| $-36 = 2x$ | Subtract 4 from each side. |
| $-18 = x$ | Divide each side by 2. |

### EXERCISES

**Solve the equation.**

SEE EXAMPLES 2 AND 3 on p. 299 for Exs. 12–18

**12.** $-7b + 10 = -11 - 4b$     **13.** $5(m - 9) = -27 - 4m$     **14.** $6(t - 5) = 2(t + 5)$

**15.** $3(11 + c) = 19 + c$     **16.** $2q + 17 = 19q - 51$     **17.** $2 - (a - 4) = -2(a - 1)$

**18. Rowing** At the Rolling River Regatta, fifty more than twice the number of women's rowing teams is equal to eighty-seven less than three times the number of women's rowing teams. Write and solve an equation to find the number of women's rowing teams at the regatta.

## 6.3 Solving Equations Involving Fractions and Decimals

pp. 303–307

### EXAMPLE

**Solve the equation.**

**a.**

| | |
|---|---|
| $\frac{1}{4}y = \frac{1}{6}y - 5 + \frac{1}{2}y$ | Original equation |
| $3y = 2y - 60 + 6y$ | Multiply each side by the LCD, 12. |
| $3y = 8y - 60$ | Combine like terms. |
| $-5y = -60$ | Subtract 8y from each side. |
| $y = 12$ | Divide each side by −5. |

**b.**

| | |
|---|---|
| $-7 + 0.03x = 0.31x$ | Original equation |
| $-700 + 3x = 31x$ | Multiply each side by 100. |
| $-700 = 28x$ | Subtract 3x from each side. |
| $-25 = x$ | Divide each side by 28. |

## EXERCISES

**Solve the equation.**

*SEE EXAMPLES*
*1, 2, AND 3*
on pp. 303–304
for Exs. 19–25

**19.** $-3.5a - 11.4 + 9.9a = 3$

**20.** $\frac{11}{16}n - 3 + \frac{1}{4}n = \frac{7}{4}$

**21.** $5s + 3\frac{1}{8} = \frac{5}{24} - 2s$

**22.** $\frac{2}{3}b + \frac{4}{5} = \frac{1}{6}b + 2\frac{3}{10}$

**23.** $16.7m - 167.2 = 60.8 + 2.45m$

**24.** $-8 + 4.6r = 4r - 2.6$

**25. Recycling** When you buy a can of seltzer water, you pay for the seltzer water and a \$.05 recycling deposit. You pay \$4.56 for a 12-pack of seltzer water. How much did each can of seltzer water cost before the deposit?

---

**6.4** ## Solving Equations Involving Circumference

*pp. 312–317*

### EXAMPLE

Find the unknown measurement, where $r$ = radius, $d$ = diameter, and $C$ = circumference. Use 3.14 or $\frac{22}{7}$ for $\pi$.

**a.** $C = \underline{\ ?\ }$, $d = 30.5$ cm

$C = \pi d$

$\approx (3.14)(30.5)$

$= 95.77$ cm

**b.** $C = 47\frac{2}{3}$ in., $r = \underline{\ ?\ }$

$C = 2\pi r$

$\frac{143}{3} \approx 2\left(\frac{22}{7}\right)r$

$r = \frac{143}{3} \cdot \frac{7}{44} = 7\frac{7}{12}$ in.

### EXERCISES

Find the unknown radius, $r$, diameter, $d$, or circumference, $C$.
Use 3.14 or $\frac{22}{7}$ for $\pi$. Round to the nearest hundredth if necessary.

*SEE EXAMPLES*
*1, 2, 3, AND 4*
on pp. 312–314
for Exs. 26–35

**26.** $C = \underline{\ ?\ }$

21 ft

**27.** $C = 62.8$ mm

$d = \ ?$

**28.** $C = 12$ in.

$r = \ ?$

**29.** $C = 66$ ft, $d = \underline{\ ?\ }$

**30.** $C = 100.48$ cm, $r = \underline{\ ?\ }$

**31.** $C = \underline{\ ?\ }$, $d = 1$ mi

**32.** $C = \underline{\ ?\ }$, $r = 7$ in.

**33.** $C = 440$ m, $d = \underline{\ ?\ }$

**34.** $C = 176$ cm, $r = \underline{\ ?\ }$

**35. Architecture** The Minnesota State Capitol has one of the largest unsupported marble domes in the world, with a diameter of 89 feet at its widest point. Find its circumference. Use 3.14 for $\pi$.

## 6.5 Solving Multi-Step Inequalities

pp. 318–322

**EXAMPLE**

| | |
|---|---|
| $-5(x + 9) \geq 30$ | Original inequality |
| $-5x - 45 \geq 30$ | Distributive property |
| $-5x \geq 75$ | Add 45 to each side. |
| $x \leq -15$ | Divide each side by $-5$ and reverse the inequality symbol. |

**SEE EXAMPLES
1 AND 2**
on pp. 318–319
for Exs. 36–38

### EXERCISES

**Solve the inequality.**

**36.** $-5 < 3x + 16$

**37.** $m + 4(5 - m) > -7$

**38.** $6 - (g - 7) \leq 6 - 8g$

## 6.6 Problem Solving and Inequalities

pp. 324–329

**EXAMPLE**

You and 3 friends plan to use a $50 gift certificate to pay for dinner. You order an appetizer to share that costs $6. What is the most each of you can spend so the total cost of the meal is no more than $50?

| | |
|---|---|
| $4x + 6 \leq 50$ | Write an inequality. |
| $4x \leq 44$ | Subtract 6 from each side. |
| $x \leq 11$ | Divide each side by 4. |

▶ **Answer** The most that each of you can spend is $11.

### EXERCISES

**Write the sentence as an inequality. Then solve the inequality.**

**SEE EXAMPLES
1 AND 2**
on pp. 324–325
for Exs. 39–41

**39.** Fourteen minus three times a number is at most eleven.

**40.** Seven times the difference of fifteen and a number is at least fifty-six.

**41. Fundraiser** The school chorus is selling $2 raffle tickets to raise money for a trip. The chorus already has $116 saved. How many tickets does the chorus need to sell in order to have at least $250 to help pay for the trip?

**Solve the equation.**

**1.** $-3z + 17 + 12z = 11$  **2.** $m - 6(m + 10) = 50$  **3.** $7(12 - r) = -84$

**4.** $3b + 4 = b - 4$  **5.** $-25 - a = 2a + 20$  **6.** $3(2x - 11) = 3(x + 10)$

**7.** $\dfrac{3x - 5}{10} = 7$  **8.** $\dfrac{-3r + 54}{5} = 2r + 3$  **9.** $\dfrac{3}{5}w = 5w + \dfrac{22}{25}$

**Find the unknown measurement, where $r$ = radius, $d$ = diameter, and $C$ = circumference. Use 3.14 or $\dfrac{22}{7}$ for $\pi$.**

**10.** $C = \underline{\ ?\ }$, $d = 12.3$ mm  **11.** $C = 22$ in., $r = \underline{\ ?\ }$  **12.** $C = 9.42$ ft, $d = \underline{\ ?\ }$

**Solve the inequality.**

**13.** $6n + 19 \le 7$  **14.** $10 - 3x > 25$  **15.** $9c - 8 \ge 3c + 16$

**16.** $3(k + 3) > k - 1$  **17.** $8y + 3y + 36 \le 124$  **18.** $w - 4(w + 5) < -8$

**Write the sentence as an inequality. Then solve the inequality.**

**19.** Nine added to the product of 11 and a number is at most 4.

**20.** Two times a number, minus 13, is less than the number plus 8.

**21.** Seven times the difference of 12 and a number is at least 14.

**22. SHOPPING** You bought a new shirt for $15.95 and 5 pairs of socks. Your friend bought 10 pairs of socks and spent $4.20 less than you. How much did each pair of socks cost?

**23. NEWSPAPERS** In 1999 there were 1647 daily and 7471 weekly newspapers published in the United States, as well as $x$ other kinds of newspapers. The total number of newspapers was 700 greater than seven times the number of other kinds of newpapers. How many newspapers were published in 1999 that were not daily or weekly?

**24. TETHERBALL** A tetherball pole is 10 feet high. The tetherball is attached to the top of the pole with a string so that the ball hangs 2 feet above the ground. The diameter of the ball is 8.4 inches. How long is the string attached to the tetherball? What is the circumference of the longest path that point $P$ could make through the air around the pole? Use 3.14 for $\pi$. Round your answer to the nearest tenth of a foot.

**25. SNACK MIX** You are buying 2.2 pounds of peanuts that cost $4.50 per pound and sesame sticks that cost $1.70 per pound. You can't spend more than $15. What are the possible numbers of pounds of sesame sticks you can buy?

# 6 TAKS PREPARATION

**TEXAS** TAKS Obj. 6
TEKS 8.16.A

## REVIEWING PATTERN PROBLEMS

You may need to look for a pattern to solve a problem. Carefully review the data given, find what the data have in common, and use the common element to continue the pattern beyond the given data.

Recall the following formulas from this chapter:

**Circumference of a Circle**

$C = \pi d$

$C = 2\pi r$

---

**EXAMPLE**

What is the circumference of the 10th circle in the pattern below?

2 cm    4 cm    6 cm    8 cm

---

### Solution

**STEP 1** **Describe** and extend the pattern. The radius of each circle is two more than the radius of the previous circle.

| Circle | 1 | 2 | 3 | 4 | 5 | 6 | 7 | 8 | 9 | 10 |
|---|---|---|---|---|---|---|---|---|---|---|
| Radius (cm) | 2 | 4 | 6 | 8 | 10 | 12 | 14 | 16 | 18 | 20 |

+2  +2  +2

Notice that the radius of the 10th circle is 20 centimeters.

**STEP 2** **Find** the circumference. To find the circumference of the 10th circle, use the formula that involves the radius.

| | |
|---|---|
| $C = 2\pi r$ | **Circumference formula** |
| $C \approx 2(3.14)(20)$ | **Substitute 3.14 for $\pi$ and 20 for $r$.** |
| $= 125.6$ | **Multiply.** |

▶ **Answer** The circumference of the 10th circle is about 125.6 centimeters.

# PATTERN PROBLEMS ON TAKS

Below are examples of pattern problems in multiple choice format. Try solving the problems before looking at the solutions. (Cover the solutions with a piece of paper.) Then check your solutions against the ones given.

**1.** A pattern of equations is shown below:

$$0.02x + 0.05 = 0.07$$
$$0.2x + 0.5 = 0.7$$
$$2x + 5 = 7$$
$$20x + 50 = 70$$

Which statement best describes this pattern of equations?

**A** The solution of each equation is 10 times the solution of the previous equation.

**B** The solution of each equation is the same.

**C** The solution of each equation is 10 more than the solution of the previous equation.

**D** The solution of the fourth equation is 1000 times the solution of the first equation.

**Solution**

Solve the first equation.

$$0.02x + 0.05 = 0.07$$
$$0.02x = 0.02$$
$$x = 1$$

Solve the second equation.

$$0.2x + 0.5 = 0.7$$
$$0.2x = 0.2$$
$$x = 1$$

Because $x = 1$ in the first two equations, substitute $x = 1$ into the third and fourth equations.

Each equation is true when $x = 1$, so the solution of each equation is the same.

The correct answer is B.

**2.** The figures below have a repeating pattern.

Which is the 13th figure in the pattern?

**F**   **G**

**H**   **J**

**Solution**

The first four figures shown are all different. The 5th figure shown is the same as the first. So, the pattern repeats after the fourth figure. The 13th figure is the same as the first.

So, the correct answer is F.

# 6 TAKS PRACTICE

## PRACTICE FOR TAKS OBJECTIVE 6

1. Blaine multiplied his age by 2, divided by 5, subtracted 4, and added 1. The result was 11. Which could be the first step in finding Blaine's age?

   **A** Add 1 to 11

   **B** Subtract 1 from 11

   **C** Multiply 11 by 2

   **D** Divide 11 by 5

2. Which statement best describes the pattern of equations shown?

   $$1 \times -9 = -9$$
   $$2 \times -9 = -18$$
   $$3 \times -9 = -27$$

   **F** When the factor being multiplied by $-9$ is increased by one, the product is decreased by one.

   **G** When the factor being multiplied by $-9$ is increased by nine, the product is decreased by nine.

   **H** When the factor being multiplied by $-9$ is increased by one, the product is decreased by nine.

   **J** When the factor being multiplied by $-9$ is increased by nine, the product is decreased by one.

3. Greta must find the next number in the pattern shown below. What strategy should she use?

   $$-4,\ 12,\ -36,\ 108,\ \underline{\ ?\ }$$

   **A** Find the sum of 16 and 108.

   **B** Find the difference of 108 and 16.

   **C** Find the product of $-3$ and 108.

   **D** Find the quotient of 108 and $-3$.

4. The table shows a pattern of the diameters of five circles.

   | Circle | Diameter (in.) |
   |--------|----------------|
   | 1 | 2 |
   | 2 | 4 |
   | 3 | 8 |
   | 4 | 16 |
   | 5 | 32 |

   What is the approximate circumference of the 8th circle in the pattern?

   **F** 256 in.

   **G** 402 in.

   **H** 804 in.

   **J** 1608 in.

## MIXED TAKS PRACTICE

5. Nancy has $10 to spend at the store. She bought 3 boxes of cereal for $2.98 each and a gallon of milk. Which equation can be used to determine the maximum cost of the milk? *TAKS Obj. 2*

   **A** $3(2.98) + 1 \leq 10$

   **B** $3(2.98 + x) \leq 10$

   **C** $10 - 3(2.98) \leq x$

   **D** $3(2.98) + x \leq 10$

6. The distance between two objects outside the Earth's atmosphere is about 270,000 meters. How can this be written in scientific notation? *TAKS Obj. 1*

   **F** $2.7 \times 10^{-6}$ m

   **G** $2.7 \times 10^{-5}$ m

   **H** $2.7 \times 10^{5}$ m

   **J** $2.7 \times 10^{6}$ m

## MIXED TAKS PRACTICE

**7.** Points *F, G, H,* and *J* are all moved 4 units to the left and 3 units up. Which point will then be in the second quadrant? *TAKS Obj. 3*

**A** *F*

**B** *G*

**C** *H*

**D** *J*

**8.** A meteorologist measured temperatures in Fahrenheit at five locations. The lowest temperature was 55°F, and the highest temperature was 63°F. The meteorologist measured the temperature at a sixth location. This measurement did not change the range of the data. Which MUST be true of *t*, the temperature at the sixth location? *TAKS Obj. 6*

**F** $t < 55°F$.

**G** $t > 63°F$.

**H** $55°F \leq t \leq 63°F$.

**J** Either $t = 55°F$ or $t = 63°F$

**9.** What fraction is between 0.3 and 0.5? *TAKS Obj. 1*

**A** $\dfrac{1}{4}$

**B** $\dfrac{3}{7}$

**C** $\dfrac{3}{5}$

**D** $\dfrac{5}{6}$

**10.** Rod must cut three rods of wood into smaller pieces of equal length. The rods measure 20 inches, 44 inches, and 64 inches. What can Rod do to find the longest each piece can be? *TAKS Obj. 6*

**F** Write the factors of 20, 44, and 64 and find one factor that they have in common.

**G** Write the factors of 20, 44, and 64 and find the greatest prime factor that they have in common.

**H** Write the factors of 20, 44, and 64 and find the factor of greatest value that they have in common.

**J** Add 20, 44, and 64 and divide by 3.

**11.** What are the coordinates of the point at the center of the square? *TAKS Obj. 3*

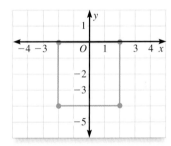

**A** $(-2, 0)$

**B** $(2, -4)$

**C** $(-2, -4)$

**D** $(0, -2)$

**12. GRIDDED ANSWER** Members of a jazz quartet in France have heights of 1.55 meters, 1.78 meters, 1.90 meters, and 1.83 meters. A fifth musician sits in with the band. What height, in meters, must the fifth musician be so that the mean of the 5 heights is 1.73 meters? *TAKS Obj. 6*

*Record your answer and fill in the bubbles on your answer document. Be sure to use the correct place value.*

# 7 Ratio, Proportion, and Percent

TEXAS

## Animated Math

at *classzone.com*

- Rates, p. 344
- Percent Applications, p. 379
- Simple Probability, p. 383

## Get-Ready Games

**Review Prerequisite Skills** by playing *Video Maze* and *Find the Path*.

**Skill Focus:** Solving equations

Find a path through the maze from start to finish.

- Then find the sum of all the solutions of the equations to find your total number of points.

- Which path has the least number of points?

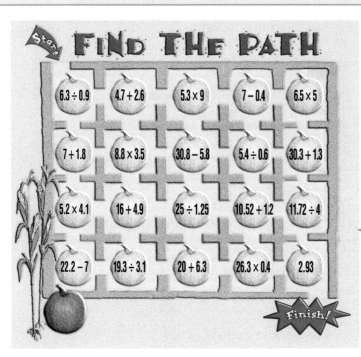

**Skill Focus:** Performing operations on decimals

Find your way from start to finish in the maze above.

- Evaluate each expression. Then move to the nearest expression that begins with the number that is the value of the previous expression.

- For example, if you start from 5.3 + 4.2 and your choices are 1.4 + 7.2 and 9.5 − 8, you would move to 9.5 − 8 because 5.3 + 4.2 = 9.5.

## Stop and Think

1. **WRITING** A student says that a decimal divided by a decimal is never a whole number. *Explain* the error in the student's reasoning.

2. **CRITICAL THINKING** How many different paths are there through the *Video Maze* that do not cover the same ground more than once?

# Review Prerequisite Skills

## VOCABULARY CHECK

**REVIEW WORDS**

- **data,** *p. 3*
- **equation,** *p. 26*
- **formula,** *p. 32*
- **simplest form,** *p. 187*
- **equivalent fractions,** *p. 187*

**Copy and complete using a review word from the list at the left.**

**1.** The fraction $\frac{1}{2}$ is in __?__, but $\frac{2}{4}$ is not.

**2.** The fractions $\frac{2}{3}$ and $\frac{4}{6}$ are __?__.

**3.** A mathematical sentence that shows two expressions have the same value is called a(n) __?__.

## SKILL CHECK

**Solve the equation.** *(p. 122)*

**4.** $\frac{x}{7} = 3$    **5.** $\frac{x}{-2} = 4$    **6.** $-9x = 108$    **7.** $8x = 56$

**8.** You have 15 pairs of socks in your drawer, including exactly 6 pairs of black socks. What fraction of your socks are black? *(p. 187)*

**Write the fraction in simplest form.** *(p. 187)*

**9.** $\frac{15}{75}$    **10.** $\frac{12}{60}$    **11.** $\frac{9ab}{36a}$    **12.** $\frac{18n^3}{36n}$

**Order the numbers from least to greatest.** *(p. 255)*

**13.** $0, -0.25, \frac{1}{3}, \frac{12}{9}, -1.11, \frac{9}{8}$    **14.** $1.28, -\frac{7}{8}, \frac{1}{12}, \frac{10}{3}, -0.02, 0.34$

**TEXAS @HomeTutor**   Prerequisite skills practice at classzone.com

## Notetaking Skills   Taking Notes in Class

In each chapter you will learn a new notetaking skill. In Chapter 7 you will apply the strategy of taking notes in class to topics such as Example 3 on p. 355.

As you participate in class, be sure to ask questions about things you don't understand. Write the answers in your notes.

Writing Decimals as Fractions

$0.007 = \frac{7}{1000}$   0.007 has 3 decimal places.
1000 has 3 zeros.

$0.13 = \frac{13}{100}$   0.13 has 2 decimal places.
100 has 2 zeros.

*Number of decimal places equals number of zeros!*

# 7.1 Ratios and Rates

**TEKS** *8.2.D, 8.3.B*

| | |
|---|---|
| **Before** | You found equivalent fractions. |
| **Now** | You'll find ratios and unit rates. |
| **Why?** | So you can compare speeds, as in Ex. 46. |

**KEY VOCABULARY**
- **ratio,** *p. 343*
- **equivalent ratios,** *p. 343*
- **rate,** *p. 344*
- **unit rate,** *p. 344*

## ACTIVITY

**You can compare side lengths and perimeters of squares.**

**STEP 1**  Copy and complete the table using the squares shown. Write the fractions in simplest form.

**STEP 2**  Describe what you notice about the fractions in the table.

**STEP 3**  Describe the relationship between the side length and the perimeter of a square with side length *s*.

| Side length | 2 | 4 | 5 |
|---|---|---|---|
| Perimeter | ? | ? | ? |
| $\dfrac{\text{Side length}}{\text{Perimeter}}$ | ? | ? | ? |

**READING**
All three ways of writing a ratio of two numbers are read in the same manner. So $\frac{9}{5}$, 9 : 5, and 9 to 5 are all read "the ratio of nine to five."

In the activity, you used a *ratio* to compare the side length of a square to its perimeter. A **ratio** uses division to compare two numbers. You can write the ratio of *a* to *b* (*b* ≠ 0) in the following three ways.

$$\frac{a}{b} \qquad\qquad a : b \qquad\qquad a \text{ to } b$$

Ratios that have the same value are called **equivalent ratios**. For example: 9 : 5, 18 : 10, and $3 : 1\frac{2}{3}$ are all equivalent ratios.

### EXAMPLE 1  Writing a Ratio

**Skiing** A ski resort has 15 easy, 25 intermediate, 7 difficult, and 11 expert-only trails. Write the ratio "intermediate trails : easy trails" in three ways.

$$\frac{\text{intermediate trails}}{\text{easy trails}} = \frac{25}{15} = \frac{5}{3} \qquad \textbf{Write as a fraction and simplify.}$$

▶ **Answer**  The ratio can be written as $\frac{5}{3}$, 5 : 3, or 5 to 3.

**Rates** A **rate** is a ratio of two quantities that have different units. Two rates are equivalent if they have the same value.

**EXAMPLE 2** Finding an Equivalent Rate

**Weather** Lightning strikes about 100 times per second around the world. About how many times does lightning strike per minute around the world?

**SOLUTION**

CONVERT UNITS
Need help with converting units? See p. 815.

Because 60 seconds = 1 minute, $\dfrac{60 \text{ sec}}{1 \text{ min}}$ is equivalent to 1.

$$\dfrac{100 \text{ times}}{1 \text{ sec}} = \dfrac{100 \text{ times}}{1 \text{ sec}} \cdot \dfrac{60 \text{ sec}}{1 \text{ min}} \quad \textbf{Multiply by a fraction that is equivalent to 1.}$$

$$= \dfrac{6000 \text{ times}}{1 \text{ min}} \quad \textbf{Simplify.}$$

▶ **Answer** Lightning strikes about 6000 times per minute around the world.

**Unit Rates** A **unit rate** is a rate that has a denominator of 1 unit. To write a unit rate, find an equivalent rate with a denominator of 1 unit.

**EXAMPLE 3** Finding a Unit Rate

WRITE EQUIVALENT FRACTIONS
Need help with equivalent fractions? See p. 187.

Write −24 feet per 5 seconds as a unit rate.

$$\dfrac{-24 \text{ ft}}{5 \text{ sec}} = -\dfrac{24 \div 5}{5 \div 5} \quad \textbf{Divide numerator and denominator by 5 to get a denominator of 1 unit.}$$

$$= \dfrac{-4.8}{1} \quad \textbf{Simplify.}$$

▶ **Answer** The unit rate is −4.8 feet per second.

*Animated* **Math**
at classzone.com

**Check** Round −4.8 feet per second to −5 feet per second. The product −5 · 5 = −25, which is about −24, so the answer is reasonable.

✓ **GUIDED PRACTICE** for Examples 1, 2, and 3

Use the information in Example 1 to write the ratio in three ways.

**1.** expert-only trails : easy trails

**2.** easy trails : difficult trails

**3. Pumping Water** A water pump moves 2 gallons of water per second. How many gallons of water are pumped per minute? Write your answer as a rate.

Write the rate as a unit rate.

**4.** $\dfrac{114 \text{ points}}{6 \text{ games}}$

**5.** $\dfrac{365 \text{ people}}{5 \text{ months}}$

**6.** $\dfrac{329 \text{ miles}}{10 \text{ gallons}}$

**7.** $\dfrac{-49 \text{ m}}{14 \text{ sec}}$

# 7.1 EXERCISES

HOMEWORK KEY

★ = **TAKS Practice and Reasoning**
Exs. 28, 42, 45, 46, and 48

◯ = **HINTS** AND **HOMEWORK HELP**
for Exs. 5, 7, 13, 19, 43 at classzone.com

## SKILL PRACTICE

**1. VOCABULARY** What is the difference between a ratio and a rate?

**2. VOCABULARY** Copy and complete: "Three gallons to $4.50" and "five gallons to $7.50" are equivalent __?__.

**WRITING AND SIMPLIFYING RATIOS** Write the ratio as a fraction in simplest form and two other ways.

**SEE EXAMPLE 1**
on p. 343
for Exs. 3–10

**3.** $\dfrac{33}{22}$      **4.** $\dfrac{20}{25}$      **⑤.** $\dfrac{27}{42}$      **6.** $\dfrac{-12}{4}$

**⑦.** 51 to 17      **8.** 26 : 39      **9.** 28 : 6      **10.** 35 to 49

**MEASUREMENT** Write the equivalent rate.

**SEE EXAMPLE 2**
on p. 344
for Exs. 11–18

**11.** $\dfrac{60 \text{ mi}}{\text{h}} = \dfrac{? \text{ mi}}{\text{min}}$      **12.** $\dfrac{32 \text{ oz}}{\text{serving}} = \dfrac{? \text{ lb}}{\text{serving}}$      **⑬.** $\dfrac{105 \text{ min}}{\text{game}} = \dfrac{? \text{ h}}{\text{game}}$      **14.** $\dfrac{\$1.44}{\text{ft}} = \dfrac{\$ ?}{\text{yd}}$

**15.** $\dfrac{50 \text{ ft}}{\text{sec}} = \dfrac{? \text{ ft}}{\text{min}}$      **16.** $\dfrac{87 \text{ cents}}{30 \text{ in.}} = \dfrac{? \text{ cents}}{\text{ft}}$      **17.** $\dfrac{15 \text{ min}}{\text{quarter}} = \dfrac{? \text{ hr}}{\text{quarter}}$      **18.** $\dfrac{20 \text{ mi}}{\text{h}} = \dfrac{? \text{ ft}}{\text{h}}$

**UNIT RATES** Write the rate as a unit rate. Check for reasonableness.

**SEE EXAMPLE 3**
on p. 344
for Exs. 19–26

**⑲.** $\dfrac{24 \text{ adults}}{6 \text{ cars}}$      **20.** $\dfrac{80 \text{ mi}}{4 \text{ h}}$      **21.** $\dfrac{18 \text{ degrees}}{6 \text{ min}}$      **22.** $\dfrac{610 \text{ rotations}}{5 \text{ min}}$

**23.** $\dfrac{50 \text{ oz}}{5 \text{ servings}}$      **24.** $\dfrac{-75 \text{ ft}}{20 \text{ sec}}$      **25.** $\dfrac{-34 \text{ m}}{8 \text{ sec}}$      **26.** $\dfrac{3 \text{ lb}}{\$2}$

**27. ERROR ANALYSIS** Your friend multiplied $\dfrac{14 \text{ times}}{\text{day}}$ by $\dfrac{1 \text{ week}}{7 \text{ days}}$ to get $\dfrac{2 \text{ times}}{\text{week}}$ as an equivalent ratio. Describe and correct the error that your friend made in writing the equivalent rate.

**28. ★ TAKS REASONING** Which rate is equivalent to 232 miles per 4 hours?

ⓐ $\dfrac{58 \text{ mi}}{4 \text{ h}}$      ⓑ $\dfrac{174 \text{ mi}}{3 \text{ h}}$      ⓒ $\dfrac{229 \text{ mi}}{1 \text{ h}}$      ⓓ $\dfrac{116 \text{ mi}}{1 \text{ h}}$

**COMPARING RATIOS** Tell whether the ratios are equivalent.

**29.** 3 to 12 and 2 to 6      **30.** 6 : 18 and 10 : 30      **31.** 15 : 35 and 18 : 42

**⊗ ALGEBRA** Find a value of the variable that makes the ratios equivalent.

**32.** $\dfrac{x}{8} = \dfrac{4}{16}$      **33.** $\dfrac{9}{c} = \dfrac{27}{30}$      **34.** $\dfrac{6}{10} = \dfrac{15}{n}$      **35.** $\dfrac{2}{12} = \dfrac{z}{18}$

**36.** $\dfrac{8}{x} = \dfrac{x}{18}$      **37.** $\dfrac{16}{y} = \dfrac{y}{4}$      **38.** $\dfrac{3}{a} = \dfrac{a}{27}$      **39.** $\dfrac{t}{2} = \dfrac{18}{t}$

**40. CHALLENGE** Write all pairs of equivalent ratios that use the numbers 6, 9, 10, and 15 exactly once.

**SEE EXAMPLE 1**
on p. 343
for Ex. 41

**41. WRITING** The aspect ratio of a TV screen is the ratio of its length to its width. The aspect ratio of a *standard* TV screen is 4 : 3. The aspect ratio of a *wide screen* TV in the United States is 16 : 9. *Describe* how to tell whether a TV has a standard or wide screen, given its length and width.

**SEE EXAMPLE 2**
on p. 344
for Exs. 42–43

**42. ⬩ TAKS REASONING** About 1 of every 10 people is left-handed. How many people in your math class would you predict are left-handed? *Explain.*

**43. CLOCKS** A clock chimes 4 times each hour. How many times does it chime in a week?

**SEE EXAMPLE 3**
on p. 344
for Ex. 44

**44. WAGES** You are paid $47.25 for 7 hours. How much are you paid per hour?

**45. ⬩ TAKS REASONING** The table shows the costs of oranges at four grocery stores. Which grocery store prices its oranges using a constant unit rate?

| Amount | Cost of Oranges at Four Stores | | | |
|---|---|---|---|---|
| | A | B | C | D |
| 10-lb bag | $11.70 | $11.70 | $12.00 | $12.00 |
| 20-lb bag | $22.90 | $23.40 | $24.00 | $22.00 |
| 30-lb bag | $33.60 | $35.10 | $35.00 | $32.00 |

   **Ⓐ** Store A      **Ⓑ** Store B

   **Ⓒ** Store C      **Ⓓ** Store D

**46. ⬩ TAKS REASONING** At top speed, a greyhound, a roadrunner, and a cheetah can achieve the following distances in the given length of time. Which animal is the fastest? Which animal is the slowest? *Explain* your reasoning.

330 ft in 5 sec

75 ft in 3 sec

198 ft in 2 sec

**47. CHALLENGE** Elliot and Colin both bring pretzels to school for a snack. The ratio of the number of pretzels Elliot brings to the number of pretzels Colin brings is 5 to 1. Elliot gives four pretzels to Colin, so the ratio is 3 to 1. How many pretzels does Elliot now have? *Explain.*

**REVIEW**
Lesson 3.4;
TAKS Workbook

**48. ⬩ TAKS PRACTICE** Six people each fill a dozen water balloons for a party. The balloons are evenly distributed among 4 teams. Which equation can be used to find $x$, the number of balloons given to each team? *TAKS Obj. 2*

   **Ⓐ** $6x = 4 \times 12$        **Ⓑ** $4x = 6 \times 12$

   **Ⓒ** $12x = 4 \times 6$       **Ⓓ** $4x = 6 \times 6$

**EXTRA PRACTICE** for Lesson 7.1, p. 807         ⬩ **ONLINE QUIZ** at classzone.com

# INVESTIGATION
*Use before Lesson 7.2*

**GOAL**
Make scale drawings.

**MATERIALS**
• ruler
• colored pencils
• grid paper
• magazine

 **TEKS** *8.6.A, 8.10.A*

## 7.2 Making a Scale Drawing

A *scale drawing* of an object preserves ratios of lengths but is either smaller or larger than the original object.

**EXPLORE** **Make an enlarged drawing of the picture.**

**STEP 1** **Draw** a grid on the original picture. Use unit squares that are smaller than the unit squares on your grid paper.

**STEP 2** **Draw** a rectangle on your grid paper that is the same number of units long and wide as the picture you want to enlarge.

**STEP 3** **Copy** the image that appears in a corner of the original onto your grid paper at the corresponding corner. Continue copying the image one block at a time until you have drawn the entire picture.

**STEP 4** **Measure** the width of the copy and of the original. The *scale* of the drawing is the ratio of corresponding measurements of the copy to the measurements of the original. What is the scale of your drawing?

**PRACTICE**

1. Cut out a picture from a magazine and create an enlarged scale drawing of it as described in Steps 1–3 above. Measure the original picture and the enlarged drawing to determine the scale.

**DRAW CONCLUSIONS**

2. **REASONING** Is the ratio of the area of a unit square in the copy to the area of a unit square in the original the same as the ratio of their sides? *Explain* using data from the scale drawing that you made.

3. **WRITING** *Explain* what would happen if different scales were used in the same drawing.

## 7.2 Writing and Solving Proportions

TEKS 8.3.B, 8.9.B

| Before | You wrote ratios. |
|---|---|
| Now | You'll write and solve proportions. |
| Why? | So you can find proportional amounts, as in Example 1. |

**KEY VOCABULARY**
- proportion, *p. 348*
- cross products, *p. 349*
- scale model, *p. 350*
- scale, *p. 350*

A **proportion** is an equation that states that two ratios are equivalent. The proportion below is read "*a* is to *b* as *c* is to *d*."

$$\frac{a}{b} = \frac{c}{d}, b \neq 0, d \neq 0$$

### EXAMPLE 1 Writing and Solving a Proportion

**Rhinoceros Beetles** An adult rhinoceros beetle weighs only 0.525 ounce but can carry about 446.25 ounces on its back. If a person were proportionately as strong as a rhinoceros beetle, how much weight could a 100 pound person carry?

**SOLUTION**

|  | Beetle | Person |
|---|---|---|
| **Carries** | 446.25 oz | *x* lb |
| **Weighs** | 0.525 oz | 100 lb |

Use a table to set up a proportion.

*ANOTHER WAY*

You can also use the following proportion in Example 1:

$$\frac{x}{446.25} = \frac{100}{0.525}$$

$$\frac{446.25}{0.525} = \frac{x}{100}$$

Write a proportion $\frac{\text{ounces}}{\text{ounces}} = \frac{\text{pounds}}{\text{pounds}}$.

$$\frac{446.25}{0.525} \cdot 100 = \frac{x}{100} \cdot 100$$

Multiply each side by 100.

$$85{,}000 = x$$

Simplify.

▶ **Answer** If human strength were proportional to that of a rhinoceros beetle, a 100 pound person could carry 85,000 pounds.

### ✓ GUIDED PRACTICE for Example 1

1. **What If?** Some ants weigh only 0.0001 ounce but can carry about 0.005 ounce. If a person were proportionately as strong as one of these ants, how much weight could a 100 pound person carry?

**Solve the proportion.**

2. $\frac{n}{12} = \frac{3}{4}$

3. $\frac{50}{20} = \frac{z}{16}$

4. $\frac{25}{3} = \frac{t}{51}$

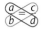
**Cross Products** The proportion $\frac{a}{b} = \frac{c}{d}$ has **cross products** $ad$ and $bc$.

$a \cdot d \qquad b \cdot c$

You can use cross products to solve a proportion. You can also use cross products to check whether two ratios form a proportion.

---

**KEY CONCEPT**                                   *For Your Notebook*

**Cross Products Property**

**Words**     The cross products of a proportion are equal.

**Numbers**   Because $\frac{3}{4} = \frac{9}{12}$, you know that $3 \cdot 12 = 4 \cdot 9$.

**Algebra**   If $\frac{a}{b} = \frac{c}{d}$, where $b$ and $d$ are nonzero numbers, then $ad = bc$.

---

## EXAMPLE 2   Using the Cross Products Property

$\frac{6.8}{15.4} = \frac{40.8}{m}$          Write original proportion.

$6.8m = 15.4(40.8)$          **Cross products property**

$6.8m = 628.32$          **Multiply.**

$\frac{6.8m}{6.8} = \frac{628.32}{6.8}$          **Divide each side by 6.8.**

$m = 92.4$          **Simplify.**

**Check** You can check your solution by finding the cross products of the proportion. If the cross products are equal, the solution is correct.

$\frac{6.8}{15.4} \stackrel{?}{=} \frac{40.8}{92.4}$          **Substitute 92.4 for m.**

$6.8(92.4) \stackrel{?}{=} 15.4(40.8)$          **Multiply.**

$628.32 = 628.32$ ✓

**Animated Math** at classzone.com

---

✓ **GUIDED PRACTICE**   for Example 2

**Solve the proportion. Then check your solution.**

**5.** $\frac{6}{c} = \frac{54}{99}$     **6.** $\frac{n}{14} = \frac{63}{84}$     **7.** $\frac{2.1}{0.9} = \frac{27.3}{y}$

**8.** $\frac{16.2}{67.4} = \frac{x}{134.8}$     **9.** $\frac{8}{a} = \frac{0.4}{0.62}$     **10.** $\frac{b}{1.8} = \frac{49.6}{14.4}$

**Scale** The dimensions of a **scale model** are proportional to the dimensions of the actual object. The relationship between the model's dimensions and the actual object's dimensions is called the **scale**. A scale can be written as a ratio with or without units. For example, the scale 1 in. : 3 ft can also be written as 1 : 36.

**EXAMPLE 3** TAKS PRACTICE: Multiple Choice

> **Sculpture** Strawberry Point, Iowa, has a strawberry sculpture that is 15 feet tall. If the scale of this model is 12 feet to 1 inch, how tall was the actual strawberry?
>
> **(A)** 1.25 inches  **(B)** 12.5 inches  **(C)** 1.25 feet  **(D)** 12.5 feet

*ELIMINATE CHOICES*
According to the scale, the actual strawberry should be smaller than the sculpture. So, you can eliminate choice D.

**SOLUTION**

STRAWBERRY POINT

$$\text{Scale} = \frac{\text{Height of strawberry model}}{\text{Height of actual strawberry}}$$

$\dfrac{12 \text{ ft}}{1 \text{ in.}} = \dfrac{15 \text{ ft}}{h \text{ in.}}$   **Write a proportion.**

$12h = 15$   **Cross products property**

$h = 1.25$   **Divide each side by 12.**

▶ **Answer** The height of the actual strawberry was 1.25 inches. The correct answer is A.  **(A)** **(B)** **(C)** **(D)**

✓ **GUIDED PRACTICE**   for Example 3

11. **What If?** Suppose the scale of the model in Example 3 is 25 feet to 3 inches. How tall was the actual strawberry?

# 7.2 **EXERCISES**

HOMEWORK KEY
= TAKS Practice and Reasoning
Exs. 7, 42, 44, 46, and 52

○ = HINTS AND HOMEWORK HELP
for Exs. 5, 9, 15, 21, 39 at classzone.com

**SKILL PRACTICE**

1. **VOCABULARY** *Describe* how to use cross products to solve a proportion.

2. **VOCABULARY** Copy and complete: The relationship between a model's dimensions and the actual object's dimensions is given by the __?__ .

*SEE EXAMPLE 1*
on p. 348
for Exs. 3–6

**SOLVING PROPORTIONS** **Solve the proportion. Then check your solution.**

3. $\dfrac{1}{2} = \dfrac{x}{6}$

4. $\dfrac{c}{10} = \dfrac{3}{5}$

5. $\dfrac{h}{4} = \dfrac{45}{20}$

6. $\dfrac{3}{8} = \dfrac{x}{32}$

**SEE EXAMPLE 1**
on p. 348
for Ex. 7

7. ⬥ **TAKS REASONING** What is the solution of the proportion $\frac{12}{15} = \frac{x}{25}$?

   Ⓐ 7.2          Ⓑ 20          Ⓒ 22          Ⓓ 31.25

**CHECKING PROPORTIONS** Tell whether the ratios form a proportion.

**SEE EXAMPLE 2**
on p. 349
for Exs. 8–24

8. $\frac{3}{4} \stackrel{?}{=} \frac{6}{8}$          9. $\frac{1}{2} \stackrel{?}{=} \frac{2}{5}$          10. $\frac{14}{21} \stackrel{?}{=} \frac{26}{39}$          11. $\frac{15}{45} \stackrel{?}{=} \frac{45}{135}$

**USING CROSS PRODUCTS** Solve the proportion.

12. $\frac{2}{3} = \frac{4}{z}$          13. $\frac{6}{a} = \frac{3}{1}$          14. $\frac{39}{13} = \frac{9}{d}$          15. $\frac{68}{12} = \frac{51}{p}$

16. $\frac{17}{12} = \frac{k}{36}$          17. $\frac{2}{5} = \frac{c}{20}$          18. $\frac{7.2}{m} = \frac{2.4}{1.8}$          19. $\frac{256}{9.6} = \frac{1.6}{g}$

20. $\frac{67.2}{g} = \frac{16.8}{3.3}$          21. $\frac{t}{29.4} = \frac{5.5}{4.2}$          22. $\frac{f}{5.4} = \frac{483}{18.9}$          23. $\frac{712}{8.8} = \frac{x}{18.7}$

24. **ERROR ANALYSIS** Describe and correct the error made in solving the proportion.

$\frac{3}{9} = \frac{12}{m}$
$9m = 3 \cdot 12$
$9m = 36$
$m = 4$

**SCALE MODELS** You use a scale of 3 inches to 50 feet to make scale models of buildings. A building's actual height is given. Find the model's height.

**SEE EXAMPLE 3**
on p. 350
for Exs. 25–28

25. $h = 100$ ft          26. $h = 240$ ft

27. $h = 316$ ft          28. $h = 545$ ft

In Exercises 29–34, find the value of $x$. Use this example to help you.

**EXTENSION** Solving Multi-Step Proportions

$\frac{30}{2 + x} = \frac{6}{7}$          Write original proportion.

$30 \cdot 7 = (2 + x) \cdot 6$          Cross products property

$210 = 12 + 6x$          Multiply and use distributive property.

$33 = x$          Solve the two-step equation for $x$.

29. $\frac{2}{x + 2} = \frac{18}{27}$          30. $\frac{x - 2}{8} = \frac{30}{40}$          31. $\frac{9}{5} = \frac{36}{x - 3}$

32. $\frac{5}{x} = \frac{7}{x + 4}$          33. $\frac{x}{5} = \frac{3x - 4}{7}$          34. $\frac{3 - 5x}{4} = \frac{x + 5}{9}$

**MULTIPLE VARIABLES** Find the value of each variable. Check your solution.

35. $\frac{4}{x - 5} = \frac{3}{2x} = \frac{y}{21}$          36. $\frac{7}{b - 36} = \frac{a}{72} = \frac{28}{b}$          37. $\frac{8}{p - 10} = \frac{16}{p - 5} = \frac{n + 8}{p}$

38. **CHALLENGE** If $\frac{a}{b} = \frac{c}{d}$, where $a, b, c,$ and $d$ are nonzero numbers, is it true that $\frac{a}{c} = \frac{b}{d}$? Is it true that $\frac{d}{a} = \frac{c}{b}$? *Justify* your answers using algebraic properties or *counterexamples* (examples of when the statement is false).

**SEE EXAMPLE 1**
on p. 348
for Exs. 39–41

**39.** **CARS** A car moving at a constant speed travels 88 feet in 2 seconds. Use a proportion to find how many feet it travels in one minute.

**40.** **EARNINGS** You earn $54 mowing 3 lawns. You charge the same amount for each lawn. How much do you earn for mowing 5 lawns?

**41.** **MENTAL MATH** Ten pounds of organic pasta cost $16. *Explain* how to use equivalent fractions and mental math to find the cost of 5 pounds of pasta.

**SEE EXAMPLE 3**
on p. 350
for Exs. 42–44

**42.** ✈ **TAKS REASONING** The Transamerica Building in San Francisco is 853 feet tall and is 145 feet wide at its widest point. You want to make a drawing of the building that has a scale of 1 in. : 80 ft. Will your drawing fit on a regular $8\frac{1}{2} \times 11$ sheet of paper? *Explain* your reasoning.

**43.** ◆ **MULTIPLE REPRESENTATIONS** You want to sketch three views of a car using a scale of 1 inch to 40 inches. The actual car is 215 inches long, 76 inches wide, and 54 inches high.

  **a.** **Calculate** Calculate the length, width, and height of the car for your drawing.

  **b.** **Draw Views** Draw rectangles for a front, side, and overhead view of the car with the dimensions you found in part (a). Then sketch the views.

**44.** ✈ **TAKS REASONING** The scale on a map is $\frac{1}{4}$ inch : 20 miles. The distance from Montgomery, Alabama, to Atlanta, Georgia, is about 2 inches on the map. About how far is it from Montgomery to Atlanta?

  **(A)** 20 miles    **(B)** 80 miles    **(C)** 160 miles    **(D)** 200 miles

**45.** **WRITING** The wingspan and length of a space shuttle orbiter model are shown. What additional pieces of information could be used to find the scale of the model? *Explain*.

13 in.

$20\frac{1}{3}$ in.

**46.** ✈ **TAKS REASONING** To produce one pound of honey, the bees from a hive fly over 55,000 miles and visit about 2 million flowers.

  **a.** Estimate how many flowers are visited to make 10 ounces of honey.

  **b.** Estimate how many miles the bees fly to make 10 ounces of honey.

  **c.** Estimate the mean number of flowers visited per mile traveled. *Explain* your reasoning.

**The Green Park** The Green Park in London, England, was given its name in 1746 and opened to the public in 1826. Once stocked with deer and used as hunting grounds, the park is presently a place used by tourists and Londoners for exercising, picnicking, and relaxing. The park is roughly the shape of a triangle, as shown in the map at the right, whose longest side is about 2600 feet long.

**47. Find a Scale** Use a ruler to find the scale of the map in centimeters to feet.

**48. Estimation** Estimate the dimensions of the triangular shaped park. Use the dimensions to estimate the perimeter and area of the park.

**49. Calculate** A type of grass seed costs about $.36 for every square yard. About how much would it cost to cover all of The Green Park with this grass seed?

**50. SOCCER** Your school's soccer team had a record of 4 wins and 6 losses after losing its last game. To make the playoffs, your team needs to win 75% of all of its games. If your team wins the rest of its games, at least how many games *must be* left in the schedule for your team to make the playoffs?

**51. CHALLENGE** A 5-inch by 8-inch photo needs to be proportionally increased in size to fit a space whose width is 5 inches less than its length. Find the perimeter and area of the enlarged photo.

 **MIXED REVIEW FOR TAKS**          **TAKS** PRACTICE at classzone.com

*REVIEW*
Lesson 1.6;
TAKS Workbook

**52.** 🔻 **TAKS PRACTICE** During a long distance bike trip in Canada, Alice biked 43 kilometers in $3\frac{1}{2}$ hours, Paula biked 47.5 kilometers in $4\frac{1}{2}$ hours, and Gail biked 52 kilometers in 4 hours. Which statement is true? *TAKS Obj. 2*

Ⓐ Alice and Paula biked at about the same average speed.

Ⓑ If they start at the same place and bike the same route at the same average speeds as above, Gail will be about 4.9 kilometers ahead of Paula after 2 hours.

Ⓒ If they start at the same place and bike the same route at the same average speeds as above, Alice will be about 9 kilometers ahead of Paula after 3 hours.

Ⓓ Alice is the fastest of the three.

# 7.3 Solving Percent Problems

**TEKS** *8.3.B, 8.4*

| Before | You solved proportions. |
|---|---|
| Now | You'll solve percent problems using proportions. |
| Why? | So you can use data to find percents, as in Example 1. |

**KEY VOCABULARY**
• percent, *p. 354*

The word *percent* means "per hundred." A **percent** is a ratio whose denominator is 100. The symbol for percent is %.

---

### KEY CONCEPT
*For Your Notebook*

**Solving Percent Problems**

To represent "*a* is *p* percent of *b*," use the proportion

$$\frac{a}{b} = \frac{p}{100}$$

where *a* is part of the base *b* and *p*%, or $\frac{p}{100}$, is the percent.

---

### EXAMPLE 1 Finding a Percent

**Environment** A service club is planting seedlings as part of an erosion prevention project. Out of 240 newly planted seedlings, 15 are laurel sumac. What percent of the seedlings are laurel sumac?

**SOLUTION**

To find the percent of seedlings that are laurel sumac, use a percent proportion.

$\frac{a}{b} = \frac{p}{100}$      **Write a percent proportion.**

$\frac{15}{240} = \frac{p}{100}$      **Substitute 15 for *a* and 240 for *b*.**

$\frac{15}{240} \cdot 100 = \frac{p}{100} \cdot 100$      **Multiply each side by 100.**

$6.25 = p$      **Simplify.**

▶ **Answer** 6.25% of the seedlings are laurel sumac.

**LOOK BACK**
Need help with multiplying a fraction by a whole number? See p. 243.

---

✓ **GUIDED PRACTICE**    for Example 1

**Use a percent proportion.**

**1.** 63 is what percent of 75?

**2.** 84 is what percent of 70?

---

## EXAMPLE 2  Finding Part of a Base

 **School Newspaper**  Your school newspaper's budget this year is 160% of last year's budget, which was $2125. What is this year's budget?

### SOLUTION

*ANOTHER WAY*
You can also solve these proportions by using cross products.

$$\frac{a}{b} = \frac{p}{100}$$  Write a percent proportion.

$$\frac{a}{2125} = \frac{160}{100}$$  Substitute 2125 for $b$ and 160 for $p$.

$$\frac{a}{2125} \cdot 2125 = \frac{160}{100} \cdot 2125$$  Multiply each side by 2125.

$$a = 3400$$  Simplify.

▶ **Answer**  This year's budget is $3400.

## EXAMPLE 3  Finding a Base

 **24 is 0.8% of what number?**

*TAKE NOTES*
In your notes, you may want to include each step needed to solve a percent proportion.

$$\frac{a}{b} = \frac{p}{100}$$  Write a percent proportion.

$$\frac{24}{b} = \frac{0.8}{100}$$  Substitute 24 for $a$ and 0.8 for $p$.

$$24 \cdot 100 = b \cdot 0.8$$  Cross products property

$$3000 = b$$  Divide each side by 0.8 and simplify.

▶ **Answer**  24 is 0.8% of 3000.

---

**CONCEPT SUMMARY**                    *For Your Notebook*

### Percent Problems

| Question | Method | Proportion |
|---|---|---|
| $a$ is what percent of $b$? | Solve for $p$. | $\frac{a}{b} = \frac{p}{100}$ |
| What number is $p\%$ of $b$? | Solve for $a$. | $\frac{a}{b} = \frac{p}{100}$ |
| $a$ is $p\%$ of what number? | Solve for $b$. | $\frac{a}{b} = \frac{p}{100}$ |

---

✓ **GUIDED PRACTICE**  for Examples 2 and 3

**Use a percent proportion.**

**3.** What number is 16% of 75?

**4.** What number is 35% of 92?

**5.** 260 is 325% of what number?

**6.** What number is 0.5% of 65?

## 7.3 EXERCISES

### SKILL PRACTICE

1. **VOCABULARY** Copy and complete: Another way to say "25 songs out of 100" is to say "25 ? of the songs."

2. **VOCABULARY** In the sentence "30 is 75% of 40," which number is the base?

**USING PROPORTIONS** Write a proportion to represent the percent problem. Then solve the proportion to answer the question.

**SEE EXAMPLES 1, 2, AND 3** on pp. 354–355 for Exs. 3–17

3. 209 is 38% of what number?

4. 6 is what percent of 75?

5. 5 is what percent of 125?

6. 481 is 52% of what number?

7. What number is 45% of 245?

8. What number is 30% of 120?

**USING PROPORTIONS** Use a percent proportion to answer the question.

9. 756 is what percent of 840?

10. 39 is what percent of 50?

11. 918 is 170% of what number?

12. 111 is what percent of 740?

13. 567 is what percent of 420?

14. What number is 520% of 150?

15. What number is 0.36% of 700?

16. 179.2 is 32% of what number?

17. ✦ **TAKS REASONING** How much is 20% of $90?

   Ⓐ $18      Ⓑ $20      Ⓒ $70      Ⓓ $72

18. **ERROR ANALYSIS** Describe and correct the error made in answering the following question: *What percent of 60 is 12?*

$$\frac{a}{b} = \frac{p}{100} \quad \times$$
$$\frac{60}{12} = \frac{p}{100}$$
$$500 = p$$
500% of 60 is 12.

19. ✦ **TAKS REASONING** Write three percent problems in which you find the percent, three in which you find the part, and three in which you find the base.

**NUMBER SENSE** Copy and complete the statement using <, >, or =.

20. 30% of 120 ? 120% of 30

21. 20% of 80 ? 40% of 50

22. 15% of 140 ? 75% of 24

23. 25% of 80 ? 125% of 12

24. 150% of 30 ? 75% of 48

25. 10% of 400 ? 25% of 160

🄧 **ALGEBRA** Solve the percent problem in terms of *y*.

26. What number is 50% of 8*y*?

27. 3*y* is 60% of what number?

**CHALLENGE** Find the unknown number.

28. 85% of 20% of what number is 34?

29. 115% of 25% of what number is 46?

SEE EXAMPLES
1, 2, AND 3
on pp. 354–355
for Exs. 30–35

**30.** **GUIDED PROBLEM SOLVING** You ask 356 people if they enjoy drawing. Of these people, 89 say they do like to draw. What percent of the people surveyed like to draw?

   **a.** Write a percent proportion.

   **b.** Substitute the known values for the variables.

   **c.** Solve the proportion.

**31.** **MARATHON** Of the 23,513 people who entered the Honolulu Marathon one year, 19,236 finished. What percent of the runners finished? Round your answer to the nearest tenth of a percent.

**32.** **TAKS REASONING** A bag of 150 stickers contains 28% blue, 26% red, 34% green, and 12% yellow stickers. Which proportion can be used to find $g$, the number of green stickers in the bag?

   **A** $\dfrac{g}{100} = \dfrac{34}{150}$      **B** $\dfrac{34}{100} = \dfrac{g}{150}$      **C** $\dfrac{100}{150} = \dfrac{g}{34}$      **D** $\dfrac{34}{100} = \dfrac{150}{g}$

**33.** **WATER** A child's body weight is approximately 75% water. About how many pounds of a 60 pound child's weight is water?

**34.** **TAKS REASONING** You read that 560 of the 875 students at your school belong to a school club. Write and solve a proportion to find the percent of students who belong to a club. *Explain* how you could use equivalent fractions and estimation to check your answer.

**35.** **REPTILES** The largest crocodiles alive today are 24 feet in length. Recently, researchers found bones of an ancient crocodile. It was 167% as long as today's longest crocodiles. How much longer was the ancient crocodile than today's longest crocodile? *Round* to the nearest foot.

**36.** **WRITING** *Explain* how you might find 10% of 400 without writing a proportion.

**37.** **NUMBER SENSE** One day, 32 of 80 people wore a red shirt to school. What percent of the 80 people did *not* wear a red shirt to school?

**38.** **QUIZ SCORES** You earned 32 points on a quiz. Your score was 80%. What was the maximum number of points on the quiz? How many more points would you have needed to earn a score of 90%? *Explain.*

**39.** **TAKS REASONING** *Describe* a real-world situation where a percent greater than 100% can be used.

**40.** **DINOSAURS** You buy a scale model of a Dilophosaurus for your brother. The scale of the model is 1 inch to 3 feet 4 inches. To the nearest percent, what percent of the actual height is the model's height?

41. **MULTI-STEP PROBLEM** Mary Anne and Josefina are mowing the lawn of their neighbor's town house to make extra money. Use the diagram below to answer the questions.

   **a.** How many square feet has each mowed so far?

   **b.** Who has mowed the greatest percent of her section so far?

   **c.** Mary Anne finishes her section while Josefina takes a break to get them both some water and helps Josefina by mowing 5% of the unmowed portion of the back lawn. Josefina mows the rest. How many square feet does Josefina mow? What percent of the entire lawn does she mow?

42. **CHALLENGE** You use a photocopier to reduce an 8 inch by 10 inch photograph. When you press the reduction button, it reduces both the length and width by the percent selected. What is the new area if you reduce the photograph to 64% of its original size and then reduce the result to 78% of its size? What is the new area if you reduce to 78% first and then to 64%? *Compare* the two values.

43. **CHALLENGE** A worker gets a raise so that his pay is now 120% of what it was. Then the employer offers the worker the option of working less time but making only 80% of the new pay rate. Would choosing this option enable the worker to make *more*, *less*, or *the same amount* as before the raise? *Explain.*

## MIXED REVIEW FOR TAKS

**TAKS** PRACTICE at classzone.com

*REVIEW*

Lesson 7.2;
TAKS Workbook

44. **TAKS PRACTICE** A mechanic makes a scale drawing of a tool shed. In the drawing, the tool shed is 4 inches wide and 5 inches long. The actual length of the shed is 20 feet. What is the actual area of the shed? *TAKS Obj. 2*

   **(A)** $20 \text{ ft}^2$

   **(B)** $80 \text{ ft}^2$

   **(C)** $320 \text{ ft}^2$

   **(D)** $500 \text{ ft}^2$

*REVIEW*

Lesson 5.5;
TAKS Workbook

45. **TAKS PRACTICE** After completing a project, a carpenter has 4 pieces of wood left. Which list shows the lengths of the pieces in order from least to greatest? *TAKS Obj. 1*

   **(F)** $0.09 \text{ m}, \frac{2}{5} \text{ m}, \frac{1}{3} \text{ m}, 0.5 \text{ m}$

   **(G)** $\frac{1}{3} \text{ m}, \frac{2}{5} \text{ m}, 0.09 \text{ m}, 0.5 \text{ m}$

   **(H)** $0.09 \text{ m}, \frac{1}{3} \text{ m}, 0.5 \text{ m}, \frac{2}{5} \text{ m}$

   **(J)** $0.09 \text{ m}, \frac{1}{3} \text{ m}, \frac{2}{5} \text{ m}, 0.5 \text{ m}$

# 7.4 Fractions, Decimals, and Percents

TEKS *8.1.A, 8.3.B*

| | |
|---|---|
| **Before** | You wrote fractions as decimals and decimals as fractions. |
| **Now** | You'll rewrite fractions, decimals, and percents. |
| **Why?** | So you can express survey data as percents, as in Example 4. |

**KEY VOCABULARY**
• circle graph, *p. 360*

The diagram below shows several ways to represent 20% using concepts from Lessons 4.3, 5.5, and 7.3.

$$20\% = \frac{20}{100} = 0.20 \qquad 20\% = \frac{20}{100} = \frac{20 \div 20}{100 \div 20} = \frac{1}{5}$$

**Percents and Decimals** To write a percent as a decimal, you can divide by 100, because $p\% = \dfrac{p}{100} = p \div 100$. Recall that dividing by 100 is the same as moving the decimal point two places to the left.

---

## EXAMPLE 1 Writing a Percent as a Decimal

*AVOID ERRORS*
Add a zero on the left if necessary to move the decimal point two places to the left.

**a.** $65\% = 65 \div 100 = .65 = 0.65$

**b.** $250\% = 250 \div 100 = 2.50 = 2.5$

**c.** $0.3\% = 0.3 \div 100 = .003 = 0.003$

---

To write a decimal as a percent, reverse the process in Example 1 and multiply by 100. Note that multiplying by 100 is the same as moving the decimal point two places to the left.

---

## EXAMPLE 2 Writing a Decimal as a Percent

*AVOID ERRORS*
Add a zero on the right if necessary to move the decimal point two places to the right.

**a.** $0.95 = (0.95 \times 100)\% = 095. = 95\%$

**b.** $2.7 = (2.7 \times 100)\% = 270. = 270\%$

**c.** $0.004 = (0.004 \times 100)\% = 000.4 = 0.4\%$

**Percents and Fractions** Since percent means per 100, to write $p\%$ as a fraction, use $p$ as the numerator and 100 as the denominator. Then simplify.

**EXAMPLE 3** Writing a Percent as a Fraction

**COMMON EQUIVALENTS**
For a list of common fraction, decimal, and percent equivalents, see p. 820

**a.** $25\% = \dfrac{25}{100} = \dfrac{25 \div 25}{100 \div 25} = \dfrac{1}{4}$

**b.** $325\% = \dfrac{325}{100} = \dfrac{325 \div 25}{100 \div 25} = \dfrac{13}{4} = 3\dfrac{1}{4}$

**c.** $0.2\% = \dfrac{0.2}{100} = \dfrac{0.2 \times 10}{100 \times 10} = \dfrac{2}{1000} = \dfrac{1}{500}$

**Circle Graphs** A **circle graph** represents data as parts of a circle, with each part labeled with its fraction or equivalent percent. Each item of data belongs in exactly one of the parts. So, the sum of the fractions equals 1, or the sum of the percents equals 100.

**EXAMPLE 4** Writing a Fraction as a Percent

**Survey** The circle graph below shows the results of a survey of how 500 students prefer to spend their time.

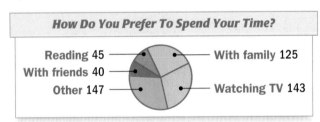

*How Do You Prefer To Spend Your Time?*

Reading 45 — With family 125
With friends 40 —
Other 147 — Watching TV 143

**a.** What percent of students prefer to spend time with friends?

$$\dfrac{40}{500} = \dfrac{p}{100}$$
$$4000 = 500p$$
$$8 = p$$

▶ **Answer** 8% of all of the students prefer to spend time with friends.

**b.** What percent of those who didn't answer "other" said "with friends"?

$$\dfrac{40}{353} = \dfrac{p}{100}$$
$$4000 = 353p$$
$$11.33 \approx p$$

▶ **Answer** About 11% of the selected group said "with friends."

**ANOTHER WAY**
You can also write fractions as percents by using equivalent fractions.
$\dfrac{40}{500} = \dfrac{8}{100} = 8\%$

✓ **GUIDED PRACTICE** for Examples 3 and 4

Write the percent as a decimal and as a fraction in simplest form.

**1.** 35%  **2.** 140%  **3.** 0.75%  **4.** 12.12%

Write the decimal or fraction as a percent.

**5.** 0.9  **6.** 5.04  **7.** $\dfrac{1}{20}$  **8.** $\dfrac{3}{8}$

**EXAMPLE 5** Ordering Fractions, Decimals, and Percents

**Sleep Habits** A survey of dog owners found the following portions represent the three most popular sleeping places for dogs: $\frac{9}{40}$ on owner's bed, 0.19 in a dog house, and 16.8% on the floor. Order these numbers from least to greatest.

**STEP 1** **Write** the numbers as decimals with the same number of decimal places.

$$\frac{9}{40} = 0.225 \qquad\qquad 0.19 = 0.190 \qquad\qquad 16.8\% = 0.168$$

**STEP 2** **Compare** the decimals: $0.168 < 0.190$ and $0.190 < 0.225$.

▶ **Answer** The numbers ordered from least to greatest are 16.8%, 0.19, and $\frac{9}{40}$.

**Check** Use a number line to order the decimals.

**Animated Math** at classzone.com

---

✓ **GUIDED PRACTICE** **for Example 5**

**Order the numbers from least to greatest.**

**9.** $41\%, \frac{9}{20}, 0.389$      **10.** $\frac{9}{10}, 0.099, 95\%$      **11.** $1.5, 145\%, \frac{7}{5}$

---

# 7.4 EXERCISES

HOMEWORK
KEY

🏴 = **TAKS Practice and Reasoning**
Exs. 58, 71, 75, 76, 78, 79, and 80

◯ = **HINTS AND HOMEWORK HELP**
for Exs. 3, 13, 23, 43, 67 at classzone.com

## SKILL PRACTICE

**1. VOCABULARY** In a circle graph, what is the sum of the percents? What is the sum of the fractions?

**SEE EXAMPLE 1**
on p. 359
for Exs. 2–11

**REWRITING PERCENTS** Write the percent as a decimal.

**2.** 80%    **3.** 12.5%    **4.** 7.5%    **5.** 110%    **6.** 1.05%

**7.** 44.55%    **8.** 0.4%    **9.** 0.78%    **10.** 187.09%    **11.** 0.08%

**SEE EXAMPLE 2**
on p. 359
for Exs. 12–21

**REWRITING DECIMALS** Write the decimal as a percent.

**12.** 0.09    **13.** 1.27    **14.** 0.7    **15.** 2.1    **16.** 4

**17.** 0.51    **18.** 0.003    **19.** 0.057    **20.** 0.039    **21.** 0.004

**SEE EXAMPLE 2**
on p. 359
for Ex. 22

**22. ERROR ANALYSIS** Describe and correct the error made in writing 0.001 as a percent.

$$\times \quad 0.001 = \frac{1}{100} = 1\%$$

**REWRITING PERCENTS** Write the percent as a fraction.

**SEE EXAMPLE 3**
on p. 360
for Exs. 23–32

**(23.)** 40%  **24.** 87%  **25.** 32.5%  **26.** 5%  **27.** 124%

**28.** 1%  **29.** 4.2%  **30.** 200.2%  **31.** 8.03%  **32.** 0.07%

**REWRITING FRACTIONS** Write the fraction as a percent.

**SEE EXAMPLE 4**
on p. 360
for Exs. 33–42

**33.** $\frac{5}{8}$  **34.** $\frac{3}{2}$  **35.** $\frac{1}{80}$  **36.** $\frac{3}{20}$  **37.** $\frac{31}{10}$

**38.** $\frac{4}{800}$  **39.** $\frac{4}{50}$  **40.** $\frac{117}{200}$  **41.** $\frac{7}{16}$  **42.** $\frac{11}{12}$

**COMPARING** Copy and complete the statement using <, >, or =.

**SEE EXAMPLE 5**
on p. 361
for Exs. 43–51

**(43.)** $\frac{1}{4}$ ? 26%  **44.** 450% ? $\frac{9}{2}$  **45.** $\frac{13}{25}$ ? 0.5

**46.** 0.0825 ? $\frac{17}{200}$  **47.** 27% ? $\frac{1}{5}$  **48.** $\frac{7}{20}$ ? 35%

**49.** 4.5% ? 0.045  **50.** 3.83% ? 0.383  **51.** 101% ? 0.101

**ORDERING NUMBERS** Order the numbers from least to greatest.

**52.** 0.3, $\frac{9}{40}$, 22%, 0.228, $\frac{41}{125}$  **53.** 6.5%, $\frac{9}{50}$, 0.65, 66%, 0.5

**54.** $\frac{4}{7}$, 0.058, 58, 58%, 0.58%  **55.** 212%, 21.2, $\frac{21}{100}$, 0.212, $\frac{21}{10}$

**56.** $\frac{11}{15}$, 0.73, 7.3%, $\frac{75}{100}$, 0.73%  **57.** $\frac{12}{25}$, 480%, 0.484, 4.84, 4.8%

**58. ★ TAKS REASONING** Which numbers are in order from least to greatest?

**(A)** 0.25, 2.5%, $\frac{2}{7}$  **(B)** 2.5%, 0.25, $\frac{2}{7}$  **(C)** 0.25, $\frac{2}{7}$, 2.5%  **(D)** 2.5%, $\frac{2}{7}$, 0.25

**59. WHICH ONE DOESN'T BELONG?** When written as a percent, which fraction is not like the others?

**A.** $\frac{9}{8}$  **B.** $\frac{5}{4}$  **C.** $\frac{7}{4}$  **D.** $\frac{31}{20}$

**60. ERROR ANALYSIS** A student says that because $\frac{1}{4}$ equals 25% and 5 is greater than 4, $\frac{1}{5}$ must be greater than 25%. Describe and correct the error in the student's reasoning.

**COMPARING PERCENTS** Use graph paper to illustrate.

**61.** 45% and 4.5%  **62.** $33\frac{1}{3}$% and $3\frac{1}{3}$%  **63.** 20% and 2%  **64.** 75% and 7.5%

**65. CHALLENGE** Is 50% of 30% of 120 the same as $\frac{3}{20}$ of 120? *Explain.*

**LANGUAGES** The circle graph shows the world languages that U.S. high school students studied in a recent year. Each fraction represents part of the total number of U.S. high school students who studied a world language.

*SEE EXAMPLE 4*
on p. 360
for Exs. 66–72

**66.** Which language was the most popular?

**67.** What percent of the students studied German?

**68.** What percent of the students studied French or German?

**69.** What percent of the students did *not* study Spanish?

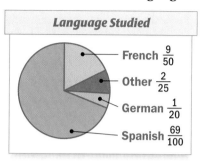

**Language Studied**

French $\frac{9}{50}$

Other $\frac{2}{25}$

German $\frac{1}{20}$

Spanish $\frac{69}{100}$

**70. SLEEPING** You survey 48 people and find that 18 of them sleep eight hours a night. What percent sleep eight hours a night?

**71.** ⬇ **TAKS REASONING** There are 25 cars in a parking lot. Nine of the cars are red. The rest of the cars are black or white.

    **a.** What percent of cars in the lot are red? *not* red?

    **b.** *Describe* two ways to determine the percent of cars that are *not* black given the number of white cars.

**72. REASONING** If a fraction is greater than 1, what do you know about the equivalent percent? *Explain.*

*SEE EXAMPLE 5*
on p. 361
for Ex. 73

**73.** ◆ **MULTIPLE REPRESENTATIONS** A survey asked fathers to name the five most indispensable products to fathers with a newborn. The results are as follows: $\frac{17}{20}$ said infant carrier/car seat, $\frac{1}{2}$ said pacifier, 0.7 said stroller, $\frac{19}{50}$ said baby monitor, and 79% said disposable diapers. Order the numbers from least to greatest. *Check* using a number line.

**74. WRITING** The table shows the percents of people who buy various types of music. *Explain* why the data should *not* be represented in a circle graph. Then display the data in an appropriate way.

| Music | Rock | Pop | Rap | R&B | Country |
|-------|------|-----|-----|-----|---------|
| Percent | 25.2% | 8.9% | 13.3% | 10.6% | 10.4% |

**75.** ⬇ **TAKS REASONING** Sometimes a percent is greater than 100. For example, a store can sell 125% of the number of sweaters it sold last year. *Describe* a situation where a percent should not be greater than 100.

**76.** ⬇ **TAKS REASONING** A football field is 100 yards long, excluding the end zones. Approximately what percent of a mile is a football field's length?

    **(A)** 1.9%      **(B)** 5.7%      **(C)** 17.6%      **(D)** 52.8%

**77. CHALLENGE** You conduct a survey about laundry detergent. Brand A is preferred by $\frac{2}{15}$ of the people. Brand B is preferred by $\frac{5}{12}$ of the people. Of the remaining people, 80% prefer Brand C and the rest have no preference. What percent of all the people surveyed have no preference?

**MIXED REVIEW FOR TAKS**  **TAKS** PRACTICE at classzone.com

*REVIEW*
Lesson 7.3;
TAKS Workbook

**78.** **TAKS PRACTICE** At a high school, ninth graders chose between three elective courses. Of 160 students, 40% elected sociology, 45% chose a media literacy class, and 15% took philosophy. Which proportion will let you find *p*, the number of students who took philosophy? *TAKS Obj. 2*

(A) $\frac{15}{100} = \frac{r}{60}$    (B) $\frac{100}{160} = \frac{r}{15}$    (C) $\frac{15}{100} = \frac{160}{r}$    (D) $\frac{15}{100} = \frac{r}{160}$

*REVIEW*
Lesson 1.6;
TAKS Workbook

**79.** **TAKS PRACTICE** How long will it take a car to travel 279 miles at a rate of 62 miles per hour? *TAKS Obj. 2*

(F) 3.3 h    (G) 3 h 30 min    (H) 4.3 h    (J) 4 h 30 min

*REVIEW*
Lesson 6.4;
TAKS Workbook

**80.** **TAKS PRACTICE** A wheel travels about 150 inches in 3 full rotations. What is the approximate radius of the wheel? *TAKS Obj. 3*

(A) 8 in.    (B) 16 in.    (C) 24 in.    (D) 50 in.

---

**QUIZ** *for Lessons 7.1–7.4*

**SIMPLIFYING RATIOS** **A box of animal crackers contains 6 gorillas, 5 bears, 4 camels, 2 monkeys, 2 sheep, and 1 lion. Write the ratio in simplest form.** *(p. 343)*

**1.** gorillas to sheep     **2.** monkeys to camels     **3.** bears to lions

**Solve the proportion.** *(p. 348)*

**4.** $\frac{a}{72} = \frac{5}{6}$       **5.** $\frac{2}{3} = \frac{7}{x}$       **6.** $\frac{18}{27} = \frac{y}{3}$

**7.** $\frac{6}{8} = \frac{b}{28}$       **8.** $\frac{12}{c} = \frac{23}{92}$       **9.** $\frac{z}{8} = \frac{95}{19}$

**10. CLOTHING SALES** You save 40% when buying a shirt that originally cost $29. How much do you save? *(p. 354)*

**GARDENING** **The circle graph shows the numbers of flowers that you planted in a flowerbed.** *(p. 359)*

**11.** How many flowers did you plant?

**12.** What percent of the flowerbed is daffodils?

**13.** What two types of flowers combine to equal 70%?

*Flowers Planted*

— Carnations **12**
— Daffodils **9**
— Tulips **6**
— Sunflowers **3**

## Lessons 7.1–7.4

**MULTIPLE CHOICE**

1. **CARS** Two cars are traveling at the rates of speed shown below. What is the speed of the car traveling the fastest? *TEKS 8.3.B*

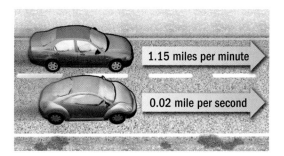

1.15 miles per minute

0.02 mile per second

Ⓐ 51 miles per hour

Ⓑ 69 miles per hour

Ⓒ 72 miles per hour

Ⓓ 115 miles per hour

2. **WATERMELON** Water makes up about 95% of the weight of a watermelon. About how much weight of a 12 pound watermelon is *not* water? *TEKS 8.3.B*

Ⓕ 6 oz          Ⓖ 10 oz

Ⓗ 6 lb          Ⓙ 11 lb 6 oz

3. **PHOTOCOPIERS** A photocopier was upgraded. The new machine outputs 223% more copies than before. The original machine produced 10 copies per minute. About how many copies per minute does the new machine produce? *TEKS 8.14.B*

Ⓐ 2          Ⓑ 12

Ⓒ 22          Ⓓ 32

4. **WEATHER** There were 3 cloudy days and 4 sunny days last week. Which is the ratio of sunny days to cloudy days? *TEKS 8.4.A*

Ⓕ 3 : 4          Ⓖ 3 : 7

Ⓗ 4 : 3          Ⓙ 4 : 7

5. **FREE THROWS** In a 3 game basketball tournament, Alma made 1 out of 4 free throws in the first game. She made 2 out of 5 free throws in the second game. In the third game, she attempted 6 free throws. If Alma made 60% of her attempted free throws during the tournament, how many free throws did she make in the third game? *TEKS 8.3.B*

Ⓐ 2          Ⓑ 4

Ⓒ 5          Ⓓ 6

6. **SURVEY** Gillian surveyed students on their favorite day of the week. Of those who replied, 0.9% said Tuesday, $\frac{1}{4}$ said Friday, 60% said Saturday, and 0.1 said Sunday. What percent of students did NOT choose the 2 most favored days of the week? *TEKS 8.1.B*

Ⓕ 11%          Ⓖ 15%

Ⓗ 30%          Ⓙ 85%

**GRIDDED ANSWER** ⊙①●③④⑤⑥⑦⑧⑨

7. **MODELS** A scale model of the Bank One Center in Dallas, Texas, has a scale of 1 in. : 100 ft. The height of the actual building is 787 feet. The width of the model is 5.16 inches less than the height of the model. What is the model's width in inches? *TEKS 8.14.C*

# 7.5 Percent of Change

TEKS *8.3.B, 8.14.A*

| | |
|---|---|
| **Before** | You solved problems with percents. |
| **Now** | You'll solve problems with percent of increase or decrease. |
| **Why?** | To find percent of change, as with tourism in Example 3. |

**KEY VOCABULARY**
- **percent of change,** *p. 366*
- **percent of increase,** *p. 366*
- **percent of decrease,** *p. 366*

A **percent of change** shows how much a quantity has increased or decreased from the original amount. When the new amount is greater than the original amount, the percent of change is called a **percent of increase**. When the new amount is less than the original amount, it is called a **percent of decrease**.

> ### KEY CONCEPT
> *For Your Notebook*
>
> **Percent of Change**
>
> Use the following equation to find the percent of change.
>
> $$\text{Percent of change, } p\% = \frac{\text{Amount of increase or decrease}}{\text{Original amount}}$$

### EXAMPLE 1 Finding a Percent of Decrease

**Bears** During the summer, a bear's heart rate is about 60 beats per minute, but it can drop to as low as 8 beats per minute during the winter. What is the percent of change in a bear's heart rate from the summer rate to the winter low rate?

#### SOLUTION

To find the percent of decrease, use the percent of change equation.

$p\% = \dfrac{60 - 8}{60}$     **Write amount of decrease and divide by original amount.**

$= \dfrac{52}{60}$     **Subtract.**

$= 0.8\overline{6}$     **Write fraction as a decimal.**

$\approx 86.67\%$     **Write decimal as a percent.**

*REVIEW DECIMALS*
Need help with repeating decimals? See p. 255.

▶ **Answer** The percent of decrease is about 86.7%.

## EXAMPLE 2 Finding a Percent of Increase

**School Enrollment** A school had 825 students enrolled last year. This year, 870 students are enrolled. Find the percent of increase to the nearest tenth.

**SOLUTION**

**AVOID ERRORS**
Make sure you use the original amount, not the new amount, in the denominator when finding a percent of change.

$$p\% = \frac{870 - 825}{825}$$    Write amount of decrease and divide by original amount.

$$= \frac{45}{825}$$    Subtract.

$$= 0.05\overline{45}$$    Write fraction as a decimal.

$$\approx 5.45\%$$    Write decimal as a percent.

▶ **Answer** The percent of increase is about 5.5%.

**Decimal Method** A shortcut to finding a percent of a number is to write the percent as a decimal and then find the product of the decimal and the number. For example, 10% of 60 = 0.10(60) = 6.

## EXAMPLE 3 Using Percent of Increase

**National Parks** From October to November one year, attendance at Everglades National Park increased about 27.4%. There were 59,084 visitors in October. To the nearest hundred, how many people visited in November?

**SOLUTION**

**ANOTHER WAY**
Using a proportion in Step 1 will give the same result as multiplying by a decimal.

$\frac{a}{60} = \frac{10}{100}$

$a = \frac{10}{100}(60)$

$a = 0.1(60)$

**STEP 1** **Find** the increase.

Increase = **27.4%** of 59,084

$$= \mathbf{0.274}(59,084)$$    Write 27.4% as a decimal.

$$\approx 16,189$$    Multiply.

**STEP 2** **Add** the increase to the original amount.

New Amount ≈ 59,084 + 16,189 = 75,273

▶ **Answer** About 75,300 people visited the park in November.

## ✓ GUIDED PRACTICE    for Examples 1, 2, and 3

**Tell whether the change is an *increase* or *decrease*. Then find the percent of change. Round to the nearest percent.**

**1.** Original amount: 50
New amount: 36

**2.** Original amount: 10
New amount: 29.5

**3.** Original amount: 90
New amount: 110

**4.** **What If?** In Example 3, suppose the attendance decreased by about 11%. Approximate, to the nearest thousand, the attendance in November.

# 7.5 EXERCISES

HOMEWORK KEY

✦ = TAKS Practice and Reasoning
Exs. 8, 27, 28, 33, and 35

○ = HINTS AND HOMEWORK HELP
for Exs. 3, 7, 9, 13, 27 at classzone.com

## SKILL PRACTICE

1. **VOCABULARY** Copy and complete: When the original amount is less than the new amount, the percent of change is called a(n) __?__ .

**FINDING PERCENT OF CHANGE** Tell whether the change is an *increase* or *decrease*. Then find the percent of change. Round to the nearest percent.

*SEE EXAMPLES 1 AND 2*
on pp. 366–367
for Exs. 2–8

2. 10 rabbits to 16 rabbits

3. 360 pounds to 352 pounds

4. $33,300 to $31,080

5. 12,200 voters to 13,908 voters

6. 50 minutes to 45 minutes

7. 350 meters to 420 meters

8. ✦ **TAKS REASONING** An increase from 1 to 3 is what percent of increase?

Ⓐ 66.7%    Ⓑ 100%    Ⓒ 200%    Ⓓ 300%

**FINDING NEW AMOUNTS** Find the new amount.

*SEE EXAMPLE 3*
on p. 367
for Exs. 9–14

9. 1100 is increased by 4%.

10. 24,700 is decreased by 13%.

11. 8 is increased by 60%.

12. 65 is decreased by 30%.

13. 88,000 is decreased by 12.5%.

14. 26,000 is increased by 14.6%.

15. **ERROR ANALYSIS** Your friend says "Multiplying a number by 5 is a 500% increase." Describe and correct the error in your friend's reasoning.

(XV) **ALGEBRA** Find the percent of increase or decrease.

16. $x$ to $4x$

17. $6b$ to $9b$

18. $d$ to $5d$

19. $4h$ to $6h$

20. $y$ to $\frac{3}{8}y$

21. $4.5a$ to $2.25a$

22. $5m$ to $4.5m$

23. $z$ to $\frac{3}{4}z$

24. **CHALLENGE** A number increases by 50%, and then decreases by 50%. What is the percent of change from the original number to the final number?

## PROBLEM SOLVING

*SEE EXAMPLE 3*
on p. 367
for Ex. 25

25. **GUIDED PROBLEM SOLVING** In 1975, there were 130,000 tennis courts in the United States. This number increased by 69% from 1975 to 1985. The number then increased by 9% from 1985 to 1995. How many tennis courts were in the United States in 1985 and in 1995?

a. Find the number of tennis courts in 1985.

b. Find the amount of the second increase.

c. Find the number of tennis courts in 1995.

**SEE EXAMPLE 3**
on p. 367
for Ex. 26

**26.** **POPULATION**  The population of the United States in 1993 was about 260,255,000. In 2003, it was about 291,049,000. Find the percent of increase to the nearest tenth of a percent.

**27.** **TAKS REASONING** A camera is on sale for 10% off $170, and you have a coupon for an extra 10% off. How much will this camera cost?

**(A)** $136  **(B)** $137.70  **(C)** $153  **(D)** $168.30

**28.** **TAKS REASONING** Oregon produces about 99% of the hazelnuts grown in the United States. Its record harvest was in 1997. In 2004 about how many tons of hazelnuts were produced in the United States? *Explain.*

**29.** **WRITING**      A friend says that multiplying a number by $\frac{1}{4}$ is a 25% decrease. *Explain* why this is *not* true.

**30.** **NUMBER SENSE**  Dividing a number by 5 is a decrease of what percent?

**31.** **ENLARGEMENT**  You have a photograph that is 6 inches by 4 inches. You want to enlarge it so that these dimensions are increased by 50%. What will the new dimensions be? Will the increase in area be *greater than*, *less than*, or *equal to* 50%? *Explain.*

**32.** **GEOMETRY**  The side lengths of the triangle at the right are increased by 100% to form a new triangle. What is the percent increase in area from the original triangle to the new triangle?

**33.** **TAKS REASONING**      The average time spent playing video games by a person in the United States was 60 hours in 2001. This time increased by about 11.7% from 2001 to 2002. At this rate, how many hours would you expect each person to spend playing video games in 2007? *Justify* your reasoning.

**34.** **CHALLENGE**  From 1990 to 2000 the population of Houston, Texas, increased by about 9.3%. In 2000, the population was 1,953,631. At this growth rate, is 1,772,000 a reasonable estimate for the population of Houston in 1990? *Explain.*

## MIXED REVIEW FOR TAKS
**TAKS** **PRACTICE** at classzone.com

**REVIEW**
Lesson 7.4;
TAKS Workbook

**35.** **TAKS PRACTICE**  One fifth of the cashiers at a supermarket have held their jobs for more than 2 years. If there are 30 cashiers working at the supermarket, which procedure will NOT yield the number of cashiers who have held their jobs for more than 2 years? *TAKS Obj. 6*

**(A)** Find the quotient of 30 and 6

**(B)** Multiply 30 by 0.2

**(C)** Find 20% of 30

**(D)** Divide 30 by 5

# 7.6 Percent Applications

| | |
|---|---|
| **Before** | You solved problems with percent of increase or decrease. |
| **Now** | You'll solve percent application problems. |
| **Why?** | So you can calculate sale prices, as in Example 1. |

**KEY VOCABULARY**
- **markup,** *p. 370*
- **discount,** *p. 370*

A retail store buys items from manufacturers at wholesale prices. The store then sells the items to customers at retail prices. The increase in the wholesale price of an item is a **markup**. A decrease in the retail price of an item is a **discount**. You can find the retail price or sale price of an item using the equations below.

$$\text{Retail price} = \text{Wholesale price} + \text{Markup}$$

$$\text{Sale price} = \text{Original price} - \text{Discount}$$

## EXAMPLE 1 Finding a Sale Price

**Guitars** You are shopping for a guitar and find one with an original price of $160. The store is offering a 30% discount on all guitars. What is the sale price of the guitar?

**SOLUTION**

**CHECK FOR REASONABLENESS**

Receiving a 30% discount is the same as paying 70% of the original price. So, you can find the sale price by multiplying its original price by 70%.

70% of 160 ≈
$\frac{3}{4} \times 160 = 120$
The answer is reasonable.

**STEP 1** **Find** the amount of the discount.

Discount = 30% of $160

$\quad = 0.3(160)$      **Write 30% as a decimal.**

$\quad = 48$      **Multiply.**

**STEP 2** **Subtract** the discount from the original price.

$160 - 48 = 112$

▶ **Answer** The sale price of the guitar is $112.

### ✓ GUIDED PRACTICE    for Example 1

**Find the sale price. Check that your answer is reasonable.**

1. Original price: $25
   Percent discount: 10%

2. Original price: $85.50
   Percent discount: 30%

3. Original price: $14.20
   Percent discount: 20%

4. Original price: $136.24
   Percent discount: 25%

## EXAMPLE 2  Finding a Retail Price

**Clothing**  A shirt has a wholesale price of $16. The percent markup is 120%. What is the retail price?

**SOLUTION**

**STEP 1**  **Find** the amount of the markup.

$$\text{Markup} = 120\% \text{ of } \$16$$
$$= 1.2(16) \qquad \textbf{Write 120\% as a decimal.}$$
$$= 19.2 \qquad \textbf{Multiply.}$$

*AVOID ERRORS*
Remember that the markup must be added to the wholesale price to find the retail price.

**STEP 2**  **Add** the markup to the wholesale price.

$$16 + 19.2 = 35.2$$

▶ **Answer**  The retail price of the shirt is $35.20.

**Sales Tax and Tips**  Sales tax and tips are amounts that are added to the price of some purchases. Sales tax and tips are usually calculated using a percent of the purchase price.

## EXAMPLE 3  Finding Sales Tax

**CD Player**  A portable CD player costs $48 before tax. The sales tax is 4.5%. What is the total cost?

*ANOTHER WAY*
Paying 4.5% tax on an item is the same as paying 104.5% of the original price. So, in Example 3 you can find the total cost of the CD player as follows.
$$1.045(48) = 50.16.$$

**SOLUTION**

**STEP 1**  **Find** the amount of the sales tax.

$$4.5\% \text{ of } \$48 = 0.045(48) = 2.16$$

**STEP 2**  **Add** the sales tax to the price of the portable CD player.

$$2.16 + 48 = 50.16$$

▶ **Answer**  The total cost of the CD player is $50.16.

---

✓ **GUIDED PRACTICE**  for Examples 2 and 3

**Find the retail price.**

5. Wholesale price: $64
   Percent markup: 85%

6. Wholesale price: $35
   Percent markup: 110%

**Find the total cost. Round to the nearest cent.**

7. Price: $8.90
   Sales tax: 5%

8. Price: $54.07
   Sales tax: 7%

**EXAMPLE 4** TAKS REASONING: Multi-Step Problem

**Restaurants** Your food bill at a restaurant is $24. You leave a 20% tip. The sales tax is 6%. What is the total cost of the meal?

**SOLUTION**

*AVOID ERRORS*
The tip at a restaurant is generally based on the food bill only. Do not include the sales tax when finding a tip.

**STEP 1** **Find** the amount of the tip.

20% of $24 = 0.20(24) = 4.8

**STEP 2** **Find** the amount of the sales tax.

6% of $24 = 0.06(24) = 1.44

**STEP 3** **Add** the food bill, tip, and sales tax.

24 + 4.8 + 1.44 = 30.24

▶ **Answer** The total cost of the meal is $30.24.

✓ **GUIDED PRACTICE** for Example 4

9. **What If?** In Example 4 suppose that your bill is $35, the sales tax is 6%, and you leave a 15% tip. What is the total cost of the meal?

# 7.6 EXERCISES

HOMEWORK KEY

 = **TAKS Practice and Reasoning**
Exs. 9, 28, 29, 31, 40, 41, and 42

○ = **HINTS** AND **HOMEWORK HELP**
for Exs. 3, 5, 15, 29, 33 at classzone.com

**SKILL PRACTICE**

VOCABULARY **Copy and complete the statement.**

1. To find the retail price, add the __?__ to the wholesale price.

2. The sale price is the original price minus the __?__.

FINDING PRICES **Find the sale price or retail price. Round to the nearest cent. Check that your answer is reasonable.**

*SEE EXAMPLES 1 AND 2*
on pp. 370–371
for Exs. 3–9

3. Original price: $60
   Percent discount: 15%

4. Original price: $28.50
   Percent discount: 60%

5. Wholesale price: $25
   Percent markup: 65%

6. Wholesale price: $14.50
   Percent markup: 140%

7. Original price: $42
   Percent discount: 30%

8. Wholesale price: $19
   Percent markup: 110%

9.  **TAKS REASONING** What is the price of a $16.49 item marked up 130%?

    (**A**) $12.68    (**B**) $21.44    (**C**) $37.93    (**D**) $146.49

**FINDING COSTS** Find the total cost. Round to the nearest cent.

SEE EXAMPLES
3 AND 4
on pp. 371–372
for Exs. 10–15

**10.** Original price: $72
Sales tax: 6%

**11.** Original price: $58.40
Sales tax: 5.5%

**12.** Original price: $8.40
Sales tax: 7%

**13.** Original price: $258.20
Sales tax: 6.5%

**14.** Food bill: $28.50
Tip: 18%
Sales tax: 4.5%

**15.** Food bill: $18
Tip: 20%
Sales tax: 5%

**16. ERROR ANALYSIS** The original cost of an item is $28. It has a 5% discount and a 5% sales tax. A friend says that the item should cost $28 after the discount and sales tax. Describe and correct the error in your friend's reasoning.

**PERCENT CHANGES** Tell whether the price is a *discount* or *markup*, and find the percent of discount or markup. Then find the new price for a $96 item, with the same percent of change.

**17.** Old price: $32
New price: $24

**18.** Old price: $45
New price: $40.50

**19.** Old price: $19
New price: $33.25

**20.** Old price: $55
New price: $121

**21.** Old price: $12.50
New price: $22.50

**22.** Old price: $199.99
New price: $119.99

**CHALLENGE** Find the indicated value.

**23.** Original price: ___?___
Discount: 20%
Sales tax: 7.5%
Final price: $43

**24.** Original price: $150
Discount: ___?___
Sales tax: 5%
Final price: $126

**25.** Original price: $75
Discount: 18%
Sales tax: ___?___
Final price: $63.96

## PROBLEM SOLVING

SEE EXAMPLES
3 AND 4
on pp. 371–372
for Exs. 26–29

**26. LAMP COSTS** A lamp costs $25.75. The sales tax is 4%. What is the total cost?

**27. RESTAURANT COSTS** Your food bill at a restaurant is $30. You leave a 20% tip. The sales tax is 6%. What is the total cost of the meal?

**28. TAKS REASONING** A book costs $12.95 and is on sale for 15% off. The sales tax is 6%. What is the total cost of the book?

**A** $11.01 **B** $11.67 **C** $11.78 **D** $13.73

**29. TAKS REASONING** You and two friends eat at a restaurant and split the total bill evenly. The food bill is $20.88. Sales tax is 5%. You leave a 20% tip. How much should each person pay?

**A** $6.96 **B** $7.31 **C** $8.35 **D** $8.70

**30. ESTIMATION** The original price of an item is $42 and the percent of discount is 25%. *Explain* how to estimate the sale price.

SEE EXAMPLE 4
on p. 372
for Ex. 31

SEE EXAMPLES
1 AND 2
on pp. 370–371
for Exs. 32–33

31. ⬥ **TAKS REASONING** Find both the 15% and 20% tips for a food bill that totals $24.20. *Explain* why people often leave a tip between 15% and 20% rather than leaving exactly 15% or 20%.

32. **GASOLINE** Though gasoline prices may change quickly, the markup is usually $.12 per gallon. What percent is that if the wholesale price is $3 per gallon?

33. **CLOTHING** The wholesale price of a shirt is $15. A store marks up the price by 75%. When the shirts don't sell, the store offers a 20% discount. What is the sale price of the shirts?

34. **TIPPING** You order a pizza to be delivered. The bill comes to $12.60. You pay $15 and tell the delivery person to keep the change. Is your tip *more* or *less* than 20%? *Explain.*

35. **DVD COSTS** A DVD has a regular price of $26 and is on sale for $16.90. What is the percent discount? How much would a $59 DVD boxed set cost if it has the same discount?

36. **SPORTING GOODS** A basketball has a wholesale price of $12 and is marked up 115%. Later it is discounted 15%. The sales tax is 4.5%. Find the final cost of the basketball including tax. Round to the nearest cent.

37. **WRITING** A store is having a sale offering a discount of 40% on all coats. One week later the store discounts the coats an extra 60%. Is the store giving away the coats for free? *Explain* your reasoning.

38. **ELECTRONICS** After a 125% markup and a 10% discount, the price of an MP3 player is $30.78 before tax. What was the wholesale price?

39. **CHALLENGE** A total bill, including sales tax and tip, is $33. The tax is 4% and the tip is 16% of the bill before tax. Find the cost before tax and tip.

## MIXED REVIEW FOR TAKS

**TAKS** PRACTICE at classzone.com

REVIEW
Lesson 1.7;
TAKS Workbook

40. ⬥ **TAKS PRACTICE** Roger evaluates the expression $2n + 5$ for several values of $n$, including $n = 1$, $n = 2$, $n = 3$, and $n = 4$. He notices a pattern in the results of 7, 9, 11, and 13. If he continues writing out this pattern, what will be the value of the ninth term? *TAKS Obj. 2*

  (A) 9      (B) 15      (C) 18      (D) 23

REVIEW
Lesson 5.8;
TAKS Workbook

41. ⬥ **TAKS PRACTICE** Vinny buys shirts for $4.99, $10.99, and $8.99. Then he buys one more shirt. If the average price of all 4 shirts was $8.24, how much did the fourth shirt cost? *TAKS Obj. 6*

  (F) $6.99      (G) $7.99      (H) $8.99      (J) $9.99

REVIEW
Lesson 7.3;
TAKS Workbook

42. ⬥ **TAKS PRACTICE** Which expression shows 4.5% of 30? *TAKS Obj. 2*

  (A) 4.5(30)                (B) 0.45(30)

  (C) 0.045(30)             (D) 30 ÷ 4.5

🔎 **ONLINE QUIZ** at classzone.com

# 7.7 Using the Percent Equation

TEKS 8.1.B, 8.3.B

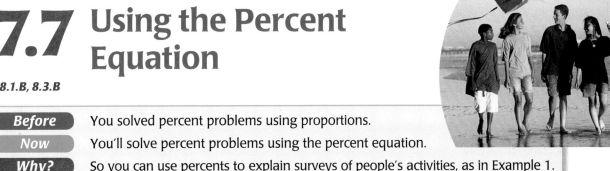

| **Before** | You solved percent problems using proportions. |
| **Now** | You'll solve percent problems using the percent equation. |
| **Why?** | So you can use percents to explain surveys of people's activities, as in Example 1. |

**KEY VOCABULARY**
- **interest,** *p. 376*
- **principal,** *p. 376*
- **annual interest rate,** *p. 376*

In Lesson 7.3, you solved percent problems using the proportion $\frac{a}{b} = \frac{p}{100}$.

If you multiply each side of this by $b$, you get the *percent equation* summarized below and used in this lesson.

---

**KEY CONCEPT** *For Your Notebook*

**The Percent Equation**

To represent the statement "$a$ is $p$ percent of $b$" use the equation:

$$a = p\% \cdot b \qquad \text{Part of the base} = \text{Percent} \cdot \text{Base}$$

---

**EXAMPLE 1** Finding Part of a Base

*ANOTHER WAY*
You could also find the answer by solving the proportion:

$$\frac{a}{2000} = \frac{26.7}{100}$$

**Beaches** In a survey of 2000 people, 26.7% said that they visited a beach during the past year. How many people said they visited a beach during the past year?

**SOLUTION**

Use the percent equation.

| $a = p\% \cdot b$ | **Write percent equation.** |
| $= 26.7\% \cdot 2000$ | **Substitute 26.7 for $p$ and 2000 for $b$.** |
| $= 0.267 \cdot 2000$ | **Write percent as a decimal.** |
| $= 534$ | **Multiply.** |

▶ **Answer** The number of people who said they visited a beach during the past year is 534.

**Check** Estimate $26.7 \approx 25$, and 25% of 2000 is 500. So the answer is reasonable.

---

 **GUIDED PRACTICE** for Example 1

**Use the percent equation.**

1. Find 45% of 700.
2. Find 110% of 320.
3. Find 0.5% of 450.

## EXAMPLE 2    Finding a Base

**Student Council** Marc received 273, or 35%, of the votes in the student council election. How many students voted in the election?

$$a = p\% \cdot b \qquad \text{Write percent equation.}$$

$$273 = 35\% \cdot b \qquad \text{Substitute 273 for } a \text{ and 35 for } p.$$

$$273 = 0.35 \cdot b \qquad \text{Write 35\% as a decimal.}$$

$$780 = b \qquad \text{Divide each side by 0.35.}$$

▸ **Answer** 780 students voted in the election.

**READING**

To set up the percent equation correctly, make sure you read the problem carefully. Then think of a question that represents what you need to find out: "273 is 35% of what number?"

---

**Simple Interest** **Interest** is an amount paid for the use of money. **Principal** is the amount you borrow or deposit. When interest is paid only on the principal, it is called *simple interest*. The percent of the principal you pay or earn per year is the **annual interest rate**.

**VOCABULARY**

When you borrow money from a bank, you pay interest on the amount you borrowed.

---

### KEY CONCEPT                                  *For Your Notebook*

**Simple Interest**

**Words**    To find simple interest $I$, find the product of the principal $P$, the *annual* interest rate $r$ written as a decimal, and the time $t$ in years.

**Algebra**    $I = Prt$

---

## EXAMPLE 3    Finding Simple Interest

**Savings** You deposit $500 in a savings account that pays a simple interest rate of 2.5% per year. How much interest will you earn after 18 months?

$$I = Prt \qquad \text{Write formula for simple interest.}$$

$$= (500)(0.025)(1.5) \qquad \text{Substitute values. 18 months} = 1.5 \text{ years.}$$

$$= 18.75 \qquad \text{Multiply.}$$

▸ **Answer** You will earn $18.75 in interest.

*Animated* **Math**
at classzone.com

**CHECK FOR REASONABLENESS**

The interest for 1 year is a little over 2% of $500, or $10. So the interest for a year and a half is a little over $15. The answer is reasonable.

---

✓ **GUIDED PRACTICE**    for Examples 2 and 3

**Solve using the percent equation.**

**4.** 6.4 is 62.5% of what number?          **5.** 15 is what percent of 120?

**6. What If?** Suppose the simple interest rate in Example 3 is 3.5%. How much interest will you earn after 24 months?

## 7.7 EXERCISES

### SKILL PRACTICE

1. **VOCABULARY** What do you call the amount earned or paid for the use of money?

2. **VOCABULARY** Copy and complete: To find simple interest, multiply the annual interest rate written as a decimal, the time in years, and the _?_.

**PERCENT EQUATION** Solve using the percent equation.

*SEE EXAMPLES 1 AND 2*
on pp. 375–376
for Exs. 3–15

3. What number is 46% of 900?

4. 205 is what percent of 250?

5. 132 is 24% of what number?

6. What number is 95% of 420?

7. What number is 120% of 55?

8. What number is 0.4% of 150?

9. 115 is 46% of what number?

10. 26 is 130% of what number?

11. 62.4 is 80% of what number?

12. 289.25 is 89% of what number?

13. 3 is what percent of 600?

14. 291.04 is what percent of 856?

15. **ERROR ANALYSIS** Describe and correct the error made in finding the solution.

> ✗ 54 is 60% of what number?
> 54 = 60 · b
> 0.9 = b

**INTEREST** Find the amount of simple interest earned. Check for reasonableness.

*SEE EXAMPLE 3*
on p. 376
for Exs. 16–18

16. Principal: $250
Annual rate: 2%
Time: 3 years

17. Principal : $940
Annual rate: 3.5%
Time: 30 months

18. Principal : $620
Annual rate: 3%
Time: 20 months

**MENTAL MATH** Solve for the unknown amount.

19. 60% of 60 = 90% of _?_

20. 20% of 70 = _?_% of 280

21. 0.5% of 140 = _?_% of 70

22. 160% of 25 = 80% of _?_

23. ◆ **TAKS REASONING** You deposit $450 into an account that earns simple interest at an annual rate of 4.5%. Which expression could be used to find the amount of money in the account after 2 years?

(A) 450(0.045)(2)

(B) 450(0.45)(2)

(C) 450 + 450(0.045)(2)

(D) 450 + 450(0.45)(2)

**USING A FORMULA** Use the formula $I = Prt$ to find the unknown value.

24. $I = \$12.50$
$P = \$500$
$r = \underline{\ ?\ }$
$t = 6$ months

25. $I = \$89.25$
$P = \$850$
$r = 5.25\%$
$t = \underline{\ ?\ }$

26. $I = \$260$
$P = \underline{\ ?\ }$
$r = 6.5\%$
$t = 4$ years

27. $I = \$320$
$P = \underline{\ ?\ }$
$r = 8\%$
$t = 2$ years

**28. CHALLENGE** Using principal = $10,000, rate = $x$%, and years = $y$, write an expression for interest. Suppose the interest rate doubles to $2x$%. What values of $y$ result in the same interest as before? more interest than before? less interest than before?

## PROBLEM SOLVING

*SEE EXAMPLE 3*
on p. 376
for Exs. 29, 33

**29. GUIDED PROBLEM SOLVING** A savings account pays a 3% simple annual interest rate. How much must you put in the savings account to earn $100 in interest in 6 months?

  **a.** Write the simple interest formula.

  **b.** Substitute known values in the formula.

  **c.** Solve the equation for *P*. Round to the nearest cent.

*SEE EXAMPLES 1 AND 2*
on pp. 375–376
for Exs. 30–32

**30. WEATHER** In Charlotte, North Carolina, an average of 30.7% of the days of a year have precipitation. How many days in a year does Charlotte have precipitation? Round to the nearest day.

**31.** 🔷 **TAKS REASONING** You save $63.60 when you purchase a jacket on sale. The jacket was discounted 30% off its regular price. What was the regular price of the jacket?

  **A** $82.68    **B** $90.86    **C** $108.12    **D** $212.00

**32.** 🔷 **TAKS REASONING** Vicki hears on the local news that 37.5% of the movie theaters in her city, or 6 theaters, offer discount tickets to students. Write and solve a percent equation to determine the number of theaters in Vicki's city. Then solve the problem using a proportion. *Compare* the methods.

**33. LOAN** You borrow $1200 from a bank that charges 9.5% simple annual interest. After 15 months you pay back the loan. How much interest do you pay on the loan? What is the total amount that you pay the bank?

**34. MULTI-STEP PROBLEM** The area of the state of Texas is 171.1 million acres. Of this, 15.7% is cropland.

  **a.** How much of Texas is cropland? Round to the nearest hundred thousand acres.

  **b.** About 10,500 acres of the cropland in Texas are planted with peppers. What percent of cropland in Texas is planted with peppers? Round to the nearest hundredth of a percent.

**35. WRITING** Are the solutions of $\frac{12}{b} = \frac{3}{100}$ and $12 = 3\% \cdot b$ the same or different? *Explain* your reasoning.

**36. SAVINGS** How much money must you deposit in a savings account that pays a 4% simple annual interest rate to earn $50 in 60 months?

**37. LOOK FOR A PATTERN** Copy and complete the table by finding the percent of each number. *Describe* the relationship you see among the three results in each row. *Explain* how you could use this relationship to help you find a percent of a number.

|    | 5% | 10% | 15% |
|----|----|-----|-----|
| 22 | ?  | 2.2 | ?   |
| 50 | ?  | ?   | ?   |
| 76 | ?  | ?   | ?   |

**38. TAKS REASONING** Give two different principals and simple interest rates for a bank account that pays $39 in interest over a 3 year period.

**CHALLENGE** *Compound interest* on a savings account is earned on both the principal and on any interest that has already been earned. Each time the interest is compounded, you multiply the amount currently in the account, including interest, by the interest rate for that time period.

**39.** You deposit $500 into an account that earns an annual interest rate of 4% compounded annually. How much will you have in your account after the third year? after the sixth year? Round your answers to the nearest cent.

**40.** You have the option to invest $1000 in a 6 month certificate of deposit that earns 3.6% simple interest or in a savings account that pays a monthly interest rate of 0.22% compounded monthly. How long would you have to leave your money in the savings account to earn the same amount as by investing in the CD?

---

## MIXED REVIEW FOR TAKS

**TAKS PRACTICE** at classzone.com

REVIEW
Lesson 7.3;
TAKS Workbook

**41. TAKS PRACTICE** Science professors decide to hold two races to raise money for high school science labs. One race is described on their fundraising flyers as a $2.0 \times 10^4$ meter race, and the other as a $2.0 \times 10^3$ meter race. The length of the second race is what percent of the length of the first race? *TAKS Obj. 2*

**(A)** 1%  **(B)** 2%  **(C)** 10%  **(D)** 20%

---

## Brain Game

### Shrink Ray

Ray invents two zappers that shrink and enlarge things.

After shrinking almost everything in the house to *40%* of its original size, Ray's mother demands that he return things to normal. What percent setting should he use to zap objects back to their original size?

The next day Ray uses the zapper to enlarge things by *60%*.
What percent setting should he use to get them back to their normal size?

*Animated Math* at classzone.com

---

**EXTRA PRACTICE** for Lesson 7.7, p. 807          **ONLINE QUIZ** at classzone.com          **379**

**GOAL**
Use a calculator to compute compound interest.

 **TEKS** *8.3.B, 8.14.D*

# 7.7 Compound Interest

*Compound interest* is interest earned on both the principal and on any interest that has already been earned.

**EXAMPLE** Mark deposits $2000 into an account that pays an annual interest rate of 3.5% compounded annually. He doesn't add or remove money from his account for 4 years. How much money will Mark have in 4 years?

**SOLUTION**

The balance of an account after a year can be found by multiplying the principal balance by the sum of 1 and the annual interest rate written as a decimal. Use the keystrokes below to find the amount of money in the account in 4 years. Round the answer only after the final 4th year, not after each year.

**Keystrokes**                                    **Display**

2000 [=] [×] 1.035 [=]              | 2070 | In 1 year

[=]              | 2142.45 | In 2 years

[=]              | 2217.43575 | In 3 years

[=]              | 2295.046001 | In 4 years

▶ **Answer** Mark will have $2295.05 in his account in 4 years.

**PRACTICE** Find the balance of the account earning compound interest.

1. Principal: $7000
   Annual rate: 2%
   Time: 4 years

2. Principal: $7000
   Annual rate: 4%
   Time: 2 years

3. Principal: $1995
   Annual rate: 6.5%
   Time: 10 years

4. **COMPARE** You deposit $1500 into an account that pays an interest rate of 4% compounded annually. Your friend deposits $1500 into an account that pays a simple annual interest rate of 4%. Compare the balances of the two accounts after 5 years.

5. **COMPARE** You deposit $9000, into an account that pays an interest rate of 3.5% compounded annually. Your sister deposits $10,000 into an account that pays a simple annual interest rate of 2.5%. Compare balances of the two accounts after 10 years.

# 7.8 Simple Probability

| | |
|---|---|
| **Before** | You found ratios. |
| **Now** | You'll find probabilities of events. |
| **Why?** | So you can make predictions, as for picking shirt colors in Ex. 37. |

**KEY VOCABULARY**

- **outcome,** *p. 381*
- **event,** *p. 381*
- **favorable outcome,** *p. 381*
- **probability of an event,** *p. 381*
- **theoretical probability,** *p. 381*
- **experimental probability,** *p. 382*

## ACTIVITY

**You can toss a coin to perform a probability experiment.**

**STEP 1** **Copy** and complete the table at the right by tossing a coin 20 times.

| Number of heads | ? |
|---|---|
| Number of tails | ? |

**STEP 2** **Use** the data to write each ratio below. Then compare the ratios.

a. $\dfrac{\text{Number of heads}}{\text{Total number of coin tosses}}$     b. $\dfrac{\text{Number of tails}}{\text{Total number of coin tosses}}$

**STEP 3** **Combine** your results with those of the other students in your class. Compare the class ratios with your own ratios.

In the activity, you performed an experiment. The possible results of an experiment are **outcomes**. An **event** is a collection of outcomes. Once you specify an event, the outcomes for that event are called **favorable outcomes**. The **probability of an event** is the likelihood that the event will occur.

Probabilities can range from 0 to 1. The closer the probability of an event is to 1, the more likely it is that the event will occur.

| $P = 0$ | $P = 0.25$ | $P = 0.5$ | $P = 0.75$ | $P = 1$ |
|---|---|---|---|---|
| Impossible | Unlikely | Likely to occur half the time | Likely | Certain |

## KEY CONCEPT                    *For Your Notebook*

### Probability of an Event

The **theoretical probability** of an event when all outcomes are equally likely is:

$$P(\text{event}) = \frac{\text{Number of favorable outcomes}}{\text{Number of possible outcomes}}$$

## EXAMPLE 1 Using Theoretical Probability

**Coin Toss** Predict the number of times a coin will land heads up in 50 coin tosses. There are two equally likely outcomes when you toss the coin, heads or tails.

$$P(\text{heads}) = \frac{\text{Number of favorable outcomes}}{\text{Number of possible outcomes}} = \frac{1}{2}$$

**▶ Answer** You can predict that $\frac{1}{2}$, or 25, of the tosses will land heads up.

*READING*
The notation "P(event)" is read "the probability of an event."

**Experimental Probability** An **experimental probability** is based on the results of a sample or experiment. Experimental probability is the ratio of number of favorable outcomes to the total number of times the experiment was performed. This ratio is sometimes called *relative frequency*.

## EXAMPLE 2 Finding Experimental Probability

**You roll a number cube 100 times. Your results are given in the table below. Find the experimental probability of rolling a 6.**

| Number | 1 | 2 | 3 | 4 | 5 | 6 |
|--------|----|----|----|----|----|----|
| Rolls | 17 | 15 | 20 | 16 | 14 | 18 |

*WRITE PROBABILITIES*
A probability can be expressed as a fraction, as a decimal, or as a percent.

$$P(\text{rolling a 6}) = \frac{18}{100} \quad\longleftarrow\quad \textbf{Number of favorable outcomes}$$
$$\longleftarrow\quad \textbf{Total number of rolls}$$

$$= 0.18 = 18\%$$

**▶ Answer** The experimental probability of rolling a 6 is 18%.

## EXAMPLE 3 TAKS PRACTICE: Multiple Choice

**Quality Control** A company manufactures buttons. A quality control inspector finds 3 defective buttons in a batch of 375 buttons. About how many buttons would you expect to be defective in a shipment of 20,450 buttons?

**(A)** 3  **(B)** 55  **(C)** 164  **(D)** 375

*ELIMINATE CHOICES*
Because about 3 buttons are defective in every batch of 375, the number of defective buttons in a shipment of 20,450 must be well over 3. So, you can eliminate choice A.

### SOLUTION

**STEP 1** **Find** the experimental probability of a button being defective.

$$P(\text{defective}) = \frac{3}{375} = \frac{1}{125}$$

**STEP 2** **Multiply** the probability by the total number of buttons in the shipment and round to the nearest whole number.

$$\frac{1}{125} \times 20{,}450 \approx 164$$

**▶ Answer** You could expect about 164 buttons in a shipment of 20,450 to be defective. The correct answer is C. **(A) (B) (C) (D)**

1. **Number Cube** Use the information given in Example 2. What is the experimental probability of rolling a number greater than 3? What is the theoretical probability of this event?

2. **What If?** Use the information in Example 3. About how many buttons would you expect to be defective in a shipment of 25,000 buttons?

# 7.8 EXERCISES

HOMEWORK KEY

🏈 = **TAKS Practice and Reasoning**
Exs. 19, 30, 32, 34, 36, 37, and 41

◯ = **HINTS AND HOMEWORK HELP**
for Exs. 5, 9, 11, 15, 29 at classzone.com

## SKILL PRACTICE

1. **VOCABULARY** Copy and complete: The favorable outcomes for rolling an even number on a number cube are ___?___ .

2. **VOCABULARY** Describe the difference between experimental and theoretical probability.

**THEORETICAL PROBABILITY** **You randomly draw a tile from a bag that contains 10 A-tiles, 7 E-tiles, 6 I-tiles, 5 O-tiles, and 2 U-tiles. Find the theoretical probability of the event. Write as a fraction in simplest form.**

**SEE EXAMPLE 1**
on p. 382
for Exs. 3–8

3. You draw an A.
4. You draw an I.
5. You draw an I or an O.
6. You draw an E or a U.
7. You draw a Z.
8. You draw a vowel.

**EXPERIMENTAL PROBABILITY** **You roll a number cube 250 times. Your results are shown in the table. Find the experimental probability of the event.**

**SEE EXAMPLE 2**
on p. 382
for Exs. 9–13

9. You roll a 4.
10. You roll a 2.
11. You roll a number greater than 3.
12. You roll an odd number.
13. You roll a number divisible by 1.

| Number | Outcomes | Number | Outcomes |
|--------|----------|--------|----------|
| 1 | 40 | 4 | 50 |
| 2 | 42 | 5 | 35 |
| 3 | 48 | 6 | 35 |

*Animated* Math at classzone.com

**USING EXPERIMENTAL PROBABILITY** **You randomly draw a marble from a bag of 120 marbles. You record its color and replace it. Use the results to estimate the number of marbles in the bag that are the given color.**

**SEE EXAMPLE 3**
on p. 382
for Exs. 14–17

14. Yellow
15. Green
16. Red
17. Blue

| Red | Yellow | Green |
|-----|--------|-------|
| 7 | 3 | 5 |

*Animated* Math at classzone.com

18. **ERROR ANALYSIS** A student spins a two-color spinner a number of times. The pointer lands on red 7 times and on blue 13 times. Describe and correct the error made in the solution.

> Experimental probability of spinning red = $\frac{7}{13}$

19. 🔸 **TAKS REASONING** What is the probability of getting a multiple of 3 when rolling a number cube?

   (A) $\frac{3}{10}$      (B) $\frac{1}{3}$      (C) $\frac{1}{2}$      (D) $\frac{2}{3}$

**FINDING PROBABILITY** In Exercises 20–23, find the probability of the event.

20. *Not* rolling a 2 on a number cube

21. *Not* rolling a number less than 3 on a number cube

22. *Not* spinning blue on the spinner shown

23. *Not* spinning blue, red, or yellow on the spinner shown

24. **REASONING** Refer to the spinner above. Is spinning green *impossible, unlikely, likely,* or *certain*? *Explain* your reasoning.

25. **CHALLENGE** You toss two coins at the same time. How likely are you to get two tails? *Justify* your answer.

26. **CHALLENGE** You roll two number cubes. What is the probability that the sum of the numbers is a multiple of 5? *Explain* your reasoning.

## PROBLEM SOLVING

SEE EXAMPLE 1
on p. 382
for Exs. 27–28

27. ♦ **MULTIPLE REPRESENTATIONS** You randomly pick one sock from a drawer that has 4 white socks, 12 black socks, and 8 brown socks.

   a. **Draw a Picture** Draw a picture that represents those probabilities.

   b. **Write** Write the probabilities of picking each color sock.

28. **REASONING** You have 15 coins in your pocket: 4 quarters, 3 pennies, 5 dimes, and 3 nickels. *Explain* why theoretical probability wouldn't be a good way to predict which coin you pull out of your pocket?

SEE EXAMPLES
2 AND 3
on p. 382
for Exs. 29–31

29. **SURVEYS** In a survey of 896 people, 409 said that their second toes are longer than their big toes. What is the probability to the nearest percent that a randomly chosen person from the survey has a longer second toe?

30. 🔸 **TAKS REASONING** In a group of 40 people, 24 prefer dogs to cats. One person is selected at random from the group. What is the probability that the person will prefer dogs to cats?

   (A) 0.24      (B) 0.4      (C) 0.6      (D) 0.67

31. **BOARD GAMES** You are playing a board game that uses a spinner like the one shown to determine how many spaces to move. Predict the number of times you would move exactly 5 spaces in 50 spins.

**32.** ⭐ **TAKS REASONING** Sharon and Erica are softball players. Out of 20 times at bat, Sharon got 7 hits. Out of 35 times at bat, Erica got 10 hits. Who do you think is more likely to get a hit her next time at bat? *Explain.*

**33.** PERFORM AN EXPERIMENT Write each of the letters of your last name on a slip of paper and perform an experiment.

    **a.** Place the slips into a bag and then randomly draw one slip. Record the result and replace it. Repeat this process 19 more times.

    **b.** What is the experimental probability of drawing the first letter of your name? *Predict* the number of times you would draw the first letter of your name out of 100 draws.

**34.** ⭐ **TAKS REASONING** *Describe* a real-life event that is certain to occur and a real-life event that cannot occur. *Explain.*

**35.** LEFT-HANDEDNESS The circle graphs below show the likelihood of each handedness for a child based on the handedness of its parents. Out of 500 pairs of parents with one child, how many of the children would you expect to be left-handed if both parents are right-handed? If only the mom is left-handed? How many of the children would you expect to be right-handed if both parents are left-handed? If only the dad is left-handed?

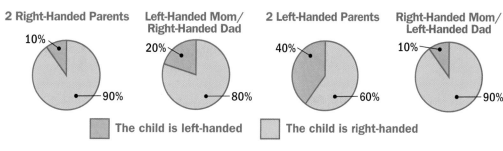

**2 Right-Handed Parents** 10% 90%   **Left-Handed Mom/ Right-Handed Dad** 20% 80%   **2 Left-Handed Parents** 40% 60%   **Right-Handed Mom/ Left-Handed Dad** 10% 90%

■ The child is left-handed     ☐ The child is right-handed

**36.** ⭐ **TAKS REASONING** Use a coin to complete the following.

    **a. Calculate** Using theoretical probability, predict the number of times a coin would land heads up in 20 tosses.

    **b. Experiment** Flip a coin 20 times and record the outcomes in a table.

    **c. Compare** Were the results from part (a) and part (b) the same?

    **d. Extend** Repeat parts (b) and (c) two more times. What does this tell you about theoretical and experimental probabilities?

**37.** ⭐ **TAKS REASONING** A clothing store surveys 100 girls ages 12 to 16 about the color of T-shirt they prefer. The results are given in the table at the right. The store uses this data to order more T-shirts. What conclusion(s) can you make about the numbers and colors of T-shirts that should be ordered?

| T-Shirt Colors | |
|---|---|
| **Color** | **Number** |
| blue | 15 |
| pink | 40 |
| purple | 35 |
| orange | 10 |

**38.** WRITING Vernon rolled a number cube 24 times and got a 6 once. He thinks that his chances of getting a 6 on his next roll are high. Is his reasoning correct? *Explain* why or why not.

**39. CHOOSING NAMES** There are exactly 20 girls and 20 boys in your gym class. The teacher writes each name on a slip of paper and places the slips in a hat. You randomly draw one slip, replace it, choose another, and record the genders of the names you drew. You repeat this 100 times. Predict the number of times you would draw two boys' names. *Explain.*

**40. CHALLENGE** You and a friend are playing a game where you take turns rolling a number cube. You gain 2 points for rolling a prime number, and your friend gains 2 points for rolling a composite number. Does this game favor you or your friend? A game is fair if each player has an equal chance of winning. *Describe* how you can change the game to make it fair.

**MIXED REVIEW FOR TAKS**                     **TAKS** PRACTICE at classzone.com

*REVIEW*
Lesson 3.4;
TAKS Workbook

**41.** ⬥ **TAKS PRACTICE** The figure shows a rectangle crossed by two diagonals. One triangle formed by the diagonals is shaded. Which of the statements is true? *TAKS Obj. 6*

Ⓐ The area of the shaded region equals 0.25 multiplied by the area of the unshaded area.

Ⓑ Less than $\frac{1}{4}$ of the rectangle is shaded.

Ⓒ The shaded area is about 33% of the unshaded area.

Ⓓ The area of the shaded region is $\frac{1}{3}$ the area of the total rectangle.

**QUIZ for Lessons 7.5–7.8**

**Tell if the change is an *increase* or *decrease*. Then find the percent of change.** *(p. 366)*

**1.** Original amount: $120
New amount: $138

**2.** Original amount: 260 miles
New amount: 169 miles

**3. RETAIL** A shirt has a $20 wholesale price and is marked up 50%. The sales tax is 5%. What is the total cost of the shirt? *(p. 370)*

**Solve using the percent equation.** *(p. 375)*

**4.** 75 is 125% of what number?

**5.** 552.5 is what percent of 85,000?

**6. KOALAS** Koalas absorb only about 25% of the fiber they eat. How much fiber is absorbed by a koala that eats 10.5 ounces of fiber per day? *(p. 375)*

**You spin the spinner at the right 40 times. Predict how many times the spinner lands on the specified color.** *(p. 381)*

**7.** Red

**8.** Blue

**9.** Yellow

**10.** White

## Lessons 7.5–7.8

**MULTIPLE CHOICE**

1. **PRICES** At a clothing store, all sweaters are the same price. You pick out a sweater and a pair of pants. When you get to the cashier, you find that sweaters are on sale for 40% off the original price and your bill is $40.40. So, you add two more sweaters to your purchase, bringing the bill to $81.20. About what percent of the final bill is the cost of the pair of pants? *TEKS 8.14.B*

Ⓐ 19%    Ⓑ 25%

Ⓒ 49.5%    Ⓓ 50.5%

2. **FISHING EQUIPMENT** A sporting goods store places a 60% markup on a tackle box for which it paid $16. The store later discounts the price so that a customer can buy the box at the store's cost. By what percent must the store discount the box? *TEKS 8.3.B*

Ⓕ 9.6%    Ⓖ 25.6%

Ⓗ 60%    Ⓙ 62.5%

3. **SAVINGS** Mark deposits $300 in a savings account that pays a simple interest rate of 2.3% per year. He doesn't add or remove money from his account. What is the total amount of money in the account after 30 months? *TEKS 8.3.B*

Ⓐ $317.25    Ⓑ $507.75

Ⓒ $617.25    Ⓓ $725.50

4. **GRATUITY** At a diner, Jay and Gia pay for their $22.20 meal with a $20 bill and a $10 bill. The change they are given consists of a $5 bill, two $1 bills, and some coins. About what percent of the bill can they leave as a tip using all of the remaining change, except for the $5 bill? *TEKS 8.14.A*

Ⓕ 13%    Ⓖ 15%

Ⓗ 18%    Ⓙ 20%

5. **SPINNERS** All sections of the spinner are of equal size. What is the probability of NOT spinning yellow on the spinner? *TEKS 8.11.B*

Ⓐ 12.5%    Ⓑ 25%

Ⓒ 75%    Ⓓ 87.5%

6. **TURTLES** Arthur grows water plants as a treat for his turtle. Properly fed, the plants can grow 50% in mass each week. Arthur plans to feed 50% of the plant mass to the turtle at the end of each week, letting the plants grow for a week in between feedings. Arthur starts this process with 5 grams of water plants. Approximately how much food is given to the turtle at the end of week 3? *TEKS 8.14.C*

Ⓕ 2.1 g    Ⓖ 3.75 g

Ⓗ 8.44 g    Ⓙ 8.66 g

**GRIDDED ANSWER** ⊙①●③④⑤⑥⑦⑧⑨

7. **MARBLES** You have 5 blue marbles, 2 red marbles, and 3 yellow marbles. You choose one marble at random. What is the probability that you will choose a red marble? Write your answer as a decimal. *TEKS 8.11.B*

## REVIEW KEY VOCABULARY

- ratio, *p. 343*
- equivalent ratios, *p. 343*
- rate, unit rate, *p. 344*
- proportion, *p. 348*
- cross products, *p. 349*
- scale model, *p. 350*
- scale, *p. 350*

- percent, *p. 354*
- circle graph, *p. 360*
- percent of change, *p. 366*
- percent of increase, *p. 366*
- percent of decrease, *p. 366*
- markup, discount, *p. 370*
- interest, *p. 376*

- principal, *p. 376*
- annual interest rate, *p. 376*
- outcome, event, *p. 381*
- favorable outcome, *p. 381*
- probability of an event, *p. 381*
- theoretical probability, *p. 381*
- experimental probability, *p. 382*

### VOCABULARY EXERCISES

**Copy and complete the statement.**

1. If you write $\dfrac{180 \text{ miles}}{3 \text{ hours}}$ as $\dfrac{60 \text{ miles}}{1 \text{ hour}}$, you have written the rate as a(n) __?__ .

2. A ratio whose denominator is 100 is a __?__ .

3. The theoretical probability of an event is the ratio of the number of __?__ to the number of __?__ when all outcomes are equally likely.

4. The increase in the wholesale price of an item is a __?__ .

5. A decrease in the price of an item is a __?__ .

**Match the definition with the correct word at the right.**

6. the amount of money that you borrow or deposit

7. the amount paid for the use of money

8. the percent of the principal that you pay or earn each year

   **A.** annual interest rate

   **B.** interest

   **C.** principal

## REVIEW EXAMPLES AND EXERCISES

### 7.1 Ratios and Rates

*pp. 343–346*

**EXAMPLE**

**Write 282 miles per 6 hours as a unit rate.**

$$\frac{282 \text{ miles}}{6 \text{ hours}} = \frac{282 \div 6}{6 \div 6} \qquad \text{Divide numerator and denominator by 6.}$$

$$= \frac{47}{1} \qquad \text{Simplify.}$$

▶ **Answer** The unit rate is 47 miles per hour.

## EXERCISES

**Write the ratio of shaded to unshaded squares in simplest form.**

SEE EXAMPLES
1, 2, AND 3
on pp. 343–344
for Exs. 9–19

9.

10.

**Write the rate as a unit rate.**

11. $\dfrac{30 \text{ feet}}{4 \text{ seconds}}$

12. $\dfrac{\$3.36}{2 \text{ gallons}}$

13. $\dfrac{72 \text{ people}}{4 \text{ groups}}$

14. $\dfrac{90 \text{ miles}}{4 \text{ hours}}$

15. $\dfrac{28 \text{ feet}}{2 \text{ seconds}}$

16. $\dfrac{48 \text{ points}}{4 \text{ quarters}}$

17. $\dfrac{356 \text{ kilometers}}{8 \text{ hours}}$

18. $\dfrac{\$17.25}{5 \text{ pounds}}$

19. **Running** Emily runs 1600 meters in 5 minutes 30 seconds, and Megan runs 800 meters in 2 minutes 40 seconds. Who has the faster average speed?

## 7.2 Writing and Solving Proportions

*pp. 348–353*

### EXAMPLE

**Solve the proportion.**

$\dfrac{7.2}{9.4} = \dfrac{36}{x}$      Write original proportion.

$7.2 \cdot x = 9.4 \cdot 36$      Cross products property

$7.2x = 338.4$      Multiply.

$\dfrac{7.2x}{7.2} = \dfrac{338.4}{7.2}$      Divide each side by 7.2.

$x = 47$      Simplify.

### EXERCISES

**Solve the proportion.**

SEE EXAMPLES
2 AND 3
on pp. 349–350
for Exs. 20–26

20. $\dfrac{5}{13} = \dfrac{18}{c}$

21. $\dfrac{48}{54} = \dfrac{x}{6}$

22. $\dfrac{n}{12} = \dfrac{7}{8}$

23. $\dfrac{25}{b+1} = \dfrac{5}{2}$

24. **Maps** A map has a scale of 1 inch : 10 miles. The actual distance between two cities is 105 miles. Write and solve a proportion to find the distance between the cities on the map.

25. **Earnings** You earn $12 walking 3 dogs. You charge the same amount for each dog. How much do you earn for walking 5 dogs?

26. **Reading** You can read 51 pages in 45 minutes. How many pages can you read in an hour?

## 7.3 Solving Percent Problems

*pp. 354–358*

**EXAMPLE**

**36 is 15% of what number?**

$$\frac{a}{b} = \frac{p}{100}$$  Write a percent proportion.

$$\frac{36}{b} = \frac{15}{100}$$  Substitute 36 for $a$ and 15 for $p$.

$36 \cdot 100 = 15b$  Cross products property

$240 = b$  Divide each side by 15.

### EXERCISES

**Use a percent proportion.**

**SEE EXAMPLES 1 AND 2**
on pp. 354–355
for Exs. 27–29

**27.** 72 is what percent of 1200?

**28.** What number is 95% of 26?

**29. Surveys** You ask 270 people if they read for fun. Of these people, 146 say they do. What percent of the people surveyed like to read for fun?

## 7.4 Fractions, Decimals, and Percents

*pp. 359–364*

**EXAMPLE**

**Write 28% as a decimal and as a fraction.**

$28\% = 28\% = 0.28$  Remove % sign. Move decimal point two places to the left.

$28\% = \frac{28}{100} = \frac{7}{25}$  Write as a fraction and simplify.

▶ **Answer** 28% can be written as 0.28 and as $\frac{7}{25}$.

### EXERCISES

**Write the percent as a decimal and as a fraction.**

**SEE EXAMPLES 1, 2, 3, AND 4**
on pp. 359–360
for Exs. 30–38

**30.** 74%

**31.** 3.8%

**32.** 16.8%

**33.** 130%

**Write the fraction or decimal as a percent.**

**34.** $\frac{3}{5}$

**35.** $\frac{5}{2}$

**36.** 0.02

**37.** 18.6

**38. Food Surveys** You survey 72 people and find that 18 of them like pork chops. What percent like pork chops?

## 7.5 Percent of Change

pp. 366–369

**EXAMPLE**

**Plant Growth** Find the percent of increase in height of a plant 60 inches tall that grows to 84 inches.

$p\% = \dfrac{84 - 60}{60}$     Write amount of increase and divide by original amount.

$= \dfrac{24}{60}$     Subtract.

$= 0.4$     Write fraction as a decimal.

$= 40\%$     Write decimal as a percent.

▶ **Answer** The percent of increase in height is 40%.

### EXERCISES

**Find the percent of increase or decrease. Round to the nearest percent.**

*SEE EXAMPLES 1 AND 2*
on pp. 366–367
for Exs. 39–41

**39.** original amount: 50; new amount: 35     **40.** original amount: 90; new amount: 220

**41. Weight** A moving van's load changes from 800 pounds to 984 pounds after picking up an appliance. Find the percent of increase.

## 7.6 Percent Applications

pp. 370–374

**EXAMPLE**

**Sale Price** A pair of shoes has an original price of $40. What is the sale price after a 15% discount?

$40 \times 0.15 = 6$     Multiply to find discount.

$40 - 6 = 34$     Subtract discount from original price.

▶ **Answer** The sale price of the shoes is $34.

### EXERCISES

**Find the sale price or retail price.**

*SEE EXAMPLES 1, 2, AND 3*
on pp. 370–371
for Exs. 42–44

**42.** wholesale price: $30; percent markup: 70%

**43.** original price: $72; percent discount: 18%

**44. Restaurant Costs** Your meal at a restaurant costs $14.99. Sales tax is 3%. You leave a 15% tip. How much did you spend?

## 7.7 Using the Percent Equation

pp. 375–379

### EXAMPLE

**What number is 26% of 300?**

| | |
|---|---|
| $a = p\% \cdot b$ | Write percent equation. |
| $a = 26\% \cdot 300$ | Substitute 26 for $p$ and 300 for $b$. |
| $a = 0.26(300)$ | Write percent as a decimal. |
| $a = 78$ | Multiply. |

### EXERCISES

**Solve using the percent equation.**

SEE EXAMPLES
1, 2, AND 3
on pp. 375–376
for Exs. 45–48

**45.** 72 is 75% of what number?

**46.** What number is 34% of 856?

**Find the amount of simple interest earned in 3 years.**

**47.** principal: $460; annual rate: 3.5%

**48.** principal: $1540; annual rate: 2.75%

## 7.8 Simple Probability

pp. 381–386

### EXAMPLE

**Probability** Rosa tosses the box 250 times and 28 tosses resulted in a 1. Find the experimental probability of the box landing on 1.

Use the results to find the experimental probability.

$$P(1) = \frac{28}{250} \quad \xleftarrow{\quad} \text{Number of favorable outcomes}$$
$$\xleftarrow{\quad} \text{Total number of tosses}$$

$$= \frac{14}{125} = 0.112 = 11.2\%$$

### EXERCISES

SEE EXAMPLES
1 AND 2
on p. 382
for Exs. 49–52

**49. Marbles** You randomly draw a marble out of a bag that contains 8 red, 5 yellow, and 4 blue marbles. Find the probability of drawing each color.

**Experimental Probability** You roll a number cube 200 times. Your results are shown in the table. Find the experimental probability of the event.

**50.** You roll a 5.

**51.** You roll a number less than 5.

**52.** You roll a number divisible by 3.

| Number | 1 | 2 | 3 | 4 | 5 | 6 |
|---|---|---|---|---|---|---|
| Outcomes | 35 | 28 | 46 | 27 | 30 | 34 |

**Write the ratio of shaded to unshaded squares in simplest form.**

**1.**    **2.**    **3.**    **4.**

**Write the rate as a unit rate.**

**5.** $\dfrac{156 \text{ miles}}{3 \text{ hours}}$   **6.** $\dfrac{18 \text{ servings}}{6 \text{ people}}$   **7.** $\dfrac{448 \text{ cycles}}{5 \text{ days}}$   **8.** $\dfrac{525 \text{ meters}}{21 \text{ seconds}}$

**Solve the proportion.**

**9.** $\dfrac{12}{16} = \dfrac{18}{a}$   **10.** $\dfrac{15}{6} = \dfrac{d}{4}$   **11.** $\dfrac{9}{n} = \dfrac{21}{14}$   **12.** $\dfrac{t-3}{12} = \dfrac{11}{6}$

**Find the missing number.**

**13.** What number is 320% of 120?   **14.** What number is 0.5% of 700?

**15.** 19 is what percent of 50?   **16.** 192 is what percent of 32?

**17.** 27 is 8% of what number?   **18.** 5.1 is 30% of what number?

**Write the percent as a decimal and as a fraction.**

**19.** 0.7%   **20.** 419%   **21.** 8%   **22.** 7.8%

**Find the percent of change. Tell whether it is an increase or decrease.**

**23.** Original amount: 40
New amount: 36

**24.** Original amount: 225
New amount: 324

**25.** Original amount: 258
New amount: 6.45

**A box contains 9 tiles that together spell the word "TENNESSEE." You draw at random one tile from the box. Find the probability of the event.**

**26.** Drawing an E   **27.** Drawing an S

**28. MAPS** The road distance from Miami, Florida, to Columbia, South Carolina, on a map is about 6.7 centimeters. The scale is 1 cm : 150 km. What is the actual distance from Miami to Columbia?

**29. SURVEY** In a survey, 34%, or 102 people, said they enjoy canoeing. How many people were surveyed?

**30. FOOD** Your food bill at a restaurant totals $26. There is a 6.5% sales tax and you leave a 16% tip. What is the total cost of the meal?

**31. RECYCLING** The average person in the United States generates about 4.5 pounds of waste per day. About 30% of this waste is recycled. About how many pounds of waste are recycled per person per week?

**TEXAS** TAKS Objs. 1 and 2
TEKS 8.1.B, 8.3.B

## REVIEWING PROPORTION PROBLEMS

In some real-life situations, you may need to compare rates such as prices or speeds. To do so, find the unit rate of each price or speed. Remember that a unit rate is a rate that has a denominator of 1 unit. Then compare these unit rates.

### EXAMPLE

**Pricing** The prices of four different packages of pencils are given in the table.

| Package Prices | |
|---|---|
| *Number of Pencils* | *Price* |
| 2 | $0.30 |
| 6 | $0.84 |
| 12 | $1.68 |
| 24 | $2.64 |

**a.** Which two packages have the same cost per pencil?

**b.** Which package offers the best deal?

### Solution

**a.** To determine which two packages have the same cost per pencil, find the unit price for all four packages.

**2-pencil package:** $\dfrac{\$0.30}{2 \text{ pencils}} = \dfrac{\$0.15}{1 \text{ pencil}}$

**6-pencil package:** $\dfrac{\$0.84}{6 \text{ pencils}} = \dfrac{\$0.14}{1 \text{ pencil}}$

**12-pencil package:** $\dfrac{\$1.68}{12 \text{ pencils}} = \dfrac{\$0.14}{1 \text{ pencil}}$

**24-pencil package:** $\dfrac{\$2.64}{24 \text{ pencils}} = \dfrac{\$0.11}{1 \text{ pencil}}$

▶ **Answer** The 6-pencil package and the 12-pencil package have the same cost per pencil.

**b.** By comparing the unit prices found in part (a), you can conclude that the 24-pencil package has the lowest cost per pencil.

▶ **Answer** The 24-pencil package is the best deal.

# PROPORTION PROBLEMS ON TAKS

Below are examples of proportion problems in multiple choice format. Try solving the problems before looking at the solutions. (Cover the solutions with a piece of paper.) Then check your solutions against the ones given.

**1.** Tara ran 175 feet in 35 seconds. Leslie ran at the same rate for 25 seconds. How much farther did Tara run than Leslie?

**A** 25 ft

**B** 50 ft

**C** 75 ft

**D** 125 ft

**Solution**

Write and solve a proportion to find the distance $d$ that Leslie ran.

$$\frac{175}{35} = \frac{d}{25} \longleftarrow \text{distance} \atop \longleftarrow \text{time}$$

$$175 \cdot 25 = 35 \cdot d$$

$$125 = d$$

Leslie ran 125 feet. Tara ran 175 feet. Tara ran 50 feet farther than Leslie, so the correct answer is B.

Ⓐ     Ⓑ     Ⓒ     Ⓓ

**2.** A bag contains 25% red marbles, 15% green marbles, 30% blue marbles, and 30% yellow marbles. There are 180 marbles total in the bag. What is the total number of green marbles in the bag?

**F** 15

**G** 27

**H** 45

**J** 54

**Solution**

Use the percent proportion $\frac{a}{b} = \frac{p}{100}$ where $a$ is part of the base $b$ and $p$ is the percent.

$$\frac{a}{180} = \frac{15}{100}$$

$$100 \cdot a = 15 \cdot 180$$

$$a = 27$$

So, the correct answer is G.

Ⓕ     Ⓖ     Ⓗ     Ⓙ

**3.** One Saturday night, a hostess at a restaurant counted 52 people entering a restaurant during the four hours that she worked. The number of people entering the restaurant per hour was the same the next Saturday night. How many people entered the restaurant during five hours that next Saturday night?

**A** 53

**B** 56

**C** 65

**D** 78

**Solution**

Write and solve a proportion to find the number of people $n$ entering the restaurant during 5 hours.

$$\frac{52}{4} = \frac{n}{5} \longleftarrow \text{number of people} \atop \longleftarrow \text{hours}$$

$$52 \cdot 5 = 4 \cdot n$$

$$65 = n$$

So, the correct answer is C.

Ⓐ     Ⓑ     Ⓒ     Ⓓ

# 7 TAKS PRACTICE

## PRACTICE FOR TAKS OBJECTIVES 1 AND 2

1. At a concert hall, there are 5 orchestra seats for every 2 balcony seats. The manager of the hall plans to renovate and add 15 more orchestra seats. The manager wants to preserve the ratio of orchestra seats to balcony seats. What proportion can be used to find $y$, the number of balcony seats the manager must add during renovation?

   **A** $\dfrac{3}{2} = \dfrac{y}{15}$

   **B** $\dfrac{2}{y} = \dfrac{15}{3}$

   **C** $\dfrac{2}{5} = \dfrac{y}{15}$

   **D** $\dfrac{5}{y} = \dfrac{15}{2}$

2. Natalie bought 5 pounds of milk chocolate for $9.45 and 3 pounds of fudge for $6.90. White chocolate in the same shop sold for $1.99 per pound and pralines sold for $0.50 an ounce. Which was cheapest per pound?

   **F** Pralines

   **G** White chocolate

   **H** Fudge

   **J** Milk chocolate

3. One hundred twenty people saw the sneak preview of a film. One third of the audience disliked the film. Thirty-five people thought the film was mediocre, and 30% of the people loved the film. Which statement is correct?

   **A** Five fewer people loved the film than the thirty-five people who thought it mediocre.

   **B** Most people loved the film.

   **C** Thirty-three people disliked the film.

   **D** Nine people didn't fall into any of the three categories of people who disliked the film, thought it mediocre, or loved the film.

4. Notebooks sell for $2.00 each, $3.00 for two, and $4.00 for four. Which describes the change in price according to the quantity purchased?

   **F** The unit price is $1.00 more when twice as many notebooks are bought.

   **G** The unit price is $0.50 less when twice as many notebooks are bought.

   **H** The unit price is the same no matter how many notebooks are bought.

   **J** The unit price is halved when twice as many notebooks are bought.

5. Angie usually bikes 16 miles in 2 hours. Pat usually bikes 18 miles in $1\frac{1}{2}$ hours. If they start in the same place at the same time and ride along the same route at their usual speeds, how far apart will they be after 6 hours?

   **A** 6 miles

   **B** 12 miles

   **C** 18 miles

   **D** 24 miles

## MIXED TAKS PRACTICE

6. Three plants have the following heights: $3\frac{1}{12}$ feet, $\frac{23}{6}$ feet, and $\frac{10}{3}$ feet. Which shows the heights in order from least to greatest?
   *TAKS Obj. 1*

   **F** $3\frac{1}{12}$ ft, $\frac{10}{3}$ ft, $\frac{23}{6}$ ft

   **G** $3\frac{1}{12}$ ft, $\frac{23}{6}$ ft, $\frac{10}{3}$ ft

   **H** $\frac{23}{6}$ ft, $\frac{10}{3}$ ft, $3\frac{1}{12}$ ft

   **J** $\frac{23}{6}$ ft, $3\frac{1}{12}$ ft, $\frac{10}{3}$ ft

## MIXED TAKS PRACTICE

**7.** Stanley has a bag of 52 tiles. Each tile has a letter of the alphabet on it. He wants to find the probability of drawing a Q from the bag if he takes out 3 tiles, leaving each tile out after he draws it. To solve his problem, what missing piece of information must he know? *TAKS Obj. 6*

  **A** Whether he drew a Q the last time he tried the same experiment

  **B** Number of tiles in the bag with the letter Q on them

  **C** Probability of drawing a tile with the letter A on it

  **D** Whether every letter of the alphabet is represented on the tiles

**8.** A circle with a radius of 5 units is shown below.

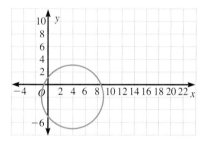

Which ordered pair represents a point on the circle? *TAKS Obj. 3*

  **F** $(9, -2)$

  **G** $(4, -2)$

  **H** $(-2, -1)$

  **J** $(3, 4)$

**9.** A wheel has a radius of 16 inches. What approximate distance will the wheel travel if it rolls straight ahead and makes a total of 3 full rotations? *TAKS Obj. 3*

  **A** 150.72 in.      **B** 200.96 in.

  **C** 301.44 in.      **D** 602.88 in.

**10.** An integer $x$ is less than the product of itself and one quarter. What must be true of the integer $x$? *TAKS Obj. 6*

  **F** $x < 0$

  **G** $0 < x < 1$

  **H** $x > 4$

  **J** $0 < x$

**11.** A fair number cube is rolled 10 times. A number less than 5 should appear about what percent of the time? *TAKS Obj. 5*

  **A** 10%

  **B** 16.5%

  **C** 40%

  **D** 67%

**12.** A survey of people's preferences for writing implements found that 22.5% liked pencils, $\frac{5}{11}$ liked ballpoint pens, and 0.32 liked felt tipped pens. Which lists these ratios in order from least to greatest? *TAKS Obj. 1*

  **F** $\frac{5}{11}$, 22.5%, 0.32

  **G** 22.5%, $\frac{5}{11}$, 0.32

  **H** 22.5%, 0.32, $\frac{5}{11}$

  **J** 0.32, $\frac{5}{11}$, 22.5%

**13. GRIDDED ANSWER** Rachel bought shoes on sale for $28. The original price of the shoes was $40. By what percent was the original price of the shoes reduced during the sale? Write the percent as a decimal. *TAKS Obj. 2*

*Record your answer and fill in the bubbles on your answer document. Be sure to use the correct place value.*

**Evaluate the expression.**

**1.** $66 - 11 \times 5$ *(p. 8)*

**2.** $8 \div (3.5 + 0.5)$ *(p. 8)*

**3.** $17 + (3 \times 4)^2$ *(p. 19)*

**4.** $8 \times 6 \div 2^4$ *(p. 19)*

**5.** $(-3 + 11) + 5$ *(p. 83)*

**6.** $(14 - 8) - 13$ *(p. 83)*

**7.** $-3(8 + 6)$ *(p. 88)*

**8.** $-5(-3 - 7)$ *(p. 88)*

**9.** $(-5 \cdot 8) \cdot 4$ *(p. 88)*

**Write the fraction in simplest form.** *(p. 187)*

**10.** $\dfrac{104}{39}$

**11.** $-\dfrac{32}{102}$

**12.** $-\dfrac{9abc}{12a}$

**13.** $\dfrac{21bcd}{7bc}$

**Write the equivalent rate.** *(p. 343)*

**14.** $\dfrac{\$5.97}{\text{yd}} = \dfrac{\$?}{\text{ft}}$

**15.** $\dfrac{30 \text{ mi}}{\text{h}} = \dfrac{? \text{ mi}}{\text{min}}$

**16.** $\dfrac{4 \text{ oz}}{\text{serving}} = \dfrac{? \text{ lb}}{\text{serving}}$

**17.** $\dfrac{180 \text{ ft}}{\text{sec}} = \dfrac{? \text{ ft}}{\text{min}}$

**Simplify. Write the expression using only positive exponents.** *(p. 208)*

**18.** $7x^{-4}$

**19.** $a^{-6} \cdot a^4$

**20.** $\dfrac{8w^{-6}}{24w^2}$

**21.** $\dfrac{16r^{-2}}{4r^3}$

**Find the sum, difference, product, or quotient.**

**22.** $-55 + (-43)$ *(p. 63)*

**23.** $0 + (-144)$ *(p. 63)*

**24.** $-21 - 33$ *(p. 68)*

**25.** $-17 - (-67)$ *(p. 68)*

**26.** $-5(-16)$ *(p. 73)*

**27.** $3(-8)(10)$ *(p. 73)*

**28.** $\dfrac{-51}{-17}$ *(p. 77)*

**29.** $\dfrac{0}{-25}$ *(p. 77)*

**30.** $-9\dfrac{3}{4} + 4\dfrac{2}{3}$ *(p. 233)*

**31.** $-\dfrac{19x}{25} - \dfrac{11x}{25}$ *(p. 233)*

**32.** $\dfrac{3}{c} - \dfrac{7}{2c}$ *(p. 238)*

**33.** $\dfrac{9}{21} \cdot \dfrac{7}{5}$ *(p. 243)*

**34.** $12\dfrac{1}{2} \cdot \dfrac{6}{25}$ *(p. 243)*

**35.** $\dfrac{13}{18} \div \dfrac{5}{6}$ *(p. 247)*

**36.** $5\dfrac{8}{11} \div \left(-\dfrac{3}{4}\right)$ *(p. 247)*

**37.** $16.7 \cdot (-3.2)$ *(p. 265)*

**38.** $43.4 \cdot 0.13$ *(p. 265)*

**39.** $3.434 \div 8.08$ *(p. 265)*

**Solve the equation or inequality.**

**40.** $8 = b - (-6)$ *(p. 117)*

**41.** $9y = -63$ *(p. 122)*

**42.** $2c - 5 = 17$ *(p. 129)*

**43.** $d + 3.4 \le 9.1$ *(p. 148)*

**44.** $\dfrac{1}{3}x > -2$ *(p. 154)*

**45.** $7 - 2y \le 11$ *(p. 154)*

**46.** $x = 5(2x + 3)$ *(p. 298)*

**47.** $6 - \dfrac{2}{5}a > 2$ *(p. 318)*

**48.** $2(3k + 1) \le 5k - 30$ *(p. 318)*

**Write the decimal or fraction as a percent.** *(p. 359)*

**49.** $0.43$

**50.** $0.003$

**51.** $\dfrac{3}{10}$

**52.** $\dfrac{29}{20}$

**Find the probability of the event.** *(p. 381)*

**53.** A vowel is randomly chosen from the letters A, B, C, D, E, and F.

**54.** A number less than 4 is randomly drawn from the numbers 1, 2, 3, and 4.

**55. CLOTHES** A sweater costs $45 and a pair of jeans cost $35. You buy 3 sweaters and 2 pairs of jeans on a sale day where sweaters are $10 off and jeans are $5 off. Write an expression for the cost of the clothes, and evaluate it. *(p. 13)*

**56. STOCK MARKET** Your uncle owns 25 shares of stock A, 45 shares of stock B, and 60 shares of stock C. In one day, the price per share changed by +$.56 for stock A, −$1.80 for stock B, and −$.50 for stock C. Find the total change in value of your uncle's stocks. *(p. 73)*

**57. SAVING** You have $80 today. You save $40 a week. How many weeks will it take to save enough to buy a camera that costs $320? How many weeks will it take if you save $35 a week? *(p. 154)*

**58. FOUNTAIN** A fountain in an amusement park has special-effect devices called *shooters*. They shoot columns of water at different time intervals. One shooter goes off every 8 seconds while another goes off every 12 seconds. How long after the fountain is turned on will both shooters go off at the same time? *(p. 192)*

**BIRTH WEIGHTS** In Exercises 59 and 60, use the table. It shows approximate weights, in pounds, of several newborn animals. *(p. 260)*

| Newborn Animal | Birth Weight (lb) |
|---|---|
| Hippopotamus | 66 |
| Giant panda | 0.25 |
| Giraffe | 150 |
| Polar bear | 1.32 |
| Gentoo penguin | 0.29 |

**59.** How much more does the hippopotamus weigh than the gentoo penguin?

**60.** How much more does the polar bear weigh than the giant panda?

**61. ICEBERGS** When an iceberg broke free from Antarctica in May of 2002, it was about 34.5 miles long and 11.5 miles wide. About how much area did the iceberg cover? *(p. 265)*

**62. SCHOOL FUNDRAISER** You are selling magazine subscriptions for a school fundraiser. If you sell at least 75 subscriptions in 2 weeks you win a prize. You sold 26 subscriptions in one week. What is the mean number of subscriptions you have to sell per day to sell at least 75 total? *(p. 324)*

**CLASS PROJECTS** In Exercises 63–65, use the circle graph. It shows the results of a survey of 300 students who were asked what they would choose for a final project. *(p. 359)*

**63.** What percent of students chose an oral report?

**64.** What fraction of students chose a visual project? Write the fraction in simplest form.

**65.** Which final project was chosen by 21% of the students?

**Final Project**

- Visual project 105
- Writing a paper 96
- Taking a test 63
- Oral report 36

# 8 Polygons and Transformations

## Before

**In previous chapters you've . . .**

- Solved equations
- Plotted points in a coordinate plane

## Now

## Why?

**So you can solve real-world problems about . . .**

- rugs, p. 404
- referees, p. 413
- origami, p. 443

 **Math**
*at classzone.com*

- Playing Golf with Angles, p. 413
- Polygons and Angles, p. 421
- Transformations and Symmetry, p. 442

---

## Get-Ready Games

**Review Prerequisite Skills** by playing *Find the Flags*.

**Skill Focus:** Plotting points on a coordinate plane

### FIND THE FLAGS

**MATERIALS**

- 2 sheets of grid paper for each player

- Pencils

**HOW TO PLAY**  Each player draws a coordinate graph on both sheets of grid paper. Each player draws squares along the grid lines passing through the points (7, 0), (0, −7), (−7, 0), and (0, 7). A player secretly marks 4 flags on one graph. A flag is three consecutive points with integer coordinates, either horizontally or vertically. Flags cannot touch the outside borders. On each turn, a player should follow the steps on the next page.

---

# Find the Flags

**1** **CALL** out a point. The other player lets you know if you hit or missed one of their flags.

**2** **MARK** a hit with an "X" and a miss with an "O" on your second graph where your flags are not marked. If you hit a flag, you get to go again.

**HOW TO WIN** Be the first player to hit all the points in the other player's flags.

## Stop and Think

1. **WRITING** How did you decide where to put your flags? Did it work? *Explain.* What strategy did you use when trying to find the other player's flags? Did it work? *Explain.*

2. **CRITICAL THINKING** How many points are there (not including any on the border) in each graph? *Explain* how you got your answer.

# Review Prerequisite Skills

### REVIEW WORDS

- **point,** *p. 773*
- **line,** *p. 773*
- **ray,** *p. 773*
- **plane,** *p. 773*
- **angle,** *p. 774*
- **vertex,** *p. 774*
- **degree,** *p. 776*

## VOCABULARY CHECK

**Identify the object with the review word from the list at the left.** *(p. 773)*

**1.** **2.** **3.**

**4.** Copy and complete with a review word from the list at the left:
A unit for measuring angles is a(n) __?__ .

## SKILL CHECK

**Use a protractor to measure the angle.** *(p. 776)*

**5.** **6.** **7.**

**8.** **9.** **10.**

**11. Scale Models** You have a giant crayon that is a scale model of a regular crayon. A regular crayon is about 0.25 inch wide and 3.5 inches long. The giant crayon is 6 inches wide. How long is it? *(p. 348)*

**TEXAS @HomeTutor** Prerequisite skills practice at classzone.com

## Notetaking Skills    Making a Concept Map

In each chapter you will learn a new notetaking skill. In Chapter 8, you can apply the strategy of making a concept map to Example 1 on page 416.

You will often learn new concepts that are related to each other. It is helpful to organize these concepts in your notes with a map or chart.

A rectangle is a figure with four sides. Its opposite sides have the same length, and its angles are right angles.

A square is a rectangle with sides that have the same length.

# 8.1 Angle Pairs

TEKS 8.15.A, 8.16.B

| | |
|---|---|
| **Before** | You solved equations to find the value of a variable. |
| **Now** | You'll solve equations to find angle measures. |
| **Why?** | So you can find angle measures in objects, such as skis as in Ex. 28. |

**KEY VOCABULARY**
- straight angle, right angle, *p. 403*
- supplementary, complementary, *p. 403*
- vertical angles, *p. 404*
- perpendicular lines, *p. 404*
- parallel lines, *p. 405*

A **straight angle** measures 180°. A **right angle** measures 90°. The mark ⌐ tells you that an angle is a right angle.

**180°**

**Straight angle**

**90°**

**Right angle**

Two angles are **supplementary** if the sum of their measures is 180°. Two angles are **complementary** if the sum of their measures is 90°. You can write "the measure of angle 1" as $m\angle 1$.

∠1 and ∠2 are supplementary.
$m\angle 1 + m\angle 2 = 180°$

∠3 and ∠4 are complementary.
$m\angle 3 + m\angle 4 = 90°$

---

### EXAMPLE 1  Finding an Angle Measure

∠1 and ∠2 are complementary, and $m\angle 2 = 32°$. Find $m\angle 1$.

**SOLUTION**

| | |
|---|---|
| $m\angle 1 + m\angle 2 = 90°$ | **Definition of complementary angles** |
| $m\angle 1 + 32° = 90°$ | **Substitute 32° for $m\angle 2$.** |
| $m\angle 1 = 58°$ | **Subtract 32° from each side.** |

*Animated* **Math**
at classzone.com

---

✓ **GUIDED PRACTICE**  for Example 1

**Tell whether ∠1 and ∠2 are *complementary, supplementary,* or *neither*.**

**1.** $m\angle 1 = 79°$
$m\angle 2 = 101°$

**2.** $m\angle 1 = 64°$
$m\angle 2 = 36°$

**3.** $m\angle 1 = 52°$
$m\angle 2 = 38°$

**4.** $m\angle 1 = 44°$
$m\angle 2 = 46°$

**5.** $m\angle 1 = 53°$
$m\angle 2 = 47°$

**6.** $m\angle 1 = 95°$
$m\angle 2 = 85°$

**Vertical Angles** When two lines intersect at a point, they form two pairs of angles that do not share a side. These pairs are called **vertical angles**, and they always have the same measure.

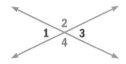

∠1 and ∠3 are vertical angles.
$m\angle 1 = m\angle 3$

∠2 and ∠4 are vertical angles.
$m\angle 2 = m\angle 4$

**EXAMPLE 2** TAKS REASONING: Multi-Step Problem

**Textiles** Find the angle measures indicated in the rug design if $m\angle 1 = 122°$.

**SOLUTION**

It is given that $m\angle 1 = 122°$.

**STEP 1** ∠1 and ∠3 are vertical angles. Their measures are equal, so $m\angle 3 = 122°$.

**STEP 2** ∠1 and ∠2 are supplementary.

| | |
|---|---|
| $m\angle 1 + m\angle 2 = 180°$ | **Definition of supplementary angles** |
| $122° + m\angle 2 = 180°$ | **Substitute 122° for $m\angle 1$.** |
| $m\angle 2 = 58°$ | **Subtract 122° from each side.** |

**STEP 3** ∠2 and ∠4 are vertical angles. Their measures are equal, so $m\angle 4 = 58°$.

▶ **Answer** $m\angle 1 = m\angle 3 = 122°$, $m\angle 2 = m\angle 4 = 58°$

✓ **GUIDED PRACTICE** for Example 2

Find the measures of the numbered angles.

7.

8.

**Lines in a Plane** Using vertical and supplementary angles, you can see that when two lines intersect to form one right angle, they form four right angles. Two lines that intersect at a right angle are called **perpendicular lines**.

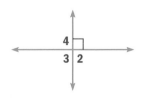

Two lines in the same plane that do not intersect are called **parallel lines**. When a line intersects two parallel lines, several pairs of angles that are formed have equal measures.

**KEY CONCEPT**                                    *For Your Notebook*

**Angles and Parallel Lines**

**Corresponding Angles**

$m\angle 1 = m\angle 5$        $m\angle 2 = m\angle 6$

$m\angle 3 = m\angle 7$        $m\angle 4 = m\angle 8$

**Alternate Interior Angles**

$m\angle 3 = m\angle 6$        $m\angle 4 = m\angle 5$

**Alternate Exterior Angles**

$m\angle 1 = m\angle 8$        $m\angle 2 = m\angle 7$

**READING**

The red arrows on the lines indicate that the lines in the diagram are parallel.

---

**EXAMPLE 3** **Using Parallel Lines**

 **Use the diagram to find the angle measure.**

**a.** $m\angle 1$

**b.** $m\angle 2$

**SOLUTION**

**a.** $\angle 1$ and $\angle 5$ are corresponding angles, so they have equal measures. You can find $m\angle 5$ because it is the supplement of the given angle.

$m\angle 5 + 125° = 180°$        **Definition of supplementary angles**

$m\angle 5 = 55°$        **Subtract 125° from each side.**

▶ **Answer** $m\angle 1 = 55°$

**b.** $\angle 2$ and the given angle are alternate exterior angles, so they have equal measures.

▶ **Answer** $m\angle 2 = 125°$

**ANOTHER WAY**

You could also find $m\angle 1$ by finding the $m\angle 7$, its alternate exterior angle.

---

✓ **GUIDED PRACTICE**    **for Example 3**

**Find the angle measure.**

**9.** $m\angle 2$        **10.** $m\angle 3$

**11.** $m\angle 4$        **12.** $m\angle 1$

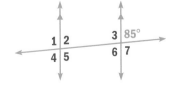

# 8.1 EXERCISES

HOMEWORK KEY

= TAKS Practice and Reasoning
Exs. 9, 31, 33, 34, 36, 42, and 43

○ = HINTS AND HOMEWORK HELP
for Exs. 3, 5, 9, 11, 29 at classzone.com

## SKILL PRACTICE

**VOCABULARY** Copy and complete the statement.

1. The sum of the measures of two __?__ angles is 180°.

2. Two lines that intersect to form a right angle are called __?__.

**CLASSIFYING ANGLES** Tell whether the angles are *complementary*, *supplementary*, or *neither*.

**SEE EXAMPLE 1**
on p. 403
for Exs. 3–9

3. $m\angle 1 = 62°$, $m\angle 2 = 118°$

4. $m\angle 1 = 51°$, $m\angle 2 = 39°$

**FINDING ANGLE MEASURES** Find the angle measure.

5. $\angle 1$ and $\angle 2$ are complementary, and $m\angle 1 = 56°$. Find $m\angle 2$.

6. $\angle 3$ and $\angle 4$ are supplementary, and $m\angle 4 = 71°$. Find $m\angle 3$.

7. $\angle 5$ and $\angle 6$ are supplementary, and $m\angle 5 = 22°$. Find $m\angle 6$.

8. $\angle 7$ and $\angle 8$ are complementary, and $m\angle 8 = 84°$. Find $m\angle 7$.

9. **TAKS REASONING** Which angles are complementary?

Ⓐ $\angle 1$ and $\angle 2$

Ⓑ $\angle 2$ and $\angle 3$

Ⓒ $\angle 3$ and $\angle 4$

Ⓓ $\angle 4$ and $\angle 1$

**ANGLE PAIRS** Find the measures of the numbered angles.

**SEE EXAMPLES
2 AND 3**
on pp. 404–405
for Exs. 10–14

10.

11.

12.

13.

14. **ERROR ANALYSIS** Describe and correct the error made in the statement.

15. **WHICH ONE DOESN'T BELONG?** Which of the angle pairs doesn't belong?

$m\angle 2 = 68°$ because the measures of vertical angles add up to 180°

A. $m\angle 1 = 21°$, $m\angle 2 = 69°$

B. $m\angle 3 = 12°$, $m\angle 4 = 68°$

C. $m\angle 5 = 79°$, $m\angle 6 = 11°$

D. $m\angle 7 = 45°$, $m\angle 8 = 45°$

**PARALLEL LINES** In Exercises 16–19, use the figure at the right. Find the measure of the angle. Tell which types of angle pairs you used.

**16.** $m\angle 1$        **17.** $m\angle 2$

**18.** $m\angle 3$        **19.** $m\angle 4$

**20. GEOMETRY** A four sided figure is formed by the intersecting lines in the diagram above. *Describe* the angle relationships in this figure, based on your answers to Exercises 16–19.

**REASONING** Copy and complete each sentence with *always*, *sometimes*, or *never*. *Explain* your reasoning.

**21.** Two angles are __?__ supplementary.

**22.** Vertical angles __?__ have different measures.

**23.** Perpendicular lines __?__ form four right angles.

**⟨xy⟩ ALGEBRA** Find the value of the variable and the angle measures.

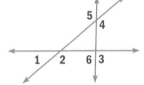

**24.** $m\angle 1 = (5x + 15)°$ and $m\angle 2 = 28x°$

**25.** $m\angle 6 = (100 - 10y)°$ and $m\angle 3 = 45y°$

**26.** $m\angle 4 = (7n + 39)°$ and $m\angle 5 = (11n - 13)°$

**27. CHALLENGE** $\angle B$ and $\angle C$ are supplementary. The measure of $\angle C$ is four times the measure of $\angle B$. Find $m\angle B$.

## PROBLEM SOLVING

**28. SKIS** One of the angle measures formed by the skis in the diagram at the right is 60°. What are the measures of the other 3 angles?

**29.** **PARALLEL LINES** A line intersects three parallel lines. How many pairs of vertical angles are formed? *Explain* your answer and include an example.

**30. STATIONERY** A student designed the stationery border shown at the right. *Explain* how to find $m\angle 2$ if $m\angle 1 = 135°$.

**31.** 🔷 **TAKS REASONING** Draw a pair of complementary angles and a pair of supplementary angles. Then draw a pair of angles that are neither complementary nor supplementary.

**32. ESTIMATION** Estimate the measure of the angle. Then approximate the measure of the complement of the angle.

**33.** ◆ **TAKS REASONING** In the diagram of the parking lot, $m\angle 1 = 120°$. What is $m\angle 1 + m\angle 3$?

   **(A)** 90°        **(B)** 120°

   **(C)** 240°      **(D)** 225°

**34.** ◆ **TAKS REASONING** Two complementary angles have the same measure. *Explain* how you can find the measure of each angle.

**35.** **INTERSECTING PATHS** Two bicycle paths intersect to form a 75° angle. Sketch the intersection and find the measure of each angle formed.

**36.** ◆ **TAKS REASONING** *Describe* three real-world situations involving perpendicular lines.

**37.** **ARCHITECTURE** The upright supports shown at the right are parallel. What are $m\angle 1$, $m\angle 2$, and $m\angle 3$? *Explain.*

**38.** **GEOMETRY** Draw two parallel lines $m$ and $n$. Then draw two more parallel lines that are perpendicular to line $m$. How many right angles are formed? *Explain* how you know they are right angles.

**39.** **GEOMETRY** Draw two parallel lines. Then draw a line that intersects the two parallel lines at a 60° angle. How many 60° angles are formed?

**40.** **ORIENTATION** A man walks with traffic toward the intersection of two perpendicular streets. He looks directly in front of him at the corner across the street. Then he turns 45° counterclockwise and looks at the northeast corner of the intersection. Using directions, describe the corner he is standing on.

**41.** **CHALLENGE** Use the diagram to find the unknown angle measure between Mulberry Street and Walnut Street.

---

◆ **MIXED REVIEW FOR TAKS**      **TAKS PRACTICE** at classzone.com

*REVIEW*
Lesson 7.7;
TAKS Workbook

**42.** ◆ **TAKS PRACTICE** The measure of a triangle's height is 62.5% of its base. The triangle's height has no factors in common with its base. Which are possible measurements for the triangle's height, $h$, and its base, $b$? *TAKS Obj. 6*

   **(A)** $h = 5, b = 8$          **(B)** $h = 10, b = 16$

   **(C)** $h = 3, b = 8$          **(D)** $h = 6, b = 16$

*REVIEW*
Lesson 7.8;
TAKS Workbook

**43.** ◆ **TAKS PRACTICE** A spinner is divided into twenty equal parts, labeled 1 through 20. What is the probability of NOT spinning a 6 or 7? *TAKS Obj. 5*

   **(F)** 10%     **(G)** 60%     **(H)** 70%     **(J)** 90%

# Constructions

**Extension**
*Use after Lesson 8.1*

**TEKS** *8.14.D, 8.15.A*

**GOAL** Copy an angle and construct perpendicular lines and parallel lines.

You can *construct* geometric figures using special tools. A *compass* is used to draw parts of circles called *arcs*. A *straightedge* is used to draw straight lines.

**EXAMPLE 1** Copying an Angle

**STEP 1** **Draw** an angle. Label its vertex *A*. Then draw a ray with endpoint *X*.

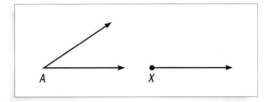

**USE A COMPASS**
Need help using a compass? See p. 777.

**STEP 2** **Draw** an arc with center *A*. Label *B* and *C* on ∠*A*. Use the same compass setting to draw an arc with center *X*. Label point *Y*.

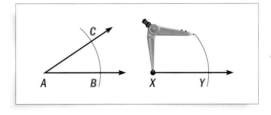

**STEP 3** **Draw** an arc with center *B* that passes through *C*. Use the same compass setting to draw an arc with center *Y*. Label point *Z*.

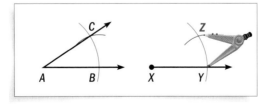

**STEP 4** **Use** a straightedge to draw a ray with endpoint *X* through *Z*.

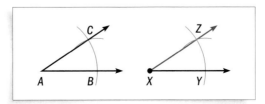

**Check** Use a protractor to check that *m*∠*A* = *m*∠*X*.

## EXAMPLE 2  Constructing a Perpendicular Line

**STEP 1** **Draw** a line and a point $P$ not on the line. Draw an arc with center $P$ that intersects the line twice. Label $A$ and $B$. Using the same compass setting, draw arcs with centers $A$ and $B$.

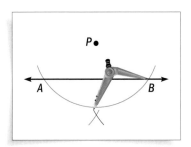

**STEP 2** **Label** point $Q$ where the last two arcs intersect. Draw a line through $P$ and $Q$. Lines $PQ$ and $AB$ are perpendicular.

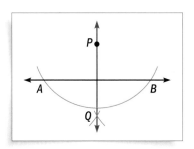

## EXAMPLE 3  Constructing a Parallel Line

**ANOTHER WAY**

In Step 1, you can make line $PQ$ intersect line $AB$ at any angle. Step 2 will still make a line parallel to line $AB$.

**STEP 1** **Follow** the steps in Example 2 to construct perpendicular lines. Label $\angle 1$.

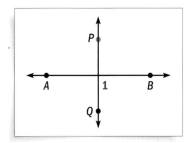

**STEP 2** **Follow** the steps in Example 1 to copy $\angle 1$ at point $P$ as shown.

## EXERCISES

In Exercises 1–4, use a protractor to draw an angle with the given measure. Then use a compass and straightedge to copy the angle.

**1.** $45°$  **2.** $120°$  **3.** $135°$  **4.** $60°$

**CONSTRUCTIONS** Use a compass and straightedge to construct the figure.

**5.** Three parallel lines  **6.** Right triangle  **7.** Rectangle

**8.** **POINT ON A LINE** Example 2 can be adjusted so you can make perpendicular lines when $P$ is on a line. Draw a line and label point $P$ on it. In Step 2, to find $Q$, open your compass wider than it was in Step 1. Draw line $PQ$, which is perpendicular to the given line.

## 8.2 Angles and Triangles

TEKS *8.15.A, 8.16.B*

| | |
|---|---|
| **Before** | You identified pairs of angles. |
| **Now** | You'll classify angles and triangles. |
| **Why?** | So you can classify triangles in architecture, as in Ex. 32. |

**KEY VOCABULARY**
• **acute, right, obtuse angle,** *p. 411*
• **acute, right, obtuse triangle,** *p. 411*
• **equilateral, isosceles, scalene triangle,** *p. 411*

An angle can be classified by its measure.

**Acute angle**

Measure is less than 90°.

**Right angle**

Measure is exactly 90°.

**Obtuse angle**

Measure is greater than 90° and less than 180°.

---

### KEY CONCEPT
*For Your Notebook*

#### Classifying Triangles

**By Angles**

An **acute triangle** has three acute angles.

A **right triangle** has one right angle.

An **obtuse triangle** has one obtuse angle.

**By Sides**

An **equilateral triangle** has three sides of equal length.

An **isosceles triangle** has at least two sides of equal length.

A **scalene triangle** has no sides of equal length.

---

A geometric figure can be named using the vertices of each of its angles. Use either a clockwise or counterclockwise order such as △ACB or △DEF.

Tick marks in a drawing show that side lengths are equal. Arc marks show that angle measures are equal.

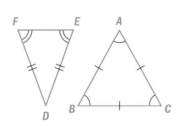

## EXAMPLE 1 Classifying a Triangle

**a.** Classify △*XYZ* by its angles.

**b.** Classify △*XYZ* by its side lengths.

### SOLUTION

**a.** The triangle has a right angle at *Y*. So, it is a right triangle.

**b.** The triangle has two sides of equal length. So, it is an isosceles triangle.

**Angles in a Triangle** From the diagram below you can see that the sum of the angle measures in the triangle is 180°. This is true for any triangle.

## EXAMPLE 2 Finding an Unknown Angle Measure

 Find the value of *x*. Then classify the triangle by its angles.

### SOLUTION

The sum of the angle measures of a triangle is 180°.

| | |
|---|---|
| $x° + 42° + 42° = 180°$ | **Write an equation.** |
| $x + 84 = 180$ | **Add.** |
| $x + 84 - 84 = 180 - 84$ | **Subtract 84 from each side.** |
| $x = 96$ | **Simplify.** |

▶ **Answer** The value of *x* is 96. The triangle has one obtuse angle, so it is an obtuse triangle.

## ✓ GUIDED PRACTICE for Examples 1 and 2

**Classify the triangle by its side lengths.**

**1.** 7 cm, 9 cm, 7 cm          **2.** 11 ft, 11 ft, 11 ft          **3.** 4 in., 5 in., 6 in.

**4.** 6 ft, 6 ft, 6 ft          **5.** 10 mm, 10 mm, 8 mm          **6.** 2 cm, 8 cm, 7 cm

**7.** Find the value of *x*. Then classify the triangle by its angles.

# 8.2 EXERCISES

HOMEWORK KEY

= TAKS Practice and Reasoning
Exs. 16, 33, 34, 39, and 40

= HINTS AND HOMEWORK HELP
for Exs. 5, 7, 11, 13, 29 at classzone.com

## SKILL PRACTICE

**VOCABULARY** Copy and complete the statement.

**1.** A(n) __?__ triangle has no sides of equal length.

**2.** A(n) __?__ triangle has at least two sides of equal length.

**VOCABULARY** The referee is making calls during a hockey game. Classify the angle made by his arms as *acute*, *obtuse*, or *right*.

**3.** Cross checking

**4.** Roughing

**5.** Delayed calling of penalty

*Animated Math* at classzone.com

**CLASSIFYING BY SIDES** Classify the triangle by its side lengths.

SEE EXAMPLE 1
on p. 412
for Exs. 6–12

**6.**

4 in.
2 in.
3 in.

**7.**

3 ft     3 ft
3 ft

**8.**

3 cm
3 cm

**9.**

**10.**

**11.**
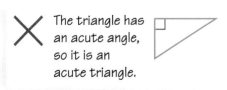
4 cm
5 cm
3 cm

**12. ERROR ANALYSIS** Describe and correct the error made in the statement.

The triangle has an acute angle, so it is an acute triangle.

**CLASSIFYING BY ANGLES** Find the value of *x*. Classify the triangle by its angles.

SEE EXAMPLES
1 AND 2
on p. 412
for Exs. 13–15

**13.**

$x°$
43°     79°

**14.**

66°     $x°$

**15.**

116°     32°
$x°$

SEE EXAMPLE 2
on p. 412
for Ex. 16–19

**16.**  **TAKS REASONING** The angles of a triangle measure 110°, 40°, and x°. What is the value of x?

(**A**) 30      (**B**) 40      (**C**) 50      (**D**) 210

**REASONING** Can the angles of a triangle have the given measures? *Explain* your reasoning.

**17.** 43°, 48°, 90°      **18.** 1.5°, 0.5°, 178°      **19.** 21.3°, 56.7°, 102°

**ISOSCELES TRIANGLES** In an isosceles triangle, the angles opposite the sides with the same length have the same measure. Find the measure of the unknown angles of the triangle and classify it by its angles.

**20.**
**21.**
**22.**

 **ALGEBRA** Find the measure of each angle of the triangle.

**23.**
**24.**
**25.**

**26. USING PARALLEL LINES** Find the measures of the numbered angles.

**27. CHALLENGE** Name all ten of the triangles in the figure and classify each triangle by its angles. Are there any triangles in the figure that are isosceles? If so, *explain* your reasoning and name the isosceles triangles.

---

## PROBLEM SOLVING

**28. ARCHITECTURE** The two side edges of the gable in the illustration at the right have the same length. What kind of triangle is formed? *Explain.*

**29.** **MENTAL MATH** An *equiangular* triangle has three angles with equal measures. Find the measures of those angles.

**30. WRITING** Can a right triangle be equilateral? *Explain* your reasoning.

**31. REASONING** Can two angles of a triangle be supplementary? *Explain.*

**32. TELESCOPE** The McMath-Pierce Solar Telescope is located at the Kitt Peak National Observatory near Tucson, Arizona. The telescope has a 100 foot tall tower and a 200 foot shaft that slants to the ground. Classify the triangle formed by the telescope and the ground by its sides and by its angles.

**33.** ⬥ **TAKS REASONING** The following statements about △ABC are true: $m\angle C$ is greater than $m\angle B$, $m\angle B$ is greater than $m\angle A$, and $m\angle A$ is greater than 40°. What are the angle measures of △ABC?

   (**A**) $m\angle A = 48°$     (**B**) $m\angle A = 36°$     (**C**) $m\angle A = 60°$     (**D**) $m\angle A = 48°$
       $m\angle B = 78°$          $m\angle B = 54°$          $m\angle B = 60°$          $m\angle B = 54°$
       $m\angle C = 54°$          $m\angle C = 90°$          $m\angle C = 60°$          $m\angle C = 78°$

**34.** ⬥ **TAKS REASONING** Try to draw each triangle whose side lengths are given at the right. Which triangles are possible to draw? *Explain* why the other triangle(s) cannot be drawn.

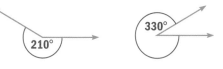

△ABC    9 cm, 8 cm, 4 cm
△DEF    9 cm, 6 cm, 4 cm
△GHI    9 cm, 2 cm, 4 cm

**REFLEX ANGLES** An angle whose measure is greater than 180°, but less than 360°, is called a *reflex angle.* Two reflex angles are shown at the right. In Exercises 35–37, find the value of *x* and classify the angle.

**35.**

**36.**

**37.**

**38. CHALLENGE** List all sets of three whole numbers that total 10 units, such as 3, 3, and 4. Which of these sets could be lengths of the sides of a triangle? How is the longest side in each of these sets related to the other two sides?

---

## MIXED REVIEW FOR TAKS

**TAKS PRACTICE** at classzone.com

*REVIEW*
Lesson 8.1;
TAKS Workbook

**39.** ⬥ **TAKS PRACTICE** $\angle 1$ and $\angle 2$ are supplementary, and $m\angle 1 = 34°$. Which procedure can be used to find $m\angle 2$? *TAKS Obj. 6*

   (**A**) Add 34 to 90              (**B**) Add 34 to 180
   (**C**) Subtract 34 from 90     (**D**) Subtract 34 from 180

*REVIEW*
Lesson 5.2;
TAKS Workbook

**40.** ⬥ **TAKS PRACTICE** One week in June, a civil engineer completed one third of the week's work on Monday, one quarter of the week's work on Tuesday, and one fifth of the week's work on Wednesday. Approximately what portion of the week's work is left? *TAKS Obj. 1*

   (**F**) $\frac{1}{6}$          (**G**) $\frac{1}{5}$          (**H**) $\frac{1}{4}$          (**J**) $\frac{2}{5}$

# 8.3 Quadrilaterals

| | |
|---|---|
| **Before** | You classified angles and triangles. |
| **Now** | You'll classify quadrilaterals. |
| **Why?** | So you can find angles of quadrilaterals, as in a compass rose in Ex. 28. |

**KEY VOCABULARY**
- **quadrilateral,** *p. 416*
- **trapezoid,** *p. 416*
- **parallelogram,** *p. 416*
- **rhombus,** *p. 416*

A **quadrilateral** is a closed figure with four sides that are line segments. The figures below are special types of quadrilaterals.

| *Special Quadrilaterals* | *Diagram* |
|---|---|
| **Trapezoid** <br> A **trapezoid** is a quadrilateral with exactly 1 pair of parallel sides. | |
| **Parallelogram** <br> A **parallelogram** is a quadrilateral with two pairs of parallel sides. | |
| **Rhombus** <br> A **rhombus** is a parallelogram with 4 sides of equal length. | |
| **Rectangle** <br> A *rectangle* is a parallelogram with 4 right angles. | |
| **Square** <br> A *square* is a parallelogram with 4 sides of equal length and 4 right angles. | |

## EXAMPLE 1   Classifying a Quadrilateral

*TAKE NOTES*

You can organize the definitions of quadrilaterals in your notebook using a concept map.

**Classify the quadrilateral.**

**a.**
5 cm   5 cm
5 cm   5 cm

The quadrilateral is a parallelogram with 4 sides of equal length. So, it is a rhombus.

**b.**

The quadrilateral is a parallelogram with 4 sides of equal length and 4 right angles. So, it is a square.

**Angles in a Quadrilateral**  A *diagonal* is a segment that joins two vertices of a quadrilateral but is not a side. You can use a diagonal of a quadrilateral to show that the sum of the angle measures in a quadrilateral is 360°.

Cut a quadrilateral along a diagonal to form two triangles.

The sum of the angle measures in each triangle is 180°.

The sum of the angle measures in a quadrilateral is 180° + 180° = 360°.

**EXAMPLE 2**  **Finding an Unknown Angle Measure**

Find the value of $x$.

**SOLUTION**

$$x° + 51° + 129° + 129° = 360°$$  The sum of the angle measures is 360°.

$$x + 309 = 360$$  Add.

$$x = 51$$  Subtract 309 from each side.

---

✓ **GUIDED PRACTICE**  for Examples 1 and 2

Use the figure at the right.

1. Classify the quadrilateral.

2. Find the value of $x$.

---

## 8.3 EXERCISES

**HOMEWORK KEY**

🌟 = **TAKS Practice and Reasoning**
Exs. 16, 29, 33, and 34

◯ = **HINTS** AND **HOMEWORK HELP**
for Exs. 3, 7, 9, 13, 27 at classzone.com

### SKILL PRACTICE

**VOCABULARY**  Copy and complete the statement.

1. A quadrilateral with exactly 1 pair of parallel sides is a __?__.

2. A parallelogram with 4 right angles is a __?__.

**CLASSIFYING QUADRILATERALS**  Classify the quadrilateral.

**SEE EXAMPLE 1**
on p. 416
for Exs. 3–5

3.

4.

5.

**SEE EXAMPLE 1**
on p. 416
for Exs. 6–8

**MEASUREMENT** Measure the side lengths. Then classify the quadrilateral.

**6.**

**7.**

**8.**

**SEE EXAMPLE 2**
on p. 417
for Exs. 9–14

**ALGEBRA** Find the values of *x* and *y*.

**9.**
110° 71°
70° x°

**10.**
60°
x°
95° 100°

**11.**
x° 140° 70°
85°

**12.**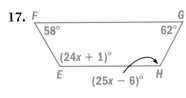
100°
80° 40°
y° x°

**13.**
y°
115° x°

**14.**
54° 110°
x°
54° y°
105°

**15. ERROR ANALYSIS** Describe and correct the error made in listing the diagonals of parallelogram *ABCD*.

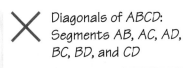
Diagonals of ABCD:
Segments AB, AC, AD,
BC, BD, and CD

**16. ⬥ TAKS REASONING** Classify the fourth angle of a quadrilateral that has three acute angles.

**(A)** Acute **(B)** Right **(C)** Obtuse **(D)** Straight

**ALGEBRA** Find the value of *x* and the unknown angle measures.

**17.** *F*      *G*
58°    62°
(24x + 1)°
*E*   (25x − 6)°   *H*

**18.** *K*   (3x + 13)°
*J*   x°   (x + 1)°   *L*
(4x − 14)°   *M*

**REASONING** Tell whether the statement is *always*, *sometimes*, or *never* true. *Justify* your reasoning.

**19.** A rhombus is a parallelogram.

**20.** A rectangle is a square.

**21.** A square is a parallelogram.

**22.** A triangle is a quadrilateral.

**23.** A trapezoid is a parallelogram.

**24.** A quadrilateral is a rectangle.

**Animated Math** at classzone.com

**25. CHALLENGE** Find the values of *x*, *y*, and *z* in the diagram. *Explain* your reasoning.

122°
60°
x°
z°
y°

⬥ = **TAKS Practice and Reasoning**     ◯ = **HINTS AND HOMEWORK HELP** *at classzone.com*

SEE EXAMPLE 1
on p. 416
for Ex. 26

**26. DESIGN** Classify the quadrilaterals of each color in the design below.

**27. REASONING** How many different diagonals can be drawn in any quadrilateral? *Justify* your answer by sketching each quadrilateral discussed on page 416 and all of its diagonals.

SEE EXAMPLE 2
on p. 417
for Ex. 28

**28. COMPASS ROSE** A compass rose is a figure used on a map to show direction. The compass rose shown includes four red rhombuses. Find the value of $x$ and the unknown angle measures.

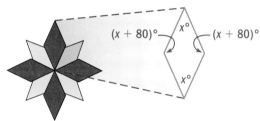

**29.** ⬥ **TAKS REASONING** Two equilateral triangles share a common side. Which quadrilateral does the figure form? *Explain.*

**30. WRITING** What is the greatest number of obtuse angles that a quadrilateral can have? *Explain* your reasoning.

**31. REASONING** Is it possible for a quadrilateral to have three 60° angles? *Explain* why or why not.

**32. CHALLENGE** Use the figure at the right.

a. A trapezoid is divided into four quadrilaterals, as shown. Classify the quadrilaterals. Then find the measure of each labeled angle. *Explain* your reasoning.

b. *Describe* the relationship between opposite angles in a parallelogram and between consecutive angles. *Justify* your reasoning.

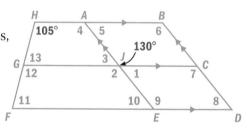

REVIEW
Lesson 7.8;
TAKS Workbook

**33.** ⬥ **TAKS PRACTICE** The probability of a coin landing heads up every time is greater than 12% if you flip it how many times? *TAKS Obj. 5*

Ⓐ At most twice      Ⓑ At most 3 times

Ⓒ At most 4 times      Ⓓ At most 5 times

REVIEW
Lesson 6.3;
TAKS Workbook

**34.** ⬥ **TAKS PRACTICE** Al is one third as old as Kay. Ray is one half as old as Kay. The sum of Al's age and Ray's age is 15. What is Kay's age? *TAKS Obj. 6*

Ⓕ 5      Ⓖ 18      Ⓗ 30      Ⓙ 45

# 8.4 Polygons and Angles

TEKS *8.16.A, 8.16.B*

| **Before** | You found angle measures in triangles and quadrilaterals. |
| **Now** | You'll find angle measures in polygons. |
| **Why?** | So you can classify polygons in nature, as in Ex. 27. |

## KEY VOCABULARY

- **polygon,** *p. 420*
- **regular polygon,** *p. 420*
- **pentagon,** *p. 420*
- **hexagon,** *p. 420*
- **heptagon,** *p. 420*
- **octagon,** *p. 420*

## ACTIVITY

**You can use triangles to find the sum of the angle measures in other figures.**

**STEP 1** **Copy** the table. Divide each figure into triangles by drawing all the diagonal lines that begin at the point marked.

**STEP 2** **Use** your drawings to complete the table.

| Shape | Quadrilateral | Pentagon | Hexagon | Heptagon | Octagon |
|---|---|---|---|---|---|
| Number of Sides | 4 | ? | ? | ? | ? |
| Number of Diagonal Lines | 1 | ? | ? | ? | ? |
| Number of Triangles Formed | 2 | ? | ? | ? | ? |
| Sum of Angle Measures | 360° | ? | ? | ? | ? |

**STEP 3** **Use** your results to complete a column for a 10-sided figure.

**Polygons** A **polygon** is a closed figure whose sides are line segments that intersect only at their endpoints. In a **regular polygon**, all the angles have the same measure and all the sides have the same length. Polygons can be identified by the number of their sides as shown in the table in the Activity.

**READING**
You can use "*n*-gon," where *n* is the number of sides, to identify a polygon if you haven't learned its name. A 13-gon is a 13-sided polygon.

**Polygons**

**Regular polygons**

**Not polygons**

**EXAMPLE 1** Identifying Figures

**Is the bottom of the box a** *polygon*, **a** *regular polygon*, **or** *not a polygon*? *Explain.*

**a.** It is not a polygon. The bottom edge does not have line segments.

**b.** It is a regular polygon. Its angles have equal measures, and its sides have equal lengths.

*Animated* **Math** at classzone.com

**Angles** In the activity on page 420, you used triangles to find the sum of the angle measures in polygons. In a regular polygon, the measure of one angle is the sum of the angle measures divided by the number of sides.

---

**KEY CONCEPT** *For Your Notebook*

**Angle Measures in a Polygon**

Sum of angle measures in an $n$-gon: $(n - 2) \cdot 180°$

Measure of one angle in a *regular* $n$-gon: $\dfrac{(n - 2) \cdot 180°}{n}$

---

**EXAMPLE 2** Finding an Angle Measure

**Find the measure of one angle in a regular octagon.**

A regular octagon has 8 sides, so $n = 8$.

$$\frac{(n - 2) \cdot 180°}{n} = \frac{(8 - 2) \cdot 180°}{8}$$    **Substitute 8 for** *n*.

$$= \frac{1080°}{8}$$    **Simplify numerator.**

$$= 135°$$    **Divide.**

▶ **Answer** The measure of one angle in a regular octagon is 135°.

---

✓ **GUIDED PRACTICE** **for Examples 1 and 2**

1. Find the sum of the angle measures in a 9-gon.

2. Find the measure of one angle in a regular heptagon. Round to the nearest tenth of a degree.

# 8.4 EXERCISES

## SKILL PRACTICE

**VOCABULARY** Copy and complete the statement.

1. A _?_ is a closed figure with sides that are line segments that intersect only at their endpoints.

2. A _?_ is a closed figure with sides that are line segments of equal length meeting only at their endpoints, and with all angles of equal measure.

*SEE EXAMPLE 1*
on p. 421
for Exs. 3–5

**CLASSIFYING FIGURES** Tell whether the figure is a *polygon*, a *regular polygon*, or *not a polygon*.

(3.)                    4.                    5.

*SEE EXAMPLE 2*
on p. 421
for Exs. 6–14

**FINDING ANGLE MEASURES** Find the sum of the angle measures in the polygon.

6. 12-gon          (7.) 16-gon          8. 11-gon          9. 20-gon

10. **ERROR ANALYSIS** Describe and correct the error made in finding the sum of the angle measures of a hexagon.

Sum of angle measures = 6 · 180°
                       = 1080°

**FINDING AN ANGLE MEASURE** Find the measure of one angle in the polygon. Round to the nearest degree if necessary.

11. Regular 10-gon          12. Regular 14-gon          13. Regular 15-gon

14.  **TAKS REASONING** Four angles in a pentagon measure 90°, 85°, 120°, and 130°. What is the measure of the fifth angle?

Ⓐ 105°          Ⓑ 115°          Ⓒ 120°          Ⓓ 165°

**ALGEBRA** Find the value of *x* and the unknown angle measures.

15.                         16.                         17.

18. **WHICH ONE DOESN'T BELONG?** Which of the following is not a regular polygon?

A.                    B.                    C.                    D.

**IDENTIFYING POLYGONS** Find the type of *n*-gon whose angle measures have the given sum.

**19.** 1980°        **20.** 2520°        **21.** 2880°        **22.** 3600°

**23. CHALLENGE** The measures of the angles of a regular polygon are whole numbers. What is the greatest number of sides that the polygon can have? *Explain.*

**PROBLEM SOLVING**

**SWIMMING POOL DESIGNS** Tell whether the swimming pool design is a polygon. *Justify* your reasoning.

**24.**

**25.**

**26.**

**27. GEOLOGY** Classify the polygons shown in the photograph of the rock formation in Yellowstone National Park at the top of page 420.

**28.**  **TAKS REASONING** A table has 7 sides of equal length and 7 angles of equal measure. What is the measure of one angle of the table?

   **A** 25.7°        **B** 128.6°        **C** 210.0°        **D** 252.0°

**29. MAKE A MODEL** You want to cut a 10-gon out of a piece of paper. You are told to first draw a pentagon on the paper and cut it out. *Explain* how you can cut your pentagon to create a 10-gon. Then follow your procedure to create a 10-gon.

**30.**  **TAKS REASONING** Sketch a polygon that is not regular, but has sides of equal length.

**31.**  **TAKS REASONING** Is a figure eight a polygon? Give two reasons to *justify* your answer.

**32.**  **TAKS REASONING** The angles marked with letters in the figures below are called *exterior angles.*

   **a. Evaluate** Find the measures of the exterior angles of each polygon.

   **b. Calculate** Find the sum of the exterior angle measures for each polygon.

   **c. Patterns** Describe a pattern in the sums you found in part (b).

**33. MAKE A CONJECTURE** Draw all diagonals of a quadrilateral, a pentagon, and a hexagon. Write the numbers of diagonals as a pattern. *Predict* the next number in the pattern. Draw a heptagon and check your predictions.

**34. BASES** You want to design a new base marker for a new type of baseball game. Is it possible to make a base marker that is a regular polygon with each angle having a measure of 135°? of 145°? *Explain*.

**35. CHALLENGE** In a regular polygon, the measure of each exterior angle, as described in Exercise 32, is 25% of the measure of each interior angle. Name this polygon.

**36. CHALLENGE** The sum of a polygon's angle measures is 15 times the measure of the exterior angle of a regular pentagon. Identify the polygon.

---

## MIXED REVIEW FOR TAKS

**TAKS PRACTICE** at classzone.com

*REVIEW*
Lesson 8.3;
TAKS Workbook

**37. TAKS PRACTICE** Which procedure can be used to find *n*? *TAKS Obj. 6*

(A) Divide 360 by 4

(B) Divide the sum of 90 and 112 by 2

(C) Subtract the sum of 90 and 112 from 360

(D) Subtract the sum of 90, 90, and 112 from 360

*REVIEW*
Lesson 7.2;
TAKS Workbook

**38. TAKS PRACTICE** A model of the Clifton Suspension Bridge has a scale of 1 inch to 26 feet. The model is about 27 inches long. Approximately how long is the actual bridge? *TAKS Obj. 1*

(F) 1 ft          (G) 26 ft          (H) 27 ft          (J) 702 ft

---

## QUIZ *for Lessons 8.1–8.4*

Tell whether the angles are *complementary*, *supplementary*, or *neither*. *(p. 403)*

**1.** $m\angle 1 = 32°, m\angle 2 = 148°$     **2.** $m\angle 3 = 59°, m\angle 4 = 41°$     **3.** $m\angle 5 = 12°, m\angle 6 = 78°$

**4.** $m\angle 7 = 116°, m\angle 8 = 64°$     **5.** $m\angle A = 73°, m\angle B = 117°$     **6.** $m\angle C = 48°, m\angle D = 42°$

Can the angles in a triangle have the measures given? *Explain* why or why not. If so classify the triangle. *(p. 411)*

**7.** 23°, 57°, 95°          **8.** 64.6°, 77.3°, 38.1°          **9.** 155°, 24.9°, 0.1°

Find the value of *x*.

**10.**  *(p. 416)*     **11.**  *(p. 403)*     **12.**  *(p. 420)*

**13.** Classify the figures in Exercises 10 and 12. *(pp. 416, 420)*

---

## Lessons 8.1–8.4

**MULTIPLE CHOICE**

1. **SCISSORS** A pair of scissors forms four angles.

   What is $m\angle 4$ if $m\angle 3$ is 30°? *TEKS 8.2.B*

   Ⓐ 30°          Ⓑ 50°

   Ⓒ 130°          Ⓓ 150°

2. **OCTAGON** A regular octagon is divided in half by drawing a segment connecting the midpoints of two opposite sides. Two new polygons are formed by this action. What is the sum of the angle measures in each polygon? *TEKS 8.14.C*

   Ⓕ 540°          Ⓖ 780°

   Ⓗ 1080°          Ⓙ 1440°

3. **DRIVING** Vida drives south on Kendell Road. She makes a 35° left (counterclockwise) turn. Then she turns left onto Linden Road, which runs parallel to Kendell. What is the measure, in degrees, of Vida's turn onto Linden Road? *TEKS 8.14.C*

   Ⓐ 35°          Ⓑ 55°

   Ⓒ 90°          Ⓓ 145°

4. **ISOSCELES TRIANGLES** What is the value of $x$? *TEKS 8.2.B*

   Ⓕ 30°          Ⓖ 60°

   Ⓗ 75°          Ⓙ 105°

5. **ANGLE EQUATION** What is the measure of $\angle A$? *TEKS 8.2.B*

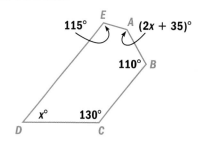

   Ⓐ 50°          Ⓑ 85°

   Ⓒ 120°          Ⓓ 135°

6. **FLAG** The flag of the Bahamas is shown below.

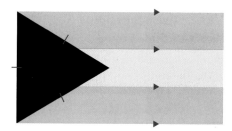

   Which does NOT describe either the black, blue, or yellow polygons? *TEKS 8.7.B*

   Ⓕ Triangle          Ⓖ Quadrilateral

   Ⓗ Pentagon          Ⓙ Hexagon

**GRIDDED ANSWER** Ⓞ①●③④⑤⑥⑦⑧⑨

7. **SIGNS** The arrow in the highway sign below is comprised of an isosceles triangle and a rectangle. Find the sum, in degrees, of the angles of the polygon formed by these two shapes. *TEKS 8.2.A*

# INVESTIGATION
*Use before Lesson 8.5*

**GOAL**
Copy a triangle.

**MATERIALS**
- compass
- straightedge
- protractor

**TEKS** *8.16.A*

# 8.5 Copying a Triangle

You can use a compass and a straightedge to copy a triangle.

**EXPLORE** **Use a compass and straightedge to copy a triangle.**

**STEP 1** **Draw** a triangle with vertices *A*, *B*, and *C*. Draw a ray with endpoint *P*. Draw an arc with center *A* through point *C*. Use the same compass setting to draw an arc with center *P*. Label point *Q*.

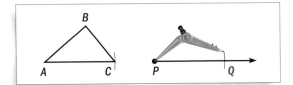

**STEP 2** **Draw** an arc with center *C* through point *B*. Use the same compass setting to draw an arc with center *Q*.

**STEP 3** **Draw** an arc with center *A* through point *B*. Use the same compass setting to draw an arc with center *P*. Label point *R*. Connect *P* and *R*. Connect *R* and *Q*.

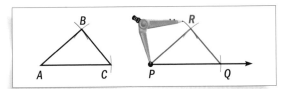

**PRACTICE** **Draw a triangle that fits the description. Then use a compass and straightedge to copy the triangle.**

1. acute

2. obtuse

3. right

**DRAW CONCLUSIONS**

4. **REASONING** Measure the angles of each triangle you drew in Exercises 1–3. Then measure the angles of the triangles you copied. What do you notice? *Explain.*

5. **WRITING** Suppose you use a compass and straightedge to copy a triangle. What angle measures of the new triangle are identical to the original triangle?

# 8.5 Congruent Polygons

TEKS 8.7.B, 8.16.B

**Before** You identified polygons.

**Now** You'll identify and name congruent polygons.

**Why?** So you can identify congruent triangles, as in Example 3.

**KEY VOCABULARY**
- **congruent segments,** *p. 427*
- **congruent angles,** *p. 427*
- **corresponding parts,** *p. 427*

**Congruent segments** have equal lengths. **Congruent angles** have equal measures. The symbol ≅ means "is congruent to."

Congruent polygons have the same shape and size. Polygons are congruent if their *corresponding* angles and sides are congruent. **Corresponding parts** are in the same position in different figures. To name congruent polygons, list their corresponding vertices in the same order. In the diagram △*KLM* ≅ △*PQR*.

**READING**

Two letters with a line over them refer to a *line segment*. For example, $\overline{PR}$ is read "segment *PR*" and means "the side with endpoints *P* and *R*."

Corresponding angles are congruent.

$$\angle K \cong \angle P \qquad \angle L \cong \angle Q \qquad \angle M \cong \angle R$$

Corresponding sides are congruent.

$$\overline{LM} \cong \overline{QR} \qquad \overline{KL} \cong \overline{PQ} \qquad \overline{KM} \cong \overline{PR}$$

## EXAMPLE 1   Name Corresponding Parts

**Picture Frames** In the frame below, quadrilateral *ABCD* ≅ quadrilateral *JKLM*. Name all pairs of corresponding angles and sides.

**SOLUTION**

Corresponding angles are congruent.

$$\angle A, \angle J \qquad \qquad \angle B, \angle K$$

$$\angle C, \angle L \qquad \qquad \angle D, \angle M$$

Corresponding sides are congruent.

$$\overline{AB}, \overline{JK} \qquad \qquad \overline{BC}, \overline{KL}$$

$$\overline{CD}, \overline{LM} \qquad \qquad \overline{AD}, \overline{JM}$$

✓ **GUIDED PRACTICE**   for Example 1

1. In Example 1, quadrilateral *EFGH* ≅ quadrilateral *QRNP*. Name all pairs of corresponding angles and sides.

**EXAMPLE 2** **Using Congruent Polygons**

△*JKL* ≅ △*TSR*. Find *m*∠*S*.

**SOLUTION**

Corresponding angles are congruent.

∠*K* and ∠*S* are corresponding angles, so they have the same measure. Find *m*∠*K*.

| | |
|---|---|
| $31° + m\angle K + 25° = 180°$ | Sum of angle measures is 180°. |
| $m\angle K + 56° = 180°$ | Add. |
| $m\angle K + 56 - 56 = 180 - 56$ | Subtract 56 from each side. |
| $m\angle K = 124°$ | Simplify. |

▶ **Answer** Because *m*∠*K* = *m*∠*S*, *m*∠*S* = 124°.

**Congruent Triangles** You can use the special rules below in the chart to tell whether triangles are congruent.

---

**Determining Whether Triangles Are Congruent**

**Side-Side-Side (SSS)**

If three sides of one triangle are congruent to three sides of another triangle, then the triangles are congruent.

△*ABC* ≅ △*DEF*

**Side-Angle-Side (SAS)**

If two sides and the angle between them in one triangle are congruent to two sides and the angle between them in another triangle, then the triangles are congruent.

△*JKL* ≅ △*MNP*

**Angle-Side-Angle (ASA)**

If two angles and the side between them in one triangle are congruent to two angles and the side between them in another triangle, then the triangles are congruent.

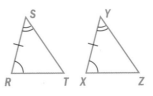

△*RST* ≅ △*XYZ*

---

✓ **GUIDED PRACTICE** **for Example 2**

**Find the value using the triangles in Example 2.**

**2.** length of $\overline{ST}$          **3.** *m*∠*T*          **4.** *m*∠*R*

EXAMPLE 3 **Identifying Congruent Triangles**

**Bridges** Name the congruent triangles formed by the bridge cables. Explain how you know they are congruent.

**SOLUTION**

Identify congruent corresponding parts.

$$\overline{CB} \cong \overline{CD}$$   Sides are congruent.

$$\overline{AC} \cong \overline{AC}$$   Side is congruent to itself.

$$\angle ACB \cong \angle ACD$$   Right angles are congruent.

▶**Answer**  $\triangle ACB \cong \triangle ACD$ by Side-Angle-Side.

---

✓ **GUIDED PRACTICE**   **for Example 3**

**Determine whether the triangles are congruent.**

5.

6.

---

## 8.5 EXERCISES

### SKILL PRACTICE

**VOCABULARY  Copy and complete the statement.**

1. Two angles with the same measure are  __?__ .

2. Sides and angles that are in the same position in different figures are called  __?__ .

**USING CONGRUENT POLYGONS  In the diagram, quadrilateral** *KLMN* ≅ **quadrilateral** *SPQR.*

*SEE EXAMPLES 1 AND 2*
on pp. 427–428
for Exs. 3–6

3. Name four pairs of congruent angles.

4. Find $m\angle S$.

5. Find the length of $\overline{NK}$.

6. Find $m\angle R$.

**MEASUREMENT** Quadrilateral *ABEF* ≅ quadrilateral *DGHC*. Find the unknown measure.

**SEE EXAMPLE 2**
on p. 428
for Exs. 7–10

**7.** m∠C

**8.** length of $\overline{AF}$

**9.** m∠A

**10.** length of $\overline{HC}$

**SEE EXAMPLE 3**
on p. 429
for Exs. 11–12

**11. IDENTIFYING CONGRUENT TRIANGLES** Name all the congruent triangles shown. *Justify* your answers.

**12. ERROR ANALYSIS** Describe and correct the error made in the solution.

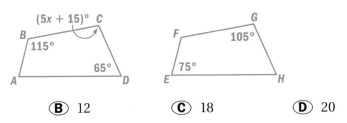

△ABC ≅ △DEF
by Side-Angle-Side.

**13.** ✦ **TAKS REASONING** Polygon *ABCD* ≅ polygon *EFGH*. Find the value of *x*.

(5*x* + 15)° C

B 115°

65°

A        D

G

F        105°

75°

E        H

**A** 10            **B** 12            **C** 18            **D** 20

**REASONING** *Explain* how you know the triangles are congruent. Then write an equation and solve for *x*.

**14.**
4 m
5 m
(*x* − 6) m

**15.**
(2*x* + 6) cm
32 cm

**16.**
*x*°
(2*x* − 24)°

**17. EXAMPLE AND NONEXAMPLES** Sketch two polygons whose corresponding angles are congruent but whose corresponding sides are *not* congruent. Sketch two polygons whose corresponding sides are congruent but whose corresponding angles are *not* congruent.

**18. CHALLENGE** Is it true that if any two sides and an angle of one triangle are congruent to any two sides and an angle of another triangle, then the triangles are congruent? *Justify* your answer with a sketch of two such triangles.

**19.** **SOCCER FIELD** In 1994, Michigan State University covered the floor of the Silverdome with natural grass for the World Cup Tournament. The pieces of sod were in the shape of regular hexagons. *Explain* how you know the regular hexagons were congruent.

**KITES** *Explain* how you know the red triangles in the kites are congruent.

**SEE EXAMPLE 3**
on p. 429
for Exs. 20–21

**20.**

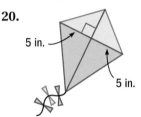

5 in.

5 in.

**21.**

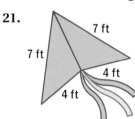

7 ft

7 ft

4 ft

4 ft

**22.** **WRITING** *Explain* how equality and congruence are similar. *Explain* how equality and congruence are different.

**23.** **CLOTHING** Two back pockets on a pair of jeans are congruent. Find $m\angle 1$.

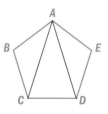

105°

1

**24.** **TAKS REASONING** What is the fewest pairs of corresponding parts that have to be congruent to establish that two triangles are congruent? Once you know that the triangles are congruent, how many pairs of corresponding parts do you know are congruent? *Explain.*

**25.** **TAKS REASONING** *ABCDE* is a regular pentagon. Which statement is not true?

Ⓐ $\overline{AC} \cong \overline{AD}$     Ⓑ $\overline{CB} \cong \overline{AD}$

Ⓒ $\overline{AB} \cong \overline{DC}$     Ⓓ $\angle BAE \cong \angle AED$

**26.** **WRITING** Use the regular pentagon in Exercise 25. *Explain* how you can show that $\triangle ACD$ is isosceles.

**27.** **REASONING** In $\triangle ABC$ and $\triangle XYZ$, $\overline{AB} \cong \overline{XY}$, $\overline{BC} \cong \overline{YZ}$, and $m\angle C \cong m\angle Z$. Can you conclude that another pair of congruent angles is present? *Explain* your reasoning.

**28.** **DIAGONALS** Draw a rectangle and mark the congruent sides and right angles. Then draw a diagonal. *Explain* how you know that the two triangles formed are congruent.

**29. POD SHELTERS** The triangles in the pod shelter shown are isosceles triangles. Two sides of each triangle are 7 feet long. What other information do you need to know to show that these triangles are congruent?

**30. DRAW A DIAGRAM** Sketch regular hexagon *LMNOPQ* and mark the congruent sides and angles. Draw three different diagonals from vertex *L* of the hexagon.

   **a.** Which triangle is congruent to △*LMN*?

   **b.** Name all the corresponding congruent parts in the two triangles in part (a).

   **c.** Which other two triangles do you now know are congruent? Which rule did you use?

**31. CHALLENGE** You are standing beside a stream at *A*. You walk off the distance shown to *C*. Your friend walks the same distance on the opposite bank from the tree to *D*. What corresponding parts of the two triangles are congruent? Are the triangles congruent? *Justify* your reasoning.

*REVIEW*
Lesson 8.4;
TAKS Workbook

**32.** **TAKS PRACTICE** The following statements are true about a polygon.

   • The number of sides is greater than 5.

   • The measure of one angle in the polygon is less than 128°.

Which type of polygon fits both statements? *TAKS Obj. 6*

   **(A)** Square             **(B)** Regular pentagon

   **(C)** Regular hexagon     **(D)** Regular heptagon

*REVIEW*
Lesson 3.5;
TAKS Workbook

**33.** **TAKS PRACTICE** The perimeter of the triangle shown is 36 meters. Which equation can be used to find the missing side length, *y*? *TAKS Obj. 2*

   **(F)** $\frac{1}{2}(9)y = 36$        **(G)** $9 + 15 + 36 = y$

   **(H)** $\frac{1}{2}(15)y = 36$      **(J)** $9 + 15 + y = 36$

# 8.6 Reflections and Symmetry

TEKS 8.6.B, 8.7.D

| Before | You plotted points in a coordinate plane. |
| Now | You'll reflect figures and identify lines of symmetry. |
| Why? | So you can find reflections, as in Example 2. |

**KEY VOCABULARY**
• **reflection,** *p. 433*
• **transformation,** *p. 433*
• **image,** *p. 433*
• **line symmetry,** *p. 435*

The photo above illustrates a *reflection*. A **reflection** creates a mirror image of each point of a figure.

A reflection is a type of **transformation**, an operation that changes a figure into another figure. The new figure created is called the **image**.

## EXAMPLE 1  Identifying a Reflection

**Tell whether the red figure is a reflection of the blue figure.**

**a.**

The figure is a reflection.

**b.**

The figure is *not* a reflection.

## EXAMPLE 2  Reflecting in the y-Axis

Quadrilateral *ABCD* is reflected in the *y*-axis. Write the coordinates of each vertex of quadrilateral *ABCD* and its image, quadrilateral *A′B′C′D′*.

**SOLUTION**

*READING*
You can describe reflections of figures in a coordinate plane using coordinate notation. The notation $A \rightarrow A'$ is read "*A* goes to *A* prime."

| Original | | Image |
|----------|----|-------|
| $A(-1, 1)$ | $\rightarrow$ | $A'(1, 1)$ |
| $B(-3, 1)$ | $\rightarrow$ | $B'(3, 1)$ |
| $C(-4, 3)$ | $\rightarrow$ | $C'(4, 3)$ |
| $D(-2, 4)$ | $\rightarrow$ | $D'(2, 4)$ |

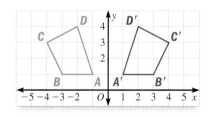

## ✓ GUIDED PRACTICE  for Examples 1 and 2

1. Tell whether the red arrow is a reflection of the blue arrow.

2. Graph the triangle with vertices $J(0, 1)$, $K(0, 4)$, and $L(5, 2)$. Reflect the triangle in the *y*-axis.

When you reflect a figure in a line, the line is called the **line of reflection**. You may have noticed in Example 2 that when the line of reflection is the *y*-axis, the *x*-coordinate of each point is multiplied by $-1$.

> **KEY CONCEPT** *For Your Notebook*
>
> ### Reflections in the *x*-axis
>
> **Words** To reflect a point in the *x*-axis, multiply its *y*-coordinate by $-1$.
>
> **Numbers** $P(2, -3) \rightarrow P'(2, 3)$ **Algebra** $(x, y) \rightarrow (x, -y)$
>
> ### Reflections in the *y*-axis
>
> **Words** To reflect a point in the *y*-axis, multiply its *x*-coordinate by $-1$.
>
> **Numbers** $P(2, -3) \rightarrow P'(-2, 3)$ **Algebra** $(x, y) \rightarrow (-x, y)$

**EXAMPLE 3** **TAKS PRACTICE: Multiple Choice**

**ELIMINATE CHOICES**
When you reflect a point in the *x*-axis, you multiply the *y*-coordinate by $-1$. So, you can eliminate choices A and B.

Reflect △*PQR* in the *x*-axis. What are the coordinates of the vertices of △*P'Q'R'*?

Ⓐ $(-2, 2), (-5, 3), (-6, 1)$

Ⓑ $(2, 2), (5, 3), (6, 1)$

Ⓒ $(2, -2), (5, -3), (6, -1)$

Ⓓ $(-2, -2), (-5, -3), (-6, -1)$

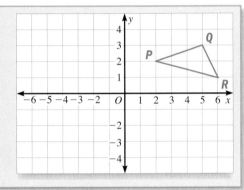

**SOLUTION**

Multiply each *y*-coordinate by $-1$.

| **Original** | | **Image** |
|---|---|---|
| $(x, y)$ | $\rightarrow$ | $(x, -y)$ |
| $P(2, 2)$ | $\rightarrow$ | $P'(2, -2)$ |
| $Q(5, 3)$ | $\rightarrow$ | $Q'(5, -3)$ |
| $R(6, 1)$ | $\rightarrow$ | $R'(6, -1)$ |

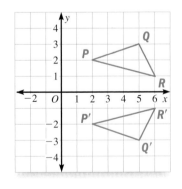

▶ **Answer** The coordinates of the vertices of △*P'Q'R'* are $(2, -2), (5, -3), (6, -1)$. The correct answer is C. Ⓐ Ⓑ **Ⓒ** Ⓓ

✓ **GUIDED PRACTICE** **for Example 3**

**3.** Graph the figure with vertices $S(-3, 2), T(-1, 4), U(-4, 5),$ and $V(-5, 3)$. Reflect the figure in the *x*-axis. Label the coordinates of the vertices of $S'T'U'V'$.

**Symmetry** A figure has **line symmetry** if one half of the figure is a mirror image of the other half. A *line of symmetry* divides the figure into two congruent parts that are mirror images of each other.

---

**EXAMPLE 4** Identifying Lines of Symmetry

**AVOID ERRORS**
Symmetry is a property of points and lines, but not of color. For example, regardless of the colorings in parts (a) and (b), the figures would still be symmetric.

**How many lines of symmetry does the picture have?**

**a.** one line of symmetry   **b.** five lines of symmetry   **c.** no lines of symmetry

*Animated* Math   at classzone.com

---

✓ **GUIDED PRACTICE**   **for Example 4**

**4.** How many lines of symmetry does a square have? a rhombus?

---

# 8.6 EXERCISES

HOMEWORK KEY

🌟 = **TAKS Practice and Reasoning**
Exs. 10, 11, 26, 27, 28, 30, and 35

◯ = **HINTS AND HOMEWORK HELP**
for Exs. 3, 7, 13, 25 at classzone.com

## SKILL PRACTICE

**VOCABULARY** Copy and complete the statement.

**1.** A(n) _?_ creates a mirror image of the original figure.

**2.** A(n) _?_ is an operation that changes a figure into another figure.

**SEE EXAMPLE 1**
on p. 433
for Exs. 3–5

**REFLECTIONS** Tell whether the red figure is a reflection of the blue figure.

**3.**    **4.**    **5.**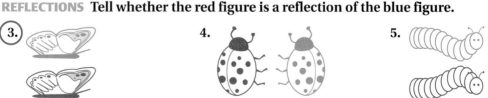

**DRAWING REFLECTIONS** Graph the polygon and its reflection in the given axis.

**SEE EXAMPLES 2 AND 3**
on pp. 433–434
for Exs. 6–8

**6.** $A(3, 6)$, $B(6, 3)$, $C(5, 0)$, $D(1, 1)$; $x$-axis

**7.** $Q(-1, 3)$, $R(-3, 6)$, $S(-6, 4)$, $T(-6, 0)$; $x$-axis

**8.** $B(2, -1)$, $C(5, 0)$, $D(7, -2)$, $E(0, -6)$; $y$-axis

**SEE EXAMPLES**
**2 AND 3**
on pp. 433–434
for Exs. 9–10

**9. ERROR ANALYSIS** Describe and correct the error made in finding the coordinates of the vertices of the image of △*ABC* after a reflection in the *x*-axis.

| | Original: | Image: |
|---|---|---|
| | *A*(4, 5) | *A*′(−4, 5) |
| | *B*(2, 0) | *B*′(−2, 0) |
| | *C*(6, 2) | *C*′(−6, 2) |

**10. ☆ TAKS REASONING** Which figure is a reflected image of figure D?

    **(A)** Figure A    **(B)** Figure B

    **(C)** Figure C    **(D)** None

**SEE EXAMPLE 4**
on p. 435
for Exs. 11–14

**11. ☆ TAKS REASONING** How many lines of symmetry does figure A have?

    **(A)** 0    **(B)** 1

    **(C)** 2    **(D)** 4

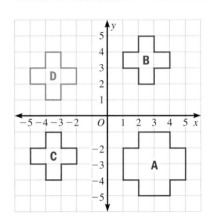

**LINE SYMMETRY** **How many lines of symmetry does the figure have?**

**12.**     **13.**     **14.**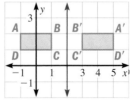

**REASONING** **Draw and classify the described polygon. Draw the lines of symmetry, if any. Is there more than one possible polygon? If so, name the polygon(s).**

**15.** Triangle with no lines of of symmetry

**16.** Triangle with exactly three lines of symmetry

**17.** Quadrilateral with exactly two lines of symmetry

**18.** Quadrilateral with only one line of symmetry

**REFLECTIONS** **In a coordinate plane you can reflect a figure in a line other than the *x*- or *y*-axis. In the diagram below, quadrilateral *ABCD* is reflected in the red line. In Exercises 19–22, copy the coordinate plane including the red line. Then graph the polygon and its reflection in the red line.**

**19.** *R*(0, 0), *S*(1, 3), *T*(2, 0)

**20.** *X*(−2, 3), *Y*(1, −2), *Z*(−2, −3)

**21.** *E*(−3, 2), *F*(1, 2), *G*(1, −1), *H*(−3, −1)

**22.** *J*(−4, 5), *K*(−1, 5), *L*(−1, 1), *M*(−4, 1)

**23. CHALLENGE** Which of the 26 capital letters in the English alphabet have no line of symmetry? one line of symmetry? two lines of symmetry? or more than two lines of symmetry?

**SEE EXAMPLES**
**2 AND 3**
on pp. 433–434
for Exs. 24,
27–28

**24. MAKE A MODEL** Write your name at the top of a piece of tracing paper. Fold the paper and trace your name to create a reflection. Unfold the paper to see your name and its reflection.

*Sara Jeanne*

**25.) WRITING** *Explain* how to determine whether two figures are reflections of one another in the *y*-axis.

**26.** ⬩ **TAKS REASONING** △*RST* is reflected in the *x*-axis to form △*R'S'T'*. The coordinates of point *R* are $(-4, 3)$. What are the coordinates of *R'*?

**(A)** $(4, 3)$ **(B)** $(4, -3)$ **(C)** $(-4, 3)$ **(D)** $(-4, -3)$

**SEE EXAMPLE 4**
on p. 435 for
Exs. 27–28

**27.** ⬩ **TAKS REASONING** Part of a pattern is shown at the right. Using grid paper, copy and transform the pattern so that it has exactly one line of symmetry. Draw the line of symmetry. *Compare* your drawing with your classmates' drawings. Is there more than one possible pattern?

**28.** ⬩ **TAKS REASONING** Use the table below.

| Sides | 3 | 4 | 5 | 6 | 8 |
|---|---|---|---|---|---|
| Regular Polygon |  | ? | ? | ? | ? |
| Lines of Symmetry | ? | ? | ? | ? | ? |

a. **Sketch** Copy the table and sketch a regular polygon with the given number of sides in each column. Draw all the lines of symmetry.

b. **Evaluate** Count the lines of symmetry. Complete the table.

c. **Look for a Pattern** How is the number of sides related to the number of lines of symmetry?

**29.** ◆ **MULTIPLE REPRESENTATIONS** Telephone companies want to place a telephone pole near the street, giving the shortest distance between house A and house B. This is accomplished by reflecting house A in the line of the street, then drawing a line that contains the image of house A and house B. The point where this line and the street meet is where the telephone pole will be placed. Draw this scenario. Give another real world situation where this reasoning can be used.

**30.** ⬩ **TAKS REASONING** The words WOW and HI have line symmetry. Write two more words that have line symmetry.

**31. GEOMETRY** Graph the polygon with vertices $S(-6, 0)$, $T(0, 6)$, $V(6, 0)$, $W(2, -4)$, and $X(-2, -4)$. Reflect the polygon in the x-axis and graph its image in the same coordinate plane. Does the figure have more than one line of symmetry? *Explain.*

**32. MULTI-STEP PROBLEM** The vertices of polygon *ABCDEF* are $A(0, 0)$, $B(0, 2)$, $C(2, 2)$, $D(2, 6)$, $E(4, 6)$, and $F(4,0)$.

  **a.** Draw polygon *ABCDEF* in a coordinate plane. Classify the polygon.

  **b.** In the same coordinate plane used in part (a), reflect polygon *ABCDEF* in the y-axis. Next, reflect the image of polygon *ABCDEF* in the x-axis. Then reflect the second image of polygon *ABCDEF* in the y-axis.

  **c.** *Describe* the figure formed by polygon *ABCDEF* and its 3 images. Is this figure a polygon?

**33. CHALLENGE** The vertices of two triangles are given below. Using graph paper, graph both triangles in the same coordinate plane. Fold the graph paper once so that $\triangle ABC$ coincides with $\triangle EFG$. Are the triangles congruent? *Describe* the fold line. How are the coordinates related?

    $\triangle ABC$: $A(2, 1)$, $B(8, 1)$, $C(7, 3)$         $\triangle EFG$: $E(1, 2)$, $F(1, 8)$, $G(3, 7)$

**34. CHALLENGE** A polygon has vertices $A(1, -2)$, $B(5, -1)$, $C(8, -4)$, $D(7, -7)$, and $E(4, -8)$. Reflect the polygon in the x-axis and find the coordinates of the vertices of its image. Then reflect the image in the y-axis. Is the third polygon a reflection of the original polygon? *Explain.*

*REVIEW*
Lesson 8.5;
TAKS Workbook

**35. TAKS PRACTICE** $\triangle ABC$ is congruent to $\triangle DEF$. Which procedure can be used to find the number of degrees in $\angle D$? *TAKS Obj. 6*

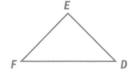

  **(A)** Subtract 44 from 180         **(B)** Subtract 134 from 180

  **(C)** Subtract 44 from 90          **(D)** Note that $\angle D$ is congruent to $\angle A$

**Brain Game**

**Deep Reflections**

Use a mirror to read this quotation from William Shakespeare.

*...understanding... / ...Theuesesnotitself / Justitionsassayount... / buthyreflection...*

# 8.7 Translations and Rotations

TEKS 8.6.B, 8.7.D

| **Before** | You reflected figures in a coordinate plane. |
| **Now** | You'll translate or rotate figures in a coordinate plane. |
| **Why?** | So you can describe transformations, as in Ex. 19. |

**KEY VOCABULARY**
- **translation,** *p. 439*
- **rotation,** *p. 440*

## ACTIVITY

**You can see how moving a triangle changes its vertices.**

**STEP 1** **Graph** an image of *A* by moving it 7 units to the right and 2 units up. Plot the new vertex and label it *A′*.

**STEP 2** **Repeat** Step 1 with *B* and *C*. Then connect the vertices to form △*A′B′C′*.

**STEP 3** **Compare** the coordinates of *A*, *B*, and *C* to those of *A′*, *B′*, and *C′*.

**Translations** In the activity, you transformed △*ABC* by *sliding* it. A **translation** is a transformation that moves each point of a figure the same distance in the same direction. The image is congruent to the original figure.

To translate a figure in a coordinate plane, you change the coordinates of its points by using the guidelines below, assuming *a* and *b* are positive.

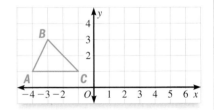

**Slide to the right *a* units**
$$x \rightarrow x + a$$

**Slide up *b* units**
$$y \rightarrow y + b$$

**Slide to the left *a* units**
$$x \rightarrow x - a$$

**Slide down *b* units**
$$y \rightarrow y - b$$

## EXAMPLE 1  Using Coordinate Notation

**Describe the translation from the blue figure to the red figure.**

**SOLUTION**

Each point moves 6 units to the right and 3 units down. The translation is

$$(x, y) \rightarrow (x + 6, y - 3)$$

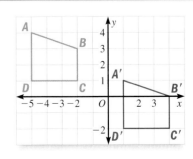

1. *Describe* the translation from the blue figure to the red figure.

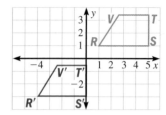

**VOCABULARY**

The angle through which a figure is rotated is called the *angle of rotation*. The common point at the rotation's center is called the *center of rotation*.

**Rotations** A **rotation** is a transformation that turns each point of a figure the same number of degrees around a common point. In this lesson, figures in a coordinate plane will always be rotated around the origin.

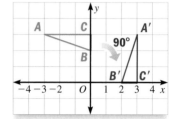

---

**KEY CONCEPT** *For Your Notebook*

**90° Clockwise Rotation**

**Words** To rotate a point $P$ 90° *clockwise*, switch the coordinates, then multiply the new $y$-coordinate by $-1$.

**Numbers** $P(6, 2) \rightarrow P'(2, -6)$ **Algebra** $P(x, y) \rightarrow P'(y, -x)$

**90° Counterclockwise Rotation**

**Words** To rotate a point $P$ 90° *counterclockwise*, switch the coordinates, then multiply the new $x$-coordinate by $-1$.

**Numbers** $P(5, 3) \rightarrow P'(-3, 5)$ **Algebra** $P(x, y) \rightarrow P'(-y, x)$

---

**EXAMPLE 2** Rotating 90° Clockwise

**READING**

Clockwise is the direction the hands on a clock turn. Counterclockwise is the opposite direction.

**Rotate quadrilateral *FGHJ* 90° clockwise.**

**SOLUTION**

| Original | | Image |
|----------|----|-------|
| $(x, y)$ | $\rightarrow$ | $(y, -x)$ |
| $F(2, 2)$ | $\rightarrow$ | $F'(2, -2)$ |
| $G(2, 4)$ | $\rightarrow$ | $G'(4, -2)$ |
| $H(4, 4)$ | $\rightarrow$ | $H'(4, -4)$ |
| $J(5, 2)$ | $\rightarrow$ | $J'(2, -5)$ |

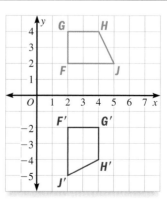

The graph shows *FGHJ* and *F'G'H'J'*.

## 180° Rotations

**Words**      To rotate a point 180°, multiply its coordinates by $-1$.

**Numbers**    $P(4, 1) \rightarrow P'(-4, -1)$     **Algebra**    $P(x, y) \rightarrow P'(-x, -y)$

---

**EXAMPLE 3**   Rotating 180°

Rotate $\triangle ABC$ 180°.

**SOLUTION**

| Original | | Image |
|---|---|---|
| $(x, y)$ | $\rightarrow$ | $(-x, -y)$ |
| $A(-6, 0)$ | $\rightarrow$ | $A'(6, 0)$ |
| $B(-5, 2)$ | $\rightarrow$ | $B'(5, -2)$ |
| $C(-1, 3)$ | $\rightarrow$ | $C'(1, -3)$ |

The graph shows $\triangle ABC$ and $\triangle A'B'C'$.

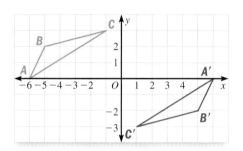

---

✔ **GUIDED PRACTICE**   **for Examples 2 and 3**

Graph $A(1, 1)$, $B(3, 1)$, $C(3, 3)$, and $D(1, 4)$. Find its image after the given rotation.

**2.** 90° clockwise          **3.** 90° counterclockwise     **4.** 180°

---

# 8.7 EXERCISES

HOMEWORK KEY

🏴 = **TAKS Practice and Reasoning**
Exs. 30, 31, 32, 35, and 36

○ = **HINTS AND HOMEWORK HELP**
for Exs. 5, 7, 11, 13, 23 at classzone.com

**SKILL PRACTICE**

**VOCABULARY** Identify the transformation shown in the graph.

**1.**

**2.**

**3.**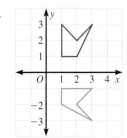

**USING COORDINATE NOTATION** Use coordinate notation to describe the translation from the blue figure to the red figure.

**SEE EXAMPLE 1**
on p. 439
for Exs. 4–7, 13

**4.**

**5.**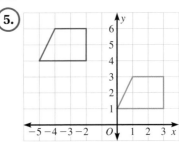

**TRANSLATING TRIANGLES** Find the coordinates of the vertices of the triangle's image after the translation. Then graph the triangle's image.

**6.** $\triangle PQR$: $P(0, -1)$, $Q(3, -1)$, $R(5, -3)$; translation: $(x, y) \rightarrow (x - 5, y + 1)$

**7.** $\triangle LMN$: $L(4, 2)$, $M(0, 3)$, $N(1, 1)$; translation: $(x, y) \rightarrow (x + 1, y - 6)$

**SEE EXAMPLE 2**
on p. 440 for
Exs. 8–12

**8. ERROR ANALYSIS** $\triangle JKL$ has vertices $J(-4, -3)$, $K(-2, 0)$, and $L(1, 2)$. Describe and correct the error made in finding the coordinates of the vertices of its image when it is rotated 90° clockwise.

**9. MULTI-STEP PROBLEM** Rotate $\triangle RST$ 90° counterclockwise.

**a.** Graph $\triangle RST$ with vertices $R(-2, -1)$, $S(-5, -2)$, and $T(-4, 2)$.

**b.** Find the coordinates of the vertices of the triangle's image.

**c.** Graph $\triangle R'S'T'$, the image of $\triangle RST$ after the rotation.

**10. ROTATING A TRIANGLE** Use the triangle described in Exercise 9. Find the coordinates of the vertices of the image after a 180° rotation and after a clockwise rotation of 90°. Graph each image.

**TRANSFORMATIONS** In Exercises 11–16, graph $\triangle LMN$ with vertices $L(2, 0)$, $M(2, 3)$, and $N(6, 0)$. Then graph its image after the transformation.

**11.** Rotate 180°.

**12.** Rotate 90° counterclockwise.

**13.** Translate using $(x, y) \rightarrow (x - 3, y - 4)$.

**14.** Rotate 180°. Then translate using $(x, y) \rightarrow (x + 1, y + 1)$.

**15.** Translate using $(x, y) \rightarrow (x + 3, y)$. Then rotate 180°.

**Animated Math**
at classzone.com

**16. TRANSFORMATIONS** Graph quadrilateral $ABCD$ with vertices $A(-4, 2)$, $B(-2, 0)$, $C(-2, -2)$, and $D(0, 2)$.

**a.** Graph $A'B'C'D'$ by reflecting $ABCD$ in the $x$-axis.

**b.** Graph $A''B''C''D''$ by translating $A'B'C'D'$ 4 units to the right.

**c.** Graph $A'''B'''C'''D'''$ by rotating $A''B''C''D''$ 180°.

17. **MULTIPLE METHODS** *Describe* one translation, one reflection, and one rotation that make the red square the image of the blue square. Then find 3 combinations of transformations that make the red square the image of the blue square.

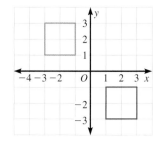

18. **CHALLENGE** Use the coordinate notation for a 180° rotation and 90° rotation clockwise. Show that combining these two gives the coordinate notation for rotating a figure 90° counterclockwise.

## PROBLEM SOLVING

19. **ORIGAMI** *Describe* all possible rotations that will produce an image identical in shape to the given figure.

**TRANSFORMATIONS** **Name the type of transformation modeled by the action.**

20. Riding down an escalator

21. Making a handprint in clay

22. Opening a combination lock

23. Going down a water slide

24. Looking in a mirror

25. Riding a carousel

26. **WRITING** Point *A* in Quadrant II is rotated 180°. Find the quadrant in which point *A'* lies. Point *B* in Quadrant IV is rotated 90° clockwise. Find the quadrant in which point *B'* lies. *Explain* your reasoning.

**READING IN MATH** **Read the information below for Exercises 28–30.**

**Kaleidoscopes** A figure has *rotational symmetry* if a turn of 180° or less about a point produces an image that fits exactly on the original figure. Kaleidoscopes use mirrors to create images with rotational symmetry. The number of repeats in a pattern depends on the angle measure of the mirrors.

27. **Interpret** Tell whether each image has rotational symmetry. If so, describe the least angle of rotation that produces each image.

28. **Predict** If you turned each image upside down, would it appear the same? *Explain.*

29. **Analyze** Can a figure have rotational symmetry without having line symmetry? *Explain.*

**30.**  **TAKS REASONING** The figures below follow a pattern.

Figure 1   Figure 2   Figure 3   Figure 4   Figure 5   Figure 6   ...

Which figure shows a 90° clockwise rotation of Figure 10 in the pattern?

Ⓐ    Ⓑ    Ⓒ    Ⓓ

**31.**  **TAKS REASONING**   Draw a polygon that appears the same when rotated clockwise or counterclockwise by angles of 45°, 90°, and 180°.

**32.**  **TAKS REASONING**   Rotate the figure at the right 90° clockwise. Reflect the image in the *y*-axis. Graph the final image. Complete the rule for the combination of transformations you performed. *Explain* your reasoning.

$$(x, y) \rightarrow (\underline{\ ?\ }, \underline{\ ?\ })$$

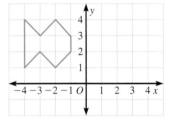

**33.** **CHALLENGE**  A line *l* passes through Quadrants I and III at a 45° angle to both axes. It is the line of reflection $(x, y) \rightarrow (y, x)$. Draw any $\triangle ABC$ and reflect it in line *l*. Then reflect the image in the *y*-axis. Which single transformation of $\triangle ABC$ will form the second image? *Justify* your answer.

**34.** **CHALLENGE**  The figure at the right is the image of a triangle rotated 90° clockwise and reflected in the *y*-axis. Graph the original figure.

---

 **MIXED REVIEW FOR TAKS**      **TAKS** **PRACTICE** at classzone.com

*REVIEW*
..................
Lesson 8.6;
TAKS Workbook

**35.**  **TAKS PRACTICE** If $\triangle PQR$ is reflected across the *x*-axis to form $\triangle P'Q'R'$, what will be the coordinates of point $Q'$? *TAKS Obj. 3*

Ⓐ (−2, −1)   Ⓑ (−2, 1)   Ⓒ (2, −1)   Ⓓ (4, −4)

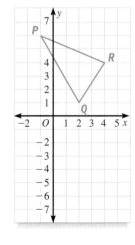

*REVIEW*
..................
Lesson 7.2;
TAKS Workbook

**36.**  **TAKS PRACTICE** A model of a 702-foot tall building is 9 inches wide and 9 inches long. What other information is necessary to find the height of the model? *TAKS Obj. 6*

Ⓕ The weight of the building

Ⓖ The number of stories in the building

Ⓗ The scale used

Ⓙ The area of the base of the model

# Tessellations

TEKS *8.6.B, 8.14.D*

**GOAL** Decide if a shape tessellates. Create tessellations.

**KEY VOCABULARY**
• tessellation, *p. 445*

You can use reflections, rotations, and translations to create a *tessellation*, like the one shown here. A **tessellation** is a repeating pattern of figures that covers a plane with no gaps or overlaps. If a figure can be used to create a tessellation, you say the figure *tessellates*.

## EXAMPLE 1  Identifying Tessellating Polygons

**Tell whether the polygon tessellates.**

a.

Yes, you can create a tessellation by translating a rectangle.

b.

No, regular pentagons will not cover the plane without gaps or overlaps.

You can create a tessellation by altering a polygon that tessellates.

## EXAMPLE 2  Creating a Tessellation

**Alter a parallelogram to create a tessellation.**

**SOLUTION**

*STEP 1*
**Cut** a triangle from the parallelogram.

*STEP 2*
**Slide** the triangle to the opposite side.

*STEP 3*
**Translate** the figure to create a tessellation.

**EXAMPLE 3** Creating a Tessellation

**Create a tessellation by altering an equilateral triangle.**

**STEP 1**
**Cut** a piece from the triangle.

**STEP 2**
**Slide** the piece to another side.

**STEP 3**
**Reflect** the figure, then translate the pair.

**EXERCISES**

**Tell whether the figure tessellates.**

1.

2.

3.

4. *Explain* how you can transform the blue shape to create the tessellation.

5. Copy and continue the pattern.

**Copy the polygon and use it to create a tessellation. Describe how the polygon was transformed in your tessellation.**

6.

7.

8.

9. Create two different tessellations using the shape at the right.

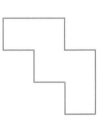

10. Create a tessellation by altering a rectangle.

11. Create a tessellation by altering a parallelogram that is not a rectangle.

# 8.8 Similarity and Dilations

TEKS *8.6.A, 8.9.B*

| Before | You used congruent polygons to find missing measures. |
| Now | You'll use similar polygons to find missing measures. |
| Why? | So you can compare real-world shapes, as in Example 1. |

**KEY VOCABULARY**
- **similar polygons,** *p. 447*
- **dilation,** *p. 449*
- **scale factor,** *p. 449*

**Similar polygons** have the same shape, but they can be different sizes. The symbol ~ means "is similar to." When you name similar polygons, list their corresponding vertices in the same order.

---

**KEY CONCEPT**                          *For Your Notebook*

**Similar Polygons**

$\triangle ABC \sim \triangle XYZ$

Corresponding angles are congruent.

$\angle A \cong \angle X \quad \angle B \cong \angle Y \quad \angle C \cong \angle Z$

Corresponding side lengths are proportional.

$\dfrac{AB}{XY} = \dfrac{BC}{YZ} \qquad \dfrac{BC}{YZ} = \dfrac{AC}{XZ} \qquad \dfrac{AC}{XZ} = \dfrac{AB}{XY}$

---

**EXAMPLE 1**  Identifying Similar Polygons

**Tell whether the television screens are similar.**

**STEP 1**  **Decide** whether corresponding angles are congruent. Each angle measures 90°.

$\angle A \cong \angle E \qquad\qquad \angle B \cong \angle F$

$\angle C \cong \angle G \qquad\qquad \angle D \cong \angle H$

**REVIEW PROPORTIONS**
For help with proportions, see p. 348.

**STEP 2**  **Decide** whether corresponding side lengths are proportional.

$$\frac{30 \text{ inches}}{18 \text{ inches}} \overset{?}{=} \frac{40 \text{ inches}}{24 \text{ inches}}$$

$$\frac{5 \cdot \cancel{6}}{3 \cdot \cancel{6}} \overset{?}{=} \frac{5 \cdot \cancel{8}}{3 \cdot \cancel{8}}$$

$$\frac{5}{3} = \frac{5}{3}$$

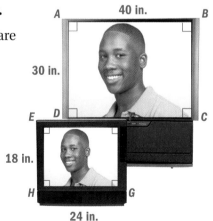

▶ **Answer**  Yes, quadrilateral *ABCD* ~ quadrilateral *EFGH*.

1. Measure the rectangles. Tell which rectangles are similar.

| A | B | C | D | E |

 **TAKS**

**EXAMPLE 2**   **TAKS PRACTICE: Multiple Choice**

*ELIMINATE CHOICES*
Because △KLM is larger than △NPQ, you know that the length of $\overline{KL}$ is greater than 12 m. So, you can eliminate choices A and B.

> In the diagram, △KLM ~ △NPQ. What is the length of $\overline{KL}$?
>
> Ⓐ 4 m   Ⓑ 12 m
>
> Ⓒ 22 m   Ⓓ 36 m

**SOLUTION**

Corresponding side lengths are proportional.

$\dfrac{KL}{NP} = \dfrac{LM}{PQ}$   **Write a proportion.**

*VOCABULARY*
$KL$ represents the length of $\overline{KL}$.

$\dfrac{\overline{KL}}{12\text{ m}} = \dfrac{15\text{ m}}{5\text{ m}}$   **Substitute given values.**

$\overline{KL} = 24$   **Solve the proportion.**

▶ **Answer** The length of $\overline{KL}$ is 36 meters. The correct answer is D.   Ⓐ Ⓑ Ⓒ Ⓓ

**EXAMPLE 3**   **Using Indirect Measurement**

 **Height** Alma is 5 feet tall and casts a 7 foot shadow. At the same time, a tree casts a 14 foot shadow. The triangles formed are similar. Find the height of the tree.

**SOLUTION**

You can use a proportion to find the height of the tree.

$\dfrac{\text{Tree's height}}{\text{Alma's height}} = \dfrac{\text{Length of tree's shadow}}{\text{Length of Alma's shadow}}$   **Write a proportion.**

$\dfrac{x \text{ feet}}{5 \text{ feet}} = \dfrac{14 \text{ feet}}{7 \text{ feet}}$   **Substitute given values.**

$x = 10$   **Solve the proportion.**

▶ **Answer** The tree is 10 feet tall.

**Dilations** A **dilation** stretches or shrinks a figure. The image created by a dilation is similar to the original figure. The **scale factor** of a dilation is the ratio of a side length after the dilation to the corresponding side length before the dilation. In this lesson, the center of a dilation will always be the origin.

---

**KEY CONCEPT** *For Your Notebook*

**Dilations**

**Words** To dilate a polygon, multiply the coordinates of each vertex by the scale factor $k$.

**Numbers** $P(4, 1) \rightarrow P'(8, 2)$ **Algebra** $P(x, y) \rightarrow P'(kx, ky)$

---

**EXAMPLE 4** **Dilating a Polygon**

Quadrilateral $ABCD$ has vertices $A(-1, -1)$, $B(0, 1)$, $C(2, 2)$, and $D(3, 0)$. Dilate using a scale factor of 3.

**SOLUTION**

Graph the quadrilateral. Find the coordinates of the vertices of the image.

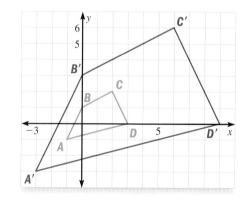

| Original | | Image |
|---|---|---|
| $(x, y)$ | $\rightarrow$ | $(3x, 3y)$ |
| $A(-1, -1)$ | $\rightarrow$ | $A'(-3, -3)$ |
| $B(0, 1)$ | $\rightarrow$ | $B'(0, 3)$ |
| $C(2, 2)$ | $\rightarrow$ | $C'(6, 6)$ |
| $D(3, 0)$ | $\rightarrow$ | $D'(9, 0)$ |

**SCALE FACTOR**
A scale factor greater than 1 results in an enlargement of the original figure. A scale factor between 0 and 1 results in a reduction of the original figure.

Graph the image of the quadrilateral.

---

✓ **GUIDED PRACTICE** **for Examples 2, 3, and 4**

**2.** At the right, $ABCD \sim FGHJ$. Find the value of $x$.

**3. What If?** Suppose the tree in Example 3 casts a shadow of 18 feet, a 6 foot tall person casts a 9 foot shadow, and the triangles are similar. Find the height of the tree. Check your answer for reasonableness.

**4.** Graph $\triangle RST$ with vertices $R(1, 1)$, $S(3, 2)$, and $T(2, 3)$. Then graph its image after a dilation using a scale factor of 2; a scale factor of $\frac{1}{3}$.

# 8.8 EXERCISES

HOMEWORK KEY

= TAKS Practice and Reasoning
Exs. 18, 27, 29, 39, and 40

= HINTS AND HOMEWORK HELP
for Exs. 5, 9, 11, 15, 27 at classzone.com

## SKILL PRACTICE

**VOCABULARY Copy and complete the statement.**

1. The ___?___ of a dilation is the ratio of corresponding side lengths.

2. A polygon and its image after dilation are always ___?___.

**IDENTIFYING SIMILAR POLYGONS Tell whether the polygons are similar.** *Justify* your reasoning.

**SEE EXAMPLE 1**
on p. 447
for Exs. 3–6

3.

4.

5.

6.

**USING SIMILAR POLYGONS Use the similar polygons to find the value of x.**

**SEE EXAMPLE 2**
on p. 448
for Exs. 7–10

7. △ABC ~ △DEF

8. △GHJ ~ △KHM

9. CDFG ~ HJLK.

10. MNPQ ~ RSTV.

**GRAPHING DILATIONS** **Graph the polygon with the given vertices. Then graph its image after dilation using a scale factor $k$.**

11. $W(2, 2)$, $X(0, 4)$, $Y(4, 6)$, $Z(6, 0)$; $k = 3$

12. $B(0, -2)$, $C(4, 2)$, $D(-, 6)$, $E(-2, 6)$, $F(-4, 2)$; $k = \frac{1}{2}$

13. $R(8, 8)$, $S(-4, 4)$, $T(-4, -4)$; $k = \frac{3}{4}$

14. $L(2, -2)$, $M(4, 2)$, $N(-3, 2)$, $P(-1, -2)$; $k = 4$

15. $G(-2, -6)$, $H(-8, -8)$, $J(-6, -2)$, $K(0, 0)$; $k = 1.5$

16. $K(24, 6)$, $L(8, 10)$, $M(8, 0)$, $N(0, 18)$, $P(20, 22)$; $k = 1.75$

17. **ERROR ANALYSIS** A student is asked to graph the image of polygon *ABCD* after a dilation using a scale factor of 3. Describe and correct the student's error.

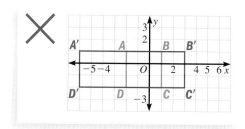

18. **TAKS REASONING** $\triangle ABC \sim \triangle DEF$ by a scale factor of $\frac{1}{2}$. How does the area of $\triangle DEF$ compare to the area of $\triangle ABC$?

(A) 4 times as great  (B) 2 times as great  (C) $\frac{1}{2}$ as great  (D) $\frac{1}{4}$ as great

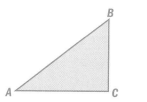

**DILATIONS** **Graph the similar figures and find the scale factor.**

19. $\triangle ABC$: $A(4, 6)$, $B(8, 8)$, $C(12, 4)$
    $\triangle DEF$: $D(2, 3)$, $E(4, 4)$, $F(6, 2)$

20. $GHIJ$: $G(1, 4)$, $H(6, 4)$, $I(6, 1)$, $J(1, 1)$
    $KLMN$: $K(3, 12)$, $L(18, 12)$, $M(18, 3)$, $N(3, 3)$

21. $PQRS$: $P(4, 8)$, $Q(8, 8)$, $R(8, 2)$, $S(4, 2)$
    $TUVW$: $T(8, 14)$, $U(16, 14)$, $V(16, 2)$, $W(8, 2)$

22. **NAMING SIMILAR POLYGONS** Name two similar polygons in the diagram. Find the scale factor.

23. **USING SIMILAR POLYGONS** Pentagon *ABCDE* ~ pentagon *FGHJK*. Find the values of *x* and *y*.

24. **CHALLENGE** Hexagon *ABCDEF* is similar to hexagon *PQRSTU*. Find the values of *x* and *y*.

---

### PROBLEM SOLVING

25. **SCALE FACTOR** *EFGH* is the image of *ABCD* after a dilation. The vertices of *ABCD* and *EFGH* are *A*(−1, 2), *B*(3, 2), *C*(3, −1), *D*(−1, −1), *E*(−4, 8), *F*(12, 8), *G*(12, −4), and *H*(−4, −4). What is the scale factor? What is the perimeter of *ABCD*? How is the ratio of the perimeter related to the scale factor?

26. **BOOKSHELF** A friend buys the bookshelf shown below for her bedroom. The assembly instructions include the diagram shown below. Is the diagram drawn to scale? *Justify* your reasoning.

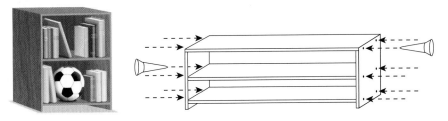

27. **TAKS REASONING** Jenny is 5 feet tall and casts a 3 foot shadow. At the same time, a flagpole casts a 15 foot shadow. What is the height of the flagpole?

   **A** 9 feet          **B** 15 feet          **C** 17 feet          **D** 25 feet

28. **ESTIMATION** Rectangle *ABCD* is similar to rectangle *EFGH*. A friend says that *EF* is about 8 meters. Is this estimate reasonable? *Explain.*

29. **TAKS REASONING** If two triangles are congruent, are they also similar? *Explain.*

★ = TAKS Practice and Reasoning          ◯ = **HINTS AND HOMEWORK HELP** *at classzone.com*

**SEE EXAMPLE 3**
on p. 448
for Ex. 30

**30. INDIRECT MEASUREMENT** Castle Fantastica on Camps Bay Beach in Cape Town, South Africa is one of the tallest sandcastles ever built. Its sculptors used over 400,000 pounds of sand. Suppose the sandcastle casts a shadow 140 feet long at the same time that your 5.5 feet tall friend casts a shadow 28 feet long. How tall is the sandcastle? Check for reasonableness.

**31. REASONING** A polygon is dilated by a scale factor of 1. Will the image be *larger than, smaller than,* or *identical to* the original polygon? *Explain.*

**32. WRITING** *Explain* why all squares are similar, but not all rectangles are similar.

**33. AREA** The area of *ABCD* is 80 square inches. *ABCD ~ WXYZ. Explain* how to find the area of *WXYZ.*

**34. PERIMETER** △*RST* is similar to △*VWX* where *RS* = 10 feet and *VW* = 30 feet. *Describe* the perimeter of △*VWX.*

**35. PHOTOGRAPHY** The dimensions of a negative made from 35 mm film are 24 mm by 36 mm. If a 100 mm by 150 mm print is made from this negative, what is the scale factor?

**36. CHALLENGE** Show that △*LMQ* is similar to △*ONQ. Justify* your reasoning.

**37. CHALLENGE** A golden rectangle is one whose length and width are in a ratio of about 8 to 5. The golden spiral is formed by drawing arcs centered at the corner of each square. These rectangles and spirals are often found in nature, art, and architecture. Measure the dimensions of the rectangles below in millimeters. Name all the golden rectangles. Are they similar? *Explain.*

**38. CHALLENGE** Polygon *ABCD* is similar to polygon *RSTU*. The area of *ABCD* is 51 square centimeters. Find the area of *RSTU*. *Explain* your method.

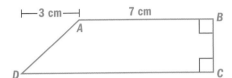

*REVIEW*
Lesson 8.7;
TAKS Workbook

**39.** **TAKS PRACTICE** Which shows the figure at the right after it is rotated 270° clockwise? *TAKS Obj. 6*

(A)   (B)

(C)   (D)

*REVIEW*
Lesson 7.2;
TAKS Workbook

**40.** **TAKS PRACTICE** A researcher surveys 1200 people in a city and finds that 450 of them visit the local library at least once every 2 weeks. There are 75,000 people living in the city. Based on the survey data, what is a reasonable estimate of the total number of city residents who visit the local library at least once every 2 weeks? *TAKS Obj. 5*

(F) 28,000   (G) 37,500

(H) 74,250   (J) 200,000

**QUIZ** *for Lessons 8.5–8.8*

**Find the value of *x*.**

**1.** $\triangle ABC \cong \triangle DEF$ *(p. 427)*

**2.** *PQRS ~ WXYZ* *(p. 447)*

**Name the type of transformation modeled by the action.** *(pp. 433, 439)*

**3.** Sledding downhill

**4.** Leaving fingerprints

**5.** Spinning in place

**6.** Opening a drawer

**7.** Graph $\triangle ABC$ with vertices *A*(1, 1), *B*(2, 3), and *C*(3, 0). Dilate the triangle using a scale factor of 4. Translate 2 units to the right and 3 units down, then reflect the triangle over the *y*-axis. *(p. 447)*

## Lessons 8.5–8.8

**MULTIPLE CHOICE**

**1. SIDE LENGTHS** In the figures below, △LMN ~ △PQR. What is the value of *x*?
*TEKS 8.9.B*

- **Ⓐ** 6 ft
- **Ⓑ** 8 ft
- **Ⓒ** 9 ft
- **Ⓓ** 10 ft

**2. REFLECTIONS** Triangle *ABC* has vertices *A*(2, 1), *B*(4, 3), and *C*(6, 2). Triangle *A′B′C′* is formed by reflecting triangle *ABC* in the *x*-axis. What are the vertices of *B′*? *TEKS 8.6.B*

- **Ⓕ** (−4, 3)
- **Ⓖ** (−3, 4)
- **Ⓗ** (3, 4)
- **Ⓙ** (4, −3)

**3. TRANSFORMATIONS** Which of the following transforms Figure A to Figure B? *TEKS 8.6.B*

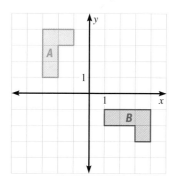

- **Ⓐ** Rotate 90° clockwise around the origin, then translate using $(x, y) \rightarrow (x, y - 3)$
- **Ⓑ** Rotate 90° clockwise around the origin, then translate using $(x, y) \rightarrow (x, y - 4)$
- **Ⓒ** Rotate 180° around the origin, then translate using $(x, y) \rightarrow (x - 1, y)$
- **Ⓓ** Rotate 180° around the origin, then translate using $(x, y) \rightarrow (x - 2, y)$

**4. MODEL CARS** You are designing a model car that is a scale replica of a full-sized car. The scale factor of the model to the actual car is $\frac{1}{24}$. The license plate on the model car is $\frac{1}{4}$ inch high and $\frac{1}{2}$ inch wide. What is the perimeter of the actual license plate? *TEKS 8.3.B*

- **Ⓕ** 24 in.
- **Ⓖ** 36 in.
- **Ⓗ** 48 in.
- **Ⓙ** 72 in.

**5. WHAT IF?** Suppose you design a second car that is $\frac{1}{4}$ the size of the model car you designed in Exercise 4. What is the perimeter of the license plate on the second model car? *TEKS 8.3.B*

- **Ⓐ** $\frac{1}{4}$ in.
- **Ⓑ** $\frac{3}{8}$ in.
- **Ⓒ** $\frac{3}{4}$ in.
- **Ⓓ** 9 in.

**6. DILATING AREAS** A rectangle has an area of 8 inches. It is dilated by a scale factor of two. What is the new area? *TEKS 8.10.A*

- **Ⓕ** 4 in.$^2$
- **Ⓖ** 8 in.$^2$
- **Ⓗ** 16 in.$^2$
- **Ⓙ** 32 in.$^2$

**GRIDDED ANSWER** ⊘①②●④⑤⑥⑦⑧⑨

**7. LINE OF SIGHT** Karen wants to find the height of a tree that is 45 feet away from a pole that is 17 feet tall. When she stands 15 feet from the pole, on the side opposite the tree, she can see the top of the tree and the top of the pole line up in her line of sight. Her eyes are 5 feet from the ground. How tall is the tree in feet? *TEKS 8.14.A*

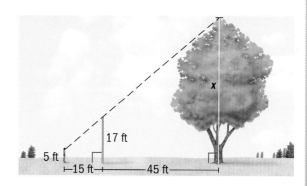

## REVIEW KEY VOCABULARY

- straight angle, *p. 403*
- right angle, *p. 403*
- supplementary, *p. 403*
- complementary, *p. 403*
- vertical angles, *p. 404*
- perpendicular lines, *p. 404*
- parallel lines, *p. 405*
- acute, obtuse angle, *p. 411*
- acute, right, obtuse triangle, *p. 411*

- equilateral, isosceles, scalene triangle, *p. 411*
- quadrilateral, trapezoid, *p. 416*
- parallelogram, rhombus, *p. 416*
- polygon, pentagon, *p. 420*
- regular polygon, *p. 420*
- hexagon, heptagon, *p. 420*
- octagon, *p. 420*
- congruent segments, *p. 427*
- congruent angles, *p. 427*

- corresponding parts, *p. 427*
- reflection, *p. 433*
- transformation, *p. 433*
- image, *p. 433*
- line symmetry, *p. 435*
- translation, *p. 439*
- rotation, *p. 440*
- similar polygons, *p. 447*
- dilation, *p. 449*
- scale factor, *p. 449*

### VOCABULARY EXERCISES

**Match each word with the correct definition.**

   **1.** Transformation     **A.** A transformation that stretches or shrinks a figure

   **2.** Reflection          **B.** A transformation that slides a figure

   **3.** Translation         **C.** A transformation that creates a mirror image of a figure

   **4.** Dilation            **D.** An operation that changes one figure into another figure

**Copy and complete the statement.**

   **5.** Two angles whose measures have a sum of 90° are   ?   angles.

   **6.** Two lines on the same plane that never intersect are   ?  .

   **7.** A(n)   ?   is a polygon with seven sides.

   **8.** A figure has   ?   if one half of the figure is a mirror image of the other half.

## REVIEW EXAMPLES AND EXERCISES

### 8.1 Angle Pairs
*pp. 403–408*

**EXAMPLE**

**The measure of ∠1 is 115°. Find the measure of ∠2.**

| | |
|---|---|
| $m\angle 1 + m\angle 2 = 180°$ | **Definition of supplementary angles** |
| $115° + m\angle 2 = 180°$ | **Substitute 115° for $m\angle 1$.** |
| $m\angle 2 = 65°$ | **Subtract 115° from each side.** |

## EXERCISES

**Find the measure of ∠1.**

SEE EXAMPLES
1, 2, AND 3
on pp. 403–405
for Exs. 9–12

**9.**

**10.**

**11.**

**12.** Find the measures of ∠1, ∠2, ∠3, ∠4, and ∠5. *Justify* your reasoning.

---

**8.2  Angles and Triangles**                                    *pp. 411–415*

### EXAMPLE

**Find the value of x.**

$$x° + 30° + 40° = 180°$$   **Sum of angle measures is 180°.**

$$x + 70 = 180$$   **Add.**

$$x = 110$$   **Subtract 70 from each side.**

## EXERCISES

SEE EXAMPLE 2
on p. 412
for Exs. 13–15

**The measures of two angles of a triangle are given. Find the value of x. Then classify the triangle by its angles.**

**13.** 90°, 64°, $x°$        **14.** 17°, 55°, $x°$        **15.** 40°, 52°, $x°$

---

**8.3  Quadrilaterals**                                          *pp. 416–419*

### EXAMPLE

**Classify the quadrilateral.**

The figure is a parallelogram with 4 sides of equal length. So, it is a rhombus.

## EXERCISES

**Classify the quadrilateral and find the value of x.**

SEE EXAMPLES
1 AND 2
on pp. 416–417
for Exs. 16–18

**16.**

**17.**

**18.**

**Polygons and Angles** *pp. 420–424*

**EXAMPLE**

Find the measure of ∠A in regular pentagon *ABCDE*.

$$m\angle A = \frac{(n-2) \cdot 180°}{n}$$   Formula for measure of one angle in regular polygon

$$= \frac{(5-2) \cdot 180°}{5}$$   Substitute 5 for *n*.

$$= 108°$$   Simplify.

**EXERCISES**

SEE EXAMPLE 2
on p. 421
for Exs. 19–20

**19.** Find the measure of one angle in a regular 12-gon.

**20.** Find the sum of the angle measures in a hexagon.

**8.5** **Congruent Polygons** *pp. 427–432*

**EXAMPLE**

Name the congruent triangles. *Explain* how you know that they are congruent.

∠M ≅ ∠R      Angles are congruent.

$\overline{LM} \cong \overline{SR}$      Sides are congruent.

∠L ≅ ∠S      Angles are congruent.

△LMN ≅ △SRT by Angle-Side-Angle.

**EXERCISES**

Name the congruent triangles. *Explain* how you know they are congruent.

SEE EXAMPLE 3
on p. 429
for Exs. 21–24

**21.**

**22.**

**23.**

**24.**

**EXAMPLE 1**

Graph △*ABC* with vertices *A*(1, 3), *B*(4, 3), and *C*(3, 1). Then graph its reflection in the *x*-axis.

| Original | | Image |
|---|---|---|
| (*x*, *y*) | → | (*x*, −*y*) |
| *A*(1, 3) | → | *A*′(1, −3) |
| *B*(4, 3) | → | *B*′(4, −3) |
| *C*(3, 1) | → | *C*′(3, −1) |

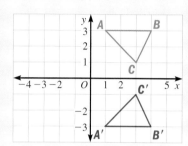

*SEE EXAMPLE 2*
on p. 433
for Ex. 25

**EXERCISES**

**25.** Graph the reflection of △*ABC* shown above in the *y*-axis.

**EXAMPLE 2**

How many lines of symmetry does the butterfly have?

The butterfly has one line of symmetry.

**EXERCISES**

How many lines of symmetry does the figure have?

*SEE EXAMPLE 4*
on p. 435
for Exs. 26–28

**26.**

**27.**

**28.**

> **EXAMPLE**

Graph $\triangle KLM$ with vertices $K(3, 1)$, $L(1, 4)$, and $M(3, 3)$. Then rotate it 90°
counterclockwise, and graph the image.

| Original | | Image |
|---|---|---|
| $(x, y)$ | $\rightarrow$ | $(-y, x)$ |
| $K(3, 1)$ | $\rightarrow$ | $K'(-1, 3)$ |
| $L(1, 4)$ | $\rightarrow$ | $L'(-4, 1)$ |
| $M(3, 3)$ | $\rightarrow$ | $M'(-3, 3)$ |

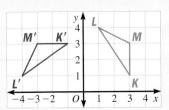

## EXERCISES

**SEE EXAMPLES
1 AND 3**
on pp. 439, 441
for Exs. 29–30

Use $\triangle KLM$ in the Example above.

**29.** Translate $\triangle KLM$ using $(x, y) \rightarrow (x - 2, y + 1)$.

**30.** Rotate $\triangle KLM$ 180° and graph its image.

8.8    **Similarity and Dilations**    *pp. 447–454*

> **EXAMPLE**

Polygons *ABCD* and *FGHJ* are similar.
Find the length of $\overline{BC}$.

| | |
|---|---|
| $\dfrac{AB}{FG} = \dfrac{BC}{GH}$ | Write a proportion. |
| $\dfrac{16}{20} = \dfrac{x}{15}$ | Substitute. |
| $x = 12$ | Solve for *x*. |

▶ **Answer**  The length of $\overline{BC}$ is 12 meters.

## EXERCISES

**SEE EXAMPLES
2 AND 3**
on p. 448
for Exs. 31–32

**31.** **Building Heights**  A 20 foot flagpole stands beside a building. The
flagpole casts a shadow that is 25 feet long. At the same time, the
building casts a shadow that is 60 feet long. How tall is the building?

**32.** Rectangle *JKLM* is the image of rectangle *PQRS* after a dilation. *PQRS*
has a length of 40 centimeters and a width of 10 centimeters. *JKLM* has
a perimeter of 20 centimeters. Find the scale factor, then find the length
and width of *JKLM*.

**Find the measures of the numbered angles.**

1.

2.

3.

**Find the measure of the numbered angle.**

4.

5.

6.

**Classify the quadrilateral.**

7.

8.

9.

**Find the measure of one angle in the polygon.**

10. Square

11. Regular octagon

12. Regular 9-gon

13. **ALGEBRA** Write and solve an equation to find the value of $x$.

**Graph the figure and its image after the given transformation.**

14. Rotate 180°.

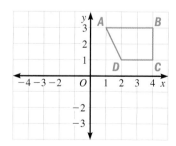

15. Translate using $(x, y) \rightarrow (x - 5, y + 3)$.

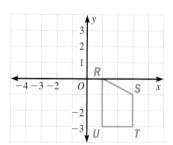

16. **SHADOWS** Joe is 72 inches tall and has a 108 inch shadow. At the same time, Martha has a 96 inch shadow. How tall is Martha?

17. The lengths of the sides of a triangle are 5 centimeters, 12 centimeters, and 15 centimeters. The shortest side of a similar triangle has a length of 12.5 centimeters. Find the lengths of the other two sides. What is the perimeter of each triangle? What is the scale factor?

## REVIEWING GEOMETRY PROBLEMS

The side lengths and heights of similar triangles are proportional. Proportions can be used to find corresponding side lengths and corresponding heights of similar triangles. Areas can be found once side lengths and heights are known.

**EXAMPLE**

Triangle *ABC* and triangle *DEF* are similar. The area of triangle *DEF* is 15 square units. What is the area of triangle *ABC*?

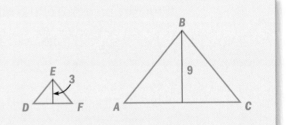

## Solution

**STEP 1**  **Find** the base of △*DEF*.

$$A = \frac{1}{2}bh \qquad \text{Write area formula.}$$

$$15 = \frac{1}{2}(b)(3) \qquad \text{Substitute values.}$$

$$15 = (b)\frac{3}{2} \qquad \text{Multiply.}$$

$$15 \cdot \frac{2}{3} = (b)\frac{3}{2} \cdot \frac{2}{3} \qquad \text{Multiply each side by } \frac{2}{3}.$$

$$10 = b \qquad \text{Simplify.}$$

**STEP 2**  **Write** a proportion to find the base of △*ABC*.

$$\frac{AC}{DF} = \frac{h_1}{h_2} \qquad \text{Write a proportion.}$$

$$\frac{y}{10} = \frac{9}{3} \qquad \text{Substitute given values.}$$

$$y = 30 \qquad \text{Solve the proportion.}$$

The base of △*ABC*, segment *AC*, is 30 units.

**STEP 3**  **Find** the area of △*ABC*.

**AVOID ERRORS**
..........................
The side lengths and height of △*ABC* are 3 times those of △*DEF*. But the area of △*ABC* is 9 times the area of △*DEF*.

$$A = \frac{1}{2}(30)(9) \qquad \text{Write area formula and substitute values.}$$

$$= 135 \qquad \text{Multiply.}$$

▶ **Answer**  The area of △*ABC* is 135 square units.

# GEOMETRY PROBLEMS ON TAKS

Below are examples of geometry problems in multiple choice format. Try solving the problems before looking at the solutions. (Cover the solutions with a piece of paper.) Then check your solutions against the ones given.

**1.** Triangle *ABC* is being dilated to form triangle *RST*. Two vertices of triangle *RST* are shown. What are the coordinates of *T*?

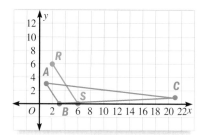

**A** (42, 2)

**B** (22, 3)

**C** (24, 2)

**D** (42, 3)

### Solution

List the vertices of the original figure and the corresponding vertices of the image that are given.

| Original | Image |
|----------|-------|
| A(1, 3)  | R(2, 6) |
| B(3, 0)  | S(6, 0) |

The coordinates of the image are found by multiplying the coordinates of the original figure by the scale factor, 2.

So, the coordinates of vertex *T* are (21 • 2, 1 • 2) or (42, 2).

The correct answer is A.

**2.** Hexagon *LMNOPQ* is similar to hexagon *UVWXYZ*. By what scale factor was hexagon *UVWXYZ* dilated to form hexagon *LMNOPQ*?

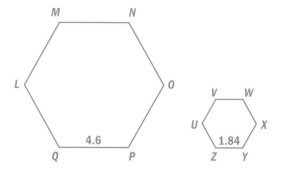

**F** 0.4

**G** 1.6

**H** 2.5

**J** 2.8

### Solution

The scale factor of a dilation is the ratio of side lengths after the dilation to corresponding side lengths before the dilation.

Here, the known side length after the dilation is the length of segment *QP*. The known side length before the dilation is the length of segment *ZY*.

To determine the scale factor, x, write and simplify the ratio.

$$x = \frac{QP}{ZY}$$

$$x = \frac{4.6}{1.84}$$

$$x = 2.5$$

The scale factor is 2.5. So, the correct answer is H.

# 8 TAKS PRACTICE

## PRACTICE FOR TAKS OBJECTIVES 3 AND 4

**1.** Pentagon *QRSTU* was dilated by a scale factor of 0.75 to form pentagon *JKLMN*.

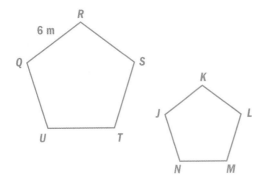

What is the length of *JK*?

**A** 4.5 m

**B** 5.25 m

**C** 6.75 m

**D** 8 m

**2.** Quadrilateral *ABCD* was dilated to form quadrilateral *WXYZ*. What scale factor was used to perform the dilation?

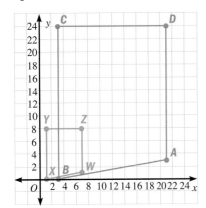

**F** $\frac{1}{3}$

**G** $\frac{1}{2}$

**H** 2

**J** 3

**3.** Rectangle *QRST* is similar to rectangle *VWXY*. If the area of rectangle *VWXY* is 48 square units, what is the area of rectangle *QRST*?

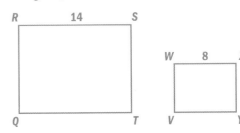

**A** 82 square units

**B** 140 square units

**C** 147 square units

**D** 154 square units

**4.** The area of square *EFGH* is 25% of the area of square *QRST*. If the side length of square *QRST* is 10 yards, what is the side length of square *EFGH*?

**F** 1.25 yd

**G** 2.5 yd

**H** 5 yd

**J** 7.5 yd

## MIXED TAKS PRACTICE

**5.** Four friends belong to a book club. They each read an average of 5 books over the summer. A fifth friend who read 10 books over the summer joins the book club. Which expression shows the average number of books read by all five friends? *TAKS Obj. 1*

**A** $\frac{5 + 10}{5}$

**B** $\frac{4(5 + 10)}{5}$

**C** $\frac{4 \cdot 5 + 10}{5}$

**D** $\frac{5 + 10}{4 \cdot 5}$

## MIXED TAKS PRACTICE

**6.** Triangle *LMN* is shown on the coordinate grid below.

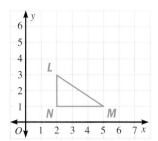

Triangle *LMN* is reflected across the *x*-axis to form triangle *L'M'N'*. What are the coordinates of *L'*? *TAKS Obj. 3*

**F** $(-5, 3)$

**G** $(-2, 3)$

**H** $(2, -3)$

**J** $(2, -1)$

**7.** Audrey hears that about 40% of the students in her school study Spanish. What information can NOT be deduced from this fact alone? *TAKS Obj. 6*

**A** Proportion of students in her school who study Spanish to those who do not study Spanish

**B** Percent of students in her school who do not study Spanish

**C** Number of students in her school who study Spanish

**D** Fraction of students who study Spanish in her school

**8.** Adam is shopping for blank CDs. He visits several shops and checks online as well. Which bulk price offers the lowest price per CD? *TAKS Obj. 2*

**F** 25 CDs for $6.25

**G** 50 CDs for $18

**H** 20 CDs for $5.40

**J** 250 CDs for $90

**9.** Brian performs several random experiments. In which experiment does the desired result have the greatest probability of occurring? *TAKS Obj. 5*

**A** Rolling a 2 on a fair number cube whose faces are labeled 1 through 6.

**B** Spinning a 2 on a spinner divided into 5 equal parts. The parts are numbered 1 through 5.

**C** Choosing a red marble from a bag containing 8 red marbles and 4 blue marbles.

**D** Picking a piece of cake without a penny in it when the cake is cut into four equal pieces and one piece has a penny in it.

**10.** $\triangle ABC$ is similar to $\triangle DEF$.

Which procedure can be used to find the number of degrees in $\angle E$? *TAKS Obj. 6*

**F** Subtract 46 from 90

**G** Subtract 46 from 180

**H** Subtract 46 from 360

**J** Subtract 136 from 360

**11. GRIDDED ANSWER** A certain historic novel costs 60% less in paperback than in hardcover. Lisa has a coupon for another 5% off. She uses the coupon to buy the paperback version of the book. If the book in hardcover costs $25, how much will Lisa pay for the paperback? *TAKS Obj. 6*

*Record your answer and fill in the bubbles on your answer document. Be sure to use the correct place value.*

# 9 Real Numbers and Right Triangles

TEXAS

### Before

In previous chapters you've . . .

• Found the square of a number
• Investigated rational numbers

### Now

**TEKS** you'll study . . .

| 8.1.C | 9.1 | Square roots |
| 8.1.C | 9.2 | Real numbers |
| 8.9.A | 9.3 | The Pythagorean theorem |
| 8.9.A | 9.4 | Pythagorean triples |
| 8.1.C | 9.5 | Special right triangles |
| 8.9.B | 9.6 | Trigonometric ratios |

### Why?

So you can solve real-world problems about . . .

• fire towers, p. 474
• parasailing, p. 483
• softball, p. 493
• totem poles, p. 504

 **Math**

*at classzone.com*

• Rational Numbers, p. 475
• The Pythagorean Theorem, p. 483
• Special Right Triangles, p. 495

## Get-Ready Games

**Review Prerequisite Skills** by playing *Spin Your Wheels and Ramp Match.*

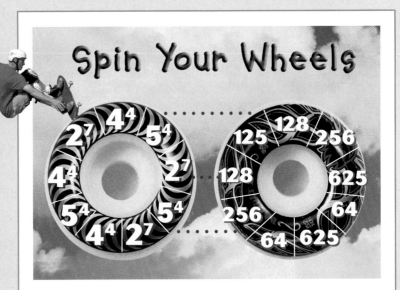

**Spin Your Wheels**

**Skill Focus:** Evaluating powers

Spin the wheels until all three red lines connect equal values.

• You can turn the wheels one click at a time. Each click moves a wheel one space clockwise.

• How many clicks do you need to turn the left wheel?

• How many clicks do you need to turn the right wheel?

**Ramp Match**

**Skill Focus:** Identifying angles in triangles

Find the ramp each bike or skateboard matches.

• Match the angle on the bike or skateboard with the ramp it fits.

## Stop and Think

1. **CRITICAL THINKING** How can you write $4^4$ as a power of 2? *Explain.*

2. **WRITING** *Explain* why a triangular ramp that has angles of 90°, 40°, and 55° cannot exist.

# Review Prerequisite Skills

**REVIEW WORDS**
- **rational number,** *p. 255*
- **right angle,** *p. 403*
- **right triangle,** *p. 411*
- **equilateral triangle,** *p. 411*
- **isosceles triangle,** *p. 411*
- **scalene triangle,** *p. 411*

## VOCABULARY CHECK

Use a review word to classify the triangle by its side lengths.

**1.**  **2.**  **3.**

**4.** A right triangle, when classified by its side lengths, may *not* be a(n) __?__ triangle.

## SKILL CHECK

Evaluate the expression. *(p. 19)*

**5.** $4^2 + 3^2$ **6.** $14^2 - 5^2$ **7.** $27^2 - 3^2$ **8.** $2^2 + 6^2$

**9.** $6^2 - 3^2$ **10.** $10^2 - 5^2$ **11.** $5^2 + 6^2$ **12.** $7^2 + 3^2$

Find the measure of each angle in the triangle. *(p. 411)*

**13.**  **14.**  **15.**

**TEXAS @HomeTutor** Prerequisite skills practice at classzone.com

# Notetaking Skills    Illustrating with Examples

In each chapter you will learn a new notetaking skill. In Chapter 9 you will illustrate new concepts with examples, as in Example 1 on p. 482.

When you learn a new concept or formula, write it in your notes along with an example and important information.

Right triangle

1 right angle (90°)
Sum of measures of other 2 angles is 90°.

Can be isosceles or scalene. Never equilateral.

# 9.1 Square Roots

TEKS 8.1.C, 8.14.D

| **Before** | You found squares of numbers. |
| **Now** | You'll find and approximate square roots of numbers. |
| **Why?** | So you can find side lengths, as in Ex. 54. |

**KEY VOCABULARY**
- square root, *p. 469*
- radical expression, *p. 469*
- perfect square, *p. 470*

## ACTIVITY

**You can find the side length of a square if you know its area.**

**STEP 1** **Copy** and complete the table using the diagram.

Area = 1   **Area = 4**   Area = 9

| Area of square (square units) | 1 | 4 | 9 | 16 | 25 | 36 |
|---|---|---|---|---|---|---|
| Side length (units) | 1 | 2 | 3 | ? | ? | ? |

**STEP 2** **Find** the length of each side of a square with an area of 49 square units, 64 square units, 100 square units, and 400 square units.

**STEP 3** **Describe** the length of a side of a square that has an area between 81 and 100 square units.

The numbers 5 and $-5$ are the *square roots* of 25 because $5^2 = 25$ and $(-5)^2 = 25$. If $m^2 = n$, then $m$ is a **square root** of $n$. Every positive number has a positive square root and a negative square root. Zero has one square root, which is zero.

The symbol $\sqrt{\phantom{x}}$ is called a *radical sign*. It is used to represent the positive square root. The symbol $-\sqrt{\phantom{x}}$ represents the negative square root. A **radical expression** is an expression that involves a radical sign.

$$\sqrt{25} = 5 \qquad \text{positive square root}$$
$$-\sqrt{25} = -5 \qquad \text{negative square root}$$

## EXAMPLE 1 Evaluating Square Roots

**a.** $\sqrt{36} = 6$ because $6^2 = 36$.

**b.** $-\sqrt{64} = -8$ because $(-8^2) = 64$.

**c.** $\sqrt{\dfrac{4}{25}} = \dfrac{2}{5}$ because $\left(\dfrac{2}{5}\right)^2 = \dfrac{4}{25}$

**d.** $\sqrt{0.81} = 0.9$ because $(0.9)^2 = 0.81$.

**Perfect Squares** A **perfect square** is any number that has integer square roots, such as 1, 4, 9, and 16. You can approximate the square roots of a number that is not a perfect square using a number line or a calculator.

**EXAMPLE 2** TAKS PRACTICE: Multiple Choice

> **Round $\sqrt{85}$ to the nearest whole number.**
>
> **(A)** 8      **(B)** 9      **(C)** 10      **(D)** 11

*ELIMINATE CHOICES*
You know that 85 is between 81 (or $9^2$) and 100 (or $10^2$), so $\sqrt{85}$ is between 9 and 10. Choices A and D can be eliminated.

**SOLUTION**

You can use a number line to approximate $\sqrt{85}$ to the nearest whole number. Because $\sqrt{85}$ is between 9 and 10, you need to decide whether $\sqrt{85}$ is closer to 9 or 10. Find $9.5^2$. You can calculate that $9.5^2 = 90.25$ and $(\sqrt{85})^2 = 85$.

$$\sqrt{81} \quad \sqrt{85} \quad \sqrt{90.25} \qquad \sqrt{100}$$

|     |     |     |
|-----|-----|-----|
| 9   | 9.5 | 10  |
| $9^2 = 81$ | $9.5^2 = 90.25$ | $10^2 = 100$ |

As shown on the number line, $\sqrt{85}$ is between $\sqrt{81}$ and $\sqrt{90.25}$, so it has a value between 9 and 9.5. Therefore, $\sqrt{85}$ is closer to 9 than it is to 10.

▶ **Answer** To the nearest whole number, $\sqrt{85} \approx 9$.
The correct answer is B. **(A) (B) (C) (D)**

✓ **GUIDED PRACTICE** for Examples 1 and 2

*USE A TABLE*
You may want to use the Table of Square Roots on p. 819.

**Find or approximate the square root to the nearest integer.**

**1.** $\sqrt{4}$      **2.** $\sqrt{0}$      **3.** $-\sqrt{36}$      **4.** $-\sqrt{81}$

**5.** $\sqrt{23}$      **6.** $\sqrt{41}$      **7.** $\sqrt{\dfrac{25}{81}}$      **8.** $\sqrt{0.36}$

**EXAMPLE 3** Using a Calculator

**Evaluate the square root. Round to the nearest tenth, if necessary.**

**a.** $-\sqrt{56.25}$      **b.** $\sqrt{8}$      **c.** $-\sqrt{1256}$

**SOLUTION**

| | Keystrokes | Display | Answer |
|---|---|---|---|
| **a.** | [(−)] [2nd] [√ ] **56.25** [=] | −7.5 | −7.5 |
| **b.** | [2nd] [√ ] **8** [=] | 2.828427125 | 2.8 |
| **c.** | [(−)] [2nd] [√ ] **1256** [=] | −35.44009029 | −35.4 |

## EXAMPLE 4 Using a Square Root Equation

**Amusement Parks** On an amusement park ride, riders stand against a circular wall that spins. At a certain speed, the floor drops out and the force of the rotation keeps the riders pinned to the wall.

The model $s = 4.95\sqrt{r}$ gives the speed needed to keep riders pinned to the wall. In the model, $s$ is the speed in meters per second and $r$ is the radius of the ride in meters. Find the speed necessary to keep riders pinned to the wall of a ride that has a radius of 2.61 meters.

### SOLUTION

| | |
|---|---|
| $s = 4.95\sqrt{r}$ | Write equation for speed of the ride. |
| $= 4.95\sqrt{\mathbf{2.61}}$ | Substitute 2.61 for $r$. |
| $\approx 4.95(1.62)$ | Approximate the square root using a calculator. |
| $= 8.019$ | Multiply. |

▶ **Answer** The speed should be about 8 meters per second.

## EXAMPLE 5 Solving Equations Using Square Roots

**a.**

| | |
|---|---|
| $x^2 = 64$ | Original equation |
| $x = \pm\sqrt{64}$ | Definition of square root |
| $x = \pm 8$ | Evaluate square roots. |

▶ **Answer** The solutions are 8 and $-8$.

*READING*
The symbol $\pm$ is read "plus or minus." The statement $x = \pm 8$ means that 8 and $-8$ are the solutions of $x^2 = 64$.

**b.**

| | |
|---|---|
| $z^2 + 14 = 20$ | Original equation |
| $z^2 + 14 - 14 = 20 - 14$ | Subtract 14 from each side. |
| $z^2 = 6$ | Simplify. |
| $z = \pm\sqrt{6}$ | Definition of square root |
| $z \approx \pm 2.4$ | Approximate square roots. |

▶ **Answer** The solutions are about 2.4 and $-2.4$.

✓ **GUIDED PRACTICE**  for Examples 3, 4, and 5

**Use a calculator to evaluate. Round to the nearest tenth.**

**9.** $\sqrt{236}$  **10.** $\sqrt{11}$  **11.** $-\sqrt{20.96}$  **12.** $-\sqrt{3590}$

**Solve the equation. Check your solutions.**

**13.** $t^2 = 36$  **14.** $k^2 = 121$  **15.** $y^2 - 15 = 10$  **16.** $x^2 + 7 = 16$

## SKILL PRACTICE

1. **VOCABULARY** Copy and complete: A number $b$ is a square root of $c$ if __?__.

2. **VOCABULARY** *Explain* why the number 121 is a perfect square.

*SEE EXAMPLE 1*
on p. 469
for Exs. 3–7

**EVALUATING SQUARE ROOTS** **Find the square root.**

3. $-\sqrt{1}$       4. $\sqrt{100}$       ⑤ $\sqrt{144}$       6. $-\sqrt{16}$

7. **ERROR ANALYSIS** Describe and correct the error made in finding the square root of $-\sqrt{49}$.

$$\times \quad -\sqrt{49} = 7$$

**APPROXIMATING SQUARE ROOTS** **Approximate the square root to the nearest whole number.**

*SEE EXAMPLE 2*
on p. 470
for Exs. 8–15

8. $\sqrt{33}$       9. $\sqrt{14}$       10. $\sqrt{117}$       11. $\sqrt{52}$

12. $\sqrt{74}$       ⑬ $\sqrt{22}$       14. $\sqrt{48}$       15. $\sqrt{123}$

*SEE EXAMPLE 3*
on p. 470
for Exs. 16–20

**USING A CALCULATOR** **Use a calculator to approximate the square root. Round to the nearest tenth if necessary.**

16. $-\sqrt{34.6}$       ⑰ $\sqrt{43.56}$       18. $\sqrt{2440}$       19. $-\sqrt{6204}$

20. ⬥ **TAKS REASONING** Which square root is closest to 13?

Ⓐ $\sqrt{165}$       Ⓑ $\sqrt{175}$       Ⓒ $\sqrt{185}$       Ⓓ $\sqrt{193}$

**SOLVING EQUATIONS** **Solve the equation. Round to the nearest hundredth if necessary. Check your solution(s).**

*SEE EXAMPLE 5*
on p. 471
for Exs. 21–35

21. $x^2 = 0$       22. $b^2 = 49$       23. $y^2 = 81$

24. $z^2 - 169 = 0$       25. $y^2 + 7 = 56$       26. $a^2 + 12 = 48$

27. $n^2 - 27 = 94$       28. $y^2 - 31 = 36$       29. $62 + z^2 = 198$

30. $c^2 - 0.35 = 1.65$       31. $58 + m^2 = 253$       32. $k^2 - 0.17 = 0.64$

33. $m^2 + 0.38 = 1.82$       34. $p^2 + 0.06 = 1.27$       35. $s^2 - 0.52 = 1.44$

**REASONING** **Complete the statement with *always*, *sometimes*, or *never*.**

36. Square roots are __?__ whole numbers.

37. Square roots of perfect squares are __?__ integers.

38. A number __?__ has more than two square roots.

🆇🆈 **ALGEBRA** **Evaluate the expression $\sqrt{a^2 - b^2}$ for the given values.**

39. $a = 5, b = 5$       40. $a = 10, b = 8$       41. $a = 15, b = 12$

**RATIONAL SQUARE ROOTS** Find the square root.

42. $-\sqrt{\dfrac{1}{4}}$

43. $\sqrt{\dfrac{16}{25}}$

44. $-\sqrt{\dfrac{81}{100}}$

45. $\sqrt{\dfrac{144}{169}}$

46. $\sqrt{1.44}$

47. $\sqrt{1.96}$

48. $-\sqrt{0.25}$

49. $\sqrt{11.56}$

**CHALLENGE** Simplify the expression. Round to the nearest hundredth if necessary.

50. $\sqrt{\sqrt{625}}$

51. $-\sqrt{\sqrt{1296}}$

52. $-\sqrt{\sqrt{\sqrt{256}}}$

53. $\sqrt{\sqrt{\sqrt{4096}}}$

## PROBLEM SOLVING

**SEE EXAMPLES 1 AND 3**
on pp. 469–470
for Exs. 54, 55

54. **GUIDED PROBLEM SOLVING** You have a square piece of fabric for the front of a square pillow. The fabric has an area of 729 square inches. You use all the fabric. What is the length of one side of the pillow?

   **a.** Write an equation using the formula for the area of a square.

   **b.** Use the definition of square root to solve the equation.

   **c.** Evaluate the positive square root.

55. **TAKS REASONING** You want to put a fence around a square plot of land that has an area of 6250 square yards. What is the length of a side, to the nearest tenth of a yard?

   (**A**) 19.8 yards     (**B**) 79.0 yards

   (**C**) 79.1 yards     (**D**) 625.0 yards

56. **TAKS REASONING** *Explain* how to find the perimeter of a square given its area. To the nearest yard, what is the perimeter of the square plot of land in Exercise 55?

57. **HOME DECORATING** A tablecloth measures 50 inches by 50 inches. Will it cover a square table with an area of 21.5 square feet? *Explain.*

58. **EXAMPLES AND NONEXAMPLES** Give three examples of numbers whose square roots are not rational numbers. Give three examples of numbers whose square roots are rational. Include at least one non-integer in each list.

59. **ROADWAYS** A road is 330 feet long. The region where the road intersects the other roads is shaded darker in the diagram. The area of each intersection is 576 square feet. Find the length $w$ in the diagram. Then find the area of the roadway.

60. **WRITING** Your friend tells you that $\sqrt{5}$ is a rational number because you can write it as $\dfrac{\sqrt{5}}{1}$. Do you agree or disagree? *Explain.*

**Fire Towers** New Hampshire lookout towers were built in the early 1900s to spot forest fires. Mount Cardigan, which has a view of the 6288 foot tall Mount Washington, was built in 1924. Many towers were constructed over the next few decades. Sixteen towers are still in operation. Ideally, the distance $d$ in miles that a person can see from a tower is given by the formula $d = \sqrt{1.5h}$, where $h$ is the height in feet above the surrounding land.

61. **Calculate** A ranger standing at Mount Cardigan is about 3100 feet above the surrounding land. How far can the ranger ideally see?

SEE EXAMPLE 4 on p. 472 for Exs. 61–63

62. **Reasoning** A person standing in the fire tower of Mount Monadnock, which is no longer in use, could see 104 miles to Mount Washington. Mount Monadnock is about 3100 feet above the surrounding land. *Explain* how it is possible to see farther than the formula suggests.

63. **Elevation** A ranger at Mount Prospect tower can see about 57.6 miles. At about what height above the surrounding land is the ranger?

64. **LOOK FOR A PATTERN** Find the positive square roots of 0.36, 0.0036, 0.000036, and 0.00000036. What pattern do you notice? Using the pattern, predict the positive square root of 0.0000000036.

65. **CHALLENGE** In Example 2, you learned how to approximate the value of a square root to the nearest whole number without using a calculator. *Explain* how to approximate the value of a square root to the nearest tenth if you do not have a calculator.

## MIXED REVIEW FOR TAKS

**TAKS PRACTICE** at classzone.com

REVIEW Lesson 8.7; TAKS Workbook

66. **TAKS PRACTICE** If $\triangle JKL$ is translated 5 units to the right and 4 units up to form $\triangle J'K'L'$, what are the coordinates of point $J'$? *TAKS Obj. 3*

(A) $(-3, -3)$
(B) $(1, 2)$
(C) $(2, 1)$
(D) $(5, 4)$

REVIEW Lesson 4.1; TAKS Workbook

67. **TAKS PRACTICE** For any integer $x$, which expression always produces an even integer? *TAKS Obj. 6*

(F) $x^2$      (G) $x + 2$      (H) $2x$      (J) $x \div 2$

# 9.2 Rational and Irrational Numbers

**TEKS** *8.1.A, 8.1.C*

| | |
|---|---|
| **Before** | You investigated rational numbers. |
| **Now** | You'll work with irrational numbers. |
| **Why?** | So you can analyze effects of weather, as in Example 4. |

**KEY VOCABULARY**
- **irrational number,** p. 475
- **real number,** p. 475

Recall that a *rational number* is a number that can be written as a quotient $\frac{a}{b}$, where $a$ and $b$ are integers and $b \neq 0$. An **irrational number** is a number that cannot be written as a quotient of two integers. If $n$ is a positive integer and is not a perfect square, then $\sqrt{n}$ and $-\sqrt{n}$ are irrational numbers.

Together, rational numbers and irrational numbers make up the set of **real numbers**. The Venn diagram shows the relationships among numbers in the real number system.

**Real Numbers**

| Rational numbers | Irrational numbers |
|---|---|
| Integers | $\sqrt{2}$  $\pi$ |
| Whole numbers | 0.1010010001 . . . |

The decimal form of a rational number is either terminating or repeating. The decimal form of an irrational number neither terminates nor repeats.

---

## EXAMPLE 1  Classifying Real Numbers

*REWRITE NUMBERS*
Need help writing a rational number as a decimal? See p. 255.

| Number | Type | Decimal Form | Type of Decimal |
|---|---|---|---|
| **a.** $\frac{3}{4}$ | Rational | $\frac{3}{4} = 0.75$ | Terminating |
| **b.** $\frac{1}{11}$ | Rational | $\frac{1}{11} = 0.0909 \ldots = 0.\overline{09}$ | Repeating |
| **c.** $\sqrt{3}$ | Irrational | $\sqrt{3} = 1.7320508 \ldots$ | Nonterminating and nonrepeating |

*Animated* **Math** at classzone.com

---

✓ **GUIDED PRACTICE**  for Example 1

**Tell whether the number is *rational* or *irrational*. *Explain* your reasoning.**

**1.** $\frac{5}{8}$    **2.** $\sqrt{7}$    **3.** $\sqrt{25}$    **4.** $\frac{2}{9}$

**EXAMPLE 2** Comparing Real Numbers

Graph $\sqrt{\dfrac{1}{2}}$ and $\dfrac{1}{2}$ on a number line. Then copy and complete the statement

$\sqrt{\dfrac{1}{2}}$ _?_ $\dfrac{1}{2}$ with <, >, or =.

**SOLUTION**

*AVOID ERRORS*
A radical sign acts as a grouping symbol. So, you must evaluate the expression under the radical sign before finding its square root.

Use a calculator to approximate the square root. Graph the decimal forms of the numbers on a number line and compare.

$\dfrac{1}{2} = 0.5$    $\sqrt{\dfrac{1}{2}} = \sqrt{0.5} \approx 0.707$

▶ **Answer** Because $\dfrac{1}{2}$ is to the left of $\sqrt{\dfrac{1}{2}}$, $\sqrt{\dfrac{1}{2}} > \dfrac{1}{2}$.

---

✔ **GUIDED PRACTICE** for Example 2

Copy and complete the statement with <, >, or =.

**5.** $4$ _?_ $\sqrt{8}$　　　**6.** $\dfrac{4}{5}$ _?_ $\sqrt{\dfrac{4}{5}}$　　　**7.** $\dfrac{1}{4}$ _?_ $\sqrt{\dfrac{1}{4}}$　　　**8.** $\sqrt{7}$ _?_ $3$

---

**EXAMPLE 3** Ordering Real Numbers

Order the numbers $0.4\overline{7}$, $0.\overline{474}$, $0.\overline{47}$, and $\sqrt{0.23}$ from least to greatest.

**SOLUTION**

**STEP 1** Write each decimal out to six decimal places.

$0.4\overline{7} = 0.477777\ldots$ — Notice that the first two digits after the decimal point are the same for each number.

$0.\overline{474} = 0.474474\ldots$

$0.\overline{47} = 0.474747\ldots$ — Use the second pair of digits to order the decimals.

$\sqrt{0.23} = 0.479583\ldots$

**STEP 2** Write the decimals in order:

$0.474474\ldots, 0.474747\ldots, 0.477777\ldots,$ and $0.479583\ldots$

▶ **Answer** From least to greatest, the order is $0.\overline{474}$, $0.\overline{47}$, $0.4\overline{7}$, and $\sqrt{0.23}$.

*Animated Math* at classzone.com

---

✔ **GUIDED PRACTICE** for Example 3

**9.** Order the decimals $0.\overline{52}$, $0.\overline{525}$, $0.52\overline{5}$, and $\sqrt{0.276}$ from least to greatest.

**10.** Order the decimals $1.7$, $\sqrt{1.7}$, $1.\overline{89}$, and $1.\overline{3}$ from least to greatest.

**EXAMPLE 4** **Using an Irrational Number**

**Waves** For large ocean waves, the wind speed $s$ in knots and the height of the waves $h$ in feet are related by the equation $s = \sqrt{\dfrac{h}{0.019}}$. If the waves are about 9.5 feet tall, what must the wind speed be? (1 knot is equivalent to 1.15 miles per hour.)

**SOLUTION**

$$s = \sqrt{\frac{h}{0.019}} \qquad \text{Write original equation.}$$

$$= \sqrt{\frac{9.5}{0.019}} \qquad \text{Substitute 9.5 for } h.$$

$$= \sqrt{500} \qquad \text{Divide.}$$

$$\approx 22.4 \qquad \text{Approximate square root.}$$

▶ **Answer** The wind speed is about 22 knots.

✓ **GUIDED PRACTICE** **for Example 4**

**11. What If?** In Example 4, suppose the waves grow to about 15 feet tall. What is the wind speed rounded to the nearest knot?

# 9.2 EXERCISES

HOMEWORK KEY

🏴 = **TAKS Practice and Reasoning**
Exs. 31, 33, 63, 65, 70, 74, and 75

◯ = **HINTS** AND **HOMEWORK HELP**
for Exs. 5, 9, 13, 27, 67 at classzone.com

## SKILL PRACTICE

**VOCABULARY** Copy and complete the statement.

**1.** Numbers that cannot be written as a quotient of two integers are __?__.

**2.** Together, rational and irrational numbers make up the set of __?__.

**CLASSIFYING REAL NUMBERS** Tell whether the number is *rational* or *irrational*. *Explain* your reasoning.

SEE EXAMPLE 1
on p. 475
for Exs. 3–15

**3.** 0.682

**4.** 0.12345 . . .

**5.** $0.\overline{2}$

**6.** 0.30311

**7.** $\sqrt{36}$

**8.** $\sqrt{62}$

**9.** $\sqrt{5}$

**10.** $\sqrt{144}$

**11.**  $\dfrac{9}{46}$

**12.** $\sqrt{\dfrac{25}{49}}$

**13.** $\sqrt{\dfrac{100}{81}}$

**14.** $\dfrac{22}{31}$

**15. WHICH ONE DOESN'T BELONG?** Tell which number does not belong. *Justify* your reasoning.

**A.** $\sqrt{\dfrac{1}{4}}$

**B.** $\sqrt{\dfrac{1}{3}}$

**C.** $\sqrt{\dfrac{2}{5}}$

**D.** $\sqrt{\dfrac{5}{6}}$

**COMPARING REAL NUMBERS** Graph the pair of numbers on a number line. Then copy and complete the statement with <, >, or =.

16. $\dfrac{5}{6}$ ? $\sqrt{\dfrac{5}{6}}$

17. $\sqrt{0.9}$ ? $0.9$

18. $\sqrt{2.25}$ ? $\dfrac{3.5}{2.4}$

19. $\sqrt{4.6}$ ? $2.5$

20. $2.6$ ? $\sqrt{6.7}$

21. $\sqrt{\dfrac{8}{11}}$ ? $\dfrac{9}{10}$

**CHOOSE A METHOD** Copy and complete with <, >, or =. Tell whether you used *mental math*, *estimation*, or a *calculator*.

22. $0.81$ ? $\sqrt{0.81}$

23. $5$ ? $\sqrt{10}$

24. $\sqrt{\dfrac{64}{121}}$ ? $\dfrac{8}{11}$

25. $\sqrt{\dfrac{16}{3}}$ ? $5$

26. $\sqrt{21}$ ? $7$

27. $-5$ ? $-\sqrt{25}$

28. $\sqrt{9.9}$ ? $3.3$

29. $1.3$ ? $\sqrt{1.7}$

30. $-0.4$ ? $-\sqrt{1.6}$

31. ⬥ **TAKS REASONING** Which statement is *not* true?

Ⓐ $\sqrt{12} < 4$ Ⓑ $8 > \sqrt{16}$ Ⓒ $\sqrt{169} = 13$ Ⓓ $\sqrt{30} < 5$

32. **GRAPHING REAL NUMBERS** Graph the numbers $-\sqrt{9}$, $8.69$, $\sqrt{45}$, and $\dfrac{141}{25}$ on a number line. Then order the numbers from least to greatest.

33. ⬥ **TAKS REASONING** Which of the following shows the numbers in order from least to greatest?

Ⓐ $\sqrt{2}$, $\sqrt{5}$, $1$, $2$, $3$  Ⓑ $1$, $\sqrt{2}$, $\sqrt{5}$, $2$, $3$

Ⓒ $1$, $\sqrt{2}$, $2$, $\sqrt{5}$, $3$  Ⓓ $1$, $\sqrt{2}$, $2$, $3$, $\sqrt{5}$

**ORDERING REAL NUMBERS** Order the numbers from least to greatest.

34. $0.1\overline{3}$, $0.\overline{131}$, $0.\overline{13}$, $0.133$

35. $0.\overline{26}$, $0.266$, $0.2\overline{6}$, $0.\overline{262}$

36. $\sqrt{0.68}$, $0.4\overline{5}$, $0.455$, $0.\overline{45}$

37. $0.3\overline{9}$, $\sqrt{0.17}$, $0.\overline{39}$, $0.399$

38. $1.5$, $\sqrt{8}$, $-4$, $-3.75$

39. $\sqrt{81}$, $10.3$, $\sqrt{220}$, $-9$

40. $-\sqrt{12}$, $-\sqrt{\dfrac{1}{4}}$, $-3.5$, $-\dfrac{3}{4}$

41. $1.02$, $\sqrt{2.5}$, $\sqrt{1.25}$, $\dfrac{2}{5}$

42. **ERROR ANALYSIS** A student says $\sqrt{64}$ is irrational because of the radical symbol. What is incorrect with this reasoning?

✕ **ALGEBRA** Evaluate when $a = 2$, $b = 4$, and $c = 9$. Classify the result as *rational* or *irrational*. Round to the nearest tenth, if necessary.

43. $\sqrt{b + c}$

44. $\sqrt{c^2 - (a + b)}$

45. $\sqrt{a^2 - b + c}$

46. $\sqrt{bc + b + c}$

47. $\sqrt{c^2 - b^2 + 1}$

48. $\sqrt{ab + bc - a^2}$

**CLASSIFYING REAL NUMBERS** Classify the value of the expression as *rational*, *irrational*, or *cannot be determined* when $\sqrt{x}$ is irrational and $n$ is an integer. *Explain* your reasoning.

49. $\sqrt{x} + n$

50. $\sqrt{x} + \sqrt{x}$

51. $n\sqrt{x}$

52. **REASONING** Is $\sqrt{-4}$ a rational number? *Explain* your reasoning.

**REASONING** Evaluate the expressions when $a = 4$, $b = 3$, $c = 9$, and $d = 5$. Then tell whether the expressions are *always*, *sometimes*, or *never* equal if $a$, $b$, $c$, and $d$ are real numbers greater than zero. *Explain* your reasoning.

**53.** $\sqrt{a + c}, \ \sqrt{a} + \sqrt{c}$

**54.** $\sqrt{a^2}, (\sqrt{a})^2$

**55.** $\sqrt{ac}, \ \sqrt{a} \cdot \sqrt{c}$

**56.** $\sqrt{a^2 + b^2}, \ \sqrt{a^2} + \sqrt{b^2}$

**57.** $\sqrt{d^2 - a^2}, \ \sqrt{d^2} - \sqrt{a^2}$

**58.** $\sqrt{\dfrac{a}{c}}, \ \dfrac{\sqrt{a}}{\sqrt{c}}$

**REASONING** Determine whether the expression is *always*, *sometimes*, or *never* irrational for whole number values of $x$.

**59.** $\sqrt{x + 3}$

**60.** $\sqrt{x^2}$

**61.** $\sqrt{x} \div 4$

**62. CHALLENGE** Describe the values of $x$ for which $\sqrt{x^2} = -x$. Give an example to support your answer.

## PROBLEM SOLVING

*SEE EXAMPLE 1*
on p. 475
for Exs. 63–64

**63.**  **TAKS REASONING** The area of a square judo mat is 400 square feet. What is *not* true about the perimeter?

**A** It is rational.  **B** It is irrational.

**C** It is an integer.  **D** It is a real number.

**64. FLOOR DIMENSIONS** The floor of a square room has an area of 212 square feet. Are the dimensions of the room *rational* or *irrational*?

**65.** **TAKS REASONING** Give an example of a rational number and an irrational number between 8 and 9.

**66. WRITING** Your aunt offers you a square piece of carpet that has an area of 110 square feet. You want to use the carpet in a bedroom that measures 10.5 feet by 11.2 feet. Will the carpet fit in the room? *Explain.*

**67. DECORATING** You are decorating your room. You have a square stencil that covers an area of 20.25 square inches. The wall you are decorating is $7\frac{1}{2}$ feet high. How many stencils fit between the floor and the ceiling?

**68.** ◆ **MULTIPLE REPRESENTATIONS** Use the numbers in the list below.

$$-0.122333\ldots, \ \sqrt{7.9}, \ \frac{3\sqrt{7}}{6}, \ \frac{\sqrt{3 + 22}}{4}, \ \frac{\sqrt{9}}{1}, \ -\frac{\sqrt{144}}{2}$$

**a. Decimals** Write each number as a decimal. If needed, round to the nearest tenth.

**b. Diagram** Draw a Venn diagram showing rational and irrational numbers. Place the numbers from the list above in your diagram.

**c. Detailed Diagram** Draw a Venn diagram showing real numbers, rational numbers, integers, irrational numbers, and positive and negative numbers. Place the numbers from the list above in your diagram.

**69. BOX KITES** To find the minimum wind speed required to fly a box kite, use the formula $m = 5\sqrt{\dfrac{w}{A}}$, where $m$ is minimum speed in miles per hour, $w$ is weight in ounces, and $A$ is the area in square feet of the surface used to lift the kite. A box kite weighs 19.6 ounces and its surface area is 11.71 square feet. The wind is blowing at 6 miles per hour. Can you fly your kite? *Explain* your reasoning.

**SEE EXAMPLE 4**
on p. 477
for Ex. 70

**70.** 🟥 **TAKS REASONING** The radius of a circle is given by the formula $r = \sqrt{\dfrac{A}{\pi}}$, where $A$ is the area of the circle.

    **a.** Find the radius of a circle to the nearest tenth when the area is 6 square feet.

    **b.** Find the radius and diameter of the circle when the area is $9\pi$ square feet.

    **c.** *Describe* the type of number the area needs to be for the radius to be an integer.

**71. REASONING** Your friend gets a result of 2.645751311 on a calculator and says that it has to be an irrational number. Is your friend right? *Explain* your reasoning.

**72. GEOMETRY** The figure is composed of one large square and four smaller congruent squares. The area of the shaded region is 45 square centimeters. Is the side length of the large square *rational* or *irrational*? *Explain* your reasoning.

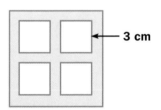

← 3 cm

**73. CHALLENGE** Find three rational numbers and three irrational numbers between $\dfrac{2}{3}$ and $\dfrac{3}{4}$. Can you write all of the rational numbers that are between these two numbers? *Explain* your reasoning.

---

## MIXED REVIEW FOR TAKS

**TAKS** PRACTICE at classzone.com

**REVIEW**
Lesson 7.4;
TAKS Workbook

**74.** 🟥 **TAKS PRACTICE** A restaurant will raise the price of lunch specials. The specials are $9.10 now. Which is the greatest increase in price? *TAKS Obj. 1*

    **(A)** 15% increase         **(B)** $1.20 increase

    **(C)** $\dfrac{1}{8}$ increase         **(D)** $\dfrac{2}{13}$ increase

**REVIEW**
Lesson 8.8;
TAKS Workbook

**75.** 🟥 **TAKS PRACTICE** $\triangle ABC$ is similar to $\triangle DEF$. What is the length of $\overline{DE}$? *TAKS Obj. 4*

    **(F)** 0.6 units

    **(G)** 3 units

    **(H)** 15 units

    **(J)** 16.6 units

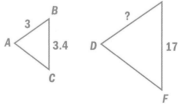

INVESTIGATION
*Use before Lesson 9.3*

**GOAL**
Use graph paper to relate the side lengths of a right triangle.

**MATERIALS**
• graph paper
• pen or pencil

TEKS *8.7.C, 8.16.A*

# 9.3 Modeling the Pythagorean Theorem

You can use graph paper to find the length of a right triangle's *hypotenuse*, which is the side opposite the right angle.

**EXPLORE** **Find the length of the hypotenuse of a right triangle with side lengths of three units and four units.**

**STEP 1** **Draw** the right triangle on graph paper. The sides of the triangle that form the right angle are called *legs*. For each leg, draw a square that has a leg as one side. What is the sum of the areas of these two squares?

**STEP 2** **Measure** the hypotenuse using graph paper. If you draw a square with the hypotenuse as one side, what is its area?

**STEP 3** **Compare** the sum of the areas you found in Step 1 to the area you found in Step 2. What do you notice?

**PRACTICE** **Repeat Steps 1–3 for right triangles with legs of the given lengths.**

1. 5, 12        2. 6, 8        3. 8, 15

**DRAW CONCLUSIONS**

4. **REASONING** Let the lengths of the legs of a right triangle be *a* and *b*, and the length of the hypotenuse be *c*. Write a conjecture about the relationship between the lengths of the legs and the length of the hypotenuse.

# 9.3 The Pythagorean Theorem

TEKS *8.9.A, 8.16.B*

| **Before** | You used formulas to solve problems. |
| **Now** | You'll use the Pythagorean Theorem to solve problems. |
| **Why?** | So you can find distances, as in Example 2. |

**KEY VOCABULARY**
- **leg**, *p. 482*
- **hypotenuse**, *p. 482*
- **Pythagorean Theorem**, *p. 482*
- **converse**, *p. 483*

In a right triangle, the sides that form the right angle are called **legs**. The side opposite the right angle, which is always the longest side, is the **hypotenuse**. As you may have observed in the Investigation on page 481, the lengths of the legs and the hypotenuse are related by the **Pythagorean Theorem**.

---

### KEY CONCEPT                    *For Your Notebook*

**Pythagorean Theorem**

**Words**    For any right triangle, the sum of the squares of the lengths of the legs equals the square of the length of the hypotenuse.

$a = 3$, $c = 5$, $b = 4$

**Algebra**    $a^2 + b^2 = c^2$        **Numbers**    $3^2 + 4^2 = 5^2$

---

### EXAMPLE 1    Finding the Length of a Hypotenuse

*TAKE NOTES*
Be sure to write the Pythagorean Theorem and a few examples in your notebook.

**Find the length of the hypotenuse of a right triangle with a 15 inch leg and a 20 inch leg.**

$$a^2 + b^2 = c^2 \qquad \text{Pythagorean Theorem}$$

$$15^2 + 20^2 = c^2 \qquad \text{Substitute 15 for } a \text{ and 20 for } b.$$

$$225 + 400 = c^2 \qquad \text{Evaluate powers.}$$

$$625 = c^2 \qquad \text{Add.}$$

$$\sqrt{625} = c \qquad \text{Take positive square root of each side.}$$

$$25 = c \qquad \text{Evaluate square root.}$$

▶ **Answer** The length of the hypotenuse is 25 inches.

---

✓ **GUIDED PRACTICE**    for Example 1

1. Find the length of the hypotenuse of a right triangle with a 28 inch leg and a 45 inch leg.

**Interpreting Results** In application problems, you usually need to take only the positive square root. For example, length, speed, and height are positive, so a negative square root would not give a reasonable answer.

**EXAMPLE 2** TAKS PRACTICE: Multiple Choice

**Parasailing** You are parasailing as shown in the diagram at the right. After getting airborne and reaching cruising speed, your position is 150 feet behind the boat. To the nearest foot, how high are you above the water?

*ELIMINATE CHOICES*
Height is positive, so choice A can be eliminated.

**(A)** −161 ft      **(B)** 161 ft

**(C)** 200 ft      **(D)** 266 ft

**SOLUTION**

| | |
|---|---|
| $a^2 + b^2 = c^2$ | **Pythagorean Theorem** |
| $150^2 + b^2 = 220^2$ | **Substitute 150 for *a* and 220 for *c*.** |
| $22{,}500 + b^2 = 48{,}400$ | **Evaluate powers.** |
| $b^2 = 25{,}900$ | **Subtract 22,500 from each side.** |
| $b = \sqrt{25{,}900}$ | **Take positive square root of each side.** |
| $b \approx 160.9348$ | **Approximate square root.** |

▶ **Answer** You are about 161 feet above the water. The correct answer is B.  (A) (B) (C) (D)

at classzone.com

✓ **GUIDED PRACTICE** for Example 2

**Find the unknown length. Round to the nearest tenth, if necessary.**

2. $c$, $a = 7.5$ in., $b = 18$ in.

3. $a$, $c = 16$ m, $b = 8$ m

4. $c = 15$ ft, $b$, $a = 9$ ft

**Converse of the Pythagorean Theorem** The Pythagorean Theorem can be written as an if-then statement with two parts.

**Theorem** If a triangle is a right triangle, then $a^2 + b^2 = c^2$.

When you reverse the parts of an if-then statement, the new statement is called the **converse** of the statement.

**Converse** If $a^2 + b^2 = c^2$, then the triangle is a right triangle.

The converse of a *true* statement may or may not be true. The converse of the Pythagorean Theorem is true. You can use the converse of the Pythagorean Theorem to decide whether a triangle is a right triangle.

EXAMPLE 3 **Identifying Right Triangles**

Use the converse of the Pythagorean Theorem to determine whether a triangle with the given side lengths is a right triangle.

**a.** $a = 6$, $b = 8$, $c = 10$

$$a^2 + b^2 \stackrel{?}{=} c^2$$

$$6^2 + 8^2 \stackrel{?}{=} 10^2$$

$$36 + 64 \stackrel{?}{=} 100$$

$$100 = 100 \checkmark$$

▶ **Answer** A right triangle

**b.** $a = 10$, $b = 12$, $c = 16$

$$a^2 + b^2 \stackrel{?}{=} c^2$$

$$10^2 + 12^2 \stackrel{?}{=} 16^2$$

$$100 + 144 \stackrel{?}{=} 256$$

$$244 \neq 256 \; ✗$$

▶ **Answer** Not a right triangle

---

✓ **GUIDED PRACTICE** for Example 3

**5.** Is a triangle with side lengths 14, 17, and 23 a right triangle? *Explain.*

---

## 9.3 EXERCISES

**HOMEWORK KEY**

⬥ = **TAKS Practice and Reasoning**
Exs. 6, 32, 34, 35, 39, and 40

○ = **HINTS AND HOMEWORK HELP**
for Exs. 3, 9, 13, 33 at classzone.com

### SKILL PRACTICE

**VOCABULARY Copy and complete the statement.**

**1.** In a right triangle, the side opposite the right angle is called the ___?___ .

**2.** The theorem that relates the lengths of the legs to the length of the hypotenuse of a right triangle is the ___?___ .

**FINDING THE HYPOTENUSE Find the length of the hypotenuse.**

**SEE EXAMPLE 1**
on p. 482
for Exs. 3–6

**3.**

**4.**

**5.**

**6.** ⬥ **TAKS REASONING** The legs of a right triangle have lengths of 24 inches and 32 inches. What is the length of the hypotenuse?

(A) 20 inches   (B) 40 inches   (C) 48 inches   (D) 56 inches

**FINDING LEGS Find the length of the unknown leg. Round to the nearest tenth if necessary.**

**SEE EXAMPLE 2**
on p. 483
for Exs. 7–10

**7.**

**8.**

**9.**

**10. ERROR ANALYSIS** Describe and correct the error made in finding the length of the third side of the right triangle. Round to the nearest tenth of a foot.

$$a^2 + b^2 = c^2$$
$$6^2 + 8^2 = c^2$$
$$36 + 64 = c^2$$
$$100 = c^2$$
$$10 = c$$

**CLASSIFYING TRIANGLES** Determine whether the given triangle side lengths form a right triangle.

**SEE EXAMPLE 3**
on p. 484
for Exs. 11–16

**11.** 4 m, 5 m, 7 m     **12.** 50 in., 64 in., 80 in.     **13.** 85 ft, 204 ft, 221 ft

**14.** 1.2 mi, 1.6 mi, 2 mi     **15.** 6.5 cm, 15.6 cm, 16.9 cm     **16.** 28.8 m, 8.4 m, 31 m

**FINDING UNKNOWN LENGTHS** Let $a$ and $b$ represent the lengths of the legs of a right triangle, and let $c$ represent the length of the hypotenuse. Find the unknown length.

**17.** $a = 1.5$, $b = \underline{\ ?\ }$, $c = 2.5$     **18.** $a = \underline{\ ?\ }$, $b = 123$, $c = 139.4$

**19.** $a = 2.8$, $b = 4.5$, $c = \underline{\ ?\ }$     **20.** $a = 4.5$, $b = \underline{\ ?\ }$, $c = 7.5$

**21.** $a = \underline{\ ?\ }$, $b = 2$, $c = \sqrt{13}$     **22.** $a = \sqrt{8}$, $b = 1$, $c = \underline{\ ?\ }$

**23.** $a = \underline{\ ?\ }$, $b = 37.5$, $c = 42.5$     **24.** $a = 2.5$, $b = 6$, $c = \underline{\ ?\ }$

**25.** $a = 2$, $b = \sqrt{21}$, $c = \underline{\ ?\ }$     **26.** $a = \sqrt{6}$, $b = \underline{\ ?\ }$, $c = \sqrt{15}$

**27. REASONING** An isosceles right triangle has a hypotenuse length of 6 feet. Find the length of each leg. Round to the nearest hundredth foot.

**28. ALGEBRA** A rectangle is $x$ feet by $3x$ feet. The length of a diagonal is $\sqrt{5}$ feet. Find the dimensions of the rectangle to the nearest hundredth of a foot.

**29. CHALLENGE** Find the length of segment $AB$ in the rectangular prism shown.

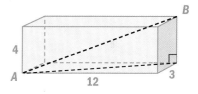

---

## PROBLEM SOLVING

**SEE EXAMPLE 1**
on p. 482
for Ex. 30

**30. VOLLEYBALL NET** You are setting up a volleyball net using two 8 foot poles to hold up the net. You are going to attach each pole to a stake in the ground using a piece of rope. Each stake should be 4 feet from the pole. Assume that the ropes are stretched tight. How long should each rope be? Round to the nearest tenth of a foot.

**31. WRITING** *Explain* the difference between the Pythagorean Theorem and the converse of the Pythagorean Theorem. Give an example to show how each is used.

**SEE EXAMPLE 2**
on p. 483
for Ex. 32

**32. TAKS REASONING** 13 foot ladder is leaning against a building. The bottom of the ladder is 5 feet from the building. How high up does the ladder meet the wall?

    **(A)** 12 feet     **(B)** 13.9 feet     **(C)** 14 feet     **(D)** 18 feet

<br>

**SEE EXAMPLE 2**
on p. 483
for Ex. 33

**33.** **UTILITY POLES** A wire with a length of 23.8 meters is attached to a utility pole. The wire is anchored to the ground 9 meters from the base of the pole. How high above the ground is the wire attached to the utility pole? Round to the nearest tenth of a meter.

**34.** **TAKS REASONING** Write a true if-then statement whose converse is also true. Then write a true if-then statement whose converse is false.

**35.** **TAKS REASONING** A rectangular window is similar to the shape of the wall in which it is located. The wall is 20 feet wide with a diagonal of 25 feet. The window is $3\frac{1}{3}$ feet wide. Find the height of the window using two different methods: (a) by first finding the height of the wall, and (b) by first finding the diagonal of the window. *Explain* your methods.

**36.** **DRAW A DIAGRAM** Eric is hiking from his campsite to a creek. He walks 3.5 miles directly south, 4 miles directly east, and then 1.5 miles directly south.

  **a.** Draw and label a triangle you can use to find the distance between the campsite and the creek.

  **b.** Find the distance from the campsite to the creek.

  **c.** Assume that the ground is flat. How much shorter is it to walk in a straight line than it is to take Eric's route?

**37.** **CHALLENGE** Draw several different obtuse triangles and measure the lengths of the sides. Let *a* and *b* represent the lengths of the two shorter sides and let *c* represent the length of the longest side. Make a conjecture about the relationship between the lengths of the sides of obtuse triangles.

**38.** **CHALLENGE** Two sides of a quadrilateral are each 5 inches long. The other two sides are each *a* inches long. One diagonal is $\sqrt{a^2 + 25}$ inches long. Can the quadrilateral be a rectangle? *Explain* your reasoning.

## MIXED REVIEW FOR TAKS

**TAKS PRACTICE** at classzone.com

**REVIEW**
Lesson 9.1;
TAKS Workbook

**39.** **TAKS PRACTICE** An accountant does some calculations and ends up with several square roots as solutions. The accountant wants to know which of the square roots is closest to 7. Which irrational number should the accountant choose? *TAKS Obj. 1*

  **A** $\sqrt{14}$      **B** $\sqrt{35}$      **C** $\sqrt{45}$      **D** $\sqrt{60}$

**REVIEW**
Lesson 7.2;
TAKS Workbook

**40.** **TAKS PRACTICE** Rob called a company with questions about a product. A recording told him that he was the sixth person waiting for information. He was put on hold for 2.5 minutes before he spoke to a customer service representative. What is the best estimate for the total length of time the fifteenth person on hold might have waited? *TAKS Obj. 2*

  **F** 6.25 min      **G** 7.5 min      **H** 11.5 min      **J** 37.5 min

# 9.4 Using the Pythagorean Theorem

TEKS *8.7.B, 8.9.A*

| Before | You found the side lengths of right triangles. |
|---|---|
| Now | You'll solve real-world problems using the Pythagorean Theorem. |
| Why? | So you can find distances indirectly, as in Example 1. |

**KEY VOCABULARY**
• **Pythagorean triple,** *p. 488*

**Boating** You and your friend live on different sides of a lake. To ride your bicycle to your friend's house, you travel 0.5 mile directly east, and then 1.2 miles directly south. How far is it to your friend's house by boat?

One way to find the distance from your house to your friend's house by boat is to measure the distance *indirectly*. Because the bicycle and boat paths form a right triangle, you can do this using the Pythagorean Theorem.

---

**EXAMPLE 1** Using Indirect Measurement

To answer the question above, let $a$ and $b$ represent the lengths of the legs (bicycle paths) of the right triangle connecting your house and your friend's house. Let $x$ represent the length of the hypotenuse (boat path).

$$a^2 + b^2 = x^2 \quad \text{Pythagorean Theorem}$$
$$0.5^2 + 1.2^2 = x^2 \quad \text{Substitute 0.5 for } a \text{ and 1.2 for } b.$$
$$0.25 + 1.44 = x^2 \quad \text{Evaluate powers.}$$
$$1.69 = x^2 \quad \text{Add.}$$
$$1.3 = x \quad \text{Take positive square root of each side.}$$

*ANOTHER WAY*
Because $a$ and $b$ are both legs, you can also substitute 1.2 for $a$ and 0.5 for $b$. The result will be the same.

▶ **Answer** It is 1.3 miles to your friend's house by boat.

---

 **GUIDED PRACTICE** for Example 1

1. **What If?** What if your friend's house is 0.5 mile east and 0.9 mile south. How far is your friend's house from your house? Round your answer to the nearest tenth of a mile.

2. **Marina** Use the map in Example 1. How far is it to the marina from your house by boat? Round your answer to the nearest tenth of a mile.

**EXAMPLE 2** Finding Perimeter and Area

**Find the perimeter and area of the triangle.**

**SOLUTION**

**STEP 1** Find the height of the triangle.

$$h^2 + 15^2 = 17^2 \qquad \text{Pythagorean Theorem}$$
$$h^2 + 225 = 289 \qquad \text{Evaluate powers.}$$
$$h^2 = 64 \qquad \text{Subtract 225 from each side.}$$
$$h = 8 \qquad \text{Take positive square root of each side.}$$

**STEP 2** Use the height to find the perimeter and area.

$$\textbf{Perimeter} = 8 + 15 + 17 = 40$$

$$\textbf{Area} = \frac{1}{2}(15)(8) = 60$$

*REVIEW FORMULAS*
Need help finding the perimeter and area of a triangle? See p. 142.

▶ **Answer** The perimeter is 40 cm and the area is 60 cm$^2$.

**Pythagorean Triples** A **Pythagorean triple** is a set of three positive integers $a$, $b$, and $c$ such that $a^2 + b^2 = c^2$. For example, the integers 3, 4, and 5 form a Pythagorean triple because $3^2 + 4^2 = 5^2$.

**EXAMPLE 3** Identifying a Pythagorean Triple

**Use the converse of the Pythagorean Theorem to determine whether the side lengths of the triangle form a Pythagorean triple.**

$$a^2 + b^2 = c^2 \qquad \text{Definition of Pythagorean triple}$$
$$12^2 + 35^2 \stackrel{?}{=} 37^2 \qquad \text{Substitute 12 for } a, \text{ 35 for } b, \text{ and 37 for } c.$$
$$144 + 1225 \stackrel{?}{=} 1369 \qquad \text{Evaluate powers.}$$
$$1369 = 1369 \qquad \text{Add.}$$

*AVOID ERRORS*
Even though a drawing of a triangle may appear to have a right angle, you should confirm this using the converse of the Pythagorean Theorem.

▶ **Answer** Because $12^2 + 35^2 = 37^2$ and the side lengths are integers, the side lengths form a Pythagorean triple.

✓ **GUIDED PRACTICE** for Examples 2 and 3

**3.** Find the perimeter and area of a right triangle that has a hypotenuse of length 74 feet and a leg of length 70 feet.

**4.** Determine whether the side lengths of the triangle form a Pythagorean triple.

# 9.4 EXERCISES

HOMEWORK KEY

✈ = **TAKS Practice and Reasoning**
Exs. 10, 34, and 37

◯ = **HINTS** AND **HOMEWORK HELP**
for Exs. 3, 5, 11, 31 at classzone.com

## SKILL PRACTICE

1. **VOCABULARY** Copy and complete: The integers 5, 12, and 13 form a __?__ because $5^2 + 12^2 = 13^2$.

**FINDING PERIMETER AND AREA** Let *a* and *b* represent the lengths of the legs of a right triangle, and let *c* represent the length of the hypotenuse. Find the unknown length. Then find the perimeter and area.

SEE EXAMPLE 2
on p. 488
for Exs. 2–9

2. $a = 12$ cm, $b = 16$ cm, $c = $ __?__

3. $a = 20$ ft, $b = $ __?__ , $c = 25$ ft

4. $a = $ __?__ , $b = 4.2$ km, $c = 5.8$ km

5. $a = 4.8$ in., $b = 3.6$ in., $c = $ __?__

6. $a = 60$ yd, $b = $ __?__ , $c = 601.5$ yd

7. $a = $ __?__ , $b = 117$ m, $c = 125$ m

8. $a = 1.1$ cm, $b = 6$ cm, $c = $ __?__

9. $a = 15$ yd, $b = $ __?__ , $c = 25$ yd

10. ✈ **TAKS REASONING** What is the perimeter of a right triangle whose leg lengths are 3.6 inches and 7.7 inches?

Ⓐ 8.5 in.     Ⓑ 18.1 in.     Ⓒ 19.8 in.     Ⓓ 27.72 in.$^2$

11. **ERROR ANALYSIS** Describe and correct the error made in finding the area of the triangle below.

Area $= \frac{1}{2}(5.3)(2.1)$
$= 5.565$ ft$^2$

2.1 ft

5.3 ft

SEE EXAMPLE 3
on p. 488
for Exs. 12–15

**IDENTIFYING PYTHAGOREAN TRIPLES** Determine whether the numbers form a Pythagorean triple.

12. 9, 36, 41     13. 55, 48, 73     14. 39, 80, 89     15. 45, 96, 104

**USING AREA** Find the perimeter of the right triangle given the length of one leg and the area.

16. $a = 6$ m
    Area $= 24$ m$^2$

17. $a = 8.8$ mi
    Area $= 46.2$ mi$^2$

18. $a = 84$ cm
    Area $= 546$ cm$^2$

**USING PERIMETER** An isosceles triangle has perimeter *P*, in yards. Exactly one side has length *c* yards. Find the lengths of the other two sides. Then determine whether the triangle is an isosceles right triangle.

19. $c = \sqrt{50}$
    $P = 10 + \sqrt{50}$

20. $c = 4$
    $P = 4 + \sqrt{32}$

21. $c = \sqrt{13}$
    $P = 5 + \sqrt{13}$

22. **REASONING** The numbers 5, 12, and 13 form a Pythagorean triple. If each number is multiplied by the same positive integer, do the new numbers form a Pythagorean triple? *Justify* your reasoning.

**23.** **XY** ALGEBRA Write an equation for the perimeter of an isosceles right triangle in terms of its leg length *a*. Evaluate the equation for *a* = 9. Round your answer to the nearest tenth.

**In Exercises 24–29, find the distance between the points. Round your answer to the nearest tenth if necessary.**

---

**EXTENSION** **Finding the Distance Between Two Points**

The distance *d* between two points (*s*, *t*) and (*u*, *v*) is given by the formula $d = \sqrt{(u-s)^2 + (v-t)^2}$. Find the distance between (2, 3) and (8, 11).

$d = \sqrt{(u-s)^2 + (v-t)^2}$    Distance formula

$\quad = \sqrt{(8-2)^2 + (11-3)^2}$    Substitute values.

$\quad = \sqrt{36 + 64}$    Simplify.

$\quad = 10$    Evaluate square root.

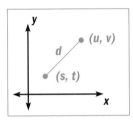

---

**24.** (0, −12), (5, 0)          **25.** (−2, 4), (5, −6)          **26.** (1, 6), (3, 4)

**27.** (−4, 7), (3, 3)          **28.** (6, −3), (−5, −1)          **29.** (−2, 0), (1, 9)

**30.** CHALLENGE Copy the diagram above in the Extension to form a right triangle with the given segment as the hypotenuse. Use the Pythagorean Theorem to derive the distance formula used above.

---

## PROBLEM SOLVING

SEE EXAMPLE 1
on p. 487
for Exs. 31–33

**31.** GUIDED PROBLEM SOLVING A rectangular swimming pool has a length of 41 feet and a width of 11 feet. Tina swims the diagonal distance across the pool. About how far does she swim?

  **a.** Draw a diagram.

  **b.** Label the known distances.

  **c.** Use the Pythagorean Theorem to find the unknown length. Round your answer to the nearest tenth of a foot.

**32.** LANDMARKS You are standing 500 feet from the Washington Monument. Using a range finder on the ground, you measure the distance from your location to the top of the monument to be 747 feet. Find the height of the Washington Monument to the nearest foot.

**33.** WRITING In what situations might it be easier to use indirect measurement than direct measurement? When might direct measurement be the better method? Give examples to justify your reasoning.

**34.** ✎ **TAKS REASONING** You are making a bookshelf, as shown. What is the value of $x$, rounded to the nearest inch?

Ⓐ 18 in.　Ⓑ 25 in.　Ⓒ 43 in.　Ⓓ 63 in.

**35.** ◆ **MULTIPLE REPRESENTATIONS** Right triangle $ABC$ has side lengths of 3 inches, 4 inches, and 5 inches. Triangle $DEF$ has double the side lengths of triangle $ABC$. Triangle $TUV$ has triple the side lengths of triangle $ABC$.

  **a. Make a Table** Make a table of the side lengths, perimeters, and areas of the three triangles. Compare the results.

  **b. Draw a Diagram** Use a ruler to draw the three triangles. *Describe* how to use the diagrams to compare the perimeters and areas of the triangles.

**36. CHALLENGE** Find the area of the shaded region given $\triangle ABC \sim \triangle ADE$, $AB = 10$ ft, $AC = 6$ ft, and $DE = 16$ ft.

---

## MIXED REVIEW FOR TAKS

**TAKS** PRACTICE at classzone.com

*REVIEW*
...........
Lesson 8.3;
TAKS Workbook

**37.** ✎ **TAKS PRACTICE** A non-square rhombus is divided into 2 triangles by connecting a pair of opposite corners. What two shapes are formed by this action? *TAKS Obj. 6*

  Ⓐ Two congruent isosceles triangles

  Ⓑ Two congruent right triangles

  Ⓒ Two isosceles triangles that are not congruent

  Ⓓ Two right triangles that are not congruent

---

## QUIZ *for Lessons 9.1–9.4*

Use a calculator to approximate the square root. Round to the nearest tenth. *(p. 469)*

**1.** $\sqrt{50}$       **2.** $\sqrt{18}$       **3.** $-\sqrt{160}$       **4.** $\sqrt{462}$

Solve the equation. Check your solutions. *(p. 469)*

**5.** $x^2 = 400$       **6.** $b^2 - 11 = -2$       **7.** $m^2 + 140 = 284$

**8.** Find the length of the hypotenuse of a right triangle with leg lengths of 12 meters and 16 meters. *(p. 482)*

**9.** Find the perimeter and area of a right triangle that has a hypotenuse of length 41 feet and one leg of length 9 feet. *(p. 487)*

Determine whether the numbers form a Pythagorean triple. *(p. 482)*

**10.** 5, 12, 15       **11.** 60, 91, 109       **12.** 11, 40, 41

## Lessons 9.1–9.4

**MULTIPLE CHOICE**

1. **INTERIOR DESIGN** Martha is purchasing an artistic rug for her den. The den is 12 feet long and 9 feet wide. A square rug with which area will fit in Martha's den? *TEKS 8.7.B*

Ⓐ 81 ft²                Ⓑ 90.25 ft²

Ⓒ 108 ft²              Ⓓ 144 ft²

2. **UTILITIES** A support wire is stretched taut from the top of a 7 meter utility pole to the ground. The distance from the base of the pole to the point where the wire meets the ground is 7.5 meters. What is the length of the wire to the nearest tenth of a meter? *TEKS 8.9.A*

Ⓕ 9.9 m                Ⓖ 10.3 m

Ⓗ 14.5 m              Ⓙ 26.25 m

3. **SCHOOL DANCE** A 3 foot tall banner is hanging on the wall of the Grand Ballroom in a hotel hosting a school dance. Jacob is standing 36 feet away from the wall where the banner is hanging. A tool is used to measure a distance of 45 feet from Jacob's eye level (6 feet) to the top of the banner. How far above the floor does the bottom of the banner hang? *TEKS 8.14.C*

Ⓐ 21 ft                Ⓑ 24 ft

Ⓒ 27 ft                Ⓓ 30 ft

4. **NUMBERS** Which of the following is an irrational number between 0.44 and 0.45? *TEKS 8.1.C*

Ⓕ $\sqrt{0.25}$                Ⓖ 0.4010010001 . . .

Ⓗ $0.\overline{45}$                Ⓙ $\sqrt{0.2}$

5. **QUILTING** You are making a quilt using a design based on the pattern shown below called the Wheel of Theodorus. This pattern is a spiral design using right triangles. What is the perimeter of the portion of the design shown? *TEKS 8.9.A*

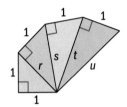

Ⓐ $\left(5 + \sqrt{2}\right)$ units        Ⓑ 7 units

Ⓒ $\left(5 + \sqrt{5}\right)$ units        Ⓓ 10 units

**GRIDDED ANSWER** ⓪①●③④⑤⑥⑦⑧⑨

6. **SPACE NEEDLE** You are standing 200 feet from the base of the towering Space Needle in Seattle, Washington. Your friend is on the observation deck platform, 520 feet above the ground. To the nearest tenth of a foot, how much greater is the distance between you and your friend than the height of the observation deck? *TEKS 8.9.A*

7. **KITES** Find the area of the kite. Round to the nearest square inch. *TEKS 8.7.B*

# 9.5 Special Right Triangles

**TEKS** *8.1.C, 8.9.B*

| **Before** | You solved real-life problems using the Pythagorean Theorem. |
| **Now** | You'll use special right triangles to solve real-life problems. |
| **Why?** | So you can find distances in sports, as in Example 1. |

**KEY VOCABULARY**

- **equilateral triangle, isosceles triangle, right triangle, scalene triangle,** *p. 411*
- **leg,** *p. 482*
- **hypotenuse,** *p. 482*

To find unknown side lengths of some right triangles, you can use special side length relationships. You can think of a 45°-45°-90° as half of a square and use the Pythagorean Theorem to get the result below.

---

**KEY CONCEPT**                                        *For Your Notebook*

### 45°-45°-90° Triangle

**Words**   In a 45°-45°-90° isosceles triangle, the length of the hypotenuse is the product of the length of a leg and $\sqrt{2}$.

**Algebra**   hypotenuse $=$ leg $\cdot \sqrt{2}$

$\qquad\qquad = x\sqrt{2}$

---

## EXAMPLE 1   Using a 45°-45°-90° Triangle

**Softball**  The infield of a softball field is a square with a side length of 60 feet. A catcher throws the ball from home plate to second base. How far does the catcher have to throw the ball?

### SOLUTION

To find the distance, use the rule for a 45°-45°-90° triangle.

$$\text{hypotenuse} = \textbf{leg} \cdot \sqrt{2}$$

$$= \textbf{60} \cdot \sqrt{2}$$

$$\approx 60(1.414)$$

$$= 84.84$$

> **Answer** A catcher has to throw the ball about 85 feet.

*ANOTHER WAY*

You can use the Pythagorean Theorem to find the hypotenuse.

$a^2 + b^2 = c^2$

$60^2 + 60^2 = c^2$

$7200 = c^2$

$84.84 \approx c$

---

✓ **GUIDED PRACTICE**   for Example 1

1. **City Parks**  A city park is shaped like a square with a side length of 150 feet. What is the distance diagonally across the park?

**30°-60°-90° Triangles** You can think of a 30°-60°-90° triangle as half of an equilateral triangle and use the Pythagorean Theorem to get the result below. To give the triangle's *exact dimensions*, you may leave your answers as a radical expression.

**KEY CONCEPT**                                *For Your Notebook*

**30°-60°-90° Triangle**

**Words**   In a 30°-60°-90° triangle, the hypotenuse is twice as long as the shorter leg. The length of the longer leg is the product of the length of the shorter leg and $\sqrt{3}$.

**Diagram**

**Algebra**   hypotenuse $= 2 \cdot$ shorter leg
$$= 2x$$
longer leg $=$ shorter leg $\cdot \sqrt{3}$
$$= x\sqrt{3}$$

---

**EXAMPLE 2**   Using a 30°-60°-90° Triangle

Find the value of each variable in the triangle. Give the exact answer.

You need to find the length of the shorter leg first in order to find the length of the longer leg.

**STEP 1**   Find the length of the shorter leg.

| | |
|---|---|
| hypotenuse $= 2 \cdot$ **shorter leg** | Rule for 30°-60°-90° triangle |
| $10 = 2 \cdot x$ | Substitute. |
| $5 = x$ | Divide each side by 2. |

**STEP 2**   Find the length of the longer leg.

| | |
|---|---|
| longer leg $=$ **shorter leg** $\cdot \sqrt{3}$ | Rule for 30°-60°-90° triangle |
| $y = 5\sqrt{3}$ | Substitute. |

**CHECK ANSWERS**
You can use the Pythagorean Theorem to check the solutions in Example 2.

▶ **Answer** The shorter leg is 5 units long. The longer leg is $5\sqrt{3}$ units long.

---

✓ **GUIDED PRACTICE**   for Example 2

Find the value of each variable. Give the exact answer.

**2.**

**3.**

**4.**

**EXAMPLE 3** Using a Special Right Triangle

**Water Ski Show** The pyramid ski show is a common attraction at water parks. Find the horizontal distance from the pyramid to the boat.

**STEP 1** **Find** the length of the shorter leg.

$$\text{hypotenuse} = 2 \cdot \text{shorter leg}$$
$$26 = 2 \cdot x$$
$$13 = x$$

**STEP 2** **Find** the length of the longer leg.

$$\text{longer leg} = \text{shorter leg} \cdot \sqrt{3}$$
$$y = 13 \cdot \sqrt{3}$$
$$\approx 22.52$$

▶ **Answer** The horizontal distance is about 23 feet.

*Animated* Math
at classzone.com

:·MULTIPLY
:·SQUARE ROOTS
·········································
You may need to
multiply square roots to
find a side length. You
can use the following
relationship:
$\sqrt{a} \cdot \sqrt{b} = \sqrt{a \cdot b}$.
For example,
$\sqrt{2} \cdot \sqrt{3} = \sqrt{2 \cdot 3} = \sqrt{6}$.

✓ **GUIDED PRACTICE** **for Example 3**

**5. What If?** In Example 3, suppose that the horizontal distance from the pyramid to the boat is $15\sqrt{3}$ feet. What is the distance from the top of the pyramid to the boat?

---

# 9.5 EXERCISES

HOMEWORK
KEY

🌟 = **TAKS Practice and Reasoning**
Exs. 16, 22, 25, 28, and 31

◯ = **HINTS** AND **HOMEWORK HELP**
for Exs. 3, 5, 11, 23 at classzone.com

## SKILL PRACTICE

**1. VOCABULARY** Copy and complete: A 45°-45°-90° triangle is a(n) __?__ triangle.

**2. VOCABULARY** *Explain* how the length of the hypotenuse in a 45°-45°-90° triangle is related to the length of a leg.

**45°-45°-90° TRIANGLES** **Find the value of the variable. Give the exact answer.**

:·SEE EXAMPLE 1
:·on p. 493
:·for Exs. 3–8

3.

4.

5.

6.

7.

8.

9. **ERROR ANALYSIS** Bailey calculated the length of the hypotenuse of an isosceles right triangle with a leg length of 8 inches. Describe and correct the error.

**30°-60°-90° TRIANGLES** Find the exact value of each variable.

10.

11.

12.

13. 

14. 

15. 

16. **TAKS REASONING** The hypotenuse of a 30°-60°-90° triangle has a length of $10\sqrt{3}$ feet. What is the length of the shorter leg?

Ⓐ $20\sqrt{3}$ feet  Ⓑ 10 feet  Ⓒ $5\sqrt{3}$ feet  Ⓓ 5 feet

**PERIMETER** Find the perimeter of the figure. Round to the nearest unit.

17. 

18. 

19. 

20. **AREA** In the diagram at the right, $\triangle ABC \sim \triangle XYZ$. Find all unknown side lengths of the triangles. What is the area of $\triangle XYZ$? Give exact answers.

21. **CHALLENGE** Find the lengths $AD$, $DC$, $BD$, and $BC$ in $\triangle ABC$. Name each 30°-60°-90° triangle in the diagram. Find and compare the areas of each 30°-60°-90° triangle.

## PROBLEM SOLVING

22. **TAKS REASONING** A flag is folded into the shape of a 45°-45°-90° triangle with a hypotenuse length of 20 inches. What is the approximate value of $x$?

Ⓐ 10 inches  Ⓑ 11.5 inches

Ⓒ 14.1 inches  Ⓓ 28.3 inches

**23.** **ESCALATOR** An escalator going down to the main floor of a subway station is 230 feet long and makes a 30° angle with the main floor. How many feet below the main floor is the subway station?

**24.** **REASONING** Is it possible to have an equilateral right triangle? *Explain* your reasoning.

**25.** **TAKS REASONING** Use a protractor to draw a 30°-60°-90° triangle. Use a ruler to measure one of the sides. Then use the 30°-60°-90° rules to find the lengths of the other two sides. Measure to check your calculations.

**26.** **QUILTING** Find the perimeters of the five squares within the diagram of the Snail's Trail quilt pattern at the right. The triangles are all 45°-45°-90° triangles. Round your answers to the nearest inch if necessary.

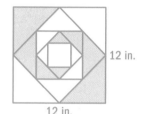

12 in.

12 in.

**27.** **TRIANGLES** Find the perimeters of the four large right triangles in the quilt pattern at the right. Then find the sum of the perimeters. Give exact answers.

**28.** **TAKS REASONING** A 45°-45°-90° triangle is drawn inside of a 30°-60°-90° triangle, as shown. Write a variable expression for the area of the shaded region. *Explain* how you found your answer.

2x meters 45°

30°

**29.** **WRITING** Use the Pythagorean Theorem to verify the 30°-60°-90° rule. Give an example.

**30.** **CHALLENGE** A regular hexagon can be divided into 6 equilateral triangles as shown. Find the perimeter and area of the hexagon.

1.5 mm

---

### MIXED REVIEW FOR TAKS

**TAKS** PRACTICE at classzone.com

REVIEW
Lesson 8.8;
TAKS Workbook

**31.** **TAKS PRACTICE** $\triangle ABC$ is equilateral and $\triangle ABC \sim \triangle JKL$. What scale factor was used to dilate $\triangle ABC$ to $\triangle JKL$? *TAKS Obj. 3*

**(A)** 0.25

**(B)** 4

**(C)** 12.6

**(D)** 21.2

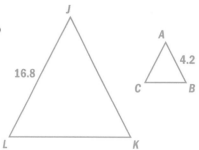

J

A

16.8

4.2

C

B

L

K

---

**EXTRA PRACTICE** for Lesson 9.5, p. 809

ONLINE QUIZ at classzone.com

**GOAL**
Find the sine and cosine ratios of right triangles.

**MATERIALS**
- metric ruler
- protractor

**TEKS** *8.6.A, 8.16.A*

# 9.6 Exploring Trigonometric Ratios

You can use a protractor and metric ruler to find the ratios of the length of each leg of a right triangle to the length of the hypotenuse.

**EXPLORE** **Find ratios of side lengths of similar right triangles.**

**STEP 1** **Draw** a 40° angle. Mark tick marks every 5 centimeters along one side.

**STEP 2** **Draw** perpendicular line segments from four of the tick marks to intersect with the other side of the angle.

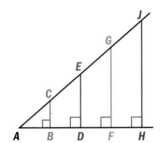

**STEP 3** **Identify** the four similar triangles in your drawing. Measure the legs of each triangle in your drawing to the nearest tenth of a centimeter. Then copy and complete the table. Round your answers to the nearest hundredth.

   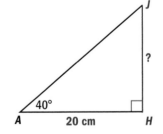

| Triangle | Leg 1 | Leg 2 | Hypotenuse | $\dfrac{\text{Leg 1}}{\text{Hypotenuse}}$ | $\dfrac{\text{Leg 2}}{\text{Hypotenuse}}$ |
|---|---|---|---|---|---|
| △ABC | 5 cm | ? | ? | ? | ? |
| △ADE | 10 cm | ? | ? | ? | ? |
| △AFG | 15 cm | ? | ? | ? | ? |
| △AHJ | 20 cm | ? | ? | ? | ? |

**STEP 4** **Describe** the pattern in the ratios $\dfrac{\text{Leg 1}}{\text{Hypotenuse}}$ in your table.

**STEP 5** **Describe** the pattern in the ratios $\dfrac{\text{Leg 2}}{\text{Hypotenuse}}$ in your table.

**STEP 6** **Repeat** Steps 1–5 using a 70° angle. Based on your results, do the ratios depend on the lengths of the right triangles' sides or on the measures of their angles?

The ratios $\dfrac{\text{Leg 1}}{\text{Hypotenuse}}$ and $\dfrac{\text{Leg 2}}{\text{Hypotenuse}}$ have special names. They are called the *sine* and *cosine* ratios and can be defined as follows:

$$\sin A = \frac{\text{length of leg opposite } \angle A}{\text{length of hypotenuse}} \qquad \cos A = \frac{\text{length of leg adjacent } \angle A}{\text{length of hypotenuse}}$$

**PRACTICE** Find the sine and cosine ratios for ∠A and ∠B.

**1.**

**2.**

**3.**

**4.**

**5.**

**6.**

**DRAW CONCLUSIONS**

**7. REASONING** Measure ∠A in each triangle in Exercises 1–6. Write the measures in order from least to greatest. Make a table that shows m∠A, sin A, and cos A. Then copy and complete the following two statements using *increases* or *decreases*.

**a.** As m∠A increases from 0° to 90°, the value of sin A __?__.

**b.** As m∠A increases from 0° to 90°, the value of cos A __?__.

# 9.6 Using Trigonometric Ratios

TEKS *8.3.B, 8.9.B*

**Before** You found the side lengths of special right triangles.

**Now** You'll use trigonometric ratios to find the side lengths.

**Why?** So you can use angles to find heights, as in Example 5.

**KEY VOCABULARY**
- **trigonometric ratio,** *p. 500*
- **sine,** *p. 500*
- **cosine,** *p. 500*
- **tangent,** *p. 500*

**Water Slide** A water slide makes an angle of about 18° with the ground. The slide extends horizontally about 64.2 meters. What is the height of the slide? You will find out how to solve this problem in Example 5.

You can find the height of the water slide using a *trigonometric ratio*. A **trigonometric ratio** is a ratio of the lengths of two sides of a right triangle. The three basic trigonometric ratios are **sine**, **cosine**, and **tangent**. These are abbreviated as sin, cos, and tan.

---

**KEY CONCEPT** *For Your Notebook*

### Trigonometric Ratios

$$\sin A = \frac{\text{side opposite } \angle A}{\text{hypotenuse}} = \frac{a}{c}$$

$$\cos A = \frac{\text{side adjacent to } \angle A}{\text{hypotenuse}} = \frac{b}{c}$$

$$\tan A = \frac{\text{side opposite } \angle A}{\text{side adjacent to } \angle A} = \frac{a}{b}$$

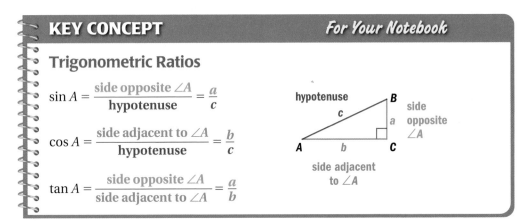

---

**EXAMPLE 1** Finding Trigonometric Ratios

**DETERMINE SIDES**
Determining the opposite and adjacent sides depends on the angle being used. For $\angle Q$, the length of the opposite side is 12 feet, and the length of the adjacent side is 5 feet.

For △*PQR*, write the sine, cosine, and tangent ratios for ∠*P*.

**SOLUTION**

For ∠*P*, the length of the opposite side is 5 feet, and the length of the adjacent side is 12 feet. The length of the hypotenuse is 13 feet.

$$\sin P = \frac{\text{opposite}}{\text{hypotenuse}} = \frac{5}{13}$$

$$\cos P = \frac{\text{adjacent}}{\text{hypotenuse}} = \frac{12}{13}$$

$$\tan P = \frac{\text{opposite}}{\text{adjacent}} = \frac{5}{12}$$

**EXAMPLE 2**  Using a Calculator

When using a calculator to find trigonometric ratios of angles measured in degrees, be sure the calculator is in *degree mode*. You can test this by checking that tan 45° = 1.

Use a calculator to find sine, cosine, and tangent of 30°.

| Keystrokes | Display | Answer |
|---|---|---|
| a. [2nd] [TRIG] [=] 30 [=] [2nd] | 0.5 | sin 30° = 0.5 |
| b. [2nd] [TRIG] [▶] [▶] [=] 30 [=] [2nd] | 0.8660254 | cos 30° ≈ 0.8660 |
| c. [2nd] [TRIG] [◀] [◀] [=] 30 [=] [2nd] | 0.5773503 | tan 30° ≈ 0.5774 |

✓ **GUIDED PRACTICE**  for Examples 1 and 2

1. For $\triangle ABC$, write the sine, cosine, and tangent ratios for $\angle A$ and $\angle C$. Which ratio has a value greater than 1?

2. Draw a 45°-45°-90° triangle. Label the legs 2 ft and the hypotenuse appropriately. Write the sine, cosine, and tangent ratios for one of the 45° angles. Does it make a difference which 45° angle you choose? *Explain.*

Use a calculator to approximate the expression. Round your answer to four decimal places.

3. cos 70°    4. tan 50°    5. sin 25°    6. tan 7°

**EXAMPLE 3**  Using a Cosine Ratio

**Find the value of $x$ in the triangle.**

The length of the hypotenuse is 8 inches. The unknown side is adjacent to the given angle. Use the cosine of $\angle K$.

$$\cos K = \frac{\text{adjacent}}{\text{hypotenuse}}$$    Definition of cosine

$$\cos 55° = \frac{x}{8}$$    Substitute.

$$8 \cdot \cos 55° = 8 \cdot \frac{x}{8}$$    Multiply each side by 8.

$$4.5886 \approx x$$    Use a calculator.

▶ **Answer**  The value of $x$ is about 4.59 inches.

✓ **GUIDED PRACTICE**  for Example 3

7. Find the value of $x$ in the triangle. Round your answer to the nearest hundredth of a foot.

**EXAMPLE 4** Using a Sine Ratio

**Ski Jump** A ski jump is 380 feet long and makes a 27.6° angle with the ground. Find the height $x$ of the ski jump.

**SOLUTION**

The unknown side is opposite the given angle. Use the sine ratio.

$$\sin 27.6° = \frac{\text{opposite}}{\text{hypotenuse}}$$     **Definition of sine**

$$\sin 27.6° = \frac{x}{380}$$     **Substitute.**

$$380 \cdot \sin 27.6° = 380 \cdot \frac{x}{380}$$     **Multiply each side by 380.**

$$176.05 \approx x$$     **Use a calculator.**

▶ **Answer** The ski jump is about 176 feet high.

**EXAMPLE 5** Using a Tangent Ratio

**Water Slide** Find the height $h$ of the water slide described on page 500.

**SOLUTION**

Use the tangent ratio.

$$\tan 18° = \frac{\text{opposite}}{\text{adjacent}}$$     **Definition of tangent**

$$\tan 18° = \frac{h}{64.2}$$     **Substitute.**

$$64.2 \cdot \tan 18° = 64.2 \cdot \frac{h}{64.2}$$     **Multiply each side by 64.2.**

$$20.85984 \approx h$$     **Use a calculator.**

▶ **Answer** The height of the water slide is about 20.9 meters.

 **GUIDED PRACTICE**    **for Examples 4 and 5**

**8. What If?** In Example 4, what is the height $x$ if the angle measure is 31°?

**9. What If?** In Example 5, what is the height $h$ if the angle measure is 16°?

## 9.6 **EXERCISES**

**HOMEWORK KEY**

⬥ = **TAKS Practice and Reasoning**
Exs. 7, 15, 34, 35, 36, and 44

◯ = **HINTS** AND **HOMEWORK HELP**
for Exs. 5, 9, 13, 31 at classzone.com

### SKILL PRACTICE

**VOCABULARY** Match the term with the correct trigonometric ratio.

**1.** sine

**2.** cosine

**3.** tangent

**A.** $\dfrac{\text{adjacent}}{\text{hypotenuse}}$

**B.** $\dfrac{\text{opposite}}{\text{hypotenuse}}$

**C.** $\dfrac{\text{opposite}}{\text{adjacent}}$

*SEE EXAMPLE 1*
on p. 500
for Exs. 4–7

**FINDING TRIGONOMETRIC RATIOS** In △*PQR*, write the sine, cosine, and tangent ratios for ∠*P* and ∠*R*.

**4.**

**5.**

**6.**

**7.** ⬥ **TAKS REASONING** What is the cosine of ∠*E*?

**(A)** $\dfrac{5}{13}$

**(B)** $\dfrac{12}{13}$

**(C)** $\dfrac{13}{5}$

**(D)** 13

*SEE EXAMPLE 2*
on p. 501
for Exs. 8–11

**USING A CALCULATOR** Use a calculator to approximate the given expression. Round your answer to four decimal places.

**8.** tan 51°

**9.** sin 80°

**10.** sin 36°

**11.** cos 76°

*SEE EXAMPLES*
*3, 4, AND 5*
on pp. 501–502
for Exs. 12–16

**USING TRIGONOMETRIC RATIOS** Find the value of *x*. Round your answer to the nearest thousandth.

**12.**

**13.**

**14.**

**15.** ⬥ **TAKS REASONING** What is the approximate length of side $\overline{AC}$?

**(A)** 7 ft

**(B)** 10 ft

**(C)** $7\sqrt{3}$ ft

**(D)** 14 ft

**16.** **ERROR ANALYSIS** Describe and correct the error made in finding the length of side *LK*.

$$\tan 25° = \frac{x}{15}$$
so $x \approx 7$ cm

**FINDING PERIMETER** Find the perimeter of the triangle. Round your answer to the nearest tenth.

**17.**

**18.**

**19.**

**20.** Ⓧ **ALGEBRA** Write the trigonometric ratios for ∠*A* and ∠*B* in △*ABC* in terms of *x*.

**FINDING ANGLES AND SIDE LENGTHS** Find the measure of the unknown angle and sides. Then use the side lengths to write three trigonometric ratios for ∠*C*.

**21.**

**22.**

**23.**

**24. REASONING** Use the definitions of the trigonometric ratios to show
$\dfrac{\sin A}{\cos A} = \tan A$.

**CHALLENGE** Given △*ABC* with ∠*C* = 90°, tell whether the statement is *always*, *sometimes*, or *never* true. *Explain* your reasoning.

**25.** $\sin A = \sin B$    **26.** $\sin A = \cos B$    **27.** $\sin A = \tan A$    **28.** $\sin A = \cos A$

## PROBLEM SOLVING

**SEE EXAMPLES 3, 4, AND 5** on pp. 501–502 for Exs. 29, 31

**29. GUIDED PROBLEM SOLVING** You stand 50 feet from a totem pole that is perpendicular to the ground. The angle from the point where you stand to the top of the totem pole is 42°. How tall is the totem pole?

  **a.** Draw a diagram and identify the sides of the triangle.

  **b.** Write an equation using a trigonometric ratio.

  **c.** Solve the equation. Round your answer to the nearest foot.

**30. DRAW A DIAGRAM** A piece of sheet metal is in the shape of right triangle *ABC* where $\tan A = \dfrac{15}{8}$ and $\cos B = \dfrac{15}{17}$. Sketch a triangle to represent the sheet metal and label each side with the appropriate length.

**31.) PET SUPPLIES** You are constructing a scratching post and platform for your cat as shown at the right. Find the length *x* of the scratching post to the nearest tenth of a foot.

**32. WRITING** *Explain* how to find the sine, cosine, and tangent ratios of an acute angle of a right triangle.

**33. MULTI-STEP PROBLEM** Some whales have been known to dive as deep as 3000 meters in search of their favorite food.

**Starting Point** 25°

? 

2000 m

?

*Not drawn to scale*

    **a.** The whale shown finds food after swimming 2000 meters. About how far is the whale's starting point from the point on the water's surface directly above its food?

    **b.** To the nearest meter, at what depth did the whale find its food?

    **c.** Did this whale dive more or less than half of the deepest known dive?

**34. ✈ TAKS REASONING** What is the approximate area of the boat sail?

    **Ⓐ** $5.77 \text{ ft}^2$      **Ⓑ** $17.32 \text{ ft}^2$

    **Ⓒ** $28.87 \text{ ft}^2$   **Ⓓ** $57.74 \text{ ft}^2$

10 ft

60°

x

**35. ✈ TAKS REASONING** Describe a real-world situation that can be modeled by $\sin 10° = \dfrac{x}{20}$.

**36. ✈ TAKS REASONING** A tethered hot air balloon is released from point *B* and rises straight upward. You are standing at point *A*, which is 30 meters from point *B*.

    **a.** Write the tangent ratio for each height of the balloon shown in the diagram.

    **b.** Would you expect the value of tan *A* to *increase* or *decrease* as the balloon rises to 60 meters? *Explain* your reasoning.

    **c.** As the balloon lands, it travels straight downward. How does *m∠A* change? Does cos *A increase* or *decrease*? *Explain* your reasoning.

60 m

30 m

A   30 m   B

**37. REASONING** Jared is standing about 400 feet from an office building and about the same distance from an apartment complex. The apartment complex is half the height of the office building. To see the top of the office building, Jared looks up about 60° from horizontal. Will the angle Jared looks up from horizontal to see the top of the apartment complex be half the previous angle measure? *Explain* your reasoning.

**REASONING Is there a value of *x* which makes the equation true? *Explain* your reasoning.**

**38.** $\sin x° > 1$        **39.** $\tan x° > 1$        **40.** $\sin x° = 1$        **41.** $\cos x° = 1$

**42. CHALLENGE** Find the area of an isosceles triangle that has two 50° angles and two sides of length 6 meters.

**43. CHALLENGE** An airplane is at an altitude of 33,000 feet when the pilot starts the descent to the airport. The pilot wants the plane to descend at an angle of 3°. How many miles away from the airport must the descent begin? Round your answer to the nearest mile.

*REVIEW*
Lesson 3.5;
TAKS Workbook

**44.** ◆ **TAKS PRACTICE** Which procedure should be used to find the area of the figure at the right? *TAKS Obj. 6*

Ⓐ Find the area of the triangles using the Pythagorean theorem. Add the area of the rectangle to the area of the triangles.

Ⓑ Find the area of the triangles using the Pythagorean theorem. Subtract the area of the rectangle from the area of the triangles.

Ⓒ Find the area of the triangles using the given lengths. Subtract the area of the rectangle from the area of the triangles.

Ⓓ Find the area of the triangles using the given lengths. Add the area of the rectangle to the area of the triangles.

---

## QUIZ *for Lessons 9.5–9.6*

**Find the value of each variable. Give exact answers.** *(p. 493)*

**1.**

**2.**

**3.**

**In △ABC, write the sine, cosine, and tangent ratios for ∠A and ∠B.** *(p. 500)*

**4.**

**5.**

**6.**

**7.** **AVIATION** A plane flies 1° off course for 2000 miles. To the nearest tenth of a mile, how far will the plane be from its course? *(p. 500)*

---

## BrainGame

### A Real Winner

Replace each expression with the letter of its decimal approximation to find the name of a person who won the Nobel Prize in both physics and chemistry.

cos 15°   sin 52°   cos 85°   sin 60°   cos 45°

tan 30°   tan 12°   sin 5°   cos 30°   sin 45°

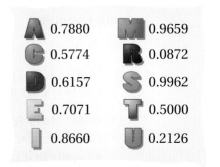

A 0.7880    M 0.9659
C 0.5774    R 0.0872
D 0.6157    S 0.9962
E 0.7071    T 0.5000
I 0.8660    U 0.2126

---

**TEKS** *8.3.B, 8.14.D*

# 9.6 Finding an Angle Measure

You can use the *inverse* of a trigonometric ratio to find the measure of an angle in a right triangle. For example, you can use the inverse tangent feature of your calculator to solve the following problem. The inverse tangent formula is:

If $\tan x° = \dfrac{a}{b}$, then $x° = \tan^{-1}\left(\dfrac{a}{b}\right)$.

Read this as "the angle whose tangent is $\dfrac{a}{b}$."

**EXPLORE** In the 1870s, a cable car system was built in San Francisco. A section of California Street has a vertical height of 76 feet and a horizontal length of 420 feet. Find the angle of the hill, $x°$.

**Solution** To find the angle, use inverse tangent.

$\tan x° = \dfrac{\text{opposite}}{\text{adjacent}}$ **Definition of tangent**

$\tan x° = \dfrac{76}{420}$ **Substitute.**

$x° = \tan^{-1}\left(\dfrac{76}{420}\right)$ **Definition of inverse tangent**

$x \approx 10.3$ **Use your calculator to approximate.**

Press the **2nd** key and then press the **TRIG** key. Highlight the inverse tangent feature and then press **=**. Enter the ratio and press **=** again.

▸ **Answer** The angle of the hill is about 10°.

**PRACTICE** Use a calculator to approximate the expression. Round to the nearest tenth of a degree.

**1.** $\tan^{-1}(0.25)$      **2.** $\tan^{-1}(0.14)$      **3.** $\tan^{-1}(0.92)$

**4.** $\tan^{-1}(1.05)$      **5.** $\tan^{-1}(24.65)$      **6.** $\tan^{-1}(64.25)$

**DRAW CONCLUSIONS**

**7.** **REASONING** Given $\tan^{-1}(0.18)$ and $\tan^{-1}(32.46)$, which one would you expect to represent the larger angle? Why?

**8.** **OPEN-ENDED** Write a positive ratio and its reciprocal in fraction form. Find the inverse tangent of each ratio. How are the two angles related?

## Lessons 9.5–9.6

**MULTIPLE CHOICE**

1. **WALLPAPER** A wallpaper designer draws triangle *A* as a 45°-45°-90° triangle. Triangle B has the hypotenuse of Triangle A as one leg, and the other leg has length 2. If you continue the pattern by drawing one more right triangle C with one leg of length 2 and the other leg the hypotenuse of the previous triangle, what is the hypotenuse of right triangle *D*? *TEKS 8.7.B*

**A** $2\sqrt{2}$      **B** $2\sqrt{3}$

**C** 4      **D** $2\sqrt{5}$

2. **DISTANCE** Kirsten and Madison are both on a city sidewalk looking up at their friend Jan in a restaurant at the top of a skyscraper, 500 feet above the ground. The angle of elevation is 45° for Kirsten and 30° for Madison. Which expression can be used to find how much farther Madison is from Jan than Kirsten is from Jan? *TEKS 8.2.A*

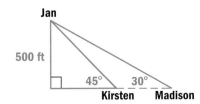

**F** $1000 - 500\sqrt{2}$

**G** $500\sqrt{3} - 500$

**H** $500\sqrt{2} - 500$

**J** $500 - 500\sqrt{3}$

3. **EXERCISE** The directions for doing abdominal crunches say "*Legs bent; arms back, supporting head and neck; chin up. Lift shoulders and back about 30° off the floor.*" Sheri read these directions and wondered how high, in inches, she should lift her shoulders. Sheri's shoulder-to-hip length is 28 inches. How high should she lift her shoulders to do this exercise correctly? *TEKS 8.14.A*

**A** 14 in.      **B** 24.2 in.

**C** 48.5 in.      **D** 56 in.

4. **ROLLER COASTER** A roller coaster climbs 300 feet above ground on a 45° inclined track and descends sharply as shown in the diagram. Approximate the length of the track to the nearest foot through the ascent and descent. *TEKS 8.1.C*

**F** 353 ft      **G** 424 ft

**H** 758 ft      **J** 2152 ft

**GRIDDED ANSWER** ⊙①●③④⑤⑥⑦⑧⑨

5. **SKATEBOARDING** You are constructing a skateboard ramp like the one shown in the diagram. Find *x*, the height of the top edge of the ramp. Round your answer to the nearest tenth of a foot. *TEKS 8.7.B*

## REVIEW KEY VOCABULARY

- square root, *p. 469*
- radical expression, *p. 469*
- perfect square, *p. 470*
- irrational number, *p. 475*
- real number, *p. 475*

- leg, *p. 482*
- hypotenuse, *p. 482*
- Pythagorean Theorem, *p. 482*
- converse, *p. 483*
- Pythagorean triple, *p. 488*

- trigonometric ratio, *p. 500*
- sine, *p. 500*
- cosine, *p. 500*
- tangent, *p. 500*

### VOCABULARY EXERCISES

1. Describe the difference between a rational number and an irrational number.

2. Give three examples of rational numbers and three examples of irrational numbers.

3. Describe how the lengths of the legs and the length of the hypotenuse of a right triangle are related.

4. Give three examples of a perfect square and its roots. Write a product equation for each as proof.

**Copy and complete the statement.**

5. A(n) __?__ is any number that has an integer as its square root.

6. In a right triangle, the side opposite the right angle is the __?__.

7. In a 30°-60°-90° triangle, the __?__ leg is opposite the 30° angle.

8. Sine, cosine, and tangent are __?__ ratios.

9. Reversing the parts of an if-then statement produces a(n) __?__ statement.

## REVIEW EXAMPLES AND EXERCISES

### 9.1 Square Roots

*pp. 469–474*

**EXAMPLE**

**Solve the equation $x^2 - 18 = 4$.**

| | |
|---|---|
| $x^2 - 18 = 4$ | Original equation |
| $x^2 = 22$ | Add 18 to each side. |
| $x = \pm\sqrt{22}$ | Definition of square root |
| $x \approx \pm 4.69$ | Approximate square root. |

## EXERCISES

**Use a calculator to approximate the square root. Round to the nearest tenth, if necessary.**

*SEE EXAMPLES 1, 3, 4, AND 5*
on pp. 470–471
for Exs. 10–27

**10.** $\sqrt{94.09}$     **11.** $-\sqrt{784}$     **12.** $-\sqrt{2125}$     **13.** $\sqrt{941}$

**14.** $\sqrt{63.42}$     **15.** $-\sqrt{1200}$     **16.** $\sqrt{861}$     **17.** $-\sqrt{306.12}$

**Solve the equation using mental math.**

**18.** $a^2 = 169$     **19.** $b^2 - 20 = 101$     **20.** $c^2 + 25 = 89$     **21.** $15 + x^2 = 51$

**22.** $y^2 - 12 = 13$     **23.** $40 + z^2 = 56$     **24.** $v^2 + 36 = 85$     **25.** $214 - w^2 = 60$

**26. Architecture** The area of the square base of a building is 2025 square feet. Write and solve a square root equation for the length of one side of the base.

**27. Distance** Ken is 2 miles east and $n$ miles north of Central Square. The distance $d$ from the square is given by the formula $d = \sqrt{2^2 + n^2}$. To the nearest tenth mile, how far away from Central Square is Ken if $n = 5$?

## 9.2 Rational and Irrational Numbers
*pp. 475–480*

### EXAMPLE

**Graph the numbers $\sqrt{7}$ and 3 on a number line. Then complete the statement $\sqrt{7}$ _?_ 3 with <, >, or =.**

Use a calculator to approximate the square root. Then graph the numbers on a number line and compare.

$$\sqrt{7} \approx 2.6458 \qquad 3$$

2.5  2.6  2.7  2.8  2.9  3  3.1     So, $\sqrt{7} < 3$.

### EXERCISES

**Tell whether the number is *rational* or *irrational*. *Explain* your reasoning.**

*SEE EXAMPLES 1 AND 2*
on pp. 475–476
for Exs. 28–39

**28.** $\sqrt{100}$     **29.** $0.\overline{6}$     **30.** $\dfrac{16}{25}$     **31.** $\sqrt{6}$

**32.** $\dfrac{1}{3}$     **33.** $\sqrt{\dfrac{27}{3}}$     **34.** $5.\overline{8}$     **35.** $\sqrt{44}$

**Graph the pair of numbers on a number line. Then complete the statement with <, >, or =.**

**36.** $\sqrt{31}$ _?_ 4     **37.** 7 _?_ $\sqrt{59}$     **38.** $-9$ _?_ $-\sqrt{81}$     **39.** $\sqrt{48}$ _?_ 6.3

## 9.3 The Pythagorean Theorem

*pp. 482–486*

**EXAMPLE**

**Find the unknown length.**

22 in.

20 in.

$a$

$$a^2 + b^2 = c^2 \qquad \text{Pythagorean Theorem}$$

$$a^2 + 20^2 = 22^2 \qquad \text{Substitute 20 for } b \text{ and 22 for } c.$$

$$a^2 = 84 \qquad \text{Simplify.}$$

$$a \approx 9.2 \text{ in.} \qquad \text{Take positive square root of each side.}$$

### EXERCISES

The lengths of the legs of a right triangle are $a$ and $b$, and $c$ is the length of the hypotenuse. Find the unknown length.

*SEE EXAMPLE 1*
on p. 482
for Exs. 40–45

**40.** $a = 2.4$, $b = 0.7$, $c = \underline{\ ?\ }$  **41.** $b = 24$, $c = 40$, $a = \underline{\ ?\ }$  **42.** $a = 8$, $c = 17$, $b = \underline{\ ?\ }$

Determine whether the given triangle side lengths form a right triangle.

**43.** 12, 35, 37  **44.** 15, 48, 50  **45.** 10, 24, 26

## 9.4 Using the Pythagorean Theorem

*pp. 487–491*

**EXAMPLE**

**Find the perimeter and area of the triangle.**

61

60

$b$

$$a^2 + b^2 = c^2 \qquad \text{Perimeter} = a + b + c$$

$$60^2 + b^2 = 61^2 \qquad \qquad = 60 + 11 + 61 = 132 \text{ units}$$

$$b^2 = 121 \qquad \text{Area} = \frac{1}{2}ab = \frac{1}{2} \times 60 \times 11$$

$$b = 11 \qquad \qquad = 330 \text{ square units}$$

### EXERCISES

The lengths of the legs of a right triangle are $a$ and $b$, and $c$ is the length of the hypotenuse. Find the unknown length, the perimeter, and area.

*SEE EXAMPLE 2*
on p. 488
for Exs. 46–50

**46.** $a = 21$ in., $b = 50.4$ in., $c = \underline{\ ?\ }$ in.  **47.** $a = \underline{\ ?\ }$ cm, $b = 63$ cm, $c = 225$ cm

**48.** $a = 12$ m, $b = \underline{\ ?\ }$ m, $c = 25.5$ m  **49.** $a = 44$ ft, $b = 33$ ft, $c = \underline{\ ?\ }$ ft

**50. National Parks** A tree in Sequoia National Park in California is about 250 feet tall. You are standing 50 feet away. To the nearest foot, how far away is the top of the tree?

**Special Right Triangles**

pp. 493–497

**EXAMPLE**

Find the length of the hypotenuse. Give the exact answer.

$$\text{hypotenuse} = \text{leg} \cdot \sqrt{2} \qquad \text{Rule for } 45°\text{-}45°\text{-}90° \text{ triangle}$$
$$= 26\sqrt{2} \qquad\qquad \text{Substitute.}$$

▶ **Answer** The length of the hypotenuse is $26\sqrt{2}$ feet.

**EXERCISES**

Find the value of each variable. Give the exact answer.

*SEE EXAMPLES 1 AND 2* on pp. 493–494 for Exs. 51–54

**51.**

**52.** **53.**

**54. Pyramid** Four sides of a pyramid are congruent equilateral triangles. The side lengths of the triangles are 6 inches. Find the area of one triangle.

**Using Trigonometric Ratios**

pp. 500–505

**EXAMPLE**

In $\triangle ABC$, write the sine, cosine, and tangent ratios for $\angle A$.

$$\sin A = \frac{\text{opposite}}{\text{hypotenuse}} = \frac{12}{37}$$

$$\cos A = \frac{\text{adjacent}}{\text{hypotenuse}} = \frac{35}{37}$$

$$\tan A = \frac{\text{opposite}}{\text{adjacent}} = \frac{12}{35}$$

**EXERCISES**

In $\triangle ABC$, write the sine, cosine, and tangent ratios for $\angle A$ and $\angle B$. Simplify if necessary.

*SEE EXAMPLE 1* on p. 500 for Exs. 55–57

**55.**

**56.** **57.**

**Solve the equation.**

**1.** $x^2 = 49$    **2.** $m^2 + 41 = 162$    **3.** $n^2 - 63 = 162$    **4.** $a^2 + 88 = 232$

**Tell whether the number is *rational* or *irrational*. *Explain* your reasoning.**

**5.** $\sqrt{16}$    **6.** $\dfrac{23}{24}$    **7.** $\sqrt{39}$    **8.** $\sqrt{\dfrac{1}{4}}$

**Graph each pair of numbers on a number line. Then copy and complete the statement with <, >, or =.**

**9.** $\sqrt{9}$ _?_ 3    **10.** $-11$ _?_ $-\sqrt{11}$    **11.** $\sqrt{12}$ _?_ 4

**Find the length of the unknown side of the right triangle. Round to the nearest tenth, if necessary. Then find the area and perimeter.**

**12.**

6.4 m

8 m

**13.**

11 ft    11 ft

**14.**

122 mm

120 mm

**Determine whether the given side lengths can form a right triangle.**

**15.** 15, 24, 25    **16.** 28, 96, 100

**17.** 3.6, 5.8, 5.9    **18.** 22.5, 30, 37.5

**Find the value of the unknown variables. Give the exact answer.**

**19.**

y    7 cm
45°
x

**20.**

x    13$\sqrt{2}$ ft
45°
x

**21.**

6$\sqrt{3}$ in.
30°
x
60°    y

**22. ZOOLOGY** A study of animal motion determined that the maximum walking speed $s$, in feet per second, that an animal can walk is $s = 5.66\sqrt{l}$, where $l$ is the animal's leg length, in feet. What is the maximum walking speed for an ostrich with a leg length of 4 feet?

**23. INCLINE** In the 1870s, a motorized incline was built in Pittsburgh, PA, to climb the steep hill known as Mt. Washington. The track of the incline is 793 feet long and makes a 30° angle with the ground, as shown at the right. Find the height of the boarding platform at the top of the incline.

793 ft
x
30°

TEXAS TAKS Objs. 3 and 4
TEKS 8.7.C, 8.9.A

## REVIEWING GEOMETRY PROBLEMS

Earlier in this chapter, you learned to find missing lengths in right triangles using the *Pythagorean Theorem* ($a^2 + b^2 = c^2$) and *trigonometric ratios*. The following example is solved in two different ways using the Pythagorean Theorem.

### EXAMPLE

**Geometry** The figure at the right shows a rectangle divided into 3 triangles. What is the length of $\overline{AB}$?

### Solution

**METHOD 1** Use the Pythagorean Theorem to find the length of $\overline{AB}$.

Notice that $\triangle ADE \cong \triangle BCE$ by Side-Angle-Side. So, $\overline{AB} \cong \overline{BE}$.

| | |
|---|---|
| $a^2 + b^2 = c^2$ | **Pythagorean Theorem** |
| $(5\sqrt{2})^2 + (5\sqrt{2})^2 = c^2$ | **Substitute values.** |
| $50 + 50 = c^2$ | **Evaluate powers.** |
| $100 = c^2$ | **Add.** |
| $10 = c$ | **Take positive square roots.** |

**METHOD 2** Use the Pythagorean Theorem to find the length of $\overline{EC}$. Then use the result to find the length of $\overline{AB}$.

Notice that the side lengths of $\triangle BCE$ are equal. Let the side lengths be $x$.

| | |
|---|---|
| $a^2 + b^2 = c^2$ | **Pythagorean Theorem** |
| $x^2 + x^2 = (5\sqrt{2})^2$ | **Substitute values.** |
| $2x^2 = 50$ | **Simplify.** |
| $x^2 = 25$ | **Divide each side by 2.** |
| $x = 5$ | **Take positive square roots.** |

Because $\overline{DE} \cong \overline{EC}$, they are both 5 inches long. So, the length of $\overline{DC}$ is 10 inches. Because $ABCD$ is a rectangle, $\overline{AB} \cong \overline{DC}$.

▶ **Answer** The length of $\overline{AB}$ is 10 inches.

# GEOMETRY PROBLEMS ON TAKS

Below are examples of geometry problems in multiple choice format. Try solving the problems before looking at the solutions. (Cover the solutions with a piece of paper.) Then check your solutions against the ones given.

**1.** Which diagram shows enough information to find the length of the unknown line segment?

**A**

9 cm

**B**

**C**

**D**

**Solution**

The diagonals in choices A and C do not form a right triangle, so those lengths cannot be determined. Choices A and C can be eliminated.

The diagonal in choice B forms a right triangle, but only one leg length is known (5 cm). The measure of the other angles in this right triangle are not given, so you cannot find the length of the other leg or the hypotenuse. Choice B can be eliminated.

The diagonal in choice D divides the rectangle into two right triangles. One leg length and the hypotenuse are given, so you can find the other leg length using the Pythagorean Theorem.

$$5^2 + b^2 = 10^2$$

So, the correct answer is D.

Ⓐ  Ⓑ  Ⓒ  **Ⓓ**

**2.** A 10-foot high set of stairs needs to be built. The stairs will extend horizontally for 12.8 feet, as shown in the diagram below. Which equation is true for the length, *s*, of the ascending staircase?

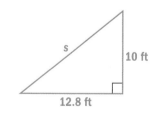

**F**  $s^2 = 12.8 + 10$

**G**  $s^2 + 10^2 = 12.8^2$

**H**  $s^2 = (12.8 + 10)^2$

**J**  $s^2 - 12.8^2 = 10^2$

**Solution**

The diagram shows that the rising staircase forms a right triangle. The length *s* of the staircase is the hypotenuse of the triangle.

Use the Pythagorean Theorem to find one equation that you know is true.

$$a^2 + b^2 = c^2$$
$$10^2 + 12.8^2 = s^2$$

Look carefully at the four possible answers to see if one of them can be derived from the above equation. By subtracting $12.8^2$ from both sides of the equation, you can see that $s^2 - 12.8^2 = 10^2$. So, the correct answer is J.

Ⓕ  Ⓖ  Ⓗ  **Ⓙ**

# 9 TAKS PRACTICE

## PRACTICE FOR TAKS OBJECTIVES 3 AND 4

**1.** Which relationship is NOT always true for the triangle shown below?

- **A** $a^2 + b^2 = c^2$
- **B** $a^2 = c^2 - b^2$
- **C** $b^2 = c^2 + a^2$
- **D** $-a^2 = b^2 - c^2$

**2.** A diagram of a roof is shown below. What is the approximate length of line segment $b$?

- **F** 12 ft
- **G** 19 ft
- **H** 24 ft
- **J** 38 ft

**3.** What is the area of *ABCD*?

- **A** $\sqrt{85}$ in.$^2$
- **B** 36 in.$^2$
- **C** 49 in.$^2$
- **D** 85 in.$^2$

**4.** An architect designed a stone table in a city park in the shape of an equilateral triangle. What is the length of each side of the stone table if the height of the triangle is $2\sqrt{3}$ feet?

- **F** $\sqrt{6}$ ft
- **G** 4 ft
- **H** $2\sqrt{6}$ ft
- **J** $2\sqrt{3}$ ft

**5.** Joan must find the length of certain line segments in geometric problems. Which drawing shows enough information to find the length of line segment $a$?

**A**

**B**

**C**

**D**

## MIXED TAKS PRACTICE

**6.** Which number is between $\sqrt{8}$ and $\sqrt{10}$?
*TAKS Obj. 1*

- **F** 2.8
- **G** $\pi$
- **H** $\dfrac{16}{5}$
- **J** 4

## MIXED TAKS PRACTICE

**7.** A triangle is inscribed in a rectangle as shown. Which expression represents the area of the shaded region? *TAKS Obj. 2*

5 cm

8 cm

**A** $8 \cdot 5 - \frac{1}{2} \cdot 8 \cdot 5$

**B** $\frac{1}{2}(8 \cdot 5 - 8 \cdot 5)$

**C** $\frac{1}{2} \cdot 8 \cdot 5 - 8 \cdot 5$

**D** $8 \cdot 5 - 2.5 \cdot 4$

**8.** In the sequence below, which expression can be used to find the value of the term in the $n$th position? *TAKS Obj. 2*

| Position | Value of Term |
|----------|---------------|
| 1 | 0.5 |
| 2 | 1.5 |
| 3 | 2.5 |
| 4 | 3.5 |

**F** $\dfrac{n}{2}$

**G** $n - 0.5$

**H** $0.5n$

**J** $2n$

**9.** Sara's friend says the expression "you know" about 3 times every 15 minutes. What is the best estimate for the number of times her friend uses this phrase in 5 hours of conversation? *TAKS Obj. 1*

**A** 1 time

**B** 15 times

**C** 20 times

**D** 60 times

**10.** A ruler in the shape of a right triangle measures inches along each of its sides. About how many inches can it measure on its longest side? *TAKS Obj. 4*

4 in.

4 in.

**F** 4 in.

**G** 5.7 in.

**H** 8 in.

**J** 32 in.

**11.** Which point will form a 45°-45°-90° triangle with the points plotted below? *TAKS Obj. 3*

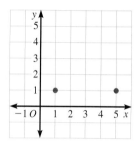

**A** (1, 4)

**B** (1, 5)

**C** (5, 4)

**D** (3, 4)

**12. GRIDDED ANSWER** One measure of the base for a large public monument is shown below. What is the circumference of the base? Round your answer to the nearest hundredth of a yard. *TAKS Obj. 3*

3 yd

*Record your answer and fill in the bubbles on your answer document. Be sure to use the correct place value.*

# 10 Measurement, Area, and Volume

TEXAS

## Before

In previous chapters you've ...

- Found the areas of rectangles
- Identified and sketched polygons

## Now

 you'll study ...

| 8.10.A | 10.1 Areas of quadrilaterals |
| 8.1.C | 10.2 Areas of circles |
| 8.7.A | 10.3 Solid figures |
| 8.8.A | 10.4 Surface areas |
| 8.8.C | 10.5 More surface areas |
| 8.10.B | 10.6 Volumes |
| 8.8.B | 10.7 More volumes |

## Why?

So you can solve real-world problems about ...

- architecture, p. 522
- hockey, p. 528
- recycling, p. 556
- swimming pools, p. 559

 **Math**
at classzone.com

- Areas of Parallelograms and Trapezoids, p. 522
- Classifying Solids, p. 535
- Volume of a Prism, p. 554

## Get-Ready Games

**Review Prerequisite Skills** by playing *Measure Match.*

**Skill Focus:** Finding the perimeter, area, or circumference of squares, rectangles, triangles, and circles

## MEASURE MATCH

### MATERIALS

- 15 Picture Cards
- 15 Measure Cards

**HOW TO PLAY** Place all cards face down and mix them up. On your turn follow the steps on the next page.

**TURN** over two cards.

**2** **DECIDE** whether the two cards match. Cards match when you turn over a Picture Card and a Measure Card that describes the picture. If the cards match, you may keep them. Otherwise, turn them back over.

**3** **REMEMBER** where the cards are so you can find matching pairs on future turns.

## HOW TO WIN

Be the player with the most cards once all the cards have been matched.

### Stop and Think

1. **WRITING** If the Measure Cards did not have *A*, *P*, or *C* on them, would you still be able to tell what was being measured? *Explain.*

2. **EXTENSION** Design six new cards for *Measure Match.* Three should be Picture Cards and three should be Measure Cards. Make sure each Picture Card matches a Measure Card.

# Review Prerequisite Skills

## VOCABULARY CHECK

**REVIEW WORDS**

- **area,** *p. 32*
- **base,** *p. 142*
- **height,** *p. 142*
- **circle,** *p. 312*
- **radius,** *p. 312*
- **pi (π),** *p. 312*
- **trapezoid,** *p. 416*
- **parallelogram,** *p. 416*
- **rhombus,** *p. 416*

Classify the figure using a review word from the list at the left.

**1.** quadrilateral *ABCD*

**2.** $\overline{PQ}$

**3.** quadrilateral *JKLM*

## SKILL CHECK

Find the area of the shaded region. *(p.142)*

**4.**

4 ft
4 ft
8 ft
4 ft
7 ft

**5.**

5 cm
5 cm

**6.**

3 in.
3 in.
6 in.

**TEXAS @HomeTutor**  Prerequisite skills practice at classzone.com

# Notetaking Skills  Using a Concept Grid

In each chapter you will learn a new notetaking skill. In Chapter 10 you will apply the strategy of using a concept grid to circles in Example 1 on p. 527.

You can use a *concept grid* to organize what you know about a topic.

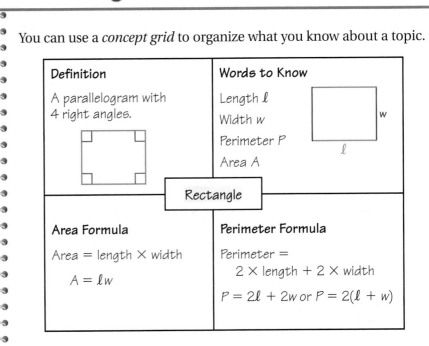

| Definition | Words to Know |
|---|---|
| A parallelogram with 4 right angles. | Length $\ell$ <br> Width $w$ <br> Perimeter $P$ <br> Area $A$ |

Rectangle

| Area Formula | Perimeter Formula |
|---|---|
| Area = length × width <br><br> $A = \ell w$ | Perimeter = <br> 2 × length + 2 × width <br> $P = 2\ell + 2w$ or $P = 2(\ell + w)$ |

# 10.1 Areas of Parallelograms and Trapezoids

**TEKS** *8.7.B, 8.10.A*

| | |
|---|---|
| **Before** | You found the areas of triangles and rectangles. |
| **Now** | You'll find the areas of parallelograms and trapezoids. |
| **Why?** | So you can find areas of surfaces, such as golf greens in Ex. 38. |

**KEY VOCABULARY**
- **base of a parallelogram,** *p. 521*
- **height of a parallelogram,** *p. 521*
- **bases of a trapezoid,** *p. 522*
- **height of a trapezoid,** *p. 522*

The **base of a parallelogram** is the length of any one of its sides. The perpendicular distance between the base and the opposite side is the **height of a parallelogram**. The diagram below shows how to change a parallelogram into a rectangle with the same base, height, and area.

Start with any parallelogram.

Cut the parallelogram to form a right triangle and a trapezoid.

Move the triangle to form a rectangle.

The area of the rectangle is the product of the base and the height, so the formula for the area of the parallelogram is $A = bh$.

---

**KEY CONCEPT** *For Your Notebook*

**Area of a Parallelogram**

**Words** The area of a parallelogram is the product of the base and the height.

**Algebra** $A = bh$

**Numbers** $A = 5 \cdot 3 = 15 \text{ cm}^2$

---

**EXAMPLE 1** Finding the Area of a Parallelogram

**Find the area of the parallelogram.**

**SOLUTION**

$A = bh$      **Write formula for area.**

$\quad = 8 \cdot 10$      **Substitute 8 for *b* and 10 for *h*.**

$\quad = 80$      **Multiply.**

▶ **Answer** The parallelogram has an area of 80 square inches.

**READING**

The bases of a trapezoid are labeled $b_1$ and $b_2$. You read these labels as "*b* sub one" and "*b* sub two." Need more help with trapezoids? See p. 416

**Trapezoids** The **bases of a trapezoid** are its two parallel sides. The perpendicular distance between the bases is the **height of a trapezoid**. The diagram below shows how two congruent trapezoids with height *h* and bases $b_1$ and $b_2$ can form a parallelogram with height *h* and base $b_1 + b_2$.

The area of the parallelogram is $(b_1 + b_2)h$, so the area of each trapezoid is $\frac{1}{2}(b_1 + b_2)h$.

---

**KEY CONCEPT**                                   *For Your Notebook*

**Area of a Trapezoid**

**Words**   The area of a trapezoid is one half the product of the sum of the bases and the height.

$b_1 = 4$ m
$h = 3$ m
$b_2 = 8$ m

**Algebra**   $A = \frac{1}{2}(b_1 + b_2)h$   **Numbers**   $A = \frac{1}{2}(4 + 8)3 = 18$ m$^2$

---

**EXAMPLE 2**   **Finding the Area of a Trapezoid**

**Architecture** The Winslow House in River Forest, Illinois, was designed by Frank Lloyd Wright. The front part of the roof is a trapezoid, as shown. What is its area?

31 ft
25 ft
77 ft

**SOLUTION**

$A = \frac{1}{2}(b_1 + b_2)h$   Write formula for area of a trapezoid.

$= \frac{1}{2}(31 + 77)25$   Substitute values for $b_1$, $b_2$, and *h*.

$= 1350$   Multiply.

▶ **Answer** The front of the roof has an area of 1350 square feet.

*Animated* Math
at classzone.com

---

✔  **GUIDED PRACTICE**   **for Examples 1 and 2**

**Sketch the quadrilateral and find its area.**

1. A parallelogram with a base of 20 meters and a height of 9 meters

2. A trapezoid with bases of 14 feet and 17 feet and a height of 6 feet

**EXAMPLE 3** TAKS PRACTICE: Multiple Choice

> **Geometry** The dimensions of trapezoid *ABCD* are shown below. A similar trapezoid can be produced by doubling the dimension of the trapezoid. How does the area change when the dimensions are doubled?

ELIMINATE CHOICES
Because doubling the side lengths of trapezoid *ABCD* increases its size, its area will also increase. You can eliminate choice A.

> Ⓐ The area is cut in half.
>
> Ⓑ The area is 2 times greater.
>
> Ⓒ The area is 3 times greater.
>
> Ⓓ The area is 4 times greater.

**SOLUTION**

*STEP 1* **Find** the area of trapezoid *ABCD* and the enlarged trapezoid.

$$A = \frac{1}{2}(b_1 + b_2)h \qquad\qquad A = \frac{1}{2}(b_1 + b_2)(h)$$

$$= \frac{1}{2}(4 + 12)2 \qquad\qquad = \frac{1}{2}(2 \cdot 4 + 2 \cdot 12)(2 \cdot 2)$$

$$= 16 \text{ m}^2 \qquad\qquad\qquad = 64 \text{ m}^2$$

*STEP 2* **Compare:** $\frac{64 \text{ m}^2}{16 \text{ m}^2} = 4$.

▶ **Answer** When the side lengths of trapezoid *ABCD* are doubled, the area becomes 4 times the original area. The correct answer is D. Ⓐ Ⓑ Ⓒ Ⓓ

---

✓ **GUIDED PRACTICE** for Example 3

3. **What If?** Suppose the side lengths of trapezoid *ABCD* in Example 3 are tripled. How does the area change?

---

# 10.1 EXERCISES

HOMEWORK KEY 🗺 = **TAKS Practice and Reasoning**
Exs. 8, 37, 40, 43, 47, and 48

◯ = **HINTS AND HOMEWORK HELP**
for Exs. 5, 9, 15, 19, 39 at classzone.com

**SKILL PRACTICE**

**VOCABULARY** Write the area formula for the polygon.

1. parallelogram 　　　　 2. triangle 　　　　 3. trapezoid

**FINDING AREA** Find the area of the parallelogram.

SEE EXAMPLE 1
on p. 521
for Exs. 4–6

**SEE EXAMPLE 1**
on p. 521
for Exs. 7–14

**7. ERROR ANALYSIS** Describe and correct the error made in finding the area of a parallelogram.

$A = bh$
$= 7 \cdot 10$
$= 70 \text{ in.}^2$

5 in.    7 in.
10 in.

**8. ★ TAKS REASONING** What is the area of the parallelogram?

  **A** $20 \text{ ft}^2$      **B** $25 \text{ ft}^2$

  **C** $40 \text{ ft}^2$      **D** $50 \text{ ft}^2$

10 ft
5 ft   4 ft

**SKETCHING PARALLELOGRAMS** Sketch a parallelogram with base $b$ units and height $h$ units. Then find its area.

**9.** $b = 12$, $h = 8$      **10.** $b = 9$, $h = 14$      **11.** $b = 10$, $h = 22$

**12.** $b = 2$, $h = 1.5$      **13.** $b = 3.2$, $h = 5$      **14.** $b = 12$, $h = 18$

**FINDING AREA** Find the area of the trapezoid.

**SEE EXAMPLE 2**
on p. 522
for Exs. 15–21

**15.**

18 in.
12 in.
9 in.

**16.**

13 yd
10 yd
5 yd
12 yd

**17.**

54 m
39 m
15 m
17 m   10 m

**SKETCHING TRAPEZOIDS** Sketch a trapezoid with bases $b_1$ units and $b_2$ units and height $h$ units. Then find its area.

**18.** $b_1 = 13$, $b_2 = 7$, $h = 6$      **19.** $b_1 = 8$, $b_2 = 16$, $h = 11$

**20.** $b_1 = 5.5$, $b_2 = 2.5$, $h = 3$      **21.** $b_1 = 16.2$, $b_2 = 10$, $h = 4$

**COMPARING AREAS** Quadrilateral *EFGH* is similar to quadrilateral *ABCD*. Find and compare the areas of the quadrilaterals.

**SEE EXAMPLE 3**
on p. 523
for Exs. 22–23

**22.**

A   8 m   B
10 m
D   14 m   C
E   4 m   F
5 m
H   7 m   G

**23.**

E   12 ft   F
9 ft
H   G
A   4 ft   B
3 ft
D   C

**FINDING AREA** Find the area of the polygon.

**24.**

45 in.   37 in.
16 in.

**25.**

21 ft
9 ft
24 ft

**26.**

1 cm
2 cm
2 cm
3 cm

**GRAPHING** Plot the points in a coordinate plane and connect them to form a parallelogram. Then find the area of the parallelogram.

**27.** $(-3, -1)$, $(0, 4)$, $(6, 4)$, $(3, -1)$      **28.** $(8, 0)$, $(11, -5)$, $(-2, -5)$, $(-5, 0)$

**ALGEBRA** Write and solve an equation to find the unknown dimension of the quadrilateral.

29. parallelogram: $A = 84$ cm$^2$, $b = $ _?_ , $h = 12$ cm

30. parallelogram: $A = 105$ m$^2$, $b = 15$ m, $h = $ _?_

31. trapezoid: $A = 100$ in.$^2$, $b_1 = 10$ in., $b_2 = 15$ in., $h = $ _?_

32. trapezoid: $A = 78$ ft$^2$, $b_1 = 12$ ft, $b_2 = $ _?_ , $h = 6$ ft

**FINDING AREA** Find the area of the parallelogram or trapezoid.

33.
18 in.
15 in.
27 in.

34.
5 m
13 m
30 m

35.
40 cm
34 cm
30 cm

36. **CHALLENGE** The area of the trapezoid is 225 square inches. Find the values of $x$ and $y$. Round to the nearest tenth if necessary.

$y$
$x$
10 in.
$2y$

---

## PROBLEM SOLVING

SEE EXAMPLES
1 AND 2
on pp. 521–522
for Exs. 37–39

37. **TAKS REASONING** The front of an audio speaker is the shape of a trapezoid. Its top edge is 14 inches wide, its bottom edge is 16 inches wide, and its height is 23 inches. What is the area of the front of the speaker?

(A) 173 in.$^2$   (B) 345 in.$^2$   (C) 368 in.$^2$   (D) 5152 in.$^2$

38. **GUIDED PROBLEM SOLVING** You are designing a putting green for a miniature golf course, as shown. What is the area of the green?

$4\frac{1}{2}$ ft
12 ft
6 ft
12 ft
6 ft
12 ft

   a. Copy the shape and divide the putting green into a trapezoid and a parallelogram.

   b. Find the area of each quadrilateral.

   c. Add the two areas to find the total area.

39. **FURNITURE** Alice is making an end table with a top surface in the shape of a trapezoid. If the parallel sides have lengths 18 inches and 24 inches, and the perpendicular distance between them is 15 inches, how many square inches of tile does Alice need for the table top?

40. **TAKS REASONING** Sketch a trapezoid and a parallelogram, each with an area of 54 square feet. Label the dimensions needed to find each area.

41. **MEASUREMENT** Use a metric ruler to measure the dimensions of the parallelogram in millimeters. Then find the area.

**42. WRITING** What do you think an isosceles trapezoid is? *Explain* your reasoning. Include a drawing with your answer.

*SEE EXAMPLE 3*
on p. 523
for Ex. 43

**43.** ◆ **TAKS REASONING** Use the parallelogram shown.

   **a. Calculate** Find the area of the parallelogram.

   **b. Compare** What happens to the area when the dimensions of the parallelogram are doubled? tripled?

2 cm
5 cm

   **c. Predict** Suppose you multiply each dimension of a parallelogram by a positive number $k$. Write a formula for the area of the new parallelogram. Test your formula for several values of $k$. How does this formula compare with the original formula? How will the areas compare?

   **d. Compare** Suppose you multiply each dimension of a trapezoid by a positive number $k$. Write a formula for the area of the new trapezoid. Test your formula for several values of $k$. How does this formula compare with the original formula? How will the areas compare?

**ESTIMATION Use the given scale and the formula for the area of a trapezoid or a parallelogram to estimate the area of the state.**

**44.** Nevada

0 mi     200 mi

**45.** Tennessee

0 mi          200 mi

**46. CHALLENGE** The floor of a gazebo is in the shape of a regular hexagon with sides that are each 6 feet long. Find the area of the floor to the nearest tenth of a square foot.

## MIXED REVIEW FOR TAKS
**TAKS** PRACTICE at classzone.com

*REVIEW*
Lesson 9.1;
TAKS Workbook

**47.** ◆ **TAKS PRACTICE** A physicist has made four measurements during experiments involving optics. The physicist tries to determine which measurement is not close to the number 4.5. Which irrational number is farthest from 4.5? *TAKS Obj. 1*

   **(A)** $\sqrt{15}$     **(B)** $\sqrt{18}$     **(C)** $\sqrt{20}$     **(D)** $\sqrt{22}$

*REVIEW*
Lesson 6.4;
TAKS Workbook

**48.** ◆ **TAKS PRACTICE** Wright is fashioning jewelry from copper. He needs to know the diameter of a bracelet that has a circumference of 6.3 inches. What procedure can he use? *TAKS Obj. 6*

   **(F)** Find the quotient of 6.3 and $\pi$, then divide by 2

   **(G)** Find the product of 6.3 and $\pi$, then divide by 2

   **(H)** Find the quotient of 6.3 and $\pi$

   **(J)** Find the product of 6.3 and $\pi$

⟳ **ONLINE QUIZ** at classzone.com

# 10.2 Areas of Circles

TEKS *8.1.C, 8.7.B*

**Before** You found the areas of parallelograms and trapezoids.

**Now** You'll find the areas of circles.

**Why?** So you can find areas of regions, as in a hockey rink in Example 3.

**KEY VOCABULARY**

• **area,** *p. 32*

• **circle, radius, diameter, circumference,** *p. 312*

• **pi (π),** *p. 312*

---

**ACTIVITY**

You can use a model to find a formula for the area of a circle.

**STEP 1** **Draw** a circle and cut it into 8 congruent sections. Arrange the sections of the circle to resemble a parallelogram, as shown. How are the base and height of the "parallelogram" related to the circumference and the radius of the circle?

**STEP 2** **Write** a formula for the area of the circle in terms of *r*. Use your results from Step 1 and the formulas for the area of a parallelogram and the circumference of a circle.

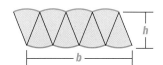

---

**KEY CONCEPT** *For Your Notebook*

**Area of a Circle**

**Words** The area of a circle is the product of π and the square of the radius.

*r = 6 cm*

**Algebra** $A = \pi r^2$   **Numbers** $A = \pi(6)^2 = 36\pi$ cm$^2$

---

**EXAMPLE 1** **Finding the Area of a Circle**

*TAKE NOTES*

To help organize information about circles in your notebook, make a concept grid. Be sure to include approximations for π, as shown on p. 312.

**Find the area of a circle with a diameter of 10 inches.**

$A = \pi r^2$   **Write formula for area.**

$\approx 3.14(5)^2$   **Substitute 3.14 for π and 5 for *r*.**

$= 78.5$   **Evaluate using a calculator.**

10 in.

▶ **Answer** The area is about 78.5 square inches.

 at classzone.com

## EXAMPLE 2 · Finding the Radius of a Circle

**Find the radius of a circle that has an area of 530.66 square feet.**

### SOLUTION

| | |
|---|---|
| $A = \pi r^2$ | Write formula for area of a circle. |
| $530.66 \approx (3.14)r^2$ | Substitute 530.66 for $A$ and 3.14 for $\pi$. |
| $169 = r^2$ | Divide each side by 3.14. |
| $\sqrt{169} = r$ | Take positive square root of each side. |
| $13 = r$ | Evaluate square root. |

**AVOID ERRORS**
Make sure you use the correct units when writing your answer. Linear units should be used to describe the radius of a circle.

▶ **Answer** The radius of the circle is about 13 feet.

---

 **GUIDED PRACTICE** for Examples 1 and 2

**Find the unknown area or radius of the circle. Use 3.14 for $\pi$.**

**1.** $r = 7$ ft, $A = $ ___?___    **2.** $d = 3$ km, $A = $ ___?___    **3.** $A = 628$ cm$^2$, $r = $ ___?___

---

**TAKS**

## EXAMPLE 3 · TAKS REASONING: Multi-Step Problem

**Hockey** Find the combined area of the two face-off circles of the ice hockey rink shown.

### SOLUTION

**STEP 1** **Find** the radius. The distance between the centers is 44 feet and the gap between the circles is 14 feet. So,

$r + 14 + r = 44$ and $r = 15$.

**STEP 2** **Calculate** the area. Use the formula for the area of a circle.

| | |
|---|---|
| $A = 2\pi r^2$ | Area of two circles |
| $\approx 2(3.14)(15)^2$ | Substitute 3.14 for $\pi$ and 15 for $r$. |
| $= 1413$ | Evaluate using a calculator. |

**CHECK REASONABLENESS**
Estimate to check your answer.
$2\pi(15)^2 \approx 2(3)(225)$
$\approx 1350$

▶ **Answer** The area of the circles is about 1413 square feet.

**Animated Math**
at classzone.com

---

 **GUIDED PRACTICE** for Example 3

**Find the area of the shaded region. Use 3.14 for $\pi$.**

**4.**

**5.**

(4.) 12 in., 36 in.

(5.) 6 ft, 10 ft

# 10.2 EXERCISES

HOMEWORK KEY

 = **TAKS Practice and Reasoning**
Exs. 28, 38, 44, 48, and 49

○ = **HINTS** AND **HOMEWORK HELP**
for Exs. 3, 11, 13, 17, 37 at classzone.com

## SKILL PRACTICE

**VOCABULARY** **Copy and complete the statement.**

1. The area of a circle is the product of $\pi$ and the square of the __?__.

2. The circumference of a circle is the product of $\pi$ and the __?__.

**USING DRAWINGS** **Find the area of the circle. Use 3.14 for $\pi$.**

*SEE EXAMPLE 1*
on p. 527
for Exs. 3–15

3.
2 ft

4.
10 cm

5.
13.3 m

6.
50 yd

7.
17 mm

8.
20.8 cm

9. **ERROR ANALYSIS** Describe and correct the error made in finding the area of the circle.

11 yd

$$
\begin{aligned}
A &= \pi r^2 \\
&\approx (3.14)(11)^2 \\
&= 379.94 \text{ yd}^2
\end{aligned}
$$

**FINDING AREA** **Find the area of the circle with the given radius or diameter. Use 3.14 for $\pi$. Estimate to check your answer.**

10. $r = 9$ cm

11. $r = 17$ ft

12. $r = 30.4$ m

13. $d = 28$ mm

14. $d = 6$ yd

15. $d = 40.2$ in.

**FINDING THE RADIUS** **Find the radius of the circle with the given area $A$. Use 3.14 for $\pi$.**

*SEE EXAMPLE 2*
on p. 528
for Exs. 16–24

16. $A = 28.26$ ft$^2$

17. $A = 3.14$ m$^2$

18. $A = 200.96$ yd$^2$

19. $A = 113.04$ in.$^2$

20. $A = 12.56$ mm$^2$

21. $A = 254.34$ cm$^2$

22. $A = 907.46$ mi$^2$

23. $A = 4069.44$ cm$^2$

24. $A = 1808.64$ ft$^2$

**ALGEBRA** **Find the area of the circle with the given circumference $C$. Use 3.14 for $\pi$.**

25. $C = 18.84$ ft

26. $C = 81.64$ m

27. $C = 37.68$ cm

28. **TAKS REASONING** What is the approximate area of a circle with a circumference of 50.24 millimeters? Use 3.14 for $\pi$.

Ⓐ 8 mm    Ⓑ 16 mm    Ⓒ 200.96 mm$^2$    Ⓓ 803.84 mm$^2$

**29. MEASUREMENT** Use a ruler to measure the radius of the circle in millimeters. Then find the area of the circle. Use 3.14 for $\pi$.

**30. MENTAL MATH** The area of a circle is $25\pi$ square feet. What is the radius?

*SEE EXAMPLE 3*
on p. 528
for Exs. 31–34

**31. AREA** Find the area of the shaded region. Use $\frac{22}{7}$ for $\pi$.

7 mm

**FINDING AREA** Find the area of the shaded region. Use 3.14 for $\pi$.

**32.**
9 m
4 m

**33.**
8 in.
20 in.
22 in.

**34.**
4 km
7 km
10 km

**35.** ⓍⓎ **REASONING** A circle has a circumference of $c$ units and an area of $a$ square units. What is the radius of the circle if $c = a$? *Explain.*

**36. CHALLENGE** The circles in the pattern shown share the same center, and every other circle is shaded. The radii of the circles, going from the innermost to the outermost, are $1, \sqrt{2}, \sqrt{3}, 2, \sqrt{5}, \sqrt{6}$, and so on. Assume the pattern continues to $n$ circles, where $n$ is even. Write a formula for the area of the shaded region.

## PROBLEM SOLVING

*SEE EXAMPLE 1*
on p. 527
for Exs. 37–38

**37. SPRINKLERS** You are using a rotating sprinkler to water your yard. The sprinkler rotates in a complete circle. It sprays water at most 12 feet. Find the area of the yard that is watered. Use 3.14 for $\pi$.

**38.** 🏴 **TAKS REASONING** A circular swimming pool has a diameter of 18 feet. To the nearest square foot, what is the smallest amount of material needed to cover the surface of the pool? Use 3.14 for $\pi$.

    Ⓐ 57 ft$^2$      Ⓑ 113 ft$^2$

    Ⓒ 254 ft$^2$      Ⓓ 1017 ft$^2$

*SEE EXAMPLE 3*
on p. 528
for Exs. 39–40

**39. TENNIS CENTER** The roof of the New South Wales Tennis Center in Sydney, Australia, can be approximated by a circle. A level of seats is covered by the ring-shaped roof shown in the photo, whose outer diameter is about 100 meters and inner diameter is about 65 meters. What is the area covered by the roof? Use 3.14 for $\pi$.

**40. WRITING** The rectangle intersecting the circle passes through the center of the circle. *Explain* how to find the area of the shaded region.

1.5 m
3 m

**Energy Savings** The type of windows in a home affects heating costs. Double-paned windows will reduce the amount of heat lost during the winter. They cost about $1.50 more per square foot than single-paned windows. Low-emissivity windows have an invisible coating on the glass that reflects heat. They cost about $3.00 more per square foot than double-paned windows.

41. **Calculate** You want to install the window shown. Find its area to the nearest square foot. Use the area to calculate the additional cost of installing a double-paned window instead of a single-paned window.

42. **Calculate** Find the additional cost of installing a double-paned window with the low-emissivity coating instead of a single-paned window.

43. **Analyze** Double-paned windows offer an annual energy savings of $.60 per square foot. Low-emissivity windows save an additional $.50 per square foot annually. After how many years is the extra cost of the double-paned low-emissivity window offset by the energy savings?

44. **TAKS REASONING** Copy and complete the table. Leave your answers in terms of $\pi$. What happens to the area of a circle when the radius is multiplied by a positive number $k$? *Justify* your reasoning.

| Radius r | Area of a circle with radius r | Area of a circle with radius 2r | Area of a circle with radius 3r | Area of a circle with radius 4r |
|---|---|---|---|---|
| 2 in. | $4\pi$ in.$^2$ | ? | ? | ? |
| 3 in. | ? | ? | ? | ? |
| 5 in. | ? | ? | ? | ? |

45. **MULTI-STEP PROBLEM** You are using a disk sander to sand a porch that has an area of 11,520 square inches. One disk for the sander has a diameter of 7 inches. Another disk has a diameter of 10 inches.

 a. You can sand a section of the porch with an area equal to that of five disks in one minute. Find the area that you can sand in one minute with each size disk. Use 3.14 for $\pi$.

 b. About how much time would you save by sanding the entire porch with the larger disk? Round your answer to the nearest minute.

46. **ESTIMATION** The diameter of the circle in the diagram is 20 centimeters. Find the area of each square to the nearest tenth and use the areas to estimate the area of the circle. Then calculate the area of the circle and compare it to your estimate. Use 3.14 for $\pi$.

**47. CHALLENGE** You cut a circle of radius *r* out of a square piece of paper as shown. You want the area of the shaded region to be (4 − π) square inches. Find the value of *r*.

 **MIXED REVIEW FOR TAKS** ⬤ **TAKS** **PRACTICE** at classzone.com

*REVIEW*
······················
Lesson 10.1;
TAKS Workbook

**48.** 🏴 **TAKS PRACTICE** The table below shows the dimensions of several parallelograms. Which parallelogram has an area less than 575 square meters? *TAKS Obj. 2*

|  | Height | Base |
|---|---|---|
| **Parallelogram A** | 24 m | 24 m |
| **Parallelogram B** | 16 m | 36 m |
| **Parallelogram C** | 32 m | 18 m |
| **Parallelogram D** | 20 m | 28 m |

(A) Parallelogram A

(B) Parallelogram B

(C) Parallelogram C

(D) Parallelogram D

*REVIEW*
······················
Lesson 5.7;
TAKS Workbook

**49.** 🏴 **TAKS PRACTICE** Nikki is at a carnival and has $6. She would like to buy some cotton candy for $2.25 and use the rest of her money to go on the rides. Each ride costs $0.75. To find the number of rides she can go on, she subtracts 2.25 from 6, then she— *TAKS Obj. 6*

(F) multiplies the result by 0.75.

(G) divides the result by 0.75.

(H) multiplies 0.75 by itself.

(J) finds 75% of the result.

---

**BrainGame**

# What's the Score?

The center circle of the target has a radius of 3 inches and each ring is 3 inches wide. Find the area of each region in terms of π. Then use the formula below to find the score for each region. Round to the nearest whole number.

$$score = \frac{225\pi}{area}$$

For example, the yellow region has an area of π(3)², or 9π square inches. The score in the yellow region is

$$\frac{225\pi}{area} = \frac{225\pi}{9\pi} = 25.$$

Who has a higher score, Greg or Jamie?

 |

Greg | Jamie

**TEKS** *8.10.A, 8.16.A*

# 10.2 Comparing Radii of Circles

**EXPLORE** How does the radius of a circle change when its area is multiplied by 4?

**STEP 1** **Create** a spreadsheet with an original circle area in cell A1 and the multiplier 4 in cell A2. Enter formulas for the Area column that refer to these cells, as shown.

**STEP 2** **Enter** formulas for the Radius column, as shown. The radius of a circle with area $A$ is given by $\sqrt{\frac{A}{\pi}}$.

| | Comparing Radii | | |
|---|---|---|---|
| | **A** | **B** | **C** |
| **1** | 1 | Original circle area | |
| **2** | 4 | Multiplier | |
| **3** | | | |
| **4** | Area | Radius | Ratio |
| **5** | =A1 | =SQRT(A5/PI()) | |
| **6** | =A5*A2 | =SQRT(A6/PI()) | =B6/B5 |

**STEP 3** **Compare** the radii of the two circles by dividing the second radius by the first radius. Enter a formula for this quotient in the Ratio column.

**STEP 4** **Change** the value of the original circle area in cell A1 several times. What do you notice about the ratio of the radii?

| | **A** | **B** | **C** |
|---|---|---|---|
| **1** | 1 | Original circle area | |
| **2** | 4 | Multiplier | |
| **3** | | | |
| **4** | Area | Radius | Ratio |
| **5** | 1 | 0.564190 | |
| **6** | 4 | 1.128379 | 2 |

| | **A** | **B** | **C** |
|---|---|---|---|
| **1** | 5 | Original circle area | |
| **2** | 4 | Multiplier | |
| **3** | | | |
| **4** | Area | Radius | Ratio |
| **5** | 5 | 1.261566 | |
| **6** | 20 | 2.523133 | 2 |

| | **A** | **B** | **C** |
|---|---|---|---|
| **1** | 15 | Original circle area | |
| **2** | 4 | Multiplier | |
| **3** | | | |
| **4** | Area | Radius | Ratio |
| **5** | 15 | 2.185097 | |
| **6** | 60 | 4.370194 | 2 |

▶ **Answer** When the area of a circle is multiplied by 4, the radius is multiplied by 2.

**PRACTICE** **Find how the radius of a circle changes when its area is multiplied by the given number.**

**1.** 9 **2.** 16 **3.** 25 **4.** 36

**DRAW CONCLUSIONS**

5. **REASONING** How does the radius of a circle change when its area is doubled? tripled? *Explain.*

6. **ANALYZE** *Explain* why $r = \sqrt{\frac{A}{\pi}}$ is the formula for the radius of a circle with area $A$.

# 10.3 Three-Dimensional Figures

TEKS  *8.7.A, 8.16.B*

| Before | You classified and sketched polygons. |
|---|---|
| Now | You'll classify and sketch solids. |
| Why? | So you can classify solids that form structures, as in Exs. 14–16. |

**KEY VOCABULARY**

- **solid, polyhedron, face,** *p. 534*
- **prism,** *p. 534*
- **pyramid,** *p. 534*
- **cylinder,** *p. 534*
- **cone,** *p. 534*
- **sphere,** *p. 534*
- **edge, vertex,** *p. 534*

A **solid** is a three-dimensional figure that encloses a part of space. A **polyhedron** is a solid that is enclosed by polygons. A polyhedron has only flat surfaces. The polygons that form a polyhedron are called **faces**.

---

### Classifying Solids

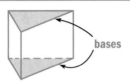

A **prism** is a polyhedron. Prisms have two congruent bases that lie in parallel planes. The other faces are rectangles. A *cube* is a prism with six square faces.

A **pyramid** is a polyhedron. Pyramids have one base. The other faces are triangles.

A **cylinder** is a solid with two congruent circular bases that lie in parallel planes.

A **cone** is a solid with one circular base.

A **sphere** is a solid formed by all points in space that are the same distance from a fixed point called the center.

---

### EXAMPLE 1 Classifying Solids

**Classify the solid. Tell whether it is a polyhedron.**

The solid has two congruent circular bases that lie in parallel planes, so it is a cylinder. It is not a polyhedron, because circles are not polygons.

*Animated* **Math**
at classzone.com

**Edges and Vertices** The segments where faces of a polyhedron meet are called **edges**. A **vertex** is a point where three or more edges meet. The plural of vertex is *vertices*.

## EXAMPLE 2  Counting Faces, Edges, and Vertices

**Classify the solid. Then count the number of faces, edges, and vertices.**

### SOLUTION

The solid is a pentagonal pyramid.

Remember to include the base when counting faces.

**6 faces**          **10 edges**          **6 vertices**

*Animated* Math
at classzone.com

 **VOCABULARY**

You can name a prism or pyramid using the shape of its base. For example, in Example 2 the base is a pentagon, so the solid is called a *pentagonal pyramid*.

## EXAMPLE 3  Sketching a Solid

**Show two ways to represent a triangular prism.**

**METHOD 1** Sketch the solid.

**STEP 1  Sketch** two congruent bases.

**STEP 2  Connect** the vertices.

**STEP 3  Make** any hidden lines dashed.

**ANOTHER WAY**

You can draw other views of the triangular prism in Example 3 by using a different perspective.

**METHOD 2** Sketch the top, front, and side views of the solid.

**top**

**front**

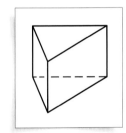

**side**

*Animated* Math
at classzone.com

✓ **GUIDED PRACTICE**  **for Examples 1, 2, and 3**

**Classify the solid. Then tell whether it is a polyhedron.**

**1.**

**2.**

**3.**

**4.** Show two ways to represent a rectangular pyramid. Then count the number of faces, edges, and vertices.

# 10.3 EXERCISES

## SKILL PRACTICE

**VOCABULARY Match the description with the solid.**

**1.** two rectangular bases

**2.** three rectangular faces

**3.** four triangular faces

**A.** triangular prism

**B.** rectangular pyramid

**C.** rectangular prism

**CLASSIFYING SOLIDS Classify the solid. Then tell whether it is a polyhedron.**

*SEE EXAMPLE 1*
on p. 534
for Exs. 4–6

**4.**

**5.**

**6.**

**COUNTING FACES, EDGES, AND VERTICES Classify the solid. Then count the number of faces, edges, and vertices.**

*SEE EXAMPLES 2 AND 3*
on p. 535
for Exs. 7–13

**7.**

**8.**

**9.**

**10. ERROR ANALYSIS** A student says that because a hexagon has 6 sides, a hexagonal pyramid has 6 edges. What is wrong with this statement?

**SKETCHING SOLIDS Show two ways to represent the solid.**

**11.** rectangular prism

**12.** hexagonal prism

**13.** cylinder

**CLASSIFYING SOLIDS Classify the solids that form the structure.**

**14.**

**15.**

**16.**

**17. ✦ TAKS REASONING** What is the name of the solid with the given views?

Ⓐ triangle

Ⓑ triangular prism

Ⓒ triangular pyramid

Ⓓ rectangular pyramid

top     front     side

**SKETCHING SOLIDS** Sketch the solid with the given views.

18.

top    front    side

19.
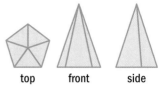

top    front    side

**CHALLENGE** Classify the quadrilateral outlined in green, formed by the intersection of a cube and a plane.

20.

21.

22.

23. **CHALLENGE** Sketch a cube and a plane whose intersection is (a) a triangle and (b) a hexagon.

## PROBLEM SOLVING

24. **GUIDED PROBLEM SOLVING** Sketch a square pyramid.

   **a.** Sketch a parallelogram for the square base.

   **b.** Draw a dot centered above the parallelogram.

   **c.** Connect the vertices of the parallelogram to the dot. Make any hidden lines dashed.

SEE EXAMPLE 1
on p. 534
for Exs. 25–27

25.  **TAKS REASONING** Which of the following solids is a polyhedron?

Ⓐ     Ⓑ     Ⓒ     Ⓓ

26. **WRITING** *Explain* how a pyramid and a prism with congruent bases are alike and how they are different.

27.  **TAKS REASONING** Give an example of a cylinder, a cone, and a square prism that you find in your classroom or at home.

28. **LOOK FOR A PATTERN** Copy and complete the table. Use the pattern to write a formula that gives the number of edges of a polyhedron in terms of the number of faces and vertices. This is called *Euler's Formula*.

| Figure | Number of faces F | Number of vertices V | Number of edges E | F + V |
|---|---|---|---|---|
| pentagonal pyramid | 6 | 6 | 10 | 12 |
| rectangular pyramid | ? | ? | ? | ? |
| triangular prism | ? | ? | ? | ? |
| rectangular prism | ? | ? | ? | ? |

**29. CHALLENGE** The polyhedron shown is a cube. Find the length $AB$ in terms of $s$.

**30. CHALLENGE** Describe how you could divide a cube into congruent square pyramids.

*REVIEW*
Lesson 10.2;
TAKS Workbook

**31.** 🔻 **TAKS PRACTICE** The diagram at the right shows a circle that fits exactly inside a square. The radius of the circle is represented by $r$. This radius is exactly half the length of the side length of the square. If the area of the square is 50 square meters, what is the area of the circle? *TAKS Obj. 2*

**(A)** $(12.5)\pi\,\text{m}^2$   **(B)** $\frac{1}{2}\sqrt{50}\,\pi\,\text{m}^2$   **(C)** $\frac{1}{4}\sqrt{50}\,\pi\,\text{m}^2$   **(D)** $25\pi\,\text{m}^2$

*REVIEW*
Lesson 8.8;
TAKS Workbook

**32.** 🔻 **TAKS PRACTICE** Rectangle $ABCD$ is similar to rectangle $RSTU$. The area of rectangle $ABCD$ is 144 square feet. What is the area of rectangle $RSTU$? *TAKS Obj. 4*

**(F)** $2\,\text{ft}^2$   **(G)** $16\,\text{ft}^2$   **(H)** $48\,\text{ft}^2$   **(J)** $192\,\text{ft}^2$

## QUIZ *for Lessons 10.1–10.3*

**Find the area of the parallelogram or trapezoid.** *(p. 521)*

**1.**

**2.**

**3.**

**4.** A trapezoid has a height of 8 feet. The lengths of the bases are 10 feet and 14 feet. Find the area of the trapezoid. *(p. 521)*

**5.** Find the area of a circle with diameter 22 feet. Use 3.14 for $\pi$. *(p. 527)*

**Find the radius of the circle with the given area. Use 3.14 for $\pi$.** *(p. 527)*

**6.** $A = 254.34\,\text{ft}^2$      **7.** $A = 452.16\,\text{cm}^2$      **8.** $A = 78.5\,\text{m}^2$

**9.** The triangular faces of the solid are all congruent. Classify the solid in as many ways as possible. Then tell whether it is a polyhedron. *(p. 534)*

**10.** Show two ways to represent a triangular pyramid. Then count the number of faces, edges, and vertices. *(p. 534)*

# Sketching Solids

**Use after Lesson 10.3**

TEKS 8.7.A

**GOAL** Draw views of solids and make isometric drawings.

**KEY VOCABULARY**
• isometric drawing, *p. 539*

In Lesson 10.3, you drew the top, front, and side views of common solids. In the following examples, you will see how to draw the top, front, and side views of more complicated solids.

**EXAMPLE 1** Drawing Views of a Solid

**Draw the top, front, and side views of the solid.**

**SOLUTION**

top     front     side

The interior lines represent edges of faces.

**Isometric Drawings** An **isometric drawing** is another way to make a two-dimensional drawing of a three-dimensional figure. It is created using a grid of dots and a set of three axes that intersect to form 120° angles. Use the dots to guide your drawing and give depth to the figure.

**EXAMPLE 2** Creating an Isometric Drawing

**Create an isometric drawing of the solid from Example 1.**

**SOLUTION**

The isometric drawing is shown at the right. Each vertical edge of the solid is represented by a vertical line segment.

Add depth to the drawing by shading the top, front, and sides differently.

## EXAMPLE 3   Interpreting an Isometric Drawing

Draw the top, front, and side views of the solid.

**SOLUTION**

You can arrange the views in the following way.

top

front

side

## EXERCISES

Draw the top, front, and side views of the solid.

1.

2.

3.

Create an isometric drawing of the solid.

4.

5.

6.

Draw the top, front, and side views of the solid. Assume no cubes, except those needed to support the visible ones, are hidden from view.

7.

8.

9.

## Lessons 10.1–10.3

**MULTIPLE CHOICE**

1. **REAL ESTATE** A rectangular house is built on a lot that is shaped like a trapezoid. The house is completely surrounded by a grass lawn. The house is 55 feet long and 35 feet wide. The lot has base lengths of 75 feet and 125 feet, and a height of 65 feet. Which expression can be used to find the area of the lot covered by grass in square feet? *TEKS 8.15.A*

   **(A)** $0.5(65)(75 + 125)$

   **(B)** $65(75 + 125) - 35(55)$

   **(C)** $0.5(65)(75 + 125) - 35(55)$

   **(D)** $0.5(65)(75 + 125) + 35(55)$

2. **EQUAL AREAS** The dimensions of two polygons are given below. For what value of $b_2$ is the area of the trapezoid equal to the area of the parallelogram? *TEKS 8.16.A*

   Parallelogram: $b = 20$ m, $h = 30$ m

   Trapezoid: $b_1 = 10$ m, $b_2 = \underline{\ ?\ }$, $h = 30$ m

   **(F)** 2 m          **(G)** 10 m

   **(H)** 20 m         **(J)** 30 m

3. **SKETCHING VIEWS** The crystal below is a composite of several solids. Which represents the top view of the crystal? *TEKS 8.7.A*

   **(A)**           **(B)**

   **(C)**

   **(D)**

4. **SEALANT** The diagram below shows the dimensions of a pool and an attached deck. You want to protect the deck by covering it with two coats of a waterproof sealant. One half-gallon can of sealant covers 160 square feet and costs $4.50. How much should you expect to pay, including tax, for enough sealant to complete the deck? Assume the sales tax is 6%. *TEKS 8.7.B*

   **(F)** $4.50          **(G)** $4.77

   **(H)** $9.00          **(J)** $9.54

5. **SPRINKLERS** You water two areas of your yard with rotating sprinklers. One sprinkler rotates in a complete circle and sprays water up to 10 feet. The other sprinkler rotates only half of a circle and sprays water up to 15 feet. About how much more area does the second sprinkler cover than the first? *TEKS 8.14.A*

   **(A)** $10 \text{ ft}^2$          **(B)** $25 \text{ ft}^2$

   **(C)** $39 \text{ ft}^2$          **(D)** $393 \text{ ft}^2$

**GRIDDED ANSWER** ⊙①●③④⑤⑥⑦⑧⑨

6. **ART** An art piece has the shape of a pentagonal prism. How many faces does it have? *TEKS 8.7.B*

7. **PARKING** The total area of the four congruent parking spaces below is 72 square meters. How long is each line dividing the spaces, in meters? *TEKS 8.2.B*

# 10.4 Surface Areas of Prisms and Cylinders

TEKS 8.8.A, 8.8.C

| Before | You classified prisms and cylinders. |
| Now | You'll find the surface areas of prisms and cylinders. |
| Why? | So you can find areas of objects, as the mailbox in Ex. 33. |

**KEY VOCABULARY**
- net, *p. 542*
- surface area, *p. 542*

One way to represent a solid is to use a *net*. A **net** is a two-dimensional pattern that forms a solid when it is folded.

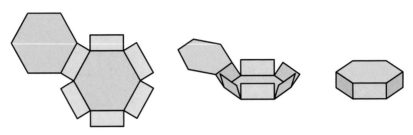

Each polygon of the net represents one face of the solid. For a given solid, several arrangements of these polygons are usually possible.

## EXAMPLE 1 Drawing a Net

**Draw a net of the triangular prism.**

### SOLUTION

**METHOD 1**
Draw one base with a rectangle adjacent to each side. Draw the other base adjacent to one of the rectangles.

**METHOD 2**
For the rectangular faces, draw adjacent rectangles. Draw the bases on opposite sides of one rectangle.

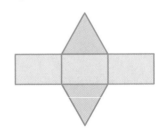

**Surface Area** The **surface area** of a polyhedron is the sum of the areas of its faces. To find the surface area of the triangular prism above, find the sum of the areas of the two triangular faces and the three rectangular faces.

## EXAMPLE 2 Using a Net to Find Surface Area

**Storage Chest** You are painting a storage chest with the given dimensions. Find the surface area to be painted.

15 in.

30 in.                    15 in.

**ANOTHER WAY**
Any pair of parallel faces in a rectangular prism can be considered the bases of the solid. Another way to draw a net for the storage chest is:

### SOLUTION

Draw a net of the chest.

The area of each square face is 15 in. • 15 in. = **225 in.²**

The area of each rectangular face is 30 in. • 15 in. = **450 in.²**

225 in.²   450 in.²   225 in.²

15 in.   450 in.²   450 in.²

15 in.   450 in.²   15 in.

30 in.

There are two square faces and four rectangular faces, so the surface area is 2 • **225 in.²** + 4 • **450 in.²** = 2250 in.²

▶ **Answer** The surface area of the storage chest is 2250 square inches.

Notice that in Example 2 the four blue faces form a large rectangle that has length equal to the perimeter of the red base.

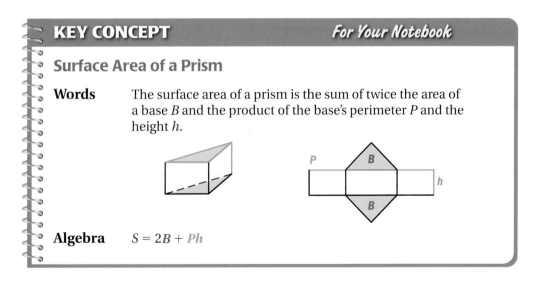

### KEY CONCEPT                                        *For Your Notebook*

### Surface Area of a Prism

**Words**     The surface area of a prism is the sum of twice the area of a base $B$ and the product of the base's perimeter $P$ and the height $h$.

$P$          $B$

$h$

$B$

**Algebra**     $S = 2B + Ph$

## EXAMPLE 3 Using a Formula to Find Surface Area

**Find the surface area of the triangular prism.**

$$S = 2B + Ph$$

$$= 2\left(\frac{1}{2} \cdot 10 \cdot 12\right) + (13 + 13 + 10)15$$

$$= 660$$

12 cm   13 cm

13 cm

15 cm

10 cm

**CHECK FOR REASONABLENESS**
Round each length to its leading digit. Then, $S \approx 2\left(\frac{1}{2}\right)(10^2) + 30 \cdot 20 = 100 + 600 = 700 \text{ cm}^2.$

▶ **Answer** The surface area of the prism is 660 square centimeters.

**Cylinders** The net of a cylinder has two circles for the bases. The curved surface of the cylinder becomes a rectangle in the net. The width of the rectangle is the height of the cylinder, and the length of the rectangle is the circumference of the base.

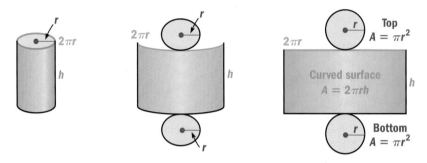

---

### KEY CONCEPT
*For Your Notebook*

#### Surface Area of a Cylinder

**Words**  The surface area of a cylinder is the sum of twice the area of a base $B$ and the product of the base's circumference $C$ and the height $h$.

**Algebra**  $S = 2B + Ch = 2\pi r^2 + 2\pi rh$

---

### EXAMPLE 4  Finding the Surface Area of a Cylinder

**Packaging**  Find the surface area of the can of sloppy joe sauce.

10.7 cm

8 cm

#### SOLUTION

The radius is one half the diameter, so $r = 4$ cm.

| | |
|---|---|
| $S = 2\pi r^2 + 2\pi rh$ | Write formula for surface area. |
| $= 2\pi(4)^2 + 2\pi(4)(10.7)$ | Substitute 4 for $r$ and 10.7 for $h$. |
| $\approx 369.45$ | Evaluate using a calculator. |

▶ **Answer**  The surface area of the can is about 369 square centimeters.

*USE A CALCULATOR*
You can use the [π] key on your calculator instead of 3.14 when evaluating formulas.

---

✓ **GUIDED PRACTICE**  for Examples 1, 2, 3, and 4

Draw a net of the solid. Then find the surface area. Round to the nearest tenth. Check your answer for reasonableness.

**1.**

3 ft
5 ft
12 ft

**2.**
10 m
6 m
14 m
8 m

**3.**

8 in.
20 in.

**Lateral Surface Area** The *lateral surface area* of a three-dimensional figure is the surface area of the figure excluding the area of its bases.

**EXAMPLE 5** **TAKS PRACTICE: Multiple Choice**

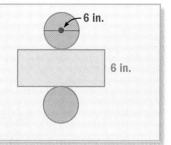

**Storage Container** A net for a cylindrical paint can is shown at the right. Approximate the lateral surface area of the container.

Ⓐ 28 in.²      Ⓑ 113 in.²

Ⓒ 170 in.²      Ⓓ 226 in.²

6 in.

6 in.

**ELIMINATE CHOICES**
The height of the rectangle is 6 in. and the length is greater than 6 in. So, the area must be greater than $A = (6)(6) = 36$ in.² You can eliminate choice A.

**SOLUTION**

The lateral surface area of a cylinder is equal to the area of its curved surface. The surface becomes a rectangle in the net of the cylinder, with length equal to the circumference of the base.

$$\text{Lateral surface area} = 2\pi r h \qquad \text{Multiply circumference and height.}$$

$$= 2\pi(3)(6) \qquad \text{Substitute 3 for } r \text{ and 6 for } h.$$

$$\approx 113.04 \qquad \text{Evaluate using a calculator.}$$

▶ **Answer** The lateral surface area of the container is about 113 cm². The correct answer is B. Ⓐ Ⓑ Ⓒ Ⓓ

✓ **GUIDED PRACTICE** **for Example 5**

**4. What If?** Suppose the radius of the cylinder in Example 5 is 5 inches and the height is 10 inches. Approximate the lateral surface area.

# 10.4 **EXERCISES**

HOMEWORK KEY

= **TAKS Practice and Reasoning**
Exs. 13, 28, 30, 31, 37, and 38

○ = **HINTS** AND **HOMEWORK HELP**
for Exs. 3, 7, 9, 15, 29 at classzone.com

**SKILL PRACTICE**

1. **VOCABULARY** In your own words, explain what surface area is.

2. **VOCABULARY** Copy and complete: The net of a cylinder is made up of two ___?___ and one ___?___.

**DRAWING NETS** Draw a net of the prism.

**SEE EXAMPLE 1**
on p. 542
for Exs. 3–5

3.

4.

5.

**USING NETS** Draw a net. Then use the net to find the surface area.

SEE EXAMPLE 2
on p. 543
for Exs. 6–8

**6.**
10 in.
10 in.
10 in.

**7.**
12 ft
20 ft
13 ft
15 ft
21 ft

**8.**
5 m
2 m
4 m
3 m

**USING FORMULAS** Find the surface area of the prism given *B*, *P*, and *h*.

SEE EXAMPLE 3
on p. 543
for Exs. 9–13

**9.** $B = 4$ in.$^2$, $P = 8$ in., $h = 5$ in.

**10.** $B = 20$ cm$^2$, $P = 12$ cm, $h = 3$ cm

**11.** $B = 45$ yd$^2$, $P = 30$ yd, $h = 2.8$ yd

**12.** $B = 19.3$ m$^2$, $P = 16$ m, $h = 0.5$ m

**13.** ✏ **TAKS REASONING** What is the surface area of a rectangular prism that is 3 feet long, 2 feet wide, and 9 feet high?

**(A)** 14 ft$^2$     **(B)** 54 ft$^2$     **(C)** 61 ft$^2$     **(D)** 102 ft$^2$

**SURFACE AREA OF CYLINDERS** Draw a net. Then use the net to find the surface area of the cylinder. Round to the nearest tenth.

SEE EXAMPLE 4
on p. 544
for Exs. 14–16

**14.**
13 mm
2 mm

**15.**
14 in.
6 in.

**16.**
8 ft
16 ft

**SKETCHING CYLINDERS** Sketch a cylinder with radius *r* and height *h*. Then find its surface area and lateral surface area. Round to the nearest tenth.

SEE EXAMPLE 5
on p. 545
for Exs. 17–19

**17.** $r = 6$ m, $h = 2$ m

**18.** $r = 1$ ft, $h = 7$ ft

**19.** $r = 10$ cm, $h = 20$ cm

**20. INTERPRETING NETS** Find the area of the net shown. Will the net form a closed figure when folded? If not, copy and complete the net so it will form a closed figure.

12 m
7 m

**LATERAL SURFACE AREA** Find the lateral surface area of the prism given *B*, *P*, and *h*. Check that your answer is reasonable.

**21.** $B = 56$ ft$^2$, $P = 30$ ft, $h = 5$ ft

**22.** $B = 27$ in.$^2$, $P = 24$ in., $h = 12$ in.

**23.** $B = 42$ cm$^2$, $P = 34$ cm, $h = 6$ cm

**24.** $B = 24$ m$^2$, $P = 20$ m, $h = 7$ m

**25. ERROR ANALYSIS** Describe and correct the error made in finding the lateral surface area of the cylinder.

3 in.
7 in.

$$S = 2\pi r^2 + 2\pi rh$$
$$= 2\pi(3)^2 + 2\pi(3)(7)$$
$$\approx 188.5 \text{ in.}^2$$

**26. CHALLENGE** Draw a net of the triangular prism shown whose edge lengths are all 1 foot. *Explain* how to find the height of the triangular bases. Then find its surface area and lateral surface area. Round to the nearest tenth.

1 ft
1 ft
1 ft
1 ft

**27. CHALLENGE** The height of a cylinder is 2 feet. Its lateral surface area is $4\pi^2$ square feet. What is its radius?

**28.** ▲ **TAKS REASONING** Draw a net of a cylindrical object at home or at school. Find the surface area of the object.

*SEE EXAMPLE 4*
*on p. 544*
*for Ex. 29*

**29.** **CRYSTAL BRIDGE** At the Myriad Botanical Gardens in Oklahoma City, a tropical conservatory bridges a small lake. The Crystal Bridge is a cylinder 224 feet long and 70 feet in diameter. Find the surface area of the Crystal Bridge, including bases. Round to the nearest tenth.

*SEE EXAMPLE 3*
*on p. 543*
*for Ex. 30*

**30.** ▲ **TAKS REASONING** A cubic package has side lengths of 2 feet. What is the least amount of wrapping paper needed to wrap the package?

**(A)** $8 \text{ ft}^2$  **(B)** $16 \text{ ft}^2$  **(C)** $24 \text{ ft}^2$  **(D)** $48 \text{ ft}^2$

**31.** ▲ **TAKS REASONING** You are dipping pieces of bread into fondue. The fondue coats the outside of the bread. Some of the pieces of bread are 1 inch cubes. Others are cylinders that are 1 inch high and 1 inch in diameter. Which uses more fondue? *Explain.*

**BREAK INTO PARTS** **Draw a net of the solid with the correct proportions. Then find the surface area. Round to the nearest tenth if necessary.**

**32.**

1 in.
3 in.
1 in.
3 in.
3 in.
3 in.

**33.**

3 in.
8 in.
18 in.
6 in.

**34.** **WRITING** *Explain* why you can multiply the perimeter of the base times the height to find the lateral surface area of a prism.

**35.** **XV ALGEBRA** Each edge of a cube has length $s$. Write and simplify an expression for the surface area of a cube in terms of $s$.

**36.** **CHALLENGE** Does doubling the height of a prism or cylinder result in a doubling of the surface area? of the lateral surface area? *Explain.*

*REVIEW*
*Lesson 10.2;*
*TAKS Workbook*

**37.** ▲ **TAKS PRACTICE** The circumference of a nickel is about $2\pi$ centimeters. What is the approximate area of one side of the coin? *TAKS Obj. 2*

**(A)** $3.14 \text{ cm}^2$  **(B)** $12.56 \text{ cm}^2$  **(C)** $25.12 \text{ cm}^2$  **(D)** $50.24 \text{ cm}^2$

*REVIEW*
*Lesson 7.4;*
*TAKS Workbook*

**38.** ▲ **TAKS PRACTICE** Between 60% and 65% of a coastline has been built on. The rest is preserved as wetlands. If the total length of the coast is written as $c$, what possible length of the coast might be preserved? *TAKS Obj. 1*

**(F)** $\frac{1}{3}c$  **(G)** $(0.345)c$  **(H)** $\frac{3}{8}c$  **(J)** $(0.64)c$

# 10.5 Surface Areas of Pyramids and Cones

TEKS *8.8.A, 8.8.C*

| Before | You found the surface areas of prisms and cylinders. |
| Now | You'll find the surface areas of pyramids and cones. |
| Why? | So you can find the surface area of buildings, as the pyramid in Ex. 33. |

**KEY VOCABULARY**
• slant height, *p. 548*

The height *h* of a pyramid is the perpendicular distance between the vertex and the base.

The **slant height** *l* of a regular pyramid is the height of a *lateral* face, that is, any face that is not the base.

*TAKE NOTES*
All the pyramids in this lesson are regular. For a regular pyramid, the slant height is the same on any face that is not the base.

The net for a regular pyramid has a regular polygon as the base and congruent isosceles triangles on each side of the base.

You can use the net of a pyramid to find the surface area of the pyramid.

| | | **Base area** | | **Area of lateral faces** | |
|---|---|---|---|---|---|
| Surface area | = | Area of base | + | Number of triangles | × | Area of each triangle |

$$= \quad B \quad + \quad 4 \quad \times \quad \left(\tfrac{1}{2}sl\right)$$

$$= \quad B + \tfrac{1}{2}(4s)l$$

$$= \quad B + \tfrac{1}{2}Pl$$

The product of the number of triangles and the side length of the base is the perimeter of the base.

---

**KEY CONCEPT** *For Your Notebook*

### Surface Area of a Pyramid

**Words**    The surface area of a regular pyramid is the sum of the area of the base *B* and one half the product of the base perimeter *P* and the slant height *l*.

**Algebra**    $S = B + \tfrac{1}{2}Pl$

---

**EXAMPLE 1** Finding the Surface Area of a Pyramid

Find the surface area of the regular pyramid. Round to the nearest tenth.

6 m

8 m    8 m

$B \approx 27.7 \text{ m}^2$

**SOLUTION**

**STEP 1** **Find** the perimeter of the base.

$$P = 8 + 8 + 8 = 24$$

*AVOID ERRORS*

Remember to include the area of the base since the question does not ask for lateral surface area.

**STEP 2** **Substitute** into the formula for surface area.

$S = B + \frac{1}{2}Pl$          Write formula for surface area of a pyramid.

$\approx 27.7 + \frac{1}{2}(24)(6)$     Substitute 27.7 for *B*, 24 for *P*, and 6 for *l*.

$= 99.7$          Simplify.

▶ **Answer** The surface area is about 99.7 square meters.

✓ **GUIDED PRACTICE** for Example 1

Draw a net. Use it to find the surface area. Round to the nearest tenth.

1.
12 ft

8 ft
8 ft

2. 10 in.
12 in.
12 in.
$B \approx 62.4 \text{ in.}^2$

3.
9 mm

6 mm

4. Find the lateral surface area of a square pyramid with a base side length of 12.5 centimeters and a slant height of 8.4 centimeters.

**Cones** You can use the net of a cone to find its surface area. The curved surface of a cone is a section of a circle with radius *l*, the slant height of the cone.

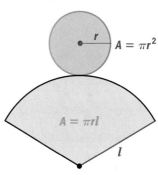

$r$    $A = \pi r^2$

$A = \pi r l$

$l$

The area of the curved, lateral surface, called the *lateral surface area* of the cone, is $A = \pi r l$, where *r* is the radius of the base of the cone.

**EXAMPLE 2**   Finding the Surface Area of a Cone

**Find the surface area of a cone with radius 4 m and slant height 9 m.**

| | |
|---|---|
| $S = \pi r^2 + \pi r l$ | Write formula for surface area of a cone. |
| $= \pi(4)^2 + \pi(4)(9)$ | Substitute 4 for *r* and 9 for *l*. |
| $\approx 163.4$ | Evaluate using a calculator. |

▶ **Answer**   The surface area is about 163.4 square meters.

✓ **GUIDED PRACTICE**   **for Example 2**

**5.** Find the surface area and lateral surface area of a cone with radius
6 meters and slant height 12 meters. Round to the nearest tenth.

---

# 10.5 EXERCISES

**SKILL PRACTICE**

**1. VOCABULARY** Draw a square pyramid. Label *h*, *l*, and *B*.

**NETS AND SURFACE AREA** Sketch a net of the solid. Then find the surface
area. Round to the nearest tenth if necessary.

*SEE EXAMPLE 1*
on p. 549
for Exs. 2–4

**2.**
11 m
15 m
15 m

**3.** 5 ft
4 ft
4 ft
$B \approx 6.9 \text{ ft}^2$

**4.** 1.5 mm
1.5 mm
1.5 mm

*SEE EXAMPLE 2*
on p. 550
for Exs. 5–7

**5.**
10 cm
6 cm

**6.**
8 in.
14 in.

**7.**
13 in.
3 in.

**SEE EXAMPLES**
**1 AND 2**
·············
on pp. 549–550
for Exs. 8–13

8. ✦ **TAKS REASONING** What is the surface area of a square pyramid with a base side length of 7 meters and a slant height of 5 meters?

(A) 70 m²      (B) 95 m²      (C) 119 m²      (D) 150.5 m²

**FINDING SURFACE AREA** Find the surface area of the square pyramid with base side length *s* and slant height *l*, or of the cone with radius *r* and slant height *l*. Round to the nearest tenth if necessary.

9. $s = 5$ cm
$l = 4.2$ cm

10. $s = 15$ yd
$l = 10$ yd

11. $r = 12$ m
$l = 6.5$ m

12. $r = 4$ mm
$l = 5.5$ mm

13. **ERROR ANALYSIS** Describe and correct the error made in finding the surface area of the solid.

$$S = \pi r^2 + \pi r l$$
$$= \pi(6)^2 + \pi(6)(8)$$
$$\approx 263.89 \text{ ft}^2$$

**REASONING** *Explain* how to find the slant height of the solid. Then find it and calculate the surface area. Round to the nearest tenth if necessary.

14.

15.

16.

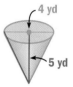

**SPHERES** The surface area $S$ of a sphere is $S = 4\pi r^2$ where $r$ is the radius of the sphere. Find the surface area of the sphere. Round to the nearest tenth.

17.

18.

19.

**XV** **CHALLENGE** The surface area $S$, base side length $b$, and slant height $l$ of a square pyramid are given. Find the value of $x$.

20. $S = 555$ m²
$b = 15$ m
$l = (2x + 1)$ m

21. $S = 460$ cm²
$b = 10$ cm
$l = (3x - 3)$ cm

22. $S = 125.6$ in.²
$b = 5$ in.
$l = (x + 2)$ in.

## PROBLEM SOLVING

**SEE EXAMPLES**
**1 AND 2**
·············
on pp. 549–550
for Exs. 23–24

23. **SET DESIGN** Your school needs a square pyramid with a base for a play. Each side of the base will have a length of 10 feet. The slant height will be 15 feet. How many square feet of material are needed to build this pyramid?

24. ✦ **TAKS REASONING** Approximate the lateral surface area of the ice cream cone shown with an open base.

(A) 13.4 in.²      (B) 16.5 in.²

(C) 26.7 in.²      (D) 39.3 in.²

**25. WRITING** *Describe* the difference between the *slant height* and the *height* of a pyramid and of a cone.

SEE EXAMPLE 2
on p. 550
for Exs. 26–30

**26. MULTI-STEP PROBLEM** Pablo makes a paper cone with no base. It has a radius of 4 inches and a slant height of 7 inches.

   **a.** What is the surface area of Pablo's cone? Round to the nearest tenth.

   **b.** Monica makes a larger cone that has a radius and slant height that are twice the lengths of those on Pablo's cone. *Compare* the surface area of Monica's cone to that of Pablo's cone.

**ICICLES** **Icicles are shaped like cones. As they melt, icicles change size but stay similar in shape. Find the lateral surface area of an icicle with the given dimensions in terms of $\pi$.**

**27.** $r = 1$ in., $l = 6$ in.     **28.** $r = 2$ in., $l = 12$ in.

**29.** $r = 3$ in., $l = 18$ in.     **30.** $r = 4$ in., $l = 24$ in.

**31. LOOK FOR A PATTERN** *Describe* the pattern developed in Exercises 27–30. Then predict the surface area of an icicle with a radius of 5 inches and a slant height of 30 inches.

**32. NUMBER SENSE** Predict which solid has a greater surface area: a *square pyramid* with a slant height of 12 units and a base side length of 10 units or a *cone* with a slant height of 12 units and a diameter of 10 units. *Explain* your reasoning. Then check your answer.

**33.** ⬥ **TAKS REASONING** The Rainforest Pyramid in Galveston Island, Texas, is a square pyramid with a height of 100 feet. Each side of its base measures 200 feet. *Explain* how to find the slant height. Then find the slant height and the lateral surface area of the pyramid.

**34. CHALLENGE** Find the surface area of the regular hexagonal pyramid shown. In the diagram of its base, all the triangles are equilateral and congruent. *Explain* how you found your answer.

15 cm

6 cm

3 cm  3 cm

---

## MIXED REVIEW FOR TAKS

**TAKS** PRACTICE at classzone.com

REVIEW
Lesson 10.4
TAKS Workbook

**35.** ⬥ **TAKS PRACTICE** A net for a cylindrical candle is shown at the right. What is the approximate lateral surface area of the candle? *TAKS Obj. 4*

  **(A)** $220$ cm$^2$

  **(B)** $440$ cm$^2$

  **(C)** $500$ cm$^2$

  **(D)** $600$ cm$^2$

10 cm

14 cm

# INVESTIGATION
*Use before Lesson 10.6*

**GOAL**
Find the volume of a
rectangular prism.

**MATERIALS**
• sugar cubes

**TEKS** *8.8.B, 8.16.A*

## 10.6 Exploring Volume

The *volume* of a solid is a measure of how much space it occupies. Volume is
measured in cubic units. One cubic unit is the amount of space occupied by
a cube that measures one unit on each side. This cube is called the *unit cube*.

**EXPLORE** **Find the volume of the rectangular prism.**

To find the volume of the prism shown, first build the prism using sugar
cubes to represent unit cubes. Then count the number of cubes you used.

$h = 3$ units
$w = 2$ units
$l = 4$ units

**STEP 1**

It takes 2 rows of 4 cubes, or 8 cubes,
to make the bottom of the prism.

4 units
2 units

**STEP 2**

It takes 3 layers of 8 cubes, or 24 cubes,
to make the prism the right height.

3 units
4 units
2 units

**STEP 3** Because each cube is 1 cubic unit, the prism's volume is
24 cubic units.

**PRACTICE** **Use cubes to model the volume of rectangular prisms.**

1. Copy and complete the table to find the volume of the rectangular
   prism with the given dimensions.

| Dimensions of the prism | Cubes to cover the bottom of the prism | Layers of cubes to make the prism | Volume of the prism |
|---|---|---|---|
| $4 \times 2 \times 3$ | 8 | 3 | 24 |
| $6 \times 1 \times 2$ | ? | ? | ? |
| $7 \times 5 \times 3$ | ? | ? | ? |
| $4 \times 2 \times 8$ | ? | ? | ? |

**DRAW CONCLUSIONS**

2. **REASONING** Write a formula for the area $B$ of the base of a rectangular
   prism. Then write a formula for the volume of the prism.

# 10.6 Volumes of Prisms and Cylinders

TEKS 8.8.B, 8.10.B

| Before | You found the surface areas of prisms and cylinders. |
| Now | You'll find the volumes of prisms and cylinders. |
| Why? | So you can compare capacities, as in Example 3. |

**KEY VOCABULARY**
• volume, *p. 554*

**Recycling** Residents of a community can choose between two recycling bins. Which recycling bin holds more? You will find the answer in Example 3 by comparing the *volumes* of the containers.

The **volume** of a solid is a measure of the amount of space it occupies. Volume is measured in *cubic units*. One cubic unit is the amount of space occupied by a cube that measures one unit on each side.

---

### KEY CONCEPT                                    *For Your Notebook*

**Volume of a Prism**

**Words**  The volume of a prism is the product of the area of the base $B$ and the height $h$.

**Algebra**  $V = Bh$

---

### EXAMPLE 1   Finding Volumes of Prisms

**Find the volume of the prism.**

**a.**

2 in.
8 in.
12 in.

Base is a rectangle, so $B = lw$.

$V = Bh$

$\phantom{V} = lwh$

$\phantom{V} = 12(8)(2)$

$\phantom{V} = 192$

▶ **Answer**  The volume is 192 cubic inches.

 **Animated Math** at classzone.com

**b.**

3 m          10 m
4 m

Base is a triangle, so $B = \frac{1}{2}bh'$.

$V = Bh$

$\phantom{V} = \frac{1}{2}(4)(3)(10)$

$\phantom{V} = 60$

▶ **Answer**  The volume is 60 cubic meters.

---

**AVOID ERRORS**

In the triangular prism, be careful not to confuse the height of the prism with the height of the triangular base. In part (b) of Example 1, the height of the triangle is $h' = 3$ m, but the height of the prism is $h = 10$ m.

**Volumes of Cylinders** As you discovered in the Investigation on p. 553, the volume of a prism can be calculated by finding the number of square units in the base and multiplying by the height. The formula for the volume of a cylinder is similar to the formula for the volume of a prism.

Volume of a cylinder = Area of base × Height

**REVIEW CYLINDERS**
Remember, the base of the cylinder is a circle. So its area is $\pi r^2$.

---

**KEY CONCEPT**      *For Your Notebook*

### Volume of a Cylinder

**Words**    The volume of a cylinder is the product of the area of a base $B$ and the height $h$.

**Algebra**    $V = Bh$

           $= \pi r^2 h$

height $h$

base $B$    radius $r$

---

**EXAMPLE 2**   Finding the Volume of a Cylinder

**Find the volume of the cylinder.**

**SOLUTION**

The radius is one half the diameter, so $r = 3$ cm.

6 cm
9 cm

| | |
|---|---|
| $V = Bh$ | Write formula for volume. |
| $= \pi r^2 h$ | Write formula for volume of a cylinder. |
| $= \pi(3)^2(9)$ | Substitute 3 for $r$ and 9 for $h$. |
| $= 81\pi$ | Simplify. |
| $\approx 254.469$ | Evaluate using a calculator. |

▶ **Answer** The volume is about 254 cubic centimeters.

---

✓ **GUIDED PRACTICE**    **for Examples 1 and 2**

**Find the volume of the solid. Round to the nearest tenth if necessary.**

1.
3 ft
11 ft
6 ft

2.
6 mm
8 mm
12 mm

3.
10 in.
$1\frac{1}{2}$ in.

## EXAMPLE 3 Comparing Capacities

**Recycling** To decide which recycling bin shown on page 554 can hold more, find the volume of each bin.

16 in.

23 in.

14 in.

9 in.

23 in.

$$V = Bh$$
$$= lwh$$
$$= 23(14)(16)$$
$$= 5152 \text{ in.}^3$$

$$V = Bh$$
$$= \pi r^2 h$$
$$= \pi(9)^2(23)$$
$$\approx 5852.8 \text{ in.}^3$$

▶ **Answer** The cylindrical recycling bin holds more.

**Similar Solids** As with polygons, two solids are similar if they have the same shape but not necessarily the same size. The corresponding linear measures of similar solids are proportional.

 TAKS

## EXAMPLE 4 TAKS PRACTICE: Multiple Choice

The dimensions of a prism are shown below. A *similar prism* can be produced by multiplying each dimension by the same factor. What happens to the volume when the dimensions are doubled?

**Ⓐ** The volume is cut in half.

**Ⓑ** The volume is multiplied by 2.

**Ⓒ** The volume is multiplied by 4.

**Ⓓ** The volume is multiplied by 8.

3 m

2 m

6 m

### SOLUTION

**STEP 1** **Find** the volume of the original prism.

$$V = Bh$$
$$= (6 \cdot 2)(3)$$
$$= 36 \text{ m}^3$$

**STEP 2** **Find** the volume of the similar prism

$$V = Bh$$
$$= [(6 \cdot 2) \cdot (2 \cdot 2)](3 \cdot 2)$$
$$= 288 \text{ m}^3$$

**STEP 3** **Compare** the volumes: $\frac{288 \text{ m}^3}{36 \text{ m}^3} = 8$.

▶ **Answer** When the dimensions are doubled, the volume is multiplied by 8. The correct answer is D. Ⓐ Ⓑ Ⓒ **Ⓓ**

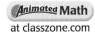

*Animated* Math

at classzone.com

**4.** Which solid has the greater volume? *Explain* your answer.

**5. What If?** Suppose the dimensions of the original prism in Example 4 were tripled. What would happen to its volume?

# 10.6 **EXERCISES**

HOMEWORK KEY

★ = **TAKS Practice and Reasoning**
Exs. 26, 32, 34, 37, 39, and 40

○ = **HINTS AND HOMEWORK HELP**
for Exs. 3, 7, 15, 17, 33 at classzone.com

## SKILL PRACTICE

**1. VOCABULARY** *Explain* the difference between surface area and volume.

**2. VOCABULARY** Copy and complete: The volume of a prism or cylinder is the area of the __?__ times the __?__.

**PRISMS** Find the volume of the rectangular prism with length *l*, width *w*, and height *h*.

*SEE EXAMPLE 1*
on p. 554
for Exs. 3–6

**3.** $l = 6$ m, $w = 2$ m, $h = 11$ m

**4.** $l = 7$ in., $w = 7$ in., $h = 7$ in.

**5.** $l = 3.8$ cm, $w = 3$ cm, $h = 1.2$ cm

**6.** $l = 16$ ft, $w = 3$ ft , $h = 2\frac{1}{2}$ ft

**VOLUMES OF CYLINDERS** Find the volume of the cylinder with radius *r* and height *h*. Round to the nearest tenth.

*SEE EXAMPLE 2*
on p. 555
for Exs. 7–12

**7.** $r = 4$ ft, $h = 11$ ft

**8.** $r = 3$ cm, $h = 9$ cm

**9.** $r = 1.2$ m, $h = 4.5$ m

**10.** $r = 6.4$ in., $h = 12$ in.

**11.** $r = 7$ m, $h = 15$ m

**12.** $r = 8.3$ yd, $h = 1.6$ yd

**FINDING VOLUMES** Find the volume of the solid. Round to the nearest tenth.

*SEE EXAMPLES 1 AND 2*
on pp. 554–555
for Exs. 13–19

**13.**

2 yd
4 yd
8 yd

**14.**

12 cm
2 cm

**15.**

7 m
15 m
24 m

**16.**

8 cm
$B = 60$ cm$^2$

**17.**

6 cm
3 cm

**18.**

5 mm
3 mm
6 mm

**19. ERROR ANALYSIS** Describe and correct the error in finding the volume of the cylinder.

$$V = Bh$$
$$= 2\pi rh$$
$$= 2\pi(4)(5)$$
$$\approx 125.66 \text{ m}^3$$

4 m
5 m

**FINDING VOLUME** Find the volume of the solid. Round to the nearest tenth. Give your answer in the smaller units.

20.
15 in.
2 ft
18 in.

21.
11 ft
4 ft
17 ft
2 yd

22.
3 ft
5 ft
3 yd
7 ft

**SIMILAR SOLIDS** Solid A is similar to solid B. Find the unknown height. Then find the volumes of the solids. How are they related?

**SEE EXAMPLE 4**
on p. 556
for Exs. 23–25

23.
Solid A
Solid B
3 m
5 m
4 m
9 m
?

24.
Solid A
5 m
6 m
Solid B
2.5 m
?

25. **NUMBER SENSE** Which has a greater effect on the volume of a cylinder: *doubling the height* or *doubling the radius*? Which has a greater effect on the volume of a rectangular prism that is longer than it is wide: *doubling the length* or *doubling the width*? *Explain.*

26. 🔺 **TAKS REASONING** The volume of a solid is 6 cubic yards. What is the volume of the solid in cubic feet?

   (A) 2 ft³    (B) 18 ft³    (C) 54 ft³    (D) 162 ft³

**CHALLENGE** Find the volume. Round to the nearest tenth if necessary.

27.
3 ft
3 ft
3 ft
9 ft
7 ft    5 ft

28.
5 in.
3 in.
6 in.
1 in.

## PROBLEM SOLVING

**REASONING** In Exercises 29–31, tell whether you would need to calculate *surface area* or *volume* to find the quantity.

29. The amount of wrapping paper needed to wrap a gift

30. The amount of cereal that will fit in a box

31. The amount of water needed to fill a watering can

**SEE EXAMPLE 2**
on p. 555
for Ex. 32

32. 🔺 **TAKS REASONING** A paint can is a cylinder 19 centimeters tall and 16 centimeters in diameter. What is the volume of the paint can?

   (A) 955 cm³    (B) 3820 cm³    (C) 4536 cm³    (D) 15,281 cm³

**SEE EXAMPLE 3**
on p. 556
for Exs. 33–35

**33.** **SWIMMING POOLS** A rectangular in-ground pool is 40 feet long, 16 feet wide, and 4 feet deep. A cylindrical above-ground pool is 6 feet deep and has a radius of 12 feet. Which pool holds more water? About how much more? *Explain*.

**34.** **TAKS REASONING** Find the volume of each eraser to the nearest tenth. How many pencil-top erasers would you use in the time it takes you to completely use the larger eraser? *Explain* your answer.

*Not drawn to scale*

**35.** **SALT SHAKERS** You buy a cylindrical box of salt that has a diameter of 4 inches and a height of 6 inches. Your salt shaker is a rectangular prism that is $1\frac{1}{2}$ inches by $1\frac{1}{2}$ inches by 3 inches. Estimate how many times the salt in the box can fill the salt shaker.

**36.** **WRITING** Two prisms have different surface areas. Can they have the same volume? *Explain*.

**37.** **TAKS REASONING** Use the cylinder at the right.

**a.** What is the effect of tripling the radius on the surface area and volume of the cylinder?

**b.** What is the effect of tripling the height on the surface area and volume of the cylinder?

**c.** What is the effect of tripling *both* the height and the radius on the surface area and volume of the cylinder?

**38.** **CHALLENGE** Find the surface area $S$ and volume $V$ of the cube at the right. Give the dimensions of another prism with a square base such that the ratio of the surface area to $S$ is equal to the ratio of the volume to $V$.

---

## MIXED REVIEW FOR TAKS

**TAKS** **PRACTICE** at classzone.com

**REVIEW**
Lesson 9.4;
TAKS Workbook

**39.** **TAKS PRACTICE** Nick and Eve walk their dogs in a park. Nick walks from A to B and then from B to C. Eve walks directly from A to C. About how much farther does Nick walk than Eve? *TAKS Obj. 4*

**(A)** 450 ft      **(B)** 550 ft

**(C)** 950 ft      **(D)** 1660 ft

**REVIEW**
Lesson 1.5;
TAKS Workbook

**40.** **TAKS PRACTICE** You are drawing a triangle so that the base and height of the triangle have the same length, $x$. The area $A$ of the triangle can be found using the equation $A = \frac{1}{2}x^2$. Find the area of the triangle when the base is 4 meters long. *TAKS Obj. 2*

**(F)** $2\ m^2$      **(G)** $4\ m^2$      **(H)** $8\ m^2$      **(J)** $16\ m^2$

**MATERIALS**
• tape • thin cardboard
• scissors • popcorn kernels
• metric ruler • protractor

**TEKS** *8.8.B, 8.16.A*

# 10.7 Comparing Volumes

Compare the volume of a pyramid to the volume of a prism.

**EXPLORE** **Compare pyramids and prisms.**

**STEP 1** **Draw** the nets shown on cardboard. Then cut out the nets and use tape to make an open square prism and an open square pyramid.

**STEP 2** **Compare** the height of the prism to the height of the pyramid. Then compare the base of the prism to the base of the pyramid. What do you notice?

**STEP 3** **Fill** the pyramid with popcorn kernels and pour the contents into the prism. Repeat until the prism is full. How many times did you have to empty the pyramid into the prism? Use this number to write the ratio of the volume of the pyramid to the volume of the prism.

**PRACTICE** **Use the formula for the volume of a rectangular prism and the ratio found in the activity to find the volume of the square pyramid.**

1.

2.

3.

**DRAW CONCLUSIONS**

4. **MAKE A MODEL** Draw the nets shown on cardboard. Use the nets to make an open cylinder and an open cone. Repeat steps 2 and 3 above using the cylinder and cone.

# 10.7 Volumes of Pyramids and Cones

| **Before** | You found the volumes of prisms and cylinders. |
| **Now** | You'll find the volumes of pyramids and cones. |
| **Why?** | So you can find the volume of structures, as in Example 3. |

**KEY VOCABULARY**
- pyramid, *p. 534*
- cone, *p. 534*
- volume, *p. 554*

The volumes of a pyramid and a prism with the same base area and the same height are related. As you may have discovered in the Investigation on p. 560, the volume of the pyramid is exactly one third the volume of the prism.

---

**KEY CONCEPT** *For Your Notebook*

### Volume of a Pyramid

**Words**    The volume $V$ of a pyramid is one third the product of the area of the base $B$ and the height $h$.

**Algebra**    $V = \frac{1}{3}Bh$

---

### EXAMPLE 1   Finding the Volume of a Pyramid

Find the volume of the square pyramid.

15 ft
30 ft

**SOLUTION**

> **CONNECT THE MODEL AND THE FORMULA**
> Because the base is a square, $B = s^2$.

$V = \frac{1}{3}Bh$      Write formula for volume of a pyramid.

$= \frac{1}{3}(30^2)(15)$      Substitute $30^2$ for $b$ and 15 for $h$.

$= 4500$      Evaluate using a calculator.

▶ **Answer** The pyramid has a volume of 4500 cubic feet.

---

✓ **GUIDED PRACTICE**   for Example 1

Find the volume of the square pyramid with base side length $s$ and height $h$.

**1.** $s = 4$ cm, $h = 5$ cm      **2.** $s = 6$ in., $h = 15$ in.      **3.** $s = 8$ mm, $h = 27$ mm

**4.** $s = 3$ yd, $h = 3$ yd      **5.** $s = 7$ m, $h = 9$ m      **6.** $s = 12$ ft, $h = 21$ ft

10.7 Volumes of Pyramids and Cones   **561**

Notice that the volume formula for pyramids does not require that the pyramid be regular, unlike the surface area formula.

### EXAMPLE 2  Finding the Volume of a Pyramid

**Find the volume of the pyramid.**

12 cm
10 cm
24 cm

**SOLUTION**

$V = \frac{1}{3}Bh$      Write formula for volume of a pyramid.

$= \frac{1}{3}\left(\frac{1}{2} \cdot 24 \cdot 10\right)(12)$      The base is a triangle, so $B = \frac{1}{2}bh$.

$= 480$      Multiply.

▶ **Answer** The pyramid has a volume of 480 cubic centimeters.

---

✓ **GUIDED PRACTICE**    **for Example 2**

**Find the volume of the pyramid given the area of the base $B$ and the height $h$.**

**7.** $B = 8\text{ cm}^2$, $h = 4$ cm     **8.** $B = 81\text{ in.}^2$, $h = 12$ in.     **9.** $B = 21\text{ yd}^2$, $h = 5$ yd

**Find the area of the base and volume of the pyramid.**

**10.**

9 in.
8 in.
8 in.

**11.**

10 ft
12 ft
5 ft

**12.**

15 m
8 m
20 m

**Volumes of Cones** The volume of a cone is related to the volume of a cylinder in the same way the volumes of a pyramid and a prism are related. That is, the volume of a cone is one third the volume of a cylinder with the same base and height.

---

**KEY CONCEPT**             *For Your Notebook*

### Volume of a Cone

**Words**      The volume of a cone $V$ is one third the product of the area of the base $B$ and the height $h$.

**Algebra**    $V = \frac{1}{3}Bh = \frac{1}{3}\pi r^2 h$

**EXAMPLE 3** Finding the Volume of a Cone

**Native Americans** Many Native American tribes built tepees that were similar to a cone in shape. A tepee has a height of 12 feet and a base diameter of 12 feet. Approximate the volume of the tepee.

12 ft

12 ft

**SOLUTION**

The radius is one half the diameter, so $r = 6$ ft.

$V = \frac{1}{3}\pi r^2 h$      Write formula for volume of a cone.

$= \frac{1}{3}\pi(6)^2(12)$      Substitute 6 for $r$ and 12 for $h$.

$= 144\pi$      Simplify.

$\approx 452.389$      Evaluate using a calculator.

▶ **Answer** The tepee has a volume of about 452 cubic feet.

**Check** Because $\frac{1}{3}\pi \approx 1$, $V \approx 36 \cdot 12 \approx 40 \cdot 10 = 400$ ft³. The answer is reasonable.

*Animated* **Math**
at classzone.com

✓ **GUIDED PRACTICE**    **for Example 3**

**Find the volume of the cone with radius $r$ and height $h$.**

**13.** $r = 24$ m, $h = 18$ m      **14.** $r = 4$ in., $h = 16$ in.      **15.** $r = 15$ ft, $h = 28$ ft

# 10.7 EXERCISES

HOMEWORK KEY

🔺 = **TAKS Practice and Reasoning**
Exs. 17, 39, 41, 45, and 46

◯ = **HINTS AND HOMEWORK HELP**
for Exs. 5, 9, 15, 19, 39 at classzone.com

## SKILL PRACTICE

**VOCABULARY** Match each solid with the *best* formula for its volume.

**1.** prism      **2.** cylinder      **3.** pyramid      **4.** cone

**A.** $V = \frac{1}{3}Bh$      **B.** $V = \pi r^2 h$      **C.** $V = \frac{1}{3}\pi r^2 h$      **D.** $V = Bh$

**VOLUME OF A PYRAMID** Find the volume of the pyramid given the area of the base $B$ and the height $h$.

**SEE EXAMPLES 1 AND 2**
on pp. 561–562 for Exs. 5–10

**5.** $B = 9$ in.², $h = 4$ in.      **6.** $B = 12$ ft², $h = 15$ ft      **7.** $B = 1.5$ m², $h = 0.6$ m

**VOLUME OF A SQUARE PYRAMID** Find the volume of the square pyramid with base side length $s$ and height $h$.

**8.** $s = 15$ m, $h = 4$ m      **9.** $s = 12$ yd, $h = 3$ yd      **10.** $s = 6$ in., $h = \frac{1}{2}$ in.

**VOLUME OF A SOLID** Find the volume of the solid. Round to the nearest tenth if necessary. Check that your answer is reasonable.

**SEE EXAMPLE 2**
on p. 562
for Exs. 11–13

**11.**
20 m
24 m
16 m

**12.**
17 in.
29 in.
25 in.

**13.**
11 ft
15 ft
9 ft

**SEE EXAMPLE 3**
on p. 563
for Exs. 14–23

**14.**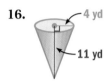
27 cm
11 cm

**15.**
45 ft
45 ft

**16.**
4 yd
11 yd

**17.** ⚑ **TAKS REASONING** What is the volume of the cone?

**A** $10\pi$ ft$^3$    **B** $21\pi$ ft$^3$

**C** $49\pi$ ft$^3$    **D** $147\pi$ ft$^3$

3 ft
7 ft

**VOLUME OF A CONE** Find the volume of the cone with the given dimensions. If two units of measure are used, give your answer in the smaller units. Round to the nearest tenth.

**18.** $r = 3$ in., $h = 7$ in.

**19.** $r = 11$ ft, $h = 4$ ft

**20.** $d = 1.2$ m, $h = 4.5$ m

**21.** $r = 83$ cm, $h = 2.8$ m

**22.** $d = 5$ m, $h = 492$ cm

**23.** $d = 3$ ft, $h = 10$ yd

**VOLUME OF A PYRAMID** Find the area of the base and volume of the pyramid with the given height $h$ and base shown.

**24.** $h = 1.8$ cm

1.3 cm
1.2 cm

**25.** $h = 8$ m

6 m  12 m
5.2 m
5.2 m

**26.** $h = 18$ in.

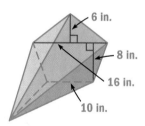
6 in.
8 in.
16 in.
10 in.

**⟨xy⟩ ALGEBRA** Find the unknown dimension using the given information.

**27.** Square pyramid
volume = 156 yd$^3$
base side length = 6 yd
height = _?_

**28.** Cone
volume = $216\pi$ ft$^3$
height = 8 ft
radius = _?_

**29.** Right triangular pyramid
volume = 28 in.$^3$
legs = 3 in., 4 in.
height = _?_

**FINDING VOLUME** Find the volume of the solid. Round to the nearest tenth.

**30.**
15 ft
20 ft
20 ft
20 ft

**31.**
10 cm
6 cm
14 cm

**32.**
2 in.
2 in.
2 in.
7 in.

33. **ERROR ANALYSIS** Harry says that when you double the dimensions of a square pyramid, you double the volume. *Describe* and correct his error.

🕸 **ALGEBRA** **Write a formula for the volume of the solid.**

34.

35.

36.

37. **CHALLENGE** Find the volume of a regular hexagonal pyramid with a height of 6 meters and a base side length of 4 meters. Round to the nearest tenth.

## PROBLEM SOLVING

**SEE EXAMPLE 3**
on p. 563
for Ex. 38

38. **SPOTLIGHT** The light from a spotlight extends out in a cone shape from the bulb. The light of the beam extends 24 feet before it hits the floor under the spotlight and creates a circle with a radius of 10 feet. What is the volume of the space directly lit by the spotlight? Round to the nearest tenth.

39. 🐾 **TAKS REASONING** Each of four wooden models has a height of 6 inches. Which has the greatest volume?

  **A** a square pyramid with base side length 8 in.

  **B** a rectangular pyramid with base side lengths 8 in. and 6 in.

  **C** a cylinder with diameter 8 in.

  **D** a cone with diameter 8 in.

40. **REASONING** Which would change the volume of a cone more: *doubling the height* or *doubling the radius*? *Explain* your reasoning.

41. 🐾 **TAKS REASONING** A rectangular prism-shaped hole 10 feet by 12 feet by 8 feet is dug into the ground. Which is the taller solid that can be formed with the excavated dirt: a *square pyramid* with a base side length of 10 feet or a *cone* with a radius of 5 feet? *Explain* your reasoning.

42. **HISTORY** Early civilizations in the Andes Mountains in Peru used cone-shaped bricks to build homes. Find the volume of a brick with a diameter of 8.3 centimeters and a slant height of 10.1 centimeters. How much space would 27 of these bricks occupy?

43. **MULTI-STEP PROBLEM** A diagram of an hourglass is shown.

  **a.** Find the volume of the cone-shaped pile of sand.

  **b.** If this is an accurate hourglass, at what rate does the sand fall through the opening? Give your answer in cubic inches per minute.

  **c.** The sand in the hourglass falls into a conical shape with a 3 to 2 ratio between the radius and the height. How many minutes have passed when the pile of sand is about 2 inches tall?

3 in.

9 in.

**44. CHALLENGE** A cone-shaped cup has a height of 11 centimeters and a radius of 4 centimeters. You pour water into the cup until it is 2 centimeters from the top. Sketch the cone. How many fluid ounces of water are in the cup? Round to the nearest tenth. (*Hint:* Use similar triangles and the fact that $1 \text{ cm}^3 \approx 0.0338 \text{ fl oz.}$)

## MIXED REVIEW FOR TAKS

**TAKS PRACTICE** at classzone.com

*REVIEW*
Lesson 10.6;
TAKS Workbook

**45.** ✏ **TAKS PRACTICE** The dimensions of two cubes are shown. The volume of the larger cube is 729 cubic inches. Find the volume of the smaller cube. *TAKS Obj. 4*

Ⓐ 9 in.³

Ⓑ 27 in.³

Ⓒ 243 in.³

Ⓓ 19,683 in.³

x          3x

*REVIEW*
Lesson 8.8;
TAKS Workbook

**46.** ✏ **TAKS PRACTICE** In the diagram shown at right, triangle I is similar to triangle II. The area of triangle I is 12 square meters. What is the area of triangle II? *TAKS Obj. 6*

Ⓕ 4.5 m²        Ⓖ 6.75 m²

Ⓗ 9 m²          Ⓙ 13.5 m²

Triangle I          Triangle II

4 m          3 m

## QUIZ for Lessons 10.4–10.7

**Find the surface area of the solid. Round to the nearest tenth.**

**1.** *(p. 542)*

6 m
10 m
24 m

**2.** *(p. 542)*
7 yd
14 yd

**3.** *(p. 548)*

8 cm
5 cm

**Find the volume of the solid. Round to the nearest tenth.**

**4.** *(p. 554)*

32 yd
150 yd

**5.** *(p. 561)*

3 ft
3 ft

**6.** *(p. 561)*

2 m
3 m
1.5 m

**7. ACCESS RAMPS** How many cubic feet of cement are needed to make the access ramp shown? *(p. 554)*

2 ft
10 ft
25 ft

# Volume of a Sphere

**TEKS** *8.8.C*

**GOAL** Find the volumes of spheres.

**KEY VOCABULARY**
- **sphere,** *p. 534*
- **volume,** *p. 554*

From Lesson 10.3, you know that a sphere is a solid formed by all points in space that are the same distance from a fixed point (the center). You can find the volume of a sphere using the following formula.

---

**KEY CONCEPT** *For Your Notebook*

**Volume of a Sphere**

**Words** The volume $V$ of a sphere is four thirds the product of $\pi$ and the cube of the radius $r$.

**Algebra** $V = \frac{4}{3}\pi r^3$

---

**EXAMPLE** **Finding the Volume of a Sphere**

Find the volume of a sphere with a radius of 5 inches.

$V = \frac{4}{3}\pi r^3$  **Write formula for volume of a sphere.**

$= \frac{4}{3}\pi(5)^3$  **Substitute 5 for r.**

$\approx 523.6$  **Evaluate using a calculator.**

▶ **Answer** The volume of the sphere is about 523.6 cubic inches.

---

**EXERCISES**

**Find the volume of the sphere. Round to the nearest tenth.**

1.

2 ft

2.

4 mm

3.

2 yd

4. radius = 9 in.

5. diameter = 12 m

6. diameter = 16 km

7. **Reasoning** What is the volume of each figure at the right? Write a word equation that relates the three volumes.

## Lessons 10.4–10.7

**MULTIPLE CHOICE**

1. **CONTAINERS** A company is making two types of covered aluminum containers. One is a cylinder with a height of 1.25 feet and a diameter of 1 foot. The other is a rectangular prism with a length of 0.75 foot, a width of 0.75 foot, and a height of 1 foot. To the nearest tenth of a cubic foot, how much greater is the cylinder's capacity? *TEKS 8.8.C*

   **A** 0.4 ft³   **B** 0.5 ft³

   **C** 1.0 ft³   **D** 1.4 ft³

2. **ALGAE** A pool service is treating algae in a rectangular pool that is 40 feet long, 20 feet wide, and 4 feet deep using sodium hypochlorite. The company uses 10 parts of sodium hypochlorite per million parts of water. Given that 1 cubic foot of water contains about 7.5 gallons, about how many cups of sodium hypochlorite are needed? *TEKS 8.14.A*

   **F** 0.384 cup

   **G** 3.84 cups

   **H** 38.4 cups

   **J** 384 cups

3. **SIMILAR PYRAMIDS** Find the volume of a pyramid with any whole number dimensions. Then find the volume of a similar pyramid whose dimensions are 1.5 times as large as the original pyramid. Which statement can be made about the larger pyramid? *TEKS 8.10.B*

   **A** The volume is 1.5 times greater.

   **B** The volume is 2.25 times greater.

   **C** The volume is 3 times greater.

   **D** The volume is 3.375 times greater.

4. **CONSTRUCTION** You are making cone-shaped paper cups. A small cup has a radius of 1.2 inches and a slant height of 3.2 inches. A large cup has a radius of 1.5 inches and a slant height of 3.5 inches. How much more paper does it take to make the larger cup than the smaller cup? *TEKS 8.2.B*

   **F** $1.09\pi$ in.²   **G** $1.41\pi$ in.²

   **H** $3.27\pi$ in.²   **J** $6.97\pi$ in.²

5. **GIFT WRAPPING** Lee is wrapping a gift in a box 8 inches long, 4 inches wide, and 2 inches high. Lee wants to tie a ribbon around the length of the box. He leaves an extra 10 inches to tie it. How long is the ribbon? *TEKS 8.14.B*

   2 in.
   4 in.
   8 in.

   **A** 16 in.   **B** 20 in.

   **C** 26 in.   **D** 30 in.

**GRIDDED ANSWER** ⊙①②●③④⑤⑥⑦⑧⑨

6. **FIREWOOD** Leon weighs a log of firewood that is one foot long and one foot in diameter. It weighs 36 pounds. He estimates that after being split, the wood will take up four thirds as much space as it does before being split. A cord of split firewood is 128 cubic feet. His truck has a capacity of 1200 pounds. How many trips must he make to deliver a cord of split firewood? *TEKS 8.14.C*

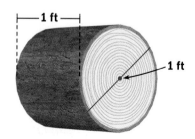
1 ft
1 ft

## REVIEW KEY VOCABULARY

- base of a parallelogram, *p. 521*
- height of a parallelogram, *p. 521*
- bases of a trapezoid, *p. 522*
- height of a trapezoid, *p. 522*
- solid, polyhedron, *p. 534*
- face, *p. 534*

- prism, *p. 534*
- pyramid, *p. 534*
- cylinder, *p. 534*
- cone, *p. 534*
- sphere, *p. 534*
- edge, vertex, *p. 534*

- net, *p. 542*
- surface area, *p. 543*
- slant height, *p. 548*
- volume, *p. 554*

### VOCABULARY EXERCISES

**Match the figure with its name.**

**1.**

**2.**

**3.**

**4.**

**A.** parallelogram     **B.** prism     **C.** sphere     **D.** trapezoid

## REVIEW EXAMPLES AND EXERCISES

### 10.1 Areas of Parallelograms and Trapezoids

*pp. 521–526*

**EXAMPLE**

**Find the area of the trapezoid.**

$A = \frac{1}{2}(b_1 + b_2)h$     **Formula for area of a trapezoid**

$= \frac{1}{2}(12 + 18)(5) = 75$     **Substitute and evaluate.**

The area of the trapezoid is 75 square inches.

12 in.

5 in.

18 in.

### EXERCISES

SEE EXAMPLES
*1, 2, AND 3*
on pp. 521–523
for Exs. 5–7

**5.** Find the area of a trapezoid with bases of 6 yards and 9 yards and a height of 8 yards.

**6.** Find the area of a parallelogram with a base of 20 feet and a height of 8 feet.

**7.** A parallelogram has a base of 36 centimeters and a height of 21 centimeters. A similar parallelogram has dimensions one third of the original dimensions. Find and compare the areas of the parallelograms.

## 10.2 Areas of Circles

*pp. 527–532*

**EXAMPLE**

Find the area of the circle. Use 3.14 for $\pi$.

$$A = \pi r^2 \qquad \text{Formula for area of a circle}$$
$$\approx 3.14(3)^2 \qquad \text{Substitute.}$$
$$= 28.26 \qquad \text{Evaluate.}$$

6 cm

The area of the circle is about 28.26 square centimeters.

### EXERCISES

Find the area of the circle with the given radius or diameter. Use 3.14 for $\pi$.

**SEE EXAMPLES 1 AND 2**
on pp. 527–528
for Exs. 8–13

**8.** $r = 2.5$ mm  **9.** $r = 3.7$ mi  **10.** $d = 7$ km

Find the radius of the circle with the given area. Use 3.14 for $\pi$.

**11.** $A = 1808.64$ in.$^2$  **12.** $A = 50.24$ mm$^2$  **13.** $A = 254.34$ yd$^2$

## 10.3 Three-Dimensional Figures

*pp. 534–538*

**EXAMPLE**

Classify the solid. Then count the number of faces, edges, and vertices.

4 faces

6 edges

4 vertices

The solid has 4 triangular faces, so it is a triangular pyramid. It is a polyhedron.

### EXERCISES

Classify the solid. Then tell whether it is a polyhedron.

**SEE EXAMPLES 1 AND 2**
on pp. 534–535
for Exs. 14–17

**14.**

**15.**

**16.**

**17.** Count the number of faces, edges, and vertices in the figure in Exercise 14.

## 10.4 Surface Areas of Prisms and Cylinders

*pp. 542–547*

**EXAMPLE**

**Find the surface area of the cylinder.**

9 cm

26 cm

$$S = 2\pi r^2 + 2\pi rh \qquad \text{Formula for surface area of a cylinder}$$

$$= 2\pi(9)^2 + 2\pi(9)(26) \qquad \text{Substitute.}$$

$$\approx 1979.203 \qquad \text{Evaluate using a calculator.}$$

The surface area of the cylinder is about 1979 square centimeters.

### EXERCISES

**SEE EXAMPLES
2, 3, AND 4**

on pp. 543–544
for Exs. 18–20

**18.** Find the surface area of the net. Identify the solid it forms.

13 in.

10 in.

12 in.

13 in.

23 in.

**Find the surface area of the solid. Round to the nearest tenth.**

**19.** a rectangular prism with a length of 5 feet, a width of 2 feet, and a height of 9 feet

**20.** a cylinder with a radius of 5 meters and a height of 10 meters

## 10.5 Surface Areas of Pyramids and Cones

*pp. 548–552*

**EXAMPLE**

**Find the surface area of the square pyramid.**

9 ft

12 ft

12 ft

$$S = B + \frac{1}{2}Pl \qquad \text{Formula for surface area of a pyramid}$$

$$= 12^2 + \frac{1}{2}(4 \cdot 12)(9) \qquad \text{Substitute.}$$

$$= 360 \qquad \text{Evaluate.}$$

The surface area of the pyramid is 360 square feet.

### EXERCISES

**SEE EXAMPLES
1 AND 2**

on pp. 549–550
for Exs. 21–23

**Find the surface area of the solid. Round to the nearest tenth.**

**21.** a square pyramid with a base area of 49 square meters and a slant height of 4 meters

**22.** a cone with a diameter of 20 feet and a slant height of 15 feet

**23. Gifts** You are wrapping a square pyramid puzzle. The base side lengths are 4 inches and the slant height is 5 inches. How much wrapping paper do you need?

## 10.6 Volumes of Prisms and Cylinders

*pp. 554–559*

**EXAMPLE**

**Find the volume of the prism.**

$V = Bh$     Formula for volume of a prism

$= \dfrac{1}{2}(7 \cdot 14)(21)$     Substitute.

$= 1029$     Evaluate.

The volume of the prism is 1029 cubic inches.

### EXERCISES

**Find the volume of the solid. Round to the nearest tenth if necessary.**

**SEE EXAMPLES**
*1 AND 2*
on pp. 554–555
for Exs. 24–26

**24.**

**25.**

**26.**

## 10.7 Volumes of Pyramids and Cones

*pp. 561–566*

**EXAMPLE**

**Find the volume of the cone.**

$V = \dfrac{1}{3}\pi r^2 h$     Formula for volume of a cone

$= \dfrac{1}{3}\pi (7)^2 (18)$     Substitute.

$\approx 923.628$     Evaluate using a calculator.

The volume of the cone is about 924 cubic feet.

### EXERCISES

**Find the volume of the solid. Round to the nearest tenth.**

**SEE EXAMPLES**
*1, 2, AND 3*
on pp. 561–563
for Exs. 27–29

**27.** a rectangular pyramid with base side lengths of 6 centimeters and 9 centimeters and a height of 7 centimeters

**28.** a cone with a radius of 4 inches and a height of 8 inches

**29. Candles** You have 12 cubic inches of candle wax. You have a mold for a square pyramid candle that has a base side length of 3 inches and a height of 5 inches. Do you have enough wax to make this candle? *Explain.*

**Find the area of the parallelogram or trapezoid.**

**1.**
7 cm
13 cm

**2.**
26 m
18 m
16 m

**3.**
21 in.
15 in.
32 in.

**Find the area of the circle given its radius or diameter. Use 3.14 for $\pi$.**

**4.** $r = 4$ ft

**5.** $d = 14$ yd

**6.** $r = 9$ mm

**Determine the radius of the circle given its area. Use 3.14 for $\pi$.**

**7.** $A = 3.7994$ ft$^2$

**8.** $A = 0.785$ m$^2$

**9.** $A = 94.985$ yd$^2$

**Classify the solid. Then tell whether it is a polyhedron.**

**10.**

**11.**

**12.**

**13.** Count the number of faces, edges, and vertices in the figure in Exercise 11.

**Find the surface area of the solid. Round to the nearest tenth if necessary.**

**14.**
60 m
8 m

**15.**
16 in.
15 in.
15 in.

**16.**
6.5 mm
21 mm

**Find the volume of the solid. Round to the nearest tenth if necessary.**

**17.**
3 ft
2 ft
4 ft

**18.**
2 mm
3 mm

**19.**
9 in.
8 in.
13 in.

**20. PAINTING** You plan to paint the 4 walls and ceiling of a rectangular room. The dimensions of the floor are 15 feet by 12 feet. The height of the room is 8 feet. A can of paint covers 400 square feet. How many cans of paint will you need to buy?

**21. FOOD PREPARATION** A stick of pepperoni is a cylinder, with a radius of 2 centimeters and a length of 12 centimeters. If a slice of pepperoni is 2 cubic centimeters, how many whole slices can be cut from the stick?

# REVIEWING PROBLEMS INVOLVING SOLIDS

You have seen the effect on the volume of certain prisms and cylinders when their dimensions are doubled or tripled. A general rule for the effect on the volume of prisms is shown below.

---

**EXAMPLE**

The dimensions of any rectangular prism are doubled or tripled.

**a.** Use the formula for the volume of a rectangular prism to show that its volume will increase by a factor of 8 when its dimensions are doubled.

**b.** Use the formula for the volume of a rectangular prism to show that its volume will increase by a factor of 27 when its dimensions are tripled.

---

## Solution

**REVIEW VARIABLES**
........................
The example has been solved for any rectangular prism of length *l*, width *w*, and height *h*. So, the answer holds true for any rectangular prism.

Find the volume, $V$, of any rectangular prism with length $l$, width $w$, and height $h$.

$V = lwh$     **Write formula for volume of a rectangular prism.**

**a.** The dimensions of the prism are doubled. So, the new length $l'$ is $2l$, the new width $w'$ is $2w$, and the new height $h'$ is $2h$. To find the volume, $V'$, after the dimensions are doubled, substitute these values into the volume formula.

$V' = l'w'h'$     **Write formula for volume of a rectangular prism.**

$\quad = (2l)(2w)(2h)$     **Substitute the new dimensions in the formula for volume.**

$\quad = 8lwh$     **Simplify.**

▸ **Answer** The volume of the new prism is $8lwh$. The volume of the original prism was $lwh$. So, the volume of the new prism is 8 times the volume of the original prism.

**b.** The dimensions of the prism are tripled. So, the new length $l'$ is $3l$, the new width $w'$ is $3w$, and the new height $h'$ is $3h$. To find the volume, $V'$, after the dimensions are tripled, substitute these values into the volume formula.

$V' = (3l)(3w)(3h)$     **Substitute the new dimensions in the formula for volume.**

$\quad = 27lwh$     **Simplify.**

▸ **Answer** The volume of the new prism is $27lwh$. The volume of the original prism was $lwh$. So, the volume of the new prism is 27 times the volume of the original prism.

# PROBLEMS INVOLVING SOLIDS ON TAKS

Below are examples of problems involving solids in multiple choice format. Try solving the problems before looking at the solutions. (Cover the solutions with a piece of paper.) Then check your solutions against the ones given.

**1.** A farmer is planning to paint the roof of his silo, which is cone-shaped as shown. What is the best estimate for the number of square feet the farmer must paint?

**A** 250 ft²

**B** 500 ft²

**C** 750 ft²

**D** 1000 ft²

**Solution**

Because only the lateral surface of the cone is to be painted, use the formula for the lateral surface area of a cone.

$$S = \pi r l$$
$$= \pi(8)(10)$$
$$\approx 251$$

So, the area he must paint is about 251 square feet. The correct answer is A.

**2.** The net of a rectangular prism is shown below. What is the volume of the rectangular prism?

15 cm

15 cm

9 cm

**F** 135 cm³

**G** 225 cm³

**H** 990 cm³

**J** 2025 cm³

**Solution**

Use the formula for the volume of a prism.

$$V = Bh$$
$$V = (lw)h$$
$$V = (15 \cdot 15)(9)$$
$$V = 2025$$

The volume of the rectangular prism is 2025 cubic centimeters. So, the correct answer is J.

**3.** Sadie is making a spherical model of the moon for a science project. Which best describes the front view of the model?

**A** Triangle

**B** Circle

**C** Sphere

**D** Cylinder

**Solution**

The top, front, and side views of a sphere are circles, as are views from any other angle.

Sadie's model is spherical. So, the correct answer is B.

## PRACTICE FOR TAKS OBJECTIVES 3 AND 4

1. The drawings below show the front, side, and top views of a solid figure built from cubes. Which drawing shows a 3-dimensional view of the solid figures?

Front view   Side view   Top view

**A**

**B**

**C**

**D**

2. The net of a square pyramid is shown below. What is the approximate lateral surface area of the square pyramid?

**F** $2.3 \text{ m}^2$

**G** $3.5 \text{ m}^2$

**H** $7 \text{ m}^2$

**J** $7.5 \text{ m}^2$

3. A cylinder has a radius of 5 inches and a height 14 inches. Its volume is $350\pi$. If the radius of the cylinder is doubled, then the volume of the cylinder will—

**A** double.

**B** triple.

**C** quadruple.

**D** be 5 times greater.

4. Kaleb wrapped a birthday gift in the box below.

2.5 in.

12 in.

14 in.

What is the total surface area of the gift box?

**F** $420 \text{ in.}^2$

**G** $456 \text{ in.}^2$

**H** $466 \text{ in.}^2$

**J** $500 \text{ in.}^2$

## MIXED TAKS PRACTICE

5. There are 15 players on a baseball team, including 2 co-captains. This season, the captains have produced a total of 82 hits between the two of them. The combined number of hits for the rest of the team is 455. Which equation can be used to find $a$, the average number of hits per player this season? Assume that the measure of average used is the mean. *TAKS Obj. 1*

**A** $a = \dfrac{(455 + 82 + 82)}{15}$

**B** $a = \dfrac{455}{13} + 82$

**C** $a = \dfrac{82}{2} + \dfrac{455}{13}$

**D** $a = \dfrac{(455 + 82)}{15}$

## MIXED TAKS PRACTICE

6. Justin has $150 in his savings account. He earns $125 each week. He plans on adding 45% of each week's earnings to the account. His bank account earns no interest. Which equation can be used to find the number of weeks, $x$, it will take the account balance to reach $800? *TAKS Obj. 2*

   **F** $125 + 0.45x = 800$

   **G** $150 + 0.45(125)x = 800$

   **H** $125(150 + 0.45x) = 800$

   **J** $0.45(150 + 125x) = 800$

7. Kolbe washes windows as a part-time job. The money he earns from one job can be found by evaluating the expression $4x + 2$, where $x$ represents the number of windows he washes. How can he find his earnings if he washes 3 windows on a job? *TAKS Obj. 6*

   **A** Multiply 4 by 3 and then multiply by 2

   **B** Multiply 4 by 3 and then add 2

   **C** Add 4 and 2 and then multiply by 3

   **D** Add 4 and 3 and then multiply by 2

8. Ms. Stockton is shopping for groceries. She plans on buying the items listed below. If she estimates her cost by rounding to the nearest fifty cents, what will be her estimate? *TAKS Obj. 1*

   | Grocery list: | |
   |---|---|
   | cereal | $2.88 |
   | apples | $4.15 |
   | milk | $3.10 |
   | loaf of bread | $1.99 |
   | laundry detergent | $5.55 |

   **F** $17.00

   **G** $17.50

   **H** $17.75

   **J** $18.00

9. Jasmine and her friends set up a badminton net, as shown below. She ties a rope at the end of each pole to secure the net. Which is closest to the length of each rope? *TAKS Obj. 4*

   **A** 10 in.

   **B** 48 in.

   **C** 70 in.

   **D** 96 in.

10. Andre wants to find the surface area of the cube shown below, but he is not sure how to do so. Which procedure can he use? *TAKS Obj. 6*

   **F** Square the side length and multiply the result by 6

   **G** Cube the side length

   **H** Multiply the side length by itself

   **J** Multiply the area of a lateral face by four

11. **GRIDDED ANSWER** A parallelogram drawn on a field for a summer camp racing tournament has an area of 44.625 square yards and a base length of 10.5 yards. What is the height in yards of the parallelogram on the field? *TAKS Obj. 3*

    *Record your answer and fill in the bubbles on your answer document. Be sure to use the correct place value.*

**Evaluate the expression when $a = 3$, $b = -15$, $c = 15$, $x = 7$, and $y = 5$.**
*(pp. 13, 77)*

**1.** $3x + 2$

**2.** $30 - 2x$

**3.** $2c - y$

**4.** $8a - 3c$

**5.** $\dfrac{y + x}{x - y}$

**6.** $\dfrac{6b}{2c}$

**7.** $\dfrac{c}{-5a}$

**8.** $\dfrac{b^2}{a^2}$

**Write the prime factorization of the number.** *(p. 176)*

**9.** 54

**10.** 70

**11.** 150

**12.** 184

**Use a percent proportion.** *(p. 354)*

**13.** What number is 500% of 16?

**14.** 200.2 is 65% of what number?

**15.** 44 is what percent of 80?

**16.** 1.7 is what percent of 340?

**Classify the polygon.**

**17.**
*(p. 411)*

**18.**
*(p. 416)*

**19.**
*(p. 411)*

**Solve the equation or inequality.** *(pp. 129, 318, 469)*

**20.** $\dfrac{d}{5} + 13 = -10$

**21.** $17 = \dfrac{x}{12} - 31$

**22.** $-21 - \dfrac{t}{3} = -6$

**23.** $\dfrac{2}{3}h - 3 \geq 1$

**24.** $\dfrac{1}{2}x + 4 \leq 7$

**25.** $-\dfrac{3}{4}x - 10 \geq 8$

**26.** $m^2 = 196$

**27.** $a^2 - 1296 = 0$

**28.** $c^2 - 28 = 36$

**Find the area of the figure.**

**29.**
*(p. 142)*

**30.**
*(p. 521)*

**31.**
*(p. 142)*

**32.**
*(p. 521)*

**33.**
*(p. 527)*

**34.**
*(p. 527)*

**Find the volume of the figure. Round to the nearest tenth if necessary.**

**35.**
*(p. 554)*

**36.**
*(p. 554)*

**37.**
*(p. 561)*

**38. WEATHER** The data show the daily high temperature in degrees Fahrenheit for two weeks.

67, 76, 78, 62, 58, 64, 70, 74, 78, 69, 68, 76, 67, 62

Make a histogram of the data. *Explain* your choice of intervals. *(p. 3)*

**39. CLASSROOM** A classroom is 25 feet by 40 feet and has seating for 28 students. Each student has a desk and chair that take up 9 square feet. There also is one large table that takes up 20 square feet. How many square feet of walking space does the classroom have? *(p. 142)*

**40. CALORIES** One serving of rice pilaf has 220 calories, including 35 calories from fat. One serving of soup has 70 calories, including 15 calories from fat. Write the calories from fat as a fraction of the total calories for each food. Which food has a greater fraction of calories from fat? *(p. 198)*

**41. COINS** A quarter's width is about $\frac{15}{16}$ inch. A dime's width is about $\frac{11}{16}$ inch. How many inches wider is a quarter? *(p. 233)*

**42. INTEREST** You invest $300 at a simple annual interest rate of 3.5% for one year. How much would you need to invest at a 2% simple annual interest rate to earn the same amount of interest that year? *(p. 375)*

**43. HIKING** Two hiking trails meet at a 24° angle. Sketch the intersection and label the measure of each angle formed. *(p. 403)*

**44. HOME PLATE** A rulebook specifies the shape of home plate as shown. Find the value of *x*. Round to the nearest whole number. *(p. 487)*

**45. SKATEBOARD RAMP** You are constructing a skateboard ramp as shown in the diagram. Find the lengths of the legs of the triangle that supports the ramp. Round your answers to the nearest tenth of a foot. *(p. 500)*

**46. CONTAINERS** A cylinder with a radius of 6 centimeters and a height of 7 centimeters has about the same volume as a rectangular prism with a length of 9 centimeters, a width of 8 centimeters, and a height of 11 centimeters. Which container uses less material to hold the same amount? About how much less material? Round to the nearest tenth. *(pp. 542, 554)*

**TEXAS**

## Before

In previous chapters you've . . .

- Translated verbal sentences into mathematical statements
- Solved one-variable equations

## Now

**TEKS** you'll study . . .

| | | |
|---|---|---|
| 8.5.B | **11.1** | Relations and functions |
| 8.12.B | **11.2** | Scatter plots |
| 8.5.A | **11.3** | Two-variable equations |
| 8.4 | **11.4** | Linear equation graphs |
| 8.4 | **11.5** | Using intercepts |
| 8.14.A | **11.6** | Slope |
| 8.5.A | **11.7** | Slope-intercept form |
| 8.4 | **11.8** | Linear inequality graphs |

## Why?

So you can solve real-world problems about . . .

- gray whales, p. 587
- elevators, p. 597
- hiking, p. 623

**Animated Math**
*at classzone.com*

- Relations and Functions, p. 586
- Slope, p. 612
- Slope-Intercept Form, p. 623

# Get-Ready Games

**Review Prerequisite Skills** by playing *Sidewalk Scramble* and *Plot the Picture*.

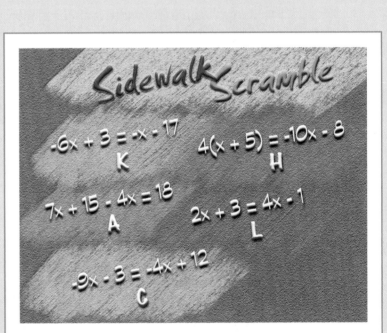

Sidewalk Scramble

$-6x + 3 = -x - 17$   **K**

$4(x + 5) = -10x - 8$   **H**

$7x + 15 - 4x = 18$   **A**

$2x + 3 = 4x - 1$   **L**

$-9x - 3 = -4x + 12$   **C**

**Skill Focus:** Solving equations in one variable

Solve the scramble to spell a word associated with sidewalk art.

- Find the solution of each equation.

- Order the equations so that the one with the least solution is first and the one with the greatest solution is last. This will unscramble the letters.

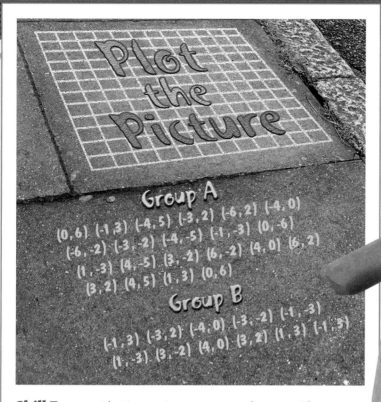

**Skill Focus:** Plotting points on a coordinate grid

Create a piece of sidewalk art.

- Plot the points listed in Group A on a coordinate grid. Connect each point with a line to the point that follows it.

- Now find and connect the points in Group B in order.

## Stop and Think

1. **WRITING** A student says that in *Sidewalk Scramble* the first step in solving the equation $-6x + 3 = -x - 17$ is to subtract $x$ from both sides. *Explain* why the student is wrong.

2. **EXTENSION** Design your own piece of sidewalk art. Write directions for making your sidewalk art using points on a coordinate grid.

# Review Prerequisite Skills

## VOCABULARY CHECK

**1.** Draw a coordinate plane and label the *x*-axis, *y*-axis, origin, and Quadrant III.

**2.** In the inequality $x \geq 8$, what does the symbol $\geq$ mean?

**3.** Describe the meaning of the numbers in the ordered pair $(-3, 2)$.

## SKILL CHECK

**4.** Write the ordered pair for each labeled point in the coordinate plane at the right. *(p. 94)*

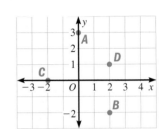

**Plot the point in a coordinate plane.** *(p. 94)*

**5.** $(0, 4)$        **6.** $(-2, 3)$

**7.** $(5, -4)$       **8.** $(-2, -3)$

**Solve the equation.** *(p. 129)*

**9.** $3 = 9x - 24$     **10.** $7 - 8x = 3$     **11.** $6x + 9 = -45$

**12.** $\dfrac{x}{4} - 1 = 6$     **13.** $15 - x = -22$     **14.** $-9 = \dfrac{x}{2} + 4$

**Solve the inequality.** *(p. 318)*

**15.** $3x - 4 \leq 5$     **16.** $-4x - 3 \geq 12$     **17.** $6 + 2x < 2$

**TEXAS @HomeTutor**   Prerequisite skills practice at classzone.com

## Notetaking Skills   Write Down Your Questions

In each chapter you will learn a new notetaking skill. In Chapter 11 you will apply the strategy of writing questions about homework to exercises on pp. 590–592.

If you don't know how to solve a homework problem, make a note in your notebook. Leave room to write the answer to your question.

What is the distance from A to C?

> I can't use the grid to count along a diagonal, so how do I solve this?

Use the Pythagorean Theorem. $AB = 3$, $BC = 4$, and $\triangle ABC$ is a right triangle, so $AC = 5$.

# 11.1 Relations and Functions

TEKS 8.5.A, 8.5.B

| **Before** | You translated verbal sentences into algebraic models. |
| **Now** | You'll use tables to represent functions. |
| **Why?** | So you can write real-world function rules, as for feeding whales in Ex. 23. |

**KEY VOCABULARY**
- **relation,** *p. 583*
- **input,** *p. 583*
- **output,** *p. 583*
- **function,** *p. 583*
- **domain,** *p. 584*
- **range,** *p. 584*

A **relation** is a set of ordered pairs that relates an **input** to an **output**. A relation can be written as a set of ordered pairs or by using an *input-output table*.

| (**Input**, **Output**) |
| :---: |
| (**2**, **5**) |
| (**4**, **7**) |
| (**−1**, **15**) |
| (**0**, **0**) |

| **Input** | **Output** |
| :---: | :---: |
| 2 | 5 |
| 4 | 7 |
| −1 | 15 |
| 0 | 0 |

A relation is a **function** if for each input there is exactly one output. In a function, you can say that the output is a *function of* the input.

---

**EXAMPLE 1** **Identifying Functions**

**AVOID ERRORS**
In a function, two different inputs can have the same output, but each input must have *exactly one* output.

Tell whether the relation is a function. *Explain* your answer.

**a.** (0, 2), (1, 4), (2, 6), (3, 8)

▸ **Answer** The relation is a function. Each input has exactly one output.

**b.**

| **Input** | 9 | 9 | 25 | 25 |
| :---: | :---: | :---: | :---: | :---: |
| **Output** | 3 | −3 | 5 | −5 |

▸ **Answer** The relation is a *not* a function. The inputs 9 and 25 both have two outputs.

at classzone.com

---

✓ **GUIDED PRACTICE** **for Example 1**

Tell whether the relation is a function. *Explain* your answer.

**1.** (−2, 4), (2, 4), (4, 2), (−2, −4)

**2.** (3, −2), (6, 1), (−3, 5), (4, 1)

**3.**

| **Input** | −4 | 0 | 4 | 8 |
| :---: | :---: | :---: | :---: | :---: |
| **Output** | 8 | 0 | 8 | 32 |

Domain and Range  The **domain** of a function is the set of all possible input values. The **range** of a function is the set of all possible output values. A *function rule* assigns each number in the domain to exactly one number in the range.

## EXAMPLE 2  Evaluating a Function

**Fundraising**  Your soccer team is selling glow sticks to raise money. The team paid $50 for a case of 48 glow sticks and sells each glow stick for $3. How many glow sticks does the team need to sell to start earning a profit? Use the function rule $P = 3g - 50$, where $P$ is the profit in dollars and $g$ is the number of glow sticks your team sells.

**SOLUTION**

*READING*
The domain and range of a function can be represented using *set notation*. In Example 2, the domain is $\{0, 1, 2, \ldots, 48\}$ and the range is $\{-50, -47, \ldots, 94\}$.

Make a table to determine how many glow sticks your soccer team needs to sell to start earning a profit.

| Input g | Function | Output P |
|---------|----------|----------|
| 0 | $P = 3(0) - 50$ | −50 |
| 10 | $P = 3(10) - 50$ | −20 |
| 16 | $P = 3(16) - 50$ | −2 |
| 17 | $P = 3(17) - 50$ | 1 |

There are 48 glow sticks, so the domain is 0, 1, 2, 3, . . ., 48. The range is −50, −47, −44, −41, . . ., 94.

▶ **Answer**  Your soccer team needs to sell 17 glow sticks.

## EXAMPLE 3  Writing a Function Rule

**Write a function rule that relates $x$ and $y$.**

| | +2 | +2 | +2 | +2 | |
| **Input x** | −4 | −2 | 0 | 2 | 4 |
| **Output y** | 1 | 3 | 5 | 7 | 9 |
| | +2 | +2 | +2 | +2 | |

**SOLUTION**

To write a function rule, try to find an equation of the form $y = ax + b$. You can look at differences in the function to find the values of $a$ and $b$.

**STEP 1**  The value of $a$ is $\dfrac{\text{change in output}}{\text{change in input}}$.

$a = \dfrac{2}{2} = 1$, so $y = 1x + b$.

**STEP 2**  To find $b$, substitute an input-output pair for $x$ and $y$.

Let $(x, y) = (0, 5)$.          $5 = 1(0) + b$, so $b = 5$.

▶ **Answer**  A function rule that relates $x$ and $y$ is $y = x + 5$.

**Check**  Substitute a different input-output pair in the function rule to check.

$3 \overset{?}{=} -2 + 5$      **Substitute (−2, 3) in function rule.**

$3 = 3$ ✓

**Sequences** A *sequence* is an ordered list of numbers. It is a special type of function whose domain includes only positive integers such as 1, 2, 3, and so on. Each sequence is made up of $n$ numbers, or *terms*, and the value of each term is $A$. In an *arithmetic sequence*, the difference between consecutive terms is constant. Its function rule has the form $A = an + b$.

**EXAMPLE 4** TAKS PRACTICE: Multiple Choice

Which function rule relates $n$ and $A$ in the arithmetic sequence: 3, 7, 11, 15, . . .?

  **A** $A = n + 4$    **B** $A = 4n$    **C** $A = 4n - 1$    **D** $A = -4n + 7$

*ELIMINATE CHOICES*
The terms of the sequence are increasing in value. So, the ratio of the change in output to the change in input must be positive. You can eliminate choice D.

**SOLUTION**

Find an equation of the form $A = an + b$.

**STEP 1** The value of $a$ is $\dfrac{\text{change in output}}{\text{change in input}}$.

$a = \dfrac{4}{1} = 4$, so $A = 4n + b$.

| | +1 | +1 | +1 | |
| --- | --- | --- | --- | --- |
| **Position** | 1 | 2 | 3 | 4 | $n$ |
| **Value of term** | 3 | 7 | 11 | 15 | $A$ |

+4  +4  +4

**STEP 2** To find $b$, substitute an input-output pair for $A$ and $n$.

Let $(n, A) = (1, 3)$      $3 = 4(1) + b$, so $b = -1$.

▸**Answer** A function rule relating $n$ and $A$ is $A = 4n - 1$. The correct answer is C.   Ⓐ Ⓑ ● Ⓓ

---

✔ **GUIDED PRACTICE**    for Examples 2, 3, and 4

**4. What If?** In Example 2, suppose each glow stick sells for $4. How many glow sticks would the team need to sell to start earning a profit?

**5.** Write a function rule that relates $x$ and $y$ in the table at the right.

| **Input x** | 1 | 2 | 3 | 4 |
| --- | --- | --- | --- | --- |
| **Output y** | −7 | −6 | −5 | −4 |

---

# 11.1 EXERCISES

HOMEWORK KEY
  = TAKS Practice and Reasoning
    Exs. 12, 24, 26, and 28

◯ = HINTS and HOMEWORK HELP
    for Exs. 7, 9, 13, 21 at classzone.com

**SKILL PRACTICE**

**1. VOCABULARY** Copy and complete: For a function, the set of all possible input values is its __?__ and the set of all possible output values is its __?__ .

*SEE EXAMPLE 1*
on p. 583
for Exs. 2–5

**IDENTIFYING FUNCTIONS** Tell whether the relation is a function. *Explain.*

**2.** $(4, 5), (2, -3), (4, 9), (-2, -3)$      **3.** $(-3, 7), (3, 7), (7, 3), (-7, -3)$

**4.** $(2, 3), (1, -6), (5, 3), (-1, -6)$      **5.** $(-8, 10), (9, 2), (2, 11), (-8, -4)$

SEE EXAMPLE 1
on p. 583
for Exs. 6–7

**IDENTIFYING FUNCTIONS** Tell whether the relation is a function. *Explain.*

**6.**

| Input | −3 | −2 | 0 | 2 |
|--------|----|----|---|---|
| Output | 9 | 4 | 0 | 4 |

**7.**

| Input | 4 | 4 | 2 | 5 |
|--------|---|----|---|----|
| Output | 2 | −2 | 5 | −5 |

SEE EXAMPLE 2
on p. 584
for Exs. 8–11

**EVALUATING FUNCTIONS** Make an input-output table for the function rule. Use the domain −2, −1, 0, 1, and 2. Identify the range.

**8.** $y = x - 1$  **9.** $y = -\frac{1}{4}x$  **10.** $y = 5x$  **11.** $y = x^2$

SEE EXAMPLE 3
on p. 584
for Exs. 12–16

**12.** ◆ **TAKS REASONING** Which function rule relates $x$ and $y$ for the set of ordered pairs (3, 1), (6, 2), (9, 3)?

**A** $y = \frac{1}{3}x$  **B** $y = 3x$  **C** $y = x - 2$  **D** $y = x - 6$

**WRITING FUNCTION RULES** Write a function rule that relates $x$ and $y$.

**13.**

| Input x | −1 | 0 | 1 | 2 |
|----------|----|---|---|---|
| Output y | 5 | 6 | 7 | 8 |

**14.**

| Input x | 0 | 1 | 2 | 3 |
|----------|---|----|-----|-----|
| Output y | 0 | −5 | −10 | −15 |

**15.**

| Input x | 1 | 2 | 3 | 4 |
|----------|---|---|---|----|
| Output y | 1 | 4 | 7 | 10 |

**16.**

| Input x | 0 | 1 | 2 | 3 |
|----------|---|-----|---|-----|
| Output y | 2 | 1.5 | 1 | 0.5 |

**Animated Math** at classzone.com

SEE EXAMPLE 4
on p. 585
for Exs. 17–18

**ARITHMETIC SEQUENCES** Write a function rule that relates $n$ and $A$ in the arithmetic sequence.

**17.** 3, 7, 11, 15, . . .  **18.** 7, 10, 13, 16, . . .

**19.** **ERROR ANALYSIS** A student says that in order to write a function rule that relates input $x$ to output $y$, the change in output must be the same as the change in input. Create an input-output table and write the related function rule to show that this statement is incorrect.

**20.** **CHALLENGE** Find the missing terms and write a function rule that relates $n$ and $A$ in the arithmetic sequence: $-\frac{1}{6}, \underline{?}, \frac{1}{2}, \underline{?}, \frac{7}{6}$.

## PROBLEM SOLVING

SEE EXAMPLE 2
on p. 584
for Ex. 21

**21.** **RECYCLING** Stanley receives $.40 per pound of aluminum cans he recycles. A function rule for this situation is $E = 0.40p$, where $E$ is the amount he earns in dollars and $p$ is the number of pounds of cans. Make an input-output table to find the number of pounds of cans Stanley needs to recycle to earn $6.

◆ = TAKS Practice and Reasoning  ○ = **HINTS AND HOMEWORK HELP** *at classzone.com*

**22. TICKETS** Ashley buys movie tickets that are all the same price. Is the total cost a function of the number of tickets? *Explain.*

SEE EXAMPLE 3
on p. 584
for Ex. 23

**23. WHALES** A gray whale calf is nursed back to health with milk-based formula. The table shows the total gallons of formula consumed over the course of $f$ feedings. Use the table to write a function rule. Then use your function rule to find how much the whale consumes in 7 feedings.

| Feedings (f) | Gallons consumed (g) |
|:---:|:---:|
| 1 | 2 |
| 2 | 4 |
| 3 | 6 |
| 4 | 8 |

**24. ✦ TAKS REASONING** Your friend says that the set of ordered pairs $(-9, 81)$, $(-4, 16)$, $(0, 0)$, $(4, 16)$, and $(-9, -81)$ is a function. Is your friend correct? If not, what is your friend's likely mistake? *Explain.*

**25. WRITING** *Explain* why the output $a$ is *not* a function of the input $b$ in the equation $a = \pm\sqrt{b}$.

**26. ✦ TAKS REASONING** *Describe* a real-world relation that is a function. *Describe* a real-world relation that is *not* a function.

**27. CHALLENGE** On a road trip, you stop every 90 minutes for a total of 4 stops. The speed you travel between stops is shown below. Assume the car travels at a constant speed between stops.

Start    1st stop    2nd stop    3rd stop    End

⊢— 35 mi/h —⊣— 40 mi/h —⊣— 45 mi/h —⊣— 50 mi/h —⊣

**a.** Write a function rule that relates the speed $x$, in miles per hour, to the distance $y$, in miles, traveled between stops.

**b.** How long, in hours and minutes, would it take to complete the entire trip at 60 miles per hour with no stops?

**MIXED REVIEW FOR TAKS**  **TAKS PRACTICE** at classzone.com

REVIEW
Lesson 9.3;
TAKS Workbook

**28. ✦ TAKS PRACTICE** In which figure with lengths $a$, $b$, and $c$ is the relationship $a^2 + b^2 = c^2$ NOT true? *TAKS Obj. 3*

Ⓐ     Ⓑ

Ⓒ     Ⓓ

# 11.2 Scatter Plots

| Before | You found a function rule given a table of values. |
| Now | You'll make and interpret scatter plots. |
| Why? | So you can compare data, such as quantity and cost of cereal in Example 2. |

**KEY VOCABULARY**
• scatter plot, *p. 588*

**NASA** NASA's Crawler Transporter is a large vehicle that moves the space shuttle and its launch platform to the launch pad. The crawler uses about 126 gallons of fuel to travel 1 mile.

The table below shows the amount of fuel, in gallons, that is used to travel different numbers of miles. How can you present this information using a graph?

| Distance (miles) | 1 | 2 | 3 | 4 | 5 | 6 |
|---|---|---|---|---|---|---|
| Fuel used (gallons) | 126 | 252 | 378 | 504 | 630 | 756 |

You can represent the information using a *scatter plot*. A **scatter plot** is a graph of a collection of ordered pairs.

## EXAMPLE 1   Making a Scatter Plot

**Make a scatter plot of the data given above.**

**SOLUTION**

**STEP 1**   **Plot** the ordered pairs from the table.

(1, 126), (2, 252), (3, 378),

(4, 504), (5, 630), (6, 756)

**STEP 2**   **Label** the horizontal and vertical axes.

Put *Distance (mi)* on the horizontal axis and *Fuel used (gal)* on the vertical axis.

*NASA Crawler Transporter*

✓ **GUIDED PRACTICE**   **for Example 1**

**Make a scatter plot of the data.**

1.
| c | −2 | −1 | 0 | 1 |
|---|---|---|---|---|
| d | −5 | −4 | −3 | −2 |

2.
| x | 0 | 3 | 6 | 9 |
|---|---|---|---|---|
| y | −2 | −4 | −6 | −8 |

**Interpreting Scatter Plots** Scatter plots show what kind of relationship exists between two sets of data.

| Positive relationship | Negative relationship | No relationship |
|---|---|---|
|  |  | 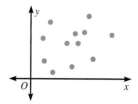 |
| The *y*-coordinates tend to increase as the *x*-coordinates increase. | The *y*-coordinates tend to decrease as the *x*-coordinates increase. | No obvious pattern exists between the coordinates. |

### EXAMPLE 2  Interpreting a Scatter Plot

**Unit Cost** The table shows the cost per ounce *y* of breakfast cereal when you buy *x* ounces. Make a scatter plot of the data. Predict whether the cost per ounce for a 22 ounce box of cereal will be *more than* or *less than* $.22. *Explain.*

| Number of ounces x | 9.6 | 11.4 | 18.2 | 18.3 | 24 | 25.5 |
|---|---|---|---|---|---|---|
| Cost per ounce y | $.44 | $.33 | $.25 | $.22 | $.17 | $.16 |

**SOLUTION**

*STEP 1* **Make** a scatter plot of the data from the table.

*STEP 2* **Describe** the relationship between the variables. The *y*-coordinates decrease as the *x*-coordinates increase. So, the quantities have a *negative relationship.*

▶ **Answer** The cost per ounce of a 22 ounce box of cereal will be less than $.22. The quantities have a negative relationship and a 22 ounce box weighs less than a 24 ounce box.

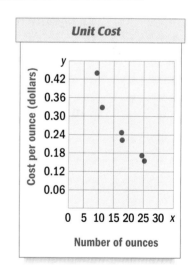

---

✓ **GUIDED PRACTICE**  for Example 2

Make a scatter plot of the data. Tell whether *x* and *y* have a *positive relationship*, a *negative relationship*, or *no relationship.*

**3.**

| x | 0 | 1 | 2 | 3 | 4 |
|---|---|---|---|---|---|
| y | 3 | 6 | 12 | 15 | 20 |

**4.**

| x | 5 | 10 | 15 | 20 | 25 |
|---|---|---|---|---|---|
| y | 24 | 18 | 25 | 15 | 22 |

# 11.2 EXERCISES

HOMEWORK KEY

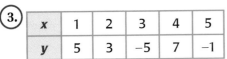

= TAKS Practice and Reasoning
Exs. 14, 19, 20, 21, 26, and 27

= HINTS AND HOMEWORK HELP
for Exs. 3, 7, 9, 19 at classzone.com

## SKILL PRACTICE

**1. VOCABULARY** What type of graph is a collection of ordered pairs?

**2. VOCABULARY** In what type of relationship do both coordinates increase?

**MAKING SCATTER PLOTS** Make a scatter plot of the data.

*SEE EXAMPLE 1*
on p. 588
for Exs. 3–4

**3.**

| x | 1 | 2 | 3 | 4 | 5 |
|---|---|---|---|---|---|
| y | 5 | 3 | −5 | 7 | −1 |

**4.**

| x | 1 | 2 | 3 | 4 | 5 |
|---|---|---|---|---|---|
| y | −2 | −1 | 0 | 1 | 2 |

**IDENTIFYING RELATIONSHIPS** Tell whether *x* and *y* have a *positive relationship*, a *negative relationship*, or *no relationship*.

*SEE EXAMPLE 2*
on p. 589
for Exs. 5–9

**5.**

**6.**

**7.**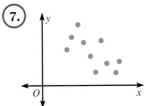

**INTERPRETING** Make a scatter plot of the data. Tell whether *x* and *y* have a *positive relationship*, a *negative relationship*, or *no relationship*.

**8.**

| x | 1 | 2 | 3 | 4 | 5 |
|---|---|---|---|---|---|
| y | 5 | 6 | 15 | 18 | 26 |

**9.**

| x | 3 | 4 | 5 | 6 | 7 |
|---|---|---|---|---|---|
| y | 3 | 6 | 10 | 7 | 16 |

**10. ERROR ANALYSIS** Describe and correct the error made in determining the relationship between the variables.

| x | −4 | −3 | −2 | −1 | 0 | 1 |
|---|----|----|----|----|---|---|
| y | 3 | 2 | 0 | 4 | 2 | 3 |

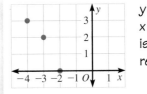

y decreases as x increases. There is a negative relationship.

**REASONING** Predict the type of relationship the data have. *Explain.*

**11.** The height of a student in 8th grade and a test score of the student

*TAKE NOTES*
As you work on the exercises, write down any questions you want to ask your teacher.

**12.** The size of a pizza and the price of a pizza

**13.** The amount of money you pay and the amount you still owe

**14.** 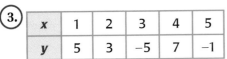 **TAKS REASONING** The variables *m* and *n* have a positive relationship. What conclusion can you make?

    **(A)** *m* is a function of *n*.
    **(B)** *n* is a function of *m*.
    **(C)** *n* increases as *m* increases.
    **(D)** *n* increases as *m* decreases.

**15. CHALLENGE** Make an input-output table for $y = (-1)^x$. Use the domain 0, 1, 2, 3, 4, 5, and 6. Then make a scatter plot of the data. What do you think the value of $y$ will be when $x = 500$? *Explain* your reasoning.

**In Exercises 16 and 17, use a scatter plot to estimate the value of the output when the input is 6.**

---

**EXTENSION** **Drawing Trend Lines**

**Basketball** The table relates the height of a basketball player and the average number of rebounds per game. Use a scatter plot to estimate the number of rebounds that a 78 inch tall player makes.

| Height (inches) | 76 | 77 | 79 | 80 | 83 | 84 |
|---|---|---|---|---|---|---|
| Average rebounds per game | 4.2 | 4 | 5.2 | 5.4 | 6.8 | 10 |

**SOLUTION**

Plot the data as shown. There appears to be a positive relationship. Use a ruler to draw a line showing the trend in the data.

The line appears to pass through (78, 4.8). You can estimate that a 78 inch tall player averages about 4.8 rebounds per game.

*Player Statistics*

---

**16.**

| Year | 1 | 9 | 15 | 19 | 32 |
|---|---|---|---|---|---|
| Mean winter temp. (°F) | 21 | 25 | 24 | 28 | 30 |

**17.**

| Week | 1 | 3 | 4 | 5 | 7 |
|---|---|---|---|---|---|
| Amount owed ($) | 30 | 25 | 20 | 16 | 5 |

---

## PROBLEM SOLVING

*SEE EXAMPLE 2*
on p. 589
for Ex. 18

**18. GUIDED PROBLEM SOLVING** The table shows the number of cookbooks sold at a bookstore in the first 6 years. Make a prediction about the number of cookbooks that will be sold in year 9.

| Year x | 1 | 2 | 3 | 4 | 5 | 6 |
|---|---|---|---|---|---|---|
| Books y | 450 | 650 | 700 | 800 | 1100 | 1250 |

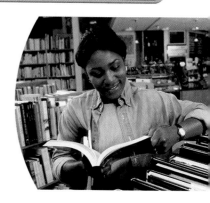

**a.** Make a scatter plot of the data.

**b.** Tell whether $x$ and $y$ have a *positive relationship*, a *negative relationship*, or *no relationship*.

**c.** In year 9, would you expect to sell *more than* or *fewer than* 1250 books?

**19.** ![Texas icon] **TAKS REASONING** *Describe* a real-world set of data that have a positive relationship at one time of the year and a negative relationship at a different time of the year.

*SEE EXAMPLE 2*
on p. 589
for Exs. 20–21

**20.** ![Texas icon] **TAKS REASONING** Make a scatter plot of the data at the right. *Describe* the relationship between the time spent studying for a test and the test score. *Predict* what will happen as study time continues to increase.

| Study time (hours) | Test score (percent) |
|---|---|
| 1 | 70 |
| 2 | 80 |
| 3 | 85 |

**21.** ![Texas icon] **TAKS REASONING** A scatter plot of the amount of bottled water sold each month from August through December shows a negative relationship. Which conclusion is valid based on the plot?

**(A)** the most water is sold in July

**(B)** as months pass, less water is sold

**(C)** the most water is sold in December

**(D)** as months pass, more water is sold

**22. REASONING** A table relates the time after which a vehicle starts traveling and its distance from point A. A scatter plot of the data shows a negative relationship. Is the vehicle traveling *toward* or *away from* point A? *Explain* your reasoning.

**23. WRITING** A newspaper claims there is a strong relationship between the weather on the day of an election and voter turnout. What do you think the newspaper means? Could the newspaper use a scatter plot to support its claim? If so, what would the labels on each axis be? *Explain*.

**24. GEOMETRY** Make a table showing the lengths and widths of four different rectangles with perimeters of 16 inches. Make a scatter plot of the data. Estimate the width of a rectangle when the length is 5.5 inches. *Explain* how you made your estimate.

**25. CHALLENGE** For the top eight teams during the regular season of the National Football League in 2004, there was a positive relationship between the average margin of victory (points scored − points allowed) and the number of wins. There was *no* relationship between points scored and number of wins. *Explain* how this is possible.

---

## MIXED REVIEW FOR TAKS

**TAKS** PRACTICE at classzone.com

*REVIEW*
Lesson 7.2;
TAKS Workbook

**26.** ![Texas icon] **TAKS PRACTICE** A scale drawing of a new train station shows a waiting room of length 20 centimeters. The actual length of the room is 75 feet. If the actual length of the information desk in the station is 4 feet, about how long will it be in the scale drawing? *TAKS Obj. 2*

**(A)** −51 cm     **(B)** 1.1 cm     **(C)** 1.6 cm     **(D)** 12 cm

*REVIEW*
Lesson 5.5;
TAKS Workbook

**27.** ![Texas icon] **TAKS PRACTICE** Which list shows the weights of four packages in order from greatest to least? *TAKS Obj. 1*

**(F)** 3.48 lb, 3.45 lb, 3.05 lb, 3.55 lb     **(G)** 3.55 lb, 3.48 lb, 3.45 lb, 3.05 lb

**(H)** 3.05 lb, 3.45 lb, 3.48 lb, 3.55 lb     **(J)** 3.55 lb, 3.05 lb, 3.48 lb, 3.45 lb

# 11.3 Equations in Two Variables

TEKS *8.4, 8.5.A*

| | |
|---|---|
| **Before** | You found solutions of equations in one variable. |
| **Now** | You'll find solutions of equations in two variables. |
| **Why?** | So you can find costs, such as rental costs in Example 1. |

**KEY VOCABULARY**
• solution of an equation in two variables, *p. 593*

A **solution of an equation in two variables** is an ordered pair whose values make the equation true. For example, (2, 3) is a solution of $x + y = 5$ because $2 + 3 = 5$.

**EXAMPLE 1** TAKS PRACTICE: Multiple Choice

> **In-line Skates** At a sports store, it costs $8 per hour to rent in-line skates plus $12 for the safety equipment. The total cost can be modeled by the equation $C = 12 + 8h$, where $C$ is the total cost in dollars and $h$ is the number of hours skated. Which table shows some possible total costs for renting in-line skates and safety equipment?

**ELIMINATE CHOICES**
You know that a one hour rental will cost $8 plus $12, or $20. So, you can eliminate choices A and B.

**(A)**

| Hours *h* | 1 | 2 | 3 | 4 |
|---|---|---|---|---|
| Cost *C* | $8 | $16 | $24 | $32 |

**(B)**

| Hours *h* | 1 | 2 | 3 | 4 |
|---|---|---|---|---|
| Cost *C* | $8 | $20 | $32 | $44 |

**(C)**

| Hours *h* | 1 | 2 | 3 | 4 |
|---|---|---|---|---|
| Cost *C* | $20 | $28 | $36 | $44 |

**(D)**

| Hours *h* | 1 | 2 | 3 | 4 |
|---|---|---|---|---|
| Cost *C* | $20 | $40 | $60 | $80 |

**SOLUTION**

Substitute several values of $h$ into the equation $C = 12 + 8h$ and solve for $C$. Then identify the table that contains the solutions.

| $h$-value | Substitute for $h$. | Evaluate. | Solution ($h$, $C$) |
|---|---|---|---|
| $h = 1$ | $C = 12 + 8(1)$ | $C = 20$ | (1, 20) |
| $h = 2$ | $C = 12 + 8(2)$ | $C = 28$ | (2, 28) |
| $h = 3$ | $C = 12 + 8(3)$ | $C = 36$ | (3, 36) |
| $h = 4$ | $C = 12 + 8(4)$ | $C = 44$ | (4, 44) |

▶ **Answer** The correct answer is C. (A) (B) (C) (D)

---

✓ **GUIDED PRACTICE** for Example 1

1. **What If?** In Example 1, the sports store will allow you to rent skates in 30 minute increments. About how much time can you skate if you have $41?

**EXAMPLE 2** Checking Solutions

**Tell whether $(7, -6)$ is a solution of $x + 3y = 14$.**

| | |
|---|---|
| $x + 3y = 14$ | Write original equation. |
| $7 + 3(-6) \stackrel{?}{=} 14$ | Substitute 7 for $x$ and $-6$ for $y$. |
| $7 + (-18) \stackrel{?}{=} 14$ | Simplify. |
| $-11 \neq 14$ ✗ | Solution does not check. |

▶ **Answer** The ordered pair $(7, -6)$ is *not* a solution of $x + 3y = 14$.

**Function Form** When you are finding solutions of an equation, it can be helpful to rewrite the equation in *function form*. To write an equation in function form, solve for $y$.

| Function form | Not function form |
|---|---|
| $y = -2x + 15$ | $2x + y = 15$ |

**EXAMPLE 3** Finding Solutions of an Equation

**Write the equation $4x + y = 15$ in function form. Then list four solutions.**

**SOLUTION**

**STEP 1** **Rewrite** the equation in function form.

| | |
|---|---|
| $4x + y = 15$ | Write original equation. |
| $y = 15 - 4x$ | Subtract $4x$ from each side. |

*SUBSTITUTE FOR X*
Generally, an equation involving two variables has an infinite number of solutions. When finding solutions, you can choose any $x$-value that is in the domain.

**STEP 2** **Choose** several values to substitute for $x$. Then solve for $y$.

| $x$-value | Substitute for $x$. | Evaluate. | Solution |
|---|---|---|---|
| $x = -1$ | $y = 15 - 4(-1)$ | $y = 19$ | $(-1, 19)$ |
| $x = 0$ | $y = 15 - 4(0)$ | $y = 15$ | $(0, 15)$ |
| $x = 1$ | $y = 15 - 4(1)$ | $y = 11$ | $(1, 11)$ |
| $x = 2$ | $y = 15 - 4(2)$ | $y = 7$ | $(2, 7)$ |

▶ **Answer** Four solutions are $(-1, 19)$, $(0, 15)$, $(1, 11)$, and $(2, 7)$.

✓ **GUIDED PRACTICE** for Examples 2 and 3

**Tell whether the ordered pair is a solution of the equation.**

**2.** $y = 3x - 7$; $(6, 5)$        **3.** $-2x - 4y = 12$; $(-4, -1)$

**List four solutions of the equation.**

**4.** $y = -2x + 6$        **5.** $3x + y = 4$

### SKILL PRACTICE

**VOCABULARY** Copy and complete the statement.

**1.** A(n) __?__ of an equation in two variables is an ordered pair.

**2.** When an equation is solved for $y$, the equation is in __?__ form.

**CALCULATING Y-VALUES** Copy and complete the table for the equation.

*SEE EXAMPLE 1*
on p. 593
for Exs. 3–5

**3.** $y = x + 8$

**4.** $y = 4 - 3x$

| $x$ | −5 | 0 | 5 | 10 |
|---|---|---|---|---|
| $y$ | ? | ? | ? | ? |

**5.** $y = -20 + x$

**CHECKING SOLUTIONS** Tell whether the ordered pair is a solution of the equation.

*SEE EXAMPLE 2*
on p. 594
for Exs. 6–13

**6.** $y = 4x + 2$; $(2, 10)$

**7.** $2x + y = 5$; $(7, 5)$

**8.** $y = 6 - x$; $(-3, 3)$

**9.** $x + 8y = 2$; $(10, -1)$

**10.** $y = 6x + 7$; $(2, 21)$

**11.** $3x - y = 26$; $(6, -8)$

**12. ERROR ANALYSIS** Describe and correct the error made in deciding whether $(-5, 4)$ is a solution of $2x + 3y = -7$.

$$2x + 3y = -7$$
$$2(4) + 3(-5) \stackrel{?}{=} -7$$
$$8 + (-15) \stackrel{?}{=} -7$$
$$-7 = -7 \checkmark \quad \text{So, } (-5, 4) \text{ is a solution.}$$

**13. 🔷 TAKS REASONING** Which ordered pair is a solution of $y = -3x + 11$?

**A** $(-2, 17)$    **B** $(0, -11)$    **C** $(2, 3)$    **D** $(-1, -14)$

**FINDING SOLUTIONS** List four solutions of the equation.

*SEE EXAMPLE 3*
on p. 594
for Exs. 14–31

**14.** $y = -2x + 5$

**15.** $y = -51 - 6x$

**16.** $16x + 24 = y$

**17.** $-5x + 3 = y$

**18.** $y = \frac{1}{2}x - 1$

**19.** $y = \frac{1}{3}x - 5$

**SOLVING FOR Y** Write the equation in function form. Then list four solutions of the equation.

**20.** $x + y = 8$

**21.** $42 = 4x + y$

**22.** $33 = -3x + y$

**23.** $5x + y = 10$

**24.** $12 = 3x + y$

**25.** $19 = -2x + y$

**26.** $4y = 8x + 12$

**27.** $5y + 15x = 10$

**28.** $-32 = 4x - 12y$

**29.** $8y = 16x - 10$

**30.** $-6y + 3x = 9$

**31.** $42 - 7y = 15x$

**32. EXAMPLES AND NONEXAMPLES** Give two ordered pairs that are solutions of the equation $-24 = 6x - y$ and two ordered pairs that are *not* solutions of the equation.

**33. ESTIMATION** Estimate the values of $9x$ and $8y$ for the ordered pair $\left(\frac{7}{3}, \frac{5}{8}\right)$. *Explain* why the ordered pair cannot be a solution of $9x + 8y = 16$.

**WRITING EQUATIONS** Write an equation for the values in the table. Then list four solutions with $x$-values greater than 100.

**34.**

| x | −1 | 0 | 1 | 2 |
|---|----|----|----|----|
| y | 2 | 4 | 6 | 8 |

**35.**

| x | 0 | 2 | 4 | 6 |
|---|----|----|----|----|
| y | 2 | 3 | 4 | 5 |

**36.**

| x | −1 | 0 | 1 | 2 |
|---|----|----|----|----|
| y | −8 | −5 | −2 | 1 |

**37.**

| x | 0 | 4 | 8 | 12 |
|---|----|----|----|----|
| y | 6 | 7 | 8 | 9 |

**CHALLENGE** Find the ordered pair that is a solution of both equations.

**38.** $y = -2x + 3$
$y = 0.5x - 2$

**39.** $y = 6x - 10$
$y = -3x + 26$

**40.** $x + 2y = 4$
$x + y = -2$

**41.** $-x - 4y = 4$
$x - 2y = 14$

---

## PROBLEM SOLVING

**SEE EXAMPLE 1**
on p. 593
for Exs. 42–44

**42. LOAN** Your friend agrees to lend you $15 to buy a model rocket. You promise to pay your friend $2.50 each week until you have paid back the full $15. Use the equation $P = 15 - 2.5n$, where $P$ is the number of dollars that you have left to pay and $n$ is the number of weeks. Find the number of weeks it takes to pay back your friend.

**43. SKATEBOARD WHEELS** Your skateboard club decides to replace each club member's wheels for a competition. A set of four wheels sells for $24 plus a $14 shipping and handling cost.

a. Use the equation $C = 24n + 14$, where $C$ is the total cost in dollars and $n$ is the number of sets of wheels ordered. What is the total cost of 4 sets of wheels?

b. The total cost of your club's order is $182. How many sets of wheels are purchased?

c. Suppose your club doubles the order. Will the total cost be $364 ($182 × 2)? *Explain*.

**44. TAKS REASONING** You pay $25 to join the summer movie club at your local theater. Each movie you see costs only $3. You can model this situation with the equation $C = 25 + 3m$, where $C$ is the total cost in dollars and $m$ is the number of movies you see. You have $60 to spend on the movie club. What is the greatest number of movies you can see?

(A) 10 movies    (B) 11 movies    (C) 28 movies    (D) 205 movies

**45. WRITING** *Explain* why it can be helpful to rewrite equations in function form when finding solutions of an equation.

**46. GLASS ELEVATOR** A glass elevator is at a height of 1200 feet. It is descending at a rate of 1000 feet per minute.

    **a.** Use the equation $h = 1200 - 1000m$, where $h$ is the height of the elevator in feet and $m$ is the time in minutes. What is the height of the elevator after 1 minute?

    **b.** How long, in minutes and seconds, will it take the elevator to reach a height of 0 feet?

**47. ✦ TAKS REASONING** You want to buy $x$ bottles of water and $y$ bottles of sports drink. Each bottle of water costs $1 and each bottle of sports drink costs $2. You have $9. Write an equation in two variables to model the total cost. Can you buy 3 bottles of sports drink and 4 bottles of water? *Explain*.

**48. REASONING** In Example 3 on page 594, you solved the equation for $y$ before substituting the $x$-values. Will you get the same solutions if you substitute the $x$-values before solving for $y$? *Justify* your reasoning.

**49. CARNIVAL** You have 2 hours to spend at a carnival where you plan to go on rides and play games. You know that each ride takes about 10 minutes, including the wait in line. Write an equation in two variables to model this situation, where $x$ is the number of rides and $y$ is the number of minutes spent playing games. You plan to go on 8 rides. How long can you play games?

**50. ⓧⓨ ALGEBRA** Write the equation $ax + by = c$ in function form.

**51. CHALLENGE** As part of a class project, you simulate a dog walking-and-feeding service. In week one, you charge $2 per walk and $4 per meal. In week two, you charge $4 per walk and $2 per meal. In week three, you charge $4 per walk and $4 per meal. You collect $38, $40, and $52 respectively for the three weeks. Each week had the same combination of walks and meals. Find the numbers of walks and meals per week.

## MIXED REVIEW FOR TAKS

**TAKS** PRACTICE at classzone.com

*REVIEW*
Lesson 10.6;
TAKS Workbook

**52. ✦ TAKS PRACTICE** Which of the following statements is true of the prisms? *TAKS Obj. 6*

    Prism A

    Prism B

    Ⓐ Prism A and Prism B have equal volumes.

    Ⓑ Prism A and Prism B have equal surface areas.

    Ⓒ Prism A has a greater surface area than Prism B.

    Ⓓ Prism B has a greater surface area than Prism A.

*REVIEW*
Lesson 7.1;
TAKS Workbook

**53. ✦ TAKS PRACTICE** Ms. Levy bought 6.5 pounds of peaches for $5.72. What was the price per pound? *TAKS Obj. 2*

    Ⓕ $0.09        Ⓖ $0.88        Ⓗ $0.94        Ⓙ $36.53

# 11.4 Graphs of Linear Equations

TEKS *8.4, 8.7.D*

| Before | You found solutions of equations in two variables. |
| Now | You'll learn to sketch the graph of a linear equation. |
| Why? | So you can recognize linear patterns, as in Ex. 42. |

**KEY VOCABULARY**
• linear equation,
  *p. 598*

## ACTIVITY

**You can graph a function by plotting ordered pairs from a table.**

**STEP 1** **Copy** and complete the table of values using the equation $y = 3x + 2$.

| x | −4 | −2 | 0 | 2 | 4 |
|---|----|----|---|---|---|
| y | −10 | ? | ? | ? | ? |

**STEP 2** **Plot** each ordered pair $(x, y)$ from the table in a coordinate plane like the one shown.

$(−4, −10), (−2, ?), (0, ?), (2, ?), (4, ?)$.

**STEP 3** **Connect** the points. What pattern do you notice?

**STEP 4** **Find** several more solutions of $y = 3x + 2$. Locate each solution in your coordinate plane. What do you notice?

**STEP 5** **Make** a conjecture about the graph of all solutions of $y = 3x + 2$.

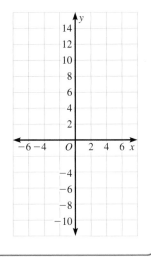

**Linear Equations** In the activity, you graphed solutions of a *linear equation*. A **linear equation** in two variables has the two variables in separate terms with each variable occurring only to the first power. The graph is a line.

| Linear equations | Not linear equations |
|---|---|
| $y = x − 1$ | $24 = rt$ |
| $3p + 5q = 16$ | $a^2 + b^2 = c^2$ |
| $s = 0.2t$ | |

The equation $24 = rt$ is not linear because it has two variables in the same term. The equation $a^2 + b^2 = c^2$ is not linear because the variables are squared.

**EXAMPLE 1** Graphing a Linear Equation

**Graph $y = \frac{1}{2}x + 1$.**

**STEP 1** **Choose** several values to substitute for $x$. Then evaluate to find $y$ and make a table of values.

| $x$ | $-4$ | $-2$ | $0$ | $2$ | $4$ |
|---|---|---|---|---|---|
| $y$ | $-1$ | $0$ | $1$ | $2$ | $3$ |

**STEP 2** **List** the solutions as ordered pairs.
$(-4, -1)$, $(-2, 0)$, $(0, 1)$, $(2, 2)$, $(4, 3)$

**READING GRAPHS**

The arrowheads on the graph in Example 1 indicate that the line extends forever in both directions.

**STEP 3** **Plot** the ordered pairs and draw a line through them. The line is the graph of $y = \frac{1}{2}x + 1$.

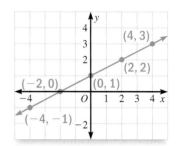

**Animated Math** at classzone.com

---

**EXAMPLE 2** Using the Graph of a Linear Equation

**Growth Rate** Sue's hair is 3 inches long and grows $\frac{1}{2}$ inch per month. The length $l$, in inches, of her hair can be modeled by the equation $l = \frac{1}{2}m + 3$, where $m$ is the time in months. Use a graph to estimate how long it will take Sue to grow her hair to a length of $5\frac{1}{2}$ inches.

**SOLUTION**

Make a table of values and plot each solution. Draw a ray through the points. Then locate the point on the ray where $l = 5\frac{1}{2}$.

**AVOID ERRORS**

In real-world contexts, be sure to choose domain values that make sense in real-world situations. In Example 2, the domain should include only positive numbers.

| $m$ | $0$ | $1$ | $2$ | $3$ |
|---|---|---|---|---|
| $l$ | $3$ | $3\frac{1}{2}$ | $4$ | $4\frac{1}{2}$ |

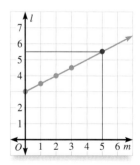

▶ **Answer** The graph shows that it will take about 5 months for Sue to grow her hair to a length of $5\frac{1}{2}$ inches.

---

✓ **GUIDED PRACTICE**  for Examples 1 and 2

**Graph the linear equation.**

**1.** $y = x + 4$    **2.** $y = x + 6$    **3.** $y = \frac{1}{2}x - 7$    **4.** $y = -2x - 3$

**5. What If?** In Example 2, suppose Sue's hair is 4 inches long. The length $l$, in inches, of her hair can be modeled by the equation $l = \frac{1}{2}m + 4$, where $m$ is the time in months. Use a graph to estimate how long it will take Sue to grow her hair to a length of $5\frac{1}{2}$ inches.

**Vertical and Horizontal Lines** Some linear equations have only one variable. The graphs of these equations are vertical or horizontal lines.

> **KEY CONCEPT** *For Your Notebook*
>
> **Vertical and Horizontal Lines**
>
> The graph of $x = a$ is the vertical line passing through $(a, 0)$.
>
> The graph of $y = b$ is the horizontal line passing through $(0, b)$.

**EXAMPLE 3** **Graphing Vertical and Horizontal Lines**

*AVOID ERRORS*
The graph of a linear equation may not be a function. A vertical line does *not* represent a function, because one input has infinitely many outputs. A horizontal line *does* represent a function.

**a.** The graph of $x = -2$ is the vertical line through $(-2, 0)$.

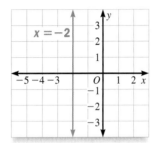

For all values of $y$, the $x$-value is $-2$.

**b.** The graph of $y = 4$ is the horizontal line through $(0, 4)$.

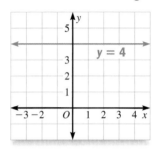

For all values of $x$, the $y$-value is 4.

✓ **GUIDED PRACTICE** **for Example 3**

**6.** Graph $y = -3$.

**7.** Graph $x = 1$.

# 11.4 EXERCISES

HOMEWORK KEY
 = **TAKS Practice and Reasoning**
Exs. 6, 42, 43, 50, and 51

○ = **HINTS AND HOMEWORK HELP**
for Exs. 3, 13, 15, 17, 41 at classzone.com

> **SKILL PRACTICE**

1. **VOCABULARY** Copy and complete: The graph of the solutions of a linear equation is a(n) __?__ .

**VOCABULARY** Tell whether the equation is a linear equation.

**2.** $3x + y = 8$     **3.** $2y - 5x = 10$     **4.** $9x^2 = y + 4$     **5.** $y = -4$

*SEE EXAMPLE 1*
on p. 599
for Ex. 6

**6.** ◤ **TAKS REASONING** Which equation's graph includes the point $(0, 0)$?

**A** $y = \frac{1}{2}x + 6$     **B** $2x + 3y = 6$     **C** $y = \frac{1}{2}x$     **D** $2x = 6 - 3y$

**GRAPHING WITH TWO VARIABLES** Graph the linear equation.

**SEE EXAMPLE 1**
on p. 599
for Exs. 7–15

**7.** $y = x + 9$         **8.** $y = x - 14$         **9.** $y = x - 17$

**10.** $y = -2x + 1$     **11.** $y = -4x + 8$     **12.** $y = 8x$

**13.** $y = -3x$        **14.** $y = \frac{1}{2}x + 5$      **15.** $y = -\frac{1}{4}x + 12$

**GRAPHING WITH ONE VARIABLE** Graph the vertical or horizontal line.

**SEE EXAMPLE 3**
on p. 600
for Exs. 16–22

**16.** $x = 2$         **17.** $y = 6$         **18.** $y = -9$

**19.** $y = -1.5$      **20.** $x = 1.5$      **21.** $x = 3.5$

**22. ERROR ANALYSIS** A student says that the equation of the line shown at the right is $y = 5$. Describe and correct the error made in the student's statement.

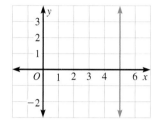

**SOLVING FOR Y** Solve the linear equation for $y$ and then graph.

**23.** $16x - 4y = 8$      **24.** $9x + 3y = 18$      **25.** $10x = -2y$

**WRITING EQUATIONS** Write the equation of the line.

**26.**     **27.**     **28.**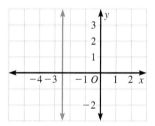

**COMPARING GRAPHS** Graph the equations in Exercises 29–32 in the same coordinate plane. How are the graphs alike? How are they different?

**29.** $y = x$       **30.** $y = x + 7$       **31.** $y = x - 5$       **32.** $y = x - 9$

**COMPARING GRAPHS** Graph the equations in Exercises 33–36 in the same coordinate plane. How are the graphs alike? How are they different?

**33.** $y = x$       **34.** $y = 3x$       **35.** $y = -x$       **36.** $y = -4x$

**CHALLENGE** Write the equation of the line.

**37.**     **38.**     **39.**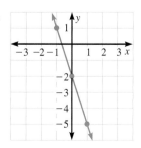

**SEE EXAMPLE 2**
on p. 599
for Exs. 40–41

**40. PHOTOGRAPHY** You need a digital camera for a photography class. The payment plan for the camera can be modeled by the equation $C = 10m + 50$, where $C$ is the total cost, in dollars, and $m$ is the number of months. Graph the equation and use your graph to estimate how much you pay in 12 months.

**41. SAVINGS** Janet is saving money for a trip. She has $80 saved and plans to add $15.50 to her savings each month. This situation can be modeled by the equation $y = 15.50x + 80$, where $y$ is the amount of money saved and $x$ is the number of months. Graph the equation and use your graph to estimate when Janet will have $250.

**42. ✦ TAKS REASONING** A deep-sea diver is 160 feet below the surface of the water. The diver is ascending at a rate of 20 feet every 4 minutes.

| Time (minutes) | 4 | 8 | 12 | 16 |
|---|---|---|---|---|
| Depth (feet) | ? | ? | ? | ? |

a. Copy and complete the table.

b. Is the relationship between depth and time linear? *Explain.*

**43. ✦ TAKS REASONING** The total cost $C$ of a cell phone plan with unlimited minutes $m$ is $40 a month. Which equation models this situation?

**(A)** $C = 40$      **(B)** $m = 40$      **(C)** $C = 40m$      **(D)** $m = 40C$

**READING IN MATH** **Read the information below for Exercises 44–46.**

**Temperature** Temperature can be measured in degrees Fahrenheit or degrees Celsius. On the Fahrenheit scale, the difference between the freezing point and boiling point of water is 180°. On the Celsius scale, the difference is 100°.

Because these differences represent the same change in temperature, every change of 9°F equals a change of 5°C. This ratio appears in fraction form in the formula for changing degrees Celsius to degrees Fahrenheit: $F = \frac{9}{5}C + 32$.

| Common Temperatures | |
|---|---|
| Freezing point of water | 32°F |
| Ideal room temperature | 70°F |
| Normal body temperature | 98.6°F |
| Boiling point of water | 212°F |

**44. Graph** Graph the equation that relates degrees Celsius to degrees Fahrenheit. Use $C = 0°, 10°, 20°, 30°,$ and $40°$ in your table of values.

**45. Interpret** Use the Common Temperatures table and your graph. Approximate the normal body temperature in degrees Celsius.

**46. Analyze** Is 10°C *warmer* or *colder* than room temperature? *Explain* how you can use your graph to answer this question.

    ✦ = **TAKS Practice and Reasoning**     ◯ = **HINTS AND HOMEWORK HELP** *at classzone.com*

47. ◆ **MULTIPLE REPRESENTATIONS** Max teaches youth swimming lessons. He starts students with 1 minute of treading water and then adds 2 minutes each month.

   a. **Write an Equation** Model this situation with an equation, where $y$ is the total time spent treading water and $x$ is the number of months.

   b. **Draw a Graph** Graph the equation and estimate the number of months it will take for the students to tread water for 13 minutes.

   c. **Evaluate Results** Use your equation from part (a) to confirm the estimate you made in part (b).

48. **REASONING** *Explain* how to find the equation of a line that is parallel to the $x$-axis and lies 8.6 units below it.

49. **CHALLENGE** Jared's age $j$ is seven years more than his sister Karen's age $k$. Write and graph an equation in two variables to model this situation. *Explain* how to use your graph to find out how old they will be when Jared is twice as old as Karen.

━━━━━ **MIXED REVIEW FOR TAKS** ━━━━━ **TAKS** **PRACTICE** at classzone.com

*REVIEW*
Lesson 11.1;
TAKS Workbook

50. ◆ **TAKS REASONING** An arithmetic sequence is shown. The term in position 1 is 5. Which expression can be used to find a term in the sequence whose position is represented by $n$? *TAKS Obj. 2*

| Position in Sequence | 1 | 2 | 3 | 4 | $n$ |
|---|---|---|---|---|---|
| Term | 5 | 7 | 9 | 11 | ? |

   **(A)** $n + 4$       **(B)** $n + 2$       **(C)** $2n + 3$       **(D)** $3n + 2$

*REVIEW*
Lesson 10.7;
TAKS Workbook

51. ◆ **TAKS PRACTICE** A cone has a height of 11 centimeters and a radius of 6 centimeters. Which is closest to the volume of the cone? *TAKS Obj. 4*

   **(F)** $69.1 \text{ cm}^3$       **(G)** $132 \text{ cm}^3$       **(H)** $414.7 \text{ cm}^3$       **(J)** $622 \text{ cm}^3$

**QUIZ** *for Lessons 11.1–11.4*

1. Make an input-output table for $y = -\frac{1}{3}x$. Use the domain 0, 1, 2, and 3. Identify the range. *(p. 583)*

**List three solutions of the equation. Then graph the equation.** *(pp. 593, 598)*

2. $7y + x = 21$       3. $-5x - 2y = -20$       4. $-3x + 9y = -18$

**Write a function rule that relates $x$ and $y$.** *(p. 583)*

5. $(-2, 0), (-1, 1), (0, 2), (1, 3), (2, 4)$       6. $(-3, -5), (0, 1), (3, 7), (6, 13), (9, 19)$

7. **FUNDRAISING** An art club raised $120 for supplies by selling pottery. Mugs cost $4 and bowls cost $2. Graph the equation $4x + 2y = 120$, where $x$ is the number of mugs sold and $y$ is the number of bowls sold. Is there a *positive relationship*, a *negative relationship*, or *no relationship* between number of mugs sold and number of bowls sold? *Explain.* *(pp. 588, 598)*

**TEKS** *8.4*

# 11.4 Graphing Linear Functions

**EXAMPLE** Use a calculator to graph $x - 2y = 6$.

**SOLUTION**

**STEP 1** **Rewrite** the equation so that it is in function form: $y = \frac{1}{2}x - 3$.

**STEP 2** **Use** the following keystrokes on a graphing calculator to enter the function:

**Keystrokes**

  1  2

x — 3

**Display**

```
Y1■(1/2)X-3
Y2=
Y3=
Y4=
```

**STEP 3** **Use** the WINDOW feature to set the viewing window for the graph. Then view the graph by pressing the GRAPH button.

```
WINDOW
 Xmin=-5
 Xmax=10
 △X=.1595...
 Xscl=1
 Ymin=-5
 Ymax=5
 Yscl=1
```

**PRACTICE** Use a calculator to graph the equation.

**1.** $y = 2x - 5$    **2.** $y = -x + 10$    **3.** $x - y = 11$    **4.** $x + y = 6$

**Tell whether the viewing window is appropriate for the graph of the equation. If not, give an appropriate window.**

**5.** $y = 4x + 5$
```
Xmin=-5
Xmax=5
△X=.1063...
Ymin=-5
Ymax=5
```

**6.** $y = 2x + 14$
```
Xmin=-5
Xmax=5
△X=.1063...
Ymin=-5
Ymax=5
```

## Lessons 11.1–11.4

**MULTIPLE CHOICE**

1. **HOT-AIR BALLOONS** A hot-air balloon is 5 feet off the ground and starts rising at a rate of 2 feet per second. The height *h*, in feet, of the balloon can be modeled by the equation $h = 5 + 2t$, where *t* is the time in seconds. Approximately how many seconds will it take for the balloon to be 8 feet off the ground? *TEKS 8.5.A*

   (A) 0.2 sec      (B) 0.7 sec

   (C) 1.5 sec      (D) 6.5 sec

2. **RUNNING** The table below shows the number of miles you run in the first four weeks of training for a 10-mile race.

   | Week *w* | 1 | 2 | 3 | 4 |
   |---|---|---|---|---|
   | Distance *d* (miles) | 3 | 3.5 | 4 | 4.5 |

   If this pattern continues, how many weeks will you need to train to run 10 miles? *TEKS 8.5.A*

   (F) 5 weeks      (G) 7.5 weeks

   (H) 8 weeks      (J) 15 weeks

3. **LAUNDRY** An electric clothes dryer costs $300 and uses $.43 worth of electricity per hour. Each load of laundry takes 45 minutes to dry. What is the total cost of drying the first 200 loads of laundry, including the initial cost of purchasing the dryer? *TEKS 8.2.B*

   (A) $300.32      (B) $357.60

   (C) $364.50      (D) $386.00

4. **CARS** A car moving at 8 feet per second begins increasing speed by 4 feet per second each second. How many seconds will it take for the car to reach a speed of 60 miles per hour? *TEKS 8.14.A*

   (F) 5 sec      (G) 10 sec

   (H) 13 sec      (J) 20 sec

5. **DVD PLAYER** Lou and Jo each save money to buy the DVD player shown. Lou already has $36 saved. He will add $2 per week to his fund. Jo has no money saved. She will put $5 in her fund each week until she can afford it.

   The first person to save the necessary amount will have how much more money than the other person at that time? *TEKS 8.5.A*

   (A) $6      (B) $8

   (C) $30      (D) $52

6. **LINES** Which point does NOT lie on the line $y = 6x + 2$? *TEKS 8.16.B*

   (F) (1, 8)      (G) (−1, −4)

   (H) (0, 2)      (J) (−2, 10)

**GRIDDED ANSWER** ⊙①②③④⑤⑥⑦⑧⑨

7. **MODEL PLANES** A $45 model plane requires $8 of new batteries each month. The total cost *C*, in dollars, is $C = 45 + 8m$, where *m* is the number of months. You receive a gift of $25 to put toward the purchase and operation of the plane. How much more money, in dollars, will you need for the plane in the first year? *TEKS 8.5.A*

# 11.5 Using Intercepts

TEKS *8.4, 8.5.A*

| Before | You graphed linear equations. |
| Now | You'll find *x*- and *y*-intercepts of lines. |
| Why? | So you can find options for exercising, as in Example 3. |

**KEY VOCABULARY**
• *x*-intercept, *p. 606*
• *y*-intercept, *p. 606*

The **x-intercept** of a graph is the *x*-coordinate of the point where the graph crosses the *x*-axis. The graph of $2x + 3y = 12$ crosses the *x*-axis at (6, 0), so its *x*-intercept is 6.

The **y-intercept** of a graph is the *y*-coordinate of the point where the graph intersects the *y*-axis. The graph of $2x + 3y = 12$ crosses the *y*-axis at (0, 4), so its *y*-intercept is 4.

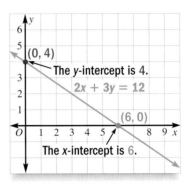

The *y*-intercept is 4.
$2x + 3y = 12$
The *x*-intercept is 6.

---

**KEY CONCEPT**                    *For Your Notebook*

## Finding Intercepts

**x-intercept**   To find the *x*-intercept of a graph, substitute 0 for *y* into the equation of the line and solve for *x*.

**y-intercept**   To find the *y*-intercept of a graph, substitute 0 for *x* into the equation of the line and solve for *y*.

---

**EXAMPLE 1**   Finding Intercepts

Find the intercepts of the graph of $y = \frac{1}{2}x - 5$.

**STEP 1**  To find the *x*-intercept, let $y = 0$ and solve for *x*.

$$y = \frac{1}{2}x - 5$$

$$0 = \frac{1}{2}x - 5$$

$$5 = \frac{1}{2}x$$

$$10 = x$$

**STEP 2**  To find the *y*-intercept, let $x = 0$ and solve for *y*.

$$y = \frac{1}{2}x - 5$$

$$y = \frac{1}{2}(0) - 5$$

$$y = 0 - 5$$

$$y = -5$$

▶ **Answer**  The *x*-intercept is 10 and the *y*-intercept is −5. The graph of the equation crosses the *x*-axis at (10, 0) and the *y*-axis at (0, −5).

**Graphing Lines** The intercepts indicate the points where a line intersects the *x*-axis and the *y*-axis. You can use these points to graph a line.

## EXAMPLE 2 Using Intercepts to Graph a Line

**Graph the line with an *x*-intercept of −3 and a *y*-intercept of 2.**

The *x*-intercept is −3, so plot the point $(-3, 0)$. The *y*-intercept is 2, so plot the point $(0, 2)$. Then draw a line through the two points.

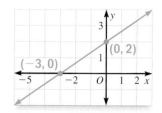

## EXAMPLE 3 Using and Interpreting Intercepts

**Fitness** Deena runs and walks with her dog on a trail that is 8 miles long. She can run 4 miles per hour and walk 2 miles per hour. Graph the equation $4x + 2y = 8$, where *x* is the number of hours she runs and *y* is the number of hours she walks. What do the intercepts represent?

### SOLUTION

**STEP 1** Find the *x*-intercept.

$$4x + 2y = 8$$
$$4x + 2(0) = 8$$
$$4x = 8$$
$$x = 2$$

**STEP 2** Find the *y*-intercept.

$$4x + 2y = 8$$
$$4(0) + 2y = 8$$
$$2y = 8$$
$$y = 4$$

**STEP 3** The *x*-intercept is 2 and the *y*-intercept is 4. So the points $(2, 0)$ and $(0, 4)$ are on the graph. Plot these points and draw a line through them.

▶ **Answer** The *x*-intercept represents the number of hours it takes Deena to run the entire time. The *y*-intercept represents the number of hours it takes Deena to walk the entire time.

✓ **GUIDED PRACTICE** for Examples 1, 2, and 3

**Find the intercepts of the graph of the equation. Then graph the line using the intercepts.**

**1.** $y = 2x - 10$　　　　**2.** $3x + y = -1$　　　　**3.** $5x + 3y = 18$

**4. What If?** In Example 3, suppose Deena runs and walks with her dog on a trail that is 12 miles long. Graph the equation $4x + 2y = 12$, where *x* is the number of hours she runs and *y* is the number of hours she walks. How are the intercepts affected by the change in the trail length?

# 11.5 EXERCISES

HOMEWORK KEY

✦ = TAKS Practice and Reasoning
Exs. 9, 31, 34, and 36

◯ = HINTS AND HOMEWORK HELP
for Exs. 5, 13, 15, 31 at classzone.com

## SKILL PRACTICE

**VOCABULARY** Identify the *x*-intercept and the *y*-intercept.

**1.**

**2.**

**FINDING INTERCEPTS** Find the intercepts of the graph of the equation.

*SEE EXAMPLE 1*
on p. 606
for Exs. 3–10

**3.** $y = 6x - 3$

**4.** $x + 4y = 12$

**5.** $5x - 2y = 10$

**6.** $x + 9y = 18$

**7.** $4x + 5y = 20$

**8.** $7x - 9y = -63$

**9.** ✦ **TAKS REASONING** What is the *y*-intercept of the graph of $2x - y = 4$?

**Ⓐ** $-4$      **Ⓑ** $-1$      **Ⓒ** $2$      **Ⓓ** $4$

**10. ERROR ANALYSIS** Describe and correct the error made in finding the intercepts of the graph of $4x - 3y = 12$.

$$4x - 3y = 12$$
$$4(0) - 3(0) \stackrel{?}{=} 12$$
$$0 \neq 12 \text{ There are no intercepts.}$$

**GRAPHING WITH INTERCEPTS** Graph the line that has the given intercepts.

*SEE EXAMPLE 2*
on p. 607
for Exs. 11–13

**11.** *x*-intercept: 9
*y*-intercept: 4

**12.** *x*-intercept: $-3$
*y*-intercept: 1

**13.** *x*-intercept: 6
*y*-intercept: $-10$

**FINDING INTERCEPTS TO GRAPH** Find the intercepts of the graph of the equation. Then graph the equation.

*SEE EXAMPLES 1 AND 2*
on p. 607
for Exs. 14–19

**14.** $y = 5x - 15$

**15.** $y = -2x + 7$

**16.** $8x + 10y = 30$

**17.** $7.5x + 3y = 19.5$

**18.** $-\frac{3}{4}x + y = -\frac{1}{2}$

**19.** $-\frac{1}{6}x + \frac{1}{3}y = \frac{1}{3}$

**COMPARING INTERCEPTS** Tell which intercept(s), if any, of the graphs of the two equations are equal.

**20.** $x + 2y = 5$
$x - 2y = 5$

**21.** $3x - 2y = 6$
$-3x - 2y = 6$

**22.** $7x + 5y = 35$
$7x + 5y = -35$

**FINDING INTERCEPTS** Find the intercepts of the graph of the equation.

**23.** $y = 9$

**24.** $y = 14$

**25.** $x = 21$

**CHALLENGE** Graph the line and its reflection in the given axis. *Describe how the intercepts change due to the reflection.*

**26.** $-3x + y = 12$; *x*-axis

**27.** $-4x + 6y = 20$; *x*-axis

**28.** $3x - 8y = 32$; *y*-axis

**SEE EXAMPLE 3**
on p. 607
for Exs. 29–31

**29. GUIDED PROBLEM SOLVING** You have $60 to spend. CDs are $12 each and videos are $10 each. The equation $12x + 10y = 60$ models this situation. Graph the equation and explain what the intercepts represent.

   **a.** Decide what $x$ and $y$ represent in the equation.

   **b.** Find the intercepts. Then graph the equation.

   **c.** *Explain* what the intercepts represent in this situation.

**30. PRIZES** You need to buy 12 prizes for a school contest. T-shirts come in packs of 4, and DVD gift certificates come in packs of 2. The number of packs you can buy of each item is represented by the equation $4x + 2y = 12$. What does the $x$-intercept tell you in this situation?

**31. TAKS REASONING** You are riding the bus home from school. After $x$ minutes, the number of miles from home $y$ is given by $2x + 3y = 18$. Find the intercepts. Then graph the equation. *Explain* what the points along the graph and the intercepts represent.

**32. WRITING** Do all graphs of linear equations have a $y$-intercept? *Explain* why or why not.

**33. REASONING** The $x$-intercept of a line is positive and the $y$-intercept is negative. Does the line slant *up* or *down* from left to right? Through which quadrant(s) does the line pass? *Explain* your reasoning.

**34. TAKS REASONING** A bank offers a savings account at a 2% simple interest rate and a certificate of deposit at a 5% simple interest rate. The equation $0.02s + 0.05c = 100$ models ways to earn $100 in interest in 1 year. What do the intercepts represent in this situation? *Describe* one way you can invest $3500 and earn exactly $100 interest.

**35. CHALLENGE** Find the intercepts of the graphs of $y = 0.5x$, $y = 3x$, and $y = 5x$. Using your results, write a conjecture about the intercepts and the graph of $y = kx$, where $k$ is a nonzero number. *Justify* your reasoning.

**MIXED REVIEW FOR TAKS**

**TAKS PRACTICE** at classzone.com

**REVIEW**
Lesson 11.4;
TAKS Workbook

**36. TAKS PRACTICE** Which equation could be used to generate the table of values at the right? *TAKS Obj. 2*

   **(A)** $y = x + 2$

   **(B)** $y = x + 4$

   **(C)** $y = 2x - 4$

   **(D)** $y = 2x + 4$

| x | y |
|---|---|
| 0 | 4 |
| 1 | 6 |
| 2 | 8 |
| 3 | 10 |

**GOAL**
Understand slope as a measure of steepness.

**MATERIALS**
• pencil
• straightedge
• graph paper

**TEKS** *8.7.D, 8.16.A*

# 11.6 Finding the Slope of a Line

You can describe the steepness of a line using its *slope,* or ratio of vertical change (rise) to horizontal change (run) between any two points on a line. You can find the slope using the formula $slope = \dfrac{rise}{run}$.

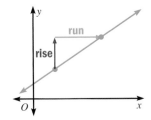

**EXPLORE 1** **Find the slope of the line passing through the points (3, 3) and (7, 5).**

**STEP 1** **Plot** the points (3, 3) and (7, 5) in a coordinate plane. Draw a line through the points.

**STEP 2** **Find** the rise. Then find the run. Substitute for rise and run in the formula for slope.

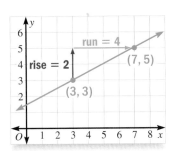

$$slope = \frac{rise}{run} = \frac{2}{4} = \frac{1}{2}$$

The slope of the line passing through the points (3, 3) and (7, 5) is $\dfrac{1}{2}$.

**PRACTICE** **Use the formula for slope.**

1. Find the slope of the line passing through the points (−1, 1) and (−3, 5). Follow the same steps as in Explore 1.

   • Plot the points (−1, 1) and (−3, 5) in a coordinate plane. Draw a line through the points.

   • Find the rise. Then find the run. Substitute for rise and run in the formula for slope.

2. Using the same points, (−1, 1) and (−3, 5), what operation can you perform on the *y*-coordinates to find the rise? What operation can you perform on the *x*-coordinates to find the run?

3. Find the slope of the line passing through the points (5, 6) and (−2, 3).

## EXPLORE 2  Use two points to find the slope of a line.

**STEP 1** **Copy** the graph at the right.

**STEP 2** **Choose** two points on the line. Find the rise and run. Calculate the slope.

**STEP 3** **Choose** a different pair of points on the line. Find the rise and run. Calculate the slope.

**STEP 4** **Describe** a pattern in your answers to Steps 2 and 3. Make a conjecture about the slope of a line.

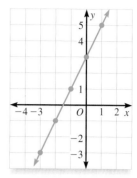

## PRACTICE  Find the slope of the line passing through the points.

**4.** $(1, 4)$, $(4, 2)$

**5.** $(1, -3)$, $(5, -2)$

**6.** $(-3, 4)$, $(0, 6)$

**7.** $(7, 8)$, $(-1, -5)$

**8.** $(-2, 6)$, $(0, -3)$

**9.** $(-9, 3)$, $(3, -9)$

**10.** If a line slants down from left to right, what can you say about the rise and run?

**11.** If a line slants up from left to right, what can you say about the rise and run?

**12.** *Compare* a line that has a slope greater than 1 with a line that has a slope between 0 and 1.

**Find the slope of the line.**

**13.**

**14.**

**15.**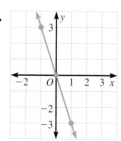

## DRAW CONCLUSIONS

**16.** **REASONING** What is the slope of the line passing through the points $(a, b)$ and $(c, d)$?

# 11.6 Slope

TEKS 8.7.D, 8.14.A

| | |
|---|---|
| **Before** | You graphed linear equations. |
| **Now** | You'll find and interpret slopes of lines. |
| **Why?** | So you can describe steepness, as of a railway in Example 1. |

**KEY VOCABULARY**
- **slope,** *p. 612*
- **rise,** *p. 612*
- **run,** *p. 612*

**Cogwheel Railway** The Mount Pilatus Railway in the Swiss Alps is the steepest cogwheel railway in the world. The track rises about 20 feet vertically for every 50 feet it runs horizontally. How can you describe the steepness of the track?

You can describe steepness using *slope*. The **slope** of a nonvertical line is the ratio of its vertical change, the **rise**, to its horizontal change, the **run**.

## EXAMPLE 1  Finding Slope

The diagram shows the rise and the run of the Mount Pilatus Railway described above.

$$\text{slope} = \frac{\text{rise}}{\text{run}} = \frac{\overset{2}{\cancel{20}} \text{ft}}{\underset{5}{\cancel{50}} \text{ft}} = \frac{2}{5}$$

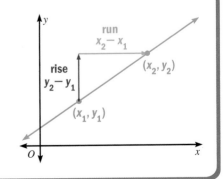

rise = 20 ft

run = 50 ft

▶ **Answer** The track has a slope of $\frac{2}{5}$.

 at classzone.com

## ✓ GUIDED PRACTICE  for Example 1

1. **Ramps** Using slope, describe the steepness of a ramp that rises 6 feet vertically for every 18 feet it reaches horizontally.

---

### KEY CONCEPT                            *For Your Notebook*

#### Slope of a Line

The slope $m$ of a nonvertical line passing through the points $(x_1, y_1)$ and $(x_2, y_2)$ is

$$m = \frac{\text{rise}}{\text{run}} = \frac{\text{change in } y}{\text{change in } x} = \frac{y_2 - y_1}{x_2 - x_1}$$

The slope of a line is the same no matter which two points on the line you choose to use in the formula.

**EXAMPLE 2** Positive and Negative Slope

Find the slope of the line.

**a.**

**b.**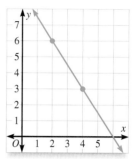

**AVOID ERRORS**
When finding the slope of a line, make sure that you are using the *x*- and *y*-coordinates in the same order.

$$m = \frac{\text{rise}}{\text{run}} = \frac{y_2 - y_1}{x_2 - x_1}$$

$$= \frac{7 - 2}{5 - 1}$$

$$= \frac{5}{4}$$

$$m = \frac{\text{rise}}{\text{run}} = \frac{y_2 - y_1}{x_2 - x_1}$$

$$= \frac{3 - 6}{4 - 2}$$

$$= \frac{-3}{2} \text{ or } -\frac{3}{2}$$

**EXAMPLE 3** Zero and Undefined Slope

Find the slope of the line.

**a.**

**b.**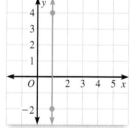

**REVIEW RULES OF DIVISION**
Remember that zero divided by any nonzero number is zero and that any number divided by zero is *undefined*.

$$m = \frac{\text{rise}}{\text{run}} = \frac{y_2 - y_1}{x_2 - x_1}$$

$$= \frac{3 - 3}{6 - 2}$$

$$= \frac{0}{4}$$

$$= 0$$

$$m = \frac{\text{rise}}{\text{run}} = \frac{y_2 - y_1}{x_2 - x_1}$$

$$= \frac{4 - (-2)}{1 - 1}$$

$$= \frac{6}{0}$$

The slope is undefined.

✓ **GUIDED PRACTICE** for Examples 2 and 3

Find the slope of the line passing through the points.

**2.** $(2, 1), (6, 4)$

**3.** $(0, 6), (10, 0)$

**4.** $(-3, -4), (5, 2)$

**5.** $(1, 5), (-3, 5)$

**6.** $(1, 6), (1, 2)$

**7.** $(-8, 3), (8, 3)$

### Slope of a Line

A line with *positive* slope rises from left to right.

A line with *negative* slope falls from left to right.

A line with *zero* slope is horizontal.

A line with *undefined* slope is vertical.

## 11.6 EXERCISES

### SKILL PRACTICE

**VOCABULARY** Copy and complete the statement.

1. Between two points, the change in the *y*-coordinate is called the __?__ .

2. Between two points, the change in the *x*-coordinate is called the __?__ .

3. The ratio of vertical change to horizontal change between any two points on a line is the __?__ of the line.

**SLOPE FROM A GRAPH** Write the coordinates of the two given points on the line. Then find the slope of the line.

*SEE EXAMPLES 2 AND 3*
on p. 613
for Exs. 4–6

4.

5.

6.

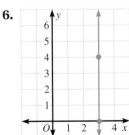

**SLOPE FROM POINTS** Find the slope of the line through the points.

**7.** $(-4, 8), (6, 6)$  **8.** $(1, 4), (1, -7)$  **9.** $(-5, 4), (3, 4)$

**10.** $(-2, -4), (4, 2)$  **11.** $(-3, 1), (-3, -2)$  **12.** $(5, 8), (0, 5)$

**13.** $(-6, -2), (6, -7)$  **14.** $(9, -8), (15, -8)$  **15.** $(12, 22), (-20, 19)$

**16. ERROR ANALYSIS** Describe and correct the error made in finding the slope of the line shown at the right.

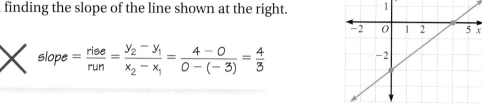

$$slope = \frac{rise}{run} = \frac{y_2 - y_1}{x_2 - x_1} = \frac{4 - 0}{0 - (-3)} = \frac{4}{3}$$

**SKETCHING LINES** Sketch a line with the given type of slope.

**17.** negative  **18.** undefined  **19.** positive  **20.** zero

**USING TRIANGLES** The given points are vertices of a triangle. Plot and connect the points. Then find the slope of each side of the triangle.

**21.** $A(0, 0), B(0, 8), C(6, 0)$  **22.** $D(-3, 4), E(4, 1), F(-1, -7)$

**23.** $G(0, 6), H(4, 0), J(-4, 0)$  **24.** $K(-5, 1), L(-1, -4), M(-2, 4)$

**COMPARING SLOPES** The greater the absolute value of a line's slope, the *steeper* the line is. The lines *a* and *b* pass through the given points. Determine which line, *a* or *b*, is steeper.

**25.** line *a*: $\left(\frac{1}{2}, -\frac{3}{2}\right), (1, 0)$

line *b*: $(4, 10), \left(-\frac{1}{2}, 1\right)$

**26.** line *a*: $(2, -9), (-11, 3)$

line *b*: $\left(\frac{5}{8}, -\frac{1}{4}\right), \left(-\frac{5}{8}, 6\right)$

**27.** ★ **TAKS REASONING** A line passing through the point $(-7, -3)$ has a slope of 0. Which point is *not* on the line?

**(A)** $(-3, 3)$  **(B)** $(-145, -3)$  **(C)** $(756, -3)$  **(D)** $\left(\frac{2}{9}, -3\right)$

 **ALGEBRA** Find the unknown value using the given slope and points on the line.

**28.** $m = \frac{7}{4}; (x, -7), (16, 0)$  **29.** $m = 0; (0, 7), (3, y)$

**30.** ⟨XY⟩ **ALGEBRA** A line contains the points $(p, q)$ and $(p + 2, q + 2)$. Find the slope of the line.

**31. GEOMETRY** A triangle has vertices $R(a, b)$, $S(c, b)$, and $T(c, d)$. Classify the triangle by its angles. Write and simplify an expression for the slope of each side of the triangle.

⟨XY⟩ **CHALLENGE** Find the unknown values using the given slope and points on the line.

**32.** $m = \frac{1}{2}; (-8, 4), (x, 2), (6, y)$  **33.** $m = -4; (2, y), (-1, 1), (x, -19)$

*SEE EXAMPLE 1*
on p. 612
for Exs. 34–38

**BIRDHOUSE** Use the red line on the diagram of a birdhouse.

**34.** What is the rise of the roof?

**35.** What is the run of the roof?

**36.** What is the slope of the roof?

**37.** ⬇ **TAKS REASONING** A roof rises 6 feet over a horizontal distance of 14 feet. What is the slope of the roof?

(A) $-8$　　　(B) $\dfrac{3}{7}$　　　(C) $\dfrac{7}{3}$　　　(D) $8$

**38.** **TIDES** The images below show a floating dock at low and high tide. Find the slope of the ramp in both images. Is the ramp steeper at high tide or at low tide? *Explain.*

**39.** **WRITING** One line passes through the points $M(1, 1)$ and $N(3, 4)$. Another line passes through the points $P(2, 5)$ and $Q(5, 8)$. Which line has a greater slope? *Explain* how you can tell by graphing the two lines. *Explain* how you can tell by calculating the slopes of the lines.

**40.** ⬇ **TAKS REASONING** Find the coordinates of the endpoints of a line segment that has a slope of $\dfrac{5}{7}$.

**41.** ⬇ **TAKS REASONING** You have selected two points on a line to find its slope. Does it matter which point is $(x_1, y_1)$ and which point is $(x_2, y_2)$? *Justify* your reasoning using examples.

**42.** **SKIING** A ski slope has a starting altitude of 2800 meters and an ending altitude of 1886 meters. The horizontal length of the ski slope is about 3299 meters. Approximate its slope. Round to the nearest hundredth.

*FIND VOLUME*
Need help
finding the
volume of
a cylinder?
See p. 555.

**43.** **REASONING** You pour a solution into a cylindrical beaker that has a 30 mm radius. Find the volume of the solution when you fill the beaker to heights of 20 mm, 40 mm, 100 mm, and 120 mm. Graph the ordered pairs (height, volume). Choose two points and find the slope of the line passing through the points. Will the slope be the same if you choose two other points? *Justify* your reasoning.

**44.** ![TAKS arrow] **TAKS REASONING** Most states' standards require that wheelchair ramps have a slope no greater than $\frac{1}{12}$.

**a.** A ramp is designed to be 2 feet high and have a horizontal length of 45 feet. Does this ramp meet standards? *Explain.*

**b.** What is the minimum horizontal length a 2 foot high ramp can have to meet standards? *Explain.*

**c.** Handrails are generally required on ramps that have a slope greater than $\frac{1}{20}$. If a 2 foot high ramp is built with a horizontal length between the lengths in (a) and (b), will it need a handrail? *Justify* your reasoning.

**45. CHALLENGE** A car travels 1613 meters on a road with a 6.21% grade. Use the Pythagorean Theorem and slope to find the meaning of road grade. *Explain* your reasoning.

1613 m

100 m

**46. CHALLENGE** A highway off-ramp takes cars from the top of a bridge to a road that is 16 feet beneath the bridge. The ramp is $\frac{3}{4}$ of a circle that has a radius of 200 feet. Find the slope of the ramp to the nearest thousandth.

---

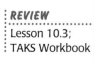 **MIXED REVIEW FOR TAKS** | **TAKS** **PRACTICE** at classzone.com

*REVIEW*
Lesson 10.4;
TAKS Workbook

**47.** ![TAKS arrow] **TAKS PRACTICE** The net of a cylindrical can of pet food is shown. Which is closest to the total surface area of the can? *TAKS Obj. 4*

**(A)** 80 cm$^2$

**(B)** 251.2 cm$^2$

**(C)** 351.9 cm$^2$

**(D)** 502.6 cm$^2$

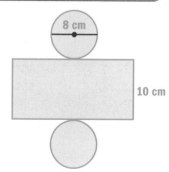

8 cm

10 cm

*REVIEW*
Lesson 10.3;
TAKS Workbook

**48.** ![TAKS arrow] **TAKS PRACTICE** Which figure best describes the side view of the drinking glass shown? *TAKS Obj. 3*

**(F)** Circle  **(G)** Trapezoid

**(H)** Rectangle  **(J)** Triangle

# Direct and Inverse Variation

**TEKS** 8.3.A, 8.5.A

**GOAL** Identify direct and inverse variation in tables and equations.

**Direct Variation** Two variables $x$ and $y$ show **direct variation** if $y = kx$ for some nonzero number $k$. The direct variation equation can also be written in the form $\frac{y}{x} = k$. So, $x$ and $y$ show direct variation if the ratio of $y$ to $x$ is constant.

## EXAMPLE 1  Identifying Direct Variation

**Tell whether the equation represents direct variation.**

**a.** $-2x + y = 0$

**b.** $-2x + y = 3$

**SOLUTION**

**a. METHOD 1**
Make a table of values and find the ratios of $y$ to $x$.

| $x$ | 1 | 2 | 3 | 4 | 5 |
|---|---|---|---|---|---|
| $y$ | 2 | 4 | 6 | 8 | 10 |
| Ratio $\frac{y}{x}$ | 2 | 2 | 2 | 2 | 2 |

The ratio is constant.

**METHOD 2**
Write the equation in function form.

$-2x + y = 0$

$\quad\quad y = 2x$

The equation can be written in the form $y = kx$, where $k = 2$.

▶ **Answer** The equation represents direct variation.

**b. METHOD 1**
Make a table of values and find the ratios of $y$ to $x$.

| $x$ | 1 | 2 | 3 | 4 | 5 |
|---|---|---|---|---|---|
| $y$ | 5 | 7 | 9 | 11 | 13 |
| Ratio $\frac{y}{x}$ | 5 | $\frac{7}{2}$ | 3 | $\frac{11}{4}$ | $\frac{13}{5}$ |

The ratio is *not* constant.

**METHOD 2**
Write the equation in function form.

$-2x + y = 3$

$\quad\quad y = 2x + 3$

The equation *cannot* be written in the form $y = kx$.

▶ **Answer** The equation does *not* represent direct variation.

**VOCABULARY**

If two quantities show direct variation, they are said to be *directly proportional* to one another.

**Direct Variation Graphs** The graph shows the linear equations from Example 1. Both graphs have a slope of 2, but only the graph of the direct variation equation from part (a) of Example 1 passes through the origin. All direct variation equations $y = kx$ are lines, with slope $m = k$, that pass through the origin.

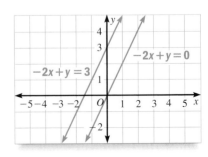

**Inverse Variation** Two variables $x$ and $y$ show **inverse variation** if $y = \frac{k}{x}$ for some nonzero number $k$. The inverse variation equation can be written in the form $xy = k$. So, $x$ and $y$ show inverse variation if the product $xy$ is constant.

**EXAMPLE 2** Identifying Inverse Variation

Tell whether the equation $y = \frac{4}{x}$ represents inverse variation.

**SOLUTION**

Make a table of values for the equation and find the products $xy$.

▶ **Answer** The products are equivalent, so the equation represents inverse variation.

| $x$ | 1 | 2 | 3 | 4 | 5 |
|---|---|---|---|---|---|
| $y$ | 4 | 2 | $1.\overline{3}$ | 1 | 0.8 |
| $xy$ | 4 | 4 | 4 | 4 | 4 |

**VOCABULARY**

If two quantities show indirect variation, they are said to be *inversely proportional* to one another.

**Inverse Variation Graphs** The graph shows the equation from Example 2. The graph is *not* a line. So, the ratio of the change in $y$ to the change in $x$, or *rate of change*, is not constant as in direct variation.

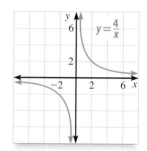

**EXERCISES**

Tell whether the table represents *direct variation*, *inverse variation*, or *neither*. *Justify* your answer.

1.
| $x$ | 1 | 2 | 3 | 4 |
|---|---|---|---|---|
| $y$ | 2 | 3 | 4 | 5 |

2.
| $x$ | 1 | 2 | 3 | 4 |
|---|---|---|---|---|
| $y$ | 3 | 6 | 9 | 12 |

3.
| $x$ | 1 | 2 | 4 | 5 |
|---|---|---|---|---|
| $y$ | 2 | 1 | 0.5 | 0.4 |

Tell whether the equation represents *direct variation*, *inverse variation*, or *neither*. *Justify* your answer.

4. $xy = 8$

5. $11x - 2.2y = 0$

6. $y + 5x = -3$

7. $y = -\frac{x}{3}$

8. $y = -\frac{3}{x}$

9. $y = -\frac{3}{x} + 1$

10. **Raffle** Anthony is selling $4 raffle tickets. Write an equation representing the amount of money $m$, in dollars, that he will have by selling $t$ tickets. Is the amount of money Anthony has *directly proportional* to the number of tickets he sells? *Justify* your answer.

11. **What If?** In Exercise 10, suppose Anthony already has $20 when he begins selling raffle tickets. Is the total amount of money Anthony has *directly proportional* to the number of tickets he sells? *Justify* your answer.

**GOAL**
Find how slope,
*y*-intercept, and an
equation are related.

**MATERIALS**
• pencil
• straightedge
• graph paper

**TEKS** *8.4, 8.16.A*

# 11.7 Slope-Intercept Form

You can find the slope and *y*-intercept of a line by looking at its equation in
*slope-intercept form.*

**EXPLORE 1** **Use a graph to find the slope and *y*-intercept of $y = 4x + 3$.**

**STEP 1** **Make** a table of values for the equation
$y = 4x + 3$.

| x | 0 | 1 | 2 |
|---|---|---|---|
| y | 3 | 7 | 11 |

**STEP 2** **Plot** the points and draw a line.

**STEP 3** **Use** the graph to find the slope and
*y*-intercept of $y = 4x + 3$.

slope $= \dfrac{4}{1} = 4$         *y*-intercept $= 3$

**PRACTICE** **In Exercises 1–3, use the table at the right.**

1. Copy and complete the table of values for the
   equation $y = -2x - 1$.

| x | −1 | 0 | 1 |
|---|---|---|---|
| y | ? | ? | ? |

2. Plot the points and draw a line.

3. Use the graph to find the slope and *y*-intercept.

4. Copy and complete the table below.

| Equation | Slope | y-intercept |
|----------|-------|-------------|
| $y = 4x + 3$ | ? | ? |
| $y = -2x - 1$ | ? | ? |

**EXPLORE 2**    Calculate the slope and *y*-intercept of $y = 3x + 5$.

**STEP 1**   **Make** a table of values for the equation $y = 3x + 5$.

| x | 1 | 2 | 3 |
|---|---|---|---|
| y | 8 | 11 | 14 |

**STEP 2**   **Calculate** the slope of the line using two points from the table.

$$m = \frac{y_2 - y_1}{x_2 - x_1} = \frac{11 - 8}{2 - 1} = 3$$

**STEP 3**   **Calculate** the *y*-intercept by substituting 0 for *x*.

$$y = 3x + 5 = 3(0) + 5 = 5$$

**PRACTICE**    **Graph the line using a table of values. Then use the graph to find the slope and *y*-intercept.**

**5.** $y = 5x - 7$      **6.** $y = -3x + 2$      **7.** $y = -\frac{2}{3}x - 6$      **8.** $y = \frac{5}{4}x + 1$

**Solve the equation for *y*. Make a table of values for the equation. Calculate the slope and *y*-intercept.**

**9.** $y + 2 = \frac{1}{2}x$      **10.** $3y = -2x + 9$      **11.** $y + 4x = -5$      **12.** $6x - 2y = 10$

**DRAW CONCLUSIONS**

**13. LOOK FOR A PATTERN**

   **a.** Include a row for $y = 3x + 5$ in your table from Exercise 4 on page 620.

   **b.** Use your table to make a conjecture about how to use the equation of a line to find the slope and *y*-intercept of the line.

   **c.** Does your conjecture in part (b) seem to be true for the equations in Exercises 5–12?

**14.**   **ALGEBRA**   What does *m* stand for in the equation $y = mx + b$? What does *b* stand for in the equation $y = mx + b$?

# 11.7 Slope-Intercept Form

TEKS *8.4, 8.5.A*

| | |
|---|---|
| **Before** | You graphed equations using intercepts. |
| **Now** | You'll write and graph equations in slope-intercept form. |
| **Why?** | So you can predict values, such as mountain temperatures in Example 3. |

**KEY VOCABULARY**
• **slope-intercept form,** *p. 622*

In Investigation 11.7 on pages 620–621, you may have observed that you can solve a linear equation for $y$ to help you identify the slope and $y$-intercept, as summarized below.

---

**KEY CONCEPT** *For Your Notebook*

### Slope-Intercept Form

**Words** The linear equation $y = mx + b$ is written in **slope-intercept form**. The slope is $m$. The $y$-intercept is $b$.

**Algebra** $y = mx + b$      **Numbers** $y = 3x + 2$

---

### EXAMPLE 1 Identifying Slopes and y-intercepts

**Find the slope and $y$-intercept of the graph of the equation.**

**a.** $y = x - 3$             **b.** $-4x + 2y = 16$

**SOLUTION**

**a.** The equation $y = x - 3$ can be written as $y = 1x + (-3)$.

▶ **Answer** The line has a slope of 1 and a $y$-intercept of $-3$.

**AVOID ERRORS**

When you rewrite the equation in part (b) of Example 1, be sure to divide *both* terms of $4x + 16$ by 2.

**b.** Write the equation $-4x + 2y = 16$ in slope-intercept form.

| | |
|---|---|
| $-4x + 2y = 16$ | **Write original equation.** |
| $2y = 4x + 16$ | **Add 4x to each side.** |
| $y = 2x + 8$ | **Divide each side by 2.** |

▶ **Answer** The line has a slope of 2 and a $y$-intercept of 8.

---

✓ **GUIDED PRACTICE** for Example 1

**Find the slope and $y$-intercept of the graph of the equation.**

**1.** $y = 6x + 1$      **2.** $y = \dfrac{1}{4}x$      **3.** $-2x + 3y = 6$

EXAMPLE 2 **Graphing Using Slope-Intercept Form**

Graph the equation $y = \frac{1}{2}x + 3$.

**STEP 1**   The *y*-intercept is 3, so plot the point (0, 3).

**STEP 2**   The slope is $\frac{1}{2}$, so plot a second point by moving up 1 unit and right 2 units.

**STEP 3**   Draw a line through the points.

*Animated* **Math**   at classzone.com

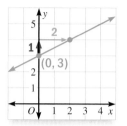

**EXAMPLE 3**   **Writing a Function Rule**

**Hiking**   You are at the base of a trail on Mount Rainier in Washington. The temperature is 50.9°F. The temperature changes at a rate of −0.005°F per foot of elevation as you hike up. What is the temperature 1000 feet above the base?

**SOLUTION**

**STEP 1**   **Write** a verbal model.

$$\boxed{\text{Temperature}} = \boxed{\substack{\text{Rate of} \\ \text{temperature change}}} \cdot \boxed{\substack{\text{Increase in} \\ \text{elevation}}} + \boxed{\substack{\text{Initial} \\ \text{temperature}}}$$

**STEP 2**   **Write** an algebraic model in slope-intercept form.

The temperature changes at a rate of −0.005°F per foot, so $m = -0.005$. The initial temperature is 50.9°F, so $b = 50.9$. Let *y* be the temperature and *x* be the change in elevation.

$y = mx + b$        **Write slope-intercept form.**

$y = -0.005x + 50.9$        **Substitute −0.005 for *m* and 50.9 for *b*.**

**STEP 3**   **Find** the value of *y* when $x = 1000$.

$y = -0.005x + 50.9$        **Write the equation.**

$\phantom{y} = -0.005(1000) + 50.9$        **Substitute 1000 for *x*.**

$\phantom{y} = 45.9$        **Simplify.**

▶ **Answer**   The temperature 1000 feet above the base is 45.9°F.

✓ **GUIDED PRACTICE**   **for Examples 2 and 3**

Use the slope and *y*-intercept to graph the equation.

**4.** $y = 2x + 5$        **5.** $y = 7x$        **6.** $-x + y = 6$

**7. What If?**  In Example 3, suppose the temperature at the base of the trail is 55.2°F. What is the temperature 2500 feet above the base?

## 11.7 EXERCISES

HOMEWORK KEY

🌟 = TAKS Practice and Reasoning
Exs. 16, 39, 40, 42, 44, 45, and 48

◯ = HINTS AND HOMEWORK HELP
for Exs. 3, 9, 19, 41 at classzone.com

### SKILL PRACTICE

**VOCABULARY** Copy and complete the statement.

**1.** For the graph of the linear equation $y = -5x + 7$, $-5$ is the  ? .

**2.** The linear equation $y = mx + b$ is in  ?  form.

**REWRITING EQUATIONS** Rewrite the equation in slope-intercept form.

**SEE EXAMPLE 1**
on p. 622
for Exs. 3–16

**3.** $2x = y + 5$

**4.** $8x - 4y = 32$

**5.** $x - y = -2$

**6. WHICH ONE DOESN'T BELONG?** Which of the following equations does not belong? *Explain* your choice.

**A.** $y = 3x - 1$    **B.** $y = -4x - 2$    **C.** $3x + y = 5$    **D.** $y = 2x - 9$

**SLOPES AND Y-INTERCEPTS** Find the slope and *y*-intercept of the graph of the equation.

**7.** $y = x + 3$

**8.** $y = 6 - x$

**9.** $1 = 2x - y$

**10.** $6x = 10 - y$

**11.** $y - 9 = -\frac{3}{4}x$

**12.** $\frac{2}{3}x - y = 3$

**13.** $2y - 6 = 0$

**14.** $y + 12x = 0$

**15.** $13x - 11y = 143$

**16. 🌟 TAKS REASONING** What is the slope of the graph of $3x + y = 4$?

**A** $-4$    **B** $-3$    **C** $3$    **D** $4$

**GRAPHING EQUATIONS** Use the slope and *y*-intercept to graph the equation.

**SEE EXAMPLE 2**
on p. 623
for Exs. 17–23

**17.** $y = x - 8$

**18.** $y = -x + 7$

**19.** $y = 3$

**20.** $2x - 2y = 1$

**21.** $-2x + 3y = -12$

**22.** $y = \frac{1}{5}x$

**23. ERROR ANALYSIS** Describe and correct the error made by a student in graphing the equation $y = -2x - 1$ using the slope and *y*-intercept.

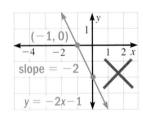

**INTERPRETING GRAPHS** Write the equation of the line in slope-intercept form.

**24.**

**25.**

**26.**

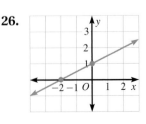

**27. NUMBER SENSE** Which equation has a steeper graph, $y = 3x - 1$ or $y = 2x - 1$? *Justify* your answer.

**WRITING EQUATIONS** Use the point on the line and the slope of the line to find the $y$-intercept of the line. Then write the slope-intercept form of the equation of the line.

**28.** $(1, 4)$; $m = 4$

**29.** $(3, -4)$; $m = 0$

**30.** $(9, 0)$; $m = \dfrac{1}{3}$

**31.** $(-2, 2)$; $m = -\dfrac{1}{2}$

**32.** $(-5, 6)$; $m = 0$

**33.** $\left(\dfrac{1}{2}, 6\right)$; $m = 2$

**WRITING EQUATIONS FROM TWO POINTS** Write the equation of the line passing through the given points.

**34.** $(-2, 9)$ and $(-4, -1)$

**35.** $(6, 10)$ and $(3, 12)$

**36.** $(-4, 4)$ and $(6, 7)$

**37.** **CHALLENGE** Find the slope and $y$-intercept of the graph of $ax + by + c = 0$, in terms of $a$, $b$, and $c$, where $b$ is not equal to 0.

## PROBLEM SOLVING

*SEE EXAMPLE 3* on p. 623 for Exs. 38–40

**38. PARACHUTING** The graph shows the altitude $y$, in feet, of a parachutist $x$ seconds after opening the parachute. Find the slope and $y$-intercept of the graph. Write the equation for the altitude in slope-intercept form. What do the slope and $y$-intercept represent in this situation?

**39. TAKS REASONING** You pay by the hour to rent a canoe. The cost for a ride back to the starting point is \$12. The total cost $C$, in dollars, of renting the canoe for $h$ hours can be modeled by $C = 9h + 12$. How much does the rental cost per hour?

**(A)** \$3      **(B)** \$9      **(C)** \$12      **(D)** \$21

**40. TAKS REASONING** The number of chirps per minute made by a cricket can be modeled by the equation $y = 4x - 156$, where $y$ is the number of chirps per minute and $x$ is the temperature in degrees Fahrenheit.

  **a.** Graph the equation.

  **b.** What does the $x$-intercept mean in this situation?

  **c.** What does the $y$-intercept mean in this situation? Does it make sense? *Explain.*

**41. WRITING** On a math test, students are asked to graph $y = \dfrac{2}{3}x + 1$. One student plots a point at $(0, 1)$, moves up 2 units and right 3 units, and then plots another point. Another student plots a point at $(0, 1)$, moves down 2 units and left 3 units, and then plots another point. Which student's graph is correct? *Explain* your reasoning.

SEE EXAMPLE 3
on p. 623
for Ex. 42

**42.** ⬥ **TAKS REASONING**      You make and sell bracelets. You spend $28 for supplies and sell the bracelets for $3.50 each.

   **a.** Write an equation to model your profit. Use *P* for profit and *b* for the number of bracelets sold.

   **b.** Graph the equation.

   **c.** How many bracelets do you need to exactly cover your expenses? to make a profit?

**43.** **REASONING** When two lines are perpendicular, and neither has a slope of zero, the product of their slopes is $-1$. What is the slope-intercept form of the equation of the line that is perpendicular to and has the same *y*-intercept as the graph of $y = 2x + 8$? *Justify* your answer.

**44.** ⬥ **TAKS REASONING**      *Describe* a real-world situation that can be represented by the graph at the right. What do the *x*- and *y*-intercepts mean in the situation?

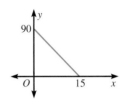

**45.** ⬥ **TAKS REASONING**      Use the equations $4x - 6y = -18$ and $-2x + 3y = 15$.

   **a.** Rewrite the equations in slope-intercept form. *Describe* any similarities.

   **b.** Graph the equations on the same coordinate plane. *Describe* how the graphs relate to each other.

   **c.** Use your answers from parts (a) and (b) to make a conjecture about how the graphs of $y = -2x - 8$ and $y = -2x - 1$ are related. *Explain* your reasoning.

**46.** **GEOMETRY** Find the area of the triangle formed by the *x*-axis, the *y*-axis, and the line $y = -2x + 6$.

**47.** **CHALLENGE** The line $y = 3x - 3$ forms one side of a rectangle. Write the equations of 3 lines that could form the other sides.

---

### 🔳 MIXED REVIEW FOR TAKS        **TAKS** PRACTICE at classzone.com

REVIEW
Lesson 11.4;
TAKS Workbook

**48.** ⬥ **TAKS PRACTICE** Which table of ordered pairs contains at least one point that does NOT lie on the line $y = 4x - 1$? *TAKS Obj. 2*

Ⓐ

| x  | y  |
|----|----|
| −1 | −5 |
| 0  | −1 |
| 1  | 3  |
| 3  | 11 |
| 4  | 15 |

Ⓑ

| x | y  |
|---|----|
| 1 | 3  |
| 2 | 7  |
| 3 | 11 |
| 4 | 15 |
| 5 | 19 |

Ⓒ

| x  | y   |
|----|-----|
| −5 | −21 |
| −4 | −17 |
| −3 | −13 |
| −2 | −9  |
| −1 | −5  |

Ⓓ

| x  | y  |
|----|----|
| 8  | 31 |
| 9  | 35 |
| 10 | 38 |
| 11 | 43 |
| 12 | 47 |

# Systems of Equations

**TEKS** 8.4

**GOAL** Solve systems of linear equations.

A **system of linear equations** in two variables is a set of two linear equations with the same variables. A **solution of a linear system** in two variables is an ordered pair that is a solution of each equation in the system.

In the system of equations below, (3, 2) is a solution.

| System of equations | Check |
|---|---|
| $2x + 4y = 14$ | $2(3) + 4(2) = 6 + 8 = 14$ ✓ |
| $3x - 5y = -1$ | $3(3) - 5(2) = 9 - 10 = -1$ ✓ |

If a system of linear equations has a solution, then the graphs of the equations intersect.

## EXAMPLE 1 Solving Linear Systems by Graphing

**Solve the linear system.**  **Equation 1**  $x + y = 5$

**Equation 2**  $y = 2x - 1$

**SOLUTION**

**STEP 1** **Write** each equation in slope-intercept form.

| Equation 1 | Equation 2 |
|---|---|
| $x + y = 5$ | $y = 2x - 1$ |
| $y = -x + 5$ | |

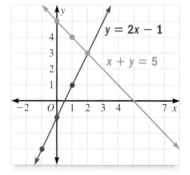

**STEP 2** **Graph** both equations.

**STEP 3** **Estimate** the point of intersection using the graph. It appears that the point of intersection is (2, 3).

**STEP 4** **Check** whether (2, 3) is the solution by substituting 2 for $x$ and 3 for $y$ in each of the equations.

| Equation 1 | Equation 2 |
|---|---|
| $x + y = 5$ | $y = 2x - 1$ |
| $2 + 3 \stackrel{?}{=} 5$ | $3 \stackrel{?}{=} 2(2) - 1$ |
| $5 = 5$ ✓ | $3 = 3$ ✓ |

▶ **Answer** The solution is (2, 3).

## EXAMPLE 2  Solving Linear Systems by Substitution

**Solve the linear system.**

Equation 1  $x + 4y = 4$

Equation 2  $x - y = -6$

**SOLUTION**

**SOLVE FOR A VARIABLE**

When solving by substitution, solve for the variable that is easier to isolate. You will get the same solution whether you begin by solving for *x* or for *y*.

**STEP 1**  **Choose** an equation to solve for one of the variables.

$$x - y = -6 \qquad \text{Write Equation 2.}$$

$$x = y - 6 \qquad \text{Add } y \text{ to each side.}$$

**STEP 2**  **Substitute** $y - 6$ for $x$ in Equation 1. Then solve for $y$.

$$x + 4y = 4 \qquad \text{Write Equation 1.}$$

$$(y - 6) + 4y = 4 \qquad \text{Substitute } y - 6 \text{ for } x.$$

$$5y - 6 = 4 \qquad \text{Combine like terms.}$$

$$5y = 10 \qquad \text{Add 6 to each side.}$$

$$y = 2 \qquad \text{Divide each side by 5.}$$

**STEP 3**  **Substitute** 2 for $y$ in the original Equation 2 and solve for $x$.

$$x - y = -6 \qquad \text{Write Equation 2.}$$

$$x - 2 = -6 \qquad \text{Substitute 2 for } y.$$

$$x = -4 \qquad \text{Add 2 to each side.}$$

▶ **Answer**  The solution is $(-4, 2)$.

---

## EXERCISES

**Solve the linear system by graphing. Then check the solution in both equations.**

**1.** $y = -x + 3$
   $y = x + 1$

**2.** $x - y = 1$
   $5x - 4y = 0$

**3.** $y = 2x - 15$
   $x = -2y$

**Solve the linear system by substitution.**

**4.** $x = 4$
   $x + y = 2$

**5.** $x + y = 4$
   $4x + y = 1$

**6.** $2x - y = -2$
   $4x + y = 20$

**7.** Graph the linear system at the right.
   *Explain* why there is *no* solution.

   $x + y = 8$
   $3x + 3y = 6$

**8.** **Trading Cards** You have 100 trading cards and your friend has 20. Every day you give your friend one card. Use the equations $c = 100 - d$ and $c = 20 + d$ to model this situation. Solve this system. *Explain* what the solution means in this situation.

# 11.8 Graphs of Linear Inequalities

TEKS 8.4, 8.5.A

| | |
|---|---|
| **Before** | You graphed linear equations. |
| **Now** | You'll graph linear inequalities. |
| **Why?** | So you can compare choices, as for buying art supplies in Example 3. |

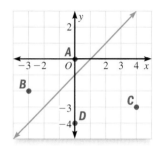

### KEY VOCABULARY
- **linear inequality,** *p. 629*
- **solution of a linear inequality,** *p. 629*
- **half-plane,** *p. 630*

## ACTIVITY

**You can use a graph to model linear inequalities.**

**STEP 1** **Sketch** the graph of $y = x - 1$.

**STEP 2** **Plot** and label the following points:

$A(0, 0), B(-3, -2), C(4, -3), D(0, -4)$

**STEP 3** **Draw** a circle around the points in Step 2 that make the inequality $y < x - 1$ true. Draw a square around the points that make the inequality $y > x - 1$ true.

**STEP 4** **Make** an observation about the solutions of $y < x - 1$ and the solutions of $y > x - 1$.

In the activity, you explored solutions of *linear inequalities*. Two examples of **linear inequalities** in two variables are $y \le 2x + 5$ and $2x + 5y < 7$. An ordered pair $(x, y)$ is a **solution of a linear inequality** if the inequality is true when the values of $x$ and $y$ are substituted into the inequality.

---

### EXAMPLE 1  Checking Solutions of a Linear Inequality

**READING**

The symbol $\nleq$ means *not less than or equal to.* It is equivalent to the symbol >, which means *greater than.*

**Tell whether the ordered pair is a solution of $3x - 4y \le -8$.**

| $(x, y)$ | $3x - 4y$ | $3x - 4y \overset{?}{\le} -8$ | Conclusion |
|---|---|---|---|
| **a.** $(0, 0)$ | $3(0) - 4(0) = 0$ | $0 \nleq -8$ | $(0, 0)$ is *not* a solution. |
| **b.** $(-1, 4)$ | $3(-1) - 4(4) = -19$ | $-19 \le -8$ | $(-1, 4)$ is a solution. |

---

✓ **GUIDED PRACTICE**  **for Example 1**

**Tell whether the ordered pair is a solution of $2x + 3y < 5$.**

**1.** $(0, 0)$      **2.** $(-4, 2)$      **3.** $(5, -1)$      **4.** $(1, 1)$

A line divides a coordinate plane into two half-planes.

**Graphing Linear Inequalities** The graph of a linear inequality in two variables is a **half-plane**. The shaded region includes all the solutions of the inequality.

A solid line indicates that points on the line *are* solutions of an inequality. A dashed line indicates that points on the line are *not* solutions.

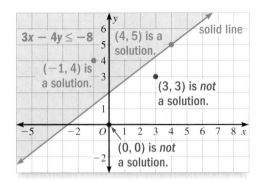

**KEY CONCEPT**                              *For Your Notebook*

### Graphing Linear Inequalities

1. Change the inequality symbol to "=". Graph the equation. Use a dashed line for < or >. Use a solid line for ≤ or ≥.

2. Test a point in one of the half-planes to check whether it is a solution of the inequality.

3. If the test point is a solution, shade the half-plane that contains the point. If the test point is not a solution, shade the other half-plane.

---

**EXAMPLE 2** Graphing a Linear Inequality

**Graph** $y - 2x > 3$.

**STEP 1** **Change** > to = and write the equation in slope-intercept form.

$$y - 2x = 3 \qquad \text{Replace > with = sign.}$$

$$y = 2x + 3 \qquad \text{Add 2x to each side.}$$

Graph the line that has a slope of 2 and a *y*-intercept of 3. Because the inequality is >, use a dashed line.

Using (0, 0) is convenient because 0 is substituted for each variable. However, you can use any point *not* on the line as a test point.

**STEP 2** **Use** (0, 0) as a test point. Substitute the point into the original inequality.

$$y - 2x > 3$$

$$0 - 2(0) \overset{?}{>} 3$$

$$0 \not> 3 \qquad \text{(0, 0) is not a solution.}$$

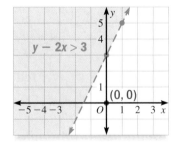

**STEP 3** **Shade** the half-plane that does *not* contain (0, 0).

---

✓ **GUIDED PRACTICE**   for Example 2

**Graph the inequality.**

**5.** $y < x + 1$ **6.** $3x + y \geq 3$ **7.** $x - 2y \geq -1$ **8.** $y \geq -2$

**EXAMPLE 3** Using the Graph of a Linear Inequality

**Art Supplies** You have at most $40 to buy art supplies. Tubes of paint cost $6 each and brushes cost $4 each. This situation can be modeled by the inequality $6x + 4y \leq 40$, where $x$ represents the number of tubes of paint and $y$ represents the number of brushes.

**a.** Graph the inequality.

**b.** How many tubes of paint and how many brushes can you buy with $40?

**SOLUTION**

**a.** Change $\leq$ to $=$ and write the equation in slope-intercept form: $y = -\dfrac{3}{2}x + 10$.

Graph the equation using a solid line.

Use (0, 0) as a test point: $6(0) + 4(0) \overset{?}{\leq} 40$

$$0 \leq 40 \checkmark$$

Shade the half-plane that contains (0, 0).

**INTERPRET A GRAPH**
All the points in the shaded region and on the line are solutions of the inequality. However, negative and fractional solutions do not make sense in this situation.

**b.** Many solutions are possible, such as (4, 4) and (2, 5). You could buy 4 tubes of paint and 4 brushes or 2 tubes of paint and 5 brushes.

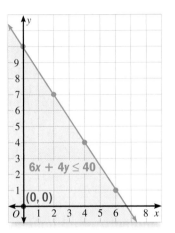

$6x + 4y \leq 40$

(0, 0)

---

✔ **GUIDED PRACTICE** for Example 3

**9. What If?** In Example 3, suppose you have at most $36 to spend. Graph the inequality $6x + 4y \leq 36$ and find two possible solutions.

---

## 11.8 EXERCISES

HOMEWORK KEY

⬐ = **TAKS Practice and Reasoning**
Exs. 24, 37, 38, 39, 40, and 42

◯ = **HINTS** AND **HOMEWORK HELP**
for Exs. 3, 9, 17, 35 at classzone.com

### SKILL PRACTICE

1. **VOCABULARY** Copy and complete: When graphing $y < 2x + 1$, the dashed line on the graph divides the coordinate plane into two __?__.

2. **VOCABULARY** Copy and complete: All the points in the shaded region of the graph of an inequality are __?__ of the inequality.

**SEE EXAMPLE 1**
on p. 629
for Exs. 3–6

**CHECKING** Tell whether the ordered pair is a solution of the inequality.

3. $5x + y \leq 17$; (1, 2)

4. $3x + 7y < 20$; $(-11, 2)$

5. $9x + 12y > 26$; $(3, -4)$

6. $11x + 18y \geq 31$; $(-6, -7)$

SEE EXAMPLE 2
on p. 630
for Exs. 7–24

**GRAPHING INEQUALITIES** Graph the inequality.

**7.** $y > 14 - 4x$    **8.** $y < x + 5$    **9.** $3x - 4 \geq y$    **10.** $y + 3 \geq 4x$

**11.** $-96 \leq -3x$    **12.** $6y > 36$    **13.** $y \geq 3x - 7$    **14.** $y \leq 4x - 12$

**15.** $y < 7x + 19$    **16.** $4x - 13 > y$    **17.** $y > 9 - 2x$    **18.** $22 < 2x$

**19.** $-2y \geq 74$    **20.** $4x - 3y \geq 12$    **21.** $-2x - 4y > 8$    **22.** $6x + 3y \leq -12$

**23. ERROR ANALYSIS** Describe and correct the error made in graphing $y \leq 2x + 1$.

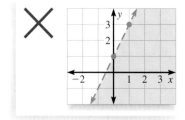

**24. ◆ TAKS REASONING** Which inequality describes the graph?

**A** $y \leq 2x + 200$    **B** $y \geq 2x + 200$

**C** $y \leq -2x + 200$    **D** $y \geq -2x + 200$

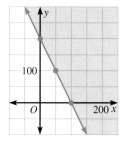

**WRITING INEQUALITIES** Write the sentence as an inequality. Then graph the inequality in a coordinate plane.

**25.** The sum of $x$ and $y$ is greater than 10.    **26.** $y$ is no more than 15.

**27.** $x$ is at least 20.    **28.** The difference of $x$ and $y$ is at most 15.

**29.** $y$ is more than two times $x$.    **30.** $x$ is no more than three times $y$.

**ALGEBRA** Let $a$ be a nonzero whole number. Tell whether a point of the given form is *always, sometimes,* or *never* a solution of the inequality.

**31.** $y \leq 5x - a$; $(a, 2a)$    **32.** $3y > x + a$; $(a, a + 1)$    **33.** $10x > a - 2y$; $(-a, 5a)$

**34. CHALLENGE** Graph the shaded region bounded by $y < \frac{2}{3}x + 5$, $y > -\frac{1}{3}x - 7$, and $y < \frac{8}{3}x - 1$. Find two ordered pairs that are solutions of all three inequalities. *Justify* your answers.

## PROBLEM SOLVING

SEE EXAMPLE 3
on p. 631
for Ex. 35

**35. TRAIL MIX** You are making a trail mix of peanuts and raisins. You have $6.00 to spend. Peanuts cost $2.00 per pound and raisins cost $1.50 per pound. Graph the inequality $2x + 1.5y \leq 6$ to find two possible combinations of pounds of peanuts $x$ and pounds of raisins $y$ that you could buy for your trail mix.

**36. WRITING** If you graph the inequalities $y < x + 3$ and $y > x + 3$, are there any points in the coordinate plane that are *not* solutions? *Explain* your reasoning.

SEE EXAMPLE 3
on p. 631
for Ex. 37

**37.** ⚑ **TAKS REASONING** Sonya can spend up to $125 on decorations for a dance. A bag of balloons costs $4 and a roll of streamers costs $2. To find how much she can buy she uses the inequality $4x + 2y \leq 125$, where $x$ is the number of bags of balloons and $y$ is the number of rolls of streamers. Which of the following is a solution of the inequality?

    **A** (30, 6)     **B** (30, 4)     **C** (25, 15)     **D** (25, 12)

**38.** ⚑ **TAKS REASONING** Write an inequality whose graph is a half-plane shaded above a dashed line. Then write an inequality whose graph is a half-plane shaded below a solid line.

**39.** ⚑ **TAKS REASONING** Write an inequality whose graph is the half-plane that contains all the points that are *not* the solutions of the inequality $5x + y \geq 2$. *Explain* your method.

**40.** ⚑ **TAKS REASONING** Catherine is going on a canoe trip. She has to carry a backpack containing the meals and water she will need. Catherine can take no more than 10 pounds in her backpack. One bottle of water weighs 16 ounces and one meal weighs 10 ounces.

  **a.** Write an inequality to model the situation, where $x$ is the number of water bottles and $y$ is the number of meals.

  **b.** Graph the inequality. Use your graph to find the maximum number of water bottles she can carry when she packs 4 meals. *Explain* how you found your answer.

  **c.** Can she take 5 water bottles and 6 meals? *Explain* how your graph helps you answer this question.

**41.** **CHALLENGE** Lee sells 6 videos and 3 CDs at a yard sale and makes at most $12. Vivian sells 4 videos and 2 CDs and makes at least $10. Write an inequality to model each situation, where $x$ is the price of a video and $y$ is the price of a CD. Graph both inequalities in the same coordinate plane. Is it possible that Lee and Vivian charge the same prices? *Explain*.

## MIXED REVIEW FOR TAKS

**TAKS** PRACTICE at classzone.com

REVIEW
Lesson 10.6;
TAKS Workbook

**42.** ⚑ **TAKS PRACTICE** The dimensions of two cubes are shown. The volume of the larger cube is 216 cubic meters. What is the volume of the smaller cube? *TAKS Obj. 4*

  **A** 27 m$^3$

  **B** 54 m$^3$

  **C** 72 m$^3$

  **D** 108 m$^3$

2x      x

**Find the intercepts of the graph of the equation.** *(p. 606)*

**1.** $y = 2x + 3$

**2.** $2y + x = 6$

**3.** $x = 3$

**Find the slope of the line passing through the points.** *(p. 612)*

**4.** $(3, 4), (5, 7)$

**5.** $(-1, -3), (0, 0)$

**6.** $(-5, 3), (4, 3)$

**Find the slope and $y$-intercept of the graph of the equation. Then graph the equation.** *(p. 622)*

**7.** $y = \dfrac{6}{5}x - 2$

**8.** $-5x - 5y = -20$

**9.** $y = -x$

**Graph the inequality. Then list three solutions of the inequality.** *(p. 629)*

**10.** $y > x - 3$

**11.** $x - 3y \le -9$

**12.** $6x + 7y < -21$

**13. CAR WASH** Your club holds a car wash to raise money for a charity. In 180 minutes, the club members can wash $x$ small vehicles and $y$ large vehicles. The equation $10x + 15y = 180$ models this situation. Find the intercepts. Then graph the equation. What do the intercepts represent in this situation? *(p. 606)*

**14. LEMONADE STAND** Some children on your street are selling lemonade. They charge $.50 for a small lemonade and $1 for a large lemonade. Graph the inequality $0.5x + y \ge 20$ to find two possible combinations of small lemonades $x$ and large lemonades $y$ they could sell to make at least $20. *(p. 629)*

**Brain Game**

## Late Night Show

Each slope or $y$-intercept can be matched with exactly one lettered equation. Write the appropriate letters in the blanks to find what kind of show is being advertised.

$\underline{\ ?\ }$ $\quad$ $\underline{\ ?\ }$ $\quad$ $\underline{\ ?\ }$ $\quad$ $\underline{\ ?\ }$ $\quad$ $\underline{\ ?\ }$ $\quad$ $\underline{\ ?\ }$ $\quad$ $\underline{\ ?\ }$ $\quad$ $\underline{\ ?\ }$ $\quad$ $\underline{\ ?\ }$ $\quad$ $\underline{\ ?\ }$ $\quad$ $\underline{\ ?\ }$

$m = \dfrac{3}{2}$ $\quad$ $b = -6$ $\quad$ $m = -1$ $\quad$ $m = 3$ $\quad$ $b = 1$ $\quad$ $m = -4$ $\quad$ $b = 10$ $\quad$ $m = 1$ $\quad$ $b = -18$ $\quad$ $b = 2$ $\quad$ $m = -\dfrac{1}{3}$

**E.** $y = 2x + 1$

**L.** $2x - y = 6$

**P.** $4y = 6x - 20$

**S.** $2x + 4y = 12$

**U.** $y = \dfrac{1}{3}x + 2$

**N.** $2y = 6x - 14$

**A.** $2x + 2y = 20$

**O.** $y = 5x + 9$

**T.** $4x + y = 20$

**I.** $6x - y = 18$

**R.** $5x - 5y = 40$

**M.** $x + 3y = 18$

## Lessons 11.5–11.8

**MULTIPLE CHOICE**

1. **ICE SKATING** Dara spends 24 hours a month at ice skating lessons. In one month, she can attend 12 individual lessons and 8 partner lessons. The number of hours Dara spends in each lesson can be modeled by the equation $12x + 8y = 24$. What does the $y$-intercept of this equation represent? *TEKS 8.15.A*

Ⓐ The duration in hours of each lesson if Dara attends only individual lessons.

Ⓑ The duration in hours of each lesson if Dara attends only partner lessons.

Ⓒ The number of individual lessons Dara attends.

Ⓓ The number of partner lessons Dara attends.

2. **INEQUALITIES** The graph at the right represents all the points that are solutions to four inequalities. The equations used to graph the inequalities are

$y = -\frac{1}{3}x + 5$,

$y = \frac{1}{3}x - 5$,

$y = \frac{2}{3}x - 6$, and

$y = -\frac{2}{3}x + 6$.

Which of the following is NOT one of the inequalities? *TEKS 8.4.A*

Ⓕ $y + 5 > \frac{1}{3}x$

Ⓖ $y - 5 > -\frac{1}{3}x$

Ⓗ $y + 6 > \frac{2}{3}x$

Ⓙ $y - 6 < -\frac{2}{3}x$

3. **CURRIES** Yen buys sweet curry powder at $1.10 per ounce and hot curry powder at $1.30 per ounce. Yen wants a total of 10 ounces of curry powder. Which equation models the total cost $y$ of the curry powder if $x$ represents the number of ounces of sweet curry powder? *TEKS 8.4.A*

Ⓐ $y = 1.1x + 1.3(10 - x)$

Ⓑ $y = 1.3x + 1.1(10 - x)$

Ⓒ $y = 1.1x + 1.3(10 + x)$

Ⓓ $y = 1.3x + 1.1(10 + x)$

4. **SNACKS** Paul is buying food at a baseball game. He has at most $10 to buy popcorn and drinks. Boxes of popcorn cost $2.50 each, and drinks cost $2.00 each. What is the maximum number of boxes of popcorn he can buy if he buys 2 drinks? *TEKS 8.2.B*

Ⓕ 1   Ⓖ 2   Ⓗ 3   Ⓙ 4

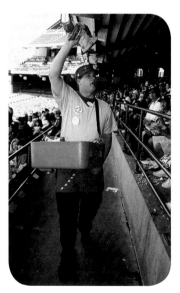

**GRIDDED ANSWER** ⓪①②●④⑤⑥⑦⑧⑨

5. **LINES** Ruth is asked to draw a line that passes through the points $(5, -1)$ and $(x, 3)$ and has an undefined slope. What must be the value of $x$? *TEKS 8.7.D*

TEXAS @*HomeTutor*

**classzone.com**
Vocabulary Practice

## REVIEW KEY VOCABULARY

- relation, *p. 583*
- input, *p. 583*
- output, *p. 583*
- function, *p. 583*
- domain, *p. 584*
- range, *p. 584*

- scatter plot, *p. 588*
- solution of an equation in two variables, *p. 593*
- linear equation, *p. 598*
- *x*-intercept, *p. 606*
- *y*-intercept, *p. 606*

- slope, *p. 612*
- rise, run, *p. 612*
- slope-intercept form, *p. 622*
- linear inequality, solution, *p. 629*
- half-plane, *p. 630*

### VOCABULARY EXERCISES

1. A relation that has exactly one output for each input is a(n) __?__.

2. The graph of a linear inequality in two variables is a(n) __?__.

3. For a function, the set of all possible __?__ values is the domain, and the set of all possible __?__ values is the range.

4. The slope of a nonvertical line is the ratio of its __?__ to its __?__.

5. *Explain* how to find the *x*-intercept and the *y*-intercept of the graph of an equation.

6. *Describe* a real-world situation that can be represented by a linear equation. What does the slope of the line tell you about the situation?

7. Write the steps you would take to graph a linear inequality.

## REVIEW EXAMPLES AND EXERCISES

### 11.1 Relations and Functions

*pp. 583–587*

**EXAMPLE**

**Tell whether the relation is a function. If so, write a function rule that relates *x* and *y*.**

**a.** (3, 2), (5, 3), (5, 5), (6, 7)

**b.**

| Input x  | −4 | −3 | −2 | −1 |
|----------|----|----|----|----|
| Output y | 4  | 3  | 2  | 1  |

▶ **Answer** The relation is *not* a function because 5 has two outputs.

▶ **Answer** The relation is a function because each input has exactly one output. Each *y* is the opposite of *x*, so the function rule is $y = -x$.

## EXERCISES

**Tell whether the relation is a function. If so, write a function rule that relates $x$ and $y$.**

**SEE EXAMPLES 1 AND 3**
on pp. 583–584
for Exs. 8–11

**8.** $(0, 6), (2, 6), (4, 7), (0, 3), (2, 3)$

**9.** $(-5, 1), (-2, 4), (1, 7), (2, 8), (5, 11)$

**10.**

| Input x | Output y |
|---------|----------|
| −8      | 4        |
| −2      | 1        |
| 4       | −2       |
| 10      | −5       |

**11.**

| Input x | Output y |
|---------|----------|
| 0       | −8       |
| 1       | −11      |
| 2       | −14      |
| 3       | −17      |

## 11.2 Scatter Plots

pp. 588–592

### EXAMPLE

**Make a scatter plot of the data. Then describe the relationship.**

| x | −1 | 0  | 1  | 2  |
|---|----|----|----|----|
| y | −6 | −5 | −4 | −3 |

To make a scatter plot, plot the ordered pairs from the table.

$(-1, -6), (0, -5),$
$(1, -4), (2, -3)$

The $y$-coordinates increase as the $x$-coordinates increase. So, the quantities have a positive relationship.

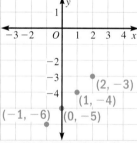

## EXERCISES

**Make a scatter plot of the data. Then describe the relationship.**

**SEE EXAMPLES 1 AND 2**
on pp. 588–589
for Exs. 12–14

**12.**

| Muffins sold | 12  | 24   | 36   | 48   |
|--------------|-----|------|------|------|
| Profit       | $6  | $12  | $18  | $24  |

**13.**

| Speed (mi/h) | 30 | 40 | 50  | 60 |
|--------------|----|----|-----|----|
| Time (h)     | 4  | 3  | 2.4 | 2  |

**14.**

| Age           | 8  | 14  | 19  | 31  |
|---------------|----|-----|-----|-----|
| Bowling score | 77 | 237 | 125 | 149 |

## 11.3 Equations in Two Variables

*pp. 593–597*

**EXAMPLE**

List three solutions of the equation $y = 2x + 3$.

| $x$-value | Substitute for $x$. | Evaluate. | Solution |
|-----------|---------------------|-----------|----------|
| $x = -2$ | $y = 2(-2) + 3$ | $y = -1$ | $(-2, -1)$ |
| $x = 0$ | $y = 2(0) + 3$ | $y = 3$ | $(0, 3)$ |
| $x = 2$ | $y = 2(2) + 3$ | $y = 7$ | $(2, 7)$ |

### EXERCISES

*SEE EXAMPLE 3*
on p. 594
for Exs. 15–16

**15.** List three solutions of the equation $x + 4y = 16$.

**16. Temperature** The temperature is 81°F as Ella begins climbing a mountain. The temperature $t$ in degrees Fahrenheit after climbing $a$ feet is approximated by $t = 81 - 0.005a$. Ella can climb 800 feet per hour. What will the temperature be if Ella climbs for 4 hours?

## 11.4 Graphs of Linear Equations

*pp. 598–603*

**EXAMPLE**

Graph $y = 2x + 2$.

**STEP 1** **Choose** several values to substitute for $x$. Then evaluate to find $y$ and make a table of values.

| $x$ | $-2$ | $-1$ | 0 | 1 | 2 |
|-----|------|------|---|---|---|
| $y$ | $-2$ | 0 | 2 | 4 | 6 |

**STEP 2** **List** the solutions as ordered pairs.
$(-2, -2), (-1, 0), (0, 2), (1, 4), (2, 6)$

**STEP 3** **Plot** the ordered pairs and draw a line through them.

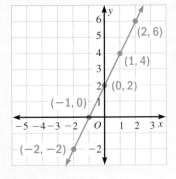

### EXERCISES

*SEE EXAMPLES*
*1 AND 3*
on pp. 599–600
for Exs. 17–19

**Graph the linear equation.**

**17.** $y = x + 2$

**18.** $3x + 2y = -2$

**19.** $y = 8$

## 11.5 Using Intercepts

pp. 606–609

**EXAMPLE**

**Find the intercepts of the graph of $y = 5x + 20$.**

To find the $x$-intercept,
let $y = 0$ and solve for $x$.

$$y = 5x + 20$$
$$0 = 5x + 20$$
$$-20 = 5x$$
$$-4 = x$$

To find the $y$-intercept,
let $x = 0$ and solve for $y$.

$$y = 5x + 20$$
$$y = 5(0) + 20$$
$$y = 0 + 20$$
$$y = 20$$

▶ **Answer** The $x$-intercept is $-4$ and the $y$-intercept is 20.

### EXERCISES

*SEE EXAMPLES 1 AND 3*
on pp. 606–607
for Exs. 20–21

**20.** Find the intercepts of the graph of $-6x + 2y = 9$.

**21.** **Taxes** The approximate amount of taxes collected by the Internal Revenue Service from 1980 to 1990 can be modeled by $y = 57.1x + 488$, where $y$ represents taxes, in billions of dollars, and $x$ represents the number of years since 1980. What is the $y$-intercept of the graph of this equation? What does the $y$-intercept mean in this situation?

## 11.6 Slope

pp. 612–617

**EXAMPLE**

**Find the slope of the line passing through $(0, 3)$ and $(4, 6)$.**

$$m = \frac{\text{rise}}{\text{run}} = \frac{y_2 - y_1}{x_2 - x_1} = \frac{6 - 3}{4 - 0} = \frac{3}{4}$$

### EXERCISES

**Write the coordinates of two points on the line. Then find the slope of the line.**

*SEE EXAMPLES 2 AND 3*
on p. 613
for Exs. 22–23

**22.**

**23.**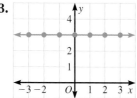

Chapter Review **639**

**EXAMPLE**

**Find the slope and $y$-intercept of the graph of $-9x + 3y = 21$.**

Write the equation $-9x + 3y = 21$ in slope-intercept form.

$$-9x + 3y = 21 \qquad \text{Write original equation.}$$
$$3y = 9x + 21 \qquad \text{Add 9x to each side.}$$
$$y = 3x + 7 \qquad \text{Divide each side by 3.}$$

▸ **Answer** The line has a slope of 3 and a $y$-intercept of 7.

**EXERCISES**

*SEE EXAMPLE 1*
on p. 622
for Exs. 24–29

**Find the slope and $y$-intercept of the graph of the equation.**

**24.** $y = 6x - 1$

**25.** $y = -\dfrac{2}{3}x + 4$

**26.** $y = 8$

**Rewrite the equation in slope-intercept form. Then find the slope and $y$-intercept of the graph of the equation.**

**27.** $y - 4x = 10$

**28.** $2y + 6 = x$

**29.** $-3x - 7y = 21$

**EXAMPLE**

**Graph $y > -2x + 4$.**

The graph of $y = -2x + 4$ has a slope of $-2$ and a $y$-intercept of 4.

Because the inequality is $>$, use a dashed line.

Use $(0, 0)$ as a test point:

$$0 \overset{?}{>} -2(0) + 4$$
$$0 \not> 4$$

Shade the half-plane that does *not* contain $(0, 0)$.

**EXERCISES**

*SEE EXAMPLE 2*
on p. 630
for Exs. 30–32

**Graph the inequality.**

**30.** $y < -\dfrac{3}{5}x - 3$

**31.** $3x - 7y \geq 21$

**32.** $4x + 8y \leq 32$

In Exercises 1 and 2, tell whether the relation is a function. If so, write a function rule that relates $x$ and $y$.

1.

| Input x | 0 | 1 | 2 | 3 |
|---------|---|---|---|---|
| Output y | 0 | −0.25 | −0.5 | −0.75 |

2.

| Input x | −2 | −1 | 0 | 1 |
|---------|----|----|---|---|
| Output y | −9 | −3 | 3 | 9 |

Tell whether the ordered pair is a solution of the equation $12x + 3y = 21$.

3. $(-1, 11)$      4. $(-4, -9)$      5. $(2, -15)$      6. $(6, -17)$

Find the slope and $y$-intercept of the graph of the equation. Then graph the equation.

7. $y = 6x - 3$      8. $-5x + y = 1$      9. $y = -\frac{1}{4}x$

Graph the inequality.

10. $3x + 6y \geq 12$      11. $7x - y \leq 49$      12. $8x - 15y > 30$

For Exercises 13–15, use the diagram of a seesaw.

13. What is the run of the seesaw?

14. What is the rise of the seesaw?

15. What is the slope of the seesaw?

5 ft

12 ft

16. What type of relationship do you expect to find in a scatter plot when comparing the number of math problems assigned and the time spent doing the assignment?

17. **YARD WORK** You have a job raking leaves. You charge $10 plus $.50 for each bag you fill with leaves. The equation $y = 0.50x + 10$ models this situation, where $x$ is the number of bags and $y$ is the total amount, in dollars, you earn. Your friend tells you that you will make $16 if you fill 8 bags. Is your friend correct? If not, find the amount you will make for filling 8 bags.

18. **GASOLINE** A scooter uses 1 gallon of gasoline per 60 miles. The equation $n = 60g$ models this relationship, where $n$ is the number of miles driven and $g$ is the number of gallons of gas used. Graph the equation and use the graph to estimate the number of miles traveled using 12 gallons of gasoline.

19. **GIFT CARD** Ken received a $25 movie gift card. Matinee shows cost $4 each and evening shows cost $8 each. The inequality $4x + 8y \leq 25$ models this situation, where $x$ is the number of matinees and $y$ is the number of evening shows. Graph the inequality and use the graph to find the greatest number of evening shows Ken can see if he sees 3 matinees.

**TEXAS** TAKS Objs. 2 and 5
TEKS 8.4.A, 8.12.B

# REVIEWING PROBLEMS INVOLVING EQUATIONS AND GRAPHS

The line $y = mx + b$ is written in *slope-intercept form* where the slope is $m$ and the $y$-intercept is $b$. Another form in which lines can be written is *standard form*. The line $Ax + By = C$ is written in standard form where $A$ and $B$ are not both zero. You may choose different strategies when graphing or identifying lines depending on the form of the linear equation that is given.

**EXAMPLE**

**Identify the graph(s) of the linear equations (a) $3x - 2y = 6$ and (b) $y = \frac{3}{2}x - 3$ below.**

**A**     **B**     **C**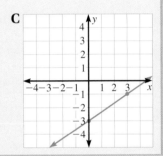

## Solution

**a.** The equation is written in standard form. One way to identify a line written in standard form is to find the intercepts.

To find the $x$-intercept, let $y = 0$ and solve for $x$.

$$3x - 2(0) = 6$$
$$x = 2$$

To find the $y$-intercept, let $x = 0$ and solve for $y$.

$$3(0) - 2y = 6$$
$$y = -3$$

The $x$-intercept is 2 and the $y$-intercept is $-3$, so the graph of the equation contains the points $(2, 0)$ and $(0, -3)$. Graph A above shows the line that contains these points.

▶ **Answer** Graph A shows the graph of the linear equation $3x - 2y = 6$.

*EQUATION IN DIFFERENT FORMS*
Notice that the equations in parts (a) and (b) have different forms but describe the same line.

**b.** The equation is written in slope-intercept form. One way to identify a line written in slope-intercept form is to identify the slope and $y$-intercept. The line has a slope of $\frac{3}{2}$ and a $y$-intercept of $-3$. Graph A above shows the line with the correct slope and $y$-intercept.

▶ **Answer** Graph A shows the graph of the linear equation $y = \frac{3}{2}x - 3$.

# PROBLEMS INVOLVING EQUATIONS AND GRAPHS ON TAKS

Below are examples of problems in multiple choice format. Try solving the problems before looking at the solutions. (Cover the solutions with a piece of paper.) Then check your solutions against the ones given.

**1.** Which equation has a linear graph that includes the points $(0, 2)$, $(1, 4)$, and $(-1, 0)$?

   **A**   $2x + y = -2$

   **B**   $-2x^2 - 2y = -2$

   **C**   $-x + 2y = -2$

   **D**   $2x - y = -2$

**Solution**

Use any two of the three points given to graph the line. The slope of the line is 2, and the y-intercept is 2. So, the slope-intercept form of the equation for the line is $y = 2x + 2$.

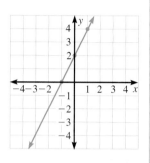

This equation rewritten in standard form is $2x - y = -2$. So, the correct answer is D.

  Ⓐ    Ⓑ    Ⓒ    **Ⓓ**

**2.** The scatterplot shows the cost for ladders in relation to the length of the ladders.

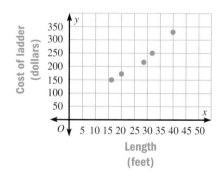

Which statement best describes the relationship on the scatterplot?

   **F**   The price of ladders decreases as the length increases.

   **G**   The price of ladders increases as the length increases.

   **H**   The price of ladders first increases and then decreases as the length increases.

   **J**   The price of ladders shows no relationship with the length.

**Solution**

The y-coordinates increase as the x-coordinates increase. The scatterplot shows a positive relationship, so the price of ladders increases as the length increases.

The correct answer is G.

  Ⓕ    **Ⓖ**    Ⓗ    Ⓙ

# 11 TAKS PRACTICE

## PRACTICE FOR TAKS OBJECTIVES 2 AND 5

1. Which graph shows the line described by the equation $2x - y = 24$?

**A**

**B**

**C**

**D**

2. A scatterplot shows a positive relationship in the data. What is true of a line drawn to show the trend in the data?

   **F** The slope is 0.

   **G** The slope is negative.

   **H** The slope is positive.

   **J** The slope is undefined.

3. The scatterplot below shows the number of deciduous teeth a dog had at the end of each month in the 2- to 6-month age range. What relationship exists between the two sets of data?

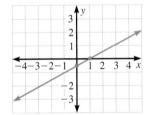

   **A** No relationship

   **B** Negative relationship

   **C** Positive relationship

   **D** Negative relationship then positive relationship

4. Which point lies on the line shown?

   **F** $\left(1\frac{1}{2}, 1\right)$

   **G** $\left(1, 1\frac{1}{2}\right)$

   **H** $(-1, -1)$

   **J** $(0, 1)$

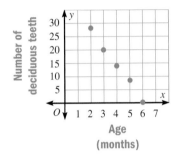

## MIXED TAKS PRACTICE

5. A shark can produce about 20,000 teeth in a lifetime. How is this expressed in scientific notation? *TAKS Obj. 1*

   **A** $2 \times 10^{-5}$

   **B** $2 \times 10^{-4}$

   **C** $2 \times 10^{4}$

   **D** $2 \times 10^{5}$

## MIXED TAKS PRACTICE

**6.** The graph of the line $y = \frac{1}{2}x + 1$ is drawn on the coordinate grid below.

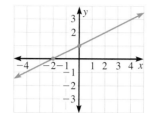

Which list of ordered pairs shows points that are NOT on the line? *TAKS Obj. 2*

**F** (4, 3), (0, 1), (10, 6)

**G** (2, 2), (−2, 0), (−10, −4)

**H** $\left(5, 2\frac{1}{2}\right), \left(1, \frac{1}{2}\right), (-8, -5)$

**J** $\left(-15, -6\frac{1}{2}\right), (-20, -9), (12, 7)$

**7.** Mrs. Pulaski has been receiving compound interest in a savings account for several years. She never places money into the account, but simply lets it collect interest. The account balance for four years is shown in the table below. What is a reasonable prediction for the approximate amount of money that will be in the account in 2010? *TAKS Obj. 1*

| Year | Balance |
|------|---------|
| 2004 | $8,000 |
| 2005 | $8,360 |
| 2006 | $8,736.20 |
| 2007 | $9,129.33 |

**A** $9,511

**B** $10,418

**C** $13,324

**D** $18,260

**8.** A line contains the points (−2, 4) and (3, −1). Which expression can be used to find the slope of the line? *TAKS Obj. 1*

**F** $\dfrac{4 + 1}{3 + 2}$

**G** $\dfrac{-1 - 4}{3 - (-2)}$

**H** $\dfrac{-1 - 4}{3 - 2}$

**J** $\dfrac{3 - (-1)}{-2 - 4}$

**9.** △*ABC* is similar to △*DEF*.

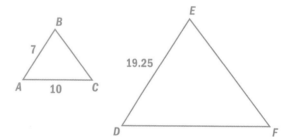

Find the length of $\overline{DF}$. *TAKS Obj. 4*

**A** 3.6 units

**B** 13.5 units

**C** 27.5 units

**D** 30 units

**10.** Which value of *x* will make the set of ordered pairs (*x*, 5), (1, −1), (−1, −7) a linear function? *TAKS Obj. 6*

**F** 1

**G** 2

**H** 3

**J** 4

**11.** **GRIDDED ANSWER** What is the value of *m* when writing $6x - 3y = 11$ in the form $y = mx + b$? *TAKS Obj. 2*

*Record your answer and fill in the bubbles on your answer document. Be sure to use the correct place value.*

# 12 Data Analysis and Probability

TEXAS

## Before

**In previous chapters you've . . .**

- Found the median and range of a data set
- Found probabilities of events

## Now

## Why?

**So you can solve real-world problems about . . .**

- skateboards, p. 671
- poetry, p. 676
- archery, p. 689

 **Math**

at *classzone.com*

- Stem-and-Leaf Plots, p. 649
- Box-and-Whisker Plot, p. 654
- Finding Outcomes, p. 670

## Get-Ready Games

**Review Prerequisite Skills** by playing *Galapagos Graphs.*

**Skill Focus:** Interpreting bar and circle graphs

### GALAPAGOS GRAPHS

#### HOW TO PLAY

 **USE** the data displays to answer each question. Record the letter for each correct answer.

About how many times larger is Santa Cruz than San Cristobal?

**A.** 2      **B.** 3      **C.** 4

What is the area of Isabela?

**D.** 1680 mi$^2$    **E.** 1771 mi$^2$    **F.** 1800 mi$^2$

What percent of the land vertebrate species in the Galapagos Islands are reptiles?

**G.** 10%      **H.** 26%      **I.** 30%

2 **WRITE** the letters of the correct answers to the questions in order. Find the number that corresponds to the letter. Put all three numbers together in the order of the answers. This will tell you the age of the oldest Galapagos tortoise on record.

**A.** 1   **B.** 2   **C.** 0   **D.** 9   **E.** 5

**F.** 2   **G.** 7   **H.** 2   **I.** 5

## Areas of Largest Galapagos Islands

Island (vertical axis): Isabela, Santa Cruz, Fernandina, Santiago, San Cristobal

Square miles (horizontal axis): 0 200 400 600 800 1000 1200 1400 1600 1800

**Great Frigatebird**

### Land Vertebrate Species

Birds 57
Reptiles 23
Mammals 9

**Giant Galapagos Tortoise**

**Galapagos Sea Lion**

## Stop and Think

1. **WRITING** *Describe* one way the circle graph would change if you included the ocean life of the Galapagos Islands.

2. **CRITICAL THINKING** Is the area of Isabela greater than the total area of the next four largest islands? *Explain.*

# Review Prerequisite Skills

## REVIEW WORDS

- **data,** *p. 3*
- **mean,** *p. 272*
- **median,** *p. 272*
- **range,** *p. 273*
- **outcome,** *p. 381*
- **probability of an event,** *p. 381*

## VOCABULARY CHECK

**Copy and complete using a review word from the list at the left.**

1. When you flip a coin, heads and tails are the two possible __?__.

2. Find the sum of the values of a set of data and then divide by the number of data values to find the __?__ of the data.

3. The __?__ is a measure of how likely it is that the event will occur.

## SKILL CHECK

**Find the mean and the median of the data set.** *(p. 272)*

4. 23, 27, 13, 24, 19, 21, 25, 25, 12    5. 0.2, 0.35, 1.33, 1.32, 0.05, 0.5

**Find the probability of the event.** *(p. 381)*

6. You roll a number cube and get a number greater than 4.

7. You randomly choose the letter A from a bag holding the eight lettered tiles that spell ARKANSAS.

**TEXAS @HomeTutor** Prerequisite skills practice at classzone.com

## Notetaking Skills     Contrasting Terms

In each chapter you will learn a new notetaking skill. In Chapter 12 you will apply the strategy of contrasting terms to Example 3 on p. 682.

When words have similar meanings, you should emphasize their differences in your notes.

**Pairs of Angles**

Complementary Angles: The sum of the angle measures is 90°.

Supplementary Angles: The sum of the angle measures is 180°.

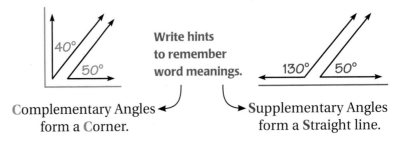

Write hints to remember word meanings.

Complementary Angles form a Corner.

Supplementary Angles form a Straight line.

In Lesson 12.6, you should note the difference between combinations and permutations.

# 12.1 Stem-and-Leaf Plots

TEKS *8.12.C, 8.14.A*

| Before | You organized data using bar graphs and histograms. |
| Now | You will make and interpret stem-and-leaf plots. |
| Why? | So you can organize sports data, as in Example 1. |

**KEY VOCABULARY**
• **stem-and-leaf plot,**
  *p. 649*

**Track**  Hurdlers entering the 200 meter hurdles at a track meet were ranked according to their qualifying times, in seconds, shown below.

$$28.6 \quad 29.2 \quad 28.1 \quad 27.5 \quad 29.8 \quad 28.7$$
$$30.2 \quad 29.3 \quad 28.3 \quad 28.9 \quad 29.9 \quad 28.4$$

How can the data be displayed to show the distribution of the times?

A **stem-and-leaf plot** is a data display that helps you see how data are distributed. A stem-and-leaf plot is useful for ordering large sets of data like the one above.

---

**EXAMPLE 1**  **Making a Stem-and-Leaf Plot**

**STEP 1**  **Identify** the stems. The times range from 27.5 seconds to 30.2 seconds. Let the **stems** be the digits in the tens' and ones' places. Then the **leaves** are the tenths' digits.

**STEP 2**  **Write** the stems first. Then record each time by writing its tenths' digit on the same line as its corresponding stem. Include a key that shows what the stems and leaves represent.

**STEP 3**  **Make** an ordered stem-and-leaf plot.

**Unordered Plot**

*READING*
In a stem-and-leaf plot, a stem can be one or more digits. A leaf is usually a single digit.

| 27 | 5 |
| 28 | 6 1 7 3 9 4 |
| 29 | 2 8 3 9 |
| 30 | 2 |

Key: 27 | 5 = 27.5

**Ordered Plot**

| 27 | 5 |
| 28 | 1 3 4 6 7 9 |
| 29 | 2 3 8 9 |
| 30 | 2 |

Key: 27 | 5 = 27.5

> The leaves for each stem are listed in order from least to greatest.

**Animated Math** at classzone.com

---

✓ **GUIDED PRACTICE**  **for Example 1**

**1.** Make an ordered stem-and-leaf plot of the video game prices: $40, $15, $10, $19, $12, $24, $15, $39, $51, $50, $35, $20, $47, $36, $30, $25, $27, $29, $24, $43, $29.

## EXAMPLE 2  Interpreting a Stem-and-Leaf Plot

*AVOID ERRORS*

Read the key carefully so you understand the data in a stem-and-leaf plot. In Example 2, 6│8 means 68, not 6.8.

**Biology** The stem-and-leaf plot at the right shows the lengths, in millimeters, of fish in a tank. Use the stem-and-leaf plot to describe the data. What interval includes the most lengths?

```
4 │ 9
5 │ 7 7 9
6 │ 1 2 4 4 7 8 8 9
7 │ 6 8
8 │ 4      Key: 6 │ 8 = 68
```

### SOLUTION

The longest fish is 84 millimeters and the shortest fish is 49 millimeters. So the range of lengths is 35 millimeters. Most of the lengths are in the 60–69 interval.

**Double Stem-and-Leaf Plots**  A double stem-and-leaf plot can be used to compare two sets of data. You read to the left of the stems for one set of data and to the right for the other.

## EXAMPLE 3  Making a Double Stem-and-Leaf Plot

**Test Scores** The data below show the test scores for Beth's class and Marisa's class. Overall, which class had the better test scores?

Beth's class:  95, 86, 79, 79, 58, 68, 90, 63, 71, 81, 82, 94, 64, 76, 77, 79, 83, 91, 83, 68, 74, 71

Marisa's class:  95, 73, 76, 84, 84, 89, 67, 82, 88, 86, 93, 97, 96, 84, 60, 75, 91, 87, 89, 86, 76, 93

### SOLUTION

You can use a double stem-and-leaf plot to compare the test scores.

```
    Beth's Class       Marisa's Class

               8 │ 5 │
         8 8 4 3 │ 6 │ 0 7
   9 9 9 7 6 4 1 1 │ 7 │ 3 5 6 6
         6 3 3 2 1 │ 8 │ 2 4 4 4 6 6 7 8 9 9
         5 4 1 0 │ 9 │ 1 3 3 5 6 7    Key: 0 │ 9 │ 1 represents 90 and 91
```

▶ **Answer** Marisa's class had better scores, because her class had more scores in the eighties and nineties.

✓ **GUIDED PRACTICE**   for Examples 2 and 3

2. Make an ordered double stem-and-leaf plot to compare the lengths, in minutes, of the last 15 phone calls made by two friends. In general, who made longer calls, Kenyon or Jason? *Justify* your reasoning.

Kenyon:  8, 12, 8, 17, 5, 28, 16, 23, 29, 14, 21, 34, 16, 28, 31
Jason:  31, 16, 24, 28, 7, 12, 5, 11, 5, 13, 14, 6, 11, 19, 24

# 12.1 EXERCISES

HOMEWORK KEY

🔶 = **TAKS Practice and Reasoning**
Exs. 14, 15, 26, 28, and 33

⬤ = **HINTS** AND **HOMEWORK HELP**
for Exs. 5, 9, 11, 15, 27 at classzone.com

## SKILL PRACTICE

1. **VOCABULARY** Copy and complete: The key for a stem-and-leaf plot says 7 | 4 = 74. In the plot, 7 is the __?__ and 4 is the __?__.

2. **VOCABULARY** Why is it important to include a key in a stem-and-leaf plot?

**SEE EXAMPLE 1**
on p. 649
for Exs. 3–13

**STEMS AND LEAVES** Write the number as it would appear in a stem-and-leaf plot. Identify the stem and the leaf.

3. 80        4. 117        (5.) 12.9        6. 4.6

**STEM-AND-LEAF PLOTS** Make an ordered stem-and-leaf plot of the data. Identify the interval that includes the most data values.

7. 45, 48, 65, 50, 67, 82, 74, 63, 52, 61, 84, 66, 40

8. 33, 12, 8, 14, 35, 9, 26, 37, 4, 6, 8, 20, 15, 32, 29

(9.) 108, 95, 89, 112, 109, 94, 103, 115, 105, 92

10. 461, 492, 439, 467, 501, 485, 475, 451, 510, 468, 494, 461

(11.) 20.2, 22.6, 18.3, 18.7, 22.5, 18.1, 18.6, 21.9, 18.4, 22.8

12. 5.1, 4.0, 5.3, 3.2, 5.7, 6.9, 5.3, 4.6, 5.2, 6.7, 4.9, 4.7, 5.5

13. **ERROR ANALYSIS** Describe and correct the error made in making a stem-and-leaf plot for the data set:

115, 111, 108, 95, 91, 83

```
8 | 3
9 | 1 5        ✕
1 | 8 11 15   Key: 1 | 15 = 115
```

**SEE EXAMPLE 2**
on p. 650
for Exs. 14–15

14. 🔶 **TAKS REASONING** What is the range of the data in the stem-and-leaf plot?

(A) 3        (B) 3.7

(C) 7        (D) 37

```
10 | 1 4
11 | 2 3 5 5 9
12 | 0 0
13 | 1 6 8 8    Key: 12 | 0 = 120
```

(15.) 🔶 **TAKS REASONING** Use the stem-and-leaf plot from Exercise 14. Which interval has the most data values?

(A) 100–109    (B) 110–119    (C) 120–129    (D) 130–139

**DOUBLE STEM-AND-LEAF PLOTS** Make an ordered double stem-and-leaf plot of the two sets of data.

**SEE EXAMPLE 3**
on p. 650
for Exs. 16–19

16. Set A: 16, 19, 8, 22, 18, 20, 32, 5
    Set B: 12, 8, 25, 42, 31, 15, 16, 9

17. Set C: 102, 98, 111, 70, 118, 92, 77
    Set D: 115, 88, 87, 102, 65, 95, 93

18. Set A: 24, 27, 28, 32, 58, 32, 32, 25
    Set B: 22, 31, 43, 22, 21, 55, 36, 29

19. Set C: 8.8, 9.8, 4.7, 6.3, 6.8, 8.0, 7.7
    Set D: 9.5, 6.8, 7.8, 10, 5.5, 9.1, 9.3

**AVERAGES** Find the mean, median, and mode(s) of the data.

**20.**

```
5 | 0 0 1 6
6 | 5 9 9
7 | 1 1 2 4 4 4 8    Key: 5 | 3 = 53
```

**21.**

```
0 | 1 1
1 | 4 5 9
2 | 0 0 5 8 8
3 | 0 9         Key: 1 | 4 = 1.4
```

**CHALLENGE** Make an ordered stem-and-leaf plot with data that have the given characteristics. The display should have at least 8 data values.

**22.** a range of 52 and a mode of 30

**23.** a mean of 10 and a median of 15

## PROBLEM SOLVING

SEE EXAMPLES 1 AND 2 on pp. 649–650 for Ex. 24

**24. GUIDED PROBLEM SOLVING** The times, in minutes, it takes fifteen students to get ready for school are as follows: 25, 10, 25, 15, 30, 18, 35, 40, 28, 20, 28, 17, 12, 22, 32. Make an ordered stem-and-leaf plot of the data. What interval includes the most time values?

   **a.** Identify the highest and lowest data values.

   **b.** Make an ordered stem-and-leaf plot. Include a key.

   **c.** Use the plot to find where most of the times fall.

SEE EXAMPLE 2 on p. 650 for Exs. 25–28

**25. RESTAURANTS** The stem-and-leaf plot shows the average waiting times, in minutes, to be seated for fifteen restaurants. What are the shortest and longest waiting times? Which interval has the fewest number of waiting times?

```
0 | 5 6 9
1 | 2 5 5
2 | 0 0 5 8
3 | 2 8
4 | 0 5 5      Key: 2 | 5 = 25
```

**26. TAKS REASONING** The stem-and-leaf plot shows the ages of several people. What is the median age?

   **(A)** 25          **(B)** 30

   **(C)** 31          **(D)** 37

```
1 | 3 7 9
2 | 0 1 4 5
3 | 7 9
4 | 0 1 2 2 2  Key: 4 | 1 = 41
```

**ELECTRIC BILLS** In Exercises 27 and 28, use the line graph. It shows the cost of a family's electric bills for each of 11 months.

**27.** Make an ordered stem-and-leaf plot of the monthly costs. Find the median and the range of the data.

**28. TAKS REASONING** Which display is more useful for finding the range? the median? *Explain.*

= **TAKS Practice and Reasoning**      ◯ = **HINTS AND HOMEWORK HELP** *at* classzone.com

**29. WRITING** Can you make a stem-and-leaf plot from a frequency table? *Explain* why or why not.

*SEE EXAMPLE 3*
on p. 650
for Ex. 30

**30. FOOTBALL** The total points that the Cleveland Browns scored in each game of a recent season are given below. Red numbers represent wins, and blue numbers represent losses. Make an ordered double stem-and-leaf plot of the data. *Describe* the relationship between points scored and the outcome of the game.

6  24  23  20  14  24  21  12
27  18  15  16  10  7  41  7

**31.** ◆ **MULTIPLE REPRESENTATIONS** The average monthly temperatures in degrees Fahrenheit (°F) for Los Angeles, California, are given below.

56.8, 57.6, 58.0, 60.1, 62.7, 65.7, 69.1, 70.5, 69.9, 66.8, 61.6, 56.9

**a. Display** Make an ordered stem-and-leaf plot of the data. What is the range?

**b. Convert** Convert the data to degrees Celsius (°C) using the formula $C = \frac{5}{9}(F - 32)$. Round to the nearest tenth of a degree.

**c. Compare** Make an ordered stem-and-leaf plot of the converted data. *Describe* how the plots are alike and how they are different.

**32. CHALLENGE** For an awards banquet, you are making a highlight video that can last no more than 15 minutes. Use the following lengths, in minutes, of the video segments you'd like to include.

2:30, 2:29, 2:14, 2:19, 1:49, 2:30, 2:57, 2:30, 2:01, 2:21, 1:53

Make an ordered stem-and-leaf plot of the data. *Explain* how you chose a key. What is the greatest and least number of segments that you can show without leaving time for another? *Justify* your reasoning.

## MIXED REVIEW FOR TAKS

**TAKS PRACTICE** at classzone.com

*REVIEW*
Lesson 11.2;
TAKS Workbook

**33.** **TAKS PRACTICE** The scatterplot shows the number of people, in millions, who attended symphony orchestra concerts in the United States each year from 1998 to 2002. Which best describes the data over the 5 years? *TAKS Obj. 5*

Symphony Orchestra Attendance

**A** Attendance decreased about 6%

**B** Attendance increased about 6%

**C** Attendance decreased about 50%

**D** Attendance increased about 50%

# 12.2 Box-and-Whisker Plots

 TEKS *8.12.A, 8.12.C*

**Before** You found the median and range of a data set.
**Now** You will make and interpret box-and-whisker plots.
**Why?** So you can show data distribution, as in Example 1.

**KEY VOCABULARY**
• box-and-whisker plot, *p. 654*
• lower quartile, *p. 654*
• upper quartile, *p. 654*
• lower extreme, *p. 654*
• upper extreme, *p. 654*

**Bridges** The lengths, in meters, of the world's ten longest suspension bridges are listed below. How can you display these data to show how the lengths are distributed?

1280  1490  1991  1377  1298  1210  1624  1158  1385  1410

A **box-and-whisker plot** is a data display that organizes data values into four parts. Ordered data are divided into lower and upper halves by the median.

The **lower quartile** is the median of the lower half of the data set. The median of the upper half of the data set is the **upper quartile**.

The **lower extreme** is the least data value and the **upper extreme** is the greatest data value.

---

**EXAMPLE 1** **Making a Box-and-Whisker Plot**

*FIND QUARTILES*
If a data set has an odd number of values, then the median is not included in either half of the data when finding the quartiles. For help with finding a median, see p. 272.

Display the bridge lengths above in a box-and-whisker plot.

**STEP 1** **Order** the data to find the median, the quartiles, and the extremes.

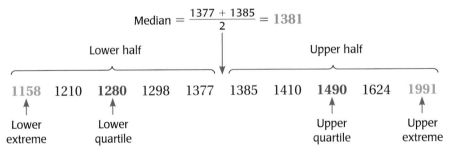

$$\text{Median} = \frac{1377 + 1385}{2} = 1381$$

**STEP 2** **Plot** these values below a number line.

Draw a box with sides at both quartiles.   Draw a vertical line through the median.   Draw "whiskers" from the box to both extremes.

*Animated* **Math** at classzone.com

**Interpreting a Box-and-Whisker Plot** A box-and-whisker plot helps to show how varied, or spread out, the data are. The points divide the data into four parts. Each part represents about one quarter of the data. The *interquartile range* is the difference of the upper quartile and the lower quartile.

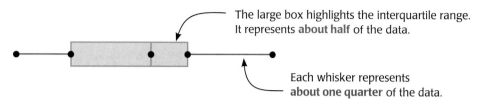

The large box highlights the interquartile range. It represents **about half** of the data.

Each whisker represents **about one quarter** of the data.

You can use box-and-whisker plots to compare two or more data sets.

## EXAMPLE 2 Interpreting Box-and-Whisker Plots

**Food Science** You are testing whether a fertilizer helps tomato plants grow. You divide the plants into two equal groups, and give fertilizer to the plants in Group 2, but not to Group 1. The box-and-whisker plots show how much the plants grew, in centimeters, for each group of plants after two weeks.

a. About what fraction of the unfertilized plants grew as much as any of the fertilized plants?

b. About what fraction of the fertilized plants grew 4 to 8 centimeters?

### SOLUTION

a. The right whisker for Group 1 overlaps the left whisker for Group 2. So about one quarter of the unfertilized plants grew as much as any of the fertilized plants.

b. The large box in the plot for Group 2 ranges from 4 to 8, so about one half of the fertilized plants grew 4 to 8 centimeters.

✓ **GUIDED PRACTICE**    **for Examples 1 and 2**

**Exercising** Over a period of ten days, Ming exercised for 34, 27, 26, 15, 24, 21, 30, 23, 24, and 35 minutes. Chantelle exercised for 26, 33, 36, 21, 41, 36, 29, 25, 34, and 35 minutes.

1. Make a box-and-whisker plot of the data for each person.

2. Who usually exercised longer? *Explain.*

3. About how often did each person exercise for 25–35 minutes?

# 12.2 EXERCISES

HOMEWORK KEY

= TAKS Practice and Reasoning
Exs. 14, 20, 22, 27, 28, 31, and 32

○ = HINTS AND HOMEWORK HELP
for Exs. 3, 9, 13, 23 at classzone.com

## SKILL PRACTICE

**VOCABULARY** **Copy and complete the statement.**

1. The median of the lower half of a data set is the __?__.

2. The upper and lower __?__ of a data set are the greatest and least data values.

**MAKING BOX-AND-WHISKER PLOTS** **Make a box-and-whisker plot of the data.**

*SEE EXAMPLE 1*
on p. 654
for Exs. 3–7

3. $67, $53, $41, $33, $52, $28, $70, $56, $54, $48, $65, $72, $44, $59, $62

4. 327 ft, 419 ft, 9 ft, 299 ft, 111 ft, 0 ft, 254 ft, 126 ft, 192 ft, 284 ft

5. 26 m, 389 m, 878 m, 144 m, 515 m, 404 m, 423 m, 357 m, 421 m, 593 m

6. 92 cm, 106 cm, 84 cm, 120 cm, 12 cm, 256 cm, 396 cm, 1024 cm, 297 cm

7. **ERROR ANALYSIS** You are analyzing the data set 23, 25, 29, 31, 33, 35.
Your friend says that because the greatest data value is 35, the upper
quartile is 35. Describe and correct the error made by your friend.

*SEE EXAMPLE 2*
on p. 655
for Exs. 8–14

**ESTIMATION** **The box-and-whisker plot shows the lengths, in inches, of
the jumps in a frog-jumping contest. Estimate the following values.**

8. median          9. lower quartile          10. range          11. upper extreme

**USING A BOX-AND-WHISKER PLOT** **In Exercises 12–15, use the plot below.**

12. About what fraction of the data values are in the interval from 40 to 50?

13. Between what two values are the median and about half of the data located?

14. **TAKS REASONING** About what percent of the data values are *not* in
the range from 15 to 25?

Ⓐ 25%          Ⓑ 50%          Ⓒ 75%          Ⓓ 100%

15. **WHICH ONE DOESN'T BELONG?** Which number below must be a data
value from which the box-and-whisker plot was made?

**A.** 25          **B.** 40          **C.** 50          **D.** 75

**REASONING** Tell whether the statement is *true* or *false*. *Justify* your reasoning.

**16.** The interquartile range includes about half of the data.

**17.** There are more data values from the lower extreme to the lower quartile than there are from the median to the upper quartile.

**18.** The range of a data set is twice the interquartile range.

**19. CHALLENGE** Change one value in the data set below so that the median of the data becomes 13, the lower quartile becomes 7, and the upper quartile becomes 17. *Explain* your reasoning.

3, 4, 5, 7, 9, 11, 13, 15, 17, 18, 21

## PROBLEM SOLVING

*SEE EXAMPLE 1*
on p. 654
for Exs. 20–21

**20.** **TAKS REASONING** The data below are the weights, in pounds, of 10 giant pumpkins.

853, 811.5, 785, 1020, 826.5, 789, 838, 810, 731, 822.5

What is the upper quartile of the data?

**(A)** 789  **(B)** 810  **(C)** 817  **(D)** 838

**21. GUIDED PROBLEM SOLVING** You had the following scores while playing a math game: 306, 211, 235, 197, 351, 141, 227, 296, 159, 324, 280, and 267. Make a box-and-whisker plot of your scores.

  **a.** Find the range and draw a number line.

  **b.** Find the median, quartiles, and extremes.

  **c.** Draw the box-and-whisker plot.

**22.** **TAKS REASONING** *Explain* how making a line plot or stem-and-leaf plot can help you to make a box-and-whisker plot. When would a line plot be a better choice?

*SEE EXAMPLE 2*
on p. 655
for Exs. 23–24

**23.** **BASKETBALL** The box-and-whisker plots show the points scored in several games for two players. What conclusions can you make about the players' performances? Which player is more consistent? *Explain*.

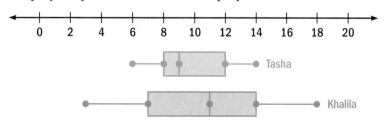

**24. CAMERA PRICES** The prices of several cameras are $179.99, $329.99, $229.99, $284.99, $399.99, $379.99, $299.99, $259.99, and $259.99. Order the list of prices from least to greatest. Then make a box-and-whisker plot of the data. What conclusions can you make?

**LAKE AREA** Use the following areas, in square kilometers, of the world's ten largest lakes: 371,000, 82,100, 69,500, 64,500, 59,600, 57,800, 32,900, 31,500, 31,300, 28,900.

**25.** An *outlier* is a data value that is much less or much greater than all or most of the other values in a data set. Make a box-and-whisker plot of the data above. Which value is an outlier?

**26.** **WRITING** Remove the outlier and then make another box-and-whisker plot. *Describe* how an outlier affects a box-and-whisker plot.

**27.** **TAKS REASONING** Choose three exercises from Exercises 20–30 in this lesson. Count the number of words in each sentence. Record this data in a stem-and-leaf plot or a line plot. Repeat using a long newspaper article. Make a box-and-whisker plot comparing the two sets of data. What conclusions can you make?

**28.** **TAKS REASONING** The masses, in grams, of 10 sample bolts from two factories are shown. The masses should be between 198.5 and 202 grams.

> Factory A: 199, 201, 200, 198.5, 200.5, 202, 201, 200.8, 200.9, 198.5
> Factory B: 201, 200.4, 203, 200.8, 201, 203.4, 200.6, 201, 200.9, 203.1

**a.** Make box-and-whisker plots using the same number line to compare the samples.

**b.** *Describe* how well each factory makes bolts within the desired mass range, based on the samples.

**CHALLENGE** For Exercises 29 and 30, use the circle graph. It displays the age groups of 16 people in a club.

*Age of Attendees*

— 13–15 years 25%
— 19–47 years 25%
— 16–18 years 50%

**29.** Make two sets of data that could be represented by the circle graph. Make each set have different medians and quartiles. Then make box-and-whisker plots of each set.

**30.** In a friend's answer to Exercise 29, one data set has 13 ages ranging from 13 to 19. In the other, one age is 18 and four are greater than 40. *Explain* how the upper quartiles of these data sets vary.

---

## MIXED REVIEW FOR TAKS

**TAKS** **PRACTICE** at classzone.com

*REVIEW*
Lesson 11.1;
TAKS Workbook

**31.** **TAKS PRACTICE** The $n$th term of a sequence equals $n + 2(n - 3)$. What are the 7th and 8th terms in the sequence? *TAKS Obj. 2*

**(A)** 7, 8    **(B)** 15, 18    **(C)** 18, 21    **(D)** 36, 50

*REVIEW*
Lesson 8.6;
TAKS Workbook

**32.** **TAKS PRACTICE** $\triangle ABC$ has vertices $A(2, 1)$, $B(4, 3)$, and $C(6, 2)$. $\triangle A'B'C'$ is formed by reflecting $\triangle ABC$ across the $x$-axis. Point $B'$ lies in which quadrant? *TAKS Obj. 3*

**(F)** Quadrant I    **(G)** Quadrant II

**(H)** Quadrant III    **(J)** Quadrant IV

 **ONLINE QUIZ** at classzone.com

# 12.3 Using Data Displays

TEKS *8.12.C, 8.15.A*

| | |
|---|---|
| **Before** | You organized data using box-and-whisker plots. |
| **Now** | You will organize data using circle graphs and line graphs. |
| **Why?** | So you can analyze data, such as for insect species in Example 2. |

**KEY VOCABULARY**
- **circle graph,** *p. 659*
- **line graph,** *p. 660*

**Whistling Survey** A survey asked, "How well can you whistle?" The results are shown in the *circle graph* below.

A **circle graph** represents data as sections of a circle. Each section can be labeled with its data value or with the data value's portion of the whole written as a fraction, decimal, or percent. Because the graph represents all the data, the sum of the portions must equal 1, or 100%.

**How Well Can You Whistle?**
- Can whistle a tune 75%
- Can whistle a note 12%
- Can't whistle 13%

To make a circle graph, find the angle measure, to the nearest degree, that represents each data value's portion of the whole. The sum of all the angle measures must equal 360°, the number of degrees in a circle.

## EXAMPLE 1  Making a Circle Graph

**E-mail** A survey asked, "How often do you check your e-mail?" Of the 100 people asked, 4 responded *less than weekly*, 23 responded *weekly*, and 73 responded *every day*. Display the data in a circle graph.

**STEP 1** Use a proportion to find the number of degrees you should use to represent each response as a section of a circle graph.

| **Less than weekly** | **Weekly** | **Every day** |
|---|---|---|
| $\dfrac{4}{100} = \dfrac{a}{360°}$ | $\dfrac{23}{100} = \dfrac{b}{360°}$ | $\dfrac{73}{100} = \dfrac{c}{360°}$ |
| $a = 14.4° \approx \mathbf{14°}$ | $b = 82.8° \approx \mathbf{83°}$ | $c = 262.8° \approx 263°$ |

**STEP 2** Draw a circle. Show its center.

**STEP 3** Use a protractor to draw the first angle measure. Label the section.

**STEP 4** Draw and label remaining sections. Include a title.

*Check Your E-mail?*
- Less than weekly 4
- Weekly 23
- Every day 73

> **DRAW SECTIONS**
> In Example 1, you can draw the 14° and 83° angles first. Then the remaining section of the circle will have a measure of 263°.

The graph shows that most people check their e-mail every day.

**Line Graphs** A **line graph** uses line segments to connect data points. A line graph is often used to represent data that change over time.

---

**EXAMPLE 2** Making a Line Graph

**Environment** The table shows the number of insect species on the United States endangered species list. Make a line graph of the data.

| Year | 1994 | 1996 | 1998 | 2000 | 2002 | 2004 |
|------|------|------|------|------|------|------|
| Number | 19 | 20 | 28 | 33 | 35 | 35 |

**AVOID ERRORS**
Make sure you choose the horizontal and vertical scales carefully so that the data are not distorted.

**STEP 1** **Draw** and label the horizontal and vertical scales.

**STEP 2** **Plot** a point for each data pair.

**STEP 3** **Draw** line segments to connect the points. Include a title.

The graph shows an increase over time.

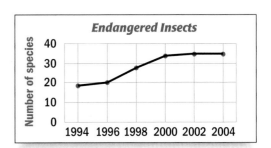

---

✓ **GUIDED PRACTICE** for Examples 1 and 2

**Use the table of polling data.**

1. Make a circle graph of the data for Week 1. What does the graph show?

2. Make a line graph of the data for Ben. What does the graph show?

| Who Will You Vote For? | | | |
|------|------|------|------|
| Week | 1 | 2 | 3 |
| Ben | 55% | 50% | 40% |
| Alice | 45% | 50% | 60% |

---

**CONCEPT SUMMARY** *For Your Notebook*

**TAKING NOTES**
For each type of data display you study, include an example in your notebook along with a summary of the information that you can read from the display.

**Using Appropriate Data Displays**

Using appropriate data displays helps you analyze data.

Use a *circle graph* to represent data as parts of a whole.

Use a *line graph* to display data over time.

Use a *stem-and-leaf plot* to order a data set.

Use a *box-and-whisker plot* to show the data's distribution in quarters, using the median, quartiles, and extremes.

Use a *bar graph* to display data in distinct categories.

Use a *Venn diagram* to display data in overlapping categories.

Use a *histogram* to compare the frequencies of data that are grouped in equal intervals.

---

EXAMPLE 3 **Choosing a Data Display**

**Choose an appropriate display for the data.**

**a.** The table shows the results of a survey that asked students if they are going away during summer vacation.

| Response | Percent |
|----------|---------|
| Yes | 48% |
| No | 37% |
| Don't know | 15% |

**b.** The table shows the results of a survey that asked students why they use the Internet.

| Purpose | Percent |
|---------|---------|
| Research | 62% |
| Shopping | 34% |
| E-mail | 45% |
| Browsing | 18% |

**AVOID ERRORS**
You can only display data with a circle graph if the categories don't overlap and the percents add up to 100%, as in part (a) of Example 3.

**SOLUTION**

**a.** The percents total 100%, so a circle graph is appropriate.

**b.** The percents total more than 100%. An appropriate display is a bar graph.

✓ **GUIDED PRACTICE** for Example 3

**3. Surveys** Choose an appropriate display for the results of a survey asking "How often do you finish your homework before dinner?" The results were: *always*, 25%; *sometimes*, 45%; *never*, 30%. *Explain* your choice.

# 12.3 EXERCISES

HOMEWORK KEY
= **TAKS Practice and Reasoning**
Exs. 15, 16, 25, 26, and 35

○ = **HINTS AND HOMEWORK HELP**
for Exs. 3, 5, 7, 11, 25 at classzone.com

## SKILL PRACTICE

1. **VOCABULARY** Copy and complete: Use a __?__ to display data as parts of a whole, and a __?__ to display changes in a quantity over time.

**FINDING ANGLES** Find the angle measure in a circle graph for the given ratio.

**SEE EXAMPLE 1**
on p. 659
for Exs. 2–8

**2.** 31%          **3.** $\frac{3}{8}$          **4.** 14%          **5.** 27 out of 60

**MAKING CIRCLE GRAPHS** A survey asked 200 students "How often do you snack during the day?" Make a circle graph of the survey data.

**6.**
| Answer | Students |
|--------|----------|
| *Never* | 20 |
| *Rarely* | 90 |
| *Sometimes* | 70 |
| *Often* | 20 |

**7.**
| Answer | Students |
|--------|----------|
| *Never* | 0 |
| *Rarely* | 50 |
| *Sometimes* | 120 |
| *Often* | 30 |

**8.**
| Answer | Students |
|--------|----------|
| *Never* | 40 |
| *Rarely* | 20 |
| *Sometimes* | 85 |
| *Often* | 55 |

**MAKING LINE GRAPHS** Make a line graph of the data.

**SEE EXAMPLE 2**
on p. 660
for Exs. 9–11

**9.**

| Day | Mon | Tue | Wed | Thu | Fri |
|---|---|---|---|---|---|
| Distance (mi) | 480 | 400 | 355 | 350 | 402 |

**10.**

| Month | Jan | Feb | Mar | Apr | May | Jun |
|---|---|---|---|---|---|---|
| Sales | $4500 | $4800 | $6250 | $5000 | $5400 | $7300 |

**11.**

| Year | 2000 | 2001 | 2002 | 2003 | 2004 |
|---|---|---|---|---|---|
| Rainfall (in.) | 8.5 | 6.8 | 2.4 | 2.4 | 8.2 |

**SEE EXAMPLE 1**
on p. 659
for Ex. 12

**12. ERROR ANALYSIS** A survey asked 75 students "Do you like the new lunch menu?" The responses were: *yes*, 50; *no*, 10; *undecided*, 15. Describe and correct the error made in finding the angle measures for a circle graph of the data.

$\times$ Yes = 50%, or 180°
No = 10%, or 36°
Undecided = 360 − (180 + 36)
= 144°

**CHOOSING APPROPRIATE DISPLAYS** Choose an appropriate display for the data. *Justify* your choice.

**SEE EXAMPLE 3**
on p. 661
for Exs. 13–19

**13.**

| Response | Students |
|---|---|
| Yes | 240 |
| No | 640 |
| Not sure | 120 |

**14.**

| Week | Percent |
|---|---|
| 1 | 50% |
| 2 | 59% |
| 3 | 53% |

**15. TAKS REASONING** You polled 30 students in your class about how much their families pay for Internet service. Twelve of the 30 pay more than $25 per month. Which proportion could you use to find the number of degrees in the section of a circle graph that represents these results?

**A** $\frac{12}{30} = \frac{x}{360}$     **B** $\frac{12}{30} = \frac{360}{x}$     **C** $\frac{12}{25} = \frac{x}{30}$     **D** $\frac{12}{25} = \frac{30}{x}$

**16. TAKS REASONING** *Write* a survey question that meets the condition. *Justify* your answer.

  **a.** The results can be displayed in a circle graph.

  **b.** The results cannot be displayed in a circle graph.

**REASONING** In Exercises 17–19, tell which type of display you would use for the data described. *Explain* your reasoning.

**17.** You record the temperature at noon every day for a month.

**18.** You record the temperature at five locations at a given time.

**19.** You record the high temperature every day for a month, and find how often the daily high temperature falls within each 10 degree temperature interval.

**20. CHALLENGE** *Describe* a set of data that could be displayed in three types of data displays. *Explain* how to display it in each.

SEE EXAMPLES
1 AND 2
on pp. 659–660
for Exs. 21–22

**THEATER** Use the table showing attendance at your school play.

21. Make a circle graph to display each attendance number as a portion of the total attendance.

22. Tickets cost $7 each. Make a line graph that shows how much money was collected from each performance.

| Play Attendance | |
|---|---|
| *Friday* | 130 |
| *Saturday (2:00 P.M.)* | 231 |
| *Saturday (8:00 P.M. )* | 291 |
| *Sunday* | 185 |

**NEW YORK CITY** In Exercises 23 and 24, use the map. It shows the land area in square miles of each of the five boroughs of New York City.

23. To the nearest whole percent, find the total area of New York City that each borough covers.

24. Represent the data using a circle graph. Then compare the areas of the boroughs.

25. ✦ **TAKS REASONING** You ask 100 people a yes or no question. The possible answers are *yes*, *no*, and *no answer*. What types of displays would be appropriate for this type of data? *Explain* your reasoning.

26. ✦ **TAKS REASONING** Use the whistling graph on page 659. Which is a reasonable estimate of the number of people out of 500 who will be unable to whistle?

   Ⓐ 375       Ⓑ 65       Ⓒ 60       Ⓓ 13

**TELEPHONE SALES** Use the table showing the number, in thousands, of corded and cordless telephones sold to dealers from 1999 to 2004.

| | *1999* | *2000* | *2001* | *2002* | *2003* | *2004* |
|---|---|---|---|---|---|---|
| *Corded* | 34,486 | 29,670 | 24,957 | 23,813 | 21,918 | 20,051 |
| *Cordless* | 39,654 | 39,042 | 40,000 | 36,556 | 37,998 | 33,809 |

27. Make a double line graph showing these data. *Explain* how you chose the scale you used on the vertical axis.

28. Between which two consecutive years did the number of cordless telephones sold increase the most? Is this easier to tell from the *table* or the *graph*? *Justify* your answer.

29. What is the mean of the annual decreases in sales of corded telephones from 1999 to 2004?

30. **WRITING** What can you conclude about the trends in sales of each type of telephone? *Justify* your answer using the graph.

**Football** Barry Sanders was a running back for the Detroit Lions from 1989 to 1998. He was inducted into the Professional Football Hall of Fame in 2004. During his career, he rushed for a total of 15,269 yards and led the league in rushing yards four times. The table below shows his rushing attempts and average rushing yards per attempt.

| Season | 1989 | 1990 | 1991 | 1992 | 1993 | 1994 | 1995 | 1996 | 1997 | 1998 |
|---|---|---|---|---|---|---|---|---|---|---|
| Attempts | 280 | 255 | 342 | 312 | 243 | 331 | 314 | 307 | 335 | 343 |
| Average Yards | 5.25 | 5.10 | 4.53 | 4.33 | 4.59 | 5.69 | 4.78 | 5.06 | 6.13 | 4.35 |

31. **Calculate** Copy the table. Add a third row showing Sanders's *total* career rushing yards at the end of each season. Round to the nearest yard.

32. **Decide** Choose an appropriate display for the data calculated in Exercise 31. *Explain* why you chose the display.

33. **Analyze** *Explain* how you can use the display to determine if Sanders accumulated more rushing yards from 1989–1993 or 1994–1998.

34. **CHALLENGE** A circle graph has 4 sections formed using an obtuse angle, a right angle, and two acute angles. *Describe* two data sets that could be represented by such a graph.

## MIXED REVIEW FOR TAKS

**TAKS** PRACTICE at classzone.com

*REVIEW*
Lesson 12.1;
TAKS Workbook

35. **TAKS PRACTICE** The stem-and-leaf plot shows the duration, in minutes, of each movie in your DVD collection. Use this data to find the probability that a movie chosen at random is more than 2 hours long. *TAKS Obj. 6*

Ⓐ $\frac{2}{5}$   Ⓑ $\frac{9}{20}$   Ⓒ $\frac{1}{2}$   Ⓓ $\frac{2}{3}$

```
10 | 2 6 8 9
11 | 0 1 4 4 7 9 9
12 | 0 1 1 2 3 5 9
13 |
14 | 7 8          Key: 12 | 1 = 121
```

## QUIZ for Lessons 12.1–12.3

1. **ATTENDANCE** Make an ordered double stem-and-leaf plot comparing the ballpark attendance data below for April and June. Then make a pair of box-and-whisker plots that compare the data. Use the displays to compare April attendance to June attendance. *(p. 649)*

   April: 1025, 1058, 1030, 997, 990, 1116, 1001, 995, 1122, 1099
   June: 1056, 1125, 1151, 1048, 1123, 1097, 1042, 1164, 1125, 1131

2. **FOOD** Consumption of peanuts per person in the United States was as follows: 1999, 6 lb; 2000, 5.8 lb; 2001, 5.9 lb; 2002, 5.8 lb; 2003, 6.3 lb. Make a circle graph or a line graph of the data. *Explain* your choice. *(p. 659)*

**ONLINE QUIZ** at classzone.com

**TEKS** *8.12.C*

# 12.3 Making Data Displays

**EXAMPLE 1** The table shows the cost, in dollars, of a phone call based on the length, in minutes, of the call. Make a scatter plot or a line graph using a calculator.

| Minutes | Cost |
|---------|------|
| 5 | 0.5 |
| 10 | 1 |
| 15 | 1.5 |
| 20 | 2 |
| 25 | 2.4 |
| 30 | 2.7 |

**SOLUTION**

**STEP 1** **Enter** the data into two lists.

**STEP 2** **Choose** maximums and minimums for the window.

**STEP 3** **Choose** a display from the PLOT menu and set the Xlist and Ylist.

Choose ⊾⋅ː for a scatter plot or ⟋ for a line graph.

**STEP 4** **Press** GRAPH to show the display you have chosen.

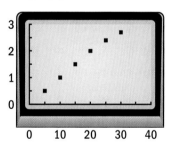

**PRACTICE** Make a scatter plot and a line graph of the data.

1.

| Year | 2000 | 2001 | 2002 | 2003 | 2004 | 2005 |
|------|------|------|------|------|------|------|
| Rainfall (in.) | 21.4 | 39.8 | 34.5 | 26.1 | 44.9 | 38.7 |

*Continued on next page*

**EXAMPLE 2** The table shows the number of people out of 200 surveyed who prefer each type of music. Use a graphing calculator to make a circle graph of the data.

| Favorite Music | |
|---|---|
| *Pop* | 75 |
| *Rock* | 62 |
| *Country* | 43 |
| *Classical* | 20 |

**SOLUTION**

**STEP 1** **Press** LIST . Then use the TEXT menu to name a list and its categories. Use quotation marks for the first item, so the calculator recognizes that the list is *categorical* (contains words).

Use quotation marks for categorical data.

Enter the numerical data into a second list.

**STEP 2** **Use** the PLOT menu to choose the two lists.

You can display the data as numbers or as percents.

**STEP 3** **Press** GRAPH to display the circle graph.

number display

**PRACTICE** Make a circle graph of the survey data.

2.

| Did You Get Enough Sleep? | |
|---|---|
| *Need more* | 541 |
| *Need less* | 167 |
| *Just right* | 282 |
| *Don't know* | 21 |

3.

| The Last Movie I Saw I Watched ... | |
|---|---|
| *in a theater.* | 410 |
| *on television.* | 483 |
| *on a computer.* | 21 |

# Misleading Graphs

TEKS *8.13.B, 8.15.B*

**GOAL** Identify and analyze misleading graphs.

**KEY VOCABULARY**
• **bar graph,** *p. 3*
• **line graph,** *p. 660*

When you analyze a graph to make conclusions about the data, be aware that the display may be misleading.

**EXAMPLE 1** Identifying a Misleading Graph

**Attendance** Which of the bar graphs that show attendance at an annual rock festival from 2006 to 2010 could be misleading?

*READING*
.....................
Remember that the broken axis symbol ⤴ indicates that some of the values in the axis have been left out.

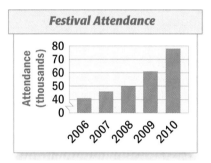

The first graph has a break in the vertical axis, so comparing the bars may lead to incorrect conclusions. It looks as if attendance in 2010 was three or four times as great as in 2006, but attendance only doubled during this time. The second graph is less likely to mislead.

**EXAMPLE 2** Analyzing Misleading Graphs

**Business** The line graphs below display a company's profits and sales for each year from 2006 to 2010. What is misleading about each graph?

**a.**

**b.**
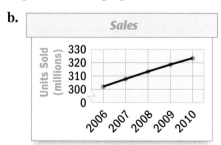

**SOLUTION**

**a.** The range on the vertical scale is greater than needed. The graph suggests that profits have decreased only slightly, when they have decreased by a third.

**b.** Because the vertical axis starts at 300, sales seem to have risen rapidly. An unbroken axis would show that sales have risen slowly, at less than 2% per year.

**EXAMPLE 3**  **Misleading Comparisons**

**Resorts** Compare the average monthly temperatures at two resorts.

**SOLUTION**

At a glance, the displays suggest that the temperatures are about the same, but the vertical axes are different.

When data for both resorts are graphed together, it becomes clear that Sunny Vista has warmer temperatures.

## EXERCISES

**Tell whether the data are represented clearly. If the graph is misleading, explain why. Then redraw the graph so that it is not misleading.**

**1.**

**2.**

**3. Baseball** The table below shows a baseball pitcher's wins and losses per season. Make a graph that suggests a positive performance. Then make another graph that suggests a negative performance.

| Year | 2000 | 2001 | 2002 | 2003 | 2004 |
|------|------|------|------|------|------|
| **Wins** | 6 | 8 | 10 | 12 | 16 |
| **Losses** | 7 | 9 | 9 | 13 | 14 |

## Lessons 12.1–12.3

**MULTIPLE CHOICE**

1. **SOFTBALL** The stem-and-leaf plot shows the number of home runs for each player on a softball team. Which measure of data is represented by 21? *TEKS 8.12.A*

   **Home Runs**

   ```
   0 | 4 5 7 8
   1 | 2 4 5 6 6 8
   2 | 1 4 5        Key: 1|2 = 12
   ```

   **(A)** Mean     **(B)** Median

   **(C)** Mode     **(D)** Range

2. **CAMERAS** You have two sets of data. Each set consists of 15 camera prices. Both data sets have identical box-and-whisker plots. Which statement must be true? *TEKS 8.15.A*

   **(F)** The prices in one set of data are identical to the prices in the other set of data.

   **(G)** The means of both data sets are equal.

   **(H)** The highest and lowest prices in both data sets are the same.

   **(J)** The ranges of both data sets equal 15.

3. **AGES** Which set of data values representing people's ages has a range of 23, an upper quartile of 45, an interquartile range of 10, and a median of 41? *TEKS 8.16.B*

   **(A)** {23, 26, 32, 36, 41, 42, 42, 45, 45, 46}

   **(B)** {23, 26, 32, 36, 41, 41, 33, 54, 54, 35}

   **(C)** {19, 25, 32, 31, 40, 42, 33, 24, 19, 35}

   **(D)** {55, 39, 43, 36, 44, 32, 33, 54, 45, 35}

4. **VIDEO GAMES** The numbers of minutes that you and a friend played a video game are given below. Red numbers represent your times, and blue numbers represent your friend's times. Which graph best represents the data? *TEKS 8.15.B*

   12, 10, 26, 22, 18, 17, 5, 20, 22, 18, 15, 8, 14, 19, 22, 23, 25, 8, 16, 20

   **(F)**

   **(G)**

   | Your times | | Your friend's times |
   |---|---|---|
   | 8 8 5 | 0 | 3 7 9 |
   | 8 2 0 | 1 | 4 5 6 7 8 9 |
   | 0 | 2 | 0 2 2 2 3 5 6 |

   Key: 1 | 4 = 14

   **(H)** *Video Game Times*

   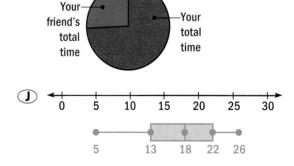

   **(J)**

**GRIDDED ANSWER** ⓪①●③④⑤⑥⑦⑧⑨

5. **CIRCLE GRAPH** Your class has 18 males and 30 females. You want to display this information in a circle graph. What angle, in degrees, should you use to represent the portion of your class that is male? *TEKS 8.12.C*

# 12.4 Counting Methods

| | |
|---|---|
| **Before** | You found theoretical and experimental probability. |
| **Now** | You will use counting methods to count the number of choices. |
| **Why?** | So you can count the number of skateboard designs, as in Example 2. |

**KEY VOCABULARY**
• tree diagram, *p. 670*

## ACTIVITY

**You can count choices using an organized list.**

You are choosing an outfit. You can choose a T-shirt (T), a button-down shirt (B), or a sweater (S) as a top, and jeans (J) or khakis (K) for pants.

 T-shirt **(T)**    button-down **(B)**    sweater **(S)**    jeans **(J)**    khakis **(K)**

**STEP 1** **Make** a list of all possible outfits. Use the letters to represent possible outfits. One possible outfit is TJ, which means a T-shirt and jeans.

**STEP 2** **Add** dress pants (D) in addition to jeans and khakis as a choice for pants. How many outfits are possible now?

*Animated* Math
at classzone.com

In the activity, you made lists to count the number of choices. Another way to count the number of choices is to use a **tree diagram**.

## EXAMPLE 1 Making a Tree Diagram

You can make a tree diagram to count the number of possible outfits after adding a green polo shirt (P) following Step 2 of the activity above. Use branches to match each type of shirt with each type of pants.

T          B          S          P

J  K  D    J  K  D    J  K  D    J  K  D

There are 12 different possible outfits.

Another way to count choices is to use the *counting principle.*

**EXAMPLE 2** Using the Counting Principle

**Skateboards** To build a skateboard, you can choose one deck and one type of wheel assembly from those shown. To count the number of different skateboards you can build, use the counting principle.

Decks

Wheel Assemblies

$$5 \quad \cdot \quad 3 \quad = \quad 15 \qquad \text{Counting principle}$$

**decks**     **wheel assemblies**

▶**Answer** You can build 15 different skateboards.

**EXAMPLE 3** Using the Counting Principle

**Passwords** You are choosing a password that starts with 3 letters and then has 2 digits. How many different passwords are possible?

**SOLUTION**

$$\underbrace{26 \cdot 26 \cdot 26}_{\text{letters}} \cdot \underbrace{10 \cdot 10}_{\text{digits}} = 1{,}757{,}600 \qquad \text{Counting principle}$$

▶**Answer** There are 1,757,600 different possible passwords.

✓ **GUIDED PRACTICE**     for Examples 1, 2, and 3

1. **What If?** You decide to include socks as part of the outfit in Example 1. You can choose between red (R) and green (G). How many outfits are possible?

2. **Soccer Uniforms** Your soccer team's uniform choices include yellow and green shirts, white, black, and green shorts, and four colors of socks. How many different uniforms are possible?

3. **What If?** In Example 3, suppose that the passwords may *not* start with an A or use the letter Q. How many different passwords are possible? *Explain.*

**EXAMPLE 4** TAKS REASONING: Multi-Step Problem

**Number Cubes** You and three friends each roll a number cube. What is the probability that you each roll the same number?

**STEP 1** List the favorable outcomes. There are 6:

1-1-1-1   2-2-2-2   3-3-3-3   4-4-4-4   5-5-5-5   6-6-6-6

**STEP 2** Find the number of possible outcomes using the counting principle.

$$6 \cdot 6 \cdot 6 \cdot 6 = 1296$$

4 number cubes

**REVIEW PROBABILITY**
For help with probability, see p. 381.

**STEP 3** Find the probability: $\dfrac{\text{Number of favorable outcomes}}{\text{Number of possible outcomes}} = \dfrac{6}{1296} = \dfrac{1}{216}$

▶ **Answer** The probability that you each roll the same number is $\dfrac{1}{216}$.

---

✓ **GUIDED PRACTICE** for Example 4

4. **Coins** Six people each flip a coin. What is the probability of 6 heads?

---

# 12.4 EXERCISES

HOMEWORK KEY

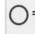 = **TAKS Practice and Reasoning**
Exs. 7, 19, 21, 25, and 26

○ = **HINTS AND HOMEWORK HELP**
for Exs. 3, 5, 7, 17 at classzone.com

## SKILL PRACTICE

**VOCABULARY Copy and complete the statement.**

1. If one event can occur in *m* ways and for each of those a second event can occur in *n* ways, then the two events can occur together in __?__ ways.

2. The probability of an event when all outcomes are equally likely is the number of __?__ outcomes divided by the number of __?__ outcomes.

**SOLVING TWO WAYS Use the counting principle to find the number of choices that are possible. Then check your answer using a tree diagram.**

**SEE EXAMPLES 1, 2, AND 3**
on pp. 670–671 for Exs. 3–7

3. Choose apple, blueberry, lemon, or cherry pie with juice or tea.

4. Choose a small, medium, or large shirt in red, yellow, or blue.

5. Choose a hat or scarf in gray, white, or black.

6. Choose one of 5 essays and one of 2 extra credit questions.

7. ✦ **TAKS REASONING** A license plate is composed of 3 letters followed by 4 digits. How many different license plates are possible?

(A) 7        (B) 12        (C) 175,760,000        (D) 456,976,000

**8. ERROR ANALYSIS** Describe and correct the error in solving the following problem: *A snack stand sells small and large drinks in 3 flavors. How many drink choices are available?*

$$\times \begin{array}{l} m = 2 \\ n = 3 \\ 2 + 3 = 5 \end{array}$$

**PROBABILITY** A website randomly generates a confirmation code after purchases. The code consists of 4 letters. Find the probability that the code fits the given description. Count only *a*, *e*, *i*, *o*, and *u* as vowels.

SEE EXAMPLE 4
on p. 672
for Exs. 9–12

**9.** starts with a consonant

**10.** contains only vowels

**11.** code is MNYR

**12.** uses the same letter in each spot

**COUNTING OUTCOMES** You have 4 U.S. coins, 8 foreign coins, and 3 U.S. currency bills at home. Find how many different outcomes are possible if the following are chosen at random.

**13.** 2 U.S. bills and 2 U.S. coins from your U.S. bills and coins

**14.** 2 U.S. coins and 3 foreign coins from your U.S. coins and foreign coins

**15. CHALLENGE** A password with 5 numbers has $10^5$ possible choices, from 00000 to 99999. How does the number of possible passwords change if no password may use a digit more than once? *Explain.*

## PROBLEM SOLVING

SEE EXAMPLES
1 AND 2
on pp. 670–671
for Exs. 16–18

**16. WEEKEND PLANS** You would like to go to the movies, a play, or the zoo. You can invite your cousin or your best friend. You can go on Friday or Saturday. Make a tree diagram to list all of the possibilities. Then use the counting principle to check your answer.

**17. WRITING** You are interested in 5 CDs and 4 books. *Describe* how to find the number of different pairs of 1 CD and 1 book that you can buy.

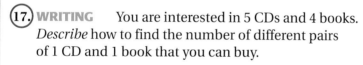

**18. CLASS ELECTION** The ballot shows the candidates in a class election. Make a tree diagram to find the number of different ways a president, treasurer, and secretary can be chosen. Use the counting principle to check your answer.

| President | Treasurer | Secretary |
|---|---|---|
| ☐ Amy | ☐ Jessica | ☐ Scott |
| ☐ Hector | ☐ Michael | ☐ Nicole |
| | ☐ Carson | ☐ Thomas |
| | | ☐ Angela |
| | | ☐ Isabel |

SEE EXAMPLE 4
on p. 672
for Exs. 19–20

**19. TAKS REASONING** You and three friends each pick a movie at random from four choices. What is the probability that you all pick the same movie?

**A** $\frac{1}{27}$  **B** $\frac{1}{64}$  **C** $\frac{1}{81}$  **D** $\frac{1}{256}$

**20. STATES** You and Terry randomly choose the name of a state. What is the probability that you both choose a state whose name starts with a T? (Tennessee and Texas are the two states that start with the letter T.)

**21.** ⚓ **TAKS REASONING** You want a sandwich, a side order, and a drink from a lunch cart that offers 3 sandwiches, 2 side orders, and 5 drink choices. Draw two different tree diagrams that show how many lunches are possible. Do both tree diagrams yield the same result? *Explain.*

**22. REASONING** A restaurant has 36 possible meals that you can choose. A meal has a main course, a salad, and a dessert. The menu lists 6 main courses and 2 salads. How many desserts are available? *Explain.*

**BRAILLE** **In Exercises 23 and 24, use the following information.**

Braille uses arrangements of raised dots to form symbols that represent letters, numbers, and punctuation marks. Braille is read by touching the symbols. Each symbol is a cell of 6 dots arranged in 3 rows of 2. In the cell, certain dots are raised to make a particular symbol.

**23.** How many different Braille symbols are possible? How many symbols are possible with no raised dots? With 6 raised dots?

**24.** Is the number of symbols possible with one raised dot the same as with 5 raised dots? *Explain.*

**25.** ⚓ **TAKS REASONING** You are at a grocery store buying flavored water. You can choose lime, lemon, cherry, or orange. You can choose a 0.5 liter, 1 liter, or 2 liter bottle.

   **a. Draw** Make a tree diagram that shows all of the different bottles of flavored water that you can choose.

   **b. Calculate** How many different bottles can you choose from if 5 new flavors become available?

   **c. Challenge** The sign shows the prices for each bottle size. What are the different total prices that you could be charged for three bottles? What is the greatest total quantity of water you can buy if you have only $2.60?

   | Water Sale |
   |---|
   | 0.5 liter – $0.59 |
   | 1 liter – $0.69 |
   | 2 liter – $0.99 |

---

⭐ **MIXED REVIEW FOR TAKS**          **TAKS** **PRACTICE** at classzone.com

**REVIEW**
Lesson 11.3;
TAKS Workbook

**26.** ⚓ **TAKS PRACTICE** A sports store charges $15 per day to rent snowshoes plus $120 for the security deposit. The initial payment is given by the equation $C = 120 + 15d$, where $C$ is the total cost, in dollars, and $d$ is the number of days the snowshoes are expected to be rented. Which table shows some possible initial payments? *TAKS Obj. 2*

**(A)**

| $d$ | 1 | 2 | 3 | 4 |
|---|---|---|---|---|
| $C$ | 15 | 30 | 45 | 60 |

**(B)**

| $d$ | 1 | 2 | 3 | 4 |
|---|---|---|---|---|
| $C$ | 135 | 150 | 165 | 180 |

**(C)**

| $d$ | −1 | 0 | 1 | 2 |
|---|---|---|---|---|
| $C$ | 105 | 120 | 135 | 150 |

**(D)**

| $d$ | 1 | 3 | 5 | 7 |
|---|---|---|---|---|
| $C$ | 135 | 150 | 165 | 180 |

# 12.5 Permutations

TEKS *8.2.B, 8.14.A*

| **Before** | You used the counting principle to count possibilities. |
|---|---|
| **Now** | You will use permutations to count possibilities. |
| **Why?** | So you can count color possibilities, as in Ex. 32. |

**KEY VOCABULARY**
• **permutation,** *p. 675*
• **factorial,** *p. 675*

In some arrangements of groups, order is important. For example, the diagram shows the different ways that a group of three dogs could finish first, second, and third at a dog show.

Each arrangement lists the same dogs, but the orders are different. Arrangements such as these are called *permutations*. A **permutation** is an arrangement in which order is important. You can use the counting principle to count permutations.

---

**EXAMPLE 1** **Counting Permutations**

**Music** You have five CDs. You can use the counting principle to count the number of permutations of 5 CDs. This is the number of different orders in which you can listen to the CDs.

| Choices for 1st CD | Choices for 2nd CD | Choices for 3rd CD | Choices for 4th CD | Choices for 5th CD | |
|---|---|---|---|---|---|
| 5 • | 4 • | 3 • | 2 • | 1 | = 120 |

▶ **Answer** You can listen to the CDs in 120 different orders.

---

**USE A FACTORIAL**
You can use *n*! to find the number of permutations of *n* objects, where *n* is a positive integer.

**Factorials** In Example 1, you evaluated $5 \cdot 4 \cdot 3 \cdot 2 \cdot 1$. You can write $5 \cdot 4 \cdot 3 \cdot 2 \cdot 1$ as 5!, which is read "5 **factorial**."

> **Numbers** $5! = 5 \cdot 4 \cdot 3 \cdot 2 \cdot 1$
>
> **Algebra** $n! = n \cdot (n - 1) \cdot (n - 2) \cdot \ldots \cdot 1$

The value of 0! is defined to be 1.

EXAMPLE 2 **Counting Permutations**

**Band Competition** Twelve marching bands are entered in a competition. You can use the counting principle to count how many ways first, second, and third places can be awarded.

| Choices for<br>1st place | | Choices for<br>2nd place | | Choices for<br>3rd place | | | |
|:---:|:---:|:---:|:---:|:---:|:---:|:---:|:---|
| 12 | • | 11 | • | 10 | = 1320 | | Counting principle |

▶ **Answer** There are 1320 ways to award the three places.

✓ **GUIDED PRACTICE** for Examples 1 and 2

1. Evaluate 3!.  2. Evaluate 6!.  3. Evaluate 1!.

4. Chris wants to see four movies that were released in the past month. In how many different orders can Chris watch the movies?

5. In how many ways can 7 runners finish in first, second, and third place?

**Permutation Notation** Example 2 shows how to find the number of permutations of 12 objects taken 3 at a time. This is written $_{12}P_3$.

---

**KEY CONCEPT** *For Your Notebook*

**Permutations**

**Algebra**  The number of permutations of $n$ objects taken $r$ at a time can be written as $_nP_r$ and evaluated using $\dfrac{n!}{(n-r)!}$.

**Numbers**  $_7P_3 = \dfrac{7!}{(7-3)!} = \dfrac{7!}{4!} = \dfrac{7 \cdot 6 \cdot 5 \cdot \cancel{4} \cdot \cancel{3} \cdot \cancel{2} \cdot \cancel{1}}{\cancel{4} \cdot \cancel{3} \cdot \cancel{2} \cdot \cancel{1}} = 7 \cdot 6 \cdot 5$

---

**EXAMPLE 3** **Evaluating a Permutation**

**Poetry** Two students are chosen from a group of 6 to read the first and second poems at the school's poetry reading. To find how many different ways the students can be chosen, find $_6P_2$.

**ANOTHER WAY**

In Example 3, you can also write 6! as 6 • 5 • 4! and divide out 4!.

$\dfrac{6 \cdot 5 \cdot 4!}{4!} = 6 \cdot 5.$

$_6P_2 = \dfrac{6!}{(6-2)!} = \dfrac{6!}{4!}$  **Use permutation formula.**

$= \dfrac{6 \cdot 5 \cdot \cancel{4} \cdot \cancel{3} \cdot \cancel{2} \cdot \cancel{1}}{\cancel{4} \cdot \cancel{3} \cdot \cancel{2} \cdot \cancel{1}}$  **Divide out common factors.**

$= 30$  **Multiply.**

▶ **Answer** The students can be chosen in 30 ways.

**Find the number of permutations.**

**6.** $_5P_3$        **7.** $_6P_6$        **8.** $_8P_7$        **9.** $_{100}P_2$

**10. What If?** Suppose 3 students are chosen from a group of 8 to read in Example 3. In how many different ways can the students be chosen?

# 12.5 EXERCISES

HOMEWORK KEY

🟫 = **TAKS Practice and Reasoning**
Exs. 16, 31, 32, 37, 41, and 42

⭕ = **HINTS AND HOMEWORK HELP**
for Exs. 5, 7, 13, 15, 33 at classzone.com

## SKILL PRACTICE

**VOCABULARY Copy and complete the statement.**

**1.** The number of permutations of 15 objects taken 7 at a time is written __?__ .

**2.** The product of all integers from 1 to a number $n$ is written __?__ .

SEE EXAMPLE 1
on p. 675
for Exs. 3–6

**EVALUATING FACTORIALS Evaluate the factorial.**

**3.** $2!$        **4.** $0!$        **⑤** $7!$        **6.** $9!$

SEE EXAMPLES
2 AND 3
on p. 676
for Exs. 7–15

**EVALUATING PERMUTATIONS Find the number of permutations.**

**⑦** $_4P_2$        **8.** $_9P_6$        **9.** $_{10}P_7$        **10.** $_5P_5$

**11.** $_{12}P_6$        **12.** $_7P_4$        **⑬** $_{15}P_5$        **14.** $_{20}P_3$

**⑮ ERROR ANALYSIS** Describe and correct the error made in evaluating $_5P_3$.

$$_5P_3 = \frac{5!}{3!} = \frac{5 \cdot 4 \cdot \cancel{3} \cdot \cancel{2} \cdot \cancel{1}}{\cancel{3} \cdot \cancel{2} \cdot \cancel{1}}$$
$$\cancel{\phantom{X}} = 5 \cdot 4$$
$$= 20$$

SEE EXAMPLE 1
on p. 675
for Exs. 16–21

**16. 🟫 TAKS REASONING** You go to the cafeteria with five friends. Which expression can you use to find how many different ways you and your friends can stand in the lunch line?

     **Ⓐ** $_6P_1$      **Ⓑ** $_6P_5$      **Ⓒ** $_5P_5$      **Ⓓ** $_6P_6$

**FINDING PERMUTATIONS Describe the permutation you need to evaluate to find the answer. Then solve the problem.**

**17.** How many different ways can you arrange the letters in the word HOLIDAY?

**18.** There are 8 students in the school play. How many different ways can 6 of the cast members be arranged in a row?

**19.** A deck of cards has 52 cards. How many different arrangements of 5 cards can be made from the deck?

**20.** You borrow 5 books. In how many different orders can you read the books?

**21.** The German Club has 24 members. In how many ways can the club select a president, vice president, secretary, and treasurer from its members?

**COMPARING** Copy and complete the statement with <, >, or =.

**22.** $_8P_5 \, \underline{?} \, _8P_1$

**23.** $_6P_2 \, \underline{?} \, _6P_4$

**24.** $_{10}P_{10} \, \underline{?} \, _9P_9$

**25.** $_5P_1 \, \underline{?} \, _8P_1$

**26.** $_7P_7 \, \underline{?} \, 7!$

**27.** $_4P_3 \, \underline{?} \, _6P_2$

**28. CHALLENGE** Why do you think that 0! = 1? *Explain.* (Hint: Try to write this statement as a permutation in words.)

## PROBLEM SOLVING

**SEE EXAMPLES 2 AND 3**
on p. 676
for Exs. 29–30, 32–33, 35

**29. SUMMER CAMP** You are given a list of 10 activities you can do while camping. You are asked to pick your first, second, third, and fourth choices. How many different permutations are possible?

**30. SOFTBALL** Your softball team has 15 players. Find the number of different ways that the first, second, third, fourth, and fifth batters can be chosen.

**31.** ⤶ **TAKS REASONING** Your friend says that 11! = 11 · 10!. Is your friend correct? *Explain.*

**32.** ⤶ **TAKS REASONING** You are knitting a stocking hat, and you want it to have 4 different colored stripes of equal width. You have 6 colors of yarn. How many different hats can you knit?

**(A)** 24 **(B)** 30 **(C)** 360 **(D)** 720

**33. GARDENING** You are planning a garden with 3 rows. Each row will have one type of flower, and none of the rows will be the same. You can choose from the flowers below. Find the number of permutations.

Day Lily   Poppy   Gladiolus   Daffodil   Rose   Sunflower   Tulip

**SEE EXAMPLE 3**
on p. 676
for Ex. 34

**34. WRITING** In Example 1 on page 675, you found the number of permutations of 5 CDs taken how many at a time? *Explain.*

**35. PHONE CALLS** When you come back from vacation, you want to call Ed, Sue, Ty, and Nestor. You have time to make only two calls. Find the number of different ways in which you can call two friends. Then make an organized list to show all the different ways to make 2 calls.

**36. MULTI-STEP PROBLEM** There are 50 people entered in a drawing to win three door prizes. Only 1 prize will be awarded to each winner.

　**a.** How many different ways can the winners be chosen?

　**b.** Another prize is added to the drawing. How many different ways can four winners be chosen?

　**c.** Compare the number of permutations in parts (a) and (b). *Explain* any differences.

**37.**  **TAKS REASONING** Your school team is 1 of 15 in a cheerleading competition.

**a.** Trophies are awarded for first, second, third, and fourth places. In how many different ways can the trophies be awarded?

**b.** Suppose the four teams that perform best are all given *excellence* medals instead of first, second, third, and fourth place trophies. In this case, are there more or fewer ways to give the awards than in part (a)? *Explain.*

**XV** **FUNCTIONS** In Exercises 38 and 39, consider the functions $_6P_r$, $_7P_r$, and $_8P_r$.

**38.** Make an input-output table for each of the 3 functions. The domain of each is $r = 1, 2, 3, \ldots n$. The range consists of the values of $_6P_r$, $_7P_r$, and $_8P_r$. Describe any patterns that you see.

**39.** **CHALLENGE** Predict which of these expressions has the greatest value: $_{23}P_6$, $_{23}P_{12}$, $_{23}P_{18}$, $_{23}P_{23}$. *Justify* your reasoning using the patterns in your tables.

**40.** **CHALLENGE** For a science fair, 20 students submit a project. The top $r$ projects can be awarded ribbons in $_{20}P_r$ ways. If one more project is awarded a ribbon, how many times greater is the number of permutations of ribbons awarded?

## MIXED REVIEW FOR TAKS

**TAKS** **PRACTICE** at classzone.com

**REVIEW**
Lesson 12.3;
TAKS Workbook

**41.**  **TAKS PRACTICE** The bar graph shows the number of international travelers visiting the United States over a span of ten years. Jerry maintains that the number of tourists doubled from 1995 and 1996 to 1999 and 2000. Why might he have come to this incorrect conclusion? *TAKS Obj. 5*

**(A)** There is a break in the vertical axis.

**(B)** The overall trend is not increasing.

**(C)** The bar graph shows data from two years together.

**(D)** Intervals of 5 million on the vertical scale make it difficult to read the data for certain years.

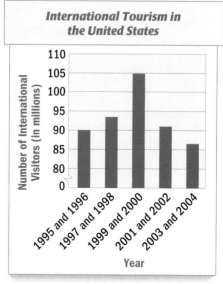

*International Tourism in the United States*

**REVIEW**
Lesson 9.1;
TAKS Workbook

**42.**  **TAKS PRACTICE** The area of a square is 175 square inches. Which best represents the length of a side of the square? *TAKS Obj. 1*

**(F)** 12.9 in.    **(G)** 13.2 in.    **(H)** 13.9 in.    **(J)** 14 in.

# 12.6 Combinations

TEKS *8.2.A, 8.14.A*

| | |
|---|---|
| **Before** | You used permutations to count possibilities. |
| **Now** | You will use combinations to count possibilities. |
| **Why?** | So you can count possible groups, as for a fair in Example 1. |

**KEY VOCABULARY**
• **combination,** *p. 680*

In Lesson 12.5, you studied permutations, which are arrangements in which order is important. A **combination** is a group of items whose order is *not* important. For example, suppose you go to lunch with a friend. You choose milk, soup, and a salad. Your friend chooses soup, a salad, and milk. The order in which the items are chosen does not matter. You both have the same meal.

The two meals are the same.

## EXAMPLE 1  Listing Combinations

**County Fair**  You have 4 tickets to the county fair and can take 3 of your friends. You can choose from Abby (A), Brian (B), Chloe (C), and David (D). How many different choices of groups of friends do you have?

**SOLUTION**

List all possible arrangements of three friends. Then cross out any duplicate groupings that represent the same group of friends.

**ANOTHER WAY**
The answer makes sense because you can leave out Abby, Brian, Chloe, or David with each choice.

(ABC)  A̶C̶B̶  B̶A̶C̶  B̶C̶A̶  C̶A̶B̶  C̶B̶A̶ ◄─── ABC, ACB, BAC, BCA, CAB, and CBA all represent the same group.
(ABD)  A̶D̶B̶  B̶A̶D̶  B̶D̶A̶  D̶A̶B̶  D̶B̶A̶
(ACD)  A̶D̶C̶  C̶A̶D̶  C̶D̶A̶  D̶A̶C̶  D̶C̶A̶
(BCD)  B̶D̶C̶  C̶B̶D̶  C̶D̶B̶  D̶B̶C̶  D̶C̶B̶

▶**Answer**  You have 4 different choices of groups to take to the fair.

## ✓ GUIDED PRACTICE  for Example 1

1. **What If?**  In Example 1, suppose you have only 3 tickets and can take 2 of your friends. Now how many different choices of groups do you have?

**Combination Notation** In Example 1, after you cross out the duplicate groupings, you are left with the number of combinations of 4 items chosen 3 at a time. Using combination notation, this is written $_4C_3$.

---

**KEY CONCEPT**  *For Your Notebook*

### Combination Notation

**Words**  To find the number of combinations of $n$ objects taken $r$ at a time, divide the number of permutations of $n$ objects taken $r$ at a time by $r!$.

**Algebra**  $_nC_r = \dfrac{_nP_r}{r!}$    **Numbers**  $_9C_4 = \dfrac{_9P_4}{4!}$

---

**EXAMPLE 2**  **Evaluating Combinations**

Find the number of combinations.

**a.** $_8C_3$                              **b.** $_9C_7$

**SOLUTION**

**a.** $_8C_3 = \dfrac{_8P_3}{3!}$     **Combination formula**

$= \dfrac{8 \cdot 7 \cdot 6}{3!}$     $_8P_3 = \dfrac{8!}{(8-3)!} = 8 \cdot 7 \cdot 6$

$= \dfrac{8 \cdot 7 \cdot \cancel{6}}{\cancel{3} \cdot \cancel{2} \cdot 1}$     **Expand. $3! = 3 \cdot 2 \cdot 1$. Divide out common factors.**

$= 56$     **Simplify.**

**b.** $_9C_7 = \dfrac{_9P_7}{7!}$     **Combination formula**

$= \dfrac{9 \cdot 8 \cdot 7 \cdot 6 \cdot 5 \cdot 4 \cdot 3}{7!}$     $_9P_7 = \dfrac{9!}{(9-7)!} = 9 \cdot 8 \cdot 7 \cdot 6 \cdot 5 \cdot 4 \cdot 3$

$= \dfrac{9 \cdot \overset{4}{\cancel{8}} \cdot \cancel{7} \cdot \cancel{6} \cdot \cancel{5} \cdot \cancel{4} \cdot \cancel{3}}{\cancel{7} \cdot \cancel{6} \cdot \cancel{5} \cdot \cancel{4} \cdot \cancel{3} \cdot \underset{1}{\cancel{2}} \cdot 1}$     **Expand 7!. Divide out common factors.**

$= 36$     **Simplify.**

---

✓ **GUIDED PRACTICE**  **for Example 2**

Find the number of combinations.

**2.** $_8C_8$          **3.** $_8C_7$          **4.** $_7C_2$          **5.** $_6C_1$

**6. Bookstore** You are shopping at a bookstore. You have enough money to buy 4 books. There are 7 books at the store that you want to read. How many combinations of books can be purchased?

EXAMPLE 3 **Permutations and Combinations**

VOCABULARY

*Mutate* means to change. For *permutations*, you count changes in the order of items. For *combinations*, objects *combined* in any order represent the same group.

**Tell whether the possibilities can be counted using a *permutation* or *combination*. Then write an expression for the number of possibilities.**

**a. Swimming** There are 8 swimmers in the 400 meter freestyle race. In how many ways can the swimmers finish first, second, and third?

**b. Track** Your track team has 6 runners available for the 4 person relay event. How many different 4 person teams can be chosen?

**SOLUTION**

a. Because the swimmers can finish first, second, or third, order is important. So the possibilities can be counted by evaluating $_8P_3$.

b. Order is not important in choosing the team members, so the possibilities can be counted by evaluating $_6C_4$.

✓ **GUIDED PRACTICE** **for Example 3**

**Tell whether the possibilities can be counted using a *permutation* or *combination*. Then write an expression for the number of possibilities.**

7. **Pizza Toppings** A pizza shop offers 12 different pizza toppings. How many different 3-topping pizzas are possible?

8. **Student Council** There are 15 members on the student council. In how many ways can they elect a president and a vice president for the council?

# 12.6 **EXERCISES**

HOMEWORK KEY

= **TAKS Practice and Reasoning**
Exs. 4, 31, 32, and 38

◯ = **HINTS** AND **HOMEWORK HELP**
for Exs. 3, 7, 9, 15, 29 at classzone.com

## SKILL PRACTICE

**VOCABULARY  Copy and complete the statement.**

1. The expression $_9C_5$ represents the number of combinations of __?__ objects taken __?__ at a time.

2. To find the number of combinations of *n* objects taken *r* at a time, divide the number of __?__ of *n* objects taken *r* at a time by *r*!.

SEE EXAMPLE 1
on p. 680
for Ex. 3

3. **LISTING COMBINATIONS** For a test, you can choose any 2 essay questions to answer from the 5 questions asked. Make a list and cross out the duplicate choices to show how many different pairs of essay questions you could answer.

SEE EXAMPLE 2
on p. 681
for Ex. 4

4.  **TAKS REASONING** Which expression is equivalent to $_6C_3$?

**A** $\dfrac{6!}{(6-3)!}$    **B** $6 \cdot 5 \cdot 4$    **C** $\dfrac{_6P_3}{6!}$    **D** $\dfrac{6 \cdot 5 \cdot 4}{3!}$

SEE EXAMPLE 2
on p. 681
for Exs. 5–16

**COMBINATIONS** **Find the number of combinations.**

**5.** $_4C_1$

**6.** $_4C_4$

**7.** $_7C_6$

**8.** $_5C_2$

**9.** $_8C_6$

**10.** $_8C_1$

**11.** $_{10}C_8$

**12.** $_9C_5$

**13.** $_{11}C_3$

**14.** $_{13}C_{11}$

**15.** $_9C_2$

**16.** $_{100}C_{99}$

**17. ERROR ANALYSIS** Your class is voting for the
new school colors. You are asked to choose
2 colors from a list of 8 colors. *Describe* and
correct the error made in counting the color
pairs you can choose.

$$_8P_2 = \frac{8!}{(8-2)!}$$
$$= \frac{8 \cdot 7 \cdot 6 \cdot 5 \cdot 4 \cdot 3 \cdot 2 \cdot 1}{6 \cdot 5 \cdot 4 \cdot 3 \cdot 2 \cdot 1}$$
$$= 56 \text{ color pairs}$$

**COUNTING CHOICES** **Answer the question. Tell
whether you used a *permutation* or *combination*.**

SEE EXAMPLE 3
on p. 682
for Exs. 18–21

**18.** How many groups of 2 colors of balloons can you choose from
4 colors of balloons?

**19.** How many ways can you do your homework for 4 subjects?

**20.** How many ways can you play your 5 favorite songs?

**21.** How many groups of 3 vegetables can you choose from 5 vegetables
to make vegetable soup?

**22. LOOK FOR A PATTERN** Copy and complete the table by finding the
number of combinations. Then describe the pattern.

| $_7C_0$ | $_7C_1$ | $_7C_2$ | $_7C_3$ | $_7C_4$ | $_7C_5$ | $_7C_6$ | $_7C_7$ |
|---|---|---|---|---|---|---|---|
| ? | ? | ? | ? | ? | ? | ? | ? |

**CHALLENGE** **Solve the inequality for *n* or *r*.**

**23.** $_nC_3 \geq 20$

**24.** $_nC_2 < 21$

**25.** $_6C_r \leq 15$

**26.** $_8C_r > 28$

## PROBLEM SOLVING

SEE EXAMPLES
2 AND 3
on pp. 681–682
for Exs. 27–30

**27. ART** An art instructor must choose 2 art projects for students
to complete from this list: clay, plaster, wood, wire, drawing,
painting. How many combinations of 2 projects are possible?

**28. HOCKEY** Your hockey team is choosing 2 team captains from
its 18 members. Find the number of combinations that are
possible.

**29. DEBATING** A debate team has 5 members. Your debating club
has 12 students. How many different teams can be chosen?

**30. GARDENING** You want to grow 4 different vegetables. You can
choose from 9 types of vegetable seed. How many different
groups of 4 types of seed can you choose?

**31.** ★ **TAKS REASONING** You are at a fair with 4 friends. All of you want to ride the roller coaster, but only 3 people can fit in the first car. How many different groups of 3 can you and your friends make?

Ⓐ 60 Ⓑ 15 Ⓒ 10 Ⓓ 4

**32.** ★ **TAKS REASONING** Is it possible to evaluate a combination such as $_3C_4$, $_2C_6$, or $_1C_{10}$? *Explain* why or why not.

**33.** **WRITING** *Describe* the difference between a permutation and a combination using real-world examples.

**34.** **NUMBER SENSE** Tell whether the value of $_nP_r$ is *always*, *sometimes*, or *never* greater than the value of $_nC_r$. *Explain* your reasoning.

**SEE EXAMPLES 2 AND 3**
on pp. 681–682 for Ex. 35

**35.** **MULTI-STEP PROBLEM** You are coloring the map shown at the right. You want each state to be a different color.

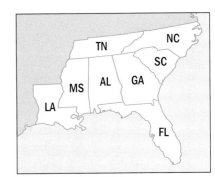

   **a.** In how many ways can you color the map if you have 8 colors?

   **b.** How many 8-color groups can you choose from 10 colors?

   **c.** In how many ways can you color the map using 8 out of 10 colors? *Explain.*

**36.** **VIDEO GAMES** You want to borrow 4 out of 20 video games from a friend. How many different groups of four games can you choose? Suppose you are already sure about two of the game choices. How many different groups of four games can you choose? *Explain.*

**37.** **CHALLENGE** What is the value of $_nC_r$ when $r = n$? What is the value of $_nC_r$ when $n - r = 1$? *Explain.*

---

## MIXED REVIEW FOR TAKS

**TAKS PRACTICE** at classzone.com

**REVIEW**
Lesson 11.2;
TAKS Workbook

**38.** ★ **TAKS PRACTICE** The scatter plot shows the average high temperatures in Alexandria, Egypt, from April through September. Anne concludes that the average high temperature will be between 90°F and 95°F in October. Why might her conclusion be incorrect? *TAKS Obj. 5*

   Ⓐ She underestimated the increasing trend of the data.

   Ⓑ She overestimated the increasing trend of the data.

   Ⓒ It is not appropriate to make this type of conclusion because the relationship between months and temperature is not linear.

   Ⓓ The scatter plot shows a negative trend.

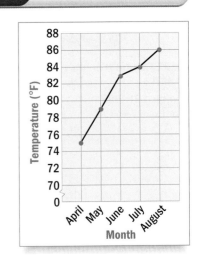

**ONLINE QUIZ** at classzone.com

# 12.7 Probability and Odds

TEKS 8.2.B, 8.11.A

| | |
|---|---|
| **Before** | You found the probability of events. |
| **Now** | You will find the odds in favor of events. |
| **Why?** | So you can find odds in sports, as in Example 3. |

**KEY VOCABULARY**
- **complementary events,** *p. 685*
- **unfavorable outcome,** *p. 686*
- **odds,** *p. 686*

### ACTIVITY

**Use the spinner at the right.**

**STEP 1** **Decide** whether it is more likely for the spinner to land on blue or red. *Explain* your reasoning.

**STEP 2** **Find** each ratio. Use the ratios to compare the chance of landing on red to the chance of landing on blue.

    **a.** $\dfrac{\text{number of red sections}}{\text{number of blue sections}}$   **b.** $\dfrac{\text{number of blue sections}}{\text{number of red sections}}$

**STEP 3** **Explain** how to find the probability of the spinner *not* landing on red.

In the activity, the spinner will land on either red or blue. Two events are **complementary** when one event or the other (but not both) must occur. The sum of the probabilities of complementary events is always 1.

When Events A and B are complementary, $P(\text{Event A}) = 1 - P(\text{Event B})$.

---

### EXAMPLE 1   Finding Probabilities

*USE PROBABILITY*
The probability that Event A occurs and the probability that Event A does *not* occur have a sum of 1 because they are complementary events. For help with probability, see p. 381.

**Gifts** You and seven friends contribute money for a gift. Everyone's name is put in a hat. The person whose name is chosen at random picks the gift.

  **a.** What is the probability that your name is chosen?

  **b.** What is the probability that your name is *not* chosen?

**SOLUTION**

  **a.** $P(\text{your name is chosen}) = \dfrac{\text{Number of favorable outcomes}}{\text{Number of possible outcomes}} = \dfrac{1}{8}$

  **b.** $P(\text{your name is not chosen}) = 1 - P(\text{your name is chosen})$

$$= 1 - \frac{1}{8}$$

$$= \frac{7}{8}$$

**Odds** Once you specify the event for which you are finding the probability, outcomes for that event are called *favorable outcomes*. The other outcomes are **unfavorable outcomes**.

When all outcomes are equally likely, the **odds** in favor of an event are equal to the ratio of favorable outcomes to unfavorable outcomes.

$$\text{Odds in favor} = \frac{\text{Number of favorable outcomes}}{\text{Number of unfavorable outcomes}}$$

---

### EXAMPLE 2    Finding Odds

**Vacation Survey** You do a survey asking your class to rank three vacation choices. Results for "the beach" are shown at the right. What are the odds in favor of a randomly chosen student from your class ranking a beach vacation first?

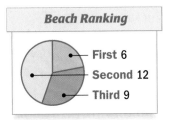

**Beach Ranking**

First 6
Second 12
Third 9

#### SOLUTION

The beach was ranked first by 6 students, so there are 6 favorable outcomes. It was ranked second by 12 students, and ranked third by 9 students, so there are $12 + 9 = 21$ unfavorable outcomes.

$$\text{Odds in favor} = \frac{\text{Number of favorable outcomes}}{\text{Number of unfavorable outcomes}}$$

$$= \frac{6}{21}$$

$$= \frac{2}{7}$$

▶ **Answer** The odds in favor of a randomly chosen student ranking a beach vacation first are 2 to 7.

> **READING**
> Odds are always read as a ratio. For example, $\frac{5}{2}$ is read "five to two," not "five halves."

---

### ✓ GUIDED PRACTICE    for Examples 1 and 2

**You are given the probability that event A will occur. Find the probability that event A will *not* occur.**

**1.** $P(A) = \frac{3}{4}$      **2.** $P(A) = 0.45$      **3.** $P(A) = 32\%$      **4.** $P(A) = \frac{7}{10}$

**5.** The 11 letters in the word MISSISSIPPI are each written on pieces of paper and randomly chosen from a bag. What is the probability of drawing an S from the bag? What is the probability of *not* drawing an S?

**You choose a card at random from a set of cards numbered 1 to 24. Find the odds in favor of the event.**

**6.** You choose a 10.                    **7.** You choose an odd number.

**8.** You choose an even number greater than 8.

**Probability and Odds** If you know the probability of an event, you can use the following formula to find the odds in favor of that event.

$$\text{Odds} = \frac{\text{Probability event will occur}}{\text{Probability event will not occur}} = \frac{\text{Probability event will occur}}{1 - \text{Probability event will occur}}$$

**EXAMPLE 3** Finding Odds Using Probability

**Basketball** Sean makes 65% of his free throws. What are Sean's odds in favor of making a free throw?

**SOLUTION**

$$\text{Odds} = \frac{0.65}{1 - 0.65} \qquad \text{Write percents as decimals.}$$

$$= \frac{0.65}{0.35} \qquad \text{Subtract.}$$

$$= \frac{65}{35}, \text{ or } \frac{13}{7} \qquad \text{Multiply by } \frac{100}{100}. \text{ Then simplify.}$$

▶ **Answer** Sean's odds in favor of making a free throw are 13 to 7.

✓ **GUIDED PRACTICE** for Example 3

**9. What If?** In Example 3, suppose Sean makes 85% of his free throws. What are Sean's odds in favor of making a free throw?

# 12.7 EXERCISES

HOMEWORK KEY
= TAKS Practice and Reasoning
Exs. 20, 32, 33, 38, and 39

○ = HINTS and HOMEWORK HELP
for Exs. 5, 9, 11, 15, 31 at classzone.com

**SKILL PRACTICE**

**VOCABULARY** Copy and complete the statement.

**1.** Find the ratio of the number of favorable outcomes to the number of unfavorable outcomes to find the __?__ of an event.

**2.** Two events are __?__ when one event or the other (but not both) must occur.

*SEE EXAMPLE 1*
*on p. 685*
*for Exs. 3–6*

**COMPLEMENTARY EVENTS** You are given the probability that event A will occur. Find the probability that event A will *not* occur.

**3.** $P(A) = 84\%$  **4.** $P(A) = \frac{2}{5}$  **5.** $P(A) = 0.37$  **6.** $P(A) = \frac{9}{10}$

*SEE EXAMPLES*
*1 AND 2*
*on pp. 685–686*
*for Exs. 7–10*

**MARBLES** You randomly choose a marble from the given group. Find the probability of choosing a red marble, and of *not* choosing a red marble. Then find the odds in favor of choosing a blue marble.

**7.** 3 red and 7 blue marbles

**8.** 4 red and 9 blue marbles

**9.** 6 red and 5 blue marbles

**10.** 6 red, 5 blue, and 3 green marbles

**SEE EXAMPLE 2**
on p. 686
for Exs. 11–15

**ODDS** **You roll a number cube. Find the odds in favor of the given event.**

**11.** Roll a 3.

**12.** Roll a number less than 6.

**13.** Roll a number greater than 2.

**14.** Roll an odd number less than 5.

**15.** **ERROR ANALYSIS** Describe and correct the error made in finding the odds in favor of rolling a number greater than 4 on a number cube.

$$\times \quad \text{Odds} = \frac{4}{2} = \frac{2}{1}$$
The odds in favor are 2 to 1.

**LETTERED TILES** **You are randomly selecting lettered tiles. Use the given probability to find the odds in favor of selecting the letter.**

**SEE EXAMPLE 3**
on p. 687
for Exs. 16–20

**16.** $P(\text{letter I}) = 5\%$   **17.** $P(\text{letter E}) = 55\%$   **18.** $P(\text{letter S}) = 12\%$   **19.** $P(\text{letter R}) = 8\%$

**20.** **TAKS REASONING** The probability of an event is 60%. What are the odds in favor of the event?

**A** 3 to 5     **B** 2 to 3     **C** 5 to 3     **D** 3 to 2

**ODDS** **Use the odds in favor of an event to find the probability of the event.**

**21.** 1 to 3     **22.** 1 to 1     **23.** 27 to 23     **24.** 7 to 13

**25.** **ALGEBRA** The odds in favor of an event are $a$ to $b$. Write an expression for the probability of the event.

**26.** **CHALLENGE** You spin a spinner with $n$ equal-sized sections numbered 1 through $n$. The probability of getting a number greater than 9 is 25%. What are the odds in favor of getting a number less than 5? *Explain.*

## PROBLEM SOLVING

**SEE EXAMPLE 1**
on p. 685 for
Exs. 27–28

**27.** **CLOTHING** You randomly pull a sock from a drawer with 4 patterned socks, 8 gym socks, 6 striped socks, and 2 red socks. What is the probability that you do *not* choose a gym sock?

**PIZZA** **Use the circle graph. It shows the number of pizza orders for each type of crust.**

**28.** What is the probability that a randomly chosen pizza order is *not* for thin crust?

**SEE EXAMPLE 2**
on p. 686 for
Exs. 29–31

**29.** What are the odds in favor of a randomly chosen pizza order being for regular crust?

**30.** What are the odds in favor of a randomly chosen pizza order *not* being for stuffed crust?

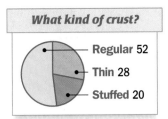

**What kind of crust?**

Regular 52
Thin 28
Stuffed 20

**31.** **HOCKEY** A hockey goalie has a save percentage of 93%. What are the goalie's odds in favor of making a save?

**SEE EXAMPLE 3**
on p. 687
for Ex. 32

**32.** **TAKS REASONING** The weather forecast says that there is a 30 percent probability of rain. What are the odds in favor of rain?

**A** 3 to 7     **B** 3 to 10     **C** 7 to 3     **D** 10 to 3

= TAKS Practice and Reasoning          = HINTS AND HOMEWORK HELP *at classzone.com*

**33.** ✒ **TAKS REASONING** Sam finds the probability of Event A is 0.2. Jan finds the odds in favor of Event A are 1 to 4. Are they both right? *Explain.*

**ODDS AGAINST** **In Exercises 34 and 35, use the following information.**

In this lesson, you learned how to find the *odds in favor* of an event. You can also find the *odds against* an event.

$$\text{Odds against} = \frac{\text{Number of unfavorable outcomes}}{\text{Number of favorable outcomes}}$$

**34.** You randomly choose a chip from a bag of 6 blue, 3 red, and 5 green chips. Find the odds in favor of choosing a green chip. Then find the odds against choosing a green chip.

**35.** **WRITING** You hear a friend claim that "the odds that you get hit by lightning are a million to one." Is your friend talking about *odds in favor* or *odds against*? *Explain* your reasoning.

**36.** **MULTI-STEP PROBLEM** Assume that when an arrow hits the target shown at the right, the arrow is equally likely to hit any point on the target. The probability $P$ that an arrow lands within the red bull's-eye circle is given by $P = \dfrac{\text{Area of bull's-eye}}{\text{Area of target}}$.

3 in.
9 in.
15 in.

  **a.** **Geometry** What is the area of the bull's-eye? What is the total area of the target? Write your answers in terms of $\pi$.

  **b.** **Probability** What is the probability that an arrow hitting the target lands within the bull's-eye?

  **c.** **Odds** What are the odds that an arrow hitting the target lands on the blue region?

**37.** **CHALLENGE** Beverage A includes a bottle cap with 1 to 11 odds in favor of winning a free bottle. Beverage B's bottle cap includes an $x$% probability of winning. After opening 132 bottles of each drink, you win 1 more time with beverage B than with beverage A. Find $x$.

---

**MIXED REVIEW FOR TAKS**   **TAKS** **PRACTICE** at classzone.com

*REVIEW*
Lesson 7.8;
TAKS Workbook

**38.** ✦ **TAKS PRACTICE** The probability that a bottle of juice sold in grocery stores contains a prize is $\dfrac{1}{50}$. About how many bottles with prizes will be delivered to a grocery that receives 925 bottles of juice to sell? *TAKS Obj. 5*

  **(A)** 9    **(B)** 19    **(C)** 28    **(D)** 50

*REVIEW*
Lesson 11.1;
TAKS Workbook

**39.** ✦ **TAKS PRACTICE** Which expression shows the $n$th term in the sequence: $-3, -5, -7, -9, \ldots$? Assume the first number shown is the first term, the second number shown is the second term, and so forth. *TAKS Obj. 2*

  **(F)** $n - 1$    **(G)** $-2n$    **(H)** $-2n - 1$    **(J)** $-2n + 1$

**Extension**

*Use after Lesson 12.7*

# Number Sets and Probability

**TEKS** *8.11.A, 8.12.C*

**GOAL** Apply set theory to numbers and probability.

**KEY VOCABULARY**
• **set,** *p. 690*
• **element,** *p. 690*
• **empty set,** *p. 690*
• **universal set,** *p. 690*
• **union,** *p. 690*
• **intersection,** *p. 690*
• **complement,** *p. 690*

A **set** is a collection of distinct objects. Each object in a set is called an **element** or *member* of the set. You can use set notation to write a set by enclosing the elements of the set in braces. For example, the set $A$ of positive even numbers less than 20 can be written as

$$A = \{2, 4, 6, 8, 10, 12, 14, 16, 18\}.$$

The **empty set** is the set with no elements and is written as $\varnothing$. The **universal set** is the set of all elements under consideration and is written as $U$. Sets can be related to one another in a variety of ways, as shown below.

---

**KEY CONCEPT**                    *For Your Notebook*

### Union, Intersection, and Complement

The **union** of two sets $A$ and $B$ is the set of all elements in *either* $A$ or $B$, and is written $A \cup B$.

The **intersection** of two sets $A$ and $B$ is the set of all elements in *both* $A$ and $B$, and is written $A \cap B$.

The **complement** of set $A$ is the set of all elements in $U$ that are *not* in $A$ and is written $\sim\!A$.

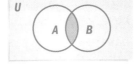

---

**EXAMPLE 1** **Finding Complements of Sets**

Let $U$ be the integers from 0 to 10. Let $A = \{1, 2, 3, 4, 5\}$ and $B = \{2, 4, 6, 8, 10\}$.

**a.** Find $\sim\!A$.

**b.** Find $\sim\!(A \cup B)$.

*VENN DIAGRAMS*
When drawing diagrams for the complement of a set, be sure to shade everything that is not included in the set.

**SOLUTION**

**a.** The set $\sim\!A$ consists of all the elements in $U$ that are not in $A$.

$\sim\!A = \{0, 6, 7, 8, 9, 10\}$

**b.** The complement of $A \cup B$ is the set of all elements in neither $A$ nor $B$.

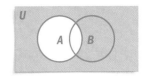

$\sim\!(A \cup B) = \{0, 7, 9\}$

**Probability and Sets** You can find the probability that an element of set $A$ is in $U$ as you did for other probabilities.

$$P(\text{set } A) = \frac{\text{Number of favorable outcomes}}{\text{Total number of outcomes}} = \frac{\text{Number of elements in set } A}{\text{Number of elements in } U}$$

**EXAMPLE 2** **Finding Probabilities for Complements of Events**

Consider the universal set $U$ to be the whole numbers from 15 to 25. Let $A$ be the set of even numbers and $B$ be the set of perfect squares. Find $P(\sim(A \cap B))$ and $P(\sim(A \cup B))$ when an element is chosen at random from $U$.

**SOLUTION**

**STEP 1** **List** the elements of $A$ and $B$.

$A = \{16, 18, 20, 22, 24\}$ $\qquad\qquad$ $B = \{16, 25\}$

**STEP 2** **Find** $\sim(A \cap B)$ and $\sim(A \cup B)$.

$A \cap B = \{16\}$, so $\sim(A \cap B) = \{15, 17, 18, 19, 20, 21, 22, 23, 24, 25\}$

$A \cup B = \{16, 18, 20, 22, 24, 25\}$, so $\sim(A \cup B) = \{15, 17, 19, 21, 23\}$

**STEP 3** **Calculate** the probabilities.

$$P(\sim(A \cap B)) = \frac{\text{Number of elements in } \sim(A \cap B)}{\text{Number of elements in } U} = \frac{10}{11}$$

$$P(\sim(A \cup B)) = \frac{\text{Number of elements in } \sim(A \cup B)}{\text{Number of elements in } U} = \frac{5}{11}$$

**EXERCISES**

Let $U$ be the set of integers from $-7$ to $7$, $A$ be the set of multiples of 3, and $B$ be the set of whole numbers from 2 to 5. List the elements in the given set. Draw a Venn diagram to represent it.

SEE EXAMPLE 1
on p. 690 for
Exs. 1–8, 13

**1.** $\sim A$ $\qquad$ **2.** $\sim B$ $\qquad$ **3.** $\sim(A \cup B)$ $\qquad$ **4.** $\sim(A \cap B)$

**5.** $\sim A \cup B$ $\qquad$ **6.** $A \cap \sim B$ $\qquad$ **7.** $\sim A \cap \sim B$ $\qquad$ **8.** $\sim A \cup \sim B$

Let $U$, $A$, and $B$ be the sets described for Exercises 1–8. Find the probability that an element chosen at random from $U$ belongs to the set described.

SEE EXAMPLE 2
on p. 691 for
Exs. 9–12

**9.** $\sim A \cup B$ $\qquad$ **10.** $A \cap \sim B$ $\qquad$ **11.** $\sim A \cap \sim B$ $\qquad$ **12.** $\sim A \cup \sim B$

**13. Reasoning** What is the intersection of a set $A$ and its complement? What is the union of these two sets? *Justify* your reasoning.

**CHALLENGE** Two sets are equal if they contain the same elements. For example for every set $A$, $\sim(\sim A) = A$. Use a Venn diagram to show that the sets are equal for all sets $A$ and $B$.

**14.** $\sim A \cup \sim B = \sim(A \cap B)$ $\qquad\qquad$ **15.** $\sim A \cap \sim B = \sim(A \cup B)$

**16.** $A \cap \sim B = \sim(\sim A \cup B)$ $\qquad\qquad$ **17.** $A \cup \sim B = \sim(\sim A \cap B)$

# INVESTIGATION
*Use before Lesson 12.8*

**GOAL**
Use a simulation to explore probability.

**MATERIALS**
• index cards
• calculator

**TEKS** *8.11.A, 8.11.C*

## 12.8 Probability and Simulations

You can use a simulation to explore probability. A *simulation* is an experiment done to explore the probability of an event.

**EXPLORE 1**  **Simulate a real-world situation.**

**Do a simulation to find an experimental probability that you and a friend are the 2 students randomly chosen from a group of 8 students.**

**STEP 1** **Label** eight index cards as shown. Use 1 to represent yourself, 2 to represent your friend, and 3, 4, 5, 6, 7, and 8 to represent the other students.

| 1 | 2 | 3 | 4 |
| 5 | 6 | 7 | 8 |

**STEP 2** **Shuffle** the cards. Randomly draw a card, and then another, without replacing the first. Record your results. Decide whether or not the results represent you and your friend being chosen. Replace the cards.

**STEP 3** **Repeat** drawing a pair of cards. Draw a total of 10 pairs. For each pair of cards drawn, record the results.

Use the ratio $\dfrac{\text{you and friend are chosen}}{\text{total number of pairs drawn}}$ to find the

experimental probability that you and your friend are chosen.

| Pair | Times Drawn |
|------|-------------|
| 1, 4 | I |
| 7, 2 | II |
| 5, 8 | I |

**PRACTICE**

1. Use your results from the simulation above. Combine all the class results. Based on these results, what is the experimental probability that you and your friend are chosen?

2. The die at the right has 8 sides numbered 1–8. Each outcome is equally likely when the die is rolled. *Describe* how you can use this die to simulate the event above. *Explain* why each pair *n, n* must be disregarded.

## EXPLORE 2  Use technology to simulate a real-world situation.

**Use your calculator's random integer function to simulate randomly choosing 1 student from a group of 8. Find the experimental probability that any of the students is randomly chosen twice in a row.**

**STEP 1** Use 1, 2, 3, 4, 5, 6, 7, and 8 to represent the students.

**STEP 2** **Clear** your calculator screen. Press **MATH** and choose the PRB menu. Select *randInt(*, the random integer function.

**STEP 3** Enter **1** **,** **8** **)** **ENTER** to select an integer at random from 1 to 8. Press **ENTER** again to simulate choosing a student again. Record whether your results represent a match.

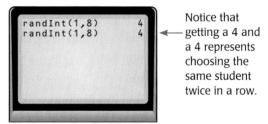

Notice that getting a 4 and a 4 represents choosing the same student twice in a row.

**STEP 4** **Complete** the simulation a total of 10 times. Record your results. What is the experimental probability that any of the students is randomly chosen twice in a row?

## PRACTICE  Design a simulation of the situation.

**3.** You randomly choose to go to the library, from the choices mall, library, or bowling lanes.

**4.** You and your friend Chris are randomly chosen from a group of 10 team members to be co-captains.

## DRAW CONCLUSIONS

**5.** **REASONING** Refer to Exercise 1 on page 692. Which results do you think are more likely to be closer to the theoretical probability that you and your friend are chosen, your results or the class results? *Explain.*

**6.** **WRITING** *Explain* how the simulation in Explore 2 above would be different if you wanted to find the probability that *you* are randomly chosen twice in a row from a group of eight people.

# 12.8 Independent and Dependent Events

TEKS 8.11.A, 8.14.A

| | |
|---|---|
| **Before** | You found the probability of an event. |
| **Now** | You will study independent and dependent events. |
| **Why?** | So you can find probabilities of games, as in Example 2. |

**KEY VOCABULARY**
- compound events, *p. 694*
- independent events, *p. 694*
- dependent events, *p. 694*

When you consider the outcomes of two events, the events are called **compound events**. Compound events are **independent events** if the occurrence of one event does *not* affect the likelihood that the other event will occur. Compound events are **dependent events** if the occurrence of one event *does* affect the likelihood that the other will occur.

Suppose you randomly choose two gumballs one at a time from the jar below. The probability of choosing two red gumballs with replacement is different than the probability without replacement.

| **Independent Events** | **Dependent Events** |
|---|---|

| First Event | Second Event | First Event | Second Event |
|---|---|---|---|

$$P(\text{red}) = \frac{2}{5} \qquad P(\text{red}) = \frac{2}{5} \qquad P(\text{red}) = \frac{2}{5} \qquad P(\text{red}) = \frac{1}{4}$$

If you replace the gumball, the probability of choosing a red one is the same each time.

If you don't replace the gumball after choosing, the probability changes.

## EXAMPLE 1  Independent and Dependent Events

**Tell whether the events are *independent* or *dependent*.**

**a.** You roll a number cube. Then you roll the number cube again.

**b.** You randomly draw a number from a bag. Then you randomly draw a second number without putting the first number back.

**SOLUTION**

**a.** The result of the first roll does not affect the result of the second roll, so the events are independent.

**b.** There is one fewer number in the bag for the second draw, so the events are dependent.

**Multiple Events** To find the probability that Event A *and* Event B happen, you multiply probabilities. Because the occurrence of an event may affect the probability of another event, you should determine whether the events are independent or dependent before multiplying.

> **KEY CONCEPT** *For Your Notebook*
>
> ### Probability of Independent Events
>
> **Words**  For two independent events, the probability that both events occur is the product of the probabilities of the events.
>
> **Algebra**  If events A and B are independent, then
> $P(A \text{ and } B) = P(A) \cdot P(B)$.

 **EXAMPLE 2**  **TAKS PRACTICE: Multiple Choice**

> **School Fair**  Your class is raising money by operating a ball toss game. You estimate that about 1 out of every 15 balls tossed results in a win. What is the probability that someone will win two tosses in a row?
>
> **(A)** $\dfrac{1}{225}$  **(B)** $\dfrac{1}{30}$  **(C)** $\dfrac{2}{15}$  **(D)** $\dfrac{15}{2}$

*ELIMINATE CHOICES*
The probability of an event must be between 0 and 1. Choice D can be eliminated.

**SOLUTION**

The tosses are independent events, because the outcome of a toss does not affect the probability of the next toss resulting in a win.

So the probability of each event is $\dfrac{1}{15}$.

$$P(\text{win and win}) = P(\text{win}) \cdot P(\text{win}) = \dfrac{1}{15} \cdot \dfrac{1}{15} = \dfrac{1}{225}$$

▶ **Answer**  The probability of two winning tosses in a row is $\dfrac{1}{225}$.
The correct answer is A.  Ⓐ Ⓑ Ⓒ Ⓓ

✓ **GUIDED PRACTICE**  for Examples 1 and 2

**In Exercises 1 and 2, tell whether the events are *independent* or *dependent*. *Explain* your reasoning.**

1. You toss a coin. Then you roll a number cube.

2. You randomly choose 1 of 10 marbles. Then you randomly choose one of the remaining 9 marbles.

3. You toss a coin twice. Find the probability of getting two heads.

**Dependent Events** If A and B are dependent events, the probability that B occurs given that A also occurs is not the same as the probability of B. So, you should use *P*(B given A) instead of *P*(B) to represent the probability that B occurs given that A also occurs.

---

**KEY CONCEPT**                                      *For Your Notebook*

**Probability of Dependent Events**

**Words**     For two dependent events, the probability that both
              events occur is the product of the probability of the first
              event and the probability of the second event given that
              the first event also occurs.

**Algebra**   If events A and B are dependent,
              then $P(A \text{ and } B) = P(A) \cdot P(B \text{ given } A)$.

---

**EXAMPLE 3**  Finding Probability of Dependent Events

**Bingo** You are playing the bingo card shown. The caller has 50 numbers left to call. What is the probability that you will get bingo with the next 2 numbers called?

**SOLUTION**

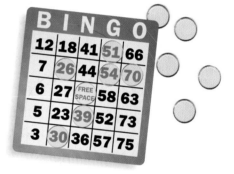

You need B7 and N44 for bingo. Find the probability of success when each of the next 2 numbers is drawn. Then multiply.

$$P(\text{B7 or N44}) = \frac{2}{50} = \frac{1}{25}$$     **There are 50 numbers left to call.**

$$P(\text{remaining number}) = \frac{1}{49}$$     **There are 49 numbers left to call.**

$$P(\text{both numbers}) = \frac{1}{25} \cdot \frac{1}{49} = \frac{1}{1225}$$     **Multiply the probabilities.**

▶ **Answer** The probability that you will get bingo when the next 2 numbers are called is $\frac{1}{1225}$, or about 0.0008.

*Animated* **Math**
at classzone.com

---

✓ **GUIDED PRACTICE**   **for Example 3**

 **4. What If?** In Example 3, suppose 36 numbers are left to call. Find the probability.

 **5. Prizes** You are randomly choosing 2 business cards from a dish with 40 cards, each from a different business, to win prizes. What is the probability you choose the cards for the dry cleaners and the hair salon?

# 12.8 EXERCISES

HOMEWORK
KEY

= **TAKS Practice and Reasoning**
  Exs. 13, 15, 28, 29, and 34

○ = **HINTS** AND **HOMEWORK HELP**
  for Exs. 3, 5, 9, 11, 25 at classzone.com

## SKILL PRACTICE

**VOCABULARY** **Copy and complete the statement.**

**1.** When the occurrence of an event does not affect the probability of the next event, the events are __?__.

**2.** Two events are __?__ events if the occurrence of one event affects the probability that the other event will occur.

**IDENTIFYING EVENTS** **Tell whether the events are *independent* or *dependent*.**

SEE EXAMPLE 1
on p. 694
for Exs. 3–6

**3.** You randomly choose a marble from a jar. You replace the marble and randomly choose another marble.

**4.** Your teacher randomly chooses you to give a report. The teacher then randomly chooses Pam from the remaining students.

**5.** You randomly choose a password from a list of words. Then your friend randomly chooses a password from the remaining words.

**6.** You randomly draw a card from a deck of cards. You replace the card and then randomly draw another card.

**FINDING PROBABILITIES** **Events A and B are independent. Events C and D are dependent. Find the missing probability.**

SEE EXAMPLES
2 AND 3
on pp. 695–696
for Exs. 7–14

**7.** $P(A) = 0.4$
$P(B) = 0.6$
$P(A \text{ and } B) =$ __?__

**8.** $P(A) = 0.9$
$P(B) =$ __?__
$P(A \text{ and } B) = 0.09$

**9.** $P(A) =$ __?__
$P(B) = 0.6$
$P(A \text{ and } B) = 0.12$

**10.** $P(C) = 0.75$
$P(D \text{ given } C) = 0.5$
$P(C \text{ and } D) =$ __?__

**11.** $P(C) = 0.8$
$P(D \text{ given } C) =$ __?__
$P(C \text{ and } D) = 0.32$

**12.** $P(C) =$ __?__
$P(D \text{ given } C) = 0.3$
$P(C \text{ and } D) = 0.039$

**13.** ✦ **TAKS REASONING** You spin the spinner at the right twice. What is the probability of getting blue both times?

**(A)** $\frac{1}{16}$  **(B)** $\frac{1}{8}$  **(C)** $\frac{1}{4}$  **(D)** $\frac{1}{2}$

**14.** **ERROR ANALYSIS** Describe and correct the error made in finding $P(A \text{ and } B)$.

$$P(A) = 0.2$$
$$P(B \text{ given } A) = 0.25$$
$$P(A \text{ and } B) = 0.2 + 0.25 = 0.45$$

**15.** ✦ **TAKS REASONING** Create two probability problems, one for a situation involving independent events, and the other for a situation involving dependent events. Then calculate the probabilities. Show your work.

**16. CHECKING REASONABLENESS** A friend looks at the spinner and says that the probability of the spinner landing on the blue region and then the red region is about 0.5 • 0.25, or 0.125. Is this a reasonable estimate? *Explain.*

**SELECTING LETTERS** A bag contains 100 lettered tiles. The number of tiles that show various letters is given in the table. Find the probability of randomly choosing two letters with the given characteristics.

**17.** both A's if you replace the first before choosing the second

**18.** both A's without replacement

**19.** a T followed by an H, with replacement

**20.** a T followed by an H, without replacement

| Letter | Number of Tiles |
|--------|-----------------|
| A | 9 |
| H | 2 |
| T | 6 |

**CHALLENGE** Refer to the bag of 100 lettered tiles in Exercises 17–20.

**21.** The probability of choosing a D first and then an A without replacing the D is $\frac{1}{275}$. How many D's are in the bag?

**22.** The probability of choosing an E first, replacing it, and then choosing a T is $\frac{9}{1250}$. How many E's are in the bag?

## PROBLEM SOLVING

In Exercises 23–25, tell whether the events are *independent* or *dependent.* Then find the probability.

*SEE EXAMPLES 1, 2, AND 3*
on pp. 694–696 for Exs. 23–25

**23. BUTTONS** You draw a button at random from the jar at the right. Without replacing the first button, you draw another. What is the probability that you draw a red button and then a yellow button? a yellow button and then a blue button?

**24. BANQUET** At a banquet, you can order a main course of a chef's salad, salmon and potatoes, ham and beans, or steak and rice. You can drink water, juice, milk, coffee, or iced tea. All choices are equally likely. What is the probability that a randomly chosen person orders a chef's salad and juice?

**(25.) BAKING** You have a basket of rolls: 5 wheat, 6 sourdough, 8 sesame, and 9 cheese. You randomly choose a roll, keep it, and then choose another. What is the probability that you pick a sesame roll and then a cheese roll?

*SEE EXAMPLES 2 AND 3*
on pp. 695–696 for Exs. 26–28

**26. LUCKY PLATE** Each day, the person who gets the lucky plate wins a free snack from the school cafeteria. The cafeteria sells 127 lunches on Wednesday and 134 lunches on Thursday. You buy a lunch both days. What is the probability that you win on both days?

 = TAKS Practice and Reasoning     ◯ = HINTS AND HOMEWORK HELP *at classzone.com*

**27. ERROR ANALYSIS** A deck of 10 cards is numbered with the integers from 1 to 10. You randomly pick a card, and then another, without replacement. Describe and correct the error made in finding the probability of selecting 2 prime numbers.

$$\times \quad P(A) = \frac{4}{10}$$
$$P(B \text{ given } A) = \frac{3}{10}$$
$$P(A \text{ and } B) = \frac{4}{10} \cdot \frac{3}{10} = \frac{12}{100} = \frac{3}{25}$$

**28. TAKS REASONING** Your teacher is giving away two prizes by random drawing. She puts the class's 25 names into a hat. She draws the first name. Then she draws a second name without replacing the first name.

What is the probability that your name will be chosen first? Does the probability that your name will be chosen second depend on the first outcome? *Explain.*

**29. TAKS REASONING** You are choosing an outfit at random. You can choose a red, blue, or green shirt as a top and jeans or khakis for pants.

  **a.** Make a tree diagram to find the number of possible outfits. *Describe* the relationship between the number of possible outfits and the probability of choosing one outfit.

  **b.** Find *P*(red shirt), *P*(jeans), *P*(red shirt and jeans).

  **c.** If *P*(red shirt and jeans) $= \frac{1}{10}$, how many shirts do you have to choose from if you still have only 2 pairs of pants? *Explain.*

**30. WRITING** Tennis player A wins a match 80% of the time when she serves first and 50% of the time when her opponent serves first. Player A serves first in the first match and the probability of her winning 2 matches in a row is 40%. Who served first in the second match? *Explain* your reasoning.

**31. REASONING** You toss a coin. What is the probability that you get heads 7 times in a row? Suppose you have already tossed heads 6 times in a row. What is the probability that you will get heads on the next toss? *Explain.*

**32. INVESTING** A brochure says, "If you invested money with us 5 years ago, that money grew by an average of 20%." The brochure also says, "Past performance is no guarantee of future results." Which statement leads you to think that investing money today is independent of past events? Which statements suggests the opposite? *Explain.*

**33. CHALLENGE** A town's election for mayor drew 75% of the town's 800 eligible voters. What is the probability that two different randomly selected people both voted in the election?

*REVIEW*
Lesson 12.3;
TAKS Workbook

**34.** 🏵 **TAKS PRACTICE** The table shows the percent of certain species of fish caught on a fishing trip out of all fish caught on the trip. Which circle graph best represents the data? *TAKS Obj. 5*

| Fish species | Rainbow Trout | Brown Trout | Grayling | Other |
|---|---|---|---|---|
| **Percent of fish caught** | 40% | 35% | 15% | 10% |

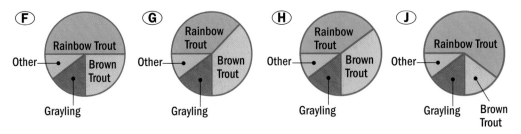

---

**QUIZ** *for Lessons 12.4–12.8*

1. **SHOES** You can buy sandals or sneakers in black, brown, tan, or white. Make a tree diagram to show the possible choices for shoes. *(p. 670)*

2. **CAMP** You are scheduling swimming, crafts, canoeing, and softball. How many different schedules of four different activities are possible? *(p. 675)*

3. **HOCKEY** Find the number of ways two players can be chosen from 20 team members. *(p. 675)*

4. **RAIN** The probability that it will rain today is 0.4. What are the odds in favor of rain? What is the probability that it will *not* rain? *(p. 685)*

**Find the probability.** *(p. 694)*

5. You roll a 5 on a 6-sided number cube. Then you roll another 5.

6. A bag holds 3 red and 5 blue tiles. You randomly draw a red tile, keep it, and then randomly draw a blue tile.

---

**Brain Game**    *Lucky Numbers*

Two balls will be randomly chosen without replacement from the bowl shown.

- Bo wins if the first ball is blue, and the next ball is a 3 or a 4.

- Sherry wins if the first ball is an even number and the next ball is green.

- Eva wins if both balls are red.

Who has the best chance of winning?

# Extension

*Use after Lesson 12.8*

# Samples

**TEKS** *8.13.A*

**GOAL** Identify biased samples and surveys.

**KEY VOCABULARY**
• **population,** *p. 701*
• **sample,** *p. 701*
• **random sample,** *p. 701*
• **biased sample,** *p. 701*

One way to collect data about a group is by doing a survey. A **population** is the entire group of people or objects that you want information about. When it is difficult to survey an entire population, a **sample**, or a part of the entire group, is surveyed.

The size of a sample affects the reliability of the results. Larger samples are considered to be more reliable than smaller samples. A larger sample size decreases the probability that you will get misleading results due to chance. For example, suppose you are flipping a coin. You will get 7 out of 10 heads more often than 70 out of 100 or 700 out of 1000.

In a **random sample**, each person or object has an equally likely chance of being selected. A non-random sample can result in a **biased sample** that is not representative of the population.

---

**EXAMPLE 1** **Identifying Potentially Biased Samples**

**Costume Dance** The student council wants students to help decide on a theme for a costume dance. Students can choose one of the council's three ideas from the options listed at the right.

Surveying all of the students will take too long, so a sample will be surveyed. Tell whether the survey method could result in a biased sample. *Explain* your reasoning.

**a.** Survey members of the movie club.

**b.** Survey students as they enter the school.

**c.** Survey students on the football team.

**SOLUTION**

**a.** This method could result in a biased sample because this group is more likely to favor the movie theme.

**b.** This method is not likely to result in a biased sample because a wide range of students will be surveyed.

**c.** This method could result in a biased sample because the football players are more likely to favor sports and games.

*Continued on next page*

**Survey Questions** When you create a survey, you need to phrase the questions so that the responses accurately reflect the views of the people surveyed. If not, the survey results may be misleading.

**EXAMPLE 2** Identifying Potentially Biased Questions

**Tell whether the question could produce biased results.** *Explain.*

a. Do you support the unfair policy of requiring students to do a time-consuming community project? YES ☐ NO ☐

b. Do you like our new apple-nut yogurt flavor, now on sale in stores everywhere? YES ☐ NO ☐

**SOLUTION**

a. This question states that the policy is unfair and that the project is time-consuming. It encourages a response of *no*. So, the question could lead to biased results.

b. The question assumes that the person responding has tried the new yogurt flavor. Those who have not tried the new flavor may not give an accurate opinion. So, the question could lead to biased results.

**EXERCISES**

**Stadiums** A city survey plans to ask residents whether they favor using public funds to pay for a new baseball stadium. Tell whether the method could result in a biased sample. *Explain.*

1. Ask people that call in to a sports radio talk show.

2. Ask every tenth person listed in the phone book.

3. Ask every fifth person who enters the sporting goods store in town.

4. **Menus** A restaurant wants to know what kinds of food to add to its menu to attract new customers. *Describe* a sampling method that the restaurant can use that is not likely to result in a biased sample.

**Tell whether the survey question could produce biased results.** *Explain* **your reasoning.**

5. Would you rather relax at home while reading a book, or go to a noisy, crowded mall?

6. Allowing messy, dangerous dogs into the park will cause safety and health problems. Will you vote to allow dogs into the park?

7. How often do you buy lunch in the school cafeteria?

8. Do you agree with this store's policy for returning purchases?

## Lessons 12.4–12.8

**MULTIPLE CHOICE**

1. **FAMILY** The probability that a person is a boy is 0.5. What is the probability that all four cousins in a family are boys? *TEKS 8.11.A*

   (A) 0.0625　　(B) 0.25

   (C) 0.5　　(D) 1

2. **NUMBER CUBES** You roll a number cube 5 times. The first 4 times you roll a three. What is the probability that you roll a three on your last roll? *TEKS 8.11.A*

   (F) $\frac{1}{7776}$　　(G) $\frac{1}{3125}$

   (H) $\frac{1}{216}$　　(J) $\frac{1}{6}$

3. **WEATHER** The weather forecast says that there is a 40% probability of rain. What are the odds in favor of NOT raining? *TEKS 8.4.A*

   (A) 2 to 3　　(B) 3 to 2

   (C) 3 to 5　　(D) 5 to 3

4. **TELEPHONE NUMBERS** A certain town can use the digits 0, 1, 2, 6, 7, and 8 for its telephone prefixes. How many three digit telephone prefixes are possible for this town if each digit can be used only once in a prefix and the first digit cannot be a 1 or a 0? *TEKS 8.14.C*

   (F) 60　　(G) 80

   (H) 100　　(J) 120

5. **SANDWICHES** Zach goes to a restaurant for a sandwich. Each sandwich comes with one meat, one cheese, and one dressing.

| Meat | Cheese | Dressing |
|------|--------|----------|
| Ham | American | Italian |
| Roast Beef | Mozzarella | Mayonnaise |
| Turkey | Provolone | Oil and Vinegar |
| | Swiss | Vinaigrette |

   Salami is added to the choices of meat. How many more types of sandwiches are possible after salami is added to the choices of meat? *TEKS 8.14.B*

   (A) 12　　(B) 16

   (C) 48　　(D) 64

6. **NEW PROBABILITY** Meg has a bag with 3 pink marbles, 4 red marbles, 3 yellow marbles and 8 blue marbles. Meg will draw one marble from the bag. Which action will increase the probability of drawing a pink marble the most? *TEKS 8.16.B*

   (F) Removing a pink marble from the bag before the drawing.

   (G) Adding a pink marble to the bag before the drawing.

   (H) Removing a red marble and a blue marble from the bag before the drawing.

   (J) Removing a yellow marble from the bag before the drawing.

**GRIDDED ANSWER** ⊘①②●④⑤⑥⑦⑧⑨

7. **BASEBALL TOURNAMENT** The first team to win 3 out of 5 possible games will be the winner of a baseball tournament. In how many ways can a team win 3 out of 5 games? *TEKS 8.2.A*

## REVIEW KEY VOCABULARY

- stem-and-leaf plot, *p. 649*
- box-and-whisker plot, *p. 654*
- lower quartile, *p. 654*
- upper quartile, *p. 654*
- lower extreme, *p. 654*
- upper extreme, *p. 654*

- circle graph, *p. 659*
- line graph, *p. 660*
- tree diagram, *p. 670*
- permutation, *p. 675*
- factorial, *p. 675*
- combination, *p. 680*

- complementary events, *p. 685*
- unfavorable outcome, *p. 686*
- odds, *p. 686*
- compound events, *p. 694*
- independent events, *p. 694*
- dependent events, *p. 694*

### VOCABULARY EXERCISES

**In Exercises 1–6, match the description with the correct vocabulary item from the list above.**

1. An arrangement in which order is important

2. An arrangement in which order is *not* important

3. A graph that displays data in distinct categories

4. A graph used to display changes in a quantity over time

5. A plot used to order a data set

6. A plot that divides a data set into 4 quarters

## REVIEW EXAMPLES AND EXERCISES

### 12.1 Stem-and-Leaf Plots
*pp. 649–653*

**EXAMPLE**

**Make a stem-and-leaf plot of the data below:**

$$24, 29, 35, 32, 22, 20, 43, 27, 41, 31, 26$$

**STEP 1** **Record** the data set in an unordered stem-and-leaf plot.

| 2 | 4 9 2 0 7 6 |
|---|---|
| 3 | 5 2 1 |
| 4 | 3 1 |

**STEP 2** **Order** the leaves. Include a key.

| 2 | 0 2 4 6 7 9 |
|---|---|
| 3 | 1 2 5 |
| 4 | 1 3 |

Key: 4 | 1 = 41

## EXERCISES

**Make an ordered stem-and-leaf plot of the data. Identify the interval that includes the most data values.**

SEE EXAMPLES
1 AND 2
on pp. 649–650
for Exs. 7–10

7. 20, 25, 36, 16, 29, 32, 27, 42, 28, 31, 15, 19, 21, 37, 22

8. 11.2, 7.5, 15.1, 15.7, 15.0, 6.7, 11.3, 8.4, 7.3, 10.6, 9.2, 15.6, 11.9, 15.8

9. 81, 100, 94, 97, 86, 100, 97, 96, 84, 99

10. **Wind Speed** Make an ordered stem-and-leaf plot of the wind speed data, given in miles per hour: 9, 15, 8, 19, 11, 18, 11, 24, 7, 14, 21, 2, 7, 15, 12.

---

## 12.2 Box-and-Whisker Plots

*pp. 654–658*

### EXAMPLE

**Make a box-and-whisker plot of the data below:**

$$70, 69, 75, 65, 64, 85, 61, 66, 73, 61, 84.$$

**STEP 1** **Order** the data to find the median, quartiles, and extremes.

**STEP 2** **Plot** these values below a number line.

---

## EXERCISES

**Make a box-and-whisker plot of the data.**

SEE EXAMPLES
1 AND 2
on pp. 654–655
for Exs. 11–13

11. 5, 13, 9, 31, 25, 21, 25, 18, 23, 14, 32, 3, 22, 11, 16

12. 62, 41, 65, 76, 68, 83, 81, 80, 70, 85, 79, 42, 61, 74, 68

13. **Chess** The prices of several chess sets are $15, $20, $38, $95, $60, $45, $40, $35, and $50. Make a box-and-whisker plot of the data. *Describe* how the data are distributed.

## 12.3 Using Data Displays

pp. 659–664

### EXAMPLE

**Election** A survey indicates 35% of students do not know who they will vote for in a school election, 38% will vote for Wong, and 27% will vote for Nelson. Display the data in a circle graph.

**STEP 1** **Find** the number of degrees to use to represent each response as a section in a circle graph.

**Not sure**

$0.35(360°) = 126°$

**Wong**

$0.38(360°) \approx 137°$

**Nelson**

$0.27(360°) \approx 97°$

**STEP 2** **Draw** a circle and use the angle measures to draw the sections.

**Who Will You Vote For?**

Not sure 35%

Wong 38%

Nelson 27%

### EXERCISE

SEE EXAMPLE 1
on p. 659
for Ex. 14

**14. Dessert** The results of a student survey on favorite summer drinks were as follows: *iced tea*, 50%; *lemonade*, 25%; *limeade*, 10%; *other*, 15%. Display the data in a circle graph.

## 12.4 Counting Methods

pp. 670–674

### EXAMPLE

**Construction** To build a birdhouse, you can choose from 3 designs and 6 colors. How many different birdhouses can you build?

$3 \cdot 6 = 18$    **Counting principle**

designs   colors

▶ **Answer** You can build 18 different birdhouses.

### EXERCISE

SEE EXAMPLES
1 AND 2
on pp. 670–671
for Ex. 15

**15. Clothing** You need to choose one of 4 hats and one of 3 shirts to wear. Make a tree diagram to find the number of different hat-shirt pairs. Use the counting principle to check your answer.

## 12.5 Permutations

pp. 675–679

### EXAMPLE

**Swimming** At a swim meet, 10 swimmers are in an event. In how many ways can first, second, third, and fourth place medals be awarded?

$$_{10}P_4 = \frac{10!}{(10-4)!} = \frac{10!}{6!}$$ Use permutation formula.

$$= \frac{10 \cdot 9 \cdot 8 \cdot 7 \cdot \cancel{6} \cdot \cancel{5} \cdot \cancel{4} \cdot \cancel{3} \cdot \cancel{2} \cdot \cancel{1}}{\cancel{6} \cdot \cancel{5} \cdot \cancel{4} \cdot \cancel{3} \cdot \cancel{2} \cdot \cancel{1}}$$ Divide out common factors.

$$= 5040$$ Multiply.

▶ **Answer** There are 5040 ways to award the medals.

### EXERCISES

**Find the number of permutations.**

**SEE EXAMPLE 3**
on p. 676
for Exs. 16–20

**16.** $_8P_4$      **17.** $_{10}P_3$      **18.** $_{12}P_1$      **19.** $_{13}P_5$

**20.** The Griffiths have six children. In how many ways can they line up their children for a picture?

## 12.6 Combinations

pp. 680–684

### EXAMPLE

**Evaluate $_7C_5$.**

$$_7C_5 = \frac{_7P_5}{5!}$$ Combination formula

$$= \frac{7 \cdot 6 \cdot 5 \cdot 4 \cdot 3}{5!}$$     $_7P_5 = \frac{7!}{(7-5)!} = 7 \cdot 6 \cdot 5 \cdot 4 \cdot 3$

$$= \frac{7 \cdot \overset{3}{\cancel{6}} \cdot \cancel{5} \cdot \cancel{4} \cdot \cancel{3}}{\cancel{5} \cdot \cancel{4} \cdot \cancel{3} \cdot 2 \cdot 1}$$ Expand 5! Divide out common factors.

$$= 21$$ Simplify.

### EXERCISES

**Find the number of combinations.**

**SEE EXAMPLES
2 AND 3**
on pp. 681–682
for Exs. 21–25

**21.** $_9C_2$      **22.** $_6C_1$      **23.** $_9C_9$      **24.** $_{12}C_8$

**25. MP3 Players** Your MP3 player holds 15 songs and you have 30 songs in your collection. Can the number of possible groups of 15 songs be counted using a *permutation* or a *combination*? Find the number of groups possible.

## 12.7 Probability and Odds

*pp. 685–689*

### EXAMPLE

**Shopping Spree** A customer is chosen at random from a group of 10 males and 15 females to win a shopping spree. What is the probability that the winner is *not* male? What are the odds in favor?

$$P(\text{not male}) = 1 - P(\text{male})$$

$$= 1 - \frac{10}{25}$$

$$= \frac{15}{25}, \text{ or } \frac{3}{5}$$

$$\text{Odds} = \frac{\text{Number of favorable outcomes}}{\text{Number of unfavorable outcomes}}$$

$$= \frac{\text{Number that are not male}}{\text{Number that are male}}$$

$$= \frac{15}{10}$$

$$= \frac{3}{2}$$

▶ **Answer** The probability that the winner is not male is $\frac{3}{5}$. The odds in favor of not choosing a male are 3 to 2.

### EXERCISE

SEE EXAMPLES
1, 2, AND 3
on pp. 685–687
for Ex. 26

26. **Contest** The probability that you will win a contest is 76%. What is the probability that you will lose the contest? What are the odds in favor of losing the contest?

## 12.8 Independent and Dependent Events

*pp. 694–699*

### EXAMPLE

**Lettered Tiles** Tiles with each of the 11 letters in PROBABILITY are in a bag. You randomly draw a tile, do not replace it, and then randomly draw a second tile. What is the probability that both tiles are I's?

$$P(\text{I and I}) = P(\text{I}) \cdot P(\text{I given I}) = \frac{2}{11} \cdot \frac{1}{10} = \frac{1}{55}$$

### EXERCISES

SEE EXAMPLES
2 AND 3
on pp. 695–696
for Exs. 27–28

27. If you replace the first tile in the example above, what is the probability that the first tile is B and the second is L?

28. **Weather** A weather forecaster says there is a 60% chance that it will snow on Wednesday and a 25% chance that it will snow on Thursday. Find the probability that it will snow on both Wednesday and Thursday.

**Make a stem-and-leaf plot of the data. Identify the interval that includes the most values. Then make a box-and-whisker plot.**

1. 46 kg, 70 kg, 21 kg, 136 kg, 55 kg, 60 kg, 72 kg, 104 kg, 52 kg, 96 kg, 43 kg, 59 kg, 88 kg, 56 kg

2. 12.1 in., 13.5 in., 12.8 in., 10 in., 7 in., 11.2 in., 12.9 in., 11.1 in., 12 in., 13.7 in., 8.2 in., 10.1 in., 13.3 in., 12.5 in., 11.7 in.

**Use the circle graph. It shows student replies to *Which animal career would you most enjoy*?**

3. What is the probability that a randomly chosen student replied *rodeo star*?

4. What is the probability that a randomly chosen student did *not* reply *veterinarian*?

5. What are the odds in favor of a randomly chosen student replying *zookeeper*?

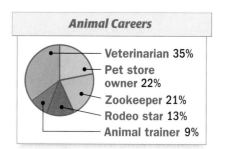

*Animal Careers*

- Veterinarian 35%
- Pet store owner 22%
- Zookeeper 21%
- Rodeo star 13%
- Animal trainer 9%

**In Exercises 6 and 7, tell whether the events are *independent* or *dependent*. Then find the probability.**

6. You roll a 6 on a number cube. Then you roll a 2.

7. You have 8 blue marbles and 12 red marbles in a bag. You randomly pick a blue marble on the first draw. Then you randomly pick another blue marble without replacing the first one.

8. **ACADEMY AWARDS** The lengths, in minutes, of the Best Picture Academy Award winning movies for the years 1990–1999 are 99, 118, 122, 131, 142, 160, 177, 183, 194, and 197. Make a box-and-whisker plot of the data. *Describe* how the data are distributed.

9. **TEMPERATURE** The record low temperatures in Miami, Florida, are given in the table. Display the data in an appropriate graph. *Justify* your choice of display.

| Month | Ja | Fe | Mr | Ap | Ma | Jn | Jl | Au | Se | Oc | No | De |
|---|---|---|---|---|---|---|---|---|---|---|---|---|
| Temp (°F) | 30 | 32 | 32 | 46 | 53 | 60 | 69 | 68 | 68 | 51 | 39 | 30 |

10. **MOVIES** You and four friends are going to a movie. In how many different orders can you pick your friends up? List all the possible orders.

11. **SCHOOL DANCE** You are making a banner for a school dance and have a choice of 8 colors. You want to use 4 different colors. How many different combinations are possible?

## REVIEWING DATA ANALYSIS PROBLEMS

Earlier in this chapter, you learned about misleading graphs. The following example and problems will explore other ways that data displays can mislead. Invalid conclusions may result from these displays.

**EXAMPLE**

**Sleep Patterns** The bar graph shows the average number of hours per day that different animals sleep. Why might a person reading the graph get an incorrect idea about the differences in the number of hours slept in a day by the animals in the graph?

### Solution

The height of the bars may lead to the conclusion that a pig sleeps about half as many hours per day as a brown bat. A person reading the graph at a glance may also conclude that the combined number of hours that a cow and a pig sleep per day is about the same as the number of hours that a tiger sleeps in a day.

These conclusions are false. The height of the bars cannot be compared because the intervals on the vertical scale are inconsistent. The graph at the right is less likely to mislead because it has consistent intervals on the vertical scale.

# DATA ANALYSIS PROBLEMS ON TAKS

Below are examples of data analysis problems in multiple choice format. Try solving the problems before looking at the solutions. (Cover the solutions with a piece of paper.) Then check your solutions against the ones given.

**1.** Steven glanced at the graph below.

He concluded that there were no passengers under the age of 20 on the plane. Why might he be incorrect?

**A** The bars of the graph fall between the numbers shown in the vertical scale.

**B** The graph divides the passengers into too few age groups.

**C** The vertical scale starts at 10.

**D** The vertical scale ends too low.

**Solution**

The vertical scale of the graph starts at 10. So, if there are ten or fewer passengers in an age group this information will not appear on the graph.

It is possible that there are as many as 10 passengers in the 0- to 19-year-old range.

The most likely explanation of Steven's incorrect conclusion is that he failed to notice the vertical scale of the graph starts at 10. The correct answer is C.

**2.** Ray surveyed students in his school to determine their favorite sport. He listed hockey, softball, soccer, and golf on the survey. The results are shown below.

| Sports | Hockey | Softball | Soccer | Golf |
|---|---|---|---|---|
| Students | 54 | 77 | 83 | 21 |

Ray says soccer is the students' favorite sport out of all sports. Why might he be incorrect?

**F** Students may be biased toward one sport.

**G** The captain of the softball team was absent.

**H** He did not include the choice of "other."

**J** Golf is not a team sport like the others.

**Solution**

Because the survey only gave four choices and no option of "other," students answering the question had to pick one of the sports listed. Their favorite sport may not be on the list.

So, the survey only reveals the students' favorite sport out of those listed, not their favorite sport in general.

The correct answer is H.

# 12 TAKS PRACTICE

## PRACTICE FOR TAKS OBJECTIVE 5

1. The misleading bar graph shows the average number of hours per week that four students studied.

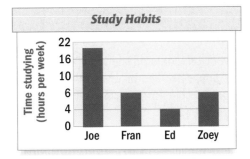

**Study Habits**

What true conclusion can be drawn from the graph despite its misleading design?

**A** Joe spends less time studying than Fran, Ed, and Zoey combined.

**B** Ed studies half as much as Fran.

**C** Joe studies 4.5 times as much as Ed.

**D** Fran and Zoey study the same amount of time.

2. The graph below displays the amounts of gasoline sold at a gas station on Friday. Which conclusion CANNOT be drawn from the misleading graph?

**Gasoline Sales**

**F** No purchases of 16 or more gallons were made.

**G** More purchases were in the range of 6 to 10 gallons than in other ranges.

**H** The range of 16 or more gallons accounted for the fewest purchases.

**J** Fifteen purchases were made for 1 to 5 gallons.

3. Janie surveyed the members of her extended family about which of two intersections had more traffic. The results are shown in the table below.

| Intersection | 26th and Peninsula | Pine and Norcross |
|---|---|---|
| Votes | 17 | 11 |

From these results, Janie concluded that people in her city believe the intersection at 26th & Peninsula has more traffic than the intersection at Pine & Norcross. Which is the best explanation for why her conclusion might be invalid?

**A** The survey should have included more than two intersections.

**B** The sample was not representative of her family.

**C** The survey should have included people outside of her family.

**D** No information on the intersections was included in her survey.

## MIXED TAKS PRACTICE

4. When making sugar water for a bird feeder, Randy adds 1 cup of sugar for every 4 cups of boiling water. If he boils 14 cups of water, which proportion can he use to find $x$, the number of cups of sugar he should add? *TAKS Obj. 2*

**F** $\dfrac{1}{4} = \dfrac{x}{14}$

**G** $\dfrac{1}{4} = \dfrac{14}{x}$

**H** $\dfrac{14}{4} = \dfrac{1}{x}$

**J** $\dfrac{4}{14} = \dfrac{4}{x}$

## MIXED TAKS PRACTICE

**5.** A password consists of 5 letters. Cheri says that there are less than 15 million possible passwords. Why is she correct? *TAKS Obj. 6*

**A** Because there are $10^5 = 100,000$ possible passwords.

**B** Because there are $26 \cdot 5 = 130$ possible passwords.

**C** Because there are $26 \cdot 25 \cdot 24 \cdot 23 \cdot 22 = 7,893,600$ possible passwords.

**D** Because there are $26^5 = 11,881,376$ possible passwords.

**6.** In a school parking lot, there are 16 red cars, 25 gray cars, and 9 green cars. Which circle graph best represents the data? *TAKS Obj. 5*

**F**

**G**

**H**

**J**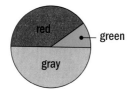

**7.** Ali plants a flower garden in a circle around a tree. The circle formed by the outer edge of the garden has twice the radius of the circle formed by the inner edge. What is the approximate area of the flower garden? *TAKS Obj. 3*

**A** $12.56 \text{ ft}^2$

**B** $25.12 \text{ ft}^2$

**C** $37.68 \text{ ft}^2$

**D** $50.24 \text{ ft}^2$

**8.** Lars rolls a six-sided number cube 3 times. What is the probability that he rolls the same number all 3 times? *TAKS Obj. 5*

**F** $\frac{1}{216}$

**G** $\frac{5}{216}$

**H** $\frac{1}{36}$

**J** $\frac{1}{6}$

**9.** When making a stuffed animal, Jerome can choose between 8 animals, 4 colors, and 15 outfits. How many different stuffed animals are possible? *TAKS Obj. 6*

**A** 27

**B** 47

**C** 480

**D** 560

**10. GRIDDED ANSWER** Reggie plans to buy a digital camera that is on sale for 15% off the regular price. If the regular price is $140, what is the sale price in dollars? *TAKS Obj. 2*

*Record your answer and fill in the bubbles on your answer document. Be sure to use the correct place value.*

# 13 Polynomials and Functions

## Before

In previous chapters you've . . .

• Simplified expressions by combining like terms
• Graphed linear functions

## Now

**TEKS** you'll study . . .

| | | |
|---|---|---|
| 8.5.A | **13.1** | Polynomials |
| 8.7.B | **13.2** | Adding polynomials |
| 8.8.C | **13.3** | Monomials and powers |
| 8.7.B | **13.4** | Multiplying binomials |
| 8.4 | **13.5** | Non-linear functions |

## Why?

So you can solve real-world problems about . . .

• treehouses, p. 723
• baseball, p. 737
• stage design, p. 737
• juggling, p. 739

Math
at classzone.com

• Polynomials, p. 719
• Adding and Subtracting Polynomials, p. 722
• Multiplying Binomials, p. 733

## Get-Ready Games

**Review Prerequisite Skills** by playing *Piñata Punch* and *Unmasking Expressions.*

### PIÑATA PUNCH

$(5 - 11)^3 \cdot 2 \cdot (-6)^{-2}$

$\dfrac{4^7}{(9 - 5)^3}$

$3^{-3} \cdot 3^8 + 5$

$2^5 \cdot 7 \cdot 2^{-1}$

$\dfrac{(7 + 1)^6}{8^4}$

18   12   250   112   8   -64

**Skill Focus:** Using properties of exponents

To break open the piñata on your turn, you need to pick the right stick.

• Evaluate the expression under each stick.

• A stick breaks the piñata if it has the same value as one of the spots.

• Which stick breaks the piñata? Which spot should you hit?

# Unmasking Expressions

$x - 4x + 3 + 9x$

$-7x + 8 - 2(3x + 4)$

$5(x - 6) + 10x - 3$

$8x - 3 - 4(2x + 3)$

$4 - (3x - 1) + x$

$17 - 4x - 13 + 2x$

| John | Maria | Sam | Carol | Vincent | Sophie |
|------|-------|-----|-------|---------|--------|
| $6x + 3$ | $-2x + 4$ | $-13x$ | $-15$ | $-2x + 5$ | $15x - 33$ |

**Skill Focus:** Combining like terms

Find who is behind each of the masks.

- Match the expression under the mask with the correct simplified expression below a name.

## Stop and Think

1. **WRITING** *Explain* the steps for simplifying the expression that is given under the mask worn by Sam in *Unmasking Expressions*.

2. **CRITICAL THINKING** Write another expression whose value would allow you to break the piñata in *Piñata Punch*.

# Review Prerequisite Skills

## VOCABULARY CHECK

**REVIEW WORDS**
- **power,** *p. 19*
- **exponent,** *p. 19*
- **like terms,** *p. 89*
- **terms,** *p. 89*
- **coefficient,** *p. 89*
- **monomial,** *p. 178*
- **function,** *p. 583*

Copy and complete using a review word from the list at the left.

**1.** In the monomial $2x^3$, the 2 is the __?__ and the 3 is the __?__.

**2.** A relation that assigns exactly one output value to each input value is a(n) __?__.

**3.** A number, a variable, or a product of a number and one or more variables is a(n) __?__.

## SKILL CHECK

**Simplify the expression.** *(p. 88)*

**4.** $6x - 4 + 4x - 3$  **5.** $-5(2x + 3) - 4x$  **6.** $7(3x - 5) - (-x)$

**7.** $-2x - (-5x)$  **8.** $-2(-4x - 8)$  **9.** $-3(3x) + 18x$

**Simplify. Write the expression using only positive exponents.** *(p. 208)*

**10.** $\dfrac{y^4}{y^6}$  **11.** $\dfrac{5^{37}}{5^{35}}$  **12.** $x^4 \cdot x^5$

**List four solutions of the equation.** *(p. 593)*

**13.** $y = 3x - 5$  **14.** $y = -2x + 1$  **15.** $y = \dfrac{1}{2}x$

**TEXAS** *@HomeTutor*  Prerequisite skills practice at classzone.com

## Notetaking Skills    Summarizing Material

A summary of the property of exponents is shown at the right. In Chapter 13 you will apply the strategy of summarizing material to Example 1 on p. 734.

In your notebook, summarize the main ideas from each lesson. This will help you to see how key ideas are related.

### Exponent Rules

**Product of Powers**

$x^2 \cdot x^3 = x^{2+3} = x^5$

**Quotient of Powers** $(x \neq 0)$

$\dfrac{x^5}{x^2} = x^{5-2} = x^3$

**Zero Exponent** $(x \neq 0)$

$x^0 = 1$

**Negative Exponent** $(x \neq 0)$

$x^{-4} = \dfrac{1}{x^4}$

# 13.1 Polynomials

TEKS 8.5.A

| Before | You simplified expressions by combining like terms. |
|---|---|
| Now | You will simplify polynomials by combining like terms. |
| Why? | So you can apply polynomials, as with finding heights in Example 3. |

**KEY VOCABULARY**
- **monomial,** *p. 178*
- **polynomial,** *p. 717*
- **binomial,** *p. 717*
- **trinomial,** *p. 717*
- **standard form,** *p. 717*

In Lesson 4.1 you were introduced to monomials. A **polynomial** is a monomial or a sum of monomials. Each monomial in a polynomial is called a *term*. Polynomials are classified by the number of their terms when they are in simplified form. If a polynomial has more than three terms, it is simply called a polynomial.

| Monomial (1 term) | Binomial (2 terms) | Trinomial (3 terms) |
|---|---|---|
| $-2x$ | $3x - 2$ | $-2a^2 + 3a + 1$ |
| $4$ | $-s^4 + 6s^3$ | $3 + 5r - 7r^2$ |

A polynomial in one variable is written in **standard form** if the exponents of the variable decrease from left to right.

| Standard Form | Not Standard Form |
|---|---|
| $3x^3 - 2x^2 + 4$ | $3 + 5y$ |
| $-2m^6 + 5m^3 - m$ | $7t^4 - t^7 - 2t^2 + 3t$ |

## EXAMPLE 1 Writing Polynomials in Standard Form

 **Write the polynomial in standard form. Classify the polynomial.**

**AVOID ERRORS**
If you do not see an exponent with a variable, then the exponent of the variable is 1.
$2x = 2x^1$

**a.** $x - 9 + 5x^2 = x + (-9) + 5x^2$     **Write subtraction as addition.**

                $= 5x^2 + x + (-9)$     **Order terms with decreasing exponents.**

▸ **Answer** The polynomial $5x^2 + x - 9$ has 3 terms, so it is a trinomial.

**b.** $2x - 3x^3 = 2x + (-3x^3)$     **Write subtraction as addition.**

             $= -3x^3 + 2x$     **Order terms with decreasing exponents.**

▸ **Answer** The polynomial $-3x^3 + 2x$ has 2 terms, so it is a binomial.

 **GUIDED PRACTICE**    **for Example 1**

**Write the polynomial in standard form and classify it.**

**1.** $4 + b^2 - 8b$        **2.** $11 + 2n^4 - 7n + 5n^2$      **3.** $-5 + 3x^2$

**Simplifying Polynomials** Remember that *like terms* have the same variables raised to the same powers. To simplify a polynomial, combine like terms by adding their coefficients.

**EXAMPLE 2** **Simplifying Polynomials**

Simplify the polynomial and write it in standard form.

**a.** $3x^2 - 2x + 4x^2 - 3$ $\quad = 3x^2 + 4x^2 - 2x - 3$ $\qquad$ **Group like terms.**

$\qquad\qquad\qquad\qquad\quad = 7x^2 - 2x - 3$ $\qquad$ **Simplify.**

*REVIEW LIKE TERMS*
For help with like terms, see p. 88. Remember that $x^2 = 1x^2$.

**b.** $x^2 + 2 + 4(x^2 - 2x)$ $\quad = x^2 + 2 + 4(x^2) - 4(2x)$ $\qquad$ **Distributive property**

$\qquad\qquad\qquad\qquad\qquad = x^2 + 2 + 4x^2 - 8x$ $\qquad$ **Multiply.**

$\qquad\qquad\qquad\qquad\qquad = x^2 + 4x^2 + 2 - 8x$ $\qquad$ **Group like terms.**

$\qquad\qquad\qquad\qquad\qquad = 5x^2 + 2 - 8x$ $\qquad$ **Simplify.**

$\qquad\qquad\qquad\qquad\qquad = 5x^2 - 8x + 2$ $\qquad$ **Write in standard form.**

**EXAMPLE 3** **Evaluating a Polynomial Expression**

**Falling Objects** You drop a pinecone from a bridge that is 150 feet high. The height, in feet, of the pinecone after $t$ seconds of falling, can be found using the polynomial $-16t^2 + 150$. Find the pinecone's height after 2 seconds.

**SOLUTION**

$-16t^2 + 150 = -16(2)^2 + 150$ $\qquad$ **Substitute 2 for $t$.**

$\qquad\qquad\quad = -16(4) + 150$ $\qquad$ **Evaluate the power.**

$\qquad\qquad\quad = -64 + 150$ $\qquad$ **Multiply.**

$\qquad\qquad\quad = 86$ $\qquad$ **Add.**

▶ **Answer** The pinecone's height after 2 seconds is 86 feet.

✓ **GUIDED PRACTICE** **for Examples 2 and 3**

Simplify the polynomial and write it in standard form.

**4.** $7p + 5p^2 - 2 - 3p^2$

**5.** $10s^4 - 3s + s^4 - 1$

**6.** $2(a^2 + 3a - 1) + 2a^2$

**7.** $8x + 3(2x^2 - x + 1)$

**8.** $6d^3 - 4d - 4d^3 - 6d$

**9.** $-5x^2 + 7 + 2(-6 + 7x^2)$

Find the height of the pinecone in Example 3 after it falls for the given number of seconds.

**10.** 0.5 sec $\qquad$ **11.** 1 sec $\qquad$ **12.** 1.5 sec $\qquad$ **13.** 3 sec

# 13.1 EXERCISES

HOMEWORK KEY  = **TAKS Practice and Reasoning**
Exs. 22, 37, 41, and 44

○ = **HINTS AND HOMEWORK HELP**
for Exs. 7, 9, 13, 17, 33 at classzone.com

## SKILL PRACTICE

**VOCABULARY** Classify the polynomial.

**1.** $x^2 + 3x - 7$      **2.** $y - 5$      **3.** $8s^2t$      **4.** $2a^2 + 9a^3 + a$

**CLASSIFYING** Write the polynomial in standard form and classify it.

*SEE EXAMPLE 1*
on p. 717
for Exs. 5–12

**5.** $7 + 3m$      **6.** $8 - n + 2n^2$      **7.** $5n - 1 - n^2$      **8.** $4b - 4 + 6b^3$

**9.** $2 - 5y + y^2$      **10.** $z^3 + 4z^2 + 7z^7$      **11.** $-13x^3 + 4x^{10}$      **12.** $3 - r^4 + r + 2r^3$

**SIMPLIFYING** Simplify the polynomial and write it in standard form.

*SEE EXAMPLE 2*
on p. 718
for Exs. 13–22

**13.** $2c^2 - c^2 + 5c$          **14.** $4q^3 - 7q^5 + 3q - q^3$

**15.** $g^3 - 10 + 2g^2 - 5g^3$      **16.** $1 + 12m^2 - 5m + 6m - 7$

**17.** $3x^2 + 5(x^2 - 3x + 6)$      **18.** $-6(2y^3 - 4y^2 + 1) + 10y^2$

**19.** $-4(t - 3t^2 + 8 - 4t) + 6t^2 - 5$      **20.** $-3(-s^4 + 2s - 6 - s) - 8s + s^4$

**21. ERROR ANALYSIS** Describe and correct the error
made in simplifying the polynomial.

*Animated Math* at classzone.com

$$-3x^2 - 4(5x + 1)$$
$$\times \begin{aligned} &= -3x^2 - 20x - 4 \\ &= -23x - 4 \end{aligned}$$

**22.**  **TAKS REASONING** Simplify the polynomial $5(x^2 - 2x - 3) - 9x^2$.

    Ⓐ $4x^2 + 10x - 15$          Ⓑ $-4x^2 + 10x - 15$

    Ⓒ $-4x^2 - 15x - 10x$      Ⓓ $-4x^2 - 10x - 15$

**SIMPLIFYING POLYNOMIALS** Simplify the polynomial.

**23.** $5a - 4(3b + 6) + 4b$          **24.** $-z^2 + 3z - 2(4y - 5z)$

**25.** $-3ab^2 + 2ab + 5a^2b^2 - 3ab^2 + 4ab$      **26.** $3xy + 2xy^2 - 5x^2y^2 + 3x^2y - 4xy - 7xy^2$

**27. EXAMPLES AND NONEXAMPLES** Give examples of three polynomials
that are in standard form and three that are *not* in standard form.

**GEOMETRY** Write an expression for the perimeter in standard form.

**28.**
$2x + 3$

**29.**
$x$
$2(x + 1)$

**CHALLENGE** Find the expression that makes the equation true.

**30.** $3xy + 6y - 2x^2 + 4 + \underline{\ ?\ } = 3x^2 - 5y - 7xy - 4x$

**31.** $4y^2 + 2x^2 + 9 + \underline{\ ?\ } = 3y^2 + x^2 + 5xy + 6$

**BASEBALL** **Use the following information.**

A player hits a ball 60 mi/h, or 88 ft/sec, upward. Evaluate $-16t^2 + 88t + 2$ to find the ball's height, in feet, after the given number of seconds.

*SEE EXAMPLE 3*
on p. 718
for Exs. 32–36

**32.** $t = 1.5$      **33.** $t = 2$

**34.** $t = 2.5$      **35.** $t = 3$

**36.** **WRITING**   Find the meaning of the prefix *poly-* in a dictionary. *Explain* what this tells you about the words *polygon* and *polynomial*.

**37.** **TAKS REASONING** The height, in feet, of a falling pebble after $t$ seconds of falling from a height of 45 feet can be found using the polynomial $-16t^2 + 45$. What is the pebble's height after 1.5 seconds?

  **(A)** 9 feet      **(B)** 21 feet      **(C)** 24 feet      **(D)** 36 feet

**REASONING** **Tell whether the statement is *always*, *sometimes*, or *never* true. *Justify* your reasoning.**

**38.** The terms of a trinomial are monomials.

**39.** A monomial has one factor.

**40.** A binomial has more than two terms.

**41.** **TAKS REASONING** The longer leg of a right triangle is four more than twice the shorter leg. The hypotenuse is four less than three times the shorter leg. Write a simplified expression for the perimeter of the right triangle. Find the perimeter when the shorter leg is 10 inches long.

**42.** **REASONING** If a polynomial in one variable is written in standard form with all nonzero coefficients and it has $n$ terms, what is the value of the greatest exponent? *Justify* your answer.

**43.** **CHALLENGE** Determine whether the equation $4g^2 + 3g = 7g^3$ is *always*, *sometimes*, or *never* true. *Explain* your reasoning.

**MIXED REVIEW FOR TAKS**          **TAKS PRACTICE** at classzone.com

*REVIEW*
Lesson 10.4;
TAKS Workbook

**44.** **TAKS PRACTICE** Alonzo shipped a poster to his brother in the cylindrical shipping container shown below. Which is closest to the lateral surface area of the container? *TAKS Obj. 4*

—0.25 ft

3 ft

  **(A)** 0.75 ft²      **(B)** 1.18 ft²      **(C)** 2.36 ft²      **(D)** 2.45 ft²

# 13.2 Adding and Subtracting Polynomials

TEKS *8.7.B, 8.14.D*

**Before** You simplified polynomials.

**Now** You'll add and subtract polynomials.

**Why?** So you can find the area of a surface, such as the floor space in Example 4.

**KEY VOCABULARY**
• **opposite,** *p. 58*
• **like terms,** *p. 89*

## ACTIVITY

You can model polynomial addition with algebra tiles.

$x^2$-tile  $x$-tile  1-tile

**STEP 1** **Write** the two polynomials represented by the two groups of algebra tiles below.

**STEP 2** **Group** *like* algebra tiles to model the sum of the polynomials. Draw your model. Write the polynomial that your drawing represents.

**STEP 3** **Use** algebra tiles to model the sum of the polynomials below. Write the polynomial that your model represents.

a. $(3x^2 + 6x + 1) + (x^2 + x)$    b. $(2x^2 + 3x + 1) + (4x^2 + x)$

In the activity, you used algebra tiles to add two polynomials. You add polynomials by combining like terms.

## EXAMPLE 1  Adding Polynomials Vertically

Find the sum $(-4x^3 + x^2 - 3x - 1) + (4x^2 - 7x + 5)$.

$$
\begin{array}{lr}
\quad -4x^3 + \ x^2 - \ 3x - 1 & \text{Write the second polynomial under the first.} \\
+ \qquad\quad 4x^2 - \ 7x + 5 & \text{Arrange like terms in columns.} \\
\hline
\ -4x^3 + 5x^2 - 10x + 4 & \text{Add like terms.}
\end{array}
$$

In Example 1, you combined like terms vertically. You can also add polynomials by combining like terms horizontally.

**EXAMPLE 2** Adding Polynomials Horizontally

**XY** Find the sum $(2y^2 - 4y + 6) + (y^2 + 3y - 2)$.

**SOLUTION**

*REGROUP TERMS*
When you regroup terms, move a subtraction or addition sign with the term that follows it.

$(2y^2 - 4y + 6) + (y^2 + 3y - 2)$

$= 2y^2 + y^2 - 4y + 3y + 6 - 2$  **Group like terms.**

$= 3y^2 - y + 4$  **Combine like terms.**

*Animated* **Math** at classzone.com

✓ **GUIDED PRACTICE** for Examples 1 and 2

**Find the sum.**

1. $(6x^2 - 3x + 1) + (3x^3 + 4x^2 - 5x)$  2. $(5n^2 + 2n - 9) + (3n^2 - 4)$

3. $(y^2 - y + 1) + (-2y^2 + 2y - 1)$  4. $(3p^2 - p - 1) + (p^2 + p - 4)$

**Subtracting Polynomials** You can subtract a polynomial by adding its *opposite*. To find the opposite of a polynomial, multiply each of its terms by $-1$. You can subtract polynomials vertically or horizontally.

**EXAMPLE 3** Subtracting Polynomials Vertically

**XY** Find the difference $(4x^3 + 5x^2 - 2x - 5) - (3x^3 - 4x + 2)$.

**SOLUTION**

*AVOID ERRORS*
Be sure to write the opposite of every term in the second polynomial, not just the first term.

**STEP 1** Find the opposite of the second polynomial.

$-(3x^3 - 4x + 2) = -3x^3 + 4x - 2$

**STEP 2** Find the sum $(4x^3 + 5x^2 - 2x - 5) + (-3x^3 + 4x - 2)$.

$$4x^3 + 5x^2 - 2x - 5$$  **Write the second polynomial under the first.**

$$+ \; -3x^3 \qquad + 4x - 2$$  **Arrange like terms in columns.**

$$x^3 + 5x^2 + 2x - 7$$  **Add like terms.**

✓ **GUIDED PRACTICE** for Example 3

**Find the difference.**

5. $(4r^2 - r + 8) - (r^2 + 6r - 1)$  6. $(6m^2 + 2m - 3) - (7m^2 + 4)$

**EXAMPLE 4** Finding Area

**Tree House** The design for a tree house calls for a rectangular hole in the floor. Write a polynomial expression for the area of the tree house floor.

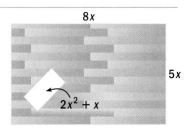

8x

5x

$2x^2 + x$

**SOLUTION**

To find the area of the floor, use the area of the two rectangles.

**Area of Large Rectangle**          **Area of Small Rectangle**

$8x \cdot 5x = 40x^2$                         $2x^2 + x$

$$= 40x^2 - (2x^2 + x)$$

$$= 40x^2 - 2x^2 - x \qquad \text{Add the opposite.}$$

$$= 38x^2 - x \qquad \text{Combine like terms.}$$

*AVOID ERRORS*
Be sure to write the second polynomial in parentheses when subtracting.

▶ **Answer** A polynomial expression for the area of the floor is $38x^2 - x$.

---

✓ **GUIDED PRACTICE** for Example 4

**7. What If?** Suppose the tree house in Example 4 has a length of $10x$ and a width of $6x$, and the area of the rectangular hole is $4x^2 - 2x$. Write a polynomial expression for the area of the tree house floor.

---

## 13.2 EXERCISES

HOMEWORK KEY

▼ = **TAKS Practice and Reasoning**
Exs. 12, 34, 35, 36, 37, 41, and 42

◯ = **HINTS AND HOMEWORK HELP**
for Exs. 3, 7, 13, 17, 33 at classzone.com

### SKILL PRACTICE

**VOCABULARY** **Copy and complete the statement.**

1. To add polynomials, you should combine __?__.

2. To find the __?__ of a polynomial, multiply each of its terms by $-1$.

**ADDING POLYNOMIALS** **Find the sum.**

*SEE EXAMPLES 1 AND 2*
on pp. 721–722
for Exs. 3–10

**3.** $(8y + 5) + (4y - 3)$

**4.** $(x - 6) + (2x + 9)$

**5.** $(4x + 7) + (x - 3)$

**6.** $(-2a - 9) + (a + 4)$

**7.** $(-g^2 + g + 9) + (7g^2 - 6)$

**8.** $(3z^2 - 2z + 1) + (4z^3 + 3z)$

**9.** $(2k^2 + 5k) + (4k^2 - 5k)$

**10.** $(6x^3 - 12x + 1) + (8x^2 - 4)$

SEE EXAMPLES
1 AND 2
..............
on pp. 721–722
for Exs. 11–12

**11. ERROR ANALYSIS** Describe and correct the error(s) in the solution.

$$\begin{array}{r} -4x^3 + 5x^2 - 7x + 2 \\ + \ \ 2x^3 \ \ - 6x \ + 10 \\ \hline -2x^3 - \ \ x^2 + 3x + 2 \end{array}$$

**12.** ✦ **TAKS REASONING** Find the sum of the expressions $(-7x^3 + 4x^2 - 1)$ and $(x^3 - 9x + 3)$.

**Ⓐ** $-6x^3 + 4x^2 - 9x + 2$      **Ⓑ** $-8x^3 + 4x^2 - 9x - 4$

**Ⓒ** $-6x^3 + 5x^2 + 2$      **Ⓓ** $-8x^3 - 5x^2 + 4$

**SUBTRACTING POLYNOMIALS** Find the difference.

SEE EXAMPLE 3
..............
on p. 722
for Exs. 13–20

**⑬** $(7x + 10) - (x - 2)$      **14.** $(4p + 1) - (p - 7)$

**15.** $(-5d - 1) - (5d + 6)$      **16.** $(7y + 1) - (3y - 2)$

**⑰** $(6r^2 + 2r - 5) - (3r^2 - 9)$      **18.** $(-4b^3 - 9b + 2) - (b^3 - b + 3)$

**19.** $(5a^2 + 3a + 8) - (2a^2 - 2a - 9)$      **20.** $(4p^3 + p^2 - 8) - (7p^3 + 2p + 5)$

**SIMPLIFYING EXPRESSIONS** Simplify the expression.

**21.** $(4n - 3) + (9n + 5) - (n - 1)$      **22.** $(-8m + 1) - (2m - 6) + 5m$

**23.** $-2(5y + 3) - 9(y + 1)$      **24.** $4(-3s^2 + s - 4) + (5s^2 + s + 7)$

**25.** $3(q^2 - q) + 2(7q^2 - 2q)$      **26.** $6(t^3 - t^2 + 3t) - 4(5t^3 + t^2 - t)$

**27.** $5(4x^3 - 2x^2 + 1) + 3(7x^2 - 5x)$      **28.** $-7(2v^4 + 3v^2 - 1) - 5(-3v^3 - 6)$

**SOLVING EQUATIONS** Solve the equation.

**29.** $(2x^2 - 3x + 4) - (x^2 - 3x + 13) = 0$      **30.** $(-6x^2 + 7x - 5) - (-6x^2 - 5x + 7) = 0$

**31. CHALLENGE** Let $A$ and $B$ represent polynomial expressions. Find $A$ and $B$ when $A + B = 5z - 4$ and $A - B = 3z + 10$. *Explain* your reasoning.

## PROBLEM SOLVING

**GEOMETRY** Write a polynomial expression for the perimeter of the figure. Simplify the polynomial.

SEE EXAMPLE 4
..............
on p. 723
for Exs. 32–35

**32.**

$-x^2 + 11x + 8$    $x^2 + 3x - 4$    $2x^2 - x + 10$

**㉝**

$2x^2 - 2x + 3$    $-x^2 + 10x + 1$

**34.** ✦ **TAKS REASONING** The perimeter of the rectangle shown is 118 feet. What is the value of $x$?

(3x + 4) ft

(2x + 5) ft

**Ⓐ** 10      **Ⓑ** 21.8

**Ⓒ** 29.5      **Ⓓ** 38

**REVIEW FORMULAS**

Need help with geometry formulas? See p. 142.

**35.** ✈ **TAKS REASONING** *Explain* how to find the area of wallboard needed to cover the wall shown, not including the window. Then find the area as a polynomial in standard form.

**36.** ✈ **TAKS REASONING** Give three examples of two trinomials in standard form whose sum is a binomial.

**37.** ✈ **TAKS REASONING** To make a set of coasters, you cut identical circles out of a piece of clay rolled into a flat square.

   **a.** Write a polynomial expression for the area of clay that remains after you remove the circles as shown below.

   **b.** Simplify the polynomial in part (a), using 3.14 for $\pi$.

   **c.** Is there enough clay left over to make another coaster of the same radius and thickness? *Explain* your answer.

**38.** **GEOMETRY** You are constructing two wooden pyramids with square bases using the designs shown. Write a simplified polynomial expression for the total surface area of the two pyramids.

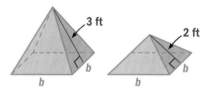

**39.** **WRITING** *Describe* the similarities and differences between adding and subtracting integers and adding and subtracting polynomials.

**40.** **CHALLENGE** Find the values of $x$ and $y$ in the parallelogram. *Explain* the properties of the parallelogram you used to write your equations.

---

## MIXED REVIEW FOR TAKS

**TAKS** **PRACTICE** at classzone.com

**REVIEW**

Lesson 11.3;
TAKS Workbook

**41.** ✈ **TAKS PRACTICE** Which equation could be used to generate the table of values at the right? *TAKS Obj. 2*

| $x$ | −1 | 0 | 2 | 5 |
|---|---|---|---|---|
| $y$ | 9 | 7 | 3 | −3 |

   **Ⓐ** $y = -x + 7$   **Ⓑ** $y = -2x + 6$   **Ⓒ** $y = -2x + 7$   **Ⓓ** $y = 2x + 11$

**REVIEW**

Lesson 12.8;
TAKS Workbook

**42.** ✈ **TAKS PRACTICE** So far this season, a baseball player has 7 hits in 21 at-bats. Based on that performance, what is the probability that the player will NOT have any hits either of the next 2 at-bats? *TAKS Obj. 5*

   **Ⓕ** $\dfrac{1}{9}$     **Ⓖ** $\dfrac{1}{3}$     **Ⓗ** $\dfrac{4}{9}$     **Ⓙ** $\dfrac{2}{3}$

# 13.3 Monomials and Powers

TEKS 8.8.C, 8.16.A

| Before | You added and subtracted polynomials. |
| Now | You will apply properties of exponents to monomials. |
| Why? | So you can compare measures, such as volumes in Ex. 59. |

**KEY VOCABULARY**
- **power,** *p. 19*
- **exponent,** *p. 19*
- **coefficient,** *p. 89*
- **monomial,** *p. 178*

## ACTIVITY

You can use the properties of exponents to simplify monomials.

**STEP 1** **Copy** and complete the table by expanding, regrouping, and simplifying each expression. What patterns do you notice?

| Expression | Expand | Regroup | Simplify |
|---|---|---|---|
| $(3x)(4x^2)$ | $3 \cdot x \cdot 4 \cdot x \cdot x$ | $3 \cdot 4 \cdot x \cdot x \cdot x$ | $12x^3$ |
| $(-2x)(5x^4)$ | ? | ? | ? |
| $(xy)^3$ | $xy \cdot xy \cdot xy$ | $x \cdot x \cdot x \cdot y \cdot y \cdot y$ | $x^3y^3$ |
| $(4x)^2$ | ? | ? | ? |
| $(-3x)^3$ | ? | ? | ? |

**STEP 2** **Use** your results to simplify the expressions $(5x)(2x^3)$ and $(3pq)^2$.

**REVIEW MULTIPLYING POWERS**
Need help with rules of exponents? See p. 202.

In the activity, you expanded powers to multiply monomials. You can also multiply monomials by first multiplying their coefficients and then using the product of powers property to multiply variables.

## EXAMPLE 1 Multiplying Monomials

 Simplify the expression $(2x^3)(-3x)$.

$$(2x^3)(-3x) = 2 \cdot x^3 \cdot (-3) \cdot x \qquad \text{Expand the expression.}$$
$$= 2 \cdot (-3) \cdot x^3 \cdot x \qquad \text{Regroup factors.}$$
$$= -6 \cdot x^3 \cdot x \qquad \text{Multiply coefficients.}$$
$$= -6x^4 \qquad \text{Product of powers property}$$

✓ **GUIDED PRACTICE** for Example 1

Simplify the expression.

**1.** $4a(a^2)$     **2.** $(-2m)(7m^2)$     **3.** $(-x)(8x^2)$     **4.** $(y^5)(5y^3)$

**Distributive Property** You can use the distributive property and the properties of exponents to find the product of a monomial and a binomial.

**EXAMPLE 2** **Using the Distributive Property**

 Simplify the expression $2n(4n^2 - 5)$.

$$2n(4n^2 - 5) = (2n)(4n^2) - (2n)(5) \qquad \text{Distributive property}$$
$$= 8 \cdot n \cdot n^2 - 10 \cdot n \qquad \text{Multiply coefficients.}$$
$$= 8n^3 - 10n \qquad \text{Product of powers property}$$

In the activity on page 726, you found powers of products. You can use the rule below to simplify a power of a product.

**KEY CONCEPT** *For Your Notebook*

**Power of a Product Property**

**Words** To simplify a power of a product, find the power of each factor and multiply.

**Algebra** $(ab)^m = a^m \cdot b^m$ **Numbers** $(5 \cdot 2)^3 = 5^3 \cdot 2^3$

**EXAMPLE 3** **Simplifying a Power of a Product**

**TAKE NOTES**
You will learn many new properties about exponents in this lesson. Be sure to write all the properties and a corresponding example of each in your notebook.

**Container** The radius of a container is twice its height. Write an expression for the volume of the container. Use the formula $V = \pi r^2 h$ in the table of formulas on p. 816.

**SOLUTION**

$$V = \pi(2h)^2 h \qquad \text{Substitute } 2h \text{ for } r.$$
$$= \pi(2^2 \cdot h^2)\, h \qquad \text{Power of a product property}$$
$$= \pi \cdot 4 \cdot h^2 \cdot h \qquad \text{Evaluate each power.}$$
$$= 4\pi h^3 \qquad \text{Product of powers property}$$

▶ **Answer** An expression for the volume of the container is $4\pi h^3$.

✓ **GUIDED PRACTICE** for Examples 2 and 3

Simplify the expression.

**AVOID ERRORS**
Remember that
$(-x)^4 = (-1x)^4 = (-1)^4(x)^4.$

**5.** $p(2p + 3)$ **6.** $-t^2(-2t + 8)$ **7.** $(5yz)^3$ **8.** $(-xy)^2$

**9. What If?** Suppose the radius of the container in Example 3 is three times its height. Write an expression for the volume of the container.

**Power of a Power Property**

**Words**    To simplify a power of a power, multiply exponents.

**Algebra**    $(a^m)^n = a^{mn}$        **Numbers**    $(5^3)^2 = 5^{3 \cdot 2} = 5^6$

---

**EXAMPLE 4**   **Simplifying a Power of a Power**

*ANOTHER WAY*

You can also expand $(2y^2)^3$ by multiplying the monomial by itself 3 times.
$(2y^2)^3 = 2y^2 \cdot 2y^2 \cdot 2y^2$
$= 8y^6$

 **Simplify the expression $(2y^2)^3$.**

$(2y^2)^3 = 2^3 \cdot (y^2)^3$    **Power of a product property**

$= 8 \cdot y^{2 \cdot 3}$    **Power of a power property**

$= 8y^6$    **Simplify.**

---

✓ **GUIDED PRACTICE**    **for Example 4**

**Simplify the expression.**

**10.** $(2^4)^2$        **11.** $(x^6)^2$        **12.** $(5m^3)^2$        **13.** $(a^2b)^2$

---

# 13.3 EXERCISES

HOMEWORK KEY

**= TAKS Practice and Reasoning**
**Exs. 33, 56, 57, 59, 62, and 63**

○ **= HINTS AND HOMEWORK HELP**
**for Exs. 5, 13, 19, 29, 53** at classzone.com

## SKILL PRACTICE

**VOCABULARY  Match the expression with the property used to simplify it.**

**1.** $(2y)^5$            **A.** power of a power property

**2.** $(x^2)^7$            **B.** power of a product property

**3.** $3 \cdot x^4 \cdot x^6$        **C.** product of powers property

**MULTIPLYING MONOMIALS  Simplify the expression by multiplying the monomials.**

*SEE EXAMPLE 1*
on p. 726
for Exs. 4–9

**4.** $(-4x)(5x^3)$        **5.** $(-16t)(-3t^9)$        **6.** $(-x^2)(-3x)$

**7.** $(3s)(-2s^3)$        **8.** $(-b^3)(-b^8)$        **9.** $(-y^2)(y^3)$

**USING THE DISTRIBUTIVE PROPERTY  Simplify the expression by using the distributive property.**

*SEE EXAMPLE 2*
on p. 727
for Exs. 10–15

**10.** $2w(3w + 1)$        **11.** $-t(t^2 - 4)$        **12.** $-8x(x^5 + x)$

**13.** $3k^2(12 - k^5)$        **14.** $4q^3(3q + 6)$        **15.** $-7a^2(5a^3 - 9a)$

**SEE EXAMPLES
3 AND 4**
on pp. 727–728
for Exs. 16–31

**APPLYING POWER PROPERTIES** Simplify the expression by using the power of a product property or by using the power of a power property.

**16.** $(5z)^3$

**17.** $(xyz)^5$

**18.** $(2ab)^4$

**19.** $(-6z)^3$

**20.** $(-dt)^4$

**21.** $(3rs)^2$

**22.** $(-3xy)^3$

**23.** $(10bh)^5$

**24.** $(t^4)^2$

**25.** $(y^2)^2$

**26.** $(c^2)^9$

**27.** $(-x^2)^{10}$

**28.** $(ab^3)^2$

**29.** $(x^2y^2)^3$

**30.** $(3a^2)^2$

**31.** $(2r^3)^3$

**32. ERROR ANALYSIS** Describe and correct the error made in simplifying the expression.

$$\times \quad (3x^3)^2 = 3x^{3 \cdot 2}$$
$$= 3x^6$$

**33. TAKS REASONING** Simplify the expression $(-2b^4)^3$.

**(A)** $-8b^{12}$

**(B)** $-2b^{12}$

**(C)** $-8b^7$

**(D)** $-2b^7$

**SCIENTIFIC NOTATION** Simplify the expression and write it in scientific notation.

**34.** $(3 \times 10^4)^3$

**35.** $(9 \times 10^{10})^3$

**36.** $(5 \times 10^7)^4$

**SIMPLIFYING EXPRESSIONS** Simplify the expression.

**37.** $2(5mn^4)^3$

**38.** $-3a^{10}(a^4b^2c)^4$

**39.** $(-2x^4)^3(x^4yz^8)$

**40.** $3[(r^4s^3)^4 \cdot r^8s]^3$

**41.** $2[(c^2d)^3 \cdot (c^3d^4)^4]^2$

**42.** $\left(\dfrac{2x^2}{x}\right)^3$

**43.** $\left(\dfrac{9h^5}{h^7}\right)^2$

**44.** $\dfrac{(4x^2)^3}{(2x)^4}$

**45.** $\dfrac{(-3mn)^2}{(n^2)^3}$

**CHALLENGE** Copy and complete the statement with a monomial.

**46.** $8a^6 + 64a^3 = \underline{\ ?\ }(a^3 + 8)$

**47.** $12b^2 - 9b^2c^4 = \underline{\ ?\ }(4 - 3c^4)$

**48.** $18x^2y - 9xy^2 = \underline{\ ?\ }(2x - y)$

**49.** $12x^3y^6 + 20x^5y^2 = \underline{\ ?\ }(3y^4 + 5x^2)$

## PROBLEM SOLVING

**SEE EXAMPLES
1, 2, AND 3**
on pp. 726–727
for Exs. 50–51

**50. PHOTO ALBUMS** You are making photo albums in different sizes. The photo area on each page is twice as long as it is wide and needs a 2 inch margin for binding. Write a polynomial expression for the total area of one page.

**51. GEOMETRY** A cube has side length of $5x$. Write an expression in simplest form for the volume of the cube.

**52. GUIDED PROBLEM SOLVING** Simplify the expression $\left(\dfrac{x}{y}\right)^4$.

  **a.** Write the expression in expanded form.

  **b.** Simplify by multiplying numerators and multiplying denominators.

  **c.** Write a rule to simplify a quotient raised to a power.

**53.** **SEAT CUSHION** You need fabric for a window seat cushion. Use the trapezoid pattern shown to write a polynomial expression for the area of the top of the cushion. Simplify the expression.

**54.** **WRITING** *Explain* why $(4y)^2$ is different from $4y^2$.

**55.** **GEOMETRY** The volume of a cone is given by the expression $\frac{1}{3}\pi r^2 h$. Write the expression for the volume of a cone with twice the radius and *compare* it to the original expression.

**56.** ☟ **TAKS REASONING** A circle has radius $r$ and a square has a side length twice the radius of the circle. Write and simplify expressions for the areas of the figures. Then write and simplify a ratio comparing the area of the circle to the area of the square. Leave your answer in terms of $\pi$.

**57.** ☟ **TAKS REASONING** The diameter of a cylindrical canister is four times its height $h$. Which expression represents its surface area?

(**A**) $4\pi h^2$      (**B**) $12\pi h^2$      (**C**) $16\pi h^2$      (**D**) $20\pi h^2$

**58.** **GEOMETRY** Write and simplify a polynomial expression for the volume of the square pyramid.

**59.** ☟ **TAKS REASONING** You can use the formula for the volume of a sphere to approximate the volumes of spherical objects in our solar system. The volume $V$ of a sphere is given by $V = \frac{4}{3}\pi r^3$.

  **a.** **Calculate** The radius of Saturn is about $6.0 \times 10^4$ kilometers. Approximate the volume of Saturn. Write your answer in scientific notation.

  **b.** **Calculate** The radius of Saturn's moon Dione is about 560 kilometers. Approximate the volume of Dione. Write your answer in scientific notation.

  **c.** **Estimate** Write a ratio comparing the volume of Saturn to the volume of Dione. About how many times larger is Saturn than Dione?

**60.** **DECIBELS** A decibel (dB) is a measure of the intensity (or volume) of sound. For each increase in 10 dB, the intensity is 10 times as great. You are trying to have a conversation at a stadium where the noise level is 110 dB. Your conversation is at a volume of 60 dB. How many times greater is the volume of the crowd than the volume of your conversation? *Explain.*

**61.** **CHALLENGE** Use the properties of exponents to show that $\left(\dfrac{a}{b}\right)^m = \dfrac{a^m}{b^m}$ when $b$ is a nonzero real number. (Hint: Use the definition of negative exponents). *Justify* each step.

*REVIEW*
Lesson 5.2;
TAKS Workbook

**62.** ✏ **TAKS PRACTICE** Abe talks on the phone for one quarter of his free hour, reads for one third of the hour, and goes online for one eighth of the hour. About how much free time does he have left? *TAKS Obj. 1*

(**A**) 1 min          (**B**) 7 min          (**C**) 18 min          (**D**) 43 min

*REVIEW*
Lesson 7.6;
TAKS Workbook

**63.** ✏ **TAKS PRACTICE** The sale price for 5 equally-priced CDs is 85% of the pre-sale price. By what percent is the price of one CD reduced? *TAKS Obj. 2*

(**F**) 15%          (**G**) 17%          (**H**) 85%          (**J**) 97%

---

**QUIZ** *for Lessons 13.1–13.3*

**Simplify the polynomial and write it in standard form.** *(p. 717)*

**1.** $5x^2 + 4x - 3x^2 - 11x$

**2.** $-5k^3 - 2(3k^3 + k - 4)$

**Find the sum or difference.** *(p. 721)*

**3.** $(6n^3 - 2n^2) + (n^3 + 7n^2 - 4n)$

**4.** $(4b^2 - 3b + 8) - (2b^2 - 6)$

**5.** $(x^2 + 6x + 1) - (2x^2 - 8x + 4)$

**6.** $(3m^2 + m - 9) + (7m^2 + 2)$

**7. AREA** Write a polynomial expression for the area of the floor surrounding the rug in the diagram. Simplify the polynomial. *(p. 726)*

$x$
$2x$   $x - 3$
$3x$

**Simplify the expression.** *(p. 726)*

**8.** $(3t^4)(4t^2)$          **9.** $(2c^3)^4$          **10.** $(-2y)^4$          **11.** $-5d(3d^2 + 2)$

---

**Brain Game**

## *Polynomial Potions*

You need to make six perfumes using the six ingredients in the laboratory. Each perfume is made by adding two fragrances together. Use the ingredients listed below and the perfume labels to find the secret formulas.

**Fragrance A**
$x^2 - 2x + 2$

**Fragrance B**
$-x^2 - 6x - 2$

**Fragrance C**
$2x^2 - 3x + 1$

**Fragrance D**
$-3x^2 + 2x - 1$

**Fragrance E**
$3x^2 + 5x - 4$

**Fragrance F**
$-2x^2 + x - 3$

$-2x - 2$
$x^2 - 9x - 1$
$-8x$
$5x^2 + 2x - 3$
$7x - 5$
$x^2 + 6x - 7$

---

## Lessons 13.1–13.3

**MULTIPLE CHOICE**

1. **ECONOMICS** A T-shirt company has operating expenses of $3000 per month. Each shirt needs $3 of fabric and is sold for $12. Which expression represents the profit from selling $x$ shirts? (Hint: Profit = Revenue − Cost.) *TEKS 8.15.A*

Ⓐ $3x + 3000 − 12x$

Ⓑ $3x − (3000 + 12x)$

Ⓒ $12x − 3x + 3000$

Ⓓ $12x − (3x + 3000)$

2. **PROFIT** A restaurant sells half and whole hoagies. Each half hoagie costs $1.50 to make and is sold for $3. Each whole hoagie costs $3 to make and is sold for $5. The manager says that if the restaurant sells 200 half hoagies this week, it will need to sell 100 whole hoagies to make a profit of $500. Why is the manager correct? *TEKS 8.16.B*

Ⓕ Because 100 whole hoagies are sold for a total of $500.

Ⓖ Because 200 half hoagies are sold for more than $500.

Ⓗ Because 200 half hoagies create a profit of $200 and 100 whole hoagies create a profit of $300.

Ⓙ Because 200 half hoagies create a profit of $300 and 100 whole hoagies create a profit of $200.

3. **BALLOONS** For a spherical balloon with radius $r$, the volume is given by the formula $V = \frac{4}{3}\pi r^3$. Uma has a spherical balloon of radius $r$. Which expression can she use to represent the volume of the balloon after the radius of the balloon is tripled, if the variable $r$ in the expression represents the original radius of the balloon? *TEKS 8.10.B*

Ⓐ $\frac{4}{3}\pi r^3$      Ⓑ $4\pi r^3$

Ⓒ $36\pi r^3$      Ⓓ $36\pi r^9$

4. **GRAVITY** A walnut falls out of a tree from a height of 75 feet. Its height in feet after $t$ seconds of falling is given by the polynomial $−16t^2 + 75$. About how many seconds pass from the moment the nut begins to fall until it hits the ground? *TEKS 8.5.A*

Ⓕ 2.2 sec      Ⓖ 2.3 sec

Ⓗ 3 sec      Ⓙ 4.7 sec

**ANGLES** In Exercises 5 and 6, use the triangle below.

5. Find the value of $x$. *TEKS 8.2.B*

Ⓐ 20      Ⓑ 38

Ⓒ 63      Ⓓ 74

6. Find the possible values of $y$. *TEKS 8.2.B*

Ⓕ ±3      Ⓖ ±9

Ⓗ ±27      Ⓙ ±81

**GRIDDED ANSWER** ⓞ①❷③④⑤⑥⑦⑧⑨

7. **KITCHEN** The perimeter of a square kitchen floor is 36 feet. The length of each wall is 1 foot more than twice the length $x$, in feet, of the sink. How many feet long is the sink? *TEKS 8.7.B*

**TEKS** *8.15.A, 8.16.B*

# 13.4 Multiplying Binomials

You can model binomial multiplication with algebra tiles.

**EXPLORE** Model the product $(x + 3)(3x + 2)$ with algebra tiles.

**STEP 1** **Model** each binomial with algebra tiles. Arrange the first binomial vertically and the second binomial horizontally, as shown.

**STEP 2** **Notice** that the binomials define a rectangular area with length $(3x + 2)$ units and width $(x + 3)$ units. Fill in the region with the appropriate tiles, as shown.

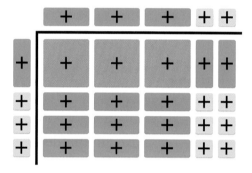

**STEP 3** **Add** the areas of the rectangles on the inside of the model to see that the total area is $3x^2 + 11x + 6$. This is the product of the binomials.

**PRACTICE** Find the product with algebra tiles. Draw your model.

**1.** $(x + 1)(x + 2)$ **2.** $(x + 4)(x + 4)$ **3.** $(x + 2)(2x + 2)$

*Animated Math* at classzone.com

**DRAW CONCLUSIONS**

Model the expression with algebra tiles. Arrange the tiles in a rectangle.
Find the two binomials that have this product.

**4.** $x^2 + 5x + 6$ **5.** $x^2 + 2x + 1$ **6.** $3x^2 + 8x + 4$

**7. REASONING** *Describe* how these models relate to the distributive property.

# 13.4 Multiplying Binomials

TEKS **8.5.A, 8.7.B**

| | |
|---|---|
| **Before** | You multiplied monomials and polynomials. |
| **Now** | You'll multiply binomials. |
| **Why?** | So you can find the area of a surface, such as a stage in Ex. 48. |

**KEY VOCABULARY**
- **polynomial,** *p. 717*
- **binomial,** *p. 717*

In the Investigation on page 733 you used a visual model to multiply binomials. The model below shows that $(x + 2)(3x + 1) = 3x^2 + 7x + 2$.

You can multiply two binomials using a table or a vertical method.

## EXAMPLE 1  Multiplying Binomials with a Table

Find the product $(-3x + 2)(8x + 7)$ and simplify.

Write the first polynomial on the left of the table.

Write the second polynomial above the table.

| | $8x$ | $7$ |
|---|---|---|
| $-3x$ | $-24x^2$ | $-21x$ |
| $2$ | $16x$ | $14$ |

Multiply to fill in the table.

The product is $-24x^2 - 21x + 16x + 14$. Combine like terms.

▶ **Answer** The product is $-24x^2 - 5x + 14$.

## EXAMPLE 2  Multiplying Binomials Vertically

Find the product $(2x - 5)(3x + 4)$ and simplify.

$$
\begin{array}{r}
2x - 5 \\
\times \quad 3x + 4 \\
\hline
8x - 20 \\
6x^2 - 15x \\
\hline
6x^2 - 7x - 20
\end{array}
$$

Write the first binomial.

Write the second binomial.

Multiply $4(2x - 5)$.

Multiply $3x(2x - 5)$. Line up like terms.

Add $8x - 20$ and $6x^2 - 15x$.

**Distributive Property** Another way to multiply binomials is to use the distributive property.

**EXAMPLE 3** Multiplying Polynomials Horizontally

**VOCABULARY**
*Compound interest* is earned on the original amount of money in an account and on the interest already earned.

**Banking** You deposit $1 into a savings account with interest compounded annually. The balance of the account after two years can be found using the expression $(1 + r)^2$, where $r$ represents the annual interest rate. Expand this expression and simplify.

**SOLUTION**

To expand the expression, multiply two binomials.

$$(1 + r)^2 = (1 + r)(1 + r) \qquad \text{$(1 + r)^2$ means $(1 + r)(1 + r)$.}$$
$$= 1(1 + r) + r(1 + r) \qquad \text{Distributive property}$$
$$= 1 + r + r + r^2 \qquad \text{Distributive property}$$
$$= 1 + 2r + r^2 \qquad \text{Combine like terms.}$$
$$= r^2 + 2r + 1 \qquad \text{Write in standard form.}$$

**The FOIL Method** The letters in the word FOIL can help you remember how to multiply binomials. The letters should remind you to multiply the First pair, Outer pair, Inner pair, and Last pair.

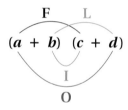

**EXAMPLE 4** Multiplying with the FOIL Method

Find the product $(2x + 3)(3x - 1)$ and simplify.

**ANOTHER WAY**
Another way to find the product in Example 4 is to either use a table or use the distributive property.

| **F** | | **O** | | **I** | | **L** | |
|---|---|---|---|---|---|---|---|
| First | + | Outer | + | Inner | + | Last | |
| $2x \cdot 3x$ | + | $2x \cdot (-1)$ | + | $3 \cdot 3x$ | + | $3 \cdot (-1)$ | **Group terms.** |
| $6x^2$ | + | $(-2x)$ | + | $9x$ | + | $(-3)$ | **Multiply.** |
| | | $6x^2 + 7x - 3$ | | | | | **Combine like terms.** |

✓ **GUIDED PRACTICE** for Examples 1, 2, 3, and 4

**Find the product and simplify.**

**1.** $(x + 1)(x + 3)$      **2.** $(b - 4)(b - 3)$      **3.** $(3t - 4)(t + 2)$

**4.** $(d + 6)(d + 5)$      **5.** $(x - 3)(x - 1)$      **6.** $(5s + 3)(2s - 4)$

# 13.4 EXERCISES

## SKILL PRACTICE

1. **VOCABULARY** Copy and complete: A polynomial with two terms is called a __?__ .

2. **VOCABULARY** *Describe* the FOIL method in your own words.

*SEE EXAMPLES*
*1 AND 2*
on p. 734
for Exs. 3–8

**MAKE A TABLE** Use a table to find the product. Simplify the result. Then multiply vertically to check the result.

3. $(y - 4)(y + 1)$
4. $(g + 3)(g + 7)$
5. $(x - 4)(x + 4)$
6. $(2m + 3)(m - 7)$
7. $(3q - 1)(5q - 1)$
8. $(7b - 3)(9b + 4)$

**MULTIPLYING BINOMIALS** Find the product and simplify.

*SEE EXAMPLES*
*1, 2, 3, AND 4*
on pp. 734–735
for Exs. 9–25

9. $(x + 9)(x - 2)$
10. $(x + 3)(x - 3)$
11. $(a + 10)(a - 4)$
12. $(6r + 7)(r - 1)$
13. $(t - 1)(-3t - 4)$
14. $(-2x - 5)(11x - 12)$
15. $(3x + 1)(3x - 1)$
16. $(3x - 1)(5x - 4)$
17. $(2m + 7)(3m + 1)$
18. $(7b - 3)(-2b + 5)$
19. $(6z + 5)(6z + 5)$
20. $(2g + 9)(2g - 9)$
21. $\left(\frac{1}{2}x + 2\right)(4x - 6)$
22. $(9b - 12)\left(\frac{1}{3}b - 6\right)$
23. $(n^2 - 2)(n^2 + 1)$

24. **ERROR ANALYSIS** Describe and correct the error made in multiplying the binomials.

$$\begin{aligned}(x + 2)(x - 4) &= x \cdot x + x \cdot 4 + 2 \cdot x + 2 \cdot (-4) \\ &= x^2 + 4x + 2x - 8 \\ &= x^2 + 6x - 8\end{aligned}$$

25. **TAKS REASONING** What is the product $(x + 6)(x - 2)$?

Ⓐ $x^2 - 4x - 12$   Ⓑ $x^2 - 4x + 4$   Ⓒ $x^2 + 4x + 12$   Ⓓ $x^2 + 4x - 12$

**MULTIPLYING TRINOMIALS** Find the product and simplify.

26. $(x + 5)(2x^2 + 5x + 7)$
27. $(x - 4)(x^2 + 3x + 9)$
28. $(x + 6)(3x^2 - 4x + 1)$
29. $(2x + 1)(4x^2 - x + 5)$
30. $(3x + 2)(2x^2 + 6x - 4)$
31. $(4x - 3)(-x^2 - 5x - 6)$

**MEASUREMENT** Write the figure's area as a polynomial in standard form.

32.

33.

34.

**CHALLENGE** Copy and complete the statement with the correct binomial.

35. $x^2 + 8x + 7 = (\_\,?\,\_)(x + 7)$
36. $x^2 + 6x + 8 = (x + 2)(\_\,?\,\_)$
37. $x^2 - 9x + 14 = (\_\,?\,\_)(x - 2)$
38. $x^2 - 7x - 18 = (x - 9)(\_\,?\,\_)$

## PROBLEM SOLVING

**SEE EXAMPLE 3**
on p. 735
for Exs. 39, 47

**39. COMPOUND INTEREST** You deposit $50 into a savings account with interest compounded annually. The expression $50(1 + r)^2$, where $r$ is the interest rate, gives the account balance after 2 years. Expand this expression and simplify. Find the account balance when $r = 0.03$.

**40. ✦ TAKS REASONING** Which product gives the area of the photograph and frame?

  Ⓐ $(x + 18)(x + 8)$

  Ⓑ $(2x - 18)(2x - 8)$

  Ⓒ $(2x + 18)(2x + 8)$

  Ⓓ $(x - 18)(x - 8)$

**41. ✦ TAKS REASONING** *Describe* the pattern in the products of binomials like $(x - a)(x + a)$.

**42. REASONING** *Explain* why the expression $(x + 3)^2$ does not equal $x^2 + 9$. Include the correct simplification in your answer.

**43. WRITING** How is finding the product of two binomials like finding the product of a monomial and a polynomial? How is it different?

**44. SWIMMING POOL** A swimming pool is surrounded by a walkway as shown. Write and simplify a polynomial expression for the area of the pool and walkway.

**45. ✦ TAKS REASONING** Write a binomial that contains a variable $x$ raised to the first power and another binomial that contains the variable $x$ raised to a power other than 1. Then find their product.

**46. BASEBALL** The middle of a baseball is a sphere made of cork and two layers of rubber with a radius of 0.6875 inch. Use the surface area formula $S = 4\pi r^2$ to write a polynomial expression in terms of $x$ for the amount of leather needed to cover the ball. Expand the expression and simplify.

0.6875 in.

**47. COMPOUND INTEREST** You deposit $20 into a savings account with interest compounded annually. The expression $20(1 + r)^3$, where $r$ is the interest rate, gives the account balance after 3 years. Expand this expression and simplify. Find the account balance when $r = 0.05$.

**48. STAGE DESIGN** You are building a platform on a 30 foot by 20 foot stage for a school talent show as shown. Write and simplify a polynomial expression for the area of the platform using the design shown. Then find the area when $x$ is 5 feet.

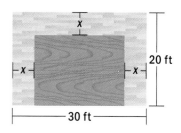

**49. GEOMETRY** The base of a triangle is 6 inches less than twice a number $n$. The height of the triangle is 6 inches more than 6 times the number $n$.

   **a.** Write a simplified polynomial for the area of the triangle in terms of $n$.

   **b.** If $n$ is one fourth of the mean of the base and height, what is the area when the mean is 20 inches? Check the result.

**50. MULTI-STEP PROBLEM** You want to make a box with no lid out of a 17 inch by 11 inch piece of cardboard. You cut out squares of the same size from each corner. Then you fold the sides up and tape them together.

   **a.** Write polynomials for the length, width, and height of the box.

   **b.** Write a polynomial for the volume of the box in standard form.

   **c.** Find the volume of the box for $x$ values of 1 inch, 2 inches, 3 inches, and 4 inches. Which value gives the greatest volume?

   **d.** Could a box be formed using cut out squares with side lengths of 6 inches? *Explain* why or why not.

**51. CHALLENGE** A rectangular house is twice as long as it is wide. It is surrounded by a lawn that extends 15 feet from the house on all sides. There is a 3 foot wide brick path from the street to the door.

   **a.** Find and simplify expressions in terms of the width $x$, in feet, of the house for the total area of the house and yard, and for the area of the lawn.

   **b.** Suppose the house is 60 feet long. Find the total area of the house and yard, and just the area of the lawn.

---

## MIXED REVIEW FOR TAKS

**TAKS PRACTICE** at classzone.com

*REVIEW*
Lesson 5.8;
TAKS Workbook

**52. TAKS PRACTICE** Thirty apartments are being rented in an apartment complex. The average number of cars per apartment is 1.8. If an apartment becomes vacant whose inhabitants had 3 cars, which equation can be used to find $n$, the new average number of cars per apartment? *TAKS Obj. 1*

  **(A)** $n = \dfrac{(30 \times 1.8) - 3}{29}$

  **(B)** $n = \dfrac{30 - 3}{29}$

  **(C)** $n = \dfrac{(30 \times 1.8) - 3}{30}$

  **(D)** $n = \dfrac{1.8(30 - 3)}{30}$

---

**EXTRA PRACTICE** for Lesson 13.4, p. 813

**ONLINE QUIZ** at classzone.com

# 13.5 Nonlinear Functions

TEKS 8.4, 8.5.A

**Before** You wrote function rules and graphed linear functions.

**Now** You'll use function notation and graph nonlinear functions.

**Why?** So you can write a function, as for e-mail sent in Ex. 49.

**KEY VOCABULARY**
- function notation, *p. 739*
- vertical line test, *p. 740*

In Lesson 11.1, you wrote functions as equations in $x$ and $y$. You used $x$ to name the input and $y$ to name the output. Sometimes it is useful to use **function notation** instead. The symbol $f(x)$ is read as "the function of $f$ at $x$" or "$f$ of $x$."

| function in $x$ and $y$ | function notation |
|---|---|
| $y = 3x - 4$ | $f(x) = 3x - 4$ |
| $y = 2x^2 + 2$ | $f(x) = 2x^2 + 2$ |

---

## EXAMPLE 1  Using Function Notation

**Juggling** You are juggling three balls. The height $h$, in feet, of the ball can be found using the equation $h = -16t^2 + 20t + 3$, where $t$ is the number of seconds after you let go of the ball.

**a.** Write a function that models the height of a ball $x$ seconds after you let go of it. Use function notation.

**b.** Evaluate for $x = 0.5$.

**SOLUTION**

**a.** Let $f(x)$ = height in feet and $x$ = time in seconds.

$$f(x) = -16x^2 + 20x + 3$$    Write the height equation shown above in function notation.

**AVOID ERRORS**
$f(x)$ does not mean "$f$ times $x$." It means "the value of the function $f$ at $x$."

**b.**   $f(0.5) = -16(0.5)^2 + 20(0.5) + 3$    Substitute 0.5 for $x$.

$= -16(0.25) + 10 + 3$    Evaluate.

$= 9$    Simplify.

▶ **Answer** The function is $f(x) = -16x^2 + 20x + 3$. The height of the ball 0.5 second after you let go of it is 9 feet.

---

✓ **GUIDED PRACTICE**   for Example 1

**Rewrite using function notation. Evaluate for $x = 3$.**

**1.** $y = x^2$

**2.** $y = 3x^2 + 4$

**3.** $y = -\frac{1}{2}x^2$

**Graphing Functions** The function in Example 1 is nonlinear. A nonlinear function has a graph that is not a straight line. In Lesson 11.4, you graphed linear functions using a table of values. You can also graph nonlinear functions by first making a table of values.

**EXAMPLE 2** TAKS PRACTICE: Multiple Choice

Which is the graph of the function $f(x) = x^2 - 2$?

**ELIMINATE CHOICES**
You know that the graph passes through $(0, -2)$. So you can eliminate choice A.

**SOLUTION**

**STEP 1** **Choose** several $x$-values and make a table of values.

| $x$ | $-2$ | $-1$ | $0$ | $1$ | $2$ |
|---|---|---|---|---|---|
| $f(x)$ | $2$ | $-1$ | $-2$ | $-1$ | $2$ |

**STEP 2** **List** the solutions as ordered pairs.
$(-2, 2), (-1, -1), (0, -2), (1, -1), (2, 2)$

**STEP 3** **Plot** the ordered pairs. Then draw a smooth curve through the points, as shown.

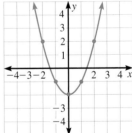

▶ **Answer** The graph that contains the points is graph B. The correct answer is B.
Ⓐ Ⓑ Ⓒ Ⓓ

✓ **GUIDED PRACTICE** for Example 2

**Graph the function using a table of values.**

**4.** $f(x) = -x^2 + 4$     **5.** $f(x) = x^2 + 1$     **6.** $f(x) = 2x^2$

**Vertical Line Test** You can use the **vertical line test** to tell whether a graph represents a function. If any vertical line intersects the graph at more than one point, then the graph does *not* represent a function. Remember, a function has exactly one output value for each input value.

**EXAMPLE 3** Using the Vertical Line Test

 **Tell whether the graph represents a function.**

**AVOID ERRORS**

Consider *all* possible vertical lines by passing a straight edge across the entire graph. If any line intersects two or more points on the graph, the equation is not a function.

a.

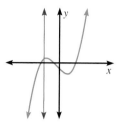

No vertical line intersects the graph at more than one point. So, the graph represents a function.

b.

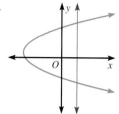

A vertical line intersects the graph at more than one point. So, the graph does *not* represent a function.

✓ **GUIDED PRACTICE** for Example 3

**Tell whether the graph represents a function.**

7.

8.

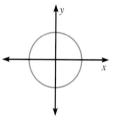

# 13.5 EXERCISES

HOMEWORK KEY

🌟 = **TAKS Practice and Reasoning**
Exs. 10, 11, 42, 47, 49, 51, 57, and 58

◯ = **HINTS AND HOMEWORK HELP**
for Exs. 7, 13, 17, 21, 41 at classzone.com

**SKILL PRACTICE**

1. **VOCABULARY** *Explain* why $f = 2x + 4$ is not in function notation.

2. **VOCABULARY** Copy and complete: You can use the __?__ to determine whether a graph represents a function.

**EVALUATING FUNCTIONS** Rewrite the equation using function notation. Then evaluate the function for $x = -2, 0,$ and 2.

*SEE EXAMPLE 1*
on p. 739
for Exs. 3–9

3. $y = x^2$

4. $y = 4x^2$

5. $y = -3x^2$

6. $y = -x^2 + 10$

7. $y = x^2 - 5$

8. $y = 2x^2 - x$

9. **ERROR ANALYSIS** Describe and correct the error made in evaluating $f(x) = x^2 - 3$ for $x = -5.$

 $f(-5) = -5^2 - 3$
$= -25 - 3$
$= -28$

**SEE EXAMPLE 1**
on p. 739
for Ex. 10

**10.**  **TAKS REASONING** Which equation is written in function notation?

**A** $2(f) + 4 = x$  **B** $f(x) = x^2 + 7$  **C** $y - 7 = x^2$  **D** $y = x^2 + 7$

**SEE EXAMPLE 2**
on p. 740
for Exs. 11–20

**11.**  **TAKS REASONING** Which is the graph of the function $y = \frac{1}{2}x^2$?

**GRAPHING FUNCTIONS** Graph the function using a table of values with $x = -3, -2, -1, 0, 1, 2,$ and $3$.

**12.** $f(x) = 4x^2$  **13.** $f(x) = x^2 + 8$  **14.** $f(x) = -x^2 + 5$

**15.** $f(x) = -2x^2$  **16.** $f(x) = 3x^2 - 4$  **17.** $f(x) = -\frac{1}{2}x^2$

**18.** $f(x) = 5 - 5x^2$  **19.** $f(x) = 4x^2 + x$  **20.** $f(x) = x^2 - 3x$

**VERTICAL LINE TEST** Tell whether the graph represents a function. Tell whether the graph is nonlinear.

**SEE EXAMPLE 3**
on p. 741
for Exs. 21–24

**21.**

**22.**

**23.**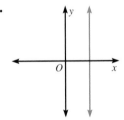

**24. WHICH ONE DOESN'T BELONG?** Which graph doesn't belong? *Explain.*

**A.**

**B.**

**C.**

**D.**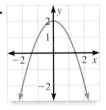

**GRAPHING FUNCTIONS** Graph the function using a table of values.

**25.** $f(x) = (x - 1)^2$  **26.** $f(x) = (x + 2)^2$  **27.** $f(x) = x^3 - 2$

**28.** $f(x) = 2x^3 - 3x$  **29.** $f(x) = -x^4$  **30.** $f(x) = 1 - \frac{1}{5}x^5$

**SOLVING FOR X** Find the value(s) of $x$ for which $f(x) = 4$.

**31.** $f(x) = x^2$

**32.** $f(x) = 5x^2 - 6$

**33.** $f(x) = 8 - 4x^2$

**34.** $f(x) = (x + 7)^2$

**35.** $f(x) = (1 - x)^2$

**36.** $f(x) = x^3 + 4$

**WORK BACKWARD** Write an equation in function notation for the given values.

**37.**

| x | −4 | −2 | 0 | 2 | 4 |
|------|------|------|------|------|------|
| f(x) | −64 | −8 | 0 | 8 | 64 |

**38.**

| x | −5 | −2 | 0 | 3 | 6 |
|------|------|------|------|------|------|
| f(x) | 5 | 2 | 0 | 3 | 6 |

**39. ROTATION** Let $c$ be a real number. Is the graph of $y = c$ a function? Is the graph a function after it is rotated 90° in either direction? *Explain.*

**40. CHALLENGE** Write an equation in function notation for the values in the table.

| x | −2 | −1 | 0 | 1 | 2 |
|------|------|------|------|------|------|
| f(x) | −2 | −5 | −6 | −5 | −2 |

## PROBLEM SOLVING

**SEE EXAMPLE 1**
on p. 739
for Exs. 41−43

**41. REFLECTING POOL** A rectangular reflecting pool is 50 feet long and 30 feet wide. The depth $d$, in feet, of the water is constant across the pool. Write a function that you can use to find the volume of water in the pool. Is the function *linear* or *nonlinear*?

**42. TAKS REASONING** You drop a coin into a well. It hits water after 3 seconds. The elevation $d$, in feet, of the coin after it falls for $t$ seconds in the air is given by $d = -16t^2 + 4$. Write the equation in function notation. How far does the coin fall before hitting the water? *Explain* your reasoning.

**43. ACCOUNT BALANCES** You deposit $20 into a savings account that earns 2.4% interest compounded monthly. The expression $20(1.002)^t$ gives the account balance after $t$ months. Write a function for the account balance, and find the balance after 1, 2, and 3 months.

**SEE EXAMPLE 2**
on p. 740
for Exs. 44, 45

**44. DRAW A GRAPH** Write a function for the area of the triangle shown at the right. Graph the function using a table of values. Estimate, to the nearest whole number, the value of $x$ when the area of the triangle is 30 square inches.

**45. GEOMETRY** Write in function notation an equation for the area of a circle with diameter $x$. Find the area when the diameter is 8 inches. Graph the equation.

**SEE EXAMPLE 3**
on p. 741
for Ex. 46

**46. WRITING** *Describe* how to use the vertical line test and explain why it is used to determine whether a graph is a function.

**47. TAKS REASONING** Write an equation for a nonlinear function. Graph the equation. Rotate the graph 90° clockwise and tell whether the rotated graph is a function.

**48. GRAPH AND COMPARE** Graph the function $f(x) = x^3$ using a table of values. Be sure to include negative and positive $x$-values in your table. *Describe* how this graph is different from the graph of the function $f(x) = x^2$.

**49. TAKS REASONING** You e-mail two copies of a joke on January 1. Each recipient e-mails two copies of the joke the day after receiving it. Which function gives the number of e-mails sent on day $d$, where $d = 1$ represents January 1, $d = 2$ represents January 2, and so on?

    **A** $f(d) = 2d$     **B** $f(d) = 2^d$     **C** $f(d) = d^2$     **D** $f(d) = d + 2$

**50. MULTIPLE REPRESENTATIONS** In 2004, the United States population was about 292.8 million people and growing at 0.9% each year. You can predict the future population $y$ with the equation $y = (292,800,000)(1.009)^t$, where $t$ is the number of years since 2004.

   a. **Write a Function** Write the equation as a function.

   b. **Make a Table** Use the function in part (a) to create a table of values.

   c. **Draw a Graph** Draw a graph from the table in part (b). Predict the population of the United States in 2010.

**51. TAKS REASONING** Graph the four functions below using tables of values and describe their differences. *Explain* the effect of a negative coefficient on a graph.

$$f(x) = x^2 \qquad f(x) = -x^2 \qquad f(x) = \frac{1}{2}x \qquad f(x) = -\frac{1}{2}x$$

**READING *IN* MATH** **Read the information below for Exercises 52–54.**

**Physics in Baseball** The distance that a baseball flies in a home run is often estimated using physics, because using a measuring tape is often not reasonable. The major things that impact the distance that a hit baseball travels are the speed, the angle, and the height of the ball immediately after it leaves the bat. Because of other forces on the ball, the best angle to hit a home run has been proven to be about 35 degrees.

**52. Time** If a baseball were hit at a 35° angle and a speed of 110 feet per second from a height of 2.5 feet above the ground, it would travel about 90 feet per second horizontally. Write an equation in function notation for the horizontal distance traveled by the ball in $x$ seconds.

**53. Distance** Under the conditions described in Exercise 52, the height of the ball is approximated by the function $f(x) = -16x^2 + 63x + 2.5$. When the ball is at a distance of 315 feet from the plate, is it high enough to go over the left field wall, shown above, and be a home run? *Explain.*

**54. Number Sense** *Describe* the domain of the function $f(t)$. Would this player have hit a home run if the ball had been hit to left-center field? *Explain.*

**55. CHALLENGE** Write a function for the area of the rectangle shown. Find the length and width of the rectangle when the area is *maximized*. *Explain* how you found your answers.

$10 - x$

**56. CHALLENGE** Using tables of values, graph $f(x) = (x - 7)(x + 4)$, $g(x) = (x - 5)(x + 1)$, and $h(x) = (x - 2)(x + 3)$. Use your three graphs to predict the *x*-intercepts of the function $k(x) = (x - a)(x + b)$.

 **MIXED REVIEW FOR TAKS**  **TAKS** PRACTICE at classzone.com

REVIEW
Lesson 8.8;
TAKS Workbook

**57.** ☆ **TAKS PRACTICE** $\triangle DEF$ is similar to $\triangle GHI$. Which information would be enough on its own to allow you to find the length of $\overline{DF}$? *TAKS Obj. 6*

**A** The proportion of the side lengths of $\triangle DEF$ to $\triangle GHI$.

**B** The proportion of the side lengths of $\triangle DEF$ to $\triangle GHI$ and the length of side $\overline{GH}$.

**C** The lengths of sides $\overline{IG}$ and sides $\overline{GH}$.

**D** The lengths of sides $\overline{IG}$ and sides $\overline{HI}$.

REVIEW
Lesson 7.5;
TAKS Workbook

**58.** ☆ **TAKS PRACTICE** Hugh drove 110 miles from his house to Austin, Texas, in 2 hours 20 minutes. His average speed on the way back, taking the same route, was 20% slower. How long was the drive back? *TAKS Obj. 2*

**F** 1 h 52 min  **G** 2 h 55 min  **H** 3 h 22 min  **J** 11 h 40 min

**QUIZ for Lessons 13.4–13.5**

**Find the product and simplify.** *(p. 734)*

**1.** $(x - 1)(x + 9)$  **2.** $(a + 4)(a + 9)$  **3.** $(m - 2)(m - 8)$

**4.** $(4y + 5)(y - 2)$  **5.** $(b + 3)(4b - 3)$  **6.** $(3z - 2)(2z - 7)$

**Rewrite using function notation.** *(p. 739)*

**7.** $y = 3x + 9$  **8.** $y = -2x^2 - 4$  **9.** $y = 19 - x + x^2$

**Evaluate the function for $x = -2, -1, 0, 1,$ and 2.** *(p. 739)*

**10.** $f(x) = 2 - x^2$  **11.** $f(x) = \frac{1}{2}x^2 - 6$  **12.** $f(x) = x^2 + x$

**Graph the function using a table of values.** *(p. 739)*

**13.** $f(x) = -x^2 + 1$  **14.** $f(x) = \frac{1}{4}x^2$  **15.** $f(x) = -3x^2 - 4$

EXTRA PRACTICE for Lesson 13.5, p. 813     ONLINE QUIZ at classzone.com     **745**

**GOAL**
Use a graphing calculator to graph nonlinear functions.

TEKS 8.4

# 13.5 Graphing Nonlinear Functions

**EXAMPLE** Use a graphing calculator to compare the functions.

$$y_1 = x^2 \qquad y_2 = 2x^2 \qquad y_3 = 3x^2 \qquad y_4 = 4x^2$$

**SOLUTION**

Use the following keystrokes to enter the functions into a graphing calculator.

**Keystrokes**　　　　　　　　　　　　　　　**Display**

Y=

$Y_1$　　Y= X x² ENTER

$Y_2$　　Y= 2 X x² ENTER

$Y_3$　　Y= 3 X x² ENTER

$Y_4$　　Y= 4 X x²

GRAPH

▶ **Answer** The graphs are curves, called *parabolas*, that pass through (0, 0). As the coefficient of $x^2$ increases, the curve gets narrower.

**PRACTICE** Graph the functions using a graphing calculator. *Describe the pattern in the graphs.*

**1.** $y = x^2 + 5$ 　　**2.** $y = x^2 - 5$ 　　**3.** $y = x^2 + 7$ 　　**4.** $y = x^2 - 7$

**GRAPH THE FUNCTIONS** *Compare* each graph to the graphs in the Example above.

**5.** $y = -x^2$ 　　**6.** $y = -2x^2$ 　　**7.** $y = -3x^2$ 　　**8.** $y = -4x^2$

**9.** $y = 3 - x^2$ 　　**10.** $y = 3 + x^2$ 　　**11.** $y = 8 - x^2$ 　　**12.** $y = 8 + x^2$

## Lessons 13.4 and 13.5

**MULTIPLE CHOICE**

1. **CUBIC TUNNEL** A smaller cube is removed from a larger cube, as shown. Which polynomial expression represents the volume of the solid? *TEKS 8.4.A*

$x + 1$
$x$ $x$
$x$
$x + 1$
$x + 1$
$x + 1$

   **A** $x^3$

   **B** $x^3 + 3x^2 + 3x + 1$

   **C** $3x^2 + 3x + 1$

   **D** $x^3 + 2x^2 + 3x + 1$

2. **THROWN OBJECT** The height, in feet, of a thrown object is given by the function $f(x) = -16x^2 + vx + c$, where $x$ is time in seconds, $v$ is the initial upward speed in feet per second, and $c$ is the initial height in feet. A ball is thrown from a height of 5 feet at an initial upward speed of 48 feet per second. Which best describes the ball's motion one second after it is thrown? *TEKS 8.14.A*

   **F** The ball is falling.

   **G** The ball is rising.

   **H** The ball stops rising and is about to fall.

   **J** The ball has hit the ground.

3. **FALLING FRUIT** A bird drops an apricot while flying. The height of the apricot in feet can be modeled by $f(x) = -16x^2 + 90$, where $x$ is the number of seconds after the apricot is dropped. From what height was the apricot dropped? *TEKS 8.14.B*

   **A** 2.4 feet      **B** 16 feet

   **C** 64 feet       **D** 90 feet

4. **PROFIT MARGIN** A company manager predicts that $P_1(t) = (5t - 3)^2 - 50$ models the company's profit, in thousands of dollars, for the next 5 years, assuming $t$ is the number of years from today. The accountant predicts the model is $P_2(t) = 16t^2 - 12t - 41$. Which statement explains the meaning of $P_1(4) - P_2(4) = 72$? *TEKS 8.15.A*

   **F** The manager's prediction for the profit after 4 years is $72 more than the accountant's prediction.

   **G** The manager's prediction for the profit after 4 years is $72,000 more than the accountant's prediction.

   **H** The accountant's prediction for the profit after 4 years is $72,000.

   **J** The accountant's prediction for the profit after 4 years is $72 more than the manager's prediction.

5. **SKID LENGTH** A vehicle is decelerating at a certain rate. The equation $f(x) = \sqrt{18x}$ describes the speed of the vehicle in miles per hour when it starts its skid as a function of $x$, the skid length in feet. The skid length that the vehicle made was 7 feet. What was the approximate speed of the vehicle when it began its skid? *TEKS 8.1.C*

   **A** 6 miles per hour      **B** 7 miles per hour

   **C** 11 miles per hour     **D** 14 miles per hour

**GRIDDED ANSWER** ⊙①●③④⑤⑥⑦⑧⑨

6. **DEPRECIATION** The value, in dollars, of a $2400 computer $t$ years after it is bought is $2400(0.5)^t$. If the computer was purchased in 2005, what is the first year that the value will be less than 5% of its original value? *TEKS 8.5.A*

## REVIEW KEY VOCABULARY

- polynomial, *p. 717*
- binomial, *p. 717*
- trinomial, *p. 717*
- standard form, *p. 717*
- function notation, *p. 739*
- vertical line test, *p. 740*

### VOCABULARY EXERCISES

**Copy and complete the statement.**

1. The sum of two or more monomials is called a __?__.

2. The polynomial $x^3 - 2x + 1$ is a __?__.

3. A polynomial in one variable is written in __?__ if the exponents of the variable decrease from left to right.

4. You can use the __?__ to tell whether a graph represents a function.

**Classify the polynomial as a *monomial*, a *binomial*, or a *trinomial*.**

5. $5x^3 + 2x + 3$
6. $5a^3$
7. $5y + 3$
8. $-r + 3$

## REVIEW EXAMPLES AND EXERCISES

### 13.1  Polynomials
*pp. 717–720*

**EXAMPLE**

**Simplify the polynomial $4x^2 - 5(x^2 - x + 3 - 2x)$.**

$4x^2 - 5(x^2 - x + 3 - 2x)$

$= 4x^2 - 5x^2 + 5x - 15 + 10x$      **Distributive property**

$= -x^2 + 15x - 15$      **Combine like terms.**

**EXERCISES**

**Simplify the polynomial and write it in standard form.**

*SEE EXAMPLES 1, 2, AND 3 on pp. 717–718 for Exs. 9–15*

9. $8k + 1 + 3k + k^2 - 4$
10. $5w - 2w + 2w^2 - 8$
11. $6p^2 + 9(2p^3 + 3 + p^2)$
12. $3x^2 + 4(7 - x^2 + 4x)$
13. $-8(2s - 3s^2 + 7) + 4s^3$
14. $4(5y - 2y^2 + 11) - 2y^2$

15. **Height** The height, in feet, of a falling acorn after $t$ seconds of falling from a height of 70 feet can be found using the polynomial $-16t^2 + 70$. What is the acorn's height after 2 seconds of falling?

## 13.2 Adding and Subtracting Polynomials

pp. 721–725

### EXAMPLE

**Find the sum $(3x^2 - 2x + 7) + (5x - 9)$.**

$$
\begin{array}{ll}
\quad 3x^2 - 2x + 7 & \text{Write the second polynomial under the first.} \\
+ \quad\quad\ 5x - 9 & \text{Arrange like terms in columns.} \\
\hline
\quad 3x^2 + 3x - 2 & \text{Combine like terms.}
\end{array}
$$

### EXERCISES

**Find the sum or difference.**

SEE EXAMPLES
1, 2, 3, AND 4
on pp. 721–723
for Exs. 16–20

**16.** $(10q^2 - 6) - (q^2 + 1)$

**17.** $(7y^2 + y - 4) + (y^2 - y - 1)$

**18.** $4(m^2 - 3m) + 5(2m^2 - m)$

**19.** $-2(v^3 - v^2 + v) - 3(v^3 + 4v^2)$

**20. Perimeter** Write a polynomial expression for the perimeter of the quadrilateral. Simplify the polynomial.

## 13.3 Monomials and Powers

pp. 726–731

### EXAMPLE

**Simplify the expression $(x^3)(3x)^2$.**

$$
\begin{aligned}
(x^3)(3x)^2 &= x^3(3^2 \cdot x^2) && \text{Power of a product property} \\
&= x^3 \cdot 9 \cdot x^2 && \text{Evaluate the power.} \\
&= 9x^5 && \text{Product of powers property}
\end{aligned}
$$

### EXERCISES

**Simplify the expression.**

SEE EXAMPLES
1, 2, 3, AND 4
on pp. 726–728
for Exs. 21–27

**21.** $(-6a^2b^4)^3$

**22.** $x^2(5x - 7)$

**23.** $-3a(a^2 - 2a)$

**Write a polynomial expression for the area of the figure and simplify.**

**24.**

**25.** $3x + 9$ \ $6x$

**26.** $x - 5$ \ $4x$

**27. Volume** Write the expression for the volume of a sphere with a radius of $3x$.

## 13.4 Multiplying Binomials

pp. 734–738

### EXAMPLE

**Find the product** $(x + 3)(x + 2)$ **and simplify.**

$$(x + 3)(x + 2) = x(x + 2) + 3(x + 2) \quad \text{Distributive property}$$
$$= x^2 + 2x + 3x + 6 \quad \text{Distributive property}$$
$$= x^2 + 5x + 6 \quad \text{Combine like terms.}$$

### EXERCISES

*SEE EXAMPLES 1, 2, 3, AND 4 on pp. 734–735 for Exs. 28–30*

**Find the product and simplify.**

**28.** $(t + 3)(t - 4)$　　　**29.** $(q - 7)(q - 9)$　　　**30.** $(2k - 9)(-4k - 1)$

## 13.5 Nonlinear Functions

pp. 739–745

### EXAMPLE

**Graph** $f(x) = -2x^2 + 5.$

**STEP 1**　**Choose** several $x$-values and make a table of values.

| x | −2 | −1 | 0 | 1 | 2 |
|---|---|---|---|---|---|
| f(x) | −3 | 3 | 5 | 3 | −3 |

**STEP 2**　**List** the solutions as ordered pairs.
$(-2, -3), (-1, 3), (0, 5), (1, 3), (2, -3)$

**STEP 3**　**Graph** the ordered pairs. Draw a smooth curve through the points, as shown.

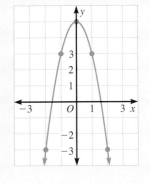

### EXERCISES

*SEE EXAMPLES 2 AND 3 on pp. 740–741 for Exs. 31–37*

**Graph the function using a table of values.**

**31.** $f(x) = x^2 + 3$　　**32.** $f(x) = 7 - x^2$　　**33.** $f(x) = x^2 - 4$　　**34.** $f(x) = 3x^2 + 1$

**Tell whether the graph represents a function.**

**35.**　　　**36.**　　**37.**　

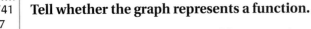

**Simplify the polynomial and write it in standard form.**

**1.** $10x - 7x + 4 + x^2 - 3x + 4$

**2.** $-y + 6(y^2 - y^3 + 1)$

**Find the sum or difference.**

**3.** $(3r^2 + 4r - 7) + (-r^2 - r + 11)$

**4.** $(4s^2 - 11s) - (s^2 - 6s + 21)$

**5.** $(4a^5 - a) + (-3a^5 + 1)$

**6.** $(-y^2 + 12) + (8y^2 - 10)$

**7.** $(5x^6 - 3x^2 + x) - (4x^2 + 2x)$

**8.** $(-7z^3 + z^2 - 5) - (z^3 - 3z^2 + 1)$

**Simplify the expression.**

**9.** $(3a^2)(5a^2b)$

**10.** $(9z)^2$

**11.** $(3d^2)^4$

**12.** $(-2w^4)^3$

**13.** $(-2p^2)^4$

**14.** $(x^4y)^8$

**15.** $(4n^2)(-3n)$

**16.** $(3r)^3(3r)$

**Find the product and simplify.**

**17.** $m(3m + 8)$

**18.** $7n(n^2 - 2)$

**19.** $3p(2p^2 + 3p)$

**20.** $(2x + 7)(3x + 2)$

**21.** $(4y + 12)(y - 3)$

**22.** $(z - 9)(5z + 8)$

**23.** $(4k + 5)(2k + 8)$

**24.** $(7b + 9)(b - 4)$

**25.** $(t - 6)(3t + 12)$

**Graph the function using a table of values.**

**26.** $f(x) = -5x^2$

**27.** $f(x) = x^2 + 3$

**28.** $f(x) = x^2 - 1$

**Tell whether the graph represents a function.**

**29.**

**30.**

**31.**
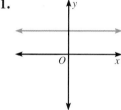

**32. APPLE PICKING** An apple falls from a 28 foot tall tree. The height, in feet, of the apple after $t$ seconds of falling can be found using the polynomial $-16t^2 + 28$. Find the apple's height after 0.5 second.

**33. PERIMETER** Write a polynomial expression for the perimeter of the triangle. Simplify the polynomial.

**34. SPEED SKIING** A speed skier is accelerating at a rate of $a$ ft/sec$^2$ for a period of $t$ seconds. The function $f(t) = \frac{1}{2}at^2$ models the distance, in feet, traveled by the skier. Graph the function that models an acceleration of 15 ft/sec$^2$.

TAKS Obj. 6
TEKS 8.14.B,
8.15.A

## REVIEWING POLYNOMIAL AND FUNCTION PROBLEMS

In the following example, you must understand what information is needed to solve a real-world problem involving polynomials.

---

**EXAMPLE**

**Porch** The length of Maya's porch is twice as long as its width. The area of the porch floor is 72 square feet. This year, she'll extend the width of the porch by 4 feet, and she plans to paint the entire surface of the porch floor. What additional information is needed to find the number of cans of paint she must use?

**(A)** The area of the new porch floor

**(B)** The area covered by a can of paint

**(C)** The volume of a paint can

**(D)** The width of the old porch

---

### Solution

**Make a Plan** The problem involves area. If you had enough information and wanted to find the number of cans of paint that Maya must use to paint the porch floor, you would normally find the area of the new porch floor. Then you would divide it by the area covered by one can of paint.

**Solve the Problem** The two main pieces of information needed to solve the problem are the area of the new porch floor and the area covered by one can of paint.

Enough information is already given to find the area of the new porch floor. Use the information given about the area of the old porch to solve for $w$, the original width.

| | |
|---|---|
| $72 = (2w)(w)$ | **Substitute values in area formula.** |
| $72 = 2w^2$ | **Evaluate.** |
| $w = 6$ | **Solve for w.** |

The width of the old porch is 6 feet. The area of the new porch floor is the product of its length and width, $(w + 4)(2w) = 2w^2 + 8w$. Substitute 6 for $w$ to find that the area is 120 square feet.

▶ **Answer** You need to know the area covered by one can of paint. No information given allows you to find this information. The correct answer is B.  Ⓐ Ⓑ Ⓒ Ⓓ

# POLYNOMIAL AND FUNCTION PROBLEMS ON TAKS

Below are examples of polynomial and function problems in multiple choice format. Try solving the problems before looking at the solutions. (Cover the solutions with a piece of paper.) Then check your solutions against the ones given.

**1.** Kat used algebra tiles to model the product $(x + 2)(x + 4)$. Which expression best represents the product in simplest terms?

**A** $x^2 + 6x + 8$

**B** $x^2 + 4x + 8$

**C** $x^2 + 2x + 8$

**D** $x^2 + 8x + 8$

### Solution

The model suggests that the product $(x + 2)(x + 4)$ is equivalent to the expression $x^2 + 4x + 2x + 8$, or simply $x^2 + 6x + 8$.

You can check the model by algebraically finding the product of the two factors.

$$(x + 2)(x + 4) = x \cdot x + x \cdot 4 + 2 \cdot x + 2 \cdot 4$$
$$= x^2 + 4x + 2x + 8$$
$$= x^2 + 6x + 8$$

So, the correct answer is A.

Ⓐ   Ⓑ   Ⓒ   Ⓓ

**2.** The side length of a square plot of land is represented by the expression $4rs^3$. Which expression gives the area of the land?

**F** $4rs^6$

**G** $4r^2s^6$

**H** $16rs^3$

**J** $16r^2s^6$

### Solution

Substitute the side length into the formula for the area of a square and simplify.

$$A = s^2 = (4rs^3)^2 = 4^2r^2s^{3 \cdot 2} = 16r^2s^6$$

So, the correct answer is J.

Ⓕ   Ⓖ   Ⓗ   Ⓙ

**3.** A diagram of a boat dock is shown below. Which expression best represents the perimeter of the dock in simplest terms?

**A** $5x - 8$

**B** $6x + 7$

**C** $10x - 16$

**D** $6x^2 - 17x + 7$

### Solution

Substitute the dimensions into the formula for the perimeter of a rectangle and simplify.

$$P = 2l + 2w$$
$$= 2(3x - 7) + 2(2x - 1)$$
$$= (6x - 14) + (4x - 2)$$
$$= (6x + 4x) + (-14 - 2)$$
$$= 10x - 16$$

So, the correct answer is C.

Ⓐ   Ⓑ   Ⓒ   Ⓓ

## PRACTICE FOR TAKS OBJECTIVE 6

**1.** The view from above a new square wrestling ring is shown. What piece of information is NOT enough to find the distance, $x$, between opposite corners?

**A** Sum of interior angles of the ring

**B** Perimeter of the ring

**C** Area of the ring

**D** Side length of the ring

**2.** The dimensions of a cube are given in the diagram below.

Which expression represents the volume of the cube?

**F** $6x^2 - 48x + 96$

**G** $x^3 - 64$

**H** $x^3 - 12x^2 - 48x - 64$

**J** $x^3 - 12x^2 + 48x - 64$

$x - 4$

**3.** Henry has a bag of 10 marbles. Some are blue, some green, some pink, and some red. He plans to draw one marble from the bag. Without replacing the first marble, he will draw a second marble. What information is NOT enough to find the probability that he draws a red marble from the bag both times?

**A** Number of red marbles in the bag

**B** Proportion of red marbles to blue and green marbles

**C** Probability of drawing a red marble the first time he draws a marble

**D** Proportion of blue, green, and pink marbles to total marbles

**4.** Mr. Fitzgerald is laying rectangular linoleum tiles on his rectangular kitchen floor. The tiles will be laid flush, with no space between them. He knows the length and width of the floor and the length and width of the linoleum tiles. If an exact number of tiles will cover the entire floor, what must also be true?

**F** The length of the tiles is a factor of the length of the floor and the width of the tiles is a factor of the width of the floor.

**G** The area of the tiles is a factor of the area of the floor.

**H** The rectangular tiles are similar to the rectangular floor.

**J** Both the tiles and the floor must be not only rectangular but square.

## MIXED TAKS PRACTICE

**5.** The picture below shows a metal storage box.

Which drawing best represents a top view of the object? *TAKS Obj. 3*

**A**

**B**

**C**

**D**

## MIXED TAKS PRACTICE

6. Jacob has $500 in his bank account. He plans on adding 20% of each pay check to the account. He earns $150 each week. Which inequality can be used to find the number of weeks, *x*, it will take the balance to surpass $800? *TAKS Obj. 2*

   **F**  $500 + 0.20x > 800$

   **G**  $500 + 0.20(150)x > 800$

   **H**  $150(500 + 0.2x) > 800$

   **J**  $0.2(500 + 150x) > 800$

7. The probability of a memory stick being defective is $\frac{1}{40}$. About how many of 4250 memory sticks should be defective? *TAKS Obj. 5*

   **A**  40

   **B**  95

   **C**  106

   **D**  170,000

8. Alejandro surveyed all the boys in his class about their favorite sport. The results are shown below. Alejandro concluded that football was the favorite sport among students in his class. Which is the best explanation for why his conclusion might not be valid? *TAKS Obj. 5*

   | Favorite sport | Football | Soccer | Rugby | Other |
   |---|---|---|---|---|
   | Students | 6 | 4 | 1 | 5 |

   **F**  Alejandro may have phrased the question in the survey incorrectly.

   **G**  The survey was not representative of all students in his class.

   **H**  The survey should have been done with girls only.

   **J**  The survey should not have included rugby.

9. Which table of ordered pairs contains only points on the curve $y = x^2 - 9$? *TAKS Obj. 2*

   **A**
   | x | 0 | 0 | 1 | 2 |
   |---|---|---|---|---|
   | y | 3 | −3 | −8 | −5 |

   **B**
   | x | −1 | 0 | 1 | 2 |
   |---|---|---|---|---|
   | y | −8 | −9 | −8 | −5 |

   **C**
   | x | 0 | 1 | 2 | 3 |
   |---|---|---|---|---|
   | y | −9 | −8 | −7 | −6 |

   **D**
   | x | −8 | −5 | 0 | 7 |
   |---|---|---|---|---|
   | y | 1 | 2 | 3 | 4 |

10. Kelly bought a cake pan for $7.35 and 4 equally priced cake mixes. She paid a total of $11.55. To find the cost of each cake mix, you find the difference of 11.55 and 7.35, then— *TAKS Obj. 6*

    **F**  find the sum of the result and 7.35.

    **G**  find the difference of the result and 11.55.

    **H**  find the product of the result and 4.

    **J**  find the quotient of the result and 4.

11. **GRIDDED ANSWER** What is the area in square centimeters of the triangle, when $x = 5$? *TAKS Obj. 2*

    *Record your answer and fill in the bubbles on your answer document. Be sure to use the correct place value.*

**Order the numbers from least to greatest.**

**1.** $-45, 45, 43, -43, -43.5$ *(p. 57)*

**2.** $-25, -(-25), |35|, -|20|, |-16|$ *(p. 57)*

**3.** $2\frac{3}{10}, 2.32, \frac{11}{5}, 2.25, \frac{5}{2}$ *(p. 255)*

**4.** $0.45, \frac{3}{8}, 0.4, \frac{5}{12}, 0.46$ *(p. 255)*

**5.** $0.\overline{18}, 0.\overline{181}, 0.1\overline{88}, 0.188$ *(p. 475)*

**6.** $2.\overline{7}, 2.7\overline{2}, 2.\overline{727}, 2.72$ *(p. 475)*

**Give the coordinates of the point.** *(p. 94)*

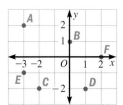

**7.** $A$

**8.** $B$

**9.** $C$

**10.** $D$

**11.** $E$

**12.** $F$

**Evaluate the expression $\sqrt{x^2 - y^2}$ for the given values.** *(p. 469)*

**13.** $x = 5, y = 3$

**14.** $x = 10, y = 8$

**15.** $x = 15, y = 12$

**Find the perimeter of the triangle.** *(p. 487)*

**16.**
9 in.
40 in.

**17.**
24 ft
32 ft

**18.**
60 cm
61 cm

**Graph the equation or inequality.**

**19.** $y = 4 + \frac{2}{3}x$ *(p. 622)*

**20.** $x + y = 6$ *(p. 622)*

**21.** $2y + 6x = 10$ *(p. 622)*

**22.** $y < x - 4$ *(p. 622)*

**23.** $y \geq 2x - 3$ *(p. 629)*

**24.** $x + y > 6$ *(p. 629)*

**Make a stem-and-leaf plot. Tell which stem includes the most values. Then make a box-and-whisker plot.** *(pp. 649, 654)*

**25.** 46 kg, 70 kg, 21 kg, 136 kg, 55 kg, 60 kg, 72 kg, 104 kg, 52 kg

**26.** 12.1 in., 13.5 in., 12.8 in., 10 in., 7 in., 11.2 in., 12.9 in., 11.1 in., 12 in., 13.7 in.

**Evaluate the expression.**

**27.** $_{11}P_5$ *(p. 675)*

**28.** $_{13}P_4$ *(p. 675)*

**29.** $_{10}C_3$ *(p. 680)*

**30.** $_{12}C_7$ *(p. 680)*

**Simplify.**

**31.** $(10q^2 - 6) + (q^2 + 1)$ *(p. 721)*

**32.** $(7y^2 + y - 4) + (y^2 - y - 1)$ *(p. 721)*

**33.** $(3x^3 + 4x - 1) + (x^3 - x^2 - 8)$ *(p. 721)*

**34.** $(4x^2 - 2x + 5) - (x^2 - 6x + 8)$ *(p. 721)*

**35.** $(2xy)^3$ *(p. 726)*

**36.** $(7z)(-4z)^2$ *(p. 726)*

**37.** $(-c^3)(2c^4)$ *(p. 726)*

**38.** $-y^3(-y^2 + 11y)$ *(p. 726)*

39. **LANDSCAPING** A lawn cart can haul a maximum of 300 pounds. You are hauling logs across your yard for a landscaping project. Using 15 pounds as the average weight per log, write an inequality that models the situation. Solve the inequality and interpret the solution. *(p. 154)*

40. **WALKING** You take a break after walking $3\frac{3}{4}$ miles of a 5 mile trail. How much of the trail is left? You walk $\frac{1}{2}$ of the remaining portion of the trail, then it starts to rain so you run to the end of the trail. How far did you run? *(p. 238)*

41. **FUNDRAISER** At a school fundraiser, the science club made 58% of its money selling juice, 27% selling cookies, and 15% selling apples. The club made $87 selling juice. How much did the club make selling cookies? How much did it make selling apples? *(p. 375)*

42. **BUILDINGS** The area of the square base of a building is 3721 square feet. Find the perimeter of the base of the building and the length of the diagonal of the base to the nearest foot. *(p. 482)*

43. **DRAWING NETS** Draw a net for an octagonal pyramid. How many faces, edges, and vertices does the octagonal pyramid have? *(p. 534)*

44. **BASEBALL** You have $60 to spend. Baseballs are $6 each and sunflower seeds are $3 per package. The number of each item you can buy is modeled by the equation $6x + 3y = 60$. Graph the equation and explain what the intercepts represent. *(p. 606)*

45. **GROCERY SHOPPING** You have $20 to spend on peppers for a big pot of chili you are making. Jalapeno peppers cost $3.00 per pound and red bell peppers cost $4.00 per pound. The amount of each pepper you can buy is modeled by the inequality $3x + 4y \le 20$ where $x$ is the number of pounds of jalapeno peppers, and $y$ is the number of pounds of red bell peppers. Graph the inequality. *(p. 629)*

46. **PHOTOGRAPHY** You and six friends line up for a photograph in one row. In how many ways can you line up for the photograph? *(p. 675)*

47. **SOFTBALL** A softball player has a batting average of .350, which means she gets a hit 35% of her times at bat. What are the odds that she will get a hit in her next at bat? *(p. 685)*

48. **DISTANCE** The height, in feet, of a projectile $t$ seconds after it was launched can be found by evaluating the expression $-16t^2 + 64t + 5$. Find the height of the projectile when $t = 1$ and $t = 3$. What do you notice? *Explain* how this is possible. *(p. 717)*

49. **INTEREST** You deposit $25 into a savings account with interest compounded annually. The account balance after 2 years is given by the expression $25(r + 1)^2$. Expand this expression and simplify. *(p. 734)*

# Contents of Student Resources

# Skills Review Handbook

## Place Value

The **whole numbers** are the numbers 0, 1, 2, 3, . . . . A **digit** is any of the numbers 0, 1, 2, 3, 4, 5, 6, 7, 8, or 9. The decimals are numbers such as 121.32, 25.6, and 3.456. For example, the decimal 4.5 has the digits 4 and 5. The place value of each digit in a whole number or a decimal depends on its position within the number. For example, in the number 491,037.892, the 8 has a value of 0.8 or $8 \times 0.1$ because it is in the tenths' place.

ten millions | millions | hundred thousands | ten thousands | thousands | hundreds | tens | ones | tenths | hundredths | thousandths

,  4  9  1,  0  3  7.  8  9  2

### EXAMPLE 1

**Write the number 27,037.6 in expanded form.**

$$27,037.6 = 20,000 + 7000 + 30 + 7 + 0.6$$

**The zero in the hundreds' position is a placeholder.**

$$= 2 \times 10,000 + 7 \times 1000 + 3 \times 10 + 7 \times 1 + 6 \times 0.1$$

### EXAMPLE 2

**Write the number in standard form.**

**a.** $4 \times 1000 + 5 \times 10 + 6 \times 0.1 + 8 \times 0.01$

**b.** Four million, sixty thousand, five and two thousandths

**SOLUTION**

**a.** $4 \times 1000 + 5 \times 10 + 6 \times 0.1 + 8 \times 0.01 = 4000 + 50 + 0.6 + 0.08$

$$= 4050.68$$

**b.** Write 4 in the millions' place, 6 in the ten thousands' place, 5 in the ones' place, and the 2 in the thousandths' place. Use zeros as placeholders for the other places. The answer is 4,060,005.002.

### PRACTICE

**Write the number in expanded form.**

**1.** 56,809      **2.** 3.075      **3.** 1002.003      **4.** 306.405

**Write the number in standard form.**

**5.** $5 \times 100,000 + 6 \times 10 + 9 \times 1 + 7 \times 0.001$      **6.** Five million, ten and thirty-six thousandths

# Rounding

To **round** a number means to approximate the number to a given place value. When rounding, look at the digit to the right of that place value. If the digit to the right is less than 5 (0, 1, 2, 3, or 4), round down. If the digit to the right is 5 or greater (5, 6, 7, 8, or 9), round up.

## EXAMPLE 1

**Round the number to the place value of the red digit.**

**a.** 6932

**b.** 45.674

### SOLUTION

**a.** Because the 9 is in the hundreds' place, round 6932 to the nearest hundred. Notice that 6932 is between 6900 and 7000, so it will round to one of these two numbers.

Notice that 6932 is closer to 6900 than to 7000.

The digit to the right of the 9 in the hundreds' place is the 3 in the tens' place. Because 3 is less than 5, round down.

▶ **Answer** 6932 rounded to the nearest hundred is 6900.

**b.** Because 6 is in the tenths' place, round 45.674 to the nearest tenth. Notice that 45.674 is between 45.6 and 45.7, so it will round to one of these two numbers.

Notice that 45.674 is closer to 45.7 than to 45.6.

The digit to the right of the 6 in the tenths' place is the 7 in the hundredths' place. Because 7 is 5 or greater, round up.

▶ **Answer** 45.674 rounded to the nearest tenth is 45.7.

## PRACTICE

**Round the number to the place value of the red digit.**

| | | |
|---|---|---|
| **1.** 1253 | **2.** 57,309 | **3.** 8.183 |
| **4.** 32.76 | **5.** 44,380 | **6.** 12.535 |
| **7.** 452.84 | **8.** 998,543 | **9.** 62,847 |
| **10.** 640,796 | **11.** 164.479 | **12.** 1209.4 |
| **13.** 52.961 | **14.** 12,742.5 | **15.** 3,501,652 |

# Divisibility Tests

When two nonzero whole numbers are multiplied together, each number is a **factor** of the product. A number is **divisible** by another number if the second number is a factor of the first. For example, $2 \times 5 = 10$, so 2 and 5 are factors of 10, and 10 is divisible by both 2 and 5.

You can use the following tests to test a whole number for divisibility by 2, 3, 4, 5, 6, 8, 9, and 10.

Divisible by 2:   The last digit of the number is 0, 2, 4, 6, or 8.

Divisible by 3:   The sum of the digits of the number is divisible by 3.

Divisible by 4:   The last two digits of the number are divisible by 4.

Divisible by 5:   The last digit of the number is 0 or 5.

Divisible by 6:   The number is divisible by both 2 and 3.

Divisible by 8:   The last three digits of the number are divisible by 8.

Divisible by 9:   The sum of the digits of the number is divisible by 9.

Divisible by 10:  The last digit of the number is 0.

## EXAMPLE 1

**Test the number for divisibility by 2, 3, 4, 5, 6, 8, 9, and 10.**

  **a.** 2736                              **b.** 74,420

### SOLUTION

  **a.** The last digit of 2736 is 6, so it is divisible by 2 but not by 5 or 10. The sum of the digits is $2 + 7 + 3 + 6 = 18$, so it is divisible by 3 and 9. The last two digits, 36, are divisible by 4, so 2736 is divisible by 4. Because 2736 is divisible by both 2 and 3, it is divisible by 6. The last three digits, 736, are divisible by 8, so 2736 is divisible by 8.

     ▶ **Answer**  2736 is divisible by 2, 3, 4, 6, 8, and 9.

  **b.** The last digit of 74,420 is 0, so it is divisible by 2, 5, and 10. The sum of the digits is $7 + 4 + 4 + 2 + 0 = 17$, so it is not divisible by 3 or 9. The last two digits, 20, are divisible by 4, so 74,420 is divisible by 4. Because 74,420 is divisible by 2, but not by 3, it is not divisible by 6. The last three digits, 420, are not divisible by 8, so 74,420 is not divisible by 8.

     ▶ **Answer**  74,420 is divisible by 2, 4, 5, and 10.

## PRACTICE

**Test the number for divisibility by 2, 3, 4, 5, 6, 8, 9, and 10.**

| | | | | |
|---|---|---|---|---|
| **1.** 34 | **2.** 84 | **3.** 285 | **4.** 560 | **5.** 972 |
| **6.** 4210 | **7.** 2815 | **8.** 6390 | **9.** 88,004 | **10.** 75,432 |

# Mixed Numbers and Improper Fractions

 **TEKS** *7.1.B*

A **fraction** is a number of the form $\frac{a}{b}$ ($b \neq 0$) where $a$ is called the **numerator** and $b$ is called the **denominator**.

A number $1\frac{3}{5}$, read as "one and three fifths," is a *mixed number*. A **mixed number** is the sum of a whole number part and a fraction part.

An **improper fraction**, such as $\frac{21}{8}$ is any fraction in which the numerator is greater than or equal to the denominator.

## EXAMPLE 1

**Write $3\frac{2}{5}$ as an improper fraction.**

$$3\frac{2}{5} = \frac{15 + 2}{5} \qquad \text{1 whole} = \frac{5}{5}, \text{ so 3 wholes} = \frac{3 \times 5}{5}, \text{ or } \frac{15}{5}.$$

$$= \frac{17}{5} \qquad \text{Add.}$$

## EXAMPLE 2

**Write $\frac{13}{4}$ as a mixed number.**

1. Divide 13 by 4.

$$\begin{array}{r} 3\text{R}1 \\ 4\overline{)13} \\ \underline{12} \\ 1 \end{array}$$

2. Write the mixed number. $\qquad 3 + \frac{1}{4} = 3\frac{1}{4}$

## PRACTICE

**Copy and complete the statement.**

**1.** $7\frac{3}{5} = \frac{?}{5}$      **2.** $3\frac{1}{6} = \frac{?}{6}$      **3.** $\frac{23}{4} = 5\frac{?}{4}$      **4.** $\frac{17}{7} = 2\frac{?}{7}$

**Write the mixed number as an improper fraction.**

**5.** $3\frac{1}{2}$      **6.** $1\frac{5}{6}$      **7.** $4\frac{3}{8}$      **8.** $8\frac{5}{7}$      **9.** $10\frac{3}{4}$

**Write the improper fraction as a mixed number.**

**10.** $\frac{11}{4}$      **11.** $\frac{15}{2}$      **12.** $\frac{25}{6}$      **13.** $\frac{17}{3}$      **14.** $\frac{33}{8}$

# Ratio and Rate

One way to compare numbers is to use a ratio. The **ratio** uses division to compare two numbers. You can write the ratio of $a$ to $b$ as $\frac{a}{b}$, as $a : b$, or as "$a$ to $b$."

## EXAMPLE 1

There are 15 boys and 17 girls in the band. Write the ratio of the number of boys to girls in the band in three ways.

$$\frac{\text{Number of boys}}{\text{Number of girls}} = \frac{15}{17} = 15 \text{ to } 17 = 15 : 17$$

A **rate** is a ratio of two quantities that have different units, such as $\frac{150 \text{ miles}}{3 \text{ hours}}$.

A **unit rate** is a rate with a denominator of 1 unit.

## EXAMPLE 2

Write the rate $\frac{150 \text{ miles}}{3 \text{ hours}}$ as a unit rate.

$$\overset{\div \, 3}{\frac{150 \text{ mi}}{3 \text{ h}} = \frac{50 \text{ mi}}{1 \text{ h}}} \underset{\div \, 3}{} \qquad \text{Divide 3 by 3 to get 1, so divide 150 by 3 also.}$$

▶ **Answer** The unit rate is 50 miles per hour.

## PRACTICE

The table shows the numbers of boys and girls in Mr. Smith's class and in Ms. Jung's class. Use the table to write the specified ratio.

1. Boys in Mr. Smith's class to girls in Mr. Smith's class

2. Boys in Mr. Smith's class to boys in Ms. Jung's class

3. Girls in Ms. Jung's class to all girls

|  | Boys | Girls |
|---|---|---|
| **Mr. Smith's class** | 13 | 12 |
| **Ms. Jung's class** | 17 | 11 |

**Write the rate and unit rate.**

4. 8 feet in 2 seconds

5. $24 for 8 pens

6. 333 miles in 6 hours

7. 280 words in 5 minutes

8. 3 quarts for $2.50

9. 8 inches in 6 days

# Adding and Subtracting Decimals

**TEKS** *7.2.B*

To add and subtract decimals, start with the digits in the place on the right. Moving to the left, add or subtract the digits one place value at a time, regrouping as needed.

## EXAMPLE 1

**Find the sum 0.157 + 0.663.**

**STEP 1** Add the thousandths. Regroup 10 thousandths as 1 hundredth and 0 thousandths.

$$\begin{array}{r} {\scriptstyle 1} \\ 0.157 \\ + \ 0.663 \\ \hline 0 \end{array}$$

**STEP 2** Add the hundreths. Regroup 12 hundredths as 1 tenth and 2 hundredths.

$$\begin{array}{r} {\scriptstyle 1\ 1} \\ 0.157 \\ + \ 0.663 \\ \hline 20 \end{array}$$

**STEP 3** Add the tenths. Place the decimal point in the answer.

$$\begin{array}{r} {\scriptstyle 1\ 1} \\ 0.157 \\ + \ 0.663 \\ \hline 0.820 \end{array}$$

## EXAMPLE 2

**Find the difference 30.7 − 3.8.**

**STEP 1** Start with the tenths. There are not enough tenths in 30.7 to subtract 8 tenths.

$$\begin{array}{r} 30.7 \\ - \ 3.8 \\ \hline \end{array}$$

**STEP 2** Move to the ones. There are no ones in 30.7, so regroup 1 ten as 9 ones and 10 tenths.

$$\begin{array}{r} {\scriptstyle 9} \\ {\scriptstyle 2\ 10\ 17} \\ 30.7 \\ - \ 3.8 \\ \hline \end{array}$$

**STEP 3** Subtract. Place the decimal point in the answer.

$$\begin{array}{r} {\scriptstyle 9} \\ {\scriptstyle 2\ 10\ 17} \\ 30.7 \\ - \ 3.8 \\ \hline 26.9 \end{array}$$

**Check** Because addition and subtraction are inverse operations, you can check your answer by adding: 26.9 + 3.8 = 30.7.

## PRACTICE

**Find the sum or difference.**

**1.** 3.56 + 2.74

**2.** 12.7 + 93.8

**3.** 27.5 + 3.6

**4.** 0.923 + 0.179

**5.** 4.217 + 6.739

**6.** 9.3 − 2.8

**7.** 4.56 − 1.65

**8.** 13.64 − 5.85

**9.** 38.45 − 19.57

**10.** 741.52 − 48.66

**11.** 56.98 + 0.82

**12.** 100.476 − 4.989

**13.** 365.57 − 79.38

**14.** 49.86 + 2.65

**15.** 97.156 − 9.092

**16.** 232.543 − 209.692

# Adding and Subtracting Fractions

To add two fractions with a common denominator, write the sum of the numerators over the denominator.

**Numbers** $\dfrac{2}{5} + \dfrac{1}{5} = \dfrac{3}{5}$       **Algebra** $\dfrac{a}{c} + \dfrac{b}{c} = \dfrac{a+b}{c}$ $(c \neq 0)$

## EXAMPLE 1

Find the sum $\dfrac{4}{7} + \dfrac{6}{7}$.

$\dfrac{4}{7} + \dfrac{6}{7} = \dfrac{4+6}{7}$       **Write sum of numerators over denominator.**

$= \dfrac{10}{7}$       **Add.**

$= 1\dfrac{3}{7}$       **Write the improper fraction as a mixed number.**

To subtract two fractions with a common denominator, write the difference of the numerators over the denominator.

**Numbers** $\dfrac{7}{9} - \dfrac{2}{9} = \dfrac{5}{9}$       **Algebra** $\dfrac{a}{c} - \dfrac{b}{c} = \dfrac{a-b}{c}$ $(c \neq 0)$

## EXAMPLE 2

Find the difference $\dfrac{10}{11} - \dfrac{4}{11}$.

$\dfrac{10}{11} - \dfrac{4}{11} = \dfrac{10-4}{11}$       **Write difference of numerators over denominator.**

$= \dfrac{6}{11}$       **Subtract.**

## PRACTICE

**Find the sum or difference.**

**1.** $\dfrac{1}{3} + \dfrac{1}{3}$    **2.** $\dfrac{8}{9} + \dfrac{5}{9}$    **3.** $\dfrac{6}{7} - \dfrac{3}{7}$    **4.** $\dfrac{11}{12} - \dfrac{4}{12}$    **5.** $\dfrac{1}{8} + \dfrac{7}{8}$

**6.** $\dfrac{8}{11} + \dfrac{7}{11}$    **7.** $\dfrac{13}{15} - \dfrac{2}{15}$    **8.** $\dfrac{5}{6} - \dfrac{4}{6}$    **9.** $\dfrac{1}{9} + \dfrac{1}{9}$    **10.** $\dfrac{10}{11} - \dfrac{2}{11}$

**11.** $\dfrac{11}{12} + \dfrac{8}{12}$    **12.** $\dfrac{9}{10} - \dfrac{6}{10}$    **13.** $\dfrac{5}{9} - \dfrac{4}{9}$    **14.** $\dfrac{9}{16} + \dfrac{12}{16}$    **15.** $\dfrac{11}{14} - \dfrac{2}{14}$

**16.** $\dfrac{8}{15} - \dfrac{8}{15}$    **17.** $\dfrac{5}{12} + \dfrac{2}{12}$    **18.** $\dfrac{8}{10} + \dfrac{1}{10}$    **19.** $\dfrac{6}{7} + \dfrac{5}{7}$    **20.** $\dfrac{5}{8} - \dfrac{2}{8}$

# Estimation in Addition and Subtraction

To **estimate** a solution means to find an approximate answer. When numbers being added have about the same value, you can use *clustering* to estimate their sum. Another way to estimate is to add the digits in the greatest place, then round the remaining parts of the numbers and add. Finally, add the sums together.

## EXAMPLE 1

**Estimate the sum 3836 + 4235 + 3982.**

$$
\begin{array}{r} 3836 \\ 4235 \\ + \ 3982 \\ \hline \end{array}
\qquad
\begin{array}{r} 4000 \\ 4000 \\ + \ 4000 \\ \hline 12{,}000 \end{array}
$$
The numbers all cluster around the value 4000.

▶ **Answer** The sum 3836 + 4235 + 3982 is *about* 12,000.

To estimate a difference, first subtract the digits in the greatest place. Then round the remaining parts of the numbers and subtract the lesser number from the greater number. Finally, combine the two differences using addition or subtraction as shown below.

## EXAMPLE 2

**Estimate the difference 68,453 − 32,792.**

**STEP 1** First subtract the digits in the ten thousands' place.

$$
\begin{array}{r} 68{,}453 \\ - \ 32{,}792 \\ \hline \end{array}
\qquad
\begin{array}{r} 60{,}000 \\ - \ 30{,}000 \\ \hline 30{,}000 \end{array}
$$

**STEP 2** Then round the remaining digits to the nearest thousand. Subtract the lesser number from the greater number.

$$
\begin{array}{r} 8{,}000 \\ - \ 3{,}000 \\ \hline 5{,}000 \end{array}
$$

**STEP 3** Because the greater remaining number was originally on the *top*, you *add* the differences.

$$30{,}000 + 5{,}000 = 35{,}000$$

Note that if the greater remaining number had originally been on the *bottom*, you would *subtract* the differences.

## PRACTICE

**Estimate the sum or difference.**

**1.** 935 + 887 + 912

**2.** 4967 + 4802 + 5218

**3.** 5971 + 6032 + 7865

**4.** 8891 − 4932

**5.** 4373 − 2158

**6.** 449,739 − 285,921

# Solving Problems Using Addition and Subtraction

TEKS 7.2.B

You can use the following guidelines to tell whether to use addition or subtraction to solve a word problem.

- Use addition when you need to combine, join, or find a total.

- Use subtraction when you need to separate, compare, take away, find how many are left, or find how many more are needed.

## EXAMPLE 1

**You have 36 stamps in your stamp collection. You want to collect 18 more stamps. How many stamps will you have in all?**

You need to combine, so you need to add.

$$36 + 18 = 54$$

▶ **Answer**  You will have 54 stamps in your stamp collection.

## EXAMPLE 2

**Your total bill for lunch is \$4.78. You pay with a \$5 bill. How much change do you receive?**

You need to take away, so you need to subtract.

$$\$5.00 - \$4.78 = \$.22$$

▶ **Answer**  You receive \$.22 in change.

## PRACTICE

1. You spend \$48 for a coat and \$45 for a pair of shoes. How much do you spend in all?

2. You bought a box of 96 pencils. You gave 28 of the pencils to your friend. How many pencils do you have left?

3. You have \$18. You buy a video for \$15.99. How much money do you have left?

4. You have 24 country CDs and 18 pop CDs. How many country and pop CDs do you have in all?

5. You have 900 minutes a month on your cell phone plan. You have used 652 minutes so far this month. How many minutes do you have left?

6. You have \$149. You make \$24 babysitting. How much money do you have?

# Multiplying Fractions

TEKS **7.2.B**

To multiply a fraction by a whole number, multiply the numerator of the fraction by the whole number and write the product over the denominator of the fraction. Simplify if possible.

## EXAMPLE 1

**Find the product.**

**a.** $3 \times \dfrac{2}{7} = \dfrac{3 \times 2}{7}$   Write the product of the whole number and the numerator over the denominator.

$= \dfrac{6}{7}$   Multiply.

**b.** $\dfrac{3}{8} \times 5 = \dfrac{3 \times 5}{8}$   Write the product of the whole number and the numerator over the denominator.

$= \dfrac{15}{8}$, or $1\dfrac{7}{8}$   Multiply. Then write as a mixed number.

To multiply two fractions, write the product of the numerators over the product of the denominators. Simplify if possible.

$$\text{product of fractions} = \frac{\text{product of numerators}}{\text{product of denominators}}$$

## EXAMPLE 2

**Find the product.**

$\dfrac{4}{5} \times \dfrac{2}{3} = \dfrac{4 \times 2}{5 \times 3}$   Use rule for multiplying fractions.

$= \dfrac{8}{15}$   Multiply.

## PRACTICE

**Find the product. Simplify if possible.**

**1.** $6 \times \dfrac{2}{15}$   **2.** $2 \times \dfrac{6}{11}$   **3.** $4 \times \dfrac{5}{9}$   **4.** $8 \times \dfrac{5}{9}$   **5.** $\dfrac{3}{4} \times 7$

**6.** $\dfrac{4}{7} \times 5$   **7.** $\dfrac{6}{7} \times 3$   **8.** $\dfrac{3}{7} \times \dfrac{6}{11}$   **9.** $\dfrac{2}{3} \times \dfrac{4}{5}$   **10.** $\dfrac{3}{4} \times \dfrac{1}{7}$

**11.** $\dfrac{1}{8} \times \dfrac{3}{5}$   **12.** $\dfrac{7}{9} \times \dfrac{5}{8}$   **13.** $\dfrac{5}{9} \times \dfrac{2}{3}$   **14.** $\dfrac{3}{8} \times \dfrac{4}{5}$   **15.** $\dfrac{5}{12} \times \dfrac{5}{6}$

# Multiplication of a Decimal by a Whole Number  TEKS *7.2.B*

To multiply a decimal by a whole number, multiply the entire first number (ignoring the decimal point) by the digit in each place value of the second number to get partial products. Add the partial products. Then place the decimal point in the answer, showing the same number of decimal places as in the decimal.

## EXAMPLE 1

**Find the product 31.5 × 206.**

**STEP 1**

Multiply 31.5 by the ones' dig in 206. Ignore the decimal point.

$$
\begin{array}{r}
3\phantom{0} \\
31.5 \\
\times\ 206 \\
\hline
1890
\end{array}
$$

**STEP 2**

Skip the 0 in the tens' place, and multiply by the hundreds' digit. Start the partial product in the hundreds' place.

$$
\begin{array}{r}
1\phantom{0} \\
31.5 \\
\times\ 206 \\
\hline
1890 \\
630\phantom{0}
\end{array}
$$

**STEP 3**

Add the partial products. The decimal has one decimal place, so show one decimal place in the answer.

$$
\begin{array}{r}
31.5 \\
\times\ 206 \\
\hline
1890 \\
630\phantom{0} \\
\hline
6489.0
\end{array}
$$

## PRACTICE

**Find the product.**

| | | | | |
|---|---|---|---|---|
| **1.** 2.3 × 98 | **2.** 0.62 × 46 | **3.** 85 × 7.9 | **4.** 0.56 × 63 | **5.** 2.08 × 14 |
| **6.** 6.52 × 36 | **7.** 7.24 × 89 | **8.** 8.35 × 16 | **9.** 77.6 × 22 | **10.** 3.45 × 105 |
| **11.** 453 × 41.2 | **12.** 614 × 6.71 | **13.** 32.6 × 463 | **14.** 71.8 × 934 | **15.** 90.5 × 407 |
| **16.** 15.36 × 123 | **17.** 3.442 × 276 | **18.** 93.08 × 306 | **19.** 5.436 × 682 | **20.** 60.97 × 708 |
| **21.** 142.82 × 35 | **22.** 25.987 × 76 | **23.** 32.903 × 55 | **24.** 243.72 × 38 | **25.** 75.032 × 73 |
| **26.** 380.77 × 114 | **27.** 508.25 × 237 | **28.** 15.456 × 591 | **29.** 36.902 × 205 | **30.** 8257.6 × 459 |

# Dividing Decimals

TEKS 7.2.B

In a division problem, the number being divided is called the **dividend** and the number it is being divided by is called the **divisor**. The result of the division is called the **quotient**. To **divide** two numbers, you start with the leftmost digit of the dividend and move to the right. Before you start dividing decimals, place the decimal point in the quotient.

## EXAMPLE 1

**Find the quotient 5.2 ÷ 8.**

**STEP 1**
Place the decimal point in the quotient directly above the decimal point in the dividend. Then divide as with whole numbers. Because 8 is greater than 5, place a zero above the 5.

$$
\begin{array}{r}
0. \\
\text{divisor} \rightarrow 8\overline{)5.2} \leftarrow \text{dividend}
\end{array}
$$

**STEP 2**
Because 8 × 6 = 48, estimate that 8 divides 52 about 6 times. Multiply 6 and 8. Then subtract 48 from 52. Be sure the difference is less than the divisor: 4 < 8.

$$
\begin{array}{r}
0.6 \\
8\overline{)5.2} \\
-48 \\
\hline
4
\end{array}
$$

**STEP 3**
Add zero as a placeholder. Bring down the zero. Divide 40 by 8 to get 5. Multiply 5 and 8. Subtract 40 from 40. The remainder is zero.

$$
\begin{array}{r}
0.65 \\
8\overline{)5.20} \\
-48 \\
\hline
40 \\
-40 \\
\hline
0
\end{array}
$$

## EXAMPLE 2

**Find the quotient 12 ÷ 2.8.**

**STEP 1**
To multiply the divisor and the dividend by 10, move both decimal points 1 place to the right. Then divide as with whole numbers.

$$
\text{divisor} \rightarrow 28\overline{)120} \leftarrow \text{dividend}
$$

**STEP 2**
Because 28 × 4 = 112, estimate that 28 divides 120 about 4 times. Multiply 4 and 28. Then subtract 112 from 120.

$$
\begin{array}{r}
4 \\
28\overline{)120} \\
-112 \\
\hline
8
\end{array}
$$

**STEP 3**
Be sure the difference is less than the divisor: 8 < 28. So 12 ÷ 2.8 is equal to $4\frac{8}{28}$, or $4\frac{2}{7}$.

$$
\begin{array}{r}
4R8 \\
28\overline{)120} \\
-112 \\
\hline
8
\end{array}
$$

## PRACTICE

**Find the quotient.**

**1.** 2.7 ÷ 6  **2.** 3.8 ÷ 4  **3.** 6.8 ÷ 8  **4.** 46.9 ÷ 7  **5.** 13.71 ÷ 3

**6.** 15 ÷ 2.5  **7.** 8 ÷ 1.3  **8.** 32 ÷ 5.46  **9.** 63 ÷ 7.12  **10.** 75 ÷ 6.357

# Estimation in Multiplication and Division

TEKS 7.2.F

One way to estimate a product or a quotient is to find a range for the product or quotient by finding a low estimate and a high estimate. A low estimate and a high estimate can be found by using *compatible numbers,* which are numbers that make a calculation easier.

### EXAMPLE 1

**Find a low and high estimate for the product 56 × 35 using compatible numbers.**

For a low estimate, round both factors *down.*   $50 \times 30 = 1500$

For a high estimate, round both factors *up.*   $60 \times 40 = 2400$

▸ **Answer**  The product $56 \times 35$ is between 1500 and 2400.

### EXAMPLE 2

**Find a low and high estimate for the quotient 23,400 ÷ 45 using compatible numbers.**

When the divisor has more than one digit, round it.

For a *low* estimate, round the divisor *up* and choose a compatible dividend that is *lower* than the original dividend.

$$50\overline{)20,000}^{\,400}$$

For a *high* estimate, round the divisor *down* and choose a compatible dividend that is *higher* than the original dividend.

$$40\overline{)24,000}^{\,600}$$

▸ **Answer**  The quotient $23,400 \div 45$ is between 400 and 600.

### PRACTICE

**Find a low and high estimate for the product or quotient using compatible numbers.**

1. $43 \times 16$
2. $359 \times 28$
3. $852 \times 53$
4. $734 \times 76$
5. $225 \div 6$
6. $2795 \div 7$
7. $17,934 \div 77$
8. $41,042 \div 92$
9. $326 \times 48$
10. $612 \times 273$
11. $745 \times 158$
12. $905 \times 657$
13. $625 \times 28$
14. $809 \times 97$
15. $742 \div 8$
16. $231 \div 38$
17. $5421 \div 7$
18. $4972 \div 18$
19. $1583 \div 82$
20. $43,789 \div 64$

# Solving Problems Using Multiplication and Division

TEKS 7.2.B, 7.2.D

You can use the following guidelines to tell whether to use multiplication or division to solve a word problem.

- Use multiplication when you need to find the total number of objects that are in groups of equal size or to find a fractional part of another number.

- Use division when you need to find the number of equal groups or the number in each equal group.

## EXAMPLE 1

**You baked 48 muffins. You give $\frac{1}{3}$ of them to your friend. How many muffins did you give to your friend?**

You need to find the fractional part of another number, so you need to multiply.

$$48 \cdot \frac{1}{3} = 16$$

▶ **Answer** You gave 16 muffins to your friend.

## EXAMPLE 2

**You bought 4 cans of soup for a total of $3.56. How much did you pay for each can of soup?**

You need to find the amount in each equal group, so you need to divide.

$$3.56 \div 4 = 0.89$$

▶ **Answer** You paid $.89 for each can of soup.

## PRACTICE

1. You bought 6 notebooks. Each notebook cost $1.58. How much did you pay for all of the notebooks?

2. You have 92 baseball cards. You give $\frac{1}{4}$ of your cards to your friend. How many cards did you give your friend?

3. You have 12 flats of flowers. If each flat contains 48 flowers, how many flowers do you have?

4. You paid $22.95 for the plates for your party. If you bought 9 packages of plates, how much did you pay for each package?

# Points, Lines, and Planes

In geometry, a **point** is usually labeled with an uppercase letter, such as *A* or *B*. Points are used to name *lines*, *rays*, and *segments*. A **plane** is a flat surface that extends without end in all directions. You can represent a plane by a figure that looks like a floor or a wall.

| Words | Diagram | Symbols |
|---|---|---|
| A **line** extends without end in two *opposite* directions. | X Y | $\overleftrightarrow{XY}$ or $\overleftrightarrow{YX}$ |
| A **ray** has one **endpoint** and extends without end in *one* direction. | X Y | $\overrightarrow{XY}$ |
| A **segment** has two endpoints. | X Y | $\overline{XY}$ or $\overline{YX}$ |

## EXAMPLE 1

**Identify and name the *line, ray,* or segment.**

**a.**
*A*     *B*

**b.**
*M*   *N*

**c.**
*P*     *Q*

**SOLUTION**

**a.** The figure is a segment that can be named $\overline{AB}$.

**b.** The figure is a line that can be named $\overleftrightarrow{MN}$.

**c.** The figure is a ray that can be named $\overrightarrow{PQ}$.

## PRACTICE

**Match the name with the correct figure.**

**1.** $\overline{CD}$

**2.** $\overleftrightarrow{CD}$

**3.** $\overrightarrow{CD}$

**A.**
*D*     *C*

**B.**
*C*           *D*

**C.**
*C*     *D*

**In Exercises 4–7, use the diagram.**

**4.** Name three points.

**5.** Name two rays.

**6.** Name two lines.

**7.** Name a segment that has *S* as an endpoint.

# Angles

An **angle** is formed by two rays with the same endpoint. The endpoint is called the **vertex**. The symbol ∠ is used to represent an angle.

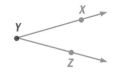

## EXAMPLE 1

**Name the angle above in three ways.**

Name the angle by its vertex alone: ∠Y

Name the angle by its vertex and two points, with the vertex as the middle point: ∠XYZ

Name the angle by its vertex and two points, but reverse the order of the points: ∠ZYX

## PRACTICE

**Match the name with the correct angle.**

**1.** ∠ABC

**2.** ∠RST

**3.** ∠MNP

**A.**

**B.**

**C.**

**Name the angle in three ways.**

**4.**

**5.**

**6.**

**7.**

**8.**

**9.**

**10.** Draw a triangle with vertices P, Q, and R. Name each angle of the triangle in three ways.

# Using a Ruler

TEKS 7.9.A

An **inch ruler** has markings for inches, halves of an inch, fourths of an inch, eighths of an inch, and sixteenths of an inch. As the lengths get shorter, so do the markings.

A **centimeter ruler** has markings for centimeters, halves of a centimeter, and tenths of a centimeter (also called *millimeters*). Like an inch ruler, as the lengths get shorter, so do the markings.

## EXAMPLE 1

**Use a ruler to draw a segment with the given length.**

**a.** $2\frac{1}{8}$ inches

**b.** 3.8 centimeters

### SOLUTION

**a.** Start at the leftmost mark on the ruler.

Draw a segment so that the other end is at the first $\frac{1}{8}$ in. mark after 2.

**b.** Start at the leftmost mark on the ruler.

Draw a segment so that the other end is at the 3.8 cm mark.

## PRACTICE

**Use a ruler to draw a segment with the given length.**

**1.** $\frac{7}{16}$ inch

**2.** $4\frac{5}{8}$ inches

**3.** 4.3 centimeters

**4.** 2.7 centimeters

**5.** $2\frac{5}{16}$ inches

**6.** 6.5 centimeters

**7.** 2.9 centimeters

**8.** $1\frac{1}{4}$ inches

# Using a Protractor

A **protractor** is a tool you can use to draw and measure angles. A unit of measure for angles is the **degree** (°). To measure an angle, place the center of the protractor on the vertex of the angle and line up one ray with the 0° line. Then read the measure where the other ray crosses the protractor.

The measure of ∠XYZ is 135°. You can write this as *m*∠XYZ = 135°.

## EXAMPLE 1

**Use a protractor to draw an angle that has a measure of 48°.**

**STEP 1**   Draw and label a ray.

**STEP 2**   Place the center of the protractor at the endpoint of the ray. Line up the ray with the 0° line. Then draw and label a point at the 48° mark on the inner scale.

**STEP 3**   Remove the protractor and draw $\overrightarrow{KL}$ to complete the angle.

## PRACTICE

**Use a protractor to measure the angle.**

**1.**   **2.**   **3.**

**4.** Use a protractor to draw angles measuring 46°, 125°, and 73°.

# Using a Compass

A **compass** is an instrument used to draw circles. A **straightedge** is any object that can be used to draw a segment.

## EXAMPLE 1

**Use a compass to draw a circle with radius 3 cm.**

Recall that the *radius* of a circle is the distance between the center of the circle and any point on the circle.

Use a metric ruler to open the compass so that the distance between the point and the pencil is 3 cm.

Place the point on a piece of paper and rotate the pencil around the point to draw the circle.

3 cm

## EXAMPLE 2

**Use a straightedge and a compass to draw a segment whose length is the sum of $\overline{MN}$ and $\overline{PQ}$.**

$M \qquad\qquad N \quad P \qquad\qquad Q$

### SOLUTION

Use a straightedge to draw a segment longer than both given segments.

Open your compass to measure $\overline{MN}$. Using this compass setting, place the point at the left end of your segment and make a mark that crosses your segment.

Then open your compass to measure $\overline{PQ}$. Using this compass setting, place the point at the first mark you made on your segment and make another mark that crosses your segment.

length of segment *MN* · length of segment *PQ*

sum of lengths

## PRACTICE

1. Use a compass to draw a circle with radius 4 cm.

2. Use a straightedge and a compass to draw a segment whose length is the *sum* of the lengths of the two given segments.

3. Use a straightedge and a compass to draw a segment whose length is the *difference* of the lengths of the two given segments in Exercise 2.

SKILLS REVIEW HANDBOOK

# Solving Problems Involving Time

 TEKS 7.13.A

When you have a start time and an end time that are both before or both after noon, you can find the *elapsed time* by subtracting the start time from the end time. When you have a start time before noon and an end time after noon, you can find the elapsed time by adding 12 hours to the end time, then subtracting.

## EXAMPLE 1

A seminar started at 8:30 A.M. and ended at 4:15 P.M. How long did the seminar last?

**STEP 1** **Add** 12 to the later time.

$$\begin{array}{r} 4:15 \\ + \ 12:00 \\ \hline 16:15 \end{array}$$

**STEP 2** **Subtract** to find the elapsed time.

You cannot subtract 30 from 15. Rename 1 hour as 60 minutes. Then subtract.

$$\begin{array}{r} {\scriptstyle 15 \ \ 75} \\ \cancel{16}:\cancel{15} \\ - \ \ 8:30 \\ \hline 7:45 \end{array}$$

▶ **Answer** The seminar lasted 7 hours 45 minutes.

## EXAMPLE 2

Morgan spends 20 minutes on her math homework and studies 55 minutes for a science test. She starts at 4:45 P.M. When does she finish?

**STEP 1** **Add** to find the elapsed time.

| | |
|---|---|
| 0:20 | Time for math |
| + 0:55 | Time for science |
| 0:75 | Elapsed time |
| 1:15 | Rewrite. 60 min = 1 h |

**STEP 2** **Add** to find the end time.

| | |
|---|---|
| 4:45 | Start time |
| + 1:15 | Elapsed time |
| 5:60 | End time |
| 6:00 | Rewrite. 60 min = 1 h |

▶ **Answer** Morgan finished her math and science homework at 6:00 P.M.

## PRACTICE

1. How long was a concert that started at 7:13 P.M. and ended at 9:24 P.M.?

2. How long was a school day that started at 8:10 A.M. and ended at 3:15 P.M.?

3. A soccer practice began at 2:45 P.M. The players warmed up for 10 minutes and scrimmaged for 40 minutes. What time did the practice end?

4. Jeff began watching a DVD at 7:25 P.M. He spent 1 hour 39 minutes watching the movie and 25 minutes watching the extra features on the DVD. What time did he finish watching the DVD?

# Converting Customary Units

To convert customary units, multiply by a convenient form of 1. For example:

- To convert inches to feet, multiply by $\dfrac{1 \text{ ft}}{12 \text{ in.}}$.

- To convert feet to inches, multiply by $\dfrac{12 \text{ in.}}{1 \text{ ft}}$.

For a listing of customary units and time, see the Table of Measures on page 815.

## EXAMPLE 1

**Copy and complete the statement.**

   **a.** 13,200 ft = _?_ mi     **b.** 6 c = _?_ fl oz     **c.** 78 h = _?_ d

**SOLUTION**

   **a.** $13{,}200 \text{ ft} \times \dfrac{1 \text{ mi}}{5280 \text{ ft}} = \dfrac{\overset{5}{\cancel{13200 \text{ ft}}} \times 1 \text{ mi}}{\underset{2}{\cancel{5280 \text{ ft}}}} = \dfrac{5}{2} \text{ mi, or } 2\dfrac{1}{2} \text{ mi}$    So, 13,200 ft = $2\dfrac{1}{2}$ mi.

   **b.** $6 \text{ c} \times \dfrac{8 \text{ fl oz}}{1 \text{ c}} = \dfrac{6 \cancel{\text{c}} \times 8 \text{ fl oz}}{1 \cancel{\text{c}}} = 48 \text{ fl oz}$    So, 6 c = 48 fl oz.

   **c.** $78 \text{ h} \times \dfrac{1 \text{ d}}{24 \text{ h}} = \dfrac{\overset{13}{\cancel{78 \text{ h}}} \times 1 \text{ d}}{\underset{4}{\cancel{24 \text{ h}}}} = \dfrac{13}{4} \text{ d, or } 3\dfrac{1}{4} \text{ d}$   So, 78 h = $3\dfrac{1}{4}$ d.

## EXAMPLE 2

**Convert 82 ounces into pounds and ounces.**

**STEP 1**   **Convert** 82 ounces to pounds.

$$82 \text{ oz} \times \frac{1 \text{ lb}}{16 \text{ oz}} = \frac{\overset{41}{\cancel{82 \text{ oz}}} \times 1 \text{ lb}}{\underset{8}{\cancel{16 \text{ oz}}}} = \frac{41}{8} \text{ lb, or } 5\frac{1}{8} \text{ lb}$$

**STEP 2**   **Convert** the fractional part from pounds to ounces.

$$\frac{1 \text{ lb}}{8} \times \frac{16 \text{ oz}}{1 \text{ lb}} = \frac{1 \cancel{\text{lb}} \times \overset{2}{\cancel{16}} \text{ oz}}{\underset{1}{\cancel{8 \text{ lb}}}} = 2 \text{ oz}$$

▶ **Answer** So, 82 ounces = 5 lb 2 oz.

## PRACTICE

**Copy and complete the statement.**

   **1.** 23 yd = _?_ ft     **2.** 4 lb = _?_ oz     **3.** 42 qt = _?_ gal

   **4.** 18 in. = _?_ yd     **5.** 3 gal = _?_ pt     **6.** 32 oz = _?_ lb

   **7.** 26 fl oz = _?_ c _?_ fl oz    **8.** 165 min = _?_ h     **9.** 75 in. = _?_ ft _?_ in.

# Converting Metric Units

The metric system is a base-ten system. Metric prefixes are associated with decimal place values.

| thousands: | hundreds: | tens: | ones: | tenths: | hundredths: | thousandths: |
|---|---|---|---|---|---|---|
| kilo- | hecto- | deka-<br>liter,<br>gram | meter, | deci- | centi- | milli- |

To convert from large to small metric units, multiply by a multiple of 10.

To convert from small to large metric units, divide by a multiple of 10.

For a listing of metric units, see the Table of Measures on page 815.

## EXAMPLE 1

**Copy and complete the statement.**

**a.** $5.75 \text{ kg} = \underline{\ ?\ } \text{ g}$

**b.** $44 \text{ m} = \underline{\ ?\ } \text{ cm}$

**c.** $110 \text{ mL} = \underline{\ ?\ } \text{ L}$

**SOLUTION**

**a.** To convert from kilograms to grams, multiply by 1000.

$5.75 \times 1000 = 5750$, so $5.75 \text{ kg} = 5750 \text{ g}$.

**b.** To convert from meters to centimeters, multiply by 100.

$44 \times 100 = 4400$, so $44 \text{ m} = 4400 \text{ cm}$.

**c.** To convert from milliliters to liters, divide by 1000.

$110 \div 1000 = 0.11$, so $110 \text{ mL} = 0.11 \text{ L}$.

## EXAMPLE 2

**Copy and complete using <, >, or = : 160 mg $\underline{\ ?\ }$ 16 g.**

$160 \text{ mg} \underline{\ ?\ } 16 \text{ g}$     **Strategy: Convert grams to milligrams.**

$160 \text{ mg} \underline{\ ?\ } 16,000 \text{ mg}$     $16 \times 1000 = 16,000$, so $16 \text{ g} = 16,000 \text{ mg}$.

$160 \text{ mg} < 16,000 \text{ mg}$     **Compare.**

▸ **Answer** $160 \text{ mg} < 16 \text{ g}$

## PRACTICE

**Copy and complete the statement.**

**1.** $6.42 \text{ kL} = \underline{\ ?\ } \text{ L}$

**2.** $4 \text{ cm} = \underline{\ ?\ } \text{ m}$

**3.** $5.5 \text{ g} = \underline{\ ?\ } \text{ mg}$

**Copy and complete the statement using <, >, or =.**

**4.** $8 \text{ km} \underline{\ ?\ } 8000 \text{ m}$

**5.** $1200 \text{ mg} \underline{\ ?\ } 12 \text{ g}$

**6.** $9.2 \text{ L} \underline{\ ?\ } 0.0092 \text{ mL}$

# Converting Between Metric and Customary Units

TEKS 7.2.D

To convert between metric and customary units, use the approximate relationships shown below.

| Length | Capacity | Weight |
|---|---|---|
| 1 mm ≈ 0.0394 in. | 1 mL ≈ 0.0338 fl oz | 1 g ≈ 0.0353 oz |
| 1 m ≈ 3.28 ft | 1 L ≈ 1.06 qt | 1 kg ≈ 2.2 lb |
| 1 km ≈ 0.621 mi | 1 kL ≈ 264 gal | |

## EXAMPLE 1

**Copy and complete the statement. Round to the nearest whole number.**

**a.** 127 km ≈ __?__ mi
**b.** 116 lb ≈ __?__ kg
**c.** 50 mL ≈ __?__ fl oz

### SOLUTION

**a.** $127 \text{ km} \times \dfrac{0.621 \text{ mi}}{1 \text{ km}} = \dfrac{127 \text{ km} \times 0.621 \text{ mi}}{1 \text{ km}} = 78.867 \text{ mi} \approx 79 \text{ mi}$  So, 127 km ≈ 79 mi.

**b.** $116 \text{ lb} \times \dfrac{1 \text{ kg}}{2.2 \text{ lb}} = \dfrac{116 \text{ lb} \times 1 \text{ kg}}{2.2 \text{ lb}} = \dfrac{116}{2.2} \text{ kg} = 52.72 \text{ kg} \approx 53 \text{ kg}$  So, 116 lb ≈ 53 kg.

**c.** $50 \text{ mL} \times \dfrac{0.0338 \text{ fl oz}}{1 \text{ mL}} = \dfrac{50 \text{ mL} \times 0.0338 \text{ fl oz}}{1 \text{ mL}} = 1.69 \text{ fl oz} \approx 2 \text{ fl oz}$  So, 50 mL ≈ 2 fl oz.

## EXAMPLE 2

**Copy and complete using < or > =: 210 m __?__ 670 ft.**

| | |
|---|---|
| 210 m __?__ 670 ft | **Strategy: Convert meters to feet.** |
| 688.8 ft __?__ 670 ft | **210 × 3.28 = 688.8, so 210 m ≈ 688.8 ft.** |
| 688.8 ft > 670 ft | **Compare.** |

▶ **Answer**  210 m > 670 ft

## PRACTICE

**Copy and complete the statement. Round to the nearest whole number.**

**1.** 80 kg ≈ __?__ lb
**2.** 56 mi ≈ __?__ km
**3.** 24 qt ≈ __?__ L

**Copy and complete the statement using < or >.**

**4.** 808 mm __?__ 33 in.
**5.** 40 gal __?__ 0.5 kL
**6.** 1 oz __?__ 20 g

# Reading and Making Line Plots

TEKS 7.11.A

A **line plot** uses a number line to show how often data values occur.

## EXAMPLE

**You surveyed 20 of your friends and asked them how many pets they have. Their responses were:**

$$6, 2, 3, 1, 5, 0, 2, 4, 1, 1, 6, 2, 0, 3, 1, 4, 3, 2, 1, 1.$$

**a.** Make a line plot of the data.

**b.** What was the most frequent response?

### SOLUTION

**a.**

**b.** The greatest number of ×s is above 1, so 1 was the most frequent response.

## PRACTICE

**Make a line plot of the data.**

1. In a survey, 15 people were asked how many TVs they own.
   Their responses were: 1, 2, 1, 4, 3, 2, 1, 5, 1, 2, 3, 1, 2, 1, 2.

2. In a survey, 18 people were asked how many times they eat out each week.
   Their responses were: 2, 4, 1, 3, 5, 6, 3, 7, 2, 1, 4, 8, 5, 4, 3, 4, 1, 2.

**Use the line plot below. It shows the results of a questionnaire asking people how many hours they exercise each week.**

3. How many people completed the questionnaire?

4. How many more people exercise 4 hours each week than exercise 6 hours each week?

5. How many people exercise less than 3 hours each week?

# Reading and Making Bar Graphs

TEKS 7.11.A

Data are numbers or facts. A **bar graph** is one way to display data. A bar graph uses bars to show how quantities in categories compare.

**EXAMPLE 1**

**The bar graph shows the results of a survey on favorite flavors of ice cream. Which flavor was chosen the most? Which flavor was chosen the least?**

The longest bar on the graph represents the 11 people who chose chocolate. So, chocolate was chosen the most.

The shortest bar represents the 2 students who chose strawberry. So, strawberry was chosen the least.

To make a bar graph, choose a title and a scale. Draw and label the axes. Then draw bars to represent the data given.

**EXAMPLE 2**

**Draw a bar graph for the data given.**

| Subject | Number of Students |
|---------|-------------------|
| Math | 8 |
| English | 15 |
| History | 20 |
| Science | 16 |

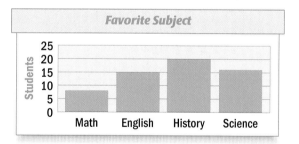

**PRACTICE**

**In Exercises 1–3, use the bar graph of ice cream flavors above.**

1. How many students chose butter pecan as a favorite ice cream flavor?

2. How many students chose vanilla as a favorite ice cream flavor?

3. Which two flavors were chosen by the same number of students?

4. Suppose 8 more students took the survey shown in the second example. Draw a new bar graph if 3 of the students chose math, 4 chose history, and 1 chose science.

# Reading and Making Line Graphs

Another way to display data is to use a *line graph*. A **line graph** uses line segments to show how a quantity changes over time.

## EXAMPLE 1

**The line graph shows plant growth data collected by students every day for 7 days. The greatest increase in growth occurred between what two days? What was the amount of the increase?**

The steepest segment in the line graph is from Monday to Tuesday. The students recorded a height of 1 inch on Monday and a height of 3.5 inches on Tuesday, for an increase of 2.5 inches.

To make a line graph, choose a title and scales. Draw and label the axes. Then plot and connect points to represent the data given.

## EXAMPLE 2

**Draw a line graph for the data given.**

| Month | Weight of Puppy (pounds) |
|-------|--------------------------|
| 1     | 3                        |
| 2     | 5.5                      |
| 3     | 7                        |
| 4     | 11                       |

## PRACTICE

**In Exercises 1 and 2, use the plant growth line graph above.**

1. Between which two days was the growth 1 inch?

2. Between which two days did the height remain the same?

3. Suppose in month 5 the puppy in the second example weighed 15 pounds. Copy the graph and add this data to it.

# Venn Diagrams and Logical Reasoning

 TEKS *7.11.A*

A **Venn diagram** uses shapes to show how sets are related.

**EXAMPLE 1**

**Draw and use a Venn diagram.**

**a.** Draw a Venn diagram of the whole numbers from 6 through 19 where set *A* consists of even numbers and set *B* consists of multiples of 5.

**b.** Is the following statement *true* or *false*? Explain. *No even whole number from 6 through 19 is a multiple of 5.*

**c.** Is the following statement *always*, *sometimes*, or *never* true? Explain. *A multiple of 5 from 6 through 19 is even.*

**SOLUTION**

**a.**

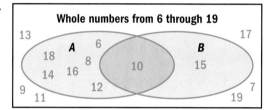

**b.** False. 10 is an even whole number that is a multiple of 5.

**c.** Sometimes. It is true that 10 is a multiple of 5 that is even, but 15 is a multiple of 5 that is odd.

**PRACTICE**

**Draw a Venn diagram of the sets described.**

**1.** Of the whole numbers less than 12, set *A* consists of numbers that are greater than 8 and set *B* consists of odd numbers.

**2.** Of the whole numbers less than 10, set *C* consists of multiples of 3 and set *D* consists of even numbers.

**Use the Venn diagrams you drew in Exercises 1 and 2 to answer the question. Explain your reasoning.**

**3.** Is the following statement *true* or *false*?
*There is only one odd number greater than 8 and less than 12.*

**4.** Is the following statement *always*, *sometimes*, or *never* true?
*A whole number less than 10 is both a multiple of 3 and even.*

TEKS *7.13.B, 7.13.C*

## Make a Model

**Problem** The width of a rectangular flag is $\frac{2}{3}$ its length. The flag is folded in half lengthwise. Then the flag is repeatedly folded into triangles, as shown, as many times as possible. How many layers thick will the resulting folded flag be?

| Make a Model |
| --- |
| Draw a Diagram |
| Guess, Check, and Revise |
| Work Backward |
| Make a List or Table |
| Look for a Pattern |
| Break into Parts |
| Solve a Simpler Problem |
| Use a Venn Diagram |
| Act It Out |

### 1 Read and Understand

You need to find the number of layers thick a flag will be when folded as described.

### 2 Make a Plan

It is hard to tell how many layers the flag will have. Making a model of the flag will allow you to perform the folds and count how many layers there are.

### 3 Solve the Problem

Cut a rectangle out of graph paper whose width is $\frac{2}{3}$ its length. Make the length of the rectangle 12 units and the width of the rectangle $\frac{2}{3} \cdot 12 = 8$ units.

Fold the rectangle in half lengthwise. Then repeatedly fold triangles.

Open the paper up and count the number of triangles. There are 12 small triangles, so the folded flag is 12 layers thick.

### 4 Look Back

Check your answer by making and folding another model for the flag, but one that has a different length and width.

### Practice the Strategy

You are deciding between buying two frozen pizzas. One pizza is circular and has a diameter of 8 inches. The other pizza is rectangular with a length of 8 inches and a width of 5 inches. Without performing any calculations, tell which pizza has the greater area.

*(See p. 796 for more practice.)*

# Draw a Diagram

TEKS 7.13.B, 7.13.C

**Problem** Steve is hanging two large rectangular posters on one wall of his room. The width of the wall is $6\frac{1}{4}$ feet. Steve aligns the edge of one poster with the left edge of the wall. He aligns the edge of the other poster with the right edge of the wall. The posters overlap by 5 inches. If the posters are the same size and have the same orientation, what is the width of each poster?

| |
|---|
| Make a Model |
| **Draw a Diagram** |
| Guess, Check, and Revise |
| Work Backward |
| Make a List or Table |
| Look for a Pattern |
| Break into Parts |
| Solve a Simpler Problem |
| Use a Venn Diagram |
| Act It Out |

## ① Read and Understand

You need to find the width of each poster.

## ② Make a Plan

Drawing a diagram can help you visualize how the posters are hung on the wall and how the given distances relate.

## ③ Solve the Problem

The outside edges of the posters align with the edges of the wall, and the posters overlap. Draw a diagram of this situation.

The length of the wall is $6\frac{1}{4}$ feet and the posters overlap by 5 inches. Label these distances. The diagram shows that the parts of the posters that do not overlap must measure

$6\frac{1}{4}$ ft − 5 in. = 75 in. − 5 in. = 70 in.

The posters have the same width, so the part of each poster that does not overlap measures 70 ÷ 2 = 35 in.

The width of each poster is 35 + 5 = 40 in.

$6\frac{1}{4}$ ft

5 in.

## ④ Look Back

Reread the problem and check that your diagram is consistent with each piece of the given information.

## Practice the Strategy

In town, the post office is $1\frac{3}{8}$ miles south of the town hall. The town hall is $\frac{3}{4}$ mile north of the bank. How far and in what direction would you have to travel to get from the bank to the post office?
*(See p. 796 for more practice.)*

# Guess, Check, and Revise

TEKS 7.13.B, 7.13.C

**Problem** In a certain arcade game, you roll each of 3 balls up a ramp and into rings of different sizes. For every 25 points you score, you get one ticket. In the first game you score 130 points by getting 2 balls in the inner ring and 1 ball in the outer ring. In the second game you score 110 points by getting 1 ball in the inner ring and 2 balls in the outer ring. How many points would you score by getting 3 balls in the inner ring?

| |
|---|
| Make a Model |
| Draw a Diagram |
| **Guess, Check, and Revise** |
| Work Backward |
| Make a List or Table |
| Look for a Pattern |
| Break into Parts |
| Solve a Simpler Problem |
| Use a Venn Diagram |
| Act It Out |

**1 Read and Understand**

You need to find the points you would score by getting 3 balls in the inner ring. To find this, you first need to find the point value of the inner ring.

**2 Make a Plan**

You are given information about the combined number of points scored by getting balls in the two different rings. You are not given information on the individual point values of the rings. This suggests the strategy of guessing, checking, and then revising an answer.

**3 Solve the Problem**

Try guessing that the inner ring is worth 60 points and the outer ring is worth 10 points.

**First game:** $2(60) + 1(10) = 130$ ✓       **Second game:** $1(60) + 2(10) = 80$ ✗

Now try guessing 50 points for the inner ring and 30 points for the outer ring.

**First game:** $2(50) + 1(30) = 130$ ✓       **Second game:** $1(50) + 2(30) = 110$ ✓

The inner ring is worth 50 points and the outer ring is worth 30 points.

Since $3 \cdot 50 = 150$, getting 3 balls in the inner ring would result in a score of 150 points.

**4 Look Back**

Reread the problem to make sure that you answered the question being asked. Notice that the question asks for the points you would score by getting 3 balls in the inner ring, not the point values of the rings.

**Practice the Strategy**

The product of two numbers is 64. The difference of the same two numbers is 12. What is the sum of the two numbers?
*(See p. 797 for more practice.)*

# Work Backward

TEKS 7.13.B, 7.13.C

**Problem** Kristin brought some picture frames to sell at a two-day craft fair. On the first day of the fair, Kristin sold $\frac{1}{4}$ of her picture frames. On the second day, Kristin sold $\frac{2}{3}$ of the remaining picture frames. If Kristin sold 30 picture frames on the second day of the fair, how many picture frames did she bring to sell at the craft fair?

| |
|---|
| Make a Model |
| Draw a Diagram |
| Guess, Check, and Revise |
| **Work Backward** |
| Make a List or Table |
| Look for a Pattern |
| Break into Parts |
| Solve a Simpler Problem |
| Use a Venn Diagram |
| Act It Out |

**1 Read and Understand**

You need to find the number of picture frames that Kristin brought to the craft fair.

**2 Make a Plan**

You are given the number of frames sold during the second day of the fair, so you can work backward to find the number of frames remaining after the first day. Continue to work backward to find the number of frames brought to the fair.

**3 Solve the Problem**

Work backward from the 30 picture frames that were sold on the second day.

• Ask yourself: 30 is $\frac{2}{3}$ of what?    Answer: 30 is $\frac{2}{3}$ of 45.

Work backward from the 45 picture frames remaining after the first day.

• Ask yourself: 45 is $\frac{3}{4}$ of what?    Answer: 45 is $\frac{3}{4}$ of 60.

Kristin brought 60 picture frames to the craft fair.

**4 Look Back**

Work forward to check that your answer is correct. Kristin sold $\frac{1}{4} \cdot 60 = 15$ frames the first day. So she had $60 - 15 = 45$ remaining. She sold $\frac{2}{3} \cdot 45 = 30$ frames the second day.

**Practice the Strategy**

Mrs. O'Neil gives stickers to reward her students for good behavior. On Wednesday Mrs. O'Neil gave out 3 fewer stickers than on Tuesday. On Tuesday she gave out three times as many stickers as on Monday. If Mrs. O'Neil gave out 4 stickers on Monday, how many stickers did she give out on Wednesday?
*(See p. 797 for more practice.)*

# Make a List or Table

TEKS *7.13.B, 7.13.C*

**Problem** You get a haircut every 5 months. If you got a haircut in January of this year, in how many years will you next get a haircut in January? You get a haircut in January, in June, in November, and so on.

| |
|---|
| Make a Model |
| Draw a Diagram |
| Guess, Check, and Revise |
| Work Backward |
| **Make a List or Table** |
| Look for a Pattern |
| Break into Parts |
| Solve a Simpler Problem |
| Use a Venn Diagram |
| Act It Out |

**1 Read and Understand**

You need to find how many years it will be until you again have a haircut in the month of January.

**2 Make a Plan**

You need to keep track of both the month in which you get a haircut and the number of years that have passed. Making a table is a good way to organize this information.

**3 Solve the Problem**

Make a table of the months in which you get a haircut. Remember that there are 4 months between months in which you get a haircut. Use a new column for each new year.

| Year 1 | Year 2 | Year 3 | Year 4 | Year 5 | Year 6 |
|--------|--------|--------|--------|--------|--------|
| January | April | February | May | March | January |
| June | September | July | October | August | June |
| November | | December | | | November |

1 year  2 years  3 years  4 years  5 years

Your next haircut in January will take place in 5 years.

**4 Look Back**

Make sure that your answer seems reasonable. Since you get a haircut every 5 months, the total number of months between January haircuts should be divisible by 5. There are 12 months in a year, so there are 5 • 12 = 60 months in 5 years. Since 60 is divisible by 5, the answer seems reasonable.

**Practice the Strategy**

Sam does his laundry every 5 days. If he does his laundry on Tuesday of this week, in how many weeks will he next do his laundry on a Tuesday?
*(See pp. 797–798 for more practice.)*

# Look for a Pattern

TEKS 7.13.B, 7.13.C

**Problem** A landscaper charges the prices shown in the table for mowing lawns of different sizes. How much would you expect the landscaper to charge for mowing a lawn that is 55,000 square feet?

| Lawn size | Cost |
|-----------|------|
| 10,000 ft² | $20 |
| 20,000 ft² | $28 |
| 30,000 ft² | $36 |
| 40,000 ft² | $44 |

LEN'S LAWN CARE

| |
|---|
| Make a Model |
| Draw a Diagram |
| Guess, Check, and Revise |
| Work Backward |
| Make a List or Table |
| **Look for a Pattern** |
| Break into Parts |
| Solve a Simpler Problem |
| Use a Venn Diagram |
| Act It Out |

**PROBLEM SOLVING HANDBOOK**

## 1 Read and Understand

You need to predict the cost of mowing a lawn with an area of 55,000 square feet.

## 2 Make a Plan

Since you are not given any information about the cost of mowing a lawn that is 55,000 square feet in size, you have to look for a pattern in the costs of the lawn sizes you are given.

## 3 Solve the Problem

Look for a pattern in the way the cost increases as the lawn size increases.

For each additional 10,000 square feet, the cost of mowing the lawn increases by $8. It can be expected that the cost of mowing a lawn that is 50,000 square feet will be $52 and the cost of mowing a lawn that is 60,000 square feet will be $60. Since 55,000 is halfway between 50,000 and 60,000, the cost of mowing 55,000 square feet should be halfway between $52 and $60.

You can expect the cost of mowing 55,000 square feet to be $56.

| Lawn Size | Cost | |
|-----------|------|------|
| 10,000 ft² | $20 | + $8 |
| 20,000 ft² | $28 | + $8 |
| 30,000 ft² | $36 | + $8 |
| 40,000 ft² | $44 | |

## 4 Look Back

Make sure that you performed your calculations correctly and that you answered the question being asked.

## Practice the Strategy

Roland teaches piano lessons. All the lessons are the same length. On Saturday, the first lesson starts at 9:15 A.M., the second lesson starts at 9:50 A.M., the third lesson starts at 10:25 A.M., and the fourth lesson starts at 11:00 A.M. At what time will Roland begin teaching the seventh lesson?

*(See p. 798 for more practice.)*

# Break into Parts

TEKS 7.13.B, 7.13.C

**Problem** Dara is planning to wallpaper one wall of her living room. A diagram of her living room is given at the right. How many square feet of wallpaper will Dara need?

19 ft
3 ft
3 ft
4 ft
8 ft
2.5 ft
2.5 ft
3.5 ft

| Make a Model |
| Draw a Diagram |
| Guess, Check, and Revise |
| Work Backward |
| Make a List or Table |
| Look for a Pattern |
| **Break into Parts** |
| Solve a Simpler Problem |
| Use a Venn Diagram |
| Act It Out |

## ① Read and Understand

You need to find the area of Dara's living room wall.

## ② Make a Plan

Since wallpaper will not be placed everywhere, break the problem into parts by finding the overall area and subtracting the area of the windows and fireplace.

## ③ Solve the Problem

The overall area of the living room wall is:

$8(19) = 152$ square feet.

The area that will not be covered with wallpaper is:

$(2.5)(3) + (3.5)(4) + (2.5)(3) = 7.5 + 14 + 7.5 = 29$ square feet.

The area that will be covered with wallpaper is $152 - 29 = 123$ square feet.

## ④ Look Back

Check for reasonableness by estimating. The overall area of the living room is about $8(20) = 160$ square feet.

The area that will not be covered with wallpaper is about
$3(3) + 4(4) + 3(3) = 34$ square feet.

The answer is reasonable since
$160 - 34 = 126$.

## Practice the Strategy

Rockford Middle School is organizing a 3-hour ice-skating dance for its 280 students. Ice skates will be provided for every student. The costs associated with having an ice-skating dance are given. How much will the dance cost?

| | |
|---|---|
| **Rink rental** | $125 an hour |
| **Dj** | $80 an hour |
| **Skate rental** | $2 per person |

*(See p. 799 for more practice.)*

# Solve a Simpler Problem

**TEKS** 7.13.B, 7.13.C

**Problem** The Rios family is having a family reunion with 40 families. The first family to arrive puts 2 dimes in a jar to be given to a charity. The second family puts in 4 dimes, the third family puts in 6 dimes, and so on. The last family to arrive puts in 80 dimes. How much money is given to the charity?

| Make a Model |
| Draw a Diagram |
| Guess, Check, and Revise |
| Work Backward |
| Make a List or Table |
| Look for a Pattern |
| Break into Parts |
| **Solve a Simpler Problem** |
| Use a Venn Diagram |
| Act It Out |

### 1 Read and Understand

You need to find the sum of the even numbers from 2 though 80 and find the value of that number of dimes.

### 2 Make a Plan

To solve the problem, you could add every even number from 2 through 80, but this would take a long time. Instead, you can look for a simpler problem whose solution can help you find an answer.

### 3 Solve the Problem

Solve a simpler problem by grouping the even numbers from 2 through 80 into pairs of numbers whose sum is 82.

$$2 + 80 = 82$$
$$2 + 4 + 6 + \ldots + 76 + 78 + 80$$
$$4 + 78 = 82$$

The last pair of numbers is 40 and 42.

Since the numbers are even only, this means that there must be $40 \div 2 = 20$ pairs of numbers. So the sum of the even numbers from 2 through 80 is $20 \cdot 82 = 1640$. The amount of money given to charity is $1640 \times \$.10 = \$164$.

### 4 Look Back

Check that your answer is reasonable. There are a total of 40 numbers. Since the middle number is about 40, you can expect that the sum of the numbers would be about $40 \cdot 40 = 1600$. The answer is reasonable.

## Practice the Strategy

A caterer uses square tables for dinner events. Each table can seat 4 people, with one person on each side. Tables can also be pushed together to seat more people. If the caterer needs to create one long table that can seat 30 people for dinner, how many square tables does he need to use?

*(See p. 799 for more practice.)*

**PROBLEM SOLVING HANDBOOK**

# Use a Venn Diagram

**Problem** In a survey about phone service, 205 people said they have a home phone only, and 40 said they have a cell phone only. 173 people said they have both a home phone and a cell phone, but no beeper, and 20 said they have a home phone, a cell phone, and a beeper. 24 people said they have a home phone and a beeper, but no cell phone, and 36 said they have a cell phone and a beeper, but no home phone. How many of the people surveyed have a cell phone?

| |
|---|
| Make a Model |
| Draw a Diagram |
| Guess, Check, and Revise |
| Work Backward |
| Make a List or Table |
| Look for a Pattern |
| Break into Parts |
| Solve a Simpler Problem |
| **Use a Venn Diagram** |
| Act It Out |

## ① Read and Understand

You need to find the number of people surveyed who have a cell phone.

## ② Make a Plan

The answer is not obvious because some people have more than one type of service. Use a Venn diagram to organize the information.

## ③ Solve the Problem

Draw a Venn diagram to represent the given information.

The diagram shows that 269 people have cell phones.

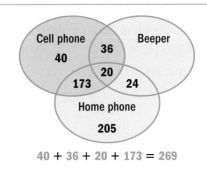

$$40 + 36 + 20 + 173 = 269$$

## ④ Look Back

Make sure that you placed the numbers in the correct places in the Venn diagram. Also check your addition.

### Practice the Strategy

The tulips in a garden are yellow, white, red, or a mixture of these colors. There are 20 yellow tulips, 15 white tulips, and 12 red tulips. There are 8 yellow and white tulips, 10 yellow and red tulips, and 5 tulips with all three colors. There are no red and white tulips. How many tulips have at least some red?

*(See pp. 799–800 for more practice.)*

# Act It Out

TEKS 7.13.B, 7.13.C

**Problem** You are in a lunch line with 4 students in front of you and 6 students behind you. You let a friend into the line in front of you, who then lets 2 students get in line behind her. Then 2 students join the end of the lunch line. How many students are now in the lunch line? What is your new position in the lunch line?

| Make a Model |
|---|
| Draw a Diagram |
| Guess, Check, and Revise |
| Work Backward |
| Make a List or Table |
| Look for a Pattern |
| Break into Parts |
| Solve a Simpler Problem |
| Use a Venn Diagram |
| **Act It Out** |

### 1 Read and Understand

You need to place a number of people in a line. Find the number of people in line and your place in line after people have joined the line.

### 2 Make a Plan

You can solve the problem by using slips of paper to represent people. Then follow the directions in the problem.

### 3 Solve the Problem

Begin by placing a slip of paper labeled with your name on it, then placing 4 slips to the left of it and 6 slips to the right of it.

Start of line ☐ ☐ ☐ ☐ you ☐ ☐ ☐ ☐ ☐ ☐

Then place 3 slips to the left of the one representing you and two slips at the end of the line.

Start of line ☐ ☐ ☐ ☐ ☐ ☐ ☐ you ☐ ☐ ☐ ☐ ☐ ☐ ☐ ☐

▶ **Answer** There are 16 people in line, and you are eighth in line.

### 4 Look Back

You can solve the problem a different way. Draw a diagram of the line as it is. Add to the diagram to show people joining it. Then count to find how many people are in line and what your position is.

### Practice the Strategy

You have 8 quarters, 10 dimes, and 7 nickels. You give half your dimes and 2 nickels to a friend. Then you spend one fourth of your quarters and one nickel. How much money do you have left?
*(See p. 800 for more practice.)*

**Solve the problem and show your work.**

## Make a Model

1. Each page of a photo album is 8 inches wide by 12 inches long. You have photos that are 4 inches wide by 6 inches long that you want to display in the album. Can you display 4 photos vertically on a single page? Can you display 3 photos horizontally? Can you display 2 photos vertically and 1 photo horizontally? *(Problem Solving Strategy Review, p. 786)*

2. Joe is making cellophane wrappers for pieces of his homemade saltwater taffy. He has 3 sheets of cellophane wrap that are each 9 inches wide and 10 inches long. How many 3 inch by 2 inch wrappers can Joe make? *(Problem Solving Strategy Review, p. 786)*

3. Elizabeth is making a 16 page booklet. She takes a piece of paper and folds it in half three times, as shown. Elizabeth then plans to staple the paper on the left edge, and trim the top and side of the booklet with scissors. She first wants to unfold the paper and number the pages of the book. Show how she should do this so that each page number appears in the lower right-hand corner of every page after the book is made. *(Problem Solving Strategy Review, p. 786)*

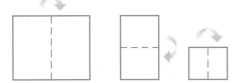

## Draw a Diagram

4. Andy hung two dartboards directly across from each other on opposite walls in his basement. The walls are 15 feet apart. A toe line is a line marking where a player should stand to throw darts. Andy wants to mark a toe line exactly 7 feet $9\frac{1}{4}$ inches from the base of the wall on which each dartboard is hung. How far apart will the two toe lines be? *(Problem Solving Strategy Review, p. 787)*

5. Thomas is covering the wall area above his kitchen stove with square ceramic tiles. The square tiles have side lengths of 4 inches. The wall area above Thomas's stove is 2 feet by $2\frac{1}{2}$ feet. Thomas can cut tiles for an exact fit. What is the least number of tiles Thomas needs to cover the wall? *(Problem Solving Strategy Review, p. 787)*

6. You are making a beaded bracelet that is 7 inches long. You have 7 beads that you want to place on the bracelet. Each bead is $\frac{1}{2}$ inch long. You want equal amounts of space between each of the beads and between the end of the bracelet and the first bead and the end of the bracelet and the last bead. How far apart should the beads be? *(Problem Solving Strategy Review, p. 787)*

7. Marco and Ali deliver newspapers in the same neighborhood. They each start their paper route at home. Marco's route takes him 2 blocks north, 3 blocks west, and then 5 blocks south. Ali's route takes her 4 blocks west, 3 blocks north, and then 5 blocks east. Marco lives 2 blocks north of Ali. How many times do their routes cross? *(Problem Solving Strategy Review, p. 787)*

Solve the problem and show your work.

# Guess, Check, and Revise

**8.** The sum of two three-digit numbers is 534. Each number contains the digits 1, 2, and 3. What are the numbers? *(Problem Solving Strategy Review, p. 788)*

$$\begin{array}{r} \boxed{?}\ \boxed{?}\ \boxed{?} \\ +\ \boxed{?}\ \boxed{?}\ \boxed{?} \\ \hline 5\quad 3\quad 4 \end{array}$$

**9.** Seven children in a neighborhood are riding bicycles and tricycles. If there are a total of 17 wheels, how many children are riding each type of cycle? *(Problem Solving Strategy Review, p. 788)*

**10.** Dina bought a small plant, a medium plant, and a large plant for $37.50. The medium plant cost $5.00 more than the small plant, and the large plant cost $5.00 more than the medium plant. How much did the small plant cost? *(Problem Solving Strategy Review, p. 788)*

**11.** Consecutive numbers are numbers that follow one after another. The numbers 1, 2, and 3 are consecutive numbers. The sum of three consecutive numbers is 66. What are the numbers? *(Problem Solving Strategy Review, p. 788)*

**12.** You are playing a game where you collect blue chips and green chips. For every blue chip you get one point. For every green chip you lose a point. You have a total of 20 chips and 14 points. How many blue chips do you have? How many green chips do you have? *(Problem Solving Strategy Review, p. 788)*

# Work Backward

**13.** Mr. Sanchez drove a rental car on a 3 day vacation. He drove twice as many miles on the first day as he drove on the second day. He drove 7 more miles on the second day than he drove on the third day. Mr. Sanchez drove 12 miles on the third day. How many miles did he drive during his vacation? *(Problem Solving Strategy Review, p. 789)*

**14.** Aisha runs every 3 days. She also does sit-ups every other day. If today is Tuesday and Aisha both ran and did sit-ups, on what day of the week did Aisha last do both activities on the same day? *(Problem Solving Strategy Review, p. 789)*

**15.** A dance company held auditions to fill 3 spots in the company. After the first round of auditions, $\frac{2}{3}$ of the dancers were cut. After the second round of auditions, $\frac{1}{4}$ of the remaining dancers were asked back for the third round. Five dancers made it to the third round of auditions. How many dancers were there in the first round of auditions? *(Problem Solving Strategy Review, p. 789)*

**16.** Andrew works out at a gym three times a week. He always starts with 15 minutes of stretching, followed by 50 minutes of cardiovascular exercise, and then 35 minutes of weightlifting. Andrew finishes his workouts at 7:15 P.M. What time does he start his workouts? *(Problem Solving Strategy Review, p. 789)*

**17.** At the beginning of the school year, your class was divided into seven equal groups. Later in the year, your group joined another group, and then two students left your group. Now there are four students in your group. How many students were in your class at the beginning of the year? *(Problem Solving Strategy Review, p. 789)*

# Make a List or Table

**18.** Amy calls a store to order a tote bag with her initials ABC embroidered on it. The store employee she talks to later forgets the order of the initials. How many bags would the employee have to make to be sure that one bag has the initials in the correct order? *(Problem Solving Strategy Review, p. 790)*

*Continued*

**Solve the problem and show your work.**

**19.** Ben has a $5 bill and a $10 bill. He decides to buy 2 souvenirs at an airport shop. The prices of various souvenirs are given below. Ben has $5.50 after his purchase. Which souvenirs did he buy? *(Problem Solving Strategy Review, p. 790)*

> **Souvenir Price List**
>
> Pen ........................ $2.50
> Keychain ............... $4.75
> Hat ........................ $6.25

**20.** Six cheerleaders form a pyramid. Suzie is always on the top, Diane and Avril are always in the middle row, and Monique, Olivia, and Tyra are always in the bottom row. How many different ways can the six cheerleaders form a pyramid? *(Problem Solving Strategy Review, p. 790)*

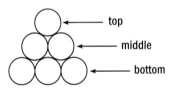

## Look for a Pattern

**21.** Two grocery stores send discount coupons through the mail. Store A sends a $5 off coupon every other week. Store B sends a $10 off coupon every third week. Veronica does her weekly grocery shopping at whichever store has the better coupon. If both stores send coupons the first week of the year, how much will Veronica save with the coupons that year? *(Problem Solving Strategy Review, p. 791)*

**22.** At track practice, the girls and the boys do a "leapfrog" drill. Six girls run in a single-file line next to 8 boys in a single-file line. Every quarter-lap around the track, the last runner in each line sprints to the front of the line. At the start of the drill, Mara is in the front of the girls' line and Dan is in the front of the boys' line. After how many laps will Mara and Dan both start sprinting at the same time? *(Problem Solving Strategy Review, p. 791)*

**23.** A commuter rail has its fares based on the number of zones traveled. The individual and family fares for a one-way ride within the first four numbers of zones are given in the table. The individual fare for traveling 6 zones is $4.50. What is the family fare for traveling 6 zones? If a family of 3 people is traveling on the commuter rail, is it cheaper for them to pay the individual fares or the family fare? *(Problem Solving Strategy Review, p. 791)*

| Number of zones | Individual fare | Family fare |
|---|---|---|
| 1 | $2.25 | $9.00 |
| 2 | $2.50 | $10.00 |
| 3 | $3.25 | $13.00 |
| 4 | $3.50 | $14.00 |

**24.** Manny is stacking wooden crates to make a staircase, as shown below. He keeps adding crates to increase the height of the staircase. Each crate has a height of 1 foot. How many crates will Manny use to make a staircase that reaches a height of 9 feet? *(Problem Solving Strategy Review, p. 791)*

**Solve the problem and show your work.**

# Break Into Parts

**25.** Auditions are being held for the school play. It takes 5 minutes to audition for an acting part and 3 minutes to audition for a chorus part. Only one student can audition at a time. There are 22 students auditioning for a chorus part and 25 students auditioning for an acting part. How long, in hours and minutes, will the auditions last? *(Problem Solving Strategy Review, p. 792)*

**26.** How many different rectangles are in the figure below? *(Problem Solving Strategy Review, p. 792)*

**27.** Your school is having a party. The party costs are given below. If 150 people are expected, how much will the party cost? *(Problem Solving Strategy Review, p. 792)*

| Decorations | $42 |
|---|---|
| Appetizers | $5 per person |
| Drinks | $1.75 per person |

# Solve a Simpler Problem

**28.** Bridget decides to do her summer reading in the following way.

- The first day she will read 2 pages.

- The second day she will read 4 pages.

- The third day she will read 6 pages.

If Bridget continues increasing reading until she reads 100 pages in one day, how many pages will she read in all? *(Problem Solving Strategy Review, p. 793)*

**29.** Matt is making confetti to throw at a surprise party. He uses a hole punch to punch holes that are $\frac{1}{4}$ inch in diameter. About how many holes can be punched out of one sheet of $8\frac{1}{2}$ inch by 11 inch paper? *(Problem Solving Strategy Review, p. 793)*

**30.** Jorie Middle School is having a slide show during the final assembly of the year. The slide show will have 200 photos taken throughout the year. The first photo will be of eighth graders, the second of sixth graders, the third of eighth graders, the fourth of seventh graders, the fifth of eighth graders, and so on. How many of the 200 photos will be of sixth graders? *(Problem Solving Strategy Review, p. 793)*

**31.** The manager of an apartment complex is painting parking space numbers in the parking lot. The manager lost the stencil for the number 2. Instead of buying a new stencil, the manager decides to use the stencil for the number 5 and flip it upside down. The parking spaces are numbered from 1 to 300. How many times will the manager need to use the number 5 stencil? *(Problem Solving Strategy Review, p. 793)*

# Use a Venn Diagram

**32.** Of the 500 people with cameras at a high school graduation, 120 people used both a digital camera and a film camera. There were 208 people who used a film camera, but not a digital camera. How many people used only a digital camera? *(Problem Solving Strategy Review, p. 794)*

*Continued*

**Solve the problem and show your work.**

33. On Saturday, several people fished from one pier. There were 11 people who caught only brown trout. There were 7 people who caught both brown trout and rainbow trout, and 13 people who caught only rainbow trout. How many people caught rainbow trout that day? *(Problem Solving Strategy Review, p. 794)*

34. There are 18 students in your class. Eight students have a cat and five students have a dog. Two students have both a cat and a dog. How many students have neither a cat nor a dog? *(Problem Solving Strategy Review, p. 794)*

35. At one high school there are 45 teachers who teach freshmen and sophomores, and 39 teachers who teach juniors and seniors. If there are 77 teachers at the high school, how many of them teach students in all four grade levels? *(Problem Solving Strategy Review, p. 794)*

36. Twenty-four cats are in a shelter. Ten cats are black, and six cats have short tails. Three cats are black and have short tails. How many cats are neither black nor have short tails? *(Problem Solving Strategy Review, p. 794)*

## Act It Out

37. Justin, Bob, Kelly, Michelle, and Rebecca are all different heights. Kelly is taller than Michelle and Justin. Rebecca is shorter than Justin but taller than Michelle. Bob is the tallest of the five. List the students in order from tallest to shortest. *(Problem Solving Strategy Review, p. 795)*

38. Four sets of twins are at a party. Each person shakes hands one time with every other person except his or her twin. How many handshakes take place? *(Problem Solving Strategy Review, p. 795)*

39. The area of a poster board is 1000 square inches. You cut it in half repeatedly, setting aside one half each time. How many cuts will you make before the area of the remaining piece is less than 1 square inch? *(Problem Solving Strategy Review, p. 795)*

40. You are dividing a sheet of paper into rectangles by folding it in thirds. You fold the paper 3 times into thirds without opening it. How many rectangles do you have? How many rectangles will you have if you fold the paper in thirds one more time? *(Problem Solving Strategy Review, p. 795)*

41. Three boxes of different sizes are stacked on a table, with the largest box on the bottom and the smallest box on the top. You need to move the whole stack of boxes onto another table, but you can only move one box at a time. Also, no box can touch the floor, and no box can support a larger box without breaking. In addition to the table the boxes will be moved to, there is one other table in the room. All the tables are just large enough to hold the stack of boxes. List the moves it takes you to transfer the boxes. *(Problem Solving Strategy Review, p. 795)*

Table 1     Table 2     Table 3

42. You have an ATM card for your savings account, but you forgot your four-digit personal identification number (PIN). You know that the first digit is a 4 and the last three digits include a 4, a 2, and a 6. How many possibilities are there for your PIN? *(Problem Solving Strategy Review, p. 795)*

43. Darryl, Carlene, Tyrone, and Penelope are in line in that order for lunch at the cafeteria. Carlene lets Penelope cut in front of her. Darryl lets Tyrone cut in back of him. Tyrone then lets Carlene cut in front of him. In what order are they now? *(Problem Solving Strategy Review, p. 795)*

# Extra Practice

## Chapter 1

**1.1**  **The frequency table shows the heights of 30 students.**

| Height (inches) | 54–55.9 | 56–57.9 | 58–59.9 | 60–61.9 | 62–63.9 | 64–65.9 | 66–67.9 | 68–69.9 |
|---|---|---|---|---|---|---|---|---|
| Frequency | 1 | 2 | 4 | 5 | 7 | 6 | 3 | 2 |

1. Make a histogram of the data shown in the frequency table.

2. Which height interval has the greatest number of students?

3. Can you use the histogram to determine the number of students who are between 60 and 69.9 inches tall? *Explain.*

**1.2**  **Evaluate the expression.**

4. $15 - 3 \cdot 2 + 4$

5. $42 \div [(5 - 2) \cdot (1 + 1)]$

6. $2 + \dfrac{100 - 36}{7 + 9}$

7. $4 \cdot 7 - 8 \cdot 3$

8. $3 + 10 \cdot 5 \div 2$

9. $(11 - 56 \div 8) \cdot 9$

**1.3**  **Evaluate the expression when $r = 1.5$ and $s = 2.4$.**

10. $10r + s$

11. $\dfrac{7s}{r + 0.5}$

12. $8rs$

13. $3(r + s)$

**1.4**  **Evaluate the expression.**

14. $24 - (2^3 + 1) \cdot 2$

15. $6^3 \div (2 + 1)^2 + 3$

16. $(8 - 5)^4 + 7 \cdot 5^2$

**1.5**  **In Exercises 17–24, solve the equation using mental math.**

17. $5n = 35$

18. $\dfrac{60}{t} = 4$

19. $12 + w = 75$

20. $41 - a = 23$

21. $9 + b = 17$

22. $63 - c = 10$

23. $6x = 54$

24. $\dfrac{m}{12} = 9$

**1.6**  25. Find the perimeter and area of a rectangular garden with a length of 13 feet and a width of 8 feet.

26. Ramon jogs at a rate of 5 miles per hour. How far does he jog in 1.5 hours?

27. Find the side length of a square that has a perimeter of 32 centimeters.

**1.7**  28. You do 5 hours of yard work each day for 4 days and earn $6 per hour. Then you buy 2 concert tickets for $12 each. Use the problem solving plan to find how much money you have left.

# Chapter 2

**2.1**  **Use a number line to order the integers from least to greatest.**

**1.** $33, -24, -43, 7, 19, -2$

**2.** $-230, 157, -68, -146, 5, 94$

**Write the opposite and the absolute value of the integer.**

**3.** $-25$

**4.** $467$

**5.** $0$

**6.** $|-2|$

**2.2**  **Find the sum.**

**7.** $342 + (-751)$

**8.** $-147 + 71$

**9.** $-89 + 268$

**10.** $-29 + (-51) + 36$

**11.** $-78 + 65 + 13$

**12.** $93 + (-57) + (-102)$

**2.3**  **Find the difference.**

**13.** $-12 - 4$

**14.** $10 - 13$

**15.** $34 - (-17)$

**16.** $-18 - (-17)$

**17.** $23 - 38$

**18.** $81 - (-16)$

**19.** $-9 - (-77)$

**20.** $-63 - 19$

**2.4**  **Find the product.**

**21.** $(-7)(-50)$

**22.** $25(-7)$

**23.** $-4(16)$

**24.** $(-12)(-21)$

**25.** $-95(0)(-58)$

**26.** $54(-1)(5)$

**27.** $8(-2)(-3)(5)$

**28.** $(-14)(4)(6)(9)$

**2.5**  **In Exercises 29–32, find the quotient.**

**29.** $\dfrac{96}{-8}$

**30.** $\dfrac{-48}{-12}$

**31.** $\dfrac{0}{4}$

**32.** $\dfrac{-80}{5}$

**33.** Find the mean of the data: $-8, 6, 3, -20, -9, 4$.

**2.6**  **Evaluate the expression. Justify each step.**

**34.** $-28 + (74 - 32)$

**35.** $7\left(2 \cdot \dfrac{3}{7}\right)$

**36.** $(-7.2 + 3.5) + (-3.5)$

**2.7**  **Use the distributive property to evaluate or simplify the expression.**

**37.** $-5(-3 + 8)$

**38.** $3(m - 4)$

**39.** $-1(4 + 9r)$

**40.** $8(-4j - 3)$

**Simplify the expression by combining like terms.**

**41.** $-x + 3y - 5y + 6x$

**42.** $2(3k - 6) + 4 + 5k$

**43.** $5a - 3(2a + b) - 7b$

**2.8**  **Plot the point in a coordinate plane and describe its location.**

**44.** $A(3, -2)$

**45.** $B(5, 1)$

**46.** $C(0, -4)$

**47.** $D(-1, -3)$

# Chapter 3

### 3.1 Solve the equation. Check your solution.

**1.** $n - 3 = 5$

**2.** $36 = p + 20$

**3.** $-4 = h - 9$

**4.** $27 + z = 51$

### 3.2 Solve the equation. Check your solution.

**5.** $32 = \dfrac{x}{2}$

**6.** $11k = -55$

**7.** $76 = 19r$

**8.** $\dfrac{y}{-1.4} = -5$

### 3.3 Solve the equation. Check your solution.

**9.** $5a - 2 = 33$

**10.** $\dfrac{d}{3} + 8 = -6$

**11.** $-1 = 14 - 2h$

**12.** $84 - z = 96$

**13.** $\dfrac{c}{4} + 7 = 12$

**14.** $47 = -6y + 5$

**15.** $73 = 15 - b$

**16.** $55 = 7t - 8$

### 3.4 In Exercises 17 and 18, translate the statement into an equation. Then solve the equation.

**17.** Five less than the product of 6 and a number is 13.

**18.** The sum of 5 and the quotient of a number and 3 is $-1$.

**19.** An auto repair shop charges \$48 per hour for labor plus the cost of parts. Your car needs new parts that cost \$129, and the total cost is \$201. How much time is required to repair the car?

### 3.5 Find the area and perimeter of the triangle.

**20.**

**21.**

**22.**

**23.** A rectangle has an area of 60 square meters and a length of 12 meters. What is the width of the rectangle? What is the perimeter?

**24.** A square has an area of 81 square feet. What is the length of each side?

### 3.6 Solve the inequality. Then graph its solution.

**25.** $4 + j \geq -1$

**26.** $0 < m - 6$

**27.** $z + 4.5 \leq 2$

**28.** $-38 > t - 46$

### 3.7 Solve the inequality. Then graph its solution.

**29.** $5x < -25$

**30.** $3 \leq -\dfrac{1}{3}y$

**31.** $2 \geq \dfrac{s}{4}$

**32.** $-13k > -65$

# Chapter 4

**4.1** **Write the prime factorization of the number.**

**1.** 72      **2.** 65      **3.** 153      **4.** 196

**Factor the monomial.**

**5.** $25pq$      **6.** $7a^3$      **7.** $22xy^2$      **8.** $54s^2t$

**4.2** **Find the greatest common factor of the numbers or monomials.**

**9.** 45, 75      **10.** 108, 162

**11.** $6bc,\ 35abc^2$      **12.** $4p^2,\ 18qr$

**13.** $21mn,\ 9km^2$      **14.** $14x^2y^3,\ 28xy^2$

**15.** $34w^2z^2,\ 51w^5z^4$      **16.** $abcdf,\ a^2d^3gh$

**4.3** **Write the fraction in simplest form.**

**17.** $\dfrac{32}{64}$    **18.** $\dfrac{-15}{39}$    **19.** $\dfrac{-22}{77}$    **20.** $\dfrac{17}{51}$

**21.** $\dfrac{10x}{45xy}$    **22.** $\dfrac{-16mn}{40mn}$    **23.** $\dfrac{-6ab}{4bc}$    **24.** $\dfrac{28rs}{7rst}$

**4.4** **Find the least common multiple of the numbers or monomials.**

**25.** 30, 60      **26.** $4x,\ 18xy^2$

**27.** $5ab^2,\ 3bc^2$      **28.** $12x^3y,\ 8x^2y^4$

**4.5** **Copy and complete the statement with <, >, or =.**

**29.** $\dfrac{7}{8}\ \underset{?}{\_}\ \dfrac{9}{11}$    **30.** $3\dfrac{3}{5}\ \underset{?}{\_}\ \dfrac{11}{3}$    **31.** $\dfrac{17}{6}\ \underset{?}{\_}\ 2\dfrac{13}{18}$    **32.** $1\dfrac{10}{15}\ \underset{?}{\_}\ \dfrac{35}{21}$

**33.** $\dfrac{11}{10}\ \underset{?}{\_}\ 1\dfrac{1}{8}$    **34.** $\dfrac{4}{5}\ \underset{?}{\_}\ \dfrac{6}{11}$    **35.** $\dfrac{50}{9}\ \underset{?}{\_}\ 5\dfrac{2}{7}$    **36.** $\dfrac{63}{15}\ \underset{?}{\_}\ 4\dfrac{5}{12}$

**4.6** **Simplify the expression. Write your answer as a power.**

**37.** $z^5 \cdot z$    **38.** $5^8 \cdot 5^4$    **39.** $(-7)^6 \cdot (-7)^3$    **40.** $a^2 \cdot a^4$

**41.** $\dfrac{6^9}{6^5}$    **42.** $\dfrac{(-8)^{12}}{(-8)^2}$    **43.** $\dfrac{(-v)^7}{(-v)^4}$    **44.** $\dfrac{c^9}{c}$

**4.7** **Simplify. Write the expression using only positive exponents.**

**45.** $6k^{-1}$    **46.** $a^3 \cdot a^{-3}$    **47.** $\dfrac{s^{-3}}{s^4}$    **48.** $n^{-4} \cdot n^{-2}$

**4.8** **Write the number in scientific notation.**

**49.** 124,000,000    **50.** 0.0000005    **51.** 0.0000791    **52.** 32,100

**Write the number in standard form.**

**53.** $2.7 \times 10^{-3}$    **54.** $9.09 \times 10^2$    **55.** $5.88 \times 10^{11}$    **56.** $6.2 \times 10^{-8}$

# Chapter 5

**5.1** **Find the sum or difference.**

1. $\dfrac{7}{8} + \dfrac{5}{8}$

2. $5\dfrac{1}{5} - 3\dfrac{4}{5}$

3. $-\dfrac{11m}{15} + \dfrac{m}{15}$

4. $-\dfrac{5a}{9b} - \dfrac{4a}{9b}$

**5.2** **Find the sum or difference.**

5. $\dfrac{9}{10} - \dfrac{5}{6}$

6. $\dfrac{2}{5} - \dfrac{3}{7}$

7. $4\dfrac{1}{4} + 3\dfrac{7}{8}$

8. $-\dfrac{5}{12} + \dfrac{11}{16}$

**5.3** **Find the product.**

9. $\dfrac{7}{8} \cdot \dfrac{3}{14}$

10. $5 \cdot \left(-3\dfrac{1}{4}\right)$

11. $-\dfrac{5}{18} \cdot 1\dfrac{1}{3}$

12. $-1\dfrac{3}{5} \cdot \left(-2\dfrac{1}{4}\right)$

**5.4** **Find the quotient.**

13. $\dfrac{5}{9} \div 2$

14. $-\dfrac{7}{12} \div \dfrac{2}{3}$

15. $4\dfrac{1}{8} \div \left(-1\dfrac{1}{3}\right)$

16. $-2\dfrac{1}{2} \div (-10)$

**5.5** **Write the fraction or mixed number as a decimal. Write the decimal as a fraction or mixed number.**

17. $-\dfrac{48}{125}$

18. $4\dfrac{11}{12}$

19. $-0.28$

20. $0.\overline{72}$

21. $0.006$

22. $-8.34$

23. $3\dfrac{7}{8}$

24. $-\dfrac{16}{250}$

**Order the numbers from least to greatest.**

25. $-\dfrac{7}{3}, -2\dfrac{5}{12}, -2.43, -2.5, -2\dfrac{2}{5}$

26. $\dfrac{18}{5}, 3\dfrac{1}{3}, 3.8, 3.55, 3\dfrac{7}{12}$

27. $\dfrac{26}{5}, 5.3, 5\dfrac{2}{9}, 5.21, 5\dfrac{3}{8}$

28. $-4.2, -4\dfrac{1}{6}, -\dfrac{59}{14}, -4\dfrac{3}{7}, -4.04$

**5.6** **Find the sum or difference.**

29. $7.21 + (-3.4)$

30. $-9.8 + (-3.7)$

31. $0.8 - (-12.3)$

32. $8.217 - 9.68$

33. $-10.2 + (-6.35)$

34. $-8.78 + 3.9$

35. $3.28 - 11.395$

36. $-0.04 - 5.789$

**5.7** **Find the product or quotient.**

37. $-8.32 \cdot (-0.47)$

38. $-20.51 \cdot 3.14$

39. $0.435 \div 0.29$

40. $2.072 \div (-0.74)$

41. $4.7 \cdot (-6.78)$

42. $-0.14 \cdot (-9.43)$

43. $-19.27 \div 2.35$

44. $0.224 \div 5.6$

**5.8** **Find the mean, median, mode(s), and range of the data.**

45. Finishing times for a race in minutes: 24, 37, 57, 81, 31, 25, 43, 39, 33, 40, 34, 65, 50

46. Daily low temperatures: $-6°F, -7°F, -6°F, 5°F, 3°F, 0°F, -3°F$

47. Grades on quizzes: 93, 84, 100, 95, 89, 78, 78, 85, 83, 95

# Chapter 6

**6.1** **Solve the equation. Then check the solution.**

**1.** $6k - 8 - 4k = 6$　　　**2.** $16 = 2(s + 9) - 4$　　　**3.** $5(n + 7) + 1 = -9$

**4.** $-8 = -3m + 2 + 5m$　　**5.** $\dfrac{7a - 2}{3} = 4$　　　**6.** $2 = \dfrac{3 - 4t}{5}$

**6.2** **Solve the equation. Then check the solution.**

**7.** $3a + 2 = 7a + 10$　　　**8.** $9y - 8 = 6y + 7$　　　**9.** $5x + 7 = 8(x - 1)$

**10.** $13v = 7(9 - v)$　　　**11.** $5(w + 3) = -10w$　　　**12.** $2(z + 5) = 3z + 14$

**6.3** **Solve the equation. Then check the solution.**

**13.** $2.8y + 8.6 = 9.12 - 1.2y$　　**14.** $7.25p - 3 + p = 14.325$　　**15.** $7 - 2.65z = -4.4z$

**16.** $x - \dfrac{2}{3}x = \dfrac{3}{4}$　　　**17.** $\dfrac{9}{10}n + \dfrac{1}{5} = \dfrac{7}{10}n - \dfrac{3}{5}$　　　**18.** $\dfrac{6}{4}r - \dfrac{21}{8} = \dfrac{3}{4}r$

**6.4** **Find the indicated measurement, where $r$ = radius, $d$ = diameter, and $C$ = circumference. Use 3.14 or $\dfrac{22}{7}$ for $\pi$. Explain your choice of value for $\pi$.**

**19.** $r = \underline{\ ?\ }$　　　**20.** $C = \underline{\ ?\ }$　　　**21.** $r = \underline{\ ?\ }$　　　**22.** $d = \underline{\ ?\ }$

**6.5** **Solve the inequality. Then graph the solution.**

**23.** $19 - 8c > 3$　　　　　　　　**24.** $2(7 + n) \le -10$

**25.** $5s + 3 \ge -7 - 5s$　　　　　　**26.** $20 - 11x \ge -2$

**27.** $4(b - 3) > 20$　　　　　　　　**28.** $-6y - 13 < 11 + 2y$

**6.6** **In Exercises 29–32, write the sentence as an inequality. Let $n$ represent the unknown number. Then solve the inequality.**

**29.** Twelve more than half a number is at most 8.

**30.** The difference of 3 times a number and 2 is greater than 7.

**31.** Four times a number is no less than 16.

**32.** The quotient of 18 and 6 times a number is less than 3.

**33.** You want to ride your bike for at least 28 miles. You have already biked for 10 miles. If you bike at a speed of 12 miles per hour, how much longer do you need to bike?

**34.** Nathan has $20 to spend at a carnival. The carnival has a $10 entrance fee. Ride tickets cost $.75 each. What number of tickets can Nathan buy?

# Chapter 7

**7.1**  **A baseball team had 12 wins, 4 losses, and 2 ties in one season. Write the ratio as a fraction in simplest form and two other ways.**

**1.** wins to losses

**2.** losses to games played

**3.** wins to games played

**Write the equivalent rate.**

**4.** $\dfrac{9000 \text{ tickets}}{6 \text{ hours}} = \dfrac{? \text{ tickets}}{\text{hour}}$

**5.** $\dfrac{240 \text{ tickets}}{\text{hours}} = \dfrac{? \text{ tickets}}{\text{minute}}$

**6.** $\dfrac{7 \text{ meters}}{\text{second}} = \dfrac{? \text{ meters}}{\text{minute}}$

**7.2**  **Solve the proportion. Then check your solution.**

**7.** $\dfrac{x}{18} = \dfrac{25}{2}$

**8.** $\dfrac{4}{9} = \dfrac{5}{y}$

**9.** $\dfrac{3.6}{n} = \dfrac{4.8}{12.4}$

**10.** $\dfrac{m}{6} = \dfrac{35}{42}$

**7.3**  **Use a percent proportion.**

**11.** 9 is what percent of 75?

**12.** 42 is 25% of what number?

**13.** What number is 7% of 128?

**14.** 7 is what percent of 56?

**7.4**  **Write the decimal or fraction as a percent.**

**15.** 0.125

**16.** 1.42

**17.** $\dfrac{18}{25}$

**18.** $\dfrac{197}{200}$

**Write the percent as a decimal and as a fraction.**

**19.** 31%

**20.** 55%

**21.** 175%

**22.** 1.28%

**7.5**  **In Exercises 23–25, tell whether the change is an *increase* or *decrease*. Then find the percent of change.**

**23.** Original amount: 25
New amount: 28

**24.** Original amount: 144
New amount: 126

**25.** Original amount: 5000
New amount: 4950

**7.6**  **26.** A pair of shoes has a wholesale price of $28. The percent markup is 110%. What is the retail price?

**27.** Your food bill at a restaurant is $18.40. You leave a 15% tip. The sales tax is 5%. Find the total cost of the meal.

**7.7**  **Solve using the percent equation.**

**28.** What number is 121% of 412?

**29.** 13 is 15.6% of what number?

**30.** 57 is what percent of 76?

**31.** What number is 0.3% of 28?

**7.8**  **A bag contains 12 slips of paper numbered from 1 through 12. A slip of paper is chosen at random. Find the probability of the event.**

**32.** Drawing a number greater than 4

**33.** Drawing a number that is divisible by 5

# Chapter 8

**8.1** Find the measure(s) of the numbered angle(s).

**1.**

**2.**

**3.**

**8.2** Find the value of *x*. Classify the triangle by its angles.

**4.**

**5.**

**6.**

**8.3** In Exercises 7–9, classify the quadrilateral.

**7.**

**8.**

**9.**

**8.4** **10.** Find the sum of the angle measures in an 11-gon.

**11.** Find the measure of one angle in a regular 18-gon.

**8.5** In Exercises 12–14, use the diagrams.

**12.** Name all pairs of congruent sides.

**13.** Name all pairs of congruent angles.

**14.** Explain how you know that $\triangle ABC \cong \triangle PQR$.

In Exercises 15–21, graph $\triangle ABC$ with vertices $A(-2, 4)$, $B(0, 2)$, and $C(-2, -6)$. Then graph its image after the given transformation.

**8.6** **15.** Reflect $\triangle ABC$ in the *x*-axis.

**16.** Reflect $\triangle ABC$ in the *y*-axis.

**8.7** **17.** Translate $\triangle ABC$ using $(x, y) \rightarrow (x - 1, y + 4)$.

**18.** Translate $\triangle ABC$ using $(x, y) \rightarrow (x + 2, y - 3)$.

**19.** Rotate $\triangle ABC$ 90° clockwise.

**8.8** **20.** Dilate $\triangle ABC$ by a scale factor of 2.

**21.** Dilate $\triangle ABC$ by a scale factor of $\frac{1}{2}$.

# Chapter 9

**9.1** Use a calculator to approximate the square root. Round to the nearest tenth.

**1.** $\sqrt{52}$         **2.** $\sqrt{9.6}$         **3.** $-\sqrt{738}$         **4.** $-\sqrt{2037}$

Solve the equation. Check your solutions.

**5.** $k^2 = 900$                       **6.** $h^2 - 5 = 44$

**7.** $153 + z^2 = 378$             **8.** $168 = v^2 - 1$

**9.** $a^2 + 7 = 88$                 **10.** $m^2 = 3600$

**11.** $x^2 - 11 = 53$              **12.** $w^2 + 78 = 478$

**9.2** In Exercises 13–16, graph the pair of numbers on a number line. Then copy and complete the statement with <, >, or =.

**13.** $\sqrt{18}$ ? 4      **14.** $\sqrt{\dfrac{9}{16}}$ ? $\dfrac{3}{4}$      **15.** $-8$ ? $-\sqrt{70}$      **16.** $\dfrac{2}{3}$ ? $\sqrt{\dfrac{1}{9}}$

**17.** Order the decimals $0.12$, $0.\overline{1}$, $0.\overline{12}$, $0.123$, and $0.\overline{123}$ from least to greatest.

**18.** Order the decimals $0.34$, $0.\overline{3}$, $0.\overline{34}$, and $0.334$ from least to greatest.

**9.3** Let $a$ and $b$ represent the lengths of the legs of a right triangle, and let $c$ represent the length of the hypotenuse. Find the unknown length.

**19.** $a = 21$, $b = 28$, $c = $ __?__      **20.** $a = $ __?__, $b = 63$, $c = 65$

**21.** $a = 56$, $b = $ __?__, $c = 65$      **22.** $a = 1.5$, $b = 3.6$, $c = $ __?__

**23.** $a = $ __?__, $b = 100$, $c = 125$      **24.** $a = 32$, $b = $ __?__, $c = 68$

**9.4** Determine whether the numbers form a Pythagorean triple.

**25.** 40, 42, 58                      **26.** 37, 39, 54

**27.** 15, 112, 113                 **28.** 12, 35, 38

**9.5** Find the values of the variables. Give exact answers.

**29.**

**30.**

**31.**

**9.6** In $\triangle ABC$, write the sine, cosine, and tangent ratios for $\angle A$ and $\angle B$.

**32.**

**33.**

**34.**

**35.** Use a calculator to approximate the sine, cosine, and tangent of $62°$. Round your answers to four decimal places.

# Chapter 10

**10.1**  **Sketch a parallelogram with base _b_ and height _h_ and find its area.**

**1.** $b = 15$ in., $h = 13$ in.    **2.** $b = 9.4$ ft, $h = 4.8$ ft    **3.** $b = 8\frac{1}{3}$ cm, $h = 1\frac{1}{5}$ cm

**Sketch a trapezoid with bases $b_1$ and $b_2$ and height _h_ and find its area.**

**4.** $b_1 = 9$ m, $b_2 = 16$ m, $h = 18$ m    **5.** $b_1 = 40$ yd, $b_2 = 28$ yd, $h = 10.5$ yd

**10.2**  **In Exercises 6–13, find the area of the circle given its radius _r_ or diameter _d_. Use 3.14 for $\pi$.**

**6.** $r = 18$ mi    **7.** $d = 80$ in.

**8.** $d = 11$ mm    **9.** $r = 2.9$ ft

**10.** $d = 7.8$ in.    **11.** $r = 0.3$ cm

**12.** $r = 11$ ft    **13.** $d = 16$ mi

**10.3**  **14.** How many faces, edges, and vertices does a hexagonal pyramid have?

**15.** Show two ways to represent a cylinder. Tell whether it is a polyhedron.

**10.4**  **Draw a net for the solid. Then find the surface area. Round to the nearest tenth.**

**16.**     **17.**     **18.**

**10.5**  **Find the surface area of the solid. Round to the nearest tenth.**

**19.** A square pyramid with base side length 12 m and slant height 9 m

**20.** A cone with radius 8 cm and slant height 9 cm

**21.** A cone with diameter 15 m and slant height 8.2 m

**10.6**  **Find the volume of the solid. Round to the nearest tenth.**

**22.** The prism in Exercise 16

**23.** The prism in Exercise 17

**24.** The cylinder in Exercise 18

**10.7**  **Find the volume of the solid. Round to the nearest tenth.**

**25.** A square pyramid with base side length 10 ft and height 8 ft

**26.** A cone with radius 18 m and height 6 m

**27.** The triangular pyramid shown at the right

# Chapter 11

**11.1**    **1.** Decide whether the relation $(-3, 3)$, $(-2, 2)$, $(-1, 1)$, $(0, 0)$, $(1, 1)$ is a function. Explain your answer.

       **2.** Make an input-output table for the function $y = 0.5x$. Use a domain of $-4$, $-2$, $0$, $2$, and $4$. Identify the range.

       **3.** Write a function rule that relates $x$ and $y$.

| Input x | −5 | −3 | −1 | 1 |
|---------|----|----|----|---|
| Output y | −6 | −4 | −2 | 0 |

**11.2**    **4.** Make a scatter plot of the data in Exercise 3. Describe the relationship between $x$ and $y$.

**11.3**    **Tell whether the ordered pair is a solution of the equation.**

       **5.** $y = 3x - 7$; $(1, 4)$        **6.** $4x + y = 5$; $(2, -1)$        **7.** $y = \frac{1}{2}x + \frac{1}{2}$; $(-3, -1)$

       **List four solutions of the equation.**

       **8.** $y = -x - 3$                       **9.** $y = 7 + 2x$

       **10.** $y = -\frac{2}{3}x$                     **11.** $y = -x$

       **12.** $-x + y = 1$                    **13.** $3x + y = -2$

       **14.** $x + 2y = 8$                     **15.** $-3y + 4x = 7$

**11.4**    **Graph the linear equation.**

       **16.** $y = -3$        **17.** $y = \frac{1}{4}x - 2$        **18.** $x = 4$        **19.** $3x + y = 4$

**11.5**    **In Exercises 20–23, find the intercepts of the graph of the equation.**

       **20.** $y = -2x + 4$        **21.** $y = 5x - 1$        **22.** $x + 5y = -5$        **23.** $2x - 3y = 12$

       **24.** Graph the line with an $x$-intercept of 4 and a $y$-intercept of $-1$.

       **25.** Graph the line with an $x$-intercept of $-2$ and a $y$-intercept of 10.

**11.6**    **Find the slope of the line passing through the points.**

       **26.** $(-2, 3)$, $(6, 1)$                 **27.** $(5, 0)$, $(5, -9)$

       **28.** $(6, -4)$, $(2, -4)$             **29.** $(7, -5)$, $(-2, -14)$

       **30.** $(-7, 8)$, $(-9, 5)$             **31.** $(-3, -2)$, $(-7, 2)$

       **32.** $(4, 9)$, $(3, 13)$               **33.** $(0, 7)$, $(-3, -10)$

**11.7**    **Find the slope and $y$-intercept of the graph of the equation.**

       **34.** $y = 3x - 5$        **35.** $y = 2$        **36.** $y = -\frac{1}{3}x + 1$        **37.** $2x - y = 8$

**11.8**    **Graph the inequality.**

       **38.** $y > -x - 3$        **39.** $6 \le 3y$        **40.** $5 + 2x > y$        **41.** $4x + 3y \le -12$

# Chapter 12

**In Exercises 1–3, use the following lengths, in inches, of alligators at an alligator farm: 140, 127, 103, 140, 118, 100, 117, 101, 116, 129, 130, 105, 99, 143.**

**12.1**

1. Make an ordered stem-and-leaf plot of the data. Identify the interval that includes the most data values.

2. Find the median and range of the data.

**12.2**

3. Make a box-and-whisker plot of the data. What conclusions can you make?

**12.3**

4. In a survey about favorite kinds of movies, 20 people chose dramas, 4 chose horror movies, 8 chose science fiction, and 18 chose comedies. Represent the data in a circle graph.

5. You want to display the average monthly price of a stock for each month in 2001. What type of display would you use? Explain.

**12.4**

6. You can take one of three different classes in the morning or the afternoon. Make a tree diagram to find the number of choices that are possible.

7. A license plate has 3 digits followed by 3 letters. How many different license plates are possible?

**12.5** **In Exercises 8–11, find the number of permutations.**

8. $_7P_2$

9. $_{11}P_1$

10. $_8P_5$

11. $_{10}P_3$

12. There are 8 students in the school play. How many different ways can the cast be arranged in a row?

**12.6** **In Exercises 13–16, find the number of combinations.**

13. $_5C_4$

14. $_{20}C_2$

15. $_6C_3$

16. $_{12}C_9$

17. A CD case holds 30 CDs. How many ways can you select 3 CDs from the case?

**12.7**

18. A telephone number is chosen at random. Find the odds that the last digit is greater than 3.

**12.8**

19. You flip two coins. Find the probability that you do *not* get two heads.

20. You and two friends each roll a number cube. What is the probability that all of you roll a 3?

21. Ten slips of paper numbered 1 through 10 are placed in a bag. You draw a slip at random and draw another without replacing the first. Find the probability that both numbers are odd.

# Chapter 13

**13.1**  In Exercises 1–3, simplify the polynomial and write it in standard form.

**1.** $3 + 5x - x^2 - 7x + 4$      **2.** $2t^4 + t^3 - 6 - 3t^3 + t^2$      **3.** $4(5 - k) + 4k - k^2 + 1$

**4.** The height, in feet, of a falling pebble after $t$ seconds of falling from a height of 45 feet can be found using the polynomial $-16t^2 + 45$. Find the pebble's height after 1.5 seconds.

**13.2**  Find the sum or difference.

**5.** $(3x^2 + 5x - 4) + (-2x^3 + x^2 + 9x)$      **6.** $(-8x^2 - x + 1) - (7x^2 - 5x + 1)$

**7.** $(4x^3 - 8x^2 + 2) - (x^3 + x^2 - 6x + 5)$      **8.** $(-x^2 - 3x + 7) + (x^2 + 4x - 9)$

**9.** $(2x^3 - 2x^2 + 1) + (-x^3 + 9x + 5)$      **10.** $(3x^2 - 5x - 10) - (5x^3 + x - 2)$

**13.3**  Simplify the expression.

**11.** $(4z)(-7z^5)$                            **12.** $(-r^2)(-3r^2)$

**13.** $-3n(2n - 5)$                     **14.** $q^3(-q + 2)$

**15.** $(5ab)^3$                                 **16.** $(-rst)^4$

**17.** $(p^6)^4$                                  **18.** $(3y^5)^2$

**13.4**  Find the product and simplify.

**19.** $(2x + 1)(x - 5)$                   **20.** $(m - 3)(-m + 4)$

**21.** $(d + 6)(d + 4)$                   **22.** $(4y - 3)(4y + 3)$

**23.** $(a - 8)(a - 7)$                   **24.** $(5x + 2)(2x - 1)$

**13.5**  Rewrite using function notation.

**25.** $y = 2x - 5$          **26.** $y = 3x^2$               **27.** $y = 5x^2 + 1$

Evaluate the function for $x = -2, -1, 0, 1,$ and 2.

**28.** $f(x) = 2x^2 + x$       **29.** $f(x) = \frac{1}{4}x^2$          **30.** $f(x) = \frac{1}{2}x^2 - x$

**31.** $f(x) = -3x^2 + 2x$     **32.** $f(x) = x^2 + 4x$       **33.** $f(x) = -x^2 - 3$

Graph the function using a table of values.

**34.** $f(x) = 3x^2$          **35.** $f(x) = -x^2 + 2$      **36.** $f(x) = 2x^2 - 4$

Tell whether the graph represents a function.

**37.**             **38.**             **39.**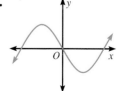

# Tables

## Table of Symbols

| Symbol | Meaning | Page |
|---|---|---|
| 26.10 | decimal point | **2** |
| $=$ | equals, is equal to | **8, 26** |
| $3 \cdot x$ <br> $3(x)$ <br> $3x$ | 3 times $x$ | **8, 13** |
| $\dfrac{14}{2}$ | 14 divided by 2 | **9** |
| ( ) | parentheses—a grouping symbol | **9** |
| [ ] | brackets—a grouping symbol | **9** |
| $4^3$ | $4 \cdot 4 \cdot 4$ | **19** |
| $\stackrel{?}{=}$ | is equal to? | **27** |
| $\neq$ | is not equal to | **27** |
| ⌐ | right angle | **32, 403** |
| $\approx$ | is approximately equal to | **38** |
| . . . | continues on | **57** |
| $-3$ | negative 3 | **57** |
| $-3$ | the opposite of 3 | **58** |
| $|a|$ | the absolute value of a number $a$ | **58** |
| $(x, y)$ | ordered pair | **94** |
| $<$ | is less than | **148, 324** |
| $>$ | is greater than | **148, 324** |
| $\leq$ | is less than or equal to | **148, 324** |
| $\geq$ | is greater than or equal to | **148, 324** |
| $1.1\overline{6}$ | repeating decimal $1.16666\ldots$ | **255** |

| Symbol | Meaning | Page |
|---|---|---|
| $\pi$ | pi—a number approximately equal to 3.14 | **312** |
| $a : b, \dfrac{a}{b}$ | ratio of $a$ to $b$ | **343** |
| $\%$ | percent | **354** |
| $\circ$ | degree(s) | **403, 776** |
| $\angle A$ | angle with vertex point $A$ | **403, 774** |
| $m\angle B$ | the measure of angle $B$ | **403** |
| $\perp$ | is perpendicular to | **404** |
| $\parallel$ | is parallel to | **405** |
| $\longleftrightarrow \longleftrightarrow$ | parallel lines | **405** |
| $\cong$ | is congruent to | **427** |
| $\overline{AB}$ | line segment $AB$ | **427** |
| $\triangle ABC$ | triangle with vertices $A$, $B$, and $C$ | **428** |
| $A'$ | the image of point $A$ | **433** |
| $\sim$ | is similar to | **447** |
| $\sqrt{a}$ | the positive square root of a number $a$ where $a \geq 0$ | **469** |
| $\pm$ | plus or minus | **471** |
| $\nleq$ | is not less than or equal to | **629** |
| $3!$ | 3 factorial, or $3 \cdot 2 \cdot 1$ | **675** |
| $f(x)$ | the function of $f$ at $x$ | **739** |
| $\overleftrightarrow{AB}$ | line $AB$ | **773** |
| $\overrightarrow{AB}$ | ray $AB$ | **773** |

# Table of Measures

## Time

60 seconds (sec) = 1 minute (min)
60 minutes = 1 hour (h)
24 hours = 1 day (d)
7 days = 1 week (wk)
4 weeks (approx.) = 1 month

$\left.\begin{array}{l}\text{365 days} \\ \text{52 weeks (approx.)} \\ \text{12 months}\end{array}\right\} = 1 \text{ year}$

10 years = 1 decade
100 years = 1 century

## Metric

### Length

10 millimeters (mm) = 1 centimeter (cm)

$\left.\begin{array}{l}\text{100 cm} \\ \text{1000 mm}\end{array}\right\} = 1 \text{ meter (m)}$

1000 m = 1 kilometer (km)

### Area

100 square millimeters $(\text{mm}^2)$ = 1 square centimeter $(\text{cm}^2)$
10,000 $\text{cm}^2$ = 1 square meter $(\text{m}^2)$
10,000 $\text{m}^2$ = 1 hectare (ha)

### Volume

1000 cubic millimeters $(\text{mm}^3)$ = 1 cubic centimeter $(\text{cm}^3)$
1,000,000 $\text{cm}^3$ = 1 cubic meter $(\text{m}^3)$

### Liquid Capacity

$\left.\begin{array}{l}\text{1000 millimeters (mL)} \\ \text{1000 cubic centimeters (cm}^3\text{)}\end{array}\right\} = 1 \text{ liter (L)}$

1000 L = 1 kiloliter (kL)

### Mass

1000 milligrams (mg) = 1 gram (g)
1000 g = 1 kilogram (kg)
1000 kg = 1 metric ton (t)

### Temperature  Degrees Celsius (°C)

0°C = freezing point of water
37°C = normal body temperature
100°C = boiling point of water

## United States Customary

### Length

12 inches (in.) = 1 foot (ft)

$\left.\begin{array}{l}\text{36 in.} \\ \text{3 ft}\end{array}\right\} = 1 \text{ yard (yd)}$

$\left.\begin{array}{l}\text{5280 ft} \\ \text{1760 yd}\end{array}\right\} = 1 \text{ mile (mi)}$

### Area

144 square inches (in.$^2$) = 1 square foot (ft$^2$)
9 ft$^2$ = 1 square yard (yd$^2$)

$\left.\begin{array}{l}\text{43,560 ft}^2 \\ \text{4840 yd}^2\end{array}\right\} = 1 \text{ acre (A)}$

### Volume

1728 cubic inches (in.$^3$) = 1 cubic foot (ft$^3$)
27 ft$^3$ = 1 cubic foot (yd$^3$)

### Liquid Capacity

8 fluid ounces (fl oz) = 1 cup (c)
2 c = 1 pint (pt)
2 pt = 1 quart (qt)
4 qt = 1 gallon (gal)

### Weight

16 ounces (oz) = 1 pound (lb)
2000 lb = 1 ton

### Temperature  Degrees Fahrenheit (°F)

32°F = freezing point of water
98.6°F = normal body temperature
212°F = boiling point of water

TABLES

# Table of Formulas

# Table of Properties

| **Number Properties** |
|---|

### Identity Properties *(pp. 64, 74)*

**Addition** The sum of a number and the additive identity, 0, is the number.

**Numbers** $7 + 0 = 7$
**Algebra** $a + 0 = a$

**Multiplication** The product of a number and and the multiplicative identity, 1, is the number.

**Numbers** $3 \cdot 1 = 3$
**Algebra** $a \cdot 1 = a$

---

### Inverse Properties *(pp. 64, 247)*

**Addition** The sum of a number and its additive inverse, or opposite, is 0.

**Numbers** $4 + (-4) = 0$

**Algebra** $a + (-a) = 0$

**Multiplication** The product of a nonzero number and its multiplicative inverse, or reciprocal, is 1.

**Numbers** $\dfrac{2}{3} \cdot \dfrac{3}{2} = 1$

**Algebra** $\dfrac{a}{b} \cdot \dfrac{b}{a} = 1 \ (a, b \neq 0)$

---

### Commutative Property *(p. 83)*

**Addition** In a sum, you can add terms in any order.

**Numbers** $-2 + 5 = 5 + (-2)$
**Algebra** $a + b = b + a$

**Multiplication** In a product, you can multiply factors in any order.

**Numbers** $3(-6) = -6(3)$
**Algebra** $ab = ba$

---

### Associative Property *(p. 84)*

**Addition** Changing the grouping of terms in a sum will not change the sum.

**Numbers** $(2 + 4) + 6 = 2 + (4 + 6)$
**Algebra** $(a + b) + c = a + (b + c)$

**Multiplication** Changing the grouping of factors in a product will not change the product.

**Numbers** $(6 \times 2.5) \times 4 = 6 \times (2.5 \times 4)$
**Algebra** $(ab)c = a(bc)$

---

### Distributive Property *(p. 88)*

You can multiply a number and a sum by multiplying each term of the sum by the number and then adding these products. The same property applies to subtraction.

**Numbers** $3(4 + 6) = 3(4) + 3(6)$
**Algebra** $a(b + c) = a(b) + a(c)$

$2(8 - 5) = 2(8) - 2(5)$
$a(b - c) = a(b) - a(c)$

---

### Properties of Exponents *(pp. 202, 203)*

To find the *product of powers* with the same base, add their exponents

**Numbers** $5^2 \cdot 5^3 = 5^{2+3} = 5^5$
**Algebra** $a^b \cdot a^c = a^{b+c}$

To find the *quotient of powers* with the same nonzero base, subtract the denominator's exponent from the numerator's exponent.

**Numbers** $\dfrac{7^4}{7^2} = 7^{4-2} = 7^2$ **Algebra** $\dfrac{a^b}{a^c} = a^{b-c}$

---

### Cross Products Property *(p. 349)*

The cross products of a proportion are equal.

**Numbers** Because $\dfrac{3}{4} = \dfrac{6}{8}$, $3 \cdot 8 = 4 \cdot 6$.

**Algebra** If $\dfrac{a}{b} = \dfrac{c}{d}$, then $ad = bc$, $b, d \neq 0$.

**TABLES**

# Finding Squares and Square Roots

## EXAMPLE 1  Finding a Square

**Find $54^2$.**

Find 54 in the column labeled *No.* (an abbreviation for *Number*). Read across to the column labeled *Square*.

| No. | Square | Sq. Root |
|-----|--------|----------|
| 51 | 2601 | 7.141 |
| 52 | 2704 | 7.211 |
| 53 | 2809 | 7.280 |
| 54 | 2916 | 7.348 |
| 55 | 3025 | 7.416 |

▶ **Answer**  So, $54^2 = 2916$.

## EXAMPLE 2  Finding a Square Root

**Find a decimal approximation of $\sqrt{54}$.**

Find 54 in the column labeled *No.* Read across to the column labeled *Sq. Root*.

| No. | Square | Sq. Root |
|-----|--------|----------|
| 51 | 2601 | 7.141 |
| 52 | 2704 | 7.211 |
| 53 | 2809 | 7.280 |
| 54 | 2916 | 7.348 |
| 55 | 3025 | 7.416 |

▶ **Answer**  So, to the nearest thousandth, $\sqrt{54} \approx 7.348$.

## EXAMPLE 3  Finding a Square Root

**Find a decimal approximation of $\sqrt{3000}$.**

Find the two numbers in the *Square* column that 3000 is between. Read across to the column labeled *No.*; $\sqrt{3000}$ is between 54 and 55, but closer to 55.

| No. | Square | Sq. Root |
|-----|--------|----------|
| 51 | 2601 | 7.141 |
| 52 | 2704 | 7.211 |
| 53 | 2809 | 7.280 |
| 54 | 2916 | 7.348 |
| 55 | 3025 | 7.416 |

▶ **Answer**  So, $\sqrt{3000} \approx 55$. A more accurate approximation can be found using a calculator: 54.772256.

# Table of Squares and Square Roots

| No. | Square | Sq. Root | No. | Square | Sq. Root | No. | Square | Sq. Root |
|---|---|---|---|---|---|---|---|---|
| 1 | 1 | 1.000 | 51 | 2601 | 7.141 | 101 | 10,201 | 10.050 |
| 2 | 4 | 1.414 | 52 | 2704 | 7.211 | 102 | 10,404 | 10.100 |
| 3 | 9 | 1.732 | 53 | 2809 | 7.280 | 103 | 10,609 | 10.149 |
| 4 | 16 | 2.000 | 54 | 2916 | 7.348 | 104 | 10,816 | 10.198 |
| 5 | 25 | 2.236 | 55 | 3025 | 7.416 | 105 | 11,025 | 10.247 |
| 6 | 36 | 2.449 | 56 | 3136 | 7.483 | 106 | 11,236 | 10.296 |
| 7 | 49 | 2.646 | 57 | 3249 | 7.550 | 107 | 11,449 | 10.344 |
| 8 | 64 | 2.828 | 58 | 3364 | 7.616 | 108 | 11,664 | 10.392 |
| 9 | 81 | 3.000 | 59 | 3481 | 7.681 | 109 | 11,881 | 10.440 |
| 10 | 100 | 3.162 | 60 | 3600 | 7.746 | 110 | 12,100 | 10.488 |
| 11 | 121 | 3.317 | 61 | 3721 | 7.810 | 111 | 12,321 | 10.536 |
| 12 | 144 | 3.464 | 62 | 3844 | 7.874 | 112 | 12,544 | 10.583 |
| 13 | 169 | 3.606 | 63 | 3969 | 7.937 | 113 | 12,769 | 10.630 |
| 14 | 196 | 3.742 | 64 | 4096 | 8.000 | 114 | 12,996 | 10.677 |
| 15 | 225 | 3.873 | 65 | 4225 | 8.062 | 115 | 13,225 | 10.724 |
| 16 | 256 | 4.000 | 66 | 4356 | 8.124 | 116 | 13,456 | 10.770 |
| 17 | 289 | 4.123 | 67 | 4489 | 8.185 | 117 | 13,689 | 10.817 |
| 18 | 324 | 4.243 | 68 | 4624 | 8.246 | 118 | 13,924 | 10.863 |
| 19 | 361 | 4.359 | 69 | 4761 | 8.307 | 119 | 14,161 | 10.909 |
| 20 | 400 | 4.472 | 70 | 4900 | 8.367 | 120 | 14,400 | 10.954 |
| 21 | 441 | 4.583 | 71 | 5041 | 8.426 | 121 | 14,641 | 11.000 |
| 22 | 484 | 4.690 | 72 | 5184 | 8.485 | 122 | 14,884 | 11.045 |
| 23 | 529 | 4.796 | 73 | 5329 | 8.544 | 123 | 15,129 | 11.091 |
| 24 | 576 | 4.899 | 74 | 5476 | 8.602 | 124 | 15,376 | 11.136 |
| 25 | 625 | 5.000 | 75 | 5625 | 8.660 | 125 | 15,625 | 11.180 |
| 26 | 676 | 5.099 | 76 | 5776 | 8.718 | 126 | 15,876 | 11.225 |
| 27 | 729 | 5.196 | 77 | 5929 | 8.775 | 127 | 16,129 | 11.269 |
| 28 | 784 | 5.292 | 78 | 6084 | 8.832 | 128 | 16,384 | 11.314 |
| 29 | 841 | 5.385 | 79 | 6241 | 8.888 | 129 | 16,641 | 11.358 |
| 30 | 900 | 5.477 | 80 | 6400 | 8.944 | 130 | 16,900 | 11.402 |
| 31 | 961 | 5.568 | 81 | 6561 | 9.000 | 131 | 17,161 | 11.446 |
| 32 | 1024 | 5.657 | 82 | 6724 | 9.055 | 132 | 17,424 | 11.489 |
| 33 | 1089 | 5.745 | 83 | 6889 | 9.110 | 133 | 17,689 | 11.533 |
| 34 | 1156 | 5.831 | 84 | 7056 | 9.165 | 134 | 17,956 | 11.576 |
| 35 | 1225 | 5.916 | 85 | 7225 | 9.220 | 135 | 18,225 | 11.619 |
| 36 | 1296 | 6.000 | 86 | 7396 | 9.274 | 136 | 18,496 | 11.662 |
| 37 | 1369 | 6.083 | 87 | 7569 | 9.327 | 137 | 18,769 | 11.705 |
| 38 | 1444 | 6.164 | 88 | 7744 | 9.381 | 138 | 19,044 | 11.747 |
| 39 | 1521 | 6.245 | 89 | 7921 | 9.434 | 139 | 19,321 | 11.790 |
| 40 | 1600 | 6.325 | 90 | 8100 | 9.487 | 140 | 19,600 | 11.832 |
| 41 | 1681 | 6.403 | 91 | 8281 | 9.539 | 141 | 19,881 | 11.874 |
| 42 | 1764 | 6.481 | 92 | 8464 | 9.592 | 142 | 20,164 | 11.916 |
| 43 | 1849 | 6.557 | 93 | 8649 | 9.644 | 143 | 20,449 | 11.958 |
| 44 | 1936 | 6.633 | 94 | 8836 | 9.695 | 144 | 20,736 | 12.000 |
| 45 | 2025 | 6.708 | 95 | 9025 | 9.747 | 145 | 21,025 | 12.042 |
| 46 | 2116 | 6.782 | 96 | 9216 | 9.798 | 146 | 21,316 | 12.083 |
| 47 | 2209 | 6.856 | 97 | 9409 | 9.849 | 147 | 21,609 | 12.124 |
| 48 | 2304 | 6.928 | 98 | 9604 | 9.899 | 148 | 21,904 | 12.166 |
| 49 | 2401 | 7.000 | 99 | 9801 | 9.950 | 149 | 22,201 | 12.207 |
| 50 | 2500 | 7.071 | 100 | 10,000 | 10.000 | 150 | 22,500 | 12.247 |

# Equivalent Fractions, Decimals, and Percents

| Fraction | Decimal | Percent |
|:---:|:---:|:---:|
| $\frac{1}{10}$ | 0.1 | 10% |
| $\frac{1}{8}$ | 0.125 | $12\frac{1}{2}\%$ |
| $\frac{1}{5}$ | 0.2 | 20% |
| $\frac{1}{4}$ | 0.25 | 25% |
| $\frac{3}{10}$ | 0.3 | 30% |
| $\frac{1}{3}$ | $0.\overline{3}$ | $33\frac{1}{3}\%$ |
| $\frac{3}{8}$ | 0.375 | $37\frac{1}{2}\%$ |
| $\frac{2}{5}$ | 0.4 | 40% |
| $\frac{1}{2}$ | 0.5 | 50% |
| $\frac{3}{5}$ | 0.6 | 60% |
| $\frac{5}{8}$ | 0.625 | $62\frac{1}{2}\%$ |
| $\frac{2}{3}$ | $0.\overline{6}$ | $66\frac{2}{3}\%$ |
| $\frac{7}{10}$ | 0.7 | 70% |
| $\frac{3}{4}$ | 0.75 | 75% |
| $\frac{4}{5}$ | 0.8 | 80% |
| $\frac{7}{8}$ | 0.875 | $87\frac{1}{2}\%$ |
| $\frac{9}{10}$ | 0.9 | 90% |
| 1 | 1 | 100% |

# English-Spanish Glossary

## A

**absolute value** (p. 58) The absolute value of a number $a$ is the distance between $a$ and 0 on a number line. The absolute value of $a$ is written $|a|$.

**valor absoluto** (pág. 58) El valor absoluto de un número $a$ es la distancia entre $a$ y 0 en una recta numérica. El valor absoluto de $a$ se escribe $|a|$.

$$|4| = 4 \qquad |-7| = 7 \qquad |0| = 0$$

---

**acute angle** (p. 411) An angle whose measure is less than 90°.

**ángulo agudo** (pág. 411) Un ángulo que mide menos de 90°.

---

**acute triangle** (p. 411) A triangle with three acute angles.

**triángulo acutángulo** (pág. 411) Un triángulo que tiene tres ángulos agudos.

---

**addition property of equality** (p. 118) Adding the same number to each side of an equation produces an equivalent equation.

**propiedad de igualdad en la suma** (pág. 118) Al sumar el mismo número a cada lado de una ecuación se produce una ecuación equivalente.

If $x - 5 = 2$, then $x - 5 + 5 = 2 + 5$, so $x = 7$.
If $x - a = b$, then $x - a + a = b + a$.

Si $x - 5 = 2$, entonces $x - 5 + 5 = 2 + 5$, por lo tanto $x = 7$.
Si $x - a = b$, entonces $x - a + a = b + a$.

---

**additive identity** (p. 64) The number 0 is the additive identity because the sum of any number and 0 is the original number.

**identidad de la suma** (pág. 64) El número 0 es la identidad de la suma porque la suma de cualquier número y 0 es el número original.

$$-7 + 0 = -7$$
$$a + 0 = a$$

---

**additive inverse** (p. 64) The additive inverse of a number $a$ is the opposite of the number, or $-a$. The sum of a number and its additive inverse is 0.

**inverso aditivo** (pág. 64) El inverso aditivo de un número $a$ es el opuesto del número, o $-a$. La suma de un número y su inverso aditivo es 0.

The *additive inverse* of 6 is $-6$, so $6 + (-6) = 0$.

El *inverso aditivo* de 6 es $-6$, por lo tanto $6 + (-6) = 0$.

---

**angle** (p. 774) A figure formed by two rays that begin at a common point, called the vertex.

**ángulo** (pág. 774) Figura formada por dos semirrectas que comienzan en un punto común, llamado vértice.

ray/semirrecta
vertex/vértice
ray/semirrecta

**angle of rotation** (p. 440) In a rotation, the angle formed by two rays drawn from the center of rotation through corresponding points on the original figure and its image.

**ángulo de rotación** (pág. 440) En una rotación, el ángulo formado por dos semirrectas trazadas desde el centro de rotación a través de puntos correspondientes en la figura original y su imagen.

*See* rotation.

*Véase* rotación.

---

**annual interest rate** (p. 376) In simple interest, the percent of the principal earned or paid per year.

**tasa de interés anual** (pág. 376) En interés simple, el porcentaje sobre el capital ganado o pagado por año.

*See* simple interest.

*Véase* interés simple.

---

**area** (p. 32) The number of square units covered by a figure.

**área** (pág. 32) La cantidad de unidades cuadradas que cubre una figura.

2 units/2 unidades

7 units/7 unidades

*Area* = 14 square units

*Área* = 14 unidades cuadradas

---

**associative property of addition** (p. 84) Changing the grouping of terms in a sum does not change the sum.

**propiedad asociativa de la suma** (pág. 84) Cambiar la manera en que se agrupan los términos en una suma no cambia la suma.

$$(9 + 4) + 6 = 9 + (4 + 6)$$
$$(a + b) + c = a + (b + c)$$

---

**associative property of multiplication** (p. 84) Changing the grouping of factors in a product does not change the product.

**propiedad asociativa de la multiplicación** (pág. 84) Cambiar la manera en que se agrupan los factores en un producto no cambia el producto.

$$(2 \cdot 5) \cdot 3 = 2 \cdot (5 \cdot 3)$$
$$(ab)c = a(bc)$$

---

**B**

**bar graph** (p. 3) A type of graph in which the lengths of bars are used to represent and compare data in categories.

**gráfica de barras** (pág. 3) Un tipo de gráfica en el que las longitudes de las barras se usan para representar y comparar datos.

**Annual Sales at an Automobile Dealership**
**Ventas anuales en concesionario automotriz**

Automobiles / Automóviles

400
300
200
100
0

Cars / Carros    Trucks / Camiones    SUVs / SUVs

| | |
|---|---|
| **base of a parallelogram** (p. 521) The length of any side of the parallelogram can be used as the base.<br><br>**base de un paralelogramo** (pág. 521) La longitud de cualquier lado del paralelogramo puede usarse como la base. | <br>height/altura, $h$<br>base/base, $b$ |
| **base of a power** (p. 19) The number or expression that is used as a factor in a repeated multiplication.<br><br>**base de una potencia** (pág. 19) El número o la expresión que se usa como factor en una multiplicación repetida. | In the power $5^3$, the *base* is 5.<br><br>La *base* de la potencia $5^3$ es 5. |
| **base of a triangle** (p. 142) The length of any side of the triangle can be used as the base.<br><br>**base de un triángulo** (pág. 142) La longitud de cualquier lado de un triángulo puede usarse como base. | height/altura, $h$<br>base/base, $b$ |
| **bases of a trapezoid** (p. 522) The lengths of the parallel sides of the trapezoid.<br><br>**bases de un trapecio** (pág. 522) Las longitudes de los lados paralelos de un trapecio. | base/base, $b_1$<br>height/altura, $h$<br>base/base, $b_2$ |
| **biased sample** (p. 702) A sample that is not representative of the population from which it is selected.<br><br>**muestra parcial** (pág. 702) Una muestra que no es representativa de la población de la cual fue seleccionada. | The members of a soccer team are a *biased sample* if you want to find the average time students spend playing sports each week.<br><br>Los miembros de un equipo de fútbol son una *muestra parcial* para determinar la cantidad promedio de tiempo a la semana que los estudiantes practican deportes. |
| **binomial** (p. 717) A polynomial with two terms.<br><br>**binomio** (pág. 717) Polinomio que tiene dos términos. | $7y^4 + 9$ |
| **box-and-whisker plot** (p. 654) A data display that divides a data set into four parts using the lower extreme, lower quartile, median, upper quartile, and upper extreme.<br><br>**diagrama de líneas y bloques** (pág. 654) Diagrama que divide un conjunto de datos en cuatro partes usando el extremo inferior, el cuartil inferior, la mediana, el cuartil superior y el extremo superior. | 0  10  20  30  40  50<br><br>8  19  26  37  45 |

**center of a circle** (p. 312) The point inside the circle that is the same distance from all points on the circle.

**centro de un círculo** (pág. 312) El punto en el interior del círculo que está a la misma distancia de todos los puntos del círculo.

*See* circle.

*Véase* círculo.

---

**center of a rotation** (p. 440) The point about which a figure is turned when the figure undergoes a rotation.

**centro de rotación** (pág. 440) El punto alrededor del cual gira una figura cuando la figura sufre una rotación.

*See* rotation.

*Véase* rotación.

---

**circle** (p. 312) The set of all points in a plane that are the same distance, called the radius, from a fixed point, called the center.

**círculo** (pág. 312) El conjunto de todos los puntos en un plano que están a la misma distancia, llamada radio, de un punto fijo, llamado centro.

---

**circle graph** (p. 360, 659) A circle graph displays data as sections of a circle. The entire circle represents all the data. Each section is labeled using the actual data or using data expressed as fractions, decimals, or percents of the sum of the data.

**gráfica circular** (pág. 360, 659) Una gráfica circular representa los datos como secciones de un círculo. El círculo completo representa todos los datos. Cada sección está rotulada con los datos reales o usando datos expresados como fracciones, decimales o porcentajes de la suma de los datos.

---

**circumference** (p. 312) The distance around a circle.

**circunferencia** (pág. 312) La distancia alrededor de un círculo.

*See* circle.

*Véase* círculo.

---

**coefficient** (p. 89) The number part of a term that includes a variable.

**coeficiente** (pág. 89) La parte numérica de un término que incluye una variable.

The *coefficient* of 7$x$ is 7.

El *coeficiente* de 7$x$ es 7.

---

**combination** (p. 680) A grouping of objects in which the order is not important.

**combinación** (pág. 680) Agrupación de objetos en la que el orden no es importante.

There are 6 *combinations* of 2 letters chosen from VASE:
  VA  VS  VE  AS  AE  SE

Existen 6 *combinaciones* de 2 letras tomadas de la palabra VASO:
  VA  VS  VO  AS  AO  SO

| | |
|---|---|
| **common factor** (p. 181)  A whole number that is a factor of two or more nonzero whole numbers. | The *common factors* of 8 and 12 are 1, 2, and 4. |
| **factor común** (pág. 181)  Un número natural que es factor de dos o más números naturales distintos de cero. | Los *factores comunes* de 8 y 12 son 1, 2 y 4. |
| **common multiple** (p. 192)  A multiple that is shared by two or more numbers. | The *common multiples* of 4 and 6 are 12, 24, 36, . . . . |
| **múltiplo común** (pág. 192)  Un múltiplo compartido por dos o más números. | Los *múltiplos comunes* de 4 y 6 son 12, 24, 36, … |
| **commutative property of addition** (p. 83)  In a sum, you can add terms in any order.  **propiedad conmutativa de la suma** (pág. 83)  En una suma, puedes sumar los términos en cualquier orden. | $$4 + 7 = 7 + 4$$ $$a + b = b + a$$ |
| **commutative property of multiplication** (p. 83)  In a product, you can multiply factors in any order.  **propiedad conmutativa de la multiplicación** (pág. 83) En un producto, puedes multiplicar los factores en cualquier orden. | $$5(-8) = -8(5)$$ $$ab = ba$$ |
| **complementary angles** (p. 403)  Two angles whose measures have a sum of 90°.  **ángulos complementarios** (pág. 403)  Dos ángulos cuyas medidas suman 90°. | |
| **complementary events** (p. 685)  Two events are complementary when one event or the other (but not both) must occur.  **eventos complementarios** (pág. 685)  Dos eventos son complementarios cuando un evento o el otro (no ambos) debe ocurrir. | When rolling a number cube, the events "getting an odd number" and "getting an even number" are *complementary events*.  Al lanzar un cubo numerado, los eventos "obtener un número par" y "obtener un número impar" y son *eventos complementarios* o *complementos*. |
| **complement** (p. 690)  The set of all elements that are in universal set $U$ that are not in set $A$, written as $\sim A$.  **complemento** (pág. 690)  El conjunto de todos los elementos que están en el conjunto universal $U$ y no están en el conjunto $A$, que se expresa como $\sim A$. | |
| **composite number** (p. 177)  A whole number greater than 1 that has positive factors other than 1 and itself.  **número compuesto** (pág. 177)  Un número natural mayor que 1 que tiene factores positivos distintos a 1 y a sí mismo. | 6 is a *composite number* because its factors are 1, 2, 3, and 6.  6 es un *número compuesto* porque sus factores son 1, 2, 3, y 6. |

**compound events** (p. 694) Two or more events that can happen either at the same time or one after the other.

**eventos compuestos** (pág. 694) Dos o más eventos que pueden ocurrir al mismo tiempo o uno después del otro.

*See* independent events *and* dependent events.

*Véase* eventos independientes *y* eventos dependientes.

---

**compound interest** (p. 380) Interest earned on both the principal and on any interest that has already been earned.

**interés compuesto** (pág. 380) Interés que se gana sobre el capital y sobre cualquier interés que ya se ha ganado.

You deposit $250 in an account that earns 4% interest compounded yearly. After 5 years, your account balance is
$y = 250(1 + 0.04)5 \approx $304.16$.

Depositas $250 en una cuenta que gana 4% de interés compuesto anualmente. Después de 5 años, el balance de tu cuenta es
$y = 250(1 + 0.04)5 \approx $304.16$.

---

**cone** (p. 534) A solid with one circular base.

**cono** (pág. 534) Un cuerpo geométrico que tiene una base circular.

base/base

---

**congruent angles** (p. 427) Angles that have the same measure.

**ángulos congruentes** (pág. 427) Ángulos que tienen medidas iguales.

*See* congruent polygons.

*Véase* polígonos congruentes.

---

**congruent polygons** (p. 427) Similar polygons that have the same size. For congruent polygons, corresponding angles are congruent and corresponding sides are congruent. The symbol $\cong$ indicates congruence and is read "is congruent to."

**polígonos congruentes** (pág. 427) Polígonos similares que tienen el mismo tamaño. Para polígonos congruentes, los ángulos correspondientes son congruentes y los lados correspondientes son congruentes. El signo $\cong$ indica congruencia y se lee "es congruente con".

$\triangle ABC \cong \triangle DEF$

---

**congruent segments** (p. 427) Segments that have the same length.

**segmentos congruentes** (pág. 427) Segmentos que tienen igual longitud.

*See* congruent polygons.

*Véase* polígonos congruentes.

---

**constant term** (p. 89) A term that has a number but no variable.

**término constante** (pág. 89) Un término que tiene un número pero no una variable.

In the expression $5y + 9$, the term 9 is a *constant term.*

En la expresión $5y + 9$, el término 9 es un *término constante.*

**converse** (p. 483) An if-then statement where the hypothesis and conclusion of the original statement have been reversed.

Original: If you clean your room, then it will be neat.
*Converse*: If your room is neat, then you cleaned it.

**recíproco** (pág. 483) Un enunciado de tipo si-entonces en el cual la hipótesis y la conclusión del enunciado original se han intercambiado.

Original: Si ordenas tu habitación, entonces estará arreglada.
*Recíproco*: Si tu habitación está arreglada, entonces es que la ordenaste.

---

**coordinate plane** (p. 94) A coordinate system formed by the intersection of a horizontal number line, called the *x*-axis, and a vertical number line, called the *y*-axis.

**plano de coordenadas** (pág. 94) Un sistema de coordenadas formado por la intersección de una recta numérica horizontal, llamada eje *x*, y una recta numérica vertical, llamada eje *y*.

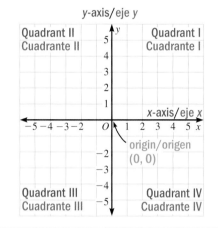

---

**corresponding angles** (p. 427) Angles that occupy corresponding positions when a line intersects two other lines.

**ángulos correspondientes** (pág. 427) Ángulos que ocupan posiciones correspondientes cuando una recta interseca otras dos rectas.

∠1 and ∠2 are *corresponding angles*.

∠1 y ∠2 son *ángulos correspondientes*.

---

**corresponding parts** (p. 427) Pairs of sides and angles of polygons that are in the same relative position.

**elementos correspondientes** (pág. 427) Pares de lados y ángulos de polígonos que están en la misma posición relativa.

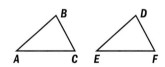

∠A and ∠E are corresponding angles.
$\overline{AB}$ and $\overline{ED}$ are corresponding sides.

∠A y ∠E son ángulos correspondientes.
$\overline{AB}$ y $\overline{ED}$ son lados correspondientes.

---

**cosine** (p. 500) The cosine of any acute angle *A* of a right triangle is the ratio of the adjacent leg to the hypotenuse.

**coseno** (pág. 500) El coseno de cualquier ángulo agudo *A* de un triángulo rectángulo es la razón entre el cateto adyacente y la hipotenusa.

$\cos A = \dfrac{b}{c}$

**counting principle** (p. 671) If one event can occur in $m$ ways, and for each of these a second event can occur in $n$ ways, then the number of ways that the two events can occur together is $m \cdot n$. The counting principle can be extended to three or more events.

**principio de conteo** (pág. 671) Si un evento puede ocurrir de $m$ maneras, y para cada una de éstas un segundo evento puede ocurrir de $n$ maneras, entonces el número de maneras en las que pueden ocurrir ambos eventos juntos es $m \cdot n$. El principio de conteo puede extenderse a tres o más eventos.

If a T-shirt is made in 5 sizes and in 7 colors, then the number of different T-shirts that are possible is $5 \cdot 7 = 35$.

Si una camiseta se hace en 5 tallas y 7 colores, entonces el número de camisetas diferentes posibles es $5 \cdot 7 = 35$.

---

**cross products** (p. 349) For the proportion $\frac{a}{b} = \frac{c}{d}$, where $b \neq 0$ and $d \neq 0$, the cross product are $ad$ and $bc$.

**productos cruzados** (pág. 349) Para la proporción $\frac{a}{b} = \frac{c}{d}$, donde $b \neq 0$ y $d \neq 0$, los productos cruzados son $ad$ y $bc$.

The *cross products* of the proportion $\frac{2}{3} = \frac{4}{6}$ are $2 \cdot 6$ and $3 \cdot 4$.

Los *productos cruzados* de la proporción $\frac{2}{3} = \frac{4}{6}$ son $2 \cdot 6$ y $3 \cdot 4$.

---

**cylinder** (p. 534) A solid with two congruent circular bases that lie in parallel planes.

**cilindro** (pág. 534) Un cuerpo geométrico que tiene dos bases circulares congruentes que se ubican en planos paralelos.

bases/bases

---

# D

**data** (p. 3) Information, facts, or numbers that describe something.

**datos** (pág. 3) Información, hechos o números que describen algo.

Numbers of cars sold annually at a dealership: 340, 350, 345, 347, 352, 360, 365

Número de carros que se venden anualmente en el concesionario: 340, 350, 345, 347, 352, 360, 365

---

**degrees** (p. 776) Unit of measure for angles. The symbol for degrees is °. There are 360° in a circle.

**grados** (pág. 776) Unidad de medida para ángulos. El símbolo para los grados es °. Hay 360° en un círculo.

---

**dependent events** (p. 694) Two events such that the occurrence of one affects the likelihood that the other will occur.

**eventos dependientes** (pág. 694) Dos eventos tales que la ocurrencia de uno afecta la probabilidad de que ocurra el otro.

A bag contains 5 red and 8 blue marbles. You randomly choose a marble, do not replace it, then randomly choose another marble. The events "first marble is red" and "second marble is red" are *dependent events*.

Una bolsa contiene 5 canicas rojas y 8 azules. Tomas una canica al azar y no la reemplazas, luego tomas otra canica al azar. Los eventos "primera canica es roja" y "segunda canica es roja" son *eventos dependientes*.

**diagonal** (p. 417) A segment, other than a side, that connects two vertices of a polygon.

**diagonal** (pág. 417) Un segmento, distinto de un lado, que conecta dos vértices de un polígono.

diagonals/
diagonales

**diameter of a circle** (p. 312) The distance across the circle through the center.

**diámetro de un círculo** (pág. 312) La distancia que atraviesa el círculo por el centro.

*See* circle.

*Véase* círculo.

**dilation** (p. 449) A transformation that stretches or shrinks a figure.

**dilatación** (pág. 449) Una transformación que estira o encoge una figura.

The scale factor is $\frac{1}{2}$.

El factor de escala es $\frac{1}{2}$.

**direct variation** (p. 618) The relationship of two variables $x$ and $y$ if there is a nonzero number $k$ such that $y = kx$ or $k = \frac{y}{x}$.

**variación directa** (pág. 618) La relación entre dos variables $x$ e $y$ cuando hay un número $k$ distinto de cero, de manera tal que $y = kx$ ó $k = \frac{y}{x}$.

$$y = 5x$$
$$y = kx$$

**discount** (p. 370) A decrease in the price of an item.

**descuento** (pág. 370) Una disminución en el precio de un artículo.

The original price of a pair of jeans is $42 but the store sells it for $29.99. The *discount* is $12.01.

El precio original de un par de pantalones es $42, pero la tienda los vende a $29.99. El *descuento* es $12.01.

**distributive property** (p. 88) For all numbers $a$, $b$, and $c$, $a(b + c) = ab + ac$ and $a(b - c) = ab - ac$.

**propiedad distributiva** (pág. 88) Para todos los números $a$, $b$ y $c$, $a(b + c) = ab + ac$ y $a(b - c) = ab - ac$.

$$8(10 + 4) = 8(10) + 8(4)$$
$$3(4 - 2) = 3(4) - 3(2)$$

**division property of equality** (p. 123) Dividing each side of an equation by the same nonzero number produces an equivalent equation.

**propiedad de igualdad en la división** (pág. 123) Al dividir cada lado de una ecuación por el mismo número distinto de cero se obtiene una ecuación equivalente.

If $6x = 54$, then $\frac{6x}{6} = \frac{54}{6}$, so $x = 9$.
If $ax = b$ and $a \neq 0$, then $\frac{ax}{a} = \frac{b}{a}$.

Si $6x = 54$, entonces $\frac{6x}{6} = \frac{54}{6}$, por lo tanto $x = 9$.
Si $ax = b$ y $a \neq 0$, entonces $\frac{ax}{a} = \frac{b}{a}$.

**domain of a function** (p. 584)  The set of all possible input values for the function.

**dominio de una función** (pág. 584)  El conjunto de todos los valores de entrada posibles para la función.

*See* function.

*Véase* función.

---

### E

**edge of a polyhedron** (p. 534)  A line segment where two faces of the polyhedron meet.

**arista de un poliedro** (pág. 534)  Un segmento de recta donde se encuentran dos caras del poliedro.

face
cara

edge
arista

vertex
vértice

---

**element** (p. 690)  An object in a set.

**elemento** (pág. 690)  Un objeto en un conjunto.

5 is an *element* of the set of whole numbers, $W = \{0, 1, 2, 3, 4, 5, \ldots\}$.

5 es un *elemento* en el conjunto de los números naturales $N = \{0, 1, 2, 3, 4, 5, \ldots\}$.

---

**empty set** (p. 690)  The set with no elements, written as $\varnothing$.

**conjunto vacío** (pág. 690)  El conjunto que no tiene elementos, que se expresa como $\varnothing$.

The set of negative whole numbers $= \varnothing$.

El conjunto de los números naturales negativos $= \varnothing$.

---

**equation** (p. 26)  A mathematical sentence formed by setting two expressions equal.

**ecuación** (pág. 26)  Un enunciado matemático que se forma al establecer como iguales dos expresiones.

$3 \cdot 6 = 18$ and $x + 7 = 12$ are *equations*.

$3 \cdot 6 = 18$ y $x + 7 = 12$ son *ecuaciones*.

---

**equilateral triangle** (p. 411)  A triangle with three congruent sides.

**triángulo equilátero** (pág. 411)  Un triángulo que tiene tres lados congruentes.

---

**equivalent equations** (p. 117)  Equations that have the same solution(s).

**ecuaciones equivalentes** (pág. 117)  Ecuaciones que tienen la misma solución o soluciones.

$2x - 6 = 0$ and $2x = 6$ are *equivalent equations* because the solution of both equations is 3.

$2x - 6 = 0$ y $2x = 6$ son *ecuaciones equivalentes* porque la solución de ambas ecuaciones es 3.

---

**equivalent fractions** (p. 187)  Fractions that represent the same part-to-whole relationship. Equivalent fractions have the same simplest form.

**fracciones equivalentes** (pág. 187)  Fracciones que representan la misma relación entre la parte y el todo. Las fracciones equivalentes tienen la misma mínima expresión.

$\frac{6}{8}$ and $\frac{9}{12}$ are *equivalent fractions* that both represent $\frac{3}{4}$.

$\frac{6}{8}$ y $\frac{9}{12}$ son *fracciones equivalentes* porque ambas representan $\frac{3}{4}$.

---

| | |
|---|---|
| **equivalent inequalities** (p. 149) Inequalities that have the same solution.<br><br>**desigualdades equivalentes** (pág. 149) Desigualdades que tienen la misma solución. | $3x \le 12$ and $x \le 4$ are *equivalent inequalities* because the solution of both inequalities is all numbers less than or equal to 4.<br><br>$3x \le 12$ y $x \le 4$ son *desigualdades equivalentes* porque la solución de ambas desigualdades es todos los números menores que o iguales a 4. |
| **equivalent ratios** (p. 343) Ratios that have the same value.<br><br>**razones equivalentes** (pág. 343) Razones que tienen el mismo valor. | $\frac{15}{12}$ and $\frac{25}{20}$ are *equivalent ratios* because $\frac{15}{12} = 1.25$ and $\frac{25}{20} = 1.25$.<br><br>$\frac{15}{12}$ y $\frac{25}{20}$ son *razones equivalentes* porque $\frac{15}{12} = 1.25$ y $\frac{25}{20} = 1.25$. |
| **evaluate** (p. 8) To find the value of an expression with one or more operations.<br><br>**hallar el valor** (pág. 8) Encontrar el valor de una expresión que tiene una o más operaciones. | $$4(3) + 6 \div 2 = 15$$ |
| **event** (p. 381) A collection of outcomes of an experiment.<br><br>**evento** (pág. 381) Un conjunto de resultados de un experimento. | An *event* for rolling a number cube is "getting a number divisible by 3."<br><br>Al lanzar un cubo numerado, "obtener un número divisible por 3" es un *evento*. |
| **experimental probability** (p. 382) A probability based on a sample or repeated trials of an experiment. The experimental probability of an event is given by:<br><br>$P(\text{event}) = \dfrac{\text{Number of favorable outcomes}}{\text{Number of trials or items in sample}}$<br><br>**probabilidad experimental** (pág. 382) Una probabilidad basada en el número de ensayos de un experimento. La probabilidad experimental de un evento se expresa:<br><br>$P(\text{evento}) = \dfrac{\text{Número de resultados favorables}}{\text{Número de ensayos}}$ | During one month, your school bus is on time 17 out of 22 school days. The *experimental probability* that the bus is on time is:<br><br>$P(\text{bus is on time}) = \frac{17}{22} \approx 0.773$<br><br>Durante un mes, tu autobús llega a tiempo 17 de 22 días escolares. La *probabilidad experimental* de que el autobús llegue a tiempo es:<br><br>$P(\text{autobús a tiempo}) = \frac{17}{22} \approx 0.773$ |
| **exponent** (p. 19) A number or expression that represents how many times a base is used as a factor in a repeated multiplication.<br><br>**exponente** (pág. 19) Un número o expresión que representa cuántas veces una base se usa como factor en una multiplicación repetida. | In the power $5^3$, the *exponent* is 3.<br><br>El *exponente* de la potencia $5^3$ es 3. |

**F**

| | |
|---|---|
| **face of a polyhedron** (p. 534) A polygon that is a side of the polyhedron.<br><br>**cara de un poliedro** (pág. 534) Un polígono que forma un lado del poliedro. | *See* edge of a polyhedron.<br><br>*Véase* arista de un poliedro. |

**factor tree** (p. 177) A diagram that can be used to write the prime factorization of a number.

**árbol de factores** (pág. 177) Un diagrama que puede usarse para escribir la descomposición de un número en factores primos.

$$54$$
$$6 \times 9$$
$$2 \times 3 \times 3 \times 3$$

---

**factorial** (p. 675) The expression $n!$ is read "$n$ factorial" and represents the product of all integers from 1 to $n$.

**factorial** (pág. 675) La expresión $n!$ se lee "factorial $n$" y representa el producto de todos los números enteros desde 1 hasta $n$.

$$4! = 4 \cdot 3 \cdot 2 \cdot 1 = 24$$

---

**favorable outcomes** (p. 381) Outcomes corresponding to a specified event.

**resultados favorables** (pág. 381) Los resultados correspondientes a un evento determinado.

When rolling a number cube, the *favorable outcomes* for the event "getting a number greater than 4" are 5 and 6.

Al lanzar un cubo numerado, los *resultados favorables* para el evento "obtener un número mayor que 4" son 5 y 6.

---

**formula** (p. 32) An equation that relates two or more quantities such as perimeter, length, and width.

**fórmula** (pág. 32) Una ecuación que relaciona dos o más cantidades tales como perímetro, longitud y ancho.

$$P = 2l + 2w$$

---

**fraction** (p. 762) A number of the form $\frac{a}{b}$ ($b \neq 0$) where $a$ is called the numerator and $b$ is called the denominator.

**fracción** (pág. 762) Un número de la forma $\frac{a}{b}$ ($b \neq 0$) donde $a$ es el numerador y $b$ es el denominador.

$\frac{5}{7}$ and $\frac{18}{10}$ are *fractions*.

$\frac{5}{7}$ y $\frac{18}{10}$ son *fracciones*.

---

**frequency** (p. 4) The number of data values that lie in an interval of a frequency table or histogram.

**frecuencia** (pág. 4) El número de valores en un conjunto de datos que se ubican en un intervalo de una tabla de frecuencias o histograma.

*See* frequency table *and* histogram.

*Véase* tabla de frecuencias *e* histograma.

---

**frequency table** (p. 4) A table used to group data values into intervals.

**tabla de frecuencias** (pág. 4) Una tabla que se usa para agrupar valores de un conjunto de datos en intervalos.

| Interval Intervalo | Tally Marca | Frequency Frecuencia |
|---|---|---|
| 0–9 | II | 2 |
| 10–19 | IIII | 4 |
| 20–29 | JHT | 5 |

**front-end estimation** (p. 261) A method for estimating the sum of two or more numbers. In this method, you add the front-end digits, estimate the sum of the remaining digits, and then add the results.

**estimación por la izquierda** (pág. 261) Un método para estimar la suma de dos o más números. En este método, se suman los dígitos de la izquierda, se estima la suma de los dígitos restantes y luego se suman los resultados.

To estimate 3.81 + 1.32 + 5.74, first add the front-end digits: 3 + 1 + 5 = 9.
Then estimate the sum of the remaining digits:
0.81 + (0.32 + 0.74) ≈ 1 + 1 = 2.
The sum is about 9 + 2 = 11.

Para estimar la suma de 3.81 + 1.32 + 5.74, suma primero los dígitos de la izquierda:
3 + 1 + 5 = 9.
Luego estima la suma de los dígitos restantes:
0.81 + (0.32 + 0.74) ≈ 1 + 1 = 2.
La suma es aproximadamente 9 + 2 = 11.

---

**function** (p. 583) A pairing of each number in a given set with exactly one number in another set. Starting with a number called an input, the function associates with it exactly one number called an output.

**función** (pág. 583) La asociación de cada número en un conjunto dado con exactamente un número de otro conjunto. Comenzando con un número llamado de entrada, la función asocia con él exactamente un número llamado de salida.

| Input/Entrada, $x$ | 1 | 2 | 3 | 4 |
|---|---|---|---|---|
| Output/Salida, $y$ | 2 | 4 | 6 | 8 |

The input-output table above represents a *function*.

La tabla anterior de entrada y salida representa una *función*.

---

**function notation** (p. 739) An equation that uses $f(x)$ to represent the output of the function $f$ for an input of $x$.

**notación de función** (pág. 739) Una ecuación que usa $f(x)$ para representar la salida de la función $f$ para una entrada de $x$.

$f(x) = 5x + 13$ is written using *function notation*.

$f(x) = 5x + 13$ está escrita según la *notación de función*.

---

# G

**graph of an inequality** (p. 148) On a number line, the set of points that represents the solution of the inequality. (*See* half-plane.)

**gráfica de una desigualdad** (pág. 148) En una recta numérica, el conjunto de puntos que representa la solución de la desigualdad. (*Véase* semiplano.)

The *graph of the inequality* $x < 2$ is shown below.

La recta numérica es la *gráfica de la desigualdad* $x < 2$.

---

**greatest common factor (GCF)** (p. 181) The greatest whole number that is a factor of two or more nonzero whole numbers.

**máximo común divisor (MCD)** (pág. 181) El mayor número natural que es un factor de dos o más números naturales distintos de cero.

The *GCF* of 18 and 27 is 9.
The *GCF* of 48, 24, and 36 is 12.

El *MCD* de 18 y 27 es 9.
El *MCD* de 48, 24 y 36 es 12.

**half-plane** (p. 630) The graph of a linear inequality in two variables.

**semiplano** (pág. 630) La gráfica de una desigualdad lineal en dos variables.

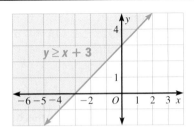

$$y \geq x + 3$$

---

**height of a parallelogram** (p. 521) The perpendicular distance between the side whose length is the base and the opposite side.

**altura de un paralelogramo** (pág. 521) La distancia perpendicular entre el lado cuya longitud es la base y el lado opuesto.

*See* **base of a parallelogram.**

*Véase* **base de un paralelogramo.**

---

**height of a trapezoid** (p. 522) The perpendicular distance between the bases of the trapezoid.

**altura de un trapecio** (pág. 522) La distancia perpendicular entre las bases de un trapecio.

*See* **bases of a trapezoid.**

*Véase* **bases de un trapecio.**

---

**height of a triangle** (p. 142) The perpendicular distance between a side whose length is the base and the vertex opposite that side.

**altura de un triángulo** (pág. 142) La distancia perpendicular entre el lado cuya longitud es la base y el vértice opuesto a esa base.

*See* **base of a triangle.**

*Véase* **base de un triángulo.**

---

**heptagon** (p. 420) A polygon with seven sides.

**heptágono** (pág. 420) Polígono que tiene siete lados.

---

**hexagon** (p. 420) A polygon with six sides.

**hexágono** (pág. 420) Polígono que tiene seis lados.

---

**histogram** (p. 4) A graph that displays data from a frequency table. A histogram has one bar for each interval of the frequency table. The height of the bar indicates the frequency for the interval.

**histograma** (pág. 4) Una gráfica que muestra datos de una tabla de frecuencias. Un histograma tiene una barra para cada intervalo de la tabla de frecuencias. La longitud de la barra indica la frecuencia para el intervalo.

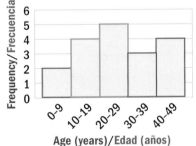

**Library Visitors on a Saturday**
**Visitantes a la biblioteca los sábados**

**hypotenuse** (p. 482) The side of a right triangle that is opposite the right angle.

**hipotenusa** (pág. 482) El lado de un triángulo rectángulo que está opuesto al ángulo recto.

## I

**identity property of addition** (p. 64) The sum of a number and the additive identity, 0, is the number.

**propiedad de identidad de la suma** (pág. 64) La suma de un número y la identidad de la suma, 0, es el mismo número.

$$8 + 0 = 8$$
$$a + 0 = a$$

**identity property of multiplication** (p. 74) The product of a number and the multiplicative identity, 1, is the number.

**propiedad de identidad de la multiplicación** (pág. 74) El producto de un número y la identidad de la multiplicación, 1, es el mismo número.

$$4 \cdot 1 = 4$$
$$a \cdot 1 = a$$

**image** (p. 433) The new figure formed by a transformation.

**imagen** (pág. 433) La figura nueva formada por una transformación.

*See* reflection, rotation, *and* translation.

*Véase* reflexión, rotación *y* traslación.

**improper fraction** (p. 762) A fraction whose numerator is greater than or equal to its denominator.

**fracción impropia** (pág. 762) Una fracción en la cual el numerador es mayor que el denominador o igual a él.

$\frac{8}{7}$ is an *improper fraction.*

$\frac{8}{7}$ es una *fracción impropia.*

**independent events** (p. 694) Two events such that the occurrence of one does not affect the likelihood that the other will occur.

**eventos independientes** (pág. 694) Dos eventos tales que la ocurrencia de uno no afecta la probabilidad de que ocurra el otro.

You toss a coin and roll a number cube. The events "getting heads" and "getting a 6" are *independent events.*

Lanzas una moneda y después lanzas un cubo numerado. Los eventos "obtener cara" y "obtener 6" son *eventos independientes.*

**inequality** (p. 148) A mathematical sentence formed by placing an inequality symbol between two expressions.

**desigualdad** (pág. 148) Un enunciado matemático formado colocando un símbolo de desigualdad entre dos expresiones.

$3 < 5$ and $x + 2 \geq -4$ are *inequalities.*

$3 < 5$ y $x + 2 \geq -4$ son *desigualdades.*

**input** (p. 583) A number on which a function operates. An input value is in the domain of the function.

**entrada** (pág. 583) Un número sobre el que opera una función. Un valor de entrada está en el dominio de la función.

*See* function.

*Véase* función.

| | |
|---|---|
| **integers** (p. 57) The numbers . . . , $-4, -3, -2, -1, 0, 1, 2,$ $3, 4, \ldots,$ consisting of the negative integers, zero, and the positive integers. | $-8$ and $14$ are *integers*. $-8\frac{1}{3}$ and $14.5$ are not *integers*. |
| **números enteros** (pág. 57) Los números ..., $-4, -3, -2,$ $-1, 0, 1, 2, 3, 4, ...,$ que constan de los números enteros negativos, cero y los números enteros positivos. | $-8$ y $14$ son *números enteros*. $-8\frac{1}{3}$ y $14.5$ no son *números enteros*. |
| **interest** (p. 376) The amount earned or paid for the use of money. | *See* **simple interest.** |
| **interés** (pág. 376) La cantidad ganada o pagada por el uso de dinero. | *Véase* **interés simple.** |
| **interquartile range** (p. 655) The difference between the upper and lower quartiles in a box-and-whisker plot. **rango entre cuartiles** (pág. 655) La diferencia entre los cuartiles superior e inferior en un diagrama de líneas y bloques. | The *interquartile range* is $37 - 19$, or $18$. El *rango entre cuartiles* es $37 - 19$, ó $18$. |
| **intersection** (p. 690) The set of all elements in *both* set $A$ and set $B$, written as $A \cap B$. **intersección** (pág. 690) El conjunto de todos los elementos que están tanto en el conjunto $A$ como en el conjunto $B$, que se expresa como $A \cap B$. | |
| **inverse operations** (p. 117) Operations that "undo" each other. **operaciones inversas** (pág. 117) Operaciones que se "deshacen" mutuamente. | Addition and subtraction are *inverse operations*. Multiplication and division are also *inverse operations*. La suma y la resta son *operaciones inversas*. La multiplicación y la división también son *operaciones inversas*. |
| **inverse property of addition** (p. 64) The sum of a number and its additive inverse, or opposite, is 0. **propiedad inversa de la suma** (pág. 64) La suma de un número y su inverso aditivo u opuesto, es cero. | $5 + (-5) = 0$ $a + (-a) = 0$ |
| **inverse property of multiplication** (p. 249) The product of a nonzero number and its multiplicative inverse, or reciprocal, is 1. **propiedad inversa de la multiplicación** (pág. 249) El producto de un número distinto de cero y su inverso multiplicativo, o recíproco, es 1. | $\frac{3}{4} \cdot \frac{4}{3} = 1$ $\frac{a}{b} \cdot \frac{b}{a} = 1 \quad (a, b \neq 0)$ |

**inverse variation** (p. 619)  The relationship of two variables $x$ and $y$ if there is a nonzero number $k$ such that $xy = k$ or $y = \frac{k}{x}$.

$\frac{x}{y} = k$ or $y = \frac{k}{x}$

$\frac{x}{y} = 8$ or $y = \frac{8}{x}$

**variación inversa** (pág. 619)  La relación entre dos variable $x$ e $y$ cuando hay un número $k$ distinto de cero, de manera tal que $xy = k$ ó $y = \frac{k}{x}$.

$\frac{x}{y} = k$ ó $y = \frac{k}{x}$

$\frac{x}{y} = 8$ ó $y = \frac{8}{x}$

---

**irrational number** (p. 475)  A real number that cannot be written as a quotient of two integers. The decimal form of an irrational number neither terminates nor repeats.

$\sqrt{2}$ and $0.313113111\ldots$ are *irrational numbers.*

**número irracional** (pág. 475)  Un número real que no puede escribirse como un cociente de dos números enteros. La forma decimal de un número irracional no termina ni se repite.

$\sqrt{2}$ y $0.313113111\ldots$ son *números irracionales.*

---

**isometric drawing** (p. 539)  A two-dimensional drawing of a three-dimensional figure that can be created using a grid of dots and a set of three axes that intersect to form 120° angles.

**dibujo isométrico** (pág. 539)  Un dibujo bidimensional de una figura tridimensional que se puede crear a partir de una cuadrícula de puntos y un conjunto de tres ejes para formar ángulos de 120°.

---

**isosceles triangle** (p. 411)  A triangle with at least two congruent sides.

**triángulo isósceles** (pág. 411)  Un triángulo que tiene al menos dos lados congruentes.

---

 **L**

**lateral surface area** (p. 545)  Surface area of a figure excluding the area of its base(s).

**área de superficie lateral** (pág. 545)  Área de la superficie de una figura que excluye el área de su(s) base(s).

lateral surface
superficie lateral

base
base

---

**leading digit** (p. 265)  The first nonzero digit in a number.

**dígito dominante** (pág. 265)  El primer dígito distinto de cero en un número.

The *leading digit* of 725 is 7.
The *leading digit* of 0.002638 is 2.

El *dígito dominante* de 725 es 7.
El *dígito dominante* de 0.002638 es 2.

| | |
|---|---|
| **least common denominator (LCD)** (p. 198) The least common multiple of the denominators of two or more fractions. | The *LCD* of $\frac{7}{10}$ and $\frac{3}{4}$ is 20, the least common multiple of 10 and 4. |
| **mínimo común denominador (m.c.d.)** (pág. 198) El mínimo común múltiplo de los denominadores de dos o más fracciones. | El *m.c.d.* de $\frac{7}{10}$ y $\frac{3}{4}$ es 20, que es el mínimo común múltiplo de 10 y 4. |
| **least common multiple (LCM)** (p. 192) The least number that is a common multiple of two or more whole numbers. | The *LCM* of 4 and 6 is 12. The *LCM* of 3, 5, and 10 is 30. |
| **mínimo común múltiplo (m.c.m.)** (pág. 192) El menor de los múltiplos comunes de dos o más números naturales. | El *m.c.m.* de 4 y 6 es 12. El *m.c.m.* de 3, 5 y 10 es 30. |
| **legs of a right triangle** (p. 482) The two sides of a right triangle that form the right angle. | *See* hypotenuse. |
| **catetos de un triángulo rectángulo** (pág. 482) Los dos lados de un triángulo rectángulo que forman el ángulo recto. | *Véase* hipotenusa. |
| **like terms** (p. 89) Terms that have identical variable parts raised to the same power. (Two or more constant terms are considered like terms.) | In the expression $x + 4 - 2x + 1$, $x$ and $-2x$ are *like terms*, and 4 and 1 are *like terms*. |
| **términos semejantes** (pág. 89) Términos que tienen partes variables idénticas elevadas a la misma potencia. (Dos o más términos constantes se consideran términos semejantes.) | En la expresión $x + 4 - 2x + 1$, $x$ y $-2x$ son *términos semejantes*, y 4 y 1 son *términos semejantes*. |
| **line** (p. 773) A figure that extends without end in two opposite directions. | |
| **recta** (pág. 773) Una figura que se extiende infinitamente en dos direcciones opuestas. | |
| **line plot** (p. 782) A number line diagram that uses X marks to show the frequencies of items or categories being tallied. | |
| **diagrama lineal** (pág. 782) Un diagrama de recta numérica que usa marcas X para mostrar las frecuencias con las que se marcan artículos o categorías. | |
| **linear equation** (p. 598) An equation in which the variables appear in separate terms and each variable occurs only to the first power. | $7y = 14x + 21$ is a *linear equation*. |
| **ecuación lineal** (pág. 598) Una ecuación en la que las variables aparecen en términos separados y cada variable se eleva sólo a la primera potencia. | $7y = 14x + 21$ es una *ecuación lineal*. |

**linear function** (p. 604)  A function whose graph is a line or a part of a line.

**función lineal** (pág. 604)  Una función cuya gráfica es una recta o parte de una recta.

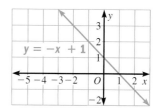

**linear inequality** (p. 629)  An inequality in which the variables appear in separate terms and each variable occurs only to the first power.

**desigualdad lineal** (pág. 629)  Una desigualdad en la que las variables aparecen en términos separados y cada variable se eleva sólo a la primera potencia.

$y \leq 2x + 5$ is a *linear inequality*.

$y \leq 2x + 5$ es una *desigualdad lineal*.

**line graph** (p. 660)  A type of graph in which points representing data pairs are connected by line segments. A line graph is used to show how a quantity changes over time.

**gráfica lineal** (pág. 660)  Un tipo de gráfica en la que los puntos que representan pares de datos se conectan por segmentos de recta. Se usa una gráfica lineal para mostrar cómo una cantidad cambia en el tiempo.

**line of reflection** (p. 434)  The line over which a figure is flipped when the figure undergoes a reflection.

**línea de reflexión** (pág. 434)  La recta sobre la que se invierte una figura cuando dicha figura se refleja.

*See* reflection.

*Véase* reflexión.

**line of symmetry** (p. 435)  A line that divides a figure into two parts that are mirror images of each other.

**línea de simetría** (pág. 435)  Una recta que divide una figura en dos partes que son imágenes reflejas entre sí.

*See* line symmetry.

*Véase* simetría lineal.

**line symmetry** (p. 435)  A figure has line symmetry if it can be divided by a line, called a line of symmetry, into two parts that are mirror images of each other.

**simetría lineal** (pág. 435)  Una figura tiene simetría lineal si puede dividirse por una recta, llamada línea de simetría, en dos partes que son imágenes reflejas entre sí.

A square has 4 lines of symmetry.

Un cuadrado tiene 4 líneas de simetría.

| | |
|---|---|
| **lower extreme** (p. 654) The least value in a data set. | *See* box-and-whisker plot. |
| **extremo inferior** (pág. 654) El valor menor en un conjunto de datos. | *Véase* diagrama de líneas y bloques. |
| **lower quartile** (p. 654) The median of the lower half of a data set. | *See* box-and-whisker plot. |
| **cuartil inferior** (pág. 654) La mediana de la mitad inferior de un conjunto de datos. | *Véase* diagrama de líneas y bloques. |

**M**

| | |
|---|---|
| **markup** (p. 370) The increase in the wholesale price of an item. | The wholesale price of a loaf of bread is $1 but the store sells it for $1.59. The *markup* is $.59. |
| **margen** (pág. 370) El aumento con respecto al precio de venta por mayor de un artículo. | El precio de venta al por mayor de una hogaza de pan es de $1, pero la tienda la vende a $1.59. El *margen* es de $.59. |
| **mean** (pp. 78, 272) The sum of the values in a data set divided by the number of values. | The *mean* of the data set<br>$$85, 59, 97, 71$$<br>is $\frac{85 + 59 + 97 + 71}{4} = \frac{312}{4} = 78.$ |
| **media** (págs. 78, 272) La suma de los valores en un conjunto de datos dividida por el número de valores. | La *media* del conjunto de datos<br>$$85, 59, 97, 71$$<br>es $\frac{85 + 59 + 97 + 71}{4} = \frac{312}{4} = 78.$ |
| **median** (p. 272) The middle value in a data set when the values are written in numerical order. If the data set has an even number of values, the median is the mean of the two middle values. | The *median* of the data set<br>$$8, 17, 21, 23, 26, 29, 34, 40, 45$$<br>is the middle value, 26. |
| **mediana** (pág. 272) El valor que está en el medio de un conjunto de datos cuando los valores están escritos en orden numérico. Si el conjunto de datos tiene un número par de valores, la mediana es la media de los dos valores que están en el medio. | La *mediana* del conjunto de datos<br>$$8, 17, 21, 23, 26, 29, 34, 40, 45$$<br>es 26, el valor que está en el medio. |
| **mixed number** (p. 762) A number that has a whole number part and a fraction part. | $3\frac{2}{5}$ is a *mixed number*. |
| **número mixto** (pág. 762) Un número que tiene una parte que es un número natural y una parte que es una fracción. | $3\frac{2}{5}$ es un *número mixto*. |
| **mode** (p. 272) The value in a data set that occurs most often. A data set can have no mode, one mode, or more than one mode. | The *mode* of the data set<br>$$73, 42, 55, 77, 61, 55, 68$$<br>is 55 because it occurs most often. |
| **moda** (pág. 272) En un conjunto de datos, el valor que ocurre con mayor frecuencia. Un conjunto de datos puede no tener moda, o puede tener una moda o más de una moda. | La *moda* del conjunto de datos<br>$$73, 42, 55, 77, 61, 55, 68$$<br>es 55 porque es el valor que aparece más veces. |

| | |
|---|---|
| **monomial** (p. 178) A number, a variable, or a product of a number and one or more variables. | $3xy$, $8x^2$, $x$, and 14 are *monomials*. |
| **monomio** (pág. 178) Un número, una variable o un producto de un número y una o más variables. | $3xy$, $8x^2$, $x$ y 14 son *monomios*. |
| **multiple** (p. 192) A multiple of a number is the product of the number and any nonzero whole number. | The *multiples* of 3 are 3, 6, 9, .... |
| **múltiplo** (pág. 192) Un múltiplo de un número es el producto del número y cualquier número natural distinto de cero. | Los *múltiplos* de 3 son 3, 6, 9, ... |
| **multiplication property of equality** (p. 122) Multiplying each side of an equation by the same nonzero number produces an equivalent equation. | If $\frac{x}{3} = 7$, then $3 \cdot \frac{x}{3} = 3 \cdot 7$, so $x = 21$. If $\frac{x}{a} = b$ and $a \neq 0$, then $a \cdot \frac{x}{a} = a \cdot b$. |
| **propiedad de igualdad en la multiplicación** (pág. 122) Al multiplicar cada lado de una ecuación por el mismo número distinto de cero se obtiene una ecuación equivalente. | Si $\frac{x}{3} = 7$, entonces $3 \cdot \frac{x}{3} = 3 \cdot 7$, por lo tanto $x = 21$. Si $\frac{x}{a} = b$ y $a \neq 0$, entonces $a \cdot \frac{x}{a} = a \cdot b$. |
| **multiplication property of zero** (p. 74) The product of a number and 0 is 0. | |
| **propiedad del cero de la multiplicación** (pág. 74) El producto de un número y 0 es 0. | $-4 \cdot 0 = 0$<br>$a \cdot 0 = 0$ |
| **multiplicative identity** (p. 74) The number 1 is the multiplicative identity because the product of any number and 1 is the original number. | |
| **identidad de la multiplicación** (pág. 74) El número 1 es la identidad de la multiplicación porque el producto de cualquier número y 1 es el número original. | $9 \cdot 1 = 9$<br>$a \cdot 1 = a$ |
| **multiplicative inverse** (p. 247) The multiplicative inverse of a number $\frac{a}{b}$ ($a, b \neq 0$) is the reciprocal of the number, or $\frac{b}{a}$. The product of a number and its multiplicative inverse is 1. | The *multiplicative inverse* of $\frac{3}{2}$ is $\frac{2}{3}$, so $\frac{3}{2} \cdot \frac{2}{3} = 1$. |
| **inverso multiplicativo** (pág. 247) El inverso multiplicativo de un número $\frac{a}{b}$ ($a, b \neq 0$) es el recíproco de dicho número, es decir $\frac{b}{a}$. El producto de un número y su inverso multiplicativo es 1. | El *inverso multiplicativo* de $\frac{3}{2}$ es $\frac{2}{3}$, por lo tanto $\frac{3}{2} \cdot \frac{2}{3} = 1$. |

**N**

| | |
|---|---|
| **negative integers** (p. 57) The integers that are less than zero. | The *negative integers* are $-1, -2, -3, -4, \ldots$. |
| **números enteros negativos** (pág. 57) Números enteros menores que cero. | Los *números enteros negativos* son $-1, -2, -3, -4, \ldots$ |

**net** (p. 542) A two-dimensional representation of a solid. This pattern forms a solid when it is folded.

**red** (pág. 542) Representación bidimensional de un cuerpo geométrico. Este patrón forma un cuerpo geométrico cuando se dobla.

---

**numerical expression** (p. 8) An expression consisting of numbers and operations.

**expresión numérica** (pág. 8) Una expresión compuesta por números y operaciones.

$$4(3) + 24 \div 2$$

---

## O

**obtuse angle** (p. 411) An angle whose measure is greater than 90° and less than 180°.

**ángulo obtuso** (pág. 411) Un ángulo cuya medida es mayor que 90° y menor que 180°.

---

**obtuse triangle** (p. 411) A triangle with one obtuse angle.

**triángulo obtusángulo** (pág. 411) Triángulo que tiene un ángulo obtuso.

---

**octagon** (p. 420) A polygon with eight sides.

**octágono** (pág. 420) Polígono que tiene ocho lados.

---

**odds in favor of an event** (p. 686) The ratio of favorable outcomes to unfavorable outcomes.

**probabilidades a favor de un evento** (pág. 686) La razón entre los resultados favorables y los resultados desfavorables.

The odds of rolling an even number on a six sided number cube is $\frac{3}{3}$, or 1.

Las probabilidades de obtener un número par en un cubo numerado de seis lados son $\frac{3}{3}$, ó 1.

---

**opposites** (p. 58) Two numbers that are the same distance from 0 on a number line but are on opposite sides of 0.

**opuestos** (pág. 58) Dos números que están a la misma distancia de 0 en una recta numérica pero en lados opuestos de 0.

−3 and 3 are *opposites*.

−3 y 3 son *opuestos*.

---

**order of operations** (p. 8) A set of rules for evaluating an expression involving more than one operation.

**orden de las operaciones** (pág. 8) Conjunto de reglas para hallar el valor de una expresión que tiene más de una operación.

To evaluate $3 + 2 \cdot 4$, you perform the multiplication before the addition:
$$3 + 2 \cdot 4 = 3 + 8 = 11$$

Para hallar el valor de $3 + 2 \cdot 4$, haz la multiplicación antes que la suma:
$$3 + 2 \cdot 4 = 3 + 8 = 11$$

**ordered pair** (p. 94) A pair of numbers $(x, y)$ that can be used to represent a point in a coordinate plane. The first number is the $x$-coordinate, and the second number is the $y$-coordinate.

**par ordenado** (pág. 94) Un par de números $(x, y)$ que se puede usar para representar un punto en un plano de coordenadas. El primer número es la coordenada $x$ y el segundo número es la coordenada $y$.

**origin** (p. 94) The point $(0, 0)$ where the $x$-axis and the $y$-axis meet in a coordinate plane.

**origen** (pág. 94) El punto $(0, 0)$ donde se encuentran el eje $x$ y el eje $y$ en un plano de coordenadas.

*See* coordinate plane.

*Véase* plano de coordenadas.

**outcomes** (p. 381) The possible results when an experiment is performed.

**resultados** (pág. 381) Resultados posibles cuando se realiza un experimento.

**When tossing a coin, the *outcomes* are heads and tails.**

Al lanzar una moneda, los *resultados* son cara y cruz.

**output** (p. 583) A number produced by evaluating a function using a given input. An output value is in the range of the function.

**salida** (pág. 583) Número producido al hallar el valor de una función utilizando una entrada dada. Un valor de salida está dentro del rango de la función.

*See* function.

*Véase* función.

**P**

**parallel lines** (p. 405) Two lines in the same plane that do not intersect. The symbol ‖ is used to indicate parallel lines.

**rectas paralelas** (pág. 405) Dos rectas en el mismo plano que no se intersecan. Se usa el símbolo ‖ para indicar rectas paralelas.

**parallelogram** (p. 416) A quadrilateral with both pairs of opposite sides parallel.

**paralelogramo** (pág. 416) Un cuadrilátero que tiene dos pares de lados opuestos paralelos.

**pentagon** (p. 420) A polygon with five sides.

**pentágono** (pág. 420) Polígono que tiene cinco lados.

**percent** (p. 354) A ratio whose denominator is 100. The symbol for percent is %.

**porcentaje** (pág. 354) Razón cuyo denominador es 100. El símbolo de porcentaje es %.

$$\frac{17}{20} = \frac{17 \cdot 5}{20 \cdot 5} = \frac{85}{100} = 85\%$$

**percent of change** (p. 366) A percent that shows how much a quantity has increased or decreased in comparison with the original amount:

Percent of change $p = \dfrac{\text{Amount of increase or decrease}}{\text{Original amount}}$

**porcentaje de cambio** (pág. 366) Porcentaje que muestra cuánto ha aumentado o disminuido una cantidad en comparación con la cantidad original:

Porcentaje de cambio $p = \dfrac{\text{Cantidad de aumento o disminución}}{\text{Cantidad original}}$

The *percent of change p* from 15 to 19 is:
$$p = \frac{19 - 15}{15} = \frac{4}{15} \approx 0.267 = 26.7\%$$

El *porcentaje de cambio p* de 15 a 19 es:
$$p = \frac{19 - 15}{15} = \frac{4}{15} \approx 0.267 = 26.7\%$$

---

**percent of decrease** (p. 366) The percent of change in a quantity when the new amount of the quantity is less than the original amount.

**porcentaje de disminución** (pág. 366) Porcentaje de cambio en una cantidad cuando el valor nuevo de una cantidad es menor que la cantidad original.

*See* **percent of change.**

*Véase* **porcentaje de cambio.**

---

**percent of increase** (p. 366) The percent of change in a quantity when the new amount of the quantity is greater than the original amount.

**porcentaje de aumento** (pág. 366) Porcentaje de cambio en una cantidad cuando el valor nuevo de una cantidad es mayor que la cantidad original.

*See* **percent of change.**

*Véase* **porcentaje de cambio.**

---

**perfect square** (p. 470) A number that is the square of an integer.

**cuadrado perfecto** (pág. 470) Un número que es el cuadrado de un número entero.

49 is a *perfect square* because $49 = (\pm 7)^2$.

49 es un *cuadrado perfecto* porque $49 = (\pm 7)^2$.

---

**perimeter** (p. 32) The distance around a figure. For a figure with straight sides, the perimeter is the sum of the lengths of the sides.

**perímetro** (pág. 32) La distancia alrededor de una figura. Para una figura de lados rectos, el perímetro es la suma de las longitudes de los lados.

7 ft/7 pies

4 ft/4 pies    4 ft/4 pies

7 ft/7 pies

*Perimeter* = 22 ft

*Perímetro* = 22 pies

---

**permutation** (p. 675) An arrangement of a group of objects in a particular order.

**permutación** (pág. 675) Disposición de un grupo de objetos en un orden particular.

There are 6 *permutations* of the 3 letters in the word CAT:

CAT   ACT   TCA   CTA   ATC   TAC

Hay 6 *permutaciones* de las 3 letras de la palabra MAR:

MAR   AMR   RMA   MRA   ARM   RAM

**perpendicular lines** (p. 404) Two lines that intersect to form a right angle. The symbol ⊥ is used to indicate perpendicular lines.

**rectas perpendiculares** (pág. 404) Dos rectas que se intersecan formando un ángulo recto. El símbolo ⊥ se usa para indicar rectas perpendiculares.

$a \perp b$

---

**pi** ($\pi$) (p. 312) The ratio of the circumference of a circle to its diameter.

**pi** ($\pi$) (pág. 312) La razón entre la circunferencia de un círculo y su diámetro.

You can use 3.14 or $\frac{22}{7}$ to approximate $\pi$.

Puedes usar 3.14 ó $\frac{22}{7}$ como el valor aproximado de $\pi$.

---

**plane** (p. 773) A plane can be thought of as a flat surface that extends without end.

**plano** (pág. 773) Se puede pensar en un plano como una superficie plana que se extiende infinitamente.

---

**point** (p. 773) A figure without dimensions that is represented by a dot.

**punto** (pág. 773) Una figura sin dimensiones que se representa con un punto.

•A

---

**polygon** (p. 420) A closed geometric figure made up of three or more line segments that intersect only at their endpoints.

**polígono** (pág. 420) Figura geométrica cerrada compuesta de tres o más segmentos de recta que se intersecan sólo en sus extremos.

Polygon
Polígono

Not a polygon
No polígono

---

**polyhedron** (p. 534) A solid that is enclosed by polygons.

**poliedro** (pág. 534) Cuerpo geométrico encerrado por polígonos.

---

**polynomial** (p. 717) A monomial or a sum of monomials.

**polinomio** (pág. 717) Un monomio o una suma de monomios.

*See* binomial, trinomial, monomial.

*Véase* binomio, trinomio, monomio.

---

**population** (p. 702) In statistics, the entire group of people or objects about which you want information.

**población** (pág. 702) En estadística, todo el grupo de personas u objetos sobre los que se busca información.

If a biologist wants to determine the average age of the elephants in a wildlife refuge, the *population* consists of every elephant in the refuge.

Si un biólogo quiere determinar la edad promedio de los elefantes de un santuario animal, la *población* consiste en cada elefante del santuario.

| | |
|---|---|
| **positive integers** (p. 57) The integers that are greater than zero.<br><br>**números enteros positivos** (pág. 57) Números enteros mayores que cero. | The *positive integers* are 1, 2, 3, 4, . . . .<br><br>Los *números enteros positivos* son 1, 2, 3, 4, ... |
| **power** (p. 19) A product formed from repeated multiplication by the same number or expression. A power consists of a base and an exponent.<br><br>**potencia** (pág. 19) Producto que se obtiene de la multiplicación repetida por el mismo número o expresión. Una potencia está compuesta de una base y un exponente. | $2^4$ is a *power* with base 2 and exponent 4.<br>$2^4 = 2 \cdot 2 \cdot 2 \cdot 2 = 16$<br><br>$2^4$ es una *potencia* con base 2 y exponente 4.<br>$2^4 = 2 \cdot 2 \cdot 2 \cdot 2 = 16$ |
| **prime factorization** (p. 177) Expressing a whole number as a product of prime numbers.<br><br>**descomposición en factores primos** (pág. 177) Expresar un número natural como producto de números primos. | The *prime factorization* of 54 is $2 \times 3 \times 3 \times 3 = 2 \times 3^3$.<br><br>La *descomposición en factores primos* de 54 es $2 \times 3 \times 3 \times 3 = 2 \times 3^3$. |
| **prime number** (p. 177) A whole number greater than 1 whose only positive factors are 1 and itself.<br><br>**número primo** (pág. 177) Un número natural mayor que 1 cuyos únicos factores positivos son 1 y él mismo. | 5 is a *prime number* because its only positive factors are 1 and 5.<br><br>5 es un *número primo*, porque sus únicos factores que son números naturales son 1 y 5. |
| **principal** (p. 376) An amount of money that is deposited or borrowed.<br><br>**capital** (pág. 376) Una cantidad de dinero que se deposita o se solicita en préstamo. | *See* **simple interest.**<br><br>*Véase* interés simple. |
| **prism** (p. 534) A solid, formed by polygons, that has two congruent bases lying in parallel planes.<br><br>**prisma** (pág. 534) Cuerpo geométrico formado por polígonos, que tiene dos bases congruentes ubicadas en planos paralelos. | bases/bases<br><br>**Rectangular prism** **Triangular prism**<br>**Prisma rectangular** **Prisma triangular** |
| **probability of an event** (p. 381) A number from 0 to 1 that measures the likelihood that the event will occur.<br><br>**probabilidad de un evento** (pág. 381) Número de 0 a 1 que mide la posibilidad de que ocurra un evento. | *See* experimental probability *and* theoretical probability.<br><br>*Véase* probabilidad experimental y probabilidad teórica. |
| **proportion** (p. 348) An equation stating that two ratios are equivalent.<br><br>**proporción** (pág. 348) Una ecuación que establece que dos razones son equivalentes. | $\frac{3}{5} = \frac{6}{10}$ and $\frac{x}{12} = \frac{25}{30}$ are *proportions*.<br><br>$\frac{3}{5} = \frac{6}{10}$ y $\frac{x}{12} = \frac{25}{30}$ son *proporciones*. |

**pyramid** (p. 534) A solid, formed by polygons, that has one base. The base can be any polygon, and the other faces are triangles.

**pirámide** (pág. 534) Cuerpo geométrico, formado por polígonos, que tiene una base. La base puede ser cualquier polígono y las otras caras son triángulos.

base/base

**Pythagorean theorem** (p. 482) For any right triangle, the sum of the squares of the lengths $a$ and $b$ of the legs equals the square of the length $c$ of the hypotenuse: $a^2 + b^2 = c^2$.

**teorema de Pitágoras** (pág. 482) Para cualquier triángulo rectángulo, la suma de los cuadrados de las longitudes $a$ y $b$ de los catetos es igual al cuadrado de la longitud $c$ de la hipotenusa: $a^2 + b^2 = c^2$.

15    25
20

$15^2 + 20^2 = 25^2$

**Pythagorean triple** (p. 488) A set of three positive integers $a$, $b$, and $c$ such that $a^2 + b^2 = c^2$.

**triple de Pitágoras** (pág. 488) Conjunto de tres números enteros positivos $a$, $b$ y $c$ de modo que $a^2 + b^2 = c^2$.

**5, 12, and 13 is a *Pythagorean triple*.**

5, 12 y 13 es un *triple de Pitágoras.*

# Q

**quadrant** (p. 94) One of the four regions that a coordinate plane is divided into by the $x$-axis and the $y$-axis.

**cuadrante** (pág. 94) Una de las cuatro regiones en las que el eje $x$ y el eje $y$ dividen un plano de coordenadas.

*See* coordinate plane.

*Véase* plano de coordenadas.

**quadrilateral** (p. 416) A closed geometric figure made up of four line segments, called sides, that intersect only at their endpoints; a polygon with four sides.

**cuadrilátero** (pág. 416) Figura geométrica cerrada formada por cuatro segmentos de recta, llamados lados, que se intersecan sólo en sus extremos; polígono de cuatro lados.

# R

**radical expression** (p. 469) An expression involving a radical sign, $\sqrt{\ }$.

**expresión radical** (pág. 469) Expresión que tiene un signo radical, $\sqrt{\ }$.

$\sqrt{3(22 + 5)}$ is a *radical expression.*

$\sqrt{3(22 + 5)}$ es una *expresión radical.*

**radius of a circle** (p. 312) The distance between the center and any point on the circle.

**radio de un círculo** (pág. 312) Distancia entre cualquier punto del círculo y su centro.

*See* circle.

*Véase* círculo.

**random sample** (p. 702) A sample selected in such a way that each member of the population has an equally likely chance to be part of the sample.

**muestra aleatoria** (pág. 702) Muestra seleccionada de tal manera que cada miembro de la población tiene la misma probabilidad de formar parte de la muestra.

A *random sample* of 5 eighth graders can be selected by putting the names of all eighth graders in a hat and drawing 5 names without looking.

Una *muestra aleatoria* de 5 estudiantes de octavo grado puede seleccionarse colocando los nombres de todos los alumnos de octavo grado en un sombrero y sacando 5 nombres sin mirar.

---

**range of a data set** (p. 273) The difference of the greatest and least values in the data set.

**rango de un conjunto de datos** (pág. 273) La diferencia entre el valor mayor y el valor menor en un conjunto de datos.

The *range of the data set*
$$60, 35, 22, 46, 81, 39$$
is $81 - 22 = 59$.

El *rango del conjunto de datos*
$$60, 35, 22, 46, 81, 39$$
es $81 - 22 = 59$.

---

**range of a function** (p. 584) The set of all possible output values for the function.

**rango de una función** (pág. 584) Conjunto de todos los valores de salida posibles para la función.

*See* function.

*Véase* función.

---

**rate** (p. 344) A ratio of two quantities measured in different units.

**tasa** (pág. 344) Razón entre dos cantidades medidas en unidades diferentes.

An airplane climbs 18,000 feet in 12 minutes. The airplane's *rate* of climb is $\frac{18,000 \text{ ft}}{12 \text{ min}} =$ 1,500 ft/min.

Un avión asciende 18,000 pies en 12 minutos. La *tasa* de ascenso del avión es $\frac{18,000 \text{ pies}}{12 \text{ min}} =$ 1,500 pies/min.

---

**rate of change** (p. 619) A comparison of a change in one quantity with a change in another quantity. In real-world situations, you can interpret the slope of a line as a rate of change.

**tasa de cambio** (pág. 619) Una comparación entre un cambio en una cantidad y un cambio en otra cantidad. En situaciones reales, puedes interpretar la pendiente de una recta como una tasa de cambio.

You pay $7 for 2 hours of computer use and $14 for 4 hours of computer use. The *rate of change* is
$$\frac{\text{change of cost}}{\text{change in time}} = \frac{14 - 7}{4 - 2} = 3.5$$
or $3.50 per hour.

Pagas $7 por usar la computadora durante 2 horas y $14 por usar la computadora por 4 horas. La *tasa de cambio* es
$$\frac{\text{cambio en el costo}}{\text{cambio en el tiempo}} = \frac{14 - 7}{4 - 2} = 3.5$$
o $3.50 por hora.

---

**ratio** (p. 343) A comparison of two numbers using division. The ratio of $a$ to $b$ (where $b \neq 0$) can be written as $a$ to $b$, as $\frac{a}{b}$, or as $a : b$.

**razón** (pág. 343) Comparación entre dos números usando la división. La razón de $a$ a $b$ (donde $b \neq 0$) puede escribirse como $a$ a $b$, como $\frac{a}{b}$ o como $a : b$.

The *ratio* of 17 to 12 can be written as 17 to 12, as $\frac{17}{12}$, or as $17 : 12$.

La *razón* de 17 a 12 puede escribirse como 17 a 12, como $\frac{17}{12}$ o como $17 : 12$.

| | |
|---|---|
| **rational number** (p. 255) A number that can be written as $\frac{a}{b}$ where $a$ and $b$ are integers and $b \neq 0$. | $6 = \frac{6}{1}$, $-\frac{3}{5} = \frac{-3}{5}$, $0.75 = \frac{3}{4}$, and $2\frac{1}{3} = \frac{7}{3}$ are all *rational numbers*. |
| **número racional** (pág. 255) Un número que se puede escribir como $\frac{a}{b}$ donde $a$ y $b$ son números enteros y $b \neq 0$. | $6 = \frac{6}{1}$, $-\frac{3}{5} = \frac{-3}{5}$, $0.75 = \frac{3}{4}$ y $2\frac{1}{3} = \frac{7}{3}$ son todos *números racionales*. |
| **ray** (p. 773) A figure that has one endpoint and extends without end in one direction. | |
| **semirrecta** (pág. 773) Una figura con un extremo que se extiende infinitamente en una dirección. | |
| **real numbers** (p. 475) The set of all rational numbers and irrational numbers. | $0$, $-\frac{5}{9}$, $2.75$, and $\sqrt{3}$ are all *real numbers*. |
| **números reales** (pág. 475) Conjunto de todos los números racionales e irracionales. | $0$, $-\frac{5}{9}$, $2.75$ y $\sqrt{3}$ son todos *números reales*. |
| **reciprocals** (p. 247) Two nonzero numbers whose product is 1. | $\frac{2}{3}$ and $\frac{3}{2}$ are *reciprocals*. |
| **recíprocos** (pág. 247) Dos números distintos de cero cuyo producto es 1. | $\frac{2}{3}$ y $\frac{3}{2}$ son *recíprocos*. |
| **reflection** (p. 433) A transformation that creates a mirror image of each point of a figure; also known as a *flip*. | |
| **reflexión** (pág. 433) Transformación que crea una imagen refleja de cada punto de una figura; también llamada *inversión*. | |
| **reflex angle** (p. 415) An angle greater than 180° but less than 360°. | |
| **ángulo cóncavo** (pág. 415) Un ángulo mayor que 180° pero menor que 360°. | |
| **regular polygon** (p. 420) A polygon with all sides equal in length and all angles equal in measure. | |
| **polígono regular** (pág. 420) Un polígono cuyos lados tienen igual longitud y cuyos ángulos tienen la misma medida. | **Regular pentagon** **Pentágono regular** |
| **relation** (p. 583) A set of ordered pairs. | $(5, 7), (6, 5), (0, 5), (6, 0)$ is a *relation*. |
| **relación** (pág. 583) Conjunto de pares ordenados. | $(5, 7), (6, 5), (0, 5), (6, 0)$ es una *relación*. |

| | |
|---|---|
| **relative frequency** (p. 382) The ratio of number of favorable outcomes to the total number of times the experiment was performed. | *See* **experimental probability.** |
| **frecuencia relativa** (pág. 382) La razón entre el número de resultados favorables y el número de veces que se llevó a cabo un experimento. | *Véase* **probabilidad experimental.** |
| **relatively prime numbers** (p. 182) Two or more nonzero whole numbers whose greatest common factor is 1. | **9 and 16 are *relatively prime* because their GCF is 1.** |
| **números relativamente primos** (pág. 182) Dos o más números naturales distintos de cero cuyo máximo común divisor es 1. | **9 y 16 son *relativamente primos* porque su MCD es 1.** |
| **repeating decimal** (p. 255) A decimal that has one or more digits that repeat without end. | **0.7777. . . and 1.$\overline{29}$ are *repeating decimals*.** |
| **decimal periódico** (pág. 255) Decimal que tiene uno o más dígitos que se repiten infinitamente. | **0.7777... y 1.$\overline{29}$ son *decimales periódicos*.** |
| **rhombus** (p. 416) A parallelogram with four congruent sides. | |
| **rombo** (pág. 416) Paralelogramo que tiene cuatro lados congruentes. | |
| **right angle** (p. 403) An angle whose measure is exactly 90°. | |
| **ángulo recto** (pág. 403) Un ángulo que mide exactamente 90°. | |
| **right triangle** (p. 411) A triangle with one right angle. | |
| **triángulo rectángulo** (pág. 411) Un triángulo que tiene un ángulo recto. | |
| **rise** (p. 612) The vertical change between two points on a line. | *See* **slope.** |
| **distancia vertical** (pág. 612) El cambio vertical entre dos puntos en una recta. | *Véase* **pendiente.** |
| **rotation** (p. 440) A transformation that rotates a figure through a given angle, called the angle of rotation, and in a given direction about a fixed point, called the center of rotation; also known as a *turn*. | |
| **rotación** (pág. 440) Transformación que rota una figura por un ángulo dado, llamado ángulo de rotación, en una dirección dada alrededor de un punto fijo, llamado centro de rotación; también se conoce como *giro*. | |

**rotational symmetry** (p. 443)  A figure has rotational symmetry if a turn of 180° or less produces an image that fits exactly on the original figure.

**simetría de rotación** (pág. 443)  Una figura tiene simetría de rotación si un giro de 180° o menor produce una imagen que es igual a la figura original.

90°

180°

A square has *rotational symmetry*.

Un cuadrado tiene *simetría de rotación*.

---

**run** (p. 612)  The horizontal change between two points on a line.

**distancia horizontal** (pág. 612)  El cambio horizontal entre dos puntos en una recta.

*See* slope.

*Véase* pendiente.

---

# S

**sample** (p. 702)  A part of a population.

**muestra** (pág. 702)  Una parte de una población.

To predict the results of an election, a survey is given to a *sample* of voters.

Para predecir los resultados de unas elecciones, se encuesta a una *muestra* de votantes.

---

**scale** (p. 350)  In a scale drawing, the scale gives the relationship between the drawing's dimensions and the actual dimensions.

**escala** (pág. 350)  En un dibujo a escala, la escala muestra la relación entre las dimensiones del dibujo y las dimensiones reales.

The *scale* "1 in. : 10 ft" means that 1 inch in the scale drawing represents an actual distance of 10 feet.

La *escala* "1 pulg. : 10 pies" significa que una pulgada en el dibujo a escala representa una distancia real de 10 pies.

---

**scale drawing** (p. 347)  A diagram of an object in which the dimensions are in proportion to the actual dimensions of the object.

**dibujo a escala** (pág. 347)  Un diagrama de un objeto cuyas dimensiones están en proporción con las dimensiones reales del objeto.

1 cm : 12 m

---

**scale factor** (p. 449)  The ratio of corresponding side lengths of a figure and its image after dilation.

**factor de escala** (pág. 449)  La razón entre las longitudes de los lados correspondientes de una figura y su imagen después de una dilatación.

*See* dilation.

*Véase* dilatación.

---

**scale model** (p. 350)  A model of an object in which the dimensions are in proportion to the actual dimensions of the object.

**modelo a escala** (pág. 350)  Un modelo de un objeto cuyas dimensiones están en proporción con las dimensiones reales del objeto.

A *scale model* of the White House appears in Tobu World Square in Japan. The scale used is 1 : 25.

En Tobu World Square, en Japón, hay un *modelo a escala* de la Casa Blanca. La escala utilizada es de 1 : 25.

**scalene triangle** (p. 411) A triangle with no congruent sides.

**triángulo escaleno** (pág. 411) Un triángulo cuyos lados no son congruentes.

**scatter plot** (p. 588) The graph of a set of data pairs $(x, y)$, which is a collection of points in a coordinate plane.

**diagrama de dispersión** (pág. 588) La gráfica de un conjunto de pares de datos $(x, y)$, que es un grupo de puntos en un plano de coordenadas.

**scientific notation** (p. 212) A number is written in scientific notation if it has the form $c \times 10^n$, where $c$ is greater than or equal to 1 and less than 10, and $n$ is an integer.

**notación científica** (pág. 212) Un número está escrito en notación científica si tiene la forma $c \times 10^n$ donde $c$ es mayor que o igual a 1 y menor que 10, y $n$ es un número entero.

In *scientific notation*, 328,000 is written as $3.28 \times 10^5$, and 0.00061 is written as $6.1 \times 10^{-4}$.

En *notación científica*, 328,000 se escribe como $3.28 \times 10^5$ y 0.00061 se escribe como $6.1 \times 10^{-4}$.

**sequence** (p. 585) An ordered list of numbers.

**secuencia** (pág. 585) Una lista ordenada de números.

1, 2, 3, 4, . . . is a *sequence*.

1, 2, 3, 4, ... es una *secuencia*.

**set** (p. 688) A collection of distinct objects.

**conjunto** (pág. 688) Una agrupación de objetos distintos.

The set of whole numbers is $W = \{0, 1, 2, 3, 4, 5, \dots\}$.

El conjunto de los números naturales es $N = \{0, 1, 2, 3, 4, 5, \dots\}$.

**similar polygons** (p. 447) Polygons that have the same shape but not necessarily the same size. Corresponding angles of similar polygons are congruent, and the ratios of the lengths of corresponding sides are equal. The symbol ~ is used to indicate that two polygons are similar.

**polígonos semejantes** (pág. 447) Polígonos que tienen la misma forma pero no necesariamente el mismo tamaño. Los ángulos correspondientes de los polígonos semejantes son congruentes y las razones de las longitudes de los lados correspondientes son iguales. Se utiliza el símbolo ~ para indicar que dos polígonos son semejantes.

$\triangle LMN \sim \triangle PQR$

**simple interest** (p. 376) Interest that is earned or paid only on the principal. The simple interest $I$ is the product of the principal $P$, the annual interest rate $r$ written as a decimal, and the time $t$ in years: $I = Prt$.

**interés simple** (pág. 376) El interés ganado o pagado sólo sobre el capital. El interés simple $I$ es el producto del capital $P$, la tasa de interés anual $r$ escrita en forma decimal y el tiempo $t$ en años: $I = Prt$.

You deposit $700 in a savings account that pays a 3% *simple annual interest* rate. After 5 years, the interest is
$I = Prt = (700)(0.03)(5) = \$105$, and your account balance is $700 + $105 = $805.

Depositas $700 en una cuenta de ahorros que genera un *interés anual simple* del 3%. Después de 5 años, el interés es
$I = Prt = (700)(0.03)(5) = \$105$, y el saldo de tu cuenta es $700 + $105 = $805.

---

**simplest form of a fraction** (p. 187) A fraction is in simplest form if its numerator and denominator have a greatest common factor of 1.

**mínima expresión de una fracción** (pág. 187) Una fracción está en su mínima expresión si el máximo común divisor del numerador y del denominador es 1.

The *simplest form of the fraction* $\frac{6}{8}$ is $\frac{3}{4}$.

La *mínima expresión de la fracción* $\frac{6}{8}$ es $\frac{3}{4}$.

---

**sine** (p. 500) The sine of any acute angle $A$ of a right triangle is the ratio of the opposite leg to the hypotenuse.

**seno** (pág. 500) El seno de cualquier ángulo agudo $A$ de un triángulo rectángulo es la razón entre el cateto opuesto y la hipotenusa.

side opposite $\angle A$
lado opuesto a $\angle A$

hypotenuse
hipotenusa

side adjacent to $\angle A$
lado adyacente a $\angle A$

$\sin A = \frac{a}{c}$

---

**slant height** (p. 548) The height of any face that is not the base of a regular pyramid.

**altura inclinada** (pág. 548) En una pirámide regular, la altura de cualquier cara que no sea la base.

slant height
altura inclinada

---

**slope** (p. 612) The slope of a nonvertical line is the ratio of the rise (vertical change) to the run (horizontal change) between any two points on the line.

**pendiente** (pág. 612) La pendiente de una recta no vertical es la razón entre la distancia vertical (cambio vertical) y la distancia horizontal (cambio horizontal) entre dos puntos cualesquiera de la recta.

run
distancia horizontal

rise
distancia vertical

The *slope* of the line above is:
$$\text{slope} = \frac{\text{rise}}{\text{run}} = \frac{2}{5}$$

La *pendiente* de la recta anterior es:
$$\text{pendiente} = \frac{\text{distancia vertical}}{\text{distancia horizontal}} = \frac{2}{5}$$

---

**slope-intercept form** (p. 622) The form of a linear equation $y = mx + b$ where $m$ is the slope and $b$ is the $y$-intercept.

**forma de pendiente e intersección** (pág. 622) La forma de una ecuación lineal $y = mx + b$, donde $m$ es la pendiente y $b$ es la intersección en $y$.

$y = 6x + 8$ is in *slope-intercept form*.

$y = 6x + 8$ está en la *forma de pendiente e intersección*.

| | |
|---|---|
| **solid** (p. 534) A three-dimensional figure that encloses a part of space. | *See* **cone, cylinder, prism, pyramid,** *and* **sphere.** |
| **cuerpo geométrico** (pág. 534) Figura tridimensional que encierra una parte del espacio. | *Véase* **cono, cilindro, prisma, pirámide** *y* **esfera.** |
| **solution of a linear system** (p. 627) An ordered pair that is a solution of each equation in a system of linear equations. | The *solution of the linear system* below is (3,3).<br>$3y - x = 6$<br>$3y + 2x = 15$ |
| **solución de un sistema lineal** (pág. 627) Un par ordenado que es la solución de cada ecuación en un sistema de ecuaciones lineales. | La *solución del sistema lineal* a continuación es (3,3).<br>$3y - x = 6$<br>$3y + 2x = 15$ |
| **solution of an equation** (p. 26) A number that makes the equation true when substituted for the variable in the equation. | The *solution of the equation* $n - 3 = 4$ is 7. |
| **solución de una ecuación** (pág. 26) Número que hace verdadera la ecuación cuando sustituye la variable en la ecuación. | La *solución de la ecuación* $n - 3 = 4$ es 7. |
| **solution of an equation in two variables** (p. 593) An ordered pair $(x, y)$ that makes the equation true when the values of $x$ and $y$ are substituted into the equation. | $(3, 8)$ is a *solution* of $y = 3x - 1$. |
| **solución de una ecuación con dos variables** (pág. 593) Un par ordenado $(x, y)$ que hace verdadera la ecuación cuando se sustituyen los valores de $x$ e $y$ en la ecuación. | $(3, 8)$ is a *solution* of $y = 3x - 1$. |
| **solution of an inequality** (p. 148) The set of all numbers that make the inequality true when substituted for the variable in the inequality. | The *solution of the inequality* $y + 2 > 5$ is $y > 3$. |
| **solución de una desigualdad** (pág. 148) Conjunto de todos los números que hacen verdadera la desigualdad cuando sustituyen la variable en la desigualdad. | La *solución de la desigualdad* $y + 2 > 5$ es $y > 3$. |
| **solution of a linear inequality** (p. 629) An ordered pair $(x, y)$ that makes the inequality true when the values of $x$ and $y$ are substituted into the inequality. | A *solution* of $y \geq 2x - 9$ is $(5, 1)$. |
| **solución de una desigualdad lineal** (pág. 629) Un par ordenado $(x, y)$ que hace verdadera la desigualdad cuando los valores de $x$ e $y$ se sustituyen en la desigualdad. | La *solución* de $y \geq 2x - 9$ es $(5, 1)$. |
| **solving an equation** (p. 26) Finding all solutions of the equation by using mental math or the properties of equality. | To *solve the equation* $4x = 20$, find the number that can be multiplied by 4 to equal 20; $4(5) = 20$, so the solution is 5. |
| **resolver una ecuación** (pág. 26) Hallar todas las soluciones de la ecuación usando el cálculo mental o las propiedades de igualdad. | Para *resolver la ecuación* $4x = 20$, halla el número que multiplicado por 4 sea igual a 20; $4(5) = 20$, por lo tanto la solución es 5. |

**sphere** (p. 534) A solid formed by all points in space that are the same distance from a fixed point called the center.

**esfera** (pág. 534) Cuerpo geométrico formado por todos los puntos en el espacio que se encuentran a la misma distancia de un punto fijo llamado centro.

center
centro

---

**square root** (p. 469) A square root of number $n$ is a number $m$ which, when multiplied by itself, equals $n$.

**raíz cuadrada** (pág. 469) La raíz cuadrada de un número $n$ es un número $m$, el cual, cuando se multiplica por sí mismo, es igual a $n$.

The *square roots* of 81 are 9 and $-9$ because $9^2 = 81$ and $(-9)^2 = 81$.

Las *raíces cuadradas* de 81 son 9 y $-9$ porque $9^2 = 81$ y $(-9)^2 = 81$.

---

**standard form** (p. 717) A polynomial written with the exponents of the variable decreasing from left to right.

**forma estándar** (pág. 717) Polinomio escrito con los exponentes de la variable en orden descendente de izquierda a derecha.

$3x^5 - 8x^3 + 5x^2 + x - 2$ is in *standard form.*

$3x^5 - 8x^3 + 5x^2 + x - 2$ está en *forma estándar.*

---

**stem-and-leaf plot** (p. 649) A data display that helps you see how data values are distributed. Each data value is separated into a leaf (the last digit) and a stem (the remaining digits). In an ordered stem-and-leaf plot, the leaves for each stem are listed in order from least to greatest.

**diagrama de tallo y hojas** (pág. 649) Diagrama que muestra cómo se distribuyen los valores en un conjunto de datos. Cada valor está separado en una hoja (el último dígito) y un tallo (los dígitos restantes). En un diagrama de tallo y hojas ordenado, las hojas para cada tallo están en orden de menor a mayor.

| stems/tallos | leaves/hojas |
|---|---|
| 10 | 8 |
| 11 | 2 2 5 |
| 12 | 1 3 |

Key/Clave: 10 | 8 = 108

---

**straight angle** (p. 403) An angle whose measure is exactly 180°.

**ángulo llano** (pág. 403) Ángulo que mide exactamente 180°.

---

**subtraction property of equality** (p. 117) Subtracting the same number from each side of an equation produces an equivalent equation.

**propiedad de igualdad en la resta** (pág. 117) Al restar el mismo número de cada lado de la ecuación se obtiene una ecuación equivalente.

If $x + 7 = 9$, then $x + 7 - 7 = 9 - 7$, so $x = 2$.
If $x + a = b$, then $x + a - a = b - a$.

Si $x + 7 = 9$, entonces $x + 7 - 7 = 9 - 7$, por lo tanto $x = 2$.
Si $x + a = b$, entonces $x + a - a = b - a$.

---

**supplementary angles** (p. 403) Two angles whose measures have a sum of 180°.

**ángulos suplementarios** (pág. 403) Dos ángulos cuyas medidas suman 180°.

79° 101°

**surface area of a polyhedron** (p. 543) The sum of the areas of the faces of the polyhedron.

**área de la superficie de un poliedro** (pág. 543) La suma de las áreas de las caras del poliedro.

3 in./3 pulg.
4 in./4 pulg.
6 in./6 pulg.

*Surface area*
$$= 2(6)(4) + 2(6)(3) + 2(4)(3)$$
$$= 108 \text{ in.}^2$$

*Área de la superficie*
$$= 2(6)(4) + 2(6)(3) + 2(4)(3)$$
$$= 108 \text{ pulg.}^2$$

---

**system of linear equations** (p. 627) A set of two or more linear equations with the same variables.

**sistema de ecuaciones lineales** (pág. 627) Un conjunto de dos o más ecuaciones lineales con las mismas variables.

$$3y - x = 6$$
$$3y + 2x = 15$$

---

## T

**tangent** (p. 500) The tangent of any acute angle A of a right triangle is the ratio of the opposite leg to the adjacent leg.

**tangente** (pág. 500) La tangente de cualquier ángulo agudo A de un triángulo rectángulo es la razón entre el cateto opuesto y el cateto adyacente.

side opposite $\angle A$
lado opuesto a $\angle A$

*B*

*c* hypotenuse
hipotenusa

*a*

*C*     *b*     *A*

$\tan A = \dfrac{a}{b}$

side adjacent to $\angle A$
lado adyacente a $\angle A$

---

**terminating decimal** (p. 255) A decimal that has a final digit.

**decimal exacto** (pág. 255) Decimal que tiene un dígito final.

0.4 and 3.6125 are *terminating decimals*.

0.4 y 3.6125 son *decimales exactos*.

---

**terms of an expression** (p. 89) The parts of an expression that are added together.

**términos de una expresión** (pág. 89) Las partes de una expresión que se suman entre sí.

The *terms* of $2x + 3$ are $2x$ and 3.

Los *términos* de $2x + 3$ son $2x$ y 3.

---

**tessellation** (p. 445) A covering of a plane with congruent copies of the same pattern so that there are no gaps or overlaps.

**teselado** (pág. 445) La cobertura de un plano con copias congruentes del mismo patrón de modo que no haya huecos o superposiciones.

**theoretical probability** (p. 381) When all outcomes are equally likely, the theoretical probability of an event is the ratio of the number of favorable outcomes to the number of possible outcomes.

**probabilidad teórica** (pág. 381) Cuando todos los resultados son igualmente probables, la probabilidad teórica de un evento es la razón entre el número de resultados favorables y el número de resultados posibles.

A bag of 20 marbles contains 7 red marbles. The *theoretical probability* of randomly choosing a red marble is:

$$P(\text{red}) = \frac{7}{20} = 0.35$$

Una bolsa de 20 canicas contiene 7 canicas rojas. La *probabilidad teórica* de tomar al azar una canica roja es:

$$P(\text{roja}) = \frac{7}{20} = 0.35$$

---

**transformation** (p. 433) An operation that changes a figure into another figure, called the image.

**transformación** (pág. 433) Operación que convierte una figura en otra figura, llamada imagen.

*See* **translation, reflection,** *and* **rotation.**

*Véase* **traslación, reflexión** *y* **rotación.**

---

**translation** (p. 439) A transformation that moves each point of a figure the same distance in the same direction; also known as a *slide*.

**traslación** (pág. 439) Transformación que mueve cada punto de una figura la misma distancia en la misma dirección.

---

**trapezoid** (p. 416) A quadrilateral with exactly one pair of parallel sides.

**trapecio** (pág. 416) Cuadrilátero que tiene exactamente un par de lados paralelos.

---

**tree diagram** (p. 670) A branching diagram that shows all the possible choices or outcomes of a process carried out in several stages.

**diagrama de árbol** (pág. 670) Diagrama ramificado que muestra todas las opciones o resultados posibles de un proceso llevado a cabo en varias etapas.

Outcomes: HH, HT, TH, TT

Resultados: HH, HT, TH, TT

---

**trigonometric ratio** (p. 500) A ratio of the lengths of two sides of a right triangle.

**razón trigonométrica** (pág. 500) Razón entre las longitudes de dos lados de un triángulo rectángulo.

*See* **sine, cosine,** *and* **tangent.**

*Véase* **seno, coseno** *y* **tangente.**

---

**trinomial** (p. 717) A polynomial with three terms.

**trinomio** (pág. 717) Polinomio que tiene tres términos.

$$3x^2 + 2x - 4$$

**unfavorable outcome** (p. 686) An outcome that is not a favorable outcome.

*See* **favorable outcome.**

**resultado desfavorable** (pág. 686) Resultado que no es un resultado favorable.

*Véase* **resultado favorable.**

---

**union** (p. 690) The set of all elements in *either* set *A* or set *B*, written as $A \cup B$.

**unión de conjuntos** (pág. 690) El conjunto que incluye todos los elementos del conjunto *A* y el conjunto *B*, que se expresa como $A \cup B$.

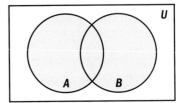

---

**unit analysis** (p. 39) Evaluate expressions with units of measure and check that your answer uses correct units.

**análisis de unidades** (pág. 39) Hallar el valor de expresiones con unidades de medida y comprobar que la respuesta usa unidades correctas.

$\frac{\text{miles}}{\text{hour}} \cdot \text{hours} = \text{miles}$

$\frac{\text{millas}}{\text{hora}} \cdot \text{horas} = \text{millas}$

---

**unit rate** (p. 344) A rate that has a denominator of 1 unit.

**tasa unitaria** (pág. 344) Una tasa cuyo denominador es 1 unidad.

$9 per hour is a *unit rate.*

$9 por hora es una *tasa unitaria.*

---

**universal set** (p. 688) The set of all elements under consideration, written as *U*.

**conjunto universal** (pág. 688) El conjunto de todos los elementos bajo consideración que se expresa como *U*.

If the universal set is the set of positive integers, then $U = \{1, 2, 3, \ldots\}$.

Si el conjunto universal es el conjunto de los números enteros positivos, entonces $U = \{1, 2, 3, \ldots\}$.

---

**upper extreme** (p. 654) The greatest value in a data set.

**extremo superior** (pág. 654) El valor mayor en un conjunto de datos.

*See* **box-and-whisker plot.**

*Véase* **diagrama de líneas y bloques.**

---

**upper quartile** (p. 654) The median of the upper half of a data set.

**cuartil superior** (pág. 654) La mediana de la mitad superior de un conjunto de datos.

*See* **box-and-whisker plot.**

*Véase* **diagrama de líneas y bloques.**

---

**variable** (p. 13) A symbol, usually a letter, that is used to represent one or more numbers.

**variable** (pág. 13) Símbolo, usualmente una letra, que se usa para representar uno o más números.

In the expression $m + 5$, the letter *m* is the *variable.*

En la expresión $m + 5$, la letra *m* es la *variable.*

**variable expression** (p. 13) An expression that consists of numbers, variables, and operations.

**expresión variable** (pág. 13) Expresión compuesta de números, variables y operaciones.

$n - 3, \frac{2s}{t}$, and $x + 4yz + 1$ are *variable expressions*.

$n - 3, \frac{2s}{t}$ y $x + 4yz + 1$ son *expresiones variables*.

---

**Venn diagram** (p. 785) A diagram that uses shapes to show how sets are related.

**diagrama de Venn** (pág. 785) Un diagrama que usa formas para mostrar cómo se relacionan los conjuntos.

---

**verbal model** (p. 9) A word equation that represents a real-world situation.

**modelo verbal** (pág. 9) Ecuación en palabras que representa una situación de la vida real.

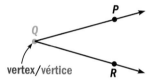

---

**vertex** (p. 759) The endpoint of the rays that form an angle.

**vértice** (pág. 759) El extremo de las semirrectas que forman un ángulo.

---

**vertex of a polyhedron** (p. 534) A point at which three or more edges of a polyhedron meet.

**vértice de un poliedro** (pág. 534) Punto en el que se juntan tres o más aristas de un poliedro.

*See* edge of a polyhedron.

*Véase* arista de un poliedro.

---

**vertical angles** (p. 404) A pair of opposite angles formed when two lines meet at a point.

**ángulos opuestos por el vértice** (pág. 404) Par de ángulos opuestos entre sí formados por dos rectas que se intersecan.

∠1 and ∠3 are *vertical angles*.
∠2 and ∠4 are also *vertical angles*.

∠1 y ∠3 son *ángulos opuestos por el vértice*.
∠2 y ∠4 también son *ángulos opuestos por el vértice*.

---

**vertical line test** (p. 740) If the vertical line intersects a graph at more than one point, then the graph does not represent a function.

**prueba de la línea vertical** (pág. 740) Si una recta vertical interseca una gráfica en más de un punto, entonces la gráfica no representa una función.

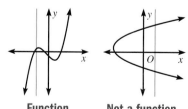

**Function**
**Función**

**Not a function**
**No es una función**

**volume of a solid** (p. 554)  The amount of space the solid occupies.

**volumen de un cuerpo geométrico** (pág. 554)  Cantidad de espacio que ocupa un cuerpo geométrico.

$Volume = \pi r^2 h \approx (3.14)(2)^2(3) \approx 37.7 \text{ m}^3$

$Volumen = \pi r^2 h \approx (3.14)(2)^2(3) \approx 37.7 \text{ m}^3$

# W

**whole numbers** (p. 759)  The numbers 0, 1, 2, 3, . . .

**números naturales** (pág. 759)  Los números 0, 1, 2, 3, ...

# X

**x-axis** (p. 94)  The horizontal number line in a coordinate plane.

**eje x** (pág. 94)  La recta numérica horizontal en un plano de coordenadas.

*See* coordinate plane.

*Véase* plano de coordenadas.

---

**x-coordinate** (p. 94)  The first number in an ordered pair representing a point in the coordinate plane.

**coordenada x** (pág. 94)  El primer número en un par ordenado que representa un punto en un plano de coordenadas.

The *x-coordinate* of the ordered pair $(-2, 1)$ is $-2$.

La *coordenada x* del par ordenado $(-2, 1)$ es $-2$.

---

**x-intercept** (p. 606)  The *x*-coordinate of the point where the graph intersects the *x*-axis.

**intersección en x** (pág. 606)  La coordenada *x* del punto donde la gráfica interseca el eje *x*.

The *x*-intercept is **4**.
La intersección en *x* es **4**.

# Y

**y-axis** (p. 94)  The vertical number line in a coordinate plane.

**eje y** (pág. 94)  La recta numérica vertical en un plano de coordenadas.

*See* coordinate plane.

*Véase* plano de coordenadas.

---

**y-coordinate** (p. 94)  The second number in an ordered pair representing a point in a coordinate plane.

**coordenada y** (pág. 94)  El segundo número en un par ordenado que representa un punto en un plano de coordenadas.

The *y-coordinate* of the ordered pair $(-2, 1)$ is 1.

La *coordenada y* del par ordenado $(-2, 1)$ es 1.

**y-intercept** (p. 606)  The *y*-coordinate of the point where the graph intersects the *y*-axis.

**intersección en y** (pág. 606)  La coordenada *y* del punto donde la gráfica interseca el eje *y*.

The *y*-intercept is **2**.
La intersección en *y* es **2**.

# Index

writing, 150–153, 319–321, 324–329
monomial, 178, 717
  factoring, 178–180
  greatest common factor of, 183, 184, 221
  least common multiple of, 193–195
  multiplying, 726–730, 749
  powers and, 726–730, 749
numerical expressions, 8
  evaluating, 8–12, 20–24, 46, 83–86, 90, 105–106, 202–207
  with exponents, 202–211
  factorial, 190
order of operations, 8–12, 20, 46, 235
polynomials, 717
  adding, 721–725, 749
  binomial, 717
  classifying, 717, 719
  evaluating, 718–720
  monomial, 178, 717
  multiplying, 726–730, 733–738, 749, 750
  non-standard form, 717
  powers and, 721–725
  simplifying, 718–720, 748
  standard form, 717–720
  subtracting, 722–725, 749
  trinomial, 717
properties
  addition property of equality, 118
  associative property of addition, 84
  associative property of multiplication, 84
  commutative property of addition, 83
  commutative property of multiplication, 83
  cross products, 349
  distributive, 88–92
  division property of equality, 123
  identity property of addition, 64
  identity property of multiplication, 74
  of inequality, 149, 154, 155
  inverse property of addition, 64
  inverse property of multiplication, 249
  multiplication property of equality, 122
  multiplication property of zero, 74
  power of a product, 727
  product of powers, 202
  quotient of powers, 203
  subtraction property of equality, 117

using
  examples, *Throughout. See for example* 13, 14, 15, 33, 69, 74, 78, 117, 118, 122, 123, 129, 130, 135, 178, 183, 189, 193, 203, 204
  exercises, *Throughout. See for example* 21, 22, 35, 40, 49, 66, 70, 75, 79, 86, 107, 120, 179, 183, 184, 190, 194, 200, 205, 206, 210
variable expression
  constant term of, 89
  evaluating, 13–18, 69, 70, 74, 75, 78, 79, 189–191, 202–211, 244–246, 718–720
  with exponents, 202–211
  like terms in, 89
  simplifying, 90–92, 106, 189–190, 234–237, 239–242, 718–720, 726–730
  terms of, 89
  writing, 14–18
**Algebra tiles**
  to model
    binomial multiplication, 733, 753
    equations with variables on both sides, 298
    one-step equations, 26, 115–116
    polynomial addition, 721
    two-step equations, 127–128
**Algorithm**
  for adding
    decimals, 260
    fractions, 234, 238
    integers, 64
    mixed numbers, 234
  for changing among fractions, decimals, and percents, 255, 359, 360
  for comparing
    fractions, 198
    fractions, decimals, and percents, 361
    mixed numbers, 199
    real numbers, 476
  for creating the Sieve of Eratosthenes, 175
  for dividing
    decimals, 266
    fractions, 247
    integers, 77
  for finding greatest common factor, 181
  for finding least common multiple, 193
  for finding mean, median, and mode, 270
  for finding retail price, 371

  for finding sale price, 370
  for finding sales tax, 371
  for graphing functions, 740
  for graphing a linear equation, 599
  for graphing a linear inequality, 630
  for making
    a circle graph, 659
    a frequency table, 4
    a histogram, 4
    a line graph, 660
    a scatter plot, 588
    a stem-and-leaf plot, 649
  for multiplying
    decimals, 265
    fractions, 243
    integers, 73
  for ordering
    fractions, decimals, and percents, 361
    real numbers, 476
  for order of operations, 8, 20
  for solving an equation, 594
  for solving problems, 38
  for subtracting
    decimals, 260
    fractions, 234, 238
    integers, 68
    mixed numbers, 234
  for writing a fraction in simplest form, 187
  for writing a function rule, 584
**Alternate exterior angles,** 405
**Alternate interior angles,** 405
**Alternative method,** *See* Another way
**Angle(s)**
  acute, 411
  alternate exterior, 405
  alternate interior, 405
  classifying, 403–408
  classifying triangles by, 411–415, 457
  complementary, 403, 648
  congruent, 427
  copying, 409
  corresponding, 405, 427
  exterior, 423
  included, 428
  inverse trigonometric ratios and, 507
  measuring with a protractor, 776
  naming, 774
  obtuse, 411
  pairs of, 403–408, 456–457
  parallel lines and, 405–408
  polygons and, 420–424, 458
  quadrilaterals and, 416–419, 457
  reflex, 415
  right, 403, 411

space flight, 60, 216, 588
speed, 34, 35, 36, 44, 344, 346, 352, 365, 513, 514, 587, 605, 705, 720, 747, 751, 763
structures, 92, 141, 157, 316, 352, 365, 399, 432, 460, 474, 492, 497, 513, 516, 530, 547, 552, 579, 597, 612, 616, 617, 723, 738, 743, 757
surveys, 357, 360, 361, 363, 364, 384, 390, 393, 399, 659, 661, 663, 666, 686, 782, 783, 794
swimming, 196, 490, 530, 603, 682, 707, 737
telephone, 133, 279, 301, 309, 437, 663, 665, 678, 703, 767, 794
television, 17, 201, 277, 782
temperature, 71, 72, 76, 78, 80, 107, 108, 110, 120, 251, 262, 264, 602, 638, 645, 653, 709
time, 285, 309, 778, 791
toys, 480, 641
track, 237, 251, 263, 330, 649, 682
travel, 36, 41, 43, 48, 53, 110, 125, 140, 141, 269, 279, 309, 317, 330, 425, 587
triathlon, 37, 44
vehicles, 25, 152, 171, 237, 253, 352, 365, 505, 605, 612, 641, 747
volleyball, 485
volunteering, 30, 237, 295, 297
water sports, 22, 265, 495, 500, 502
weather, 29, 264, 278, 322, 344, 378, 579, 700, 703
winter sports, 152, 303, 343, 407, 502, 616, 635, 751
**Approximately equal to,** 38
**Approximation,** *See also* Estimation
using a linear graph, 599, 602
of square root, 470–474, 495–497, 509–510
using trigonometric ratios, 501–507
of the value of pi, 310–311, 312
**Arc,** 409
**Arc notation,** to show angle measures are equal, 411
**Area,** 32, *See also* Lateral area; Surface area
of a circle, 527–533, 570, 816
modeling, 527
of composite figures, 35, 88, 89, 92, 144–147, 524–526, 528, 530–532
geometric probability and, 689
maximizing, 745
of a parallelogram, 521–527, 569, 816
modeling, 521

of a rectangle, 31, 143–147, 244, 816
modeling, 31
of a right triangle, 488–491
of similar triangles, 462
of a square, 31, 816
modeling, 31
of a trapezoid, 522–527, 569, 816
modeling, 522
of a triangle, 142–147, 816
modeling, 142
**Area models**
to compare fractions, 198
for geometric probability, 689
scale drawing and, 347
to show addition of fractions, 233
to show area
of a circle, 527
of a parallelogram, 521
of a rectangle, 31
of a square, 31
of a trapezoid, 522
of a triangle, 142
to show division by fractions, 247
to show equivalent fractions, 186
to show fractions, 174
to show multiplication with fractions, 243
to show percent, 359, 363, 364
to show the Pythagorean Theorem, 481
to show ratio, 389, 393
to show square root, 469
**Arithmetic sequence,** 585, 586
**Arrangements**
combinations, 680–684, 707
permutations, 675–679, 707
**Assessment,** *See also* Online Quiz
Chapter Test, 49, 107, 165, 225, 285, 335, 393, 461, 513, 573, 641, 709, 751
Guided Practice, *Throughout. See for example* 3, 4, 8, 9, 13, 14, 15, 19, 20, 27, 28, 33, 34, 37, 38, 39, 57, 58, 63, 65, 69, 74, 77, 78, 84, 85, 89, 90, 94, 95, 118, 123, 129, 130, 134, 135, 143, 144, 149, 150, 155
Problem Solving Practice, 796–800
Problem Solving Strategy Review, 786–795
Quiz, *Throughout. See for example* 24, 43, 81, 100, 139, 159, 196, 217, 252, 278, 308, 329
Skill Check, 2, 56, 114, 174, 232, 292, 342, 402, 468, 520, 582, 648, 716
Skill Practice, *Throughout. See for example* 5, 10, 15–16, 21–22,

28–29, 34–35, 40, 59–60, 65–66, 70, 75, 79, 85–86, 90–91, 96–97, 119–120, 124–125, 131–132, 136, 145–146, 150–151, 156–157
TAKS Practice, 52–53, 110–111, 168–169, 228–229, 288–289, 338–339, 396–397, 464–465, 516–517, 576–577, 644–645, 712–713, 754–755
**Associative property**
for addition, 84
using, 84–86, 105
for multiplication, 84
using, 84–86, 105
**Average(s),** 272, *See also* Mean; Median; Mode
representative, 272–277
**Avoid Errors,** *See* Error analysis
**Axes**
for line graphs, 660
$x$-axis, 94
$y$-axis, 94

## B

**Bar graph,** *See also* Histogram
choosing a data display, 660
exercises, 45, 61, 110
interpreting, 3, 5–7, 45, 710, 783
making, 783
misleading, 667
triple, 6
**Bar notation,** for repeating decimals, 255
**Base(s)**
of a cone, 534
of a cylinder, 534, 544
of a parallelogram, 521
of a percent equation, 375
in a percent problem, 354
of a power, 19
of a prism, 534, 553
of a pyramid, 534
of a trapezoid, 522
of a triangle, 142
**Biased sample,** 701
**Biased survey question,** 702
**Binomial(s),** 717
multiplying, 733–738, 750
using FOIL method, 735–738
using models, 733, 734
**Box-and-whisker plot,** 654–658, 705
choosing a data display, 660
comparing data on, 655–658
extremes of, 654
interpreting, 655–658
interquartile range, 655
making, 654–658, 705

**Equiangular triangle,** 414
**Equilateral triangle,** 411
**Equivalent equations,** 117
**Equivalent fractions,** 187
  finding, 187–191, 232
  modeling, 186
  writing, 188–191
**Equivalent inequalities,** 148
**Equivalent ratios,** 343–346
**Eratosthenes,** 175
**Error analysis**
  Avoid Errors, 4, 19, 74, 77, 90, 118,
    130, 176, 181, 182, 193, 203, 204,
    209, 214, 234, 239, 266, 273, 294,
    304, 319, 367, 371, 372, 435,
    476, 488, 501, 528, 554, 583,
    599, 600, 613, 622, 650, 660,
    661, 717, 722, 727, 739, 741
  exercises, *Throughout. See for*
    *example* 5, 10, 16, 21, 29, 34,
    40, 59, 65, 70, 75, 79, 86, 91,
    96, 119, 120, 124, 131, 136,
    145, 151, 156
**Estimation,** *See also* Approximation
  to check solutions, 248, 265, 266,
    312, 344, 375
  differences, 766
  exercises, 18, 267, 307, 316, 353,
    373, 407, 452, 526, 531, 596,
    656, 730, 755
  high and low estimates, 771
  products, 771
  quotients, 771
  square root, 470–474, 509–510
  sums, 766
  techniques
    clustering, 766
    compatible numbers, 771
    front-end, 261, 263–264
    leading digit, 265, 266
    rounding, 766
**Euler's Formula,** 537
**Evaluating**
  numerical expressions, 8–12, 19–
    23, 46, 47, 83–86, 90, 105–106,
    202–207
  radical expressions, 469, 471–474
  variable expressions, 13–18, 69,
    70, 74, 75, 78, 79, 189–191,
    202–207, 244–246, 718–720
**Event(s),** 381
  complementary, 685–689
  dependent, 694–699, 708
  independent, 694–699, 708
  likelihood of, 381
  odds of, 686–689
  probability of, 381–386
**Examples and nonexamples,** 92,
    320, 420, 473, 595, 598, 717,
    719, 740–741, 742, 750

**Expanded form**
  of a decimal, 759
  of an exponential expression, 202
  of a whole number, 759
**Experiment,** using simulation,
    692–693
**Experimental probability,** 381, 382,
    383, 385, 392
**Exponent(s),** 19, *See also* Powers
  adding to multiply powers, 202–
    207
  negative, 208–211, 224
  notation, 19
  powers and, 19
  rules of, 202–207, 223, 716
  scientific notation and, 212–218,
    224
  subtracting to divide powers,
    203–207, 223
  zero, 209–211, 224
**Expression,** *See* Numerical
    expression; Radical
    expression; Variable
    expression
**Extensions**
  compound inequalities, 151
  constructions, 409–410
  direct and inverse variation,
    618–619
  distance between two points, 490
  drawing trend lines, 591
  misleading graphs, 667–668
  number sets and probability,
    690–691
  samples, 701–702
  sketching solids, 539–540
  solving multi-step proportions, 351
  systems of equations, 627–628
  tessellations, 445–446
  volume of a sphere, 567
**Exterior angles,** 423
**Extra Practice,** 801–813
**Extremes,** data, 654

**F**

**Face(s),** of a polyhedron, 534–535
**Factor(s),** 176–180, 220
  common, 181–185
  divisibility tests and, 761
  factor tree, 177, 178, 220
  greatest common, 181–185, 221
  prime, 177–180, 220–221
  relatively prime numbers and, 182
  scale, 449–454
  Sieve of Eratosthenes and, 175
  writing, 176–180
**Factor tree,** 177, 178, 220
**Factorial(s),** 190, 675–679
  notation, 675

**Factoring**
  a monomial, 178–180
  a number, 176–180, 220–221
**Favorable outcome,** 381
  probability of, 381–386
**FOIL method,** 735
  using, 735–738
**Formulas,** 32
  angle measures in a polygon, 421
  applying, 142–147, 163
  area
    of a circle, 527, 816
    of a parallelogram, 521, 816
    of a rectangle, 32, 48, 816
    of a square, 32, 816
    of a trapezoid, 522, 816
    of a triangle, 142, 816
  circumference, 312, 816
  combination, 681
  distance, 33, 816
  distance between two points,
    490
  lateral area
    of a cone, 549
    of a cylinder, 545
  odds, 687
  percent of change, 366
  perimeter
    of a rectangle, 32, 48, 816
    of a square, 32, 816
    of a triangle, 142, 816
  permutation, 676
  probability, 381, 392, 691
  Pythagorean Theorem, 482, 816
  retail price, 370
  sale price, 370
  simple interest, 376, 816
  slope, 610, 612
  on a spreadsheet, 323
  surface area
    of a cone, 550, 816
    of a cylinder, 544, 816
    of a prism, 543, 816
    of a pyramid, 548, 816
    of a sphere, 551, 737, 816
  table of, 816
  temperature conversion
    Celsius/Fahrenheit, 35, 81, 251,
      602, 815
    Celsius/Kelvin, 262
    Kelvin/Fahrenheit, 264
  volume
    of a cone, 562, 730, 816
    of a cube, 219
    of a cylinder, 555, 727, 816
    of a prism, 554, 816
    of a pyramid, 561, 816
    of a rectangular prism, 180
    of a sphere, 567, 730, 732, 816
  writing, 311

**45°-45°-90° right triangle,** 493–497, 512

**Four-step problem solving plan,** *See* Problem solving plan

**Fraction(s),** 174, 187, 762, *See also* Mixed numbers

adding
common denominators, 233–237, 280, 765
different denominators, 238–242, 281
clearing, 304, 305
comparing, 198–201, 223
decimals and, 255–259, 283, 342, 359–364, 390, 820
denominator of, 187, 762
dividing, 247–252, 282
equations with, 304–307, 332–333
equivalent, 187
finding, 187–191, 232
modeling, 186
improper, 762
least common denominator, 198
mixed numbers and, 199–201, 223, 762
multiplying, 243–246, 281–282, 768
negative, 233
numerator of, 187, 762
order of operations and, 235
ordering, 198–201, 361
percent and, 359–364, 390, 820
rate and, 344–346
ratio and, 343–346
repeating decimals and, 255–259, 283
simplest form, 187, 222
simplifying, 187–191, 222, 226
with powers, 204–207
subtracting
common denominators, 233–237, 280, 765
different denominators, 238–242, 281
with variables, 234–237

**Frequency,** relative, 382

**Frequency table**
intervals in, 4
making, 4–7, 271

**Front-end estimation,** 261, 263–264

**Function(s),** 583
arithmetic sequences and, 585, 586
domain of, 584
evaluating, 584, 586–587
graphing, 598–604, 638
identifying, 583, 585–586, 600
nonlinear, 739–745, 750
graphing, 740–745, 750
range of, 584
relations and, 583, 585–586, 636–637

rule, 584
writing, 584–587, 623
truth, 323
vertical line test for, 740–745
writing rules for, 584–587, 623

**Function form,** 594

**Function notation,** 739

**Function rule,** 584
writing, 584–587, 623

# G

**Games**
Brain Games, 43, 100, 139, 185, 278, 308, 379, 438, 506, 532, 634, 700, 731
Get-Ready Games, xxii–1, 54–55, 112–113, 172–173, 230–231, 290–291, 340–341, 400–401, 466–467, 518–519, 580–581, 646–647, 714–715

**Geometric probability,** 689

**Geometry,** *See also* Area; Measurement; Perimeter; Surface area; Volume

angles
acute, 411
alternate exterior, 405
alternate interior, 405
classifying, 403–408
classifying triangles by, 411–415, 457
complementary, 403, 648
congruent, 427
copying, 409
corresponding, 405, 427
exterior, 423
included, 428
inverse trigonometric ratios and, 507
measuring with a protractor, 776
naming, 774
obtuse, 411
pairs of, 403–408, 456–457
parallel lines and, 405–408
polygons and, 420–424, 458
quadrilaterals and, 416–419
reflex, 415
right, 403, 411
straight, 403
sum in a polygon, 421
sum in a quadrilateral, 417
sum in a triangle, 412, 457
supplementary, 403, 648
triangles and, 411–415, 457
trigonometric ratios and, 498–507
vertex of, 774
vertical, 404

arc, 409
circle, 310–317, 333, 409, 527–533, 570
circumference, 310–317, 333, 336
classifying
angles, 403–408
polygons, 420
quadrilaterals, 416–419, 457
solids, 534–535, 536, 570
triangles, 411–415, 457
compass use, 409–410, 426, 777
constructions, 409, 410, 426, 777
corresponding angles, 405
corresponding parts, 427
endpoint, 773
half-plane, 630
parallel lines, 405
parallelogram, 416, 521–527, 569
perpendicular lines, 404
plane, 773
point, 773
polygon, 420–424, 427–432, 447–454, 458
protractor use, 409, 426, 498–499, 560, 776
Pythagorean Theorem, 481–491, 511, 816
quadrilateral, 416–420, 457
ray, 773
rectangle, 31–36, 143–147, 416, 453
segment, 773
similarity, 447–454, 460, 462, 556, 557, 558
solids, 534–538
classifying, 534–535, 536, 570
composite, 536, 541
faces, edges, and vertices of, 534–535
similar, 556, 557, 558
sketching, 535, 539–540
views of, 535, 536, 539–540
square, 31–36, 343, 416
symmetry
line, 435–438, 459
rotational, 443
tessellation, 445–446
transformations, 433
dilation, 449–454, 460
multiple, 438, 442, 445–446
reflection, 433–438
rotation, 440–444, 460
tessellation, 445–446
translation, 439–444, 460
trapezoid, 416, 522–527, 569
triangles
acute, 411
angle-side-angle congruence, 428–432
angle sum, 412, 457

INDEX

relationship to rational numbers
and whole numbers, 255
subtracting, 68–72, 103–104
**Intercept(s),** 606
finding, 606, 608
using to graph a line, 607–609
interpreting, 607, 609
**Interest**
compound, 379, 380, 735
simple, 376–379, 392, 816
**Interest rate,** 376
annual, 376
**Internet,** *See also* Animated
math; Online Quiz; Texas
@HomeTutor
searching for information on,
140
**Interquartile range,** 655
**Intersection,** of two sets, 690–691
**Interval,** in a frequency table, 4
**Inverse,** of a trigonometric ratio,
507
**Inverse operation,** 117
**Inverse property of addition,** 64
**Inverse property of multiplication,**
249
**Inverse variation,** 619
graphs, 619
**Investigations**
algebra
multiplying binomials, 733
one-step equations, 115–116
slope-intercept form, 620–621
two-step equations, 127–128
data, collecting and analyzing,
270–271
finding the slope of a line, 610–
611
geometry
copying a triangle, 426
diameter and circumference,
310–311
integers, adding, 62
measurement
area, 31
comparing volumes, 560
volume, 553
number sense
equivalent fractions, 186
factors, 175
probability, simulations and,
692–693
the Pythagorean Theorem, 481
scale drawing, 347
trigonometric ratios, 498–499
**Irrational numbers,** 475–480, 510
**Isometric drawing,** 539–540
**Isosceles triangle,** 411

**Justify results,** *Throughout. See for
example* 22, 36, 60, 66, 70, 71,
86, 93, 100, 132

**Key Concept,** 8, 20, 32, 33, 38, 64, 68,
73, 74, 77, 83, 84, 88, 117, 118,
122, 123, 130, 142, 149, 154,
155, 202, 203, 208, 209, 212,
233, 243, 247, 265, 266, 272,
312, 349, 354, 366, 375, 376,
405, 411, 421, 434, 440, 441,
447, 449, 482, 493, 494, 500,
521, 522, 527, 543, 544, 548,
550, 554, 555, 561, 562, 600,
606, 612, 622, 630, 671, 676,
681, 690, 695, 696, 727, 728

**Lateral area,** 545
of a cone, 549
of a cylinder, 545, 546
**Leading digit,** 265
rounding to, 265, 266
**Least common denominator (LCD),**
198
for adding fractions, 238–242, 281
to compare fractions, 198–201, 226
for subtracting fractions, 238–242,
281
**Least common multiple (LCM),** 192
finding, 192–196, 222
of monomials, 193–195
**Leg(s),** of a right triangle, 482
**Length**
on the coordinate plane, 95, 97, 98
measuring, 775
**Like terms,** 89
combining, 89–92, 293–297, 298–
302, 319
**Likelihood,** of an event, 381
**Line(s),** 773
parallel, 405
perpendicular, 404
**Line graph,** 660, 662–664, 784
choosing a data display, 660
double, 663, 668
on a graphing calculator, 665
interpreting, 652, 784
making, 660, 662–664, 784
misleading, 667–668
**Line plot**
making, 782
reading, 782
**Line symmetry,** 435–438, 459

**Line of symmetry,** 435
**Linear equation(s),** 598
graphing
using a graphing calculator, 604
horizontal lines, 600, 601
using intercepts, 607–609, 639
using ordered pairs, 598–603,
638
using slope-intercept form,
620–626, 640, 642
vertical lines, 600, 601
growth rate and, 599
systems of, 627–628
**Linear function,** *See* Linear equation
**Linear inequality**
graph of, 629–633, 640
solution of, 629
**Linear relationships**
non-proportional, 81, 134–139,
142–147, 251, 262, 293–297,
584–587, 593–604, 606–617,
620–626
proportional, 186–191, 310–316,
343–364, 447–454, 493–507
**Linear system,** 627–628
solution of, 627
**List,** *See* Make a list; Organized list
**Logical reasoning,** *See* Error analysis;
Games; Number sense;
Problem solving; Reasoning
**Look for a pattern,** *See also* Patterns
problem solving strategy, 791
**Lower extreme,** 654
**Lower quartile,** 654

**Make a list,** 179, 192, 670, *See also*
Organized list
problem solving strategy, 790
**Make a model,** *See also* Modeling;
Models
problem solving strategy, 786
**Make a table,** problem solving
strategy, 790
**Manipulatives,** *See also* Calculator;
Graphing calculator;
Modeling
algebra tiles, 26, 115–116, 127–128,
298, 721, 733
compass, 409–410, 426, 777
cubes, 553
index cards, 692
magazines, 347
measuring tape, 310–311
number cubes, 270–271
popcorn, 560
protractor, 409, 498–499, 560, 776
ruler, 310–311, 347, 353, 498–499,
560

**Multiple choice questions,** *Throughout. See for example* 6, 7, 10, 11, 16, 17, 18, 21, 22, 24, 25, 29, 30, 35, 36, 40, 41, 43, 44, 51, 52, 53, 59, 60, 61, 66, 67, 70, 71, 72, 75, 76, 79, 80, 81, 82, 86, 87, 90, 91, 92, 96, 97, 99, 101, 109, 110, 111, 119, 120, 121, 124, 125, 131, 133, 136, 137, 139, 141, 145, 146, 147, 151, 152, 153, 156, 157, 158, 159, 160, 167, 168, 169

**Multiple representations,** 192, *See also* Manipulatives; Modeling
examples, 39, 192, 256, 298, 361, 535
exercises, 7, 23, 211, 327, 352, 363, 384, 437, 479, 491, 603, 653, 744

**Multiplication**
binomial, 733–738, 750
to convert among units of measure, 779–781
cross products and, 349
decimal, 265–269, 284, 769
of dimensions, 556, 557, 558
estimating products, 771
exponents and, 19
to find the probability of compound events, 695–699
of fractions, 243–246, 281–282, 768
integer, 73–76, 104
of mixed numbers, 244–246
monomial, 726–730, 749
order of operations and, 8–12
phrases suggesting, 14
with powers, 202–207, 223
in problem solving, 772
properties
associative, 84
commutative, 83
equality, 122
identity, 74
inequality, 154
inverse, 249
product of powers, 202
zero, 74
in scientific notation, 214–217
to solve equations, 122–126, 162
to solve inequalities, 154–159, 164
symbols for, 8

**Multiplication property of inequality,** 154
using, 154–159

**Multiplication property of equality,** 122
using, 122–126

**Multiplication property of zero,** 74

**Multiplicative inverse,** 247
using to divide, 247–252

**Multi-step problems**
examples, *Throughout. See for example* 182, 372, 404, 528, 672
exercises, *Throughout. See for example* 5, 11, 22, 25, 44, 61, 67, 82, 98, 101, 125, 141, 157, 160

# N

***n* factorial,** 190, 675
***n*-gon,** 420
**Negative exponent,** 208–211, 224
**Negative integer,** 57
**Negative slope,** 613–615
**Negative square root,** 469
**Net,** 542–547, 560
**Nonexamples,** *See* Examples and nonexamples
**Nonlinear function,** 739–745, 750
graphing, 740–746, 750
using a graphing calculator, 746

**Notation**
arc, to show angle measures, 411
bar, for repeating decimals, 255
combination, 681
coordinate
to show a reflection, 433–438
to show a rotation, 440–444
to show a translation, 439–444
factorial, 675
function, 739
permutation, 676

**Notetaking,** student help with, 20, 89, 155, 189, 233, 257, 303, 355, 360, 416, 482, 527, 548, 590, 660, 727, 734

**Notetaking skills**
using a concept grid, 520
contrasting terms, 648
illustrating with examples, 468
including vocabulary in notes, 56
keeping a notebook, 2
making a concept map, 402
organizing information, 114
previewing the chapter, 174
recording the process, 292
summarizing material, 716
taking notes in class, 342
writing down your questions, 582
writing helpful hints, 232

**Number line**
to approximate square roots, 470
to compare and order integers, 57
to compare real numbers, 476, 510
to graph compound inequalities, 151
to graph inequalities, 148–151, 154, 156, 318, 320
to model integer addition, 62–64, 103

to order decimals, 361
to order rational numbers, 256
to show absolute value, 58
to show opposites, 58
to show probability, 381
to show time, 72

**Number sense,** *See also* Changing dimensions; Comparing; Estimation; Ordering; Properties
absolute value, 58–61, 102–103
choose a representative average, 273–277
common factors, 181–185
common multiples, 192
composite number, 175, 177
consecutive numbers, 30
divisibility tests, 761
exercises, 10, 42, 60, 157, 180, 195, 205, 259, 268, 322, 327, 356, 357, 558, 625, 684, 744
expanded form, 202, 759
exponents, 19, 202–207, 212–217
factor, 176–180, 220
factorial, 675–679
greatest common divisor (GCD), 181
greatest common factor (GCF), 181–185, 220–221
irrational number, 475–480, 510
leading digit, 265
least common denominator (LCD), 198–201
least common multiple (LCM), 192–196
multiplicative inverse, 247
opposites, 58, 102
outlier, 273
percent, 354, 359–364, 366–374, 376–379
perfect number, 180
perfect square, 470
place value, 759
prime factorization, 177–180, 220–221
prime number, 175, 177
Pythagorean Theorem, 482–491, 511
Pythagorean triple, 488, 489
range, 273–277
rational numbers, 255, 475–480, 510
real numbers, 475–480
relationship between circumference and diameter, 310–311
relationship of rational numbers, integers, and whole numbers, 255
relatively prime numbers, 182–185

rounding, 760
scientific notation, 212–217, 224
Sieve of Eratosthenes, 175
square root, 469–474, 509–510, 818
standard form, 212–217, 759
terminating decimal, 255
twin primes, 180
whole numbers, 759
**Numerator,** 187, 762
**Numerical expression(s),** 8
evaluating
with a calculator, 12
using order of operations, 8–12, 20–23, 46, 47
using properties, 83–86, 90, 105–106, 202–207
with exponents, 202–207
negative, 208–211
factorial, 190, 675

## O

**Obtuse angle,** 411
**Obtuse triangle,** 411
**Octagon,** 420
**Odds,** 686–689
**Online Quiz,** *Throughout. See for example* 7, 11, 18, 24, 30, 36, 43, 61, 67, 72, 76, 81, 87, 92, 99, 121, 126, 133, 139, 147, 153, 159
**Open-ended exercises,** *Throughout. See for example* 6, 7, 11, 17, 25, 30, 35, 44, 66, 70, 82, 97, 101, 121, 125, 132, 137, 141, 145, 151, 152, 157, 160
**Opposite integers,** 58, 102
**Order of operations,** 8–12, 20, 46
on a calculator, 12
for fractions, 235
**Ordered pair,** 94
to graph a linear equation, 598–603, 638
to plot a point, 94–99, 106
**Ordering,** *See also* Comparing
data
in a box-and-whisker plot, 654–658, 705
in a line plot, 782
in a stem-and-leaf plot, 649–653, 704–705
factors, 177
fractions, 198–201, 361
integers, 57–61, 102–103
mixed numbers, 199–201
percents, fractions, and decimals, 361, 362
rational numbers, 256, 258–259
real numbers, 476, 478

**Organized list**
of combinations, 680, 682
to count choices, 670
making to solve a problem, 192, 790
**Origin**
coordinate plane, 94
rotation around, 440–444
**Outcome,** 381, *See also* Event
favorable, 381
odds of, 686–689
probability of, 381–386
**Outlier,** 273, 658
**Output,** 583

## P

**Parabola,** as graph of a nonlinear function, 746
**Parallel lines,** 405
angles and, 405–408
construction, 410
**Parallelogram,** 416
area of, 521–527, 569, 816
base of, 521
height of, 521
**Patterns**
finding, 22, 23, 40, 68, 76, 98, 184, 259, 268, 336, 379, 474, 537, 552, 621, 679, 683, 726
problem solving strategy, 791
rules for multiplying powers and, 202
sequences, 585, 586
tessellations, 445–446
writing function rules from, 584–587
**Pentagon,** 420
**Percent,** 354
applications
discount, 370, 372–374, 391
markup, 371, 373–374, 391
sale price, 370, 372–374, 391
sales tax, 371, 373–374
simple interest, 376–379
tips, 372–374, 391
of change, 366–369, 391
circle graphs and, 360, 363, 364
decimals and, 359–364, 390, 820
decrease, 366–369, 391
equation, 375–379, 392
fractions and, 359–364, 390, 820
increase, 366–369, 391
ordering, 361
proportion and, 354–358, 390
types of problems, 355
**Perfect number,** 180
**Perfect square,** 470
**Perimeter,** 32
of composite figures, 315, 330
in the coordinate plane, 95–99

of a rectangle, 32–36, 143–147, 301, 816
of a right triangle, 488–491
of similar figures, 449
of a square, 32–36, 816
of a triangle, 142–147, 299, 301
**Permutations,** 675–679, 707
combinations and, 680–684, 707
**Perpendicular lines,** 404
construction, 410
**Pi,** 312
equations involving, 312–317
as relationship between circumference and diameter, 310–311
**Pie chart,** *See* Circle graphs
**Place value,** 759
decimals and, 256
**Plane,** 773
**Plot(s)**
box-and-whisker, 654–658, 705
choose a data display, 660
line, 782
scatter, 98, 588–592, 637, 665
stem-and-leaf, 649–653, 704–705
**Point,** 773
coordinate, 94–99, 106
**Polygon(s),** 420–424, 458, *See also* specific polygons
angle measures in, 420, 421
angle sums for, 421
congruent, 427–432, 458
dilations, 449–454
quadrilaterals, 416–419, 420
regular, 420
similar, 447–454
triangles, 411–415, 457
**Polyhedron(s),** 534, *See also* Solids
**Polynomial(s),** 717, *See also* Binomial; Monomial
adding, 721–725, 749
binomial, 717
classifying, 717, 719
evaluating, 718–720
monomial, 717
multiplying
binomials, 733–738, 750
monomials, 726–730, 749
non-standard form, 717
powers and, 726–730
simplifying, 718–720, 748
standard form, 717–720
subtracting, 722–725, 749
trinomial, 717
**Population,** 701
**Positive integers,** 57
**Positive slope,** 613–615
**Positive square root,** 469
**Power of a power property,** 728
using, 728–730

equation, 471–474
multiplying, 495
negative, 469
perfect squares and, 470
radical sign, 469
table of, 819
**Square unit,** 32
**Standard form**
of a decimal, 213–217, 759
of a polynomial, 717–720
of a whole number, 212–217, 759
**Statistics,** *See also* Data; Graphs;
Plots; Probability
choosing a representative average,
273–277
experimental probability, 382, 383,
385
extremes, 654
mean, 78–81, 105, 270, 272
median, 270, 272
mode, 270, 272
outliers, 273, 658
quartiles, 654
range, 273–277, 284
interquartile, 655
surveys, 701–702
theoretical probability, 381–386
trend lines, 591
**Stem-and-leaf plot,** 649–653, 704–705
choosing a data display, 660
double, 650–653, 664
interpreting, 650–653
making, 649–653, 704–705
**Straight angle,** 403
**Straightedge,** 409–410, 426, 610, 620,
777
**Strategies,** *See* Problem Solving
Strategy Review; Test-taking
strategies
**Substitution,** to check solutions, 27,
29, 118, 122, 130, 293, 318,
324, 349, 584, 594, 627
**Subtraction**
commutative property and, 84
decimal, 260–264, 283, 764
estimating differences, 766
to find elapsed time, 778
of fractions
common denominators, 233–
237, 280, 765
different denominators, 238–
242, 281
integer, 68–72, 103–104
as inverse of addition, 117
of mixed numbers
common denominators, 233–
237
different denominators, 239–
242
order of operations and, 8–12

phrases suggesting, 14
polynomial, 722–725, 749
properties
of equality, 117
of inequality, 149
to solve equations, 115–121, 161
to solve inequalities, 148–153, 164
**Subtraction property of equality,**
117
using, 117–121
**Subtraction property of inequality,**
149
using, 149–153
**Supplementary angles,** 403, 648
**Surface area,** 542
of a composite solid, 547
of a cone, 549–552, 571, 816
of a cylinder, 544–547, 571, 816
nets and, 542–547
of a prism, 542–543, 545–547, 571,
816
of a pyramid, 548–552, 571, 816
of a sphere, 551
**Survey**
biased question, 702
biased sample, 701
conducting, 701–702
population, 701
question, 702
random sample, 701
sample, 701–702
**Symbols**
broken axis, 667
degree, 776
factorial, 675
function notation, 739
inequality, 148
is approximately equal to, 38
is greater than, 629
is not equal to, 27
is not less than or equal to, 629
is similar to, 447
*n* factorial, 190
plus or minus, 471
radical sign, 469
right angle, 32
table of, 814
**Symmetry**
line of, 435–438, 459
rotational, 443
**System of linear equations,** 627–628
solution of, 627

### T

**Table**
frequency, 4–7
graphing a nonlinear function
with, 740–745
input-output, 583–586

interpreting, 226–227
multiplying binomials with, 734,
736
organizing information in, 114
**Tables of reference,** 814–817
Table of Formulas, 816
Table of Measures, 815
Table of Properties, 817
Table of Squares and Square
Roots, 819
Table of Symbols, 814
**TAKS,** Grade 8 Mathematics, TEKS4,
*See also* Mixed Review for
TAKS; TAKS Practice; TAKS
Preparation; TAKS Reasoning
**TAKS Practice,** 52–53, 110–111,
168–169, 228–229, 288–289,
338–339, 396–397, 464–465,
516–517, 576–577, 644–645,
712–713, 754–755
examples, 28, 34, 69, 134, 143, 199,
213, 262, 273, 295, 313, 350,
382, 434, 448, 470, 483, 523,
545, 556, 585, 593, 645, 740
exercises
for Obj. 1, 7, 11, 18, 24, 25, 52,
53, 61, 67, 72, 81, 82, 92, 109–
111, 121, 133, 141, 159, 185,
191, 196, 197, 207, 217, 219,
229, 242, 246, 254, 269, 278,
279, 287–289, 297, 307, 309,
330, 338, 339, 358, 364, 365,
395, 396, 415, 424, 425, 464,
480, 486, 492, 508, 516, 517,
526, 541, 547, 568, 576, 577,
592, 605, 635, 644, 645, 679,
703, 731, 732, 738, 747
for Obj. 2, 24, 25, 30, 44, 51, 52,
61, 76, 82, 92, 101, 111, 141,
147, 160, 168, 169, 211, 228,
229, 237, 254, 259, 279, 289,
302, 309, 322, 329, 330, 338,
346, 353, 358, 364, 365, 374,
379, 387, 395–397, 425, 432,
445, 465, 486, 517, 532, 538,
547, 559, 577, 592, 597, 603,
605, 609, 626, 635, 643–645,
658, 674, 689, 703, 712, 713,
725, 731, 732, 745, 747, 755
for Obj. 3, 44, 53, 81, 99, 101,
111, 121, 133, 141, 160, 169,
185, 217, 229, 279, 307, 309,
322, 330, 339, 364, 397, 425,
444, 445, 463–465, 474, 492,
497, 508, 515–517, 541, 575–
577, 587, 617, 635, 658, 713,
732, 754
for Obj. 4, 53, 111, 169, 219, 229,
254, 455, 463, 464, 480, 492,
515–517, 538, 552, 559, 566,

568, 575–577, 603, 617, 633, 645, 720, 725

for Obj. 5, 51, 52, 110, 168, 207, 279, 289, 302, 387, 397, 408, 419, 454, 465, 568, 643, 644, 653, 669, 679, 684, 689, 700, 703, 711–713, 732, 755

for Obj. 6, 7, 25, 30, 36, 43, 44, 53, 72, 82, 87, 99, 101, 111, 126, 139, 141, 153, 159, 160, 167–169, 180, 197, 201, 217, 227–229, 237, 252, 254, 264, 269, 279, 289, 297, 309, 317, 330, 337–339, 365, 369, 374, 386, 387, 397, 408, 415, 419, 424, 425, 432, 438, 444, 454, 455, 465, 474, 491, 492, 506, 508, 526, 532, 541, 566, 568, 577, 597, 605, 635, 645, 664, 669, 703, 713, 732, 745, 747, 753–755

**TAKS Preparation,** 50–51, 108–109, 166–167, 226–227, 286–287, 336–337, 394–395, 462–463, 514–515, 574–575, 642–643, 710–711, 752–753

**TAKS Reasoning**

examples, *Throughout. See for example* 182, 372, 404, 528, 672

exercises, *Throughout. See for example* 6, 7, 10, 11, 16, 17, 21, 22, 23, 29, 30, 35, 36, 40, 41

**Tally mark,** 4

**Tangent ratio,** 500–507, 512

inverse, 507

**Technology activities**

calculator

compound interest, 380

evaluate integer expressions, 93

inverse tangent, 507

operations with fractions, 253

order of operations, 12

scientific notation, 218

graphing calculator

graphing linear functions, 604

graphing nonlinear functions, 746

making data displays, 665–666

Internet, searching for information, 140

spreadsheet

comparing radii of circles, 533

solving inequalities, 323

**Technology support,** *See* Animated Math; Online Quiz; Texas @HomeTutor

**TEKS,** Grade 8, TEKS1–TEKS3

correlations of lessons,

investigations, and technology activities to, *Throughout. See for example* 3, 8, 12, 13, 19, 26, 31, 32, 37, 57, 62, 63, 68, 73, 77, 83, 88, 93, 94

Mixed Review for TEKS, 25, 44, 82, 101, 141, 160, 197, 219, 254, 279, 309, 330, 365, 387, 425, 455, 492, 508, 541, 568, 635, 669, 703, 732, 747

**Temperature**

conversion

Celsius/Fahrenheit, 35, 81, 251, 602, 815

Celsius/Kelvin, 262

Kelvin/Fahrenheit, 264

**Term**

coefficient of, 89

constant, 89

of an expression, 89

of a polynomial, 717

**Terminating decimal(s),** 255

fractions and, 255–259, 283

rational numbers and, 475

**Tessellation,** 445–446

**Tests,** *See* Assessment

**Test-taking strategies,** eliminate choices, 28, 34, 69, 134, 143, 199, 213, 273, 295, 313, 350, 382, 434, 448, 470, 483, 523, 545, 556, 585, 593, 695, 740

**Texas @HomeTutor,** *Throughout. See for example* 2, 45, 49, 56, 102, 107, 114, 161, 165, 174

**Theorem,** triangle inequality, 153

**Theoretical probability,** 381–386, 392, *See also* Probability

**30°-60°-90° right triangle,** 494–497

**Three-dimensional figures,** 534, *See also* Solids; specific solids; Surface area; Volume

**Tick marks,** 411

**Tiling patterns,** *See* Tessellation

**Tip,** percent, 372–374, 391

**Transformations,** 433

dilation, 449–454, 460

multiple, 438, 442, 445–446

reflection, 433–438

rotation, 440–444, 460

tessellation, 445–446

translation, 439–444, 460

**Translating**

verbal phrases, 14–18, 325–329

verbal sentences, 325–329

**Translation,** 439–444, 460

coordinate notation for, 439–444

tessellation and, 445–446

**Trapezoid,** 416

area of, 522–527, 569, 816

base of, 522

height of, 522

**Tree diagram**

factor tree, 177, 178, 220

making, 670, 672–674

**Trend line,** 591

**Triangle(s),** *See also* Right triangle

acute, 411

angle-side-angle congruence, 428–432

angle sum, 412, 457

area of, 142–147, 163, 816

base of, 142

classifying, 411–415, 457

congruent, 428–432, 458

copying, 426

equiangular, 414

equilateral, 411

height of, 142

isosceles, 411

naming, 411

obtuse, 411

perimeter of, 142–147, 299, 301

right, 411

scalene, 411

side-angle-side congruence, 428–432

side-side-side congruence, 428–432

**Triangle inequality theorem,** 153

**Trigonometric ratios,** 498–507, 512

cosine, 498–506, 512

inverse, 507

sine, 498–506, 512

tangent, 500–507, 512

**Trinomial,** 717

**Truth function,** 323

**Twin primes,** 180

**Two-dimensional figures,** *See* Geometry; Polygons; Quadrilaterals; Triangles

**U**

**Undefined slope,** 613–615

**Union,** of two sets, 690–691

**Unit analysis,** 39

**Unit conversion**

customary/customary, 779

metric/customary, 781

metric/metric, 780

rate and, 344–346

temperature

Celsius/Fahrenheit, 35, 81, 251, 602, 815

Celsius/Kelvin, 262

Fahrenheit/Kelvin, 264

**Unit cube,** 553

**Unit price,** 589

**Unit rate,** 344–346, 388–389, 763

**Universal set,** 690
**Upper extreme,** 654
**Upper quartile,** 654

**Variable(s),** 13
  on both sides of an equation, 298–302, 332
  coefficient of, 89
**Variable expression(s)**
  constant term of, 89
  evaluating, 13–18, 189–191, 202–207
    integer, 69, 70, 74, 75, 78, 79
    using multiplication, 244–246
    polynomial, 718–720
  with exponents, 202–207
    negative, 208–211
  like terms in, 89
  simplifying
    by adding and subtracting fractions, 234–237, 239–242
    by combining like terms, 89–92, 106
    using the distributive property, 727–730
    by multiplying monomials, 726–730
    using prime factorization, 188–190
    using properties of powers, 726–730
  terms of, 89
  writing, 14–18
**Variation**
  direct, 618–619
  inverse, 619
**Venn diagram**
  choosing a data display, 660
  exercises, 42
  logical reasoning and, 785
  sets and, 690–691
  showing relationships among numbers, 255, 475
  using to solve a problem, 794
**Verbal model,** 9
  in problem solving, 9, 11, 12, 27, 28, 40, 83, 123, 125, 129, 134, 135, 140, 144, 150, 155, 163, 239, 249, 293, 296, 300, 303, 319, 321, 324, 325, 326, 327, 328, 334, 623
**Vertex (vertices)**
  angle, 774
  of a polyhedron, 534–535
  of a triangle, 411
**Vertical angles,** 404
**Vertical line,** graph of, 600, 601

**Vertical line test,** 740
  using, 740–745
**Views,** of a solid, 535, 536, 539–540
**Vocabulary**
  exercises, *Throughout. See for example* 2, 5, 10, 15, 21, 28, 34, 40, 56, 59, 65, 70, 75, 79, 85, 90, 96, 119, 124, 131, 136, 145, 150, 156
  prerequisite, 2, 56, 114, 174, 232, 292, 342, 402, 468, 520, 582, 648, 716
  review, 45, 102, 161, 220, 280, 331, 388, 456, 509, 569, 636, 704, 748
**Volume(s),** 553, 554
  comparing, 560
  of a composite figure, 558, 564, 565
  of a cone, 562–566, 572, 816
  of a cube, 219
  of a cylinder, 555–559, 572, 816
  modeling, 553
  of a prism, 180, 553–559, 572, 816
  of a pyramid, 560–566, 572, 816
  of a sphere, 567

**What If? questions,** 9, 13, 20, 28, 38, 39, 65, 74, 84, 129, 135, 144, 150, 176, 182, 193, 209, 239, 249, 273, 300, 313, 314, 319, 348, 350, 367, 372, 376, 383, 449, 477, 487, 495, 502, 523, 545, 557, 585, 593, 599, 607, 623, 631, 671, 677, 680, 687, 696, 723, 727
**Wheel of Theodorus,** 492
**Which one doesn't belong? questions,** 79, 190, 267, 301, 422, 477, 624, 656, 742
**Whole number(s),** 759
  expanded form of, 759
  place value, 760
  relationship to integers and rational numbers, 255
  standard form of, 759
**Work backward,** problem solving strategy, 128, 743, 789
**Writing,** *See also* Verbal model
  using coordinate notation, 433–444
  decimals as fractions, 256–259
  equations, 27–30, 123, 125–126, 134–139, 163
  equivalent fractions, 188–191
  a formula, 31, 311
  fractions as decimals, 255–259

function rules, 584–587
  inequalities, 150–153, 166, 319, 321, 324–329
  mixed numbers as improper fractions, 762
  multi-step equations, 293–297
  multi-step inequalities, 319, 321, 324–329
  numbers in scientific notation, 212–217
  percents, decimals, and fractions, 359–364
  polynomials in standard form, 717–720
  probabilities, 382–386
  proportions, 348–353, 389
  rates, 343–346, 389
  ratios, 343–346, 389
  variable expressions, 14–18
**Writing in math,** exercises, 11, 17, 22, 30, 35, 41, 61, 62, 67, 71, 76, 80, 87, 91, 98, 121, 125, 133, 137, 146, 152, 157, 175, 180, 185, 186, 191, 195, 201, 207, 216, 237, 241, 251, 259, 264, 268, 271, 275, 297, 301, 306, 316, 317, 321, 328, 346, 347, 352, 357, 363, 378, 385, 414, 419, 426, 431, 437, 443, 473, 479, 480, 485, 490, 497, 504, 526, 530, 537, 547, 552, 559, 587, 592, 609, 616, 625, 632, 653, 658, 663, 673, 684, 689, 693, 699, 720, 725, 730, 737, 743

**x-axis,** 94
  reflection in, 434
**x-coordinate,** 94
**x-intercept,** 606

**y-axis,** 94
  reflection in, 433, 434
**y-coordinate,** 94
**y-intercept,** 606

**Zero**
  division by, 613
  as an exponent, 209–211
  multiplication property of, 74
  as placeholder, 266
  square root of, 469
**Zero slope,** 613–615

# Credits

**Cover** Yellow Dog Productions/Image Bank/Getty Images; **v** *top* Meridian Creative Group, *top center* Robert C. Jenks, Jenks Studio, *bottom center* McDougal Littell, *bottom* Jerry Head Jr.; **ix** PunchStock; **x** Associated Press, Rockwell; **xi** John Warden/Getty Images; **xii** Getty Images; **xiii** Peter Adams/Index Stock Imagery/PictureQuest; **xiv** Alan Schein Photography/Corbis; **xv** David Kelly Crow/PhotoEdit; **xvi** Royalty-Free/Corbis; **xvii** Craig Tuttle/Corbis; **xviii** Mark Antman/The Image Works; **xix** Myrleen Ferguson Cate/PhotoEdit; **xx** Paul Nicklen/National Geographic/Getty Images; **xxi** Getty Images; **xxiv** Corbis; **1** *left* Joseph Sohm/Chromosohm, Inc./Corbis, *right* Royalty-Free/Corbis; **3** Diaphor Agency/Index Stock Photography, Inc.; **4** Alan Schein/Corbis/Stock Market; **7** The Press-Enterprise, Silvia Flores/AP Wide World Photos; **8** Getty Images; **11** Columbus Telegram/Julie Blum/AP Wide World Photos; **13** *top* PunchStock, *center* Zefa Visual Media—Germany/Index Stock Photography, Inc.; **15** Gérard Villaréal/Photo Researchers, Inc.; **17** James Meyer/The Image Bank/Getty Images; **18** Creatas; **19** Greer & Associates, Inc./Superstock Inc.; **20** Ron Watts/Corbis; **22** Bob Krist/Corbis; **23** Getty Images; **25** Royalty-Free/Corbis; **26** AFP/Corbis; **27** Reuters Newmedia, Inc./Corbis; **29** Lenard Sanders; **30** Getty Images; **32** Johner/Photonica; **34** Barbara Strnadova/Photo Researchers, Inc.; **35** Larry West/Photo Researchers, Inc.; **37** Kevork Djansezian/AP Wide World Photos; **38** Ted S. Warren/AP Wide World Photos; **41** Tony Freeman/PhotoEdit; **44** Royalty-Free/Corbis; **57** Associated Press, Rockwell; **58** Artville, LLC.; **60** Ken O'Donoghue; **61** Bob Daemmrich/The Image Works; **63** Bob Daemrich/PictureQuest; **65** Kwame Zikomo/Superstock Inc.; **67** Gianni Dagli Orti/Corbis; **68** Tim Haske/Index Stock Imagery; **71** Jeff Hunter/The Image Bank/Getty Images; **72** Arthur Morris/Corbis; **73** Stephen Frink/Corbis; **76** *left* PhotoDisc, *right* Corbis; **77** PhotoDisc; **78** Dean Conger/Corbis; **81** Paul A. Souders/Corbis; **82** Caron P./Corbis Sygma; **83** *top* Steve Casimiro/Getty Images, *center* School Division/Houghton Mifflin; **86** Steven Senne/AP Wide World Photos; **87** PhotoDisc; **88** Jim Schwabel/Index Stock Photography, Inc.; **91** Ken O'Donoghue; **94** PhotoDisc/Getty Images; **97** Masterfile (RM); **101** Richard Cummins/SuperStock; **112** NASA; **113** *left* NASA, *right* NASA/Corbis; **117** Bobby Model/National Geographic/Getty Images; **120** Ken O'Donoghue; **121** Darryl Torckler/Getty Images; **122** G.D.T./Getty Images; **123** Peter Hvizdak/The Image Works; **129** Dennis O'Clair/Getty Images; **132** Colin Young-Wolff/PhotoEdit; **134** Getty Images; **135** Gabe Palmer/Corbis; **137** Syracuse Newspapers/The Image Works; **138** *top* Getty Images, *center* Ken O'Donoghue; **141** BananaStock/Alamy; **142** John Warden/Getty Images; **148** Kurt Wittman/Corbis; **150** Ken O'Donoghue; **152** Adrian Weinbrecht/Getty Images; **153** Getty Images; **154** Art Wolfe/Getty Images; **157** Pablo Corral V/Corbis; **158** Tom Prettyman/PhotoEdit; **160** Andre Jenny/Alamy; **172** Alistair Corwin/Index Stock; **173** *background* Benelux Press/Index Stock, *top left* Stephen Simpson/Taxi/Getty Images, *top right* Tom Stewart/Corbis, *bottom left* Benelux Press/Index Stock; **176** Phil Schermeister/Corbis; **179** School Division/Houghton Mifflin; **180** Tom Carter/PhotoEdit; **181** Masterfile (RM); **182** School Division/Houghton Mifflin; **184** Bob Torrez/Stone/Getty Images; **185** Corbis; **187** *top* Erich Lessing/Art Resource, NY, *ruby, sapphire, spinel, emerald* Christie's Images, *pearl* Eric Kamp/Index Stock Photography, Inc.; **191** Claus Meyer/Minden Pictures; **192** Guy Cali/PictureQuest; **195** David Young-Wolff/PhotoEdit; **196** Mark Richards/PhotoEdit; **197** Getty Images; **198** Steve Miller/AP Wide World Photos; **199** Konrad Wothe/Minden Pictures; **201** Tom Stewart/Corbis; **202** Corbis; **206** H. Mark Helfer/NIST; **208** *top* M. Hans/Vandystadt/Photo Researchers, Inc., *bottom* Roger Holden/Index Stock/PictureQuest; **211** Microfield Scientific Ltd./Photo Researchers, Inc.; **212** Getty Images; **213** International Stock/ImageState; **215** NASA; **216** SuperStock, Inc./SuperStock; **219** Ed Bock/Corbis; **230** David Brooks/Corbis; **231** *left* Don Mason/Corbis, *right* School Division/Houghton Mifflin; **233** Donna Day/Stone/Getty Images; **234** Shawn Lockhart, courtesy of Southwest Wisconsin Reptiles; **237** David Madison/Stone/Getty Images; **238** Ryan McVay/PhotoDisc/PictureQuest; **239** Ken O'Donoghue; **241** AP Photo/Todd Bissonette; **243** PunchStock; **244** EyeWire Collection/Getty Images; **246** Gianni Cigolini/Image Bank/Getty Images; **247** Phil Schermeister/Corbis; **249** Tom Stewart/Corbis; **255** G.K. & Vikki Hart/The Image Bank/Getty Images; **256** Steve Maslowski/Photo Researchers, Inc.; **259** Tom Bean/Stone/Getty Images; **260** Chuck Savage/Corbis; **261** Ken O'Donoghue; **263** Peter Adams/Index Stock Imagery/PictureQuest; **265** Bruce Leighty/Index Stock Photography, Inc.; **268** Michael K. Nichols/National Geographic/Getty Images; **269** Brad Lewis/Adventure Photography/ImageState; **272** Ralph White/Corbis; **275** PhotoDisc; **276** Kevin Schafer/The Image Bank/Getty Images; **277** Jon Feingersh/Corbis; **279** Masterfile (RM); **291** Ken O'Donoghue; **293** *both* Ken O'Donoghue; **295** Getty Images; **296** Neo Vision/Photonica; **297** Ken O'Donoghue; **298** ThinkStock/SuperStock; **300** Stockbyte; **303** *top* Gary Bell/Taxi/Getty Images, *center* Georgette Douwma/Taxi/Getty Images; **306** Tony Anderson/Taxi/Getty Images; **309** Picture Quest; **310** Ken O'Donoghue; **311** *top left and top center* Ken O'Donoghue, *top right* PhotoDisc, *bottom left and bottom right* Ken O'Donoghue, *bottom center* Comstock;

312 Alan Schein Photography/Corbis; 314 Jonathan Nourok/PhotoEdit; 316 Getty Images; 317 NASA/USGS/ Stockli, Nelson, Hasler/Laboratory for Atmospheres/ Goddard Space Flight Center; 318 Charles Krupa/AP Wide World Photos; 319 Comstock; 321 Brooklyn Productions/The Image Bank/Getty Images; 324 Duomo/Corbis; 326 Ken O'Donoghue; 327 Bob Daemmrich/The Image Works; 328 Josef Peter Fankhauser/Getty Images; 330 *both* Getty Images; 341 Ken O'Donoghue; 343 Minden Pictures; 347 PhotoDisc; 348 Wolfgang Kaehler/Corbis; 350 Courtesy of the City of Strawberry Point, Iowa; 352 age fotostock/SuperStock; 354 *top* Lee Celano/ AP Wide World Photos, *bottom* PhotoDisc; 357 Kelvin Aitken/Peter Arnold, Inc.; 359 Phillip Lee Harvey/Getty Images; 361 Getty Images; 363 David Young-Wolff/ PhotoEdit; 365 IndexStock; 366 *top* Nik Wheeler/Corbis, *bottom* PhotoDisc; 368 Patrik Giardino/Corbis; 370 *top* Richard Heinzen/SuperStock, *center* Darrell Gulin/ Stone/Getty Images; 372 Horst Herget/Masterfile 373 Ken O'Donoghue; 374 Daniel Allan/Taxi/Getty Images; 375 *top* David Young-Wolff/Photo Edit, *center* PhotoDisc; 376 PhotoDisc; 378 Inga Spence/Index Stock Photography, Inc.; 381 David Young-Wolff/PhotoEdit; 382 Ken O'Donoghue; 385 Don Smetzer/Stone/Getty Images; 387 Creatas; 401 Ken O'Donoghue; 403 Mike Chew/Corbis; 407 Ken O'Donoghue; 408 Index Stock; 409 Ken O'Donoghue; 411 Dean Conger/Corbis; 415 Index Stock; 416 Nikreates/Alamy; 420 Inga Spence/Visuals Unlimited; 421 *top* Ken O'Donoghue, *bottom* PhotoDisc; 425 *top* Stockfolio/Alamy, *bottom* Alan Schein Photography/Corbis; 427 Richard Cummins/Corbis; 431 Courtesy of Michigan State University, Department of Crop and Soil Sciences; 432 Sanford Ponder www.thepod.net; 433 Ken O'Donoghue; 435 *all* PhotoDisc; 439 Michael Newman/ PhotoEdit; 443 *top* Ken O'Donoghue, *bottom left* Masterfile (RM), *bottom center* Royalty-Free/Corbis, *bottom right* Age fotostock/SuperStock; 445 Ken O'Donoghue; 447 *top* Frank Siteman, *screens* Frank Siteman, *televisions* PhotoDisc; 453 *top* EPA/Wayne Conradie/Landov, *bottom* PhotoDisc; 465 PhotoDisc; 466 *top left* ImageState, *center* PhotoDisc/Ken O'Donoghue; 467 *top left* Joe McBride/Stone/Getty Images, *top right* PhotoDisc/Getty Images, *center* PhotoDisc, *bottom right* Royalty-Free/Corbis; 469 Getty Images; 471 Eunice Harris/Photo Researchers, Inc.; 473 Ed Elberfeld/Index Stock Photography, Inc.; 474 Jerry and Marcy Monkman/EcoPhotography.com/ Alamy; 475 Goran Stenberg/AP Wide World Photos; 477 Craig Tuttle/Corbis; 479 Getty Images; 480 Ken O'Donoghue; 482 Royalty-Free/Corbis; 487 Tony Freeman/PhotoEdit; 490 Royalty-Free/Corbis; 492 Werner Foreman/Topham/The Image Works;

493 Cleve Bryant/PhotoEdit; 497 Superstock Inc.; 500 Jeff Greenberg/eStock Photography/PictureQuest; 504 Harvey Lloyd/Taxi/Getty Images; 521 Royalty-Free/ Corbis; 522 Arcaid/Alamy; 527 Mark Antman/The Image Works; 530 Australian Picture Library/Corbis; 534 Index Stock; 536 *all* Ken O'Donoghue; 537 *left* Royalty-Free/Corbis, *second and third from left* Getty Images; 542 Royalty-Free/Corbis; 543 Ken O'Donoghue; 547 Dave G. Houser/Corbis; 548 Kevin Bartram/The Galveston County Daily News/AP Wide World Photos; 551 *left and center* Corbis, *right* PhotoDisc; 552 Royalty Free/Corbis; 554 Mark Gibson/Corbis; 561 Eyewire Collection/Getty Images; 565 Ace Stock Limited/Alamy; 568 Elena Rooraid/PhotoEdit; 581 *left* Jason Hindley/ Stone/Getty Images, *right* Ken O'Donoghue; 583 Lonely Planet Images; 586 Peter Beck/Corbis; 588 Bill Aron/ PhotoEdit; 591 Charles Gupton/Corbis; 593 Merritt Vincent/PhotoEdit; 596 Ken O'Donoghue; 597 Index Stock; 598 Corbis; 602 Antonio Mo/Taxi/Getty Images; 603 Getty Images; 605 Craig Lovell/Corbis; 606 Myrleen Ferguson Cate/PhotoEdit; 609 Tom Stewart/Corbis; 612 Jim Schwabel/Index Stock Photography, Inc.; 616 Nancy R. Cohen/PhotoDisc/Getty Images; 617 Michael Newman/PhotoEdit; 622 RO-MA Stock/ IndexStock; 625 J. H. Robinson/Photo Researchers, Inc.; 626 Ken O'Donoghue; 629 Michael Booth/Alamy; 631 Ken O'Donoghue; 633 Scott Spiker/ImageState; 635 Spencer Grant/PhotoEdit; 646–647 Tui De Roy/ Minden Pictures; 647 *left* Tui De Roy/Minden Pictures, *center* Michio Hoshino/Minden Pictures, *right* Franz Lanting/Minden Pictures; 649 David Young Wolff/ PhotoEdit; 653 Getty Images; 654 Paul Nicklen/National Geographic/Getty Images; 657 Associated Press, AP Photographer Victoria Arocho, Staff; 658 The Time Herald, Tony Pitts/AP Wide World Photos; 659 A. H. Rider/Photo Researchers, Inc.; 669 Jeff Greenberg/ PhotoEdit; 670 David Young-Wolff/PhotoEdit; 673 Jeff Greenberg/The Image Works; 674 Billy Hustace/Stone/ Getty Images; 675 Masterfile (RM); 678 *top* Antonio Mo/ Taxi/Getty Images, *center* PhotoDisc; 680 *top* Index Stock, *center row* Ken O'Donoghue; 683 Ken O'Donoghue; 685 David Gray/Reuters; 689 Stephen Simpson/Taxi/Getty Images; 694 *top* Jeff Greenberg/ PhotoEdit, *bottom* School Division/Houghton Mifflin; 698 David Young-Wolff/PhotoEdit; 699 Frank Siteman; 701 Ken O'Donoghue; 703 Masterfile (RM); 714 *both* Ken O'Donoghue; 715 Comstock; 717 Matthias Clamer/ Stone/Getty Images; 718 Masterfile; 720 Getty Images; 721 Royalty-Free/Corbis; 725 Ken O'Donoghue; 726 SPL/Photo Researchers, Inc.; 729 Getty Images; 730 Reuters/Corbis; 732 PhotoEdit; 734 Tom Carter/ PhotoEdit; 737 Royalty-Free/Corbis; 739 Getty Images; 743 M. Dillon/Corbis

# Selected Answers

## Chapter 1

**1.1 Skill Practice (p. 5)**   **1.** intervals   **3.** restaurant   **5.** about 9 more stores

**7. a.**

| Hours spent on the Internet | Frequency |
|---|---|
| 0-1.9 | 4 |
| 2-3.9 | 6 |
| 4-5.9 | 9 |
| 6-7.9 | 5 |
| 8-9.9 | 4 |
| 10-11.9 | 2 |

**b.**

| Hours spent on the Internet | Frequency |
|---|---|
| 0-2.9 | 7 |
| 3-5.9 | 12 |
| 6-8.9 | 7 |
| 9-11.9 | 4 |

**c.** Part (a); The intervals are smaller.

**9.**

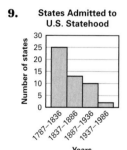

States Admitted to U.S. Statehood

**1.1 Problem Solving (pp. 6 – 7)**   **11. a.** 355, 385, 415, 445, 475, 505

**b.**

Movies Rated and Released

**c.** *Sample answer:* Overall the number of movies has increased but not at a consistent rate.   **15.** 50 years   **17.** No, there does not appear to be a pattern.   **19.** frequency table; A frequency table gives exact numbers of high tides, whereas you have to estimate the number in a histogram.

**1.2 Skill Practice (p. 10)**   **1.** Multiply 2 by 5. Add the result 10 to 8. Subtract 4 from this sum, 18, to obtain the final result, 14.   **5.** 12   **7.** 18   **9.** 6   **11.** 4   **13.** 5   **15.** 12   **17.** 7   **19.** 30   **21.** 1.2   **23.** 3   **27.** $5 \cdot (2 + 3) - 8 = 17$   **29.** $13 - 5 \cdot (8 - 6) = 3$   **31.** $(12 \div 3) \cdot (4 + 1) = 20$

**1.2 Technology Activity (p. 12)**   **1.** 106.8   **3.** 7   **5.** 5   **7.** 2   **9.** \$10.44   **11.** \$65.68

**1.3 Skill Practice (pp. 15 – 16)**   **1.** variable; numerical   **3.** 23   **5.** 15   **7.** 30   **9.** 28   **11.** 3   **13.** 4 must be multiplied by 7 before 5 is added; $5 + 28 = 33$   **15.** $10 - x$

**17.** $\dfrac{x}{7}$   **19.** $x - 15$   **21.** $22x$   **23.** 32.8; increased, 60.8 $>$ 32.8   **25.** 96; not changed, $96 = 96$   **27.** 1.6; increased, $29.6 > 1.6$   **29.** 10; decreased, $0.9 < 10$   **31.** 2.87   **33.** 3.74

**1.3 Problem Solving (pp. 16 – 18)**   **39.** 31.5 mi   **41.** $30x + 60y - 3z$   **43.** $20 - (2.75p + 2.5d)$; \$1.75   **49.** 1.8 cm; 3.6 cm   **51.** *Sample answer:* The temperature of the room or the thickness of different parts of the sculpture could affect the melting rate.

**1.4 Skill Practice (pp. 21 – 22)**   **1.** *Sample answer:* $4^5$ $_{\text{base}}$ $^{5\text{ exponent}}$   **3.** $9^5$; 9 to the fifth power   **5.** $n^6$; n to the sixth power   **7.** 1331   **9.** 64   **11.** 0   **13.** 121   **15.** 1000   **17.** 400   **19.** 16   **21.** 119   **23.** 432   **25.** 5   **27.** 221   **29.** 100   **31.** 49   **33.** 54   **35.** 7   **39.** $<$   **41.** $<$   **43.** $=$   **45.** 159.3   **47.** 2, 4, 8, 6; 4   **49.** 4, 16, 64, 256, 1024, 4096; 6, 4; The pattern is 6 and 4 alternating.

**1.4 Problem Solving (pp. 22 – 23)**   **53.** 289 in.²   **55. a.** No, the diver has fallen only 64 ft.   **b.** 80 ft; After 3 sec the diver has fallen 144 ft. The difference of 144 and 64 is 80.   **57.** $n^2$   **61.** 48 mi/h   **65.** 1; 1; $x^1 = x$ and $\dfrac{x}{x} = 1$, so $x^0 = 1$.

**1.5 Skill Practice (pp. 28 – 29)**   **1.** solving an equation   **3.** 22   **5.** 11   **7.** 11   **9.** 29   **11.** 2   **13.** 15   **15.** 17   **17.** 2   **19.** no   **21.** no   **23.** yes   **27.** 24 divided by what number is 8? 3   **29.** 24 times what number is equal to 8? $\dfrac{1}{3}$   **31.** 3   **33.** 1   **35.** 4

**1.5 Problem Solving (pp. 29 – 30)**   **45.** $14 + x = 43$; 29 in.   **47.** $5033 + b = 5396$; 363 lb   **53.** $8h = 200 - 80$; 15 h

**1.6 Skill Practice (pp. 34 – 35)**   **1.** Area is the surface a figure covers, while perimeter is the distance around the figure.   **3.** $P = 30$ yd, $A = 54$ yd²   **5.** $P = 20$ m, $A = 25$ m²   **7.** The units should be square meters; $A = s^2 = (4)^2 = 16$ m²   **9.** 6 m   **11.** 324 in.²   **13.** 11 in.   **15.** 5 mi   **17.** 8 sec   **19.** 15 ft/sec   **21.** $P = 48$ in., $A = 126$ in.²

**1.6 Problem Solving (pp. 35 – 36)**   **27.** 68° F   **29.** about 4 h   **31.** 1560 ft

**1.7 Skill Practice (p. 40)**   **1.** Read and Understand, Make a Plan, Solve the Problem, Look Back   **3.** You know the cost of lunch and the cost of the drink. You need to find out what the customer's change is.   **5.** Find the total spent on hot dogs and add it to the ticket cost. Then compare the total to $16.   **7.** $10   **9.** $4; "Each pack of pens contains 12 pens" is unnecessary information.   **11.** $69x^5$, $66x^6$

**1.7 Skill Practice (pp. 41 – 42)**

**15. a.** $\dfrac{\text{Number of people who ride in one hour}}{5 \text{ cars} \cdot 4 \text{ passengers}}$ = Number of trains that run   **b.** 45 trains   **c.** $45 \cdot 5 \cdot 4 = 900$   **19.** 150 mi   **23.** 16 pages   **25.** 3 dimes, 7 quarters   **27.** five 3 minute acts   **29.** 8 and 13   **31.** 5.4 mi; 1.8 mi

**Chapter Review (pp. 45 – 48)**   **1.** histogram   **3.** order of operations   **5.** 35–44; 65+   **7.** 39   **9.** 22   **11.** 3   **13.** 21   **15.** 2.6   **17.** 70   **19.** $n + 12$   **21.** $2 \cdot 28.5 - 20$; $37   **23.** 1024   **25.** 6561   **27.** 1260   **29.** 144 ft   **31.** 7   **33.** no   **35.** no   **37.** 16 cm   **39.** 150 mi

# Chapter 2

**2.1 Skill Practice (pp. 59 – 60)**   **1.** absolute value   **3.** >   **5.** <   **7.** >   **9.** >   **11.** $-20, -10, 5, 13, 15, 27$   **13.** $-20, -12, 18, 44, 59, 64$   **17.** 19; $-19$   **19.** 740; 740   **21.** B   **23.** D   **25.** 32   **27.** $-29$   **29.** 81   **31.** $-3$   **33.** =   **35.** <   **37.** $-|47|, -28, |-65|, -(-73), |95|$   **39.** $-14, -8, -|6|, |-1|, -(-5)$

**2.1 Problem Solving (pp. 60 – 61)**   **45.** Gieselmann Lake, Jones Lake, Craigs Pond, Silver Lake, Seneca Lake   **49.** 0   **51.** If $a$ and $b$ are both positive, or if $a$ is negative and $b$ is positive, then $a < b$. If $a$ and $b$ are both negative, or if $a$ is positive and $b$ is negative, then $a > b$.   **53.** methanol, ethanol, propanol, water; Water will remain because it will have been boiling for the shortest time.

**2.2 Skill Practice (pp. 65 – 66)**   **1.** absolute values   **3.** $-12$   **5.** 0   **7.** $-19$   **9.** 2   **13.** $-112$   **15.** 0; Inv. Prop. of Add.   **17.** $-30$   **19.** $-8$   **21.** $-29$   **23.** 7   **25.** $-3$   **27.** $-37$   **29.** 37   **31.** 51   **33.** $-1207$   **35.** $-999$   **37.** always; The sum will have the common sign, which is negative.   **39.** sometimes; It will be negative if the number with the greater absolute value is negative.   **41.** 194   **43.** $-14$

**2.2 Problem Solving (pp. 66 – 67)**   **49.** 0   **51.** $+3$   **55. a.** 900   **b.** 300 B.C.   **c.** 1200 years   **57.** above par; $-2$ or 2 under par

**2.3 Skill Practice (p. 70)**   **1.** $-2 - 6$   **3.** $-7$   **5.** $-4$   **7.** 0   **9.** $-8$   **11.** $-27$   **13.** 44   **15.** 5   **17.** $-71$   **19.** $-15$   **21.** $-5$   **23.** $-23$   **25.** 13   **29.** 5   **31.** 8   **33.** $-12$   **35.** 101   **37.** yes; *Sample answer:* The distance between two numbers is the same regardless of the order in which you subtract them. However, the difference is positive if you start with the greater number and negative if you start with the lesser number. So, $x - y$ and $y - x$ are always opposite.

**2.3 Problem Solving (pp. 71 – 72)**   **41.** $-1000$   **45.** 43°F   **49.** Jurassic Period; $\dfrac{64}{186}$ or about $\dfrac{1}{3}$   **51.** 41°F

**2.4 Skill Practice (p. 75)**   **1.** negative   **3.** 28   **5.** $-18$   **7.** $-42$   **9.** 0; Mult. Prop. of Zero   **11.** $-18$   **13.** 180   **15.** $-6$; Ident. Prop. of Mult.   **17.** 270   **19.** 60   **21.** $-280$   **23.** The product of two integers with the same sign is positive; $-8(-12) = 96$   **25.** 49   **27.** $-48$   **29.** 196   **31.** 93   **33.** $-53$   **35.** 52   **37.** 224   **39.** 336   **41.** $-4$   **43.** $-4$   **45.** $-10$   **47.** $-4$   **49.** no; *Sample answer:* $(-3)^2 = (-3)(-3) = 9$ and $-3^2 = (-1)(3)(3) = -9$

**2.4 Problem Solving (p. 76)**   **53.** $-96$ in.   **55.** $400 + 5(-125) = -225$   **57.** $-10$; 100; $-1000$; 10,000; $-100,000$; *Sample answer:* When the exponent is even, the sign is positive. When the exponent is odd, the sign is negative.

**2.5 Skill Practice (p. 79)**   **1.** mean   **3.** 0   **5.** $-5$   **7.** $-14$   **9.** 19   **11.** undefined   **13.** $\dfrac{1}{5}$   **15.** $-1$   **17.** $-\dfrac{16}{7}$ or about $-2.29$   **19.** $-3$   **21.** $-3$   **23.** $-3$   **25.** 4   **27.** 14   **29.** $-4$   **31.** 27   **33.** 19   **35.** A

**2.5 Problem Solving (pp. 80 – 81)**   **43.** points: 21; assists: 4; rebounds: 11; *Sample answer:* If the data values are not all the same, then the mean cannot be the highest value or the lowest value, so there are actual values in the data set that are above and below the mean.   **45.** –29.2°F

**2.6 Skill Practice (pp. 85 – 86)**   **1.** E   **3.** B   **5.** D   **7.** 45; Assoc. Prop. of Add.; Comm. Prop. of Add.   **9.** $-290$; Assoc. Prop. of Mult.; Comm. Prop. of Mult.   **11.** 21; Assoc. Prop. of Add.   **13.** $-140$; Comm. Prop. of Mult.; Assoc. Prop. of Mult.   **15.** $-900$; Comm. Prop. of Mult.; Assoc. Prop. of Mult.   **17.** $16 \cdot 54$   **19.** $4 + (2 + 9)$ or $(9 + 2) + 4$   **21.** $(16 + 8) + 2$ or $2 + (8 + 16)$   **23.** 69; $45 - (-68) - 44 = 45 + 68 + (-44)$ [Change Sub. to Add.] $= (45 + 68) + (-44)$ [Comm. Prop. of Add.] $= 113 + (-44)$ [Add] $= 69$ [Add]   **25.** 3; $(-26 + 33) + (-4) = 7 + (-4) = 3$ [Add]   **27.** 6; $\left(\dfrac{2}{7} + 5\right) + \dfrac{5}{7} = \left(5 + \dfrac{2}{7}\right) + \dfrac{5}{7}$ [Comm. Prop. of Add.] $= 5 + \left(\dfrac{2}{7} + \dfrac{5}{7}\right)$ [Assoc. Prop. of Add.] $= 5 + 1$ [Add] $= 6$ [Add]   **29.** 420; $12 \cdot (7 \cdot 1 \cdot 5) = 12 \cdot (7 \cdot 5)$ [Ident. Prop. of Mult.] $= 12 \cdot 35$ [Mult.] $= 420$ [Mult.]   **31.** 57; $36 + 57 + (-36) = 36 + (57 + (-36))$ [Assoc. Prop. of Add.] $= 36 + (-36 + 57)$ [Comm. Prop. of Add.] $= (36 + (-36)) + 57$ [Assoc. Prop. of Add.] $= 0 + 57$ [Inv. Prop. of Add.] $= 57$ [Ident. Prop. of Add.]   **33.** 10; $24 + (-12 - 8) + 6 = 24 + 6 + (-12 - 8)$ [Comm. Prop. of Add.] $= 30 + (-12 - 8)$ [Add] $= 30 + [-12 + (-8)]$ [Add Opposite] $= 30 + (-20)$ [Add] $= 10$ [Add]   **35.** $70x$   **37.** $x + 70$

**2.6 Problem Solving (pp. 86 – 87)**   **41.** 15 in.³; *Sample answer:* The box is 2.5 in. · 1.5 in. · 4 in., so the unit is in. · in. · in. or in.³   **43.** no; *Sample answer:* The expressions do not have same terms; The difference is that the first expression has "$-15$" and the second has "$+15$".   **47.** discount: $15.75; purchase: $31.50

**2.7 Skill Practice (pp. 90 – 91)**   **1.** $-6$   **3.** $-6y$   **5.** B   **7.** A   **9.** $28 + 32$; 60   **11.** $15 + 18$; 33   **13.** $-30 + 60 + 12$; 42   **17.** $-40 + 8x$   **19.** $95 + 19w$   **21.** $6 + 2x$   **23.** $16w + 12z$   **25.** $5x + 3y - 3$   **27.** $4r + s$   **29.** $11z$   **31.** $8c - 14$   **33.** $2a + 8b - 14$   **35.** $-5.6x + 4.4y + 4.4z$

**39.** *Sample answer:* $9(19) = 9(20 - 1) = 180 - 9 = 171$
**41.** *Sample answer:* $65(24) = 65(10 + 10 + 4) = 650 + 650 + 260 = 1300 + 260 = 1560$

**2.7 Problem Solving (pp. 91 – 92)   47.** $786.24

**2.7 Technology Activity (p. 93)   1.** $-28,546$   **3.** $11,009$
**5.** $-2,105,804$   **7.** $-262,890,144$   **9.** $-101$   **11.** yes;
*Sample answer:* The numbers of blueberries in your
3 packages are $170 - 12 = 158$, $170 - 8 = 162$, and
$170 + 16 = 186$. The average for your 3 packages is
$\frac{158 + 162 + 186}{3} = 168\frac{2}{3}$. That is a little below the claimed
average of 170, but 3 packages is a small sample.

**2.8 Skill Practice (pp. 96 – 97)**

**1.**

**3.** $(-3, 3)$   **5.** $(-5, 0)$   **7.** $(0, -2)$   **9.** $(-2.5, 2)$   *11–19. All*
*descriptions start "Begin at the origin."*   **11.** 4 to the right,
1 up; Quadrant I   **13.** 3 to the left; on the $x$-axis   **15.** 2 to
the left, 3 up; Quadrant II   **17.** 5 down; on the $y$-axis
**19.** 8.2 to the left, 6.1 up; Quadrant II   **21.** 2.4 to the
right; on the $x$-axis   **23.** The $x$ and $y$ coordinates are
reversed. For $P(2, 3)$, start at the origin, move 2 to the
right, then 3 up. For $Q(1, -1)$, start at the origin, move 1
to the right, 1 down.

**25.** square; 20 units

**27.** rectangle; 36 units

**29.** $P = 20$ units, $A = 17$ units²;

**31.** $P = 25$ units, $A = 25$ units²;

**33.** 11 units; $(9, 12)$ and $(2, 12)$; $(9, -10)$ and $(2, -10)$

**2.8 Problem Solving (pp. 97 – 99)   37.** $(2, 5)$, $(8, -1)$,
$(2, -7)$, $(-4, -1)$   **39.** 2000 ft

**43. a.** $.70; $1.40; $2.10   **b.**

**c.** $4.20
**45.** $A(-2, 6)$, $B(1, 4)$, $C(0, 1)$, $D(-4, 1)$, $E(-5, 4)$;

**47.** *Sample answer:* It is larger than the original; The
perimeter of the second rectangle is twice the perimeter
of the original rectangle.

**49.**

| width $x$ (cm) | 1 | 2 | 3 | 4 | 5 | 6 | 7 | 8 |
|---|---|---|---|---|---|---|---|---|
| Perimeter $P$ (cm) | 18 | 20 | 22 | 24 | 26 | 28 | 30 | 32 |

The ordered pairs lie on a line. (An equation of the line is
$P = 2x + 16$.);

# Chapter Review (pp. 102 – 106)

**1.** two; 15, −15 **3.** 4;

**5.** coordinate plane **7.** −42, −31, −5, 8, 11, 53 **9.** −22; 22 **11.** 512; 512 **13.** 92; 92 **15.** −147; 147 **17.** −172 **19.** 176 **21.** 401 **23.** −48 **25.** 34 **27.** −336 **29.** −86 **31.** 79 **33.** 137 **35.** −134 **37.** −54 **39.** 0 **41.** −192 **43.** −140 **45.** 56 **47.** 160 **49.** 152 ft **51.** 14 **53.** −9 **55.** −7 **57.** 3 **59.** 1 **61.** −3 **63.** −100; Comm. Prop. of Add., Assoc. Prop. of Add. **65.** 1900; Comm. Prop. of Mult., Assoc. Prop. of Mult. **67.** 1500; Assoc. Prop. of Mult. **69.** 3; Zero Prop. of Mult., Ident. Prop. of Add. **71.** $60x − 100$ **73.** $100z − 120$ **75.** $135 − 108t$ **77.** $7x − 2y$ **79.** $−4x − 6y$ **81.** $49a + b$ **83.** $84.50 **85.** $(−4, 3)$ **87.** $(−2, −3)$

# Chapter 3

**3.1 Skill Practice (pp. 119 – 120)** **1.** inverse **3.** 6 **5.** 64

**7.** 7 **9.** 17 **11.** 40 **13.** −163 **15.** 1 **17.** 0.2 **19.** $\frac{1}{3}$

**21.** 1000 should be subtracted from both sides instead of added; $x + 1000 − 1000 = 5000 − 1000$; 4000 **23.** 8 **25.** −31 **27.** 35 **29.** $n + 12 = 25$; 13 **31.** $n − 3 = −16$; −13 **33.** $97 = 24 + 16 + k + 38$; 19 cm **35.** paper and pencil; 59 **37.** paper and pencil; 1173 **39.** negative; $−50 + 12 < 0$ **41.** 9 **43.** 3

**3.1 Problem Solving (pp. 120 – 121)** **47. a.** tax **b.** $54.99 + x = 58.29$ **c.** $3.30 **49.** not correct; $t = 29 − 3$; 26°F **53.** $45 + x = 104$; 59 in. **55.** female: 8 in./year; male: 7 in./year; female

**3.2 Skill Practice (pp. 124 – 125)** **1.** divide **3.** dividing by 5 **5.** subtracting −6 **7.** dividing by −3 **9.** 18 **11.** 13 **13.** 9 **15.** 10 **17.** 2.5 **19.** −2.1 **21.** 3 **23.** −6 **25.** −31.5 **31.** −8; simplify; divide each side by −1

**33.** 4; multiply each side by 6; simplify **35.** $12\frac{2}{3}$; multiply each side by 4; simplify

**3.2 Problem Solving (pp. 125 – 126)** **43.** $1950 = 30x$; 65

**45.** $7a = 56$; $8 **49.** $100 = \frac{1}{5}t$; 500 m **51.** 22; 5

**3.3 Skill Practice (pp. 131 – 132)** **1.** solution **3.** 3 **5.** 1 **7.** −8 **9.** 81 **11.** −5 **13.** 8 **15.** 30 **17.** 48.8 **19.** −12 **23.** equation; distributive property; subt. prop. of equality; simplify; division prop. of equality; simplify **25.** 2; Use Exercise 24 because 3 divides into 9 easily.

**27.** 3; Use Exercise 23 because $6 \times \frac{1}{3}$ eliminates the fraction. **29.** $4x + 9 = 5$; −1; $3y − 10 = 2$; 4 **31.** $4h − 6 = −24$, undo division and simplify; $4h = −18$, undo

subtraction and simplify; $h = −4.5$, undo multiplication and simplify **33.** $2w − 3 = 45$, undo division and simplify; $2w = 48$, undo subtraction and simplify; $w = 24$, undo multiplication and simplify **35.** $2(4t − 7) = −66$, undo division and simplify; $4t − 7 = −33$, undo multiplication and simplify; $4t = −26$, undo subtraction and simplify; $t = −6.5$, undo multiplication and simplify

**3.3 Problem Solving (pp. 132 – 133)** **39.** 11 **43.** 19

**3.4 Skill Practice (pp. 136 – 139)** **1.** equation **3.** D **5.** A **9.** $5n + 4 = 9$; 1 **11.** $−2n + 3.5 = 7.5$; −2

**13.** $\frac{|n|}{6} = 4$; 24, −24 **15.** $|n| + 6 = 12$; 6, −6

**3.4 Problem Solving (pp. 136 – 139)** **21. a.** profit = cash taken in − expenses **b.** $93 = 6n − 15$ **c.** 18 **d.** $93 + 15 = 108$ and $108 ÷ 18 = 6$ **23.** 7 **25.** $7 **29.** 16 **31.** 29 **33.** 10 mi; no; $2 + 30 = 32$, $32 ≠ 2 × 17$ **35.** You need to know how many hours you worked.

**3.5 Skill Practice (pp. 145 – 146)** **1.** base; height **3.** 12 cm²; 16 cm **5.** 30 ft²; 30 ft **7.** 3 ft **9.** 20 m

**11.** 504 in.² **17.** 3 m **19.** $\frac{20}{w}$ in.

**3.5 Problem Solving (pp. 146 – 147)** **23. a.** 42 yd² **b.** 9 yd² **c.** 51 yd² **29.** doubles **31.** quadruples

**3.6 Problem Solving (pp. 150 – 152)** **1.** equivalent inequalities **3.** A **5.** D **7.** $x ≥ −5$; all numbers greater than or equal to −5 **9.** $x < 6$; all numbers less than 6

**11.** $p < −5$;

**13.** $n > 9$;

**15.** $m ≤ 11$;

**17.** $b < −9$;

**19.** $t > 4\frac{3}{4}$;

**21.** 1 through 9 **23.** 1 through 9 **29.** yes; When $x$ is less than 2, 2 is greater than $x$. **35.** $t$ is greater than or equal to 7 and less than 9; $t$ is between 7 and 9, including 7.

**3.6 Problem Solving (pp. 152 – 153)** **37. a.** 360 **b.** $x + 360 ≥ 425$; $x ≥ 65$ **c.**

**39.** $x + 57 > 93.5$; $x > 36.5$m **43.** $2.5 − x < 1.9$; $x > 0.6$ h; 37 min **45.** $T − 2200 ≤ 2000$; $T ≤ 4200$; one icon

**3.7 Skill Practice (pp. 156 – 157)** **1.** reverse the direction of **3.** no **5.** yes **7.** $x ≤ 32$; D **9.** $x ≥ −2$; A

**11.** $x < 8$;

**13.** $z ≥ 3$;

**15.** $x > 4$;

**17.** $b ≤ −360$;

**19.** $g < 6$;

**21.** $c \geq -6$;

**23.** $r > -56$;

**25.** $k \geq -3$;

**27.** The inequality does not need to be reversed; $-3 < x$

**31.** $p \geq 2$;

**33.** $g < 2\frac{1}{4}$;

**35.** $a \leq 36$;

**39.** $8 < n < 16$

**3.7 Problem Solving (pp. 157 – 159)** **43.** $5.5\,x \geq 275$; $x \geq 50$ **45.** You still have to isolate the variable by performing inverse operations. If multiplying or dividing by a negative number, you must reverse the direction of the inequality. **47. a.** $150p \leq 2000$ **b.** $p \leq 13.\overline{3}$ **c.** Up to 13 average sized people can ride the elevator together. **49.** $12l > 228$; $l > 19$ **51.** You can list all the solutions to an inequality used to find the possible measurements of the width of a pool. You cannot list all the solutions to an inequality used to find the number of people at the dance. **55.** $2w + 2(2w - 20) \geq 53$; $w \geq 15.5$; 16 in. by 11 in.

**Chapter Review (pp. 161 – 164)** **1.** addition and subtraction, multiplication and division; Inverse operations undo each other. **3.** equivalent **5.** $-11$

**7.** 12 **9.** $-9$ **11.** $\frac{4}{7}$ **13.** 14.8 **15.** 27 **17.** 55 **19.** 2

**21.** 9 **23.** $-72$ **25.** 27 **27.** $4p + 3 = 55$; 13 **29.** 12 **31.** 640 **33.** 9 ft **35.** $k \leq 10$;

**37.** $d \geq -6$;

**39.** $b \leq -2$;

**41.** $p < 10.2$;

**43.** $d \leq 204$ **45.** $b > -4$ **47.** $k \geq 9$ **49.** $z < 2$

# Chapter 4

**4.1 Skill Practice (pp. 178 – 179)** **1.** prime **3.** 1, 2, 3, 6, 9, 18 **5.** 1, 2, 17, 34 **7.** 1, 29 **9.** 1, 2, 3, 4, 6, 9, 12, 18, 27, 36, 54, 108 **11.** 1, 13, 23, 299 **13.** 1, 2, 4, 5, 8, 10, 16, 20, 25, 40, 50, 80, 100, 200, 400 **15.** composite **17.** prime **19.** $8, 2, 2, 2, 11; 2^3 \cdot 11$ **21.** $2, 2, 21, 5, 3, 7; 2 \cdot 3 \cdot 5 \cdot 7$ **23.** $5 \cdot 11$ **25.** $2^5 \cdot 3$ **27.** $2^2 \cdot 3^2 \cdot 11$ **29.** $2^4 \cdot 5^3$ **31.** $3 \cdot 5 \cdot c \cdot d$ **33.** $3 \cdot 3 \cdot x \cdot x \cdot y$ **35.** $2 \cdot 2 \cdot 2 \cdot 2 \cdot 3 \cdot n \cdot n \cdot n \cdot m \cdot m \cdot m$ **37.** $2 \cdot 2 \cdot 5 \cdot a \cdot b \cdot b \cdot b \cdot b \cdot c \cdot c$ **39.** 1 does not need to be included, 6 is not factored, and there are

two factors of $x$; $18x^2y = 2 \cdot 3 \cdot 3 \cdot x \cdot x \cdot y$. **41.** $56 = 2 \cdot 2 \cdot 2 \cdot 7$; Find all other combinations of products of the prime factors. $2, 2 \cdot 2, 7, 2 \cdot 2 \cdot 2, 2 \cdot 7, 2 \cdot 2 \cdot 7$. **43.** $225 = 3 \cdot 3 \cdot 5 \cdot 5$; Find all other combinations of products of the prime factors; $3, 5, 3 \cdot 3, 3 \cdot 5, 5 \cdot 5, 3 \cdot 3 \cdot 5, 3 \cdot 5 \cdot 5$. *45–47. Sample answers are given.* **45.** $3 + 13$ **47.** $7 + 23$

**4.1 Problem Solving (pp. 179 – 180)** **49. a.** 1, 2, 3, 4, 5, 6, 8, 10, 12, 15, 20, 24, 30, 40, 60, 120 **b.** 1 and 120, 2 and 60, 3 and 40, 4 and 30, 5 and 24, 6 and 20, 8 and 15, 10 and 12 **c.** 8 and 15, 10 and 12; *Sample answer:* The other arrangements would make an unreasonably long and narrow quilt.

**4.2 Skill Practice (pp. 183 – 184)** **1.** greatest common factor, or GCF **3.** 14 **5.** 4 **7.** 3 **9.** 1 **11.** The student forgot to include 2 as a factor twice; The GCF is $2 \cdot 2 \cdot 5 = 20$. **13.** no; 5 **15.** yes **17.** no; 18 **19.** yes **21.** $3x$ **23.** $5t^4$ **25.** $6s$ **27.** $3t$ **29.** 1 **35.** sometimes; For example, the GFC of 5 and 10 is 5. **37.** always; 1 is the only factor the two numbers share. **39.** Multiply the previous monomial by $4rs^2$; $256r^5s^7$, $1024r^6s^9$, $4096r^7s^{11}$; $4r^2s$

**4.2 Problem Solving (pp. 184 – 185)** **45.** *Sample answer:* The only factors of any prime number are 1 and itself, so the only common factor any two prime numbers can have is 1. For example, $5 = 1 \cdot 5$ and $7 = 1 \cdot 7$ have only 1 as a common factor, as do $43 = 1 \cdot 43$ and $79 = 1 \cdot 79$. **47.** The GCF of $cx$, $cy$, and $cz$ is the product of $c$ and the GCF of $x$, $y$, and $z$.

**4.3 Skill Practice (pp. 189 – 190)** **1.** simplest form **3.** $\frac{3}{7}$ **5.** $\frac{2}{3}$ **7.** $\frac{-5}{8}$, or $-\frac{5}{8}$ **9.** $\frac{3}{4}$ **11.** $\frac{-7}{8}$, or $-\frac{7}{8}$ **13.** yes

**15.** yes **17.** no **19.** yes **21.** C *23–25. Sample answers are given.* **23.** $\frac{4}{9}, \frac{8}{18}$ **25.** $\frac{12}{35}, \frac{24}{70}$ **27.** $-\frac{2y}{5}$; $-2$ **29.** $\frac{x}{6}$; $\frac{1}{2}$ **31.** $\frac{5}{xy^2}$; $\frac{1}{15}$ **33.** $-\frac{5}{2x^2y^2}$; $-\frac{1}{90}$ **35.** 14 **37.** 24 **39.** no **41.** yes

**4.3 Problem Solving (pp. 190 – 191)** **45.** $\frac{6}{25}$ **47.** $\frac{13}{50}$

**4.4 Skill Practice (pp. 194 – 195)** **1.** common multiple **3.** 24 **5.** 40 **7.** 36 **9.** 24 **11.** 42 **13.** 165 **15.** 210 **17.** 420 **19.** 12 is the GCF, not the LCM; The LCM is $2 \cdot 2 \cdot 2 \cdot 3$, or 24. *21–27. Methods and explanations may vary.* **21.** mental math; 500 **23.** prime factorization; 90 **25.** prime factorization; 216 **27.** prime factorization; 630 **29.** $36y^4$ **31.** $35ab^2$ **33.** $36x^3y^5$ **35.** $120c^3d^6$

**4.4 Problem Solving (pp. 195 – 196)** **45.** 180 sec **49.** yes; The greater number is the LCM. **51.** 21; The color repeats every fourth figure, and the orientation repeats every fifth figure. The LCM of 4 and 5 is 20, and 20 figures after Figure 1 is 21.

**4.5 Skill Practice (p. 200)** **1.** least common multiple, or LCM **3.** 6 **5.** 24 **7.** $<$ **9.** $>$ **11.** $>$ **13.** $>$ **15.** You must first rewrite both fractions using the LCD and then compare numerators; $\frac{3}{5} = \frac{21}{35}$ and $\frac{4}{7} = \frac{20}{35}$. Because $21 > 20$, $\frac{3}{5} > \frac{4}{7}$. **17.** $\frac{5}{4}, 1\frac{1}{2}, \frac{11}{6}$ **19.** $\frac{5}{9}, \frac{3}{4}, 1\frac{1}{3}$ **21.** $\frac{19}{12}, 1\frac{3}{5}, 2\frac{1}{4}, \frac{7}{3}$

**23.** $\frac{34}{3}, 11\frac{7}{12}, \frac{47}{4}$  **25.** $=$  **27.** $<$

**4.5 Problem Solving (p. 201)**  **37.** Sarah

**4.6 Skill Practice (pp. 204 – 206)**  **1.** base  **3.** $4^6$  **5.** $a^{12}$
**7.** $u^8$  **9.** $b^{15}$  **11.** $3^7$  **13.** $(-4)^5$  **15.** $9a^5$  **17.** $243x^9$
**19.** $25x^{16}$  **21.** $216x^6y^4$  **23.** $5^4$  **25.** $d^7$  **27.** $w^6$  **29.** $(-7)^3$
**33.** $z^5$  **35.** $25n^3$  **37.** $2401r^4$  **39.** $y^{10}$  **41.** When dividing monomials involving exponents, subtract the exponents;
$\frac{x^{20}y^6}{x^5y^3} = x^{15}y^3$  **43.** $(-2)^6$  **45.** 2  **47.** $(-3)^5$  **49.** 1

**51.** $-4b^4$  **53.** $9n^3$  **55.** 8  **57.** 12  **59.** 4  **61.** 11  **63.** 8
**65.** 12  **67.** $3x - 3 = 12; 5$  **69.** $4x + 4 = 12; 2$  **71.** $x - 5 = 3; 8$  **73.** $2 = 4x - 2; 1$  **75.** $3^6; 729$  **77.** $4^4; 256$

**4.6 Problem Solving (pp. 206 – 207)**  **83.** $10^{12}$  **85.** $10^{12}$
**87.** $10^6$  **89. a.** 1 exameter  **b.** 21 exameters
**c.** 1,000,000,000 gigameters  **d.** 21,000,000,000
gigameters  **93.** $3^{16}$ mm²; 81; $(3^8 \cdot 9)(3^8 \cdot 9) = 3^{16} \cdot 81$

**4.7 Skill Practice (p. 210)**  **1.** 1  **3.** $\frac{1}{81}$  **5.** $-\frac{1}{16}$  **7.** $\frac{1}{36}$

**9.** $-\frac{1}{625}$  **11.** $5^{-3}$ means $\frac{1}{5^3}$; $5^{-3} = \frac{1}{5^3} = \frac{1}{125}$  **13.** 1  **15.** $\frac{1}{c^7}$

**17.** $\frac{4}{z^6}$  **19.** $\frac{6}{r^9}$  **21.** 0  **23.** $-5$  **25.** $-2$  **27.** $-7$

**29.** always; A power with an exponent of zero is equal to 1, which is positive.  **31.** sometimes; If the exponent is even, it will be positive.

**4.7 Problem Solving (p. 211)**  **39.** $10^{11}$  **41.** $10^8$

**4.8 Skill Practice (pp. 214 – 215)**  **1.** yes; 9.32 is between 1 and 10, and 5 is an integer.  **3.** yes; 7 is between 1 and 10, and $-4$ is an integer.  **5.** $4.68 \times 10^{-1}$  **7.** $8.92 \times 10^{10}$
**9.** $2.13 \times 10^6$  **11.** $4.15 \times 10^{-7}$  **15.** 4,350,000  **17.** 0.0871
**19.** 0.00000000176  **21.** 2,830,000,000,000  **23.** $6 \times 10^8$
**25.** $5.85 \times 10^{-7}$  **27.** $6.552 \times 10^{14}$  **29.** $1.066 \times 10^5$
**31.** 18.6 is not between 1 and 10, and when multiplying powers with the same base, you must add the exponents, not multiply; $(3 \times 10^2) \times (6.2 \times 10^3) = (3 \times 6.2) \times (10^2 \times 10^3) = 18.6 \times 10^5 = 1.86 \times 10^6$  **33.** $>$  **35.** $>$
**37.** $3.5 \times 10^{11}$  **39.** $3.25 \times 10^3$

**4.8 Problem Solving (pp. 215 – 217)**  **45. a.** 3.2  **b.** $10^2$
**c.** $3.2 \times 10^2$  **47.** $1.5 \times 10^7$  **53.** $7.98 \times 10^7$; $4.161 \times 10^9$
**55.** $8,600,000; $60,200,000; $3,139,000,000

**4.8 Technology Activity (p. 218)**  **1.** $2.7115 \times 10^{14}$
**3.** $1.584 \times 10^{-11}$  **5.** $8.2 \times 10^6$  **7.** $4.02 \times 10^{-7}$
**9.** $4.5 \times 10^6$  **11.** $1.4 \times 10^{-9}$  **13.** about $7.7 \times 10^{11}$ gal; about $4.015 \times 10^{13}$ gal

**Chapter Review (pp. 220 – 224)**  **1.** *Sample answer:* The greatest common factor is the largest number that is a factor of both numbers. The least common multiple is the smallest number that is a multiple of both numbers.
**3.** *Sample answer: abc*, $5x$, $12x^2y$  **5.** simplest form
**7.** equivalent fractions  **9.** composite  **11.** prime  **13.** 7
**15.** $2^3 \cdot 3 \cdot 5$  **17.** $2 \cdot 2 \cdot 7 \cdot x \cdot y \cdot y \cdot y$  **19.** $2 \cdot 2 \cdot 2 \cdot 5 \cdot p \cdot p \cdot p \cdot p \cdot q \cdot q \cdot q$  **21.** 16  **23.** $7a$  **25.** 10  **27.** $x$
**29.** yes  **31.** no  **33.** 30 baskets; 2 cans of cranberry sauce, 4 cans of canned fruit, 3 cans of corn, 2 boxes of

muffin mix  **35.** $\frac{3}{20}$  **37.** $\frac{n^2}{3}$  **39.** 270  **41.** $36n^3$  **43.** $>$

**45.** $=$  **47.** $\frac{5}{8}, \frac{7}{11}, \frac{2}{3}$  **49.** $\frac{17}{3}, 5\frac{7}{8}, \frac{53}{9}$  **51.** Joe; $\frac{1}{24}$ cup

**53.** $9^9$  **55.** $a^{23}$  **57.** $5^3$  **59.** $b^7$  **61.** $y^8$  **63.** $x^3y^2$  **65.** $\frac{1}{n^3}$

**67.** $\frac{3}{c^{13}}$  **69.** $\frac{3}{2z^2}$  **71.** 20  **73.** $9 \times 10^{-7}$  **75.** 236,000,000

**77.** 0.0094  **79.** $1.612 \times 10^9$  **81.** $3.6624 \times 10^9$

# Chapter 5

**5.1 Skill Practice (pp. 235 – 236)**  **1.** denominator;
numerator  **3.** $\frac{7}{21}; \frac{1}{3}$  **5.** $\frac{2}{18}; \frac{1}{9}$  **7.** $-1\frac{4}{14}; -1\frac{2}{7}$  **9.** $-7\frac{7}{5};$
$-8\frac{2}{5}$  **11.** $-\frac{3n}{21}; -\frac{n}{7}$  **13.** $\frac{15}{a}$  **15.** $\frac{2a}{20b}; \frac{a}{10b}$  **17.** $\frac{4a}{2b}; \frac{2a}{b}$
**19.** $1\frac{1}{2}$  **21.** $1\frac{11}{18}$  **23.** $3\frac{1}{12}$  **25.** $-3\frac{3}{16}$  **27.** $\frac{1}{9}$ must be
subtracted, not added; $1\frac{1}{3}$  **29.** $\frac{2}{17}$  **31.** $\frac{8}{9}$  **33.** 0  **35.** $\frac{8}{11}$

**37.** *Sample answer:* $1\frac{1}{5} + 2\frac{3}{5} = 3\frac{4}{5}; 1\frac{1}{4} + (-1\frac{3}{4}) = -\frac{1}{2}$

**5.1 Problem Solving (pp. 236 – 238)**  **41.** $18\frac{3}{4}$ in.

**43.** $2\frac{1}{2}$ mm  **45.** 1 ft $8\frac{1}{2}$ in.

**5.2 Skill Practice (p. 240)**  **1.** least common multiple

**3.** $\frac{5}{8}$  **5.** $\frac{13}{18}$  **7.** $-\frac{33}{40}$  **9.** $4\frac{4}{5}$  **11.** $11\frac{19}{36}$  **13.** $\frac{8}{11}$

**15.** $-\frac{33w}{40}$  **17.** $\frac{17s}{20}$  **19.** $-\frac{13}{50n}$  **21.** $\frac{54 + 11a}{21a}$

*23–27. Methods will vary.*  **23.** true; paper and pencil  **25.** false; estimation  **27.** false; paper and pencil

**29.** $3\frac{23}{70}$  **31.** $4\frac{1}{24}$

**5.2 Problem Solving (pp. 241 – 242)**  **37.** $15\frac{3}{4}$ in.

**41.** $x = 25\frac{1}{2} - 9\frac{1}{3} - 7\frac{5}{6}; 8\frac{1}{3}$ ft

**5.3 Skill Practice (p. 245)**  **1.** numerators; denominators

**3.** $-1\frac{7}{8}$  **5.** $\frac{6}{25}$  **7.** $-\frac{25}{72}$  **9.** $4\frac{1}{2}$  **11.** $-19\frac{4}{5}$  **13.** $-34$

**15.** $-\frac{15}{16}$  **17.** $\frac{245}{288}$  **19.** $1\frac{7}{8}$ in.²  **21.** $11\frac{113}{121}$ m²  **23.** $-2\frac{1}{5}$

**25.** $1\frac{13}{72}$  **27.** $2\frac{3}{8}$  **29.** $4\frac{9}{16}$

**5.3 Problem Solving (p. 246)**  **33.** $1\frac{2}{5}$ km  **35.** $2\frac{1}{5}$ sec

**37.** $13\frac{11}{18}$ ft²

**5.4 Skill Practice (pp. 249 – 250)**  **1.** the reciprocal  **3.** 6

**5.** $-2\frac{1}{2}$  **7.** $\frac{7}{9}$  **9.** $-5\frac{4}{7}$  **11.** $\frac{5}{12}$  **13.** $-\frac{3}{20}$  **15.** The wrong

fraction was inverted; $-\frac{3}{10} \div (-\frac{4}{5}) = -\frac{3}{10} \times (-\frac{5}{4}) = \frac{3}{8}$

**17.** 8  **19.** $\frac{4}{9}$  **21.** $\frac{25}{36}$  **23.** 100  **25.** $2\frac{4}{49}$  **27.** $-7\frac{1}{12}$

**29.** $1\frac{3}{13}$  **31.** $3\frac{3}{5}$  **33.** $-1\frac{9}{14}$  **35.** $-5\frac{9}{10}$  **37.** $2 \div \frac{4}{5}; 2\frac{1}{2}$

**39.**

**41.**

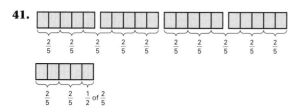

**43.** 20   **45.** $-5\frac{2}{3}$   **47.** 66   **49.** $-8$   **51.** yes; The $c$ in the numerator and denominator will divide out.

**5.4 Problem Solving (pp. 251 – 252)**   **53.** division because you are splitting 5 lb into $\frac{1}{4}$ lb sections; 20   **55.** addition because you are looking for a total of 3 different distances; $21\frac{7}{12}$ ft   **57.** multiplication because you are adding the same number of pounds repeated times; 765 lb

**5.4 Technology Activity (p. 253)**   **1.** $\frac{47}{55}$   **3.** $\frac{2}{3}$   **5.** $1\frac{1}{27}$   **7.** $\frac{2}{7}$   **9.** $11\frac{1}{5}$   **11.** $5\frac{1}{3}$   **13.** $374\frac{5}{8}$ lb

**5.5 Skill Practice (pp. 257 – 258)**   **1.** rational, integer, whole   **3.** rational, integer   **5.** 0.75   **7.** $-0.48$   **9.** $-0.16$   **11.** 3.6875   **13.** $-0.\overline{42}$   **15.** $6.5\overline{3}$   **17.** $\frac{3}{10}$ has a decimal value of 0.3 not 0.03; 2.3   **19.** $>$   **21.** $>$   **23.** $<$   **25.** $=$   **27.** $-0.4, -\frac{2}{7}, 0.1, \frac{3}{10}, \frac{5}{6}$   **29.** $\frac{3}{5}$   **31.** $\frac{12}{25}$   **33.** $\frac{73}{200}$   **35.** $-5\frac{2}{625}$   **37.** $\frac{8}{9}$   **39.** $\frac{7}{33}$   **41.** $\frac{635}{999}$   **43.** $-\frac{7}{45}$   **45.** $1.\overline{21}$, 1.21, $3^{-2}$, $\left(\frac{1}{3}\right)^3$   **47.** $0.\overline{4}, \frac{3}{7}, 4^{-2}, \left(\frac{1}{5}\right)^2$

**5.5 Problem Solving (pp. 258 – 259)**   **49.** $0.66, 2^{-4}, \frac{-1}{15}, -0.\overline{6}$   **51.** $\frac{x}{8}, \frac{x}{7}, \frac{x}{6}, \frac{x}{5}, \frac{x}{4}, \frac{x}{3}, \frac{x}{2}, x$; $x$ continues to be divided by smaller and smaller numbers, resulting in greater values.   **53.** 5

**5.6 Skill Practice (pp. 262 – 263)**   **1.** 13; 11; 25   **3.** 3.093   **5.** $-2.17$   **7.** $-10.89$   **9.** $-0.104$   **11.** 59.61   **13.** $-1.294$   **15.** 32.15   **17.** The decimals are not lined up correctly; Line up the decimal points, 17.951.   **19.** 2.4   **21.** 5.61   **23.** 7.31   **25.** $-0.17$   **27.** $-6.347$   **29.** 32   **31.** 60   **33.** 6.655   **35.** 0.1   **37.** 20.9 cm

**39.** 12.5 units;

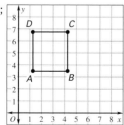

**41.** $6.\overline{224133}$   **43.** $11.\overline{1}$

**5.6 Problem Solving (pp. 263 – 264)**   **45. a.** 1.96 m   **b.** 1.31 m   **47.** yes; The sum of the whole parts is 12.

**49. a.** *Sample answer:* $123   **b.** $122.92   **c.** withdraw; $21.67

**5.7 Skill Practice (pp. 267 – 268)**   **1.** 7   **3.** 20.28   **5.** $-5.74$   **7.** 5   **9.** 12   **11.** 4   **13.** 2.5   **15.** about 1.89   **17.** $-1.5$   **19.** $-8.7$   **21.** about 290.41   **23.** The decimal in the answer was put in the wrong place; 33.252   **25.** D   **27.** $-8.1$   **29.** $-17.36$   **31.** about 0.27   **33.** about $-0.42$   **35.** about $-0.60$   **37.** $<$   **39.** 160.31   **41.** multiply by $-0.5$; 0.0625, $-0.03125$

**5.7 Problem Solving (pp. 268 – 269)**   **47.** The decimals move one place to the left;

| X | 1 | 0.1 | 0.01 | 0.001 | 0.0001 |
|---|---|---|---|---|---|
| 87 | 87 | 8.7 | 0.87 | 0.087 | 0.0087 |
| 356 | 356 | 35.6 | 3.56 | 0.356 | 0.0356 |
| 1200 | 1200 | 120 | 12 | 1.2 | 0.12 |

**51.** 1; 2; 3; 7; Each factor has one decimal place, so the products have the number of decimal places equal to the exponent value.   **53.** 87.6 mi/h; 1.2   **55.** 4548.12 ft²

**5.8 Skill Practice (pp. 274 – 275)**   **1.** mean   **3.** range   **5.** 5.875 km; 16 km; 16 km and 23 km; 17 km   **7.** $\frac{1}{4}$; 0; 0; 7   **9.** 2013; 2000; no mode; 460   **11.** 19°; 13°; none; 83°   **13.** 8 is also a mode; The modes are 5 and 8.   **15.** mean, median   **17.** mean   **19.** with red: 30, 26, 16, 85; without red: $24\frac{1}{3}$, 24.5, 16, 23; The mean and range are much smaller without the 98. The mode is unchanged, and the median is slightly lower.   **21.** 44; $58\frac{2}{7}$; 57; no mode   **23.** 7; 8; no mode; 11   **25.** 38; 27.5; no mode; 25

**5.8 Problem Solving (pp. 275 – 278)**   **31.** 52,327; 49,707; 49,646; mean; The mean takes into account the three dates with higher attendance.   **35.** $-97$ m   **37.** Jerry substituted the value of $a$ and then found the mean using the numbers. Roberta found the mean before substituting the value; Both methods are correct; Roberta's method will save time, as it takes fewer calculations.   **39.** You may not know if there are any very deep spots which would cause you to not be able to wade across.   **41.** 9.625; 9.75; 9.675; Carl; Kurt; Isaac   **43.** It removes the chance of an extremely high or low score affecting the mean.

**Chapter Review (pp. 280 – 284)**   **1.** reciprocals; multiplicative inverses   **3.** front-end estimation   **5.** rational number   **7.** $1\frac{3}{4}$   **9.** $1\frac{5}{7}$   **11.** $-\frac{n}{6}$   **13.** $-\frac{4n}{3}$   **15.** $\frac{17}{20}$   **17.** $\frac{37v}{15}$   **19.** $1\frac{5}{24}$   **21.** $-\frac{x}{34}$   **23.** $-\frac{1}{4}$   **25.** $-\frac{2}{21}$   **27.** $-26$   **29.** $-16\frac{1}{14}$   **31.** $\frac{13}{15}$   **33.** $-4$   **35.** $2\frac{1}{16}$   **37.** $-7\frac{7}{11}$   **39.** $1\frac{9}{16}$   **41.** $-0.875$   **43.** $3\frac{9}{20}$   **45.** $2\frac{65}{99}$   **47.** $-0.\overline{27}$   **49.** 42.598   **51.** 98.11   **53.** 0.803   **55.** $-12.323$   **57.** 3.0132   **59.** 2   **61.** $\frac{1}{8}$; 1; $-7$ and 2; 15   **63.** 8.25; 7; 4.8 and 7; 13.2

# Chapter 6

**6.1 Skill Practice (pp. 295 – 296)** **1.** $5x$, $-9x$; 6, $-2$ **3.** 1
**5.** $-6$ **7.** 6 **9.** 4 **11.** $-10$ **13.** $-1$ **15.** $-2$ was not
distributed correctly to $-4$; $3x - 2(x - 4) = 5$; $3x - 2x +$
$8 = 5$; $x = -3$ **17.** 1 **19.** $-37$ **21.** $-22$ **23.** $-5$

**25.** $-2$ **27.** $-11$ **29.** $-21$ **31.** $228 = \frac{1}{2}(x + 11)(19)$; 13

**33.** $x = 5$, $y = 8$; 34 units

**6.1 Problem Solving (pp. 296 – 297)** **35. a.** $8(70 + x) =$
2560 **b.** 250 tickets **37.** $P = 104$ mm; 34
**41.** $25 + (15 + 25)w - 10w = 235$; 7 weeks

**6.2 Skill Practice (pp. 300 – 301)** **1.** the distance all

around the figure **3.** 7 **5.** 27 **7.** $-8$ **9.** 9 **11.** $\frac{1}{2}$

**13.** $3\frac{1}{2}$ **15.** 36 units **17.** 132 units **19.** $-7$ **21.** $-3$

**23.** $-16$ **25.** $-7.5$ **27.** true; $x + 8 = 6x - 7$, so $x = 3$
and all 4 sides are 11. **29.** C

**6.2 Problem Solving (pp. 301 – 302)** **33.** 5 tickets
**35.** $.80; $60; *Sample answer:* If the cost of a balloon
alone is $x$, then $7 \cdot 8 + 5x = 75x$, and the solution is 0.8 or
$.80. So $7 \cdot 8 + 5x = 56 + 4 = $60.

**6.3 Skill Practice (pp. 305 – 306)** **33.** least common

denominator **3.** $-4$ **5.** $-0.34$ **7.** 3.4 **9.** 0.5 **11.** $\frac{7}{13}$

**13.** 1 **15.** 20 **17.** $-\frac{5}{4}$ or $-1\frac{1}{4}$ **19.** Some of the terms

were multiplied by 10 and some by 100; $1.5x + 0.25 =$
$1.6x$; $150x + 25 = 160x$; $25 = 10x$; $x = 2.5$ **21.** 1000; 2.5

**23.** 45; $\frac{8}{57}$ **25.** 10; $\frac{45}{4}$ or $11\frac{1}{4}$ or 11.25 **27.** 8 or 1000; $\frac{64}{9}$ or

$7\frac{1}{9}$ or $7.\overline{1}$ **29.** *Answers may vary. Sample answer:* $5x -$

$3 = 18$; $5x = 21$; $x = 4\frac{1}{5}$

**6.3 Problem Solving (pp. 306 – 307)** **35.** $3.96x +$
$4.76x = 13.08$; 1.5 lb **41.** 4950 ft²; 44 ft

**6.4 Skill Practice (pp. 314 – 316)**

**1.**

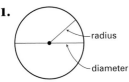

**3.** 62.8 mm; I used 3.14 because 10 is not a multiple of 7.
**5.** 314 cm; I used 3.14 because 100 is not a multiple of 7.

**7.** 44 in.; I used $\frac{22}{7}$ because 14 is a multiple of 7.

**9.** 198 mm; I used $\frac{22}{7}$ because 63 is a multiple of 7.

**11.** 264 ft; I used $\frac{22}{7}$ because 42 is a multiple of 7.

**13.** 21 in. **15.** 10.5 km **17.** 1.5 cm **19.** 25 yd
**21.** 7 m **23.** 2 cm; 6.28 cm **25.** 17 mm; 106.76 mm

**27.** 21.42 ft **29.** $\frac{C}{d}$ by the Div. Prop. of Eq. **31.** $\frac{C}{2\pi}$ by the

Div. Prop. of Eq.

**6.4 Problem Solving (pp. 316 – 317)** **37.** 22 in.; 66 in.;
The larger is 3 times as great. **39.** about 23 ft
**45.** *Sample answer:* 13 and 37; 13, because the square is
closer in size to the small circle.

**6.5 Skill Practice (pp. 320 – 321)** **1.** less than, greater
than, less than or equal to, greater than or equal to

**3.** $a \geq 1$; ![number line -2 to 4, closed at 1]

**5.** $p \leq 6$; ![number line 3 to 9, closed at 6]

**7.** $w > 2$; ![number line -1 to 5, open at 2]

**9.** $c < \frac{1}{3}$; ![number line -3 to 3, open at 1/3]

**11.** $z < -4$; ![number line -7 to -1, open at -4]

**13.** $n \leq -2$; ![number line -5 to 1, closed at -2]

**15.** $a > -2$; ![number line -5 to 1, open at -2]

**17.** $k \geq 1$; ![number line -2 to 4, closed at 1]

**21.** 21; $y \geq -10.5$ **23.** 6; $m < 24$ **25.** 100; $y < 5.1$
**27.** 100; $x \leq 49.3$
**29.** $-3 < x < 4$; ![number line -6 to 6, open at -3 and 4]

**31.** $-3 \leq x < 6$; ![number line -6 to 8, closed at -3, open at 6]

**6.5 Problem Solving (pp. 321 – 322)** **33. a.** $925 + 25p \geq$
2500 **b.** $p \geq 63$; You need at least 63 more pledges.
**35.** $16{,}000 + 150n > 18{,}550$; $n > 17$; You have to catch
more than 17 discs to have a new high score.
**39.** $h < 6000$; The base height of a *Strato* cloud is less
than 6000 ft. **41.** $6000 < h < 20{,}000$ **43.** You cannot
buy a negative number of soft drinks.

**6.5 Technology Activity (p. 323)** **1.** $y < 13$ **3.** $n \leq -1$
**5.** $t > -3$ **7.** at most 16 pencils

**6.6 Skill Practice (pp. 326 – 327)** **1.** yes; It uses *at least*.
**3.** no; It would be an equation. **5.** $x + 2 \leq 6$; $x \leq 4$
**7.** $x - 6 > 14$; $x > 20$ **9.** $x + 12 < 4$; $x < -8$
**13.** A number of ride tickets must be a whole number.
**15.** A number of hot dogs must be a whole number.

**6.6 Problem Solving (pp. 327 – 329)** **21.** $30 + 4n < 6n$;
$n > 15$; You have to attend more than 15 dances.

**25.** $\frac{90 + 92 + 115 + x}{4} \geq 100$; $x \geq 103$ **27.** $6x + 30 + 24 \leq$

$108$; $x \leq 9$; no more than 9 boxes

**Chapter Review (pp. 331 – 334)** **1.** circle **3.** B **5.** C
**7.** 6 **9.** 5 **11.** $-4$ **13.** 2 **15.** $-7$ **17.** $-4$ **19.** 2.25

**21.** $-\frac{5}{12}$ **23.** 16 **25.** $.33/can **27.** 20 mm **29.** 21 ft

**31.** 3.14 mi **33.** 140 m **35.** 279.46 ft **37.** $m < 9$
**39.** $14 - 3x \leq 11$; $x \geq 1$ **41.** at least 67 tickets

# Chapter 7

**7.1 Skill Practice (p. 345)** **1.** A rate is a ratio of two quantities that have different units. **3.** $\frac{3}{2}$, 3 to 2, 3 : 2

**5.** $\frac{9}{14}$, 9 to 14, 9 : 14 **7.** $\frac{3}{1}$, 3 to 1, 3 : 1 **9.** $\frac{14}{3}$, 14 to 3, 14 : 3

**11.** 1 **13.** 1.75 **15.** 3000 **17.** 0.25 **19.** $\frac{4 \text{ adults}}{1 \text{ car}}$

**21.** $\frac{3 \text{ degrees}}{1 \text{ min}}$ **23.** $\frac{10 \text{ oz}}{1 \text{ serving}}$ **25.** $\frac{-4.25\text{m}}{1 \text{ sec}}$

**27.** Your friend should have multiplied by

$\frac{7 \text{ days}}{1 \text{ week}} \cdot \frac{14 \text{ times}}{\text{day}} \cdot \frac{7 \text{ days}}{1 \text{ week}} = \frac{98 \text{ times}}{\text{week}}$. **29.** no **31.** yes

**33.** 10 **35.** 3 **37.** 8 **39.** 6

**7.1 Problem Solving (p. 346)** **43.** 672 times

**7.2 Skill Practice (pp. 350 – 351)** **1.** Find the cross products and solve the resulting equation to solve the proportion. **3.** 3 **5.** 9 **9.** no **11.** yes **13.** 2 **15.** 9 **17.** 8 **19.** 0.06 **21.** 38.5 **23.** 1513 **25.** 6 in. **27.** 18.96 in. **29.** 1 **31.** 23 **33.** 2.5 **35.** $x = -3$, $y = -10.5$ **37.** $n = 16$, $p = 15$

**7.2 Problem Solving (pp. 352 – 353)** **39.** 2640 ft

**41.** If you write 10 lb to $16 as a fraction $\left(\frac{10}{16}\right)$ and write an equivalent fraction with 5 in the numerator, the denominator is 8, because $\frac{10}{16} = \frac{5}{8}$, so you can see that 5 lb of pasta costs $8. **43. a.** 5.375 in., 1.9 in., 1.35 in.

**47.** $\approx \frac{1 \text{ cm}}{450 \text{ ft}}$ **49.** *Sample answer:* $72,800

**7.3 Skill Practice (p. 356)** **1.** percent **3.** $\frac{209}{b} = \frac{38}{100}$; 550

**5.** $\frac{5}{125} = \frac{p}{100}$; 4% **7.** $\frac{a}{245} = \frac{45}{100}$; 110.25 **9.** 90% **11.** 540

**13.** 135% **15.** 2.52 **21.** < **23.** > **25.** = **27.** 5y

**7.3 Problem Solving (pp. 357 – 358)** **31.** 81.8% **33.** 45 lb **35.** 16 ft **37.** 60% **41. a.** Mary Anne has mowed 960 ft² so far, and Josefina has mowed 1044 ft² so far. **b.** Mary Anne **c.** 1762.2 ft²; about 51.8%

**7.4 Skill Practice (pp. 361 – 362)** **1.** 100; 1 **3.** 0.125 **5.** 1.1 **7.** 0.4455 **9.** 0.0078 **11.** 0.0008 **13.** 127%

**15.** 210% **17.** 51% **19.** 5.7% **21.** 0.4% **23.** $\frac{4}{10}$

**25.** $\frac{13}{40}$ **27.** $1\frac{6}{25}$ **29.** $\frac{21}{500}$ **31.** $\frac{803}{10,000}$ **33.** 62.5%

**35.** 1.25% **37.** 310% **39.** 8% **41.** 43.75% **43.** <

**45.** > **47.** > **49.** = **51.** > **53.** 6.5%, $\frac{9}{50}$, 0.5, 0.65,

66% **55.** $\frac{21}{100}$, 0.212, $\frac{21}{10}$, 212%, 21.2 **57.** 4.8%, $\frac{12}{25}$,

0.484, 480%, 4.84 **59.** A

**61.**

**63.**

**7.4 Problem Solving (pp. 363 – 364)** **67.** 5% **69.** 31%

**73.** $\frac{19}{50}$, $\frac{1}{2}$, 0.7, 79%, $\frac{17}{20}$

**7.5 Skill Practice (p. 368)** **1.** increase **3.** decrease; 2% **5.** increase; 14% **7.** increase; 20% **9.** 1144 **11.** 12.8 **13.** 77,000 **15.** Your friend did not add the increase to the original number. Multiplying a number by 5 and adding the product to the original number is a 500% increase. **17.** 50% **19.** 50% **21.** 50% **23.** 25%

**7.5 Problem Solving (pp. 368 – 369)** **25. a.** 219,700 **b.** 19,773 **c.** 239,473 **31.** 9 in. by 6 in.; The increase in area will be greater than 50%. The original area is 24 in.². The area of the enlargement is 54 in.². This is a 125% increase.

**7.6 Skill Practice (pp. 372 – 373)** **1.** markup **3.** $51 **5.** $41.25 **7.** $29.40 **11.** $61.61 **13.** $274.98 **15.** $22.50 **17.** discount; 25%; $72 **19.** markup; 75%; $168 **21.** markup; 80%; $172.80

**7.6 Problem Solving (pp. 373 – 374)** **27.** $37.80 **33.** $21 **35.** 35%; $38.35

**7.7 Skill Practice (pp. 377 – 378)** **1.** interest **3.** 414 **5.** 550 **7.** 66 **9.** 250 **11.** 78 **13.** 0.5% **15.** When using 60% in an equation, the decimal needs to be moved two places to the left; $54 = 0.60b$; $90 = b$ **17.** $82.25 **19.** 40 **21.** 1 **25.** 2 yr **27.** $2000

**7.7 Problem Solving (pp. 378 – 379)** **29. a.** $I = Prt$ **b.** $100 = P(0.03)(0.5)$ **c.** $6,666.67 **33.** $142.50; $1342.50 **37.** 1.1; 3.3; 2.5; 5; 7.5; 3.8; 7.6; 11.4; *Sample answer:* 5% of a number is half of 10% of a number. 15% of a number is the sum of 5% and 10% of a number.

**7.7 Technology Activity (p. 380)** **1.** $7577.03 **3.** $3744.89 **5.** Your account balance is greater than your sister's by $195.39 after 10 years.

**7.8 Skill Practice (pp. 383 – 384)** **1.** 2, 4, and 6 **3.** $\frac{1}{3}$

**5.** $\frac{11}{30}$ **7.** $\frac{0}{30}$ **9.** 20% **11.** 48% **13.** 100% **15.** 40

**17.** 0 **21.** $\frac{2}{3}$ **23.** $\frac{1}{8}$

**7.8 Problem Solving (pp. 384 – 386)** **27. b.** white: $\frac{1}{6}$; black: $\frac{1}{2}$; brown: $\frac{1}{3}$ **29.** 46%

**31.** about 8 times **33. b.** *Sample answer:* Using the name Smith, the experimental probability of choosing the first letter was $\frac{2}{20}$; 10 times **35.** 50 children;

100 children; 300 children; 450 children
**39.** 25 times; There are 4 possible outcomes, choosing two girls, choosing two boys, choosing a girl and a boy, and choosing a boy and a girl. So, there is a 1 to 4 probability that you would choose two boys. Out of 100 times, 25 of them should be two boys.

**Chapter Review (pp. 388 – 392)** **1.** unit rate
**3.** favorable outcomes; outcomes **5.** discount **7.** B

**9.** $\frac{1}{1}$ **11.** $\frac{7.5 \text{ ft}}{1 \text{ sec}}$ **13.** $\frac{18 \text{ people}}{1 \text{ group}}$ **15.** $\frac{14 \text{ ft}}{1 \text{ sec}}$ **17.** $\frac{44.5 \text{ km}}{1 \text{ h}}$

**19.** Megan **21.** $5.\overline{3}$ **23.** 9 **25.** $20 **27.** 6% **29.** 54%

**31.** 0.038, $\frac{19}{500}$ **33.** 1.3, $\frac{13}{10}$ **35.** 250% **37.** 1860%

**39.** 30% decrease **41.** 23% **43.** $59.04 **45.** 96
**47.** $48.30 **49.** red, 47%; yellow, 29%; blue, 24%
**51.** 68%

# Chapter 8

**8.1 Skill Practice (pp. 406 – 407)** **1.** supplementary
**3.** supplementary **5.** 34° **7.** 158° **11.** $m\angle 2 = m\angle 3 = 100°$, $m\angle 1 = 80°$ **13.** $m\angle 1 = m\angle 3 = m\angle 5 = m\angle 8 = m\angle 9 = m\angle 11 = 74°$, $m\angle 2 = m\angle 4 = m\angle 6 = m\angle 7 = m\angle 10 = 106°$ **15.** B *17–19. Types may vary.* **17.** 115°; supplementary angles and corresponding angles
**19.** 115°; supplementary angles and alternate interior angles **21.** sometimes; *Sample answer:* $150° + 30° = 180°$, but $150° + 20° \neq 180°$. **23.** always; *Sample answer:* Perpendicular lines form a right angle, and angles that are supplementary to and vertical to a right angle are right angles. **25.** $y = \frac{16}{7}$; $m\angle 6 = 77\frac{1}{7}°$, $m\angle 3 = 102\frac{6}{7}°$

**8.1 Problem Solving (pp. 407 – 408)** **29.** 6 pairs; *Sample answer:* At each of the three parallel lines, 2 pairs of vertical angles are formed, so the total is 6 pairs. *Example:* See the diagram for Exercise 13 on page 406.

**35.**

105° 75°
75° 105°

**37.** Each is 67.5°; The vertical support at the peak divides the 135° angle in half, or 67.5°, and each of ∠1, ∠2, and ∠3 is a corresponding angle with the 67.5° angle.
**39.** 4 angles

**8.1 Extension (p. 410)**

**1.**

45°

**3.**

135°

**5.**

**7.**

**8.2 Skill Practice (pp. 413 – 414)** **1.** scalene **3.** acute
**5.** obtuse **7.** equilateral **9.** isosceles **11.** scalene
**13.** 58; acute **15.** 32; obtuse **17.** No, the sum must be 180°, not 181°. **19.** Yes, the sum is 180°. **21.** 70°, 70°; acute **23.** 20°, 70°, 90° **25.** 60°, 60°, 60°

**8.2 Problem Solving (pp. 414 – 415)** **29.** 60°, 60°, 60°
**31.** no; *Sample answer:* The sum of the measures of all three angles is 180°. If two angles are supplementary, then the measure of the third angle would have to be 0°, and there would not be a triangle. **35.** 295; reflex angle
**37.** 250; reflex angle

**8.3 Skill Practice (pp. 417 – 418)** **1.** trapezoid
**3.** trapezoid **5.** rhombus *7. Measurements may vary. Sample measurements are given.* **7.** 1.6 cm; rhombus
**9.** $x = 109$ **11.** $x = 65$ **13.** $x = 65, y = 115$ **15.** A diagonal is not a side; diagonals of $ABCD$: $\overline{AC}$, $\overline{BD}$
**17.** $x = 5$; $m\angle E = 121°$, $m\angle H = 119°$ **19.** always; *Sample answer:* A rhombus is a parallelogram with four equal sides. **21.** always; *Sample answer:* A square is a parallelogram with 4 equal sides and 4 right angles.
**23.** never; A trapezoid has exactly one pair of parallel sides, and a parallelogram has 2 pairs of parallel sides.

**8.3 Problem Solving (p. 419)** **27.** 2 diagonals; *Sample answer:*

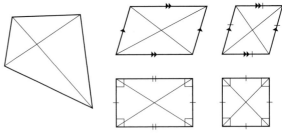

**31.** no; *Sample answer:* If the measures of three angles were 60°, then the measure of the fourth angle would have to be $360° - 3(60°) = 180°$, so the figure would not have 4 distinct sides.

**8.4 Skill Practice (pp. 422 – 423)** **1.** polygon **3.** polygon
**5.** regular polygon **7.** 2520° **9.** 3240° **11.** 144°
**13.** 156° **15.** $x = 72$; $m\angle R = m\angle N = 72°$, $m\angle L = m\angle M = m\angle P = m\angle Q = 144°$ **17.** $x = 45$; $m\angle A = m\angle D = m\angle C = 90°$, $m\angle E = m\angle ABC = 135°$
**19.** 13-gon **21.** 18-gon

**8.4 Problem Solving (pp. 423 – 424)** **25.** not a polygon; The sides are not segments. **27.** *Answers may vary. Sample answer:* Some of the rocks are pentagons and hexagons. **29.** *Answers may vary. Sample answer:* Cut off the vertices without intersecting the cuts. **33.** 2, 5, 9, …; 14 diagonals; **35.** regular 10-gon

**8.5 Skill Practice (pp. 429 – 430)** **1.** congruent **3.** $\angle K$, $\angle S$; $\angle L$, $\angle P$; $\angle M$, $\angle Q$; $\angle N$, $\angle R$ **5.** 12 in. **7.** 80° **9.** 100° **11.** $\triangle ABC \cong \triangle LKM$ by SAS; $\triangle GJH \cong \triangle PNQ$ by SSS **15.** ASA; $2x + 6 = 32$, $x = 13$ **17.** *Answers may vary. Sample answers:*

**8.5 Problem Solving (pp. 431 – 432)** **19.** Corresponding sides are equal, and corresponding angles are equal. **21.** The triangles are congruent by SSS. **23.** 127.5° **27.** no; $\triangle ABC$ is not necessarily congruent to $\triangle XYZ$, so no other pairs of angles must be congruent. **29.** *Sample answer:* You can show the triangles are congruent if you know that the third sides of the two triangles are congruent or if you know that the angles between the two 7 ft sides in each triangle are congruent.

**8.6 Skill Practice (pp. 435 – 436)** **1.** reflection **3.** no **5.** no **7.**

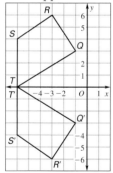

**9.** The image coordinates given are those for a reflection in the *y*-axis. The reflection of $(x, y)$ in the *x*-axis is $(x, -y)$; Original: $A(4, 5)$, $B(2, 0)$, $C(6, 2)$; Image: $A'(4, -5)$, $B'(2, 0)$, $C'(6, -2)$ **13.** 6 lines of symmetry **15.** *Sample answer:* obtuse scalene triangle; yes, any scalene triangle;

**17.** *Sample answer:* rectangle; yes, rhombus;

**19.**

**21.**

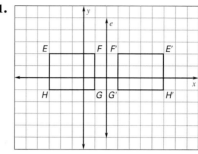

**8.6 Problem Solving (pp. 437 – 438)** **29.** *Answers may vary. Sample answer:* This method can be used in miniature golf, where you have to bounce the ball against a wall in order to go around an obstacle;

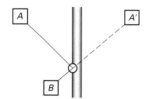

**31.** The figure has 1 line of symmetry, the *y*-axis;

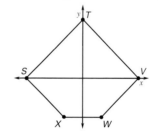

**8.7 Skill Practice (pp. 441 – 443)** **1.** reflection **3.** rotation **5.** $(x, y) \rightarrow (x - 5, y + 3)$ **7.** $L'(5, -4)$, $M'(1, -3)$, $N'(2, -5)$;

**9. a., c.**

**b.** $R'(1, -2)$, $S'(2, -5)$, $T'(-2, -4)$

**11.**

**13.** 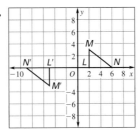 **15.**

**17.** *Blue to red* translation: $(x, y) \rightarrow (x + 4, y - 4)$; reflection: in line $y = x$; rotation: 180°; *Red to blue* (1) Reflect in *x*-axis then reflect in *y*-axis; (2) Make two 90° clockwise rotations; (3) Make two 90° counterclockwise rotations.

**8.7 Skill Practice (pp. 443 – 444)** **19.** rotations of 45°, 90°, 135°, 180°, 225°, 270°, or 315° in the clockwise or counterclockwise direction **21.** reflection **23.** translation **25.** rotation **27.** left to right; yes, 60°; yes, 72°; yes, 40° **29.** Yes; *Sample answer:* The origami pinwheel in Exercise 19 has rotational symmetry but not line symmetry.

**8.7 Extension (p. 446)** **1.** no **3.** no
**7.** translation;

**9.** *Sample answer:*

**8.8 Skill Practice (pp. 450 – 452)** **1.** scale factor **3.** yes; All regular triangles are similar. **5.** yes; Corresponding angles are congruent and $\frac{10}{5} = \frac{8}{4} = \frac{6}{3}$. **7.** 4 in. **9.** $\frac{9}{4}$ ft

**11.**

**13.**  **15.**

**17.** The student did not multiply the *y* values by 3;

**19.** scale factor: $\frac{1}{2}$;

**21.** scale factor: 2;

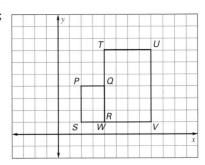

**23.** $x = 54$, $y = 6.75$ cm

**8.8 Skill Practice (pp. 452 – 454)** **25.** $\frac{4}{1}$; 14 units; the same **31.** identical; *Sample answer:* If the scale factor is 1, then the length of each edge of the second polygon will be 1 times the length of the corresponding edges of the first polygon. **33.** *Sample answer:* The area of *ABCD* is

80 in.² so $AD = 80 \div 10 = 8$ in. The scale factor is $\frac{5}{10} = \frac{1}{2}$, so $WY = \frac{1}{2}AD = \frac{1}{2}(8) = 4$ in. Then the area of $WXYZ$ is (5 in.)(4 in.) $= 20$ in.²  **35.** $\frac{25}{6}$  **37.** $ABDF \sim CDFH \sim$ $EFHJ \sim GHJL \sim IJLK \sim LKMN \sim OKMP$. They are all similar because all of their angles are equal and the sides of every rectangle are in the ratio 8 : 5.

**Chapter Review (pp. 456 – 460)**  **1.** D  **3.** B
**5.** complementary  **7.** heptagon  **9.** 109°  **11.** 25°
**13.** 26; right triangle  **15.** 88; acute triangle  **17.** 60; parallelogram  **19.** 150°  **21.** $\triangle ABC \cong \triangle GFH$; SAS
**23.** $\triangle LMN \cong \triangle PQR$; SAS

**25.**

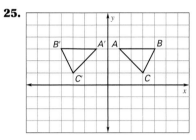

**27.** 5  **29.** $K'(1, 2)$, $L'(-1, 5)$, $M'(1, 4)$  **31.** 48 ft

# Chapter 9

**9.1 Skill Practice (pp. 472 – 473)**  **1.** $b^2 = c$  **3.** −1  **5.** 12

**7.** The answer is missing a negative sign; $-\sqrt{49} = -7$
**9.** 4  **11.** 7  **13.** 5  **15.** 11  **17.** 6.6  **19.** −78.8  **21.** 0
**23.** ±9  **25.** ±7  **27.** ±11  **29.** ±11.66  **31.** ±13.96

**33.** ±1.2  **35.** ±1.4  **37.** always  **39.** 0  **41.** 9  **43.** $\frac{4}{5}$

**45.** $\frac{12}{13}$  **47.** 1.4  **49.** 3.4

**9.1 Problem Solving (pp. 473 – 474)**  **57.** no; The tablecloth is $\frac{50}{12} = 4\frac{1}{6}$ ft by $4\frac{1}{6}$ ft. A side of the table is $\sqrt{21.5} \approx 4.6$ ft. The tablecloth is smaller than the table, so it will not cover the table.  **59.** 24 ft; 9072 ft²  **61.** 68.2 mi
**63.** about 2212 ft

**9.2 Skill Practice (pp. 477 – 479)**  **1.** irrational
**3.** rational; It is a terminating decimal.  **5.** rational; It is a repeating decimal.  **7.** rational; $\sqrt{36} = 6$, which is a terminating decimal.  **9.** irrational; $\sqrt{5}$ cannot be written as a quotient of two integers.  **11.** rational; It is the quotient of two integers.  **13.** rational; $\sqrt{\frac{100}{81}} = \frac{10}{9}$, which is the quotient of two integers.  **15.** A; It is the only rational number in the group.  **17.** >  **19.** <  **21.** <
*23–39. Methods may vary.*  **23.** >; estimation  **25.** <; estimation  **27.** =; mental math  **29.** <; calculator
**35.** $0.2\overline{62}$, $0.2\overline{6}$, 0.266, $0.2\overline{6}$  **37.** $0.\overline{39}$, 0.399, $0.3\overline{9}$,
$\sqrt{0.17}$  **39.** $-9$, $\sqrt{81}$, 10.3, $\sqrt{220}$  **41.** $\frac{2}{5}$, 1.02, $\sqrt{1.25}$,
$\sqrt{2.5}$  **43.** 3.6; irrational  **45.** 3; rational  **47.** 8.1; irrational  **49.** irrational; The sum of an irrational

number and an integer is irrational.  **51.** irrational; The product of an integer and an irrational number is irrational.  **53.** $\sqrt{13}$; 5  **55.** 6; 6; always; $(\sqrt{ac})^2 =$ $(\sqrt{ac})(\sqrt{ac}) = ac$ and $(\sqrt{a} \cdot \sqrt{c})^2 = (\sqrt{a})^2 \cdot (\sqrt{c})^2 = ac$
**57.** 3; 1; sometimes; They are equal when $a = d$.
**59.** sometimes  **61.** sometimes

**9.2 Skill Practice (pp. 479 – 480)**  **67.** yes; The carpet is $\sqrt{110} \approx 10.49$ ft by 10.49 ft. 10.49 is less than 10.5 and 11.2, so it will fit in the room.  **69.** no; The minimum wind speed required to fly the kite is $5\sqrt{\frac{19.6}{11.71}} \approx 6.5$ mi/h. A wind speed of 6 mi/h is not enough.  **71.** no; *Sample answer:* The decimal shown on the calculator screen could terminate at a higher level of accuracy, or there might be a repeating pattern in the decimal that takes more decimal places to identify than are shown.

**9.3 Skill Practice (pp. 484 – 485)**  **1.** hypotenuse
**3.** 34 ft  **5.** 104 m  **7.** 120 cm  **9.** 19.6 ft  **11.** no
**13.** yes  **15.** yes  **17.** 2  **19.** 5.3  **21.** 3  **23.** 20
**25.** 5  **27.** 4.24 ft

**9.3 Problem Solving (pp. 485 – 486)**  **33.** 22.0 m

**9.4 Skill Practice (pp. 489 – 490)**  **1.** Pythagorean triple
**3.** 15 ft; 60 ft; 150 ft²  **5.** 6 in.; 14.4 in., 8.64 in.²
**7.** 44 m; 286 m, 2574 m²  **9.** 20 yd, 60 yd, 150 yd²
**11.** The hypotenuse was used in the area formula instead of the missing leg; $a^2 + 2.1^2 = 5.3^2$, so $a \approx 4.9$ ft, and area $\approx$
$\frac{1}{2}(4.9)(2.1) \approx 5.1$ ft²  **13.** yes  **15.** no  **17.** 33 mi  **19.** 5;
5; yes  **21.** 2.5; 2.5, no  **23.** $2a + a\sqrt{2}$; 30.7 units
**25.** 12.2  **27.** 8.1  **29.** 9.5

**9.4 Problem Solving (pp. 490 – 491)**

**31. a–b.**      **c.** 42.4 ft

**35. a.**

| | $a$ | $b$ | $c$ | Perimeter | Area |
|---|---|---|---|---|---|
| $\triangle ABC$ | 3 | 4 | 5 | 12 | 6 |
| $\triangle DEF$ | 6 | 8 | 10 | 24 | 24 |
| $\triangle TUV$ | 9 | 12 | 15 | 36 | 54 |

**b.** By comparing the drawings, you can see that the perimeters are two and three times the original perimeter, but the areas are more than two and three times the original area.

**9.5 Skill Practice (pp. 495 – 496)**  **1.** isosceles right
**3.** 9 m  **5.** $30\sqrt{2}$ ft  **7.** 10 in.  **9.** She multiplied by $\sqrt{3}$ instead of $\sqrt{2}$; hypotenuse = leg $\cdot \sqrt{2} = 8\sqrt{2}$ in.

**11.** $x = 17$ cm, $z = 34$ cm  **13.** $x = 8$ m, $y = 8\sqrt{3}$ m

**15.** $x = 32\frac{1}{2}$ cm, $y = \frac{65\sqrt{3}}{2}$ cm  **17.** 4 in.  **19.** 16 mm

**9.5 Skill Practice (pp. 496 – 497)**   **23.** 115 ft
**27.** $12 + 6\sqrt{2}$ in., $48 + 24\sqrt{2}$ in.

**9.6 Skill Practice (pp. 503 – 504)**   **1.** B   **3.** C   **5.** $\sin P = \frac{11}{61}$, $\cos P = \frac{60}{61}$, $\tan P = \frac{11}{60}$, $\sin R = \frac{60}{61}$, $\cos R = \frac{11}{61}$, $\tan R = \frac{60}{11}$   **9.** 0.9848   **11.** 0.2419   **13.** 13.197 cm

**17.** 84.4 in.   **19.** 119.0 ft   **21.** $m\angle C = 60°$, $BC \approx 5$ in., $AC \approx 10$ in.; $\sin C = \frac{8.7}{10}$, $\cos C = \frac{1}{2}$, $\tan C = \frac{8.7}{5}$

**23.** $m\angle C = 70.3°$, $AB \approx 48.0$ cm, $BC \approx 17.2$ cm; $\sin C = \frac{48}{51}$, $\cos C = \frac{17.2}{51}$, $\tan C = \frac{48}{17.2}$

**9.6 Problem Solving (pp. 504 – 505)**

**29. a.**

**b.** $\tan 42° = \frac{x}{50}$   **c.** 45 ft

**31.** 3.5 ft   **33. a.** about 1813 m   **b.** about 845 m   **c.** less
**37.** no; Use the tangent ratio to find the height of the office building, about 690 ft. If you assume that the angle to the top of the apartment building is 30°, then you can use the tangent ratio to find that the apartment building is about 231 ft tall. But 231 is not half of 690, so the angle must not be 30°.   **39.** yes; for example, $\tan 60° \approx 1.7$
**41.** yes; $\cos 0° = 1$

**9.6 Technology Activity (p. 507)**   **1.** 14.0°   **3.** 42.6°
**5.** 87.7°   **7.** $\tan^{-1}(32.46)$; *Sample answer:* The greater the tangent of an angle, the larger the angle.

**Chapter Review (pp. 509 – 512)**   **1.** A rational number can be written as the ratio of two integers, while an irrational number cannot.   **3.** The sum of the squares of the lengths of the legs is equal to the square of the length of the hypotenuse.   **5.** perfect square   **7.** shortest
**9.** converse   **11.** $-28$   **13.** 30.7   **15.** $-34.6$   **17.** $-17.5$
**19.** $\pm 11$   **21.** $\pm 6$   **23.** $\pm 4$   **25.** $\pm 12$   **27.** 5.4 mi
**29.** rational; It is a repeating decimal.   **31.** irrational; $\sqrt{6}$ cannot be written as the quotient of two integers.

**33.** rational; $\sqrt{\frac{27}{3}} = \sqrt{9} = 3$, which is a terminating decimal.   **35.** irrational; $\sqrt{44}$ cannot be written as the quotient of two integers.   **37.** <   **39.** >   **41.** 32

**43.** yes   **45.** yes   **47.** 216; 504 cm, 6804 cm²   **49.** 55; 132 ft, 726 ft²   **51.** $8\sqrt{2}$ in.   **53.** $x = 6$ m, $y = 6\sqrt{3}$ m

**55.** $\sin A = \frac{3}{5}$, $\cos A = \frac{4}{5}$, $\tan A = \frac{3}{4}$, $\sin B = \frac{4}{5}$, $\cos B = \frac{3}{5}$, $\tan B = \frac{4}{3}$   **57.** $\sin A = \frac{36}{85}$, $\cos A = \frac{77}{85}$, $\tan A = \frac{36}{77}$, $\sin B = \frac{77}{85}$, $\cos B = \frac{36}{85}$, $\tan B = \frac{77}{36}$

# Chapter 10

**10.1 Skill Practice (pp. 523 – 525)**   **1.** $A = bh$   **3.** $A = \frac{1}{2}(b_1 + b_2)h$   **5.** 130 cm²   **7.** The height of the parallelogram is 5 inches, not 7 inches; $A = bh = 10(5) = 50$ in.²
**9.** 96 sq units;

**11.** 220 sq units;

**13.** 16 sq units;

**15.** 162 in.²   **17.** 480 m²

**19.** 132 sq units;

**21.** 52.4 sq units;

**23.** 12 ft²; 108 ft²; The area of *EFGH* is 9 times the area of *ABCD*.   **25.** 360 ft²

**27.** 30 sq units;

**29.** $84 = 12b$; 7 cm   **31.** $100 = \frac{1}{2}(10 + 15)h$; 8 in.
**33.** 270 in.²   **35.** 1440 cm²

**10.1 Problem Solving (pp. 525 – 526)**   **39.** 315 in.²
**41.** $b = 26$ mm, $h = 13$ mm; $A = 338$ mm²   **45.** *Sample answer:* about 43,750 mi²

**10.2 Skill Practice (pp. 529 – 530)**   **1.** radius
**3.** 12.56 ft²   **5.** about 555.43 m²   **7.** about 226.87 mm²
**9.** The radius is 5.5 yd, not 11 yd; $A = \pi r^2 \approx (3.14)(5.5)^2 \approx 95.0$ yd²   **11.** 907.46 ft²   **13.** 615.44 mm²   **15.** about 1268.59 in.²   **17.** 1 m   **19.** 6 in.   **21.** 9 cm   **23.** 36 cm
**25.** 28.26 ft²   **27.** 113.04 cm²   **29.** 10 mm; 314 mm²
**31.** 84 mm²   **33.** 239.04 in.²   **35.** 2 units; If $c = a$, then $2\pi r = \pi r^2$, and $r = 2$.

**10.2 Problem Solving (pp. 530 – 532)**   **37.** 452.16 ft²
**39.** about 4533.38 m²   **41.** 10 ft²; $15   **43.** 4 yr
**45. a.** about 192.33 in.²; 392.5 in.²   **b.** 31 min

**10.2 Technology Activity (p. 533)** **1.** multiplied by 3

**3.** multiplied by 5 **5.** multiplied by $\sqrt{2}$; multiplied by $\sqrt{3}$; *Sample answer:* If the area of a circle is multiplied by $n$, then the radius is multiplied by $\sqrt{n}$.

**10.3 Skill Practice (pp. 536 – 537)** **1.** C **3.** B
**5.** rectangular prism; yes **9.** octagonal prism; 10 faces, 24 edges, 16 vertices

**11.**  **13.**

**15.** cylinder and cone **19.**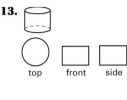

**10.3 Extension (p. 540)**

**1.** 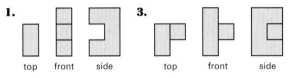 **3.**

top front side     top front side

**5.** 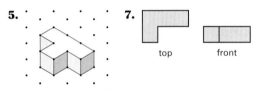 **7.**

top front side

**9.**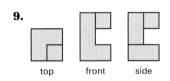

top front side

**10.4 Skill Practice (pp. 545 – 546)** **1.** *Sample answer:* Surface area is the sum of the areas of all the faces and lateral surfaces of a solid. **3.**

**5.**  **7.** 1062 ft²;

**9.** 48 in.² **11.** 174 yd²

**15.** 571.8 in.²;

**17.** 301.6 m²; 75.4 m²;

**19.** 1885.0 cm²; 1256.6 cm²;

**21.** 150 ft² **23.** 204 cm² **25.** The lateral surface area does not include the area of the bases; lateral surface area $= 2\pi rh = 2\pi(3)(7) \approx 131.9$ in.²

**10.4 Problem Solving (p. 547)** **29.** 56,957.1 ft²
**33.** 689.9 in.²;

**35.** $6s^2$

**10.5 Skill Practice (pp. 550 – 551)**

**1.**

*3–7. Sample nets are shown.*

**3.** 36.9 ft²;  **5.** 301.6 cm²;

**7.** 150.8 in.²;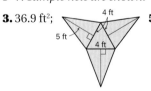

**9.** 67 cm² **11.** 697.4 m² **13.** The slant height $l$ is 10 ft, not 8 ft; $S = \pi r^2 + \pi r l = \pi(6)^2 + \pi(6)(10) \approx 301.59$ ft²
**15.** Use the Pythagorean Theorem to find the hypotenuse

of a right triangle with legs 5 ft and 12 ft; 13 ft; 282.7 ft² **17.** 19.6 in.² **19.** 153.9 in.²

**10.5 Problem Solving (pp. 551 – 552)** **23.** 400 ft²
**27.** 6π in.² **29.** 54π in.² **31.** When both *r* and *l* are multiplied by the same number, the surface area is multiplied by the square of that number; 150π in.²

**10.6 Skill Practice (pp. 557 – 558)** **1.** *Sample answer:* Surface area is the two-dimensional space surrounding a solid, while volume is the three-dimensional space inside a solid. **3.** 132 m³ **5.** 13.68 cm³ **7.** 552.9 ft³ **9.** 20.4 m³ **11.** 2309.1 m³ **13.** 64 yd³ **15.** 1260 m³ **17.** 339.3 cm³ **19.** The area of the base is $\pi r^2$, not $2\pi r$; $V = Bh = \pi r^2 h = \pi(4^2)5 \approx 251.3$ m³ **21.** 336 ft³ **23.** 15 m; 30 m³; 810 m³; The volume of *B* is 27 times the volume of *A*. **25.** doubling the radius; The effect is the same; In the volume formula for a cylinder, the radius is squared but the height is not; Since $V = lwh$ for a rectangular prism, if any dimension is doubled, the volume is doubled.

**10.6 Problem Solving (pp. 558 – 559)** **29.** surface area **31.** volume **33.** cylindrical; about 154.3 ft³; The rectangular pool has a volume of 2560 ft³, and the cylindrical pool has a volume of about 2714.3 ft³. **35.** 10–11 times

**10.7 Skill Practice (pp. 563 – 565)** **1.** D **3.** A **5.** 12 in.³ **7.** 0.3 m³ **9.** 144 yd³ **11.** 2560 m³ **13.** 247.5 ft³ **15.** 95,425.9 ft³ **19.** 506.8 ft³ **21.** 2,019,960.3 cm³ **23.** 70.7 ft³ **25.** 93.6 m²; 249.6 m³ **27.** 13 yd **29.** 14 in. **31.** 904.8 cm³ **33.** When you double the dimensions, you multiply the volume by 8. **35.** $V = lw(\frac{1}{3}h_1 + h_2)$

**10.7 Problem Solving (pp. 565 – 566)** **43. a.** 63.6 in.³ **b.** 1.06 in.³/min **c.** about 17.8 min

**10.7 Extension, p. 567** **1.** 33.5 ft³ **3.** 4.2 yd³ **5.** 904.8 m³ **7.** sphere: $V = \frac{4}{3}\pi r^3$; cone: $V = \frac{2}{3}\pi r^3$; cylinder: $V = 2\pi r^3$; volume of sphere = volume of cylinder − volume of cone

**Chapter Review (pp. 569 – 572)** **1.** B **3.** D **5.** 60 yd² **7.** 756 cm²; 84 cm²; The area of the smaller parallelogram is $\frac{1}{9}$ the area of the larger parallelogram. **9.** about 42.99 mi² **11.** 24 in. **13.** 9 yd **15.** cylinder; no **17.** 5 faces, 9 edges, 6 vertices **19.** 146 ft² **21.** 105 m² **23.** 56 in.² **25.** 135 in.³ **27.** 126 cm³ **29.** no; $\frac{1}{3}(3^2 \cdot 5) = 15 > 12$

# Chapter 11

**11.1 Skill Practice (pp. 585 – 586)** **1.** domain; range **3.** is a function; Each input has exactly 1 output. **5.** not a function; The input −8 has 2 output values. **7.** not a function; The input 4 has 2 output values.

**9.** range: $-\frac{1}{2}, -\frac{1}{4}, 0, \frac{1}{4}, \frac{1}{2}$

| x | −2 | −1 | 0 | 1 | 2 |
|---|----|----|---|---|---|
| y | $\frac{1}{2}$ | $\frac{1}{4}$ | 0 | $-\frac{1}{4}$ | $-\frac{1}{2}$ |

**11.** range: 0, 1, 4

| x | −2 | −1 | 0 | 1 | 2 |
|---|----|----|---|---|---|
| y | 4 | 1 | 0 | 1 | 4 |

**13.** $y = x + 6$ **15.** $y = 6x - 7$ **17.** $A = 4n - 1$ **19.** *Answers may vary. Sample answer:* $y = 2x$;

| x | −1 | 0 | 1 | 2 | 3 |
|---|----|---|---|---|---|
| y | −2 | 0 | 2 | 4 | 6 |

**11.1 Problem Solving (pp. 586 – 587)** **21.** *Sample answer:* 15 lb;

| p | 12 | 13 | 14 | 15 |
|---|----|----|----|----|
| E | 4.8 | 5.2 | 5.6 | 6 |

**23.** $g = 2f$; 14 gal

**11.2 Skill Practice (pp. 590 – 591)** **1.** scatter plot **3.**

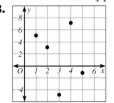

**5.** no relationship **7.** negative relationship **9.** positive relationship;

**11.** no relationship; *Sample answer:* A student's height is not related to the student's test score. **13.** negative relationship; If you have a loan, then as you pay off the loan the amount you still owe goes down. **17.** *Answers may vary. Estimate is given.* 11

**11.3 Skill Practice (pp. 595 – 596)** **1.** solution **3.** 3, 8, 13, 18 **5.** −25, −20, −15, −10 **7.** no **9.** yes **11.** yes
*15–31. Answers may vary. Sample answers are given.*
**15.** (−1, −45), (0, −51), (1, −57), (2, −63) **17.** (−1, 8), (0, 3), (1, −2), (2, −7) **19.** (−3, −6), (0, −5), (3, −4), (6, −3) **21.** $y = 42 - 4x$; (−1, 46), (0, 42), (1, 38), (2, 34) **23.** $y = 10 - 5x$; (−1, 15), (0, 10), (1, 5), (2, 0) **25.** $y = 2x + 19$; (−1, 17), (0, 19), (1, 21), (2, 23) **27.** $y = 2 - 3x$; (−1, 5), (0, 2), (1, −1), (2, −4) **29.** $y = 2x - \frac{5}{4}$; $(-1, -\frac{13}{4})$, $(0, -\frac{5}{4})$, $(1, \frac{3}{4})$, $(2, \frac{11}{4})$ **31.** $y = -\frac{15}{7}x + 6$; (−7, 21), (0, 6), (7, −9), (14, −24)

**33.** *Estimates may vary. Sample answers:* $9x = 21$; $8y = 5$; $9x + 8y$ is $21 + 5 = 26$, which is not equal to 16.   *35–37. Answers may vary. Samples are given.*

**35.** $y = \frac{1}{2}x + 2$; (102, 53), (104, 54), (106, 55), (108, 56)

**37.** $y = \frac{1}{4}x + 6$; (104, 32), (108, 33), (112, 34), (116, 35)

**11.3 Problem Solving (pp. 596 – 597)   43. a.** $110
**b.** 7 sets   **c.** No, the total cost will be $350. The total cost includes $14, which is charged only once. The shipping and handling does not double when the number of orders doubles.   **49.** $10x + y = 120$; 40 min on games

**11.4 Skill Practice (pp. 600 – 601)   1.** line   **3.** yes
**5.** yes

**7.**     **9.**

**11.**     **13.**

**15.**     **17.**

**19.**     **21.**

**23.** $y = 4x - 2$;

**25.** $y = -5x$;

**27.** $x = 3$   **29–32.** *Sample answer:* All four lines are parallel; They cross the y-axis at different points;

**33–36.** *Sample answer:* All four lines contain the origin; They have different "tilts";
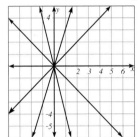

**11.4 Problem Solving (pp. 602 – 603)**
**41.** in 11 months;

**45.** *Approximations may vary. Sample answer:* 37°C
**47. a.** $y = 2x + 1$   **b.** 6 months;

**c.** $2x + 1 = 13$, $2x = 12$, $x = 6$

**11.4 Technology Activity (p. 604)**

**1.**  **3.**

**5.** yes

**11.5 Skill Practice (p. 608)** **1.** *x*-intercept: 6;

*y*-intercept: 1 **3.** *x*-intercept: $\frac{1}{2}$; *y*-intercept: –3

**5.** *x*-intercept: 2; *y*-intercept: –5
**7.** *x*-intercept: 5; *y*-intercept: 4

**11.**  **13.**

**15.** *x*-intercept: 3.5; *y*-intercept: 7;

**17.** *x*-intercept: 2.6; *y*-intercept: 6.5;

**19.** *x*-intercept: −2; *y*-intercept: 1;

**21.** *y*-intercepts **23.** *x*-intercept: none; *y*-intercept: 9
**25.** *x*-intercept: 21; *y*-intercept: none

**11.5 Problem Solving (p. 609)** **29. a.** *x* and *y* represent the numbers of CDs and videos you can buy, respectively;
**b.** *x*-intercept: 5; *y*-intercept: 6;

**c.** The intercepts indicate that you can buy 5 CDs and 0 videos or you can buy 0 CDs and 6 videos. **33.** It slants up; It goes through Quadrants I, III, and IV; *Sample answer:* Look at an example. If a line contains (1, 0) and (0, −1), it slants up from left to right and it goes through Quadrants I, III, and IV.

**11.6 Skill Practice (pp. 614 – 615)** **1.** rise **3.** slope

**5.** (−2, 6), (1, 0); −2 **7.** $-\frac{1}{5}$ **9.** 0 **11.** undefined

**13.** $-\frac{5}{12}$ **15.** $\frac{3}{32}$

**17.**  **19.**

**21.** undefined, $-\frac{4}{3}$, 0;

**23.** $-\frac{3}{2}$, 0, $\frac{3}{2}$;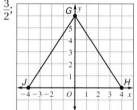

**25.** line *a* **29.** *y* = 7 **31.** right triangle; The slope of

$\overline{RT}$ is $\frac{b-d}{a-c}$; the slope of $\overline{ST}$ is $\frac{b-d}{c-c}$, which is undefined;

The slope of $\overline{RS}$ is $\frac{b-b}{a-c}$, which is 0.

**11.6 Problem Solving (pp. 616 – 617)** **35.** 3
**43.** 56,549 mm³; 113,097 mm³; 282,743 mm³; 339,292 mm³; The slope is about 2827 (which is the area of the base of the cylinder); The four points lie on a line, so any pair of points can be used to calculate the slope;

**11.6 Extension (p. 619)** **1.** neither; The data can be represented by *y* = *x* + 1, which is neither direct nor

inverse variation. **3.** inverse variation; The data can be represented by $xy = 2$. **5.** direct variation; The equation can be written as $11x = 2.2y$ or $\frac{y}{x} = 5$. **7.** direct variation; The equation can be written as $y = (-\frac{1}{3})x$. **9.** neither; The equation can be written as $xy = -3 + x$, which is neither direct nor inverse variation. **11.** no; The equation in this case is $m = 4t + 20$. The variables $m$ and $t$ do not show direct variation because the ratio of $m$ to $t$ is not constant, due to the initial 20 dollars. Also, the equation cannot be written in the form $y = kx$. So, $m$ and $t$ are not directly proportional.

**11.7 Skill Practice (pp. 624 – 625)** **1.** slope
**3.** $y = 2x - 5$ **5.** $y = x + 2$ **7.** slope: 1; $y$-intercept: 3
**9.** slope: 2; $y$-intercept: $-1$ **11.** slope: $-\frac{3}{4}$; $y$-intercept: 9
**13.** slope: 0; $y$-intercept: 3 **15.** slope: $\frac{13}{11}$; $y$-intercept: $-13$
**17.**

**19.**

**21.**

**23.** The student used the value of $b$ as the $x$-intercept, not the $y$-intercept; The line should go through $(0, -1)$ and $(-1, 1)$. **25.** $y = -\frac{3}{2}x - 3$ **27.** $y = 3x - 1$ is steeper; Its slope is 3, and the slope of $y = 2x - 1$ is 2. **29.** $-4$; $y = -4$ **31.** 1; $y = -\frac{1}{2}x + 1$ **33.** 5; $y = 2x + 5$
**35.** $y = -\frac{2}{3}x + 14$

**11.7 Problem Solving (pp. 625 – 626)**
**43.** $y = -\frac{1}{2}x + 8$;

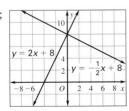

**11.7 Extension (p. 628)**
**1.** $(1, 2)$;

**3.** $(6, -3)$;

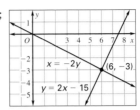

**5.** $(-1, 5)$ **7.** There is no solution because the lines are parallel;

**11.8 Skill Practice (pp. 631 – 632)** **1.** half-planes
**3.** yes **5.** no **7.**

**9.**

**11.**

**13.**

**15.**

**17.**

**19.**

**21.**

**23.** The symbol is ≤, but the graph uses a dashed line for the equation; The graph should use a solid line for the equation.

**25.** $x + y > 10$;

**27.** $x \geq 20$;

**29.** $y > 2x$;

**31.** always   **33.** never

**11.8 Problem Solving (pp. 632 – 633)**   **35.** *Answers may vary. Sample answer:* 1.5 lb of peanuts and 2 lb of raisins; 0.75 lb of peanuts and 3 lb of raisins;

**Chapter Review (pp. 636 – 640)**   **1.** function   **3.** input; output   **5.** To find the *x*-intercept, set $y = 0$ and solve for *x*. To find the *y*-intercept, set $x = 0$ and solve for *y*.
**7.** *Sample answer:* Change the inequality symbol to =. Graph the equality, using a dashed line for < or > and a solid line for ≤ or ≥. Test a point in one of the half-planes. If it satisfies the inequality, shade that half-plane. If it does not satisfy the inequality, shade the other half-plane.   **9.** yes; $y = x + 6$   **11.** yes; $y = -3x - 8$

**13.** The data represent indirect variation, with $st = 120$;

**15.** *Answers may vary. Sample answers:* $(-4, 5)$, $(0, 4)$, $(4, 3)$   **17.**

**19.**

**21.** 488; The IRS collected \$488 billion in 1980.
**23.** *Answers may vary. Sample answers are given.* $(-3, 3)$, $(0, 3)$; 0   **25.** slope: $-\frac{2}{3}$; *y*-intercept: 4   **27.** $y = 4x + 10$; slope: 4; *y*-intercept: 10   **29.** $y = -\frac{3}{7}x - 3$; slope: $\frac{3}{7}$; *y*-intercept: $-3$   **31.**

# Chapter 12

**12.1 Skill Practice (pp. 651 – 652)**   **1.** stem, leaf
**3.** 8 | 0; stem: 8, leaf: 0   **5.** 12 | 9; stem: 12, leaf: 9
**7.** 60–69;

```
4 | 0 5 8
5 | 0 2
6 | 1 3 5 6 7
7 | 4
8 | 2 4
Key: 5 | 0 = 50
```

**9.** 100–109;

```
 8 | 9
 9 | 2 4 5
10 | 3 5 8 9
11 | 2 5
Key: 11 | 2 = 112
```

**11.** 18.0–18.9;

```
18 | 1 3 4 6 7
19 |
20 | 2
21 | 9
22 | 5 6 8
Key: 21 | 9 = 21.9
```

**13.** The bottom row on the stem-and-leaf plot should be two rows with stems 10 and 11, and the key is incorrect; The key should be 11 | 5 = 115.

```
 8 | 3
 9 | 1 5
10 | 8
11 | 1 5
Key: 11 | 5 = 115
```

**17.**

| | | | |
|---|---|---|---|
| | Set C | | Set D |
| | | 6 | 5 |
| | 7 0 | 7 | |
| | | 8 | 7 8 |
| | 8 2 | 9 | 3 5 |
| | 2 | 10 | 2 |
| | 8 1 | 11 | 5 |

Key: 2 | 9 | 3 = 92 and 93

**19.**

| | | | |
|---|---|---|---|
| | Set C | | Set D |
| | 7 | 4 | |
| | | 5 | 5 |
| | 8 3 | 6 | 8 |
| | 7 | 7 | 8 |
| | 8 0 | 8 | |
| | 8 | 9 | 1 3 5 |
| | | 10 | 0 |

Key: 8 | 9 | 1 = 9.8 and 9.1

**21.** 2.0; 2.0; 0.1, 2.0 and 2.8

**12.1 Problem Solving (pp. 652 – 653)  25.** 5 min, 45 min; 30–39 minute interval

**27.** $62, $53;

| | |
|---|---|
| 4 | 3 7 |
| 5 | 5 9 |
| 6 | 2 2 |
| 7 | 2 8 |
| 8 | 4 4 |
| 9 | 6 |

Key: 8 | 4 = 84

**31. a.** 13.7°F;

| | |
|---|---|
| 56 | 8 9 |
| 57 | 6 |
| 58 | 0 |
| 59 | |
| 60 | 1 |
| 61 | 6 |
| 62 | 7 |
| 63 | |
| 64 | |
| 65 | 7 |
| 66 | 8 |
| 67 | |
| 68 | |
| 69 | 1 9 |
| 70 | 5 |

Key: 56 | 8 = 56.8

**b.** 13.8, 14.2, 14.4, 15.6, 17.1, 18.7, 20.6, 21.4, 21.1, 19.3, 16.4, 13.8  **c.** *Sample answer:* The temperatures in degrees Celsius are lower than the temperatures in degrees Fahrenheit, and temperatures in degrees Celsius are distributed over a smaller range. This is because as temperatures change by 1 degree Celsius, they change by 1.8 degrees Fahrenheit;

| | |
|---|---|
| 13 | 8 8 |
| 14 | 2 4 |
| 15 | 6 |
| 16 | 4 |
| 17 | 1 |
| 18 | 7 |
| 19 | 3 |
| 20 | 6 |
| 21 | 1 4 |

Key: 14 | 2 = 14.2

**12.2 Skill Practice (pp. 656 – 657)  1.** lower quartile

**3.**  **5.**

**7.** 35 is the upper extreme, not the upper quartile. 33 is the upper quartile.  **9.** 11 in.  **11.** 28 in.  **13.** 25 and 50  **15.** D  **17.** false; Both of these intervals include about one quarter of the data.

**12.2 Problem Solving (pp. 657 – 658)**

**21. a.** 210;

**b.** median: 251, lower quartile: 204, upper quartile: 301, extremes: 141 and 351  **c.**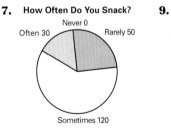

**23.** *Sample answer:* Khalila has a higher median score than Tasha, 11 points versus 9 points, but her performance is much more variable. For Khalila, it took an interval of 7, from 7 to 14, to contain half of her point totals, but for Tasha, it took only an interval of 4, from 8 to 12, to contain half of her point totals, so Tasha's scoring is more consistent. This is also shown by the fact that the extremes for Tasha are between the extremes for Khalila. Also, the range for Tasha is only 8 points, but the range is 15 points for Khalila.

**25.** 371,000;

**12.3 Skill Practice (pp. 661 – 662)  1.** circle graph, line graph  **3.** 135°  **5.** 162°

**7.**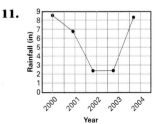

**9.**

**11.**

**13.** circle graph; The data represents parts of a whole.
**17.** line graph; The data is collected over time.

**19.** *Sample answer:* histogram; The data is the frequency of occurrence in equal intervals for a certain range.

### 12.3 Problem Solving (pp. 663 – 664)

**21.**

Play Attendance

- Sunday 185
- Friday 130
- Saturday (2 P.M.) 231
- Saturday (8 P.M.) 291

**23.** The Bronx: 14%, Queens: 36%, Brooklyn: 24%, Staten Island: 18%, Manhattan: 8%

**27.** The vertical axis is marked by 10,000's since the data is between 20,000 and 40,000.

**29.** 2887 phones per year   **31.** 1470; 2771; 4320; 5671; 6786; 8669; 10,170; 11,723; 13,777; 15,269   **33.** *Sample answer:* Subtract the total rushing yards in 1989 from the total rushing yards in 1993, and subtract the total rushing yards in 1994 from the total rushing yards in 1998. The larger number represents the interval during which Sanders accumulated more rushing yards.

### 12.3 Technology Activity (pp. 665 – 666)

**1.**

**3.**

### 12.3 Extension (p. 668)   **1.** no; *Sample answer:* There is a break in the vertical scale, so the relative change is smaller than it appears;

**3.**

### 12.4 Skill Practice (pp. 672 – 673)   **1.** $m \cdot n$   **3.** 8 choices

**5.** 6 choices   **9.** $\frac{21}{26}$   **11.** $\frac{1}{456,976}$   **13.** 18 outcomes

### 12.4 Problem Solving (pp. 673 – 674)   **17.** *Sample answer:* Draw a tree diagram to list and then count all of the possibilities, or use the counting principle.
**23.** 64 symbols; 1 symbol; 1 symbol

### 12.5 Skill Practice (pp. 677 – 678)   **1.** $_{15}P_7$   **3.** 2   **5.** 5040

**7.** 12   **9.** 604,800   **11.** 665,280   **13.** 360,360
**15.** The denominator should be $(5 - 3)!$; $_5P_3 = \frac{5!}{(5 - 3)!} =$
$\frac{5 \cdot 4 \cdot 3 \cdot 2 \cdot 1}{2 \cdot 1} = 5 \cdot 4 \cdot 3 = 60$   **17.** $_7P_7 = 5040$

**19.** $_{52}P_5 = 311,875,200$   **21.** $_{24}P_4 = 255,024$

**23.** <   **25.** <   **27.** <

### 12.5 Problem Solving (pp. 678 – 679)
**29.** 5040 permutations   **33.** 210 permutations
**35.** 12 ways; Ed and Sue, Ed and Ty, Ed and Nestor, Sue and Ed, Ty and Ed, Nestor and Ed, Sue and Ty, Ty and Sue, Sue and Nestor, Nestor and Sue, Ty and Nestor, Nestor and Ty

### 12.6 Skill Practice (pp. 682 – 683)   **1.** 9; 5
**3.** 10 pairs;

| | | | |
|---|---|---|---|
| 1, 2 | 1̶,̶3̶ | 1̶,̶4̶ | 1̶,̶5̶ |
| 2̶,̶1̶ | 2, 3 | 2̶,̶4̶ | 2̶,̶5̶ |
| 3, 1 | 3̶,̶2̶ | 3, 4 | 3̶,̶5̶ |
| 4, 1 | 4, 2 | 4̶,̶3̶ | 4, 5 |
| 5, 1 | 5, 2 | 5, 3 | 5̶,̶4̶ |

**5.** 4   **7.** 7   **9.** 28   **11.** 45   **13.** 165   **15.** 36
**17.** Order is not important, so the possibilities can be counted by evaluating $_8C_2$, not $_8P_2$; $_8C_2 = \frac{_8P_2}{2!} = \frac{8 \cdot 7}{2 \cdot 1} =$
28 possibilities   **19.** permutation; 24 orders
**21.** combination; 10 groups

**12.6 Problem Solving (pp. 683 – 684)**
**27.** 15 combinations **29.** 792 teams **35. a.** 40,320 ways
**b.** 45 ways **c.** 1,814,400 ways; Order is important, so
evaluate $_{10}P_8$.

**12.7 Skill Practice (pp. 687 – 688)** **1.** odds in favor

**3.** 16% **5.** 0.63 **7.** $\frac{3}{10}, \frac{7}{10}; \frac{7}{3}$ **9.** $\frac{6}{11}, \frac{5}{11}; \frac{5}{6}$ **11.** $\frac{1}{5}$ **13.** $\frac{2}{1}$

**15.** The student transposed the numerator and

denominator; Odds $= \frac{2}{4} = \frac{1}{2}$, so the odds in favor are

1 to 2. **17.** $\frac{11}{9}$ **19.** $\frac{2}{23}$ **21.** $\frac{1}{4}$ **23.** $\frac{27}{50}$ **25.** $\frac{a}{a+b}$

**12.7 Problem Solving (pp. 688 – 689)** **27.** $\frac{3}{5}$ **29.** $\frac{13}{12}$

**31.** $\frac{93}{7}$

**12.7 Extension, p. 691**

**1.** $\{-7, -5, -4, -2, -1, 1, 2, 4, 5, 7\}$;

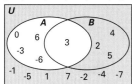

**3.** $\{-7, -5, -4, -2, -1, 1, 7\}$;

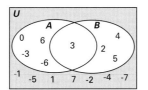

**5.** $\{-7, -5, -4, -2, -1, 1, 2, 3, 4, 5, 7\}$;

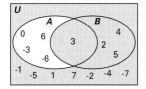

**7.** $\{-7, -5, -4, -2, -1, 1, 7\}$;

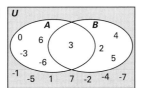

**9.** $\frac{11}{15}$ **11.** $\frac{7}{15}$ **13.** $\varnothing$; $U$; There are no elements that are

both in $A$ and not in $A$. The set of all elements in $A$ or not
in $A$ is all the elements in $U$.

**15.**

**17.**

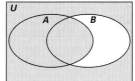

**12.8 Skill Practice (pp. 697 – 698)** **1.** independent
**3.** independent **5.** dependent **7.** 0.24 **9.** 0.2

**11.** 0.4 **17.** $\frac{81}{10,000}$ **19.** $\frac{3}{2500}$

**12.8 Problem Solving (pp. 698 – 700)**

**23.** dependent; $\frac{1}{19}$ **25.** dependent; $\frac{2}{21}$ **27.** The

probability of $B$ given $A = \frac{3}{9}$, not $\frac{3}{10}$; $P(A$ and $B) = \frac{4}{10} \cdot \frac{3}{9} =$

$\frac{12}{90} = \frac{2}{15}$ **31.** $\frac{1}{128}; \frac{1}{2}$; The probability of each toss is

independent, so the probability that you will get heads is

always $\frac{1}{2}$.

**12.8 Extension, p. 702** **1.** yes; People who call in to a
sports talk show are likely to favor sports. **3.** yes; People
who enter a sporting goods store are likely to favor sports.
*5–7. Sample explanations are given.* **5.** yes; This
question suggests the mall is noisy and crowded. It
encourages respondents to favor staying at home. So,
the question could lead to biased results. **7.** no; This
question is straightforward with no suggestions. It is not
likely to lead to biased results.

**Chapter Review (pp. 704 – 708)** **1.** permutation
**3.** circle graph **5.** stem-and-leaf plot
**7.** 20–29;
```
1 | 5 6 9
2 | 0 1 2 5 7 8 9
3 | 1 2 6 7
4 | 2
Key: 3 | 1 = 31
```
**9.** 90–99;
```
 8 | 1 4 6
 9 | 4 6 7 7 9
10 | 0 0
Key: 10 | 0 = 100
```

**11.**

**13.** *Sample answer:* About half of the chess sets are priced
between $27.50 and $55. The $95 set lies well beyond the
third quartile and appears to be an outlier;

**15.** 12 pairs;

H1  H2  H3  H4
S1 S2 S3  S1 S2 S3  S1 S2 S3  S1 S2 S3

**17.** 720 **19.** 154,440 **21.** 36 **23.** 1 **25.** combination;
155,117,520 groups **27.** 24%; $\frac{6}{19}$ **29.** 15%

# Chapter 13

**13.1 Skill Practice (p. 719)** **1.** trinomial **3.** monomial
**5.** $3m + 7$; binomial **7.** $-n^2 + 5n - 1$; trinomial
**9.** $y^2 - 5y + 2$; trinomial **11.** $4x^{10} - 13x^3$; binomial
**13.** $c^2 + 5c$ **15.** $-4g^3 + 2g^2 - 10$ **17.** $8x^2 - 15x + 30$
**19.** $18t^2 + 12t - 37$ **21.** $-3x^2$ and $-20x$ are not like
terms; $-3x^2 - 20x - 4$ is the simplest form.
**23.** $5a - 8b - 24$ **25.** $5a^2b^2 - 6ab^2 + 6ab$
**27.** *Answers may vary. Sample answer:* Standard
form: $x + 1, x^2 + x + 1, 2x^3 + 3x^2 + 4x + 1$; Not standard
form: $1 + x, x^2 + 1 + x, 1 + x + x^2$ **29.** $6x + 4$

**13.1 Problem Solving (p. 720)** **33.** 114 ft **35.** 122 ft
**39.** sometimes; The monomial 1 has one factor, but the
monomial $5x$ has two factors.

**13.2 Skill Practice (pp. 723 – 724)** **1.** like terms
**3.** $12y + 2$ **5.** $5x + 4$ **7.** $6g^2 + g + 3$ **9.** $6k^2$ **11.** The
terms were not aligned properly, and unlike terms were
combined; $-2x^3 + 5x^2 - 13x + 12$ **13.** $6x + 12$
**15.** $-10d - 7$ **17.** $3r^2 + 2r + 4$ **19.** $3a^2 + 5a + 17$
**21.** $12n + 3$ **23.** $-19y - 15$ **25.** $17q^2 - 7q$
**27.** $20x^3 + 11x^2 - 15x + 5$ **29.** $3, -3$

**13.2 Problem Solving (pp. 724 – 725)**
**33.** $2(2x^2 - 2x + 3) + 2(-x^2 + 10x + 1)$; $2x^2 + 16x + 8$

**13.3 Skill Practice (pp. 728 – 729)** **1.** B **3.** C **5.** $48t^{10}$
**7.** $-6s^4$ **9.** $-y^5$ **11.** $-t^3 + 4t$ **13.** $36k^2 - 3k^7$
**15.** $-35a^5 + 63a^3$ **17.** $x^5y^5z^5$ **19.** $-216z^3$ **21.** $9r^2s^2$
**23.** $100,000b^5h^5$ **25.** $y^4$ **27.** $x^{20}$ **29.** $x^6y^6$ **31.** $8r^9$
**35.** $7.29 \times 10^{32}$ **37.** $250m^3n^{12}$ **39.** $-8x^{16}yz^8$ **41.** $2c^{36}d^{38}$

**43.** $\dfrac{81}{h^4}$ **45.** $\dfrac{9m^2}{n^4}$

**13.3 Problem Solving (pp. 729 – 731)** **51.** $125x^3$

**53.** $\dfrac{1}{2}(b - 6)(3b + b)$; $2b^2 - 12b$ **55.** $\dfrac{4}{3}\pi r^2h$; It is 4 times
the original expression.

**13.4 Skill Practice (p. 736)** **1.** binomial **3.** $y^2 - 3y - 4$
**5.** $x^2 - 16$ **7.** $15q^2 - 8q + 1$ **9.** $x^2 + 7x - 18$
**11.** $a^2 + 6a - 40$ **13.** $-3t^2 - t + 4$ **15.** $9x^2 - 1$
**17.** $6m^2 + 23m + 7$ **19.** $36z^2 + 60z + 25$
**21.** $2x^2 + 5x - 12$ **23.** $n^4 - n^2 - 2$
**27.** $x^3 - x^2 - 3x - 36$ **29.** $8x^3 + 2x^2 + 9x + 5$
**31.** $-4x^3 - 17x^2 - 9x + 18$ **33.** $3x^2 + 16x - 35$

**13.4 Problem Solving (pp. 737 – 738)**
**39.** $50 + 100r + 50r^2$; $53.05
**47.** $20r^3 + 60r^2 + 60r + 20$; $23.15
**49. a.** $6n^2 - 12n - 18$ **b.** 72 in.²

**13.5 Skill Practice (pp. 741 – 743)** **1.** The left side
should be $f(x)$, not just $f$. **3.** $f(x) = x^2$; 4, 0, 4
**5.** $f(x) = -3x^2$; $-12$, 0, $-12$ **7.** $f(x) = x^2 - 5$; $-1$,
$-5$, $-1$ **9.** The square of $-5$ should be 25, not $-25$;
$f(-5) = (-5)^2 - 3 = 25 - 3 = 22$

**13.**  **15.**

**17.**  **19.**

**21.** yes; yes **23.** no; no

**25.**  **27.**

**29.**

**31.** $2, -2$ **33.** $1, -1$ **35.** $-1, 3$ **37.** $f(x) = x^3$
**39.** The graph of $y = c$ is a function because it is a
horizontal line. If it is rotated 90°, it is a vertical line, so it
would not represent a function.

**13.5 Problem Solving (pp. 743 – 745)** **41.** $f(d) = 1500d$;
The function is linear. **43.** $f(x) = 20(1.002)^t$; $20.04;
$20.08; $20.12

**45.** $f(x) = \dfrac{\pi x^2}{4}$; 50.3 in.²;

**49.** B  **53.** yes; *Sample answer:* $f(x) = 90x$ describes the horizontal distance in terms of time. When the distance is 315 ft, then $315 = 90x$ and $x = \frac{315}{90} = 3.5$ s. Using $f(t) = -16t^2 + 63t + 2.5$ with $t = 3.5$, the height is $-16(3.5)^2 + 63(3.5) + 2.5 = 27$ ft. The height of the wall is 21 ft and $27 \geq 21$, so the hit will be a home run.

**13.5 Technology Activity (p. 746)**  **1–4.** *Sample answer:* The graphs are all parabolas with the same shape and with vertices on the $y$-axis, but each graph moves up or down compared to the graph of $y = x^2$ by the number of units that are added to or subtracted from $x^2$. The graph moves up if this number is positive and down if this number is negative.

**1.**   **3.**

**5–8.** *Sample answer:* The graphs are the same as the graphs in the example, except they are reflected about the $x$-axis.

**5.**   **7.**

**9.** *Sample answer:* The graph is the same shape as the first graph in the example, reflected about the x-axis and shifted vertically 3 units;

**11.** *Sample answer:* The graph is the same shape as the first graph in the example, reflected about the x-axis and shifted vertically 8 units;

**Chapter Review (pp. 748 – 750)**  **1.** polynomial  **3.** standard form  **5.** trinomial  **7.** binomial

**9.** $k^2 + 11k - 3$  **11.** $18p^3 + 15p^2 + 27$  **13.** $4s^3 + 24s^2 - 16s - 56$  **15.** 6 ft  **17.** $8y^2 - 5$  **19.** $-5v^3 - 10v^2 - 2v$

**21.** $-216a^6b^{12}$  **23.** $-3a^3 + 6a^2$  **25.** $\frac{1}{2}(6x)(3x + 9) = 9x^2 + 27x$  **27.** $36\pi x^3$  **29.** $q^2 - 16q + 63$

**31.**   **33.**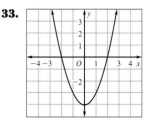

**35.** yes  **37.** no

# Skills Review Handbook

**Place Value (p. 759)**  **1.** $5 \times 10{,}000 + 6 \times 1000 + 8 \times 100 + 9 \times 1$  **3.** $1 \times 1000 + 2 \times 1 + 3 \times 0.001$  **5.** 500,069.007

**Rounding (p. 760)**  **1.** 1300  **3.** 8.2  **5.** 40,000  **7.** 450  **9.** 62.8  **11.** 164.5  **13.** 52.96  **15.** 3,501,700

**Divisibility Tests (p. 761)**  **1.** 2  **3.** 3, 5  **5.** 2, 3, 4, 6, 9  **7.** 5  **9.** 2, 4

**Mixed Numbers and Improper Fractions (p. 762)**
**1.** 38  **3.** 3  **5.** $\frac{7}{2}$  **7.** $\frac{35}{8}$  **9.** $\frac{43}{4}$  **11.** $7\frac{1}{2}$  **13.** $5\frac{2}{3}$

**Ratio and Rate (p. 763)**
**1.** $\frac{13}{12}$, 13 to 12, 13 : 12  **3.** $\frac{11}{23}$, 11 to 23, 11 : 23
**5.** $\frac{\$24}{8}$ pens $= \frac{\$3}{1}$ pen  **7.** $\frac{280 \text{ words}}{5 \text{ min}} = \frac{56 \text{ words}}{1 \text{ min}}$
**9.** $\frac{8 \text{ in.}}{6 \text{ days}} = 1\frac{1}{3}$ in. per day

**Adding and Subtracting Decimals (p. 764)**  **1.** 6.3  **3.** 31.1  **5.** 10.956  **7.** 2.91  **9.** 18.88  **11.** 57.8  **13.** 286.19  **15.** 88.064

**Adding and Subtracting Fractions (p. 765)**  **1.** $\frac{2}{3}$  **3.** $\frac{3}{7}$  **5.** 1  **7.** $\frac{11}{15}$  **9.** $\frac{2}{9}$  **11.** $1\frac{7}{12}$  **13.** $\frac{1}{9}$  **15.** $\frac{9}{14}$  **17.** $\frac{7}{12}$
**19.** $1\frac{4}{7}$

**Estimation in Addition and Subtraction (p. 766)**  *1–5. Estimates may vary.*  **1.** 2700  **3.** 20,000  **5.** 2200

**Solving Problems Using Addition and Subtraction (p. 767)**  **1.** $93  **3.** $2.01  **5.** 248 min

**Multiplying Fractions (p. 768)**  **1.** $\frac{4}{5}$  **3.** $2\frac{2}{9}$  **5.** $5\frac{1}{4}$  **7.** $2\frac{4}{7}$
**9.** $\frac{8}{15}$  **11.** $\frac{3}{40}$  **13.** $\frac{10}{27}$  **15.** $\frac{25}{72}$

**Multiplication of a Decimal by a Whole Number (p. 769)**  **1.** 225.4  **3.** 671.5  **5.** 29.12  **7.** 644.36  **9.** 1707.2  **11.** 18,663.6  **13.** 15,093.8  **15.** 36,833.5  **17.** 949.992  **19.** 3707.352  **21.** 4998.7  **23.** 1809.665  **25.** 5477.336  **27.** 120,455.25  **29.** 7564.91

**Dividing Decimals (p. 770)** **1.** 0.45 **3.** 0.85 **5.** 4.57
**7.** 6 R2 **9.** 8 R604

**Estimation in Multiplication and Division (p. 771)**
*1–19. Estimates may vary.* **1.** 400 and 1000 **3.** 40,000
and 54,000 **5.** 30 and 40 **7.** 200 and 300 **9.** 12,000
and 20,000 **11.** 70,000 and 160,000 **13.** 12,000 and
21,000 **15.** 90 and 100 **17.** 700 and 800 **19.** 10 and 20

**Solving Problems Using Multiplication and Division**
**(p. 772)** **1.** $9.48 **3.** 576 flowers

**Points, Lines, and Planes (p. 773)** **1.** B **3.** A
*5–7. Answers may vary.* **5.** $\overrightarrow{SR}$ and $\overrightarrow{ST}$ **7.** $\overline{SR}$

**Angles (p. 774)** **1.** C **3.** B **5.** ∠HJK, ∠J, ∠KJH
**7.** ∠TUV, ∠U, ∠VUT **9.** ∠FGH, ∠G, ∠HGF

**Using a Protractor (p. 776)** **1.** 110° **3.** 88°

**Using a Compass (p. 777)** **1.** A good answer will show a
circle with radius 4 cm. **3.** ────────

**Elapsed Time (p. 778)** **1.** 2 hours 11 minutes **3.** 3:35 P.M.

**Converting Customary Units (p. 779)** **1.** 69 **3.** $10\frac{1}{2}$
**5.** 24 **7.** 3; 2 **9.** 6; 3

**Converting Metric Units (p. 780)** **1.** 6420 **3.** 5500 **5.** <

**Converting Between Systems (p. 781)** **1.** 176 **3.** 23
**5.** <

**Reading and Making Line Plots (p. 782)**

**1.**

**3.** 19 people **5.** 5 people

**Reading and Making Bar Graphs (p. 783)** **1.** 9 students
**3.** Vanilla and Rocky Road

**Reading and Making Line Graphs (p. 784)**

**1.** Thursday and Friday **3.**

**Venn Diagrams and Logical Reasoning (p. 785)**

**1.**
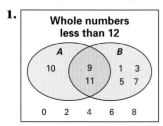

**3.** false; Both 9 and 11 are odd numbers greater than 8
and less than 12.

# Problem Solving Practice

**Make a Model (p. 796)** **1.** yes; no; yes

**3.**
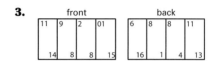

**Draw a Diagram (p. 796)** **5.** 45 **7.** 3

**Guess, Check, and Revise (p. 797)** **9.** 4 on bicycles, 3 on
tricycles **11.** 21, 22, and 23

**Work Backward (p. 798)** **13.** 69 **15.** 60 **17.** 21

**Make a List or a Table (pp. 797 – 798)** **19.** 2 keychains

**Look for a Pattern (p. 798)** **21.** $265
**23.** $18; individual fares

**Break into Parts (p. 799)** **25.** 3 hours 11 minutes
**27.** $1054.50

**Solve a Simpler Problem (p. 799)** **29.** 1496 **31.** 220

**Use a Venn Diagram (pp. 799 – 800)** **33.** 20 **35.** 7

**Act It Out (p. 800)** **37.** Bob, Kelly, Justin, Rebecca, and
Michelle **39.** 10 **41.** *Sample answer:* Move box C to
Table 3, move box B to Table 2, stack box C on top of box
B on Table 2, move box A to Table 3, move box C to Table
1, stack box B on top of box A on Table 3, and stack box C
on top of boxes B and A on Table 3. **43.** Darryl, Carlene,
Tyrone, and Penelope

# Extra Practice

**Chapter 1 (p. 801)**
**1.**
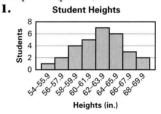

**3.** yes; You can add the frequencies for the intervals
60–61.9, 62–63.9, 64–65.9, 66–67.9, and 68–69.9. **5.** 7
**7.** 4 **9.** 36 **11.** 8.4 **13.** 11.7 **15.** 27 **17.** 7
**19.** 63 **21.** 8 **23.** 9 **25.** 42 ft; 104 ft² **27.** 8 cm

**Chapter 2 (p. 802)** **1.** −43, −24, −2, 7, 19, 33 **3.** 25; 25
**5.** 0; 0 **7.** −409 **9.** 179 **11.** 0 **13.** −16 **15.** 51
**17.** −15 **19.** 68 **21.** 350 **23.** −64 **25.** 0 **27.** 240

**29.** −12 **31.** 0 **33.** −4 **35.** $7(2 \cdot \frac{3}{7})$ [original
expression] = $7(\frac{3}{7} \cdot 2)$ [Comm. Prop. of Mult.] = $(7 \cdot \frac{3}{7}) \cdot 2$
[Assoc. Prop. of Mult.] = $3 \cdot 2$ [Multiply 7 and $\frac{3}{7}$] = 6
[Multiply 3 and 2] **37.** (−5)(−3) + (−5)(8); −25
**39.** −4 − 9r **41.** 5x − 2y **43.** −a − 10b

**44–47.**    **45.** Quadrant I

**47.** Quadrant III

**Chapter 3 (p. 803)** **1.** 8 **3.** 5 **5.** 64 **7.** 4 **9.** 7
**11.** 7.5 **13.** 20 **15.** $-58$ **17.** $6n - 5 = 13$; 3
**19.** 1.5 h **21.** 60 in.²; 36 in. **23.** 5 m; 34 m

**25.** $j \geq -5$;

**27.** $z \leq = -2.5$;

**29.** $x < -5$;

**31.** $s \leq = 8$;

**Chapter 4 (p. 804)** **1.** $2^3 \cdot 3^2$ **3.** $3^2 \cdot 17$ **5.** $5^2 \cdot p \cdot q$
**7.** $2 \cdot 11 \cdot x \cdot y \cdot y$ **9.** 15 **11.** $bc$ **13.** $3m$ **15.** $17w^2z^2$
**17.** $\frac{1}{2}$ **19.** $-\frac{2}{7}$ **21.** $\frac{2}{9y}$ **23.** $-\frac{3a}{2c}$ **25.** 60 **27.** $15ab^2c^2$
**29.** $>$ **31.** $>$ **33.** $<$ **35.** $>$ **37.** $z^6$ **39.** $(-7)^9$ **41.** $6^4$
**43.** $(-v)^3$ **45.** $\frac{6}{k}$ **47.** $\frac{1}{s^7}$ **49.** $1.24 \times 10^8$ **51.** $7.91 \times 10^{-5}$
**53.** 0.0027 **55.** 588,000,000,000

**Chapter 5 (p. 805)** **1.** $1\frac{1}{2}$ **3.** $-\frac{2m}{3}$ **5.** $\frac{1}{15}$ **7.** $8\frac{1}{8}$ **9.** $\frac{3}{16}$
**11.** $-\frac{10}{27}$ **13.** $\frac{5}{18}$ **15.** $-3\frac{3}{32}$ **17.** $-0.384$ **19.** $-\frac{7}{25}$
**21.** $\frac{3}{500}$ **23.** 3.875 **25.** $-2.5, -2.43, -2\frac{5}{12}, -2\frac{2}{5}, -\frac{7}{3}$
**27.** $\frac{26}{5}, 5.21, 5\frac{2}{9}, 5.3, 5\frac{3}{8}$ **29.** 3.81 **31.** 13.1 **33.** $-16.55$
**35.** $-8.115$ **37.** 3.9104 **39.** 1.5 **41.** $-31.866$ **43.** $-8.2$
**45.** 43; 39; no mode; 57 **47.** 88; 87; 78 and 95; 22

**Chapter 6 (p. 806)** **1.** 7 **3.** $-9$ **5.** 2 **7.** $-2$ **9.** 5
**11.** $-1$ **13.** 0.13 **15.** $-4$ **17.** $-4$ **19.** 4.5 cm

**21.** 7 yd; Use $\frac{22}{7}$ for $\pi$ since 44 is divisible by 22.

**23.** $c < 2$;

**25.** $s \geq = -1$;

**27.** $b > 8$;

**29.** $\frac{1}{2}n + 12 \leq 8$; $n \leq -8$ **31.** $4n \geq 16$; $n \geq 4$

**33.** at least $1\frac{1}{2}$ h

**Chapter 7 (p. 807)** **1.** $\frac{3}{1}$, 3 : 1, 3 to 1 **3.** $\frac{2}{3}$, 2 : 3, 2 to 3
**5.** 4 **7.** 225 **9.** 9.3 **11.** 12% **13.** 8.96 **15.** 12.5%
**17.** 72% **19.** 0.31; $\frac{31}{100}$ **21.** 1.75; $\frac{7}{4}$ **23.** increase; 12%
**25.** decrease; 1% **27.** $22.08 **29.** $83\frac{1}{3}$ **31.** 0.084 **33.** $\frac{1}{6}$

**Chapter 8 (p. 808)** **1.** $m\angle 1 = 50°$ **3.** $m\angle 5 = 50°$;
$m\angle 6 = 50°$; $m\angle 7 = 130°$ **5.** $x = 90$; right **7.** rhombus
**9.** trapezoid **11.** 160° **13.** $\angle A \cong \angle P$; $\angle B \cong \angle Q$; $\angle C \cong \angle R$

**15.**    **17.**

**19.**

**21.**

**Chapter 9 (p. 809)** **1.** 7.2 **3.** $-27.2$ **5.** 30, $-30$ **7.** 15,
$-15$ **9.** 9, $-9$ **11.** 8, $-8$ **13.** $>$ **15.** $>$ **17.** $0.\overline{1}$, 0.12,
$0.\overline{12}$, 0.123, $0.\overline{123}$ **19.** 35 **21.** 33 **23.** 75 **25.** yes
**27.** yes **29.** $x = 7\sqrt{2}$; $y = 7$ **31.** $x = 19\sqrt{3}$; $y = 38$
**33.** $\sin A = \frac{36}{85}$; $\cos A = \frac{77}{85}$; $\tan A = \frac{36}{77}$; $\sin B = \frac{77}{85}$;
$\cos B = \frac{36}{85}$; $\tan B = \frac{77}{36}$ **35.** $\sin 62° \approx 0.8829$;
$\cos 62° \approx 0.4695$; $\tan 62° \approx 1.8807$

**Chapter 10 (p. 810)** **1.** 195 in.²;

**3.** 10 cm²;

**5.** 357 yd²;

**7.** 5020 in.²   **9.** 26.4 ft²   **11.** 0.283 cm²   **13.** 201 mi²
**15.** It is not a polyhedron because circles are not polygons;

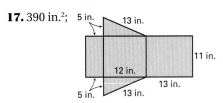

top   front   side

**17.** 390 in.²;

**19.** 360 m²   **21.** 369.9 m²   **23.** 330 in.³   **25.** 266.7 ft³
**27.** 252 cm³

## Chapter 11 (p. 811)
**1.** yes; Each input has exactly one output.   $y = x - 1$
**5.** no   **7.** yes   **9.** (−2, 3), (−1, 5), (0, 7), (1, 9)
**11.** (−2, 2), (−1, 1), (0, 0), (1, −1)   **13.** (−2, 4), (−1, 1), (0, −2), (1, −5)   **15.** (−2, −5), (1, −1), (4, 3), (7, 7)

**17.**    **19.**

**21.** $x$-intercept, $\frac{1}{5}$; $y$-intercept, $-1$   **23.** $x$-intercept, 6;
$y$-intercept, $-4$   **25.**

**27.** undefined   **29.** 1   **31.** −1   **33.** $\frac{17}{3}$   **35.** 0; 2

**37.** 2; −8   **39.**    **41.**

## Chapter 12 (p. 812)   **1.** 100–109;

| 9 | 9 |
|---|---|
| 10 | 0 1 3 5 |
| 11 | 6 7 8 |
| 12 | 7 9 |
| 13 | 0 |
| 14 | 0 0 3 |

Key: 13 | 0 = 130

**3.** *Sample answer:* About 50% of the lengths were between 103 in. and 130 in.;

100  110  120  130  140

99  103  117.5  130  143

**5.** line graph; A line graph is used to represent data that change over time.   **7.** 17,576,000 license plates
**9.** 11   **11.** 720   **13.** 5   **15.** 20   **17.** 4060 ways   **19.** $\frac{3}{4}$

**21.** $\frac{2}{9}$

## Chapter 13 (p. 813)   **1.** $-x^2 - 2x + 7$   **3.** $-k^2 + 21$
**5.** $-2x^3 + 4x^2 + 14x - 4$   **7.** $3x^3 - 9x^2 + 6x - 3$
**9.** $x^3 - 2x^2 + 9x + 6$   **11.** $-28z^6$   **13.** $-6n^2 + 15n$
**15.** $125\,a^3b^3$   **17.** $p^{24}$   **19.** $2x^2 - 9x - 5$   **21.** $d^2 + 10d + 24$   **23.** $a^2 - 15a + 56$   **25.** $f(x) = 2x - 5$   **27.** $f(x) = 5x^2 + 1$   **29.** 1; $\frac{1}{4}$; 0; $\frac{1}{4}$; 1   **31.** −16; −5; 0; −1, −8

**33.** −7; −4; −3; −4; −7

**35.**    **37.** no   **39.** yes

## Mathematics, Grade 8

### (a) Introduction

(1) Within a well-balanced mathematics curriculum, the primary focal points at Grade 8 are using basic principles of algebra to analyze and represent both proportional and non-proportional linear relationships and using probability to describe data and make predictions.

(2) Throughout mathematics in Grades 6–8, students build a foundation of basic understandings in number, operation, and quantitative reasoning; patterns, relationships, and algebraic thinking; geometry and spatial reasoning; measurement; and probability and statistics. Students use concepts, algorithms, and properties of rational numbers to explore mathematical relationships and to describe increasingly complex situations. Students use algebraic thinking to describe how a change in one quantity in a relationship results in a change in the other; and they connect verbal, numeric, graphic, and symbolic representations of relationships. Students use geometric properties and relationships, as well as spatial reasoning, to model and analyze situations and solve problems. Students communicate information about geometric figures or situations by quantifying attributes, generalize procedures from measurement experiences, and use the procedures to solve problems. Students use appropriate statistics, representations of data, reasoning, and concepts of probability to draw conclusions, evaluate arguments, and make recommendations.

(3) Problem solving in meaningful contexts, language and communication, connections within and outside mathematics, and formal and informal reasoning underlie all content areas in mathematics. Throughout mathematics in Grades 6–8, students use these processes together with graphing technology and other mathematical tools such as manipulative materials to develop conceptual understanding and solve problems as they do mathematics.

### (b) Knowledge and Skills

| | | |
|---|---|---|
| **(8.1)** | **Number, operation, and quantitative reasoning.** The student understands that different forms of numbers are appropriate for different situations. | **The student is expected to:**<br><br>**(A)** compare and order rational numbers in various forms including integers, percents, and positive and negative fractions and decimals;<br>**(B)** select and use appropriate forms of rational numbers to solve real-life problems including those involving proportional relationships;<br>**(C)** approximate (mentally and with calculators) the value of irrational numbers as they arise from problem situations (such as $\pi$, $\sqrt{2}$); and<br>**(D)** express numbers in scientific notation, including negative exponents, in appropriate problem situations. |
| **(8.2)** | **Number, operation, and quantitative reasoning.** The student selects and uses appropriate operations to solve problems and justify solutions. | **The student is expected to:**<br><br>**(A)** select appropriate operations to solve problems involving rational numbers and justify the selections;<br>**(B)** use appropriate operations to solve problems involving rational numbers in problem situations;<br>**(C)** evaluate a solution for reasonableness; and<br>**(D)** use multiplication by a constant factor (unit rate) to represent proportional relationships. |

| | | |
|---|---|---|
| **(8.3)** | **Patterns, relationships, and algebraic thinking.** The student identifies proportional or non-proportional linear relationships in problem situations and solves problems. | **The student is expected to:**<br><br>**(A)** compare and contrast proportional and non-proportional linear relationships; and<br><br>**(B)** estimate and find solutions to application problems involving percents and other proportional relationships such as similarity and rates. |
| **(8.4)** | **Patterns, relationships, and algebraic thinking.** The student makes connections among various representations of a numerical relationship. | **The student is expected to** generate a different representation of data given another representation of data (such as a table, graph, equation, or verbal description). |
| **(8.5)** | **Patterns, relationships, and algebraic thinking.** The student uses graphs, tables, and algebraic representations to make predictions and solve problems. | **The student is expected to:**<br><br>**(A)** predict, find, and justify solutions to application problems using appropriate tables, graphs, and algebraic equations; and<br><br>**(B)** find and evaluate an algebraic expression to determine any term in an arithmetic sequence (with a constant rate of change). |
| **(8.6)** | **Geometry and spatial reasoning.** The student uses transformational geometry to develop spatial sense. | **The student is expected to:**<br><br>**(A)** generate similar figures using dilations including enlargements and reductions; and<br><br>**(B)** graph dilations, reflections, and translations on a coordinate plane. |
| **(8.7)** | **Geometry and spatial reasoning.** The student uses geometry to model and describe the physical world. | **The student is expected to:**<br><br>**(A)** draw three-dimensional figures from different perspectives;<br><br>**(B)** use geometric concepts and properties to solve problems in fields such as art and architecture;<br><br>**(C)** use pictures or models to demonstrate the Pythagorean Theorem; and<br><br>**(D)** locate and name points on a coordinate plane using ordered pairs of rational numbers. |
| **(8.8)** | **Measurement.** The student uses procedures to determine measures of three-dimensional figures. | **The student is expected to:**<br><br>**(A)** find lateral and total surface area of prisms, pyramids, and cylinders using concrete models (two dimensional models);<br><br>**(B)** connect models of prisms, cylinders, pyramids, spheres, and cones to formulas for volume of these objects; and<br><br>**(C)** estimate measurements and use formulas to solve application problems involving lateral and total surface area and volume. |
| **(8.9)** | **Measurement.** The student uses indirect measurement to solve problems. | **The student is expected to:**<br><br>**(A)** use the Pythagorean Theorem to solve real-life problems; and<br><br>**(B)** use proportional relationships in similar two-dimensional figures or similar three-dimensional figures to find missing measurements. |
| **(8.10)** | **Measurement.** The student describes how changes in dimensions affect linear, area, and volume measures. | **The student is expected to:**<br><br>**(A)** describe the resulting effects on perimeter and area when dimensions of a shape are changed proportionally; and<br><br>**(B)** describe the resulting effect on volume when dimensions of a solid are changed proportionally. |

| (8.11) | **Probability and statistics.** The student applies concepts of theoretical and experimental probability to make predictions. | The student is expected to:<br><br>**(A)** find the probabilities of dependent and independent events;<br>**(B)** use theoretical probabilities and experimental results to make predictions and decisions; and<br>**(C)** select and use different models to simulate an event. |
|---|---|---|
| (8.12) | **Probability and statistics.** The student uses statistical procedures to describe data. | The student is expected to:<br><br>**(A)** select the appropriate measure of central tendency or range to describe a set of data and justify the choice for a particular situation;<br>**(B)** draw conclusions and make predictions by analyzing trends in scatterplots; and<br>**(C)** select and use an appropriate representation for presenting and displaying relationships among collected data, including line plots, line graphs, stem and leaf plots, circle graphs, bar graphs, box and whisker plots, histograms, and Venn diagrams, with and without the use of technology. |
| (8.13) | **Probability and statistics.** The student evaluates predictions and conclusions based on statistical data. | The student is expected to:<br><br>**(A)** evaluate methods of sampling to determine validity of an inference made from a set of data; and<br>**(B)** recognize misuses of graphical or numerical information and evaluate predictions and conclusions based on data analysis. |
| (8.14) | **Underlying processes and mathematical tools.** The student applies Grade 8 mathematics to solve problems connected to everyday experiences, investigations in other disciplines, and activities in and outside of school. | The student is expected to:<br><br>**(A)** identify and apply mathematics to everyday experiences, to activities in and outside of school, with other disciplines, and with other mathematical topics;<br>**(B)** use a problem-solving model that incorporates understanding the problem, making a plan, carrying out the plan, and evaluating the solution for reasonableness;<br>**(C)** select or develop an appropriate problem-solving strategy from a variety of different types, including drawing a picture, looking for a pattern, systematic guessing and checking, acting it out, making a table, working a simpler problem, or working backwards to solve a problem; and<br>**(D)** select tools such as real objects, manipulatives, paper/pencil, and technology or techniques such as mental math, estimation, and number sense to solve problems. |
| (8.15) | **Underlying processes and mathematical tools.** The student communicates about Grade 8 mathematics through informal and mathematical language, representations, and models. | The student is expected to:<br><br>**(A)** communicate mathematical ideas using language, efficient tools, appropriate units, and graphical, numerical, physical, or algebraic mathematical models; and<br>**(B)** evaluate the effectiveness of different representations to communicate ideas. |
| (8.16) | **Underlying processes and mathematical tools.** The student uses logical reasoning to make conjectures and verify conclusions. | The student is expected to:<br><br>**(A)** make conjectures from patterns or sets of examples and nonexamples; and<br>**(B)** validate his/her conclusions using mathematical properties and relationships. |

# Grade 8 TAKS Mathematics

## Objective 1

The student will demonstrate an understanding of numbers, operations, and quantative reasoning.

## Objective 2

The student will demonstrate an understanding of patterns, relationships, and algebraic reasoning.

## Objective 3

The student will demonstrate an understanding of geometry and spatial reasoning.

## Objective 4

The student will demonstrate an understanding of the concepts and uses of measurement.

## Objective 5

The student will demonstrate an understanding of probability and statistics.

## Objective 6

The student will demonstrate an understanding of the mathematical processes and tools used in problem solving.